Psychology

LEWIS BARKER
Auburn University

Upper Saddle River, New Jersey 07458

Library of Congress Cataloging-in-Publication Data

Barker, Lewis M.,
Psychology / Lewis Barker.
p. cm.
Includes bibliographical references and index.
ISBN 0-13-620816-9
1. Psychology. I. Title

BF121 .B29 2002
150–dc21 2001036797

Acquisitions Editor: Jayme Heffler
Editorial Assistant: Lauralee Lubrano
Editor in Chief of Development: Susanna Lesan
Development Editor: Elizabeth Morgan
VP/Director of Production and Manufacturing: Barbara Kittle
Senior Managing Editor: Mary Rottino
Production Editor: Kathleen Sleys
Production Assistants: Elizabeth Best / Patricia Sleys
Copyeditor: Kathy Pruno
Prepress and Manufacturing Manager: Nick Sklitsis
Prepress and Manufacturing Buyer: Tricia Kenny
AVP/Director of Marketing: Beth Gillett Mejia
Executive Marketing Manager: Sheryl Adams
Marketing Assistant: Ron Fox
Image Permissions Coordinator: Debbie Hewitson
Creative Design Director: Leslie Osher
Art Director: Maria Lange
Interior Designer: Kenny Beck
Cover Designer: Kenny Beck
Cover Art: Diane Fenster
Photo Research Supervisor: Beth Boyd
Image Permissions Supervisor: Kay Dellosa
Photo Researcher: Beaura Kathy Ringrose
Line Art Coordinator: Guy Ruggiero
Illustrations: Maria Piper / Precision Graphics / Medical and Scientific Illustration
Permissions Researcher: Lisa Black

This book was set in 10/12 Sabon by TSI Graphics and was printed and bound by Von Hoffman Press. Covers were printed by Phoenix Color Corp.

For permission to use copyrighted material, grateful acknowledgment is made to the copyright holders listed on page 682, which is considered an extension of this copyright page.

Printed in the United States of America
10 9 8 7 6 5 4 3 2 1

ISBN 0-13-620816-9

Pearson Education LTD., London
Pearson Education Australia Pty. Limited, Sydney
Pearson Education Singapore, Pte. Ltd
Pearson Education North Asia Ltd., Hong Kong
Pearson Education Canada Inc., Toronto
Pearson Education de Mexico, S.A. de C.V.
Pearson Education—Japan, Inc., Tokyo
Pearson Education Malaysia, Pte. Ltd
Pearson Education, Upper Saddle River, New Jersey

Dedication

With love and memories of my extended family, of those who lived, of those living, and of those who will follow.

Brief Contents

Part One
BACKGROUND

1 Understanding Mind and Behavior 2
2 Methodology in the Behavioral Sciences 32

Part Two
BIOLOGICAL/BEHAVIORAL PERSPECTIVE

3 Evolution and Genetics 66
4 Brain and Behavior 104
5 Motivation and Emotion 148
6 Learning and Behavior 184

Part Three
PERCEPTUAL/COGNITIVE PERSPECTIVE

7 Sensation 226
8 Perception 268
9 Consciousness 304
10 Memory 342

Part Four
DEVELOPMENTAL/INDIVIDUAL DIFFERENCES PERSPECTIVE

11 Development 378
12 Language and Thought 412
13 Intelligence 448
14 Personality 484

Part Five
SOCIAL/CULTURAL PERSPECTIVE

15 Social Psychology 510
16 Health Psychology 542
17 Abnormal Psychology 574
18 Treatment 608

Contents

Making Connections in Psychology xv

Integrated Coverage of
Evolutionary Psychology xx
Brain and Behavior xxi
Gender-Related Issues xxi
Cultural Factors xxii

Preface xxiii

To the Student xxix

About the Author xxxi

Part One

BACKGROUND

1 Understanding Mind and Behavior 2

Issues and Perspectives in Psychology 5
The Mind-Body Problem 5
An Interdisciplinary Understanding of Mind and Behavior 6
The Major Perspectives in Psychology 7
The Nature-Nurture Issue 7
The Place of Determinism 8
The Role of Common Sense 8
A Psychological Analysis of Human Behavior 11
Interim Summary 13 *For Further Thought 13*

The Roots of Psychology 13
John Locke and the British Associationists 14
The Nativists 15
Physiologists of the Mind 15
Charles Darwin's Evolutionary Theory 17
Interim Summary 18 *For Further Thought 18*

Psychology Becomes a Science 18
Structuralism: The Elements of Consciousness 19
Functionalism: The Usefulness of Consciousness 19
Behaviorism 22
Other Major Developments in 20th-Century Psychology 22
Interim Summary 23 *For Further Thought 24*

The Many Faces of Psychology 24
Occupations with Bachelor's Degrees 25
Occupations with Master's Degrees 25
Types of Psychologists 26
Specialty Areas in Psychology 27
Professional Organizations in Psychology 28
Recent Trends in Psychology 29
Interim Summary 30 *For Further Thought 30*

Concluding Thoughts 31

2 Methodology in the Behavioral Sciences 32

Curiosity and Science: A Very Human Enterprise 34

The Psychological Sciences: Philosophy and Goals 35
Psychology in Relation to Other Sciences 36
Searching for Truth? 38
Four Goals of Psychology 40
Interim Summary 42 *For Further Thought 42*

The Experimental Method 43
Questioning Behavior 43
Generating a Hypothesis 43
Designing the Experiment 44
Conducting the Experiment 45
Analyzing the Results 46
Validating the Experiment Through Peer Review 48
Publishing the Results 50
Interim Summary 51 *For Further Thought 51*

Nonexperimental Research Methods 51
Studying Individuals and Groups 52
Surveys and Case Studies 53
Correlational Research 55
Epidemiological Research 58
Psychological Inventories and Questionnaires 60

Comparison of Methods 61
Ethical Issues in Psychological Research 62
Interim Summary 63 For Further Thought 64

Concluding Thoughts 64

Part Two
BIOLOGICAL / BEHAVIORAL PERSPECTIVE

3 Evolution and Genetics 66

Human Origins 68

Evolution and Behavior 70
Distal and Proximal Causes of Behavior 70
Darwin's Theory of Evolution 71
Natural Selection 72
Interim Summary 74 For Further Thought 75

Genetics and Heredity 75
Mendel's Experiments 75
Genotypes and Phenotypes 77
Genetic Relatedness 78
Genetic Variability 82
The Influence of Genes on Behavior 83
Interim Summary 83 For Further Thought 84

Genes Meet Environment 84
Human Nature: Our Three Histories 84
The Interaction of Nature and Nurture 85
Behavioral Genetics 86
Ethology 89
Comparative Psychology 92
Neuroethology: An Interdisciplinary Approach 94
Contributions of Comparative Psychologists and Neuroethologists 94
Interim Summary 95 For Further Thought 95

Sociobiology and Evolutionary Psychology 95
Unconscious Whispering from Our Genes 96
Kin Selection and Inclusive Fitness 97
Altruism and Social Cooperation 98
Sexual Patterns 98
The Status of Evolutionary Psychology and Sociobiology 100
Interim Summary 101 For Further Thought 102

Concluding Thoughts 102

4 Brain and Behavior 104

Origins of the Human Brain 107
Brain Size in Humans and Other Animals 107
Brain Organization in Humans and Other Animals 108
The Vertebrate Plan 110
Interim Summary 112 For Further Thought 113

Overview of the Human Nervous System 113
The Peripheral Nervous System 113
The Neuroendocrine System 116
Neurons 116
The Spinal Cord and the Sensory-Motor Reflex 118
Interim Summary 120 For Further Thought 121

The Relationship of Brain and Behavior 121
Pathways Through the Spinal Cord to the Brain 121
The Reticular Formation and the Hindbrain 122
The Thalamus and Somatosensory Cortex 122
The Cerebral Cortex: Sources of Human Uniqueness 124
Brain Damage: A Clue to Brain-Behavior Relationships 127
The Mysterious Cerebellum 129
Interim Summary 131 For Further Thought 131

Left Brain, Right Brain: The Function of the Two Cerebral Hemispheres 131
Psychological Tests for the Lateralization of Function 131
The Split-Brain Procedure 132
Tests of Split-Brain Patients 134
Interim Summary 136 For Further Thought 137

Neurons, Neurotransmitters, and Drugs: The Molecular Basis of Mind and Brain 137
The Neuron's Membrane: The Key to Excitability 138
How to Excite a Neuron 139
The Action Potential 140
Neurotransmitters and Their Effects 142
The Effect of Drugs on Neurotransmitters 144
Interim Summary 145 For Further Thought 146

Concluding Thoughts 146

5 Motivation and Emotion 148

Motivation Defined 149

Physiological Bases of Motivation 151
The Neuroendocrine System 151
Homeostasis 152
Behavioral Regulation of Body States 154
Interim Summary 156 For Further Thought 156

Eating: Satisfying Hunger and Enjoying Foods 157
Multifactorial Motivation 157
Two Types of Feeding Systems 157
Nutritional Wisdom 158
Evolutionary Origins of Human Food Selection 160
Brain Mechanisms and Feeding 162
Interim Summary 165 For Further Thought 165

Pleasure 166

Brain Mechanisms Underlying Pleasure 166
Pleasure Seeking in Rats 166
Pleasure Seeking in Humans 167
Maslow's Hierarchy of Needs 168
Extrinsic Versus Intrinsic Motivators 168
The Need for Achievement 169
Interim Summary 170 For Further Thought 171

The Experience of Emotion 171

Evolutionary and Genetic Determinants of Emotion 172
Cultural Expressions of Emotion 175
Biological Bases of Emotion 176
Theories of Emotion 179
Interim Summary 182 For Further Thought 182

Concluding Thoughts 183

6 Learning And Behavior 184

Biological and Learned Behavior 186

Nature and Nurture 187
Genes and Memes 187
Interim Summary 189 For Further Thought 189

Classical, or Pavlovian, Conditioning 189

Pavlov's Influence on the Study of Learning 189
Reflexes and Conditioned Reflexes 190
The Conditioning Process 191
Habituation and Sensitization 193
Experimental Extinction 193
Higher-Order Conditioning 194
Basic Rules of Conditioning 194
Stimulus Generalization and Discrimination 195
Interim Summary 197 For Further Thought 197

Applications of Classical Conditioning 197

Emotional Responses 198
Food Preferences and Aversions 200
Morphine Tolerance 202
Interim Summary 203 For Further Thought 204

Instrumental Learning and Operant Conditioning 204

Instrumental Responses and Instrumental Learning 204
The Law of Effect 205
Behaviorism and Operant Conditioning 206
Schedules of Reinforcement 207
Interim Summary 211 For Further Thought 211

Behavior Control Through Reinforcement and Punishment 211

Environmental Determinism and Stimulus Control 212
Punishment 212
Negative Reinforcement and Avoidance Learning 214
Social Reinforcement and Observational Learning 215
Interim Summary 216 For Further Thought 216

Conditioning of Instinctive Behavior 216

Exploration, Cognitive Maps, and Latent Learning 217
Evolutionarily Prepared Learning 218
Interim Summary 221 For Further Thought 221

Conceptual Learning 221

Concept Formation in Primates 222
From Reflexes to Literacy 223
Interim Summary 224 For Further Thought 224

Concluding Thoughts 225

Part Three

PERCEPTUAL / COGNITIVE PERSPECTIVE

7 Sensation 226

Introduction to the Senses 228

The Senses as Evolved Adaptations 229
Psychophysics 231
Psychophysical Methods 232
Signal Detection Theory 233
The Two-Point Limen 234
Subliminal Perception 234
A Five-Stage Model of Sensory Systems 235
Interim Summary 236 For Further Thought 236

Seeing 236

Structure of the Eye 237
Seeing at the Level of the Retina 238
Visual Nerve Pathways 239
Nonseeing Functions of the Eye 241
Dark Adaptation 242
Color Vision 243
Color Blindness 244
Interim Summary 246 For Further Thought 247

Hearing 247

Structure of the Ear 249
Place Theory and the Traveling Wave 252
The Sensation of Loudness 252
Hearing Loss and Deafness 252
Central Auditory Processes 255
Interim Summary 257 For Further Thought 257

Tasting and Smelling: The Intimate Senses 257

What We Taste 258
How We Taste 258
Why and How We Smell 259
Interim Summary 261 For Further Thought 262

The Skin Senses: Touch, Pressure, Temperature, and Pain 262
The Human Skin 262
The Sense of Pain 264
Interim Summary 265 *For Further Thought 266*
Concluding Thoughts 266

8 Perception 268

Perception of Shapes, Edges, and Movement 271
Bottom-Up and Top-Down Processes 271
Receptive Fields and Feature Detectors 271
Cortical Processing of Features 273
Interim Summary 275 *For Further Thought 275*
Depth Perception, Perceptual Constancies, and Illusions 275
Depth Perception 276
Perceptual Constancies 278
Illusions and Ambiguous Figures 279
Interim Summary 281 *For Further Thought 282*
Conscious and Unconscious Processes in Perception 282
The Phenomenon of Blindsight 282
Seeing with the Whole Brain 284
Seeing Versus Awareness 287
The Mind-Body Problem Again 288
Interim Summary 288 *For Further Thought 289*
Perception of the Whole 289
Apparent Movement and the Phi Phenomenon 290
Principles of Perceptual Organization 291
Interim Summary 293 *For Further Thought 293*
Perception of Sound, Taste, Smell, and Touch 294
The Perception of Meaningful Sounds 294
The Perception of Odors and Tastes 295
The Perception of Touch 299
Integration Across the Senses 301
Interim Summary 301 *For Further Thought 302*
Concluding Thoughts 302

9 Consciousness 304

The Many Meanings of Mind and Consciousness 306
Mind and Consciousness in the History of Psychology 306
Biological Bases of Consciousness 307
Contemporary Thinking About Mind and Consciousness 308
Interim Summary 309 *For Further Thought 309*
Resonating with the Sun and Moon: Biological Clocks 310
Circadian Rhythms 310
Biological Clocks 311
Free-Running Rhythms and Zeitgeibers 312
Disruption of Light-Dark Cycles 313
Lunar and Seasonal Rhythms 317
Interim Summary 318 *For Further Thought 318*
Sleep and Dreams 319
Why We Sleep 319
A Normal Night's Sleep 320
REM Sleep 321
The Effects of Sleep Deprivation 323
Insomnia 324
Dreams and Dreaming 324
Interim Summary 326 *For Further Thought 326*
Alterations of the Waking State: Daydreams, Hypnotism, and Meditation 327
Daydreaming 327
Hypnosis 328
Meditation to Achieve an Altered State of Consciousness 331
Interim Summary 331 *For Further Thought 332*
Drug-Induced Alterations of Consciousness 332
Why Humans Use Drugs 332
Depressants: Alcohol and Barbiturates 333
Antianxiety Drugs 334
Stimulants, Legal and Illegal 335
Antidepressants 337
Narcotics: Heroin and Morphine 337
Hallucinogens: Marijuana and LSD 338
Drug Tolerance 338
Drug Dependence and Drug Addiction 339
Drugs and Society 339
Interim Summary 340 *For Further Thought 341*
Concluding Thoughts 341

10 Memory 342

The Evolution of Memory 344
The Adaptive Significance of Memory 344
The Evolution of Multiple Memory Systems 345
Interim Summary 346 *For Further Thought 346*
The Information-Processing Approach to Memory 346
Sensory Memory 347
Selective Attention to Information 347
Short-Term (Working) Memory 350
Long-Term Memory 353
Interim Summary 353 *For Further Thought 353*
Encoding and Short-Term Memory 354
The Recency Effect 354
The Phonological Loop 354

The Primacy Effect 356
The Process of Encoding 356
The Levels-of-Processing Hypothesis 357
Interim Summary 359 For Further Thought 359

The Enigma of Long-Term Memory 359
Implicit and Explicit Memories 359
Schemas 360
The Effect of Leading Questions 362
Remembering Versus Knowing 363
Interim Summary 363 For Further Thought 363

Memory for Movement, Events, and Words 364
Procedural Memory 364
Declarative Memory 364
Interim Summary 368 For Further Thought 368

Memorizing, Forgetting, and Improving Memory 368
Theories of Forgetting 369
Explanations for Exceptional Memory 370
The Process of Retrieval from Memory 371
Interim Summary 373 For Further Thought 373

Memory in Normal Versus Damaged Brains 374
The Case of H. M. 375
Alzheimer's Disease 375
Interim Summary 376 For Further Thought 376

Concluding Thoughts 376

Part Four
DEVELOPMENT / INDIVIDUAL DIFFERENCES PERSPECTIVE

11 Human Development 378

Conception and Prenatal Development 380
Prenatal Physical Development 380
Fetal Mind and Behavior 383
Interim Summary 385 For Further Thought 386

Birth and Early Childhood Development 386
Continuous Versus Stagelike Development 386
Perceptual Development 387
Interim Summary 391 For Further Thought 392

Cognitive Development Throughout the Life Span 392
Piaget's Stage Theory of Cognitive Development 392
Challenge to Piaget's Theory 397
Vygotsky's Sociocultural Theory of Cognitive Development 397
Cognition and Memory Throughout the Life Span 398
Kohlberg's Stage Theory of Moral Development 400
Interim Summary 402 For Further Thought 403

Psychosocial Development Throughout the Life Span 403
Infancy: Attachment and Temperament 404
Early Childhood 408
Adolescence and Adulthood 408
Bereavement: The Loss of Attachment 409
Interim Summary 410 For Further Thought 410

Concluding Thoughts 411

12 Language and Thought 412

The Origins and Nature of Human Language 414
Why Language Evolved 415
Brain Organization, Handedness, and Language 416
Language Areas in the Human Brain 417
Brain Damage and Language Loss: The Aphasias 418
Interim Summary 419 For Further Thought 420

Communication and the Question of Animal "Language" 420
Animal Communication 421
Communicating with Porpoises and Dolphins 421
Connecting with Chimpanzees and Gorillas 423
Talking with Alex, the Parrot 425
Human and Animal Language Compared 425
Interim Summary 426 For Further Thought 426

How Children Acquire Language 426
First Sounds: Crying 426
Cooing, Babbling, and Pointing 427
First Words 428
Parental Encouragement of Language Acquisition 429
The Growth of Vocabulary and Appearance of Grammar 430
A Critical Period for Language Acquisition? 431
Interim Summary 432 For Further Thought 432

Thinking Without Language 432
Thinking in Nonspeaking Humans and Nonhuman Animals 433
Problem Solving 433
Generating Solutions to Problems 435
Means-End Analyses 436
Insight 437
Interim Summary 439 For Further Thought 439

Thinking with Language 440
The Influence of Language on Perception and Thought 440
The Linguistic Relativity Hypothesis 441
The Effect of Mental Set on Problem Solving 442
Types of Thinking 442
Word Problems 444
Interim Summary 445 For Further Thought 446

Concluding Thoughts 446

13 Intelligence 448

A Brief History of Intelligence Testing 450
The Pioneering Work of Francis Galton 451
Alfred Binet's Program of Intelligence Testing 452
Spearman's Concept of General Intelligence (g) 453
The Stanford-Binet Intelligence Test 454
The Army Alpha and Beta Tests 454
The Wechsler Intelligence Tests 455
***Interim Summary* 457 *For Further Thought* 457**

IQ and Alternative Theories of Intelligence 457
The Meaning of an IQ Score 458
The Validity of IQ Tests 458
The Construct of Intelligence 459
Alternatives to IQ Tests 459
Gardner's Theory of Multiple Intelligences 460
Sternberg's Triarchic Theory of Intelligence 462
***Interim Summary* 465 *For Further Thought* 465**

The Bell Curve Wars: The Sources of Intelligence 466
Genes and Cognitive Abilities 466
Effect of the Environment on Intelligence 468
Interaction of Genes and Environment 468
Passive Versus Dynamic Exposure 470
Equal Environments and Opportunities, and Unequal Outcomes 471
The Flynn Effect 471
Biological Bases of Intelligence 472
***Interim Summary* 474 *For Further Thought* 475**

The Bell Curve Wars: Intelligence and Culture 475
Ethnic Differences in IQ 476
Educational Implications of Ethnic Differences 478
Real-World Consequences of Differences in IQ 478
***Interim Summary* 481 *For Further Thought* 481**

Concluding Thoughts 482

14 Personality 484

Personality: An Overview 485
The Adaptiveness of Personality 485
Theoretical Approaches to Personality 487

The Trait Approach 488
Greek Personality Types 488
Body Types and Personality 488
How Many Personality Types? 488
The Big Five Personality Factors 489
Genetics and Personality Types 491
***Interim Summary* 493 *For Further Thought* 493**

The Social-Learning and Social-Cognitive Approaches 493
Behavioral Conditioning of Personality 494
Cognition and Personality 494
The Interaction of Genes and Culture 495
***Interim Summary* 496 *For Further Thought* 496**

The Psychodynamic Approach 496
Freud's Psychoanalytic Theory 497
The Structure of Personality 498
Anxiety and Defense Mechanisms 499
Sexual Energy and the Death Force 500
Psychosexual Development 500
The Evaluation of Freudian Theory 502
The Analytic Theory of Carl Jung 504
Alfred Adler's Self Psychology 505
***Interim Summary* 505 *For Further Thought* 506**

Humanistic Approaches 506
Carl Rogers's Person-Centered Approach 506
Abraham Maslow's Theory of Self-Actualization 507
An Evaluation of Humanistic Personality Theories 507
***Interim Summary* 508 *For Further Thought* 508**

Concluding Thoughts 509

Part Five

SOCIAL / CULTURAL PERSPECTIVE

15 Social Psychology 510

Social Cognition: Processing Social Information 512
Attribution 513
Attitude Change and Formation 515
Cognitive Dissonance 518
***Interim Summary* 519 *For Further Thought* 520**

Social Influences on Behavior 520
Conformity 521
Obedience: Compliance with Authority 522
Group Influence on Personal Performance 524
***Interim Summary* 525 *For Further Thought* 526**

Gender, Attraction, and Love 526
Gender and Sexual Orientation 526
Genes, Hormones, and Sexual Behavior 527
Attraction and Attractiveness 529
Attractive Faces 531
Friendship and Love 532
***Interim Summary* 534 *For Further Thought* 534**

Social Relations 535
Prejudice and Stereotyping 535
Aggression 537
Interim Summary 540 *For Further Thought 540*

Concluding Thoughts 541

16 Health Psychology 542

Cultural Understandings of Health 544
Cross-Cultural Concepts of Health 545
Cross-Cultural Systems of Medicine 546
Interim Summary 547 *For Further Thought 547*

Evolutionary and Ecological Perspectives on Health 548
Why We Become Ill 548
Research on Behavioral Causes of Illness 552
Behavioral Causes of Heart Disease 554
Interim Summary 557 *For Further Thought 558*

Psychosomatic Disorders and Stress 558
Psychosomatic Disorders 558
Stress 559
Interim Summary 565 *For Further Thought 566*

Psychoneuroimmunology 566
Integrating Mind and Body 566
Functions of the Immune System 567
Conditioning of the Immune System 568
Medical Implications of Conditioning Experiments 570
Personality and the Immune System 571
Interim Summary 572 *For Further Thought 572*

Concluding Thoughts 573

17 Abnormal Psychology 574

Perspectives on Abnormal Behavior 577
What Is Abnormal Behavior? 577
A Case in Point: Jeremy 579
The Prevalence of Mental Disorders 579
Interim Summary 579 *For Further Thought 580*

Categorization of Psychological Disorders 580
The Medical Versus the Psychological Model 580
Organic Versus Functional Disorders 581
Standardization of Diagnostic Terms 581
Using the *DSM-IV* 582
Interim Summary 584 *For Further Thought 584*

Anxiety Disorders 584
Phobic Disorder 584
Generalized Anxiety Disorder 585
Panic Disorder 586
Obsessive-Compulsive Disorder 587
Interim Summary 588 *For Further Thought 588*

Somatoform Disorders 589
Hypochondriasis 589
Somatization Disorders 590
Conversion Disorders 590
Interim Summary 590 *For Further Thought 591*

Dissociative Disorders 591
Dissociative Fugue States 591
Dissociative Amnesia 591
Depersonalization Disorder 592
Dissociative Identity Disorder 592
Interim Summary 593 *For Further Thought 593*

Mood Disorders 593
Bipolar and Unipolar Disorders 594
Depression 594
The Adaptiveness of Mood Disorders 596
Interim Summary 597 *For Further Thought 597*

Schizophrenia 598
Symptoms of Schizophrenia 598
Types of Schizophrenia 599
Causes of Schizophrenia 599
Interim Summary 601 *For Further Thought 602*

Personality Disorders 602
Categories of Personality Disorders 602
Borderline Personality Disorder 603
Antisocial Personality Disorder 604
Interim Summary 605 *For Further Thought 605*

Concluding Thoughts 606

18 Treatment 608

History and Overview of Treatment 610
Treatment of Mental Illness in the 20th Century 610
The Mental Health Care System 611
Interim Summary 613 *For Further Thought 613*

The Psychoanalytic Perspective 613
Freudian Analysis 614
Other Analytical Therapies 615
Interim Summary 615 *For Further Thought 615*

Behavioral Therapies 615
Systematic Desensitization 616
Behavior Modification 616
Biofeedback Therapy 619
Interim Summary 620 *For Further Thought 620*

Insight Therapies 621
Cognitive Therapies 621
Humanistic Therapy 623

Cognitive-Behavioral Therapy 625
Group Therapy 626
Evaluating Insight Therapies 627
Interim Summary 628 *For Further Thought 629*

Medical Interventions 630

Psychosurgery: Revisiting Brain-Behavior Relationships 630
Electroconvulsive Shock Therapy 630
Drug Treatment 631
Interim Summary 634 *For Further Thought 634*

Concluding Thoughts 635

Statistical Appendix 637

Glossary 645

References 656

Photo Credits 682

Name Index 683

Subject Index 694

Making Connections in Psychology

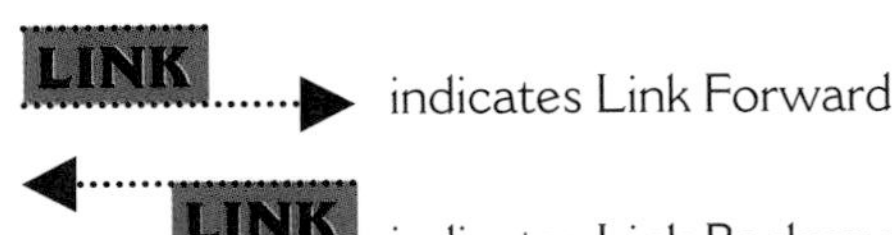

LINKs (directional arrows) are a pedagogical device found within each chapter of the text designed to help students retain the most current research and make connections in psychology.

CHAPTER 1

6 Psychology's relationship to other sciences in Ch. 2, p. 36
7 Nature-nurture in Ch. 3, p. 85
14 Development of the infant mind in Ch. 11, p. 383
16 Gray matter and white matter in Ch. 4, p. 119
17 Broca's area, and Wernicke's area in Ch. 12, p. 418

CHAPTER 2

37 Dopamine and other neurochemical pathways in Ch. 4, p. 148
38 Brain bases of reinforcement in Ch. 5, p. 166
40 Methods of measuring sleep and dreams in Ch. 9, p. 320
41 Evolution and genetics provide answers to "why" questions in Ch. 3, p. 70 and Ch. 5, p. 151
58 Epidemiological data and health psychology in Ch. 16, p. 552
60 Intelligence testing in Ch. 13, p. 452
61 Depression and abnormal psychology in Ch. 17, p. 594
61 Intelligence in Ch. 13, p. 459

CHAPTER 3

68 "Thinking" visually in Ch. 8, p. 271
71 Proximal determinants of behavior with process of habituation in Ch. 6, p. 193
85 Ontogenetic history and learning in Ch. 6, p. 187
85 Extragenetic history and memes in Ch. 6, p. 187
88 Role of genes in health in Ch. 16, p. 550
88 Heritability and twin studies of intelligence in Ch. 13, p. 466 and of personality in Ch. 14, p. 495
89 Heritability and twin studies of schizophrenia in Ch. 17, p. 600
90 Critical periods and language acquisition in Ch. 12, p. 431
90 FAPs and physiological reflexes in Ch. 4, p. 110 and in Ch. 6, p. 191
93 Social isolation and language development in Ch. 12, p. 431
94 Pair bonding and child development in Ch. 11, p. 405
98 Sociobiology and social cooperation in Ch. 15, p. 524
98 Parental investment and attachment in Ch. 11, p. 404
101 Sociobiology with *nature* in the nature-nurture argument in Ch. 6, p. 187

CHAPTER 4

107 Evolution and human ancestry in Ch. 3, p. 79
107 Human and animal consciousness in Ch. 9, p. 307
111 Role of Hypothalamus in motivated behavior in Ch. 5, p. 162
116 Role of ANS in stress and health in Ch, 16, p. 560
116 Neuroendocrine system and motivation in Ch. 5, p. 151
126 How a frog sees in Ch. 8, p. 272
126 Forebrain and consciousness in Ch. 9, p. 308
127 Brain areas for language in Ch. 12, p. 416
131 Environment affects brain during development in Ch. 11, p. 382
132 Brain control of language in Ch. 12, p. 417
134 Brain functions and consciousness in Ch. 9, p. 308
135 Conscious and unconscious seeing in Ch. 7, p. 282
135 Right hemisphere localization of emotion in Ch. 5, p. 176
142 Olds' experiments in Ch. 2, p. 33
143 Endorphins and pain in Ch. 7, p. 265
144 Drugs, brain functions and consciousness in Ch. 9, p. 332

CHAPTER 5

154 Homeostasis with ANS functioning in Ch. 4, p.114
155 Motivation and fixed action patterns in Ch. 3, p. 90
156 Acquired motives and secondary reinforcement in Ch. 6, p. 207
157 Genes and obese mice in Ch. 3, p. 87
158 Food reinforces behavior in Ch. 6, p. 207
158 Behavioral plasticity with brain plasticity in Ch. 4, p. 128

161 Cultural food practices as memes in Ch. 6, p. 187
166 Pleasure with consummatory behaviors in Ch. 3, p. 89
167 Cocaine and the brain in Ch. 9, p. 336
167 Dopamine receptors in Ch. 4, p. 143
168 Acquired motivation and secondary reinforcement in Ch. 6, p. 207
169 Effects of reinforcement on behavior in Ch. 6, p. 206
170 TAT test and projective tests in Ch. 14, p. 489
171 Emotion and abnormal psychology in Ch. 17, p. 584
172 Genetics of emotion in Ch. 3, p. 86
176 Emotions as conditioned responses in Ch. 6, p. 198
177 Emotions and the autonomic nervous system in Ch. 4, p. 116
177 Facial movements and motor homunculus in Ch. 4, p. 127
178 Surgery as treatment for mental disorders in Ch. 18, p. 629
178 Emotions and frontal lobes in Ch. 4, p. 135

CHAPTER 6

186 Learning and proximal causation in Ch. 3, p. 70
186 Behaviorism in Ch. 1, p. 22
187 Memes and extragenetic history in Ch. 3, p. 85
188 Genes and language acquisition in Ch. 12 , p. 431
190 Locke's associationism w/ Pavlov's conditioning in Ch. 1, p. 14
190 Reflexes with fixed action patterns in Ch. 3, p. 90
194 Acquired motives in Ch. 5, p. 155
198 Conditioned fear responses with phobia formation in Ch. 17, p. 585
199 Incentives in Ch. 5, p. 585
200 Association of words in semantic memory in Ch. 10, p. 365
201 Conditioned taste aversions and thiamine in Ch. 5, p. 150
206 Hedonism in Ch. 5, p. 150
207 Reinforcement, with "satisfiers" and with ESB in Ch. 2, p. 390
215 Imitation in child development in Ch. 11, p. 390
216 Observational learning with personality development in Ch. 14, p. 494
222 Compare perceptual awareness and cognition in Ch. 9, p. 308 and development of cognitive processes in Ch. 11, p. 392
223 Genes and environment in Ch. 3, p. 84

CHAPTER 7

228 Proximal and distal determinants of behavior in Ch. 3, p. 70
230 Sensorimotor for integration in the brain in Ch. 4, p. 126
233 Somatosensory cortex in Ch 4, p. 123
234 Subliminal perception with priming in Ch. 10, p. 360
235 Mind-body problem in Ch. 1, p. 5
239 Visual fields and striate cortex in split brain procedure in Ch. 4, p. 134
241 Cortical and subcortical pathways in Ch. 4, p. 119
241 Automatic movement in Ch. 4, p. 119
242 Visual attention and reticular formation in Ch. 4, p. 122
250 Transduction in vision and hearing in Ch. 7, p. 238
255 Central hearing loss and Wernick's aphasia in Ch. 12, p. 418
255 Sign language in Ch. 12, p. 430
259 Neurogenesis in Ch. 4, p. 129
259 Taste and somatosensory cortex in Ch. 4, p. 123
264 Control of pain by hypnosis in Ch. 9, p. 328
265 The PAG, drugs, and placebos in Ch. 17, p. 630

CHAPTER 8

271 Method of introspection in Ch. 1, p. 19
271 Psychophysics in Ch. 7, p. 231
275 Feature detectors with innate releasing mechanisms in Ch. 3, p. 90
281 Perception as learned associations in Ch. 6, p. 190
284 Seeing in blindsight and split brain subjects in Ch. 4, p. 133
284 Perception and emotion in Ch. 5, p. 171
288 Connected images and association formation in Ch. 6, p. 14
290 Perception and implicit memory in Ch. 10, p. 360
290 Perception and language, and thought in Ch. 12, p. 440
294 Language and temporal lobe organization in Ch. 12, p. 418
294 The role of the hippocampus in memory formation in Ch. 10, p. 374
297 Factors involved in sexual attractiveness in Ch. 15. p. 529
297 MHC complex with inbreeding in Ch. 3, p. 78
297 Recessive genes in Ch. 3, p. 77
298 Child's attraction to odors and psychosexual development in Ch. 14, p. 501
299 Teaching disgust responses and memes in Ch. 3, p. 188
299 Conditioning, and learning associations with smells in Ch. 6, p. 200
299 Infant's rooting reflex in Ch. 6, p. 191
299 Eyeblink reflex in Ch. 6, p. 191
299 Contact comfort and attachment in Ch. 11, p. 405
300 Touching and health psychology in Ch. 16, p. 533
301 Sensory association areas in parietal lobe in Ch. 4, p. 126

CHAPTER 9

307 Stream of consciousness to short-term memory in Ch. 10, p. 350
307 Watson and behaviorism in Ch. 6, p. 198

307 Brain organization and DNA in Ch. 3, p.83
311 Non-visual fibers in the retina in Ch. 7, p. 241
323 Sleep and primary drive in Ch. 5, p. 155
325 Dreams and Freud's psychoanalytic theory in Ch 14, p. 498
328 Consciousness and cocktail party phenomenon in Ch. 10, p. 349
328 Consciousness as visual consciousness in Ch. 7, p. 282
329 Tonic immobility and touching in Ch. 8, p. 300
329 Tonic immobility and SSDRs in Ch. 3, p. 91
330 Hypnotherapy as psychotherapy in Ch. 18, p. 620
331 Dissociation and depersonalization disorder in Ch. 17, p. 592
333 Adaptive characteristics of brain structures in Ch. 4, p. 107
333 Pleasure centers in the brain in Ch. 2, p. 47
333 Effect of damage to frontal cortex in Phineas Gage in Ch. 4, p. 105
336 Reuptake mechanism in Ch. 4, p. 144
336 Sympathetic nervous system in Ch. 4, p. 115
337 Glutamate receptors in Ch. 4, p. 143
338 Tolerance in Ch. 6, p. 202
339 Reinforcement in Ch. 6, p. 207

CHAPTER 10

344 Genotypic differences in Ch. 3, p. 70
345 Brain-size and psychological complexity in Ch. 3, p. 107
345 Memory and memes in Ch. 6, p. 187
356 Maintenance rehearsal and associative processes in Ch. 6, p. 190
360 Memory as a perceptual process in Ch. 8, p. 271
362 Seeing and believing in Ch. 7, p. 271
364 Procedural memory and conditioned responses in Ch. 6, p. 204
366 Frequency of association and learning in Ch. 6, p. 207
367 Memory and one-trial learning in Ch. 6, p. 201
370 Memory and intelligence in Ch. 13, p. 455
372 Context effects on memory and on conditioned tolerance in Ch. 6, p. 202
372 Effects of marijuana on memory in Ch. 9, p. 338
374 Epilepsy and cutting the corpus collossum in Ch. 4, p. 133

CHAPTER 11

380 Genes and memes in Ch. 6, p. 187
380 Nature and nurture in Ch. 3, p. 85
382 Neurogenesis in Ch. 4, p. 129
384 Auditory apparatus and hearing in Ch. 7, p. 250
385 Declarative and procedural memories in Ch. 10, p. 364
390 Locke's *tabula rasa* in Ch. 1, p. 14
391 Depth perception in Ch. 8, p. 276
392 Nativism in Ch, 1, p. 15
392 Schemas in Ch. 10, p. 360
393 Reflexive movements, and instrumental responses in Ch. 6, p. 204
396 Phonological loop and working memory in Ch. 10, p. 354
398 Language development in Ch. 12, p. 426
398 Autobiographical memory in Ch. 10, p. 366
399 Long-term memory in Ch. 10, p. 347
400 Alzheimer's disease in Ch. 17, p. 592
403 Feral children in Ch. 11, p. 171
403 The story of "Genie" in Ch. 12, p. 431
405 Contact comfort and pair bonding in Ch. 3, p. 93
405 Attachment and secondary reinforcement in Ch. 6, p. 207
407 Temperament in dogs in Ch. 3, p. 89
408 Reinforcement and social learning theory in Ch. 6, p. 215

CHAPTER 12

414 Communication by pheromone in Ch.7, p. 259
417 Language and lateralization in Ch. 4, p. 133
418 Language and brain damage in Ch. 4, p. 127
421 Alarm calls as a FAP in Ch. 3, p. 90
422 Learning conditioned responses in Ch. 6, p. 192
423 Learning about rules and concepts in Ch. 6, p. 222
425 Proximal and distal causation of behavior in Ch. 3, p. 70
428 Nativism in Ch. 1, p. 15
429 Words as operant responses that are reinforced in Ch. 6, p. 200
431 Kamala and Amala in Ch. 5, p. 171
431 Neural development in enriched environments in Ch. 4, p. 128
433 Nonverbal tests of intelligence in Ch. 13, p. 455
435 Spatial abilities and right hemisphere functioning in Ch. 4, p. 136
435 Thorndike's law of effect in Ch. 6, p. 206
435 Win-stay, lose-shift heuristic in Ch. 6, p. 222
440 Misleading language influences perception and memory in Ch. 10, p. 362
440 Language and semantic memory in Ch. 10, p. 365
442 Types of consciousness and thinking in Ch. 9, p. 306

CHAPTER 13

452 Psychological abilities are normally distributed in Ch. 2, p. 52
458 Test reliability and validity in Ch. 2, p. 60
459 Computing standard deviation in Statistical Appendix, p. 640
462 Intelligence, and individual differences in personality in Ch. 14, p. 491

463 Common sense in Ch. 1, p. 10
464 Creativity and functional fixedness in Ch. 12, p. 438
470 Genie, Amala, Kamala and critical period in Ch. 12, p. 431
470 Role of environment in instrumental learning in Ch. 6, p. 224
470 Vocabulary size and environment in Ch. 12, p. 441
471 Environmental complexity and brain organization in Ch. 4, p. 129
472 Intelligence and brain size in Ch. 3, p. 107
472 Lateralization of abilities in left and right hemispheres in Ch. 4, p. 136
473 Intelligence and short-term memory in Ch. 10, p. 356
473 Intelligence and phonological loops in Ch. 10, p. 356
473 Intelligence and fetal alcohol syndrome in Ch, 9, p. 383

CHAPTER 14

487 Genetic bases of temperament in dogs in Ch. 3, p. 89
487 Phineas Gage in Ch. 4, p. 105
491 Intelligence and creativity in Ch. 13, p. 464
491 Heritability in Ch. 3, p. 88
494 John B. Watson in Ch. 1, p. 22; B. F. Skinner and Albert Bandura in Ch. 6, pp. 206, 215
494 Schemas in Ch. 10, p. 360
495 Memes in Ch. 6, p. 187
495 Compare passive and active effects of environment in Ch. 13, p. 469
497 Conscious and unconscious processes in Ch. 9, p. 307
497 Long term and working memory in Ch. 10, p. 307
498 Psychoanalysis in Ch. 18, p. 614
498 Id and biological motivation in Ch. 5, p. 155
500 The "motives" of DNA in Ch. 3, p. 96
502 Psychosexual development with stage theories in Ch. 11, p. 386 and learning theory in Ch. 6, p. 186
503 Consummatory behaviors and evolutionary psychology in Ch. 3, p. 89
503 Priming, blindsight in Ch. 10, p. 360 and subliminal perception in Ch. 7, p. 234
503 Sociobiology in Ch. 3, p. 95
503 Acquired motivation in Ch. 5, p. 155
504 Eric Erickson, the development of identity in Ch. 11, p. 403
507 Maslow's need hierarchy in Ch. 5, p. 168

CHAPTER 15

513 Environmental determinants of behavior in Ch. 6, p. 212
516 Shaping behaviors in Ch. 6, p. 207
516 Rules for effective conditioning in Ch. 6, p. 207
518 Freudian defense mechanism in Ch. 14, p. 499
527 Intimacy vs. isolation in Ch. 11, p. 404
530 Visual development in Ch. 9, p. 389
530 Evolutionary psychology and sociobiology in Ch. 3, p. 95
531 Selfish genes in Ch. 3, p. 95
532 Gestalt Psychology in Ch. 8, p. 289
535 Proximal and distal determinants of behavior in Ch. 3, p. 70
535 Priming and implicit memory in Ch. 10, p. 360
536 Strange situation test in Ch. 11, p. 406
537 Social learning processes in Ch. 6, p. 215 and Ch. 11, p. 397
537 Freud's thanatos in Ch. 14, p. 500
537 Instinctive behaviors in Ch. 3, p. 70
537 Sexual patterns of behavior in Ch. 3, p. 98
538 Aggressive behavior and emotion in Ch. 5, p. 172
538 Brain plasticity in Ch. 4, p. 129
539 Hard and soft sciences in Ch. 2, p. 36
539 Social learning processes in Ch. 14, p. 494

CHAPTER 16

545 Descartes mind-body dualism in Ch. 1, p. 6
547 Psychotherapy in Ch. 18, p. 610
550 The smells of 18th-Century France in Ch. 7, p. 227
551 Hemoglobin and sickle cell anemia in Ch. 3, p. 83
551 The Role of memes in behavior in Ch. 6, p. 187
552 Epidemiological methods in Ch. 2, p. 53
553 Role of touch in attachment, contact comfort in Ch. 11, p. 405
554 Role of touch in adaptive social behavior in Ch. 7, p. 93
554 Stroke in Ch. 4, p. 127
556 *Ob* genes in Ch. 3, p. 87
556 Hypothalamic control of eating and drinking in Ch. 5, p. 163
556 Homeostasis and set point; insulin regulation in Ch. 5, p. 152
556 Taste receptors in Ch. 8, p. 258
557 Neurogenesis in Ch. 4, p. 129
558 Dualism in Ch. 1, p. 6
558 Glove anesthesia, and hysteria, in Ch. 14, p. 496
558 Somatoform disorders in Ch. 17, p. 589
560 Sympathetic nervous system in Ch. 4, p. 116
562 The fundamental attribution error in Ch. 15, p. 514
562 Little Albert, and learned emotional behavior in Ch. 6, p. 199
563 Maslow's *need hierarchy* in Ch. 5, p. 168 and *self-actualization* in Ch. 14, p. 507
564 Effects of alcohol and nicotine in Ch. 9, p. 333
564 Freudian defense mechanisms in Ch. 14, p. 499
565 Self-serving bias in Ch. 15, p. 514
568 Classical conditioning in Ch. 6, p. 189
570 Second signal conditioning of words in Ch. 6, p. 200

CHAPTER 17

577 Normal curve in Ch. 2 p. 53
579 Psychotherapy using drugs in Ch. 18 p. 630
579 Environmental complexity and brain organization in Ch. 4, p. 128
581 Insane asylums in Ch. 18, p. 611
581 Freud, and neurosis in Ch. 14, p. 496
585 Observational learning, and conditioned fear response in Ch. 6, p. 215
585 Prepared learning; contextual cues in Ch. 6, p. 218
585 Stress, stressors, and anxiety in Ch. 16, p. 559
589 Psychosomatic disorders in Ch. 16, p. 558
589 Pain, phantom limb in Ch. 8, p. 265
590 Freud's "glove anesthesia" in Ch. 14, p. 496
590 Blindsight in Ch. 7, p. 283
591 Autobiographical memory in Ch. 10, p. 366
592 Retrograde amnesia in Ch. 10, p. 374
593 False memories in Ch. 10, p. 345
595 Neurotransmitter serotonin in Ch. 4, p. 143 and Ch. 9, p. 337
595 Suicide as leading cause of death in Ch. 16, p. 552
596 Hedonism and the law of effect in Ch. 6, p. 206
597 Intelligence, creativity, and lateral thinking in Ch. 13, p. 464
600 Dopamine in Ch. 4, p. 143
600 Diasthesis-stress model in Ch. 16, p. 563
601 Passive and active environments in Ch. 13, p. 469

CHAPTER 18

613 Sigmund Freud in Ch. 14, p. 496
614 Defense mechanisms in Ch. 14, p. 499
615 Carl Jung, Erik Erikson, Alfred Adler in Ch. 14, p. 504
616 Conditioning and learning in Ch. 6, p. 211
616 Progressive relaxation in Ch. 9, p. 329
616 B. F. Skinner's operant condition and behavior control in Ch. 6, p. 212
618 Conditioning taste aversions in Ch. 6, p. 200
620 Progressive relaxation and hypnosis in Ch. 9, p. 329
622 Writing in a diary in Ch. 16, p. 571
623 Carl Rogers and humanistic psychology in Ch. 14, p. 506
625 Negative reinforcement in Ch. 6, p. 214
629 Trephining in Ch. 1, p. 15
629 Split-brain preparation in Ch. 4, p. 132
630 Electrical stimulation of the brain (ESB) in Ch. 2, p. 33
630 Brain seizures in Ch. 4, p. 133
630 Effects of drugs on consciousness in Table 9.1 in Ch. 9, p. 334
630 Neurogenesis in Ch. 4, p. 129
630 Neurotransmitters and drugs bind to receptor sites of neurons in Ch. 4, p. 144
632 List of neurotransmitters in Table 4.3 in Ch. 4, p. 143
632 Re-uptake, deactivation of neurotransmitters at synapse in Fig 4.25 in Ch. 4, p. 144
632 Listing of psychologically active drugs in Table 9.1 in Ch. 9, p. 334

INTEGRATED COVERAGE OF EVOLUTIONARY PSYCHOLOGY

Human genes common with non-human genes, p. 3
Genetic similarities of all humans, p. 3
Role of environment in gene expression, p. 4
Adaptation through evolutionary processes (distal, or evolutionary adaptation), p. 4
Adaptation to environment over a lifetime (proximal adaptation), p. 4
Evolutionary perspective in psychology, Table 1, p. 8
Stealing infants following death of infant, p. 9
Darwin's theory of evolution, as first comparative psychologist, p. 17
Curiosity as evolved adaptation, p. 34
Evolution answers "why" questions, p. 40
Eating, drinking, sleeping, avoiding pain, seeking pleasure as adaptive behaviors, p. 41
ESB effects and maladaptation, p. 47
Animals adapted to environment, p. 68
Evolution and extinction of species, p. 70
Humans' genetic closeness to other apes, pp. 79–81
Adaptation through evolutionary processes (distal, or evolutionary adaptation), pp. 68, 70
Adaptation to environment over a lifetime (proximal adaptation), p. 70
Continuity of species, pp. 71, 79
Physical adaptation and behavioral adaptation, p. 72
Fitness, p. 72
Adaptation to ecological niche, p. 73
Lamarkian evolution, p. 73
Genetics and heredity, pp. 73, 75, 78, 80-82
Mass extinction, p. 74
DNA, p. 77
Genotypes and phenotypes, p. 77
Genes influencing behavior, p. 83
Genes meet environment, p. 84
Phylogenetic history, p. 85
Species-specific behavior, pp. 85, 91
Zoomorphism, p. 92
Comparative psychology, p. 92
Sociobiology, p. 95
Evolutionary Psychology, p. 96
Kin selection, p. 97
Inclusive fitness, p. 97
Frontal lobes role in adaptation to changing environment, pp. 105–106,
Learning as adaptation to environment, p. 107
Language areas of brain as adaptation, p. 107
Adaptive behavior accomplished by adapted brains, p. 107
Adaptive nature of reticular formation, pp. 111–112, 122
Sensing movement, and adaptiveness, pp. 118–119
Adaptiveness of information processing, pp. 118–119
Adaptiveness of fingers, thumbs, and tongues, p. 124
Evolutionary bases of motivation and emotion, pp. 150–151
Homeostasis as adaptation, pp. 152–153
Salt- and water-seeking behavior as adaptive, pp. 154–155
Eating disorders as maladaptive, p. 150,
Food-selection and adaptation, p. 158
Nutritional wisdom as adaptation, pp. 158–159
Neophobia as adaptive eating strategy, p. 158
Sensory-specific satiety as adaptive eating strategy, p. 160
Feeding jags as adaptive eating strategy, p. 160
Adaptive food preparation, pp. 160–161
Adaptiveness of mixing protein sources in meals, p. 161
Hedonism as adaptation, pp. 166–167
Pleasure-seeking as adaptive, pp. 167–168
Biocultural evolution, p. 161
Genetic differences and lactose malabsorption, p. 162
Adaptiveness of facial expressions of emotion, pp. 172–175
Adaptiveness of emotional arousal, p. 175
Entire chapter 6, pp. 184–225
Senses as evolved adaptations promoting survival, pp. 228–231
Why we see, hear, taste, smell, and experience touch, warmth, cold, and pain, pp. 229–231
Receptors as evolved adaptations promoting fitness, pp. 229, 237, 257
Evolution of non-seeing functions of eye, p. 241
Perception of form, color, movement, and visual acuity as adaptations promoting fitness, p. 246
Chemical senses locate foods, mates; avoid prey, p. 257
Reflexive gagging as adaptation to prevent poisoning, p. 259
Adaptive function of skin senses, p. 263
Adaptiveness of sensory systems, p. 270
Pheromones, sexual behavior, and fitness, pp. 295–298
Adaptiveness of disgust responses, p. 298
Reflexes as adaptations, p. 299
Adaptive significance of touching and being touched, pp. 300–301
Consciousness as evolved adaptation, pp. 308–309
Humans' and other animals' consciousness compared, p. 308
Circadian rhythms as adaptations to light-dark cycle, pp. 310–311
Evolution of endogenous clock, p. 311
Evolutionary origins of deep sleep, pp. 319–320
Maladaptiveness of taking consciousness-altering drugs, p. 333
Evolution of opiate receptors, pp. 337–338
Memory, adaptive significance of, pp. 344–345
Evolution of multiple memory systems, pp. 345–346
Maladaptive memories, p. 345
Memory for memes, p. 345
Morning sickness as adaptation promoting fitness, p. 383
Pica as an adaptation, p. 386
Adaptiveness of neonates taste and smell preferences, pp. 387–388
Neonate prefers mother's smell, p. 388
Attachment as adaptive process, pp. 380, 404–406
Language as an evolved adaptation promoting fitness, p. 414
Why language evolved, pp. 415–416
Three stages of cognitive evolution: Prelanguage, mimesis, and voluntary retrievability, p. 415
Animal communication, p. 421
Male bird song and fitness, p. 421
Vocalizations of vervet monkeys, p. 421
Crying as an adaptation, pp. 426–427
Thinking, problem solving as adaptations, p. 433
Evolution of intelligence, pp. 450, 451
Intelligence as adaptation to environment, pp. 450, 451, 481
Intelligence as genetically determined, pp. 466–467, 477
High correlation of *g* in identical twin studies, p. 467
Personality as adaptive characteristic of humans, p. 486
Adaptive value of perceiving individual differences, p. 486
Heritability of Big 5 personality factors, pp. 491–492
Genes and environment determine personality, p. 495
Adaptive value of defense mechanisms, pp. 499–500
Freud and biological determinism, p. 503
Adaptive value of romantic love, pp. 511–512
Adaptive social interactions, p. 512
Following orders as adaptation, pp. 522, 526
Child's play as adaptive preparation for adult behaviors, pp. 526–527
Physical attraction as an adaptation promoting fitness. pp. 529–530
Symmetrical faces as adaptation promoting fitness, pp. 531–532
Deception in dating as adaptation promoting fitness, p. 531
Territorial signaling as adaptation, pp. 537–538
In-group bias as adaptation promoting fitness, pp. 535–536
Friendship, love, and kinship as adaptations promoting fitness, p. 536
Evolution of health behaviors, p. 544
Pain, fever as adaptive responses promoting fitness, p. 550
Natural selection of pathogens, p. 550
Overeating as adaptive during course of evolution, p. 556
Genetic basis for obesity, pp. 555–556
Diseases develop through coevolution with hosts, pp. 550–551
Adaptation to stress; the GAS, p. 560
Coping responses as adaptations, p. 564
Abnormal behavior as maladaptive, pp. 576, 577, 582
Anxiety disorders as exaggerated adaptations, p. 584
Phobias as evolutionarily prepared responses, p. 585
Hypochondriasis as adaptive disorder, p. 589
Mood disorders as adaptive, p. 596
Mental illness linked to creativity, p. 596
Talk therapy as adaptive intervention to effect behavioral change, p. 621
Adaptiveness of positive, self-fulfilling processes, p. 622
Use of drugs as adaptive response to pain, stress, p. 630
Drug treatment as adaptive intervention to effect behavioral change, p. 630

INTEGRATED COVERAGE OF BRAIN AND BEHAVIOR

Brain-behavior perspective, Table 1, p. 8
Olds experiment, p. 33
Brain area in rat underlying pleasure (pleasure center), p. 44
Hypothalamic areas involved in eating and drinking, p. 44
Reticular formation in rat, p. 44
Brain lesions via electrical stimulation, p. 46
Evolution of human brain, p. 68
Biochemical changes in the brain, p. 73
Brain comparisons with ancestors, p. 81
Genetically coded brain structures, p. 81
Adaptiveness of brain functioning, p. 94
Entire chapter, pp. 105–147
Role of hypothalamus in motivation, pp. 151–155
Hypothalamic control of neuroendocrine system, p. 151
Pleasure-producing areas of brain, pp. 166–168
Hypothalamic control of thirst, pp. 154–155
Role of lateral and ventromedial areas of hypothalamus in eating and drinking, p. 162
Role of subcortical and cortical areas in emotion, pp. 176–178
Amygdala and sensing of emotion, p. 177
Psychosurgery, p. 178
Brain lateralization of emotion, pp. 178–179
Brain control of smiling, pp. 177–178
Brain's bases for learning, p. 186
Brain bases for association of stimuli, p. 190
Brain basis for reflexes, pp. 190–191
Rapidity of learning, and fast conducting nerves, p. 190
Evolutionarily-prepared brains for certain types of learning, pp. 218–220
Sensory homunculus on cerebral cortex, p. 234
Brain bases for seeing, hearing, tasting, smelling, touching, and sending pain, p. 235
Retinal neurons as peripheral extension of brain, pp. 238–239
Visual nerve pathways, pp. 239–240
Lateral geniculate nucleus (LGN) and striate cortex subserving vision, p. 239
Superior colliculus as non-conscious visual pathway p. 241
Neurons in inner ear, pp. 250–251
Brainstem nuclei, medial geniculate nucleus, and temporal lobe serving auditory functioning, p. 256
Olfactory bulb and vomeral nasal organ subserves smell, p. 261
Periaquaductal gray subserving pain, p. 265
Brain bases for feature detection, p. 275
Brain bases for blindsight, for subliminal perception, pp. 271–275
Split-brain perception of visual stimuli, p. 283
Role of striate cortex in seeing, pp. 283–285
Role of extrastriate cortex in perception of color, and movements, pp. 285–286
Role of temporal lobe in visual agnosias, pp. 286–287
Role of cortical columns in perception of symmetry, p. 292
Role of Wernicke's area in perception of speech sounds, p. 294
Brain lateralization and the perception of music, p. 294
Consciousness as emergent property of large brains, p. 307
Mirror neurons and a theory of mind, p. 308
Seasonal affective disorder and brain serotonin, p. 317
Brain activity and sleep cycles, pp. 320–322
Brain bases for dreaming, pp. 321–322
Consolidation of memory in hippocampus during sleep, pp. 323–324
Activation-synthesis hypothesis of dreaming, p. 325
Brain bases for hypnosis, p. 330
Brain bases for drug effects, pp. 333–334
Role of amygdala in short-term memory, p. 374
Memory loss in Alzheimers, and brain changes, p. 375
Brain development, p. 381
Brain pruning during development, p. 382
Brain development influenced by environment, p. 382
Brain affected by teratogens, p. 382
Innate organization of neonate brain prefers viewing human faces, p. 89
Brain size, organization, and language, p. 415
Brain organization, handedness, and language, pp. 416–417
Mirror neurons in monkey brains, p. 416
Mosaic organization of brain, p. 416
Planum temporale supports communication in chimps and humans, p. 417
Lateralization of brain; Broca's area, Wernicke's area, pp. 417–418
Arcuate fasciculus, angular gyrus and language, pp. 417–418
Brain damage and aphasias, pp. 418–419
Brain areas supporting bird song, p. 421
Brain areas underlie a language acquisition device, p. 431
Brain size and intelligence, pp. 451, 472
Brain damage and intelligence, p. 465
Environment, brain, & intelligence, pp. 451, 471–472
Speed of conductance of neurons and *g*, pp. 472–473
Organizational effects of hormones on sexual development, pp. 527–528
Early gender-specific environments shape brains differently, p. 538
Role of testosterone in aggression, p. 538
Brain's involvement in psychoneuroimmunology, pp. 566–567
Touching affects brain development, p. 554
Brain cell death, and stroke, p. 554
Hypothalamic control of set point in obesity, p. 556
Medical (brain) model of mental disorders, pp. 580–581
Organic (brain) mental disorders, p. 581
Shrinkage of lobes of brain and general paresis, p. 582
Thalamic shrinkage and schizophrenia, p. 600
Dopamine hypothesis of schizophrenia, p. 600
Psychosurgery as treatment for schizophrenia, p. 629
Brain lesioning to treat depression and anxiety, p. 629
ECT (electroconvulsive therapy) as treatment for depression, pp. 629–630
Neurogenesis following ECT, possible role in benefits of treatment, p. 630
Drug therapy and effects on brain neurotransmitters, pp. 630–631

INTEGRATED COVERAGE OF GENDER-RELATED ISSUES

Individual differences perspective, Table 1, p. 8
Gender differences in heart disease, p. 35
Gender differences in performance on math test, p. 54
Gender similarities in attitudes on using animals in research, p. 62
Gender differences in birdsong, p. 94
Gender differences in reproductive strategies, pp. 97–98
Gender differences in jealousy, pp. 97–98
Gender differences in sexual behavior, pp. 98–101
Gender differences in mating patterns, pp. 100–101
Gender differences in brain size, p. 113
Male-female differences in neuroendocrine system, pp. 151–152
Secondary sex characteristics, p. 152
Gender differences in onset of presbycusis, p. 254
Role of pheromones in reproductive behavior, p. 259
Gender differences in pain perception, p. 266
Role of pheromones in regulating menstrual cycle, pp. 296–297
Gender differences in production and sensitivity to pheromones, pp. 297–298
Female smells influence fetal development, p. 295
Role of pheromones in mate selection, pp. 297–298
Gender similarities in napping, p. 316
Menstrual cycles and light conditions, p. 317
Females concealed ovulators, p. 317
Gender differences in dream content, p. 326
Gender differences in sexual fantasies, p. 327
Gender differences in daydreaming, p. 327
Recognition of gender in unshadowed ear, pp. 349–350
Morning sickness as adaptation promoting fitness, p. 383
Neonates prefer smell of lactating females, p. 388
Neonates prefer viewing mother's face, p. 389
Gender/age differences in the ability to recall words, p. 399
Strict gender roles in neonatal care, p. 404
Gender differences in the use of language, pp. 415, 420

Gender differences in brain organization of songbirds, p. 421
Galton's views on female intelligence, p. 451
Male mortality and intelligence, p. 479
Dream interpretation, and gender, p. 498
Gender differences in Freud's theories, p. 500
Oedipal and Electra complexes, pp. 502–503
Freud's denigration of women, p. 503
Gender as a Jungian archetype, p. 504
Gender effects on reception of message, p. 517
Determinants of gender identity, p. 526
Determinants of gender roles, pp. 526–527
Gender and sexual orientation, p. 526
Boys "play-fighting" and girls "parenting", pp. 526–527
Gender typing of adjectives, p. 527
Gender modeling from same-sex parents, p. 529
Gender differences in homosexual behavior, p. 529
Gender differences in attraction, pp. 530–531
Gender differences in sexual agendas, pp. 530–531
Gender difference in same-sex friendships, p. 532
Stereotypes based on gender, p. 537
Genetics and physiology of gender differences, pp. 538–539
Pseudopregnancy, pp. 543–544, 558–559
Gender differences in effects of social isolation on mortality, p. 553
Yin & Yang in Chinese medicine, p. 545
Gender differences in hardy personalities, p. 564
Sexual and gender disorders, Table 17.1, p. 583
Prevalence of panic disorder in females, p. 587
Gender differences in occurrence of dissociative identity disorder, p. 587
Gender differences in occurrence of depression, p. 595
Gender differences in suicide attempts, successful suicides, and p. 595
Gender differences in occurrence of antisocial personality disorder, p. 604

INTEGRATED COVERAGE OF CULTURAL FACTORS

Sociocultural perspective, Table 1, p. 8
Science as a culturally-defined method of acquiring knowledge, p. 34
Cultural differences in gender roles, p. 100
Cross-cultural domestication of animals, pp. 72, 86
Sexual roles differ across culture, p. 100
Sexual behavior differs across culture, p. 100
Individual differences in brain functioning compared to differences due to culture, p. 109
Sociocultural differences in motivation, p. 151
Lack of cross-cultural differences in primary motivation, p. 154
Cross-cultural differences in secondary motivation, pp. 156, 168–170
Sociocultural differences in foods/meals, pp. 160–162
Biocultural evolution of food selection and preparation, pp. 160–161
Cultural differences in cuisines and food memes, p. 161
Lack of cross-cultural differences in facial expressions of emotion, pp. 174, 176
Culture affects what is learned, pp. 185–186, 188
Tasmanian culture compared, pp. 185–186
Culture as environmental differences, p. 187
Memes - cultural transmission of information, pp. 187–188
Culture as primary mode of adaptation, p. 188
Native American culture, p. 204
Little Tree learning to handfish, p. 204
Cultural determinants and control of reinforcers, p. 216
Smells of cultures, pp. 227–228
Cultural determinants of flavor preferences, p. 258
Role of culture in perception of pain, p. 266
Culture guides top-down processes in perception, p. 271
Culture defines appropriate foods, tastes, smells, p. 295
Culture helps determine smell's influence on behavior, pp. 298–299
Culture determines what sounds are heard in language and music, pp. 270, 301
Cultural differences in use of stimulants, p. 335
Cultural differences in use of cocaine, p. 336
Cultural differences in drug use, pp. 339–340
Cognitive delays in agrarian cultures, p. 393
Cultural similarities in responses to neonates, p. 404
Cultural differences in the Strange Situation test, pp. 406–407
Cultural differences in infant expression of emotional behavior, p. 407
Cultural differences in socialization of children, pp. 407–408
Individualism vs. collectivism, p. 408
Cross-cultural similarity in expression of grief, p. 409
Cross cultural similarity, differences in language, and p. 414
Role of culture in training language skills, pp. 414, 425
Cultural differences in reinforcing/punishing infant vocalizations, p. 427
Universal grammar: cross-cultural similarities in generating grammar, pp. 430–431
Sapir-Whorf hypothesis: culture determines meaning of language, and concepts, p. 441
Role of culture in Galton's theory of intelligence, pp. 451–452
Creativity, intelligence enriches culture, p. 464
Role of culture in defining and expressing intelligence, pp. 463–464, 467
Cross cultural Flynn Effect, pp. 471–472
Cultural differences in the distribution of g, pp. 476–478
Cross-cultural applicability of Big 5 personality factors, p. 492
Social learning of personality; role of culture, p. 495
Viennese culture, and sexual repression, p. 503
Jung's collective unconscious; evidence of cross-cultural similarity, p. 504
Prejudice and stereotype; role of culture, p. 512,
Group conformity, differences in Western and non-Western cultures, p. 524
Social loafing and collectivist cultures, p. 525
Role of culture in determining gender identity, gender roles, pp. 526–527
In-group bias, and culture, pp. 535–537
Cultural differences in midwifery, p. 544
Cultural differences in conceptions of health, Table 16.1, pp. 544–546
Cultural differences in medicine, pp. 546–547
Cross-cultural use of alcohol as stress reducer, p. 564
Cross-cultural similarities in the placebo effect, p. 570
Abnormal behavior defined/categorized differently in different cultures, p. 577
DSM-IV applies to categorization of mental disorders in Western cultures, pp. 577, 582
Conversion disorders are culturally dependent, p. 590
Depression occurs cross-culturally, p. 594
Schizophrenia is interpreted differently in different cultures, p. 602
Schizophrenia treated differently in different cultures, p. 610
Cultural comparisons in the use of psychoactive drugs, Table 18.1, p. 631

Preface

A question frequently asked of authors of new introductory psychology texts is "Why another one?" "Why is this one different?"

About 30 years ago, I began reviewing introductory psychology manuscripts that were under development for various textbook publishers. Due to my teaching and research interests, I read mostly chapters on the biological bases of behavior, learning, and perception. As I matured, becoming a better teacher, publishing research, and writing and editing books, I became less satisfied with the introductory textbooks I was using. The field of psychology fascinated me because of its dynamic, interdisciplinary nature, but textbooks, on the whole, did not stress the interdisciplinary aspect, nor did they interrelate the concepts and perspectives they presented. Instead, they offered a cursory overview of seemingly separate topics.

Today, the base of knowledge in psychology is increasing geometrically with the thousands of journal articles published each year. Obviously, introductory students cannot begin to assimilate all this information. It is the author's challenge to select, interpret, and integrate the most important findings. *Psychology* is my attempt to interpret (and reinterpret), to integrate (and reintegrate) biological, behavioral, cognitive, and sociocultural knowledge into the story that *is* mainstream psychology.

As anyone can attest who attempts to fathom the implications for psychology of the human genome project, cross-disciplinary integration is not for the weak of heart. Darwin's theory of evolution has been with us for over 140 years, yet the science of applying his theory to the human mind and behavior remains in its infancy. The "cognitive revolution" is 50 years old, yet no one claims to understand all the nuances of memory, let alone what it means to be conscious. In this book I have attempted to integrate a wealth of information in a way that is meaningful to me, and I hope to others. My aim has been to lay a foundation on which future teachers and researchers in psychology can build.

ADAPTIVE THEME

In this book, an adaptive/evolutionary thread weaves together 18 chapters in 4 sections devoted to the biological/behavioral, perceptual/cognitive, developmental/individual differences, and social/cultural perspectives. The theme of the adaptive nature of behavior has both historical precedence (it is found in William James's classic text, *Principles of Psychology*, published in 1890) and currency among many of today's psychologists. To strengthen the theme, each chapter in this text opens with an attention-grabbing vignette that touches on adaptation. These brief stories are designed to attract readers, advance their understanding of adaptation, and introduce the subject at hand.

LINKS AND HIGHER-LEVEL LEARNING

Throughout the book, I have provided **LINKS** to aid students in integrating what they know with what they are learning, and to aid professors in making connections among related findings. **LINKS** are constant reminders that in psychology, simple answers are usually wrong. If not wrong, they are seldom the best answers, which are always more complicated and more interesting. **LINKS** allow students to compare the different levels of scientific analysis that are characteristic of the discipline.

For example, what attracts one person to another? Attraction has been studied in terms of physical beauty (Chapter 15, Social Psychology); in terms of attachment and an innate preference to gaze at faces (Chapter 11, Human Development); in terms of pheromones and feature detectors (Chapter 8, Perception); in terms of the compatibility of immune systems (Chapter 8, Perception); and in evolutionary terms, as an adaptation that promotes fitness (Chapter 15, Social Psychology). **LINKS** such as the ones shown here stress these connections. Knowing firsthand that there is no simple answer to the question of what attracts one person to another, students should appreciate these links. They expand the conversation and move students to a higher level of learning by promoting the analysis and synthesis of information.

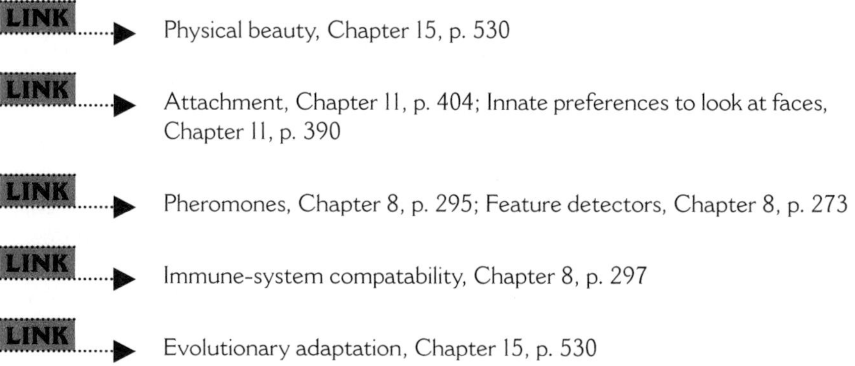

LINK
Physical beauty, Chapter 15, p. 530
LINK
Attachment, Chapter 11, p. 404; Innate preferences to look at faces, Chapter 11, p. 390
LINK
Pheromones, Chapter 8, p. 295; Feature detectors, Chapter 8, p. 273
LINK
Immune-system compatability, Chapter 8, p. 297
LINK
Evolutionary adaptation, Chapter 15, p. 530

FOR FURTHER THOUGHT

To challenge students to think more critically, I have inserted thought-provoking questions at the end of each section, under the heading For Further Thought. These questions raise thorny issues in psychology and ask students to apply the psychological data, concepts, and ideas they have learned to questions about human behavior. They are not easy questions, nor do they have just one correct answer; in fact, many can have myriad answers, depending on which factors students choose to consider. For instance, a relatively simple question from Chapter 5 (Motivation and Emotion) asks students to think about how nature and nurture interact:

> *Why do you think some people have a higher need for achievement than others?*

A more complex question from the same chapter reads:

> *In the words of a Tom Waits song, "I'd rather have a bottle in front of me than a frontal lobotomy." Such sentiment raises complex ethical issues: To what extent should inherited brain chemistry be altered to meet society's demands? What is the difference between altering emotions through the use of drugs or altering them by surgical or genetic means?*

The theme of adaptation can be expressed in a distal sense (in terms of evolution) or a proximal sense (in terms of immediate adjustment to a challenging environment). Two For Further Thought questions ask students to consider the implications of an evolved human brain, and to respond to the fact that not all people living in the United States "believe" in evolution:

Assume that the goal of psychology is a complete understanding of the human mind and behavior. What are the implications of the fact that our primate brains and behaviors have been nonhuman for a much longer period than they have been human?

Darwin asserted that humans are merely animals who evolved by natural processes. Some people find that assertion to be demeaning and contrary to their religious beliefs. What do you think?

For Further Thought questions can also be found on the text-specific Web site. This feature encourages students to go one step further in their attempt to explore the question at hand. For Further Thought questions can be used as out-of-class writing assignments, as in-class assignments for small-group discussions and problem solving, or as topics for short in-class response papers. Students' responses to these questions allow the instructor to assess what they are gaining from the text. These questions may also be useful in writing-in-the-disciplines programs.

INTERIM SUMMARIES

Research on learning and memory suggests that repetition and review are beneficial in learning new material. At the end of each major section, Interim Summaries serve as checkpoints, designed to help students organize and process what they have read before moving on to the next major section.

CONCLUDING THOUGHTS

At the end of each chapter, a short summary pulls the material together and drives home the significance of what students have learned. Connections may be made to material that will be introduced in succeeding chapters.

STUDENT SUPPLEMENTS

The following supplements are available to students who use this book:

Study Guide: Prepared by Mark Hartlaub of Texas A&M University, this student workbook is available to help students master the core concepts in each chapter. Every chapter contains a chapter overview and outline, learning objectives, key terms, labeling exercises, practice multiple-choice and true-false test questions, as well as practice essay questions. **ISBN: 013-094603-6**

Video Classics in Psychology CD-ROM: In an exclusive arrangement with the Pennsylvania State University Video Archives, Prentice Hall has created a special edition CD-ROM featuring over 25 edited video clips of original, classic research studies, including Bystander Apathy, Milgram's Obedience Study, The Bobo Doll, The Stanford Prison Study, and more.

Companion Web Site: www.prenhall.com/barker Prepared by Lawrence Symons of Western Washington University and Lynne Blesz-Vestal. This Web site offers students the ability to immediately interact with the text material. With a comprehensive online study guide, Web links, labeling exercises, a Psychology in the News feature, and access to psychology journals through ContentSelect, students will have the ability to research, learn, and expand their knowledge base of psychology and take their learning to the next level. An enhanced instructor's resource program can be accessed on Prentice Hall's *new* PsychCentral site.

Psychology on the Internet: Evaluating Online Resources: This timely supplement provides an introduction to the Internet and the numerous psychology sites on the World Wide Web. It not only describes e-mail, list servers, browsers, and how to document sources, but also provides information on how to critically evaluate those sources. Furthermore, it includes Web addresses for the most current and useful psychology Web sites. This 96-page supplementary book is free to students when shrink-wrapped to the text. **ISBN: 013-207755-X**

INSTRUCTOR SUPPLEMENTS

The following supplements are available to instructors who adopt this book: (See your Prentice Hall representative for details or log on to www.prenhall.com for further information.)

Course Compass Edition: For instructors who want course management functions, Psychology Course Compass edition is available. Offering a host of functionality, including grade book capability, interactive syllabus, test preparation and preloaded content, professors can save time preparing for class and presentations.

Distance Learning Solutions: For instructors interested in distance learning, Prentice Hall offers courses in Blackboard along with Course Compass.

Instructor's Manual: Prepared by Kerri Goodwin of Kalamazoo College. This supplement provides the following resources for each chapter of the text: summary, review of major concepts, lecture suggestions and topic outlines, suggestions for classroom discussions, additional resource materials, and a detailed content outline for lecture planning.

Powerpoint Presentation Slides: Prepared by Lawrence Symons and Lynne Blesz-Vestal. The charts and graphs of the book along with lecture outlines tied to each chapter are all available in Powerpoint slides. To preview these, go to *www.prenhall.com/barker* and click on instructor resources.

Test Item File: Prepared by Wendy Domjan of University of Texas, Austin. Completely reviewed to ensure the highest level of quality and accuracy, this test item file contains over 2,000 questions in multiple choice, true/false, and essay format, covering factual, conceptual, and applied material from the text.

Prentice Hall Custom Test: A computerized version of the test item file, this program allows full editing of questions and the addition of instructor-generated items. Other special features include random generation, scrambling question order, and test preview before printing. Available in IBM and Macintosh formats.

Films for the Humanities: With a qualifying order, a selection of films in the discipline of psychology are available. Please contact your local representative for a complete listing.

ACKNOWLEDGMENTS

Finding the courage to complete a 4-year writing project can occur only in the context of a supportive environment. A list of my strongest supporters would include my students, family, friends, and colleagues, who for many years have encouraged me to "write it the way I saw it." I am indebted, first, to Beverly, a life mate, to my father, Ronald, and my late mother, Sydona; to my brother, Richard, sister-in-law, Marilyn; to my children, Kristen, Melinda, Kira, and Jane; to my son-in-law, David; and to my two grandchildren, Sarah and Benjamin. The self-absorption of writing is extremely difficult on a family, to whom I apologize. Their support and encouragement were unwavering and always timely.

Several of my students contributed to this project, including Mark Bowman, Laura Hebert, Corinne Lambdin, and Susan Spooner. My mentors included John Flynn, James C. Smith, Herbert H. Reynolds, and the late Bruce Masterton. Colleagues who assisted me included John Batson, Bob Batsell, Elaine Brown, Bill Buskist, Mike Domjan, David Eckerman, John Fox, Jim Diaz-Granados, Tom Hanks, Peter Harzem, Jim Patton, Jim and Betsy Vardaman, Charles A. Weaver, III, and Larry Weiskrantz. My late friend Mike Best would have been proud. I would also like to thank Elliot Coups of Rutgers University for his contribution to the statistical appendix.

The personal, conversational prose I aimed for was achieved only because of the talents of Roberta Lewis and Elizabeth Morgan, working under the direction of Susanna Lesan, Editor in Chief of Development at Prentice Hall. Elizabeth Morgan expertly shaped the final draft, converting my scholarly ideas into meaningful, understandable prose. Any errors of inference, interpretation, or conjecture are mine, however. Jayme Heffler, Acquisitions Editor in Psychology, organized and coordinated the many activities of Prentice Hall staff necessary to bring a project of this magnitude into production. Her unflagging energy and enthusiasm made it possible to complete the project on time. I owe special thanks to Laura Pearson, Vice President and Editorial Director for Psychology and the Social Sciences, Karen Branson, Media Editor, and Kathy Sleys, Production Editor.

Finally, many professors of introductory psychology and experts in particular subfields reviewed one or more drafts of this book, in whole or in part. I am indebted to the following individuals for their perceptive criticism and willingness to share their expertise:

George Bagwell, *Colorado Mountain College*
Jill Becker, *University of Michigan*
Dennis Cogan, *Texas Tech University, Lubbock*
Lucinda DeWitt, *University of Minnesota*
Wendy Domjan, *University of Texas, Austin*
David Eckerman, *University of North Carolina-Chapel Hill*
Robert Emery, *University of Virginia*
Christian End, *Miami University*
Fernanda Ferreira, *Michigan State University*
Diane Gjerde, *Western Washington University*
Arnold Golub, *California State University, Sacramento*
Leonard Hamilton, *Rutgers University, New Brunswick*
Mark Hartlaub, *Texas A & M University, Corpus Christi*
John Hay, *University of Wisconsin, Milwaukee*
Tammy Ivanco, *University of Manitoba*
Robert Jensen, *California State University, Sacramento*
Pamela Keel, *Harvard University*
John Krantz, *Hanover College*
Robert Laforce, Jr., *University of New Brunswick*
David Laplante, *Univrsity of Montreal*
Steve Madigan, *University of Southern California*
Roger Mellgren, *University of Texas, Arlington*
Fathali Moghaddam, *Georgetown University*
Helen Pan, *Grand Valley State University*
Brady Phelps, *South Dakota State University*
Dana Plude, *University of Maryland, College Park*
Hillary Rodman, *Emory University*

Steve Rouse, *Pepperdine University*
Jeffrey Rudski, *Muhlenberg College*
Juan Salinas, *University of Texas, Austin*
Catherine Sanderson, *Amherst College*
H.R. Schiffman, *Rutgers University, New Brunswick*
Matthew Sopko, *Mineral Area College*
Larry Symons, *Western Washington University*
Connie Varnhagen, *Univrsity of Alberta*
A. Martin Wall, *University of Toronto*
Meg Waraczynski, *University of Wisconsin, Whitewater*

I look forward to receiving your feedback. You can email me at Barkele@Auburn.edu

—Lewis Barker

To the Student

Like many college students, I did not declare a major until my junior year. What did I want to do with the rest of my life? Psychology attracted me; I guessed it might hold clues to some of life's great mysteries. Of all the subjects I had studied, psychology had addressed the questions I was most interested in—personal ones, such as Why do I think and feel the way I do? and How can I better understand others? But as I scanned the catalog descriptions of various courses, including biological psychology, developmental psychology, and abnormal psychology, I became confused. What *was* psychology, I wondered, and why major in it?

In retrospect, the text I used many years ago as a student of introductory psychology could not have answered my questions. Only recently have psychologists begun to interrelate their wide-ranging findings and synthesize them with those of other scientists. Because your first course in psychology can have a significant impact on your future, shaping the way you think about the field, I wrote this text to give you a coherent overview of the discipline and its place in the life sciences. I wanted to introduce you to a vital and fascinating field of study, one in which researchers are breaking new ground almost every day.

To that end, I've developed several themes—threads, if you will—to weave what may seem like unrelated facts into a meaningful story. The overriding theme you'll encounter is one of *adaptation*—adaptation through evolution and adaptation to a challenging environment. But the story is even broader than that, for psychology has become an interdisciplinary science that links biology (for example, how drugs affect the brain) with behavior (why people behave differently while taking drugs) and society (what effect drugs may have on health care). To give another example, intelligence (behavior) can be linked to genes (biology) as well as to culture (society). Both these examples can be understood in terms of adaptation.

I'm sure you realize that having some insight into your past experiences and your personal history helps you to understand your present behavior. Psychology, too, has a history. Because modern psychology is best understood by knowing how the behavioral and biological sciences developed over the past century, I have placed this story within a historical and cultural context.

My adaptive theme and interdisciplinary approach may make this text sound difficult. To make it easy for students to read, understand, and remember, I have tried to write in a down-to-earth style. Reviewers have commented that this text is clear and concise, challenging without being condescending. I'm delighted to share with you, the reader, an intelligent introduction to the field.

LEARNING AIDS

I've said that this text is *interdisciplinary*, connecting ideas across several related disciplines. To highlight this feature I've added **LINKS**, or directional arrows that connect what you're reading with an idea that has already been discussed, or will be developed further in later chapters. For example, a state of consciousness that is described in Chapter 18 might be linked to an earlier discussion of the effect of drugs on consciousness:

LINK Effects of drugs on consciousness, Table 9.1, Chapter 9, p. 334

Using these links will help you in reviewing for exams, because as you'll discover in Chapter 10, the more associations you build with a term or concept, the better you will remember it.

Other features of this text are designed to help you comprehend and remember what you read. Each chapter begins with a brief story or discussion that has an adaptive theme. You will meet some interesting people in these *opening vignettes*—people we'll keep coming back to in an attempt to better understand psychological terms and concepts.

Each chapter is divided into several sections. At the end of each section, you'll find an Interim Summary and questions labeled For Further Thought. Don't be surprised if these discussion questions seem to have no easy answers, or for that matter, no correct answer. Each chapter ends with a Concluding Thoughts section that reviews what you have just read.

HOW TO STUDY FROM THIS TEXT

You can defeat the study aids in this book by misusing them. Reading only the Interim Summaries and Concluding Thoughts in order to pass an exam is like preparing for medical school entrance exams by reading *Medicine for Dummies:* It won't work. A better strategy would be to read the opening vignette, then skim the chapter, looking at the pictures, figures, and section headings to get an idea of what it is about. Why should you take the time to look closely at the figures and photographs? As you'll learn in Chapter 8, humans are primates who can process visual information quickly and effectively. Next, you might want to look at the chapter outline to see what you already know, or think you might know, about the topics covered in the chapter. Finally, read the chapter in its entirety. As you read the chapter, you should pay special attention to the boldfaced key terms, defined in the text and also in the margins. Each time you read and understand a key term concept, it is called a "rehearsal trial." Be sure to read the terms both in the text (trial 1) and in the margins (trial 2). As you will see in both Chapters 6 (Learning and Behavior) and 10 (Memory), you will have an easier time remembering items following several rehearsal trials. Trust me! When you get to the Interim Summaries, these terms will be boldfaced again—a third rehearsal trial. Reviewing before an exam is a fourth trial, and by then the terms and concepts should be familiar to you.

Additional resources to help you learn about psychology include a study guide that contains review material and sample questions; *Video Classics in Psychology,* a CD-ROM containing demonstrations of groundbreaking psychological experiments; and a comprehensive Web site, **www.prenhall.com/barker,** containing an online study guide, Web links, a Psychology in the News feature, and access to psychology journals through ContentSelect.

Welcome to *Psychology,* the fascinating study of human behavior!

—Lewis Barker

About the Author

Lewis Barker received an A.B. in Psychology from Occidental College in Los Angeles and completed an M.A. and Ph.D. in Psychology from Florida State University. His first teaching position was at Baylor University, where he discovered that he loved teaching as much as research. As a professor of Psychology and Neuroscience at Baylor University for 28 years, he has taught thousands of students in over twenty courses and laboratories. Over the years, he has published numerous research articles, authored book chapters, and contributed to edited volumes. He is also the author of *Learning and Behavior,* now in its third edition with Prentice Hall, a textbook in the general area of how humans and other animals learn.

Lewis has been the recipient of teaching awards from Psi Chi (a national honorary organization in psychology) and University teaching awards from both Baylor and FSU for dedication, persistence and effort. Currently the Chair of the Department of Psychology at Auburn University, he continues to teach a variety of courses.

Married with four daughters, Lewis reads, runs, bikes, and writes in his spare time, and travels often to keep in touch with an extended family, including his children and their significant others, and two grandchildren, all living in Texas.

Psychology

1

Understanding Mind and Behavior

Tsing-Fang Chen, B. 1930, Chinese/USA, "Human Achievement". Lucia Gallery, New York City/TF Chen/SuperStock.

Issues and Perspectives In Psychology
The Mind-Body Problem
An Interdisciplinary Understanding of Mind and Behavior
The Major Perspectives in Psychology
The Nature-Nurture Issue
The Place of Determinism
The Role of Common Sense
A Psychological Analysis of Human Behavior
Interim Summary
For Further Thought

The Roots of Psychology
John Locke and the British Associationists
The Nativists
Physiologists of Mind
Charles Darwin's Evolutionary Theory
Interim Summary
For Further Thought

Psychology Becomes a Science
Structuralism: The Elements of Consciousness
Functionalism: The Usefulness of Consciousness
Behaviorism
Other Major Developments in 20th-Century Psychology
Interim Summary
For Further Thought

The Many Faces of Psychology
Occupations with Bachelor's Degrees
Occupations with Master's Degrees
Types of Psychologists
Specialty Areas in Psychology
Professional Organizations in Psychology
Recent Trends in Psychology
Interim Summary
For Further Thought

Concluding Thoughts

In February 2001, a group of scientists gathered to announce the preliminary findings of the human genome project, which the news media had taken to calling "the book of life." When the project began several years earlier, scientists had hoped to document how genes guide human growth and development, programming everything from eye color to brain function, from intelligence to mental illness. As a psychologist, I had always seen the complex psychological processes of emotion, motivation, perceiving, learning, and remembering as the result of both genetic and environmental influences. Thus, the ambitious human genome project had caused me to wonder about my discipline's future. Would the study of psychology become irrelevant if genes turned out to determine everything important about humans?

But the "book of life" raised more questions than it answered, catapulting the study of psychology back to the forefront of the biological and social sciences. Rather than the 100,000 genes that were supposed to microprogram all aspects of a human's physical and mental life, the project showed that humans possess less than 30,000 genes. Surprisingly, most of those genes were not specific to humans; indeed, all but 300 could be found in mice. All humans, scientists found, shared 99.9 percent of their genes. Scientists could not even predict which "race" a person might belong to based solely on genes.

Was it the case, then, that an individual's genes did *not* predict that person's uniqueness? The question is important, because the study of psychology has always focused more on the influence of culture and environment of one's psychological makeup. The scientist who introduced the findings of the human genome project, Craig Venter, answered this question as follows:

> The smaller number of genes supports the notion that we're not hard-wired. We now know that the notion that one gene leads to one protein and perhaps one disease is false. . . . We know now that the environment acting on biological steps may be as important in making us what we are as the genetic code. It's clear that genes can't answer all, or even most, questions about human biology. (Allen, 2001)

Genes will continue to play a role in psychological theories of why humans behave as they do. One theory is that human behavior is adaptive. Our emotions guide our behavior in ways that help us to adapt to the world around us. Perceiving, thinking, learning, and remembering—all are adaptive behaviors.

Throughout this text, the word *adaptive* is used in two very different ways: in terms of current adaptiveness, and in evolutionary terms. Current adaptiveness refers to an individual's adaptive behavior over a lifetime. When someone who is faced with a problem adjusts or modifies his or her behavior to find a better solution or make a better decision, that person's behavior may be considered adaptive. Making poor decisions or being unaware of one's own and others' needs may be considered maladaptive. This use of the term *adaptive* raises the question: Why do people sometimes act maladaptively?

In contrast, an evolved adaptation refers to the way in which animals (including humans) adapt to their environment over many generations, through evolutionary processes. In this sense, animals' genetically determined physical forms and inborn behavioral tendencies, even as modified by the environment, may be considered adaptive. Fish are adapted to school together in water; humans and other mammals are adapted to locate water on land. In this evolutionary sense, maladaptive behavior has more dire consequences: both fish out of water and humans who cannot find water die. Thus, an *evolutionary adaptation* refers to the survival and successful reproduction of a species through inherited tendencies to behave in certain ways. Such inherited tendencies include drinking when thirsty (which bears on survival) and sexual attraction to others (which bears on reproduction).

Though the dual concept of adaptiveness is useful in the study of human behavior, psychology should not be studied solely from an adaptive perspective. This text presents many different ways in which to understand the human mind and behavior. While they are all important—at times, profound—they are not the only ways. Indeed, even broadly construed, the psychological sciences provide only limited means of understanding the human condition. In this respect they are like the biologists' book of life. However, if you are curious about human behavior (and curiosity is adaptive), you should find the study of psychology to be fulfilling and enjoyable.

This chapter will introduce the central issues and perspectives in psychology, as well as preview the content of remaining chapters. We'll begin with a discussion of what psychology is. As we will see, its integration with other disciplines, and the numerous perspectives from which it can be studied, mean that psychology cannot be simply defined. We'll explore what psychologists do, both in research settings and in clinics where patients seek their help. We'll conclude the chapter with a historical overview of the scientists who laid the foundation for our understanding of mind and behavior.

People seek meaning in life through a variety of activities. Science is only one way to understand the human condition.

ISSUES AND PERSPECTIVES IN PSYCHOLOGY

Psychology is the scientific study of mind and behavior. We'll talk about behavior at length in later chapters; here we'll concentrate on mind. The term *psyche* (from the Greek) originally meant soul, spirit, and mind. Its modern meaning is that of mind and consciousness—properties that depend on an intact, functioning brain. (After the brain dies, mind and consciousness are assumed to no longer exist.) Psychologists do not study soul and spirit, because those terms are defined without reference to the physical properties that are the subject of science. But because mind and consciousness depend on the body, they can be studied using the scientific method.

The aspects of mind psychologists study are familiar to us. They include motivation (why we do what we do); learning and memory; visual, auditory, and other forms of perception; personality; abnormal behavior; and social interaction. Because these aspects of mind cannot be measured directly, they are defined in terms of observable behavior. For example, psychologists cannot use a (hypothetical) *psychometer* to measure the strength of someone's personality. They don't use a microscope to examine the learning process, nor do they quantify memories by weighing them. These aspects of mind simply have no physical substance. Rather, they are measured by comparing what people do and how they act with norms and standards provided by the general population.

The Mind-Body Problem

Saying that aspects of mind have no physical substance brings to the fore a question that has preoccupied philosophers from prescientific times: What is the relationship between mind and body? This question has come to be known as the **mind-body problem.** The ancient Greek philosopher Aristotle (384–322 B.C.E.) proposed that the mind and body are distinct entities, a solution known as **dualism.** Centuries later the Frenchman René Descartes (1596–1650) proposed not just that the mind and body were separate entities, but that neither depended on the other for its existence, and that the two interacted in the

psychology The scientific study of mind and behavior.

mind-body problem The question of the relationship between mind and body.

dualism The idea that the mind and body are distinct entities

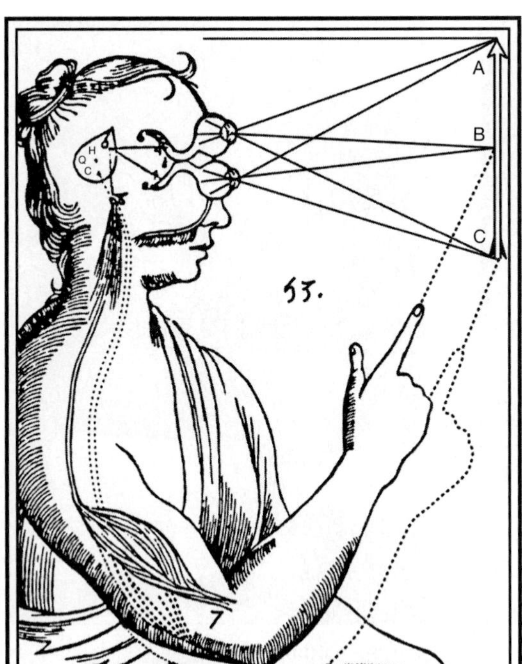

Figure 1.1 Descartes's solution to the mind-body problem. René Descartes thought that the mind and brain were separate and interacted at the pineal gland in the brain.

pineal gland of the brain (see Figure 1.1). This position is now known as *Cartesian dualism.* In Descartes's view, the mind and the soul were equivalent; unlike the body, the mind did not have substance (Descartes, 1637/1960).

In contrast to Descartes's dualism, the position of most modern psychologists (discussed in detail in Chapter 9) is that the mind depends on an intact, properly functioning brain. For reasons that remain unknown, nervous activity in some parts of the brain allows humans to see, and activity in other brain parts allows them to think, love, and feel pain. Brains that have been injured due to accident, traumatic experience, drug abuse, or genetic abnormality may produce distorted consciousness or abnormal states of mind.

Although this current understanding of the mind is based on much research, it hasn't resolved the mind-body problem. Take a second to close, then open your eyes, and marvel at the experience called seeing. Bite into a crisp apple and notice its sound, taste, and smell—each a unique experience unrelated to the apple's appearance. Remember last night's dream, the pain of a bee sting, the exhaustion at the end of a workout. Each of these experiences has an apparent reality and existence—yet opening up the brain reveals only physical matter.

An alternative to dualism, called *monism*, addresses but does not solve the mind-body problem. Monism was proposed in various forms by the ancient Greeks and by the 17th-century philosopher Baruch Spinoza (1632–1677). Spinoza's version of **monism** was that mind and body were different aspects of the same substance, the mind being its internal manifestation and the body its external manifestation (Brennan, 1998). A contemporary version holds that the mind/brain consists only of *neurons* (brain cells). Depending on how these systems of neurons are measured, they can be shown to have chemical, pharmacological, electrical, and psychological properties. But a monist would argue that these are merely different ways of measuring and experiencing the same event, the brain's activity. Needless to say, monism does not address the complexities of distinctive experiences, such as seeing and remembering and hoping. Nor does it acknowledge that such experiences seem qualitatively different from the chemical, pharmacological, and electrical activity that underlies them. For the present, at least, let's concede that the nature of mind remains an enigma, one we will explore further in the next 17 chapters.

An Interdisciplinary Understanding of Mind and Behavior

We have defined psychology as the scientific study of mind and behavior; yet by itself, psychology is not sufficient to give us a full understanding of those subjects. Over the past hundred years, psychologists have learned to exploit the methods and findings of other sciences in order to better understand the human condition. As we will see in the next chapter, psychology is flanked by biology on one side and sociology on the other. Biological sciences that are useful in understanding the human mind and behavior include evolutionary theory, genetics, physiology, anatomy, medicine, and the neurosciences (brain sciences). Sociology and anthropology are useful in understanding broad aspects of human behavior, such as interpersonal relationships, families, culture, and racial and ethnic differences.

Psychology's relationship to other sciences, Chapter 2, p. 36

But isn't psychology a discipline in its own right? The answer is that although psychology is a distinct discipline, over the past century it has also become a composite science through integration with other disciplines. That is why this book is so long, and why its subject matter can be difficult.

monism The idea that mind and body are different aspects of the same substance.

The Major Perspectives in Psychology

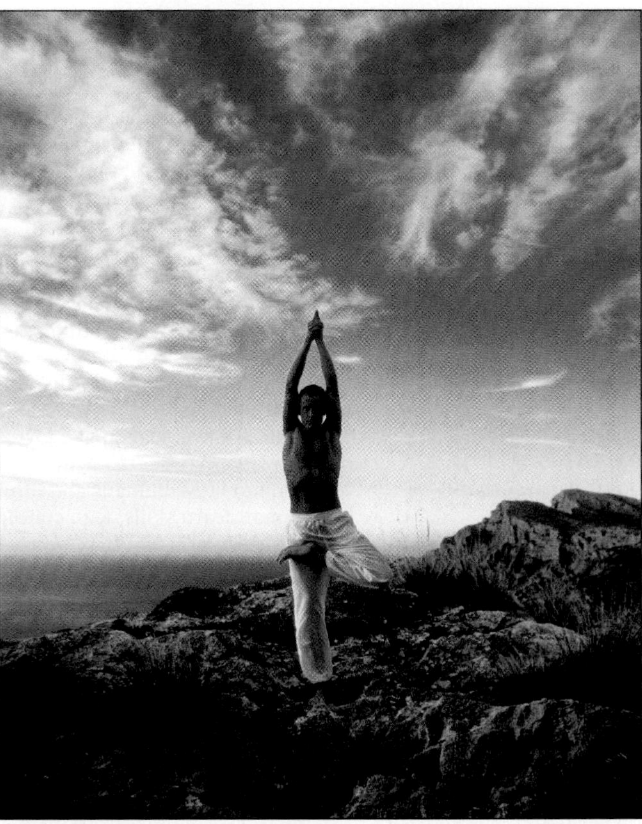

Yoga is the integration of mind and body.

Table 1.1 shows the major perspectives in psychology and the diverse methods used to study the mind, behavior, and brain processes. As it shows, there is no general agreement on what psychologists should study or the methods they should use. Those who subscribe to the biological/behavioral perspective use both humans and nonhuman animals in experiments. Their methods and results will be covered in Chapters 3 through 6, where we will seek answers to some general questions about human nature. There you are invited to wonder about how the environment you were born into has shaped the genetic endowment you inherited at conception.

Those who subscribe to the perceptual/cognitive perspective, discussed in Chapters 7 through 10, are concerned with mental events such as seeing, smelling, dreaming, thinking, remembering and forgetting, and feeling pain or pleasure. (The term *cognitive* refers to thought processes such as reason, memory, and language use.) In these chapters we will begin to explore more personal questions, such as *How did I become the kind of person I am?* and *How do I compare to other humans?* Psychologists who subscribe to the development/individual differences perspective, discussed in Chapters 11 through 14, are interested primarily in physical and cognitive development from conception through adulthood. They study the role of language in thought, as well as individual differences in intelligence, creativity, and personality.

Finally, humans are social animals who live in different cultures. The social/cultural perspective, discussed in Chapters 15 through 18, stresses that a person's behavior is influenced by others. Each of us has a unique identity, due in part to the people we know and the culture into which we were born. Ethnicity, religion, wealth, language, education, even our perceptions of physical and mental health are highly influenced by sociocultural factors. For example, we'll explore how psychologists in the Western culture categorize and treat mental illness.

Taken together, the perspectives in Table 1.1 will give us a rich understanding of an individual's unique behavior. They can also help us to sort out philosophical questions about human nature, such as the relative importance of heredity and learning in an individual's development.

The Nature-Nurture Issue

Nature-nurture issue, Chapter 3, p. 85

The interdisciplinary nature of psychology becomes clear in discussions of an issue with which you are likely to be familiar, the nature-nurture question. This issue is so important, it will come up in just about every chapter of this text. To simplify the argument, the **nature-nurture issue** is concerned with the relative importance of two broad inputs to behavior: a genetic or hereditary one (nature) and a learning or environmental one (nurture). That is, each of us is a unique combination of the influences of both our genes and our mentors—parents, teachers, and so on. What information can we use to see the effects of each of these inputs?

nature-nurture issue The question of the relative effects on behavior of genes (nature) and environment (nurture).

One approach is to use information from other disciplines, such as genetics and animal behavior. For example, we'll see in Chapter 3 that humans have evolved in ways that make them different from other animals. Because of their

Table 1.1 The Many Perspectives of Psychology

Perspective	What Is Studied	How It Is Studied
Biological/Behavioral	(Evolution) Instinctive behaviors of human and nonhuman animals	Laboratory comparisons of genes; naturalistic observation; laboratory experiments on adaptive behavior
	(Behavioral Genetics) Human intelligence and personality; behavior of nonhuman animals	Statistical comparisons of intelligence, personality, emotionality, and perception in related and unrelated people; breeding studies; genetic manipulation
	(Brain-Behavior Relationships) How brain activity is related to observable behavior, such as moving, perceiving, learning, memorizing, thinking, and so forth	Visual and electrical measurement of brain activity; effects of drugs and brain damage; behavioral and neuroscientific measures in humans and nonhuman animals
	(Motivation) Why people and animals do what they do	Physiological and psychological observation and experimentation in humans and nonhuman animals
	(Emotion) Love, fear, anger, joy	Study of facial expressions; self-report measures; effect of cognition on emotional expression
	(Learning) How humans and other animals learn skills, fear, concepts, and so forth	Classical conditioning, operant conditioning experiments; effects of reward and punishment on behavior
Perceptual/Cognitive Perspective	(Sensation and Perception) Seeing, hearing, and the other senses	Measurement of sensory functioning, depth perception, color vision, hearing, pain sensitivity, and so forth
	(Consciousness) Knowing, thinking, remembering, sleeping, and the effects of drugs	Problem-solving tests, electrophysiological monitoring of sleep and dreams; effects of drugs on mood, behavior
	(Memory) Short-term and long-term memory, attention, remembering and forgetting	Studies of list learning, selective attention, mnemonics, and the effects of brain damage
Development/Individual Differences Perspective	(Human Development) Attachment; physical and cognitive development from birth through adulthood	Sensory, perceptual, and physical capabilities; ability to solve problems, to think; strange-situation test
	(Language and Thought) Animal communication, human language, the role of language in thinking, thought processes	Comparison of humans with other animals; studies of brain damage and aphasia; cross-cultural comparison of language acquisition; studies of how people and other animals solve problems
	(Intelligence) Individual differences in intelligence; cultural differences in creativity, intelligence	Intelligence testing; twin studies; testing in the workplace and schools; brain studies; tests of reaction time
	(Personality) Individual differences in personality	Paper-and-pencil tests, factor-analytic techniques; twin studies; psychoanalysis
Social cultural/ Health Perspective	(Social Psychology) Social development from childhood through adulthood; group behavior; attitude formation	Cross-cultural comparison of male and female development; measurement of sexual orientation, attraction, and individual differences in obedience, attitudes
	(Health Psychology) Biological, psychological, and sociocultural determinants of health	Epidemiological studies; physiological monitoring of diet and exercise; measurement of stress; conditioning of the immune system
	(Abnormal Psychology) Disorders of the brain, behavior, and mind	Diagnosis and classification of disorders; twin studies
	(Treatment) Treatment of mental disorders	Comparison of psychotherapy methods; drug studies

distinctive genes, humans raised in human language environments learn to talk, but chimpanzees do not. Humans, not chimpanzees, learn to talk because their genes code for different kinds of brain organization (described in Chapter 4), one of which underlies how language is learned and generated (discussed in Chapter 12).

To take another example, consider a woman who steals another woman's newborn baby from a hospital. We might readily agree that such behavior is abnormal (Chapter 17), and suspect that something has gone dreadfully wrong in this

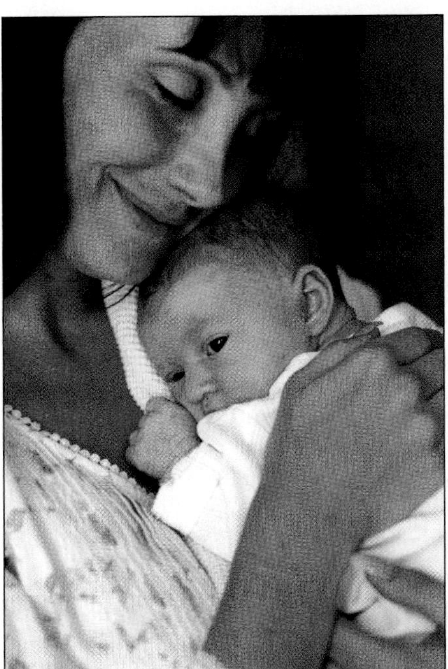

Mothering is not restricted to humans.

woman's life (that is, with her nurturing) to compel her to take such a drastic action. However, a comparative psychologist (one who compares the behavior of humans to that of other animals) might point out that both chimpanzee and orangutan mothers have been observed stealing others' babies when their own babies die (Small, 1999). Such observations force psychologists to consider that at least some human behavior can be profoundly influenced by genetic predisposition. Thus, integrating the findings of genetics, zoology, animal behavior, and the neurosciences helps psychologists to address the relative roles of nature and nurture in behavior.

The Place of Determinism

As we have seen, psychology is a science. Scientific thinking constrains how one thinks, because it is deterministic. *Determinism* is the philosophical position that reasons (causes) can be found for everything that exists and everything that happens. In other words, to a pure scientist, all instances of human behavior are determined. In the example of the woman who stole someone else's child, we can identify at least two general causes (determinants) of the child-stealing behavior: those that occurred millions of years before the woman was born and are now part of her genetic inheritance, and those that can be attributed to her immediate environment, which began at conception.

In general, people trained in the humanities (literature, history, art, the languages, and so forth) tend to be less deterministic in their thinking than people trained in the sciences. (There are many exceptions to this generalization.) Thus, in answering the question *Why is there a universe with me in it?* a psychologist is likely to arrive at somewhat different answers than a poet. The issue of determinism in psychology will be further developed over the next few chapters.

The Role of Common Sense

The mind-body problem, the nature-nurture issue, and the assumption of determinism are of interest to philosophers as well as to psychologists. But these conceptual issues may be unfamiliar to some first-year students of psychology.

What first-year students—indeed, almost all humans—*are* familiar with is human behavior. You've lived it, you've experienced it around you. For convenience, let's refer to the knowledge you bring to your study of psychology as *common sense*.

Defining Common Sense. What is common sense? One definition is that it is the shared knowledge of a culture. For example, on occasion I have heard someone dismiss a scientific finding by saying, "Oh, that's just common sense," meaning that no one would be surprised by the finding. Everyone knows animals can't talk, so why should anyone be surprised that the design of a chimpanzee's brain doesn't allow it to speak? Another meaning of the term *common sense* is that individuals have an inborn capacity to analyze a situation and come to a conclusion that others of like mind would agree with. This kind of thinking underlies our jury system, in which "reasonable" people are expected to come to a common agreement on the facts of a case and the logical and just solution.

Common Sense Is Not Always Common or Sensible. One problem with common sense is that it is often neither common nor sensible. People vary widely in what they have read, and how much they know about the world. They also vary in their intellectual abilities. Not everyone can engage in logical thinking, or as it is referred to in Chapter 11, on human development, in the *formal operations* of thinking. Consider a few examples. First, how does a hearing child of mute parents learn to talk? Common sense may hold that a child learns to talk by hearing others speak. According to logic, then, watching and listening to TV should do the trick—but it doesn't. We'll see in Chapter 12 that for reasons that are not well understood, a child must *interact* with another human being to learn to talk.

Breast-fed babies tend to be healthier than bottle-fed babies.

Similarly, in the 1960s it was common knowledge that bottle-fed babies were healthier than breast-fed babies, because mother always knew how much milk her baby had ingested. Contemporary mothers know better, however; medical research has shown that an infant's overall health is enhanced by breast milk, which contains immune-system factors as well as an optimal mix of fat and protein. Today, research has also shown that cigarette smoking is related to cancer, and that those who smoke bear a greatly increased risk of contracting both cancer and heart disease. But such was not the case 50 years ago, when the commonsense view of smoking was that it was *beneficial* to one's health!

Finally, it is common sense that more often than not, people who get good grades and score high on IQ tests have little common sense. But as we'll see in Chapter 12, there is actually a strong correlation between IQ and other measures of intelligence and success in life: Smarter people tend to do better than others.

Common Sense Is Not Enough. Actually, common sense is affected by a number of human tendencies. First, people tend to *overgeneralize*. After observing one or two socially inept nerds who happen to have high IQs, one is likely to conclude that *all* individuals with a high IQ are socially impaired. Yet all of us know some people with high IQs who are the life of the party. Each such observation violates the commonsense view.

People also tend to *oversimplify* the causes of human behavior. As we'll learn in Chapters 2 and 5, motivation and behavior have multiple causes. An individual's social behavior and intelligence are determined by a host of different factors that interact in complex ways. A third human tendency that clouds common sense, called the *self-serving bias,* is the tendency to overestimate one's own intelligence and general competence (see Chapter 15, on social psychology). Another way of explaining this pitfall is that humans tend to be subjective rather than objective in their assessments, so that each individual's common sense often reflects blatant self-interest. This dynamic may make people feel better, but it doesn't help them to draw valid conclusions.

In sum, common sense can be seen as shared cultural wisdom that can help to define society's general expectations of "the average person." But because of the human tendency to overgeneralize, oversimplify, and come to self-serving conclusions, psychologists can't rely on common sense. Science is not simply a more rigorous form of common sense: Research and logic are necessary to a scientific analysis of behavior.

A Psychological Analysis of Human Behavior

The strength of a psychology textbook is that it provides a systematic, analytical introduction to the diverse enterprise of psychology. This task is daunting: The analysis of human behavior is one of the more ambitious quests ever undertaken in *any* science. Let's consider an example of complex human social behavior that comes from a 4-week trial held in a state court. The particulars, though disguised, occurred as described.

An anthropology professor identified as Professor X had lost his tenure (a contractual employment relationship) at a university where he had taught for many years, after which he was fired. Professor X then sued the university's administration for breach of contract. He also filed a libel suit against a student who had been involved in the incident that led to his firing. She and several other female students had made a complaint claiming that he had behaved inappropriately during a summer field trip to Central America. The students testified that on more than one occasion—while drinking and dancing, escorting them home at night, and sharing sleeping quarters as a group—the professor had made them feel "uncomfortable" by standing too close to them. However, they did not charge him with sexual harassment, for he had not made sexual overtures or touched anyone inappropriately at any time.

In court, Professor X's attorney argued that the university administration had violated the rules for revoking tenure. She also claimed that the president of the university had been motivated by personal animosity toward Professor X, and had used the students' charges as a basis for firing him. The tenure committee, she charged, had also failed to consider (as they were required to) the fact that the professor was a respected and highly published academician who had provoked no prior complaints in more than 20 years of teaching. Furthermore, he had a severe hearing deficit, which forced him to stand close to other people in order to hear them. Finally, the attorney pointed out, by their admission, none of the students felt that they had been sexually harassed, and none wanted the professor to be fired. In fact, the students on the trip had not found his behavior to be unacceptable.

A Jury Begins to Deliberate. Imagine serving on the jury that had to decide Professor X's case. You might begin with questions of motivation (discussed in Chapter 5): What did the professor do and why did he do it? What kind of person is he, and what are the personalities of his accusers (Chapter 14, personality)? If he drank alcohol, was he an alcoholic (Chapters 9, altered consciousness, and 16, health)? If he made female students uncomfortable, did he do so consciously or unconsciously (Chapters 5 and 14, unconscious motivation)? Do men and women differ in their perception of sexual advances (Chapter 15, social psychology)? Did the fact that he was an older man, and

Jury decisions reflect complicated group processes.

that the students who complained were young women, contribute to their perception that his behavior was inappropriate (Chapters 11, human development, and 15, social psychology)? Were the memories of those who testified accurate (Chapter 10, memory)? Had the professor compensated for his profound hearing difficulty (Chapters 7, sensation, and 8, perception) by developing the habit of getting physically close to people—in the process making them feel uncomfortable (Chapter 15, social psychology)? Could either his behavior or that of the students who complained be considered abnormal (Chapter 17)? Why did some students see the same events differently from other students (Chapter 8, perception)?

Psychological Factors in the Jury Process. Psychologists have done formal studies of jurors and the jury process. Because a jury decision is arrived at by a group, it is highly influenced by the social process of conformity (Chapter 15, social psychology). Researchers have found that more intelligent jury members (Chapter 13, intelligence) often exercise leadership by keeping jurors focused on the issues. (On this jury, the only member who was a college graduate was selected to be foreman.) Early in the process of listening to witnesses, however, individual jurors begin to form *schemas* (Chapter 12, thought), or ideas about what might have happened. Personal characteristics such as attractiveness (Chapter 15, social psychology) can bias a juror's perception of a witness's credibility or a defendant's guilt or innocence.

The judge in Professor X's case asked the jury to decide two questions: whether the procedures by which a professor can be dismissed had been violated, and whether one of the professor's students had in fact libeled him. The jury found that the procedures the university used to fire the professor had violated his tenure contract. In a separate judgment they found that the student who complained about his behavior had not libeled him. Both sides claimed victory. As this example suggests, the many issues discussed in the chapters of this book play an important role in the analysis of human behavior.

INTERIM SUMMARY

1. The psychological sciences provide an important way, but not the only way, of understanding the human condition.
2. *Psychology* is the scientific study of mind and behavior.
3. Aspects of mind such as motivation, learning, memory, perception, personality, and intelligence are defined by reference to observable behavior.
4. The ***mind-body problem*** concerns the nature of the relationship between mind and body.
5. ***Dualism*** is the theory that body and mind are separate entities. René Descartes postulated that the body has substance but the mind doesn't, and that the two interact in the brain at the pineal gland. ***Monism*** is the theory that mind and body are different aspects of the same substance.
6. Psychology has become a composite science that integrates findings in the biological sciences, neurosciences, anthropology, and sociology.
7. Psychology can be studied from many perspectives, including the evolutionary, behavioral genetic, brain-behavior, perceptual-cognitive, personality, and sociocultural perspectives.
8. The ***nature-nurture issue*** concerns the way in which genetics and heredity (nature) and the effects of environment (nurture) interact to affect behavior.
9. Contemporary psychology integrates findings from genetics, zoology, animal behavior, and the neurosciences to address the relative roles of nature and nurture as causal determinants of behavior.
10. A commonsense understanding of human behavior facilitates day-to-day social interactions. Common sense can be misleading, however, because of the human tendencies to overgeneralize, oversimplify, and adopt a self-serving bias.
11. The analysis of human social behavior is one of the more complex undertakings in all of science. The chapter titles of this text reflect the major components in any such analysis.

For Further Thought

1. Not all people wonder "What's it all about?" How would you characterize the personalities of those who do and those who do not?
2. Why doesn't the discipline of psychology address the question of the existence of God?
3. Are you a dualist, a monist, or something else?
4. What is the wisdom of having a jury of 12 individuals analyze complex social behavior?
5. Can you think of situations in which an attorney might select jurors with common sense (who will overgeneralize and oversimplify) and other situations in which the same attorney might prefer better educated jurors?

THE ROOTS OF PSYCHOLOGY

Those who study the history of science have identified the precursors of modern science in the writings of mathematicians, astronomers, logicians, and inventors who lived several thousand years ago. These *natural philosophers* tackled problems curious humans had struggled with for centuries; in the process they discovered a variety of "thinking" tools, including mathematics and logic. Among the issues they addressed were the nature of mind and personality, two central questions in modern-day psychology. In this section we will find that people who lived hundreds of years ago had ideas that are still considered modern; they wrestled with meaningful problems that remain unsolved. Students of psychology should

John Locke (1632–1704). *Source:* Prentice-Hall College

have at least a cursory understanding of these, their intellectual forbears, for in the words of the psychologist Robert Watson (1960), "to neglect history does not mean to escape from its influence."

For example, we'll see in our study of personality (in Chapter 14) that the Greek physician Hippocrates, who lived about 2,400 years ago, thought there were four basic personality types: *choleric* (angry, violent), *melancholic* (gloomy), *phlegmatic* (calm, passive), and *sanguine* (cheerful, active). This ancient philosopher's ideas influenced the work of more recent thinkers, such as Spinoza and Descartes.

Eventually philosophers and scientists systematized their ideas, giving rise to what are called schools of psychology. We'll discuss these schools of thought later in this chapter; in this section we will look at the different ways in which they approached psychological processes. In the most general of terms, we can detect two main trunk lines in the history of psychology, a philosophical one and a biological one. In the philosophical trunk line, the debate was often between those who argued about the relative roles of experience and reason in the development of the mind. In the biological trunk line, physiologists began to devise clever experiments with laboratory animals, which complemented their observations of humans with damaged brains. We'll begin by comparing the views of two groups of philosophers, the associationists and the nativists. Then we will see how physiologists conceptualized the mind.

John Locke and the British Associationists

The British philosopher John Locke (1632–1704) may be better remembered for his contribution to constitutional law—his thinking underlies both the Declaration of Independence and the Constitution of the United States—than to psychology. We will encounter Locke's contributions to psychology in the next chapter (on the scientific method), in Chapter 6 (on learning), and in Chapters 7 and 8 (on sensation and perception). In his book *Essay Concerning Human Understanding*, published in 1690, Locke wrote at great length about **empiricism**, which he defined as a method of obtaining knowledge by observation and experimentation—in other words, through sight, hearing, and other perceptual processes. "Nothing is in the intellect that has not been in the senses," Locke asserted. He espoused this method in part because he was enamored of the successes of a contemporary scientist, Sir Isaac Newton. At that time Newton, one of the world's first and most famous experimentalists, was making startling discoveries in physics, including the way in which the eye senses light, one of Locke's interests (Fancher, 1990).

LINK
Development of the infant mind, Chapter 11, p. 383

John Locke's most enduring legacy to psychology was his proposal that infants are born devoid of any knowledge—that at birth, their minds are like a blank slate (*tabula rasa*). Whatever they experience during a lifetime—memories, aptitudes, character—is written on the slate of their minds. For Locke and others, mind was receptive and passive, fed by sensory processes that translated the environment into mental images and ideas.

Locke was the most famous philosopher of the school of British empiricists, also known as associationists. This group included, among others, George Berkeley (1685–1753), David Hume (1711–1776), and David Hartley (1705–1757). They were referred to as associationists because each espoused (in slightly different ways) the philosophy of **associationism**, or the idea that people learn and form complex ideas through the association of simpler elements. For Locke, an idea like the sun was the sum of its associative elements—its color, warmth, size, movement, and so forth. For Hume, people learned by associating events that occurred together in time or were similar to

empiricism A method of obtaining knowledge by observation and experimentation.

associationism The idea that learning, and the formation of complex ideas, is accomplished through the mental association of simpler ideas.

each other. We will see in Chapter 6 that these laws of association formed the basis of contemporary theories of learning and memory. Unlike Isaac Newton, however, none of the associationists ever tested a theory by the empirical methods they espoused. Rather, they were classic armchair philosophers.

The Nativists

The associationists' views can be contrasted with the ideas of two German philosophers, Leibniz and Kant. Both these Europeans espoused **nativism**, the idea that some kinds of perception and forms of thought are innate. Gottfried von Leibniz (1646–1716), the brilliant mathematician who discovered calculus, published a direct rebuttal of Locke's proposals. He amended Locke's assertion that there was *nothing in the intellect that had not previously been in the senses* by adding "except the intellect itself." By this statement Leibniz meant that the mind was not a passive instrument. Rather, through its structure and functions, it actively transformed sensory experiences. Among the mind's innate (inborn, hence *native*) functions he counted an understanding of unity, substance, cause, and reason. Without such native understandings in place, Leibniz reasoned, a person would be aware only of a meaningless succession of sensory impressions.

Immanuel Kant (1724–1804) took a somewhat different approach, separating the "sensible world" (the world of appearances) from the "intelligible world" (the world as seen through one's intellect and reason). In his book *Critique of Pure Reason* (1781), Kant asserted that the human mind had an innate understanding of the dimensions of space and time. Likewise, the ideas of quality, quantity, relationship, and modality were inborn; they constituted what Kant called *a priori* knowledge—knowledge for which no empirical evidence existed, and which could only be attained through pure reason. Because Kant thought these inherent properties of mind would never be subjected to scientific study, he held that psychology could never be a science (Fancher, 1990).

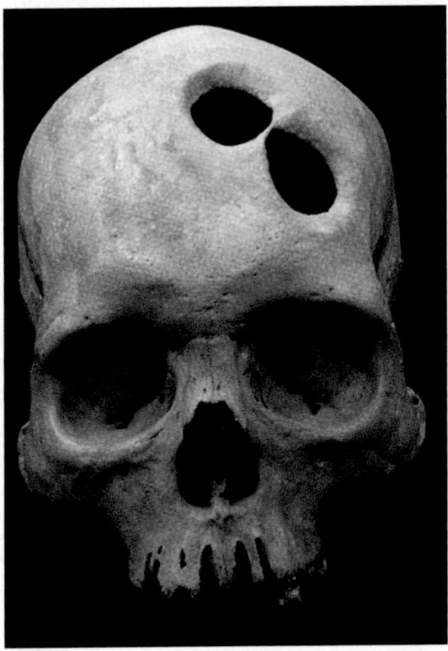

Figure 1.2 Trephination.

We will return to the nativist and empiricist positions in later chapters on perception, development, learning, language, thought, and intelligence. In these discussions we will examine 20th-century theories that suggest that the mind's *a priori* properties have a genetic basis. In this view, the mind actively rather than passively transforms sensory experiences. We'll also see that Locke's empiricism made possible the scientific study of the mind, and that his focus on the environment greatly influenced the scientific understanding of how the human mind is shaped.

Physiologists of the Mind

At about the time that British and German philosophers were writing about the nature of the mind, European scientists were beginning to investigate the physiology of the senses and the brain. Their work, which also built on the foundation laid by the Greek philosophers, represents the second of the two main trunk lines in the history of psychology, the biological one.

People of prehistoric cultures probably learned that the brain was related to the mind and behavior by observing brain-damaged individuals. Indeed, many prehistoric cultures that had no contact with golden-age Greece practiced *trephination*, the act of scraping and sawing through the cranium to the brain's surface (see Figure 1.2). From remote Polynesian islands to Brazilian rain forests, archeologists have unearthed ancient (and current!) human skulls that show evidence of trephining. These primitive surgeries were likely viewed as "treatments" for mental illness; their purpose was probably to release evil spirits. From indications

nativism The idea that some kinds of perception and forms of thinking are innate.

of new bone growth around the cut lines on many of the skulls, medical researchers have surmised that humans could survive these surgeries, performed though they were under nonsterile conditions.

Early Brain Anatomists and Physiologists. The first accurate, complete brain atlas was published in 1664 by John Willis, one of John Locke's teachers at Oxford. Willis differentiated gray matter from white matter, but wasn't sure of their functions (Fancher, 1990). A century or so later, the German physician Francis Gall (1758–1828), one of the first scientists to conduct experiments on animal brains, made great strides in understanding the structure and function of both human and nonhuman brains. Gall formulated some basic notions about the brain: that each part of the brain had a specific function; that animals with larger brains had more interesting mental lives than animals with smaller brains; that the left side of the brain controlled some functions on the right side of the body, and so forth.

LINK
Gray matter and white matter, Chapter 4, p. 119

Gall made a serious mistake, however, in promoting *phrenology*, the idea that the prominence of the bumps and indentations on an individual's skull reflect the size of the brain parts that lie beneath. Over several years Gall observed too few people and mistakenly overgeneralized from the diverse patterns of bumps he saw (see Figure 1.3). We now know that the skull's exterior surface bears little relationship to the brain's anatomy.

Through experimentation, Pierre Flourens (1794–1867) and other scientists of the day discredited phrenology. Flourens was one of the first scientists to observe the behavioral effects of systematically removing different parts of an animal's brain. Gall had proposed that a large structure at the base of the brain, called the cerebellum, was responsible for sexual desire, or "amativeness" (see Figure 1.3). But when Flourens removed successive layers of this structure in animals, he found they became uncoordinated, and eventually lost the ability to walk. He correctly concluded, as we will see in Chapter 4, that the cerebellum controls coordination and patterned movement, but has nothing to do with amativeness.

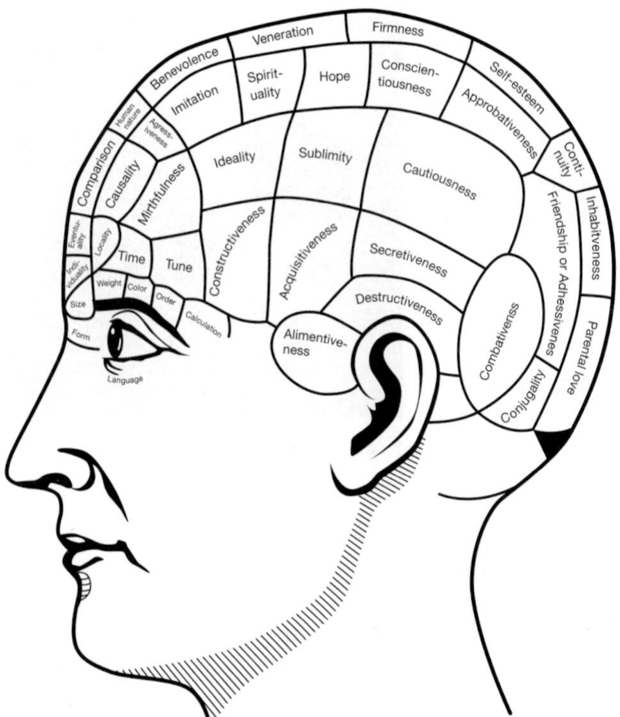

Figure 1.3 Phrenology.

Johannes Muëller and Hermann von Helmholtz. Seldom in the history of science is there a specific time and place where a sea change occurs, when one scientist's experiments herald a new way of thinking about the world. According to Boring (1929), this nexus occurred in physics and physiology during the career of Hermann von Helmholtz (1821–1894). Helmholtz's work can best be appreciated by comparing how he thought about the mind and the brain with the ideas of his teacher, Johannes Muëller (1801–1858). Muëller's research had focused on the anatomy and physiology of nerves. By electrically stimulating different nerves, Muëller had demonstrated that optic nerves produced vision; auditory nerves, hearing; and so forth. Thus, he proposed the *law of specific nerve energy:* that each sensory nerve carried information from one particular sense. Muëller, however, was a *vitalist*, a person who believes that life itself is caused by a nonphysical force. Hence, he considered some life processes, and some questions of physiology, to be beyond scientific analysis.

Helmholtz disagreed. He and other students of Muëller rejected vitalism and proposed in its place the doctrine of *mechanism:* that all physiological processes, including life itself, can be understood by the laws of physics and chemistry. Being a physicist, Helmholtz measured the amount of energy a frog used in a closed environment and found that merely by living the frog consumed energy. This result suggested to him that life could be understood in terms of the physics of energy, an idea that cemented his mechanistic views.

Helmholtz is remembered as the first scientist to imagine that nerve energy could be measured. Both Helmholtz's father (a priest) and his teacher, Muëller, assumed that nerve energy had vital properties, making nerve conduction instantaneous and unmeasurable (Koenigsberger, 1965). Indeed, Helmholtz's father became angry that his son would even *try* to measure the "spirit" in nerves, considering such probing sacrilegious as well as foolish. Nevertheless, Helmholtz invented an electrical device that indirectly measured the electrical conduction properties of nerves in both human and nonhuman subjects. (Helmholtz's other experiments and theories regarding sensory functioning—especially vision—will be discussed in Chapter 7.)

Paul Broca and Carl Wernicke. Meanwhile in Paris, Flourens was experimenting on the brains of laboratory animals, and his fellow countryman Paul Broca (1824–1880) was testing patients with brain injuries. Broca found that damage to certain areas on the left side of the brain were often correlated with difficulties in speaking. In recognition of his research, the part of the brain that is involved in the production of speech is now called *Broca's area.* In Germany, research on other brain-damaged patients led Carl Wernicke (1848–1905) to discover a similar brain-behavior relationship. Unlike Broca's patients, who could not generate language, Wernicke's patients, who had sustained damage to a different part of the left hemisphere, could speak only gibberish. That area, we will see in Chapter 4, is now called *Wernicke's area.*

Broca's area and Wernicke's area, Chapter 12, p. 418

Meanwhile, two other German scientists, Gustav Fritsch (1838–1927) and Eduard Hitzig (1838–1907), decided to observe the effect of low levels of electricity on a dog's brain. They knew from Muëller's pioneering experiments that sensory nerves could be stimulated by electricity. In a makeshift lab, Fritsch and Hitzig exposed an anesthesized dog's brain and applied current to it (a la the Baron von Frankenstein!). They found that electrical stimulation of a vertical strip of brain tissue at the side of the brain caused muscle twitches. These early experiments suggested the highly localized brain function Gall had originally proposed.

Charles Darwin's Evolutionary Theory

Another major branch on the biological trunk line in psychology can be traced to the influential theories of Charles Darwin (1809–1882). Two of Darwin's publications, *The Origin of Species* (1859) and *The Expression of Emotions in Man and Animals* (1872) changed forever the way humans thought about themselves. The first book described the biological plan for all life forms, including humans. The second established Darwin as one of the first comparative psychologists, opening the way for the psychological study of other animals. Darwin's profound influence on modern psychology is detailed in Chapter 3.

Darwin's theories, and the halting approach to the study of brain-behavior relationships in the laboratories of Western Europe, marked a turning point in the history of psychology. During the latter part of the 19th century, other philosophers would become scientists when, in laboratories designed specifically for that purpose, they began to study the human mind.

INTERIM SUMMARY

1. Before there were scientists, *natural philosophers* such as mathematicians, astronomers, logicians, and physicians addressed problems such as the nature of the human mind.
2. The history of psychology has two main trunk lines, one that originates in philosophy and one in biology.
3. For several thousand years philosophers have argued about the relative roles of *experience* and *innate reason* in the mind's development. In modern psychology, these concerns are expressed as the *nature-nurture issue*.
4. John Locke espoused ***empiricism***, the theory that knowledge is best obtained by observation and experimentation; that the newborn mind is a blank slate (*tabula rasa*); that the mind is receptive and passive; and that our ideas are the product of the ***association*** of simpler elements.
5. Gottfried von Leibniz espoused ***nativism***, the idea that some kinds of perceptions and forms of thinking are innate. Immanuel Kant, also a nativist, distinguished between sensory knowledge and *a priori* intellect and reason.
6. Evidence that prehistoric cultures understood that the mind was related to the brain can be inferred from their practice of opening the skull to release evil spirits, called *trephination*.
7. Francis Gall and Pierre Flourens were among the first scientists to conduct experiments on the animal brains, and to conclude that each part of the brain had a specific function. Gall also promoted *phrenology*, the belief that the size of the bumps on a skull are related to brain functions.
8. Johannes Muëller and his student Hermann von Helmholtz were German physiologists who studied the anatomy and physiology of nerves. Muëller was a *vitalist* who proposed the *law of specific nerve energy*; Helmholtz was a *mechanist* who measured the speed of nerve conduction.
9. Paul Broca and Carl Wernicke both found areas of the brain, now named after them, that are related to the production and comprehension of speech.
10. Charles Darwin's evolutionary theory, which outlined the origin of species and the relative place of humans in it, provided another underpinning of modern psychology.

For Further Thought

1. The Greeks proposed that each individual's personality could be characterized as a combination of four factors: *choleric* (angry, violent), *melancholic* (gloomy), *phlegmatic* (calm, passive), and *sanguine* (cheerful, active). Pick someone you know well and try to characterize her or him along these dimensions. If you cannot, what would you add?
2. Some animals can walk soon after birth, but humans take about a year before they can do so. Relate these differences to Locke's idea of a *tabula rasa* and Kant's nativist views.
3. Helmholtz's father put a lightning rod on his church's steeple (Koenigsberger, 1965), yet he objected to his son's research on nerve conduction on religious grounds. Given that religious and scientific thinking are two separate realms, is tension and conflict between them inevitable? Why or why not?

PSYCHOLOGY BECOMES A SCIENCE

We have seen that the science of psychology did not begin abruptly. Many individuals helped to lay the foundation of philosophical speculation about the mind and to provide a rudimentary understanding of brain physiology. By the time the first laboratory designed specifically to study the mind was put into operation, researchers had long been thinking in terms of brain-behavior relationships. Still, the German scientist who opened that laboratory and began the search for the "elements of mind" is remembered as the first psychologist, the first practitioner of the science of the mind.

As an assistant to Helmholtz at the University of Heidelberg, Wilhelm Wundt (1832–1920) knew how to measure the speed of nerve conduction. Could he measure the neurological activity of the brain itself, he wondered? In 1879 Wundt established a laboratory for the study of *experimental psychology* at the University of Leipzig. That act is considered to be the official beginning of the science of psychology, and Wundt the first academic psychologist (Fancher, 1990). Many other researchers traveled to Leipzig to study with Wundt, then returned home to open their own psychological laboratories. Within a couple of decades, psychologists had established more than a hundred laboratories around the world, including dozens in the United States. Wundt's influence on the developing field of psychology, then, was enormous.

Wilhelm Wundt (1832–1920)

Structuralism: The Elements of Consciousness

Fortunately, Wundt's students took psychology in many different directions, because his own attempt to measure the "contents of consciousness" never really succeeded. By relying exclusively on the method of **introspection**—verbally reporting one's conscious experience—Wundt made little progress. For years he and his student Edward Titchener (1867–1927) of Cornell University trained human "observers" to analyze their sensory perceptions, their perception of time, their attention span, and so forth. The idea of using introspection to outline the structure of consciousness in terms of its basic elements, combinations of elements, and connections among elements is now referred to as **structuralism** (Brennan, 1998). Though the attempt failed, it may have served an important function. According to Boring (1927), one of Titchener's many students, structuralism gave other psychologists both a method and a set of concepts with which to disagree. (More will be said about this method in later chapters.)

Wundt's name is linked to structuralism due more to the efforts of the historian Boring than to the nature of his research (Goodwin, 1999). In actuality, Wundt's interests were so wide ranging, they are hard to characterize. For example, he spent 20 years writing a 10-volume book entitled *Volkerpsychologie* (folk psychology). Yet Titchener translated from the German only work that related to his own structuralist interests (Goodwin, 1999). Titchener developed and promoted structuralist methods far beyond what he had learned in Wundt's laboratory.

Besides Titchener, several other students of Wundt began to do psychological research in the United States. One, G. Stanley Hall (1844–1924), returned to start the first psychological research laboratory in the United States at Johns Hopkins University. Others founded labs at Columbia and Princeton universities. Hall also started the first journal of psychology in the United States and joined with 26 other psychologists in founding the American Psychological Association. Four of his students established laboratories at Clark University in Massachusetts, Indiana University, and the Universities of Iowa and Wisconsin. Just one decade after the first psychological laboratory was founded, no fewer than 24 labs were operating in the United States and Canada, including one at Stanford University in California.

introspection The verbal reporting of one's conscious experience.

structuralism The study of consciousness in terms of its basic elements, combinations of those elements, and connections among those elements.

Functionalism: The Usefulness of Consciousness

Structuralism is sometimes referred to as a *school of psychology*, which simply means that a group of individuals conducting research within a common theoretical framework began to think about psychology in the same way. Another major

William James (1842–1910)

school of psychology, one that eventually replaced structuralism, became known as **functionalism.** Functionalists believed that researchers should focus on the usefulness of consciousness (rather than its content) and the utility of behavior. The functionalists' research was richer and broader in content than the structuralists'. For example, some functionalists began to conduct experiments on animal behavior based on Darwin's evolutionary theory.

William James and His Legacy. In large measure, functionalism can be seen as an outgrowth of the thinking of a unique individual, William James (1842–1910). James rescued American psychology from the grim structuralist experiments that were generating, in his estimation, uninteresting results. As he put it in his classic textbook (James, 1890/1950), Wundt's brand of experimental psychology "could hardly have arisen in a country whose natives could be bored."

Unlike Wundt's view, James's understanding of consciousness was a literary one. He wrote of the "stream of consciousness" that a person experiences while sitting quietly in reflection—the mind flitting here and there, back to the past and forward to the future. He wrote books on emotion and the relationship of psychology to religion, in the process inventing a psychology that was more personal, more focused on the individual, than Wundt's. Though James did not collect data himself, he trained many psychologists who did, including one of the first female psychologists, Mary Whiton Calkins (1863–1930).

Calkins' place in the history of psychology is an interesting one. In psychology's earliest days, very few women could be found in laboratories, in Germany or the United States. In the United States, higher education for women was a new concept; most universities would not allow women to take advanced degrees. Smith College and Wellesley College, among the first institutions of higher learning to be dedicated exclusively to women, were not founded until 1875.

After graduating from Smith College, Calkins took a teaching position at Wellesley. There she was offered the opportunity to develop a new course in experimental psychology—*if* she could secure a year's advanced training. Friends put Calkins in touch with William James at Harvard University. After meeting her, James enthusiastically recommended her as a student, but the president of Harvard insisted that women be educated separately from men. James was outraged. This kind of thinking, he wrote to Calkins, was "enough to make dynamiters of you and all women" (Fancher, 1990, p. 264). Under continuing pressure, Harvard's president reluctantly allowed Calkins to study informally with James. Calkins also sought out other psychologists to learn how to set up a psychological laboratory. Within a few years she had passed an unofficial doctoral exam—in James's words, "the most brilliant examination for the Ph.D. that we have had at Harvard" (Fancher, 1990, p. 266). Nevertheless, she was denied the degree.

When Calkins returned to Wellesley, she set up a laboratory and began an academic career that was distinguished by her teaching, original research, and book authorship. In 1905 she was elected the first woman president of the American Psychological Association—still without holding the degree she had earned.

Margaret Floy Washburn (1871–1939) was the first woman to receive a Ph.D. in psychology (1894), under Titchener's direction at Cornell University. Washburn later taught at Vassar College, wrote the highly influential book *The Animal Mind*, and was elected the second woman president of the APA in 1921. Both Calkins and Washburn would likely be gratified by the central position women now occupy in psychology, just a century later (see Figure 1.8 and Table 1.4).

William James is considered to be the most influential of psychology's many founders, in part because he anticipated the many directions psychology would eventually take. His two-volume textbook *Principles of Psychology* contained

functionalism The study of the usefulness of consciousness and the utility and purposefulness of behavior.

Mary Whiton Calkins (1863–1930)

Margaret Floy Washburn (1871–1939)
Source: Archives of the History of American Society—The University of Akron

chapter titles and subject matter that continue to appear in modern textbooks: the functions of the brain, habit, consciousness, attention, association, memory, sensation, perception, instinct, and emotions. James was a pragmatist, meaning that he believed people generally behave in useful and purposeful ways. His views were influenced by Charles Darwin's theory of evolution. Later functionalists would deal with the philosophical issues Darwin raised, including the similarities and differences between the human and animal minds (which are now studied by comparative psychologists) and the extent to which human motivation and social behavior reflect an evolutionary heritage (now studied by evolutionary psychologists—see Table 1.1).

Later Functionalists. One of James's students, James Angell (1869–1949), successfully developed and expanded on functionalism at the University of Chicago. He was joined there by John Dewey (1859–1952) and Harvey Carr (1873–1954). These three influential men all wrote textbooks, and over a period of many years trained a large number of Ph.D. candidates. In turn, their students took positions in departments of psychology in colleges and universities throughout the country.

Toward the end of his career, John Dewey began to apply functionalism to the design of educational systems. As Figure 1.7 (page 27) indicates, this practical application of psychology has influenced the training of large numbers of school and educational psychologists. Harvey Carr became known for integrating laboratory research on animals and humans, particularly in motivation and learning. The influence of "Chicago functionalism" became so great that without fanfare, it replaced structuralism as the defining viewpoint in American psychology.

Ironically, one applied psychologist in the functionalist camp was the student of a structuralist. James McKeen Cattell (1860–1944) studied with Wundt in Germany and taught at several universities in England and the United States before arriving at Columbia University. As we will see in Chapter 13 (on intelligence), Cattell's lifelong interest in individual differences eventually led him to devise "mental measures," or tests of students' aptitude. Cattell started his own testing company, The Psychological Corporation®, which currently markets both the SAT and the GRE tests. Needless to say, his work has profoundly shaped Western culture. One of Cattell's students, Edward Lee Thorndike (1874–1949), wrote influential texts on both educational psychology and mental measurement. (Thorndike's contributions to learning will be discussed in detail in Chapter 6.)

The pragmatic functionalism of William James and his successors persists in various forms to the present. What could be more pragmatic than a scientific discipline applied to the tasks of rearing, educating, and testing children, or to the clinical treatment of mental illness? Moreover, James's assertion that consciousness and behavior are adaptive currently finds expression in the theory and research of evolutionary psychology (Chapter 3) and physiological psychology (Chapter 4; see also the evolutionary and brain-behavioral perspectives listed in Table 1.1). Both those viewpoints are logical outgrowths of the interests of early functionalists.

Behaviorism

Another legacy of the early functionalists can be found in a movement known as *behaviorism*. According to the theory of **behaviorism,** the environment, rather than genes, is the primary determinant of both human and nonhuman behavior. In fact, the founder of behaviorism, John B. Watson (1878–1958), once a student of James Angell at the University of Chicago, defined psychology as the study of behavior, *not* the study of consciousness. Perhaps more important, Watson thought human behavior could be improved merely by improving the environment in which someone was raised.

Behaviorism incorporated the thinking of a Russian physiologist named Ivan Pavlov (1849–1936), who is remembered as the scientist who conditioned a dog to salivate at the sound of a bell. (Pavlov's work is discussed in detail in Chapter 6.) As we will see, Watson became famous as the psychologist who conditioned Little Albert, an 11-month-old infant, to fear a white rat, in much the same way as Pavlov conditioned the dog. Watson's point was that even human emotion is subject to the whims of the environment.

Behaviorism came to dominate psychological thinking in the middle decades of the 20th century. Besides Watson, the primary spokesperson for behaviorism was B. F. Skinner (1904–1990), whose ideas and research will also be covered in Chapter 6. The behaviorists' influence was so strong, many textbooks began to define psychology as the science of the analysis of behavior—and some went so far as to ignore human consciousness! As we have seen, contemporary psychology is defined in terms of both mind and behavior.

Other Major Developments in 20th-Century Psychology

The diversity of modern psychology is reflected in its many perspectives and specialty areas. The full story of the discipline will be told in coming chapters; here we can mention only a few of the most influential ideas of the last century.

Gestalt Psychology. Early in the 20th century, a group of German researchers called *Gestalt psychologists* rejected the analytical methods used by most laboratory scientists. Max Wertheimer, for example, argued that music should be studied as a whole—that its magical effect on consciousness could never be understood by analyzing individual notes. The same was true, he taught, for paintings, visual illusions, and insight learning—all suggested that the brain is wired at birth to integrate sensations and impose form on them in such a way that *the whole becomes greater than the sum of its parts.* As we will see in Chapter 8, these and other arguments of Gestalt psychologists influenced the study of learning and perception, particularly the physiological basis for perception.

behaviorism The theory that the environment rather than genes is the primary determinant of both human and nonhuman animal behavior.

Psychoanalytic Psychology. Another significant development in the history of psychology was the *psychoanalytic* approach to personality and its application in clinical psychology. Its founder, Sigmund Freud (1856–1939), is arguably the most recognizable name in all of psychology. Freud postulated that humans were more often than not unaware of why they behaved as they did. For instance, he believed they were often unconsciously motivated by sexual urges. Living and working in Vienna at the turn of the 20th century, Freud was contemporaneous with William James at Harvard. Both were free thinkers, and both unwittingly took psychology in very different directions from Wundt's German-inspired laboratory methods.

Humanistic Psychology. For the most part, experimentalists and scientific researchers shaped psychology in the 20th century. But many well-known psychologists were not scientists. Freud, who wrote case studies about his patients, lacked an empirical basis for his theory of personality. Another nonscientist who helped to shape psychology was the humanist Abraham Maslow (1908–1970). *Humanistic psychologists*, we will see in Chapter 14, first criticized and then sought to correct what they saw as the dehumanizing methods and pessimistic theories of scientific psychologists. They rejected B. F. Skinner's assertion that human behavior is determined by genes and environment, not by free will. Humans, they argued, were uniquely different from other animals, endowed with freedom and the potential for psychological growth and self-improvement.

The Neurosciences. In the 20th century, the biology of the mind found its fullest expression in what is now called neuroscience. The term, which literally means brain sciences, was coined with the founding of the Society for Neuroscience in 1970. Neuroscientists take an interdisciplinary approach to the study of the brain. Researchers who call themselves neuroscientists include psychologists, physicians, biologists, chemists, pharmacologists, and others who do research in the brain sciences.

What is the relationship of psychology to neuroscience? Think of two partially overlapping circles that share a common area. Both psychology and neuroscience include a focus on the measurement and quantification of perception, motivation, learning, and memory. But psychology also includes other subfields, such as social, personality, and abnormal psychology. As a research discipline, neuroscience lacks the breadth of psychology, especially its integration with the social sciences and the humanities.

INTERIM SUMMARY

1. In 1879 Wilhelm Wundt established a laboratory at the University of Leipzig specifically for the scientific study of the mind. Wundt is considered to be the first psychologist.
2. Wundt and his students trained observers to use the method of ***introspection***—that is, to verbally report conscious experiences such as seeing and hearing.
3. One of Wundt's students, Edward Titchener, brought his methods to the United States and developed what became known as the school of ***structuralism.*** Titchener trained several generations of American psychologists.
4. G. Stanley Hall, another student of Wundt, started the first psychological research laboratory in the United States at Johns Hopkins University.
5. William James influenced colleagues and students to focus on the usefulness of consciousness and behavior, a perspective that became known as ***functionalism.*** James's two-volume textbook *Principles of Psychology* continues to influence the direction of modern psychology.
6. Functionalism took different directions at the University of Chicago and Columbia University. The focus at Chicago was on animal learning, physiological

psychology, and educational psychology. At Columbia, James Cattell initiated research on the measurement of individual differences in intelligence and other personality characteristics.

7. The influence of structuralism effectively ended with Titchener's death, but functionalism continues to influence contemporary psychologists.
8. John B. Watson in the 1920s, and B. F. Skinner from the 1930s through the 1980s, espoused ***behaviorism***, the perspective that the environment (nurture) determines behavior and that the effects of genes (nature) are minimal.
9. Questioning the effectiveness of laboratory studies of certain aspects of behavior, *Gestalt* psychologists focused on the holistic analysis of human behavior.
10. Sigmund Freud developed the *psychoanalytic* approach to understanding mind. In part he theorized that humans are unconsciously motivated by sexual urges.
11. *Humanistic* psychologists objected to what they perceived as the dehumanizing approaches and pessimistic theories of scientific psychology. They continue to emphasize the human potential for psychological growth and self-improvement.
12. The neurosciences focus on brain-behavior relationships.

For Further Thought

1. Does the thinking of Gestalt psychologists reflect the ideas of Leibniz or Locke?
2. What are the strengths and weaknesses of a scientific discipline that entertains many different perspectives? Is psychology any different from biology or physics in that respect?
3. Was it inevitable that psychology became a science when it did? Why or why not?

THE MANY FACES OF PSYCHOLOGY

With many years of hindsight, I've concluded that my understanding of the world was significantly enhanced by my undergraduate major in psychology. And yet a bachelor's degree did not allow me to call myself a psychologist, any more than a B.A. in history allows one to be called a historian. The minimum amount of postgraduate work that qualifies one for licensing as a psychologist, typically at the state level, is a master's degree. In this section we'll look at such practical concerns, including employment considerations for psychology majors, different types of psychologists, the educational experiences and training available to psychology students, and the privileges of different psychological credentials.

Perhaps because psychology has permeated so many aspects of our culture, the number of people who study psychology has been increasing for decades. Currently, more college students take Introduction to Psychology than any other course. Psychology is now the second most common major at colleges and universities in the United States (business administration and management are first). Of the million or so students who graduate from college each year, about 70,000 major in psychology (see the American Psychological Association's Web site, listed in the references). Currently, about three of every four undergraduate psychology majors are female. Obviously, not all these students become psychologists. How are most psychology majors employed following graduation?

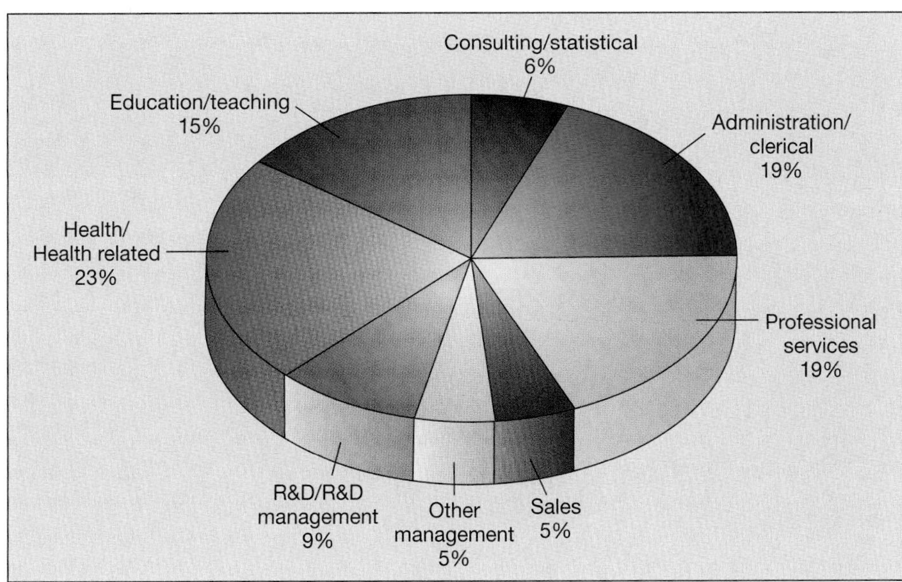

Figure 1.4 Occupations of students with bachelor's degrees in psychology in 1992. *Source:* 1994–1995 Psychology Baccalaureate Survey, Research Office, APA, 1997. *Note* Due to rounding numbers may not add to 100%. Copyright © 2001 by the American Psychological Assn. Reprinted by permission.

Occupations with Bachelor's Degrees

The most recent data on the employment of bachelor's-level psychology majors is from the mid-1990s. At the time of the survey, about 80 percent of all degree-holders were employed, and 10 percent were looking for jobs. Others who had chosen to continue their education were considered to be "in transition." Figure 1.4 shows the primary occupations of psychologists with bachelor's degrees. About one fourth go into health-related fields that do not require advanced degrees. Others can be found in the professional services, teaching, or administration and clerical work. Obviously, employment is a function of the national and world economies. At the time of this writing, employment was at an all-time high, and most college graduates of all majors who wanted to work were employed.

Let's assume you have graduated with a major in psychology and are seeking employment. Table 1.2 lists the qualities potential employers look for in psychology majors. What is interesting about this list is that with the exception of item 7, little else is specific to the methods and/or content of psychological study. Rather, the assumption seems to be that psychology majors have good people skills. Such skills translate into the ability to analyze social interactions and group behavior and to communicate successfully with team members. With these skills one can teach, conduct business, or work in information or social services.

Table 1.2 Top 10 Skills Employers Look for in Psychology Majors

1. Oral communication skills
2. Interpersonal skills
3. Analytical skills
4. Teamwork skills
5. Flexibility
6. Computer skills
7. Proficiency in field of study
8. Written communication skills
9. Leadership skills
10. Work experience

Occupations with Master's Degrees

Following another couple of years of postgraduate study, and the successful completion of degree requirements, a psychology major can earn a master's degree. Some degree programs require research, such as a master's thesis, whereas others merely require course work. In most states, professional boards set standards for the issuance of a license to practice psychology. Typically, those standards include a master's degree from an accredited university and a passing grade on a paper-and-pencil test on the content of psychology.

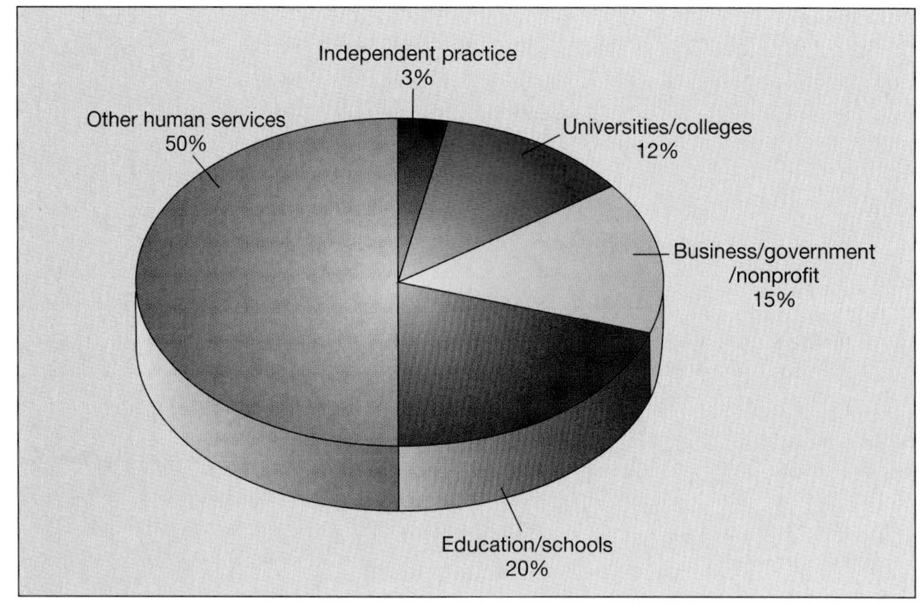

Figure 1.5 Occupations of students with master's degrees in psychology. *Source:* 1996 Employment Survey: Psychology Graduates with Master's, Specialist's, and Related Degrees. Compiled by APA Research Office, March 1999. Copyright © 2001 by American Psychological Assn. Reprinted by permission.

Figure 1.5 indicates how students with master's degrees are employed. Human services employ about half of all people with master's degrees in psychology. This category includes local, state, and federal agencies that provide diverse community services, such as job counseling, clerical help, health care, planning, personnel, criminal rehabilitation, and mental health care. Other students find employment as teachers and counselors in public schools and junior colleges. Less than 5 percent are employed privately as mental health care providers.

Types of Psychologists

Three different kinds of educational and training programs award doctoral degrees in psychology. As Figure 1.6 indicates, three-fourths of all doctorates earned are the Doctor of Philosophy in Psychology (Ph.D.) degree; about one-fifth are the Doctor of Psychology (Psy.D.) degree; and only 1 percent are the Doctor of Education (Ed.D.) degree. (These figures are for 2000.) The require-

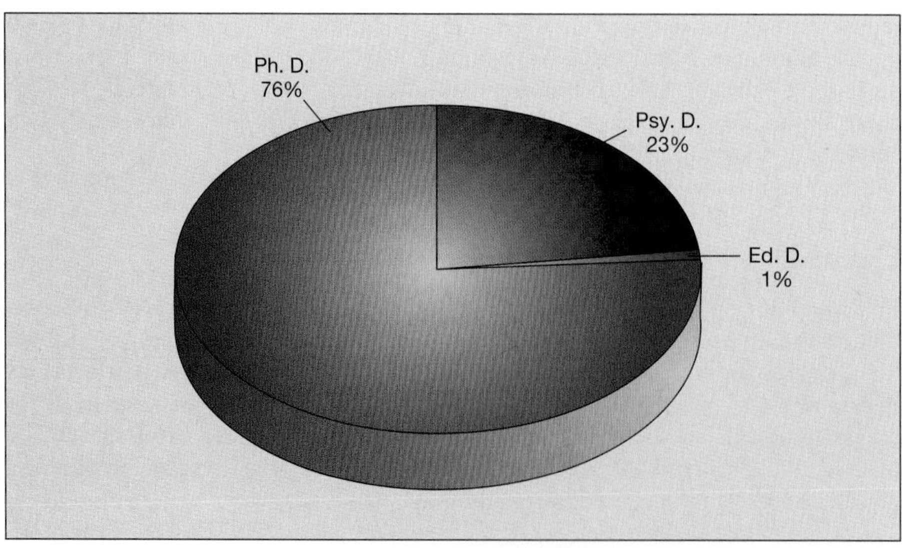

Figure 1.6 Type of doctorate awarded. *Source:* Graduate Study in Psychology 2000. Compiled by APA Research Office. Copyright © 2001 by American Psychological Assn. Reprinted by permission.

ments for a Ph.D. include the design, conduct, and defense of original research; hence, it is known as a research degree. By contrast, the requirements of most Psy.D. programs include a year of supervised practical training in an applied setting. Ph.D. programs are located in departments of psychology, whereas most Psy.D. degrees are earned in free-standing schools of psychology with a loose or nonexistent university affiliation. (Ed.D. programs are offered in schools of education.)

Psychologists can be divided into two groups: so-called pure psychologists, who do basic research in universities and in industry, and applied psychologists, whose work is aimed at solving practical problems. Today, the large majority of all applied psychologists practice **clinical psychology,** or the diagnosis and treatment of psychological disorders. Over a third of all currently trained Ph.D. psychologists specialize in clinical psychology. Add to these the Psy.D.s, and over half of all psychologists are clinical psychologists. The public's perception of psychology has been greatly influenced by this large presence of clinical psychologists, along with similarly trained counselors and social workers. These professions are now listed in the yellow pages under the generic term *psychotherapists*. The term is legally meaningless; thus when one seeks therapeutic help, it is important to determine the qualifications of the therapist.

Specialty Areas in Psychology

Figure 1.7, which shows the percentage of psychologists involved in all specialty areas, gives the truest picture of the breadth and scope of the discipline. It shows that well over half of all psychologists are involved in providing psychological services, including counseling. Some of them train counselors and clinical psychologists as well as see patients. Applied psychologists work in schools, industry, business, government, and other organizations. The rapid growth in the practice of psychology outside universities, such as in forensics, sports psychology, and industrial/organizational psychology, reflects its usefulness to society. In the words of Christine Hartel, director of the Science Directorate at the American Psychological Association, "We need people who can think logically and who can consider all the variables that define a problem. And we need such people in policy roles, as writers and in management, not just in labs" (Hartel, 1999, p. 2.).

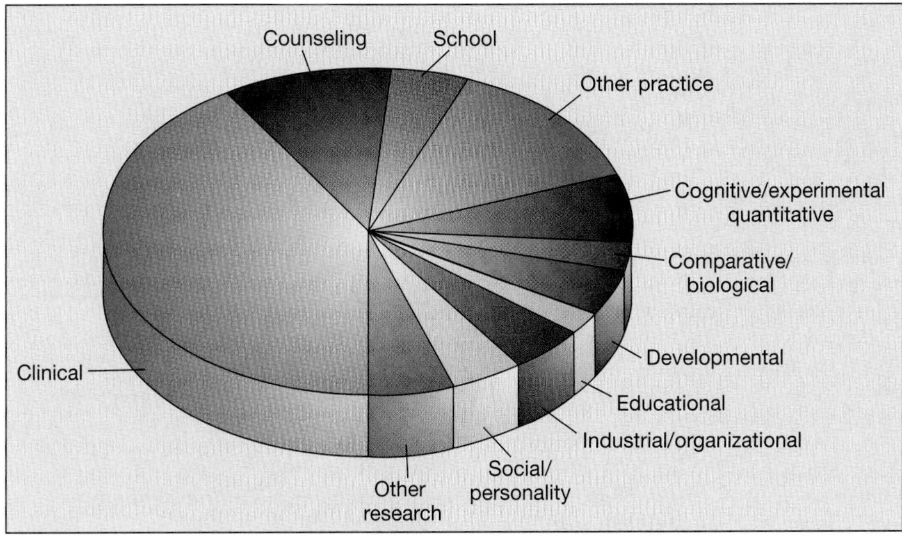

Figure 1.7 Specialty areas of earned doctorates in psychology. *Source:* Graduate Study in Psychology 2000. Compiled by APA Research Office. Copyright © 2001 by American Psychological Assn. Reprinted by permission.

clinical psychology The branch of psychology that is concerned with the diagnosis and treatment of psychological disorders.

In contrast with applied psychologists, academic psychologists teach and do research in clinical psychology and other specialty areas, including personality and social, developmental, educational, industrial/organizational, experimental, comparative, physiological, and cognitive psychology. These special research areas are described briefly in Table 1.3. Looking ahead, you might want to compare the chapter titles listed in the table of contents of this text with the doctoral specialties listed in Figure 1.7.

Professional Organizations in Psychology

Academic psychologists communicate their theories and research in classrooms, at conferences, and in scientific journals. (Scholarly publishing is an involved process that will be described in the next chapter.) At annual meetings devoted to particular specialty areas, they and others with similar interests socialize, present their research for discussion, and seek funding, typically from the federal government or private foundations. In addition to attending these special functions, most psychologists in the United States belong to one or more national organizations that represent their collective interests. Two of the most important professional organizations are the American Psychological Association (APA) and the American Psychological Society (APS).

The American Psychological Association (APA). The American Psychological Association's mission is "to advance psychology as a science, as a profession, and as a means of promoting human welfare" (American Psychological Association, 2000). Its 50 divisions represent the discipline's diverse subfields. The world's largest association of psychologists, at the end of the 20th century, the APA had a membership of about 160,000 researchers, educators, clinicians, consultants, and students.

The American Psychological Society (APS). Because the majority of the APA's members are clinical psychologists, their professional interests often differ from those of academic psychologists. In 1988, academic psychologists

Table 1.3 Specialty Areas in Psychological Research

AREA	RESEARCH FOCUS
Clinical psychology	Evaluation, diagnosis, and treatment of psychological disorders, including more or less severe behavioral and emotional problems
Cognitive psychology	Information processing, memory, thinking, problem solving, language, and creativity
Comparative psychology	Comparison of human and non human animal behavior, cognition, and brain-behavior relationships
Counseling psychology	Interviewing, testing, and therapy for individuals, families, and couples with cognitive, behavioral, and emotional disorders
Developmental psychology	Psychological development during infancy, childhood, adolescence, adulthood, and old age
Educational and school psychology	Evaluation of cognitive processes of school children, including reading and mathematics; of teaching methods; and of curriculum development and special education
General experimental psychology	Integration and teaching of research in sensation, perception, learning, motivation, emotion, and physiological psychology
Industrial/organizational psychology	Organizational structure, personnel evaluation, management, and human resources in business and government organizations
Personality psychology	Personality assessment and individual differences, including test construction for measurement of emotion, intelligence, and so forth
Neurosciences and physiological psychology	Biological underpinnings of behavior, including evolutionary/genetic considerations; brain-behavior relationships; drugs and behavior
Quantitative psychology	Measurement of psychological variables; test construction and evaluation; experimental design; statistical analysis of data
Social psychology	Interpersonal behavior, attitude formation, prejudice, group processes, attraction, sexual behavior

formed a new organization, the American Psychological Society, "to promote, protect, and advance the interests of scientifically oriented psychology in research, application, and the improvement of human welfare." The APS now has 16,000 members (American Psychological Society, 2000). Probably because the APS and the APA serve overlapping interests, many psychologists belong to both organizations, and both are thriving, successful professional groups.

Table 1.4 The Growing Role of Woman and People of Color in Psychology

WOMEN	1970s	1990s
bachelor's students	46%	73.9%
graduate students	47	72
new doctorates	33	70.3
Ph.D.s in workforce	20	46.1
People of color		
bachelor's students	11.6	24.9
graduate students	11.8	23.3
new doctorates	7.5	18.3
Ph.D.s in workforce	2.0	9.0

Sources: DOE/APA/NSF/NRC. Data compiled by the APA Research Office, 2001. Copyright © 2001 by American Psychological Assn. Reprinted by permission.

Recent Trends in Psychology

During the past couple of decades, the field of psychology has grown both in breadth and numbers, both inside and outside of universities. We have seen that three out of every four undergraduates who major in psychology are now female. Table 1.4 shows this and other trends over a 20-year period. In the 1990s women earned two-thirds of new doctorates, a dramatic increase since the 1970s. The table also shows that the field's growth reflects recent changes in the ethnic and racial makeup of the United States: people of color are becoming psychologists in greater numbers. While women still lag far behind men in the number of tenured positions they hold in colleges and universities (see Figure 1.8), the gap is beginning to narrow. Figure 1.8 shows that equal numbers of men and women are currently working toward tenure, though more women than men are employed as lecturers outside the tenure track.

In Chapter 18 we will see that the introduction of psychoactive drugs a half-century ago has revolutionized the treatment of mental illness. For historical reasons, physicians rather than clinical psychologists prescribe drugs for patients undergoing psychotherapy. Medical doctors who specialize in psychology are called *psychiatrists*. Their training begins in medical school; then, like other medical specialists, they must serve as residents in a hospital and pass special examinations in both psychology and medicine.

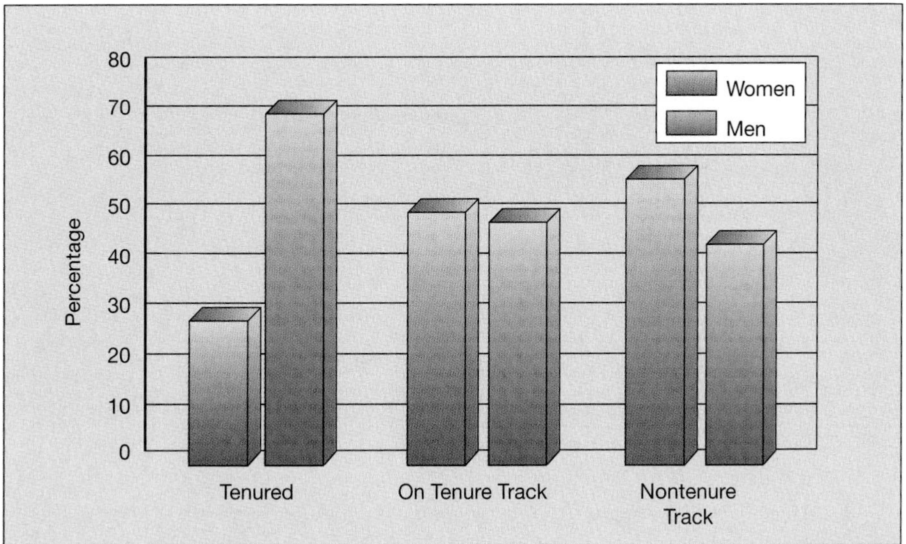

Figure 1.8 **A comparison of the employment of women and men in psychology departments in colleges and universities in the United States.** These 2001 data show that three-fourths of tenured positions are currently held by men. However, the future reversal of these numbers is indicated by the equal numbers of women on tenure track and the higher numbers of women being hired at the college level. *Source:* APA 2000–01 Faculty Salaries Survey. Compiled by APA Research Office, March 2001. Copyright © 2001 by American Psychological Assn. Reprinted by permission.

To meet all their patients' needs, many clinical psychologists, counselors, and other psychotherapists now collaborate with psychiatrists. Often, a psychiatrist will cooperate with a psychotherapist in diagnosing and developing a drug treatment program for a person suffering from a mental disorder or adjustment problem. As this book went to press, several states were experimenting with postdoctoral training programs in which psychologists could learn the skills needed to prescribe psychoactive drugs. These programs were sponsored by the American Psychological Association, in collaboration with selected schools of medicine.

INTERIM SUMMARY

1. The number of people earning both undergraduate and advanced degrees in psychology has been increasing for several decades. At present, women earn about three-fourths of all undergraduate degrees and about two-thirds of all doctorates in psychology.
2. People with bachelor's degrees in psychology work in a wide variety of fields, including health and human services, teaching, and management. They are sought after as employees because they are perceived as having people skills.
3. A master's degree in psychology requires 2 years of postgraduate work. Not many master's-level graduates work as clinical psychologists in private practice, but many are employed as community service providers at the local, state, or federal level.
4. Doctoral degrees in psychology require several additional years of education and training. Over 75 percent of doctoral degrees are Ph.D.s; about 20 percent are Psy.D.s, and 2 percent Ed.D.s.
5. *Clinical psychology* is branch of psychology devoted to the diagnosis and treatment of psychological disorders.
6. Other specialty areas in psychology include personality and social, developmental, educational, industrial/organizational, quantitative, experimental, comparative, physiological, learning, and cognitive psychology.
7. The most important professional organizations in psychology are the American Psychological Association (APA) and the American Psychological Society (APS).
8. During the 1990s increasing numbers of women and people of color earned advanced degrees in psychology.
9. *Psychiatrists* are medical doctors who specialize in psychology. At present, only physicians can prescribe psychoactive drugs, but experimental programs may lead eventually to the licensing of psychologists to prescribe drugs.

For Further Thought

1. Why do you think more women than men are currently majoring in psychology, reversing a 100-year trend toward domination of the field by men?
2. Do women have more people skills than men? Do men make better laboratory researchers than women? (For further discussion of these issues, see Chapters 13, 14, and 15.)
3. Which 2 of the 12 specialty areas listed in Table 1.3 employ more than half of all psychologists? How is this question related to questions 1 and 2?
4. At present, no matter what specialty a medical doctor has, she or he can prescribe any psychoactive drug. For example, internists and obstetrician-gynecologists routinely prescribe Prozac® (a popular antidepressant), and many pediatricians prescribe Ritalin® for children with attention deficit disorder (ADD). What are the pros and cons of this practice? What might be the benefits of allowing psychologists to prescribe psychoactive drugs?

CONCLUDING THOUGHTS

Psychology is the relatively young science of the human mind and human behavior. Academic psychologists study the processes of motivation, learning, memory, perception, personality, and intelligence from a variety of perspectives. Psychologists' interests are so varied, they defy easy comparison: Some study human relationships in social settings—marriage, for example—whereas others may be found investigating the basic processes of learning in laboratory settings. Applied psychologists work in educational settings, industry, government, and clinical settings.

The first psychologists were philosophers who adopted empirical methods. During the 1800s, these new scientists decided that theories of the nature of mind should be tested empirically, by observation and experimentation, as well as by logic and reason. They developed their methods in laboratories created for that purpose at German universities. Wilhelm Wundt is considered to be the first psychologist, not because of a unique philosophy but because he first used the experimental method. Other researchers in German laboratories studied the physiology of the brain. Hence, the roots of modern psychology lie in both philosophy and biology—that is, in Greek philosophy, British associationism, and European nativism, as well as in the evolutionary theories of Charles Darwin and the physiology of brain functions.

The early history of American psychology was shaped by Wundt's students and by William James. Wundt and his students Edward Titchener and G. Stanley Hall were structuralists who studied the structure of consciousness using the method of introspection. In turn they trained other psychologists, who at the turn of the 20th century set up laboratories in American colleges and universities. James, on the other hand, was an eclectic thinker who inspired students to think about the prospects of a scientific psychology. A diverse lot, many of his students, including some women, became interested in understanding the function rather than the structure of consciousness. To this day, researchers continue to investigate functionalist interests such as applied psychology, teaching, learning, and behavioral, physiological, and evolutionary psychology.

Some of the questions many contemporary psychologists are wrestling with have been asked for thousands of years. They include the mind-body problem: How can we best characterize mind/soul/spirit, and how is it related to the body? Rene Descartes's interactive dualism is not a satisfactory answer, nor is monism. Another issue that concerns psychologists is the relative roles of nature and nurture, a question we will deal with throughout this text. A third issue, Darwin's assertion that humans are in most respects similar to other animals, is more recent in origin. Given the biological relation between humans and animals, what is it that makes humans unique?

Common sense may explain some aspects of the human mind and behavior, but it can be misleading. Psychological conclusions must rely on logic and research, not solely on common sense. Psychology's use of the scientific method and its broad range of interests may explain its growing influence in society. Large numbers of college students now choose to major in psychology and pursue career interests in such fields as health and human services, teaching, management, and research. Women and minorities, in particular, are increasingly attracted to the study of psychology. Its diversity, its relatedness to other social sciences and the humanities, and its applications to modern culture make it an attractive discipline.

KEY TERMS

associationism *14*
behaviorism *22*
clinical psychology *27*
dualism *5*
empiricism *14*
functionalism *20*
introspection *19*
mind-body problem *5*
monism *6*
nativism *15*
nature-nurture issue *7*
psychology *5*
structuralism *19*

2

Methodology in the Behavioral Sciences

Source: Keith Haring, "Untitled," March 24, 1982. Vinyl ink on vinyl tarp, 12 × 12 ft., 144 in. × 144 in. (366 × 366 cm.). © The estate of Keith Haring. Courtesy Tony Shafrazi Gallery, New York.

Curiosity and Science: A Very Human Enterprise

The Psychological Sciences: Philosophy and Goals

Psychology in Relation to Other Sciences
Searching for Truth?
Four Goals of Psychology
Interim Summary
For Further Thought

The Experimental Method

Questioning Behavior
Generating a Hypothesis
Designing the Experiment
Conducting the Experiment
Analyzing the Results
Validating the Experiment Through Peer Review
Publishing the Results
Interim Summary
For Further Thought

Nonexperimental Research Methods

Studying Individuals and Groups
Surveys and Case Studies
Correlational Research
Epidemiological Research
Psychological Inventories and Questionnaires
Comparison of Methods
Ethical Issues in Psychological Research
Interim Summary
For Further Thought

Concluding Thoughts

In the early 1950s, Dr. James Olds and a graduate student, Mr. Peter Milner, were developing a new approach to the study of the brain. In their laboratory at McGill University in Quebec, they were attempting to stimulate an extremely small area of a rat's brain with an electrical current. Half a century ago, precise electrode placement was problematic. Each implanted electrode had to be tested, often with unpredictable results. The following conversation is a dramatization of an incident that actually happened.

"Dr. Olds, I think you might want to see this. Watch rat number 32. It keeps coming back to the corner of the table."

James Olds walked across the laboratory to observe the experiment. A suspended wire connected the brain stimulator to the electrode in the top of the rat's head, allowing the rat to creep around freely. Olds peered at the rat, sitting expectantly in one corner. He knew that rats, like cats, if fed at the same time and place each day, would return to the place where they had been fed before. This rat, however, probably had never been fed in this place. Puzzled, he asked Milner to describe what had happened.

"Well, I hooked him up and stimulated him. He shuddered, walked around, and came back to where he started. I gave him another jolt and the same thing happened, except now he doesn't move too far away, just stays in this corner."

Olds studied the rat's activity pattern, which Milner had sketched in the lab journal. "Has this rat *ever* been fed on the table?"

"No."

Rats and mice have been used in psychological research for over a century.

"Do you think the brain stimulation is paralyzing. . . ."

"I don't think so. It doesn't seem to be causing him any distress."

Later that evening, as Olds replayed the scene in his mind, the key to the puzzle hit him: *The rat kept coming back to where it was being stimulated.* Maybe, he thought, the rat wasn't trying to escape the stimulation, but was seeking it out. Maybe it *liked* the stimulation!

Arriving at the lab the next morning, Olds asked his students to help him build a new apparatus, a plastic box, open at the top, with a lever sticking through one of the walls. Olds connected the lever to a switch that controlled the brain stimulation. Now the rat could press the lever and stimulate itself. Olds placed rat number 32's paws directly on the lever, closing the switch and delivering an electrical current to the rat's brain. The rat shuddered slightly. Olds repeated the procedure. The rat shuddered, sniffed the lever repeatedly, and finally reared back and came down on the lever with its front paw, closing the switch and delivering more current to its brain. Another press, and then another followed. Within a few seconds, the rat was pressing the lever repeatedly.

"The stimulation is acting like a food pellet," Milner whispered. "The rat has learned to press the lever the same way as the ones we trained using food rewards!"

"Yes, I think so," Olds replied. "I think this electrode was placed in a part of the brain that is activated when a rat eats. I wouldn't be surprised if it turns out to be the hypothalamus."

"But we weren't aiming for the hypothalamus."

"We got lucky!"

CURIOSITY AND SCIENCE: A VERY HUMAN ENTERPRISE

As James Olds' research suggests, curiosity underlies the conduct of science. The human genome project, for example, is science that results from human curiosity about the very building blocks of our being, including the search for genes that make us curious. Curiosity is reflected in many human activities, from the creation of music to the exploration of space. For some humans, the quest for knowledge leads to the study of mathematics; for others, it leads to figuring out why a car engine won't run. *Science,* however, is one of the more complex (and curious) activities in which humans engage. It is a sophisticated method of asking questions and a way of explaining things we don't understand.

Formally defined, **science** is knowledge based on observation and experimentation and validated by other scientists. The term can be used in two ways: first, as a method of inquiry (a way to ask questions about the world and arrive at answers) and second, as a collected body of facts or knowledge about the world. (In this chapter we will be using the term in the first sense.) We tend to think of science as a detached and objective activity; yet the process is full of false starts, errors, and dead ends. A scientific **experiment** can be thought of as a test, or trial, to discover a cause-effect relationship. Hunches and intuitive

science Knowledge based on observation and experimentation and validated by other scientists.

experiment A test or trial to discover a cause-effect relationship.

guesses dot the laboratory landscape; fortuitous, unexpected events often restructure the direction of a research problem. Olds and Milner used observation and a variety of experimental procedures to test their hunches. In addition to experiments, psychologists also use nonexperimental methods, such as naturalistic observation, case studies, tests, questionnaires, and surveys, to study the human mind and behavior.

Although the experimental method has been the most successful method for psychologists—for reasons we'll pursue shortly—it is not always possible to do an experiment. For example, for ethical reasons, scientists cannot conduct human breeding experiments, but they can test for genetic effects using surveys and other behavioral tests on identical twins, as we will see later. Similarly, under normal circumstances, scientists cannot ethically implant electrodes into human brains, though they can do these invasive experiments on rats and other animals under certain conditions (see the discussion of research ethics on page 62). In the next section we will see one instance in which for medical reasons, electrodes *were* successfully implanted into the same area of the human brain that Olds and Milner studied in rats. Despite the limitations of nonexperimental methods, a lot can be learned from them. For example, from retrospective questionnaires and surveys we know a great deal about the relationship of diet and exercise to heart disease in men and women of various ages and ethnic groups. We will discuss nonexperimental research methods in the concluding section of this chapter. But first we will consider the general philosophy and goals that underlie both the experimental and nonexperimental methods.

At present, the behavioral and biological sciences cannot account for the genius of Wolfgang Amadeus Mozart.

THE PSYCHOLOGICAL SCIENCES: PHILOSOPHY AND GOALS

Can psychology be meaningfully compared with other sciences such as biology and chemistry? That is, can psychologists discover "truths" about human behavior using the scientific method in the same way that chemists successfully describe nature in terms of molecules? Although scientists don't claim to arrive at "truth," there are some commonly accepted goals of psychological research. Consider the following questions, which can be asked about both the human and the animal mind: What is the nature of the genius that underlied Mozart's musical accomplishments? Why do we sleep, and why do we dream? Does physically abusing someone make him or her violent? Psychologists seek answers to questions such as these because they, like other humans, are curious, and because they hope to solve society's problems. Because they are also skeptical, psychologists are particular about the kinds of evidence that will satisfy their curiosity.

As scientists, psychologists seek *empirical* answers to their questions. That is, the **scientific method** is based on the empirical methods of observation and experimentation. For example, a psychologist might propose that *we sleep because our brains need to rest*. If so, we might reasonably expect that relative to the waking state, the brain's metabolism, and perhaps its electrical activity, is reduced during

scientific method A method of attaining knowledge based on observation and experimentation.

sleep. A scientist might conduct a test of the brain's activity while asleep and while awake. If the experiment were conducted properly, the results of the test would either support or reject the adequacy of the proposition. In this particular example, scientists have discovered that brain activity remains high during sleep; therefore, the proposition that we sleep because our brains need to rest must be rejected. To better understand sleep, a psychologist would come up with other testable working hypotheses about how the brain functions during sleep and wakefulness.

Psychology in Relation to Other Sciences

Psychologists test an enormous range of propositions about human behavior in experiments. Figure 2.1 shows a scientific continuum, with the "hard sciences" (physics, chemistry, and biology) connecting through psychology to the "soft sciences" (sociology and anthropology). Note the central position of psychology, which itself ranges from a hard to a soft science. For example, Olds and Milner's biologically oriented research employed neurophysiological (brain functioning) and neuroanatomical (brain anatomy) methods. Their research into brain-behavior relationships is best understood as a combination of psychology and biology. In contrast, in a classic "soft" experiment discussed in Chapter 15, the social psychologist Stanley Milgram told human subjects to "follow orders" to be cruel to others (Milgram, 1963, 1974). Although Milgram found that some subjects were more likely than others to be obedient or cruel, he never investigated the reasons for their behavior in any systematic way. Unlike Olds and Milner's systematic experiments, Milgram's experiments produced only sparse observations and conjecture about the motivation of some humans in certain social situations.

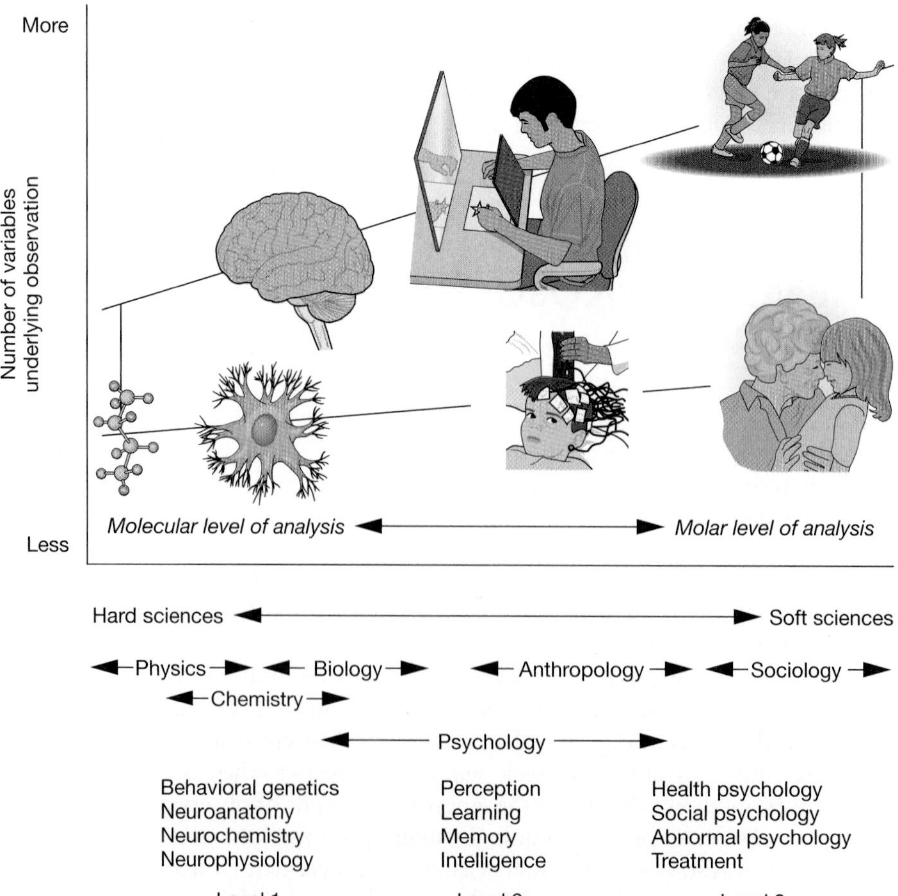

Figure 2.1 Levels of analysis in the hard and soft sciences. Psychologists observe and explain a range of events, from molecular events (as in behavioral genetics and neurochemistry) with relatively few variables to molar events (as in social psychology) with relatively more variables.

A Scientific Continuum. Note in Figure 2.1 that compared to neurophysiology and neuroanatomy, the psychological processes of learning and perception occupy a different *level of analysis*. The scientific continuum pictured in Figure 2.1 suggests that the sciences vary along a dimension labeled **molecular level** at one end and **molar level** at the other. For psychologists, biochemical and physiological analyses constitute the molecular level, and the study of the mind and behavior of whole, intact organisms, the molar level. Physics and chemistry can be thought of as molecular enterprises, because they are concerned with particles and chemical reactions. In contrast, biology, psychology, and sociology are more molar (concerned with the body as a whole). For example, biologists study specific combinations of molecular arrangements that make up genes, tissues, organs, and organ systems. Psychologists' concerns are more molar still, because they study the behavior of an intact organism. Social psychologists occupy the extreme end of this continuum, because they study the influence of other humans on human behavior. Along the continuum, psychologists pursue a wide range of research interests, using methods to match. Those with interests in the physiology and brain chemistry use different methods to investigate some of the same questions asked by social psychologists. At its best, the science of psychology can be characterized as an *interdisciplinary science*—a quest for answers to behavioral questions that range from the biological to the sociocultural.

The diagonal line displayed in Figure 2.1 suggests that the hard sciences are "hard" not because they are difficult to learn, but rather because (1) they are molecular and (2) their observations are restricted to a just few variables. For example, the hard science of chemistry deals with variables such as the concentration and state of chemicals. The variables that cause chemical reactions are said to be **antecedent conditions** to the reaction being measured—events that precede and cause another event to occur. Mixed together, chemicals x and y are the antecedents of compound z. The antecedent conditions that determine molecular arrangements often can be described by a few principles of physics. In general, fewer antecedent, causal variables underlie the observations made by physicists, chemists, and biologists than the observations made by psychologists.

In comparison, the soft sciences attempt to identify the antecedent conditions of the much more complicated responses (reactions) of behaving organisms. You can imagine, for example, the complexity of the antecedent conditions underlying Mozart's musical accomplishments, or the social relationships in his turbulent life. Because the variables underlying observations made in the hard sciences are fewer in number, the analysis of those variables is more reliable, and in a sense easier to accomplish. Physicists can theorize how electrons are arranged in an orbit around a proton; neuroscientists understand how a single neuron functions. But psychologists and sociologists attempt to understand much more complex phenomena—for example, which combinations of the billions of individually functioning neurons in the brain are responsible for memories, and how the thousands of social interactions that occur in a group affect a person's behavior. The staggering complexity of a person's psychological functioning makes difficult the accurate prediction of that person's behavior. Perhaps in some ways, social psychologists face a more daunting task than biologically oriented psychologists do.

Dopamine and other neurochemical pathways, Chapter 4, p. 143

Reductionism. Figure 2.1 suggests another important characteristic of science in general, and psychology in particular. Most psychologists—indeed, most scientists—are reductionists. **Reductionism** is an explanation of behavior by reference to molecular events—that is, by reference to physiology and ultimately to chemistry. *Why did Olds and Milner's rat press the lever?* One explanation is that the electric current stimulated neurons in the rat's brain, causing it to experience pleasure. We'll see later that these neurons are receptive to a biochemical called dopamine. Thus the behavior of lever pressing is reduced to a chemical reaction.

molecular level In research, investigations of behavior at the physiological or biochemical level.

molar level In research, investigations of the behavior of whole, intact organisms.

antecedent condition The event that precedes and causes another event to occur.

reductionism Explanation by reference to a more molecular level of analysis (such as physiology or biochemistry).

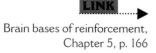

Brain bases of reinforcement, Chapter 5, p. 166

Reductionism also allows sociologists and social psychologists to explain phenomena by reference to the mind and behavior of individuals. For example, sociologists studying the role that violence plays in divorce seek to understand the determinants of violence. They might ask: *Do violent home environments produce violent individuals?* To answer this question they might compare scores on tests of impulsiveness and aggression of violent fathers and their sons with those of nonviolent fathers and their sons. They also might look for a study of the early learning experiences of a violent child to determine the extent to which excessive physical punishment was used, and under what conditions, in his home environment. Or they might compare the testosterone levels of violent and nonviolent fathers with those of their sons. Note that these psychological and biological studies constitute successively more molecular analyses of, and explanations for, the cultural phenomenon of violence (Simon, 1992). Sociologists, then, use reductionistic explanations at the level of psychology and biology in the same way that psychologists use them at the biological and biochemical levels.

Psychologists may study the upbringing of violent offenders, such as rapist/serial killer Ted Bundy, to determine whether violence during youth is a good predictor for later violent behavior.

Searching for Truth?

If scientists use a reductionistic approach to explain phenomena, does that mean that the more molecular sciences of biology and chemistry are better, or "more scientific," than the molar science of psychology? The answer to this question is not a simple one. On careful examination, experiments in biology and chemistry are not all that different from those in psychology. *All* scientific disciplines use methods that arrive at tentative conclusions rather than absolute truths—tentative, because tomorrow's experiment often forces a different understanding of today's results. Tomorrow's experiments often reveal that a particular biochemical reaction works differently than previously thought, for example. To return to Olds' experiments, he thought that he had discovered a pleasure center in the rat's brain. Did Olds *prove* that rats have "pleasure centers"? This is a difficult question to answer. Scientists no longer interpret the original experiment in the same way Olds and Milner did. It's not so much that Olds and Milner were wrong in interpreting their observations, given what was then known about brain function. Rather, additional observations from hundreds of subsequent experiments have led to the new tentative conclusion that electrical stimulation activates chemical pathways in the brain rather than neurons in specific areas located near the hypothalamus. Other experimenters, as we'll see in Chapter 5, question whether the stimulation experienced by rats is all that pleasurable. We will never know what rat number 32 experienced: Olds and Milner's experiments raised as many questions as they answered.

In their work, then, psychologists do not prove propositions to be true. But if they cannot find the absolute truth, what do they hope to accomplish? Psychologists use **probabilistic reasoning** to come to tentative conclusions that are true within a range that varies from zero to one. Consider again the question of whether children who are raised in homes with violent role models become violent themselves. You can correctly guess that collecting data on this problem from a variety of perspectives has supported the conclusion that there is a *higher probability* of violent individuals coming out of violent homes, but that violence in the home does not *cause* a child to become violent. Some aggressive fathers still manage to raise sons who are nonviolent, and some nonaggressive fathers have violent sons.

probabilistic reasoning The idea that the causes of events may not be completely determined and may be specified only within a range of probabilities.

Because the results of psychological experiments are reported in probabilistic rather than absolute terms, psychology is sometimes mistakenly referred to as an "inexact science." However, a psychologist's understanding of reality is not that different from other scientists'; a scientist's conclusions are always based on a limited number of observations. Scientists can't absolutely prove propositions about reality. Rather, they make tentative interpretations, recognizing that as more observations are made, their understanding of what is "true" will likely change. This *self-correcting* aspect of the scientific method makes it one of the very best ways humans have invented to understand the nature of reality. For example, throughout most of the 20th century various observations led to the firmly held belief that humans were born with a full complement of brain cells, and that when these cells died they were never replaced. New methods of observing and measuring brain cells in the past few years have corrected this view. Scientists now understand that under some circumstances, humans continue to grow new brain cells throughout their lifetimes. (This research will be discussed further in Chapter 4.) The tentative conclusions achieved by the scientific method are a source of concern for those who do not enjoy living with uncertainty. In recognizing how little is known for sure about the human mind and behavior, psychologists and other scientists have had to become accustomed to living with uncertainty.

Built into this process is the notion that the body of psychological knowledge may change over the years. One way to think about the conduct of psychological science is that researchers in various laboratories are testing a series of successive propositions. Over the years, an investigator's **programmatic research**—a continuing series of studies that provides partial answers to a question—begins to resemble a story. *Does violence in the home cause a child to be violent?* is an example of a starting question. In the "story line" that emerges from programmatic research, one investigation leads more or less logically to the next. Although answers to particular questions in the story about violence may come from one investigator, they may also come from several investigators. Often, researchers in two different laboratories will compete with each other to advance the story line. The conduct of science, then, is a highly social enterprise. To be believable, a researcher's scientific "stories" must meet certain standards on which the majority of other researchers can agree.

The collective judgment of scientific "referees" determines whether the reported results of an experiment are acceptable. For example, in Olds and Milner's research, did the results (a rat pressing a lever for brain stimulation) logically and reasonably follow from the reported methods and procedures used in the experiment? If judged to be sound, the results are accepted as factual. Empirical tests of propositions, then, must meet several agreed upon criteria before the test results become part of the body of knowledge of psychological science.

As previously described, science can be roughly divided into two components, *method* and *content*. Methodology refers to the plan for how an experiment is to be carried out. The content of an experiment is its result—what was discovered. The content of science as a whole refers to the **body of knowledge** that has accumulated from scientific investigations. The body of knowledge of psychology, for example, is found in the books and journals that describe the results of decades of psychological research. Unfortunately, the body of knowledge or content of psychology cannot be neatly separated from psychological methods. For example, the experimental finding that some rats will press a lever to electrically stimulate their brains (content) cannot be neatly separated from a description of the methods that were used to demonstrate the phenomenon.

To take another example, consider research on sleep and dreams (discussed in detail in Chapter 9). Imagine a sleep study in which the methodology is limited to watching a person's behavior from sundown to sunup, recording any activity—tossing and turning, for example—and perhaps writing down the verbal report of the person's dream upon awakening. This method of studying sleep would give us a veridical (truthful, accurate) but limited understanding and perspective on one of the more fascinating aspects of our lives. Other scientific methodologies bring an additional dimension to our understanding of sleep and

programmatic research A succession of experiments each aimed at solving part of a larger problem.

body of knowledge The written record of the outcomes of scientific investigations.

Prey animals sleep less, and less deeply, than do predators.

dreams. For example, electrodes might be attached to the sleeper's scalp to monitor the physiological changes that define the stages of sleep. Alternatively, a comparative psychologist might compare the sleep patterns of prey animals with those of predators, and note that the former enjoy a longer, deeper sleep. Finally, a physiologically oriented psychologist might note changes in serotonin levels during dreams and other sleep stages, and develop a hypothesis about how it and other biochemicals relate to the occurrence of sleep and dreams. Note that each experimental methodology allows only partial insight into the true nature of sleep. Each provides a different perspective, so that the content of sleep research changes with the method. It is in this sense that we can agree that "method determines content." We will see shortly that when Olds and Milner used a somewhat different methodology in follow-up experiments, their results provided an even better understanding of how the rat's brain was related to its behavior.

LINK

Methods of measuring sleep and dreams, Chapter 9, p. 320

Four Goals of Psychology

The goals of research psychologists like Olds and Milner can be pictured in pyramid form, as in Figure 2.2. There are four main goals: (1) to observe and describe behavior; (2) to determine the causes of behavior (answer the *how* questions); (3) to explain behavior (answer the *why* questions); and (4) to predict and control behavior. Let's take each in turn.

Observe and Describe. The conduct of science begins with careful observation. Peter Milner was not just watching rat number 32 as it moved around while its brain was being stimulated; he was *thinking* about what he was seeing. Olds had *expectations* about what behavior the rat might engage in next, and like all scientists, he was trying to make his observations conform to his expectations. Another way of saying this is that scientists are informed, or trained, observers, and that their observations are not "theory neutral." For example, a person with perfectly good eyesight but no knowledge of the normal behavior of rats would not know what to look for, nor be capable of interpreting and describing the complicated behavior connected with brain stimulation. A psychologist must be trained to observe and describe behavior.

Determine the Causes of Behavior. After observing and describing behavior, a psychologist next seeks answers to *how* questions. *How does the brain function? How does reinforcement work?* Different research questions and

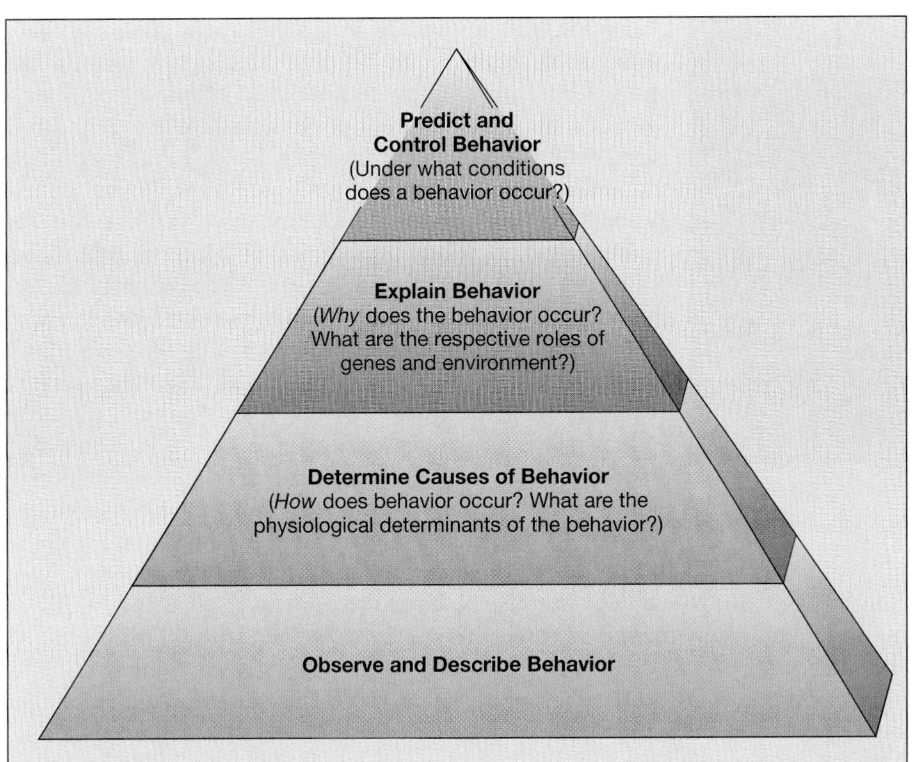

Figure 2.2 **Four goals of research psychologists.** Psychologists must observe and describe behavior before they can understand the hows and whys of behavior. At the highest level of science, psychologists can *predict* an organism's behavior.

strategies will lead to questions posed at different levels of analysis. For example, one answer to the *how* of sleep is to describe the electrical activity of the brain during waking, sleeping, and dreaming. To answer how *reinforcement* works, a researcher might measure patterns of lever pressing in rats, or changes in the behavior of prisoners in a behavior modification program. These different strategies, as shown in Figure 2.1, will lead to answers at different levels of analysis.

Explain Behavior. In addition to the physiological reductionism of *how* answers, behavior can also be explained by reference to genetic and environmental determinants. These kinds of explanations are attempts to answer *why* questions. Why do rats and humans feel pleasure and pain? Why do rats press levers and humans work from 9 to 5? Why do rats and humans have sleep and wake cycles? Even a perfect understanding of the biochemistry underlying pleasure, eating, and sleeping does *not* answer these *why* questions. We will see in Chapter 3 that some *why* questions can be answered by reference to genes that were selected over millions of years of evolution through the process of natural selection. We will find that most answers to the *why* questions of behavior involve *adaptation*. For example, animals adaptively eat, sleep, seek pleasure, and avoid pain. *Why* questions will be discussed in more detail in Chapters 3 and 5. For our present purposes, we will simply distinguish between *how* questions, which can be answered by reductionism, and *why* questions, which are answerable only by addressing the purpose of behavior in the grander scheme of things. Meeting the goals of psychological science requires answers to both *how* and *why* questions.

Evolution and genetics provide answers to *why* questions, Chapter 3, p. 70, and Chapter 5, p. 151

Predict and Control Behavior. We have seen that science begins with careful observation and experimentation to test propositions about behavior. A psychologist's curiosity eventually leads to plausible hypotheses about the causes of a behavior. With a complete understanding of how and why a behavior occurs, psychologists can begin to make accurate predictions about the causes of a

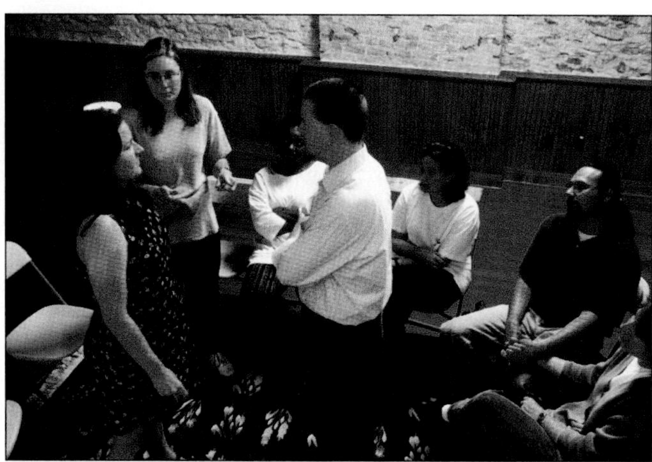

Society considers psychologists to be experts in understanding human behavior.

behavior, and ultimately act to control it. Because these latter goals have not been fully realized, some would not presume to include "prediction" and "control" of behavior on a list of the goals of psychology. Nevertheless, they are goals, for society continues to look to the psychological sciences to solve problems. For example, the courts want to know whether a defendant understands right from wrong, or is otherwise mentally fit to stand trial, because they consider psychologists to be experts in understanding abnormal behavior. Teachers want to know whether a child who is suffering from a learning disability will benefit from behavioral therapy or medication. Couples seek marital advice. Communities question whether a convict coming up for parole is a reasonable risk. Medical schools need structured interview procedures and paper-and-pencil tests that indicate which students will most likely master the curriculum *and* become effective physicians, and so on. Given the complexity of human behavior, psychologists must be careful to not oversell what is known about human behavior, and the usefulness it has in solving societal problems. At the same time, psychologists can often provide the best answers to these difficult behavioral questions. The maturing of the psychological sciences will lead to yet better prediction and control of behavior.

INTERIM SUMMARY

1. Psychology is an *interdisciplinary science* that uses the ***scientific method*** in seeking biological, behavioral, and social answers to questions about mind and behavior.
2. ***Science*** is a method of gaining knowledge about the world based on observation, *experimentation,* and reason. Experimental findings make up the content, or ***body of knowledge,*** of science.
3. ***Reductionism*** in psychology is an explanation of behavior by reference to physiology and chemistry.
4. Psychology shares features of physics, chemistry, and biology on the ***molecular level*** and the features of sociology and anthropology on the ***molar level.*** All *levels of analysis* contribute to an overall understanding of behavior.
5. In their search for causal factors, or the ***antecedent conditions*** that underlie behavior, psychologists are guided by the assumption that every behavior has a cause. Limited observation of multicausal behavioral events, however, forces them to draw conclusions using ***probabilistic reasoning.***
6. Scientific findings do not constitute "truths"; rather, science is *self-correcting* and changes with new evidence.
7. Explanations of behavior become more precise as additional observations accumulate through ***programmatic research.***
8. The four goals of psychology are (a) to observe and describe behavior; (b) to determine the causes of behavior; (c) to explain behavior, and (d) to predict and control behavior.

For Further Thought

1. Why do you suppose the rat has a brain area that is apparently devoted to "pleasure"?
2. How would you respond to the assertion that psychology is not a real science? Apply the concepts of *hard science, soft science,* and *levels of analysis* in your response.

THE EXPERIMENTAL METHOD

As indicated in Figure 2.1, the methods psychologists use produce results at a different level from those of chemistry, biology, or sociology. But while the level of analysis differs, the *methods of inquiry* into psychological processes resemble very closely those used in other scientific disciplines.

Some aspects of the experimental method are taught in elementary and secondary schools. Students learn, for example, that the experimental method is a way of stating and then attempting to solve a problem, that experiments spring from hypotheses, and that control groups are required to draw conclusions. However, the experimental method is more complex than these basic ideas suggest. For simplicity, this complex process can be divided into the following seven components:

1. Questioning behavior
2. Generating a hypothesis
3. Designing the experiment
4. Conducting the experiment
5. Analyzing the results
6. Validating the experiment through peer review
7. Publishing the results

We will work through these seven steps using Olds and Milner's research as our example.

Questioning Behavior

A cat pokes its paw into a dark opening; a curious child touches a snail's antenna to make it retract. Modern science channels such curiosity into highly specialized research through specific training. In psychology, training is accomplished in 5 to 6 years of post baccalaureate study directed by one or more faculty members in a university setting. After a graduate student (called a doctoral candidate) passes all examinations and demonstrates the ability to conduct and defend independent research in a doctoral dissertation, the university awards her or him the degree of Doctor of Philosophy (Ph.D.). James Olds was a faculty member at McGill University, and Peter Milner was his graduate student.

No research psychologist can master all there is to know about the human mind and behavior. But prior to conducting research in brain stimulation, Olds and Milner had learned a great deal about anatomy, physiology, and behavioral analysis. Their experience and training had prepared them to make skilled observations, and channeled their curiosity in studying the highly specialized problem on which they focused. Furthermore, Olds and Milner were emotionally invested in understanding their discovery. Researchers A and B have found *this,* they reasoned, and Researchers X and Y have found *that* about the brain. What do *our* observations mean? What part of the puzzle has yet to be solved? What is electrical stimulation causing in this particular rat? Their curiosity may have been innate, but their training was embedded in a continuous research tradition stretching back for decades.

Generating a Hypothesis

A scientifically trained individual begins with a hunch, or **hypothesis,** about something that isn't perfectly understood. James Olds wanted to understand the brain-behavior relationships that occurred when various parts of a rat's brain were electrically stimulated. He had read the cumulative findings of other brain researchers who worked decades earlier. Now he was faced with the task

hypothesis A hunch, idea, or theory that is formally tested in an experiment.

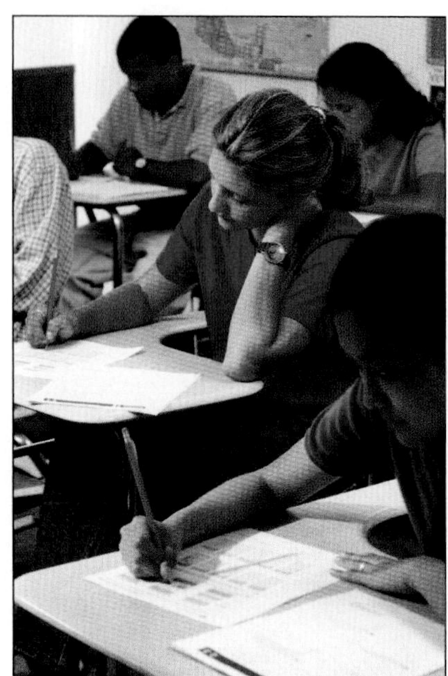

Although intelligence can be defined in many ways, most colleges use standardized test scores as an operational definition of intelligence.

of trying to understand the behavior of rat number 32. Among the thousands of details and facts he had learned, he recalled that a certain part of the brain called the hypothalamus was involved with eating and drinking. Now, when rat number 32 began to behave in an unpredictable way, Olds formed a **working hypothesis** that the brain area in question was related to food reinforcement. One characteristic of scientists, then, is that they are capable of making informed observations and sound predictions about experimental outcomes.

Sometimes luck, also known as serendipity, plays a role. Horace Walpole coined the word serendipity to describe a mythical faculty scientists possess that allows them to make important discoveries—by accident. Others have noted that a successful discovery is often best attributed to a prepared mind "being in the right place at the right time." Indeed, James Olds was just such a person. His electrode was not where he had aimed to put it—in a brainstem structure called the *reticular formation.* Because he recognized the significance of the way this particular rat was behaving, he surmised that the electrode was stimulating a different part of the brain. The result: Olds and Milner were the first researchers to observe the effects of stimulating a so-called pleasure center in the brain.

If his electrode placement had indeed produced a "good feeling" in the rat (similar to the satisfying effect of eating food when hungry), Olds still had to demonstrate the effect. First he defined "feeling good" in operational terms. He reasoned that an *operational definition* of self-reinforcement in the rat—of making itself "feel good"—was whether it would press a lever to stimulate its brain. In general, an **operational definition** defines the concept at hand ("feeling good") in terms of the operations used to measure it (that is, pressing a lever for self-stimulation).

Operational definitions are another example of the adage that "method determines content." The importance of operational definitions is that Researcher X knows exactly what Researcher Y means by psychological terms such as *pleasure, hunger, intelligence,* and *consciousness.* An operational definition makes a theoretical question an empirical one, and in doing so, serves to distinguish a scientific approach from a nonscientific one. For example, a novelist—but never a psychologist—might characterize an individual's *personality* as the "undefinable essence of a person." By contrast, a psychologist might define *intelligence* in terms of how a person scores on a series of standardized tests.

working hypothesis A simple statement of what is expected to happen in an experiment.

operational definition A definition of a concept in terms of how it is being measured.

experimental subject A human or other animal used in an experiment.

electrical stimulation of the brain (ESB) An experimental technique in which electricity is passed through an electrode into the brain.

independent variable In an experiment, a variable that is manipulated to see its effect on the dependent variable.

dependent variable A response variable that changes as a function of the independent variable.

Designing the Experiment

The best research in the psychological sciences is characterized by the testing of hypotheses through formal experimentation. Olds and Milner thought they had discovered a "pleasure center" in the brain. Now they had to prove it to the satisfaction of other researchers. They designed an experiment to test their hypothesis, that for this rat—the **experimental subject**—electrical stimulation was pleasurable.

Olds and Milner's experimental manipulation—their treatment—was to stimulate the rat's brain with electric current and observe its lever-pressing response. Their procedure is now known as **electrical stimulation of the brain,** or **ESB.** In the language of science, both the electric current and the lever-pressing response are called *variables.* Very simply, a variable is something that can stay the same or vary. For example, the voltage of the electric current used to stimulate the rat could be varied. Likewise, the rate of lever pressing could vary.

An experiment is typically designed to investigate the relationship between two variables: One—the **independent variable**—is *manipulated* by the researcher, and the other, called the **dependent variable** (in psychology experiments, most often the subject's response), depends on the independent variable. In this experiment the independent variable was the electric current delivered to the rat's brain, and the pressing of a lever was the dependent variable. (One way not to confuse these two similar-sounding terms is to remember that the dependent variable "depends on" how the subject responds to the independent variable. The rat would not have pressed the lever without the independent variable of ESB.)

Even though it may seem perfectly obvious from the description you read earlier that the brain stimulation caused the animal to press the lever, Olds and Milner realized that they had to rule out alternative explanations. Scientists are trained to be discerning, critical, and skeptical, and the requirements for scientific explanation are, therefore, quite rigorous. In designing experiments, scientists use one or more *control groups*, or conditions, to better identify and isolate the specific effects of a treatment. A **control group** is exposed to the same conditions that the treatment group experiences, but *not* to the independent variable.

Olds and Milner used several control conditions. In the first experiment they used a **within-subjects design** in which a pretreatment measure of the dependent variable is compared with a post treatment measure in the same subjects. Recall that rat number 32 did not press the lever before it received ESB (pretreatment), but did press the lever after it received the ESB (posttreatment). In another within-subjects test, the brain stimulator was turned off while the rat was pressing the lever. That is, the experimenters removed the independent variable and noted the effect on the dependent variable, lever pressing. They found that the rat quit lever pressing when the stimulator was turned off.

In a **between-groups** design, by contrast, the researcher manipulates an independent variable in a *treatment group* and compares the results to a control group that doesn't experience the independent variable. For example, Olds and Milner compared the results found in rat number 32 with the effects of stimulating other brain sites in other experimental subjects. When other rats did *not* press a lever to deliver the electric current to other brain sites, Olds and Milner safely concluded that stimulating a *specific* brain site was the causal factor. Other experimenters since Olds have introduced still other controls. Some have planted multiple electrodes in different brain sites in the same rat. They found that stimulating some sites but not others reinforces lever pressing. Why would a multiple electrode control condition be better than the within-subjects control Olds used in his original experiment? (Answer: It rules out the possibility that rat number 32 was atypical and would respond to ESB delivered anywhere in its brain.)

Conducting the Experiment

The experiment begins after the researcher formulates his or her hypothesis and double checks the experimental design. Olds and Milner began by implanting electrodes in the brains of rats. They then tested the rats by electrically stimulating their brains and observing their responses a few days after surgery. The researchers compared the stimulated rats' responses with the behavior of unoperated controls in the same situation.

Because Olds and Milner had worked with laboratory rats for many years, they knew that hungry rats will readily learn to do whatever is required of them—for example, to press a lever—to earn food. These rats were already implanted with electrodes, so all that was necessary to accomplish the experiment was to build a chamber to measure their lever-pressing response and to program the equipment so that a lever press would activate the brain stimulator. (Their stimulator, crude by today's standards, delivered a shock that could vary between 0.5 and 5.0 volts.) They next connected a hungry rat to a wire harness that allowed it to move around freely inside the chamber while connected to the stimulator. Pressing the lever stimulated a brain area near the tip of the electrode. As previously described, the rat pressed the lever repeatedly. When the stimulator was disconnected, the rat quit pressing the lever.

control group In an experiment, a comparison group exposed to all conditions of the treatment group except the independent variable.

within-subjects design The design of an experiment in which a pretreatment measure of the dependent variable is compared with a posttreatment measure in the same subjects.

between-groups design An experimental design in which the effect of manipulating an independent variable (i.e., the treatment group) is compared to that of a control group.

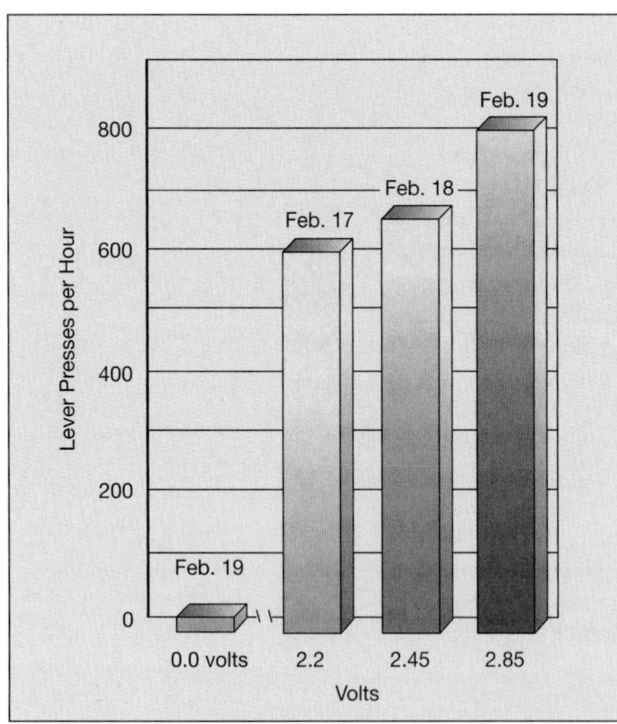

Figure 2.3 The relationship of ESB to lever pressing. Rat number 32 pressed a lever hundreds of times per hour to receive brain stimulation at three different voltages, but did not press the lever when the stimulator was turned off (0 volts). *Source:* After Olds & Milner, 1954.

After collecting behavioral data, Olds and Milner had to determine which part of the rat's brain the electrode was stimulating. They made a tiny brain lesion to mark the location of the tip of the electrode by passing a strong electrical current into the brain, which heated and destroyed the neurons the electrode touched. Next, they sacrificed the rats and removed their brains, fixed them with preservatives, and cut them into sections. Olds and Milner sliced each section thinly, stained it, and mounted it on a glass slide. Looking through a microscope, the researchers identified the path made by the electrode as it was lowered through the brain, and the tissue damaged by the tip of the electrode.

Scientists typically report on the results of a series of related experiments in their published research. Olds and Milner were no exception. Having finished the experiment, they then did a series of follow-up experiments, described in the next section.

Analyzing the Results

Figure 2.3 shows some of the results of Olds and Milner's experiments. The independent variables (ESB treatment of 2.2, 2.45, and 2.85 volts) and the control condition (0.0 volts) are arrayed on the x-axis. The levels of the independent variable—0.0, 2.2, 2.45, and 2.85 volts—are called the *parameter values* of the independent variable. The dependent variable, the rate of lever pressing, is displayed on the y-axis.

Graphs of Functional Relationships. Graphs like the one in Figure 2.3 are visual displays of the relationship of the dependent variable to the independent variable. For example, the graph in Figure 2.3 shows that at three different voltages ESB was so powerful that a rat would press the lever hundreds of times to receive it (but not at all if ESB was disconnected). Among Olds and Milner's findings was that rat number 32 responded at different rates at each of three different voltage levels of ESB, but did not respond at zero volts. Figure 2.3 shows a *functional relationship* between the voltage and the rate of lever pressing. A **functional relationship** is any orderly relationship between two variables, often an independent variable and a dependent variable.

What inference might you make from Figure 2.3? What additional details would you like to know before concluding that higher voltages of brain stimulation always lead to higher rates of lever pressing? You might have noticed that the voltage increased on three successive days (February 17, 18, and 19). Might the rate of response have increased slightly each day even if the voltage had been held constant? Let's call this the "successive days hypothesis" (as contrasted with the "increased voltage hypothesis").

The "successive days hypothesis" is a reasonable alternative to the hypothesis that increased voltage results in higher rates of self-stimulation. Perhaps the rat became increasingly sensitive to *any* voltage. In this example, then, the lever pressing might be attributed to the passage of time—a *confounding variable.* A **confounding variable** is an unknown variable that causes an observable effect. If this alternate hypothesis were true, the lever pressing might have increased even if the *same* voltage was used on each day. Can you think of an experimental design that would control for this confounding variable, allowing Olds and Milner to test the increased voltage hypothesis?

functional relationship An orderly relationship between a stimulus and response, or between two responses.

confounding variable An unknown or unidentified variable that causes an effect.

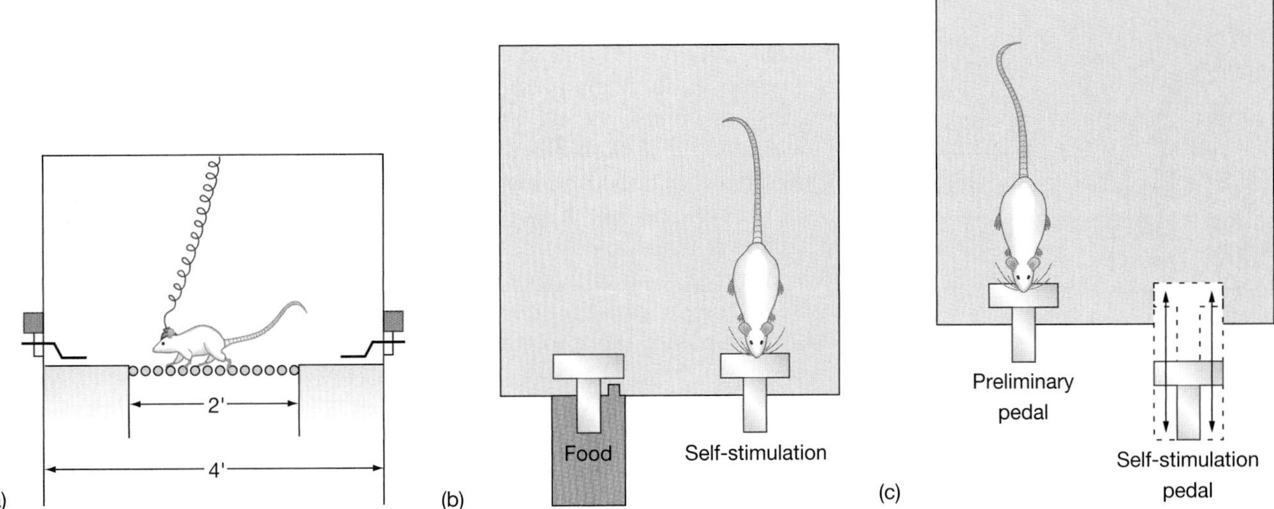

Figure 2.4 **Olds and Milners' follow-up experiments.** (a) Rats repeatedly crossed a 2-foot-long electrified grid to gain access to levers that would provide ESB. (b) When given a choice between food or ESB, starving rats chose ESB. (c) Rats would press an alternate lever 100 times to gain access to the ESB lever. *Source:* From Olds, 1969.

(Answer: Use each level of ESB briefly on the same day, varying the voltages from 0.0 to 2.2, 2.45, and 2.85). Only after an experiment had ruled out the successive day's hypothesis would the conclusion that lever pressing is related to voltage be supported.

Follow-up Experiments. Just how potent a reinforcing stimulus was ESB, Olds and Milner wondered? In follow-up experiments, they redesigned their apparatus to test various hypotheses about the motivational effects of ESB. Figure 2.4a shows that in one experiment implanted rats had to run across a 2-foot length of electrified grid—a painful experience—to gain access to a lever. After several self-stimulations on one lever, the ESB was discontinued, and the rat had to recross the grid to access ESB on another lever. Olds and Milner found that the rats would endure painful electric shocks for the opportunity to self-stimulate. In another modified chamber depicted in Figure 2.4b, a rat could choose between two levers, one that delivered ESB and a second that delivered a food pellet. Would a starving rat press a lever for food, for ESB, or for both? Olds and Milner found that the rat preferred ESB, ignoring the food lever for days.

What an amazing phenomenon! ESB seemed to be so reinforcing that rats quit eating—a highly maladaptive behavior. Perhaps, Olds thought, the ESB *made* the rat press the lever, automaton like, because it activated a motor circuit in the rat's brain that controlled lever pressing. Perhaps once started, ESB stimulation *forced* the rat to respond. To test this hypothesis, he designed the apparatus shown in Figure 2.4c. After a rat pressed the lever 100 times, a second, retractable lever was automatically inserted into the cage. Pressing the second lever produced ESB, which then retracted the second lever. Pressing the first lever 100 times repeated the process. This experiment, as well as the grid-crossing experiment, demonstrated conclusively that ESB had motivational properties and did not cause reflexive lever pressing.

Olds found himself in a most unusual position for a researcher, for seldom are results from a series of experiments so clear-cut. He and other researchers subsequently replicated the experiment in many other rats, and ultimately in other species.

Statistical Tests and the Null Hypothesis. A **statistic** is a mathematical indicator that helps a researcher make decisions about the outcome an experiment. Some experimental results, such as Olds and Milner's, are clear without statistics. The rat self-stimulated hundreds of times per hour at voltages ranging from 2.2 to 2.85 volts, but never lever pressed when the stimulator was turned off.

However, what if Olds's working hypothesis had been that rats would lever press only to a specific ESB voltage? To test this proposition, he might have used a statistical test of the **null hypothesis**, in which the researcher assumes that the independent variable has *no effect* on the treated group, and the results would be the same as those of an untreated control group. The researcher does the experiment. Next, using a statistical test, the experimenter compares the results for the treatment group with those for the control group. If the results are significantly different (that is, beyond a chance difference), the researcher can then *reject* the null hypothesis that the two groups are the same. *Rejecting the null hypothesis allows the researcher to tentatively accept the working hypothesis that a treatment effect is real.* To conclude that group differences exceed what would be expected by chance, however, is *not* the same as saying that the researcher has proved a proposition to be true. The reason is that low-probability events *do* occur: the two groups may have differed from each other *before* the experimental treatment.

Assume that Olds wanted to test the hypothesis that the observed differences in lever pressing were related to ESB voltage. The null hypothesis would be that lever pressing would not vary using 2.2, 2.4, or 2.85 volts. Olds could have conducted a statistical test of this null hypothesis using an *analysis of variance* (abbreviated ANOVA). If the test results indicated that the differences between the three groups were too large to have occurred by chance, Olds would reject the null hypothesis and conclude that rats pressed the lever at a higher rate for higher voltages. Olds (1969) did not report a statistical test of these observations on rat number 32, nor did he conclude that higher levels of ESB produced higher rates of response. Indeed, in experiments with other rats stimulated at different places in the brain, Olds found the opposite result; rats lever pressed *less* at higher voltages. In addition, an optimal voltage exists for each electrode placement.

The choice of statistical tests is closely tied to the design of the experiment. To take but one example, statistical tests that are used for data collected from within-group experimental designs (such as Olds used) differ from tests used for between-group designs. Statistical tests are of limited usefulness; they *help* but do not force researchers to arrive at conclusions about the outcomes of their experiments. By themselves, statistical analyses merely allow researchers to test certain hypotheses; they address neither the results nor the conclusions (Kirk, 1995). Therefore, even with a perfectly good statistical test that rejects the null hypothesis, an experimenter can draw the wrong conclusions about an experiment, often due to confounding variables.

After Olds concluded from his experiments that the rats' behavior could be interpreted in terms of activating a "pleasure center," he then proceeded to the next step. He tried to get his work validated by other psychologists—a process that is similar to getting a second opinion.

statistic A mathematical indicator that helps a researcher make decisions about experimental outcomes.

null hypothesis A statement that no differences exist between two groups being compared in an experiment.

Validating the Experiment Through Peer Review

Psychologists attempt to publish the results of their research for a number of reasons. One is simple: in "publish or perish" universities, professors are expected to publish to keep their jobs. A "pure" motivation is that like most people, they take pleasure in being the source of new information. Scientists who do original research are in a position of knowing something that no one else in the world may even suspect. Having satisfied *their* curiosity, most scientists take pride in having their names associated with findings they want to share with others.

A second reason that scientists submit their research for publication is that it sets in motion the process through which other researchers validate experiments. Let's say you conduct an experiment that takes 18 months from start to finish. You're excited about the outcome, and because of your genius and time invested you think it deserves the Nobel Prize. However, you now face the problem of what other people think of your work. You write your research article and submit it to a journal for publication. Journal editors and other scientists who review your research ask the following questions:

- Did you send your experiments to the appropriate journal? (Most magazines that publish science articles are called journals.) For example, because the journal *Psychological Science* publishes brief reports of general interest to all psychologists, it would be unlikely to publish your results on the differences in the habituation of neurons in the sensory ganglion cells of two species of snails. (However, the journal *Physiology and Behavior* might be interested!)
- Did you do a thorough search of the literature related to your research area, and did you carefully acknowledge the contributions of previous investigators?
- Is yours original research, or did you mistakenly do an experiment that was reported years ago by other researchers?
- Did you use reasonable methods and procedures? Do the operational definitions of your terms make sense to others?
- Are the descriptions of procedures you used and the results you obtained adequate to allow someone else to do the experiment and stand a reasonable chance of replicating it?
- Did your experimental design and statistical analysis accomplish what you set out to do? Were your control groups adequate to allow you to draw the conclusions you did? Did you consider possible confounding variables? Were your interpretation of results and the conclusions you reached valid?
- Is your research worthwhile? Do other scientists agree with you that the research you accomplished is important enough to be published?

As you can see, the review process for submitted articles is formal and uncompromising. Journal editors strive to maintain the editorial and professional standards of each one of the many psychological journals currently being published. Most read the submitted research themselves and send copies of the research to two or more other researchers, called reviewers, or referees, for their opinion. A consensus of opinion—called **validation by consensus**—guides the editor either to accept the research for publication or reject it. In addition to decisions to "accept" or "reject," a journal editor may ask for further clarification of a point or consider publishing a revised research paper.

Most journals use anonymous referees, and most referees are colleagues or peers of the person submitting the research. For this reason the process of achieving a consensus is often called **peer review**. Reviewers are typically active researchers in the same area as the research being submitted for publication. The purpose of anonymous review is to subject the submitted research to a highly critical analysis and evaluation without fear of recrimination to the reviewer. Anonymous reviews tend to be more critical and less forgiving than signed reviews. (Lest we forget, scientists are human beings who share humanity's less noble reactions, including revenge. A reviewer of his or her friend's experiments can be objective, critical, and judgmental only if the review is anonymous.)

To end on a happy note, many research findings do get published following peer review, in the last stage of the research process.

validation by consensus Support for the acceptance of an experimental finding by the agreement of other scientists who examine it.

peer review The examination of an experimental finding by other scientists.

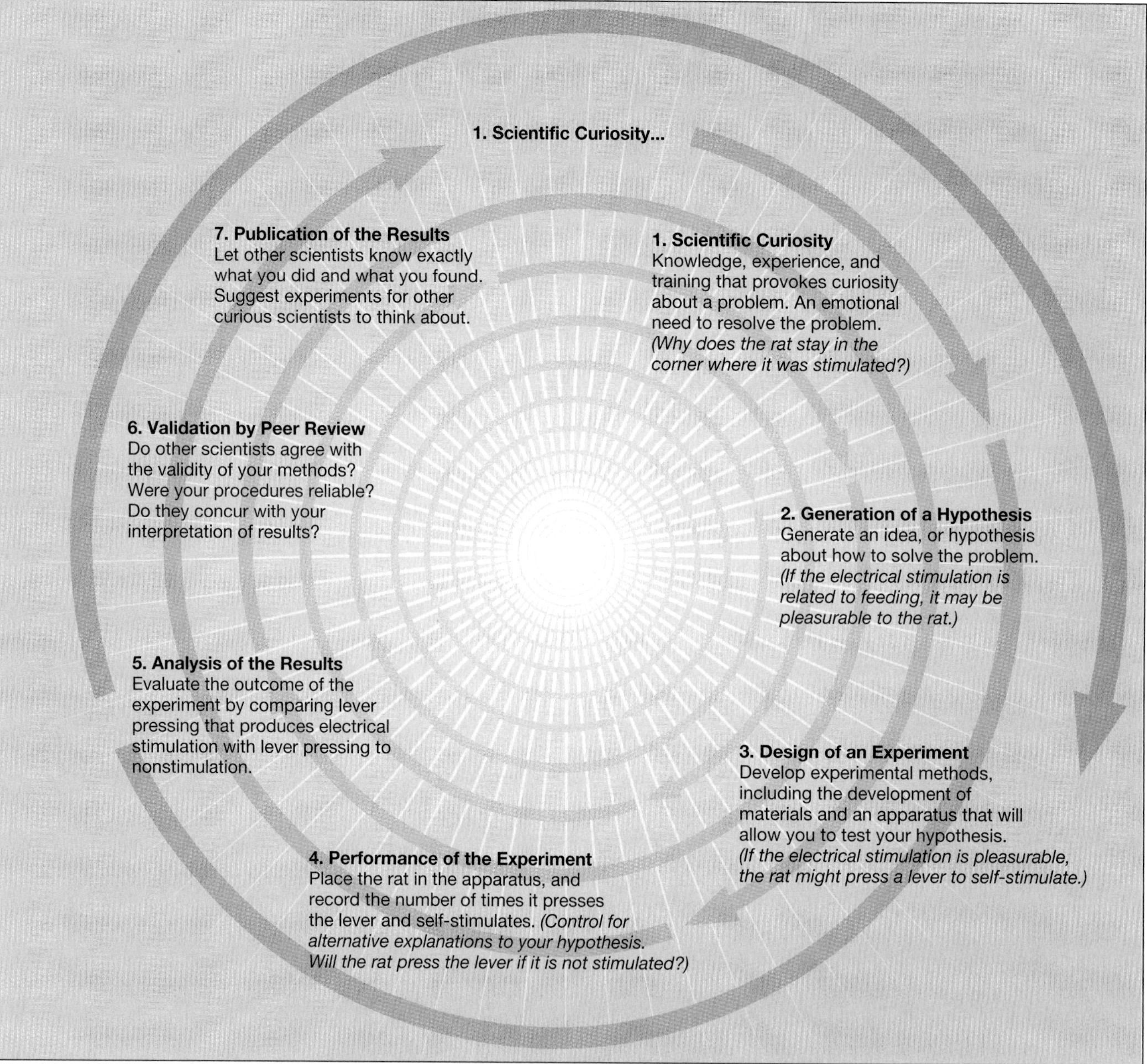

1. Scientific Curiosity...
1. Scientific Curiosity
Knowledge, experience, and training that provokes curiosity about a problem. An emotional need to resolve the problem.
(Why does the rat stay in the corner where it was stimulated?)
2. Generation of a Hypothesis
Generate an idea, or hypothesis about how to solve the problem.
(If the electrical stimulation is related to feeding, it may be pleasurable to the rat.)
3. Design of an Experiment
Develop experimental methods, including the development of materials and an apparatus that will allow you to test your hypothesis.
(If the electrical stimulation is pleasurable, the rat might press a lever to self-stimulate.)
4. Performance of the Experiment
Place the rat in the apparatus, and record the number of times it presses the lever and self-stimulates. (Control for alternative explanations to your hypothesis. Will the rat press the lever if it is not stimulated?)
5. Analysis of the Results
Evaluate the outcome of the experiment by comparing lever pressing that produces electrical stimulation with lever pressing to nonstimulation.
6. Validation by Peer Review
Do other scientists agree with the validity of your methods? Were your procedures reliable? Do they concur with your interpretation of results?
7. Publication of the Results
Let other scientists know exactly what you did and what you found. Suggest experiments for other curious scientists to think about.

Figure 2.5 The cycle of science.

Publishing the Results

In 1954 James Olds and Peter Milner published the results of their experiments in an article entitled "Positive Reinforcement Produced by Electrical Stimulation of the Septal Area and Other Regions of the Rat Brain" in the *Journal of Comparative and Physiological Psychology (JCPP)*. At the time, *JCPP* was the most appropriate and prestigious journal in this area of research. The editor of the journal and other scientists who reviewed Olds and Milner's research about half a century ago reached a consensus opinion that the results were valid and reliable, and should be published for other scientists to read. Publication of Olds and Milner's results made them a part of the body of scientific knowledge. We can say that Olds and Milner's experiments had **heuristic** value, because they led to or stimulated further research. By promoting new research, they helped to keep alive the cycle of scientific process.

heuristic Leading to or stimulating further research.

Science is a conservative enterprise; more psychological research is rejected than is accepted for publication. High standards tend to restrict the diversity of ideas entering the mainstream of psychological science. A science that restricts ideas is not necessarily bad, because the "diversity of ideas" contains a lot of nonsense. Books and magazines that do not use a rigorous review process provide other venues for alternatives to mainstream science. The result is that for the most part, the articles found in reviewed journals have come to define a vibrant, rigorous science. Scientists and the lay public alike may not agree with the observations and conclusions that constitute the subject matter of psychology, but they do agree on the method by which this knowledge was gained, including the important role of peer review. Figure 2.5 summarizes the seven steps that characterize the ongoing process of science.

INTERIM SUMMARY

1. Science grows out of human curiosity.
2. Having read the published results of related experiments, a psychologist focuses, or channels curiosity by developing a hunch, or ***hypothesis.*** Eventually this hunch becomes a ***working hypothesis***—the researcher's best guess about the probable outcome of an experiment.
3. A hypothetical term in a psychological experiment is defined by the operations used to measure it, called an ***operational definition.***
4. An experiment assesses a treatment effect in *different* subjects with a ***between-groups*** design, and compares pre- with post-treatment effects in the *same* subjects with a ***within-subjects*** design.
5. An experimenter manipulates an ***independent variable*** and measures its effect on a ***dependent variable.*** A ***confounding variable*** is an unknown variable that may cause an effect.
6. A researcher compares the results from ***experimental subjects*** of a treatment group or condition with those from an untreated ***control group*** or condition, often using a *statistical test* to compare the two groups.
7. Following a *statistical test* of the ***null hypothesis,*** an experiment often reveals a ***functional relationship*** between the independent and dependent variable.
8. Scientists submit the results of published experiments to a journal for ***peer review.*** Other researchers then analyze the details of the experiments and arrive at a ***validation by consensus*** regarding publication.
9. The results of published experiments become an accepted part of what scientists know. An experiment's ***heuristic*** value may lead to new hypotheses, new experiments, and new findings.

For Further Thought

1. How would you operationally define *consciousness*?
2. Why do nonscientists think that scientists search for and discover the truth about nature, yet, scientists hold their "truths" quite tentatively?
3. What are the strengths and weaknesses of a science that is "validated by consensus"?

NONEXPERIMENTAL RESEARCH METHODS

The experimental method is one way psychologists seek to understand the human mind and behavior. But "doing an experiment" is not always an option. In this concluding section we will look at a number of other methods psychologists use to describe, test, and measure behavior. In leaving the experimental

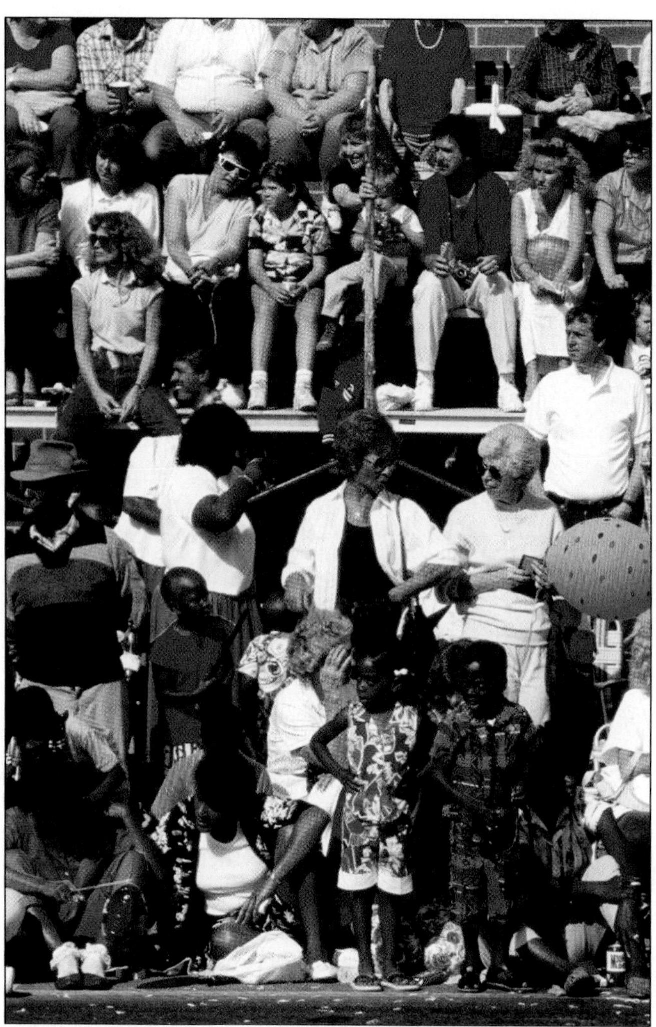
A population of humans is characterized by individual differences.

laboratory, we lose some of the power of explanation afforded by experimental analysis. Nevertheless, the nonexperimental methods described in this section provide powerful techniques that have contributed to the wealth of accumulated psychological knowledge. For example, psychologists study human behavior by asking people to respond to interviews and questionnaires, by conducting surveys, and by merely observing an individual's responses. We'll see that observations, surveys, and questionnaires provide valuable insights into psychological processes. Indeed, by measuring what most people say or are capable of doing, psychologists have defined norms of behavior—be they for emotional well-being, aptitude, or "intelligence." Such tests measure how humans sense the world, how they learn and remember. Let's look at some nonexperimental methods psychologists use, starting with the study of individual differences.

Studying Individuals and Groups

Most of us try to understand ourselves by comparing how we think and behave with how those around us think and behave. Why doesn't John cry during movies as often as Mary does? Why does Mary get better grades than Elaine? Why is Elaine a better pianist than Terry, who cries during movies even less often than John? Answers to these questions come from the study of **individual differences**—the many ways in which individuals vary within a population. Suppose, for example, that a researcher is interested in the individual differences in children's mathematical abilities. The initial question may be relatively undefined, such as "Why do some elementary students make higher math scores than others?" Let's walk through some nonexperimental methods that might be used to address this question. Then we will propose an *experiment* to show how it contrasts with the nonexperimental methods.

One of the first steps our psychological researcher might follow would be to determine the mathematical abilities of a specific group—let's say, sixth graders in the United States. She could locate data that had been gathered through a **standardized test** of mathematical aptitude given nationally to all sixth graders. The uniform procedures of a standardized test generate scores that can be meaningfully compared. The hypothetical results of such a mass testing might look like the graph in Figure 2.6, which displays a **normal distribution** (normal curve, or bell curve). A normal distribution is characterized by a **mean** (the average score) and **standard deviation** (a measure of variance, or dispersal, on both sides of the mean score). Because the normal curve represents a population of scores visually, the mean and standard deviation are called **descriptive statistics.**

Assume that the sixth graders' scores fit well with the bell-shaped curve in Figure 2.6. You can see that most scores would lie in the middle range, with few students either excelling or performing poorly. Those scores at the extremes would be found in the left and right sides (or tails) of the distribution. Note also that 95 percent of all sixth graders would lie within two standard deviations on either side of the mean. (Within three standard deviations, 99 percent of all sixth graders are accounted for.) What is intriguing about this way of

individual differences The many ways in which individuals vary within a population.

standardized test A test that is administered using uniform procedures that generates scores that can be meaningfully compared to each other.

normal distribution A normal, or bell-shaped, curve representing the frequency of occurrence of scores for a given characteristic of a population.

mean The midpoint, or arithmetic average, of a population of scores.

standard deviation A measure of variability around a mean within a population (see appendix).

descriptive statistic Simple numerical descriptions of observations, such as the mean of a distribution of scores.

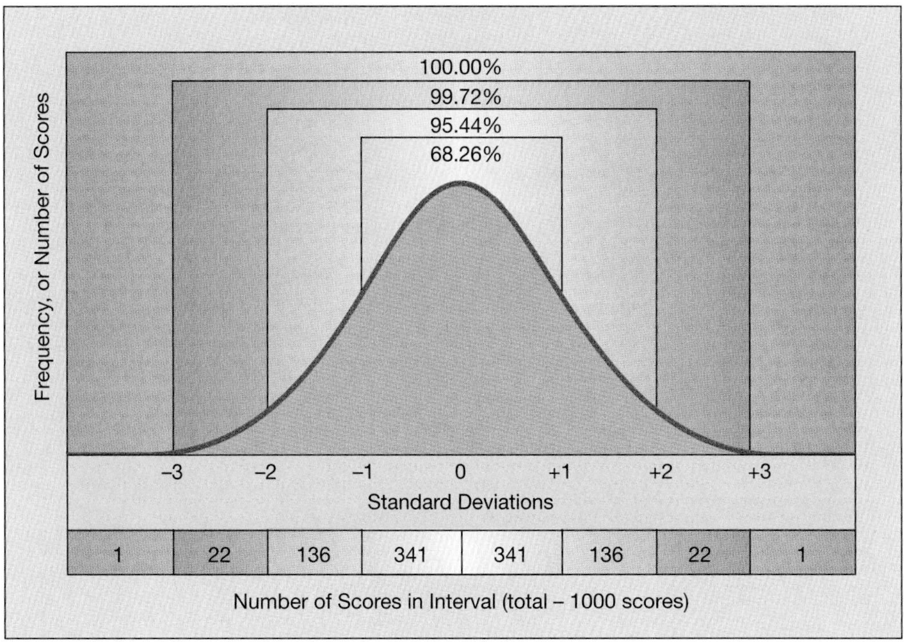

Figure 2.6 A normal distribution. A normal curve (or normal distribution of scores) showing the mean (at "0 standard deviations") and the standard deviation of a population of 1,000 scores.

comparing differences among a population of individuals is that such normal distributions are characteristic of *most* biological and psychological measurements. For example, if we measured the length of the index fingers of all sixth graders in the United States, we would find that they were also normally distributed, with most being of "average" length and a few being either extremely short or extremely long. We will see throughout this text that the psychobiological attributes of individuals, including attractiveness and intelligence, are also normally distributed.

Surveys and Case Studies

The astute reader might argue that the procedure just described *is* an experiment: The math test items can be thought of as independent variables, and the test scores of the students responding to the test are the dependent variables. Rather than comparing a treatment group with a control group, however, the standardized test presents the same math test items to everyone. Our hypothetical researcher, then, has merely collected observations and described them by counting them, a research method known as a *survey*. A **survey** is a measurement technique designed to investigate people's attitudes, aptitudes, and other behaviors. A related method, called *archival research,* is based on data collected and stored by someone other than the investigator. In fact, our understanding of the role behavior plays in health is based largely on studies that use the survey method and archival data.

Now that our researcher has found these individual differences in the mathematical ability of sixth graders, she decides to formulate a hypothesis about why these differences occur. Let's suppose her working hypothesis is that mathematical "aptitude" is really nothing more than the result of hard work: Children are better or worse at solving math problems as a function of the number of hours they study in preparation for a test. How is she to test her hypothesis? She might elect to do a **case study**—an investigation of a single individual over time. She could identify a young student and carefully examine all aspects of his or her study habits and math

survey A measurement technique designed to find out about attitudes, aptitudes, and other behaviors.

case study An investigation of a single individual over time.

The performance of these students might be studied by psychologists as a sample, from which they could draw conclusions about a population.

proficiency over a period of months or even years. One benefit of a case study is its heuristic value; study habits and math proficiency are both complex behaviors, and understanding them better in one person might lead to the generation of many hypotheses about their relation. The drawbacks of the case study are that it is time consuming and that the results are difficult to interpret. For example, are the results specific to this individual, or can they be generalized to others?

So instead of doing a case study, our researcher elects to get permission from the large public school system in the city where she lives to collect data that will allow her to better understand the math performance of her target population. Specifically, she gets the math scores of students who have taken a standardized test, and compares a *sample* of local sixth graders with the national survey results. A **sample** is a subset of scores from a population. She assumes that the normal distribution of math scores from the sample of sixth graders in her city does not differ from the distribution for the *population* of sixth graders in the national survey (see Figure 2.6). (A **population** is defined as a comprehensive set of individual scores of a particular characteristic.) She might use a statistical test to compare her sample against the national population. Should the results of this test indicate no differences between the sample and the population, she could conclude that the sixth graders in her city are representative of those in the rest of the nation. Encouraged, she decides to continue her nonexperimental study.

sample A subset of scores of a population.

population The complete set of individual scores of a particular characteristic.

Next, our researcher collects data about the sixth graders' study habits by having them complete a survey form. She asks each student to estimate how many hours each week he or she studies math. She codes each student's response to preserve its confidentiality, then compares the test scores with their self-reports of their study habits. A few of these data entries are indicated in Table 2.1. Variable 1 is the number of hours each student studied, and variable 2 is the score that student made on the math test.

Next, our researcher plots each student's estimated *study time* on the x-axis and the same student's *test score* on the y-axis. Note that one point represents

Table 2.1 Data for a Scatterplot

The number of hours spent studying and the percentage of correct items on a standardized math test for a small sample of students. In the graph in Figure 2.7, study time is plotted on the *x*-axis, and the test score is on the *y*-axis.

STUDENT ID	VARIABLE 1: STUDY TIME (HOURS)	VARIABLE 2: TEST SCORE (% CORRECT)
120	3	96
121	2.25	87
122	2	88
123	1.5	65
124	1	64
125	0	60
126	2.25	82
127	1	66
128	2.5	92
129	0.5	40
130	2.75	38

both values for each student. The resulting plot of points is called a **scatterplot** (see Figure 2.7). Note that the student with ID 129 studied for 1/2 hour and made a score of 40 on the test. The large dots plot all the scores in Table 2.1; the remaining dots are representative of data from other sixth graders.

Correlational Research

The scatterplot in Figure 2.7 allows our hypothetical researcher to visualize her hypothesis. Looking at the distribution of points, she can question whether the sixth graders' performance on this particular math test is related to how long they

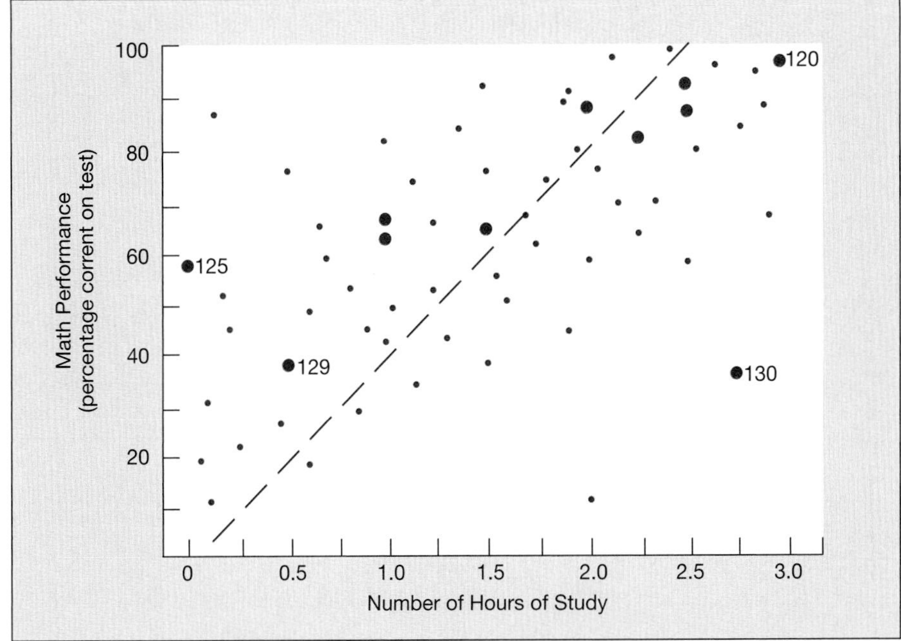

Figure 2.7 Scatterplot of a positively correlated relationship. This scatterplot of data from Table 2.1 relates students' study time to their scores on a math test. Note that student ID 125 did not study at all (0 hours) but scored a 60 on the exam. The data points from Table 2.1 are larger than the others.

scatterplot A distribution of data points that vary in two dimensions.

studied. Look at Figure 2.7 and ask yourself if there is a systematic relationship between study time and performance. That is, how well are the two variables correlated (related to each other)? One way to find out is to compute a *correlation coefficient* for the data. A **correlation coefficient** is a number that varies from +1.0—a perfect, positive relationship between two variables—to 0.0, which denotes the absence of a relationship, and –1.0—a perfect negative relationship between two variables. If every point in Figure 2.7 fell on the light blue diagonal line, the relationship between the number of hours studied and the math score achieved would be 1.0—a perfect, positive correlation. The diagonal line indicates that for each increase in value along one dimension, there is a corresponding increase in value along the other dimension. Perfect correlations are seldom seen in the behavioral and biological sciences. Strong correlations might range from .70 to .90, and weakly correlated variables often lie in the range of .10 to .20. If there is no relationship between two variables, the correlation will be close to 0.0.

An increase in one variable might also be correlated with a decrease in the other. For example, assume that a perverse researcher taught the sixth graders math procedures that would produce the wrong answers. In that case, the more they studied, the worse they would perform on the math test. Under such conditions, the correlation between time spent studying and math performance would be a negative one! Figure 2.8 shows two additional scatterplots, one indicating the absence of a relationship (correlation = 0) and the other indicating a moderately negative correlation between studying the wrong methods and subsequent math performance.

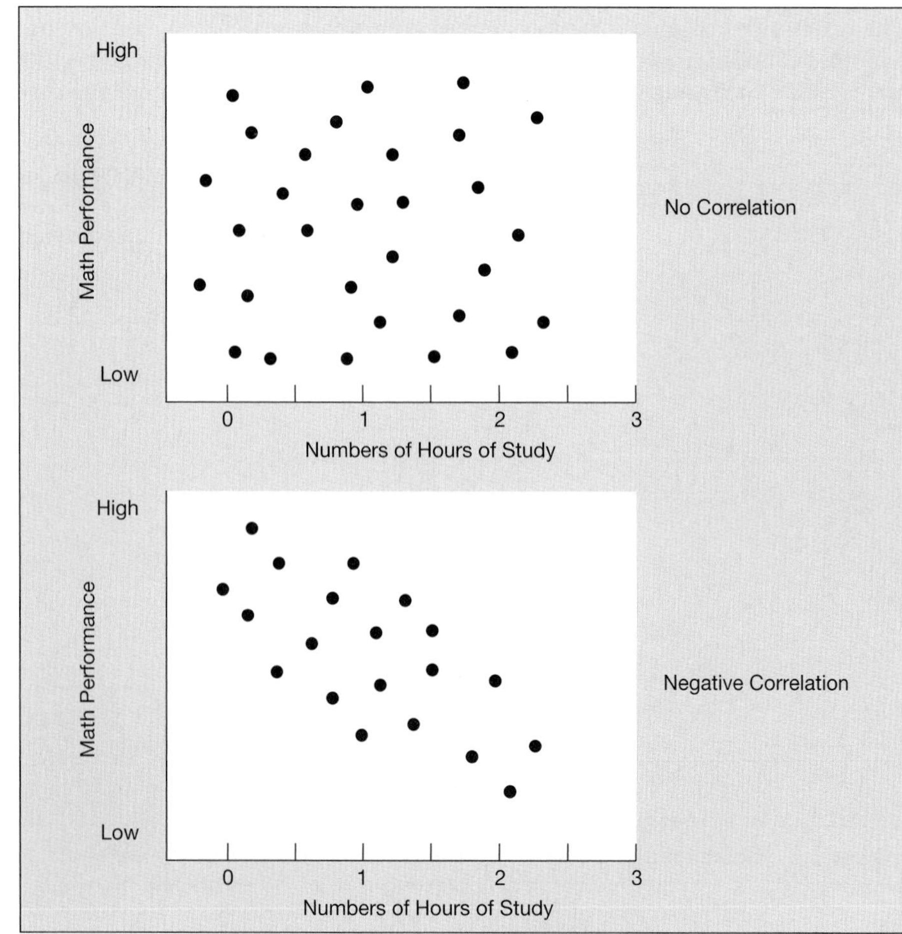

Figure 2.8 Scatterplots of random and negatively correlated relationships.

correlation coefficient A number that varies from +1.0 (a perfect, positive relationship between two variables) to 0.0 (the absence of a relationship), to –1.0 (a perfect, negative relationship between two variables).

Sports fans typically are biased in their perception of events on the field.

Note the cautious conclusion that math test scores are *influenced* by study time. The fact that two variables are correlated does not mean that they are causally related. (You may have heard this truism in the form of the expression "Correlation does not imply causation.") For example, the length of the index finger of any given sixth grader is highly correlated with the length of any other bone in that sixth grader's body. Obviously, none of those bone lengths "caused" the length of any of the other bones. Both were caused by other variables such as diet and heredity.

Does study "cause" math scores? In examining individual data points in Figure 2.7, we find that one student reported not studying for the exam, but nevertheless got a 60 percent test score (ID 125). Another (ID 130) reported studying over 2.5 hours, but scored less than 40 percent on the exam. Clearly, study time cannot be the only determinant of test performance. Other variables, including health, family life, prior learning, heredity, and so on, also affect the tendency to perform better on a test following longer study times.

Having found a positive correlation between study time and math performance, our hypothetical researcher decides to conduct an experiment to further study the relationship. In the following experiment she manipulates the independent variable, time spent studying, by assigning students to groups that differ in how long they are allowed to study. She then measures their performance on a math test. The experiment would likely confirm her finding that study time is a causal factor in math performance.

Researchers have a tendency to make biased observations that support their working hypotheses, a tendency called the **observer expectancy effect.** (An example of the observer expectancy effect is partisan fans who "see" infractions the other team has not made.) With this pitfall in mind, our hypothetical researcher attempts to design her experiment in a way that does not unduly bias its outcome. One method of minimizing observer expectancy effects is to arrange a **double-blind experiment,** in which neither the participants (the sixth graders in this example) nor the experimenter know which group they have been assigned to. The usual way double-blind experiments are designed is to have a research assistant assign coded, uninformed subjects to groups.

observer expectancy effects Observer bias—the tendency of an experimenter to make biased observations that would unduly support the working hypothesis.

double-blind experiment An experiment in which neither the researcher nor the subjects are aware of the treatment condition.

Double-blind experiments are often used in drug studies. Because subjects might expect to respond differently to receiving a drug dose specified as low, medium, or high, they are not informed of the dosage used in the treatment condition. In the present example, students would likely bring different expectancies to the math test if they knew they had studied more or less than other students. A student who knows that he or she was assigned to a low-study condition might expect to do less well than others, and might not try as hard. These **subject expectancy effects** can become confounding variables that influence the experimental results. Researchers must be careful not to introduce these expectancies—also known as *demand characteristics*—into their experiments.

Another option our researcher may exercise is to use a *matched-groups design* rather than a double-blind design. In a **matched-groups design**, subjects are assigned to groups so that a number of specified variables that might influence their performance are controlled for (matched). For example, our researcher might match her groups for sex (the same number of males and females in each group) and demonstrated math ability (equivalent numbers of high-, medium-, and low-performing students in each group). If she were testing a somewhat different hypothesis—that males and females study and perform differently on math tests—she could use sex (m or f) as a treatment variable by assigning girls to one group and boys to another. But in this case, she would merely match them by assigning equal numbers of boys and girls to each study group.

Now the researcher is ready to conduct her experiment. She allows subjects in each of three groups a different amount of time to study for a math test—for example, 0.5, 1.5, and 2.5 hours. The next day she gives them a one-hour math test. Her working hypothesis is the same as it was in the nonexperimental correlational research she conducted earlier: namely, that math performance is positively related to study time. By conducting an experiment, she can now test the null hypothesis that these groups do not differ in performance. If the groups differ to a degree that allows the null hypothesis to be rejected, she can conclude that time spent studying *is* an antecedent condition of math performance. By bringing students into a controlled testing situation using matched groups, she can reduce the variance in her observations. In addition, she need not rely on self-reports of study time; rather, she specifies, controls, and manipulates study time as an independent variable. (Students tend to over report how long they study for exams.) If the performance of these groups differs in a statistically significant way, she can safely conclude that study time *is* an antecedent condition for math performance.

LINK
Epidemiological data and health psychology, Chapter 16, p. 552

Epidemiological Research

We have seen that correlational research methods differ from experiments. To clarify the distinction between the two methods, consider the mortality rates of smokers, former smokers, and nonsmokers shown in Figure 2.9. These data are an example of *epidemiological research*, done using the survey method. In **epidemiological research**, correlational techniques are used to establish relationships between behavior and health. We will see in the study of health psychology (Chapter 16) that epidemiological research yields an understanding of health risk factors and how they are related. Epidemiological research is essential to psychologists' understanding of health behavior, because experiments with humans are ethically challenging, costly, and time consuming.

subject expectancy effects A confounding variable; the expectations a subject brings to an experiment that can influence the outcome of the experiment.

matched-groups design An experimental design in which subjects are assigned to groups so that a number of specified variables that might influence their performance are controlled.

epidemiological research The use of correlation techniques to establish relationships between behavior and health.

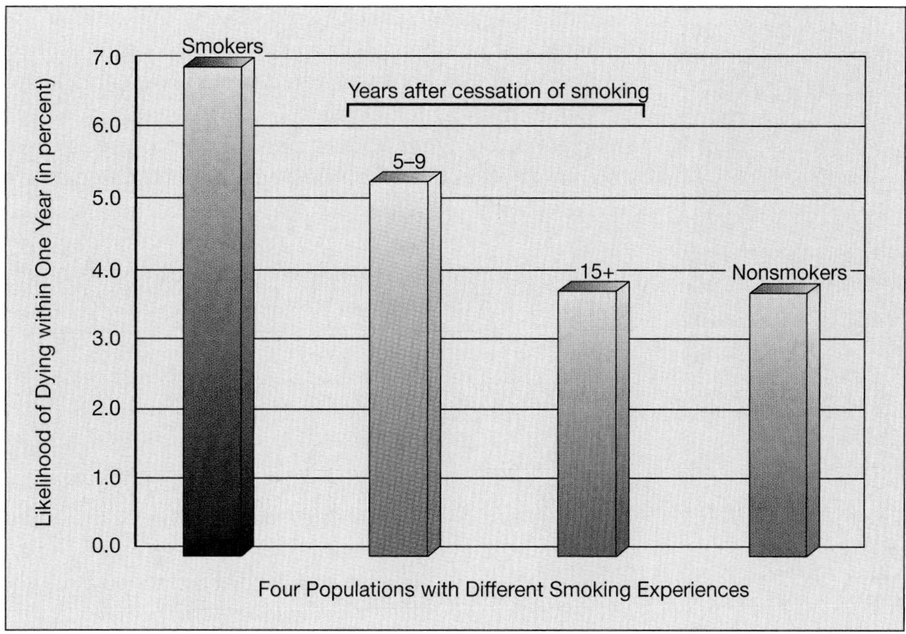

Figure 2.9 The relationship between smoking and mortality rates. *Source:* Figure from p. 200 in "Smoking and Morality Among US Veterans" by E. Roget in *Journal of Chronic Diseases*, (1974), Vol. 27. Copyright © 1974 by Elsevier Science. Reprinted by permission.

The results shown in Figure 2.9 come from a 16-year study of 250,000 U. S. veterans. What conclusions would you draw from this comparison of the death rates of cigarette smokers, former smokers, and nonsmokers? How would you answer the following questions?

(a) _____ T/F The death rate is approximately twice as high for smokers as it is for nonsmokers.

(b) _____ T/F Those who stop smoking live longer than those who continue to smoke.

(c) _____ T/F The adverse effects of cigarette smoking are reversible.

(d) _____ T/F Cigarettes kill.

Answering questions (a) and (b) "true" shows that you can read the graph and that you understand the relationship between smoking and health. You do not have to draw any inferences about this relationship, as is asked of you in questions (c) and (d). Figure 2.9 does not address the reversibility of the adverse effects of smoking. If you answered true to (c), you were making an inference that the data in Figure 2.9 do not support. The same is true of question (d). The statement that *people who smoke die at a higher rate than people who don't* is not the same as the statement *cigarettes kill.* Though smoking is correlated with a higher death rate, we cannot conclude that smoking cigarettes is the sole cause of the increased death rate. Perhaps compared to nonsmokers, smokers drive their cars more recklessly (due to nicotine?) and have more fatal accidents (because smoke gets in their eyes?). Perhaps smokers drink more alcohol and die from alcohol-related causes. Or perhaps the same genetic characteristics that predispose people to smoke also cause premature death. These are all examples of potential confounding variables—variables that may be associated with the independent variable (smoking cigarettes) and therefore cannot be ruled out as causal agents.

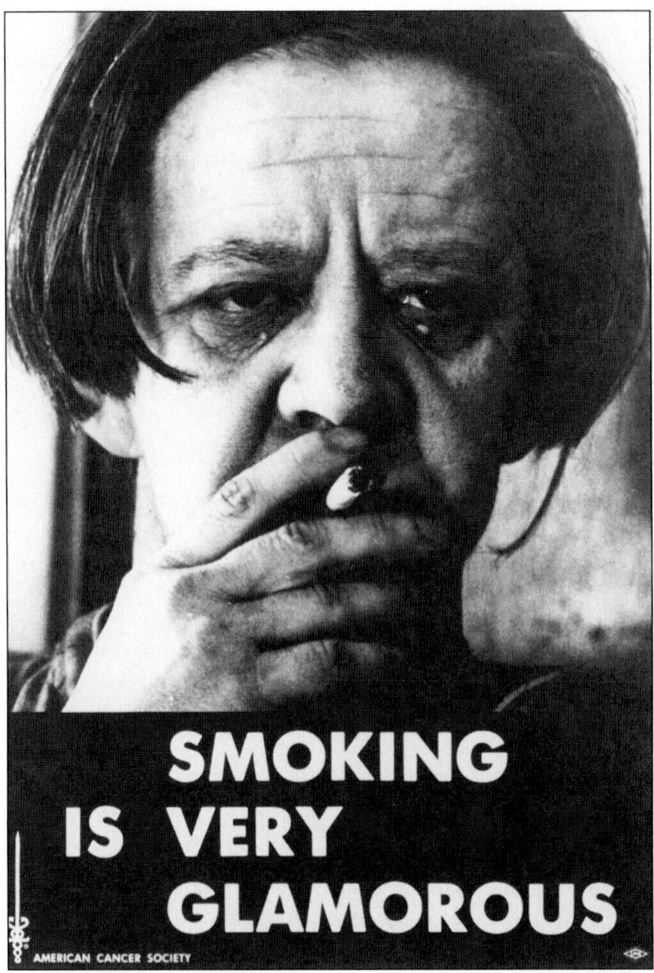
SMOKING
IS VERY
GLAMOROUS
AMERICAN CANCER SOCIETY

All confounding variables had to be ruled out as causal agents before scientists could determine that cigarette smoking resulted in higher death rates.

Epidemiological research can suggest that a relationship may exist between two variables, which opens up new questions that can be investigated by experimental methods. Other studies, for example, have shown that a high number of carcinogens (cancer-causing agents) are released by burning tobacco. In addition, we know that smoking is correlated with a higher-than-normal incidence of heart disease. This multidisciplinary pattern of results leads one to the conclusion that smoking is harmful and is highly likely to lead to increased mortality rates.

Psychological Inventories and Questionnaires

Psychologists have developed many kinds of tests, inventories, surveys, and questionnaires for a variety of purposes. For example, students are admitted to college based in part on how well they score on standardized tests such as the SAT and the ACT. These tests measure mathematical, language, and critical-thinking abilities that are correlated with success in completing coursework at the college level. In addition, you may have taken IQ tests such as the Stanford-Binet, the WISC, and/or the WAIS, described in Chapter 13.

Personnel in industry and the military often use paper-and-pencil tests to select individuals on the basis of aptitude, skill, and leadership potential. They also gather data on a person's emotional stability and other psychological and behavioral attributes. These tests, and possibly a **structured interview**—a formal procedure that allows for systematic data gathering—help to determine who will make the best pilots, mechanics, computer programmers, or mid-level managers. We will see in Chapter 14 (Personality) and Chapter 17 (Abnormal Psychology) that the health-care professions use a variety of *self-report methods* to measure personality variables. A **self-report method** is a paper-and-pencil test that can be completed by an individual. The Beck Depression Inventory (Beck, 1967) is one example; the person being tested is asked to circle the number beside the statement that best reflects how he or she feels, such as:

LINK

Intelligence testing, Chapter 13, p. 452

0 I do not feel sad.

1 I feel sad.

2 I am sad all the time and I can't snap out of it.

3 I am so sad and unhappy that I can't stand it.

We'll see in Chapter 17 that the pattern of answering such questions yields a numerical score indicative of how depressed the test taker is. Counselors and psychologists use this test, and observations from interview procedures, to assess a patient's problems and plot a course of therapy. But the question remains: How effective are psychological tests, inventories, and questionnaires?

structured interview A formal interview procedure in which specified information is obtained.

self-report method A test (such as a paper-and-pencil test) that can be completed by an individual.

psychometrics Methods of measuring psychological processes.

reliability The repeatability of an observation, experiment, or test score.

Paper-and-Pencil Test Reliability. As we saw earlier, psychological methods must be both reliable and valid. **Psychometrics** are methods of measuring psychological processes to ensure their *test* ***reliability*** and *test validity*. A reliable test is consistent—that is, it gives the same results time after time. For example, the **test-retest reliability** of the SAT (and the WAIS IQ test) is high; a person taking these tests on more than one occasion typically scores about the same at each testing. Likewise, scoring the same on two different versions of the test indicates high **alternate-form reliability.** Or a tester might compare how a person's scores on half the test items compare with the score on the other half. If the scores on two halves of a test are about the same, the test is said to have high **split-half reliability**. A test is reliable, then, if it gives the same results each time it is taken; if two forms of the test give the same results; and if the first half gives the same result as the second half. Most often, reliability is expressed as the correlation between scores earned on two administrations or two versions of a test: A correlation coefficient of 0.90 between two tests would indicate high reliability.

Paper-and-Pencil Test Validity. The **validity** of a test refers to the test's ability to measure what it is designed to measure. For a number of reasons, assessing the validity of a psychological test is more problematic than assessing its reliability. One reason is that not all investigators agree on the operational definitions of terms that describe psychological properties. For example, we will see in the chapter on intelligence that different investigators have widely differing opinions of what constitutes "intelligence." Some investigators might acknowledge the *reliability* of an intelligence test, but not its *validity*. For example, a child might reliably be able to label a red object "red" and a blue object "blue," but that ability is better related to perception than to intelligence. Likewise, not all psychologists agree that something as complex as clinical depression can be adequately assessed using the Beck Depression Inventory, a 20-item paper-and-pencil test. Finally, to the extent that test items reflect the common usage of psychological terms, the test is said to have **face validity** (validity based on surface appearance). In examining the test item from the Beck Depression Inventory on page 61, you might ask yourself whether the item corresponds to your understanding of the term *depression*.

Researchers have approached validity from a number of perspectives. For example, a test is said to have **criterion-related validity** if it is widely accepted, or correlates well with an independent assessment of the same construct. Does a patient who has been diagnosed as depressed in a structured interview also score highly on the Beck Depression Inventory? Does the aviator who scores high on a test that predicts pilot proficiency actually meet the criteria to become a pilot? Do people with high IQs behave intelligently in all aspects of their lives? The point is that for tests to be useful, they must be both valid and reliable.

Depression and abnormal psychology, Chapter 17, p. 594

Intelligence, Chapter 13, p. 459

Comparison of Methods

We have looked at both experimental and nonexperimental methods. Can we conclude from the preceding examples that *only* the experimental method provides conclusive evidence about the determinants of behavior, and that nonexperimental methods such as correlational research are fatally flawed? The answer is no, for several reasons. The first is that researchers using the experimental method can come to the wrong conclusions (Kirk, 1995). Experimental results are most often interpreted by statistical tests, which researchers can misinterpret in two ways. In comparing a treatment group with a control group, they can reject the null hypothesis (no difference between the groups) when in fact it is true; conversely, they can fail to reject it when it is false. For this reason, all experimental results are reported conditionally, meaning that there is always a slight probability that an experiment has been interpreted incorrectly.

Another reason the experimental method doesn't always identify the causes of a behavior—which typically is one goal of behavioral research—is that individual differences are *real* differences. For example, there is every reason to believe that

test-retest reliability A test is reliable if it gives the same results each time it is taken.

alternate-form reliability A test is reliable if two forms of it give the same results.

split-half reliability A test is reliable if the first half of the test gives the same result as the second half of the test.

validity The ability of a test to measure what it is designed to measure.

face validity The soundness of a test based on its surface appearance.

criterion-related validity A test is valid if it correlates well with a separate, independent assessment of the construct being measured.

were an experiment to be done in which half the human subjects smoked three packs of cigarettes a day for 60 years and a control group smoked none, some individuals in the experimental group would remain healthy, and some in the control group would not. Again, experimental results are reported tentatively because all experimental results *are* conditional.

Finally, powerful correlational techniques (such as *multivariate regression methods*) allow the analysis of behavioral complexity in ways that match or exceed the power of the experimental method. Thus, both experimental and nonexperimental methods are important in the study of behavior.

Ethical Issues in Psychological Research

Recall the hypothetical researcher who studied sixth graders' study habits. She approached her local school district to get students' math scores and asked students to fill out a form estimating how long they studied. If only research were so uncomplicated! In reality, before any data can be gathered, researchers must first get permission from one or more committees of trained professionals who consider requests to use humans and animals in research. These committees, often called Institutional Review Boards (IRBs), can be found wherever researchers conduct experiments with humans. Similar review boards regulate how animals are used in research. Each board must follow ethical guidelines designed to protect the rights of experimental subjects. In the United States, organizations such as the American Psychological Association, the National Science Foundation, and the National Institutes of Health set ethical standards.

For both humans and other animals used in research, the primary considerations are those of welfare, justifiable use, and safety: Could the procedures used in this experiment cause physical discomfort or psychological harm? If so, do the potential benefits of the experiment outweigh the costs and risks to the subject? In addition, human dignity and the right to privacy are primary considerations in regulating research with humans: Does the experimental subject understand the procedures and goals of the research? Will the results of the experiment be made public? If so, might the subject suffer embarrassment, or might his or her right to privacy be violated? Does the experiment involve deception, in which a human subject is misinformed of the main purpose of the research?

Basic to these guidelines is the underlying principle of *informed consent:* Is the subject knowledgeable about the research in question, and does the subject freely agree to participate in the experiment? One problem that arises in using human and animal subjects in research involves getting informed consent from those who cannot give it. Animals do not volunteer for the experiments in which they are used. For this and other ethical reasons, animal rights activists advocate stopping all animal research. Likewise, noncommunicative humans, such as preverbal infants, children, and severely impaired adults (including, for example, comatose patients and those suffering from Alzheimer's disease) cannot give their informed consent. In these instances, parents and legal guardians are asked to weigh the benefits of the research, and, after due consideration, to give their consent—or not.

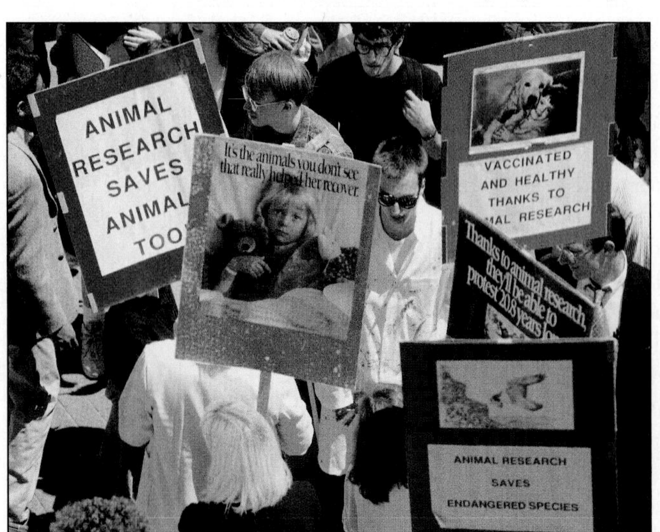

There are many good reasons to support animal research.

A recent study indicated that only 69 percent of women and 74 percent of men in the United States support using animals in medical research ("Animal Research," 1998), although higher percentages than these are reported for college students (Plaus, 1996). How do you think and feel about this issue? Here is one scientist's perspective:

> Who are the cruel and inhumane ones, the behavioral scientists whose research on animals led to the cures of the anorexic girl and the vomiting child, or those leaders of the radical animal activists who are making an exciting career of trying to stop all such research and are misinforming people by repeatedly asserting that it is without any value? (Miller, 1985)

Finally, consider the arguments of Jan Hinson, a senior at D. H. Conley High School (Pitt County, California), who captured first place at a *National Health Occupations Students of America* (NHOSA) Research Persuasive Speaking Contest. Prior to researching the speech, Ms. Hinson opposed the use of animals in research, but studying the issue changed her mind. Major points in her speech included the following:

- Animal research has extended human life spans by 20 years.
- By law, research facilities provide animals with humane living conditions that are less stressful than the struggle for survival in the wild.
- Ninety to ninety-five percent of animals suffer no pain in research.
- The majority of 20th-century medical advances have depended on animal research, such as cardiac catheterization; organ transplant techniques; discovery of insulin and DNA; treatments for tetanus, rheumatoid arthritis, whooping cough and leprosy; and development of the heart-lung machine and Salk and Sabin vaccines.
- Animal research has resulted in millions of pets that are free of heart disease, leukemia, and kidney failure.
- Five million abandoned animals are destroyed at animal shelters each year—animals that could be productively used in medical research.

The issue is joined. My personal hope is that the discriminating use of animals in research will continue.

INTERIM SUMMARY

1. Psychologists use both experimental and nonexperimental methods to study behavior.
2. Psychologists study ***individual differences*** by comparing one or more behavioral attributes in a ***sample*** or a ***population*** of individuals. Tests that use uniform procedures on specified populations are called ***standardized tests.***
3. Most biological and behavioral measurements of a population are ***normally distributed.*** Among the ***descriptive statistics*** that can be used to describe a population of scores, in addition to how they are distributed, is their ***mean*** and ***standard deviation.***
4. Observations, ***surveys,*** archival research, and ***case studies*** are nonexperimental methods commonly used to gather information, to describe, and to form preliminary hypotheses about behavior. Psychological information about an individual can be gathered using ***structured interviews*** and ***self-report methods.***
5. Correlational research attempts to discover patterns or relationships that exist among variables. ***Epidemiological research*** uses correlational methods. Two variables having a high coefficient of correlation may *not* be causally related.
6. A plot of data points that vary in two dimensions is called a ***scatterplot. Correlation coefficients*** range from 0.0 (no relationship) to +1.0 (a perfect, positive relationship) and to −1.0 (a perfect, negative relationship).
7. Researchers use ***double-blind experiments*** to minimize both ***observer*** and ***subject expectancy effects.*** Also, experimenters use ***matched-groups designs*** to control for confounding variables.
8. Researchers use ***psychometric*** methods to construct tests that must meet high standards of ***reliability. Test-retest, alternate-form,*** and ***split-half reliability*** methods are measures of a test's reliability.

9. To be meaningful, tests must have validity. ***Face validity*** and ***criterion-related validity*** are two measures of a test's meaningfulness.
10. Ethical standards in psychological research are prescribed by law and administered by review boards. Basic to ethical considerations are freedom from coercion, the right to privacy, and the informed consent of subjects. Harmful or painful procedures can be justified only within the framework of a cost-benefit analysis that favors knowledge gained.

For Further Thought

1. Think back to the last thunderstorm you were in. What was the relationship of thunder and lightning? Were they highly correlated at all times, or only as the storm drew nearby? Do you think that the causal relationship between thunder and lightning could be determined merely from observation, or would physics experiments be necessary to *prove* that lightning causes thunder?
2. Is it dehumanizing to use humans as subjects in research? Why or why not?

CONCLUDING THOUGHTS

Born of curiosity, scientific inquiry is a complex method of asking and answering questions, one that has proven to be highly adaptive. Scientific answers do not offer TRUTH, defined as the absolute right and wrong answers to questions. Rather, the current understanding of a phenomenon often changes because of new results. Is it ironic that psychologists seek precise rather than commonsense answers to questions, but must be satisfied with only tentative answers? Perhaps not. Finding adaptive solutions to problems may be easier if one holds tentative truths.

Science is a social enterprise. Through peer review, one scientist's complex decision making about the results and meaning of experimental findings is in turn judged by other scientists. Peer review makes science a conservative process. Trained reviewers are skeptical and tend to recommend for publication only those findings that are highly believable and those interpretations that fit with the current accumulation of wisdom. Again, this process may reflect earlier ways of thinking that proved adaptive. I can imagine our prescientific ancestors using a similar process—the pooling of expertise to better solve problems.

Curiosity initially takes the form of trying to understand relationships that exist in the world: Is success in school related to socioeconomic status? Is good health related to diet? and so forth. The next step is to generate testable hypotheses, and then to design and conduct experiments in which data are collected and subjected to quantitative analyses. Statistics help guide decision making. Statistical treatments of behavioral data allow experimenters to infer that a relationship exists (or not), or that a treatment variable was effective (or not). The use of statistics to test hypotheses can be viewed as an adaptive extension of basic problem solving.

The result of the scientific process is a collected body of facts—our scientific knowledge about the world. This wealth of knowledge provides an adaptive advantage to humans who possess it and greatly expands the niche that humans enjoy in competition with other animals. We'll see in the next few chapters that in addition to our genes, part of the human legacy passed on from one generation to the next is this acquired knowledge.

This chapter provides a groundwork for understanding how psychologists use different methods to study behavior. The methods of psychology are diverse; they include stimulating a small part of a rat's brain and measuring its reinforcing effects—a molecular level of inquiry—as well as measuring the math scores of sixth graders (a much more molar level of inquiry). In the next chapter we will turn our attention to a wide range of experimental methods developed by biologically oriented psychologists. You may not know yet what questions interest them, but after reading the present chapter, you should have some idea of the general methods they use to seek answers.

KEY TERMS

alternate-form reliability *61*
antecedent condition *37*
between-groups design *45*
body of knowledge *39*
case study *53*
confounding variable *46*
control group *45*
correlation coefficient *56*
criterion-related validity *61*
dependent variable *44*
descriptive statistic *52*
double-blind experiment *57*
electrical stimulation of the brain (ESB) *44*
epidemiological research *58*
experiment *34*
experimental subject *44*
face validity *61*
functional relationship *46*
heuristic *50*
hypothesis *43*
independent variable *44*
individual differences *52*
matched-groups design *58*
mean *52*
molar level *37*
molecular level *37*
normal distribution *52*
null hypothesis *48*
observer expectancy effects *57*
operational definition *44*
peer review *49*
population *54*
probabilistic reasoning *38*
programmatic research *39*
psychometrics *60*
reliability *60*
reductionism *37*
sample *54*
scatterplot *55*
science *34*
scientific method *35*
self-report method *60*
split-half reliability *61*
standard deviation *52*
standardized test *52*
statistic *48*
structured interview *60*
subject expectancy effects *58*
survey *53*
test-retest reliability *61*
validation by consensus *49*
validity *61*
within-subjects design *45*
working hypothesis *44*

3 Evolution and Genetics

Shark Dreaming/Australian Aboriginal Art Painting by Jon-Mark Semon represented by Rim Pacific

Human Origins

Evolution and Behavior
Distal and Proximal Causes of Behavior
Darwin's Theory of Evolution
Natural Selection
Interim Summary
For Further Thought

Genetics and Heredity
Mendel's Experiments
Genotypes and Phenotypes
Genetic Relatedness
Genetic Variability
The Influence of Genes on Behavior
Interim Summary
For Further Thought

Genes Meet Environment
Human Nature: Our Three Histories
The Interaction of Nature and Nurture
Behavioral Genetics
Ethology
Comparative Psychology
Neuroethology: An Interdisciplinary Approach
Contributions of Comparative Psychologists and Neuroethologists
Interim Summary
For Further Thought

Sociobiology and Evolutionary Psychology
Unconscious Whisperings from Our Genes
Kin Selection and Inclusive Fitness
Altruism and Social Cooperation
Sexual Patterns
The Status of Evolutionary Psychology and Sociobiology
Interim Summary
For Further Thought

Concluding Thoughts

The study of psychology is, among other things, a quest for self-understanding. One way to understand ourselves is to look to our beginnings. But what exactly do we mean by "our beginnings"? Although we typically think of life as beginning at either conception or birth, in this chapter we will consider the idea that a person's brain, mind, and behavior were genetically influenced long before conception. That is, the genes we inherited from our parents reflect adaptations our ancestors evolved in response to past environments. From this perspective, you and I began our existence long before we were conceived—indeed, eons before the twinkle in our grandmothers' eye.

The genes we carry reflect not just the adaptations made by ancient ancestors, but by nonhuman ancestors as well. Even a small child recognizes that compared to birds, termites, and frogs, we are more like other primates in our appearance and behavior. Perhaps that is why we recognize a kinship with chimpanzees and gorillas. Consider George Schaller's description of the gorillas he studied while living in the wild with them in Africa:

> An adult male, easily recognized by his huge size and gray back, sat among the herbs and vines. He watched me intently and then roared. Beside him sat a juvenile perhaps four years old. Three females, fat and placid, with sagging breasts and long nipples, squatted near the male, and up in the fork of a tree crouched a female with a small infant clinging to the hair on her shoulders. A few other animals moved around in the dense vegetation. Accustomed to the drab gorillas in zoos, with their pelage lusterless and scuffed by the cement floors of their cages, I was little prepared for the beauty of the beasts before me. Their hair was not merely black, but a shining blue-black, and their black faces shone as if polished.

> We sat watching each other. The large male, more than the others, held my attention. He rose repeatedly on his short, bowed legs to his full height, about six feet, whipped his arms up to beat a rapid tattoo on his bare chest, and sat down again. He was the most magnificent animal I had ever seen. His brow ridges overhung his eyes, and the crest on his crown resembled a hairy miter; his mouth when he roared was cavernous, and the large canine teeth were covered with black tartar. He lay on the slope, propped on his huge shaggy arms, and the muscles of his broad shoulders and silver back rippled. He gave an impression of dignity and restrained power, of absolute certainty in his majestic appearance. I felt a desire to communicate with him, to let him know by some small gesture that I intended no harm, that I wished only to be near him. Never before had I had this feeling on meeting an animal. As we watched each other across the valley, I wondered if he recognized the kinship that bound us. (Schaller, 1964, pp. 34–35)

The search for "our beginnings" will be told in two separate stories of adaptation, for psychology focuses both on how animals have adapted to their environment over the generations through natural selection, and on how they adapt their behavior to the environment during their lifetimes. In this chapter we will explore the biological bases of behavior—the similarities and differences between humans and other animals that are the focus of genetics, evolutionary psychology, and sociobiology. (In a later chapter we'll consider questions of adaptation during one's lifetime.) We'll find that research and theory in evolutionary psychology are yielding new insights not only into the human condition, but into that of other animals as well. Like Schaller (1964), we will wonder about the kinship that binds us to other animals.

HUMAN ORIGINS

The earliest humans to write down their thoughts wondered about the earth, the sun, and life; they pondered their own nature, including their origins. Their diverse philosophies constitute our 7,000- to 10,000-year-old historical record. For the past several hundred years scientists have provided new answers to the age-old questions about the origins of our world. The scientific method described in the previous chapter has provided solid evidence for the age of the universe, of the earth, and of the progress of life on earth. Scientific analyses tell us that the history of the earth and of life on it is a long one. Figure 3.1 illustrates this time frame. Each dot in the figure represents the passage of 10 million years; together, all 450 dots represent the 4.5-billion-year history of the earth.

Why bother with these details in a course that is concerned primarily with human thought and behavior, you may wonder. After all, psychology is the study of the mind, not the natural history of our planet. Yet in these details, we begin to appreciate the ancient origins of our minds.

What lessons might we take from Figure 3.1? First, that humans can barely fathom the length of time that the universe, the earth, and life on earth have existed. Indeed, the way humans think about time is an example of a biological limitation on the mind's functioning. Because of the way the human brain evolved, we are equipped to perceive and grasp time according to our own human scale—that is, in seconds and minutes, hours and days, and ultimately the years of our lifetime. Thinking of millions and billions of anything is difficult, because our primate ancestors were not challenged by such ideas. What our ancestors did evolve was a huge visual brain that allows us to "think" visually. The spiral of dots in

LINK
"Thinking" visually, Chapter 8, p. 271

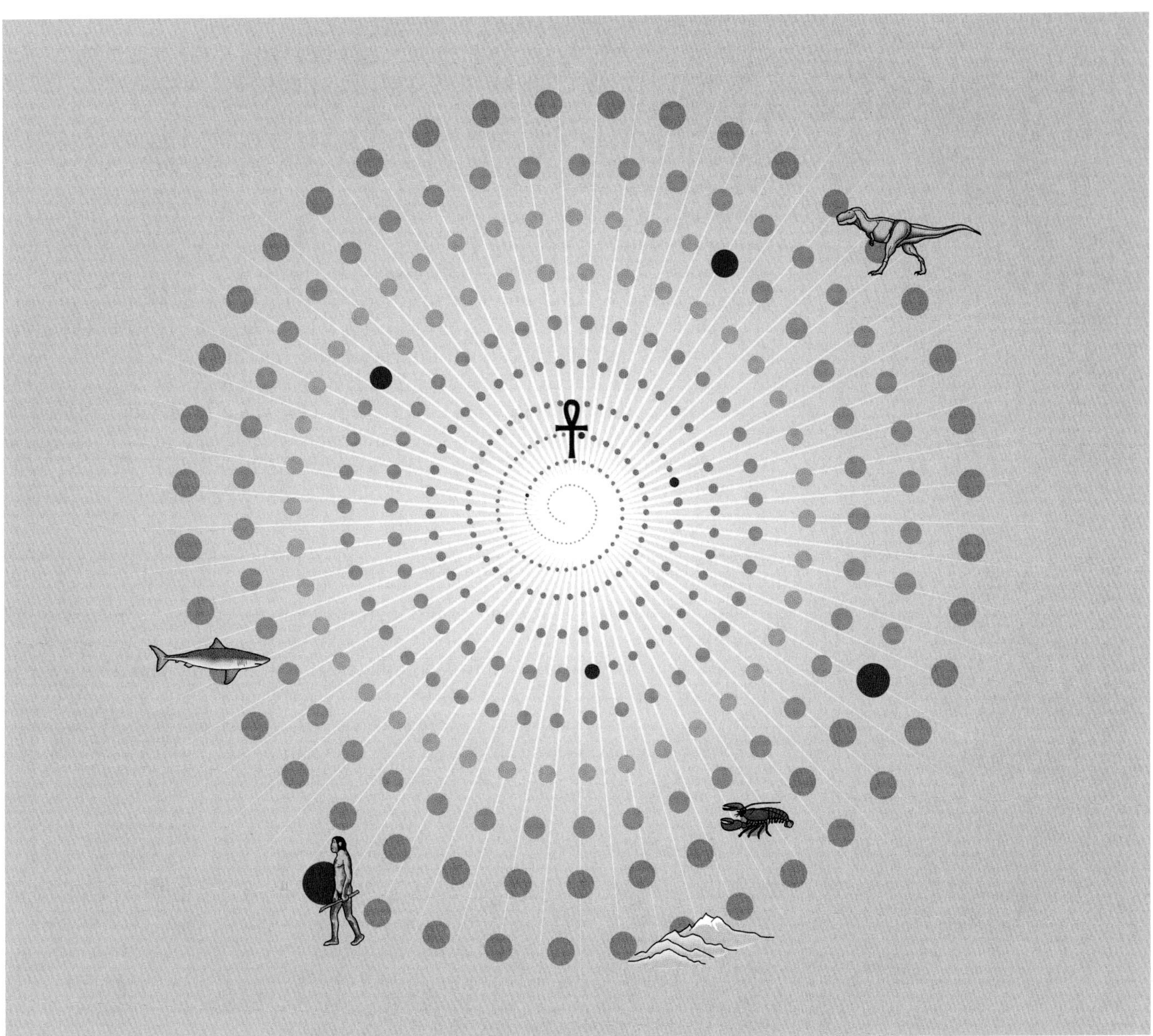

Figure 3.1 History of the earth. This 450-dot spiral symbolizes the passage of time from the earth's origin 4.5 billion years ago (center) to the present. Each dot represents the passage of 10 million years. A few features of the earth's natural history are indicated.

Figure 3.1 is a visual device that aids in this type of thinking. Yet even if you counted the 450 dots in Figure 3.1, only in the most abstract way could you "understand" that they represent 4,500,000,000 years.

A second lesson we can draw from Figure 3.1 is that humans are relative newcomers on earth. As Carl Sagan and Ann Druyan (1992) put it, "If the earth were as old as a person, a typical organism would be born, live, and die in a sliver of a second" (p. 30). Compared to many other identifiable plants and animals, humans have been on earth for only a short period. Shifts in the plates covering the earth's surface caused the formation of familiar features such as the Rocky Mountains about 65 million years ago. Over the past 7 to 8 million years, water erosion carved out the Grand Canyon. Humans did not witness either event; we have existed in our present form for only 100,000 to 200,000 years—(only a fraction of the time represented by the very last dot in Figure 3.1. (Some kinds of evidence, including the dating of human artifacts, support the 100,000-year estimate, whereas genetic models based on DNA comparisons support the 200,000-year estimate.)

A final lesson we can learn from Figure 3.1 is that species come and go. A **species** is a reproductively isolated breeding population. The general rule is that species evolve and then become extinct. One estimate is that more than 95 percent of all species that have ever lived are now extinct (Erlich & Erlich, 1981). Moreover, evolution from one life form to another is not inevitable. An example is the horseshoe crab *Limulus polyphemus,* a "living fossil" that has existed in the same form for 200 million years. That this incredible animal contains the same photopigment, *rhodopsin,* in its lateral eye as humans carry in the rods of their retinas is but one indication of our ancient evolutionary history.

In the grand scheme of things, humans may not survive as long as the dinosaurs did during their 160-million-year reign. On the other hand, as far as we know we are the only species that can contemplate our past, which should enable us to take a direct hand in our future. So how did we come about? This and other questions about evolution are central to our understanding of the human mind.

EVOLUTION AND BEHAVIOR

We saw in Chapter 1 that philosophers and psychologists have struggled with the nature-nurture question for hundreds of years. To what extent does an individual's behavior stem from inherited characteristics or environmental factors? In the interaction of the two forces, which is more important? Here we open the argument by focusing on biology. To understand the biological bases of behavior, we must consider Charles Darwin's theory of evolution and also Gregor Mendel's theory of genetics. Both have strengthened the "nature" side of the debate.

Distal and Proximal Causes of Behavior

Both Darwin's and Mendel's biological theories address the **distal** (distant, or ultimate) **causes** of behavior—that is, the evolutionary and genetic causes. According to this perspective, genes selected over millions of years predispose animals to behave reflexively and according to instinct. The term **instinct** has a long, controversial history in psychology; here it is used simply to refer to innately organized behaviors that occur without training at about the same age in most members of a species. In this view, animals behave the way they do because inborn eating, drinking, courting, and reproductive programs in their brains operate in a way that promotes their survival.

All *extant* (living, as opposed to extinct) animals have brains that successfully guide their behavior to accomplish whatever needs to be done to produce the next generation. From this perspective, the brains of all the animals studied here and in the next chapter—be they snails, monkeys, or humans—belong to successful living animals. Animals with unsuccessful brains and behavior patterns are doomed to become extinct.

Traditionally, psychologists and sociologists have focused on nurture, or the **proximal** (nearby) **causes** of behavior. Nurture is thus the effect of the local environment on the behavior of animals. From this perspective, different environments produce differences in behavior. The strength of an evolutionary approach to psychology is that it recognizes the interrelation of the ancient genetic predispositions that guide behavior with the local environments that shape behavior in the present. Consider the example of young children and young monkeys, both of whom at some point in their early development typically fear loud noises, darkness, separation, heights, empty spaces, and strange people and animals. Why do

species A reproductively isolated breeding population.

distal causes Distant causes of behavior rooted in evolutionary and genetic determinants.

instinct Innately organized behavior.

proximal causes Causes of behavior that focus on immediate, local, psychological, and sociological determinants.

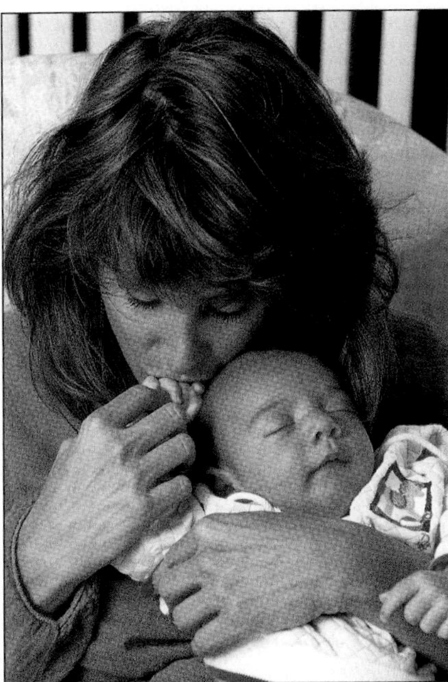

Infant primates require years of care before they can live independently.

young primates whimper, cry, and show startle reactions in these situations? An analysis of the distal causes of hiding, crouching, and crying behavior reveals that these behaviors are adaptive. Crying gets the attention of caregivers who can tend to a helpless infant. Innate tendencies or predispositions to behave in these ways, then, are thought to be genetically programmed (Young, 1978).

For the proximal causes of crying, we could examine the local environment for specific noises, persons, and objects that might provoke fear responses. All infants cry (distal causes). Some older children cry in the presence of dogs and strangers, depending on their age and the specific environment they have experienced (proximal causes). A child raised with a dog is less likely to cry in the presence of a dog. Likewise, a child raised in a household in which many people come and go is less likely to cry in the presence of other people. We will see in a later chapter that this process of habituation is itself a proximal cause of behavior, which modifies the child's distally caused innate tendencies. Let's look more closely at how evolutionary theory accounts for the distal causes of behavior.

Proximal determinants of behavior with habituation, Chapter 6, p. 193

Darwin's Theory of Evolution

Charles Darwin (1809–1882) was one of the most influential (and most controversial) individuals in human intellectual history. Today, his concept of the origin and meaning of life provides the unifying theoretical framework for the biological and behavioral sciences. In a book published in 1859, *On the Origin of Species by Means of Natural Selection,* Darwin proposed his theory of **evolution**. Simply stated, he wrote that all living forms are related to each other—that there exists a **continuity of species**. Each species, Darwin theorized, assumed its particular form due to **adaptation**, a "fit" between the plant or animal and its immediate environment. Any characteristic that improves an organism's chances of transmitting its genes to the next generation can be considered an adaptation.

Darwin's theory has generated a great deal of social as well as scientific controversy. Most scientists assume that the biological nature of an organism reflects its evolutionary history. And most psychologists assume that humans are

evolution Charles Darwin's theory that existing species of life on earth are the end result of a process of natural selection.

continuity of species (Darwin) The theory tht all living organisms are adaptations of earlier life forms and are genetically related.

adaptation Any characteristic that improves the "fit" of a plant or animal with its environment, thereby increasing its chances of transmitting genes to the next generation.

Charles Darwin (1809–1882).

no exception to this rule—that the human mind and human behavior can best be understood by examining evidence from both nature (biology) and nurture (the study of the environment and behavior).

But too often Darwin's theory is simplified and summarized to the point of absurdity: "Humans are descended from monkeys." In fact, the theory of evolution is a highly conceptual scientific analysis of life at both the molecular level and the level of natural history. As Ernst Mayr, an influential evolutionary thinker of this century, has pointed out, Darwin's theory actually encompasses several distinct subtheories (Mayr, 1991). Combined, these subtheories are sometimes referred to as the **modern synthesis**—the merging of Darwin's theory of evolution with the modern science of genetics. We will begin with the subtheory of natural selection.

Natural Selection

From their observations of the life cycles of plants and animals, the earliest thinking humans must have wondered about the different forms of life we now call species. We know that well before Darwin's time, animal breeders practiced **artificial selection**, deliberately selecting for breeding purposes plants and animals that had desired characteristics. For example, over 13,000 years ago some Stone Age humans domesticated dogs, cattle, and fowl, and planted crops (Diamond, 1997). In 19th-century England, Darwin's contemporaries recognized and bred varieties of male and female dogs, cats, cattle, pigeons, and so forth for particular colors, sizes, shapes, and temperaments. To breed larger, blacker dogs, for example, they selected for mating the largest, blackest male and female pups from litters. After several generations, more of the offspring the selected animals produced were larger and blacker. These changes across generations were accomplished artificially, by human intervention in a natural process.

To account for the tremendous variety of plant and animal species on earth, Darwin postulated that a similar selection process occurred from one generation to the next, but under natural rather than artificial conditions. He called this process **natural selection**. With other naturalists, he noted that animals and plants typically produce too many offspring in the course of a lifetime. Because the earth's resources cannot accommodate all the new lives, competition for those resources ensues. The prize of winning this competition for nature's resources is not only life, but also the opportunity to survive long enough to reproduce. The cost of losing is fewer opportunities to produce the next generation, or at the worst, death.

Darwin's theory of natural selection is as prone to misinterpretation as it is insightful and controversial. Essentially, he proposed that each species is best understood as a unique solution to specific problems of survival. Some individuals of a species are better able than others to overcome the environmental obstacles they face in day-to-day living. Such environmental obstacles, or impediments to survival, are called **selective pressures**. Drought and extremes of heat and cold are examples of selective pressures. In any species, some individual organisms will be born with adaptations that enhance their survival and ultimately their reproduction. An example is the protective coloration (camouflage) some birds exhibit, which is a physical adaptation. The ability to learn more quickly than others is an example of a behavioral adaptation. In other words, some individuals of a species may be bigger, stronger, and faster than others, whereas some may be slower but smarter.

modern synthesis The merging of Darwin's theory of evolution through natural selection with the science of genetics.

artificial selection The deliberate selection of desired characteristics in plants and animals.

natural selection (Darwin) The means by which organisms adapt to the environment and reproduce differentially.

selective pressure Any feature of an environment that allows one phenotype to have reproductive advantage over another.

fitness The reproductive success of an individual relative to other individuals; the number of reproductively fertile copies an individual contributes to the next generation.

Fitness and the Perpetuation of a Species. One way to think about protective coloration, rapid learning, and other adaptations is that they promote fitness. An individual's **fitness** is defined in terms of the number of viable, fertile offspring it produces; animals high in fitness produce many, and animals low in fitness produce few. When environmental conditions—and therefore, selective

Figure 3.2 Two different body types. A Nilotic African from the African Sudan (left) and an Aleutian from Alaska (right) both have body shapes that are adapted to their environments.

pressures—change from generation to generation, some individuals that were well adapted to the old conditions may not be able to adjust to the new conditions. Those individuals are more likely than others to die before reproducing.

The two human males in Figure 3.2 are examples of anatomical adaptations to long-term environmental extremes of heat and cold. Both girth and the length of extremities are factors in body heat loss: shorter, squatter humans retain heat better than long-limbed humans. In hot climates, tall, long-limbed humans have better survival rates than short, squat humans. Over millions of years, the better survival rate of individuals who are well adapted to their environments has produced the diversity of life forms that now inhabit different ecological niches. An animal's **ecological niche** is its environmental habitat, including resources and interactions with other animals.

The Contribution of Genetics. Before Darwin, the noted French naturalist Jean Baptiste Lamarck (1744–1829) had proposed a different theory, now known as **Lamarckian evolution**. Lamarck believed that an animal's personal experiences caused changes in its "essence." That is, he thought that (a) the slight changes an animal experienced during its lifetime gradually modified its characteristics, and (b) the next generation profited from the transmission of these *acquired characteristics*. One implication of this view is that children can benefit from the musical, mathematical, or bowling abilities of parents who patiently perfect those skills over a lifetime.

What a great idea! Unfortunately (or fortunately for the children of murderers, arsonists, and other undesirables), there is no evidence to support the theory of Lamarckian evolution. Scientific research has shown that the **genes** of individual organisms are relatively well protected from environmental influence. (Genes were unknown when Lamarck and Darwin wrote, but are now known to be the basic units of heredity.) Genes, we will see in the next section, are parts of living cells that are bathed in physiological fluids and biochemicals. The genes in sperm and eggs are *not* affected by the minute biochemical changes in the brain that underlie memory and other experiences acquired during a lifetime. Therefore, during the course of a lifetime, the only environmental factors that can grossly influence the genes that produce the next generation are certain toxic chemicals, high levels of ionizing radiation, and other known *mutagens*—substances that are responsible for genetic mutations.

ecological niche The environmental habitat of an animal, including resources and interactions with other animals.

Lamarckian evolution The theory that genetic changes can occur in populations through the inheritance of characteristics acquired during a lifetime.

gene The basic unit of heredity.

Humans comprise one species with wide genetic variability.

The Impact of Natural Calamities. Even after 140 years, Darwin's theory of natural selection remains indispensable to the biological and behavioral sciences. His conceptual framework has been remarkably successful in accounting for seemingly contradictory (and certainly puzzling) features of life on earth. But there is one influence on the evolution of life forms that Darwin did not consider. Today, scientists such as Stephen Jay Gould of Harvard University postulate that in some prehistoric periods, cataclysmic environmental changes determined which plants and animals were killed and which survived. "Blind luck" as well as natural selection, Gould argues, is responsible for the variety of life forms on earth (Gould, 1989). According to this view, natural calamities have changed the course of speciation and extinction far more rapidly than the gradual change Darwin postulated. For example, dinosaurs were well adapted to their environment for over 160 million years. Yet one large asteroid that impacted the earth 65 million years ago changed the global climate, causing the dinosaur's extinction (as well as the extinction of an estimated 90 percent of all other species of plants and animals). The asteroid's effects can be interpreted as an example of very rapid natural selection.

Gould's analysis of the extinction of the dinosaurs reinforces Darwin's view that nature seems to be blind in creating obstacles to survival. Gould holds that evolution is purposeless—a view that has been criticized on the grounds that no evidence exists to support either a purpose or a lack of purpose in the history of life on earth. Rather, that is a question better addressed by theologians.

The result of evolution is a world populated by unique living organisms. In the following section we will see that heredity successfully accounts for the similarity and continuity among life forms, and the variability introduced during reproduction accounts for the dissimilarity and diversity. Together with environmental pressures, the process of natural selection accounts for the persistence of certain living forms and the exclusion of others. There is no good reason to suspect that humans are anything other than another product of these natural processes.

INTERIM SUMMARY

1. Life has been on earth for 3.5 billion of the earth's 4.5-billion-year history. At present life is characterized by reproductively isolated breeding populations, or *species.*
2. Human life has been on earth for only 100,000 to 200,000 years, a tiny fraction of the natural history of life on earth.
3. Local, immediate environments can be seen as ***proximal*** (close) ***causes*** of an individual organism's behavior, whereas genetic programs such as reflexes and ***instincts*** can be seen as ***distal*** (distant) ***causes.***
4. According to Darwin's theory of ***evolution,*** the history of life on earth is characterized by a ***continuity of species*** that arises from the process of adaptation to the environment. Conceptually, Darwin's theory provides the theoretical basis for both a biological and a behavioral understanding of life.
5. During the early part of this century, Darwin's and Mendel's theories were connected to form the ***modern synthesis.***
6. Natural selection can be distinguished from human-directed breeding, or ***artificial selection.***
7. ***Natural selection*** refers to the process by which the next generation of offspring is produced. Organisms that successfully overcome environmental impediments, called ***selective pressures,*** will live to breed the next generation. Luck accounts for many survivors.

8. Protective coloration, rapid learning, and instincts that are matched to an individual organism's *ecological niche* are *adaptations* to an environment. When they result in more offspring, such adaptations increase the individual organism's *fitness.*
9. *Lamarckian evolution* is the discredited theory that characteristics acquired over a lifetime can affect an organism's *genes* and be transmitted to its offspring.
10. Well-adapted organisms such as dinosaurs can become extinct when a cataclysmic natural disaster occurs.

For Further Thought

1. Bring the concepts of natural selection and artificial selection to bear on your own birth.
2. Darwin asserted that humans are merely animals who evolved by natural processes. Some people find that assertion demeaning and contrary to their religious beliefs. What do you think?

GENETICS AND HEREDITY

The most obvious feature of life is physical—the way plants and animals appear. Thus early taxonomies (groupings, or arrangements) of plants and animals were based primarily on their physical features. **Genetics** is the study of patterns of heredity and variation in plants and animals. **Heredity** refers to the genetic transmission of these characteristics from one generation to the next. At its most basic, the term heredity refers to the fact that corn reproduces itself to make more corn, chickens reproduce chickens, and humans reproduce humans.

Mendel's work has allowed farmers to grow plants with predictable desired traits.

Mendel's Experiments

Scientists' first understanding of why offspring resemble their parents came from the experiments of Gregor Mendel (1822–1884). A scholarly resident of an Augustinian monastery in Czechoslovakia, Mendel experimented with the breeding of garden peas from seeds. The seeds he used had seven different pairs of characteristics. Three of the paired characteristics, for example, were the color of their seed coats (white or gray), the color of their contents (yellow or green), and their appearance (round versus wrinkled). Mendel asked basic questions about the inheritance of one or the other of the two forms of these paired traits. Because each of the characteristics appears in one of two forms, they are called **dichotomous traits.** The common garden peas Mendel used were a good choice for two reasons. First, they exhibit clearly differentiated dichotomous traits. And second, they are self-fertilizing—that is, each pea plant contains both male and female sex cells.

What exactly did Mendel do? First, he identified two varieties of peas that bred true for either round or wrinkled seeds. He then began experimenting by artificially fertilizing the blossoms of wrinkled-seed plants with pollen from round-seed plants. He found that the offspring of his experiment, the F_1 generation, all had round seeds. Mendel then planted those seeds and allowed the normal process of self-fertilization to produce the second (F_2) generation. In this group of seeds, he found that about 75 percent were round and 25 percent were wrinkled. Because the round seed characteristic showed up the most in the F_2 generation, he called it the *dominant trait,* and because the wrinkled-seed characteristic

genetics The study of patterns of heredity and variation in plants and animals.

heredity The genetic transmission of characteristics from one generation to the next.

dichotomous traits A trait, such as color, tht occurs in one or another form, but never in combination.

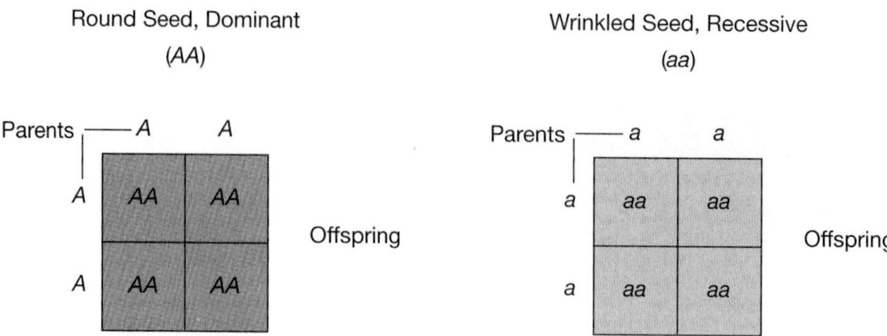

Figure 3.3 **True-breeding parent generation.** Mendel began with true-breeding round (AA) and wrinkled seeds (aa) that produced offspring exactly like their parents. Such seeds are said to be homozygous for roundness or wrinkles.

appeared only 25 percent of the time, he called it the *recessive trait*. In these and other experiments, the ratio of dominant to recessive traits was always on the order of 3:1.

Mendel's genius lies in the model of dominant and recessive traits he constructed, which predicts the ratios he observed in the F_1 and F_2 generations. His shorthand notation of capital letters for the dominant characteristic and lowercase letters for the recessive characteristic is still in use. Mendel labeled the trait for true-breeding round seeds (dominant) ***AA***, and the trait for true-breeding wrinkled seeds (recessive) ***aa***. He reasoned that round-seed plants that breed true generation after generation must have only the dominant characteristic, and wrinkled-seed plants, only the recessive characteristic.

Figure 3.3 shows the results of Mendel's true-breeding parent-generation experiments using his notation. Note that the true-breeding, self-fertilizing parent generation produced offspring that looked exactly like the parents. Figure 3.4 shows what happened when Mendel artificially fertilized the round seeds with wrinkled-seed pollen. All the offspring in this F_1 generation had the round-seed characteristic; the recessive characteristic was unexpressed. But when the F_1 generation was allowed to self-fertilize, the dominant and recessive characteristics reasserted themselves (see Figure 3.5).

Because the resulting F_2 generation produced both wrinkled and round seeds, Mendel reasoned that the numbers of each type of seed reflected the action of both traits the parent plants transmitted to their offspring. Even though three out of every four plants had round seeds, he suspected, they were round for different reasons. Twenty-five percent of the plants, he thought, had round seeds because they contained only the dominant traits, whereas 50 percent of the seeds were round because they contained one dominant and one recessive trait.

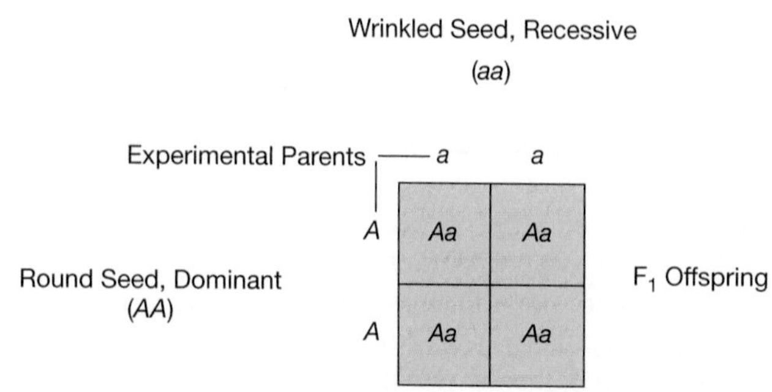

Figure 3.4 **Mendel's experimental F_1 generation.** When both parents are homozygous, one with dominant and the other with recessive alleles, the offspring are all heterozygous (Aa). In this case, all offspring would be round seeds.

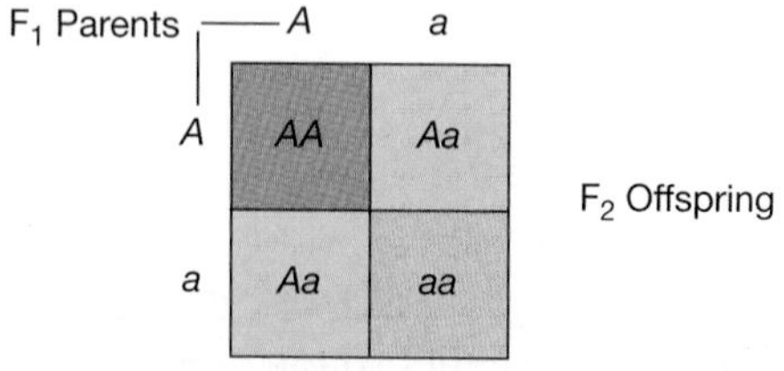

Figure 3.5 **Mendel's experimental F_2 generation.** When both parents are heterozygous, some of the offspring are heterozygous and some are homozygous. Only the homozygous recessive alleles will be expressed as wrinkled seeds (aa); the remainder are expressed as round seeds.

Mendel had discovered the basic patterns of inheritance. What he called a "trait" is now called a gene, the basic unit of the process of heredity. As our knowledge of genetics has grown since his experiments were published in 1866, other language has become necessary. The particular form of a trait (green or yellow, round or smooth) is now called an **allele.** Dominant and recessive traits are now referred to as **dominant** and **recessive alleles.** When the two alleles for a given trait are identical—a makeup that is represented as either *AA* or *aa*—a plant is said to be **homozygous** for that trait. The homozygous *aa* gene is expressed as wrinkled seeds, and the homozygous *AA* gene is expressed as round seeds. When the two alleles for a given trait are different—a makeup that is represented as *Aa*—the plant is said to be **heterozygous** for the wrinkled/smooth trait.

Identical twins have identical genotypes.

Genotypes and Phenotypes

In 1909, about 25 years after the deaths of both Darwin and Mendel, a biologist named Johannsen introduced the term *gene* and the concepts of *genotype* and *phenotype.* Johannsen defined a **genotype** as the basic combination of genes that defines a species and the individual organisms within a species. An organism's genotype is its genetic constitution. When the genotype is expressed in an environment, it is called a **phenotype.** For example, your genotype is the *potential you* at your conception, as represented by your specific genes; the *physical you,* from conception to the present, is your phenotype.

Identical twins are examples of two phenotypes with the same genotype. Although the genotypes of identical twins stay the same throughout their lifetimes, the phenotypes vary to the extent that the twins experience different environments. For example, one who routinely fasts may be thin, whereas her twin, a gourmet chef, may be overweight. We can describe Mendel's experiments, then, by saying that the phenotypic expression of 75 percent of the green peas in his F_2 generation was identical—round seeds—but that it represented two different genotypes. Twenty-five percent of round-seeded plants were of the *AA* genotype, but they looked no different from the 50 percent that were of the *Aa* genotype.

Does your schoolwork come as easily to you as it does to your roommate? Are you more athletic or less emotional than your brothers and sisters? Quite obviously, not all humans are equal, physically or psychologically. One goal of biological psychologists is to achieve a better understanding of individual differences through genetic analysis.

Consider your own human identity. As an individual you have both a unique and a shared inheritance. You are unique because of the one-of-a-kind *DNA* you got from your mother and your father. **Deoxyribonucleic acid,** or **DNA,** is a complex protein structure containing all the genetic instructions needed to make a unique individual. Your behavior is determined in part by the DNA you received from each of your biological parents. In addition, you share much of your "unique" DNA with your ancestors of the past 3.5 billion years (see Figure 3.1).

DNA is found on threadlike structures called **chromosomes** that lie within the nucleus of every cell in the body. Every human being has 46 chromosomes (23 pairs), each of which contains a separate long molecule of DNA. The basic unit of DNA, called a *nucleotide,* can exist independently of DNA—that is, as a free-floating molecule in cellular fluid. When nucleotides are strung together in sequence, they form strands of DNA. Amazingly, the diversity of all life forms arises from the arrangement of only four nucleotide bases: thymine (T), cytosine (C), adenine (A), and guanine (G).

allele A particular form of a gene at a particular place on the chromosome.

dominant allele (dominant gene) Of two alleles for the same trait, the one that is expressed in a heterozygote.

recessive allele (recessive gene) An unexpressed allele in a heterozygote, but is phenotypically expressed when homozygous.

homozygous Having the same allele for a given trait, as in the form *AA* or *aa*.

heterozygous Having two different alleles for a given trait, as in the form *Aa*.

genotype The genetic constitution of an individual organism.

phenotype The physical expression of features in an organism tht results from the interaction of its genotype with the environment.

deoxyribonucleic acid (DNA) A double-strand, helix-shaped structure containing genetic material.

chromosome A structure in the nucleus of a cell that carries genetic information in the form of a DNA molecule.

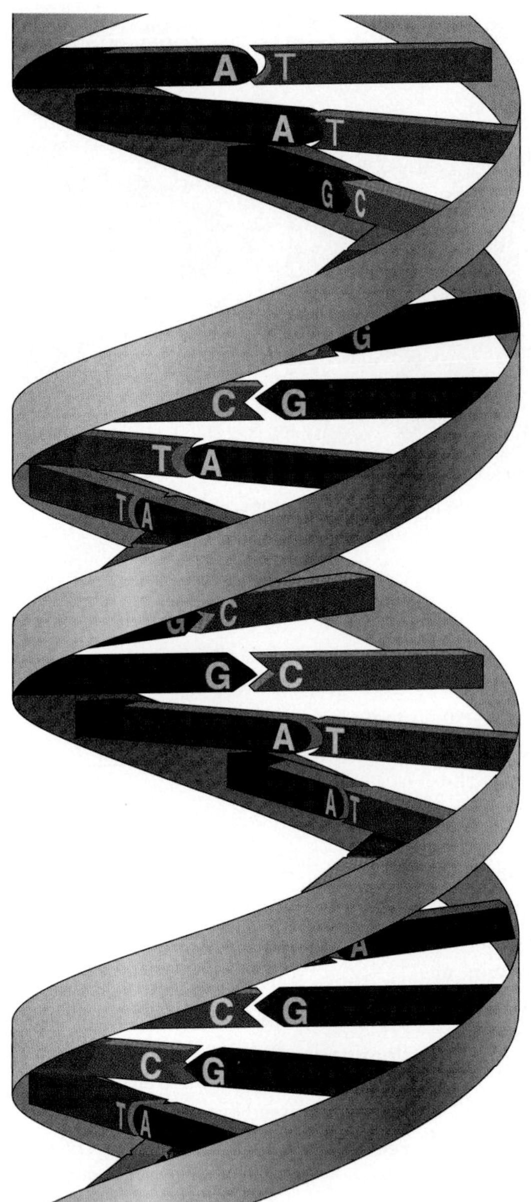

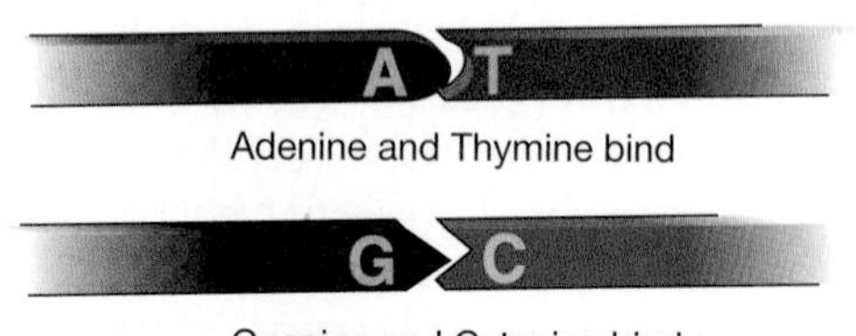

Figure 3.6 **The double-helix structure of the DNA molecule.** The distinctive shape of DNA molecules is produced by the bonding of its four nucleotide bases, adenine-thymine and guanine-cytosine.

As you can see in Figure 3.6, DNA looks like a twisted, ladderlike structure, called a double helix. The rungs of the ladder are constructed of pairs of the four nucleotide bases (also known as nucleic acids). Because the four nucleic acids have different numbers of hydrogen atoms available for bonding, only certain pairs can bond together, namely adenine with thymine and guanine with cytosine. This bonding pattern causes the DNA molecule to coil. And because of the size differences among the four nucleic acids, they stack in a distinctive manner. Adenine and guanine are too large to pair effectively, and thymine and cytosine are too small. The result is that only four pairs—A:T, T:A, C:G, and G:C—can match up.

Genetic Relatedness

We have seen that every human being has 46 chromosomes containing unique combinations of genes. If, however, you have an identical twin, you and your twin share the same genotype. In other words, the complex gene sequences that define each individual are identical in monozygotic (single-egg) twins.

Table 3.1 lists the genetic relationships within families. Notice that each of your biological parents shares 50 percent of his or her genes with you. In addition, of the thousands of copies of alleles you received from them at conception, 50 percent are also present in your brother or sister.

Genetic History Beyond Parents. Like you, each of your parents was created by a unique combination of approximately 20,000 genes on each of 23 chromosomes contributed by each one of *their* parents—and so on. The "and so on's" are intriguing! Your "shared inheritance" comes from a process of genetic transmission that has been going on in *Homo sapiens* for 100,000 to 200,000 years.

Scientists have modeled human lineages using gene-sequencing techniques. Currently their results support two quite different theories of how early humans originated. One, the "out of Africa" hypothesis, traces human origins to an extinct ancestor called *Homo erectus* who lived in Africa about 1 million years ago (Erlich, Bergstrom, Stoneking, & Gyllensten, 1996). A much more recent ancestor, now

Table 3.1 Relatives and Their Shared Genes

Degree of Relatedness	Individual Organism	Percentage of Genes Shared with You
	Identical twin	100
First degree	Sibling (brother or sister)	50
	Mother or father	50
	Child	50
Second degree	Grandparent	25
	Grandchild	25
	Half-brother or half-sister	25
	Aunt or uncle	25
	Niece or nephew	25
Third degree	First cousin	12.5
Unrelated	Stepchild	0 or ?
	Spouse	0 or ?

human, lived in Africa about 170,000 years ago (Ingman, Kaessmann, Paabo, & Gyllensten, 2000). Alternative analyses of DNA collected from genetically diverse humans support a "multiregional" theory (Wolpoff, 1989; Adcock et al., 2001). According to this theory, *Homo sapiens* evolved from regional populations of *Homo erectus* living separately in Africa, Europe, Asia, and Australia/New Guinea as many as 2 million years ago. Regardless of "racial" origin, each human shares common parents with all other humans—a great, great, great . . . great grandmother and grandfather—as well as an ancient lineage. The picture on the next page shows an artist's reconstruction, from available evidence, of what our common human ancestor *Homo ergaster* may have looked like 1.7 million years ago. Figure 3.7 shows how scientists now think we are related to our human ancestors. Continuing research in both biology and paleontology will ultimately lead to a clearer understanding of our origins.

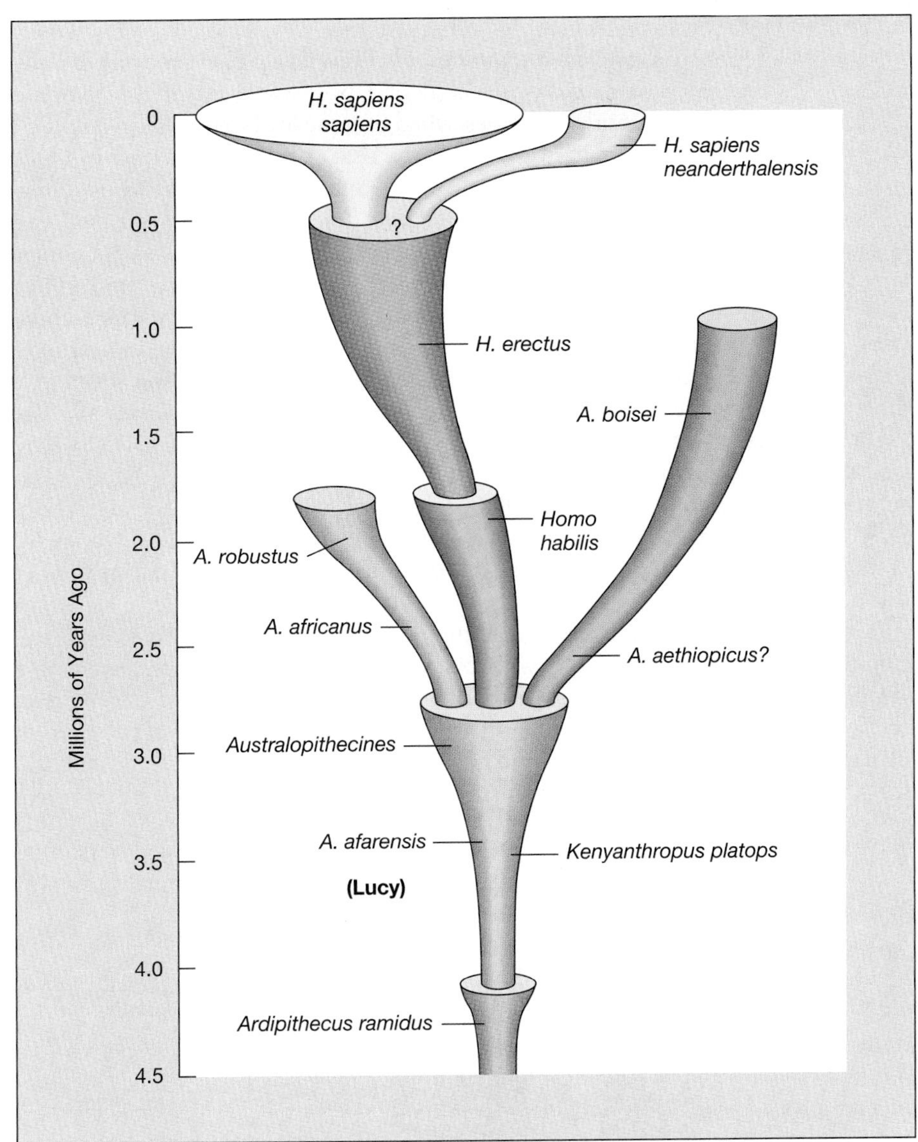

Figure 3.7 Human evolution. Human evolution over the last 4.5 million years includes *A. afarensis* (Lucy), *Homo erectus* and *Homo sapiens* (living humans), and *Homo sapiens neanderthalensis* (extinct). *Source:* From EVOLUTION 3rd ed. by M. W. Strickberger. Copyright © 1996 by Jones and Bartlett Publishers. Reprinted by permission of the publisher.

An artist's reconstruction of *Homo ergaster*, who lived 1.7 million years ago. *Source:* Natural History magazine, Vol 104, #12, (Dec '95) p. 45; John Holmes, artist.

Genetic Comparisons Across Species. Desmond Morris's classic book *The Naked Ape* begins with the assertion that "There are one hundred ninety three living species of monkeys and apes. One hundred and ninety-two of them are covered with hair." Figure 3.8 compares the body types of the only apes that have survived to the present. They are drawn without hair so you can better see the similarities and differences among them. (In fact, we probably should not make too much of our nakedness, because humans actually have a higher number of small, nearly invisible hairs per square centimeter of their bodies than most monkeys and apes.) This comparison of body structure among the great apes should help you to recognize your primate nature, for the structural similarities suggest common genes.

Our Chimpanzee Relatives. The genes of all animals are constructed of DNA, made up of the four nucleotide bases described previously. How close in structure is a human's DNA to the DNA of other primates? In 1984, scientists Charles Sibley and John Ahlquist took chimpanzee DNA and human DNA, separated the double helix of each into two strands, and allowed one strand from each species to combine. Then they measured the resulting match from one species to the other. Their experiment resulted in a 98 percent match of the nucleotide sequences of human DNA and chimpanzee DNA. Another experiment with mountain gorilla DNA produced a 97 percent match. Humans diverged from chimpanzees about 7 million years ago, Sibley and Ahlquist estimated, and from gorillas about 10 million years ago (see Figure 3.9). More recent estimates indicate that humans are genetically closer to the pygmy chimpanzee, *Pan paniscus*, than to the common chimp, *Pan troglodyte*. The two chimps share 99.3 percent of their nucleotide sequences of DNA, and we share 98.4 percent of ours with *Pan paniscus* (Sibley, Comstock, & Ahlquist, 1990). Human civilization, it seems, depends on less than 2 percent of our genetic makeup.

Here's a tough question. How can humans share about 98 percent of the nucleotide sequences of their DNA with pygmy chimpanzees, yet 0 percent with a stranger (see Table 3.1)? This question can be answered in terms of the frame of reference of the comparison. By definition, the human species shares 100 percent of its genes with other humans. Humans also share many genes with other animals; about two-thirds of all mammalian genes are held in common. A recent

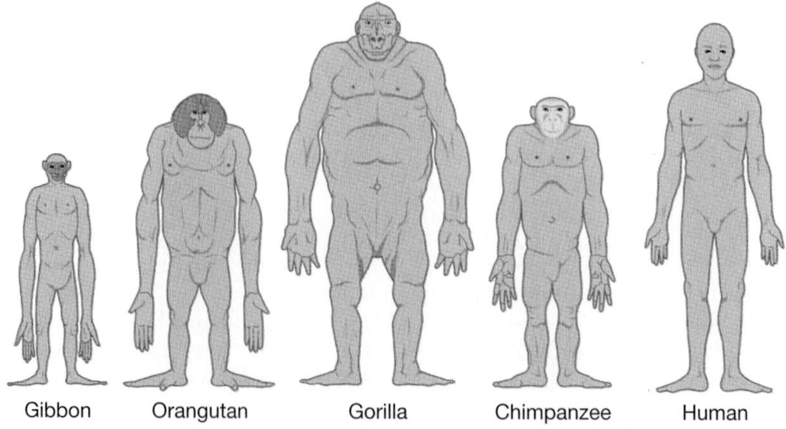

Figure 3.8 Comparative anatomy of living apes. These adult apes are drawn to scale, with their hair removed for easy comparison. *Source:* From EVOLUTION 3rd ed. by M. W. Strickberger. Copyright © 1996 by Jones and Bartlett Publishers. Reprinted by permission of the publisher.

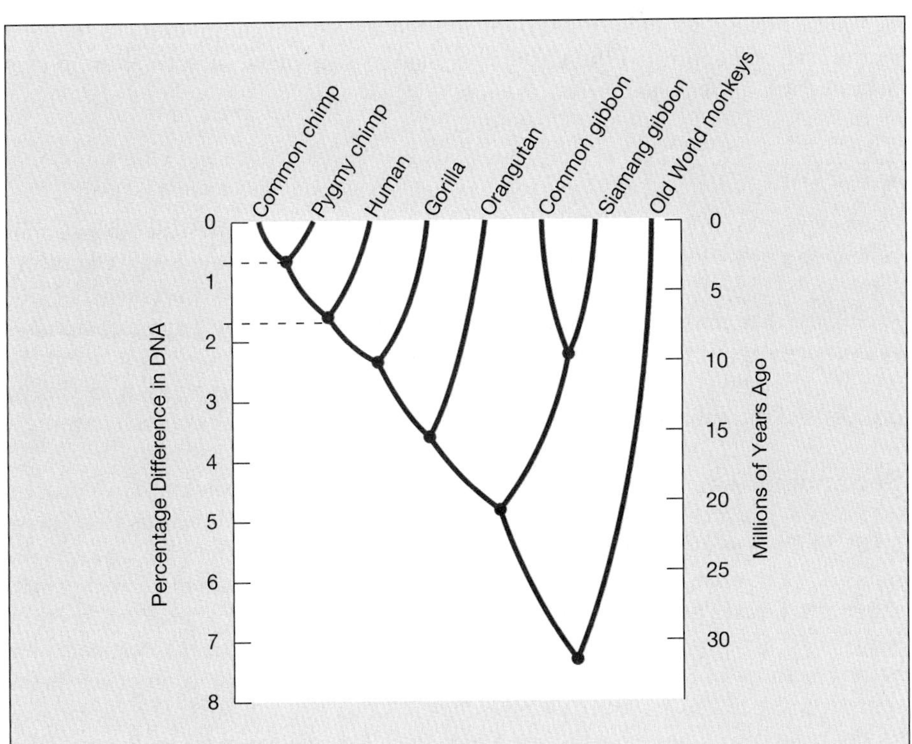

Figure 3.9 **Genetic relationships of the higher primates.** *Source:* From Diamond, 1992.

comparison of the human genome with the genome for cattle revealed that four complete chromosomes were identical (Band et al., 2000). (A genome consists of all the genes of all the members of a species.) However, in comparing humans with each other, geneticists adopt a different frame of reference. They consider that one human is related to another human if both have a common relative in the preceding three generations. So as Table 3.1 shows, a family has a higher percentage of shared genes *relative to strangers*. If two individuals are three generations removed from the parent generation, their genetic relationship is not considered a strong one.

We are not chimpanzees, nor in our present form are we psychologically much like them or any of the other living apes. So the question remains: how and when did we become so different from them? About 50,000 to 100,000 years ago, for unknown reasons, human populations increased dramatically and migrated throughout Europe and Asia. This proliferation may have been prompted by environmental changes, subtle changes in brain organization, or other factors.

The brains of our ancestors living 100,000 years ago were probably not radically different from our own. More likely, improved communication—spoken language—supported cultural advances that in turn supported larger populations. No evidence exists concerning either the presence or absence of language prior to 100,000 years ago. But the men and women who lived 50,000 years ago left evidence of ceremonial burying, and sophisticated art has survived from 25,000 to 30,000 B.C.E. Only humans possess language, representational art, a sense of being, and a concern for an afterlife. Can we speculate that our predecessors enjoyed similar sensory experiences and aspects of consciousness? With the possible exception of the elaboration of language (allowing different ways of thinking?), our remote ancestors may well have lived, learned, laughed, and loved much as we currently do.

We have seen that all humans are genetically related, and that our human ancestry can be traced through thousands of generations to an immediate precursor that was not *Homo sapiens*. Our most recent common ancestors are extinct apes;

our closest living nonhuman relatives are two species of chimpanzee. In the next section we will return to the genetic mechanisms involved in speciation, reproduction, and individual differences.

Genetic Variability

Unless you have an identical twin, you are genetically different from all other people. Where do genetic differences come from? Why are some individuals tall and others short, some happy and others morose? Why are some male and others female? The *variability* that makes individuals unique is introduced when genetic material—specifically, egg and sperm—is transmitted through sexual reproduction from the parent generation to the offspring. Genetic variation results from the genetic processes of recombination and mutation in these sex cells. Let's take each in turn.

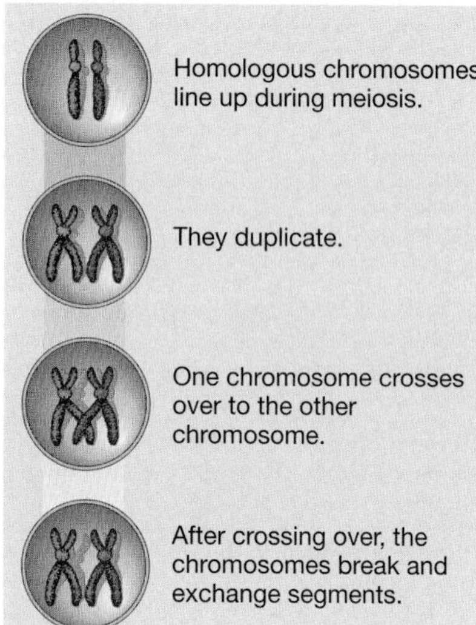
Homologous chromosomes line up during meiosis.
They duplicate.
One chromosome crosses over to the other chromosome.
After crossing over, the chromosomes break and exchange segments.

Figure 3.10 Genetic recombination. Genetic variability is introduced during sexual reproduction through the process of recombination.

Recombination. During sexual reproduction, genes are recombined in a process that begins when cells divide to produce egg and sperm, called **meiosis** (see Figure 3.10). In the egg cell, during the first stage of meiosis, chromosomes that encode the same traits, known as homologous chromosomes, line up together. Figure 3.10 shows this process of **recombination.** Then the chromosomal structures break, creating two versions of each chromosome pair, each different from the original ones. Because sections of DNA are exchanged between the paired chromosomes before the split occurs, each newly formed chromosome has a unique structure. The exchange is random and is accomplished through a process called *crossing over* (see Figure 3.10).

After the egg cell duplicates its set of chromosomes it then divides twice, making four separate cells; each of these "daughter cells" contains half the number of chromosomes as the parent cell. A similar process occurs in sperm cells, each of which also contains half the number of chromosomes as the parent cell. When the sperm and egg combine during fertilization, a new cell, known as a *zygote*, is created. The zygote is unique because it comprises spliced-together segments of the 23 chromosomes from each parent, recombined to produce offspring with 46 chromosomes each.

Mutation. A **mutation** is a random but permanent chemical change in the DNA molecule. Most mutations are harmful (often lethal), but the few that are advantageous may provide an individual with a selective edge. Mutations are the main way in which new traits are introduced into the genome of a species. Most mutations produce recessive genes. For the new characteristic to be expressed, therefore, both parents must produce the same recessive allele. This occurrence is unlikely except through common inheritance. Because related individuals have more genes in common than those who are not related, relatives have a higher probability of matching recessive genes than nonrelatives. For this reason, the offspring of close relatives, such as first cousins, have a higher chance of inheriting an expressed mutation. Ironically, because Charles and Emma Darwin were first cousins, as were one set of their grandparents, one or more of the Darwins' children probably experienced this misfortune.

meiosis The process of cell division that produces sex cells (sperm and egg) containing one of each pair of chromosomes.

recombination The process in which an organism emerges from meiosis with a combination of alleles different from that entering meiosis.

mutation A permanent, random chemical change in DNA, usually detrimental to an individual's survival.

The Role of Genetic Variation in Evolution. An old adage holds that variety is the spice of life. According to Darwin, variety literally makes life possible. The slight differences introduced from one generation to the next determine the course of evolution—which individual organisms survive and which do not. Why is this so? The answer is that some differences are advantageous to living and others are not. The significance of the concept of variability, therefore, is that some genotypes, in interaction with the environment (phenotypes), are more viable than others. In fact, at the microscopic level genes can lead to such different phenotypes as humans, dinosaurs, and mosquitoes.

The Influence of Genes on Behavior

Crying and mothering were described earlier as "genetically predisposed behaviors." The fact is, though, that genes don't behave; they code for proteins that make the cells found in muscles and spleens. These *structural proteins* are different from other proteins, called *enzymes*, which control the chemical reactions throughout an organism. How, then, can genes influence behavior?

Genetically coded structural proteins take many forms. Some become the brain cells we will study in Chapter 4. Collections of these brain cells, called brain systems, guide instinctive behavior, so we can say that brains, not genes, exhibit instinctive behavior. To take another example, the rods and cones of the retina are structural proteins that contain light-sensitive pigments. Their light-sensitive molecules evolved in response to an environment in which those wavelengths occurred. The genes themselves are insensitive to color, but because the light-sensitive cells they code for proved to be adaptive, the rod- and cone-making genes remain in the human gene pool.

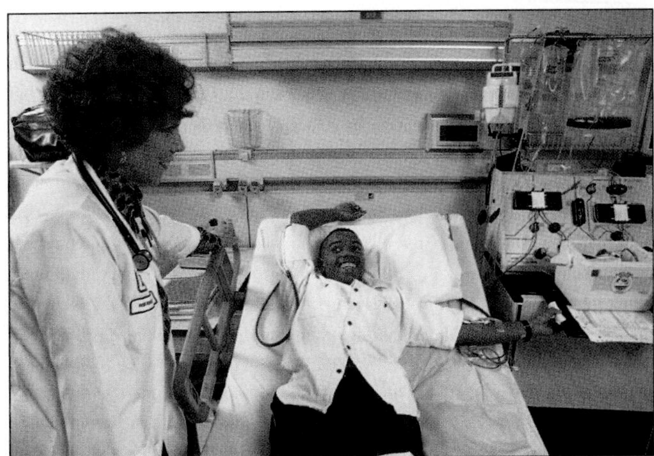

Genes that cause sickle-cell anemia are often carried by African Americans.

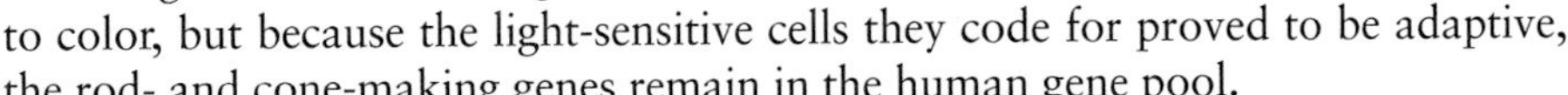

A change in only one of the amino acids in a DNA sequence can significantly affect the protein under construction. For example, consider the familiar protein hemoglobin, which carries oxygen and turns the blood red. An abnormal DNA template can cause structural changes in the 287-amino-acid sequence of this human protein. Sickle-cell disease is a genetic disorder that prevents the hemoglobin molecules in red blood cells from picking up oxygen and carrying it throughout the body. Rather than being round like normal red blood cells, sickled red blood cells are shaped like crescents. The difference between normal and sickled cells is a change in only one of the 287 amino acids that code for normal hemoglobin. In this instance, a change in just one amino acid causes a serious disorder.

The hemoglobin protein also figures in the story of our human ancestry. The 287 amino acid sequences for hemoglobin are similar among all primates, with only slight variations from species to species. Might we expect that our hemoglobin is more similar to that of chimpanzees because more of our DNA matches the chimp's than any other animal's? In fact, all 287 sequences match perfectly; the hemoglobin found in both species of chimpanzee is identical to that of humans.

INTERIM SUMMARY

1. **Genetics** is the study of patterns of heredity and variation in plants and animals. **Heredity** refers to the genetic transmission of ***deoxyribonucleic acid,*** or ***DNA,*** a complex protein structure containing genetic instructions of a species from one generation to the next.
2. Genes are found on ***chromosomes*** in every cell of the body. Genes differ in their DNA sequences. That DNA sequences are similar in all life forms attests to their common origins of those forms.
3. ***Dichotomous traits*** are caused by the same (*homozygous*) or different (*heterozygous*) forms of ***alleles*** on genes.
4. In a heterozygote, a ***dominant allele*** is expressed and a ***recessive allele*** is unexpressed.
5. A new ***genotype*** is formed at conception. Except for identical twins, each animal has a unique genotype. When a genotype is expressed in an environment, it is called a ***phenotype.***
6. Both within and between species genetic similarity, or kinship, can be measured using DNA sequencing and other gene-mapping techniques. The earliest humans evolved in Africa. Existing evidence supports both early and later migrations into Europe and Asia.

7. About 98 percent of the DNA in chimpanzees overlaps with human DNA, making them our closest living nonhuman relatives. Our most recent common ancestor with chimpanzees lived about 7 million years ago.
8. During the process of ***meiosis***, or cell division, 46 chromosomes separate to produce egg or sperm cells with 23 chromosomes each.
9. Genetic variability, or variation, results from the processes of ***recombination*** and ***mutation,*** both prior to and during sexual reproduction.
10. Genes influence our behavior by acting as templates for the coding of the proteins that make up brain cells, hormones, and all other aspects of an individual's anatomy and physiology.
11. A difference of one amino acid in the protein called hemoglobin can produce a serious abnormality known as sickle-cell anemia. The sequencing of amino acids that produce different types of hemoglobin varies little in closely related species.

For Further Thought

1. Assume that the goal of psychology is the complete understanding of the human mind and behavior. What are the implications of the fact that our primate brains and behaviors have been nonhuman for a much longer period than they have been human?
2. The next time you're at the zoo, notice how much time young children spend watching the primates as opposed to other mammals. Why the fascination with primates?

GENES MEET ENVIRONMENT

We now shift our focus from genes themselves to the interplay of genes and environment. We begin with the intriguing question of human uniqueness. To what extent do humans have a unique nature, and to what extent are they like other animals? To answer this question we must turn to the related disciplines of behavioral genetics, ethology, and comparative psychology.

Human Nature: Our Three Histories

Humans are genetically similar to one another because they share common ancestors. DNA shared over a period of just 100,000 to 200,000 years—a brief time frame by evolutionary standards—makes all humans close relatives. This shared inheritance is the physical basis for "human nature"—the tendency for humans to behave like humans and less like other species of animals. Compare, if you will, the following psychological experiences and behaviors. Humans can and do engage in the following behaviors:

Perceive	Eat	Talk
Learn	Drink	Compose symphonies
Remember	Date	Build computers
Think	Mate	Play soccer
Sleep	Care for young	Make wine
Dream	Engage in social behaviors	Appreciate the universe

Of these, most humans, other mammals, and birds engage in the behaviors listed in the first two columns. The simplest explanation for this fact is that humans share with other animals genes that determine brain organization. But human genes and brain organization are sufficiently *different* to allow them to engage in some unique behaviors—the ones indicated in column three. (We'll look at "ape language" in some detail in Chapter 12. A number of primates communicate through grunts and squeals, but none "talk.") Human nature, and only human nature, has produced human culture and civilization.

Human nature has three components. First is the history of the species contained in our genes, our **phylogenetic history**. The second component of human nature is the individual's development from fertilization through death, or one's **ontogenetic history**. The third component is our **extragenetic history**, a term coined by Carl Sagan in 1977 to represent the wisdom of earlier generations.

These three components interact. Assuming that life was created at one time and has since been continuously differentiating through the process of evolution, the human gene pool reflects the history of life during the past 3.5 billion years. And yet the amount of information contained in genes is limited. Reflexes and instincts can go only so far in terms of adaptation to the human niche. Humans therefore use large, evolved brains to learn and remember what is necessary to survive: each of us develops a unique ontogenetic history. During our lifetimes we also profit from the ontogenetic histories of other individuals in our species, especially through oral and written cross-generational communication. Our extragenetic history, then, contributes information in the form of cultural wisdom, which supplements our instinctive behavior. Together all three factors form our common human nature.

LINK
Ontogenetic history and learning, Chapter 6, p. 187

Extragenetic history and memes, Chapter 6, p. 187

If humans have a nature, of course, then there must also be a "tiger nature," a "pigeon nature," a "bee nature," and so forth. Each member of these species shares common genetic material and common inherited behavior patterns that help to define the species.

Do some aspects of human behavior resemble the behavior of other species of animals? The answer is that some do more than others. Humans behave more like other primates than like chickens because they share more genetic material with primates. Likewise, in many particulars they behave more like rats, dogs, monkeys, and cats than like chickens or manta rays, for mammals share more DNA, and hence more psychological and biological characteristics, with each other than with nonmammals.

The Interaction of Nature and Nurture

Although animals have many common properties, there is also dissimilarity and diversity among life forms. A brain organization that is unique to a species underlies a **species-specific behavior**—an adaptive, innate response pattern that is typical of that species. (For now, think of a species-specific behavior as an "instinct.") Sniffing and tasting small amounts of a new food (rats) and crawling and babbling at about 9 months of age (human infants) are examples of species-specific behavior. As innate response patterns, these behaviors support the nature side of the nature-nurture debate.

The process of learning—the *nurture side* in the nature-nurture debate—complements species-specific behaviors. Take as an example the feeding behavior of titmice (various species of birds native to England). Some individual birds of the species have been observed to remove the caps and eat the cream from the tops of bottles of home-delivered milk (Fisher & Hinde, 1949). Neither these nor any other species evolved in an ecological niche that contained bottles of milk as a food source. Such feeding behavior, therefore, is not instinctive. These birds have inherited eyes for seeing, a manipulative beak, and a physiology that regulates hunger and thirst, however. Because this basic, innately determined equipment supports feeding in a variety of environments, we can safely conclude that in their lifetimes birds *learn* to drink from milk bottles. In a behavioral analysis

phylogenetic history The evolutionary history of a specific group of organisms.

ontogenetic history The history of an animal's entire development, from fertilization through death.

extragenetic history Information in the form of cultural wisdom, including oral and written history, that is passed across generations.

species-specific behavior An adaptive, innate response pattern typical of a species.

Birds can learn to feed outside the niche in which they evolved.

of this situation, the cream would be the reinforcer (reward) for the bottle-top pecking response. With a full belly, the bird will be more likely to return for another milk-bottle meal.

A milk-drinking bird is but one example of an innate behavior that is modified by the environment. Because nature and nurture are so intertwined, behavioral scientists can approach their subject from many different perspectives. We will consider first one of the most molecular approaches, that of behavioral genetics.

Behavioral Genetics

Well before Darwin's time, artificial selection had produced systematic changes in the physical traits, temperament, and behavioral functioning of animals. Indeed, domesticated animals are the result of human intervention in and manipulation of the normal flow of genes among species. Archaeological evidence suggests that dogs were among the first animals to be domesticated; they lived with humans more than 13,000 years ago. Dogs' diverse varieties, shapes, and temperaments belie their common lineage from wolves.

Behavioral genetics is the study of how genes interact with the environment to affect an animal's behavior. Its methods include laboratory work, epidemiological studies, and survey research. A representative sampling of behavioral genetics research includes (1) the breeding of *Drosophila melanogaster* (the fruit fly) for selective physical and behavioral traits; (2) the investigation of selected behaviors in mammals, including alcohol drinking in mice, maze learning in rats, and temperamental behavior in dogs; and (3) the study of human behaviors, including the creativity and intelligence of twins and the illness Huntington's chorea.

Emotionality in Dogs. Some of the earliest laboratory experiments on behavioral characteristics were accomplished with dogs. The Russian physiologist Ivan Pavlov (1927) selectively bred dogs with *strong* and *weak* types of nervous systems. Based on laboratory tests, Pavlov defined a strong nervous system as one that could withstand high levels of sensory stimulation in conditioning experiments. John Paul Scott and John Fuller have since performed more systematic experiments involving the behavior and temperament of two breeds of dogs. Basenji hound pups are normally fearful in interactions with humans; by comparison, cocker spaniel pups are not. What might be the result of mixing their genes?

When these two types of dogs were interbred, all the offspring (the F_1 generation) were fearful. But the F_2 offspring of F_1 hybrids produced the now familiar 3:1 Mendelian pattern of inheritance. These findings can best be interpreted as meaning that the trait of fearfulness is produced by a single gene, with the fear allele being dominant (Scott & Fuller, 1965).

Appetite in Mice. My grandmother used to say that hormones are responsible for the extra weight some people gain. (Before dismissing this bit of folk wisdom, consider the fact that genes encode some proteins as hormones.) A British population geneticist, D. S. Falconer, tested this hypothesis in mice. Let's consider some details of his experiment. Beginning with a huge population of mice, he divided it into 18 separate groups, assigning the heaviest mice to 6 Heavy groups and the lightest ones to 6 Light groups. The remaining mice, which were of medium weight, filled out the 6 control groups.

behavioral genetics The study of how genes, interacting with environments, affect behavior.

For the next 23 generations, Falconer interbred the heaviest mice in each of the 6 Heavy groups, as well as the lightest mice in each of the 6 Light groups. He selected control group mice for breeding by lottery. Figure 3.11 shows his results after 23 generations. As you can see, the experiment produced noticeably heavier animals in the Heavy groups and lighter mice in the Light groups. The intermediate groups remained at about the same weight (Falconer, 1960).

A mouse (left) with *ob* recessive genes, which impair the regulation of appetite, will overeat and gain weight.

What the graph does not show is the fact that each successive Light and Heavy litter contained weaker individuals with higher infant mortality rates. At maturity, these artificially selected mice experienced decreasing fertility and smaller litter sizes. That is, their fitness suffered under artificial selection. What went wrong with these mice? Recall that the seed-coat characteristics for which Mendel bred were single-allele effects. By contrast, characteristics such as appetite and weight, called **polygenic characters**, are caused by the effects of many genes. What happened over 23 generations was that the Heavy and Light populations had the same alleles, but those alleles had been selected to occur in different frequencies. The results were the observed differences in weight and fitness, higher infant mortality, and probably other effects as well.

The loss in fitness in these populations was likely due to several factors. For example, some combinations of alleles that the experimenter selected may simply have been harmful to the mice. They might have caused adverse changes in the regulation of body temperature, hormone production, or taste sensitivity. Another factor may simply have been the result of too much inbreeding. As is suspected to have happened in Darwin's family, harmful recessive alleles may have become homozygous and been expressed phenotypically. In populations of wild mice, normal breeding patterns and natural selection would tend to keep recessive genes from being expressed. For example, a plump, less agile mouse would likely become a predator's meal, and an underweight mouse might be more susceptible to disease.

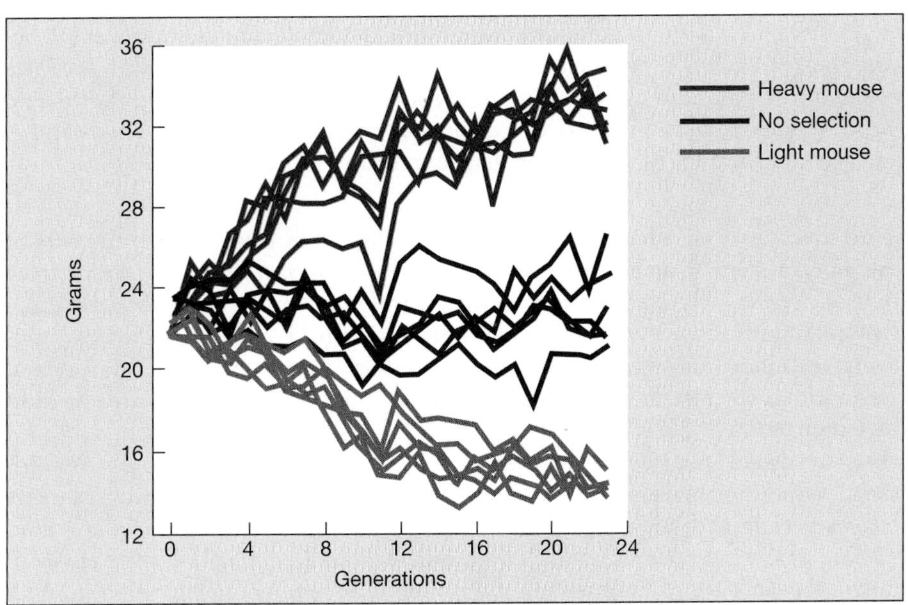

Figure 3.11 Selective breeding of mice of different weights. This figure shows the results of selectively breeding heavy with heavy mice and light with light mice. After 23 generations the average weight of the light mice was less than 16 grams, whereas the heavy mice were double that weight. *Source:* Falconer, 1960.

polygenic character A character that varies in a continous manner, presumable caused by the effects of many genes.

The Importance of the Environment in Gene Expression. In the preceding studies of temperament in dogs and appetite in mice, the environment was held constant. One might therefore think that the environment was not a factor in the observed behaviors. Yet the behavior expressed by basenji and cocker pups was *highly* dependent on the environment into which they were born. Had they been born into different environments, the expression of their respective genetic predispositions (to be fearful or not) would have varied. For example, a dog might be born into an abusive environment, the intense heat of the desert, a neighborhood near an airport with 110 dB noise levels, or a home with a playful child. Each environment would likely have interacted with the dog's genetic predisposition, and the resulting phenotypic behavior would have differed from what Scott and Fuller observed in their experiments. Likewise, mice born into an environment with limited food and water would not separate into heavy and light groups, no matter what their genetic differences were.

Furthermore, the mice in this study were homozygous for the recessive *ob* gene (*ob* for *obesity*), which was experimentally introduced. They achieved their impressive weight *only* when they were placed on an unrestricted diet. That is, their recessive gene was expressed only when they were allowed to eat whatever they wanted. Because mouse obesity did not occur in a food-restricted environment, both genes and environment must have played a role. In other experiments, obesity-prone mice failed to learn to eat *less* of a high-calorie diet or *more* of a low-calorie diet. In both these altered-food environments, the *ob* strain was unable to maintain a constant body weight, meaning that some of the *ob* genes were likely involved with caloric regulation. While on unregulated diets, these obese mice were unable to breed. Depending on the environment, therefore, inbreeding can allow recessive genes to be expressed, resulting in reduced fitness (Dewsbury & Rethlingshafer, 1973).

LINK
Role of genes in health, Chapter 16, p. 550

Researchers at Rockefeller University have since identified an *ob* gene in humans that is involved in the control and storage of fat (Zhang et al., 1994). In a later chapter we will discuss the respective roles of such "fat genes" in eating disorders and of "alcohol genes" in alcohol abuse. For now we can extrapolate from the research on obese mice that were raised in different environments this conclusion: Genes do not compel a behavior. More accurately, a behavior becomes more likely when the environment supports gene expression. The presence of unlimited food and alcohol can allow some genes to be expressed that would *not* be expressed in more restrictive environments. In this sense, the environment can account for a lot of variance in gene expression (Turkheimer, 2000).

The Concept of Heritability. Because it takes into account the role of the environment in gene expression, the idea of *heritability* is different from that of heredity. **Heritability** is a mathematical concept that expresses the relative contribution of genes and the environment to a behavior. Two assumptions are made: first, that genes and the environment are uncorrelated, and second, that the effects of genes and the environment can be measured to indicate their relative contributions. For example, assume that some phenotypical character, such as appetite, can be measured by a *heritability score*. A measured value approaching 1.0 is defined as highly heritable, meaning that the trait is determined largely by genetic and physiological variables. By contrast, a score near zero means that the trait is determined primarily by the environment. An estimate of heritability always refers to groups, never to an individual within a group.

LINK
Heritability and twin studies of intelligence, Chapter 13, p. 466

heritability The relative influence of heredity in the expression of a trait. A heritability score varies between 0 and 1, with 1 meaning that a trait is largely determined by genetic and physiological variables and 0 meaning that it is primarily environmentally caused.

Table 3.2 lists the heritability estimates for a number of psychological traits important in guide dogs for the blind. Note that the behavioral characteristic of *nervousness* is the most strongly inherited trait (.58), and *distractibility* (.08) is more environmentally determined. Assuming that both traits are undesirable in a guide dog, which trait could a good dog *trainer* correct more easily? Which could a good dog *breeder* correct more easily?

Heritability estimates have been computed for human characteristics ranging from schizophrenia to intelligence (Plomin, 1990; Bouchard, 1994). Obviously scientists cannot do selective breeding studies with humans. Instead, they estimate the effects of genes and the environment on the expression of these complex psychological and behavioral characteristics by comparing the behavior of identical twins in the same and different environments. We will explore these exciting studies in detail in later chapters.

Heritability and twin studies of personality, Chapter 14, p. 495

LINK

Heritability and twin studies of schizophrenia, Chapter 17, p. 600

Ethology

Ethologists study species-specific behaviors—how animals behave within their natural ecological niches. They propose that because free-ranging behavior is instinctive, it is lawful and therefore predictable. As mentioned earlier, *instinct* is both a useful and a slippery term. At its worst it is used with circular meaning. Ethologists use the term to describe *patterns of behavior that are common to a species,* based on systematic observation and analysis. By identifying and labeling different types of instinctive behaviors, they have gained insight into naturally occurring behaviors. Let's look at some of the ways they classify instinctive behaviors.

Table 3.2 Heritability of Traits in Guide dogs

TRAIT	HERITABILITY
Nervousness	.58
Suspicion	.10
Concentration	.28
Willingness	.22
Distractibility	.08
Dog distraction	.27
Noise distraction	.00
Sound shyness	.14
Hearing sensitivity	.00
Body sensitivity	.33

Source: From Mackenzie, Oltenacu, & Houpt, 1986.

Appetitive and Consummatory Behaviors. During the first part of the twentieth century, classical ethologists focused on the behaviors of several species of birds and fish. The questions they asked were deceptively simple: Why do certain species of animals do what they do? Among the behavioral repertoires of birds, they observed behaviors that were indispensable to survival: feeding, courting, mating, caring for offspring, and so on. In doing so they noted that these animals first engaged in preliminary activities, such as searching, by attending selectively to potential mates or food. They called these preliminary behaviors **appetitive behaviors**, and the achievement of an innate "survival" goal, such as copulating or eating, a **consummatory behavior**.

How do ethologists explain the remarkable diversity of animal behavior they observe? They first ask what selective pressures an animal faces in the niche it currently occupies. Different environments require different behaviors—the simplest examples of which are that running, flying, and swimming occur on land, in the air, and in the water, respectively. Next, ethologists ask what selective pressures must have been present in the animal's evolutionary past. Finally, they consider how a particular behavioral pattern has helped the animal to overcome a specific obstacle to survival presented by the environment. Behavior, in other words, is an adaptation to the environment, the ultimate purpose of which is to survive long enough to reproduce.

Imprinting and Critical Periods. Nobel Prize–winner Konrad Lorenz's ethological research on the graylag goose provides an example of this perspective. Lorenz found that shortly after hatching, goslings exhibited the rapid learning of a *following behavior* through a process he called **imprinting.**

In some species imprinting occurs within a few critical hours after hatching, a time known as the **critical period.** During this time an animal is particularly sensitive to certain features in the environment. In geese, *following behavior* is imprinted during such a critical period. Under normal conditions, young hatchlings will follow their mother, allowing her to take care of them.

But when Lorenz was the first moving object the goslings saw during their critical period, they followed *him* around. In time, Lorenz found that when goslings imprint to a moving human during their critical period (instead of to a

appetitive behaviors Preliminary activities (such as searching) that precede and lead to consummatory behaviors.

consummatory behaviors (Ethology) Innate "survival" behaviors such as copulating and eating.

imprinting (Ethology) A highly adaptive innate behavioral process that involves the rapid development of a response to a specific stimulus at a particular stage of development.

critical period (Ethology) A period when an animal is particularly sensitive to certain features in the environment.

Birds that imprint to humans treat humans as other birds.

moving mother goose), for the remainder of their lives they tend to treat humans as geese. At maturity, they even court and attempt to mate with humans. But he noticed that if the geese first saw him at 1 to 2 days of age rather than 1 to 2 hours, his appearance had no greater effect on their behavior than any other visual stimulus. He concluded that in geese, the critical period was 1 to 2 hours.

Other ethologists have measured the onset and duration of the critical period in several species of birds housed in laboratories. Eckhard Hess's sketch of the apparatus he used at the University of Chicago, shown in Figure 3.12, shows that a moving decoy could elicit the following behavior in newly hatched chicks. In addition to the critical period for the chicks' following behavior, the graph in the figure shows the improvements in walking and reduction in fear responses he observed during the same period.

Imprinting, then, is one of a number of instinctive behaviors that promotes survival in some birds. What do we know about imprinting and critical periods in humans? Could the period of 6 to 24 months of age be considered the critical period for humans in learning to talk? As we will see in Chapter 12, children are highly receptive to the sounds of words during this period; they rehearse these sounds without prompting, and usually master spoken grammar and syntax by 3½ years. This rapid acquisition of language during a circumscribed period appears to be highly adaptive, suggesting that it has a genetic base. In both humans who are learning to talk and goslings who are learning to follow, note the importance of the environment in eliciting the instinctive behavior. Following occurs only when the hatchling sees something to follow; likewise, children who do not hear language do not learn to speak language.

LINK
Critical periods and language acquisition, Chapter 12, p. 431

Fixed Action Patterns. Ethologists have also studied a type of instinct called a **fixed action pattern (FAP)**, which is defined as a programmed sequence of behaviors that is triggered by a specific stimulus. For example, if an egg slips out from under a brooding graylag goose and rolls from the nest, she will get up and approach the egg. The goose then uses her bill to scoop the egg back into the nest. To qualify as an FAP, a behavioral sequence must meet four criteria (Moltz, 1963). First, the behavior must be *stereotyped*—it must occur in about the same way each time, and second, once begun, the behavioral sequence should be difficult to disrupt—it should *continue to completion*. The goose's scooping action satisfies both criteria. A third characteristic of FAPs is that once they have been completed, there must be a *latent period* before they will occur again. Finally, an FAP must be innate, or *unlearned*: the animal must perform the fully integrated behavioral sequence the first time it is elicited. The egg-retrieving response of the graylag goose meets all four criteria for an FAP (Eible-Eibesfeldt, 1975).

LINK
FAPs with physiological reflexes, Chapter 4, p. 110, Chapter 6, p. 191

An FAP is triggered by a specifiable environmental stimulus, called a **sign stimulus**. In the example just given, catching sight of the egg out of the nest is a sign stimulus. Ethologists hypothesize that a genetically coded part of the visual brain, called an **innate releasing mechanism**, is particularly receptive to such sign stimuli. Metaphorically, the releasing mechanism is a "lock" to which the sign stimulus, the behavioral "key," has been perfectly fitted. When an animal encounters the sign stimulus, patterns of activity in the visual portion of its brain activate motor programs in other parts of the brain, which cause the fixed action pattern.

Fixed action patterns resemble other behaviors that we call reflexes, such as sneezing or blinking one's eyes in a dust storm. For now we may consider FAPs to be "reflexlike," and more precisely defined than the term *instinct*.

fixed action pattern (FAP) (Ethology) A programmed sequence of species-specific behaviors tht is triggered by a particular stimulus.

sign stimulus (Ethology) A specific environmental stimulus that triggers innately organized behaviors.

innate releasing mechanism (Ethology) A postulated neural mechanism tht triggers an innately organized motor program.

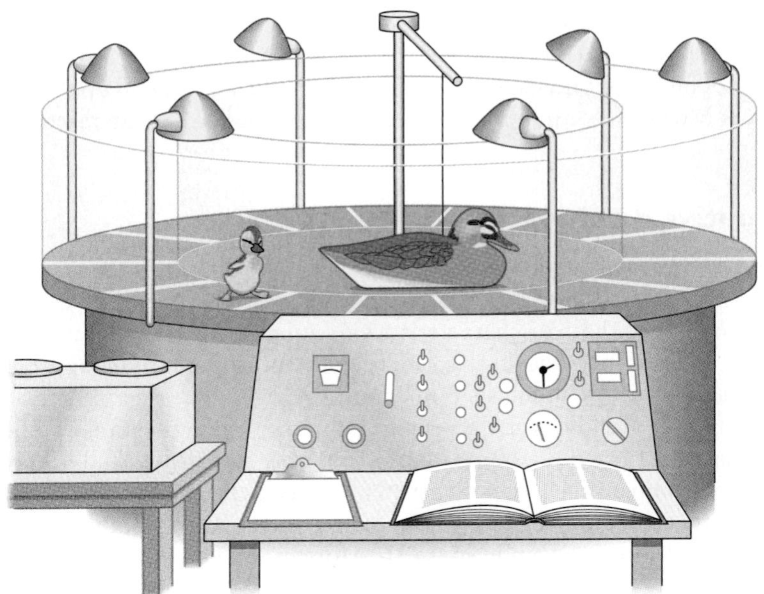

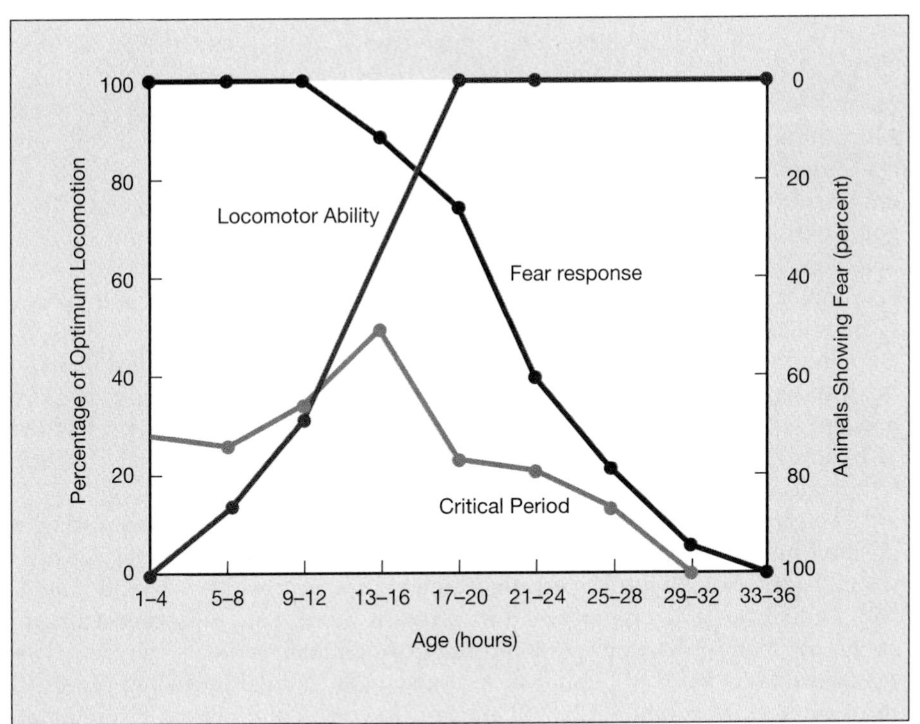

Figure 3.12 The critical period in newly hatched chicks. (a) Hess's drawing of the apparatus he used to study imprinting in the laboratory. A live duckling would follow the decoy (center) during the critical period. (b) A plot of movement (locomotor ability) and fear responses in chicks during their critical period. *Source:* Reprinted from IMPRINTING ed. by E. H. Hess and S. B. Petrovich. Copyright © 1977. Originally published by Dowden, Hutchinson and Ross, Inc.

Species-specific Defense Reactions. The study of instinctive behavior is not restricted to imprinting and FAPs in birds. For example, Robert Bolles found that both rats and birds respond to different types of aversive stimulation in predictable, characteristic ways. When given a painful electric shock, rats jump. In the presence of moving stimuli, they first freeze and then run. In contrast, pigeons flap their wings and fly in both situations (Bolles, 1971). Bolles called such innately organized defense behaviors, which are elicited by signals of potential danger, **species-specific defense reactions**, because without special training, all members of a species exhibit the same reactions.

species-specific defense reaction An innately organized hierarchy of defense behaviors elicited by signals indicating potential danger.

Even humans exhibit this type of behavior. When human infants lose support (when they are dropped, for example), they exhibit what is called a Moro reflex: they cry out, pull in their necks, scrunch up their shoulders, and pull up their hands and arms. A Moro reflex can be considered a species-specific defense reaction.

Comparative Psychology

Is there a pet owner alive who has not speculated about what animals might be thinking or dreaming about, or whether they experience emotions as we do? People who attribute human characteristics to animals, such as cunning to cats and conceit to strutting peacocks, are taking an **anthropomorphic** approach to them. Is this the way psychologists think about animals?

Comparative psychology is the scientific study of the motivation and behavior of animals for the express purpose of identifying similarities and differences among them. Comparative psychologists tend to see anthropomorphism as a pitfall. One of the first comparative psychologists was a British naturalist named Conwyn Lloyd Morgan. Writing in 1891, Morgan urged colleagues to be cautious in their interpretation of the animal mind:

> In no case may we interpret an action as the outcome of the exercise of a higher psychical faculty if it can be interpreted as the outcome of the exercise of one which stands lower in the psychological scale. (Morgan 1891, p. 53)

Cartoonists' creations are anthropomorphic.

Now known as **Morgan's canon**, this statement has been widely interpreted as an admonishment to psychologists and other researchers to avoid anthropomorphism—that is, not to attribute human characteristics to animals. However, Morgan held some unorthodox views that mingled evolutionary thinking with his Christian faith. In other writings he expressed concern about the dehumanizing implications of evolution: only humans, he thought, had the potential to be godlike. In this sense, Morgan may have been less than objective in his thinking (Morgan, 1928).

Ironically, among the earliest writings in comparative psychology was Charles Darwin's (1872) *The Expression of Emotions in Man and Animals*. Darwin's theory of evolution had rested on the continuity of life forms; he wrote this later work expressly to point out that humans, too, were animals. Darwin's position was that humans shared with other animals many psychological as well as physical characteristics. **Zoomorphism**, or the attribution of animal qualities to humans, is an implicit assumption of comparative psychology.

Which perspective is correct? Morgan assumed that humans occupy a higher position in nature than other animals. A simpler (more parsimonious) position would be to assume with Darwin that humans *are* animals, and that all animals have similarities and differences. Too often, psychologists following Morgan's canon attribute psychological simplicity to nonhuman animals. In fact, dogs, cats, porpoises, monkeys, chimpanzees, and other animals with big brains do show evidence of psychological complexity. To consistently seek the simplest explanation, psychologists would have us think differently about humans as well. Why assume cognitive complexity in humans (as Morgan did) if human thinking and behavior can be explained more simply? Interestingly, more than a century of research has not resolved these issues. Many psychologists are as reluctant to attribute psychological complexity to other animals as they are to think of the human mind in simple terms. We will rejoin this argument at various places in the text.

Historically, comparative psychologists have concentrated their research on just a few species of animals—rats, cats, dogs, pigeons, and monkeys—all of which have been domesticated for hundreds of years in various cultures. An ironic criticism of comparative psychologists is that their selection of animals for

anthropomorphism The attribution of human characteristics to animals.

comparative psychology The study of the motivation and behavior of animals in order to identify similarities and differences among them.

Morgan's canon Morgan's (1894) admonition not to attribute complex psychological processes to nonhuman animals.

zoomorphism The attribution of animal qualities to humans.

comparison with one another does not make good sense from an evolutionary perspective (Hodos & Campbell, 1969). That is, comparative psychologists typically study birds, rats, and monkeys in laboratories, often for the sake of convenience. But if they are attempting to discover the *evolution* of learning or intelligence, this argument goes, then the phylogenetic relationships of the animals they select for study make little sense. Evolution is *not* described by the simple progression of bird to rat to monkey to human.

Certainly this argument has merit. But comparative psychologists have many reasons for their choice of research animals and behaviors and the methods they use. Let's take a brief look at some representative examples of their research.

Maternal Behavior and Adult Development. In a famous series of studies using rhesus monkeys (*Macaca mulatta*), Margaret and Harry Harlow investigated the role of mother-infant feeding in **pair bonding**—the development of a strong and enduring affection between infant and parent (Harlow & Harlow, 1962). They found that when infant monkeys were taken away from their mothers, they would spend hours clinging to a wire frame covered with terry cloth (designated a "terry cloth monkey mother"). The infants would leave the terry cloth mother only long enough to nurse from a bare wire frame that held a nursing bottle. To explain these behaviors the Harlows speculated that primates had a biological need for *contact comfort*—one that was *not* met by the life-sustaining milk they sucked from an uncomfortable wire monkey mother. Later, when these motherless monkeys became adults, they neither courted the opposite sex appropriately nor copulated with them. For those who might have thought that sex was instinctive in animals, the Harlows had gathered evidence that suggested otherwise.

From this research we can see that social isolation can have severe consequences. In a later chapter we will explore the adverse effects of social isolation on intellectual development, which extend even to the acquisition of human language. The Harlows' research findings also teach us something that could not be learned using the naturalistic observation method. The courting, sexual, and maternal behaviors of humans and monkeys are not fixed action patterns that occur regardless of the environment. Rather, the environment must support and nurture their expression.

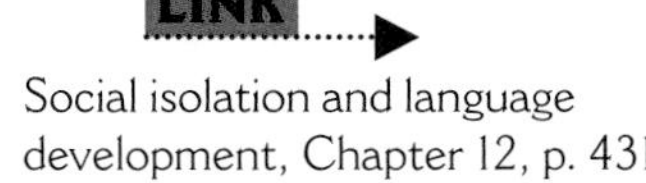

Social isolation and language development, Chapter 12, p. 431

Early Social Interaction and Adult Social Behavior. The Harlows' monkey experiments provide an effective *animal model* from which we can attain insight into the pervasive role of the environment in determining human behavior. In further research, these comparative psychologists found that the effects of raising an infant monkey without a mother could be mitigated if an infant was allowed to play with other infant monkeys for as little as an hour a day (Harlow, 1969). Total isolation, then, rather than the specific experience of not being mothered, may be critical to the development of the maladaptive behaviors these motherless monkeys displayed as adults.

Many primates engage in play.

Perhaps the recuperative effects of playing for one hour with other monkeys can be better appreciated by imagining what a roomful of infant monkeys at play looks, sounds, and smells like. As is the case with other primates, monkey play by both sexes involves wrestling, chasing, and aggressive play (Harlow, 1969). We now know that early social interactions influence both brain development and subsequent adult social behavior in adaptive ways. Likewise, early and profound social isolation is implicated in the formation of maladaptively developed

pair bonding A strong and enduring affection that unites an infant with a parent.

Pair bonding and child development, Chapter 11, p. 405

brains and ineffective behavior. One message of this research is to let the children play. Another is that pair bonding during infancy is critically important for adult human behavior, a theme we will return to in Chapter 11.

Although the Harlows did not examine the brains of the monkeys raised with surrogate mothers, research with other mammals raised in isolation has shown abnormal brain development (Rosensweig, Krech, Bennett, & Diamond, 1962). Research by neuroethologists is specifically designed to measure the effect of early environmental experience on both behavior and brain development.

Neuroethology: An Interdisciplinary Approach

Neuroethology combines research perspectives from traditional ethology with comparative studies of brain function and learning. Specifically, neuroethologists study how instinctive behaviors are modified by the environment (Nottebohm, 1991). An intriguing example of this type of research is the study of the brain mechanisms that allow birds to sing.

Male birds sing for two apparent reasons: to stake out a territory and to attract females for courting and mating. Each species has its own particular song; within species there may be several dialects. Neuroethologists have found that certain areas of the male bird's brain are genetically coded to be especially sensitive to the sounds of birdsong. Males that hear a recorded birdsong during the critical period (20 to 60 days, depending on the species) will, on maturity several months later, begin to sing the dialect they heard. If they hear nothing during the critical period, they will develop an abnormal song that contains few features characteristic of their species' song (Marler & Peters, 1988).

Research shows that certain brain structures (the song-sensing and learning pathways) allow the bird to learn what it hears during the critical period, whereas other brain structures allow it to sing. When one or the other of these two areas of the brain is damaged, the bird doesn't sing. In normal male birds, the size of these brain areas is determined by the hormone testosterone. When testosterone is injected into female birds, the appropriate brain area grows; when it becomes large enough, normally nonsinging females begin to sing (Nottebohm, 1980).

The most obvious answer to the question "why do birds sing?" is that the behavior bears on their fitness. Birds that sing mark out territory and attract mates, and in doing so successfully perpetuate their genes. But note that these territorial and communicative behaviors are more complex than the fixed action patterns that characterize "instinctive behavior." The point is that both complex human and animal *social* interactions, as well as simpler animal instincts, can be understood from an evolutionary perspective.

Contributions of Comparative Psychologists and Neuroethologists

Working from within a nature-nurture framework, comparative psychologists and neuroethologists have expanded on the basic observations that classical ethologists have made of animals living within their ecological niches. Comparative psychologists

- Brought tight experimental controls to behavioral investigations.
- Focused on *individual differences* within species.
- Promoted *animal model* research that emphasizes common learning processes and common behavior patterns among animals who share DNA.
- Furthered our understanding of the *comparative brain mechanisms* that underlie comparative behaviors.
- Struggled with the question of human uniqueness, attempting to strike a balance between zoomorphism and anthropomorphism.

neuroethology The study of the relationship between the nervous system and consummatory behaviors.

INTERIM SUMMARY

1. Every human has a unique nature that reflects his or her ***phylogenetic*** and ***ontogenetic histories,*** including experiences with our species' ***extragenetic.***
2. Each animal behaves in some ways like other animals, while also displaying unique ***species-specific behaviors.***
3. ***Behavioral genetics*** is the laboratory study of how the interaction of genes and the environment affects such diverse phenomena as temperament in dogs, obesity in mice, and intelligence and mental illness in humans.
4. Most behaviors do not result from single alleles; rather, complex behaviors are the result of many different alleles organized as ***polygenic characters.***
5. ***Heritability*** is a measure of the amount of a trait that can be attributed to genes, compared to the total effect of both genes and the environment. Heritability is a measure applied to groups, not to individuals.
6. Ethology is the study of species-specific behaviors within an animal's ecological niche. Ethologists distinguish between ***appetitive*** and ***consummatory behaviors.***
7. Konrad Lorenz found that a ***critical period*** existed in young animals' development, during which a type of rapid, long-lasting learning—***imprinting***—would occur under certain conditions.
8. ***Fixed action patterns (FAPs)*** are instinctive behaviors that (a) are innate, or unlearned; (b) occur in the same way each time; (c) are difficult to disrupt; and (d) are followed by a latent period during which the FAP cannot occur.
9. Fixed action patterns (FAPs) are released by ***sign stimuli*** that occur normally in the animal's ecological niche. Sign stimuli are detected by ***innate releasing mechanisms,*** parts of an animal's brain that are sensitive to the sign stimuli.
10. Innate responses of animals to pain or threat are called ***species-specific defense reactions.***
11. Researchers in ***comparative psychology*** work from a ***zoomorphic*** perspective, in which they compare common behavioral processes, including learning and perception, across species.
12. ***Morgan's canon*** admonishes investigators not to be ***anthropomorphic*** in their thinking. Rather, scientists should accept the simplest possible explanations for complex behaviors.
13. The Harlows' research, which showed that monkeys reared in isolation are socially deficient in courting, mating, and caring for their offspring, is an example of an *animal model* of human behavior. The Harlows' research highlighted the role of mother-infant ***pair bonding.***
14. Research in ***neuroethology*** has uncovered the brain mechanisms that underlie birdsong and demonstrated how the instinctive output of songs can be modified by the environment.

For Further Thought

1. Do humans exhibit innately organized defense reactions to pain?
2. Is it possible that humans underestimate animal intelligence and overestimate human intelligence? Can you think of examples that do not involve Lassie?
3. Is sleep an FAP according to Moltz's four criteria?
4. Birdsong is an adaptive courting behavior. Are there human parallels?

SOCIOBIOLOGY AND EVOLUTIONARY PSYCHOLOGY

Recently, the two related disciplines of sociobiology and evolutionary psychology have played an increasingly important part in the study of how genes and the environment affect the social behavior of humans and other animals. In 1975 Edward O. Wilson proposed an evolutionary model for the analysis of social behavior in his book *Sociobiology: The New Synthesis.* Though his book described the social systems of insects, Wilson's model and concepts have since been extended to humans and other animals. Formally defined, **sociobiology** is the study of the genetic determinants of social behavior. **Evolutionary psychology** is the study of the human and animal mind and behavior from the perspective of evolutionary theory. Evolutionary psychologists propose that individuals think and behave in both conscious and unconscious ways, the overall effect of which is to enhance their fitness. You have encountered evolutionary thinking throughout this chapter, so many of the arguments sociobiologists and evolutionary psychologists make will be familiar to you.

Sociobiologists and evolutionary psychologists are interested in the most basic questions that can be asked about human motivation. They ask us to think about human behavior in terms of both proximal (psychological and environmental) and distal (genetic) causes. Indeed, in emphasizing reproduction and the "shared genes" of families, sociobiologists and evolutionary psychologists have joined philosophers and theologians in addressing broad questions of the *purpose* of life and the *meaning* of human behavior.

Unconscious Whisperings from Our Genes

A satirical expression attributed to Samuel Butler (1835–1902) captures the ideas underlying evolutionary psychology. Butler turned a common expression, that "an egg is a chicken's way of making another chicken," on its head, quipping that "a chicken is an egg's way of making another egg." For evolutionary psychologists, Butler's statement is a truism. In attempting to account for animal behavior, evolutionary psychologists have shifted their focus to the egg—an animal's genetic material—and away from the adult form. From their perspective, the phenotypic forms of animals—adult frogs, chickens, and humans—are merely elaborately evolved devices for the perpetuation of the species.

The evolutionary psychologist Richard Dawkins captured and expanded on this argument in his book *The Selfish Gene*. Dawkins (1976) saw genes as living

> '. . . safe inside gigantic lumbering robots, sealed off from the outside world, communicating with it by tortuous indirect routes, manipulating it by remote control. They are in you and me; they created us, body and mind; and their preservation is the ultimate rationale for our existence. . . . [We] are their survival machines.' (p. 21)

Dawkins's writing, and David Barash's (1979) book *The Whisperings Within*, developed the idea that human behavior is unconsciously influenced by the "motivation" and "plans" contained in our genetic material. These authors and others consider adult human social behaviors to be an elaborate adaptation whose sole function is to promote one's genetic self-interest. Much of human behavior, they argue, seems to be unconsciously impelled (Barkow, Cosmides, & Tooby, 1992). All around the world, children suckle, crawl, babble, eat, drink, walk, and talk in highly similar ways. At puberty, genes cause major changes in physiology that are coincident with a new interest in sexual behavior. In most cases, attraction, courtship, the birth of offspring, and years of child rearing follow—all of which evolutionary psychologists attribute to the influence of genes.

Is this idea far-fetched? Often we find ourselves asking *Why did I do that?* or explaining an action in terms of *Something came over me*. Barash would suggest that these inexplicable actions represent the "unconscious whisperings" of genes shaped over millions of years.

Besides the large questions of the purpose and meaning of life, sociobiologists and evolutionary psychologists also address more specific questions, such as why a cowbird's social behavior includes staking out a territory and attracting a mate through song. From the perspective of evolutionary psychology, birdsong is

sociobiology The study of the genetic determinants of social behvior.

evolutionary psychology The study of human and animal minds and behavior from the perspective of evolutionary theory.

the phenotypic expression of the species' genotype, a form of communication within the species that promotes fitness. Researchers who take this perspective also seek to answer some key questions regarding kin selection, altruism, and the sexual patterns of animals. The sociobiology perspective is not without its critics; indeed, some see it as too simplistic (see Ehrlich, 2000). Fortunately, criticizing a theoretical perspective by pointing out observations, experiments, and analyses that do not support the theory in question is what science is all about.

Kin Selection and Inclusive Fitness

We have seen that the genetic relation of individuals determines the makeup of their biological families (Table 3.1, p. 78). Now we will consider the *psychology* of families. Most humans think more of, and will do more for, family members than for distant relatives or unrelated individuals. Our language and other aspects of our behavior reflect our emotional attachment to individuals with whom we share common genetic material. For example, I tell my four daughters that I love them and would do anything for them. Though I am not especially brave, I can imagine instinctively putting myself in harm's way for their benefit. I could not sleep at night knowing that any of them was gravely ill, hungry, or homeless. Yet I do sleep well knowing that around the world, many thousands of children unrelated to me suffer and die each day.

Most humans treat their kin differently from nonkin.

Most humans share these attitudes and behaviors regarding families and strangers. We may not be comfortable with the explicit expression of preference for kin and relative indifference to the mass of humanity, but these very real feelings underlie the theory of **kin selection** proposed by evolutionary psychologists. According to this theory, I love my relatives because they share my genes; in promoting their welfare, I am furthering my own self-interest by enhancing my **inclusive fitness**—that is, my own fitness and that of my relatives (Hamilton, 1964). As Table 3.1 (p. 78) indicates, an individual's inclusive fitness can be roughly determined by adding the number of genes carried by his or her relatives.

One human behavior that can be considered from the perspective of both sociobiology and evolutionary psychology is child abuse. Statistics show that a stepchild is far more likely to be abused or even murdered by a stepparent than by his or her birth parents (Daly & Wilson, 1985). In this case, evolutionary psychologists and sociobiologists reason, the lack of common genes is the distal cause of the stepparent's misbehavior. In contrast, traditional psychologists and sociologists would be more likely to emphasize the proximal causes of such abusive behavior. An example of a proximal cause of stepchild abuse might be the increased emotional and financial hardship incurred by parents of "put-together families" (families that include biologically unrelated members).

Studies of nonhuman animals also suggest the influence of distal causes. In some mammalian species, including primates, infanticide is relatively common. Langur monkeys and baboons, for example, may capture isolated females in clashes with neighboring troops. If the female has a small infant, the captors typically kill it. When the captive mother stops lactating and begins to ovulate, she is quickly impregnated by a male from the conquering troop. Sociobiologists see this behavior as part of a larger pattern of male-to-male competition for reproductive success.

Can these findings be generalized to abusive human stepparents? Only with great caution! Sociobiologists emphasize that human females are always more certain than males about the genetic makeup of a given child. According to their logic, females are certain that the fetus they are carrying is theirs, whereas males can only guess whether the fetus is theirs. A male's reluctance to accept a woman's child, and his subsequent willingness to abuse that child, may reflect an instinctive insecurity regarding his paternity.

kin selection The theory that one promotes the well-being and inclusive fitness of a genetic relative because of shared genes.

inclusive fitness The fitness of an individual and related individuals (who carry many of the same genes).

Sociobiologists extend this logic to the overwhelming differences in violent behavior between males and females. Cross-culturally, males kill males at a rate 30 times higher than females kill females, and the reason reported most often is "sexual jealousy" (Daly & Wilson, 1992). From a Darwinian perspective, the survivors of these male-male jousts can continue to produce offspring. One outcome of their triumph is the selection of stronger, more violent males who will likely continue their fathers' aggressive behaviors in the next generation.

Altruism and Social Cooperation

Surely not all human behavior is selfish and gene perpetuating, you may be thinking. What about examples of **altruism**—heroic behavior that helps others, often at the expense of the individual's survival or reproductive potential? After all, most stepparents *do not* abuse or kill their stepchildren; and on occasion, most people will incur some cost to promote the well-being of nonrelatives. Sociobiologists and evolutionary psychologists would reply that self-gain may underlie what most of us perceive as altruistic behavior. Let's look at some examples.

Many mammals and birds live in groups. Because they cooperate, these social animals live better than those who live in isolation. For example, wolves hunt in packs. Their predatory tactics demand a level of cooperation that ensures that each individual gets something to eat. It is in each wolf's self-interest, therefore, to cooperate with the others. The wolf's fitness is enhanced by a brain that learns rapidly from other wolves. Thus the wolf's cooperative behavior is both adaptive and helpful to others.

But what if an individual wolf is killed while hunting? If other group members benefit from its efforts, should its "sacrifice" be interpreted as an example of altruism? The answer is no, because other wolves in the pack are likely to share its genes. Although the wolf's death decreases its personal fitness, it does not necessarily decrease its *inclusive* fitness. Contributing to the survival of its offspring and relatives promotes the dead wolf's self-interest by fostering its inclusive fitness.

But what about the soldier who throws himself on a hand grenade to prevent his buddies from dying, you might argue. Assuming that his buddies are not relatives, he is sacrificing himself without enhancing his inclusive fitness. But consider that for millions of years, our nonhuman ancestors lived in small groups of perhaps 25 to 30 related individuals, in which sacrificing oneself for relatives and extended family was adaptive (again, because it increased inclusive fitness). Evolutionary psychologists suspect that today, the human genotype continues to promote the "adaptive" behavior of self-sacrifice, even though it may not always contribute to an individual's inclusive fitness.

Sociobiology and social cooperation, Chapter 15, p. 524

Sexual Patterns

We turn now to the supreme example of cooperation in primates, courting and mating. Relationships between the sexes can be classified a number of ways. For simplicity, we will consider here four mating patterns (Rees & Harvey, 1991): (1) **monogamy**—one female, one male; (2) **polyandry**—one female, more than one male; (3) **polygyny**—one male, more than one female; and (4) **polygandry** (or promiscuity)—more than one male, more than one female. The question is, in what frequency do these different patterns occur? Figure 3.13 indicates that species' sexual behavior patterns do vary; birds, for example, are more monogamous than mammals, which tend to be polygynous and polygandrous.

altruism A behavior that helps another individual but may diminish one's survival or reproductive potential.

monogamy A mating pattern involving one female and one male.

polyandry A mating pattern involving one female and more than one male.

polygyny A mating pattern comprised of one male and more than one female.

polygandry (or promiscuity) A mating pattern comprised of more than one male and more than one female.

Sex Roles in Reproduction and Parenting. Are human males, as movies and magazines suggest, more promiscuous than human females? The sociobio-

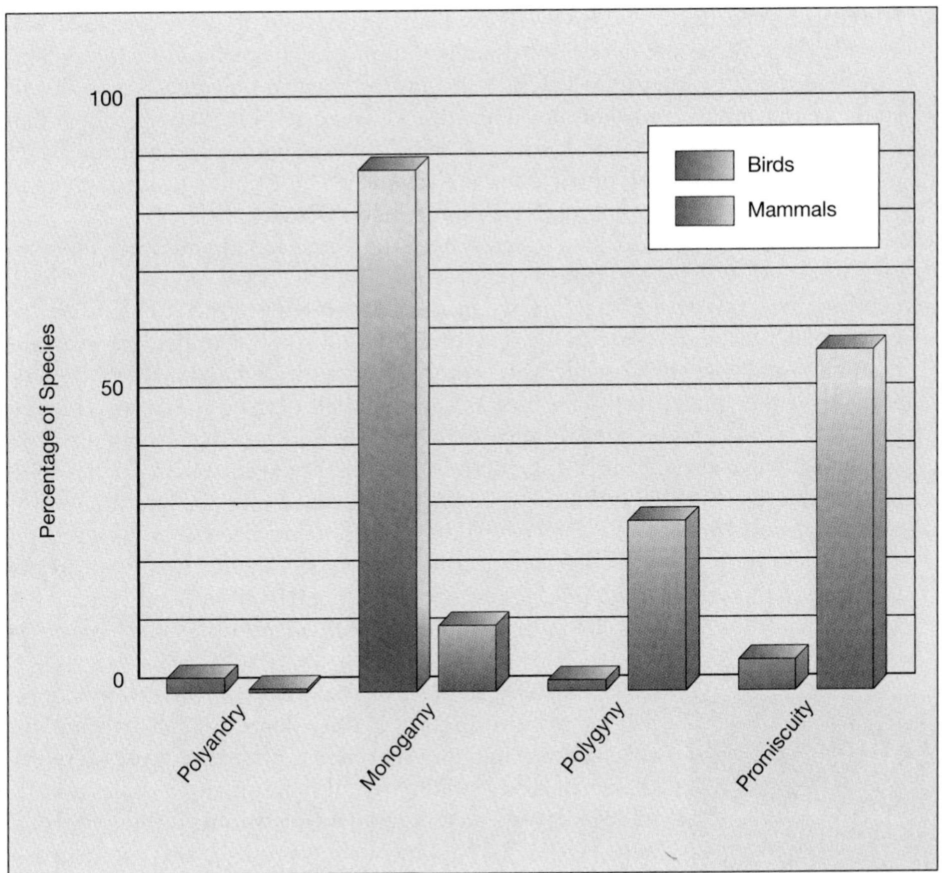

Figure 3.13 Mating patterns in mammals and birds. *Source:* From Barash, 1982, p. 277.

logical theory that addresses this issue was proposed by Robert Trivers in a 1972 research article called "Parental Investment and Sexual Selection." Trivers observed that in humans, males and females have different stakes in reproduction. Specifically, females invest more time and energy than males in carrying their offspring during gestation and caring for them after birth. Because males invest less energy in the care of their offspring, Trivers reasons, they have more free time to spend with other females. Therefore, males can have more offspring than females over the course of a lifetime.

This difference in *parental investment,* which Trivers defined as behavior that increases the chances of an offspring's survival at the cost of the parent's ability to invest in future offspring, can be seen in a comparison of the reproductive potential of human females and males. Over a lifetime, human females invest in a limited number of fertilized eggs, which they nourish for 9 months by sharing their blood supply. They then risk their lives in childbirth, expend more energy to produce milk for the newborns, and continue to care for their young for several years after birth. In contrast, males produce millions of tiny sperm that are quickly and easily replaced. They can and do walk away from the eggs they fertilize. (Males of many species abandon their offspring far more frequently than females.) One consequence of this difference in investment in parenting, according to Trivers, is that females are more discriminating in selecting their mates than males, and tend to seek individuals who will share their parental responsibilities with them.

Parental investment and attachment, Chapter 11, p. 404

Mating Systems. We can see how the male and female reproductive strategies play out in the sex lives of birds called dunnocks (*Prunella modularis*). This species is an exception to the general rule that birds are monogamous. In a 4-year study at the botanic garden at Cambridge University, N.B. Davies found that these small English birds had formed 62 monogamous pairs. He also counted 81 polyandrous females, 21 polygynous males, and 65 polygandrous groupings of two or more birds of both sexes who shared mates (Davies, 1989).

As is the case in most bird species, both male and female dunnocks help to feed the young. Monogamous pairs share in this task equally. (Indeed, monogamy tends to be the rule when the parental investment is similar for both sexes.) When two males were involved with a single female, however, the dominant male spent considerable amounts of time "guarding" the female from the other male, following her as she gathered nesting material, presumably to keep her from mating with the other male. That the dominant male was not always successful in this mission became apparent when Davies used DNA fingerprinting techniques to reveal who was doing the mating. In 11 broods of polyandrous trios, 15 of the 33 offspring had been sired by subordinate males. From the female's perspective, having *two* males help to feed her young was to her reproductive advantage. In comparison with other females, the polyandrous females' broods were larger both in numbers and in size of the offspring.

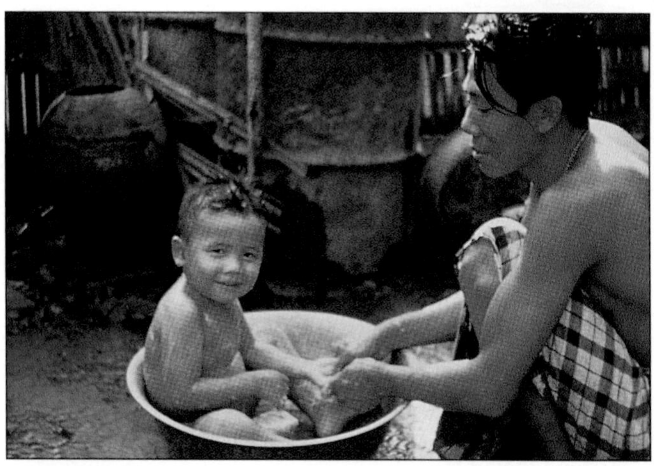

Males are less likely than females to care for young.

Compared to most bird species, human patterns of reproduction are quite variable, depending in part on the roles women and men assume in different cultures. Trivers' theory of differential parental investment by males and females suggests that human males should be polygynous, and Figure 3.14, which shows the results of a cross-cultural sampling of mating systems, supports that hypothesis. In this study polygyny was the most frequent pattern reported.

Human patterns of *sexuality* should be distinguished from human *reproductive strategies*. Indeed, many questions are raised by varieties of sexual behavior that do *not* lead to reproduction. The point is that cross-culturally (and individual differences notwithstanding), human females and males differ in their sexual behavior and child-rearing patterns.

The Status of Evolutionary Psychology and Sociobiology

The perspectives of sociobiology and evolutionary psychology continue to shape the field of psychology, though sociobiologists have been criticized for being too ambitious in their attempt to explain the human condition. Their descriptions of the sexual differences between men and women have even been seen as apologies for aggressive violent behavior, sexual promiscuity, and unequal investment in parenting. Unfortunately, sociobiological thinking has tended to fuel the political wars between the sexes.

Most evolutionary psychologists recognize that in investigating male-female differences or any other aspect of the human mind and behavior, there are no easy answers. In emphasizing the species-specific characteristics of human maleness and human femaleness, however, they tend to underestimate behavioral plasticity of women and men. Although genes might compel behavior, the particular environments in which male and female genes are expressed produce many *individual differences* in behavior. Traditional social psychologists emphasize these

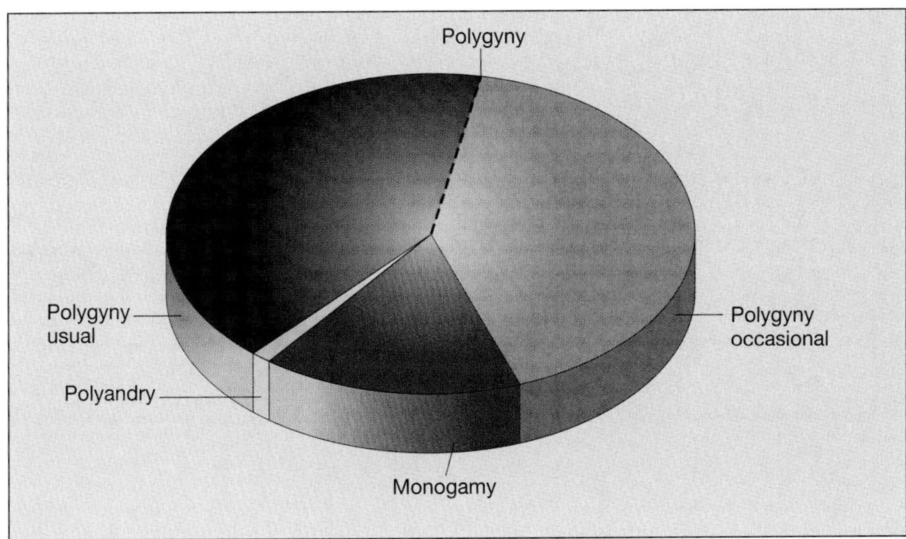

Figure 3.14 Human mating systems. This graph shows the frequency of different mating systems in 849 different humans sampled cross-culturally. Note the small percentage of polyandrous females and the high percentage of polygynous males. *Source:* Modified from Daly & Wilson, 1978.

individual differences, which can be attributed to specific learning experiences in *unique* environments.

In sum, sociobiologists and evolutionary psychologists emphasize broad patterns of male and female behaviors that exist cross-culturally (that is, *despite* unique environments). Isn't this yet another form of the continuing nature-nurture debate? As with any other scientific theory, evolutionary thinking regarding male-female differences will continue to thrive or will die depending on its usefulness in accounting for scientific observations, not on its political implications. Over time, particular theories of human behavior will be naturally selected for their usefulness or will become extinct.

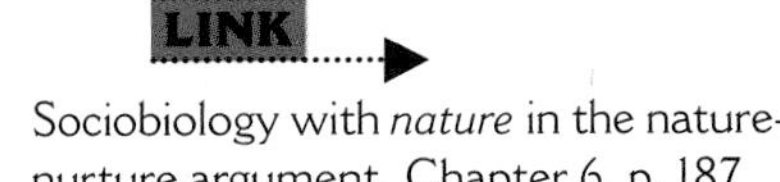

Sociobiology with *nature* in the nature-nurture argument, Chapter 6, p. 187

INTERIM SUMMARY

1. *Biological psychology* is the interdisciplinary study of the genes, brains, and behavior of human and nonhuman animals. Behavioral geneticists, ethologists, comparative psychologists, sociobiologists, and evolutionary psychologists all work from an evolutionary perspective.
2. ***Sociobiology*** is the application of evolutionary thinking to an understanding of the social behavior of animals.
3. ***Evolutionary psychology*** is the study of human and animal minds and behavior from the perspective of evolutionary theory.
4. From an evolutionary psychology perspective, animals behave in ways that maximize their **inclusive fitness,** which is measured by the number of genes they pass on to the next generation, including genes shared with close relatives.
5. Both sociobiologists and evolutionary psychologists attempt to uncover the "motives of DNA" in studies of ***kin selection, altruism,*** and cooperation in groups. Apparent altruism, they suspect, in motivated by the desire to promote genes similar to one's own.
6. Sociobiologists believe that males and females have different sexual agendas. To maximize the perpetuation of their genes, males and females favor different mating schemes: ***monogamy, polyandry, polygyny,*** and ***polygandry***
7. Sociobiologists and evolutionary psychologists describe human behavior (and human nature) in terms of inherited patterns of behavior. Traditional psychologists are interested both in understanding human nature and in accounting for individual differences in human behavior.

For Further Thought

1. Evolutionary psychologists recognize the tension created in humans when ancient genetic programs confront the powerful effects of culture and environment. Not all people cry when they are injured, and some people choose to remain celibate throughout their lives. Why?
2. Two children have been injured while swimming in a lake. Just before diving in to save them, you notice that one is your niece. Which one are you likely to try to rescue first? Why?

3. Do the sexual patterns of the people you know resemble the mating schemes of birds? Which ones?

CONCLUDING THOUGHTS

Chapter 2 described various methods scientists have developed to answer *how* questions. The *why* questions, and the search for human identity, has been our concern here. We have seen that the earth formed 4.5 billion years ago; a billion years later, the first life appeared on its surface. According to Darwin and other theorists, natural selection, including the results of cataclysmic events such as asteroids impacting the earth, has determined which species survived and which died. Humans evolved only recently, between 100,000 and 200,000 years ago. Only during the past several hundred years have humans begun to understand both our origins *and* our nature from a scientific perspective.

That all species are related has been demonstrated by an examination of their DNA. Genetics, then, has provided a means of testing Darwin's assertions and of corroborating the relationships that exist among species. Genes are the recipes for making different species of plants and animals. Each species has a unique genotype, which is more or less similar to others. The human genotype is more closely related to those of other primates than to the rest of the mammals; and mammals share more genetic sequences among themselves than they do with fish, amphibians, reptiles, and birds.

Among humans, families can be defined in terms of their genetic relationships. Identical twins are alike both physically and psychologically because they share 100 percent of their DNA—that is, they have identical genotypes. Siblings, parents, and their offspring share 50 percent of their DNA.

Because they share common genes, humans and other animals share many instincts. Ethologists and neuroethologists have shown that animal brains are organized to be innately sensitive to certain features of the environment: Birds react to sign stimuli that trigger fixed action patterns, and a songbird sings a particular dialect it hears during a critical period. Likewise, behavioral geneticists have demonstrated that some genotypes behave differently from others, depending in part on the environment in which a behavior is expressed. If an animal encounters a highly abnormal environment—a mother made of wire rather than flesh and blood, for example—genetically coded behaviors cannot be expressed and maladaptive behavior may result. Finally, evolutionary psychologists and sociobiologists have studied both kin selection and the sexual behavior patterns of males and females of different species and have proposed that individuals behave in ways that maximize their fitness. Taken together, the evidence is overwhelming that humans as well as other animals behave instinctively.

Yet we are not mindless robots; we are creative beings. We are a species that builds bridges across rivers and sends spacecrafts throughout the solar system. Human genes have produced human *brains* that interact with the environment to produce a distinctively human behavior. In the next chapter we will take a closer look at the human brain, another one of the biological bases of behavior.

KEY TERMS

adaptation *71*
allele *77*
altruism *98*
anthropomorphism *92*
appetitive behaviors *89*
artificial selection *72*
behavioral genetics *86*
chromosome *77*
comparative psychology *92*
consummatory behaviors *89*
continuity of species *71*
critical period *89*
deoxyribonucleic acid (DNA) *77*
dichotomous traits *75*
distal causes *70*
dominant allele *77*
ecological niche *73*
evolution *71*
evolutionary psychology *96*
extragenetic history *85*
fitness *72*
fixed action pattern (FAP) *90*
gene *73*
genetics *75*
genotype *77*
heredity *75*
heritability *88*
heterozygous *77*
homozygous *77*
imprinting *89*
inclusive fitness *97*
innate releasing mechanism *90*
instinct *70*
kin selection *97*
Lamarckian evolution *73*
meiosis *82*
modern synthesis *72*
monogamy *98*
Morgan's canon *92*
mutation *82*
natural selection *72*
neuroethology *94*
ontogenetic history *85*
pair bonding *93*
phenotype *77*
phylogenetic history *85*
polyandry *98*
polygandry *98*
polygenic character *87*
polygyny *98*
proximal causes *70*
recessive allele *77*
recombination *82*
selective pressure *72*
sign stimulus *90*
sociobiology *96*
species *70*
species-specific behavior *85*
species-specific defense reaction *91*
zoomorphism *92*

4

Brain and Behavior

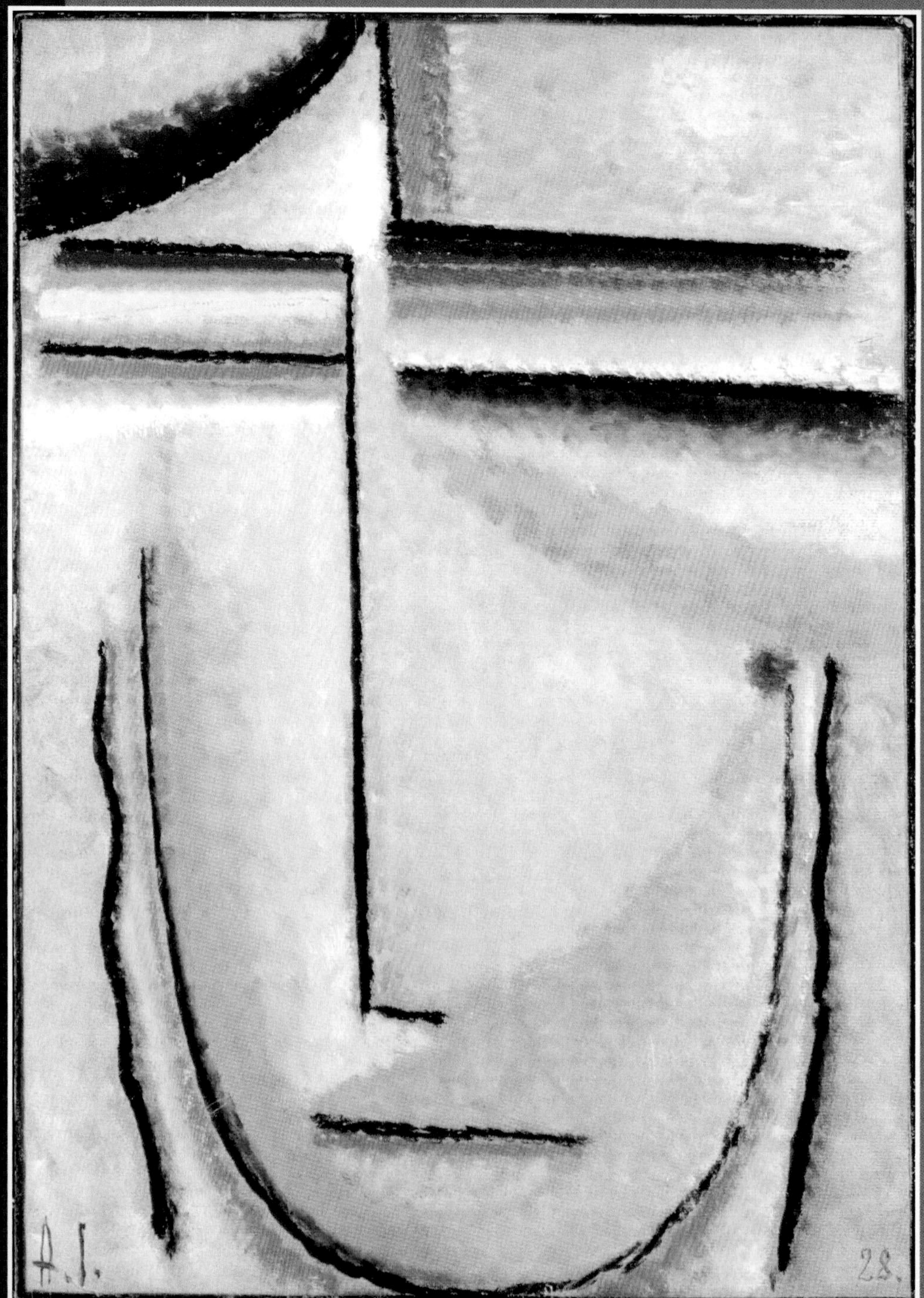

Origins of the Human Brain
Brain Size in Humans and Other Animals
Brain Organization in Humans and Other Animals
The Vertebrate Plan
Interim Summary
For Further Thought

Overview of the Human Nervous System
The Peripheral Nervous System
The Neuroendocrine System
Neurons
The Spinal Cord and the Sensory-Motor Reflex
Interim Summary
For Further Thought

The Relationship of Brain and Behavior
Pathways Through the Spinal Cord to the Brain
The Reticular Formation and the Hindbrain
The Thalamus and Somatosensory Cortex
The Cerebral Cortex: Sources of Human Uniqueness
Brain Damage: A Clue to Brain-Behavior Relationships
The Mysterious Cerebellum
Interim Summary
For Further Thought

Left Brain, Right Brain: The Function of the Two Cerebral Hemispheres
Psychological Tests for the Lateralization of Function
The Split-Brain Procedure
Tests of Split-Brain Patients
Interim Summary
For Further Thought

Neurons, Neurotransmitters, and Drugs: The Molecular Basis of Mind and Brain
The Neuron's Membrane: The Key to Excitability
How to Excite a Neuron
The Action Potential
Neurotransmitters and Their Effects
The Effect of Drugs on Neurotransmitters
Interim Summary
For Further Thought

Concluding Thoughts

In this chapter we begin the study of humans as the ultimate adaptive animal. Only humans encounter environments that include streets and submarines, fishing nets and internets, sonnets and IRS forms. Humans adapt to these inventions more or less successfully because they have evolved large brains—brains that in this instance created these very environments. Indeed, the brain may be *Homo sapiens'* most adaptive organ, in both a biological and a psychological sense.

Often the adaptiveness of the human brain is easier to see by examining the consequences of damage to the organ. Consider, for example, Phineas Gage, a 25-year-old man who was working on a railroad construction project in Vermont when he suffered a terrible accident. Gage's job was to use a 3-foot iron "tamping" rod to press gunpowder into a hole that had been drilled into a rock. Although he was described as a "most efficient and capable foreman," one day he inadvertently struck the iron rod against a rock, igniting the gunpowder. The explosion blew the bar through Gage's skull, from below the eye, where it entered, through the top of his head. Incredibly, he survived.

Before the accident Gage had "possessed a well-balanced mind [and was] a shrewd, smart businessman, very *persistent in executing all his plans of operation* [italics added]. But for 12 years after the accident, Gage lived an unemployed and directionless life. He was

> fitful, irreverent, indulging at times in the grossest profanity (which was not previously his custom). [He was] impatient of restraint or advice when it conflicts with his desires, at times . . . obstinate, yet capricious and vacillating, devising many

> plans of future operation, which are no sooner arranged than they are abandoned in turn for others appearing more feasible. To his friends and acquaintances, he was no longer Gage. (Damasio, 1994, p. 8)

Phineas Gage had suffered a massive loss of brain cells in the front part of his brain, called the frontal lobes. Without this tissue, Gage lacked one of the most adaptive functions of the human brain: He had no overall plan for living. We can infer, then, that intact frontal lobes confer on humans a continuity of personality that is both stable and predictable. Before the accident, Gage's intact brain had allowed him to make plans and set goals by which he organized his day-to-day activities; he was patient with others when he had to be, and polite when necessary. In thinking through the consequences of his actions, Gage exhibited the civilized behavior expected of an adult human. Such behavior helps not only to solve personal problems, but also to facilitate social interactions, increasing the potential of attracting a mate. In this sense, a brain that behaves normally is adaptive because it leads to reproduction and the transmission of genes to the next generation.

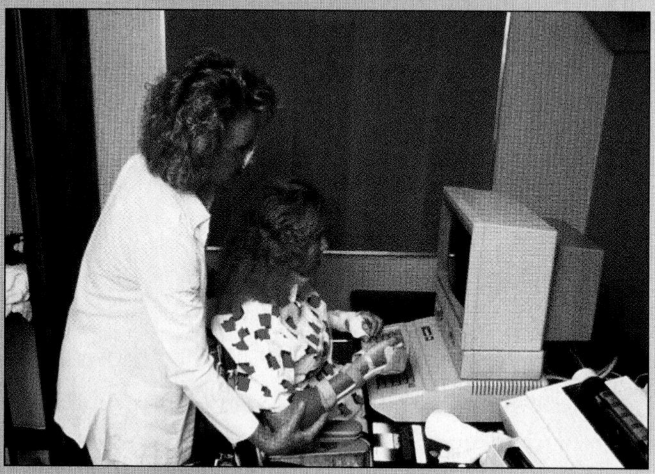

Cognitive rehabilitation following brain injury is painstakingly slow.

Scientists now know that the frontal lobes help humans to lead this kind of life by *inhibiting* behaviors that would interfere with civilized behavior. But if the frontal lobes are damaged, their inhibitory control over other parts of the brain is interrupted. Thus Gage's ability to set goals and execute plans was replaced by impulsivity; his politeness, by profanity. The cells that would normally have inhibited such primitive, brainstem-mediated behavior no longer existed. Needless to say, potential mates are repelled by such maladaptive behavior.

The premise of evolutionary psychology is that animals that behave adaptively are more likely to pass their genes on to the next generation. Adaptive behavior is accomplished through the action of adapted brains. Adapted brains promote survival and reproduction by providing each species with their unique behavioral characteristics. For example, Daniel Dennett's (1995) book *Darwin's Dangerous Idea* and Steven Pinker's (1994) *The Language Instinct* both make a compelling case that language is an adaptive characteristic that differentiates humans from other animals. The unique brain organization encoded in our genes provides the neurological basis for this characteristic, as well as for thinking and planning.

True, the brain is no more or less important for survival than a heart or lungs. Over millions of years, land-breathing vertebrates evolved arms, legs, endocrine systems, courting behavior, and patterns of sexual reproduction, all of which served to perpetuate the species. The brain, though, is more involved in generating our psychological life than is the heart. The *brain*, not the heart or spleen, is the source of human emotion and motivation. The physical brain is both the instigator of our behaviors and the repository of our memories. To better understand human nature, then, we must look inside this complicated organ.

We will begin this chapter by noting how the human brain both resembles and differs from the brains of other animals. An overview of the human nervous system will follow. We will study specific parts of the brain and their functions: How does the brain allow us to sense? to move? to speak? to remember? Next, we will touch on the functions of the two hemispheres of the brain, left and right. The chapter will conclude with a discussion of how various chemicals, including neurotransmitters, drugs, and hormones, affect the mind and behavior.

ORIGINS OF THE HUMAN BRAIN

Without question, the human brain, like every other organ, evolved in response to selective pressures presented by the earth's environment. Not surprisingly, our brains match the environmental niche we inhabit. As earth dwellers, for example, we have evolved sense organs and brains that are exquisitely sensitive to the sun's radiation. Of course, ours is not the only sun in the universe. A favorite theme of science fiction writers and moviemakers is to speculate about what types of beings (with vastly different receptors and brains) would have evolved under different suns.

Humans and other animals are adapted to the environment in similar ways. We sense the world around us using evolved receptors, and move adaptively when the brain activates muscles in our arms and legs. An evolutionary understanding of human brain functioning must begin with an examination of some of the common characteristics between humans and other animals.

Brain Size in Humans and Other Animals

Animals' brains vary in size, and to a lesser extent in their organization. With few exceptions, larger animals have larger brains. Though humans have relatively large brains (about 1,350 gm, or 3 lb), whales' and elephants' brains are four to six times larger and their bodies are larger, too. One way to compare the size of animals' brains is to plot their brain mass, in grams, against their body size (their mass in kilograms). Figure 4.1 shows that brain size is highly correlated with body size. Small animals like hummingbirds have small brains; larger animals have proportionately larger brains.

Note that while most of the animals whose measurements are shown in the figure appear close to the diagonal line, the apes are clustered well above it, with *Homo sapiens* (humans) the farthest from the line. Humans, then, have a relatively larger *brain-body ratio* than most other animals. Not surprisingly, the human brain is similar in size to the brains of genetically similar animals. The two extinct apes (*Homo habilis* and *Australopithecus aferensis*, or "Lucy") and one living ape (the chimpanzee) who are closest to humans in Figure 4.1 are also closest to humans genetically (see Chapter 3). Both "Lucy," who lived about 3.5 million years ago, and recently living chimpanzees had brains weighing about 400 to 450 gm—approximately one-third the size of an adult human brain. And the brain of our 1.5-million-year-old tool-making ancestor *Homo habilis* is estimated to have weighed about 800 gm. In contrast, the giant *Tyrannosaurus rex* lies well below the diagonal line, with a small brain relative to its large size.

Evolution and human ancestry, Chapter 3, p. 79

Do you suppose there might be a functional significance to the differences in brain-body ratios displayed in Figure 4.1? For example, might animals with relatively larger brains be more conscious of themselves and of the world than those with relatively smaller brains? We will return later to this fundamental question in psychology.

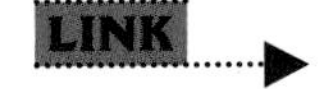

Human and animal consciousness, Chapter 9, p. 307

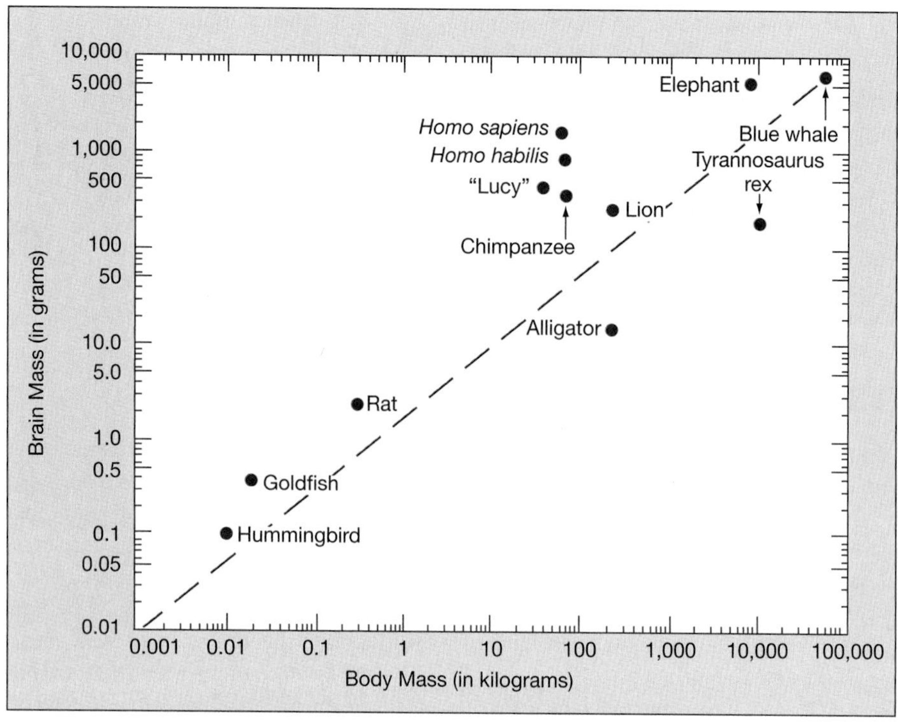

Figure 4.1 Who has the larger brain? The relationship of an animal's brain size (its mass in grams) to its body size (its mass in kilograms) can be plotted on a graph. Of the animals represented here, most lie on or near the diagonal line, indicating a close correlation between brain size and body size. The animals that fall above the diagonal line have proportionately larger brains; those that fall below the line have proportionately smaller brains. Note that while an elephant's brain weighs more than a human's brain, humans have proportionally larger brains. (*Source:* Modified from Sagan, 1977, p. 39, based on work by Jerison, 1973).

Brain Organization in Humans and Other Animals

Another way to understand the human brain is to compare its *organization* with that of other animals' brains. Figure 4.2 shows the brains of five common animals: a human, a chimpanzee, a cat, a rat, and a fish. In mammals the *cerebrum* (colored gold in the figure) covers the **forebrain** and overlays the **hindbrain** (the back part of the brain, including the cerebellum, colored red). The bass's brain is proportionately more hindbrain than forebrain; its forebrain is comprised primarily of a structure called the **thalamus**, a major sensory center. Note that the human's cerebrum is considerably larger than the others and covers all the **midbrain**, most of the hindbrain, and the thalamus as well.

Figure 4.2 illustrates two main points. The first is that these animals share common brain parts—namely, a forebrain, a midbrain, and a hindbrain. Second, mammals have relatively more of a recently evolved brain structure, the cerebrum, which overlays the more primitive (that is, phylogenetically older) midbrain and hindbrain. Of all the mammals, the primates have the most cerebrum, and among primates, humans have the largest cerebrum. This huge outer covering is divided into left and right sides, called the **cerebral hemispheres**.

Most of the cerebrum of mammals is made up of *neocortex* (neo means "new" and cortex means "bark"; thus, "new bark" surrounds the old brain). In the human brain, the neocortex is a thin layer of neurons, called the **cerebral cortex**, that covers the cerebral hemispheres. The evolutionary trend for primates—especially humans—to have relatively more cerebral cortex than other brain tissue is called **corticalization**. This feature of the human brain underlies, in Dennett's (1995) words, the "enormous elaboration of powers" that has characterized human evolution.

What is this so-called enormous elaboration of powers? What does the size and unique configuration of the human brain allow us to do? Table 4.1 lists some of the more important similarities and differences between human and nonhuman animal behavior. Beginning at the top, all vertebrates see, hear, smell,

forebrain The front part of the brain, including the cerebrum, thalamus, hypothalamus, and other structures.

midbrain The middle part of the brain, including part of the reticular formation.

hindbrain The back part of the brain, including the cerebellum and medulla.

thalamus A sensory-motor integrative center in the forebrain; in mammals, it connects the midbrain to the cerebrum.

cerebral hemispheres The two halves of the outer covering of the brain (the cerebrum).

cerebral cortex The thin layer of neocortex that covers the cerebral hemispheres.

corticalization An increase in the proportion of neocortex relative to other brain matter, a trend clearly seen in mammals.

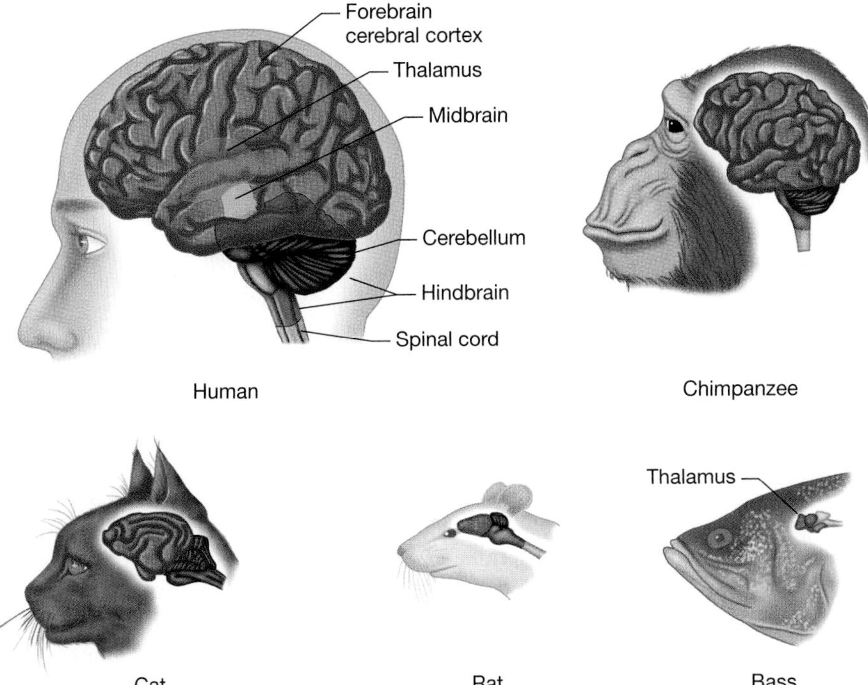

Figure 4.2 A Comparison of animal brains. Humans share with other animals a hindbrain, midbrain, and forebrain. In humans, chimpanzees, and to a lesser extent cats, a large cerebral cortex covers the brainstem. Rats, in comparison, have a tiny cerebrum, and much of their hindbrain is exposed like the cat's. A bass's forebrain consists primarily of a thalamus.

and otherwise sense their environments. All breathe, eat and drink, and survive the elements by living in caves, nests, mud-huts, or condominiums. To accomplish these consummatory behaviors, animals do *not* need to have a 1,350-gm brain (humans) or even a 450-gm brain (chimpanzees). The question, then, is what additional behaviors can humans engage in that a tiny-brained salamander,

Table 4.1 Similarities and Differences Between Human and Nonhuman Behavior

HUMANS	CHIMPANZEES, SALAMANDERS, AND OTHER NONHUMAN ANIMALS
Seeing, hearing, smelling, feeling pain	Seeing, hearing, smelling, feeling pain
Breathing, eating, drinking	Breathing, eating, drinking
Securing shelter (climate controlled)	Securing shelter (nests, caves)
Courting and mating (pheromones, Chanel No. 5®)	Courting and mating (pheromones)
Reproducing, caring for young	Reproducing, caring for young
Communicating	Communicating
Consciousness of self:	
Talking, storytelling	
Planting crops, domesticating animals	
Cooking, preserving	
Refining, distilling	
Making fashionable shoes and clothes	
Writing and performing music	
Singing, dancing	
Painting, sculpting	
Reading, writing	
Designing a curriculum, teaching	
Practicing law and medicine	
Researching in the sciences and humanities	
Selling, banking, stock brokering	
Governing	
Designing and using computers and machines	
Contemplating a Supreme Being	

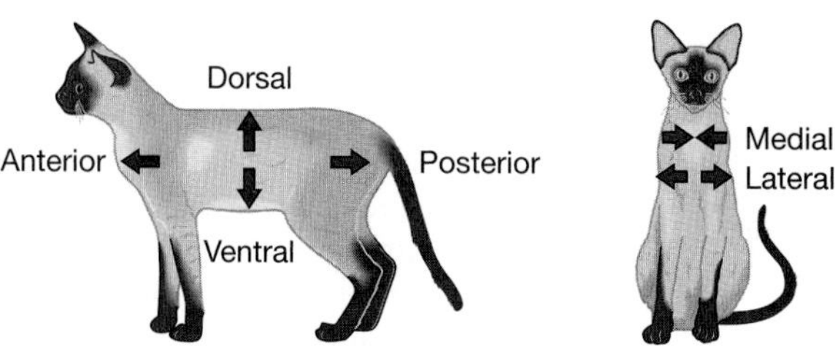

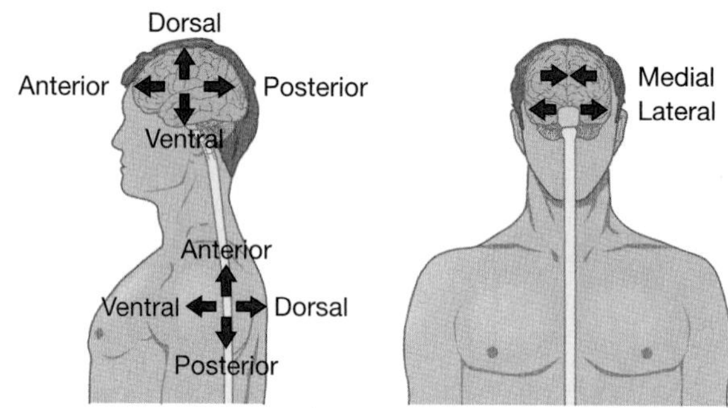

Figure 4.3 Descriptive terminology for the brain In four-legged animals (top), the brain and spinal cord lie in the same plane, so the same terms can be used for both. In upright primates (bottom), the brain and spinal cord lie in different planes, so the terminology differs. For example, *anterior* means *up* with regard to the spinal cord and *forward* with regard to the brain.

for example, could not. In fact, chimpanzees engage in limited communication and form complicated social networks with other chimpanzees. Salamanders don't. As the table shows, the tremendous size of the human neocortex is reflected in the unique ways in which humans can behave. Not only do they communicate with each other, they tell stories, solve algebra problems, and build bridges. The large human brain also supports a consciousness of self that appears to be lacking in most other animals.

The specific structures that underlie these differences will be described in a later section; here we will focus on an overview of the brain. To do that we need a vocabulary for describing the three-dimensional brain. Figure 4.3 shows that the brain sits on *top* in humans and chimpanzees, but is located at the *front* of four-legged animals. In addition to *top* and *bottom* and *front* and *back*, we can use the terms *anterior* (front of the brain), *posterior* (back of the brain), *medial* (middle), and *lateral* (side). These terms apply to humans and other vertebrates (see Figure 4.3). For both upright and four-legged animals, the belly side of the spinal cord is called *ventral*, and the back side of the spinal cord, *dorsal*. (Think of the dorsal fin of a shark.) In the sections to come, we will examine the brain from a variety of viewpoints, using this terminology to orient ourselves.

The Vertebrate Plan

Although the brains pictured in Figure 4.2 are different, they do appear to have basic structures in common. One of the first researchers to suggest that all vertebrate brains were "built" from a common plan was C. Judson Herrick. In 1948, Herrick published a book called *The Brain of the Tiger Salamander*, in which he pointed out the similarities among animal brains. Figures 4.4 and 4.5 show the important features of Herrick's so-called *vertebrate plan*. First, all fish, amphibians, reptiles, birds, and mammals have a brainstem. Located on the underside of the brain, the **brainstem** comprises all of the brain *except* the cerebral hemispheres, thalamus, **hypothalamus**, and the **cerebellum**. The brainstem includes the **medulla**, pons, and 12 pairs of **cranial nerves**. The **spinal cord** enters the lower part of the brainstem. Figure 4.4 shows where most of the cranial nerves enter the pons, medulla, and upper part of the spinal cord. Looking at the brain from underneath in Figure 4.4, neither the hypothalamus nor the thalamus is visible. Both are shown in Figure 4.5. The thalamus, like many other structures in the brain, has a left and a right side. In humans, both the thalamus and hypothalamus are covered by the cerebral hemispheres.

In all vertebrate brains, these brainstem structures are the mechanism for basic biological functioning. The brainstem helps vertebrates to maintain their balance when standing, moving, or swimming (the so-called *postural reflexes*) and regulates blood pressure, basal metabolic functioning, and breathing (*vital reflexes*). Damage to the medulla typically ends in a rapid death. The hypothalamus is also basic to other "biological" activities, such as eating, drinking, maintaining body temperature, and reproduction. It plays a prominent role in motivation and behavior, as we will see in the following chapter.

We humans are so enamored of our accomplishments—no doubt because of our huge cerebrum—that we tend to underestimate the importance of the brain-

brainstem The entire brain except for the forebrain structures.

spinal cord The part of the central nervous system that connects the brain with the lower body.

medulla The lower part of the brainstem, which connects with the spinal cord.

hypothalamus The part of the midbrain lying below the thalamus that controls biological functioning.

cerebellum The large, walnut-shaped structure located at the intersection of the hindbrain and spinal cord.

cranial nerves Twelve pairs of nerves in the CNS that serve both sensory and motor functions.

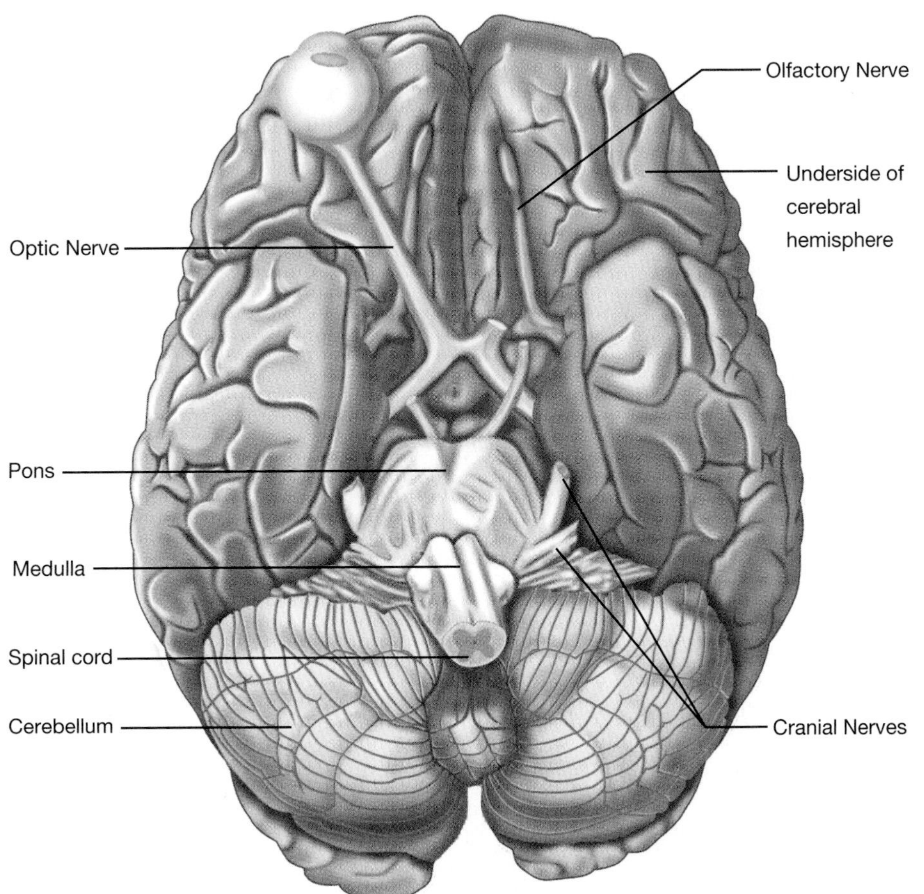

Figure 4.4 The human brainstem, viewed from below. The underside of the human brain shows the brainstem and other brain parts common to all vertebrates. (The spinal cord and cranial nerves are shown severed for the sake of simplicity.) Prominent features are the medulla, pons, and cranial nerves, as well as the cerebellum. Galen, a Roman physician who performed medical experiments about 1,800 years ago, identified the 12 pairs of cranial nerves.

stem. Herrick's analysis emphasizes how much of our behavior depends on these ancient brain structures, which are common to all vertebrates because of their shared DNA sequences.

Role of hypothalamus in motivated behavior, Chapter 5, p. 162

Figures 4.4 and 4.5 give two perspectives on the human brain, a rather typical vertebrate brain at its core, with a huge overlay of cortex on top. This brain structure has evolved from more simple brains over many millions of years. Approximately 7 million years ago humans and chimpanzees had a common ancestor. There is reason to believe that the human brain has changed more than the chimpanzee's during this period—indeed, that the living chimpanzee's brain may be representative of the brain of our human ancestors in both size and organization. Changes in both the human and the chimpanzee brain reflect the different selection pressures each species has faced over the past 7 million years.

Look again at Table 4.1. What behaviors and psychological properties are common to salamanders and humans? Do both species detect electromagnetic radiation (light) from the sun? Yes, both have functioning eyes that allow visual sensitivity as well as eye-movement and eye-blink reflexes. Do both species detect vibrations in the air (sounds)? Yes, both have an auditory apparatus. Both species also have brain mechanisms that enable them to breathe, eat, and respond to painful stimuli. But do salamanders see, hear, and experience pain in the same way as humans? Probably not. As we will see in Chapters 7 and 8, humans have developed additional brain structures that enable them to see, hear, and experience pain in a distinctively human fashion. These new structures can be thought of as "add-ons" to the basic vertebrate plan.

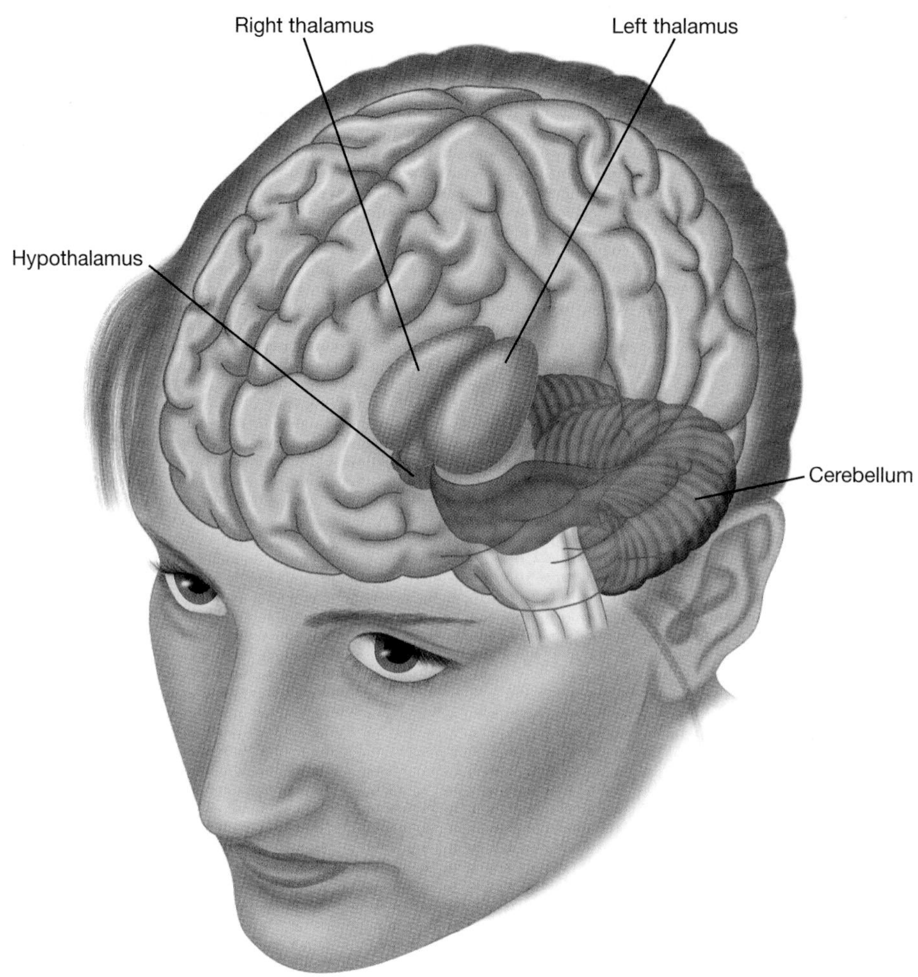

Figure 4.5 The human thalamus and brainstem. In this view of the brain, the cerebral hemispheres have been rendered transparent so that the thalamus, hypothalamus, and cerebellum can be seen. Without its cerebrum (outer covering), and excepting the enormous difference in size, the human brain resembles the bass brain shown in Figure 4.2. Both are "headed" by the thalamus, and both have a hypothalamus, cerebellum, and other midbrain and hindbrain structures (not labeled).

INTERIM SUMMARY

1. The size of an animal's brain is highly correlated with its body size.
2. The brains of prehistoric ancestors of humans ("Lucy" and *Homo habilis*) as well as those of living chimpanzees are relatively large; these primate brains most resemble those of modern humans (*Homo sapiens*).
3. Human brains and bodies are larger than chimpanzees' brains and bodies, and humans have a larger brain-size–body-size ratio than chimpanzees and other apes.
4. Adult human brains weigh on average 1,350 gm compared to the 400- to 450-gram brains of chimpanzees.
5. All vertebrates (mammals, birds, reptiles, amphibians, and fish) have a three-part brain that includes a ***forebrain,*** a ***midbrain,*** and a ***hindbrain.***
6. The left and right *cerebral hemispheres* of mammals are covered by a thin layer of neurons called *cerebral cortex.*
7. Terms used to describe the brain include *anterior* (front of brain), *posterior* (back of the brain), *medial* (toward the middle), *lateral* (toward the outside), *ventral* (belly side of the spinal cord), and *dorsal* (back side of the spinal cord).
8. All vertebrates have common brain structures (Herrick's "vertebrate plan") that reflect a common genetic heritage. These structures include the **brainstem** ***(medulla,*** **pons,** ***cranial nerves, hypothalamus, thalamus*****),** ***spinal cord,*** **and** ***cerebellum.***
9. Recently evolved mammals, such as primates, have experienced a rapid growth in the neocortex, especially the cerebral hemispheres, relative to other brain tissue, a process called *corticalization.*
10. The expansion of the neocortex is associated with uniquely human faculties, such as consciousness, language, and thought.

For Further Thought

1. On the average, human males have larger brains than human females. Why?
2. Which brain structures do you suspect are involved in individual differences in language usage and intelligence?
3. At 800 gm the brain of *Homo habilis* was intermediate in size between that of modern humans and chimpanzees. Compare the brain-body ratio of *Homo habilis* with that of modern chimpanzees. Which species do you think was smarter? Why?

OVERVIEW OF THE HUMAN NERVOUS SYSTEM

A nervous system can be thought of in a simplified way as serving three main functions: it receives information, processes it, and acts on it. The sensory systems (for seeing, feeling pain, and so forth) first detect events in the external environment and send it to the brain. After processing, neural signals from the brain to the muscles cause the arms, legs, and vocal cords to move. The nervous system accomplishes these three functions swiftly and seamlessly, so that we are seldom aware of its constant activity.

Figure 4.6 is a schematic drawing of an adult human nervous system. Together, the brain and the spinal cord make up the **central nervous system** (CNS). The brain contains upwards of 80 *billion* **neurons**, chemically sensitive brain cells that are responsible for nervous activity. The spinal cord contains approximately 1 billion. (The structure and function of neurons will be described in a later section.)

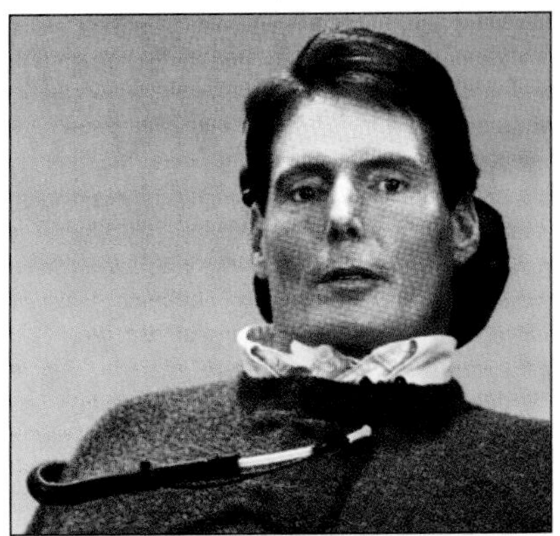

Christopher Reeve's damaged spinal cord disrupts sensory and motor information between brain and body.

The other major division of the nervous system is the **peripheral nervous system (PNS)**; (see Figure 4.6). Nerves in the PNS carry messages to and from internal organs, muscles, and glands in the periphery of the body. The spinal cord is the primary conduit that transmits information from receptors and nerves in the skin, joints, and muscles to the brain. In turn, nerves from the brain project down the spinal cord to control the muscles.

Have you ever hit your "funny bone" or had an arm or leg "go to sleep," or while riding a bicycle, hit a curb and struck your tailbone hard against the bicycle seat? If so, you have probably experienced numbness and/or excruciating pain. Because at one time or another most of us have temporarily lost either sensory or motor function in some part of the body, we can easily appreciate the normal functioning of the nerves in our spinal cords. Others are less fortunate. Too many people have experienced the permanent paralysis and loss of sensation that results from spinal cord damage as the result of an athletic injury or an automobile or riding accident. These people have tragic insight into the importance of the normal functioning of the billion or so neurons found in the spinal cord.

central nervous system (CNS) The part of the nervous system that includes the brain and spinal cord.

neurons Chemically sensitive cells in the nervous system that are responsible for nervous activity.

peripheral nervous system (PNS) The part of the nervous system that includes the somatic and autonomic nervous systems.

somatic nervous system The part of the peripheral nervous system that includes the sensory and motor nerves.

autonomic nervous system (ANS) The part of the peripheral nervous system that includes the parasympathetic division and the sympathetic division.

The Peripheral Nervous System

Figure 4.6 shows that the nerves from the brain and spinal cord extend into the periphery of the body, where they are called the *peripheral nervous system*. The PNS has two main divisions, the **somatic nervous system** and the **autonomic nervous system** (ANS).

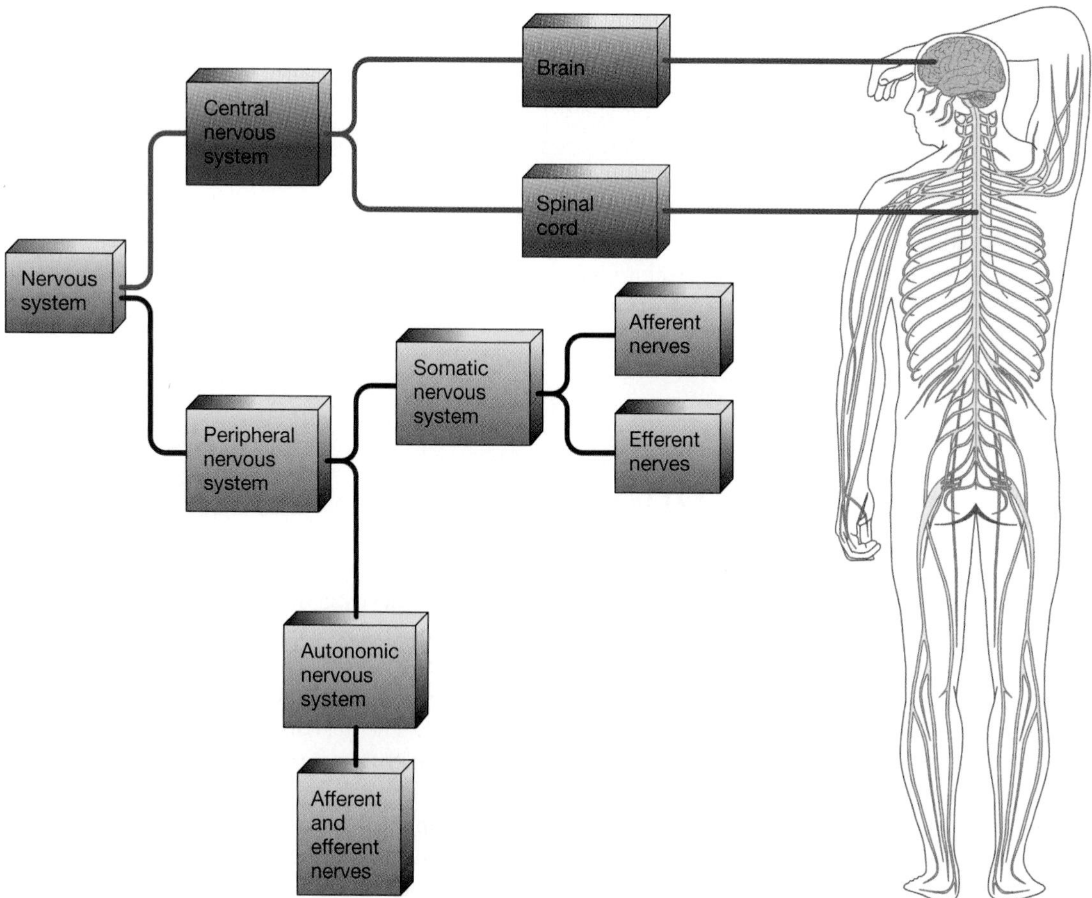

Figure 4.6 The human nervous system. The human nervous system is divided into two main branches, the *central nervous system* (CNS), shown in orange, and the *peripheral nervous system* (PNS), shown in blue here and in Figure 4.7. The peripheral nervous system is further divided into the somatic nervous system, which includes nerves that serve the periphery of the body and the autonomic nervous system (ANS), shown in detail in Figure 4.7.

The Somatic Nervous System. The word *somatic* comes from *soma,* the Greek word for "body." Somatic nerves going *to* and *from* the hands and feet of the body have two functions: they cause the muscles to move and they provide the senses of touch, temperature, and pain, respectively. Somatic nerves that run *from* the brain and spinal cord to the periphery of the body (for example, to activate the muscles) are called *efferent nerves.* Somatic nerves that bring sensory information from the periphery of the body *to* the spinal cord and brain (to communicate touch and pain, for example) are called *afferent nerves.* "Sensory afferents" and "motor efferents," then, refer to the direction of information flow, toward and away from the brain, respectively.

The Autonomic Nervous System. As Figure 4.7 shows, the autonomic nervous system (ANS) has both afferent and efferent nerves. But whereas the somatic nervous system helps the body to operate on the external environment (by sensing and acting on it), the autonomic nervous system operates on the body's "internal" environment, including the heart, lungs, stomach, and glands. Figure 4.7 shows that the autonomic nervous system has two main divisions, the *sympathetic* and *parasympathetic.* These two divisions function in a complementary

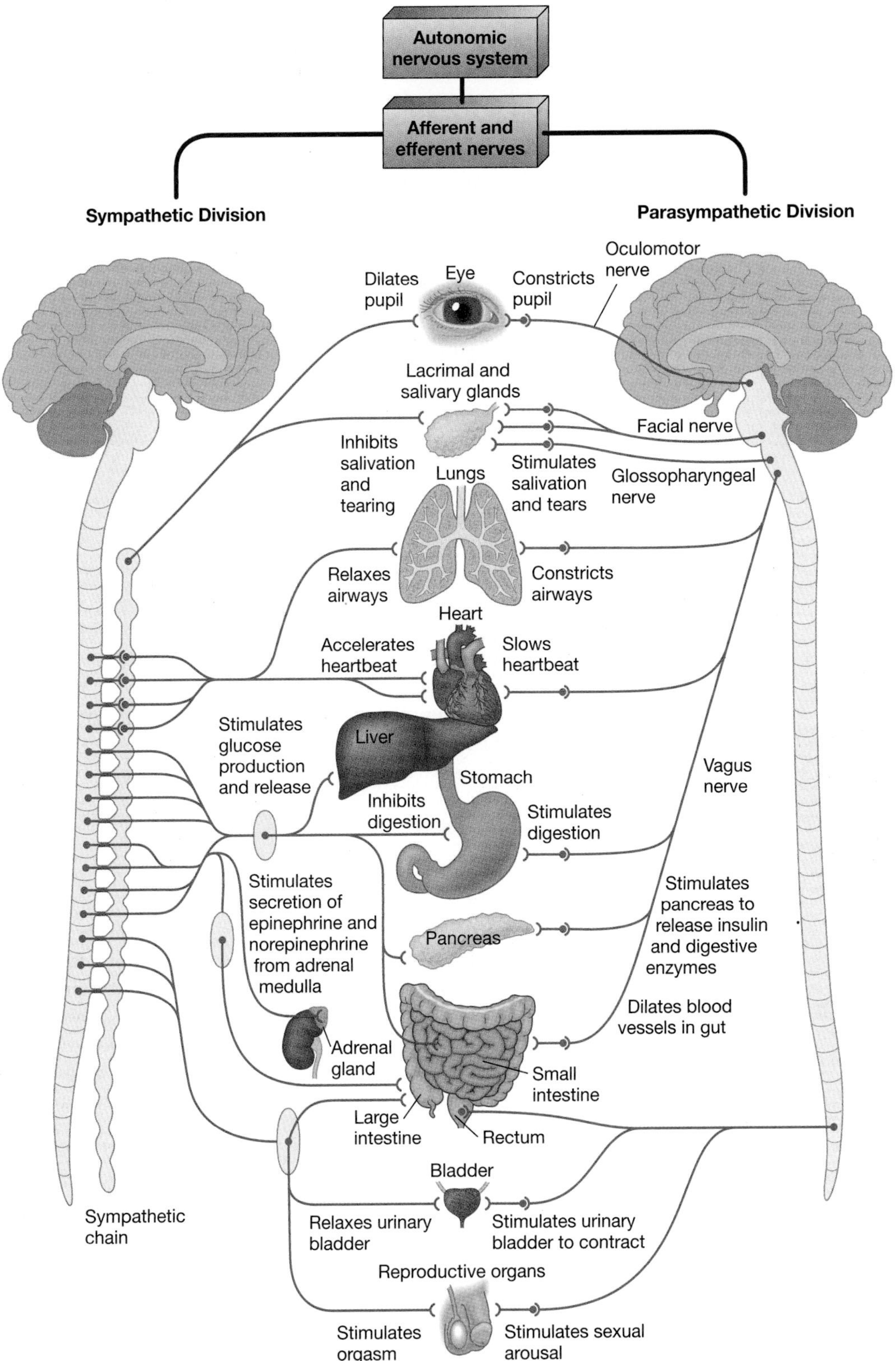

Figure 4.7 The autonomic nervous system. The two divisions of the autonomic nervous system (ANS), the sympathetic and parasympathetic, are shown here schematically. The sympathetic division arouses the body for movement, and the parasympathetic division maintains bodily functions at rest. Most of the time the two work in concert.

fashion. The **parasympathetic division** keeps the machinery of the body running smoothly when nothing much is happening; it controls breathing, heart rate, digestion, and other at-rest functions. The **sympathetic division,** in contrast, prepares the body for action. For the sake of simplicity, Figure 4.7 shows the sympathetic nerves on the left and the parasympathetic nerves on the right. In reality, however, both divisions serve both sides of the body.

These two divisions of the autonomic nervous system work together, as can be illustrated by taking them out for an evening's entertainment. Let's begin with a meal, followed by romantic dancing. Although both divisions function almost all the time, the parasympathetic division is the more active of the two during a relaxed meal. On the tongue, chemicals in foods stimulate a taste nerve to release the flow of saliva (see Figure 4.7). At peace with the world, the heart slows, diverting the flow of blood to the stomach. There, another nerve (the vagus) stimulates the digestive process and prompts the release of insulin and digestive enzymes. In sum, the parasympathetic division of the autonomic nervous system regulates the all-important vegetative functions of a resting body, contributing to a psychological state of relaxation.

Later in the evening, in response to excitement on the dance floor, the sympathetic nervous system becomes active. Also known as the "fight-or-flight" system, the sympathetic system diverts the blood away from the digestive process to the muscles. At the same time, it releases energy-producing glucose from the liver and the hormone epinephrine, also known as adrenaline, from the adrenal glands, activating the muscles. To increase the intake and utilization of oxygen, airways open wider. Sex? In both males and females the sexual response is under the control of both the sympathetic and parasympathetic systems. Sexual arousal is a parasympathetic function, whereas orgasm is controlled by the sympathetic division.

The Neuroendocrine System

LINK
Role of ANS in stress and health, Chapter 16, p. 560

Neuroendocrine system and motivation, Chapter 5, p. 151

Are eating, the action of internal organs, and sexual functioning all under the reflexive control of the peripheral nervous system, then? Nothing in human physiology and behavior could be that simple! In reality, the sympathetic and parasympathetic divisions of the ANS operate in concert with both the *neuroendocrine system* and the central nervous system. The **neuroendocrine system** is a network of neurons and glands that make and secrete hormones, chemicals that act on target tissues throughout the body. We will delay our discussion of the neuroendocrine system until the next chapter, where we will see that hormones can affect sexual desire, stress reactions, and hunger, among other behaviors.

parasympathetic division The part of the autonomic nervous system that is involved in the functioning of a body at rest.

sympathetic division The part of the autonomic nervous system that is involved in the functioning of the active body.

neuroendocrine system A network of neurons and glands that make and secrete hormones.

Neurons

The neuron is the basic functional unit of the nervous system. Besides billions of neurons, the brain and spinal cord contain an even greater number of supportive cells called *glia.* The glia support the neurons in a way similar to the way steel girders support the network of beams in a skyscraper. Glia cells are also thought to nourish healthy neurons and clear damaged neurons from the brain.

The Structure and Function of Neurons. Recall that the overall function of the nervous system is to receive information from the environment, process it, and act on it. The function of a neuron is similar. Each neuron has an input end and an output end, as well as a middle part that mediates activity between the two.

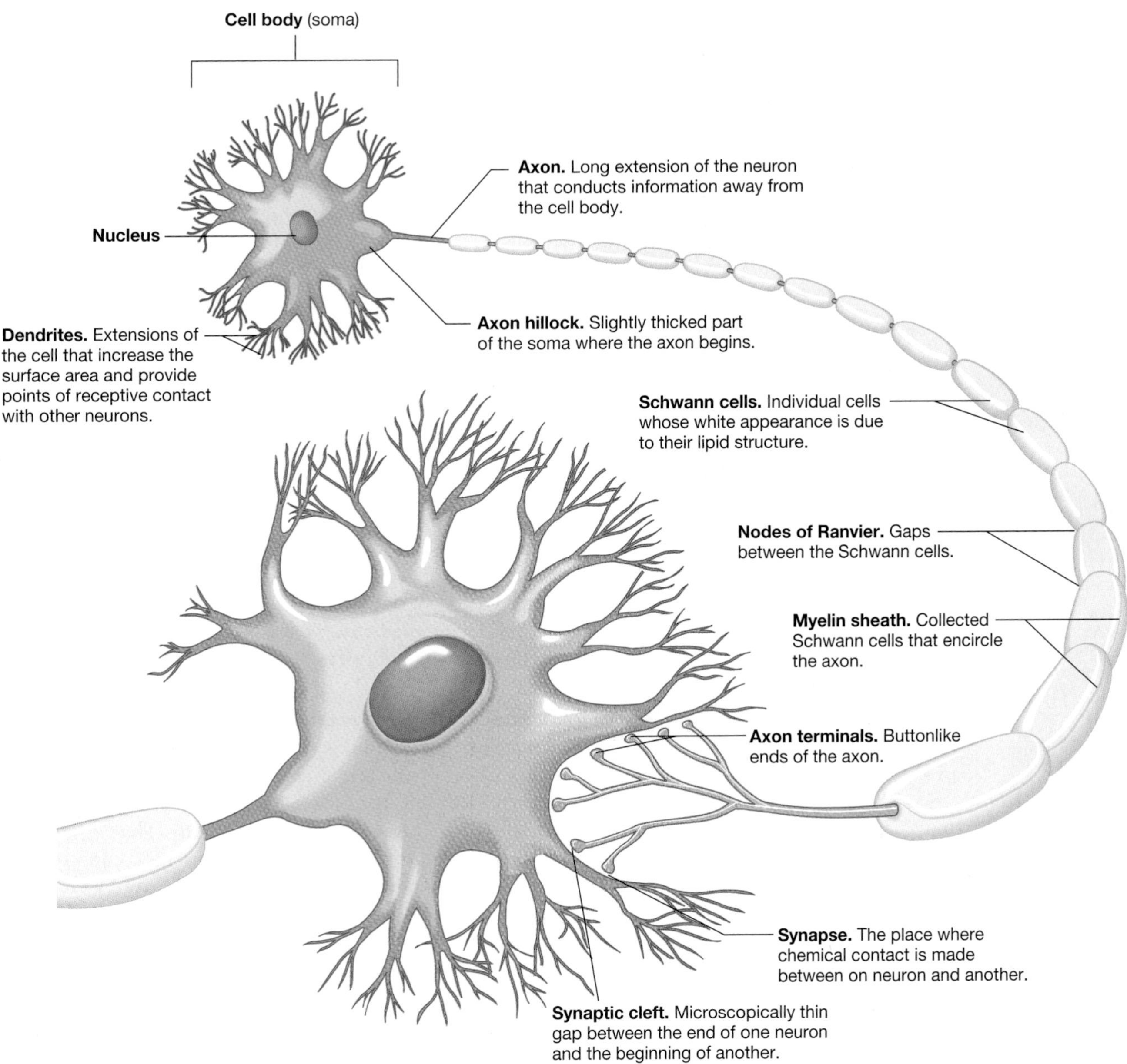
Cell body (soma)
Nucleus
Dendrites. Extensions of the cell that increase the surface area and provide points of receptive contact with other neurons.
Axon. Long extension of the neuron that conducts information away from the cell body.
Axon hillock. Slightly thicked part of the soma where the axon begins.
Schwann cells. Individual cells whose white appearance is due to their lipid structure.
Nodes of Ranvier. Gaps between the Schwann cells.
Myelin sheath. Collected Schwann cells that encircle the axon.
Axon terminals. Buttonlike ends of the axon.
Synapse. The place where chemical contact is made between on neuron and another.
Synaptic cleft. Microscopically thin gap between the end of one neuron and the beginning of another.

Figure 4.8 How neurons connect to each other. The three main parts of a neuron are its dendrites (the receiving end), its cell body (where information is processed), and its axon (the sending end). Here an axon leaves the cell body of one neuron and makes chemical contact (synapses) with another neuron. Individual Schwann cells wrap around the axon to form a myelin sheath. Note that the axon terminals do not physically touch the other neuron; the space that separates the two neurons is called the synaptic cleft.

Figure 4.8 shows two neurons interacting with each other. Like every other cell in the body, each neuron contains cytoplasm, a nucleus, mitochondria, and all the other components it needs to maintain itself. Though each neuron is designed for a particular purpose, for which there is a unique design, all neurons have three main parts that function in a similar way. In addition to a **cell body**, also known as the soma, each neuron has **dendrites**, its input devices, and an **axon**, the output device that carries nerve impulses away from the cell body. In Figure 4.8, the axon of one neuron is making contact with the dendrites and cell body of another neuron. The place at which the contact is made is called the

cell body The main part of a neuron, which contains the normal constituents of a living cell.

dendrites The receptive part of a neuron.

axon The extension of a neuron over which an action potential is conducted.

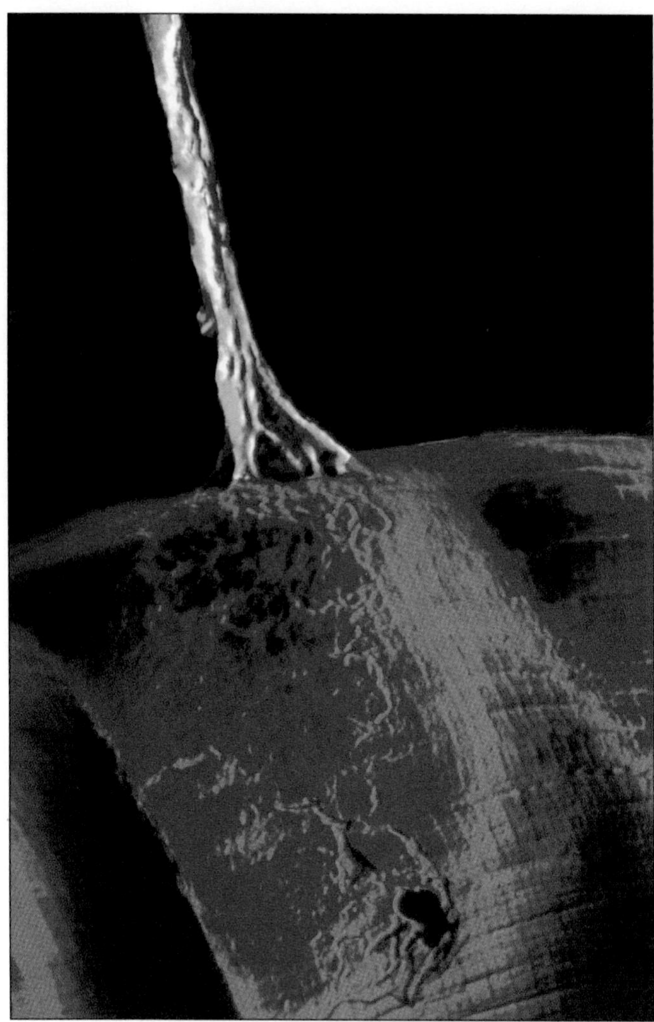

Electronmicrograph of a motor neuron making contact with muscle fibers.

synapse. (The term *synapse* also refers to the chemical processes that occur in the synapse, which we will discuss later.) Neurons that are found in the periphery of the body (such as in the retina, on the tongue, and in the skin) are called *receptors*. Receptors have specialized dendrites that are sensitive to physical energy (from the sun, from chemicals, or from being touched, for instance). For this reason, dendrites are considered the "sensory" or receiving part of a neuron.

At the other end of the neuron is the axon. Many neurons in the peripheral nervous system have axons that are wrapped with *Schwann cells,* which form what is called **myelin** (or a myelin sheath) around the axon. The gaps between adjacent Schwann cells are called the *nodes of Ranvier*. Though they are not part of a neuron, these fatty cells and the gaps between them affect how neurons transmit their signals. The myelin also gives the nervous system one of its distinctive colors: Schwann cells are white in appearance due to their lipid (fatty) membranes. Thus, the myelin-covered axons that gather in bundles called nerves, or tracts, are also white. Together these structures make up the so-called white matter of the brain. Axons with myelin covering are called *myelinated* fibers, and those with no myelin covering are called *unmyelinated* fibers.

Connections Between Neurons. A continuous *cell membrane* covers the surface of dendrites, soma, and axon. Later in this chapter we will see that events that occur on the cell membrane allow neurons to behave differently from most other cells in the body. That is, neurons are excitable; under certain conditions they can conduct nerve impulses along their axons to the buttonlike endings called *axon terminals*. Figure 4.8 shows how the terminals from one neuron make a synaptic connection—a point of chemical contact—with other neurons. Neurons do not make direct physical contact with other neurons or with the muscle fibers on which they terminate. Rather, they are separated by a small gap called the *synaptic cleft*. When they are excited, their axon terminals secrete microscopic amounts of a biochemical called a **neurotransmitter** into the synaptic cleft. The neurotransmitter can either cause the muscle fibers to contract or excite or inhibit nerve impulses in adjacent neurons.

The Spinal Cord and the Sensory-Motor Reflex

Information from the skin, joints, and muscles travel through the spinal cord to the brain; in response, nerves from the brain control the muscles. To accomplish this complicated operation, the spinal cord has several types of specialized neurons. Figure 4.9 illustrates the role of the spinal cord in a *sensory-motor reflex,* which is initiated when skin receptors that are sensitive to pressure, heat, and pain are stimulated. This information is processed in the *sensory neurons* in the *dorsal root ganglion* that lies just outside the spinal cord. In the spinal cord these sensory neurons synapse with other neurons called *interneurons,* which excite *motor neurons* connected to muscle fibers near the skin receptors (see the photograph on this page). Automatically, the muscle fibers contract, in this case moving the finger away from the flame. The sensory-motor reflex is complete.

synapse The place where one neuron makes a chemical connection with another neuron.

myelin The Schwann cells that form an outer covering on some axons.

neurotransmitter One of a variety of chemicals that neurons secrete.

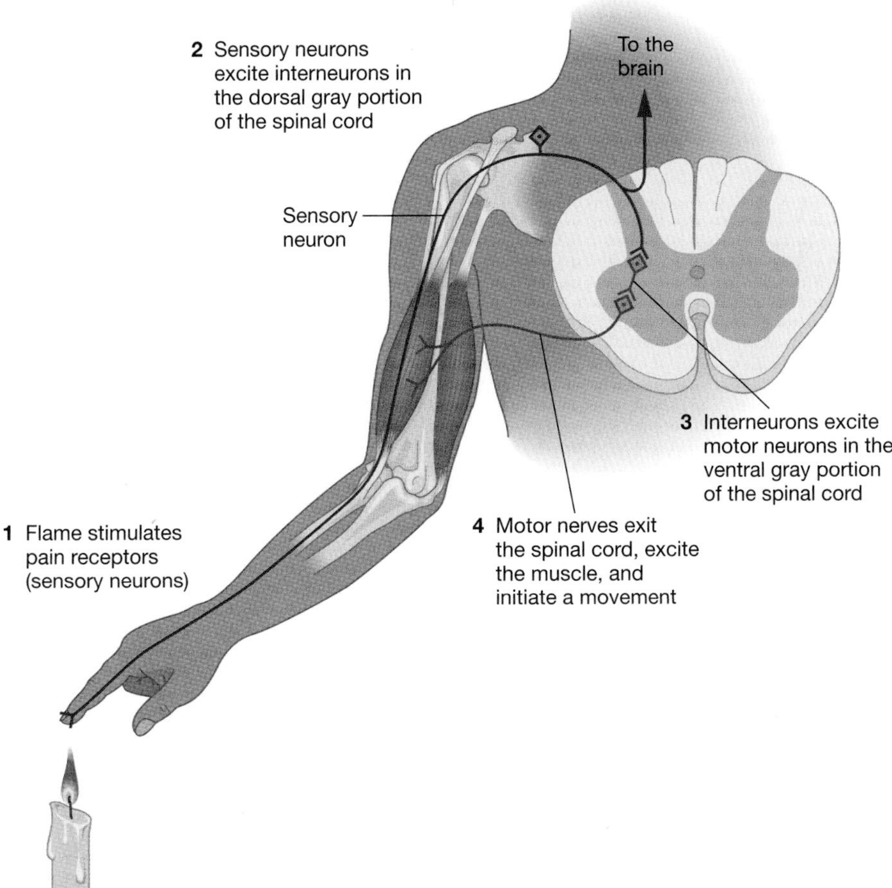
2 Sensory neurons excite interneurons in the dorsal gray portion of the spinal cord
To the brain
Sensory neuron
3 Interneurons excite motor neurons in the ventral gray portion of the spinal cord
1 Flame stimulates pain receptors (sensory neurons)
4 Motor nerves exit the spinal cord, excite the muscle, and initiate a movement

Figure 4.9 A sensory-motor reflex. A sensory-motor reflex is initiated when a sensory nerve is stimulated. Before the pain information arrives at the brain, interneurons and motor nerves in the spinal cord trigger a reflexive movement aimed at removing the source of the pain.

Although sensory-motor reflexes can occur without the brain's involvement, ascending sensory nerves inform the brain that a reflex has taken place. More often, the brain controls the muscles voluntarily by sending and receiving messages through the spinal cord. This type of functioning is called reflective (rather than reflexive) processing. Compression of the spinal cord due to injury in the lower back would interrupt the flow of sensory and motor information to the legs, causing anesthesia (loss of sensation) and paralysis, respectively. Sensory and motor functioning *above* the level of a spinal cord injury would be uninterrupted, however.

Figure 4.10 shows a cross-section through the spinal cord, with the sensory and motor nerves entering and leaving. The spinal cord's most distinctive anatomical feature is the gray H-shaped structure in the center. (If you look carefully, you will see the H in the spinal cord in Figure 4.4 as well.) The colors of the *gray matter* and the *white matter* surrounding it are due primarily to the preservatives that are used in preparing a spinal cord for study. A live, healthy spinal cord would have a *pink* "H" because of the blood that supplies the neurons found there. The surrounding white matter is composed of the cut ends of millions of myelinated nerve fibers that run in columns up and down the cord.

What is not shown in the cross-section in Figure 4.10 is the organization of the nerve fibers in the columns. The nerves that carry information about pain and temperature are located in different columns from the nerves that carry information about touch. In addition, the spinal cord, like most structures in the brain, is organized *bilaterally,* meaning that its left and right sides are mirror images, each of which serves only one side of the body.

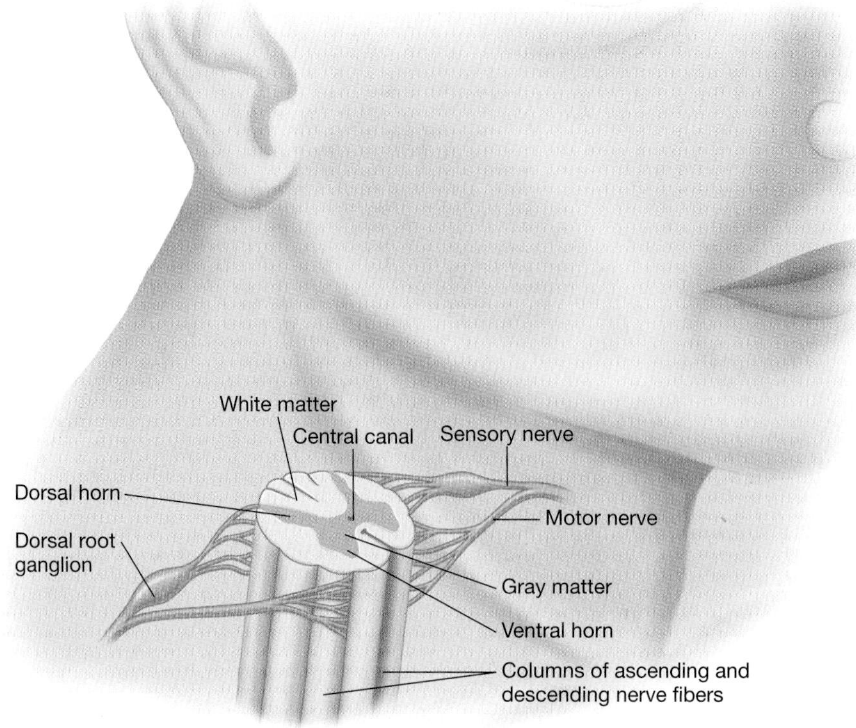

Figure 4.10 Cross-section of a human spinal cord. Sensory nerves (whose cell bodies lie in the *dorsal root ganglion)* enter the spinal cord in the dorsal horn. When stimulated, they synapse with other neurons. Motor nerves exit the spinal cord from the ventral horn. Sensory nerves enter the spinal cord at the point closest to their source; motor nerves exit at the point closest to their destination. The vertical columns of nerve fibers surrounding the "Gray H" travel to and from the brain. Breakage of these fibers can cause paralysis and/or anesthesia below the level of the break.

In the very center of the gray H is a canal filled with *cerebrospinal fluid (CSF)*. This canal connects with areas in the brain called *ventricles,* which are also filled with CSF. Notice that the gray H is skinnier in the dorsal portion (toward the back) and fatter in the ventral portion (toward the stomach). The skinny part, called the *dorsal horn,* contains interneurons, and the fatter part, called the *ventral horn,* contains motor neurons.

INTERIM SUMMARY

1. The human nervous system is divided into the ***central nervous system*** **(CNS),** which includes the *brain* and *spinal cord*; the ***peripheral nervous system*** **(PNS)**, which comprises the ***autonomic nervous system*** **(ANS)** and the ***somatic nervous system;*** and the ***neuroendocrine system.***
2. The three functions of the nervous system are to receive information about an event in the environment, to process it, and to act on it.
3. The autonomic nervous system has two main components: a ***parasympathetic division,*** which controls resting body functions (heart, lungs, stomach, muscle, liver, pancreas, adrenal glands, bladder, and reproductive organs), and a ***sympathetic division,*** which prepares the body for action.
4. The basic unit of the nervous system is the ***neuron.*** All neurons have a ***cell body, dendrites,*** and an ***axon*** that secretes a ***neurotransmitter*** at ***synapse.*** Some axons are wrapped with ***myelin.***
5. A *sensory-motor reflex* begins in the periphery of the body with stimulation of the receptive ends of *sensory neurons.* These sensory afferents in turn activate *interneurons* in the spinal cord. Finally, motor efferents stimulate muscle cells, causing a reflexive movement.
6. The spinal cord is made up of *gray matter* (cell bodies) and *white matter* (nerve fibers) that serve both sensory and motor functions at the reflexive level. Ascending and descending fibers in the spinal cord connect the periphery of the body with the brain.

For Further Thought

1. Bright light causes the iris to constrict, whereas dim light dilates it, allowing more light into the eye. In most women and men the pupil also dilates in response to pictures of nudes (Hess & Polt, 1960) and work on arithmetic problems (Hess & Polt, 1964). Notice in Figure 4.7 that the sympathetic division of the autonomic nervous system can cause the pupils to dilate. What function of the sympathetic division helps to explain dilation of the pupils in response to nude pictures and arithmetic problems?
2. Why are you more likely to have an upset stomach after arguing over dinner with your significant other than after a peaceful meal?
3. Quadriplegics have no feeling or movement in either their arms or legs, but their mental functioning is otherwise intact. What part of their brain or spinal cord has been injured?

THE RELATIONSHIP OF BRAIN AND BEHAVIOR

The burning candle we discussed in the last section is sensed not just by temperature and pain receptors, but through visual and smell receptors as well. So we might expect the brain to integrate information arriving from separate input channels—and it does. The five animals shown in Figure 4.2 each have these same sensory channels and neural pathways. Presumably, because their brains are organized *similarly*, your cat sees, smells, and feels pain from a burning candle much as you do. Any differences in the flame's appearance and smell, and the meaning your cat attaches to the pain it causes, result from *differences* between the cat's brain organization and yours.

Pathways Through the Spinal Cord to the Brain

Let's suppose *your* finger is hovering near the burning candle. How does that pain sensation reach the brain? Figure 4.11 illustrates the path of the pain fibers from the spinal cord to the brain. Before attempting to follow it, a word of advice: Because the brain is a three-dimensional structure, you can best study it by looking at it from different angles. So begin by looking at Figure 4.2 (p. 111) to recall where the forebrain is in relation to the spinal cord, hindbrain, and midbrain. Next, turn to Figure 4.4 (p. 113) and try to identify the hindbrain and the gray H of the spinal cord as it approaches the medulla.

Figure 4.11 is an "exploded" view of the brain that shows different levels of the spinal cord, hindbrain, midbrain, and forebrain. Information about pain and touch travels up the "white matter" of the spinal cord through nerves that run in tracts within the cord. Although all the pathways are bilateral, for the sake of simplicity they are drawn on one side only. After entering the spinal cord, all sensory and motor information coming from and going to the brain must cross from one side to the other. The view in Figure 4.11 is from the front, so the sensory information is shown entering the dorsal root ganglion on the *left* side of the body, crossing over, and ascending to the brain on the *right* side of the spinal cord. Information from the left side of the body, then, ends up on the right side of the brain. Later we will see that nerves that originate in the right side of the brain control muscles on the left side of the body, and vice versa.

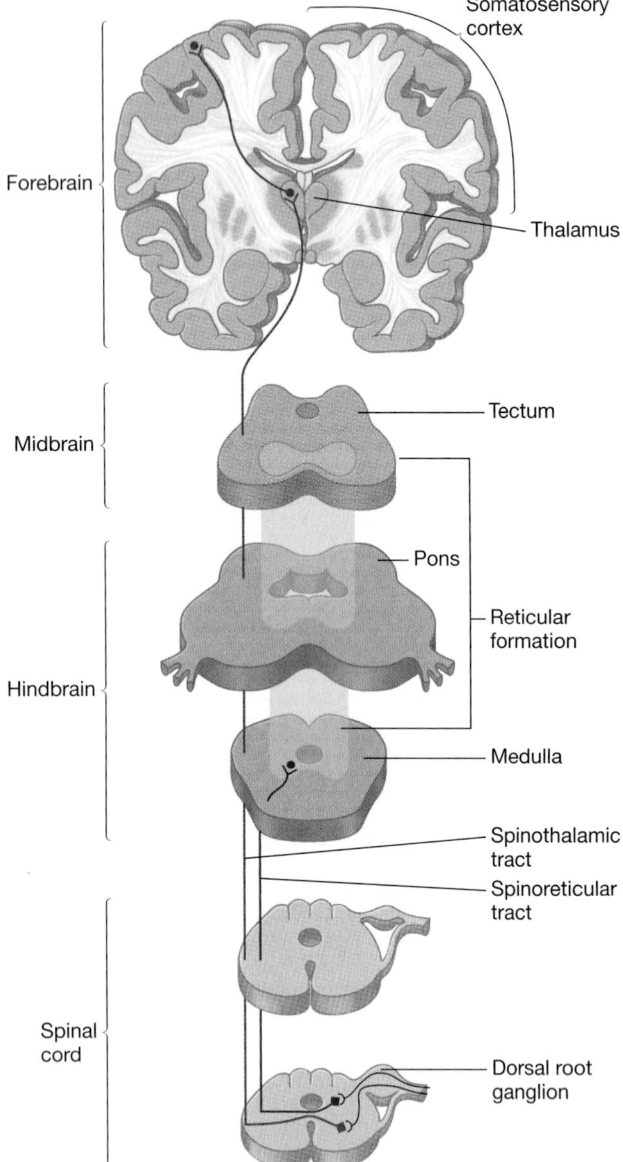

Figure 4.11 Reflexive processing of the sensation of touch. Incoming touch and pain information crosses from one side of the spinal cord to the other at the level where the sensory nerves enter the cord. It then travels to the brain through tracts in the spinal cord. (The tracts are labeled to show both their source and destination; for instance, the spinothalamic tract goes from the spine to the thalamus.) In the brain the information passes through the hindbrain and midbrain and terminates in the somatosensory cortex, part of the forebrain. A few of the structures the impulse passes through are labeled, including the reticular formation, one place where some of the nerve fibers end. Why might damage to one side of the spinal cord interrupt the sensation of touch on the other side of the body?

To simplify, only two of a number of ascending tracts are shown in Figure 4.11: the *spinothalamic track* and the *spinoreticular tract.* Their names indicate both their origin (the spine) and their destination. That is, the spinothalamic track synapses at the thalamus, and the spinoreticular tract terminates in the reticular formation of the hindbrain. Other pathways carry the information on to the neocortex in the forebrain.

The Reticular Formation and the Hindbrain

The **reticular formation** runs throughout the center of the hindbrain and midbrain. Not shown in Figure 4.11 is the fact that *all* the sensory information—seeing and hearing as well as touch and pain—travels to the reticular formation, which sends it on to other parts of the brain. What is the function of the reticular formation? Imagine a bug crawling up your back. The sensory receptors that detect this movement on your back enter the spinal cord as shown in Figure 4.10. They activate neurons in ascending nerve fibers, some of which synapse in the reticular formation. The activation of neurons in the reticular formation has an arousing, attention-getting function. These neurons, in turn, stimulate other nerve fibers that cause you to move toward the source of the stimulation. You brush off that part of your back.

Consider another example: A sharp cracking noise to your left, or a bright flash of light to your right, causes your head to turn reflexively in the correct direction. This reflexive head turning results from activation of the reticular formation and other midbrain structures to which it sends signals. Whether they realize it or not, the directors of scary movies exploit the effects of reticular activation. Specifically, they intentionally startle you by including sudden sights, sounds, and movements in their films. To scare you they must cause the reticular formation to send such information to parts of the brain that are responsible for emotion and emotional arousal.

All vertebrate brains have a reticular formation. Why? In what ways would the bass in Figure 4.2 find such a structure to be adaptive? Does the detection of a sudden movement arouse the bass to take an aggressive or defensive posture? That appears to be so. Again, we see that processing information from the environment and acting adaptively on it are two key functions of vertebrate nervous systems.

The Thalamus and Somatosensory Cortex

Figure 4.11 showed how a sensation such as being burned by a candle (or touched by a bug) arrives at the top of the brain. Nerve fibers first activate the thalamus (located just past the tip of the brainstem and covered by the cerebral hemispheres—see Figure 4.5). On both a portion of the thalamus and on the *somatosensory cortex*, the surface area of the body is laid out *somatotopically.* Somatotopic organization means that nerve fibers serving adjacent areas of the body surface—the fingers, for example—are mapped out on adjacent areas of the brain.

reticular formation A group of neurons extending from the hindbrain into the midbrain that serves to alert animals.

Figure 4.12 shows this somatotopic mapping of the body, in which nerve fibers from the fingers and the legs arrive at different places on the cortex. The strange-looking person shown in the figure is called a *sensory homunculus* (Latin for "little man"). Notice that his thumb and lips are much larger than his other body parts. The homunculus is a visual device representing the proportionate number of neurons in the cortex that are devoted to various parts of the body. Because more nerves serve the sense of touch on the face than in the middle of the back, there are more "face" neurons than "back" neurons in the somatosensory cortex. (Not shown in Figures 4.11 and 4.12 is the somatotopic organization of the body's surface on a portion of the thalamus.)

What happens when neurons in the thalamus and somatosensory cortex are activated? Simply put, they create a sense of touch and "feeling" in different parts of the body. During brain surgery, if a brief electrical impulse is applied to an exposed area of the somatosensory cortex, conscious patients will report "feeling" something on their hands, lips, or other body parts. If adjacent neurons in the arm area are stimulated, the patient may report that "something is crawling up my arm." Many years ago, Wilder Penfield, a Canadian neurosurgeon, used this technique to "map" the cortical surface of the human brain (Penfield & Boldrey,

Sensory stimulation alerts a person by activating the reticular formation.

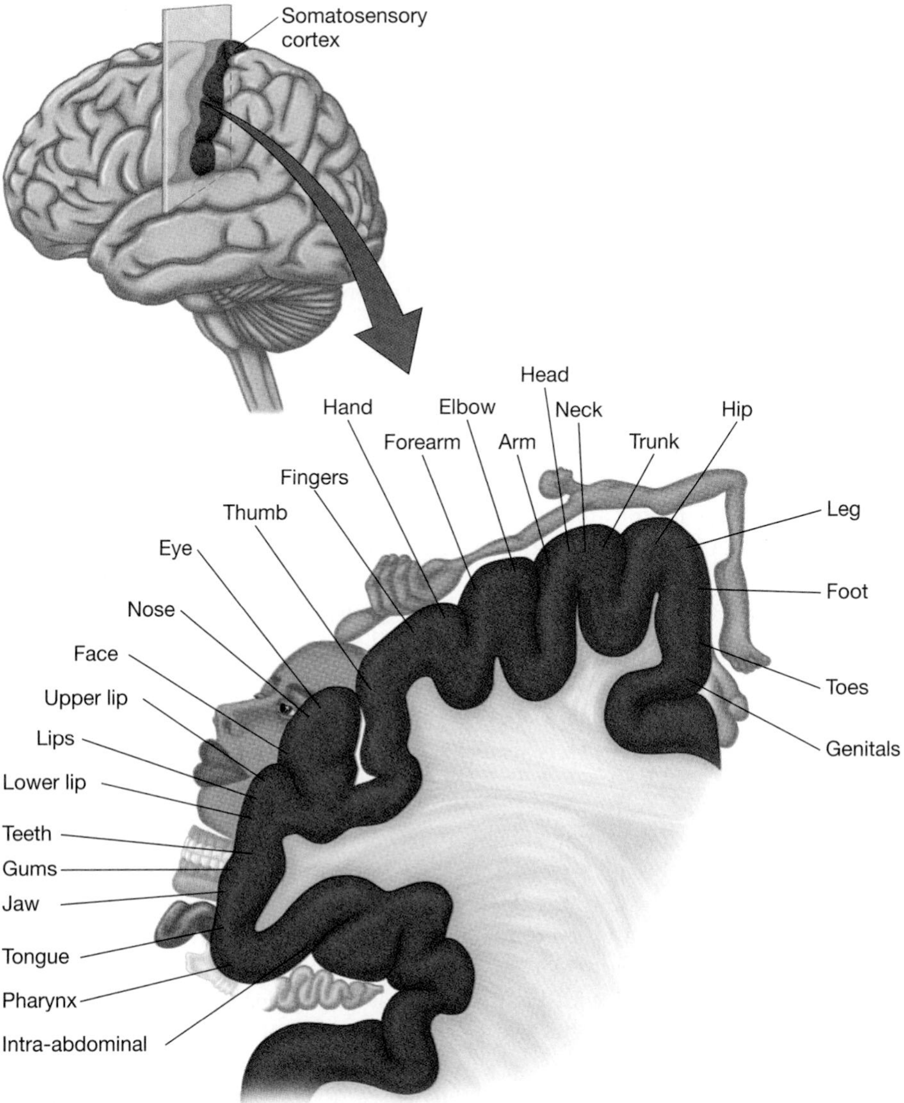

Figure 4.12 **Why the lips are more sensitive than the neck or back.** A sensory homunculus stretches across the surface of the somatosensory cortex. The disproportionately large body surface areas indicate that more sensory neurons are devoted to the hands and feet, lips and tongue than to the surface of the arms, trunk, and legs.

1937). Quite often patients are allowed to remain conscious during brain surgery, to help surgeons by reporting the sensations they experience when part of the brain is stimulated. In this way the patient "fine tunes" the surgeon's ability to locate specific brain areas. Because there are no pain receptors in the brain, patients can remain conscious without suffering when neurons are stimulated or cut.

The large numbers of cortical neurons serving the mouth area are a clue to a general rule regarding *brain-behavior relationships*. That is, the number of neurons devoted to a body part (and therefore, the size of the part of the brain devoted to it) is related to the functional importance of that part. Grasping, tool-making fingers and thumbs require more neurons than toes. Lips and tongues that chew, lick, and swallow require more neurons than the middle of the back. The emphasis on mouth may have arisen adaptively for several reasons: millions of lip and tongue neurons are necessary to guard a vulnerable opening to the body and detect the subtle mouth and larynx positions necessary to generate speech.

The Cerebral Cortex: Sources of Human Uniqueness

Let's continue our introduction to the brain by examining the function of other parts of the cerebral cortex. Figure 4.13 shows two views—one from the side, the other from overhead—of the most important surface structures of the brain. Because of its large number of convolutions (folds or wrinkles), the human cerebral cortex is much larger than its outside surface suggests. In fact, about two thirds of the area of the cerebral cortex is hidden from view. (A hidden portion of the cortex is visible in the cross-section of the somatosensory cortex in Figure 4.12.) Unfolded, the cerebral cortex would be about the size of a large road map—about 6 square feet.

The cerebral cortex, as shown in Figure 4.13, is divided into four color-coded lobes. Three of these lobes have clear boundaries formed by large grooves, or fissures, between them. The top view shows the **longitudinal fissure** that separates the left and right cerebral hemispheres. The bottom view shows the **central sulcus** and the **lateral fissure**. The four lobes of the cerebral cortex are called the **frontal lobe** (the front and top of the brain, located anterior to the central sulcus); the **parietal lobe** (the back and top part of the brain, located posterior to the central fissure); the **temporal lobe** (the side of the brain, separated from the frontal lobe by the lateral fissure); and the **occipital lobe** (the back of the brain). The precentral gyrus (the primary motor area) of the frontal lobe and the postcentral gyrus (the somatosensory area of the parietal lobe) are also labeled (compare Figure 4.12).

longitudinal fissure The main fissure or gap that separates the left and right cerebral hemispheres.

central sulcus The main fissure, or gap, that separates the frontal lobe from the parietal lobe.

lateral fissure The main fissure that separates the temporal from the frontal lobe.

frontal lobe The part of the cerebral cortex that is devoted to speech, planning, movement, association formation, and other psychological functions.

parietal lobe The part of the cerebral cortex that contains the somatosensory and associative cortex, which are involved in spatial perception and other psychological functions.

temporal lobe The part of the cerebral cortex that contains the primary auditory and associative cortex, which are involved in hearing and language.

occipital lobe The part of the cerebral cortex that contains the primary visual cortex and associative cortex, which are involved in seeing and visual consciousness.

Differences Between Humans and Other Animals. Figure 4.14 shows the highly convoluted cerebral cortexes of humans and cats, and the comparatively smooth cortical surface of a rat's brain. Because the rat's cortex lacks convolutions, it contains far fewer neurons than the cat's or human's cortex. The human brain's somatosensory area (a part of the parietal lobe discussed in the last section) and its motor (movement), visual, and auditory areas are labeled in the figure. Similar areas, as well as the area for smell (the olfactory bulb), are labeled on the cat's and rat's brains. (The olfactory bulb cannot be seen in this view of the human brain, because it lies under the frontal lobe.) Note that the cat and rat do not have separate areas devoted to the sensory and motor functions. Separate evolutionary paths led to the differentiation of those areas in the human brain, which now lie on either side of the central sulcus.

Compare Figure 4.14 with Figure 4.2 for a better idea of the different brain sizes of these animals. Figure 4.14 shows the proportional amount of sensory cortex devoted to the primary senses in each animal. Human brains contain many more neurons devoted to smell, the somatosenses, seeing, and hearing than do cat

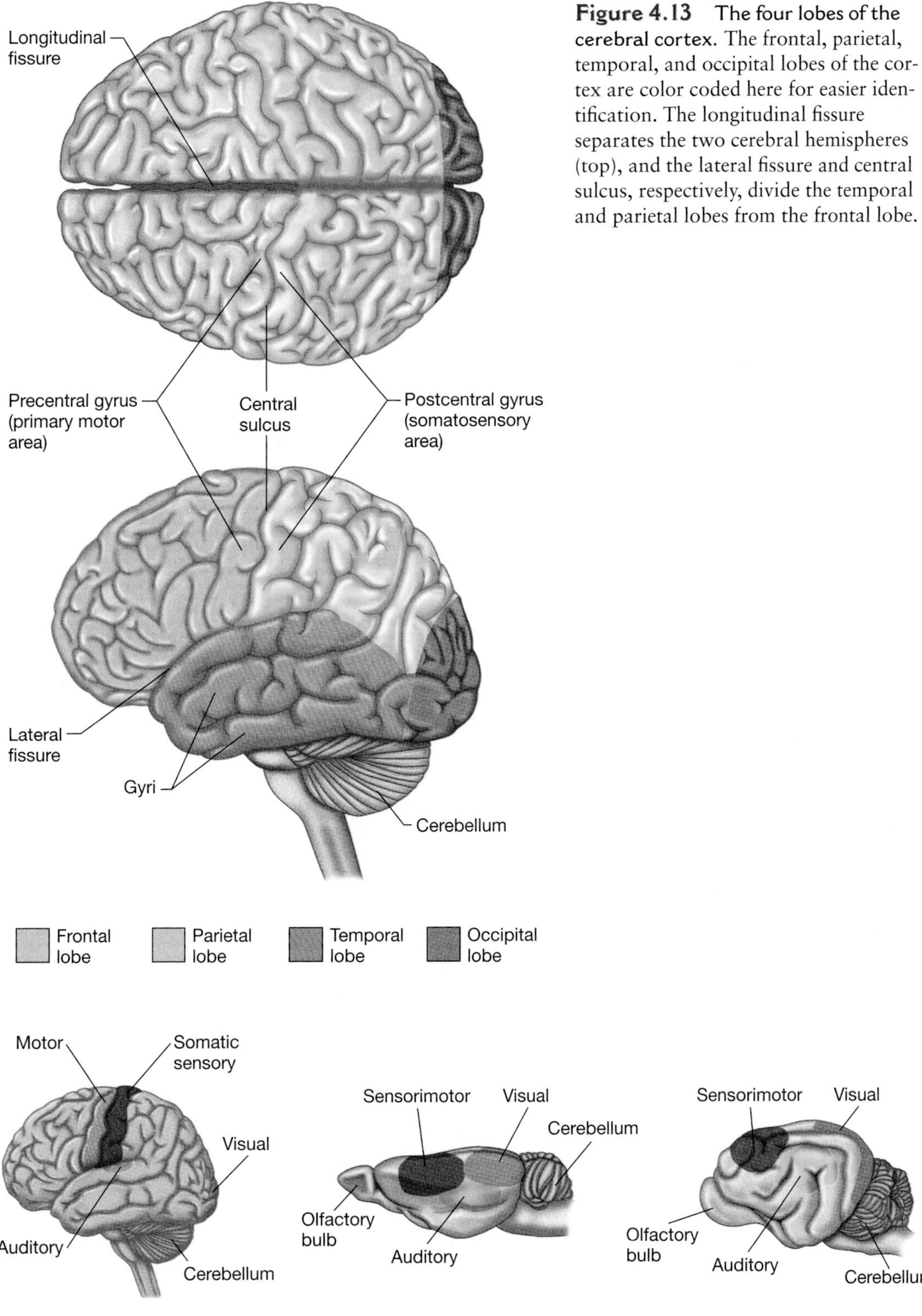

Figure 4.13 The four lobes of the cerebral cortex. The frontal, parietal, temporal, and occipital lobes of the cortex are color coded here for easier identification. The longitudinal fissure separates the two cerebral hemispheres (top), and the lateral fissure and central sulcus, respectively, divide the temporal and parietal lobes from the frontal lobe.

Figure 4.14 The cerebral cortex in humans, cats, and rats. Humans have far larger brains, and much more cerebral cortex, than cats and rats (see Figure 4.2). The human cerebral cortex also performs different functions from the nonhuman cortex. Most of the surface of the rat's brain is devoted to sensory (visual and auditory) or mixed sensory and motor functions. In contrast, the human brain has separate motor and sensory areas, as well as large areas devoted to other functions. These drawings suggest that cats and rats have larger olfactory bulbs than humans, though they do not. The human olfactory bulbs are larger, but they cannot be seen here because they are hidden under the cerebral hemispheres (see Figure 4.4).

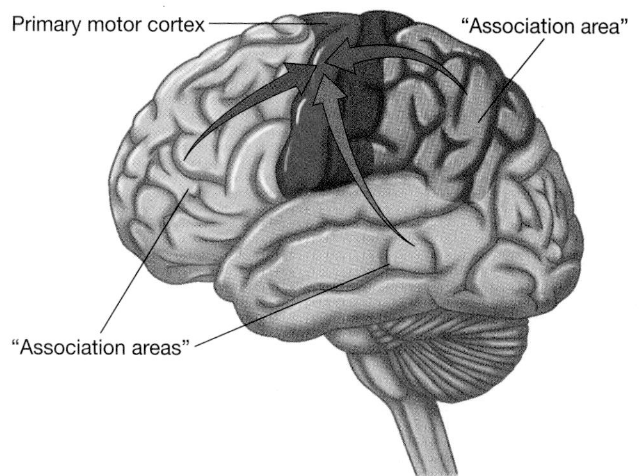

Figure 4.15 Parts of the human brain involved in movement. To initiate movement, signals from neurons in the frontal, parietal, and temporal lobes converge on the primary motor cortex in the frontal lobe.

and rat brains. Unlike cats and rats, humans have a tremendous amount of neocortex that is *not* devoted to the primary senses of seeing, hearing, touching, and smelling. In fact, the neurons responsible for the mechanics of seeing, hearing, touching, and so forth are restricted to relatively small parts of the lobes, called *primary sensory areas.* For most of the 20th century, psychologists and neurologists have been intrigued by two questions: What is the purpose of the large sensory areas of the cortex that do *not* serve primary sensory functions? and Why do humans have proportionally more nonprimary sensory cortex than other animals?

Special Functions of the Human Cortex. One answer to these questions is that the billions of neurons in a human's frontal, occipital, temporal, and parietal lobes allow sensory information to be integrated. In other words, these neurons make possible connections ("associations") among the senses as well as between the senses and motor functions. Indeed, in schematic diagrams of brain function drawn half a century ago, much of the surface of the four lobes was labeled *association area,* or "association cortex."

Figure 4.15 shows that some parts of the human cortex merge information to initiate movement. For example, the association cortex integrates the visual, auditory, and touch information necessary for skilled movement. With such a brain organization, the human can act intentionally, not just reflexively. By contrast, the frog's brain has no association cortex; visual areas of the brain are connected directly to motor areas. When a bug moves into the frog's visual field, activating neurons in the visual areas of its brain, the frog's tongue reflexively flicks out to catch the fly. Humans and other animals are not restricted to such reflexive movements, in part because their neocortical structures can make associations between sensing and moving. A human, for example, can grab a flyswatter. Other associations between the senses, such as between seeing and hearing, also take place in the cortex, in a manner that is not fully understood (Kolb & Whishaw, 1996).

LINK ▶
How a frog sees, Chapter 8, p. 272

The cortical brain areas that are involved with the association and integration of movement and the senses are the ones that afford humans a unique consciousness. Huge numbers of neurons in the frontal lobes allow humans to set goals and make plans and initiate intentional behavior. In addition to mediating the senses of touch and pain, the parietal lobe affords an "awareness" of the location of one's body parts. Likewise, neurons in the occipital, temporal, and frontal lobes allow us a consciousness, or awareness, of visual images (Weiskrantz, 1997). Other psychological functions mediated by the brain are discussed in later chapters. For example, billions of neurons located throughout the cerebral cortex enable a person to have a conversation. And when we study the brain's basis for short-term memory (Chapter 10), we'll see that damage to a specific part of the temporal lobe, called the hippocampus, impairs a human's ability to learn new ideas.

LINK ▶
Forebrain and consciousness, Chapter 9, p. 308

This comparison of the human brain with the brains of other vertebrates provides an overall picture of how our nervous system functions. We have seen that humans have evolved brain structures that allow them to sense the environment in unique ways, and move adaptively in response to it. But sensory information and movement do not dominate our lives; we think, love, remember, enjoy, and learn as well. The association cortex provides the structure that underlies the complexities of human life. Ironically, scientists can better understand the normal functioning of these structures when they fail, as we can see from an examination of the effects of brain damage.

Brain Damage: A Clue to Brain-Behavior Relationships

The vertebrate nervous system is organized into separately functioning but interconnected parts. For example, because the neocortex is in intimate communication with the brainstem, an individual's emotional behavior, which is mediated by the midbrain structures, can be affected by damage to the cortex. Likewise, voluntary movement is accomplished by the neocortex and several subcortical (literally, "beneath the cortex") structures. In fact, much of our knowledge of the higher cortical functions of the so-called association areas and their control of emotions and movement has been gleaned from humans who have survived brain damage. Recall Phineas Gage, the man who survived a vicious assault on his frontal lobes and emerged a changed person. In his case we can also infer the functions of cortical tissue that was spared from injury. Had the tamping rod damaged the nearby *primary motor cortex* of the frontal lobe (just anterior to the central sulcus—see Figure 4.13), Gage would have had difficulty controlling the movement of various parts of his body. But Gage moved normally, even though a large part of his brain had been damaged.

The Effects of Strokes. Phineas Gage's case history illustrates in dramatic fashion what is meant by the term *brain-behavior relationship*. Every day, assaults on the brain's integrity are played out in equally tragic but less dramatic fashion, in the form of strokes. Due to the high energy demands of billions of neurons, the brain receives 20 percent of the heart's blood output. Strokes are caused most often by an *aneurysm,* which occurs when the cell wall of a tiny capillary ruptures, releasing blood into the tissue that surrounds brain cells. The resulting swelling and pooling of blood can kill brain cells. In addition, the neurons' oxygen supply can be interrupted, killing more brain cells. The consequences of these ruptures, or "bleeds," is determined both by their location in the brain and by the size of the area the capillary serves.

Stroke patients must learn to use different parts of the brain to effect movement.

A person who has suffered a stroke often moves differently afterward. For example, a stroke that destroys neurons in the primary motor cortex on the left side of the brain results in a weakness or paralysis of the *right* side of the body. Figure 4.16 shows how the left side of the brain controls movement on the right side of the body, and vice versa. Nerve fibers that make up a white-matter structure called the *internal capsule* extend from the primary motor cortex down through the midbrain and medulla. At the medulla these fibers cross from one side of the brain to the other at a place called the *medullary pyramid.* (No one knows why these fibers cross between the brain and the spinal cord. The system would seem to work as effectively if the left hemisphere controlled the left side of the body, and the right hemisphere the right side.) This point, called the *decussation of the pyramids,* lies at the juncture of the medulla with the spinal cord; after crossing, the fibers enter the spinal cord. Figure 4.16 shows the entire path of the nerve fibers, called the *lateral pathway*, from the motor cortex down to the spinal cord.

Neurons in the spinal cord normally receive input from the lateral pathway; in turn, they activate the muscles, allowing the body to move. But a stroke kills the brain cells that are responsible for this cortex-initiated movement. Because a capillary typically serves only a limited brain region, the effect of a stroke is usually confined to one side of the body. Recall that the body is represented topographically on the motor cortex, in a manner similar to the adjacent somatosensory strip (see Figure 4.12). A stroke may limit paralysis to the muscles of one leg, or it might affect only the movement of one arm. A stroke that affects the part of the primary motor cortex that serves the face might leave one side of the face paralyzed. Sagging facial muscles can affect the ability to smile, and paralysis of the right or left side of the lips and tongue can impair the person's ability to speak. A stroke that affects certain parts of the frontal and left temporal lobe can also affect a person's use of language. (The language areas of the brain will be discussed in detail in a later chapter.)

Brain areas for language, Chapter 12, p. 416

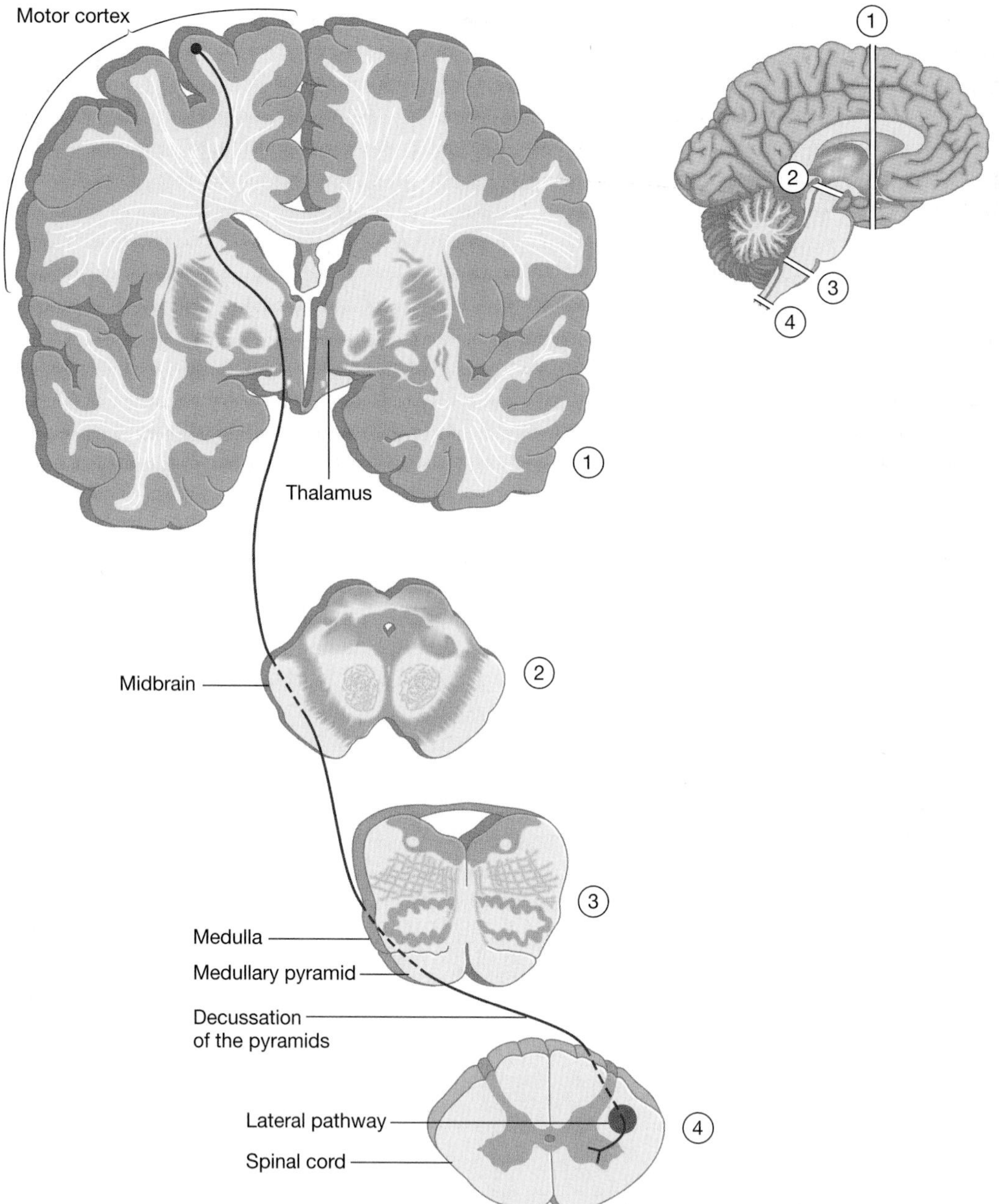

Figure 4.16 How the brain initiates intentional movements. The motor cortex of the cerebral hemispheres contains neurons that can initiate muscle movement on command, as distinct from the reflexive movements initiated by the spinal cord. (Compare this figure with Figure 4.11, which follows the movement of nerve impulses *up* the spinal cord.) The *medullary pyramid* (in the medulla) switches the descending motor nerve fibers in the lateral pathways from one side of the body to the other; hence, the left side of the brain controls the muscles on the right side of the body. The numbers correspond to the places in the brain and spinal cord that are sectioned.

Neurogenesis and Brain Plasticity. Until recently, scientists believed that humans were born with their full complement of neurons. The course of the brain's development, they thought, was characterized by cell death rather than cell growth—a pruning rather than a proliferation of neurons. But several different lines of research have dramatically changed this view. Early research (Rosenzweig, Krech, Bennett, & Diamond, 1962) had demonstrated that rats that were housed together developed neurons with more highly elaborated dendrites than rats housed individually. Group housing offers the opportunity of social interaction, which may stimulate neural growth. Findings such as these provide evidence for the brain's *plasticity,* or ability to change over a lifetime.

Recent research has extended this finding by showing that **neurogenesis**—the process of forming new neurons—occurs in the brains of senescent (old) mice who have been moved from single housing to group housing (Kemperman, Kuhn, & Gage, 1998). Mice that are allowed to exercise by running also experience neurogenesis (van Praag, Kemperman, & Gage, 1999). This additional evidence suggests that scientists have underestimated the extent of the brain's plasticity.

But what about humans? Here the evidence is more limited, because researchers cannot readily delve into live brains in search of signs of neurogenesis. However, five men did volunteer to be treated before their death with a chemical that would show changes in their brains in a postmortem examination. This research produced evidence of recent, new neuron growth in the five subjects (Eriksson et al., 1998), and subsequent research has demonstrated the growth of new neurons in the hippocampus of adult humans (Gage, 2000). These findings have caused a fundamental change in scientists' thinking about neurons. The human brain is now understood to have the potential for self-renewal (Gage, 1998, 2000).

This description of the effects of a stroke on movement of the body and on language processing is greatly simplified. In actuality, the initiation and control of voluntary movement involves many brain structures. The next section describes what can be thought of as the "loop" of brain structures that control motor responses (Kolb & Whishaw, 1996).

The Mysterious Cerebellum

Only recently has an unlikely part of the brain—the cerebellum—been shown to have a role in certain cognitive functions, including learning and memory. (To locate the cerebellum, see Figures 4.4 and 4.5.) For several hundred years, the cerebellum was believed merely to coordinate muscle movements, for people who had suffered damage to the cerebellum had been observed to move differently. For example, they couldn't touch a finger to their noses with their eyes closed; they were as likely to overshoot and hit their faces as they were to come up short. Furthermore, their movements were disjointed: shoulders, elbows, and wrists made short, uncoordinated jerks rather than smooth flowing motions.

The cerebellum accomplishes such motor tasks in part by receiving inputs from the sensory areas of the thalamus. (These pathways are not shown in Figure 4.5, but note the relative position of the thalamus and the cerebellum.) Coordinated movement requires a sense of the position of thousands of muscle fibers relative to thousands of other muscle fibers. This information is sent over thousands of motor nerve axons to other parts of the brain, including the primary motor area in the cerebrum.

This known function of the cerebellum was extended when a psychobiologist, Richard F. Thompson, and his colleagues in San Diego found that the cerebellar neurons of rabbits changed during conditioning experiments (McCormick & Thompson, 1984). The researchers hypothesized that the cerebellum stores the memory of a learned association between a tone (an auditory function) and an air puff to the eye (a sensory-motor function).

The cerebellum can "learn," then, but can it think? Using a functional MRI (a type of magnetic resonance imaging) of the cerebellum, researchers have attempted to answer this question (Parsons et al., 1997). An *f*MRI allows

neurogenesis The process of forming new neurons.

Table 4.2 Parts of the Human Brain and Their Function

PART OF BRAIN	FUNCTION
Frontal lobe	
Motor area	Initiating muscle movement throughout the body
Association areas	Planning and voluntary control of movement Goal setting Thinking Means-end analysis Language production Inhibition of spontaneous behavior
Occipital lobe	
Primary visual area	Seeing
Association areas	Perceiving and storing memories Understanding and remembering what is seen
Parietal lobe	
Somatosensory area	Sensing touch over entire body
Association areas	Perceiving and storing memories Understanding the body's location and orientation Connecting language, both seen through the eyes and heard through the ears, to speech
Temporal lobe	
Primary auditory area	Hearing sounds
Association areas	Perceiving and storing memories Understanding and remembering what is heard Hearing and understanding language
Cerebellum	Coordinating movement Integrating sensory information during conditioning Paying attention and thinking

researchers to view the activity levels of the brain's neurons on a computer screen while a subject is engaged in a task. Researchers passively brushed the fingertips of one group of subjects with sandpaper; their *f*MRIs indicated that neurons in the cerebellum responded in a way that reflected this raw sensory input. On another test, the same subjects had to decide which was the rougher of two grades of sandpaper brushed across their fingertips. Under these conditions, the *f*MRI reflected even *more* activity in the cerebellum. Researchers concluded that some aspects of "thinking" about the sandpaper were being accomplished in this "old" brain structure. Indeed, Bower (1996) has concluded that the cerebellum partially controls the "data acquisition" for seeing, hearing, touching, and so forth.

Perhaps we should not be too surprised at our emerging understanding of the cerebellum's role in cognitive functioning. Though it lies in the primitive part of the brain, the cerebellum contains more neurons than are found in all other parts of the brain combined, including the two cerebral hemispheres! Its huge size in humans may reflect its evolution to support thinking and language (Leiner, Leiner, & Dow, 1993).

The simple and not so simple functioning of the cerebellum and the four lobes of the brain are summarized in Table 4.2. The organization of these brain structures supports the use of language, which in turn allows a uniquely human consciousness. We will return to the subject of cortical functioning and consciousness at various places throughout this text.

INTERIM SUMMARY

1. Nerve pathways connect the periphery of the body to the brain through the spinal cord.
2. The ***reticular formation*** (found on the midline of the hindbrain and midbrain) alerts and arouses the organism in response to sensory input.
3. The senses (touch and pain, vision and audition) are connected to the cortex through the thalamus.
4. The cerebral hemispheres are bilateral structures, each of which has four parts: the ***frontal, parietal, temporal,*** and ***occipital lobes.***
5. Major landmarks on the surface of the *cerebral cortex* are the ***lateral fissure***, the ***central sulcus***, and the ***longitudinal fissure.***
6. The ***somatosensory cortex*** is laid out somatotopically on the parietal lobe so as to represent the sense of touch and location in the various parts of the body. The primary visual cortex and primary auditory cortex are found in the occipital and temporal lobes, respectively.
7. The so-called *association areas* in the cerebral cortex integrate seeing, hearing, language, and other cognitive functions.
8. The frontal cortex has a primary motor area; other cortical neurons have an inhibitory influence on subcortical areas of the brain.
9. Strokes are cerebral vascular accidents that result in destruction of parts of the brain, producing paralysis of the body and face, language disorders, and other effects. New neurons can form through a process called ***neurogenesis.***
10. Damage to the cerebellum results in jerky, uncoordinated movements. The cerebellum also mediates sensory associations formed during conditioning and is active during some discrimination tasks.

For Further Thought

1. Cortex in the forebrain helps humans to live in a civilized fashion by *inhibiting* behaviors generated in subcortical areas. We know that alcohol inhibits the functioning of cortical neurons. What happens when an inhibitory function is inhibited?
2. Descartes proposed that only humans exhibit voluntary behavior; other animals are merely reflexive machines. What would you need to know about your pet dog's or cat's frontal cortex, or cerebellum, to take issue with Descartes?

LEFT BRAIN, RIGHT BRAIN: THE FUNCTION OF THE TWO CEREBRAL HEMISPHERES

In addition to studying brain-damaged patients, psychologists and neurologists have developed a variety of other experimental methods that contribute to our understanding of our two-sided brain. For instance, psychological tests have revealed a **lateralization of function,** which refers to the fact that the left and right cerebral hemispheres do not function in an identical manner. Other animals (including birds and rodents) also show these differences in hemispheric specialization, which suggests that lateralization of function evolved over many millions of years (Bradshaw & Nettleton, 1989; Bradshaw, 1991).

Environment affects brain during development, Chapter 11, p. 382

Psychological Tests for the Lateralization of Function

Language, spatial abilities, emotion, and other psychological processes all seem to be lateralized in humans. Let's look at some of the clever research that has led psychologists to conclude that the two hemispheres are specialized.

lateralization of function The differences in function between the left and right cerebral hemispheres.

People can focus on one voice among many in noisy gatherings.

Dichotic Listening Tests. Most of us have had the experience of trying to sort out one voice from another at noisy parties. Imagine sitting in a laboratory, wearing earphones through which two competing messages are presented simultaneously. Which message would you hear, and why? The psychologist Doreen Kimura used this procedure, called a **dichotic listening test**, to investigate language processing. Kimura (1973) reported that when subjects hear three numbers (such as "six, nine, four") in one ear and three different numbers in the other ear simultaneously, most of them "hear" and report the numbers they heard in the right rather than the left. Other testing methods have confirmed that in the vast majority of people, spoken language is processed in the left hemisphere. Kimura's test is the easiest, cheapest, and least invasive way to determine in which hemisphere a given individual processes language. But the question is not as simple as the procedure suggests, as will become clear in an extended discussion of language issues in Chapter 12.

The Wada Test. A more invasive test—one that is used just prior to some brain surgeries—is called the *Wada test*, named after J. A. Wada, the researcher who first used it (Pinel, 1997). This test takes advantage of the fact that each hemisphere receives its main blood supply from a separate carotid artery in the neck. Sometimes referred to as the *sodium amytal test*, the Wada test begins with the injection of a small dosage of the drug sodium amytal into one of the two main arteries. Rapidly, the injected hemisphere becomes anesthetized, and for several minutes is nonfunctional. From this and other studies researchers have concluded that males are more strongly lateralized for language in one hemisphere than females, for they cannot speak when their left hemisphere is anesthetized. Females are somewhat less language impaired when their left hemisphere is anesthetized, suggesting that their language function is less strongly lateralized.

Brain control of language, Chapter 12, p. 417

PET Scans. Positron-emission tomography (PET) is a sophisticated technology that is used to locate particular functions in the brain through computer-generated images commonly called **PET scans**. PET scan images are generated by measuring the emission of electrically charged particles by a brain that has been injected with a radioactive substance. The substance—2-deoxyglucose, or 2-DG—is taken up by those neurons that are using the most energy (glucose). Light detectors built into a ring that surrounds the head capture the faint emissions from those neurons. A computer reconstructs a color picture of the neuronal activity, with the most active areas shown in red, the moderately active areas in yellow, and the least active in blue. For example, specific areas of the left hemisphere are shown to be more active than others when a human subject is engaged in various language tasks. Positron-emission tomography is also used to study other psychological functions, such as learning and memory. Even the brain activity associated with hallucinations has been recorded during the Pet scan of a schizophrenic patient.

More intriguing, however, are the results of tests done on patients whose two hemispheres have been surgically disconnected, an operation called the split-brain procedure.

dichotic listening test A test in which a subject is asked to repeat different numbers heard simultaneously in the left and right ear.

PET scan (positron-emission tomography) A method of visualizing actively functioning brain areas by measuring electrically charged particles.

The Split-Brain Procedure

Epilepsy is a term used to refer to a variety of nervous disorders characterized by spontaneous seizures, which at their worst can lead to unconsciousness, convulsions, or both. In a later section we'll see that the normal function of neurons is to transmit chemical information by means of a nervous impulse. A particularly severe form of epileptic seizure results from abnormally functioning neurons in the temporal lobe. When the discharge of these abnormal neurons spreads throughout large areas of the brain, affecting other neurons, convulsions occur. Figure 4.17 shows how the electrical discharge crosses from the left to the right hemisphere through the 200 million nerve fibers that connect the left and right hemispheres, a structure called the **corpus callosum** (from the Latin words meaning "firm body"). In severe cases, the resulting *grand mal* (French for "great evil") seizure may occur many times a day, each time causing life-threatening convulsions and unconsciousness.

Dilantin® and other medications can control epileptic seizures in many but not all patients. In the 1960s, neurosurgeons looking for an alternative to traditional drug therapy began to reevaluate an experimental surgery first performed in the 1940s. The idea underlying this surgery was to restrict the seizure to only one hemisphere by cutting the corpus callosum, the main bridge to the other hemisphere. In this **split-brain procedure,** the cortical tissue of the left and right hemispheres is carefully pulled back, exposing the white band of fibers making up the corpus callosum.

The surgeons first studied the results of a California research team (Roger Sperry, Michael Gazzaniga, and Joseph Bogen) that had measured the effects of such a procedure in monkeys (Sperry, 1964). Not only did the monkeys survive, but amazingly, their postsurgery behavior was not noticeably different. After much soul searching, Joseph Bogen and Philip Vogel cut the corpus callosum of several epileptic patients. The human patients, like the monkeys that preceded them, survived after having their cerebral hemispheres disconnected. Though the procedure did not cure their epilepsy, it did minimize both the frequency and the severity of the seizures in several dozen patients. Fortunately, antiseizure drugs developed over the past two decades have made the split-brain surgery a rare one.

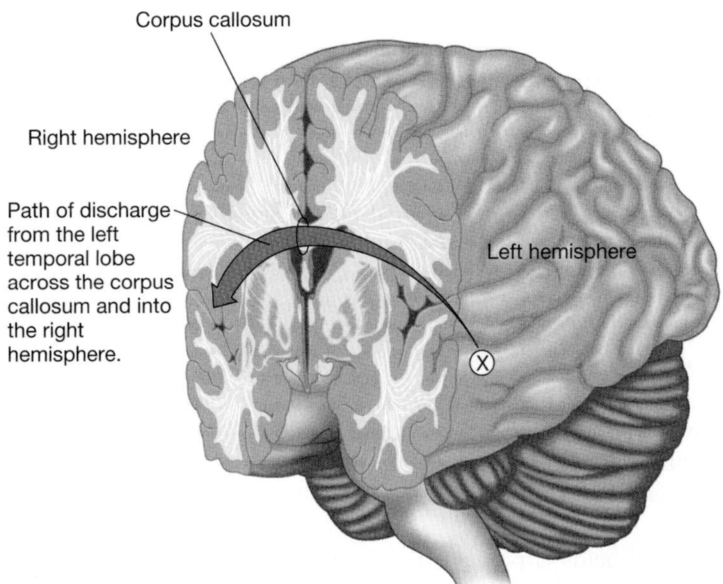

Figure 4.17 **The spread of an epileptic seizure.** The arrow shows how, during an epileptic seizure, the abnormal discharge of neurons on one side of the brain can spread to the other side through a large band of fibers called the corpus callosum. In split-brain surgery, the corpus callosum is severed to prevent transmission of the life-threatening seizures to the other side.

corpus callosum The broad band, or commissure, of fibers that connects the left and right hemispheres.

split-brain procedure Cutting the corpus callosum to disconnect the left and right cerebral hemispheres.

Careful study of the split-brain patients produced a radically different view of human consciousness and personality. So far we have studied the functions of the spinal cord, the hindbrain and midbrain structures, and the four lobes of the cerebral hemispheres, raising the issue of consciousness only occasionally. We saw, for example, that sensory input into the reticular formation, located in the brainstem, has the effect of arousing or alerting one to action. Drowsiness and alertness are certainly aspects of consciousness. We also saw that when Phineas Gage's frontal lobes were damaged, he was no longer the same person; both his behavior and his conscious experience changed. But just *where* is consciousness located?

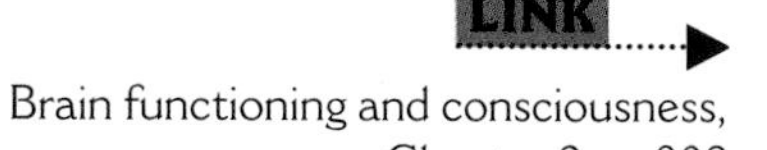
Brain functioning and consciousness, Chapter 9, p. 308

Early researchers who studied people with split brains began to suspect that human consciousness was lateralized—that is, that the left and right hemispheres expressed different kinds of consciousness. In 1968 Roger Sperry published an article titled "Hemisphere deconnection and unity in conscious awareness"; Joseph Bogen (1969) wrote another titled "The other side of the brain, II: An appositional mind." Splitting the human brain, these researchers hypothesized, split the human mind and consciousness as well. In a normal person with an intact corpus callosum, the possibility that different forms of consciousness might exist in each hemisphere was difficult to demonstrate, but in a split-brain patient, scientists might be able to do so.

Tests of Split-Brain Patients

Figure 4.18 shows a typical test used to measure the lateralization of function in a split-brain subject. A screen allows the subject to feel—but not see—a variety of test objects with one or the other hand. In addition, simple words can be flashed briefly onto a screen so that they are presented to only one hemisphere. This testing methodology allows an independent assessment of how each side of the brain processes tactile (touch) information and visual information, including words.

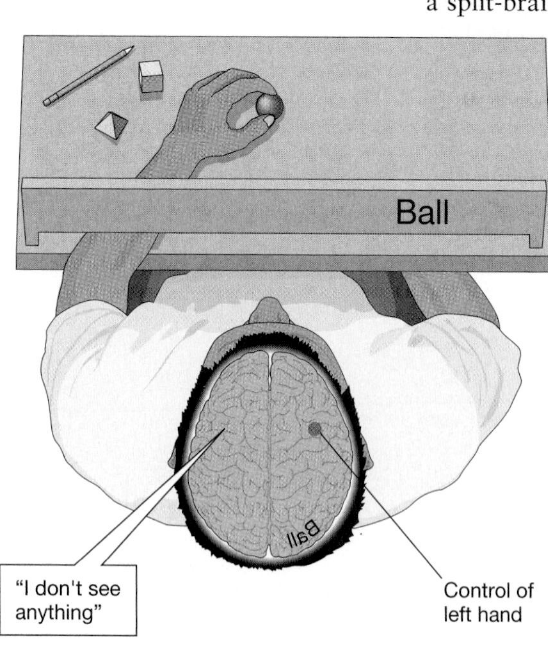

Figure 4.18 What the split-brain patient sees and hears. After recovery from split-brain surgery, patients are tested with an apparatus that restricts their visual field to one hemisphere or the other. The word *Ball* is displayed in a portion of the patient's visual field that sends information only to the right hemisphere. Patients are then asked to feel and squeeze a ball with the left hand. Under these conditions, the patient's speaking left hemisphere is not conscious of seeing the word or using the left hand. From NEUROSCIENCE: Exploring the Brain by M. F. Bear, B. W. Connors & M. A. Paradiso. Copyright © 1996. Reprinted by permission of Lippincott Williams & Wilkins.

Figure 4.18 also shows the parts of the brain a split-brain subject uses in attempting to locate an unseen ball by feeling with the left hand. Sensory nerves coming from the left hand enter and cross in the spinal cord, then ascend and arrive at the right thalamus and right somatosensory strip (you might want to review Figure 4.11). The movement of the left hand is initiated by nerves originating in the primary motor area on the right side of the brain (as seen in Figure 4.16). Sensory-motor control of the left hand, then, is accomplished by the right hemisphere.

Visual information is handled differently, however. As shown in Figure 4.18, the word *Ball* can be briefly flashed onto a screen in such a way that it is seen only in the primary visual cortex of the *right* hemisphere. This is possible because the right half of the visual field is processed only in the primary visual cortex on the right side. By asking a person to look straight ahead and focus on a fixation point, researchers can flash a word or picture onto the right visual field.

In a normal (unsplit) brain, an image visible in the right and left visual fields is processed in both hemispheres, because visual information in the right primary visual cortex is communicated to the left, and vice versa, through the corpus callosum. But when the corpus callosum is severed, peripheral vision is processed in only one hemisphere. The cortex on the opposite side of the brain cannot receive the information, because the nerve fibers that carry it have been cut.

Language and Awareness. What happened, then, to the split-brain subject when the word *Ball* was flashed to the left visual cortex? Because the left *visual* cortex is located in the same hemisphere as the left *speaking* cortex, a split-brain subject, like a normal subject, could read the word and say "ball." But what happened when the word *Ball* was flashed to right visual cortex (located in the non-speaking right hemisphere)? Although a normal subject could read the word and say "ball," a split-brain subject would say "I don't see anything." The explanation for this curious phenomenon is that in a normal person, the visual information crosses the corpus callosum and is available to the left, or "speaking" hemisphere—a brain function no longer possible when the corpus callosum has been cut. To report seeing something, a person must be "aware" of what he or she sees—which the left hemisphere in a split-brain patient is not. Thus, *seeing with awareness* depends on an intact left hemisphere. Curiously, there are people who can see without awareness; we'll learn about them in Chapter 7.

Conscious and unconscious seeing, Chapter 8, p. 282

How did researchers know that the right hemisphere saw the ball? After all, when asked, the subjects replied, "I don't see anything." Research by Mike Gazzaniga provides evidence that the right hemisphere *can* see the word *Ball*; it just can't talk about it. When the split-brain subject is asked to find an object with the name *Ball*, he or she can pick out the ball from a variety of objects, but can do so only with the left hand. The subject cannot pick out the correct object with the right hand (controlled by the left hemisphere, which never saw the word). Even though it is mute, only the right hemisphere knows what the word was, so only it can control the left hand. If an object such as a pencil or ball is covertly placed in the subject's left hand, the subject acts as if it isn't there, presumably because the subject can't talk about it. These tests indicate that although both hemispheres receive information, and each can act independently of the other (Gazzaniga, 1967, 1998), only the left hemisphere can receive information that must be talked about. They also suggest that the right hemisphere is the seat of an awareness that cannot be put into words.

The astute reader may have noticed that even if the right hemisphere can't speak, it must have *some* language capabilities. Otherwise, how could it direct the left hand to pick up the ball after the word *Ball* was flashed to it? Gazzaniga's research and other testing methods have since shown that the right hemisphere does process some language, including simple words such as the noun *ball* and some verbs. Thus subjects can respond to the researcher's simple verbal directions using only the right hemisphere. But to comprehend more complex language, they must use the left hemisphere.

Emotion and Artistic Abilities. A chance finding by Gazzaniga revealed an interesting form of nonverbal information processing (and nonverbal awareness) by the right hemisphere. During testing, photos of objects were being flashed to the nonspeaking right hemisphere of a woman whose corpus callosum had been cut. As expected, she consistently denied seeing any of them (apparently because she had no way to talk about what she was seeing). In response to a photo of a nude, however, she began to laugh. When asked what she was laughing about, she first said nothing, then said she was laughing at the researcher's "funny machine" (the slide projector). Like a ball reportedly not seen but retrieved from an assortment of objects, the nude image had an effect on the patient that she couldn't describe in words.

Right hemisphere localization of emotion, Chapter 5, p. 176

One way of interpreting this interesting finding is that language is associated with only one kind of consciousness. That is, a person can "know" and be "aware" in other ways that are inexpressible by language. In fact, the split-brain patient's right hemisphere must have had emotional knowledge about nudes. Artists and musicians, in particular, are aware of the limitations of language in expressing emotion and other forms of consciousness.

Besides emotion, the right hemisphere seems to specialize in spatial and artistic abilities. Gazzaniga (1970) reported that more than one right-handed subject could continue to write words and sentences after split-brain surgery, but could not draw very well. In fact, these subjects could draw better with the left hand after surgery, though they could not write words with it. One subject's left hand could draw a square when asked, but the right hand could draw only four disconnected corners. This and other research has revealed that the right hemisphere excels in *spatial abilities* and mechanical relationships (Levy, 1969); in judging the emotional content of mood and facial expressions (Bowers, Bauer, Coslett, & Heilman, 1985); and in the perception of melodies (Kimura, 1964).

Gazzaniga (1970) also reported that some postsurgery patients became more skilled with their hands, displaying a degree of ambidexterity that wasn't present in these patients when they had an intact corpus callosum. This positive benefit has been attributed to the removal of the inhibition each hemisphere exerts over the muscles on the opposite side of the body.

One Brain, Two Minds. Roger Sperry's and Mike Gazzaniga's most intriguing conclusion is that two minds resulted from splitting the brain. Under normal conditions—with an intact corpus callosum—the two hemispheres cooperate to make us of one mind. But as we'll see in the next chapter, the fact that people often experience conflicting thoughts, motivations, and emotions is in part due to hemispheric specialization.

One of Gazzaniga's findings, for instance, suggests the literal truth of a patient's right hand not knowing what the left is doing. The researcher noticed a male split-brain patient's left hand unbuttoning his pants and unbuckling his belt. At the same time the right hand was slapping the left hand, rebuttoning and rebuckling his pants. This finding indicates that each hemisphere can "intend" and initiate voluntary movements, which sometimes conflict. On yet another occasion, while playing horseshoes with a patient, Gazzaniga noticed that the patient's left hand had picked up and was swinging about a hand axe (out of sight, and apparently without the knowledge of, the speaking left hemisphere). The researcher intervened and disarmed the patient, musing to himself that he did not want to become the first victim of a criminal act in which the jury had to decide which hemisphere was guilty of committing a crime.

INTERIM SUMMARY

1. A variety of experimental methodologies have suggested a ***lateralization of function*** in the left and right cerebral hemispheres of the human brain.
2. When different spoken numbers are presented simultaneously into the left and right ear in a ***dichotic listening test,*** the right ear hears better than the left ear in those individuals for whom language processing is localized in the left hemisphere.
3. The Wada test, or sodium amytal test, involves anesthetizing the left or right hemisphere, temporarily blocking its normal functioning, in order to determine which hemisphere processes language.
4. Positron-emission tomography (***PET scans***) allows researchers to locate those parts of the brain that are most active during reading, dreaming, imagining, and other behavioral and psychological states.
5. In most males, language processing is more strongly lateralized than in females. Consequently, following an equivalent amount of brain damage to the left hemisphere, females have more residual language function than males.
6. In the past, some people who suffered from epilepsy had the ***corpus callosum*** cut to restrict seizures to only one hemisphere of the brain. Tests of the left and right hemispheres of such patients following this ***split-brain procedure*** have revealed a lateralization of brain function.

7. Split-brain subjects are tested by restricting the presentation of tactile and visual information to one or the other hemisphere and measuring subjects' responses. This methodology allows an assessment of how each side of the brain processes tactile (touch) and visual information, including words.
8. The right hemisphere of split-brain subjects allows them to retrieve unseen objects with the left hand, though they cannot talk about what they have successfully retrieved.
9. In most humans, language is processed in the left hemisphere; the right hemisphere appears to specialize in spatial abilities, detection of emotion, and melody recognition. Split-brain research has demonstrated that the right hemisphere does have some language abilities, however.
10. Split-brain research has provided support for a two-brain, two-mind model of consciousness. The seemingly unitary nature of consciousness is due in part to the functioning of an intact corpus callosum.

For Further Thought

1. In your experience, do males and females use language differently? How so? What might be the basis for these differences? (This topic will be further explored in Chapter 12, on language and thought.)
2. Even with an intact corpus callosum, humans often behave in ways that suggest that the right hand doesn't know what the left is doing. Can you relate such inconsistency in mood, thought, and behavior to a conflict between two different hemispheres, each with its own way of understanding the world?

NEURONS, NEUROTRANSMITTERS, AND DRUGS: THE MOLECULAR BASIS OF MIND AND BRAIN

Neurons were introduced earlier in this chapter to describe the sensory-motor reflex, one of the simplest functional units of vertebrate nervous systems. There we saw that sensory neurons detect information in the environment (touch, temperature, and so forth) and motor neurons cause muscle tissue to contract, allowing an organism to move. Perhaps because "moving a muscle" is conceptually simple, we tend to dismiss the role of neurons in accomplishing this basic *behavioral* unit. You may even think that a sensory-motor reflex is merely one of a number of rather uninteresting tasks that a living body does.

But what are we to make of the fact that similarly functioning neurons in the brain are responsible for your ability to read this text? And that other neurons are responsible for whether you are paying attention right now—or are about to nod off. Some of your neurons are helping you to tie the first part of this sentence to the last part in what is called your *short-term memory*. Yet others are responsible for your impatience with this long sentence, in a long paragraph, in a long chapter. Hope to do well on the next exam? You've got neurons responsible for your hope (or lack of it),

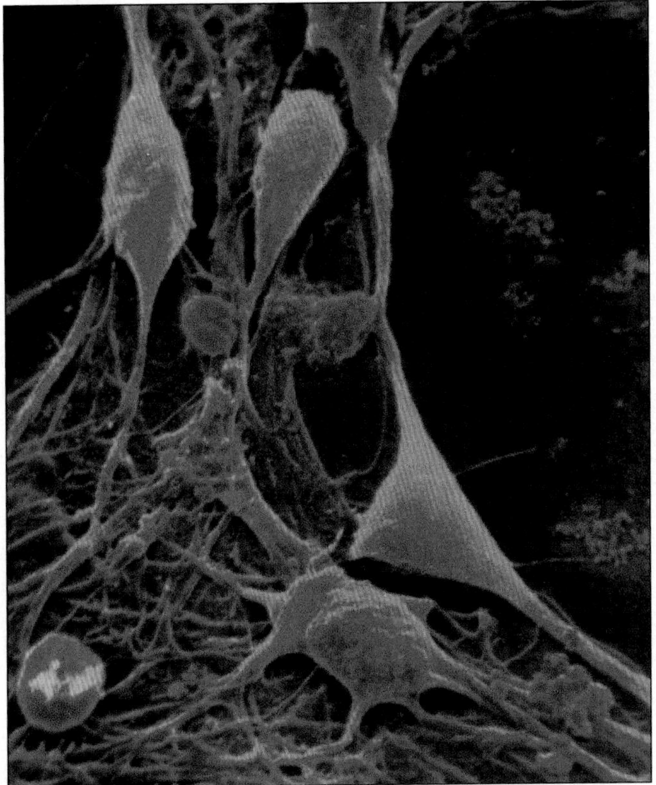

Several types of individual neurons found in different layers of the hippocampus.

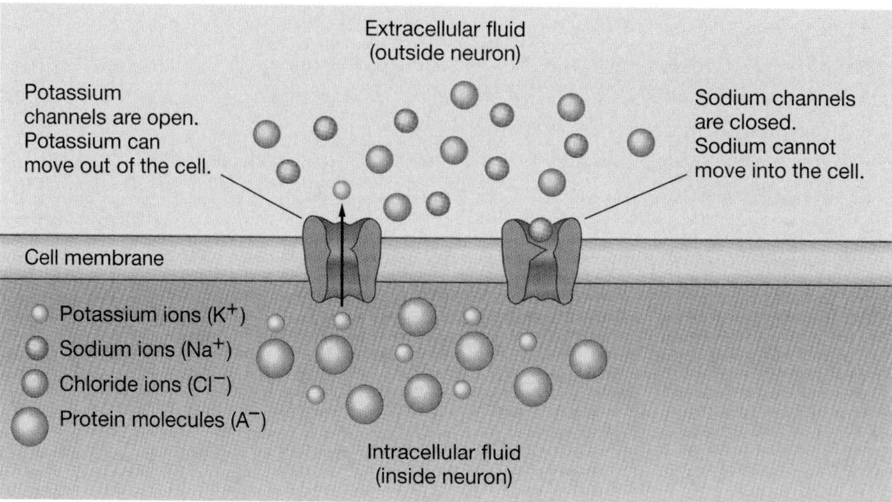

Figure 4.19 **The movement of ions through a neuron's membrane.** Channels allow the movement of ions through a neuron's membrane. Two factors determine the ions' movement: (1) whether the membrane's sodium and potassium channels are open or closed and (2) the balance of positive and negative charges of the ions and protein molecules on either side of the membrane.

your discipline in studying (or lack of it), your aptitude in psychology, and your performance on the exam. Consciousness, perception, learning, memory, personality—all are the result of the functioning of billions of neurons in your central nervous system. A few of these tiny marvels are shown in the photograph on page 137.

Neurons that sense events in the periphery of your body function somewhat differently from motor neurons. Likewise, neurons in the cerebellum are not the same as those in the temporal lobe, and all differ from the five types of neurons in the retina of your eye. Instead of describing any one of these, we'll first describe the functioning of a generic, unspecialized neuron, and then go on to discuss the way that drugs affect a neuron's functioning. Let's begin with a neuron at rest and focus on its remarkable membrane.

The Neuron's Membrane: The Key to Excitability

Actually, the membrane of a neuron is never "at rest." Figure 4.19 shows electrolytes in the form of sodium and potassium ions either moving through or trying to cross a membrane that separates the inside of a neuron from the outside. These ions, or electrolytes—so called because they carry a tiny positive or negative electric charge—are important because they are not "balanced." Their imbalance creates an electric charge across the membrane, called a *membrane potential.* Note in the figure that the potassium and sodium are both positively charged, whereas the chloride and proteins inside the cell are negatively charged. The potential across the cell membrane results from this unequal concentration of electrolytes inside the cell (in the intracellular fluid) relative to outside the cell (in the extracellular fluid).

If equal amounts of positive and negative charges existed both inside and outside the cell, the resting membrane potential would be zero. The normal **resting membrane potential,** or voltage across a resting neuron's membrane, is usually about −70 mV; it is measured by sticking an electrode through the cell wall of the neuron. The resting membrane potential is negative, not zero, because there are more negatively charged chemicals inside the cell and more positively charged chemicals outside. The cell is said to be at equilibrium (at rest) when these positive and negative charges are balanced, and there is no net movement of ions in or out of the cell.

When the resting potential is −70 mV, the neuron is "wired," or poised to discharge. Actually, one of two events can occur. A slight chemical disturbance of the membrane can cause a gradual change in the resting membrane potential (especially if the membrane in question is on either the dendrite or soma of a neuron). This effect is called a *graded potential.* The voltage may slowly increase or decrease, depending on the kind of chemical disturbance on the cell membrane.

resting membrane potential The voltage across a neuron's membrane at rest, usually about −70 mV.

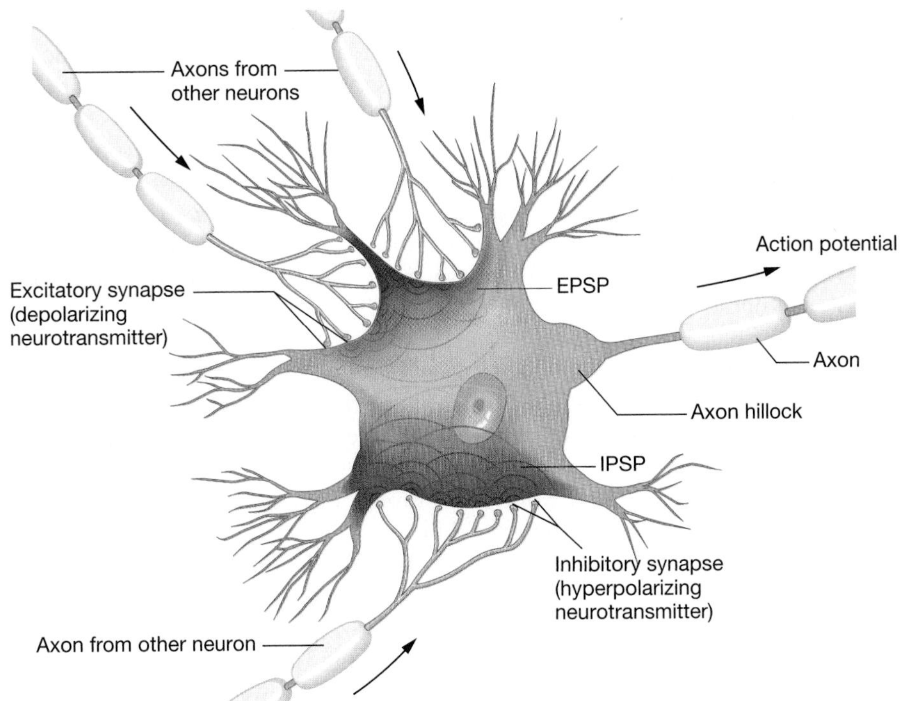

Figure 4.20 Depolarization and hyperpolarizing of a neuron. Some axon terminals secrete a neurotransmitter that depolarizes the target membrane, causing an excitatory postsynaptic potential (EPSP). Other neurotransmitters hyperpolarize the target membrane, causing an inhibitory postsynaptic potential (IPSP). These negative and positive charges spread passively across the membrane, tending to neutralize each other where they meet. Depending on the amount of neurotransmitter secreted onto the membrane, the depolarization (red) or hyperpolarization (green) may spread over the surface of the membrane by spatial or temporal summation, initiating an action potential.

However, if the graded electrical charge is great enough, the *entire neuron* can be triggered to discharge. This large nerve impulse, sometimes referred to as the firing or spiking of the neuron, is called an **action potential.**

An action potential can in turn disturb the resting membrane potential of other neurons, affecting their excitability. In fact, the action potential is one of the most important ways by which one neuron "talks" to another. Let's look more closely at the events leading up to the generation of an action potential. We will begin with a description of how a chemical disturbance can disrupt the resting membrane potential of a target neuron to produce a graded potential.

How to Excite a Neuron

Disruption of the membrane potential, and the generation of action potentials, begins with the chemical events taking place at synapse. You may want to take a second or two to review Figure 4.8, paying particular attention to how axon terminals synapse with both dendrites and the cell body of another neuron. The action takes place at the *synaptic cleft*, the microscopically thin gap that separates one neuron from another.

Figure 4.20 indicates what happens when a neurotransmitter—which can be any one of a variety of chemicals secreted by neurons—is released into the synaptic cleft. There the neurotransmitter makes contact with the membrane of another neuron. The axon terminal is sometimes referred to as *presynaptic* (because it initiates events at synapse), and the target membrane on the other side of the synaptic cleft as *postsynaptic* (because it is on the receiving end of synapse).

Depolarization and Hyperpolarization. Figure 4.20 shows how a neurotransmitter can activate another neuron (the target cell). The contact that causes the target membrane to be excited, called an *excitatory* synapse, decreases the resting membrane potential, *depolarizing* the membrane of the target neuron. This **depolarization** is localized, meaning that it affects only a small area of the target neuron's membrane. This type of graded potential is called an **excitatory postsynaptic potential,** or EPSP.

action potential A nerve impulse; the firing or spiking of a neuron.

depolarization A decrease in the membrane potential.

excitatory postsynaptic potential (EPSP) A local, graded excitatory potential that depolarizes a neuron's membrane.

Figure 4.20 shows EPSPs forming at several places of synapse on a cell membrane. Meanwhile, neurotransmitters from another neuron are producing the opposite effect where they make contact with the membrane: they are *inhibiting* the target cell's membrane potential. Like the other neurotransmitters, inhibitory neurotransmitters affect only a small area of the target neuron's membrane. Unlike the other transmitters, they tend to *hyper*polarize, or increase the resting membrane potential. For this reason **hyperpolarization**—an increase in the membrane potential—is called an **inhibitory postsynaptic potential**, or **IPSP**. Neurotransmitters that hyperpolarize the membrane, therefore, tend to work against, or inhibit, the depolarizing effects of EPSP.

How do EPSPs and IPSPs interact? Think about EPSPs and IPSPs as sexual foreplay. Some events are excitatory, bringing you closer to achieving orgasm; other events are inhibitory. EPSPs and IPSPs are the localized, graded potentials that spread passively toward the *axon hillock* (see Figure 4.20), the site that determines each neuron's threshold of excitability (approximately −65 mV in the example shown in Figure 4.21). Once this threshold is met—once the EPSP has depolarized the membrane at the axon hillock to −65mV—the neuron initiates the voltage changes known as an action potential (see Figure 4.21).

Spatial and Temporal Summation at the Axon Hillock. The axon hillock integrates the effects of multiple inputs from other neurons through the processes of *spatial* and *temporal summation*. Spatial summation (summation in space) occurs when neurotransmitters from several adjacent axon terminals excite an area of the membrane near the axon hillock. Temporal summation (summation in time) is caused by a rapidly firing neuron's excitatory neurotransmitter accumulating at the axon hillock. IPSPs, which act to block the excitatory effects on the axon hillock, can also summate spatially and temporally. If the EPSP overcomes the IPSP at the axon hillock, the neuron generates an action potential.

The Action Potential

Figures 4.19 and 4.22 show that the cell membrane of a neuron, including its axon, has pores, or channels, though which ions can pass. The rapid movement of ions through the membrane is the mechanism underlying an action potential. At rest, more sodium ions (Na^+) are outside, and more potassium ions (K^+) are inside the axon. Depolarization of the membrane to its threshold level at the axon hillock has the effect of opening both sodium and potassium channels in the membrane for about 0.5 msec. During this brief time, the Na^+ ions rush into the cell and the voltage across the membrane rises rapidly, from −70 mV (past zero volts) to about +50 mV. In response, potassium ions (K^+) rush out of the cell through their channels, eventually reversing the membrane's polarity. This K^+ ion movement triggers the adjacent Na^+ channels to close, rendering the membrane resistant to any further outflow of Na^+ ions. As Figure 4.22 shows, in another fraction of a second, the resting membrane potential is restored, and the neuron is ready to discharge again.

The All-or-None Principle. As Figure 4.22 shows, the depolarizing effect of an action potential on the cell membrane quickly spreads to adjacent areas of the axon. The result is that the action potential travels down the length of the axon, an event called a *nerve impulse* (or nerve "firing" or "spiking"). Shortly after the action potential has passed a portion of the axon, the K^+ and Na^+ ions resume their resting membrane condition, as shown in the figure. An axon cannot "half-discharge"; once the neuron's threshold has been reached, a complete action potential follows, and the nerve fires. This all-or-nothing relationship is known as the **all-or-none principle.** Following an action potential, a brief time

hyperpolarization An increase in the membrane potential.

inhibitory postsynaptic potential (IPSP) A local, graded excitatory potential that hyperpolarizes a neuron's membrane.

all-or-none principle The rule that when the electrical change in a neuron exceeds a threshold voltage, an action potential must follow.

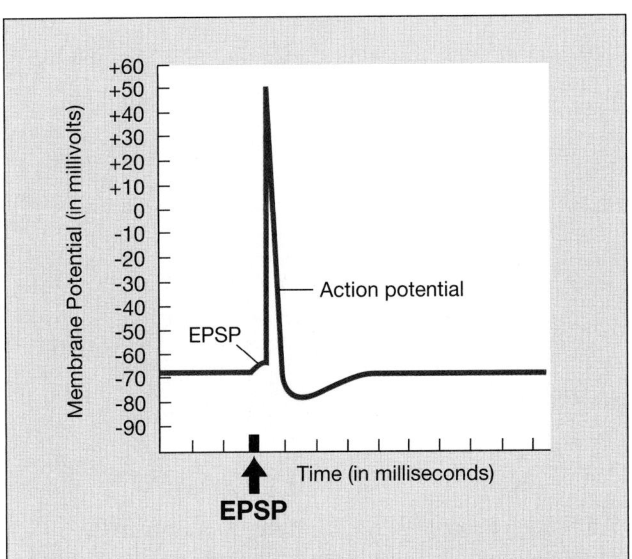

Figure 4.21 **The firing of a neuron.** An action potential results when the resting membrane potential of about –70 mV becomes depolarized (by an EPSP) beyond a threshold level of –65 mV. The sodium gates on the membrane open and sodium ions rush in, causing the voltage to rapidly approach +50 mV, an all-or-none event called a nerve spike or action potential. Then the gates close, and the resting membrane potential is quickly restored.

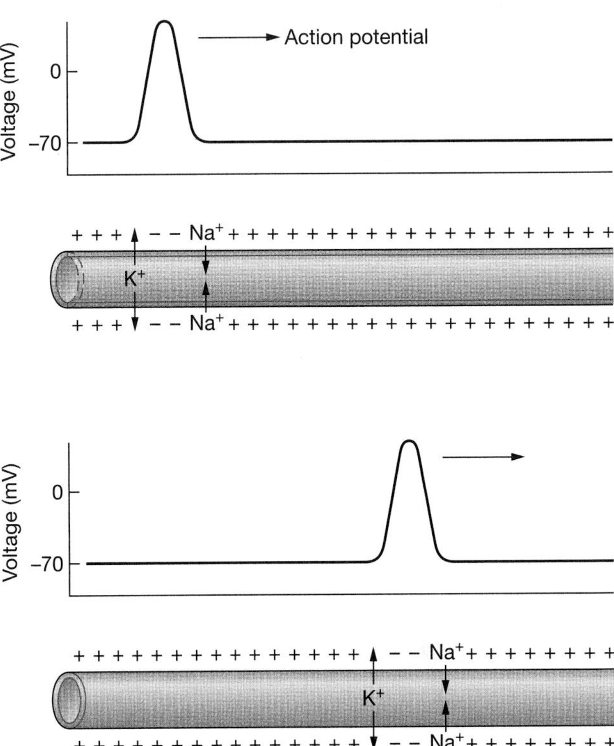

Figure 4.22 **The discharge of an action potential.** As an action potential discharges down an axon, it causes momentary changes in the movement of ions inside and outside the axon's membrane. The change in voltage from –70mV to about +50 mV is caused by sodium ions rapidly entering the cell and then exiting just as quickly.

called a *refractory period* must pass before another action potential can be generated. Nevertheless, a given neuron can discharge repeatedly if the axon hillock remains depolarized below its threshold. Some neurons can fire up to 1,000 times per second (Kolb & Whishaw, 1996).

Myelin-covered axons conduct impulses faster than unmyelinated axons. When myelin covers the axons, K^+ and Na^+ ion movement can occur *only* at the nodes of Ranvier, the gaps in the myelin-covered axon (see Figure 4.8). The result is that the action potential jumps rapidly from node to node in a process called *saltatory conduction* (saltatory from the Latin for "to leap"). The gain in speed is substantial: the one-meter-long, large-diameter myelinated axons that run from Shaquille O'Neal's toes to his spinal cord conduct nerve impulses at about 100 meters per second. In contrast, small, unmyelinated fibers conduct impulses at a rate of only 1 to 2 meters per second.

Myelinated axons allow nerve impulses to be rapidly conducted.

The Release of Neurotransmitters. Because the chemical events that occur at synapse are more complicated than the present description allows (see Kolb & Whishaw, 1996), here we will assume that each neuron makes and releases but one neurotransmitter. Figure 4.23 indicates what happens when an action potential is conducted past the myelin sheath and arrives at an axon terminal. The axon terminal makes a synaptic connection with a target neuron. Simply put, the action potential starts the release of a neurotransmitter into the synaptic cleft.

How does this event happen? First, each neuron synthesizes its own particular neurotransmitter, which is stored in *vesicles* within the axon terminal. The action potential has the effect of opening calcium (Ca^{++}) channels in the axon

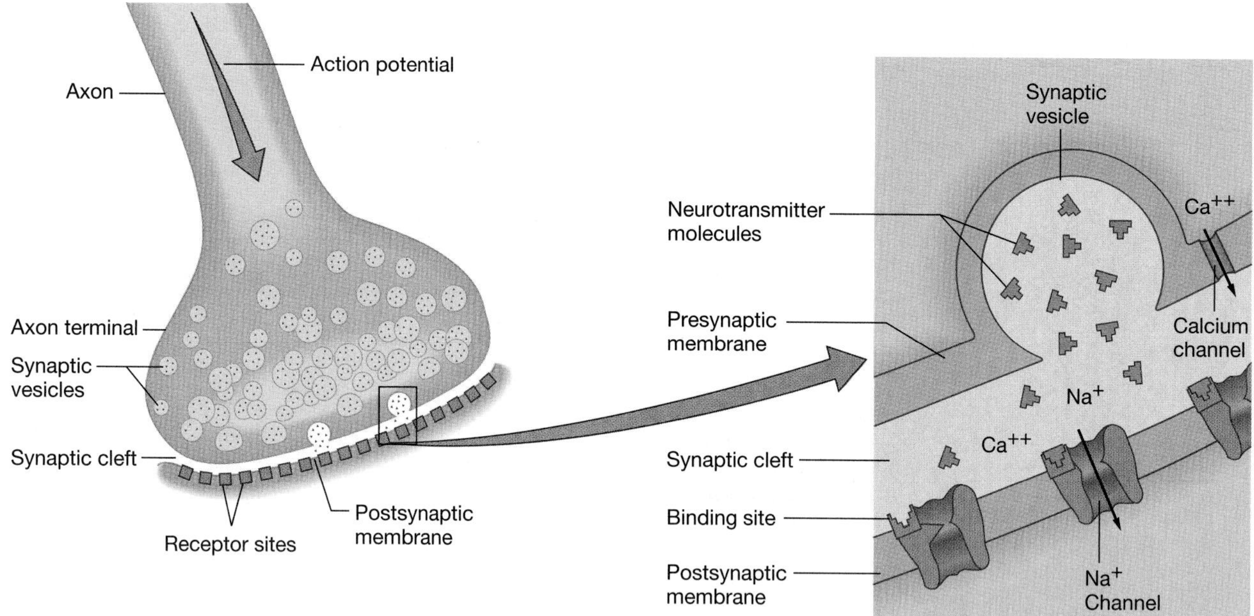

Figure 4.23 The release of neurotransmitters at synapse. An action potential pushes the synaptic vesicles to the surface of the axon terminal. There the vesicles release a neurotransmitter into the synaptic cleft. Channels in both the presynaptic membrane (the axon terminal) and the postsynaptic membrane (the target neuron) allow sodium and calcium to move in and out of the synaptic cleft. A neurotransmitter has a distinctive molecular shape that fits a receptor site on the postsynaptic membrane the way a key fits a lock. It can have either an excitatory or inhibitory effect on the target neuron.

terminals, allowing Ca^{++} to enter the cell. Figure 4.23 shows that the entry of Ca^{++} causes the vesicles to fuse with the membrane wall of the axon terminal. The vesicle's cell wall opens, spilling its contents into the synaptic cleft. Should the frequency of action potentials arriving at the axon terminals increase, more Ca^{++} would enter the cell, causing more vesicles to merge with the terminal's membrane and open, dumping more neurotransmitter into the synaptic cleft. Once the neurotransmitter is in the synaptic cleft, its distinctively shaped molecules find receptor sites located adjacent to the Na^{+} channels in the target neuron's membrane. This place on the postsynaptic membrane is called the binding site, or receptor site.

Olds' experiments, Chapter 2, p. 33

Neurotransmitters and Their Effects

To describe in detail the chemical differences of the various neurotransmitters and how they interact with drugs (a field called neuropharmacology) is beyond the scope of this text; here we can provide only an overview. Table 4.3 groups some common neurotransmitters into five classes and describes their primary functions. A given neurotransmitter can have an excitatory or inhibitory effect. Each has a particular shape that can be thought of as a key. The postsynaptic membrane has receptor sites that can be characterized as locks into which the keys may or may not fit (Changeax, 1993). The neurons that secrete different neurotransmitters differ both in their location in the brain and in their specific functioning.

Each neurotransmitter has its own special effect. For example, the neurotransmitter dopamine, listed in Table 4.3, has an effect that we discussed in connection with James Olds's self-stimulating rat experiments (see page 38). Did the rats experience "pleasure" when they pressed the bar and received brain stimulation? Olds proposed that in rats, pleasure has both an anatomical and a chemical nature. He succeeded in reinforcing the rats' behavior when he placed electrodes

Table 4.3 Neurotransmitters and Their Actions

CLASS		NEUROTRANSMITTER	ACTION
Acetylcholine		**Acetylcholine**	Contracts muscle tissue; active in ANS, CNS
Amino acids		**Glutamate**	Excitatory in CNS; EPSP
		Aspartate	Excitatory in CNS
		Glycine	Excitatory in CNS
		GABA	Inhibitory in CNS; IPSP
Monoamines		**Dopamine**	Excitatory (found primarily in the brainstem)
	Catecholamines	**Epinephrine**	Excitatory (found primarily in the brainstem)
		Norepinephrine	Excitatory (found primarily in the brainstem)
	Indolamines	**Serotonin**	Excitatory (found primarily in the brainstem)
Soluble gases		Nitric oxide	
		Carbon monoxide	Stimulates the production of other chemical messengers
Neuropeptides	**Endorphins**	ß-endorphin, others	Activates neural systems to produce analgesia, pleasure
Other peptides		Cholecystokinin	Activates neural systems to produce satiety

Source: After Pinel, 1997.

in an area of the brain called the medial forebrain bundle (MFB), whose nerve fibers pass through the hypothalamus. These fibers release the neurotransmitter *dopamine* (see Vaccarino, Schiff, & Glickman, 1989, for a review). Electrical stimulation of the brain (ESB) produces action potentials in MFB pathways, causing the release of dopamine in the brainstem—and likely an intense experience of pleasure in the rat.

Using the lock and key analogy, dopamine fits dopamine receptors, but a different neurotransmitter—acetylcholine, for example—will not; acetylcholine fits only acetylcholine receptors. Acetylcholine is the neurotransmitter neurons secrete onto muscle fibers; it is also found in both the central nervous system and the autonomic nervous system. Both dopamine and acetylcholine differ in their action from another class of neurotransmitters, amino acids, including *glutamate*. Glutamate has excitatory effects, but *GABA*, a different amino acid, is an inhibitory neurotransmitter. Other excitatory neurotransmitters include epinephrine, norepinephrine, and serotonin. A distinctive class of chemicals called *neuropeptides* also functions as a neurotransmitter. *Endorphin,* for example, is a neuropeptide that stimulates other neurons in the brain and spinal cord to produce analgesia (pain relief) and the experience of pleasure. Another neuropeptide, *cholecystokinin*, is released following a meal and produces satiety, the sensation of feeling full.

Endorphins and pain, Chapter 7, p. 265

This brief summary of the action of neurotransmitters does not do justice to the incredible stories presently unfolding in neuroscience and neuropharmacology laboratories around the world. Fifty years ago, only two transmitters, one excitatory and one inhibitory, were known to exist. Table 4.3 lists just a few of many dozens of neurotransmitters that have since been discovered in humans and other animals. Others made by other neurons in other parts of the brain are the source of our motivation and emotion, our voluntary behavior, the ways in which we learn and remember, and other aspects of our consciousness. Still other chemicals have been discovered that exhibit some but not all characteristics of a neurotransmitter. Finally, we have seen that humans share DNA with other animals

Drugs interfere with the normal actions of neurotransmitters.

and even plants. Thus we should not be surprised to learn that we also share some of the same neurotransmitters. Hsieh, Lam, van de Loo, and Coruzzi (1998) have reported finding genes in a weed, *Arabidopsis*, that encode for receptors sensitive to the neurotransmitter glutamate.

The Effect of Drugs on Neurotransmitters

When medicines and drugs (both legal and illegal) are taken into the body, they affect the processes of neurotransmitter release and reception. Many drugs and medicines come from plants; each has its own effect. For reasons that are not understood, these plant-derived substances either fit particular brain receptors or otherwise change the normal functioning of neurons at synapse. Drugs and medicines can act on both the pre- and postsynaptic membranes, speeding up or slowing down the processes that occur in the synaptic cleft. Cocaine, for example, increases the activity of two naturally occurring neurotransmitters, dopamine and norepinephrine, by interfering with the way they normally function.

Drugs, brain functioning, and consciousness, Chapter 9, p. 332

Normal Action of Neurotransmitters. To better understand how individual drugs affect neurotransmitters, we must first take a closer look at what happens in the synaptic cleft. Figure 4.24 shows an axon terminal, a target neuron, and the fate of neurotransmitters secreted into the synaptic cleft. One of three events can occur:

- The neurotransmitter can find and activate receptors in the postsynaptic membrane, resulting in either an EPSP or an IPSP.
- Unused, the neurotransmitter can reenter the presynaptic membrane, a process called *reuptake.*
- The neurotransmitter can be deactivated by enzymes already present in the synaptic cleft, a process called *enzymatic degradation.*

These three actions keep the synaptic cleft relatively clear of neurotransmitters. For example, each action potential of a neuron that secretes dopamine releases a finite amount of neurotransmitter into the synaptic cleft. Dopamine has a limited effect on the postsynaptic, or target, membrane, because the three events just described inevitably reduce the amount of the neurotransmitter available at the postsynaptic site.

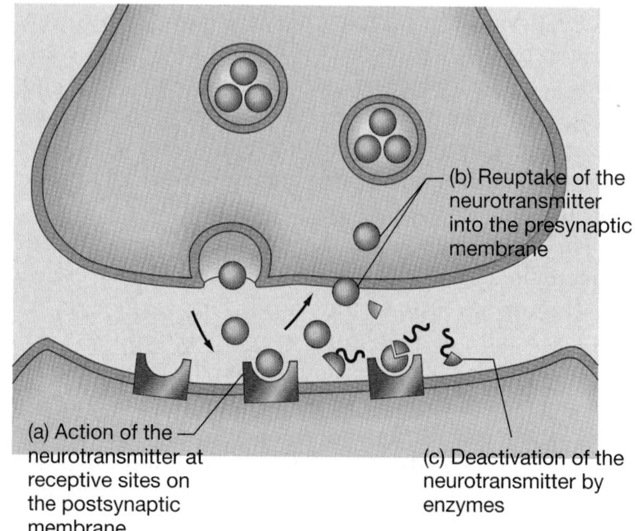

Figure 4.24 The secretion of neurotransmitters into the synaptic cleft. Once neurotransmitters have been secreted into the synaptic cleft, they can (a) act on receptive sites in the postsynaptic membrane, in either an excitatory or inhibitory way; (b) be absorbed by the presynaptic membrane, a process called reuptake; or (c) be deactivated by an enzyme.

Drug-Altered Action of Neurotransmitters. Now suppose cocaine is added to the other chemicals in the synaptic cleft. Cocaine acts by blocking the reuptake of the dopamine molecule. This artificial blockade allows the number of dopamine molecules in the cleft to rise, which tends to keep the postsynaptic membrane depolarized for extended periods. Euphoria, insomnia, and appetite suppression result. The addictive properties of cocaine are a result of the excessive stimulation of dopamine receptors.

Curare, a poison extracted from a plant, has a different mechanism of action. Long ago, indigenous South Americans discovered that curare-tipped arrows could be used to hunt animals. Normally, the neurotransmitter acetylcholine binds to receptors in muscle cells, resulting in their contraction and ultimately, in movement. But curare finds its way to the synaptic clefts and blocks the postsynaptic receptor sites on the muscle fibers, preventing the acetylcholine released by motor neurons from causing EPSPs. When the receptor sites on muscles throughout the body are blocked in this manner, the result is paralysis.

A South American man using a blowgun and curare-tipped arrow

Other drugs affect neurotransmitters in a myriad of ways. Those that either mimic or enhance the actions of neurotransmitters are called *agonists*, whereas those that block or inhibit neurotransmitters are called *antagonists*. Cocaine has an agonistic effect because it enhances the action of dopamine. Curare can be considered to have an antagonistic effect because it blocks the receptor sites for acetylcholine. Drugs can either aid or inhibit the action of neurotransmitters, then. In doing so they cause changes in behavior and psychological functioning.

INTERIM SUMMARY

1. Each neuron has a ***resting membrane potential***—an electrical voltage measuring about –70 mV that results from the presence of more positively charged sodium ions outside the cell membrane than inside.
2. A graded electrical change in a target neuron can disturb the resting membrane potential, causing either ***depolarization*** or ***hyperpolarization***.
3. Depolarization occurs when pores, or channels, in the membrane open, briefly allowing sodium (Na^+) to enter the cell. Depolarization causes an ***excitatory postsynaptic potential (EPSP)***, whereas hyperpolarization causes an ***inhibitory postsynaptic potential (IPSP)***.
4. A membrane's polarization can change as a result of both *spatial* and *temporal summation*. Such changes in polarization spread passively across the neuron's membrane toward the *axon hillock*.
5. If the threshold of depolarization at the axon hillock is exceeded, an ***action potential*** is generated. Sodium ions rush into the cell and potassium ions (K^+) exit, reversing the cell's polarity.
6. Unlike graded potentials, action potentials follow an ***all-or-none principle***. The action potential is rapidly conducted down the axon to the axon terminals. Axons that are covered in myelin sheaths conduct action potentials more quickly by allowing them to "leap" from one gap in the sheath to the next, a process called *saltatory conduction*.
7. Action potentials cause the release of neurotransmitters into the *synaptic cleft*. These neurotransmitters are synthesized in the axon, stored in *vesicles*, and released when calcium enters the presynaptic membrane, disrupting the integrity of the vesicle.
8. Various types of neurotransmitters are secreted onto target neurons. Each neurotransmitter has a molecular configuration that can be thought of as a key that activates a specific lock (receptor site) on target neurons.

9. Once a neurotransmitter has been released into the synaptic cleft, three events can follow: it can cause either an EPSP or an IPSP on the postsynaptic membrane of the target neuron; it can reenter the presynaptic membrane (*reuptake*); or it can be deactivated by *enzymatic degradation.*
10. Dopamine is a neurotransmitter that produces pleasurable sensations when it activates receptor sites in the brainstem. Cocaine blocks the reuptake of dopamine in the synaptic cleft, causing the accumulation of large amounts of dopamine, which keep the postsynaptic receptors activated.
11. Drugs can act as *agonists* or *antagonists* to the normal functioning of neurotransmitters. Drug agonists aid or mimic neurotransmitters, whereas drug antagonists block or inhibit their action by binding to the same receptor sites on the target neuron or interfering with the reuptake of the neurotransmitter.

For Further Thought

1. Now that you know how neurons function and how drugs affect neurotransmitters, are you better prepared to discuss the mind-body problem? For example, the release of dopamine and activation of the dopamine receptor are physical in nature (body), but their action seems to produce "pleasure," a characteristic of the mind. (Recall from Chapter 1 that a monist would say that both "neurotransmitter" and "pleasure" are two ways to describe the same event, whereas a dualist would say they are two separate events.)
2. The firing of a neuron was described in terms of sexual foreplay that leads to orgasm. Can you complete the analogy by explaining what is meant by a neuron's *refractory period*?
3. People whose neurons don't secrete enough dopamine tend to be unhappy and depressed. Any suggestions for therapy?
4. Why are some people quicker than others—in running, in their ability to solve problems, and in their rate of speech? Do you suspect these differences are due to differences in their brains, cultural differences, or both?
5. Should drugs, medicinal or otherwise, be used to enhance human performance? (This conversation will continue in Chapter 9.)

CONCLUDING THOUGHTS

One implication of the fact that all life on earth has a common genetic heritage is that human and animal brains share certain similarities. This chapter has extended the genetic comparison of animals to a comparison of their brain anatomy, brain physiology, and psychology. Both the human and nonhuman animal minds are the product of the way their brains function. The brains of all vertebrates—large and small—allow for sensing, moving, learning, and remembering. Humans share parts of the brain in common with these other animals, which allow each of us to see, hear, taste, smell, and experience pain. Thanks to common brain structures, fish, frogs, snakes, birds, rats, cats, dogs, monkeys, and humans all eat, sleep, reproduce, find prey, and avoid predators.

But the differences between humans and other animals are enormous. Perhaps the greatest value of the comparative method is in pinpointing and highlighting human distinctiveness. Humans not only have one of the larger brains on earth (because they are among the largest animals on earth); they also have a large brain compared to their body size. Furthermore, compared to other animals, a greater proportion of this large brain is made up of an elaborate outer covering called the cerebral hemispheres. The cerebral hemispheres have some unique properties. Unlike much of the rest of the brain, cortical neurons are designed to make new associations by connecting sensory systems with motor systems, and to exert control over impulses that arise in subcortical structures. What sets humans apart from other animals, then, is that the cerebral hemispheres allow them a capacity for thought and language that can override their instinctive tendencies.

The human brain is specialized for different functions: the left side is involved more with language and the right side more with spatial abilities and emotion. A variety of research methods, including the study of people whose brains have been split, has revealed the relationship between these aspects of mental life and different parts of the brain. The axons and dendrites of neurons that connect the separate parts of the brain—especially the millions of nerve pathways in the corpus callosum—produce a *connectedness of consciousness* that is seamless in experience.

A nervous system organizes an animal's adaptive response to the environment through its three main functions: receiving information, processing it, and acting on it. Sensory receptors take in information, after which integrative centers in the spinal cord and brain process it. Finally, an animal acts on the information by responding adaptively. The basic building block of the nervous system, the neuron, functions in a similar way: each neuron receives, processes, and acts on information. Specialized dendrites receive information in the form of neurotransmitters. The nerve cell then integrates this information in the form of EPSPs and IPSPs. Finally, the neuron acts by secreting a neurotransmitter onto another neuron or muscle tissue. The functioning of each neuron, then, is a model in miniature of the way the entire nervous system works.

Neurons and their neurotransmitters are responsible for distinct psychological states. In ways scientists are only beginning to understand, neurons in the visual system allow us to see, dopamine neurons allow us experience pleasure, and combinations of neurons in the associative cortex allow us to wonder about our existence. By enhancing or inhibiting the normal functioning of neurotransmitters, medicines and drugs affect the perception of pain, pleasure, and other psychological states. This evidence, together with the results of brain stimulation studies and an analysis of people who have sustained brain damage, leads to the conclusion that human consciousness arises from chemical events in the brain. In Dennett's (1995) words, human brains "have features lacking in other brains . . . that make possible an enormous elaboration of powers."

KEY TERMS

action potential *139*
all-or-none principle *140*
autonomic nervous system (ANS) *113*
axon *117*
brainstem *110*
cell body *117*
central nervous system (CNS) *113*
central sulcus *124*
cerebellum *110*
cerebral cortex *108*
cerebral hemispheres *108*
corpus callosum *133*
corticalization *108*
cranial nerves *110*
dendrites *117*
depolarization *139*
dichotic listening test *132*
excitatory postsynaptic potential (EPSP) *139*
forebrain *108*
frontal lobe *124*
hindbrain *108*
hyperpolarization *140*
hypothalamus *110*
inhibitory postsynaptic potential (IPSP) *140*
lateral fissure *124*
lateralization of function *131*
longitudinal fissure *124*
medulla *110*
midbrain *108*
myelin *118*
neuroendocrine system *116*
neurogenesis *129*
neurons *113*
neurotransmitter *118*
occipital lobe *124*
parasympathetic division *116*
parietal lobe *124*
peripheral nervous system (PNS) *113*
PET scan *132*
resting membrane potential *138*
reticular formation *122*
somatic nervous system *113*
spinal cord *110*
split-brain procedure *133*
sympathetic division *116*
synapse *118*
temporal lobe *124*
thalamus *108*

5

Motivation and Emotion

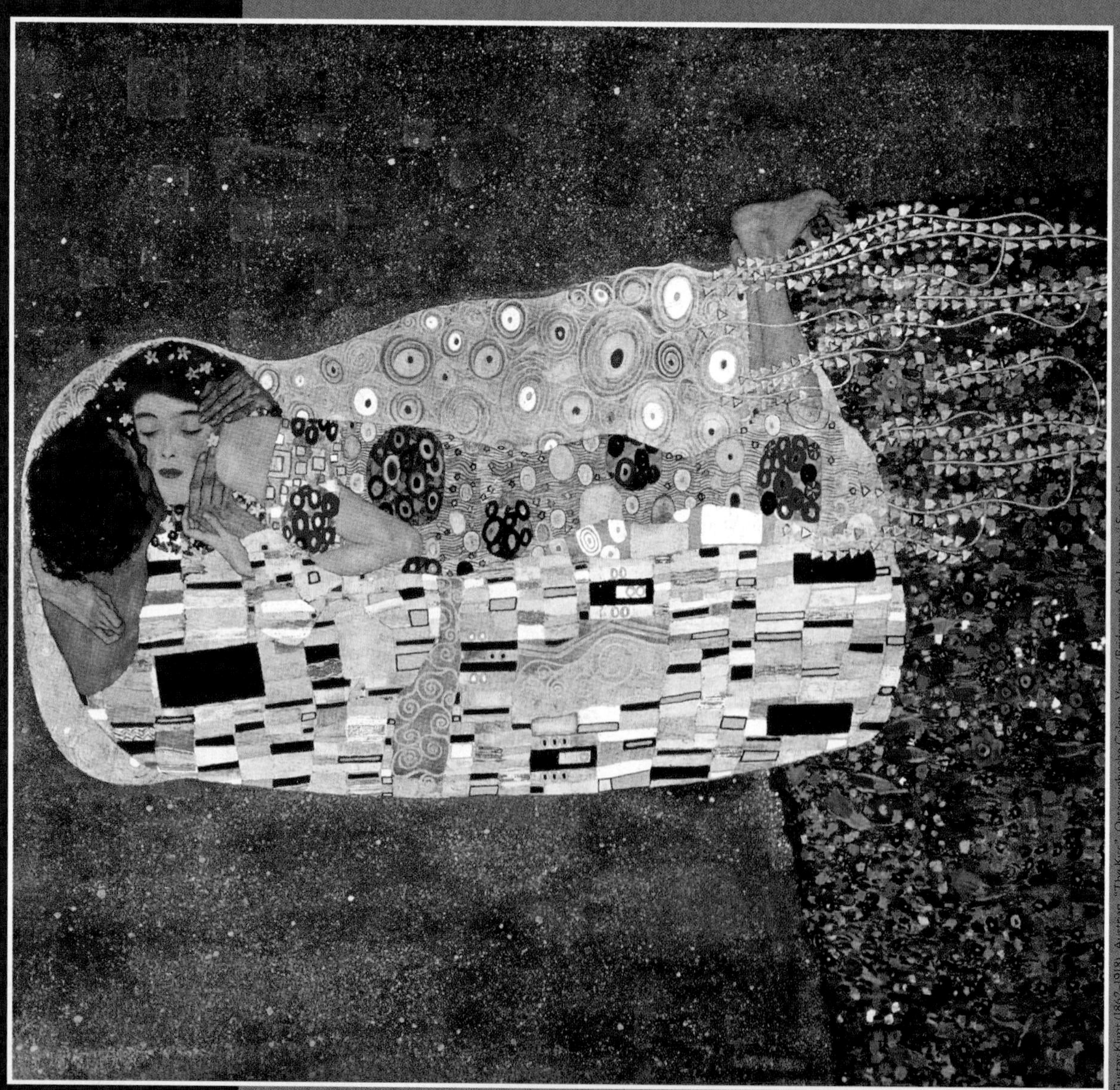

Gustav Klimt (1862–1918). Austrian, "The Kiss". Osterreichische Galerie, Vienna/Bridgeman Art Library / SuperStock.

Motivation Defined

Physiological Bases of Motivation
The Neuroendocrine System
Homeostasis
Behavioral Regulation of Body States
Interim Summary
For Further Thought

Eating: Satisfying Hunger and Enjoying Foods
Multifactorial Motivation
Two Types of Feeding Systems
Nutritional Wisdom
Evolutionary Origins of Human Food Selection
Brain Mechanisms and Feeding
Interim Summary
For Further Thought

Pleasure
Brain Mechanisms Underlying Pleasure
Pleasure Seeking in Rats
Pleasure Seeking in Humans
Maslow's Hierarchy of Needs
Extrinsic versus Intrinsic Motivators
The Need for Achievement
Interim Summary
For Further Thought

The Experience of Emotion
Evolutionary and Genetic Determinants of Emotion
Cultural Expressions of Emotion
Biological Bases of Emotion
Theories of Emotion
Interim Summary
For Further Thought

Concluding Thoughts

Born in the 1930s, a child known only by his initials, D.W., was sickly throughout his short life. Soon after birth he rejected both his mother's milk and the milk of other animals. A watery, salted gruel kept him alive his first 2 years, but the nutritionally inadequate diet slowed his physical, mental, and emotional development.

After about a year and a half, D.W. began to talk. His first words were "Ma-ma," "Wa-wa," and "Salt." His mother described D.W.'s behavior at this time:

> *. . . as soon as he knew what the word "water" meant, he would cry for it every time he heard the word mentioned. And when he saw the river or the ocean, he always thought he had to have some to drink.*

And then D.W. discovered the salt shaker:

> *He poured some out and ate it by dipping his finger in it. After this he wouldn't eat any food without having the salt, too. . . . He really cried for it and acted like he had to have it.* (Wilkins & Richter, 1940, p. 867)

D.W.'s obsession with salt and water influenced not only the first words he spoke, but also how at a very young age he looked through magazines for pictures of lakes and heavily "salted" the imaginary meals he prepared. All children drink their bath water, but D.W. had to be forcibly restrained from doing so.

These deviations from "normal" behavior can be seen as adaptive attempts to cope with a failing physiology. For unknown to his parents at the time, cancer cells were invading D.W.'s adrenal glands. The failure of his adrenal glands affected not just his appetite for

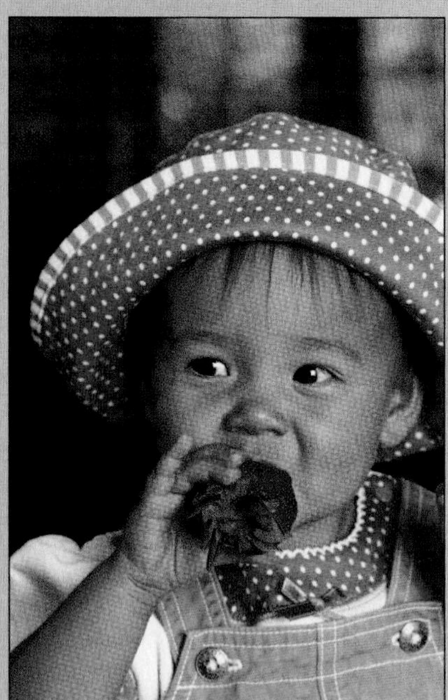

What we eat is determined by genes, physiology, and environment.

salt and water, but other aspects of his physical and emotional development as well. His parents must have been truly horrified when the 3-year-old child became *viralized:* his voice deepened and he began to grow pubic hair and an adult-sized penis.

This story does not have a happy ending. D.W. was eventually admitted to a large ward in a children's hospital for further observation and diet control. Placing him on a standard hospital diet restricted his access to salt and water. D.W.'s health soon deteriorated; he died 7 days later. With the benefit of hindsight, medical researchers can see now that the hospital environment deprived D.W. of the freedom to keep himself alive by adaptively dosing himself with salt and water.

Later in this chapter we will learn why problems with D.W.'s adrenal glands caused the child to crave salt and water, to become viralized, and to die in the absence of sufficient salt. In the process, we'll learn more about how circulating hormones affect the brain, which in turn affects behavior. We will see that under most circumstances, each of us is *motivated* to do the right thing, and that what we do has emotional consequences. Our emotions—for example, agitation, or a craving for certain substances like salt—motivate yet other behaviors, such as seeking out salt. Some aspects of motivation are innate: our genes have prepared each of us to know from birth that our bodies need air, salt and water, vitamins and minerals, and a proper mixture of protein, fat, and carbohydrates. Other aspects of motivation are learned. (Where did they hide the salt shaker *this* time?)

Throughout this chapter we'll look at examples of how genetically predisposed motivations and emotions are influenced by the cultural environment. While D.W. ultimately lost his struggle for survival, his 3-year life is a remarkable example of adapted, and adaptive, behavior. As we'll see in a later chapter, most eating disorders can be traced to maladaptively learned motivations and attitudes toward food.

MOTIVATION DEFINED

A cat stalks a bird. A student reads a chapter titled "Motivation and Emotion." What motivates these very different behaviors? **Motivation** can be broadly defined as all the factors that cause humans and other animals to behave the way they do. Remember the rat we met in Chapter 2, the one that was motivated to press a lever to stimulate certain neurons in its brain? Scientists believe that the same brain area, near the hypothalamus, provides the physical basis for pleasure in humans. This common brain structure means that rats and humans may experience a similar motivational state. Both are motivated to seek pleasure and to avoid pain, a tendency called **hedonism.**

motivation The factors that cause an animal to behave.

hedonism The basic motivation of humans and other animals to seek pleasure and avoid pain.

emotion An affective psychological experience, such as anger, joy, or fear, that is accompanied by bodily arousal.

Emotion, on the other hand, is an affective psychological experience—anger, joy, fear—that is accompanied by bodily arousal. Emotion often precedes motivation. For example, imagine that your boss told you last week that you need to show more effort. While she was talking with you your heart raced, your face flushed, and when she left, you muttered some unkind thoughts under your breath. As a result of that experience, you have stepped up your work pace. Now she tells you that you're *still* not performing as well as she would like. You begin a slow burn; even though you try not to show it, your eyes reveal anger and resentment. But then your boss pulls out a check and says that she *has* noticed your increased effort, appreciates it, and wants to reward you with a bonus. You respond with mixed emotions, but elation prevails, and in the future you are motivated to try even harder. The experience of emotion, then, often motivates a person to behave in a certain way.

These examples show that biological, psychological, and sociocultural factors all influence the great range of motivation and emotion humans experience. Evolutionary psychologists have suggested that human behavior is also influenced, or "motivated," by our genetic material (see Chapter 3). For example, Sagan and Druyan (1992) have proposed that the experiences of falling in love, separation anxiety, and jealousy are evolutionarily determined. (This theme underlies Freud's description of the *unconscious mind* as a primary source of human motivation.) To understand the full range of human motivation and emotion, then, we must account for evolutionary as well as physiological, psychological, and sociocultural factors.

PHYSIOLOGICAL BASES OF MOTIVATION

In Chapter 4 we saw that certain parts of the brain are involved in thinking and the experience of consciousness. As a result, humans can consciously experience hunger, thirst, pleasure, and other psychological states. But another less well known part of the nervous system, the neuroendocrine system, is also involved in motivation and emotion.

The Neuroendocrine System

In Chapter 4 the nervous system was described as a massive network of neurons in the brain and spinal cord, which receives and processes information and communicates with other neurons in the body through neurotransmitters. The *neuroendocrine system,* another major communication system, is a network of neurons that make and secrete neurotransmitter-like chemicals called *hormones.* Figure 5.1 shows the eight major glands of the neuroendocrine system—the

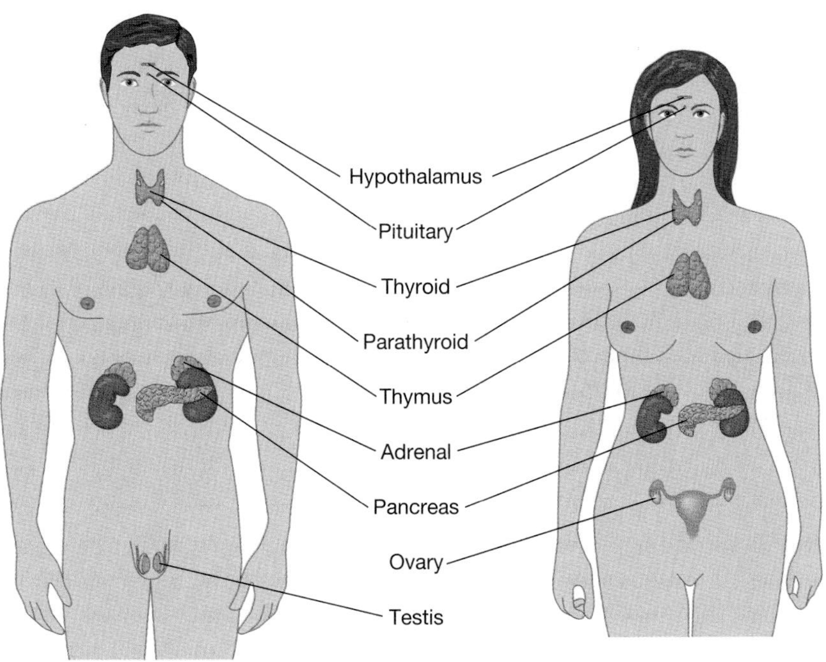

Figure 5.1 The neuroendocrine system. Each gland in the neuroendocrine system secretes a specific hormone that is detected by target tissues throughout the body. The system is controlled by the hypothalamus (see Figure 5.2).

pituitary, thyroid, parathyroid, thymus, adrenal, pancreas, ovary, and testis—along with the hypothalamus, the brain structure that regulates the system. These **endocrine glands** release hormones directly into the circulatory system.

Hormones: Messengers of Life. **Hormones** are biologically active chemicals in the form of peptides, proteins, and steroids that bind to target tissues in various organs throughout the body. Hormones regulate many physiological and behavioral functions. They are so pervasive, they are often called "messengers of life." For example, hormones known as peptides regulate hunger and thirst; they also determine rates of metabolism and bodily growth. Steroid hormones (such as *testosterone* and *estrogen*) influence the development of primary and secondary sexual characteristics, as well as courting and mating patterns. Other hormones help to regulate the immune system in fighting infections and disease. Finally, as we will see shortly, this chemical communication system is responsible for minute-by-minute regulation of blood-sugar levels, insulin, and the balance of water, sodium, calcium, potassium, and other electrolytes.

Regulation of the Neuroendocrine System. The hypothalamus, the structure that controls the endocrine glands, is located at the base of the brain (see Figure 5.1). The hypothalamus not only helps to regulate the sympathetic nervous system, but also acts as an integrative center for the regulation of sex, body temperature, hunger, and thirst. Neurons in the hypothalamus receive critical information about blood levels of hormones and nutrients such as water, salt, potassium, and calcium. Other cells in the hypothalamus signal changes that trigger voluntary and involuntary adjustments to these chemical signals.

Figure 5.2 shows how the hypothalamus, pituitary, and gonad glands work together to regulate the level of sex hormones circulating in the body. The hypothalamus is the "master" of the so-called master gland, the pituitary. It senses the level of sex hormones in the blood and directs the pituitary to secrete one of its many hormones, *gonadotropin*. When gonadotropin enters the blood stream, it circulates to target tissues in the gonads—the testis in males or the ovaries in females. The gonads in turn secrete testosterone or estrogen into the circulatory system, where they affect other target tissues. Testosterone, for example, influences the expression of the male's secondary sex characteristics, such as the growth of facial and pubic hair. As Figure 5.2 shows, nonhormonal factors, such as input from other parts of the brain to the hypothalamus, can also influence the neuroendocrine system.

The neuroendocrine system regulates bodily functions without conscious effort. This process, called homeostasis, is essential to life.

Homeostasis

To better understand the effects of the neuroendocrine system, let's look at some examples of how the body regulates itself. The term *homeostasis* was first used by Walter Cannon in his early physiology text *Wisdom of the Body* (1932). Formally defined, **homeostasis** is the process by which a physiological system maintains its equilibrium through self-regulation. Figure 5.2 shows an example of homeostasis, in which the hypothalamus senses the level of sex hormones in the blood. If the level is too low, the hypothalamus initiates a sequence of events that raises it. Water balance and body temperature are also regulated in this way.

Water Balance. The body's cells must have sufficient water to ensure that the chemicals within them remain in balance. The water level in each cell varies from low (following water use) to high (following water intake). Water content is regulated in relation to a **set point,** which is the average between the high and low values. The marvel is that each cell "knows" what its set point is.

endocrine gland An organ that produces and releases hormones.

hormone A chemical such as a peptide, protein, or steroid that is produced by glands and released into the body.

homeostasis The process in which the equilibrium of a physiological system is maintained through self-regulation.

set point The point around which a system homeostatically regulates itself.

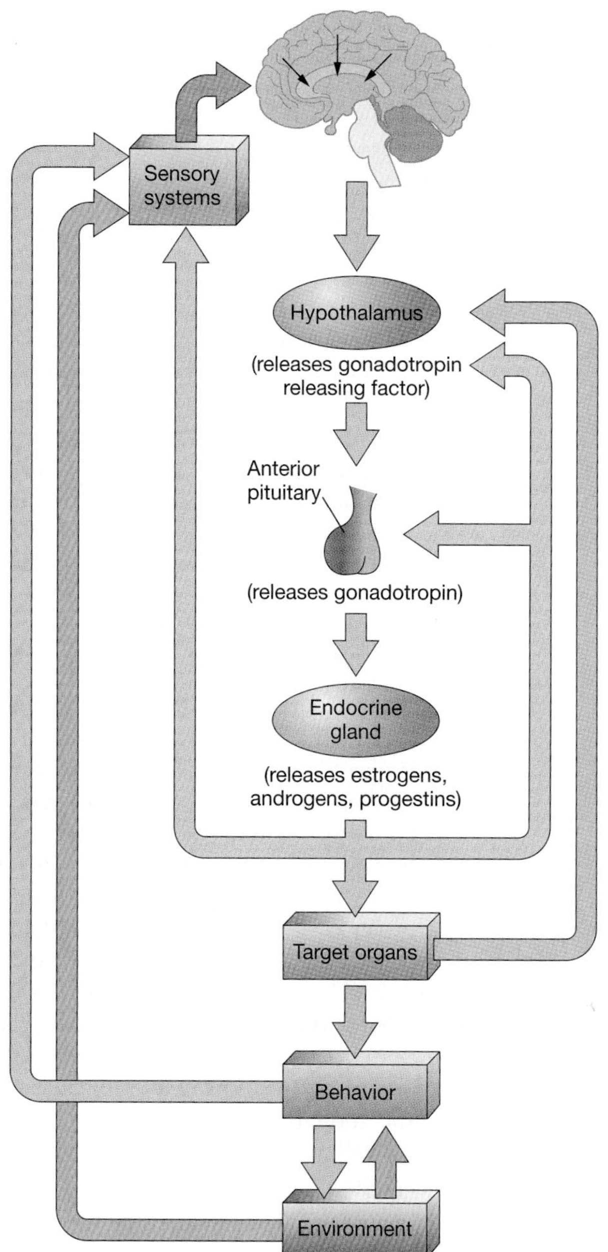

Figure 5.2 **How the neuroendocrine system functions.** This figure shows a general model for the functioning of the neuroendocrine system, using the control of gonadal hormones (estrogen, androgen, and progestin) as an example. The hypothalamus monitors the levels of circulating hormones and influences the release of gonadotropin by the pituitary. Gonadotropin then stimulates the gonads to release a hormone such as estrogen, which in turn affects target organs. Ultimately, the target organs affect behavior, and through a variety of feedback systems, signal their effects to the brain. *Source:* Modified from Rosenzweig et al., 1999, p. 131.

Self-regulation occurs through a process called **negative feedback.** Movement away from the set point triggers a counterreaction that moves the system back toward the set point. In the same way that a low level of sex hormones triggers the release of more sex hormones, too little water triggers changes in the nervous system that motivate water-seeking behavior.

Body Temperature. Besides water level, body temperature is maintained near set point through a negative feedback loop. Figure 5.3 shows that body temperature normally varies around the set point of ~98°F. Both conscious and unconscious mechanisms keep it within a comfortable range. Temperatures below the set point activate the sympathetic division of the autonomic nervous system, which conserves body heat by narrowing the blood vessels in the skin, a process called *vasoconstriction.* Another sympathetic response to the cold is shivering, an involuntary act that increases metabolic processes that raise body temperature. When

negative feedback A self-regulatory process in which movement away from a set point triggers a counteraction that moves the system back toward the set point.

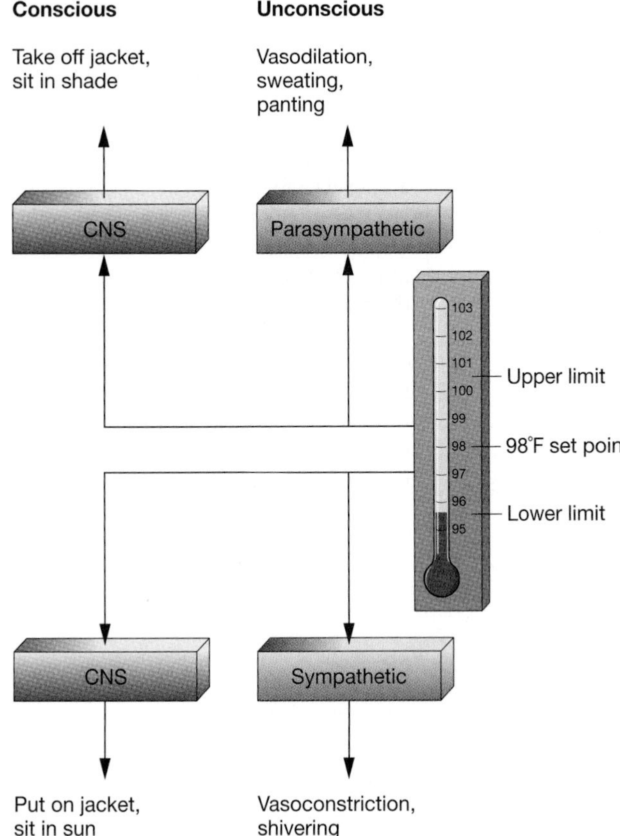

Figure 5.3 **Homeostasis and body temperature.** Body temperature varies around the set point of ~98°F through a process of negative feedback. The regulation of body temperature around this set point is accomplished unconsciously by the sympathetic and parasympathetic divisions of the ANS. Body temperature can also be consciously regulated through voluntary behavior, such as putting on or taking off extra clothing. Because the temperature shown in the figure is lower than the set point, the sympathetic system's response is to constrict the blood vessels, causing the body to shiver.

body temperature rises above the set point, the parasympathetic branch of the ANS cools the body by causing sweating and *vasodilation* of the blood vessels. As blood engorges the capillaries in the body's periphery, the skin becomes flushed and the body radiates heat into the surrounding air.

Although a person can be conscious of being too hot or too cold, and aware of sweating or shivering, these homeostatic processes are involuntary. Walter Cannon (1932) described this type of self-regulation as "body wisdom." The actions of the ANS, including vasodilation, vasoconstriction, sweating, and shivering, are involuntary and occur for the most part unconsciously. But not all bodily regulation is accomplished through such reflexes; voluntary behaviors can aid in maintaining homeostasis. For example, moving into the shade or putting on a jacket can help to regulate body temperature. Self-regulation, then, includes both conscious and unconscious processes. Animals, including humans, have physiological needs that motivate behaviors to meet those needs.

Behavioral Regulation of Body States

The nutrients needed to maintain a living cell include water, salt and other electrolytes, vitamins, minerals, and the calories derived from proteins, carbohydrates, and fats. The cycle of depletion and repletion of these cellular nutrients is adequately (if incompletely) described by the concept of homeostasis. But how did the physiological systems that regulate these nutrients evolve?

The answer to this question lies in recognizing that life began in the sea. Life forms that live in the ocean are continuously bathed in a fluid closely resembling the cytoplasm in their cells. Nevertheless, they must secure other nutrients from their environment to meet their energy needs. Land-dwelling life forms must consume both salt and water in addition to the food they need to survive. Over millions of years, land-dwelling animals have evolved physiological systems that help to regulate the salt, water, and other nutrients they require. Thus, humans continue to carry a little bit of sea with them in every cell in their bodies.

Homeostasis with ANS functioning, Chapter 4, p. 114

In addition to homeostatically regulating our internal sea, we must also replenish its basic constituents voluntarily. The term **behavioral regulation** refers to adaptive behaviors such as eating and drinking that help the body to achieve homeostasis. Behavioral regulation (which is mediated by the central nervous system) complements the basic homeostatic processes, which are mediated by the autonomic nervous system. Let's look more closely at the interplay of physiological processes and behavioral regulation.

Regulation of Water and Salt. Humans are blessedly ignorant of most of the 108 essential nutrients that are necessary for optimum health. Recently, the science of nutrition has provided names for some of them—thiamine, chromium, selenium, cholesterol. Yet every language has words for "salt" and "water," because those elements are truly special. It is no accident that most major cities in the world are located near rivers or lakes, and that many modern roads overlay ancient trails and paths to natural sources of salt. Because the continuous regulation of salt and water are critical for life, we have specific words—and appetites—for those nutrients.

behavioral regulation Adaptive behaviors that help animals achieve a homeostatic state.

Scientists have identified two types of thirst with two different causes. The thirst that 3-year-old D.W. experienced after ingesting large amounts of salt is called **osmotic thirst.** In mammals, osmotic thirst results when the concentration of solutes (dissolved substances) in the blood and other tissue fluids exceeds the normal level of 0.15M (molar). To conserve fluid, the kidneys will then secrete a more concentrated form of urine. High osmolarity of bodily fluids also triggers a **specific appetite** for fluid, resulting in an often-conscious water craving. When you eat a large bag of salted popcorn, your osmotic thirst increases, prompting you to consume some kind of beverage to relieve your thirst.

Another type of thirst, **hypovolemic thirst,** is typically triggered by an injury that causes fluid loss. (*Hypovolemic* means "low volume," as in an abnormally low fluid volume.) Hypovolemic thirst will elevate an animal's specific appetite for salt, causing it to crave slightly salty water. (An animal with osmotic thirst prefers plain water.)

Would a sailor who has been lost at sea for several days, with no drinking water, suffer from osmotic thirst or hypovolemic thirst? Answer: Unless he has lost a lot of blood through injury, the sailor will suffer extreme osmotic thirst. Drinking seawater would increase the amount of solute relative to water in the sailor's system—a potentially fatal mistake.

Low fluid volume, or hypovolemia, is sensed by so-called *volume receptors* located in large veins in the kidneys, heart, and other organs. One response to hypovolemic thirst is the secretion of *antidiuretic hormone (ADH)* by the pituitary gland. ADH (also called vasopressin) causes the kidneys to conserve water by secreting less urine. Another bodily response to hypovolemia is the release of a hormone called *renin* by the kidneys. Renin affects the production of several other hormones, including *angiotensin I* and *angiotensin II*. The main effect of angiotensin II is to constrict the blood vessels. Blood pressure can drop because of fluid loss; vasoconstriction raises it. Renin also stimulates cells around the third ventricle in the brain. These cells signal neurons in the hypothalamus to produce the psychological sensation of thirst, which motivates the animal to drink fluids to correct the hypovolemia (Ramsay & Thrasher, 1990).

Drive States and the Meeting of Needs. Our basic biological drives seem to come from within us. In Chapter 3 we studied certain instinctive behaviors called fixed action patterns (FAPs). Recall that because of an inherited behavioral program, young chicks are motivated to follow the first moving object they see. In doing so, the chicks demonstrate what is called a *primary motivation*, a biological motivation for behavior. According to Clark L. Hull, **primary motivation** is a physiological *drive* that helps an animal to meet its *needs*. A drive can be thought of as a motive that prompts an animal to act in a certain way.

Motivation and fixed action patterns, Chapter 3, p. 90

Thirst is an example of a primary motivation. Water is lost during metabolic processes; over time, it must be replaced. In Hull's analysis, a cellular need for water arouses a drive to satisfy the need. Writing in *Principals of Behavior* in 1943, Hull proposed a **drive reduction** theory of behavior: drives result in behavior that fulfills or *reduces* specific needs and achieves homeostasis by restoring the organism to a predrive state. In this example, thirst due to dehydration motivates an animal to seek water and drink it. Doing so restores homeostasis and reduces the animal's drive to drink.

Acquired Motivation and Incentives. Not all behavior can be attributed to the satisfaction of primary motivations. In fact, Hull proposed that much of human behavior is governed by what he called *acquired motivation*. **Acquired motivation** refers to motives learned over a lifetime, such as receiving praise or money. Because most people will behave in certain ways for those rewards, praise and money may be thought of as **incentives** to behave. (For this reason, acquired motivation is sometimes referred to as *incentive motivation*.)

osmotic thirst Thirst that results from an above-optimal concentration of solutes in bodily fluids.

specific appetite An innate craving for salt or water.

hypovolemic thirst Thirst that results from an abnormally low blood volume.

primary motivation Instinctive or biologically motivated behavior.

drive reduction Motivation that is based on meeting or reducing needs and restoring homeostatic balance.

acquired motivation Motives an individual learns during a lifetime.

incentive A goal or objective that motivates behavior.

LINK
Acquired motives and secondary reinforcement, Chapter 6, p. 207

Whereas primary motivation is instinctive (and as a result governs the behavior of most members of a species), acquired motivation varies from person to person. For example, one person may be motivated by language (ideas, causes, a pep talk), whereas another person might be motivated more by money and other incentives, such as a new BMW. We will return to the distinction between primary and acquired motivation later in this chapter.

INTERIM SUMMARY

1. Psychologists who study ***motivation*** recognize that biological, psychological, and sociocultural factors cause humans and other animals to behave as they do. ***Hedonism*** is a basic motivation of animals to seek pleasure and avoid pain.
2. Among the factors that motivate people are ***emotions*** such as anger, happiness, and fear.
3. The *neuroendocrine system* is a network of neurons and glands that make and secrete hormones, which provide part of the biological basis for motivation and emotion.
4. The pituitary, thyroid, parathyroid, thymus, adrenal, pancreas, ovary, and testis are all ***endocrine glands*** that release hormones into the circulatory system. ***Hormones*** are biochemicals in the form of peptides, proteins, and steroids. The hypothalamus regulates the "master gland," the pituitary.
5. Physiological systems maintain an equilibrium around a ***set point*** through self-regulation, a process called ***homeostasis***. Homeostasis occurs involuntarily through a process of ***negative feedback***, a counter-reaction that moves the system back toward the setpoint.
6. Homeostasis is aided by the conscious process of ***behavioral regulation***, such as drinking water to achieve a more optimal osmotic state.
7. Land-dwelling animals have a ***specific appetite*** for salt and water. Thirsty animals will drink water without training, and an animal with a salt deficit will innately recognize and consume salt.
8. Maintaining an optimal salt-to-water balance is critical for survival. All human cultures have words for "water" and "salt." Salt and water deficits have their conscious expression in psychological cravings.
9. ***Osmotic thirst*** occurs when too much solute (such as salt) is present in the blood; drinking water corrects the imbalance.
10. ***Hypovolemic thirst*** results from a low fluid volume, such as often follows the loss of blood from an injury. Hypovolemic thirst is sensed by *volume receptors* located in large veins in the body, which trigger corrective responses. These include the secretion of *antidiuretic hormone (ADH)* by the pituitary gland and renin by the kidneys.
11. Hypovolemic thirst is corrected by constriction of the blood vessels and increased activity of certain cells in the hypothalamus, which cause a thirst that initiates drinking.
12. The drives to eat, drink, and reproduce are examples of ***primary motivation***. These drive states motivate an animal to meet its basic needs.
13. According to Hull's ***drive reduction*** theory, animals cease to be motivated when their needs are met or reduced.
14. Words of praise and money are ***incentives***, or ***acquired*** (nonbiological) ***motivations***.

For Further Thought

1. Why do you think humans are not normally conscious of their neuroendocrine systems?
2. Some people report craving salt and others do not. Why would a person on a fast-food diet be unlikely to crave salt?
3. Pregnant women often report a craving for pickles. Why pregnant women, and why pickles?
4. Why, following major surgery, is physiological saline rather than water administered directly into the blood stream via an IV drip? (Physiological saline is a 0.15M saline solution with other electrolytes and minerals added.)

EATING: SATISFYING HUNGER AND ENJOYING FOODS

I am part of a family that gets together for meals on holidays. During these most pleasurable of times, eating and drinking specially selected and carefully prepared foods and beverages occupy our collective consciousness. As is the case with most other people around the world, these occasions help to define our family relationships and our cultural traditions. Here we see the interaction of motivation and emotion: family meals are happy times, so much so that eating meals together is one of life's great pleasures.

Multifactorial Motivation

A human's motivation to eat, then, is more complex than the homeostatic regulation of salt and water might suggest. Genetic factors are important not only in what humans eat, but also in how they select foods. Psychological factors reflecting personal experiences with foods also motivate eating. Some people, for example, prefer to eat bread made with bleached flour, and others prefer bread made with whole wheat. Finally, sociocultural factors play a role; eating with relatives on the holidays is a sociocultural motivation.

Genes and obese mice, Chapter 3, p. 87

Together, sociocultural concerns and biological and psychological factors produce the many-factored *(multifactorial)* motivation that underlies eating and other complex human behaviors. All motivated behaviors, not just food choices, are multifactorially determined. The motivation to drink alcoholic beverages and diet soft drinks, to smoke marijuana or to take aspirin, to eat meat cooked rare or well-done (or not to eat meat), to watch TV 6 hours a day (or not at all) is multifactorially determined.

Two Types of Feeding Systems

Humans are omnivores; they select from among many different food sources in the plant and animal kingdoms. Their appetites and food selections are more extensive than those of meat-eaters (carnivores) and plant-eaters (herbivores). By comparison with carnivores and herbivores, the common housefly feeds within an even more restricted niche, exhibiting what Paul Rozin at the University of Pennsylvania has called a **closed feeding system**—one that is characterized by reflexive responses to a narrow range of foods.

Closed Feeding Systems. Animals with closed feeding systems tend to have simple nervous systems. In their restricted ecological niches, these animals are not amenable to changes in diet that are based on learning. The housefly, for example, feeds reflexively when taste cells on its legs are stimulated.

In his marvelous book *To Know a Fly*, Vince Dethier describes a simple demonstration of a fly's feeding behavior. After capturing a fly, Dethier used candle wax to "glue" its back to the tip of a pencil-sized stick. The stick allowed him to carefully lower the fly's legs into various water solutions—salty, sour, sweetened, and so forth. Chemically sensitive receptors on the fly's legs alerted its brain, activating motor neurons that caused it to lower its proboscis (a tiny, trunk-like mouth). Dethier observed that when thirsty, the fly would lower its proboscis and drink the fluid. But when hungry, the fly would lower its proboscis only when the fluid was a calorie-rich sugar solution. The hungry fly would drink its fill and then retract its proboscis from the sugar solution. This simple demonstration of a closed feeding system shows that a fly's feeding behavior is reflexive (Dethier, 1962).

closed feeding system A feeding pattern characterized by reflexive responses to a narrow range of foods.

Open Feeding Systems. The **open feeding system** of humans and other omnivores is more flexible than a fly's. Animals who occupy open feeding systems *learn* what to eat from the huge variety of potential foods. Both humans and chickens are good examples of open feeding systems, because both are governed by their innate appetites *and* their early eating experiences. That is, their feeding behavior is influenced both by distal (distant) *and* by proximal (nearby) causes. Newly hatched chicks, for example, peck indiscriminately at particles of grain and sand. Such pecking behavior is instinctive and occurs in response to any small object. (Likewise, human infants will instinctively root for a nipple, and finding one, will suckle it instinctively. And snakes will instinctively feed on moving animals, but not on still ones.) However, only grain satisfies the chick's hunger. Over time chicks learn to peck only at grain and not at sand (Hogan, 1977). The grain acts as a *reinforcer* for the pecking behavior.

Food reinforces behavior, Chapter 6, p. 207

The task facing all living creatures is to find and ingest foods that provide essential nutrients and an adequate supply of energy. At first glance, omnivores appear to be ideally suited to meet these needs. If, for example, plants are unavailable during a famine, an omnivore can switch to meat. Likewise, when rabbits, fish, or eggs become scarce, an omnivore can search for edible roots. This flexibility in diet is known as *behavioral plasticity,* and it is a hallmark of our open feeding system.

Behavioral plasticity with brain plasticity, Chapter 4, p. 128

A cost-benefit analysis of open feeding systems reveals a paradox, however. The **omnivore's paradox** is that the very flexibility that is beneficial during a famine can, on other occasions, prove detrimental to the animal's health and well-being. That is because an open feeding strategy increases the risk of eating a harmful food. *Everything*—toxic plants, *salmonella*, environmentally contaminated shellfish—is available to eat. Because an open feeding system is less specialized, it contains fewer safeguards (Rozin & Kalat, 1973). The omnivore's paradox is that eating from a wide variety of food sources is nutritionally adaptive, but potentially deadly.

Open feeding systems are affected by distal causes (evolutionary and genetic determinants) as well as by proximal causes (a reliance on learning what is safe to eat). For example, many omnivores express a wariness toward new food, called **neophobia.** They have an innate tendency to cautiously approach, sniff, and taste a new food before ingesting it. Neophobia can be seen in humans who are finicky about their foods. But when humans teach their children what is and is not appropriate to put in their mouths, learning—a proximal cause—is influencing their food selection. By the time a person is an adult, he or she knows a great deal about poisons, safe food practices, and the potential of food to cause harm. We learn our lessons well: as a result of learning, young adults are more particular about what they put into their mouths than very young children.

open feeding system A feeding pattern characterized by selection from a wide variety of food choices.

omnivore's paradox The paradox that eating from a wide variety of food sources not only is nutritionally adaptive but also increases the risk of poisoning.

neophobia Fear of something new; with regard to food, finickiness, or an innate tendency to cautiously approach, sniff, and taste a new food before ingesting it.

nutritional wisdom An innate predisposition to make adaptive food choices.

Nutritional Wisdom

Neophobia shows that even open feeding systems are governed in part by instinct. Earlier we saw how the physiologically driven appetites for salt and water helped to determine the foods D.W. would eat. Other examples abound: infants innately like sweets and dislike bitter and sour tastes (Steiner, 1977). Children seem to know exactly what and when they want to eat. Could it be that humans have **nutritional wisdom**—an innate predisposition to make adaptive food choices?

The researcher Clara Davis wondered if very young children could select nutritionally appropriate foods without a caretaker's intervention. To answer this question, she studied orphaned children between 1 and 2 years of age. Some were fed an institutional diet; others were allowed to crawl around on a food-filled floor and make their own selections (Davis, 1928, 1939). Davis reported that the latter group chose cooked and fresh fruit most frequently, breads and vegetables next most often, and cooked and uncooked meats least often. (Interestingly, they were equally likely to choose cooked and uncooked meats!) Davis monitored the children's health for a year and found that their growth rates and illnesses were about the same. She concluded that toddlers could select both the type and amount of food to eat as readily as adult caretakers. However, critics of the study point out that she did not offer the children candies, cookies, or rat poison, so she really didn't test the children's nutritional wisdom!

Curiously, Davis observed that several of the children in her study selected one food and ate it nearly exclusively, then abruptly switched to another. She called this pattern a *feeding jag* (Davis, 1939). Davis wondered whether they were an example of a behavioral adaptation that helps an omnivore to select wisely from a variety of foods. We'll return to this question shortly.

Taste Cues. The acute condition of thiamine deficiency (called *Beri Beri* in humans) is a serious nutritional problem. In research laboratories, thiamine-deficient rats lose their appetite and body weight, and will die unless the thiamine they lack is replaced. Unlike foods that are innately recognized because of their sweetness or saltiness, trace amounts of thiamine have no taste. Rozin and his colleagues wondered how animals recognize trace elements such as thiamine, and somehow select the right amount from various food sources (Rozin, 1967). Animals have *not* evolved taste receptors for dozens of vitamins, minerals, and essential nutrients. How can they regulate substances they can't taste?

To find out, Rozin's team devised an experiment. First, they familiarized rats with a diet that provided optimum nutrition—a diet they labeled *familiar-safe*. Then they made the rats thiamine deficient by feeding them the same diet, but without thiamine—a diet they labeled *familiar-deficient*. Finally, they tried a new diet with thiamine, which they called a *novel diet*. They found that when the rats were given the differently flavored novel diet, they would stop eating the familiar deficient diet and begin to eat the novel diet.

But why? What motivated the rats to eat the new diet? Did they know that it contained thiamine? Figure 5.4 shows Donna Zahorik's analysis of the problem, based on research done with her colleagues (Zahorik 1977; Zahorik, Mair, & Pies, 1974). They found that lab rats preferred a familiar, safe diet. When the thiamine was removed, however (making it a *familiar, deficient* diet), the rats learned an aversion to it. At that point they overcame their neophobia and switched to a new diet. In time they learned to like the new diet, which helped them to recover from their thiamine deficiency. According to the psychologist

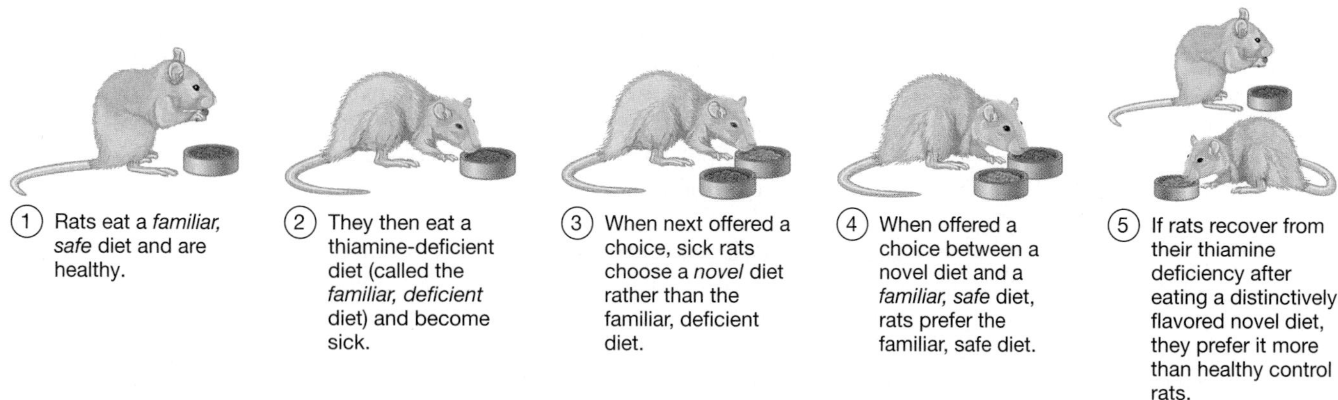

① Rats eat a *familiar, safe* diet and are healthy.
② They then eat a thiamine-deficient diet (called the *familiar, deficient* diet) and become sick.
③ When next offered a choice, sick rats choose a *novel* diet rather than the familiar, deficient diet.
④ When offered a choice between a novel diet and a *familiar, safe* diet, rats prefer the familiar, safe diet.
⑤ If rats recover from their thiamine deficiency after eating a distinctively flavored novel diet, they prefer it more than healthy control rats.

Figure 5.4 Effects of thiamine deficiency and recovery on a rat's food choices.

David Booth of the University of Birmingham, such conditioned preferences for foods that are associated with recovery provide humans and other animals with a *learned ingestive motivation* (Booth, 1991). That is, humans continue to select foods that have made them feel good in the past.

Feeding Jags. Let's reexamine children's feeding jags in the light of this research. One of my children, Jane, ate an egg each morning for months, then stopped abruptly. Other parents have reported feeding jags for peanut-butter sandwiches and macaroni and cheese. The research on thiamine deficiency suggests that in these instances, a child's preoccupation with one food is likely to decrease the probability of getting one or more essential nutrients. Omnivores get their vitamins, minerals, and other trace elements from different sources, so eating a variety of foods increases the chances of getting *all* the necessary nutrients. Thus, eating only one food during a feeding jag might induce a state of deficiency in one or more nutrients. Under these conditions, switching to a new food is adaptive, because it may replenish a needed nutrient.

A feeding jag can be interpreted in another way, however. Let's assume that my child, Jane, was protein-starved because of what she *wasn't* getting in her diet. Eggs are an excellent source of protein, so eating them exclusively would have helped her to meet her protein needs. Perhaps she came to associate the flavor of eggs with "recovery from protein deficiency," in the same way rats associate the flavor of a novel diet containing thiamine with recovery from thiamine deficiency. But after months of meeting her protein requirements by eating eggs exclusively, Jane may have incurred some other deficiency, prompting her to switch to another food. A feeding jag may at one and the same time correct a deficiency and induce another.

Sensory-Specific Satiety. We have seen that humans are leery of new foods, and that safe, familiar foods pose the least risk. But eating a variety of foods is desirable, because it increases the chances of ingesting essential nutrients. How might a person balance these competing tendencies? The psychologist Barbara Rolls and her colleagues theorize that humans experience **sensory-specific satiety**, or satiety for the foods eaten during the course of a meal, but not for other foods, such as dessert (Hetherington & Rolls, 1997; Rolls, 1986). According to this theory, animals introduce variety into their food selections because they become satiated on foods they eat repeatedly. Sensory-specific satiety is adaptive, because it counterbalances the tendency toward feeding jags.

Evolutionary Origins of Human Food Selection

All children bring innate likes and dislikes to the table, but parents select the foods they believe will meet their children's basic needs. How do parents know what to feed their children? How does anyone know which foods are safe and which should be avoided? Reading nutrition books is not the answer, because books and the science of nutrition are recent inventions. The cultural origins of our foods, though, are prehistoric. Neither my parents nor my grandparents read nutrition books, but they did have recipe boxes. Let's look at a few examples of the origin of cultural food practices.

Biocultural Evolution. Because it contains a digestible protein, corn is considered an edible plant in many cultures. Presumably, humans began eating wild corn because it tasted good, was filling, and turned out to have nutritional value. Solomon Katz, an anthropologist at the University of Pennsylvania, wondered why some Indian cultures in North, Central, and South America have traditionally boiled their corn with lime (an alkali) prior to making tortillas, while

sensory-specific satiety Satiety that is experienced for the foods eaten during a meal, but not for other foods with different sensory properties.

others have not (Katz, 1982). He found that those who *do* treat corn with alkali cultivate and eat much more corn than those who do not. Katz reasoned that the alkali method increases the nutritional value of corn, which in turn influences the extent to which corn is used as a staple in the diet.

Several points are worth stressing. First, selecting corn (or other foods) to eat is done on the basis of more than taste and smell. Presumably, the first humans who ingested corn not only did *not* become sick, but also over time became better nourished. Second, for unknown reasons, some humans began to treat corn with alkali. Perhaps an elderly person without teeth wanted to soften the dried kernels. But since early humans lacked a knowledge of nutritional chemistry, they were not likely to have done it intentionally. Over time, someone apparently recognized the value of the treatment and transmitted the information to the next generation, as part of its extragenetic history. Richard Dawkins (1976) has called such an extragenetic information transfer a *meme*—a cultural invention that is passed down through the generations. Over thousands of generations, Dawkins argues, cultures become differentiated as much by their memes as by their genes, and eventually develop distinctive cuisines. Some recipe boxes define Scandinavian cuisines, and others define Asian cuisines.

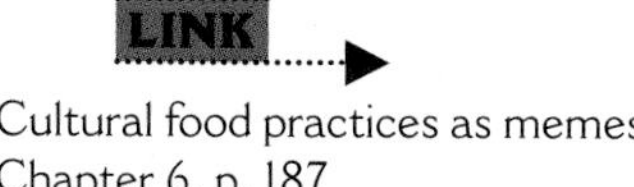

Cultural food practices as memes, Chapter 6, p. 187

Katz also studied food preparation in Africa. He was curious why certain African tribes eat bitter manioc and fava beans. Again he noted that cultural practices used to transform basic foods were sometimes surprisingly adaptive. For example, squeezing and cooking bitter manioc, a potato-like tuber, releases an anti-sickling chemical that provides some protection against *sickle-cell anemia*. Likewise, the pharmacological properties of fava beans increase the fitness of women who otherwise would be at risk for certain hereditary deficiencies (Katz, 1982). Katz called the selection of certain food preparation practices, which are memes that enhance fitness, **biocultural evolution** (Katz, 1975).

Anthropologists like Katz, then, view prehistoric human food habits in evolutionary terms. They reason that those individuals who learned how to function better than others in their omnivores' niche enjoyed a reproductive advantage. In prehistoric times, for example, humans began to group individual foods and eat them together. We now know that many protein foods do not contain all the essential amino acids necessary to maintain good health. Rather, a complementarity of foods containing proteins provides the essential mix of nutrients. Eaten separately, corn, wheat, and beans do not provide an optimal protein mix, but combined in a single meal, they do. Foods that are combined at mealtime, therefore, confer a health advantage that affects fitness. The contemporary practice of composing a meal of different food is a result of this evolutionary process. An example would be a Mexican meal that incorporates beans with corn and wheat tortillas.

Genetic Differences in Food Choices. Katz's concept of biocultural evolution is important because it suggests that genetic diversity may be due in part to different food selection strategies. If that is true, we should not be surprised that food preferences reflect genetic and ethnic heritages. Consider the fact that Asian Americans, Mexican Americans, and African Americans are more likely to get a stomach ache after drinking milk, eating cheese, or enjoying an ice cream cone than are Americans of Northern European descent. One result is that Swedish Americans and German Americans incorporate more milk products in their diet than the other groups. But why the different physiological responses to milk in different ethnic groups?

The story begins in Africa, where the anthropologist Fred Simoons decided to investigate the genetic differences among tribes who have historically used cow's milk and those who have not. He found that members of the two groups differed in the amount of the enzyme lactase that they produced. Lactase is necessary to

biocultural evolution The process by which the selection, preparation, and consumption of particular types of food enhance the fitness of individuals in a culture.

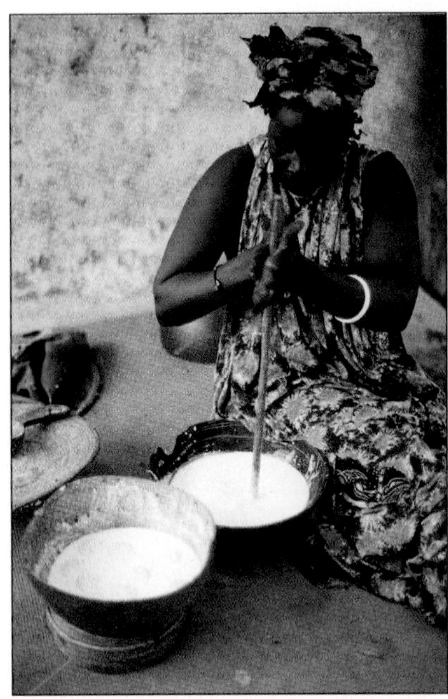

Only Africans who are lactose tolerant incorporate milk products in their diets.

digest lactose, the sugar in a mammal' s milk. In a person with insufficient lactase, milk and milk products such as cheese cause stomach aches and intestinal gas. Those who don't have enough of the enzyme are said to suffer from *lactose malabsorption* (Simoons, 1973).

A recessive gene is responsible for the low levels of lactase production in people with lactose malabsorption. Simoons theorized that in prehistoric Africa, a few individuals continued to produce lactase after being weaned from their mother's milk. Eventually they began to drink cow's milk. (This practice is weirder than it sounds. Would *you* be brave enough to be the first to drink animal secretions?) Because these lucky individuals could metabolize the lactose in cow's milk, they gained a selective advantage—an extra food source during times of famine. Over tens of thousands of years, a genetic divergence occurred between those individuals (now tribes) who tolerated lactose and those who didn't.

Simoons hypothesizes that some of these lactose-tolerant Africans migrated out of Africa into Europe. Today, their descendants, the indigenous populations of Northern Europe, have high lactose tolerance and use milk and milk products extensively. Only about one-third of the world's people have a high lactose tolerance (Flatz, 1987). Large numbers of Africans, Asians, and indigenous North and South Americans suffer from lactose malabsorption. This genetic diversity underlies the fact that some ethnic groups consume large amounts of milk products, whereas others use small amounts or none at all.

Brain Mechanisms and Feeding

Motivation is multifactorial, so no discussion of eating would be complete without mention of physiological factors. Experiments with brain stimulation, first reported in the 1940s, implicated the hypothalamus as an important determinant of both hunger and satiety. From these studies grew simple models of the hypothalamic control of eating and drinking, which have since become quite complicated. Nevertheless, this classical research in what was then called physiological psychology is instructive.

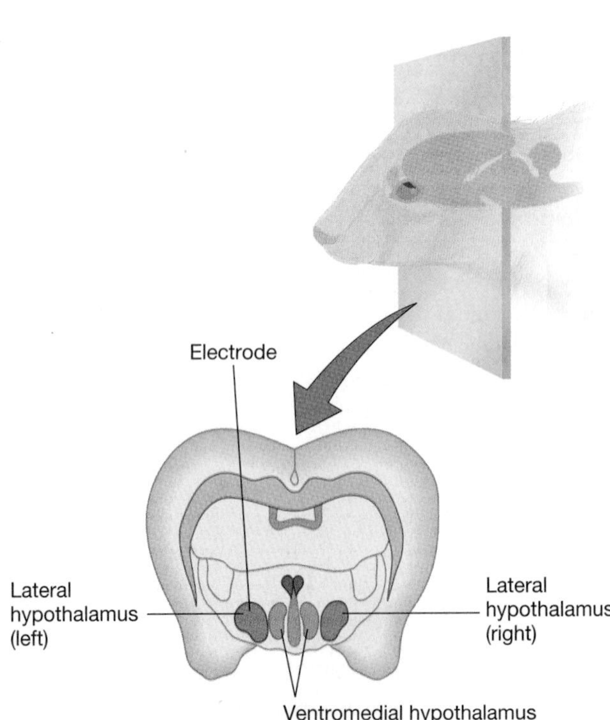

Figure 5.5 Hypothalamic control of eating. The ventromedial and lateral hypothalamus are involved in the control of eating and drinking. Here, an electrode penetrates the lateral hypothalamus at the base of the brain, on the left side.

The Role of the Hypothalamus. Figure 5.5 shows those parts of the hypothalamus that are involved in the regulation of eating. Early research with laboratory animals focused on two parts in particular, the lateral and ventromedial areas. Each can be activated by passing a small amount of electrical current through an implanted electrode. To facilitate their experiments, scientists developed a special type of electrode that can deliver a strong current to either the lateral or ventromedial area alone. The current first heats and then destroys the neurons it contacts. (Note in Figure 5.5 that the hypothalamus has left and right lateral areas and left and right ventromedial areas. Two separate electrode placements are needed to destroy all the neurons in each area.)

Many experiments have demonstrated how the stimulation and subsequent destruction of these two areas of the hypothalamus affect both eating and drinking. Let's first consider what happens when neurons in a rat's lateral hypothalamus are destroyed. The psychologist Eliot Stellar, his students, and his colleagues at the University of Pennsylvania

1

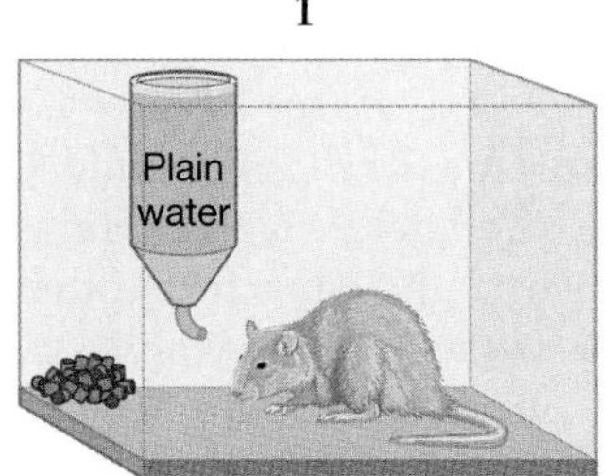

2

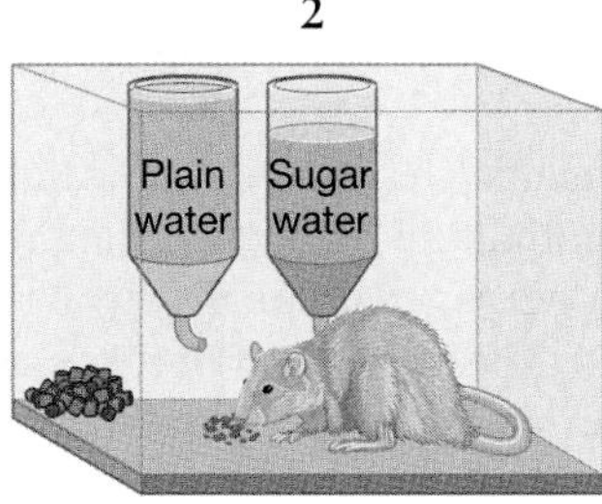

3

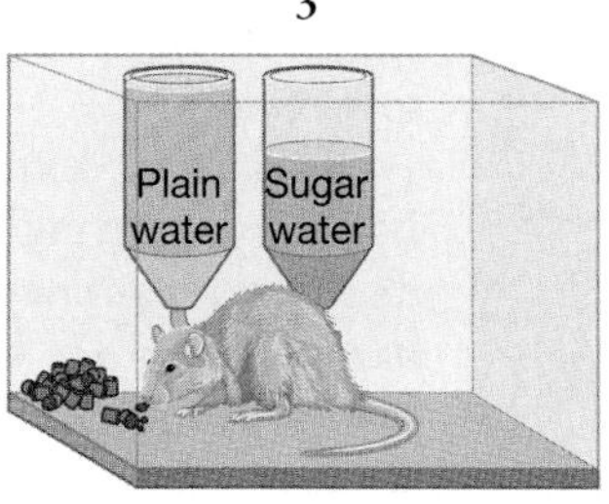

4

Figure 5.6 Recovery from damage to the lateral hypothalamus. *Source:* From "The Lateral Hypothalamic Syndrome: Recovery of Feeding and Drinking after Lateral Hypothalamic Lesions" by P. Teitelbaum and A. N. Epstein in *Psychological Review,* (1962), 69. Copyright © 1962 by American Psychological Assn. Reprinted by permission.

found that after these neurons had been destroyed, rats would not eat (they became *aphagic*) or drink (they became *adipsic*). Indeed, the rats died unless they were tube-fed. Their recovery typically followed the four-stage pattern shown in Figure 5.6 (Teitelbaum & Epstein, 1962).

In stage 1, the rats would not eat or drink voluntarily. In stage 2, they continued to reject lab chow and water but would eat more palatable food (such as a chocolate chip cookie in milk) and sweetened water. (Even for a rat, apparently, chocolate is one of life's great pleasures.) In stage 3 rats became less finicky but began to nibble at the bland lab chow and drink sweetened water. In stage 4, the rats finally ate and drank enough plain lab chow and water to keep themselves alive, but remained sickly. For example, after being deprived of food for 24 hours, normal rats adjust their appetites to make up for the meals they missed. But stage 4 rats did not engage in such compensatory eating and drinking. And when placed in a cold laboratory, they did not increase their caloric intake to raise their metabolic level, as normal rats do.

In contrast with lesions of the lateral hypothalamus, which cause rats to starve, damage to the ventromedial hypothalamus has just the opposite effect. The photo on this page shows a rat that sustained ventromedial damage 1 to 2 months before being photographed. After the surgery it began eating abnormally large amounts of lab chow, a condition called hyperphagia. At 1,000 gm, this rat weighed about three times its normal weight. After a few more months, its weight leveled off at a new set point, and the rat continued to eat enough to maintain its incredible weight.

The Dual-Center Model of Hunger. On the basis of these observations, scientists developed a dual-center model for the control of hunger. According to this theory, the lateral hypothalamus was a "start-eating" center, and the ventromedial hypothalamus a "stop-eating" center. The destruction of one or the other center would either increase or decrease an animal's eating behavior. That is, if the *start-eating center* were destroyed, the animal would cease to eat, much like the rats in Steller's experiments. Likewise, destruction of the *stop-eating center* would prevent an animal from stopping its eating, and over time, the rat would become obese. Further experiments supported the dual-center model. Stimulating the lateral hypothalamus with an implanted electrode prompted a rat to begin eating, whereas stimulating the ventromedial hypothalamus prompted an eating rat to stop (Wyrwicka & Dobrzecka, 1960).

This elegant model did not stand the test of time, however. Its demise is testimony to the inherent strength of the scientific method. The dual-center hypothesis could not account for observations made in increasingly sophisticated experiments. For example, researchers noticed that although electrical stimulation of the lateral hypothalamus would cause an animal to eat if food was available, in the absence of food it would produce other behaviors. If water was

This rat became obese after the ventromedial nucleus of its hypothalamus was destroyed.

High Insulin
Low blood glucose levels stimulate appetite. Because of high insulin levels, food is stored as fat.

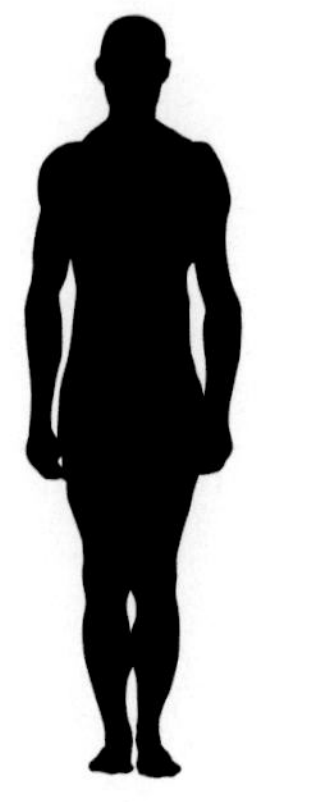

Normal Insulin
Glucose levels, appetite, and weight are all normal.

Low Insulin
Too little insulin prevents fat storage. Appetite is high but weight is low.

Figure 5.7 The effects of insulin. Too much or too little insulin can affect both appetite and overall body weight.

available, the rat would drink; if a sexual partner was available, the rat would copulate. Was the hypothalamus really a *hunger* control center, researchers began to wonder?

Still other experiments challenged the validity of the dual-center model. Besides destroying hypothalamic neurons, damage to the lateral hypothalamus disrupts dopamine-rich nerves that course through the hypothalamus from other parts of the brain. Electrical stimulation of these axons produces effects similar to that of stimulating the lateral hypothalamus. These nerves contribute both to arousal (that is, the motivation to physically approach food) and to the experience of pleasure that accompanies a meal.

These and other observations led researchers to conclude that the dual-center model was too simplistic. Nevertheless, the lateral hypothalamus *does* contribute to feeding, in several important ways: It interacts with taste areas in the brainstem, with the so-called pleasure centers in the brain, with forebrain structures that integrate the sight of food with its smell and taste (Critchley & Rolls, 1996), and with the pancreas, which releases insulin in response to food. Clearly, the lateral hypothalamus is involved with the complexities of feeding, but it is not simply a *start-eating* center.

The role of the ventromedial hypothalamus in eating is also more complicated than was originally supposed. First, the huge increases in body weight some rats displayed were found to be associated only with large brain lesions that destroyed parts of the hypothalamus *outside* the ventromedial area as well. Further experiments also revealed that damage to the ventromedial hypothalamus changed the rats' sensitivity to taste. They would overeat foods that tasted good and undereat foods that tasted bad. And though they ate about the same amount of food at each meal, they initiated many more meals than normal rats (Hoebel & Hernandez, 1993). Finally, researchers found that rats with ventromedial lesions became obese because they produced abnormally high amounts of insulin, the hormone that converts calories to fat. If these brain-damaged rats were put on a restricted diet and allowed to eat only a controlled number of calories, they nevertheless gained weight (King, Smith, & Frohman, 1984). To better understand the role of insulin in hunger, let's take a closer look at how foods provide the body with energy.

The Role of Insulin and Blood Glucose. One model of the control of feeding relates the blood levels of glucose and insulin to hunger and eating habits. Foods containing carbohydrates, fats, and proteins (amino acids) build body muscle and provide energy. One of the most important sources of energy for cells in the brain and the rest of the body is glucose. When glucose levels rise after a meal (during the *absorptive phase*), the pancreas releases *insulin,* a substance that promotes the cellular use of glucose for energy or the storage of glucose in the liver, as glycogen, or as fat. Meeting the body's needs in these ways returns the system to homeostasis, reducing hunger.

What causes hunger and initiates eating? When glucose levels are low (the *fasting phase*, before a meal), the pancreas releases *glucagon.* Glucagon prompts the kidneys to convert glycogen, the liver's stored energy reserves, back into glucose. The ratio of low glucose and insulin levels to high glucagon levels stimulates hunger, and the eating-fasting cycle repeats.

Figure 5.7 shows some long-term effects of the relationship among insulin, glucose, and hunger. Individuals with higher-than-normal insulin levels tend to store more fat than people with lower insulin levels. They also have lower glucose levels than others (Bernardis & Bellinger, 1996), which stimulate them to eat and store even more fat.

INTERIM SUMMARY

1. Biology (genetics and physiology), psychology (learned expectations), and sociocultural factors determine the food choices an individual makes. *All* motivated behaviors, such as hunger, are multifactorially determined.
2. Eating and drinking are pleasurable activities that support homeostasis through behavioral regulation.
3. As omnivores, humans have a more ***open feeding system*** (one that allows choice among alternatives based on experience) than simpler animals with a ***closed feeding system*** (a restricted food niche that allows only reflexive eating).
4. The ***omnivore's paradox*** is that while an open feeding system allows more choice among alternative foods, it contains fewer safeguards against toxic foods.
5. Sensory mechanisms that predispose an animal to detect salt, water, and other nutrients; a physiological system that regulates nutrients homeostatically; and an inborn ***neophobia,*** or fear of new foods, are all evidence of an innate ***nutritional wisdom.***
6. Changing to a new food following a *feeding jag* is evidence that animals adjust their appetites to correct nutritional deficiencies and other homeostatic imbalances.
7. Animals learn to dislike and avoid foods that make them sick. Thiamine-deficient rats learn to dislike foods that do not contain thiamine and to prefer foods that correct their thiamine deficiency. Because rats are neophobic, they prefer familiar, safe foods to novel, safe foods.
8. Eating a wide variety of foods increases the likelihood of securing all the nutrients essential to life. ***Sensory-specific satiety*** (becoming sated on a particular food during the course of a meal) introduces variety into an animal's food selections.
9. ***Biocultural evolution*** is the idea that certain food selection and preparation practices enhanced the fitness of people living in prehistoric cultures. Over generations, for example, people who were genetically predisposed to produce lactase began to use animal milk and milk products as foods. The new foods gave them an advantage during times of famine.
10. The hypothalamus is intimately involved in the control of eating and drinking.
11. Lesioning of the lateral hypothalamus and disruption of the nerves that course through that area causes rats to cease eating and drinking, conditions known as aphagia and adipsia.
12. Lesioning of the ventromedial hypothalamus causes rats to gain weight rapidly. They become more sensitive to the taste of food, initiate many more meals when palatable food is made available, and store more of the food they eat as fat.
13. Insulin helps to determine how much glucose the body stores as fat. Along with blood glucose levels, insulin levels determine whether a person is hungry or satiated.

For Further Thought

1. In Chapter 3 David Barash described genetic motivation as "The Whisperings Within" (see p. 96). The next time you order from a menu (or better, choose foods in a cafeteria line), try to sort your food selections into those that are culturally learned and those that reflect genetic whispers from your prehistoric past. Do some of your selections reveal both sources of motivation?
2. Should a toddler be expected to avoid rat poison in a test of innate nutritional wisdom? Why or why not? (HINT: Consider the selective pressures that guided the evolution of mammalian feeding systems.)
3. Given the evidence supporting the idea that humans have an inherent nutritional wisdom, and that their cuisine often reflects that wisdom, what accounts for the high-fat, high-salt diet popular in the United States?

PLEASURE

Some of the most interesting questions are those that concern the origins of pleasure. What brings us pleasure? What causes pain? Questions like these go to the very heart of the human condition. To most people, tasty food, a baby's smile, and sexual intimacy are pleasurable, whereas the death of a loved one is devastatingly painful.

Genetic predispositions and brain mechanisms underlie the human motivation to seek out pleasure and avoid pain. Both tendencies are truly ancient evolutionary adaptations that promote survival and reproduction. Eating and making love are among life's great pleasures *because* they are adaptive. We are motivated to reduce hunger, avoid pain, and find shelter from the snow *because* doing so is adaptive. Accomplishing these appetitive and consummatory behaviors activates areas in and around the hypothalamus, producing the psychological experience of pleasure.

Brain Mechanisms Underlying Pleasure

Chapter 2 detailed the findings of two psychologists, James Olds and Peter Milner, who implanted electrodes in the hypothalamus of rats to measure the effects of electrical stimulation of the brain (ESB). They quickly recognized that the conscious, free-ranging rats were motivated to self-stimulate, and that ESB seemed to produce pleasurable effects for the rats. Because the rats quickly learned to press a lever to stimulate neurons in the hypothalamus, Olds reasoned that ESB acted in the same way as food and water did in hungry and thirsty rats.

Pleasure with consummatory behaviors, Chapter 3, p. 89

Many experiments have been done since Olds first reported that he had found a "pleasure center" in the rat's brain. Recall that not all electrode placements produced the same results (see page 45). Activation of a structure called the *medial forebrain bundle (MFB)* has since been discovered to be a common factor in many successful electrode placements—that is, in those that caused a rat to self-stimulate. The MFB is a *limbic system pathway* that courses through portions of the hypothalamus. Other research has indicated that stimulation of the *mesotelencephalic dopamine system* plays a crucial role in ESB (Phillips & Fibiger, 1989). (These are the same fibers that are damaged when the lateral hypothalamus is lesioned.) Yet other brain structures and neurotransmitters have been implicated in the reinforcing effects of ESB (see Vaccarino, Schiff, & Glickman, 1989, for a review). The experience of pleasure, then, is related to both specific brain chemicals and specific brain structures.

Pleasure Seeking in Rats

How can pleasures be compared? Is eating when hungry more pleasurable than drinking when thirsty? Is 30 minutes of sexual arousal more or less pleasurable than 30 seconds of sexual orgasm? Some researchers have tried to answer these questions, and their results are quite interesting. In one experiment, a rat was offered two levers; pressing one lever produced ESB and pressing the other produced food (Routtenberg & Lindy, 1965). In daily one-hour trials, rats consistently chose ESB over food. Since they had only one hour to eat, choosing ESB meant that they died of starvation within a few days. We'll return to this amazing finding later.

In another experiment, rats were first trained to lever press for food when a light was on, and to refrain from lever pressing when a tone was sounded. Each lever press made during the time the tone sounded delayed the delivery of food for 30 seconds. After many sessions of alternating light and tone conditions, the rats learned to press the lever only when the light was on (Anderson, Ferland, & Williams, 1992). In phase two of the experiment, the food or ESB reinforcement alternated with the tone sessions. Even though the rats were hungry, and lever pressing would produce food, they ignored the opportunity to press for food, waited patiently, and responded only for ESB.

The rats who chose the pleasures of ESB over life-giving food call to mind experiments by Curt Richter (1936) who removed adrenal glands from rats. Like the child D.W., these rats excreted too much salt in their urine, and when prevented from consuming extra salt, they died in about a week. However, when such adrenalectomized rats are given a daily one-hour choice between a salt solution and a sucrose solution, some (but not all) the rats will choose the sucrose solution and die due to salt-loss (Harriman, 954). By definition, selecting sucrose or ESB in these experiments appears to be maladaptive, because each behavior resulted in death. How can we account for this apparent violation of the survival instinct?

First, rats and other animals have evolved in a way that require them to balance their nutrient intake over the course of days and weeks, not a single hour. Furthermore, to survive, rats must meet an immediate need for calories as well as salt. Normal rats prefer a sucrose solution to a salt solution, presumably because "sweet" signals a source of calories (Richter, 1942). So when faced with a choice between two short-term pleasures, some rats maladaptively chose the wrong one. (Their choice was maladaptive because they died.) However, several rats in this experiment *did* choose the salty solution over the sucrose solution, and they lived. Their choice illustrates the remarkable redundancy of salt-conserving mechanisms in animals. In most instances, hedonistic tendencies are adaptive.

But why did rats choose ESB over food in Routtenberg and Lindy's (1965) experiment? Rats have not evolved to select ESB over food (an innately predisposed behavior). One possibility is that the sensations caused by ESB are not just highly pleasurable, but are in some sense reminiscent of the pleasure of eating palatable foods (Pfaffman, 1960). So rats may simply confuse ESB sensations with eating sensations. In fact, ESB may be more pleasurable than eating lab chow, because it may elicit more potent feeding sensations. For example, ESB may produce a chocolate-chip-cookie sensation—certainly better than lab chow.

Pleasure Seeking in Humans

Humans who have experienced ESB in hypothalamic areas of the brain report that the sensation is generally pleasurable, in a sexual sort of way (Heath, 1963). There are some parallels between ESB and the effects of taking intensely pleasurable drugs, such as crack cocaine (Flynn, 1991), which commands and controls human behavior in ways that are similar to ESB in rats. Some humans totally rearrange their lives to obtain the drug, going so far as to bypass food and sex. Indeed, many cocaine addicts report a preference for the pleasures of a cocaine high over those of sexual orgasm. Their choice is similar to that of rats that prefer ESB over the opportunity to engage in sex.

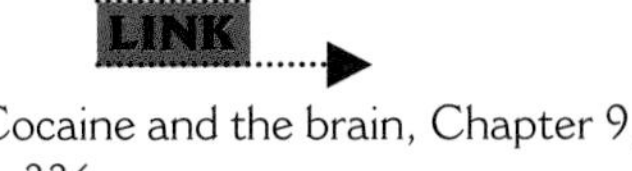

Cocaine and the brain, Chapter 9, p. 336

Dopamine receptors, Chapter 4, p. 143

The cocaine molecule is a more or less perfect key to unlock dopamine receptors in the brain, the source of cocaine's pleasure. ESB may also work on these same receptor mechanisms (Phillips & Fibiger, 1989). Humans seem to have a complex neurochemical system that when activated produces the sensation of pleasure. ESB, tasty foods, certain drugs, and sex are among the activities that stimulate this system. But how do we account for life's other pleasures—talking with friends, getting a high grade on a test, reading a novel, making money, listening to music, and so forth? Further research will likely show that these acquired activities stimulate the brain areas associated with the experience of physical pleasure.

Earlier in this chapter, a distinction was made between primary, or biological, motivation and acquired, or learned, motivation (see p. 145). Unless your life is incredibly simple, you probably are *not* motivated only by primary needs such as eating, drinking, and engaging in sex. In reading this book, for example, you're likely to be pursuing the goal of higher education. The pleasure of achieving a goal such as a college degree is an example of an acquired pleasure. We will see that *acquired pleasures* can function as *secondary reinforcers*. For example, the anticipated pleasure of achieving a long-term goal such as a college degree provides motivation; getting good grades *reinforces* studying. Achieving such goals is *not* drive reducing in the sense that Hull (1943) used the term.

LINK
Acquired motivation and secondary reinforcement, Chapter 6, p. 207

Acquired pleasures are a relative luxury; basic physical pleasures are more crucial to an animal's survival. To gain perspective on the various sources of human motivation, one psychologist developed a hierarchy of needs.

Maslow's Hierarchy of Needs

Abraham Maslow (1954, 1968) proposed that humans are motivated by a five-level *hierarchy of needs* (see Figure 5.8). Like other mammals, they have physiological (food and water), safety, and social needs; unlike other mammals, they also need esteem and the opportunity for self-actualization. But before these higher-level acquired needs can be met, humans must first meet their primary needs. They must locate food and water, find shelter from harm and bad weather, and satisfy their need to belong. The social need to be part of a group, which is exhibited by almost all mammals, is a complex biological need. With few exceptions, humans need to love others and to feel that others love them.

Once these biological needs have been met, people can turn their attention to higher needs. The need for self-esteem is the need to feel that one's existence is worthwhile. Getting an African violet to bloom, nurturing a special relationship, and earning a college degree can all contribute to a feeling of self-worth.

The highest level of motivation for humans is what Maslow calls the need for self-actualization, or the fulfillment of one's own ambitions and potential. Each person's idea of self-actualization is different. Fulfilling the life-long dream of becoming a grandparent is a self-actualizing experience for some people; holding a high office may meet the needs of another person.

Extrinsic versus Intrinsic Motivators

The distinction between primary and acquired motivations is not always clear-cut. For example, your motivation to study may reflect your curiosity about the natural world (Mays, 1991) as well as your interest in obtaining a college degree.

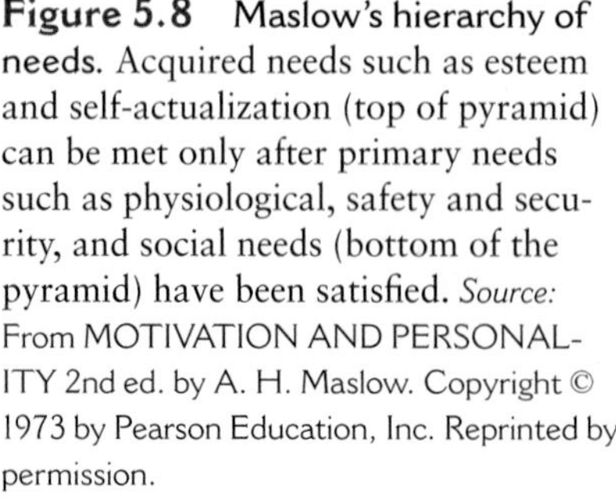

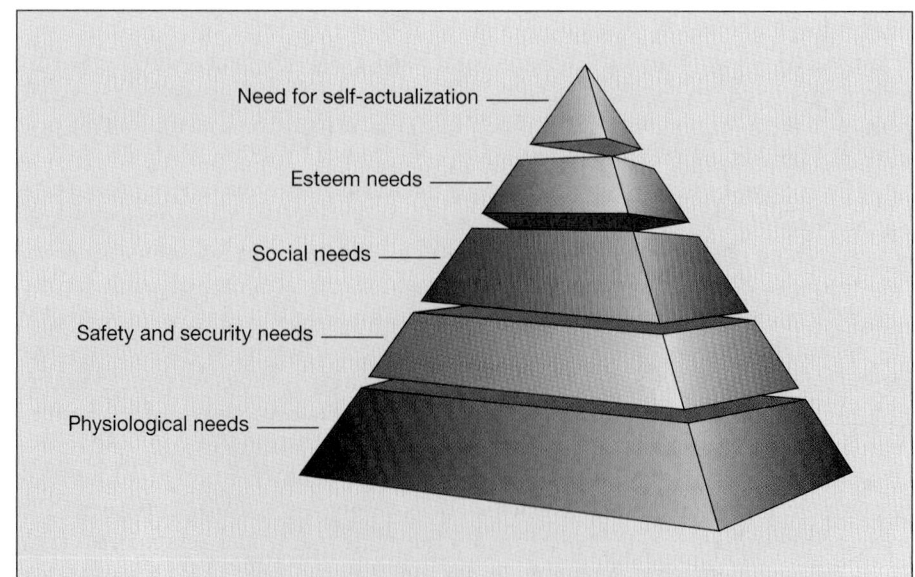

Figure 5.8 Maslow's hierarchy of needs. Acquired needs such as esteem and self-actualization (top of pyramid) can be met only after primary needs such as physiological, safety and security, and social needs (bottom of the pyramid) have been satisfied. *Source:* From MOTIVATION AND PERSONALITY 2nd ed. by A. H. Maslow. Copyright © 1973 by Pearson Education, Inc. Reprinted by permission.

Curiosity is an example of what psychologists call an **intrinsic motivation,** because meeting it is inherently satisfying to you. By contrast, attaining a college degree is an example of an **extrinsic motivation,** because it is an external incentive, a standard set by others. Likewise, a child who "runs because it feels good" is intrinsically motivated, whereas a child who runs to win a first-place medal is extrinsically motivated.

Research into extrinsic and intrinsic motivation has uncovered some interesting relationships. Many students, engineers, scientists, artists, gardeners, business people, and athletes derive tremendous satisfaction from what they do. They get so much pleasure from their work that any rewards (extrinsic motivators) they attain are secondary. Such task-focused individuals often achieve more than people who are motivated by money or other extrinsic awards (Spence & Helmreich, 1983). Researchers have further identified three qualities that contribute to the relatively greater success of task-oriented people:

- *A quest for mastery.* Some individuals internalize higher standards than others. Whether they are performing an exacting sequence of dance steps, writing a better sentence, or designing an optimal spreadsheet, these people want to get it right every time, and if possible to improve on their performance.
- *A drive to work.* Some people work harder than others to meet their internalized goals. Whether they have more energy, put more time into their work, are more focused, or exhibit a combination of these and other attributes, the end result is greater intrinsic motivation and better performance.
- *Less interest in competition.* One counterintuitive finding reported by Spence and Helmreich (1983) is that intrinsically motivated people are less competitive than extrinsically motivated people. The competitive nature of some individuals may actually interfere with their ability to achieve high standards. Intrinsically motivated people may compete with themselves to achieve their internalized standards. Thus, they have no need to compare themselves to others.

Both intrinsic and extrinsic motivators underlie most behaviors. Some research has shown that extrinsic motivators can interfere with, and sometimes undermine, intrinsic motivators—a phenomenon called the **overjustification effect.** Overjustification occurs when rewards are used to reinforce self-satisfying behavior that would have been engaged in anyway. For example, when 3- to 5-year-olds were rewarded for school activities they were engaging in for fun, they began to show less interest in the activities (Lepper, Green & Nisbett, 1973). The overjustification effect has been investigated extensively in a wide range of individuals and has generally been confirmed (Tang & Hall, 1995).

The question is, Why does this effect occur? Behaviors typically increase rather than decrease when they are tangibly reinforced with food, a prize, or good grades. One likely explanation is that people's expectations are violated when they are required to do something they would normally do anyway. Fortunately, praising a child's performance with a smile does not produce the overjustification effect (Swann & Pittman, 1977), nor does a college student's interest in a subject usually diminish with good grades.

Effects of reinforcement on behavior, Chapter 6, p. 206

intrinsic motivation Motivation to achieve self-satisfaction.

extrinsic motivation Motivation to meet the standards of others.

overjustification effect The loss of intrinsic motivation to perform a task that results from the addition of an extrinsic motivator.

need for achievement The motivation to accomplish a task quickly and effectively.

The Need for Achievement

Achieving acquired goals can become the most powerful motivator in a person's life. Hence, people "live" for their music, their profession, or their pursuit of money, to name but a few goals that motivate them. Among the better-researched esteem needs (as well as the need for self-actualization Maslow identified) is the need for achievement.

The **need for achievement** is the motivation to accomplish a challenging task quickly and effectively. David McClelland and his students and colleagues have spent 40 years studying this type of motivation (McClelland, 1985). They have

The situation shown on this TAT card is deliberately ambiguous. To explain it, the subject who views this picture must project personal motivations and emotions onto the story.

not only analyzed the personalities of individuals who demonstrated this need, but also compared the need for achievement of entire societies by analyzing their literature. Not surprisingly, they have found that individuals who score high on the need for achievement work harder than others, are more future oriented, and will delay gratification longer (Mischel, 1961). A student may demonstrate the need for achievement, for example, by spending the weekend writing a term paper instead of partying.

The need for achievement is measured by asking individuals to respond to a series of pictures showing people in a variety of ambiguous situations. The photograph on this page shows one picture from the Thematic Apperception Test (TAT), developed in the 1930s by the psychologist Henry Murray. The test subject is asked to tell a story about what is happening in each picture, including what happened before and after the event, and what the people in the picture are likely to be thinking or feeling. The TAT is an example of a *projective test*, so called because the subject is assumed to project his or her own motivation onto the people in the picture (Murray, 1938).

TAT test and personality tests, Chapter 14, p. 489

You might suspect that given a choice, people whose TAT stories reveal both a competitive nature and a high need to achieve would prefer the more challenging of two real-life tasks. Laboratory studies do not support such reasoning, however. People with a high need to achieve tend to maximize their opportunity for success by choosing intermediate-level tasks rather than the most difficult (McClelland & Koestner, 1992). The successful meeting of goals is apparently more important to these subjects than the challenge per se. Aiming unrealistically high wastes energy; accomplishing what is possible is more efficient, and in the long run more adaptive.

Achievement makes at least some people content and happy; failure can produce pain, sadness, and unhappiness. In the next section we will explore further the relationship between motivation and emotion.

INTERIM SUMMARY

1. Humans and other animals are motivated by pleasure.
2. Passing a small amount of electric current (ESB) through the *mesotelencephalic dopamine system* and other structures in and near the hypothalamus produces pleasure in rats, humans, and other animals.
3. ESB is so pleasurable that given the choice, rats will press a lever that produces ESB while ignoring a lever that yields life-sustaining food.
4. Normal rats will prefer ESB over food. Some rats that have had their adrenal glands removed prefer sucrose to a life-sustaining salt solution. Both these examples demonstrate what appears to be maladaptive behavior in short-term laboratory tests.
5. The pleasurable sensations produced by ESB are reported to be similar to sexual pleasure. A rat's preoccupation with ESB is similar to the human attraction to crack cocaine.
6. ESB, tasty foods, sex, and drugs directly stimulate the brain's pleasure-producing system. Life's other (acquired) pleasures probably do the same.
7. Acquired pleasures are among the most powerful motivators in a person's life.
8. Maslow's *hierarchy of needs* is represented by a five-level pyramid, with biological needs at the base and acquired needs at the top. The five levels are primary (food and water) needs, security needs, social needs, esteem needs, and the need for self-actualization.
9. **Intrinsic motivation** produces self-satisfaction, whereas **extrinsic motivation** brings external rewards for meeting standards set by others.

10. Two important intrinsic motivators are the quest for mastery and a high drive to work. Intrinsically motivated people are less competitive than extrinsically motivated people.
11. Extrinsic rewards that interfere with intrinsic motivation can produce an ***overjustification effect.***
12. Some people have a higher ***need for achievement*** than others. This need can be measured by the Thematic Apperception Test (TAT). Competitive and hard working, high achievers take pleasure in satisfying long-term goals.

For Further Thought

1. Comparing your culture with that of a third-world country, do you think there is a difference between the two in primary and acquired motives? In your own culture, is there a difference between the primary and acquired motives seen in infants and adults?
2. What are the intrinsic motivators in your life?
3. Why do you think some people have a higher need for achievement than others?
4. Do you think automobile advertisers should concentrate on the safety and reliability of their latest models before their styling and status? Why or why not?

THE EXPERIENCE OF EMOTION

We arrange our lives to pursue pleasure and to avoid pain, two motives that are major determinants of human behavior. The experience of pleasure—happiness—is also an *emotion*, a unique psychological state. Emotions play highly adaptive roles in our lives by allowing us to share interpretations of the environment with each other. My blush signals embarrassment and discomfort. Likewise, your laughter communicates to others a positive response to something you've experienced. Learned emotions can also be maladaptive: many common maladjustments and mental illnesses center around emotional dysfunction.

Emotion and abnormal psychology, Chapter 17, p. 584

If I were to ask you to describe the five most important events or most memorable experiences in your life, each of them would likely involve some state of emotion. For most people, life's highs and lows are measured emotionally rather than cognitively. Students are more likely to explain how happy they are to have passed an exam, for example, than to discuss the content of specific test items. Fans are more likely to attend sporting events to experience the elation of victory than to study the coach's strategy. Likewise, most people prefer to experience music emotionally rather than to analyze its structure.

In this section we'll consider not the motivating properties of emotions, but the psychological experiences of happiness and sadness, fear and anger. Among the questions we will raise is whether human emotions are innate or learned. One type of evidence that bears on this issue is the experience of feral children (Candland, 1993) who have survived after abandonment in rural areas, or less likely, after the death of their parents. Amala and Kamala, for example, were literally dug out from a wolf's den in India. Both were judged to be less than 10 years of age. Taken to an orphanage in India and raised with other children, they never learned to speak. Their adult caretakers reported that the children's emotional development remained more wolflike than human. Even with a human

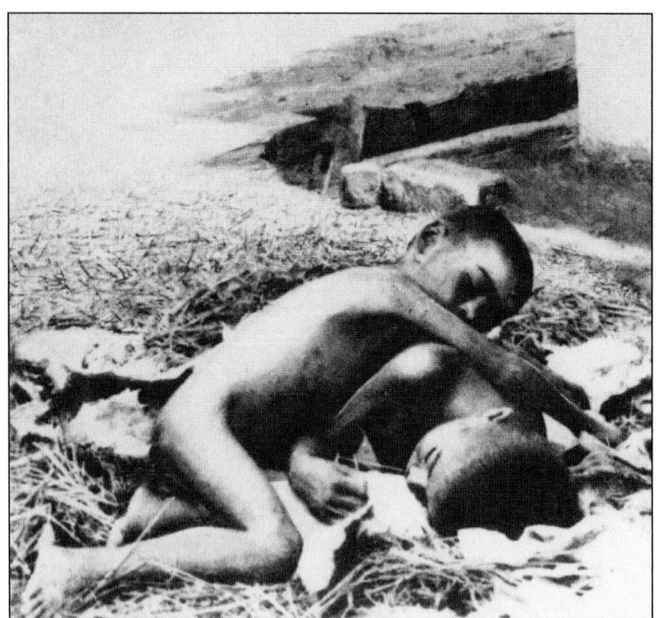

These feral children were found in a wolf's den in India. Their intellectual and emotional development were more wolflike than human.

genotype, a human brain, and human physiology, they appeared to lack the most basic of human emotions. In the words of their caretakers, "there was no sense of human emotion, except in the one case when Kamala wept when Amala died, of sorrow" (Candland, 1993, p. 67). To explain Amala and Kamala's emotional development, we must first explore the biological underpinnings of emotion.

Evolutionary and Genetic Determinants of Emotion

In *The Expression of Emotion in Man and Animals*, Charles Darwin recognized that emotional behavior is adaptive. Emotional behavior arouses an animal, helps to organize its behavior, and communicates its intentions to other animals. The drawings of the body postures of two dogs on this page were taken from Darwin's classic book (Darwin, 1872/1965). The dog on the left has assumed a threat posture; the dog on the right, a submissive posture. Both effectively communicate the dog's behavioral intentions.

Darwin proposed that the basic emotions humans experience are no different from the emotions of other animals. Humans, too, use body posture to threaten or express submission, and to communicate their sexual intentions. Darwin was especially interested in how humans' facial expressions reflect their evolutionary history. An aggressive sneer, he thought, derived from a facial threat gesture seen in many mammals, which involves pulling up a lip and exposing a canine.

Darwin's thesis that the evolutionary origins of human emotions are revealed in human facial expressions was elaborated by later researchers (Buss, 2000). Figure 5.9, for instance, traces the origins of the human smile and laughter to primitive mammals (Eibl-Eibesfeldt, 1970). To give another example, Scott and Fuller (1965) conducted breeding experiments on fearfulness in Basenji hounds and cocker spaniels (see Chapter 3, page 86). They found that fearfulness was a single-gene effect and that the fear allele was dominant. Given the similarity of brain structure in mammals (indeed, all vertebrates), emotions are likely to be primitive features of consciousness, and the expression of emotions in large part genetically determined.

Genetics of emotion, Chapter 3, p. 86

Emotions are adaptive. Positive emotions instigate approach behaviors; negative emotions lead to avoidance behaviors (see Figure 5.10). Specifically, positive emotions promote mating, deep friendship, close kinship, and cooperation (Buss,

This plate from Charles Darwin's *The Expression of Emotion in Man and Animals* shows threatening (left) and submissive postures (right) in dogs.

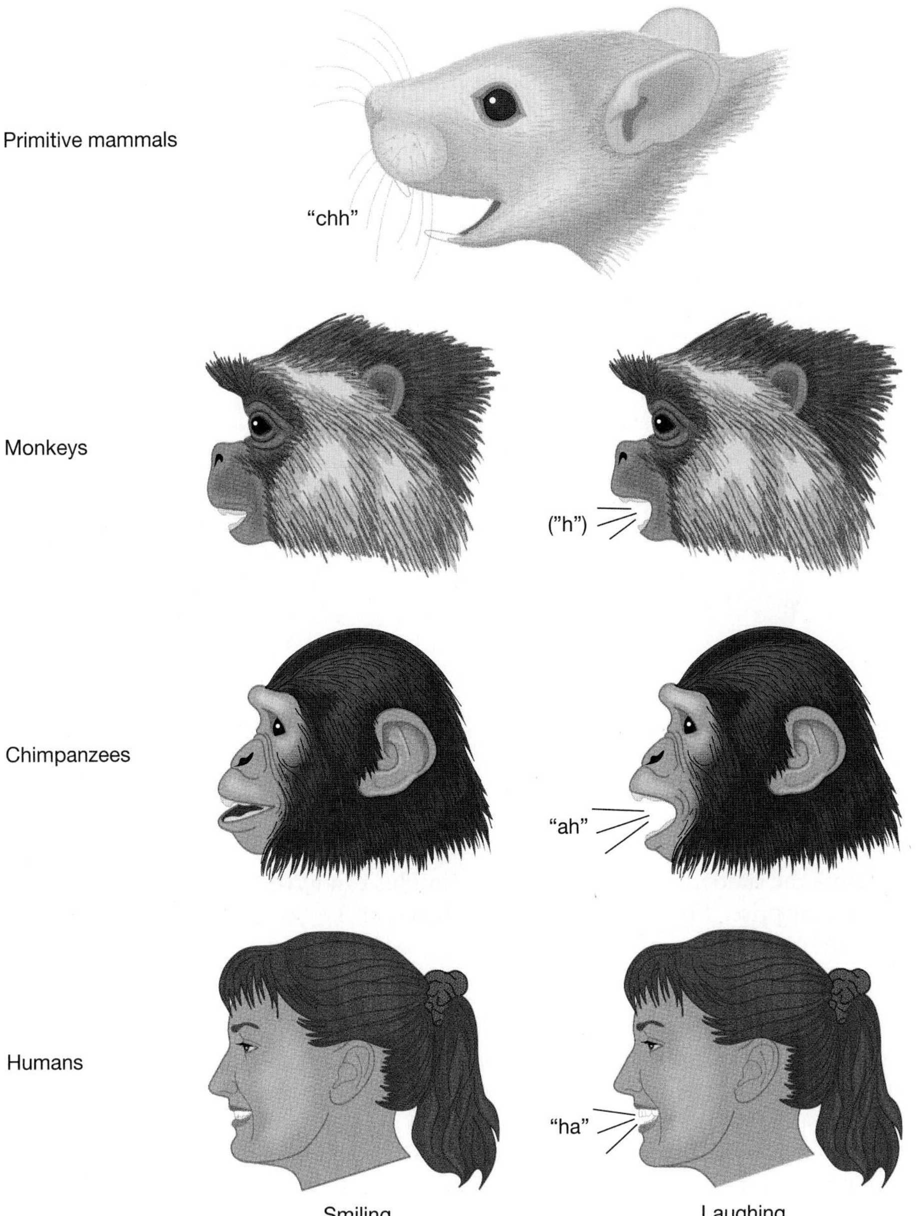

Figure 5.9 The origin of the human smile and laughter. Happiness is expressed in two ways—with a silent smile, or by laughing out loud. Similar facial expressions and vocalizations are found in other primates as well as more primitive mammals. *Source:* After Eibl-Eibesfeldt, 1970.

2000). Emotions can be experienced in varying degrees of intensity: hearts pound harder and beat faster under some conditions than others. This phenomenon is related to an animal's level of arousal, a variation indicated by the middle continuum of psychological states in Figure 5.10. For example, boredom progresses to interest and culminates in surprise.

Emotion in Wolves. The drawings on page 175 show the range of emotional intensity in a wolf. Beginning with a relaxed state (face "a"), the wolf has the option of running away or fighting when threatened. Its face expresses the combination of rage and fear that accompanies each choice. Fleeing is characterized by a flattening of the ears (faces "a" to "c"), and rage by a retracted upper lip and wrinkled nose and forehead (faces "a" to "g"). The intensity of these expressions increases with emotional arousal (face "i"). In the next chapter we'll see that low levels of stimulation tend to habituate an animal, producing boredom,

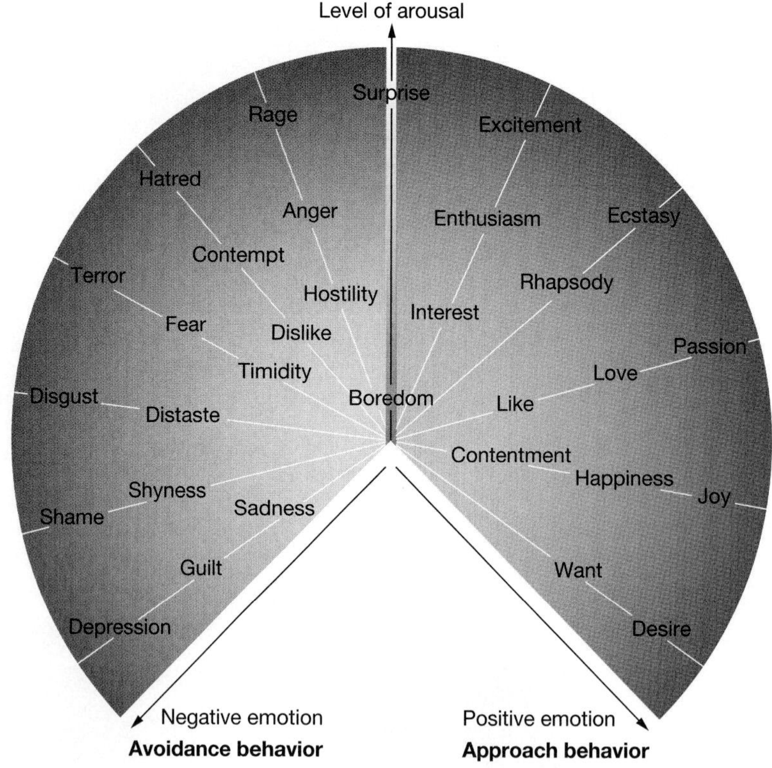

Figure 5.10 Positive and negative emotions. Negative emotions lead to avoidance behaviors, whereas positive emotions lead to approach behaviors. Here, the intensity of an emotion is indicated by the relative intensity of its color, from pastel (less bodily arousal) to full color (more bodily arousal).
Source: After Kissin, 1986.

whereas the sudden onset of an intense stimulus can have a sensitizing effect, producing surprise. Emotional responses, then, can be seen as adaptive responses elicited by the environment.

Emotion in Humans. Using different methodologies, three researchers (Plutchik, 1984; Tomkins, 1991; Izard, 1984, 1991) have recently come to many of the same conclusions as Darwin—namely, that the primary emotions are limited. Assuming as Darwin did that emotions are genetically based, and that they reflect innate tendencies, each came up with a remarkably similar list of basic emotions. All three researchers included anger, disgust, fear, interest (or anticipation), joy, and surprise on their lists. These basic emotions seem to apply to all primates and many mammals. Two investigators also listed contempt and shame as exclusively human emotions. Finally, their combined list includes sadness as a primary emotion of both humans and many mammals.

These lists are not meant to be exhaustive, but rather to suggest the wide range of subjectively experienced human feelings. As Figure 5.10 indicates, the number of emotions can be multiplied merely by considering their relative intensity, and as the drawings of wolves suggest, by blending primary emotions. Plutchik (1984), for example, has proposed that optimism is a blend of joy and anticipation, remorse a blend of sadness and disgust.

Demographic research on happiness also suggests that emotion is genetically determined. For instance, happiness is usually studied as *subjective well-being.* Some research (Okun, Stock, Haring, & Witter, 1984) has shown that subjective well-being correlates $r = .32$ with one's health. (Are healthy people happier, or does being happy make one healthy? The correlative evidence doesn't tell us.) But no single demographic variable accounts for happiness. The importance of this finding is that contrary to popular belief, a person who either inherits wealth or wins a lottery isn't necessarily a happier person for the experience (Diener, 2000).

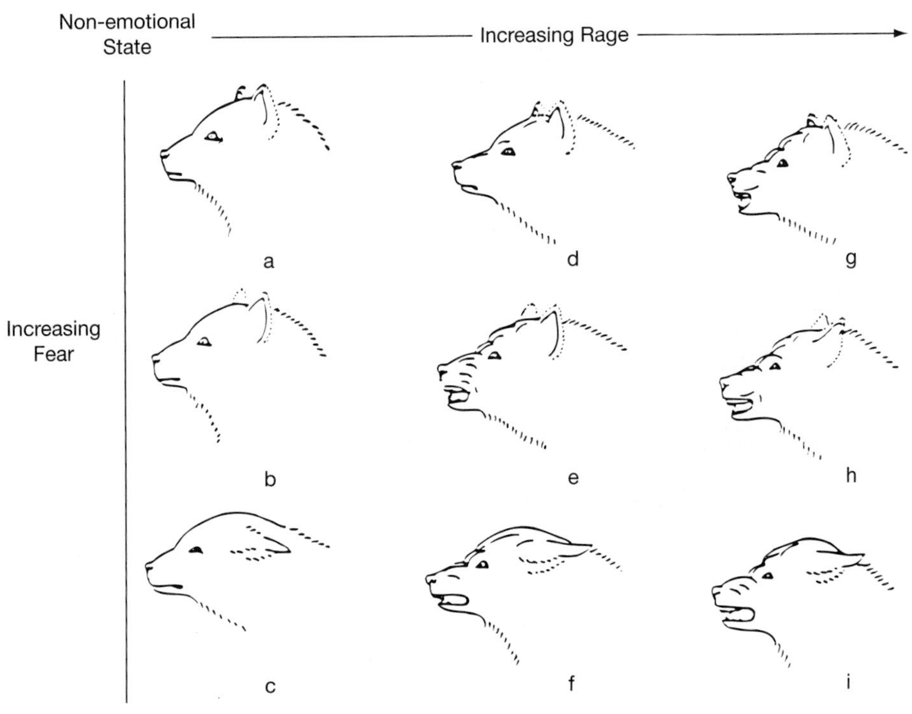

Fear, submission, and preparation for flight characterize the emotions shown on faces a to c. Faces a to g show increased anger prior to fighting. Emotions both compete with and complement each other, as shown by the expression of a wolf that is both fearful and defensively angry (face i).

Rather, happiness seems more a personality trait, something one is predisposed to at birth. As children and adults, happy people wear rose-colored glasses, and think of themselves and others in optimistic and adaptive ways (DeNeve, 1999).

LINK

Happiness and personality, Chapter 14, p. 491

Cultural Expressions of Emotion

Some research has shown that culture can modify the expression of emotion. For example, about 550 English words have emotional content, but not all of those words have equivalents in other languages, and not all cultures categorize emotions the same way (Averill, 1980). Many cultures do not have a word for either depression or anxiety; some use the words for fear, anger, and remorse in different ways than in Western culture (Russell, 1991).

Facial Expression of Emotion. Because emotions are difficult to express in language, most anthropologists and psychologists measure the behavioral expression of emotion. Not surprisingly, most researchers agree with Darwin that facial expressions are innate (that is, genetically determined) expressions of emotion. The photographs on page 176 show six facial expressions that people from different cultures identify in the same way: happiness, anger, sadness, surprise, disgust, and fear. To these six emotions more recent research has added contempt, guilt, interest, and shame (Ekman, 1993).

Display Rules. People of different cultures also wear unique "game faces" that mask their primary emotions. The look of disbelief, bemusement, and anger that a ballplayer might wear when he doesn't like a referee's call is one example; the exaggerated grimace of someone who has just heard a bad pun, another. Cultural *display rules* prescribe the appropriate body postures and facial grimaces for these game faces. Japanese who bow politely when greeting acquaintances (a primeval submissive gesture?) are conforming to elaborate cultural rules governing this ceremonial behavior. Another example of a Japanese display rule

Researchers showed these photos to test subjects and asked them to identify what emotion was being expressed. Can you match the labels anger, sadness, surprise, disgust, fear, and happiness to the correct faces? (Answer: Start with anger at 12 o'clock and read clockwise.)

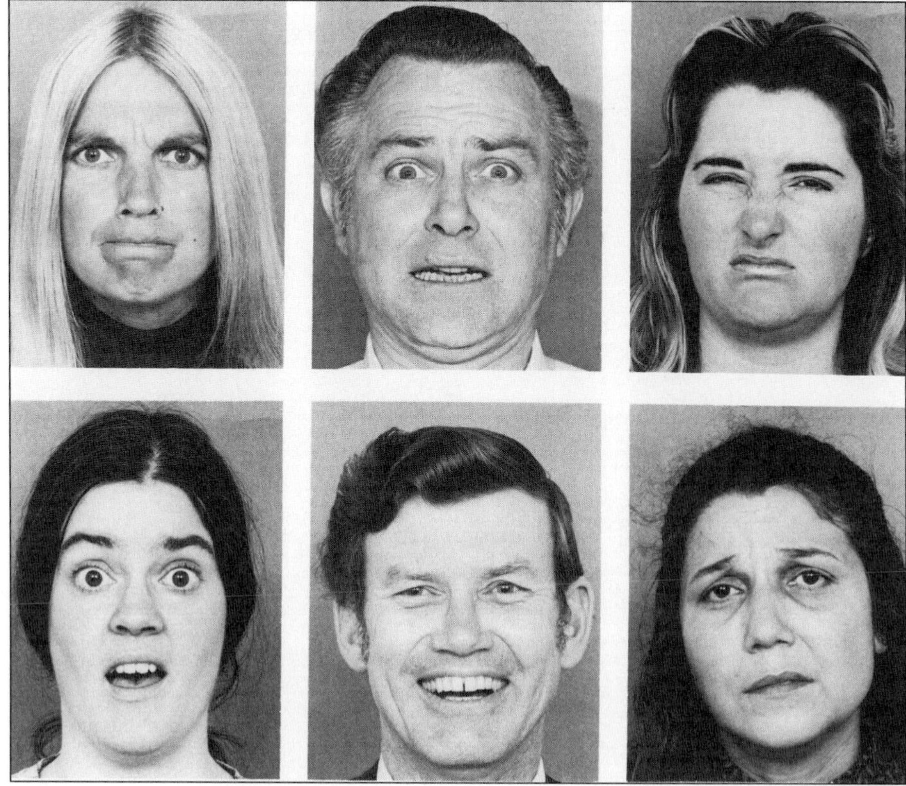

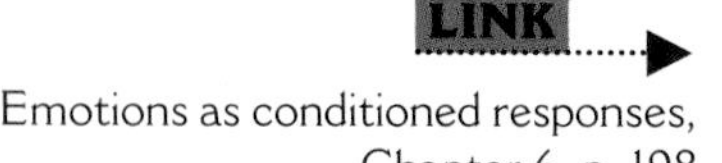

Emotions as conditioned responses, Chapter 6, p. 198

is the polite smile that substitutes for public displays of negative emotions: showing sadness or disgust is prohibited in Japanese culture. Finally, display rules governing emotional expression can become formalized as rules in law. Examples are the prohibition against excessive celebration following touchdowns, and local ordinances that prohibit saluting another person with an extended middle finger.

These culture-bound forms of emotional expression are learned. Just as a culture provides acceptable ways for people to meet their nutritional needs, it provides a framework in which people can express their innate emotions. For example, small boys are punished for crying in some cultures; they therefore learn not to express their sadness by crying. Recall the feral children, Amala and Kamala. The people who found them thought that they had been raised in a wolf-culture that prohibited the expression of emotional behavior. Thus, the two tears (*two tears*!) Kamala wept when her sister Amala died may be taken as evidence of a human essence that persisted despite the nonhuman emotional training she received.

Culture, then, provides the framework in which innate emotions are expressed. For example, the emotion of fear can be conditioned to the phrase "You didn't pass your final exam." Likewise, one person may fear a situation another does not because of different learning experiences. After a near-drowning incident, one person may fear the same ocean that someone else swims in with great delight. Like motivation, emotion has a biological basis that individuals express within the constraints of their experiences and their culture.

Leonardo daVinci (1452–1519), Mona Lisa. Louvre, Paris, France. Scala / Art Resource, N.Y.

Biological Bases of Emotion

Leonardo Da Vinci's *Mona Lisa* is among the world's most recognizable paintings. For centuries the source of her enigmatic smile has been the subject of speculation. But our interest here is more prosaic than wondering whether or not she

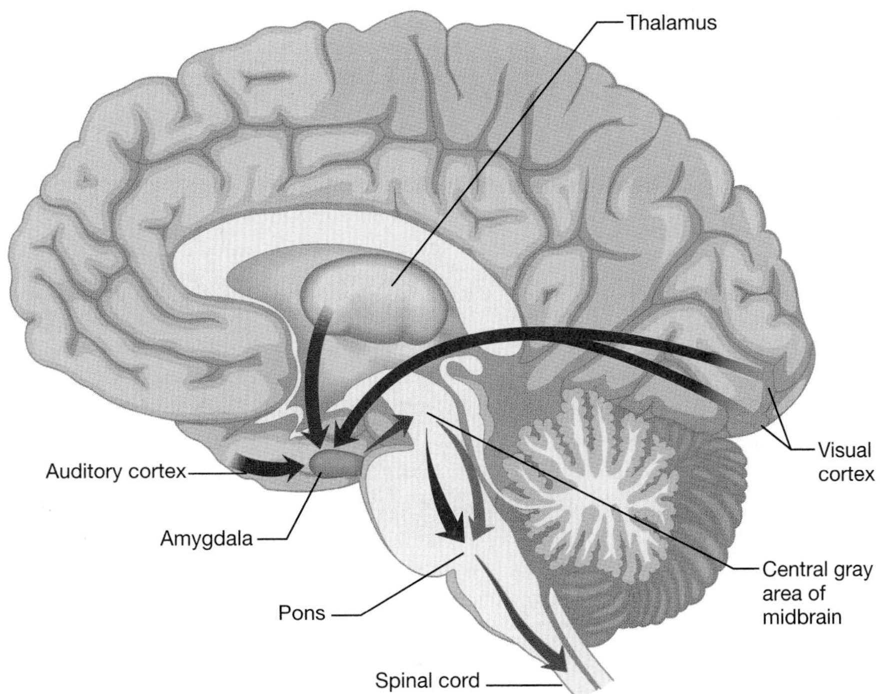

Figure 5.11 The emotional brain. A fear-inducing stimulus is perceived by subcortical brain areas (the thalamus) and cortical areas that mediate seeing and hearing (the visual and auditory cortex) and send nerve fibers to the amygdala. Movement is initiated when nerves from the amygdala synapse on midbrain structures, including the central gray area of the midbrain and pons. The information is then transmitted through the spinal cord to the body's muscles.

was happily pregnant at the time her portrait was painted! Rather, our question is how the brain generates and controls emotion and emotional expression such as Mona Lisa's, and how the brain perceives emotion in the faces of others. The physiology of emotion is not easily described; here we are particularly interested in the limbic system, where emotions begin.

The Limbic System and the Amygdala. An emotion typically begins when an environmental event triggers receptors in the eyes or ears. Hearing "WATCH OUT" or unexpectedly catching sight of one's significant other are examples of environmental stimuli that can trigger emotions. These stimuli activate the brain's limbic system. As Figure 5.11 shows, the amygdala plays a key role in interpreting events that trigger emotions and in initiating nervous activity in the medulla, pons, and spinal cord. In turn, these areas control the sympathetic division of the autonomic nervous system, which determines the appropriateness of a fight or flight response (Jansen, Nguyen, Karpitskiy, Mettenleiter, & Loewy, 1995). As we learned in Chapter 4, the sympathetic division is responsible for the pounding heart, the dilated pupils, the clammy hands, and the surge of epinephrine that characterizes intense emotion.

Emotions and the autonomic nervous system, Chapter 4, p. 116

The amygdala receives sensory input directly from receptors that are triggered by an emotion-arousing stimulus—especially those that arouse anxiety and fear. For example, PET scan studies have shown greater activity in the amygdala when subjects are looking at pictures of fearful faces than when they are looking at smiling faces (Morris et al., 1996). A person with a damaged amygdala (and immediately adjacent brain areas; see Anderson, Spencer, Fulbright, & Phelps, 2000) is impaired at interpreting facial emotions. Such a person can identify emotional expressions correctly except for a fearful one. When one patient was asked to draw faces expressing various emotions, she did fairly well, with the exception of fear (see her drawings on page 178).

Facial movements and motor homunculus, Chapter 4, p. 127

The Frontal Lobes. The expression of emotion is not limited to the amygdala and brainstem mechanisms. The frontal lobes receive information from the senses (through the thalamus) and from subcortical areas. When an oncoming

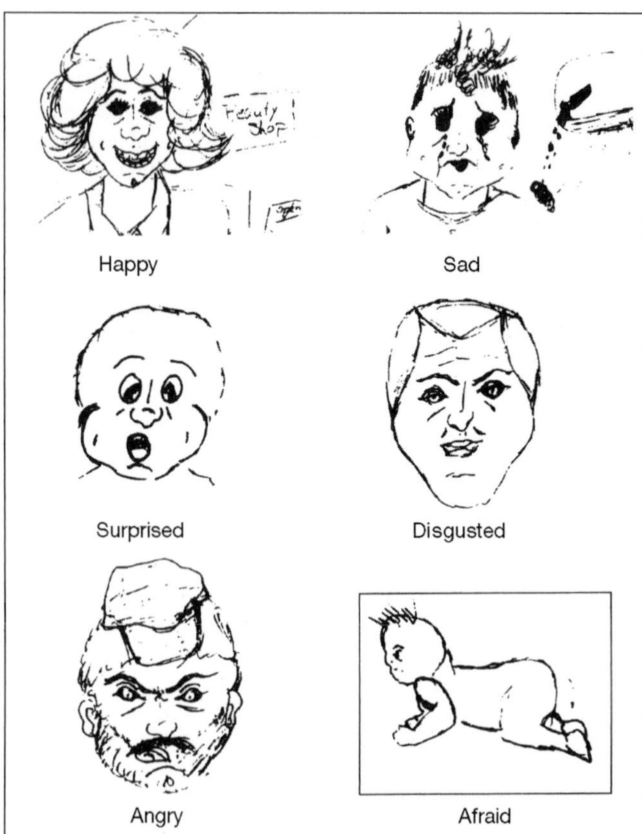

A patient suffering from a damaged amygdala drew these faces. Except for the picture of fear, all the drawings are realistic. The patient explained that she couldn't imagine fear, so she couldn't express it. Eventually she remembered that when people are afraid, their hair stands on end and they try to escape.

car crosses the double line and careens into your lane, challenging you to act, millions of neurons in your frontal lobe are activated. The frontal lobes also receive input from, and send nerve fibers to, the amygdala. Both the premotor and primary motor cortex in the frontal lobes generate movements appropriate to the emotion, including facial expressions like a reflexive or intentional grimace or smile, as well as more molar responses, such as running away, and probably the "feeling" of emotion (Damasio, 1999).

A smile is generated by two sets of facial muscles. The *orbicularis muscles* around the eyes and the *zygomatic muscles* around the mouth are both controlled unconsciously (and indirectly) by the amygdala and related limbic system structures. When a person laughs, these muscles produce a natural, uninhibited smile initiated in the subcortical structures. The cortical structures (which embody cultural mores) are responsible for "fake smiles" (Damasio, 1994). Most smiles, grimaces, and surprised expressions are the product of both voluntary and involuntary systems.

Are we now better able to understand Mona Lisa's enigmatic smile? The neuroscientist Margaret Livingston thinks that DaVinci's genius in the use of shadow causes perceptual problems for viewers: focusing on Mona Lisa's eyes with one's peripheral vision suggests a smile that disappears when the viewer's focus shifts to her mouth (Livingstone, 2000).

The role of the frontal lobes in emotion can also be seen in cases of brain damage. Recall from Chapter 4 that Phineas Gage's emotional behavior changed markedly after an exploded steel bar damaged his frontal lobes (see p. 105). After the accident his behavior was unpredictable, inappropriate, and uncontrollable. In the United States, between the 1930s and the 1950s, thousands of intentional assaults were made on the frontal lobes of people with vaguely defined emotional disorders. Before the advent of psychoactive drugs, caring for deranged people was a dangerous task. To reduce the danger, surgeons devised a form of **psychosurgery** called a *lobotomy* (or frontal lobotomy), in which nerves connecting the frontal lobes with other parts of the brain were severed. For two decades this surgery was used on 40,000 people (Shutts, 1942) because it produced the desired outcome. Lobotomized patients were more easily managed because they were apathetic and less emotional. The ethics and outcomes of this and other surgical procedures designed to change an individual's personality are discussed in Valenstein (1986). Fortunately, the advent of psychotherapeutic drugs made frontal lobotomy and its dehumanizing effects unnecessary.

LINK

Surgery as treatment for mental disorders, Chapter 18, p. 629

Emotions and frontal lobes, Chapter 4, p. 135

psychosurgery Brain surgery performed with the object of changing a person's emotional behavior.

The frontal lobes are involved not only in the expression of emotion, but also in the perception of emotional states in others. For example, subjects who viewed women's photographs in college yearbooks rated those women who expressed positive emotions (by their smiles) as more competent and more desirable as friends than others (Harker & Keltner, 2001). A number of studies of brain-damaged people (as well as the results of split-brain experiments described in Chapter 4) have implicated the *right* frontal lobe in the perception of emotion. For example, humans normally convey emotion through their tone of voice and patterns of inflection. Individuals who have suffered damage to the right frontal area, however, speak in a relatively expressionless manner and cannot pick up the emotional subtleties of humor and irony in another person's speech (Tucker, 1981). These people also have difficulty "reading" the emotional expressions in pictures of faces (Stone, Nisenson, Eliassen, & Gazzaniga, 1996). Interestingly enough, they are also less capable than others at expressing emotion through appropriate facial gestures (Rinn, 1984). The part of the brain that is apparently involved in recognizing humor (allowing a person to appreciate the punch line of a joke) has been localized in a small area of the cortex over the right eye (Shibata, 2000).

Other studies suggest that the perception of emotion is not limited to the right hemisphere, however. Using the electroencephalogram (EEG) to measure electrical activity in the frontal lobes, scientists found that subjects who viewed "happy" films of playful animals showed more responsivity in their left hemispheres, while their right hemispheres were more active when they viewed gruesome medical procedures (Davidson, 1992). The adaptive significance of such hemispheric specialization of emotion is not yet understood.

Theories of Emotion

The James-Lange Theory. A few years after Darwin (1872/1965) wrote about the adaptiveness of emotion, and the continuity of emotion among humans and other animals, two other biological theories of emotion were published. Because they shared common features, they eventually became known as the **James-Lange theory** of emotion. According to the James-Lange theory, a person becomes conscious of being in an emotional state only after the body has been aroused. Put another way, the perception of a threatening, emotionally arousing stimulus triggers the sympathetic nervous system, causing the heart to beat faster and the palms to sweat. Only then does consciousness provide an interpretation of the arousal. When confronted with a runaway car, I experience tachycardia (a fast heart beat) and therefore am afraid. In this counterintuitive, cart-before-the-horse approach, a specific biological change precedes and determines the kind of emotion that is experienced.

The Cannon-Bard Theory. Several decades later, two researchers questioned the counterintuitiveness of the James-Lange theory and proposed some changes to it. The first was William Cannon, mentioned earlier in this chapter for his development of the idea of homeostasis. Cannon argued that physiological arousal was not a sufficient trigger for emotion. For example, a person who is hard at work or running in a race is in high autonomic arousal but may be experiencing little emotion. Cannon also pointed out that very similar patterns of arousal in the autonomic nervous system (ANS) are associated with diverse emotional experiences. Fear, anger, and happiness all produce similar ANS arousal patterns (Cannon, 1927). Philip Bard elaborated on Cannon's theory, which today is known as the **Cannon-Bard theory** of emotion.

Over the years, the Cannon-Bard theory has been modified to emphasize the role of subcortical brain structures in emotion. The theory states that an emotionally arousing stimulus first activates structures in the brain, which in turn (and more or less simultaneously) arouse the ANS, producing emotion. According to the Cannon-Bard theory, then, emotion results from subcortical brain activity, which causes both the physical response and the psychological experience of emotion. Figure 5.12 contrasts the Cannon-Bard and James-Lange theories.

Which theory is right? A surprising amount of evidence supports both positions. Even though sympathetic nervous activity is similar in different emotional states (my heart beats rapidly when I'm enraged or enraptured), the body *does* feel different, as William James noted. For example, my personal experience in running a long-distance race is that my body feels different when I'm chasing someone than it does when I'm being chased. When chasing, I'm hopeful that I can catch up to the person in front of me; when being chased, I'm uneasy and fear I'll be overtaken. My *legs* seem to respond hopefully or fearfully in these situations: They feel heavy when I'm being passed and youthful when I'm catching up.

James-Lange theory The theory that emotion is the awareness of one's bodily response to a given stimulus.

Cannon-Bard theory The theory that emotion results from subcortical brain activity, which causes both a physical response and an emotional experience.

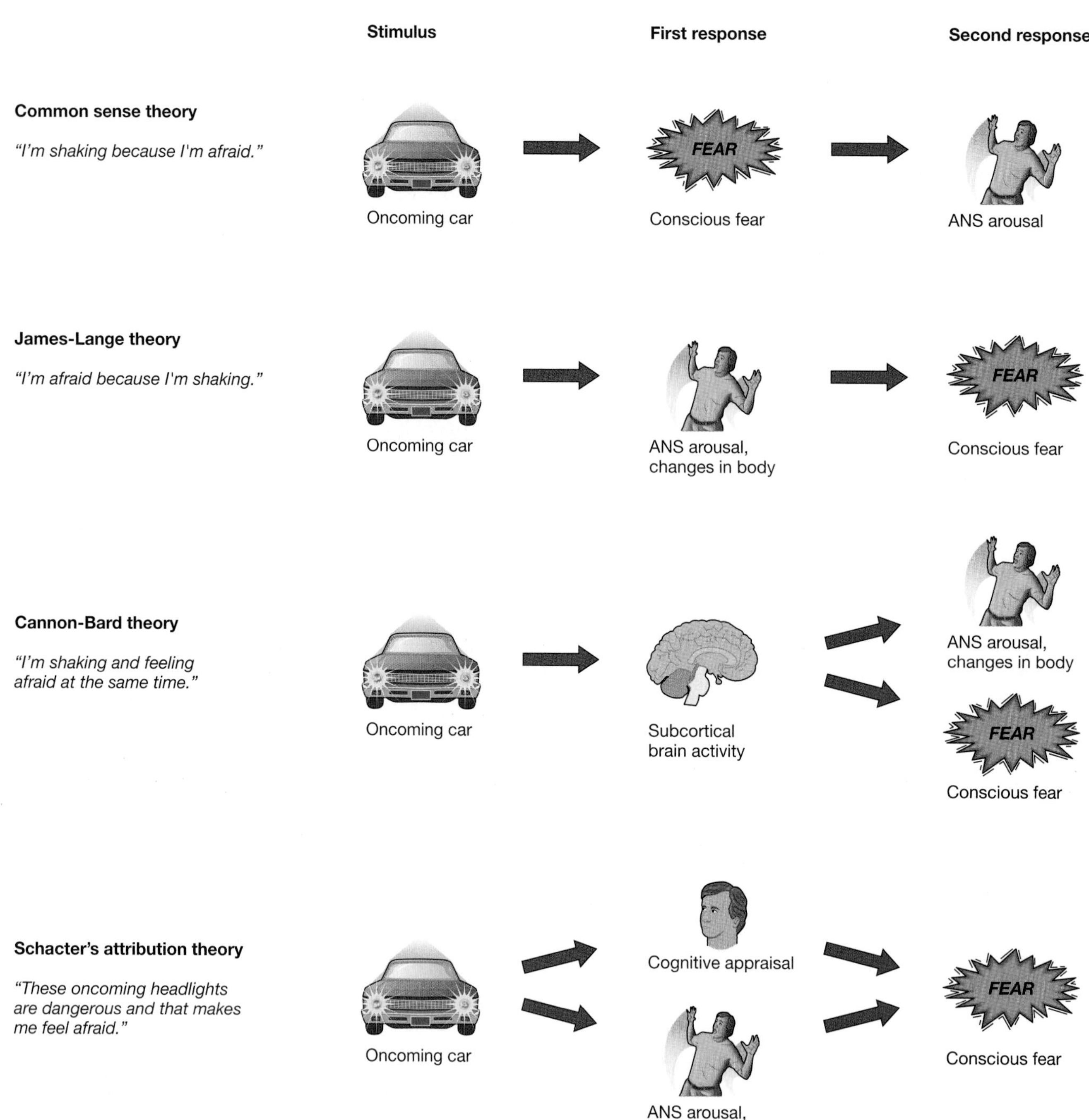

Figure 5.12 Theories of emotion. Theories of emotion differ with respect to the timing of the body's psychological and physiological responses, as well as the role of cognitive processes in interpreting emotion.

Schacter's emotional attribution theory The theory that emotion is experienced after a person appraises a stimulus and monitors the body's response.

Schacter's Emotional Attribution Theory. Stanley Schacter (1964) proposed a theory that takes into account an early cognitive interpretation of the nature of an emotion-producing situation. According to **Schacter's emotional attribution theory**, the body first becomes aroused, and then the mind thinks about what is happening. In a long-distance race, the runner's appraisal of the situation produces the emotion of hope or unease. Similarly, if after an exam you think you did well, you will feel elation—but not if you think you did poorly. And a large dog will invoke different emotions if it is seen standing behind a locked gate rather than open one. Schacter's theory, like the James-Lange theory, holds that emotion depends on a state of bodily arousal, but it also introduces a cognitive component that determines the quality of the emotion. Emotion is experienced only after a person appraises both the stimulus and the body's response.

In a classic experiment, Schacter and Singer (1962) tested the emotional attribution theory by dividing paid volunteers (college students) into three groups. Members of each group were told they would be given a vitamin injection, and sometime later a vision test. Actually, one group was injected with epinephrine, a drug that increases sympathetic nervous system activity, and the other two groups were given a control injection of saline. (This study probably could *not* be done today because it involved both gross deception and an invasive technique.) Furthermore, one of the control groups was not given any instructions about what to expect from the injection. Half the subjects in the treatment group, and half in the other control group, were told they could expect some side effects—increased heart rate, a general warming sensation, and arousal. Because those are actual effects of epinephrine, the suggested symptoms matched those they would likely experience. The other half of the subjects were told they would feel numbness, an itching sensation, and possibly a headache—all bogus effects.

After receiving the injections, subjects were tested individually in rooms in the presence of another student (called an experimental confederate), who behaved in one of two ways, as instructed by the researcher. The confederate either displayed anger or acted euphoric and goofy (mimicking a drug effect). The results, summarized in Table 5.1, were intriguing. As expected, none of the subjects who received placebo injections were affected by the confederate's behavior. Subjects who received the epinephrine injections, however, were aroused by the drug's effects. Those in the group that received accurate pretreatment instructions (Groups 1a and 1b in Table 5.1) paid no attention to the confederate's behavior. But the subjects who were injected with epinephrine and misinformed about how they would feel (Groups 1c and 1d) *were* influenced by the confederate. They displayed significantly more emotional behavior—euphoria or anger, depending on the emotion being modeled by the confederate—than control subjects. In the absence of a reason for their arousal, and without knowing how the injection was supposed to make them feel, these subjects used the information the confederates provided. As predicted by Schacter's theory, this cognitive misinformation determined the type of emotion they experienced.

Of all the various theories summarized in Figure 5.12, Schacter's attribution theory gives a better account of both the experience of emotion and observations about how the brain's activity can affect its expression. What remains to be accomplished is to incorporate both genetic and neurophysiological data into a theory of emotion.

Table 5.1 Schacter and Singer's (1962) Experiment

Group	Pretreatment Instructions	1st Independent Variable	2nd Independent Variable	Test Results
1- a, b	Accurate drug effects	Epinephrine	1- a Euphoric confederate 1- b Angry confederate	Accurate emotion Accurate emotion
1- c, d	Misleading drug effects	Epinephrine	1- c Euphoric confederate 1- d Anger confederate	Euphoria Anger
2- a,b	Accurate drug effects	Placebo	2- a Euphoric confederate 2- b Angry confederate	No effects No effects
2- c,d	Misleading drug effects	Placebo	2- c Euphoric confederate 2- d Angry confederate	No effects No effects
3- a,b	No instructions	Placebo	3- a Euphoric confederate 3- b Angry confederate	No effects No effects
2- c,d	No instructions	Placebo	3- c Euphoric confederate 3- d Angry confederate	No effects No effects

INTERIM SUMMARY

1. Emotions such as happiness and sadness, fear and anger are unique psychological and biological states. Emotions are genetically predisposed primitive features of consciousness shared by all animals.
2. Emotional behavior, elicited by environmental changes, is adaptive in arousing and helping to organize an animal's behavior, and in communicating its intentions to other animals. Positive emotions lead to approach behaviors, whereas negative emotions promote avoidance behaviors.
3. Perhaps because emotions are so poorly communicated by language, psychologists have difficulty studying them cognitively. Darwin assumed that facial expressions of emotion are innate, and with some exceptions, comparative studies of animals and cross-cultural studies of humans have supported his claims.
4. The existence of *display rules* suggests that cultural learning influences the expression of emotions. The range of emotional expression seems unlimited, as the case of two children who were raised by wolves (and expressed more wolflike than humanlike emotions) suggests.
5. The limbic system is a brain structure that mediates emotional arousal. The *amygdala*, hypothalamus, and other subcortical structures make up the limbic system.
6. The amygdala interprets whether an event has emotional significance and initiates a sympathetic (fight or flight) response by signaling the medulla, pons, and spinal cord.
7. The amygdala is a primary source of fear; an animal with a damaged amygdala does not process fearful stimuli or feel fear.
8. The frontal lobes influence the experience and interpretation of emotional responses.
9. The muscles used in a smile are under both unconscious and conscious control. An uninhibited (natural) smile is initiated by the amygdala.
10. Cases of brain damage, brain surgery, and clinical experiments on the brain show that the frontal lobe is involved in emotion.
11. A lobotomy is a type of **psychosurgery** that caused apathy and emotional blunting in thousands of hospitalized patients subjected to the procedure decades ago.
12. Several types of evidence show that the right frontal lobe is involved in emotion. Patients with damaged right frontal lobes speak without emotion, do not express emotion facially, and are insensitive to facial expressions of emotion in photographs.
13. The left hemisphere produces more EEG activity when a person is happy, and the right hemisphere, more activity when a person is unhappy.
14. The ***James-Lange theory*** of emotion is counterintuitive: a person experiences an emotion only after becoming aware that the autonomic nervous system (ANS) has been aroused to fight or flee.
15. The ***Cannon-Bard theory*** of emotion holds that an emotionally arousing stimulus simultaneously activates subcortical brain structures and arouses the ANS, producing emotion.
16. ***Schacter's emotional attribution theory*** holds that a thinking person appraises a stimulus and attributes the appropriate emotional response to ongoing ANS activity.

For Further Thought

1. Some researchers believe contempt and shame are exclusively human emotions. Do you agree? Why or why not?
2. Might there once have been adaptive value in the cultural meme of raising young boys not to cry? Is there still?
3. What part of the brain controls Mona Lisa's smile?
4. In the words of a Tom Waits song, "I'd rather have a bottle in front of me than a frontal lobotomy." Such sentiment raises a complex ethical issue: To what extent should inherited brain chemistry be altered to meet society's demands? What is the difference between altering emotions through the use of drugs and altering them by surgical means?
5. Most fans who attend sporting events and concerts are there to enjoy emotional experiences rather than to think about and analyze what is happening. Are coaches and composers interesting exceptions to this generalization?

CONCLUDING THOUGHTS

Humans are motivated to behave as they do for many reasons. In this chapter we have examined motivation in terms of biological factors (evolution, genetics, and physiology); psychological factors (hedonistic tendencies); and sociocultural factors (differences in acquired motives and in the need for achievement). The distal determinants of our behavior (genes) have endowed us with an evolved physiology that motivates us to meet our primary needs and be guided by our emotions. Most animals take pleasure in eating, drinking, and reproducing, for example. These basic motives and emotional states are adaptive; in humans, their expression is determined by culture.

Motivation and emotion have biological bases that involve both the central nervous system and the neuroendocrine system. The hormones secreted by endocrine glands are homeostatically regulated both by unconscious physiological processes and through conscious behavioral regulation.

The dietary choices of humans are determined both by their genes and by the culture's memes of the culture in which they are raised. Humans exhibit an innate nutritional wisdom that motivates them to identify, ingest, and regulate over 100 essential nutrients. They are guided by brain mechanisms that determine how foods taste and smell, by how they feel after eating a meal, and by a culture that identifies which foods are safe to eat.

Humans and other animals are motivated by pleasure. The experience of pleasure results from the activation of specific parts of the brain by tasty foods, sex, and certain drugs. Despite common origins and needs, humans are motivated differently and behave differently from other animals. For example, humans are motivated by acquired pleasures such as listening to music and reading novels. Maslow's hierarchy of needs describes how acquired pleasures and fulfilling psychological needs can become the most important motivators in a human's life. The intrinsic motivations of satisfying personal goals, meeting esteem needs, and self-actualizing depend on already having satisfied one's primary, safety, and social needs.

Happiness and sadness, fear and anger are among the emotions that help to define the human condition. Emotions are adaptive in arousing and helping animals such as ourselves to organize their behavior. They also help animals to communicate their intentions to others. The human expression of emotion is both innate and learned. Subcortical parts of the brain initiate emotional arousal, whereas the frontal lobes influence the experience and interpretation of the responses. Indeed, according to Schacter, cognitive assessment determines both the nature and depth of the emotions we experience. Emotions can be altered by drugs and surgery. More important, however, is the fact that they can be greatly influenced by the way a person is raised. In the next chapter we will explore the many ways that the environment influences and determines our behavior.

KEY TERMS

acquired motivation *155*
behavioral regulation *154*
biocultural evolution *161*
Cannon-Bard theory *179*
closed feeding system *157*
drive reduction *155*
emotion *150*
endocrine gland *152*
extrinsic motivation *169*
hedonism *150*
homeostasis *152*
hormone *152*
hypovolemic thirst *155*
incentive *155*
intrinsic motivation *169*
James-Lange theory *179*
motivation *150*
need for achievement *169*
negative feedback *153*
neophobia *158*
nutritional wisdom *158*
omnivore's paradox *158*
open feeding system *158*
osmotic thirst *155*
overjustification effect *169*
primary motivation *155*
psychosurgery *178*
Schacter's emotional attribution theory *180*
sensory-specific satiety *160*
set point *152*
specific appetite *155*

6 Learning and Behavior

Biological and Learned Behavior
Nature and Nurture
Genes and Memes
Interim Summary
For Further Thought

Classical, or Pavlovian, Conditioning
Pavlov's Influence on the Study of Learning
Reflexes and Conditioned Reflexes
The Conditioning Process
Habituation and Sensitization
Experimental Extinction
Higher-Order Conditioning
Basic Rules of Conditioning
Stimulus Generalization and Discrimination
Interim Summary
For Further Thought

Applications of Classical Conditioning
Emotional Responses
Food Preferences and Aversions
Morphine Tolerance
Interim Summary
For Further Thought

Instrumental Learning and Operant Conditioning
Instrumental Responses and Instrumental Learning
The Law of Effect
Behaviorism and Operant Conditioning
Schedules of Reinforcement
Interim Summary
For Further Thought

Behavior Control Through Reinforcement and Punishment
Environmental Determinism and Stimulus Control
Punishment
Negative Reinforcement and Avoidance Learning
Social Reinforcement and Observational Learning
Interim Summary
For Further Thought

Conditioning of Instinctive Behavior
Exploration, Cognitive Maps, and Latent Learning
Evolutionarily Prepared Learning
Interim Summary
For Further Thought

Conceptual Learning
Concept Formation in Primates
From Reflexes to Literacy
Interim Summary
For Further Thought

Concluding Thoughts

Books, movies, magazines, the Internet—all bear testimony to the variability of human behavior. Consider the experience of being born on a family farm in Iowa, in a tribal village in the Sudan, or in an inner-city neighborhood in Shanghai. These unique environments would determine much about how you behave and think, from your food, clothing, and mode of transport to your language and religious beliefs. Such cultural differences, learned over a lifetime, are examples of unique behavioral adaptations to the environment.

Suppose, for instance, that you were born 400 years ago in Tasmania, a large island near Australia. What would your life have been like? You would have grown up speaking Tasmanian, but you wouldn't have gone to school (there were none). You would have had no books, because the Tasmanians never developed a written language. As a young child, you would have learned to scavenge for food. As a young woman, you would have helped to prepare food, but not to cook it, because the Tasmanians did not know how to start a fire. You wouldn't have worked in the fields, because cultivating crops of any kind, including fruit and vegetables, hadn't been thought of. You wouldn't have milked cows or cared for a dog or cat, because the Tasmanians didn't domesticate animals. And you wouldn't have fished in a river, lake, or the surrounding ocean, because the Tasmanians had no fishing nets, or even the simplest of metal tools, such as fishhooks. Your clothing would have been limited, because no one knew how to sew. Hunting would have been difficult without bows, arrows, or boomerangs, none of which had been invented. Isolated from other human cultures, you would have had only a few memes to pass on to the next generation through your oral history.

That such a culture existed only 400 years ago is remarkable (Diamond, 1992) and illustrates that many aspects of human behavior are not instinctive, but culturally determined. In other words, they are learned. From another perspective, however, Tasmanians were clearly adapted to their environment, in the same way that people living in New York City are adapted to theirs. An adult from either of these cultures would not be likely to thrive in the other.

Differences in language, food, and religious beliefs aside, would your genetically determined "essence" be the same no matter what your culture? This question is probably unanswerable. But in most present-day cultures in the East and the West, few humans would choose to live like Tasmanians. Hence, the role of culture in the human experience looms large. Let's take a closer look at how humans learn to adapt to their environment.

In this chapter we will examine some general principles of learning that scientists have developed based on careful observation and experimentation. We will see that some forms of learning are based on innate reflexes and instincts that are genetically determined. Others, such as the concept learning that primates are capable of, depend more on culture. We will also consider some ways in which the principles of learning can be used to control and modify behavior. In studying learning and the role of the environment in learning, we will be concentrating on the proximal determinants of human behavior.

BIOLOGICAL AND LEARNED BEHAVIOR

Just how malleable *is* human behavior? In Chapter 3 we learned about two types of instinctive, or innate, behavior, fixed action patterns (FAPs) and species-specific behaviors. Besides being born with behavioral tendencies, humans and other animals can acquire new behaviors through simple methods of association formation called classical and instrumental conditioning. To a surprising extent, these methods can help to explain why people behave as they do—why they like or dislike particular foods, become fearful or remain unafraid, play soccer or perform on the piano.

Learning and proximal causation, Chapter 3, p. 70

Behaviorism, Chapter 1, p. 22

Put simply, **behavior** is what you do—the way you act and respond to your environment. It is easily seen and measured. Although some behavior is instinctive, a great deal of it is learned. **Learning** may be defined as *a more or less permanent change in behavior that results from one's personal experiences with an environment*. In defining learning this way, psychologists avoid treating it as an invisible psychological process. The fact is, even though psychologists know that brain processes underlie learning, no one has ever observed a person's brain learning something. Educators, psychologists, and parents merely observe a student's performance before and after an experience, and infer from any observed change in behavior that learning has (or has not) occurred.

behavior The ways in which animals act or respond in an environment.

learning A relatively permanent change in observable behavior that results from experience with an environment.

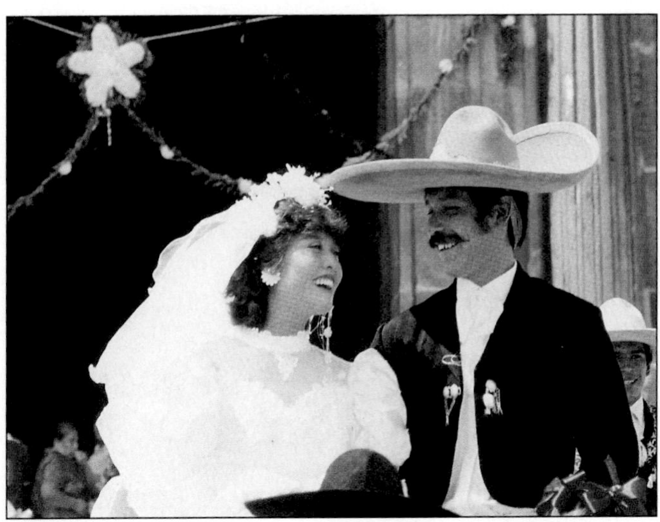

Most people select their mates from the local environment.

Nature and Nurture

Behavior has both biological and learned components, and learned, environmental experiences shape the biological behaviors as much as biology influences behaviors. Compare, for example, the different behaviors of wild mustangs and humans, which reflect both unique genotypes and learning histories. If a mustang were born into human captivity—for example, on a ranch in Wyoming—it would behave differently than if it were born into its normal ecological niche. Being touched by human hands early in its development would have a lasting impact on the mustang's behavior. No matter how "instinctive" an animal's behavior, one that is raised in captivity (and domesticated) is at a major disadvantage if it is returned to the wild. Thus, environments shape the instinctive components of behavior.

Likewise, humans would behave differently if they were raised in Washington, D.C., or on that ranch in Wyoming. All humans belong to one species, but each individual learns to like different foods, songs, books, and people, and to dislike others. Had you been raised in a different culture or subculture—that is, in a different environment—your preferences would presumably be different. To give another example, your choice of a best friend is likely to be a person who shares your own environment. Think too of acquaintances who recently became engaged or married; more than likely they met at school, at work, or in an apartment complex. Had they occupied different environments, they probably would not have become involved. Environment not only shapes behavior and learning; it determines opportunity.

Genes and Memes

What motivates humans to behave? Chapter 3 introduced Richard Dawkins's (1976) concept of a **meme,** a cultural invention that is passed from one generation to the next. Both the knowledge in a book and the skill of horse riding are bits of information that can be thought of as memes. While half the genes in a given genotype are handed down to the next generation during reproduction, memes are transmitted across generations through oral and written history. And whereas genes have only one purpose—namely, to make copies of themselves—memes are invented by the human mind for more reasons than you or I could list in a lifetime. As learned behaviors, memes may or may not contribute to our species' fitness. Nevertheless, they may be more important motivators of human behavior than genes.

Memes and extragenetic history, Chapter 3, p. 85

meme A cultural invention that is passed on from one generation to the next.

Which memes a person learns vary markedly with the person's culture.

We saw in Chapter 3 that although all mammals share some similar behaviors, only humans engage in writing, artistic expression, bridge building, soccer playing, wine making, and contemplation of the universe. By comparing your own behavior with that of other *Homo sapiens* such as the Tasmanians, you can see the importance of a cultural inheritance—memes—to human behavior. In the words of anthropologist Marvin Harris (1974), "Our primary mode of biological adaptation is cultural, not anatomical" (p. 71).

Memes and Individual Differences. The learning of memes is also an important determinant of individual differences within a culture, as well as the basis for subcultures. Which memes are learned can vary markedly within a culture, a family, or a generation. For instance, most readers of this text have learned to drive a car and to operate a computer, VCR, microwave oven, and other electronic appliances. But my grandfather never learned how to operate a computer. Likewise, I haven't a clue how to shoe a horse, or to make and throw a lariat. Though my mother spoke both German and English, only the English meme was passed on to her children, along with her genes. And though all my daughters have been exposed to algebra, some have learned it better than others. Depending on your unique *learning history,* you may or may not know how to tango or ice skate, play soccer or the piano. Your memes may include knowing how to shop for bargains, cook pasta, sing folk songs, act out or act cool, and control your temper—or not to control it.

Memes and Fitness. Do memes always promote fitness? Not necessarily, though a meme can affect fitness. Let's look at two examples. In parts of China, a law (a meme) prohibits the number of offspring a married couple may have. Such a meme directly affects fitness. Second, in most modern countries, children learn to read and write. While the ability to read and write does not affect the number of offspring a couple may have, it is an important determinant of a family's status and well-being. Arguably, literacy is a more important meme in Western culture than the number of children a couple has.

LINK
Genes and language acquisition, Chapter 12 , p. 431

The focus of this chapter is on *how* memes are transmitted from one generation to the next. Certainly language and the thought processes language supports are important to both the generation and the transmission of memes. But memes can be learned in much simpler ways. In the remainder of this chapter we will concentrate on the basic process of learning, most of which require little if any language.

INTERIM SUMMARY

1. *Behavior* is the way an animal acts; *learning* is a change in behavior that results from an animal's experiences with its environment.
2. The process of learning is inferred based on observed changes in behavior.
3. Genes contain biological information that is passed from parent to child during sexual reproduction. *Memes* are cultural inventions that are passed down from generation to generation through learning.
4. Both genes and memes determine human nature.
5. *Individual differences* in human behavior are (arguably) due more to memes than to genes.
6. Memes may or may not contribute to fitness.

For Further Thought

1. What significant aspect of the environment in which you were raised contributed most to your individuality? What significant aspect of your genes?
2. Assuming that local, immediate environments—home or apartment, friends and acquaintances, school or work—determine a person's behavior, why do you think many parents encourage their children to stay in school rather than go to work?
3. Some evolutionary psychologists have suggested that further biological evolution is unlikely for humans—that the cultural evolution of memes has largely supplanted biological adaptation. Do you agree or disagree?

CLASSICAL, OR PAVLOVIAN, CONDITIONING

The empirical study of learning began with laboratory studies performed by the Russian physiologist Ivan Pavlov (1849–1936) of St. Petersburg. Pavlov was influential both in generating new research methods and in devising a language with which to describe the effects of learning on behavior.

Pavlov's Influence on the Study of Learning

Of the 59 most important terms and concepts that describe learning, 34 can be attributed to Pavlov, and the remaining 25 to all other psychologists and physiologists. By the early 1970s, one historian reported, over 7,000 Pavlovian conditioning experiments had been published in 29 languages (Razran, 1971). Numerous journals continue to report such experiments.

Was Pavlov a genius? Perhaps in the laboratory, but outside it he was "sentimental, impractical, absent-minded, and financially negligent" (Fancier, 1990). Pavlov often forgot to pick up his paycheck; once he gave the entire amount to an irresponsible acquaintance, who could not pay it back. Yet in his research he was entirely practical, analytical, and compulsive about detail. His experiments on the physiology of learning showed that it was basically an associative process.

The Physiology of Learning. For 30 years, beginning in the late 1800s, Ivan Pavlov conducted experiments in what we now refer to as *classical conditioning*. After winning a Nobel Prize in 1906 for his research on the digestive process in dogs, Pavlov turned his attention to their "psychic secretions." He had observed that the mere sight of food caused his dogs to salivate. Countless others

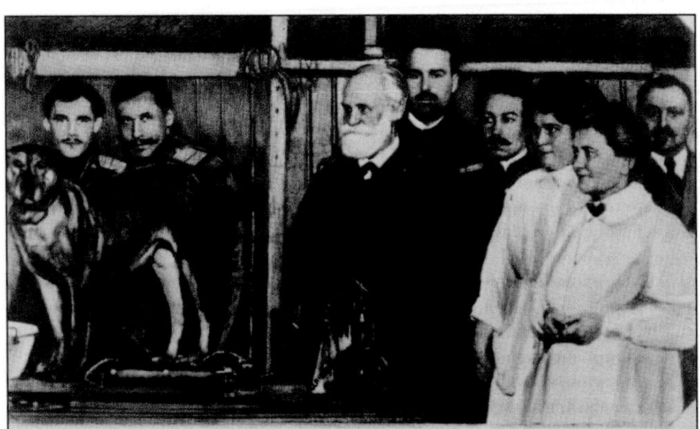

Ivan Pavlov (center) with a dog harnessed to the experimental apparatus he used in conditioning experiments.

before him had seen the same thing, but Pavlov understood its significance. He interpreted the fact that dogs apparently *learned* to salivate as a psychological phenomenon. That is, while salivation in response to the presence of food in the mouth is a physiological process, salivation in response to the mere *thought*, or *expectation*, of food is a psychological process. Pavlov set out to investigate the salivary reflex, in the hope of understanding the dog's psychological process.

Learning as an Associative Process. In his study of physiology, Pavlov had examined the functioning of a dog's salivary glands, stomach, and digestive system. He reasoned that while a dog's psychological processes were unobservable, he could study them by adapting the methods he used in his physiological research. His basic premise was that dogs learn about food by associating, or psychologically connecting, certain sights and sounds with food. The photograph on this page shows a dog in the conditioning apparatus Pavlov used to study the **associative processes** through which two or more sensations, or stimuli, became connected in a dog's mind. (John Locke, one of the British empiricists, had already formulated the rules governing how two sensations become associated; see page 40.)

Locke's associationism with Pavlov's conditioning, Chapter 1, p. 14

Pavlov recognized the adaptive nature of this type of learning. In the following passage from his book *Conditioned Reflexes* (Pavlov, 1927), he mused about the evolutionary significance of the learning process:

> It seems obvious that the whole activity of the organism should conform to definite laws. If the animal were not in exact correspondence with its environment, it would, sooner or later, cease to exist. To give a biological example: if, instead of being attracted to food, the animal were repelled by it, or if instead of running from fire the animal threw itself into the fire, then it would quickly perish. The animal must respond to changes in the environment in such a manner that its responsive activity is directed towards the preservation of its existence. (p. 9)

Reflexes and Conditioned Reflexes

The study of classical conditioning begins with an understanding of **reflexes**—innate, involuntary responses that an animal makes to specific stimuli in the environment. Table 6.1 lists some human reflexes. In a reflex, an eliciting stimulus causes a physical response. You might want to compare the concept of a *reflex* with the concept of an *instinct,* developed in Chapter 3 (see page 70). By definition, a reflex is a physiological adaptation that helps an animal to survive in its environmental niche. Although both reflexes and instinctive behaviors are naturally selected, reflexes involve fewer synapses and a simpler brain organization than instincts.

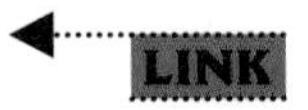

Reflexes with fixed action patterns, Chapter 3, p. 90

Reflexes may be categorized according to the eliciting stimulus and the type of response. For example, a tap on the patella (kneecap) elicits, or evokes, the motor reflex called a knee jerk. Pavlov understood reflexes as adaptive behavioral responses. For example, salivation in response to food placed on the tongue aids in an animal's digestion. Similarly, closure of the iris in response to a bright light protects the retina from heat damage. Each response to a stimulus listed in Table 6.1 evolved through the process of natural selection.

Pavlov's genius was his recognition that reflexes could be modified. That is, through the process of association formation, a new environmental signal could take the place of the original eliciting stimulus. As we will see, all the inborn reflexes in Table 6.1 can be turned into *conditioned reflexes* by being paired with a different stimulus. Let's look more closely at the conditioning process.

associative process The cognitive process that connects two stimuli, a stimulus and a response, or a response and a reinforcer.

reflex An innate, involuntary response to a specific stimulus in the environment.

Table 6.1 Types of Reflexes

ELICITING STIMULUS		REFLEXIVE RESPONSE
"Motor" (touch) reflexes		
Patellar tap	→	Knee jerk
Pressure on the surface of the eye	→	Eye blink
Touch side of infant's mouth	→	"Rooting" (search for nipple)
Touch inside of infant's palm	→	"Grasping"
Light and sound reflexes		
Loud noise, loss of equilibrium	→	Moro reflex (exaggerated in infant)
Decrease/increase in light intensity	→	Dilation/constriction of the pupil
Temperature reflexes		
Increase in body temperature	→	Sweating
Localized intense heat (burn)	→	Blister
Match burn on arm	→	Arm withdrawal
Sudden drop in body temperature	→	Goosebumps
Feeding/ingestional reflexes		
Nipple in infant's mouth	→	Sucking
Taste of food	→	Salivation
Taste of sour lemon	→	Salivation
Finger, food in throat	→	Gag reflex
Ingestion of toxin	→	Nausea, loss of appetite, vomiting
Salt loss	→	Aldosterone release
Immune system reflexes		
Cedar pollen	→	Histamine release
Antigens	→	T-lymphocyte release

Note: Eliciting stimuli originate in the environment—Darwin's "nature." Reflexes are evolved responses.

The Conditioning Process

In his experiments, Pavlov paired the taste of food with one of several distinctive sensory stimuli, including an electric bell, a metronome, "bubbling water," tuning forks, pictures, stroking of the skin, and vibrations. (For simplicity, most of the examples presented here will refer to a bell or tuning fork.) As Figure 6.1 shows, at the beginning of a typical experiment (stage 1), Pavlov noted that a dog exhibited an **orienting reflex (OR)** in response to the sound of a bell or tuning fork: it turned its head and pricked up its ears. Although the OR indicated that the sound got the dog's attention, it had no effect on the animal's reflexive behavior, such as salivation in response to food. That is, the bell or tuning fork was a *neutral stimulus* with respect to salivation.

The second reflex involved in stage 1 was the *salivary reflex,* the dog's unlearned response to the taste of food. Anticipating how this reflex would become part of the conditioning process, Pavlov referred to the food as the **unconditioned stimulus** (US) and to the dog's salivation as the **unconditioned response** (UR). For Pavlov's dog, the taste of food was a US that elicited the innate, involuntary reflex of salivation, the UR.

orienting reflex (Pavlov) An instinctive response to a stimulus, such as turning the head to locate a sound source.

unconditioned stimulus (US) (Pavlov) A stimulus that elicits an innate, involuntary, unconditioned response (UR).

unconditioned response (UR) (Pavlov) A reflexive response to an unconditioned stimulus (US).

classical conditioning A procedure in which a conditioned response results from the pairing of a conditioned stimulus with an unconditioned stimulus. (Also known as *Pavlovian conditioning*)

From Unconditioned to Conditioned Stimulus.

Stage 2 consisted of *trials* in which the sound of the bell or tuning fork preceded the presentation of food (the US). Eventually, after a number of paired presentations of the bell or tuning fork with food—a procedure now called **classical,** or **Pavlovian, conditioning**—the sound alone elicited salivation. (In stage 2 of Figure 6.1, the tuning fork is sounded; shortly thereafter, food is placed in the dog's mouth.) During and after this process, Pavlov referred to the neutral stimulus (the sound of the

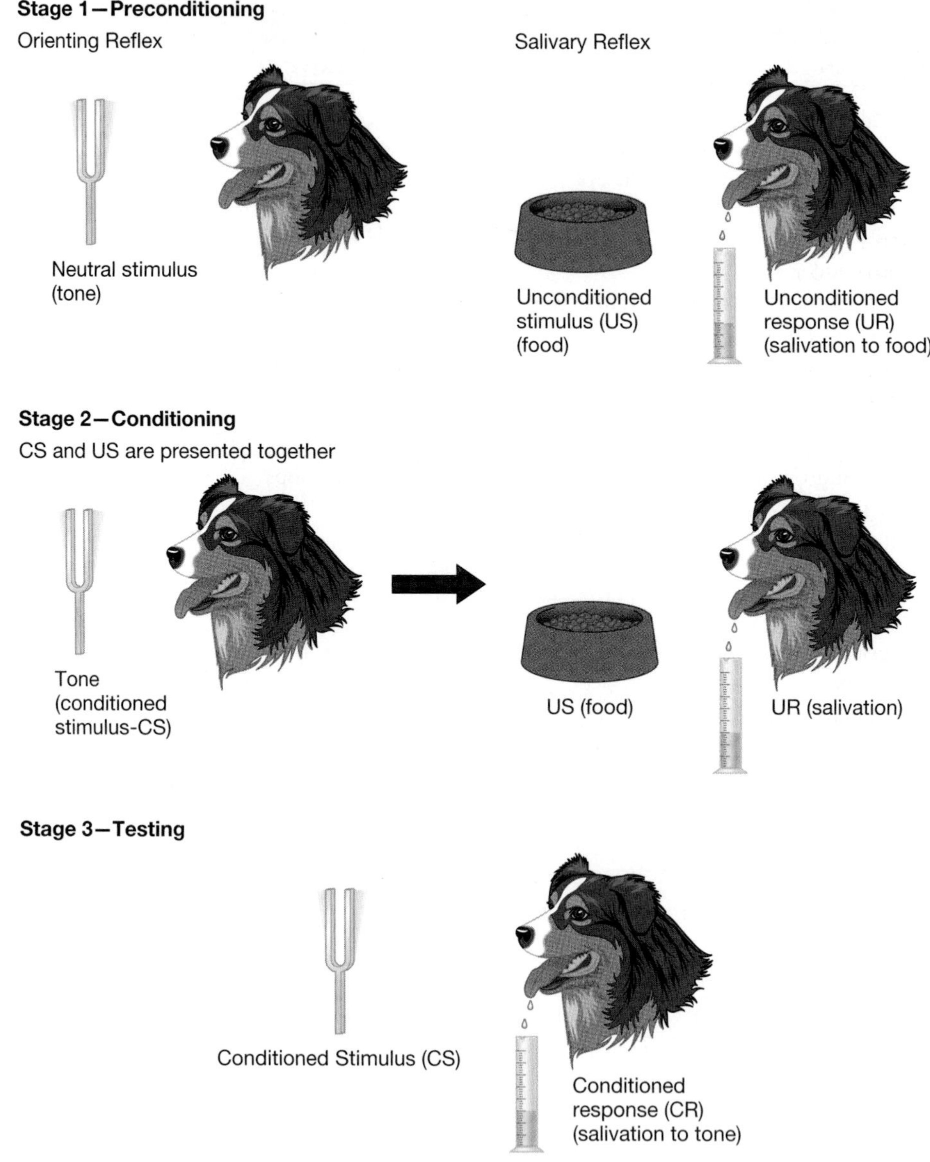

Figure 6.1 Classical (Pavlovian) conditioning. In stage 1, the dog responds reflexively to the tuning fork (with an *orienting reflex*) and the food (with a *salivary reflex*). In stage 2, the sound of the tuning fork, now called a conditioned stimulus, is paired with the food (an unconditioned stimulus) for a number of trials. In stage 3, the sound of the tuning fork alone elicits the conditioned response of salivation.

bell or tuning fork) as the **conditioned stimulus (CS).** He thought of the CS as a "signal" to the dog that something important was about to happen.

The Conditioned Response: Evidence of Learning. In stage 3 of Pavlov's experiments, the dog learned a new response to the CS. It salivated whenever the bell or tuning fork was sounded, even if no food was present. Pavlov called the dog's salivation to the sound of the tuning fork alone the **conditioned response** (**CR**). In sum, after repeated pairings of the CS (the bell or tuning fork) with the US (the taste of food), the sound alone acquired the capacity to produce the conditioned response of salivation. This change in behavior as the result of experience, Pavlov recognized, was an example of learning.

Can Pavlovian conditioning occur outside the laboratory? It certainly can. Examples of the conditioned response can be seen in the behavior of the many domestic creatures who inhabit kitchens. The rattling of a box of dry dog food or the clink of the lid on a cookie jar will often produce both an orienting response and conditioned salivation. In humans, a perfume or a distinctive voice may

conditioned stimulus (CS) (Pavlov) A stimulus (such as the sound of a bell) that can trigger a conditioned response (such as salivation).

conditioned response (CR) (Pavlov) A reflexive response that is triggered by a conditioned stimulus.

bring to mind a special person, causing the stomach to flip-flop. And the mere thought of plunging into an icy lake will raise goose bumps. All these experiences involve conditioned responses.

Habituation and Sensitization

Conditioning occurs when two stimuli, the CS and the US, become associated. What would happen if a CS or a US were presented alone? In fact, animals can learn from the presentation of a single stimulus. For example, if Pavlov's dog had heard the bell repeatedly but never received food, it would have learned to ignore the bell. Such learning is called **habituation**, a decreased responsiveness to a repetitive stimulus. Habituation is an example of *nonassociative learning*, so-called because the change in behavior occurs to a singly presented stimulus. Another form of nonassociative learning is **sensitization**, an increased responsiveness following the presentation of a single stimulus. The startle reflex in rats and other animals is an example of sensitization. Sounding a single very loud noise sensitizes an animal, so that it responds vigorously to a much weaker noise. Both sensitization and habituation are considered important forms of learning, because their effects are adaptive and long-lasting.

Experimental Extinction

If, after conditioning, the CS continues to be presented without the US, the conditioned response will weaken. This process, in which the conditioned response is reduced when the conditioned stimulus is presented without the unconditioned stimulus, is called **extinction**. For example, assume your cat has learned to associate the distinctive sound of an electric can opener (the CS) with dinner (the US). Every time she hears the can opener, she runs to the kitchen and begins to salivate.

But then you switch to a brand of cat food that comes in cans with pull-off lids. The lids make a whooshing sound when opened. Because the sound of a can opener no longer predicts dinner, it will cease to control your cat's feeding response. Her response to the can opener (CS) will *extinguish*.

Spontaneous Recovery. Pavlov studied extinction patterns in dogs. He noticed that when a dog whose conditioned behavior had been extinguished was brought back to the lab for more trials the following day, the extinction process seemed to reverse itself: the dog would again salivate to the CS. Pavlov called this reappearance of an extinguished response **spontaneous recovery**. Figure 6.2 summarizes the acquisition, extinction, and spontaneous recovery of a conditioned response.

Internal and External Inhibition. What causes spontaneous recovery? Pavlov reasoned that extinction might be hastened by a process he called *internal inhibition*, or *frustration* at not receiving a reward when expected. But the dog's frustration would tend to dissipate overnight, revealing a truer rate of extinction the next day. Thus, the dog's conditioned response reappeared. With repeated extinction trials and no reconditioning, the conditioned response will eventually extinguish completely.

Internal inhibition may be contrasted with what Pavlov called *external inhibition*—the disruptive effect of an extra stimulus on both conditioning and extinction. If, during conditioning, a bumbling aide slammed a door in Pavlov's laboratory, the dog's attention seemed to be distracted, and its learning blocked. Both internal and external inhibition interfere with the learning process. For some students, a noisy roommate is a source of external inhibition; for others, excessive worrying—a form of internal inhibition—can interfere with an assigned reading.

habituation Decreased responsiveness to a repetitive stimulus.

sensitization Increased responsiveness following the presentation of a single stimulus.

extinction *Classical conditioning:* a reduction in the conditioned response when the conditioned stimulus is presented without the unconditioned stimulus.

spontaneous recovery (Pavlov) The reappearance of an extinguished response following a delay in the extinction process.

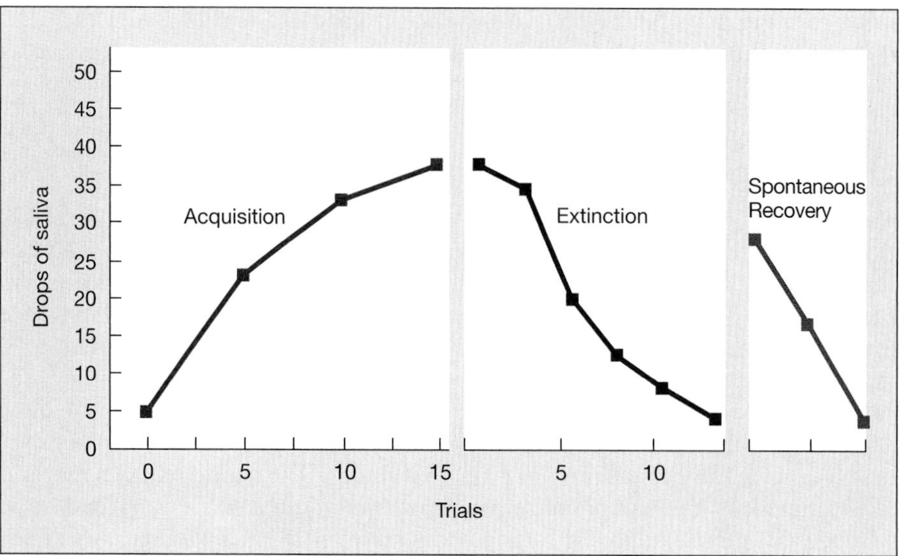

Figure 6.2 Acquisition, extinction, and spontaneous recovery. Over 15 trials (left), a dog acquired the conditioned response of salivation. But when the conditioned stimulus was presented without the unconditioned stimulus (food), the dog's salivation decreased markedly (middle). When the dog was brought back the next day for further trials, the conditioned response reappeared (dotted lines at right), a phenomenon called spontaneous recovery.

Acquired motives, Chapter 5, p. 155

Higher-Order Conditioning

Recall Pavlov's distinction between the CS and the US; the US is food or water, which meets an animal's primary biological needs; the CS is merely a signaling stimulus. In the last chapter we saw that humans are motivated by acquired incentives, such as words of praise and good grades, as well as by their primary needs. Pavlov developed a procedure to condition an arbitrary stimulus in such a way that it acquired motivating properties, becoming an acquired incentive.

Figure 6.3 illustrates the classic experiment Pavlov conducted to demonstrate **higher-order conditioning,** a procedure in which a CS acquires US properties. In stage 1, he conditioned a dog to salivate to the sound of a metronome (CS_1) when paired with food (the US). Soon the dog salivated (CR) to the sound of the metronome. Then, in Pavlov's words, ". . . a black square (CS_2) is held in front of the dog for ten seconds, and after an interval of fifteen seconds the metronome is sounded during thirty seconds. . . ."

On the tenth trial, Pavlov reported, the dog salivated 5.5 drops in response to the black square, compared to a range of 6.5 to 13.5 drops in response to the sound of the metronome. Even though the black square had never been directly associated with food, the dog had been conditioned to respond to it. The significance of higher-order conditioning is that once a "neutral" stimulus has been conditioned, it can be used to condition other responses. In Figure 6.3, once the metronome response had been conditioned, it could be used as a US to condition another response. Can you extend this concept to explain why winning a medal in the Olympics is so meaningful?

Basic Rules of Conditioning

After discovering the processes of conditioning, extinction, and spontaneous recovery, Pavlov formulated the basic rules of conditioning, which apply to most animals, not just dogs. Some of these rules of association formation are intuitively obvious, such as the fact that more trials produce better conditioning, or that the closer together the two stimuli, the more quickly the conditioned response is learned. Less obvious is Pavlov's finding that physically intense stimuli are better associated than weak stimuli, and that not all stimuli are equally conditionable. Let's look at some examples.

higher-order conditioning (Pavlov) The process through which a conditioned stimulus acquires the properties of an unconditioned stimulus.

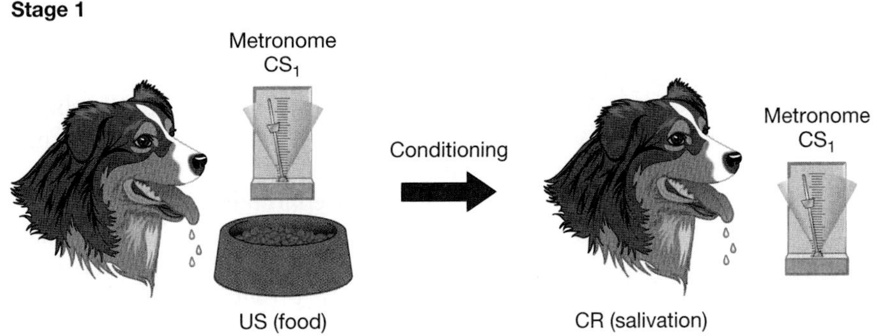

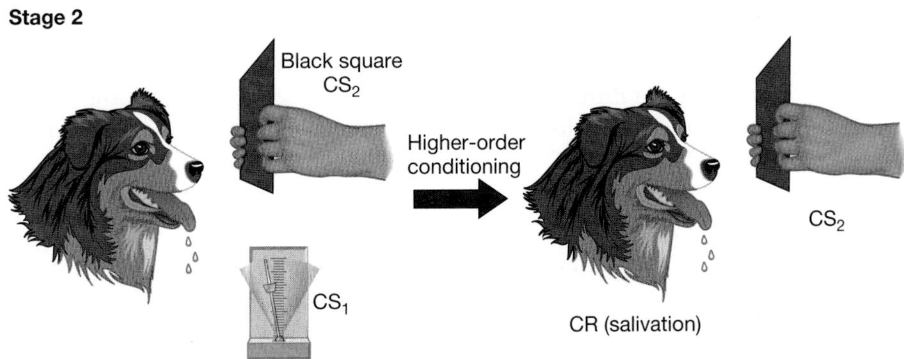

Figure 6.3 Higher-order conditioning. In stage 1, a strong salivary response is conditioned to the sound of a metronome (CS_1). In stage 2, a black square (CS_2) is repeatedly paired with the metronome (CS_1) until the dog begins to salivate to the black square alone. In this procedure, which results in higher-order conditioning, the CS_2 is never directly paired with a US (food).

Consider the use of flashcards in learning to associate Spanish vocabulary words with their English equivalents. The more trials in which you associate *bueno* with *good*, the less likely you will be to forget their association. But the time interval separating the two words is also important. If you looked at one side of the flashcard ("Bueno") and then *minutes* later looked at the other side ("Good"), you would be less likely to learn the connection between the two than if you looked quickly at the other side. The nervous system is predisposed to connect stimuli that occur close together in time (Sejnowski, Koch, & Churchland, 1988).

You might also find that some vocabulary words are more memorable (more easily learned) than others. That, too, is a common phenomenon in conditioning. Pavlov found that dogs learned more quickly when he used sounds rather than sights as signals. He also showed that the more *intense* a conditioned stimulus, the more easily it was associated with an unconditioned stimulus. (Might that be the reason advertisers tend to shout their messages?) These basic laws of learning, about which we will have more to say later, are equally applicable to salivation in dogs and vocabulary learning in humans.

Stimulus Generalization and Discrimination

Humans are not the only animals that can perceive the similarity between oranges and tangerines. The tendency to perceive stimuli that share common properties as being similar is called **stimulus generalization.** Likewise, we can easily tell the difference between onions and tomatoes based on their color, taste, and texture. This ability to perceive the difference between two stimuli is called **discrimination.** It is highly adaptive, because it allows us to recognize differences and make distinctions within our environment.

stimulus generalization The tendency to perceive stimuli that share common properties as being similar.

discrimination The ability to perceive a difference between two stimuli.

Pavlov showed that with training, animals can begin to make finer discriminations. Figure 6.4 shows the steps in one of Pavlov's experiments on stimulus generalization and discrimination. First he trained a dog to salivate to a circle, then substituted an ellipse. As we might suspect, the dog salivated to the ellipse. From its response we can infer that through stimulus generalization, the dog perceived the ellipse and the circle to be similar.

Pavlov then initiated discrimination training by continuing to pair the circle, but not the ellipse, with food. By convention, a trial of "CS with food" is designated as a *CS⁺ trial*; trials of "CS without food" are called *CS⁻ trials.* When the dog salivated to the CS⁺ (with food) but not to the CS⁻ (without food), a conditioned discrimination between the circle and the ellipse developed.

Pavlov then forced the dog to make finer and finer discriminations between the circle and an increasingly circular ellipse. The dog's salivation became less predictable. Pavlov speculated that the CS⁻ trials caused a buildup of inhibition in the dog, not unlike what happens during the extinction process. When the dog could no longer tell the difference between the CS⁺ and CS⁻ stimuli, the conditioned discrimination broke down. And so, apparently, did the dog. In Pavlov's words:

> At the same time the whole behavior of the animal underwent an abrupt change. The hitherto quiet dog began to squeal in its stand, kept wriggling about, tore off with its teeth the apparatus for mechanical stimulation of the skin . . . barked violently . . . in short, (for several weeks) it displayed all the symptoms of acute neurosis. (Pavlov, 1927, p. 291)

Pavlov thought he had discovered a way to produce an emotional disorder, which he called *experimental neurosis*, in the laboratory. Although accounting for the profound effect of this procedure on the dog's behavior is not easy, we will see in Chapter 16 that stress is a conditioned response that can have equally disturbing, long-lasting effects on human behavior.

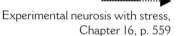

LINK ▶ Experimental neurosis with stress, Chapter 16, p. 559

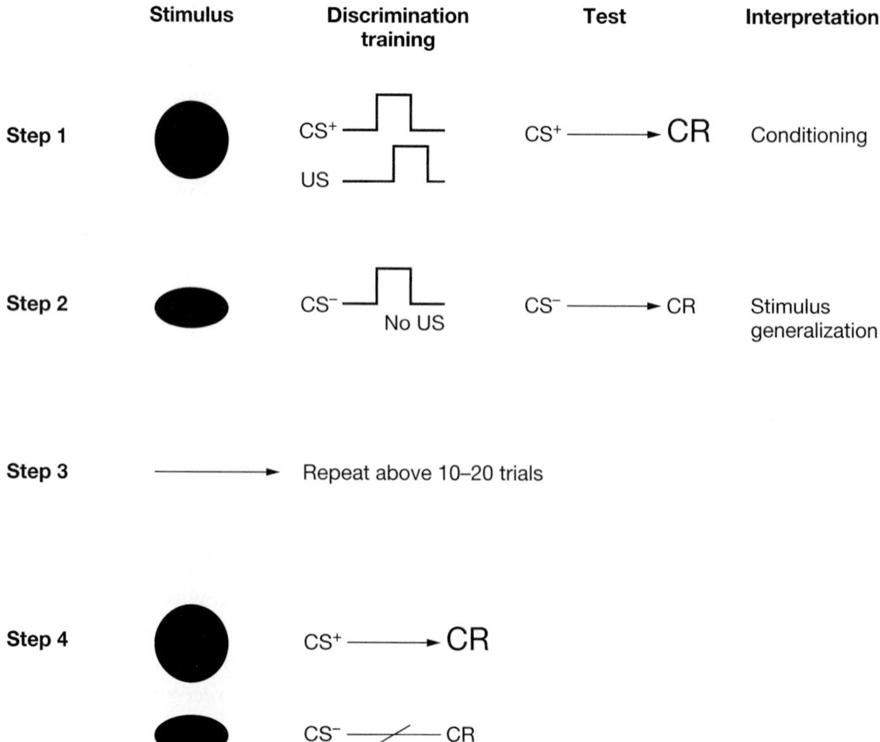

Figure 6.4 Stimulus generalization and discrimination training. In step 1, a dog is conditioned to make a salivary response to a picture of a circle that has been paired with food (CS⁺). In step 2, the dog is shown a picture of an ellipse that is not paired with food (CS⁻). The dog salivates less to the ellipse than to the circle, but more than expected, since it hasn't been conditioned to do so. Thus, the CR to the ellipse is said to have *generalized* from the CR to the circle. In step 3, the dog is repeatedly shown a circle followed by food (CS⁺), then the ellipse without food (CS⁻), a procedure called discrimination training. Finally, in step 4, the dog responds reliably to the circle but not to the ellipse; it has learned to *discriminate* between the circle and the ellipse.

Stimulus generalization and discrimination are highly adaptive processes that can be modified by learning experiences. For example, after two meals at my favorite restaurant—a bad experience with catfish and a good experience with flounder—I can still discriminate between the two stimuli. One bad experience with catfish did not overgeneralize to all fish—an especially fortunate outcome for people who live in an environment in which all food choices come from the fish family. Apparently the balance between stimulus generalization and discrimination becomes precarious under certain training conditions. Pavlov's experiment supports the notion that attempting to make too fine a discriminative response has psychological costs.

INTERIM SUMMARY

1. Pavlov's experiments were important demonstrations of the power of the environment to modify basic genotypic ***reflexes***. All dogs salivate to food, a reflex, but specific environmental experiences can produce conditioned responses by the ***associative process*** of connecting two sensations.
2. Pavlov showed that a dog's food-saliva reflex could be brought under the control of a neutral sight or sound, called a ***conditioned stimulus***, or ***(CS)***. The sound of a tuning fork, for example, does not cause salivation by itself, but does cause an ***orienting reflex (OR)*** that can be used as a conditioned stimulus.
3. By pairing a CS with food, an ***unconditioned stimulus (US)*** that elicits salivation, an ***unconditioned response (UR)*** for a number of *trials*, Pavlov discovered that the CS alone could produce the ***conditioned response (CR)*** of salivation. This process is called ***Pavlovian***, or ***classical, conditioning***.
4. When a response diminishes after repeated presentation of a stimulus, ***habituation*** to a stimulus has occurred. In contrast, ***sensitization*** occurs when an animal becomes more responsive following stimulation. Both habituation and sensitization are forms of *nonassociative learning*.
5. A conditioned response diminishes when during ***extinction***, the conditioned stimulus (CS) is presented without the unconditioned stimulus (US). If the extinction process (and the presumed buildup of *internal inhibition*) is interrupted, ***spontaneous recovery*** of the CR occurs.
6. Following ***higher-order conditioning***, a neutral stimulus, such as the sound of a word, can acquire US properties.
7. ***Stimulus generalization*** and ***discrimination*** are flip sides of the same perceptual coin. In Pavlov's classic experiment, a dog trained to respond to a circle first generalized its response to an ellipse and then was conditioned to discriminate between the two.

For Further Thought

1. Erotic daydreams can produce sexual arousal. Can you identify the unconditioned and conditioned reflexes in this example?
2. For many people, the mere mention of chicken *fajitas* sizzling over a bed of hot charcoal will cause reflexive salivation—but not for vegetarians. Why not?
3. To a novice, many tropical fish appear to be similar, but an expert can differentiate among many species. How does a novice become an expert?

APPLICATIONS OF CLASSICAL CONDITIONING

Pavlov was interested in more than when and why a dog salivates. He recognized the implication of his discoveries: that his theory could be applied to account for many types of human and nonhuman animal behavior. In this section we will see how the principles of conditioning can help to explain emotional behavior, food preferences, and drug use.

Emotional Responses

Loud noise, electric shock, and a sudden loss of support are examples of innate fear-inducing stimuli. When a normally neutral stimulus (for example, a CS in the form of words such as "Bad dog!") is repeatedly paired with an aversive stimulus (such as a swat with a rolled-up newspaper), the words will elicit a **conditioned emotional response.** (My dog, Sadie, looks really uncomfortable when I say "Bad dog!")

Laboratory Studies of Fear. The conditioning of emotional responses has been well studied in the laboratory. One of the easiest ways to produce a conditioned emotional response in a rat is to sound a tone (CS) that has been paired with an electric shock (US) while the rat was pressing a lever to obtain food. If the intensity of the shock is just strong enough to cause the rat to momentarily stop its lever pressing, after a number of tone-shock pairings, the rat will learn to associate the tone with the shock. When the tone is then sounded alone, the rat will stop lever pressing, presumably because the tone frightens it. This procedure is sometimes called *conditioned suppression,* because it suppresses the rat's lever pressing.

More than 80 years ago, in a research laboratory in the United States, a human infant was intentionally conditioned to fear a rat. The experiment remains one of the most controversial ever published. The researcher who had the audacity to try it was John B. Watson of Johns Hopkins University, who became one of the United States' most influential psychologists when he founded the behaviorist movement. Watson ignored both genetic and evolutionary considerations in the development of human behavior. Rather, as a behaviorist, he emphasized the role of the environment. Human behavior, he claimed audaciously, was directly and inevitably controlled and determined by the environment:

> Give me a dozen healthy infants, well-formed, and my own specified world to bring them up in and I'll guarantee to take anyone at random and train him to become any type of specialist I might select—doctor, lawyer, artist, merchant-chief, and yes, even beggar-man and thief, regardless of his talents, penchants, tendencies, abilities, vocations, and race of his ancestors. (Watson, 1924, p. 82)

At the pinnacle of his academic career, Watson and a graduate student, Rosalie Rayner, published the infamous "Little Albert" experiment, in which he conditioned an 11-month-old child to fear a white rat (Watson & Rayner, 1920). On several occasions over a 1-week period, Watson placed a white rat (the CS) in front of Albert and simultaneously hammered a steel bar, producing a loud clanging noise (the US). The noise startled Albert, who at first did not fear the white rat. But he soon began to respond to the rat in the same way he responded to the loud noise: he made a startle response, cried out, and tried to get away (see Figure 6.5).

Watson's theory was that like other animals, humans are buffeted on the one hand by instinct and on the other by an all-controlling environment. All emotions, he theorized, were the result of conditioning of the three basic emotions of fear, rage, and love. As children, humans were programmed by experiences such as those to which he subjected Little Albert. Despite his confident assertion that emotional and other types of behavioral conditioning were sufficient to train doctors or thieves, Watson accomplished little research to support his claims. He was even less insightful regarding the ethics of using humans in research. Today, guidelines established by the American Psychological Association forbid the kind of procedures Watson performed on Little Albert.

LINK
Conditioned fear responses with phobia formation, Chapter 17, p. 585

conditioned emotional response An emotional response (such as fear) that is triggered by a conditioned stimulus.

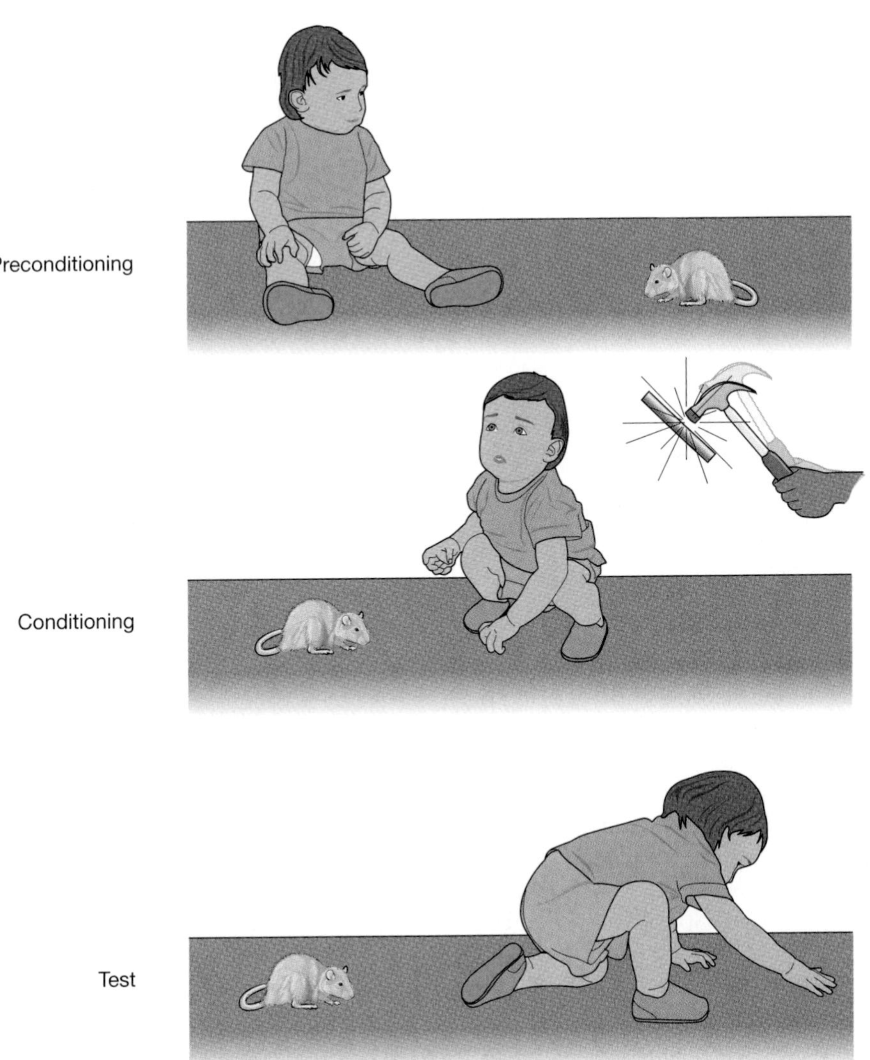

Figure 6.5 Watson's experiment with Little Albert. Prior to conditioning (top), the child known as Little Albert did not fear rats. Watson conditioned a fear response in the child (middle) by pairing a white rat (the CS) with the clang of a steel bar (the US). Finally, the rat alone elicited the fear response (bottom): Little Albert cried and turned away at the mere sight of the rat.

Real-World Applications. Few of us have been tone-shock conditioned, nor have we learned to fear rats because their appearance was paired with a loud noise. Rather, most of our emotional responses are controlled by words. Since most humans inhabit a language-rich environment, language is the foremost "neutral stimulus" for conditioning human responses, and arguably our most important meme. You may notice that your psychology professor is walking toward you, for example. Worried about the exam you took a few days ago, you reluctantly make eye contact with her. She stops; you tense. "Congratulations," she says. "You got a high B on your last exam." "Yes!" you blurt out in relief. In this example, your instructor's words conveyed an acquired incentive, evoking a conditioned emotional response from you.

LINK
Incentives, Chapter 5, p. 155

How can the words "Congratulations!" and "a high B" evoke elation? Pavlov (1927) extended his analysis of conditioned reflexes to show how humans learn the meaning of word sounds. Words, he reasoned, were like a CS that comes to control a conditioned response: they derive their meaning by being *associated* with other environmental signals. For example, an image of an apple is a signal for a real apple, one level removed from reality. The word *apple* becomes attached to the *signal* for the apple through what Pavlov called the **second-signal system**

second-signal system (Pavlov) The way in which a word (the second signal) is attached to raw sensory input (the first signal).

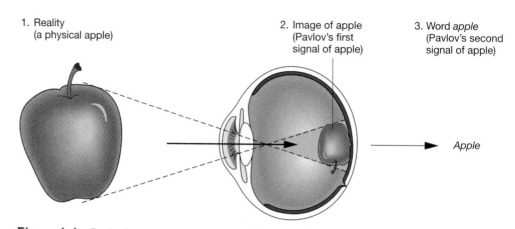

1. Reality
(a physical apple)

2. Image of apple
(Pavlov's first
signal of apple)

3. Word *apple*
(Pavlov's second
signal of apple)

Apple

Figure 6.6 Pavlov's second-signal system. Words are signals that can become associated with the sensory impressions of physical objects. A red apple is a physical object whose image (sensation) is a first-level signal for an apple. Words that describe this image are a signal for the first signal—in Pavlov's terms, a second signal.

(see Figure 6.6). In this system, a word (the second signal) is attached to raw sensory input (the first signal); seeing the apple is the first signal (CS_1) and naming it *apple* is the second signal (CS_2).

In Pavlov's schema, words can also be associated with other words. For example, both a real-world apple and the word *apple* are associated with the words *sweet, red,* and *fruit,* which are properties of apples. In fact, all words are defined in reference to other words; there are no real-world objects in a dictionary! Our understanding of the very meaning of words, then, is predicated on this association of words with other words. But how does this process occur in real life?

Association of words in semantic memory, Chapter 10, p. 365

Parents talk to their children from birth. Within months, the objects, relations, and actions in an infant's environment have been paired with their word names—*puppy* for a small dog and *hot* for a pan on the stove, for example. Some words have no specific real-world referents; the word *good*, for example, is learned through its association with a number of actions, including a loving embrace. *Good* is the CS, and the loving embrace that follows it is one of a variety of feel-good US experiences. The word *good*, then, evokes positive emotions.

To give another example, the warmth of a flame is a CS. Words that signal this CS—*hot* and *burn*—are paired with the pain of the flame. Thus the flame is associated with words that describe its properties. Under the right circumstances, *hot* and *burn* can evoke negative emotions. Later, the child learns that more complicated behavior can be signaled by the word *congratulations* and a grade of B (see Figure 6.7).

Food Preferences and Aversions

Another real-world application of classical conditioning is the development of individual food preferences. Several thousand taste experiments have been done on a variety of animals over the past 40 years. In the process, scientists have learned a lot about the *plasticity* of feeding systems. In its use here, the term *plasticity* refers to the fact that the environment can change both an animal's behavior and the physical structure of its nervous system.

Conditioned Taste Aversions. In a typical taste experiment, laboratory rats are allowed to drink a novel-flavored drink (the CS) and then are made sick by an illness-inducing drug or toxin (the US). In comparison with a control group

Figure 6.7 How words acquire emotional overtones. In early childhood, the words *no* and *bad* acquire the lifelong power to elicit emotions.

that is not made sick, the conditioned rats begin to avoid the novel-flavored drink. They are said to have developed a **conditioned taste aversion**—a disgust for a flavor that has been paired with illness. In Chapter 5, we saw that rats learned to dislike a thiamine-deficient diet through a similar method.

We humans have an intuitive grasp of this kind of conditioning, because many of us have become sick shortly after eating or drinking something. More often than not, we blame a particular flavor or food. At the age of 6, I became sick after eating fresh pineapple. I disliked pineapple for many years, and even today remember the incident all too vividly. Moreover, my taste aversion generalized to pineapple-flavored sherbet, juice, and candies.

Taste aversion learning usually takes place quickly—often in a single trial—compared to the 5 to 10 trials necessary for dogs to respond to the sound of a metronome. It may occur despite an hours-long delay between tasting a flavor and getting sick. Again, from an adaptive-evolutionary perspective, animals that can learn to associate foods with their consequences even after a lapse of several hours will survive to produce more offspring than those that continue to ingest distinctive-tasting, slow-acting toxins.

Conditioned taste aversions and thiamine, Chapter 5, p. 159

Higher-Order Conditioning of Taste Aversions. Taste aversions can also be conditioned through words. A student of mine grew up listening to her grandfather's complaints about one particular food, lamb. For weeks at a time, while he was stationed overseas during the Korean War, he had had nothing to eat except lamb. He grew to hate the taste. Years later, his granddaughter encountered the food at a formal banquet. When the host announced that they would have leg of lamb, she was overcome with a cold sweat, a churning stomach, and then nausea. Poking the food around as long as she could, she finally took a bite and gagged. The taste, she found, was fine; but the idea of it—conditioned associatively through words—had made her sick.

conditioned taste aversion A conditioning procedure in which an animal drinks a flavored solution (the CS) and is then made sick by a toxin (the US).

Morphine Tolerance

The body's responses to drugs can be conditioned. Consider the following case history:

> An elderly man in the terminal stages of cancer, suffering acute, chronic pain, was being maintained on a high dosage of morphine. Bedridden, the patient was administered the morphine on a strict schedule by a relative. On one occasion the relative was late, and the patient crawled into the next room where he administered the drug to himself. Though the drug dosage was equivalent to what he had been taking, the patient died of an "overdose." (Siegel, Hinson, Krank, & McCully, 1982)

How could the same dose of a drug produce such different effects? Classical conditioning explains how a normal dose can become an overdose. The process is similar to that in which a drug dose loses its effectiveness with repeated usage.

Behavioral and Pharmacological Tolerance. The term *tolerance* refers to the reduction of a drug's effectiveness after a person has taken it repeatedly. For example, morphine tends to warm the body, but after it has been taken repeatedly, that response diminishes. The psychologist Shepard Siegel of McMaster University devised an experiment to divide morphine tolerance into its *behavioral* and *pharmacological* components. As Figure 6.8 shows, in stage 1 of the experiment he gave rats a dose of morphine that increased their body temperature, a response called hyperthermia. In the room where the rats were injected, Siegel provided a constant background of white noise (the sound an FM radio makes when it is tuned between stations).

In stage 2, as the rats developed a tolerance for the drug, the continued administration of morphine produced less of a warming response. Siegel wanted to know how much of the reduction in warming was due to the drug's pharmacological action and how much was due to the environment. To find out, in stage 3 he injected half the rats in the usual noisy environment and half in a different room that was comparatively quiet. He found that in the new environment, the dose of morphine that had lost its effectiveness suddenly regained it.

Conditioned Compensatory Responses. How did Siegel explain these results? He reasoned that the white noise of the *familiar* room had become a conditioned stimulus that produced what he called a **conditioned compensatory response**—a physiological response that counteracted the drug's effect following repeated doses. In Chapter 5 we saw that body temperature and a variety of other physiological responses tend to vary around a set point. After morphine warms the body, homeostatic processes will bring the body back to its normal temperature. In this example the white noise signaled the rats that they were about to be warmed, so their physiological systems compensated by lowering their body temperature (Siegel, 1977).

These results elucidate the apparent morphine overdose in the elderly cancer patient. The man received daily injections in his *familiar* bedroom, but the fatal dose was self-administered in a *different* room. Taking the drug in a new room excluded familiar environmental stimuli that would have elicited a conditioned compensatory response, reducing the drug's effectiveness. In the new room, unfortunately, the drug was fully effective.

conditioned compensatory response (Siegel) A homeostatic response that counteracts a drug's effect after repeated exposures.

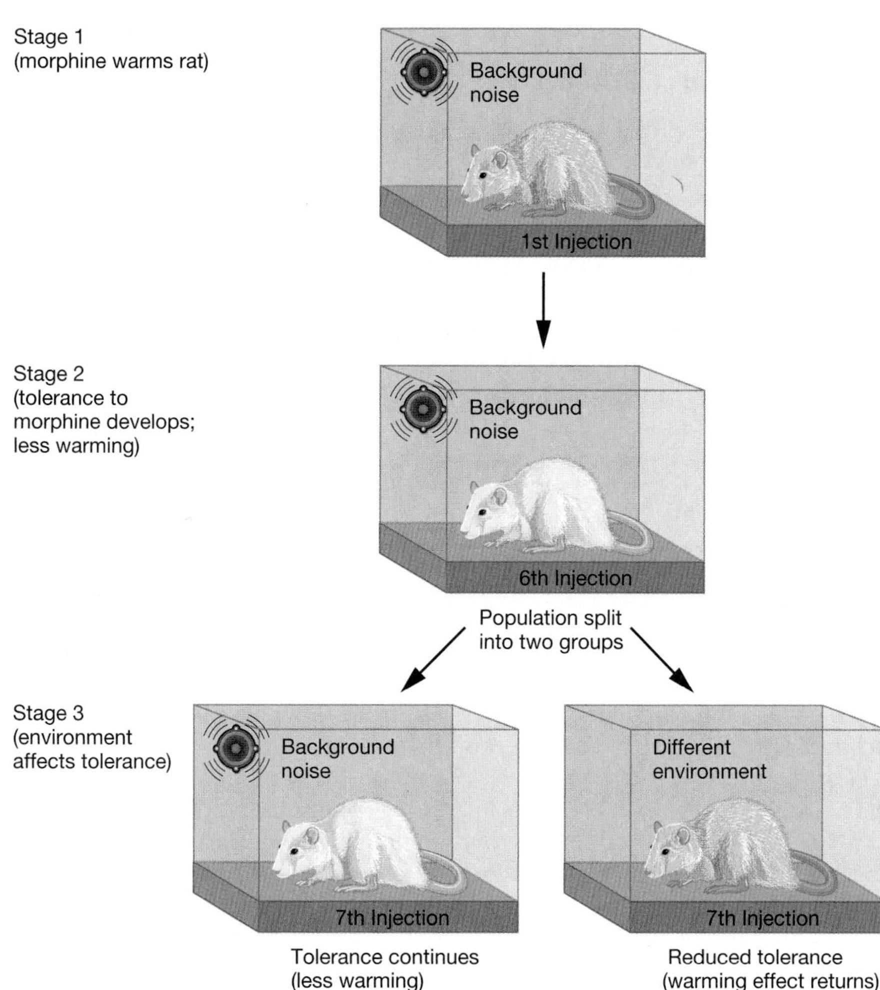

Figure 6.8 The effect of environment on the response to morphine. Rats that are injected with morphine for the first time become warm. But after six daily injections, always given in the same noisy environment, they develop a tolerance to morphine and do not become as warm when injected. If the rats are then divided into two groups, one of which gets their injection in the same noisy environment and the other of which is injected in a quiet environment, in the new environment, the regular dose of morphine will become effective again. The rats will lose their tolerance to the drug and become warm.

INTERIM SUMMARY

1. Among the most important applications of classical conditioning is the *conditioned emotional response,* in which a neutral stimulus becomes a feared stimulus after it is paired with an aversive stimulus. John B. Watson conditioned an 11-month-old child, Little Albert, to fear the sight of a white rat (the CS) by pairing it with an aversive noise (the US).
2. In a laboratory demonstration of *conditioned suppression,* a tone (CS) is paired with an electric shock (the US). Conditioning is measured by the degree to which the tone or light suppresses the lever-pressing response in rats.
3. Pavlov's *second-signal system* describes how a word can become a CS that controls emotional responses. In human behavior, words are the most important conditioned stimuli.
4. In a *conditioned taste aversion*, a flavor (CS) is paired with an illness (US). One-trial, long-delay learning can be studied using this method. Conditioned flavor preferences result from the pairing of flavors with recovery from thiamin deficiency and other illnesses.
5. Morphine tolerance can be analyzed from the perspective of Pavlovian conditioning. If an environmental stimulus (CS) enters into association with a morphine injection (US), after a number of trials, the CS will produce a *conditioned compensatory response.* When the CS is present, the morphine will be less effective (that is, a tolerance will develop).

For Further Thought

1. In what way is Pavlov's analysis of how words acquire meaning less like salivary conditioning and more like John Locke's stimulus-stimulus associationism? (See Chapter 1, page 14.)
2. A teenage daughter has an argument with her father while dining with him in a restaurant. Might she form an aversion to the restaurant as well as to the foods she ate on that occasion?
3. For several years, after arriving home each night after work, a business executive has a gin and tonic at precisely 6:30 P.M. Will she crave a drink at 6:30 on a Saturday or Sunday evening? Why or why not?

INSTRUMENTAL LEARNING AND OPERANT CONDITIONING

Classical conditioning can be thought of as the modification of basic reflexes. Yet in doing so, we run the risk of thinking of ourselves as highly interesting but nevertheless programmed, robotic creatures. The truth is, we are more than reflexive machines. Our reflexes are adaptive, and their modification, no matter how mechanical the process, is also adaptive. Moreover, the conditioning of emotional behavior to language makes humans interesting robots, indeed!

More to the point, both human and nonhuman animals engage in a variety of behaviors that seem to be initiated from within (by their internal environment, including the brain) rather than without (by their external environment). Humans, in particular, seem to exhibit volition and will—that is, to engage in spontaneous, voluntary behavior. They learn skills that complement their instincts, such as planting and harvesting, cooking and sewing, hunting and fishing. Consider, for example, how Little Tree learned to fish:

> "Granpa taught me how to hand fish. . . . This is when you lay down on the creek bank and ease your hands into the water and feel for the fish holes. When you find one, you bring your hands in easy and slow, until you feel the fish. If you are patient, you can rub your hands along the sides of the fish and he will lie in the water while you rub him. Then you take one hold behind his head, the other on his tail, and lift him out of the water. It takes some time to learn.
>
> *The Education of Little Tree* (Carter, 1976)

In Little Tree's culture, the meme of learning to hand fish had direct survival value. In today's urban culture people drive cars to shopping malls, extract money from ATMs, and decide which movie suits their fancy. Little of this behavior can be accounted for by Pavlov's theory of conditioning. What can account for it?

Instrumental Responses and Instrumental Learning

instrumental response A voluntary, nonreflexive response that acts on the environment in a meaningful way.

A distinction can be made between learning by *doing* something and being conditioned—having something done to oneself. Salivation is a reflex that can be conditioned. By contrast, an **instrumental response** is a nonreflexive behavior that acts on the environment, as in "Sara's driving skills were *instrumental* in getting her to Miami safely" or "Jaime's polite demeanor was *instrumental* in getting his teacher's attention." Rather than modifying reflexive behavior, *instrumental learning* constructs new behaviors.

Instrumental responses, although they are distinct from reflexive behavior, often work together with reflexes. A woman who is caught walking in a dust storm will both blink as the swirling cloud approaches (a reflexive response) and turn her head, pull her hat brim lower, or wrap a scarf about her face (all instrumental responses to the blast). The eye-blink response is acquired through Pavlovian conditioning (taking advantage of a reflex); the instrumental responses of bowed head and other shielding gestures are adaptively learned. Formally defined, **instrumental learning** (sometimes called instrumental conditioning) is the modification of instrumental responses using *reinforcers* and *punishers*. For example, the woman in the dust storm has learned to shield herself to avoid the punishment of the blowing dust.

Reflexes and instrumental responses interact when a person is learning a new skill. Basketball players learn to aim a basketball shot toward a hoop by taking advantage of these sensory-motor reflexes, as well as by making skeletal-muscle adjustments. Their eyes reflexively focus on the moving ball as it approaches the hoop. On the next shot, they shift their weight, make minor postural adjustments, and perhaps change their timing. Some of these adjustments are under conscious control; others are not. If a shot is successful, the posture that preceded it (including both its reflexive and voluntary components) will be reproduced on succeeding shots. Thus, instrumental learning of new behaviors, such as throwing a successful hook shot or kicking a soccer goal, is strengthened or weakened depending on whether the ball goes where it is supposed to go (that is, whether the response is *reinforced*). These skills take many thousands of trials to develop, presumably because of the many thousands of possible trajectories of soccer balls and basketballs.

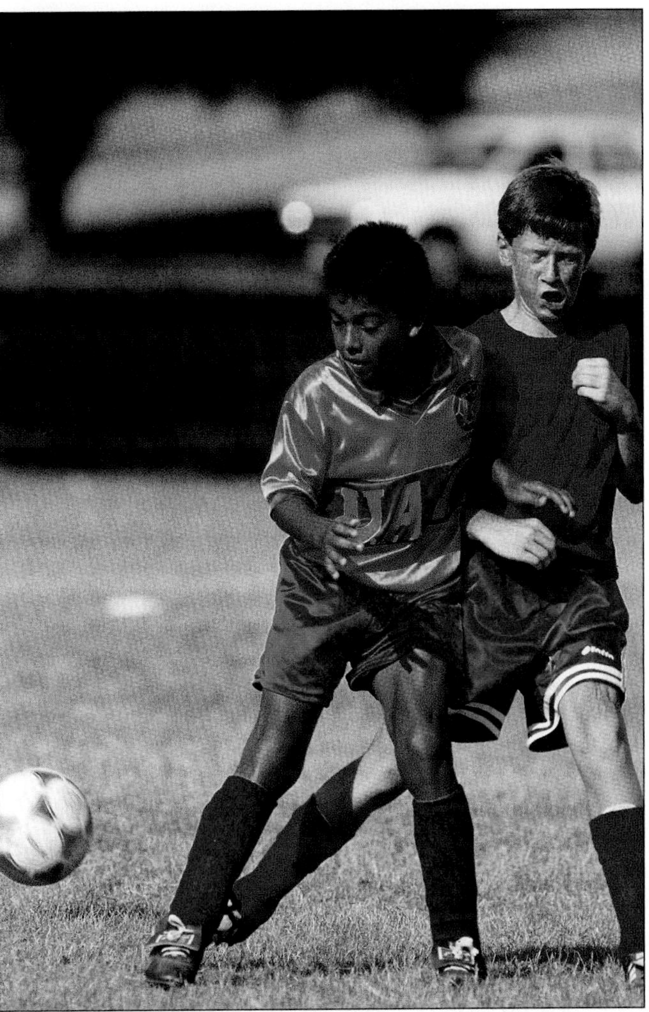

Learning to play soccer requires hours of practice. Reinforcement theory helps to account for the way in which players acquire and maintain these skilled motor behaviors.

The Law of Effect

Many people have successfully trained horses, cows, dogs, homing pigeons, and other animals to behave on cue. Not until the experiments of Edward Thorndike at Columbia University, however, did a systematic science of animal training and learning begin. Let's look at Thorndike's famous "puzzle box" studies.

Thorndike constructed an experimental chamber with a door that could be opened by animals trapped inside. He observed that when a hungry cat was placed in the box for the first time, it scratched, climbed, and bumped against the walls in a frenzied reaction both to the confinement and to the sight and smell of food just outside the box. Eventually, by accident, the cat bumped against or clawed at the simple latching mechanism. The door released, allowing the cat to escape from the box.

Later, the cat was returned to the puzzle box for a second and third trial. Thorndike found that the cat took less time to successfully locate and operate the latch on these follow-up trials. Eventually, after many more trials, the cat would unlatch the door without hesitation. Thorndike's measure of learning, then, was the reduction in the time the cat needed to escape from the puzzle box.

instrumental learning The modification of a nonreflexive behavior using reinforcers and punishers.

Thorndike also observed dogs and chickens in various boxes, and formulated some general principles of instrumental learning (Thorndike, 1911, 1932). To account for his observations, he proposed the **law of effect**, which states simply that a *response that is followed by a pleasant consequence will tend to be repeated*, whereas *a response that is followed by an unpleasant consequence will tend to decrease in frequency*. Thorndike called such pleasant and unpleasant consequences "**satisfiers**"(pleasant stimuli) and "**annoyers**" (unpleasant stimuli). His observation that successful responses increased and unsuccessful responses decreased is an operational definition of an animal that is adapting to its environment. In Thorndike's terms, the memory that formed when a hungry cat escaped from confinement tended to be "stamped in," whereas unsuccessful movements were forgotten.

Hedonism, Chapter 5, p. 150

Another way to describe the law of effect is to note that all organisms are innately endowed with hedonistic tendencies. Hedonism—the tendency to seek pleasure and avoid pain—is both adaptive and normal. Like hedonism, the law of effect is firmly grounded in biology. The brains of all animals have been selected to learn to repeat those responses that produce pleasure, presumably because pleasurable activities promote an animal's survival and reproduction (Dennett, 1975). Food, shelter, and mating (satisfiers) are all pleasurable and adaptive; hunger, pain, and adverse climate (annoyers) are all painful. For most animals, therefore, the very behaviors they engage in are instrumental in producing food, securing shelter and mates, and avoiding predators, toxins, and reproductive extinction. The *law of effect*, then, is adaptive.

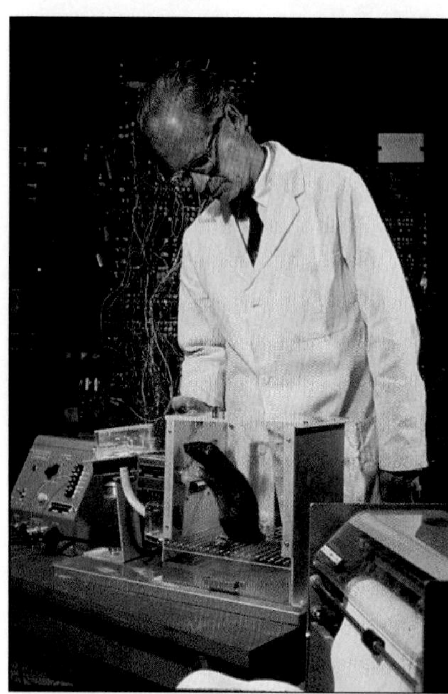

Burrhus Frederic Skinner (1904–1990) with a rat in a Skinner box.

Behaviorism and Operant Conditioning

Clearly, life-preserving behaviors are adaptive. But in what way is driving to the mall, using an ATM, or shooting a basketball adaptive? What seemed characteristic of human behavior to the Harvard behaviorist B. F. (Burrhus Frederic) Skinner (1904–1990) was how arbitrary much of it is. We humans are unlike other animals in that our behavior is idiosyncratic. Individual differences characterize our species, and the human ecological niche seems to be whatever we want to make it.

What was needed, Skinner reasoned, was a theory of learning that would account for nonreflexive, nonadaptive behavior. Skinner called the theory and the method he devised for experimentally analyzing learned behavior *operant conditioning*. Starting in the 1930s and continuing for 50 years, he and his many students made a systematic study of how animals learn in an "operant chamber" that soon became known as a *Skinner box* (Skinner, 1938, 1963). For many years, Skinner focused his research strategy on how food rewards influence the arbitrary response of lever pressing in rats (see the photograph on this page).

law of effect (Thorndike) The rule that responses that are followed by "satisfiers" tend to be repeated, whereas responses that are followed by "annoyers" tend not to be repeated.

satisfier (Thorndike) A pleasant stimulus.

annoyer (Thorndike) An unpleasant stimulus.

operant (Skinner) An instrumental response, such as a lever press, that effectively *operates* on the environment.

Reinforcing Arbitrary Responses. Skinner's operant conditioning is best thought of as a variant of Thorndike's instrumental learning. Sensitive to the ethologist's concept of innately organized behavior, Skinner sought to investigate behavior that was not so heavily influenced by instinct. He decided on a research strategy of intentionally removing animals from their natural environment. Rejecting rat mazes and Thorndike's puzzle box because they allowed animals to engage in instinctive behaviors, he set out to develop a new experimental method. Skinner selected the arbitrary response of lever pressing because it was *not* akin to fixed action patterns or other biologically prepared responses. He called the lever-pressing response an **operant**, which he defined as a response that "operates" on the environment.

Skinner showed that he could increase lever pressing in rats, and pecking in pigeons (both operant responses), by providing a *positive reinforcer* immediately following the desired response. Though he typically used food, he defined a **positive reinforcer** as *any* stimulus that followed an operant response that had the effect of increasing the rate of response. This process of *reinforcement* (or **positive reinforcement**) means providing a hungry animal with food after it makes an operant response, so that the food *reinforces* the animal's performance of the operant. Skinner used the verb *to reinforce* in the way Pavlov used the verb *to condition*. In sum, what Skinner called **operant conditioning** involved selecting an improbable response, such as lever pressing, and through the process of reinforcement, increasing the probability of its occurrence.

Reinforcement, with "satisfiers," p. 206 (this chapter), and with ESB, Chapter 2, p. 44

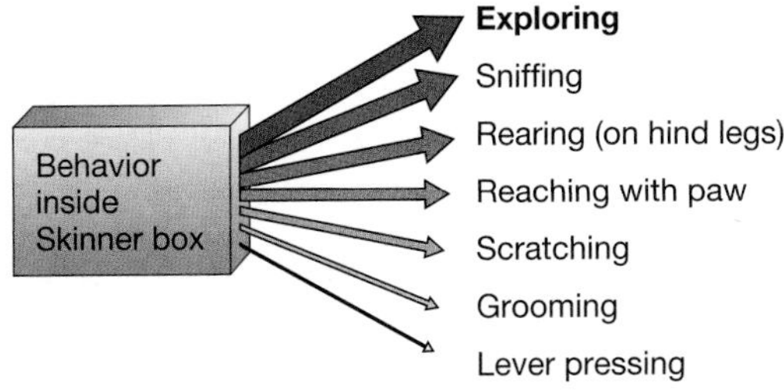

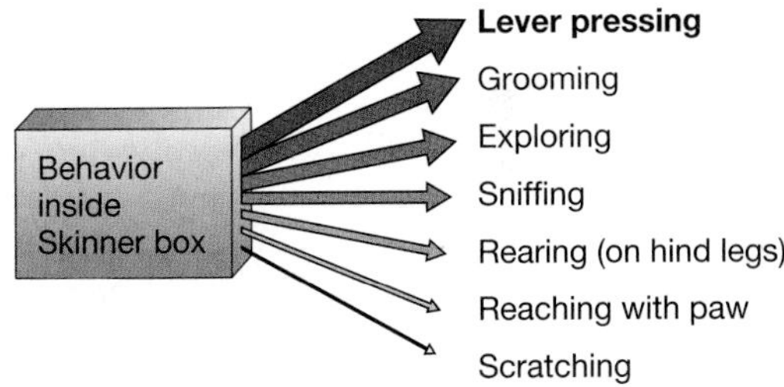

Figure 6.9 **The effect of shaping.** The amount of time a rat spends engaging in innately determined behaviors changes after it learns to press a lever for food reinforcement.

Shaping a Target Behavior. When a hungry rat is first placed in a Skinner box, it will explore the new environment for several minutes by sniffing, rearing on its hind legs, and touching objects with its front paws (see the top of Figure 6.9). When the rat sniffs or places its paw anywhere near the lever, the experimenter can activate the feeder. In this case, the target behavior—what the experimenter wants the rat to accomplish—is a lever-pressing response. In a procedure called **shaping,** the experimenter reinforces responses that approximate the target behavior, such as approaching the lever. To give a real-world example, reinforcing a small child for holding his toothbrush near his teeth is part of the process of shaping the target behavior of tooth brushing.

Eventually the target behavior emerges, and shaping is no longer necessary. The lower portion of Figure 6.9 indicates that by the 10th session in a Skinner box, the frequency of most of the rat's responses had changed. The rat now spent most of its time lever pressing for food reinforcement. Likewise, a child who is learning to brush his teeth eventually drops ineffective movements and begins to perform the toothbrushing operant effectively.

Substituting Secondary Reinforcers. We know that words of praise can act as a positive reinforcer; saying "good" can both shape and maintain the toothbrushing operant of a small child. Words, gestures, and money can become **secondary reinforcers**—neutral stimuli that acquire reinforcing properties via the process of higher-order conditioning. For example, a parent who comforts, strokes, and feeds a child is providing primary reinforcement. But stimuli that are associated with the parent, including language, eventually acquire reinforcing properties of their own.

Complex human behaviors are supported by both primary and secondary reinforcers. For example, people work to acquire money (a secondary reinforcer) so they can go on vacation. Thus reading a novel (a secondary reinforcer) while basking in the warm sun (a primary reinforcer) or munching on a tasty snack (another primary reinforcer) contribute to the positive feelings associated with the words *spring break*. Again, primary reinforcers meet biological needs, whereas secondary reinforcers acquire value through the learning process.

positive reinforcer (Skinner) Any stimulus that follows an operant response and has the effect of increasing the rate of response.

positive reinforcement (Skinner) A process in which a reward such as food is used to reinforce an operant response.

operant conditioning (Skinner) The process through which reinforcement strengthens (makes more probable) an operant response.

shaping A procedure in which responses that approximate the target behavior are reinforced.

secondary reinforcer A neutral stimulus that acquires reinforcing properties through the process of higher-order conditioning.

schedule of reinforcement The pattern according to which responses are reinforced.

Schedules of Reinforcement

Highly distinctive patterns of lever pressing result when reinforcement is delivered to animals following predetermined rules. The various ways in which responses are reinforced are called **schedules of reinforcement.** Some of the more interesting of these schedules are implemented after an animal has mastered

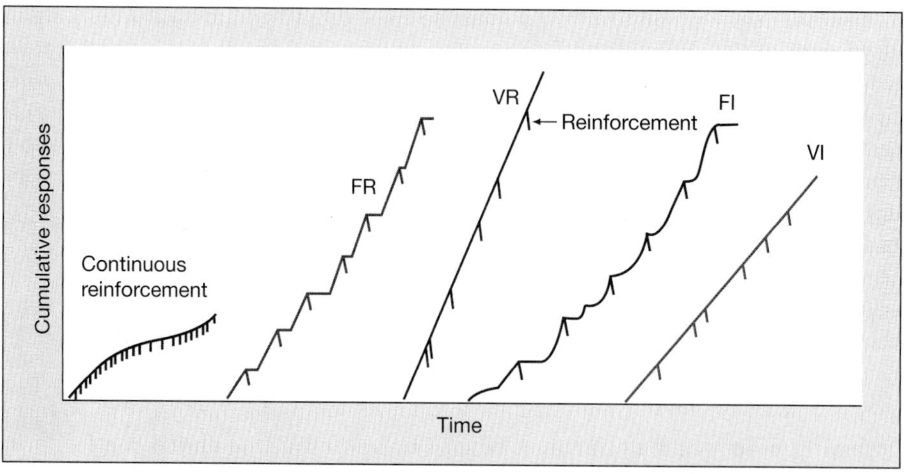

Figure 6.10 Reinforcement schedules. An animal's cumulative responses over time vary according to the type of reinforcement schedule it is on. This graph shows the effects of continuous reinforcement and fixed ratio (FR), variable ratio (VR), fixed interval (FI), and variable interval (VI) schedules. Higher rates of response are indicated by steeper slopes; hatch-marks indicate when reinforcement was delivered. *Source:* From LEARNING AND BEHAVIOR 3rd ed. by Lewis Barker. Copyright © 2001 by Pearson Education, Inc. Reprinted by permission.

continuous reinforcement, in which each correct response produces a reinforcer. When continuous reinforcement is used, animals appear to learn an "if-then" contingency. *If* I press this lever, or *if* I hold this toothbrush right, *then* a food pellet (or drink of water, or word of praise) magically appears.

The left-hand diagram in Figure 6.10 shows graphically the result of a continuous reinforcement schedule on lever pressing. After about a dozen regularly spaced responses that produced food pellets, the rat stopped and groomed itself—producing the horizontal lines on the graph—before resuming its lever pressing.

When not every response, but rather patterns of responses are reinforced, the schedule of reinforcement is called **partial reinforcement.** Many different types of partial reinforcement schedules have been studied, including the four that follow.

Fixed Ratio Schedules. In a **fixed ratio (FR) schedule**, an animal must complete a fixed number of operants before receiving reinforcement. For example, when every 10th response is reinforced, the schedule is designated an FR-10. The animal can lever press at any rate, fast or slow, but is always reinforced just after the 10th response. Obviously, the faster an animal presses the lever on an FR schedule, the more reinforcers it can earn in a given session.

You will notice several differences in the cumulative responses produced by continuous reinforcement and fixed ratio schedules, shown in Figure 6.10. Rats press the bar more often and more quickly on a partial reinforcement schedule; hence the steeper slope of the fixed ratio graph. They also tend to pause more after eating a food pellet on the fixed ratio schedule, producing what is called a *postreinforcement pause*. This pause is indicated by the horizontal line following the tick mark that indicates a reinforcer was delivered. The length of the pause increases as the number of bar presses required for reinforcement increases. For example, if 30 lever presses rather than 10 are required for reinforcement, the pause after the reinforcer will be longer. Postreinforcement pauses can be seen in everyday life. After studying many hours for an exam, students will wait a while before resuming study of that particular subject.

continuous reinforcement A procedure in which each response is followed by a reinforcer.

partial reinforcement A procedure in which *patterns* of responses (rather than single responses) are reinforced.

fixed ratio (FR) schedule A schedule of reinforcement in which a fixed number of responses must be made before a response is reinforced.

Variable Ratio Schedules. As the name implies, a **variable ratio (VR) schedule** does *not* require a fixed number of responses before a reinforcer is delivered. Rather, the number of responses an animal must make before it is reinforced varies. For example, a pigeon responding on a VR-10 schedule is reinforced for every 10th response, on average, though it may get food after just 1 or 2 responses or only after 15 or 20.

What is the effect of a variable ratio pattern of reinforcement? Let's say you have a telephone marketing job, and the number of sales you make (your reinforcer) is related to the number of calls you place (the operant response). You may make 2 or 3 sales in a row, but you may also go unrewarded for a couple of dozen calls. If you made 10 sales in a session of 100 calls, you would be on a VR-10 schedule of reinforcement. Certainly one sale out of every 10 calls, on average, will maintain a high rate of phone calling. But even infrequent VR schedules can maintain high rates of response. Some people who play slot machines in Las Vegas will pull the lever several hundred times between payoffs.

Fixed Interval Schedules. On a **fixed interval (FI) schedule,** an animal is reinforced for its first response following a specified *time interval.* For example, in a fixed 60-second interval schedule of reinforcement (abbreviated FI-60), the first response that occurs after 60 seconds has elapsed is reinforced. (The interval is measured from the time of delivery of the last reinforced response.) Even though a time contingency determines when a response is reinforced, the delivery of the reinforcement is still *response contingent:* the animal must respond to get the food. Hungry animals will make more responses if reinforcement is available after a short rather than a long interval; the response rates on an FI-10 schedule, for example, are higher than those on an FI-45 schedule.

Fixed interval schedules produce a distinctive pattern called *scalloping* (see the FI curve in Figure 6.10). Because another reinforcer is never available immediately after reinforcement, the animal doesn't resume responding immediately; thus the curve is horizontal following the hatch mark that indicates reinforcement. As the end of the fixed interval approaches (and reinforcement again becomes available), the response rate gradually increases. Similar "scallops" would appear if studying was the operant response: as the time of the exam approached, studying would become more frequent.

Variable Interval Schedules. The last pattern of reinforcement shown in Figure 6.10 is the **variable interval (VI) schedule**, in which an animal is reinforced for its first response following a varying time interval. On a variable interval schedule, the interval may vary from a few seconds to a few minutes. For example, a VI-45 schedule means that on average, a reinforcer is available during a 45-second time interval. Suppose, for example, that you are working for an advertiser who pays you $5 for each candid photograph you take of a student wearing a particular brand of jeans. You set up your camera outside the student union. Sometimes a student who is wearing the right brand walks by every few seconds; at other times you must wait several minutes between shots. But on the average, you are reinforced (you get to take a $5 photograph) every 45 seconds.

What is the effect of scheduling reinforcement so that it *averages* 45 seconds, instead of being *exactly* 45 seconds, as on a fixed interval schedule? As Figure 6.10 shows, the VI schedule eliminates the postreinforcement pause. Indeed, in both the variable interval and variable ratio schedules, reinforcement is possible with the very next response postreinforcement. So after you have just taken a photo, you immediately get ready to take another one, because the next person who walks by might be worth another $5 to you. Similarly, animals show no postreinforcement pause on these two schedules, because delaying their response could delay their reinforcement. Figure 6.10 also shows that both the

variable ratio (VR) schedule A schedule of reinforcement in which a varying number of responses must be made before a response is reinforced.

fixed interval (FI) schedule A schedule of reinforcement in which the first response made following a specified time interval is reinforced.

variable interval (VI) schedule A schedule of reinforcement in which the first response following a varying time interval is reinforced.

VI and VR schedules produce stable response rates; there are no scallops, and because the postreinforcement pause is minimal, the response patterns are relatively steady.

The Partial Reinforcement Effect. The tendency for performance that is maintained on a partial reinforcement schedule to be highly resistant to **extinction** is called the **partial reinforcement effect**, or **PRE**. To understand the partial reinforcement effect, we must reexamine the effects of continuous reinforcement schedules. Think, for example, about the last time you put a quarter into a pay telephone and came up with nothing. You probably were frustrated, because you had an *expectation* about what should have happened based on previous telephone calls you had made from pay phones. If your past experiences with pay phones have produced reliable connections, you expect the same to happen the next time. Your expectations reflect your past reinforcement history.

Now imagine living in Italy, where local phone systems are unpredictable at best. In using public phones over the years, Italians have lost many coins. That is, their telephoning operants have never been consistently reinforced. Sometimes people connect on the first coin; on other occasions they must try several times (and lose several coins) before connecting. In which phone system would you be more likely to continue feeding coins to a pay phone, the Italian system or a reliable phone system? In which system would nonreinforcement be more frustrating? With this understanding, can you explain why Italians are surprised when North Americans "become angry at telephones"?

Differential Reinforcement of Timed Responses. As with Pavlov's classical conditioning method, the results of Skinner's reinforcement studies have found wide application. One of the most interesting is their use in training highly skilled responses. A surgeon must apply just the right pressure for just the right duration in making a knife cut. A musician must make precise, timed responses within fractions of a second. Can reinforcement, which by definition *increases* the rate or probability of a response, control both fast and slow response rates?

Many skilled movements—an artist's brush strokes, a pianist's keystrokes, a student's reading and writing—require precise rhythm and pacing. For instance, a person who is developing skill as a pianist learns to play by being reinforced for hitting the correct key (which produces the correct sound) at the correct time. Two partial reinforcement schedules are useful in training such precisely timed responses. One, ***d*ifferential *r*einforcement of a *h*igh rate** of response (**DRH**), strengthens bursts of operant responses such as lever pressing. A burst may be defined as 5 or more lever presses by a rat (or 10 or more pecks by a pigeon) in a 2-second period. When a burst occurs, a food reinforcer is delivered.

If instead of speed, the desired target behavior is a slow, accurate response, ***d*ifferential *r*einforcement of *l*ow rate** of response (**DRL**) is more useful. The opposite of the DRH schedule, the DRL schedule is designed to reinforce the pauses between operant responses. An animal on a DRL-30 schedule, for example, must wait 30 seconds before a response will produce reinforcement. Each response that is made before the 30 seconds has elapsed resets the clock, so that the animal must wait an *additional* 30 seconds before reinforcement again becomes available. Because humans, like monkeys, can time their responses to within fractions of a second, both DRH and DRL schedules can shape highly skilled timed behaviors.

partial reinforcement effect (PRE) The tendency for responses that are being maintained on a partial reinforcement schedule to be highly resistant to extinction.

differential reinforcement of high rates of response (DRH) A schedule of reinforcement that is designed to reinforce bursts of operant responses.

differential reinforcement of low rates of response (DRL) A schedule of reinforcement that is designed to reinforce pauses between operant responses.

extinction *Instrumental conditioning:* a reduction in the rate of response when reinforcement is withheld.

INTERIM SUMMARY

1. In *instrumental learning*, an animal acquires adaptive, nonreflexive behaviors when its *instrumental responses* are reinforced or punished.
2. Thorndike recorded how long cats and other animals took to escape from a puzzle box. According to the *law of effect*, because of animals' hedonistic tendencies, instrumental responses that produce *satisfiers* will increase in frequency, whereas instrumental responses that produce *annoyers* will decrease in frequency and eventually stop.
3. B. F. Skinner's research strategy, called *operant conditioning*, was to pick an arbitrary response, which he called an *operant* response, and analyze how *positive reinforcement* modified and controlled that response.
4. To train operant responses in a Skinner box, a researcher uses operant conditioning to associate the delivery of food, a *positive reinforcer*, with responses that are similar to the *target response*, a process called *shaping*. *Secondary reinforcers* are formerly neutral stimuli that acquire reinforcing properties through the process of higher-order conditioning.
5. The various patterns in which responses produce reinforcement are called *schedules of reinforcement*. They include *continuous reinforcement* and a number of *partial reinforcement* schedules, such as *fixed ratio (FR)*, *variable ratio (VR)*, *fixed interval (FI)*, and *variable interval (VI) schedules*.
6. The *partial reinforcement effect (PRE)* refers to the resistance to extinction of a behavior that is maintained on a partial reinforcement schedule.
7. Depending on the schedule of reinforcement used, an animal's behavior varies with respect to rate of response, postreinforcement pauses, and the timing and patterning of skilled responses. *Differential reinforcement of a high rate* of response *(DRH)* encourages quick bursts of responses, whereas *differential reinforcement of a low rate* of response *(DRL)* encourages pauses.

For Further Thought

1. An accomplished pianist was once asked how she came to play the piano so well. She replied that she chose her parents well. Have you thought about how your genetic endowment and your early environmental experiences may have come to control your behavior in a Skinnerian sense? Or do you think that as a free agent, you can make your own way in life in spite of nature and nurture?
2. Assume you are a new parent who wants to develop lifelong habits in your child, which will persist even when you are no longer there to reinforce them. Should you worry if you miss an occasion or two on which to reinforce the child? Should you worry when your parents treat the child differently? Why or why not?

BEHAVIOR CONTROL THROUGH REINFORCEMENT AND PUNISHMENT

B. F. Skinner's analysis of behavior was similar in many respects to that of his behaviorist predecessor, John B. Watson. Both thought that emotional behavior could be conditioned. Both thought that environmental effects controlled human behavior. The difference was that Skinner and other researchers who followed him accomplished hundreds of experiments that demonstrated the power of reinforcement and punishment in controlling behavior. According to the resulting theory of **behavioral control**, the expression of a given behavior is governed by past and present reinforcement and punishment contingencies.

behavioral control The contingencies that determine the expression of a behavior through reinforcement and punishment.

Environmental Determinism and Stimulus Control

The manner in which the environment comes to control human and animal behavior has been a continuing theme in B. F. Skinner's writings. One of Skinner's best known books is *Walden Two*, a novel that describes a utopian society in which all children are raised in a highly controlled environment to become happy, productive adults (Skinner, 1948). Skinner's behaviorist philosophy, like John B. Watson's, was an extreme form of *environmental determinism*—the position that environmental stimuli exert almost total control over an animal's behavior.

To better understand how behaviorists analyze behavior, we must return to the Skinner box. Note the light next to the lever in the photograph on page 206. Skinner trained the rat to respond only when the light was on; thus, he called the light a **discriminative stimulus**, abbreviated S^d (pronounced "ess-dee"). The S^d signaled the rat when a response would be reinforced. (Notice how similar this concept is to Pavlov's CS^+, which signaled when food would be delivered.) Skinner also provided another stimulus to signal that a response such as lever pressing would *not* be reinforced; he called this stimulus a **negative discriminative stimulus**, abbreviated S^Δ (pronounced "ess-delta"). Because reinforcement ceased when the S^Δ was in effect, the rat stopped lever pressing. When trained animals responded reliably in the presence of an S^d but did *not* respond in the presence of an S^Δ, Skinner pronounced them to be under **stimulus control**.

Let's examine how environmental stimuli control my dog's behavior. Sadie will crawl up on the couch or bed in the presence of my children, but not when I'm in the room. The children are S^ds, but my presence is an S^Δ, for crawling onto the furniture. Note that Sadie is under stimulus control in the presence of both my children and me: she has been differentially reinforced, and responds predictably according to whatever stimulus is present in the environment. Another example: If you stop your automobile at a red light and go on green, Skinner would say that you are under stimulus control. The red and green traffic lights are S^ds that control the operant responses of *foot pressure on the brake* and *foot pressure on the accelerator*, respectively. The same red and green traffic lights are S^Δs for foot pressure *off* the accelerator and foot pressure *off* the brake, respectively.

Punishment

To this point, all our conditioning examples have involved reinforcement. Unfortunately, the environment that controls our behavior also includes unpleasant stimuli that we cannot avoid. Thorndike labeled them *annoyers*; Skinner called them aversive, or punishing, stimuli.

Skinner defined a *punisher* as any stimulus that decreased the rate of the response that preceded it. For humans and most other animals, common punishers include cold, heat, hunger and thirst, loud noises, and a host of other environmental stimuli that can cause pain, nausea, illness, and so on. Any stimulus that is inherently aversive is called *primary punisher*. The pain induced by a spanking is an example of a primary punisher. Neutral stimuli can acquire punishing properties through association with primary punishers. A stimulus that has acquired punishing properties through conditioning is called a *secondary punisher*. A reprimand ("No, you can't have it") is an example of a *secondary* punisher.

Punishment is formally defined as a process that decreases the rate of a response through either the delivery of an aversive stimulus or the withholding of an expected positive stimulus after a response. Punishment, then, is a singular process involving one of two procedures. Some theorists use the term *positive punishment* to describe responses that produce an aversive consequence (e.g., speeding followed by a ticket) and *negative punishment* to describe responses that do not produce expected rewards (e.g., getting a grade of 73 rather than a

discriminative stimulus (S^d) A signal that indicates when a response will be reinforced.

negative discriminative stimulus (S^Δ) A stimulus that signals that a response will not be followed by reinforcement.

stimulus control In discrimination training, the demonstration of a response in the presence of an S^d, but not in the presence of an S^Δ.

punishment The process through which an aversive stimulus decreases the rate of the response to which it is applied.

97). Because the adjectives "positive" and "negative" are confusing in this context, we will not use them. "Positive punishment" is an oxymoron, and "negative punishment" is redundant.

Emotional Consequences of Punishment. Anyone who has ever received a speeding ticket can appreciate the emotional response that accompanies punishment. There is that sinking feeling when you notice the flashing blue lights in your rearview mirror—not quite fear, perhaps, unless there is an open container of alcohol in the car, or your license has expired. A speeding ticket is an example of punishment because a response (speeding) has produced an aversive consequence (a ticket or fine, both punishers).

Let's take another example. A solid B student, you are disappointed when your exam is returned with a 73 scrawled by your name. You vaguely remember that you had two other exams the day you took the test, so instead of reading all the material in the assigned chapters, you merely skimmed it and read only your notes and the chapter summaries. But the 73 still gives you that sinking feeling, followed by confusion, anger, resignation, and so forth. One way to analyze this complex behavioral sequence is to point out that in this case you were punished for studying too little. The 73 is punishing only by comparison with the 97 you would have earned if you had read all the assigned material. Your response (reading only your notes and the chapter summaries) was punished by the withholding of a good grade. Another common example of this type of punishment is the time-out procedure used by parents and educators. Removing a child from the social environment ("Go to your room!") penalizes them by withholding available reinforcers, such as toys and friends.

Effective Use of Punishment. Punishment is in some ways like other forms of learning we have studied so far. A relatively intense punisher, applied with a short response-to-punisher interval and repeated consistently over several trials, is more effective than a mild punisher applied inconsistently over a long response-to-punisher interval. For example, a 53 exam score is more punishing than a 73; the lower grade would more effectively punish the behavior of reading only the chapter summaries. Likewise, a $500 fine would be more likely to reduce speeding than a $50 fine.

Punishment can be useless or even counterproductive if it is weak, delayed, and applied inconsistently. A 53 exam grade—certainly a punisher for a serious student—is not likely to be effective in changing your study behavior if it is delivered three weeks after the exam. As with food-reinforced lever pressing, a response-to-punisher association is better made over short time intervals.

Punishment *can* be an adaptive process that changes a person's behavior, however. Like reinforcement, punishment can shape behavior by selecting from alternative responses those that produce the most pleasure and/or avoid the most pain. If you slap the hand of a child who is reaching for a hot stove, and simultaneously say the words *no* and *hot*, you will shape an important aspect of the child's behavior. The human brain is designed to accomplish this type of learning rapidly under certain conditions. For example, some pain fibers are especially fast conducting. Being stung by a bee or touching a hot curling iron will produce a rapid reflexive response and equally rapid association formation.

Punishment, however, is too often misunderstood and misused by parents. As a child, Henry VIII of England was beaten every morning for the sins he would commit that day. Such nonspecific punishment can only have the effect of pairing the sights and sounds of the person doing the beating with the pain being induced. Because no specific response is being punished, the child will learn only to fear and hate the person administering the punishment.

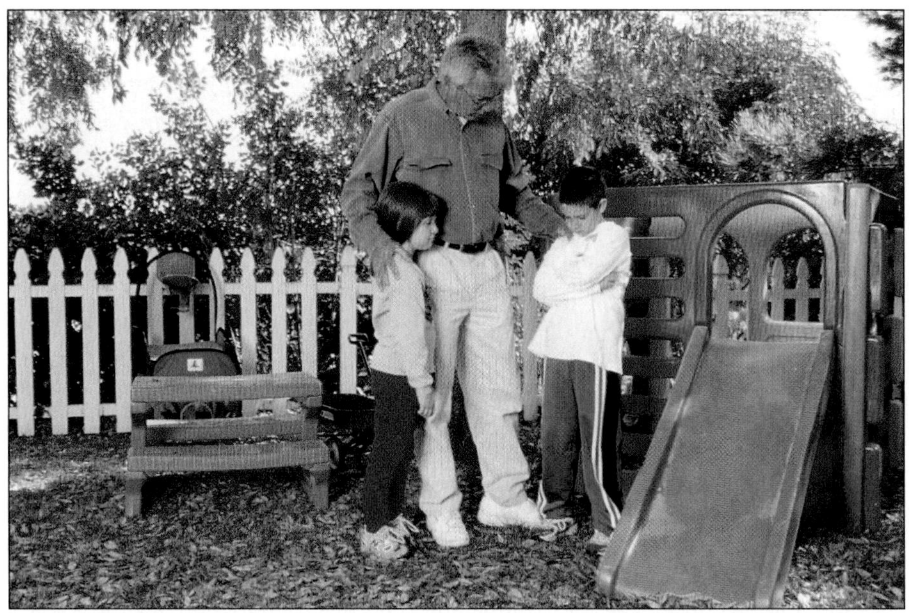

Too many parents misuse punishment in their attempt to control their children's behavior.

Negative Reinforcement and Avoidance Learning

Like rats, children, college students, and parents learn to behave in interesting ways to *avoid* punishers. Imagine being trapped barefooted in a dimly illuminated Skinner box with a steel grid for a floor. Unable to escape, you decide to relax and make the best of it—when suddenly you feel an electric shock on the soles of your feet. Aroused, you begin hopping around, and accidentally bump against a lever. The shock stops. Just about the time you start to relax, the scenario repeats itself. Jumping around, you again hit the lever and escape the shock. The third time the shock occurs, you make a beeline for the lever, hit it, and terminate the shock.

Murray Sidman did this experiment with rats and found they learned an **escape** procedure—an instrumental response that terminated the aversive stimulus. Sidman then reprogrammed his apparatus so that the lever-pressing response would both terminate the shock *and* delay the onset of the next one. This procedure resulted in **avoidance learning**, or the acquisition of an instrumental response that *prevents* an aversive stimulus. Sidman's rats eventually learned to avoid shock altogether by responding *before* its onset (Sidman, 1953).

The rats learned their avoidance responses through **negative reinforcement**, a process in which the absence of an aversive event is reinforcing. Hitting a lever to avoid a shock is similar to turning the steering wheel to avoid hitting another auto. The reinforcement you receive is *negative* because the response avoids a bad outcome. Avoiding something bad is good, and is therefore reinforcing. Thus, the behavior of turning the steering wheel in just the right way at the right moment will persist because of negative reinforcement.

Now assume that you turn the steering wheel the wrong way and hit a parked car. When a bad outcome occurs (that is, a punishing event), you are not likely to turn the steering wheel the same way in the future. Because punishment makes a response less likely to occur in the future, the *effect of punishment is the opposite of the effect of negative reinforcement.* That is, punishment *decreases* the punished response. In contrast, responding in a way that avoids or prevents an aversive stimulus or punisher is negatively reinforcing and has the effect of *increasing* that response.

escape A procedure in which an animal makes an instrumental response that terminates an aversive stimulus.

avoidance learning A procedure in which an instrumental response prevents an aversive stimulus.

negative reinforcement A process in which responses that prevent aversive events are learned, presumably because the absence of an aversive event is reinforcing.

Positive and Negative Reinforcement Combined. Now that you know the difference between punishment and reinforcement, let's analyze some common examples of human behavior. Small children learning to play soccer often turn their heads and bodies when an opposing player kicks the ball at them. Getting hit in the face hurts, so it constitutes punishment for *not* turning your head. In contrast, turning your head so that the ball doesn't hit your face is negatively reinforcing, because it is instrumental in avoiding the punishing stimulus.

Consider another example: Both skiing and riding a bicycle require small behavioral adjustments to maintain one's balance. Why, after learning to ride a bike or to ski—both highly skilled acts—do people seldom fall? The answer contains elements of both positive and negative reinforcement as well as the avoidance of punishment. First, skilled bikers and skiers engage in these activities because they feel good (positive reinforcement). Maintaining their balance prevents the punishment of falling and getting hurt (negative reinforcement). Falls are punishing events; thus, behaving in a way that produces pleasure *and* prevents falls is reinforcing.

Consider one last example: Mozart is playing a piano concerto. He presses middle C on the keyboard at the right time and in the right sequence. We can safely say that hearing middle C when it is appropriate is positively reinforcing to Mozart. Hitting middle C at the right time is also negatively reinforcing, because it avoids the disharmony of hitting the wrong note. So playing the appropriate note is maintained by both positive *and* negative reinforcement.

The Persistence of Avoidance Learning. Curiously, negatively reinforced responses extinguish more slowly than positively reinforced responses. That is, a rat trained to lever press for food will stop responding much more quickly when food is discontinued than will a rat trained to lever press to avoid an electric shock when the shocks are discontinued. The reason is that each avoidance response is at one and the same time *being reinforced* and *not being punished*. The response is reinforced, first, because it produces the desired outcome, avoiding a shock (or a fall on the ski slopes, an F on a test, or a D-note when you wanted a C). And second, it prevents the undesirable, punishing outcome of an electric shock (or a fall, a failing grade, or a sour note).

Social Reinforcement and Observational Learning

Parents, teachers, bosses, and friends—not scientists in laboratories—control the reinforcing and punishing stimuli that effectively shape human behavior. Indeed, we readily work for paychecks, grades, and *social* approval, which Albert Bandura suggested may be among the most effective reinforcers for both children and adults (Bandura & Walters, 1963). Arguing that much of human behavior is imitative and will persist in the absence of Skinner's overt reinforcers, Bandura proposed a theory of behavior called **observational learning**, or learning by watching others (Bandura, 1971). For example, mothers who urge their children to brush their teeth "like this" first model the behavior by showing how to hold and move the toothbrush. A coach may demonstrate how to swing a bat, and then physically position the elbows of little leaguers as they attempt to model what they have seen. Verbal instructions ("Hold it higher," "Keep it level") accompany the coach's words of praise and punishment.

LINK ▶
Imitation in child development, Chapter 11, p. 390

Neither Skinner nor Bandura addressed why children and other animals imitate behavior in the first place. For example, if a 2-week-old infant were to see you stick out your tongue, he or she would likely return the favor. The appearance of this behavior at such an early age indicates that imitation is probably unlearned—yet another example of a species-specific behavior. The imitative

observational learning Learning by watching others; imitation.

response may be thought of as an instrumental or operant response that can be manipulated by reinforcement or punishment. From an instrumental learning perspective, learned secondary reinforcers—smiling, verbal encouragement, and so forth—are the *social reinforcers* parents, teachers, and coaches use to promote observational learning. In this sense, Bandura's social reinforcers are equivalent to Skinner's secondary reinforcers.

Observational learning with personality development, Chapter 14, p. 494

INTERIM SUMMARY

1. ***Behavior control*** occurs when one environmental stimulus, called a ***discriminative stimulus,*** or S^d, reinforces a response, while at the same time another stimulus, called a ***negative discriminative stimulus,*** or S^{Δ}, does not. An animal is said to be under ***stimulus control*** if, after S^d-S^{Δ} training, a response occurs reliably to the S^d but not to the S^{Δ}. In such cases the discriminative stimulus is said to *control* the response.
2. A response that is punished decreases in frequency. The process of ***punishment*** is most effective when the punisher is appropriately intense and the delay between the response and the punishing stimulus (*punisher*) is minimal. The effects of punishment result from both pain and emotional conditioning.
3. ***Negative reinforcement*** is a process through which a response that is instrumental in either escaping or avoiding an aversive event is strengthened. A *negative reinforcer* increases the rate of the preceding response, as in ***escape*** and ***avoidance learning.***
4. Human skills such as skiing and bike riding are maintained by negative reinforcement. These avoidance responses are not easily extinguished, because when they are executed they are at once reinforced and not punished.
5. Bandura's theory of ***observational learning*** stresses that much of human behavior is imitative and influenced by social reinforcers.

For Further Thought

1. In his book *Beyond Freedom and Dignity*, Skinner (1971) proposed that human behavior is effectively controlled by culture—by parents, schools, governments, laws, churches, and so forth. Culture organizes environmental stimuli and doles out reinforcers and punishers. In his analysis of environmental determinism, free will is an illusion. What do you think?
2. Why, other than the reasons already described, might a one-week suspension from school be an ineffective punishment? Can you make the case that a suspension may function as a negative reinforcer?
3. What motivates you to study for exams? Why do so many people watch so much TV? Can you identify both positive and negative reinforcers for each behavior?

CONDITIONING OF INSTINCTIVE BEHAVIOR

Marian and Keller Breland learned operant conditioning techniques from B. F. Skinner while they were graduate students at Harvard. Later, in the 1960s, they started Animal Behavior Enterprises, a company that trained pigs, raccoons, chickens, and other animals for circus acts and TV programs. In a typical act, a raccoon would perform an instrumental response to earn a token, which it would then pick up and drop into a "bank." The target response of depositing the coin resulted in the delivery of food reinforcement.

The *law of effect* predicts that a hungry animal should learn a food-reinforced operant behavior, such as dropping a coin, quickly and efficiently. Many of the Brelands' trained animals did something else, however. Instead of depositing the coin, they played with it, delaying reinforcement for minutes on end. Listen to the Brelands describing a raccoon that was required to drop *two* coins into the bank to secure reinforcement:

> Not only (would) he not let go of the coins, but he spent seconds, even minutes, rubbing them together . . . and dipping them into the (bank). . . . The rubbing behavior became worse as time went on, in spite of non-reinforcement. (Breland & Breland, 1961)

Likewise, pigs would repeatedly push coins along the floor with their snouts rather than deposit them in the bank, as they had been trained to do. These behavior patterns became worse, not better, with repeated trials.

How did the Brelands explain these instances of "misbehavior"? First, they reasoned that in the natural environment, raccoons routinely "wash" their food before eating, and pigs innately "root" with their snouts. These species-specific feeding patterns appear to intrude on newly learned, highly arbitrary operants that are maintained by food reinforcement. The Brelands' term **instinctive drift** captures the most important aspects of the "misbehavior" they observed: namely, that an arbitrarily established operant response will erode (drift) in the face of more innately organized behavior, such as rooting.

The Brelands' observations are important in that they pit evolution and genetics (nature) against learning and the environment (nurture). Nature and nurture usually cooperate rather than compete. The statement made earlier in this chapter, that most learning is adaptive, reflects their mutual interaction. B. F. Skinner was especially sensitive to nature-nurture arguments. Recall that he invented the relatively arbitrary operant of lever pressing as an alternative to maze learning in hopes of avoiding this type of complication (see page 206). Skinner assumed that rats would bring innate foraging skills to maze-learning tasks, which would interfere with his study of "pure" associations. He sought instead to investigate the effects of reinforcement on "uncontaminated" responses, such as lever pressing in rats or pecking at a lighted disc in pigeons. (We'll soon see that these simple responses are not so simple.) The Brelands' findings remind us that an animal's biologically determined behavior might render reinforcement less effective. Let's look at a few more examples of the interaction of instinctive behavior with operant conditioning.

Exploration, Cognitive Maps, and Latent Learning

Edward Tolman of the University of California at Berkeley was investigating animal learning in runways and mazes. In one of his experiments, rats apparently learned a maze even though they weren't given a food reward (Tolman & Honzik, 1930a). Figure 6.11 compares the performance of three groups of rats in this experiment. Notice that all made fewer and fewer errors over the first 10 trials: the average number of errors (wrong turns and incorrect entries) dropped from about 10 per trial to about 6. The group that was always rewarded with food at the end of the maze made the fewest errors. But another group that received food for the first time on the 11th trial performed better thereafter than the group that had always been reinforced.

On the basis of this experiment, Tolman concluded that all three groups learned equally well whether or not they received a food reinforcer. They were exploring their environment, he thought, the way rats do in the natural world, and forming a *cognitive map* of the maze in the process (Tolman & Honzik, 1930b). A **cognitive map**, according to Tolman, was a mental representation of

instinctive drift (Breland) The theory that arbitrarily established responses erode (drift) in the face of more innate (instinctive) behavior.

cognitive map (Tolman) A mental representation of the route or shortest path to a target destination.

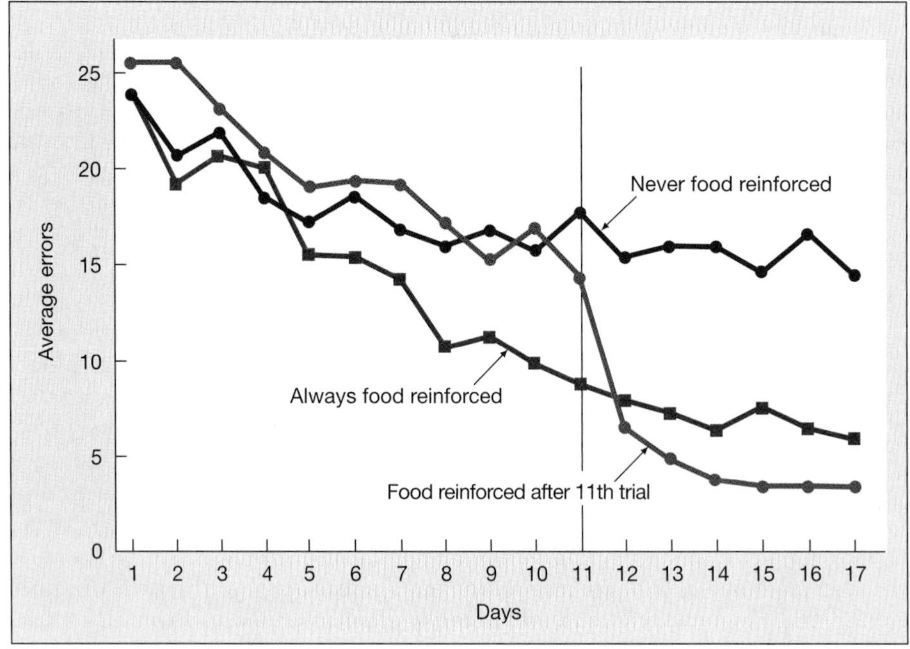

Figure 6.11 Results of Tolman's latent learning experiment. Rats learned their way through a maze by foraging for and finding food (dark dotted line) or not finding it (light dotted line, solid line). Although the rats that received food made fewer mistakes than those that did not, they all learned their way through the maze by engaging in the innate behavior of foraging.

the route or shortest path to a destination. Adding a food reward, then, increased only the animals' performance, not their learning. Tolman used the term **latent learning** to describe learning that occurred in the absence of food rewards.

A rat in a radial maze. Rats will forage systematically through all the arms, seldom retracing their steps.

Recent research by Michael Renner and his students has demonstrated that nonhungry rats bring the unlearned tendency to *explore* and *investigate* to new environments (Renner & Pierre, 1998). Using an eight-arm radial maze, they found that rats would use innate food-searching behaviors called **foraging patterns** to conduct a systematic search of each of the eight arms. In fact, the rats were experts in exploring spatial relationships involving food. If we define an error as reentry of an arm the rats had previously searched for food, *the rats seldom made errors.*

With this understanding of the innate tendencies a rat brings to a maze, how should we interpret the rapid learning demonstrated by the rats that were food-reinforced beginning on the 11th trial in Figure 6.11? First, these rats learned where food *wasn't* while foraging on trials 1 through 10. They were then reinforced for getting through the maze more and more quickly on trials 1 through 10 by being removed from an environment with no food and returned to their home cage for feeding. Therefore, we can't say that the rats learned the maze in the absence of reinforcement. Rather, their learning must be understood as the result of both innate foraging tendencies and reinforcement.

In sum, rats that learn mazes whether or not they are fed, as well as pigs and raccoons that play with tokens rather than trade them for food, may be thought of as challenges to the general learning theories proposed by Pavlov and Skinner. Another such challenge can be found in earlier experiments on the effects of ionizing radiation on rats.

latent learning (Tolman) Learning that occurs in the absence of specific food rewards.

foraging pattern An innately determined food-searching behavior.

Evolutionarily Prepared Learning

Two researchers named John Garcia and Robert Koelling developed an ingenious demonstration that is now known as the "bright, noisy, tasty water" experiment (Garcia & Koelling, 1966). When rats licked a tube containing saccharin dissolved in water ("tasty" water), they completed an electric circuit that briefly flashed a light ("bright water"). The same circuit also produced a brief clicking noise—hence the conditioned stimulus consisted of bright, noisy, tasty water. After drinking the bright, noisy, tasty water (the CS), half the rats were punished by being briefly shocked (a US); the other half were exposed to a sickening ionizing radiation (also a US). To assess the results of the conditioning, the researchers then gave the rats a choice of drinking either bright, noisy water or tasty water during extinction tests (Garcia & Koelling, 1966). Figure 6.12 shows the results.

In this experiment, the rats associated the sight and sound components of the CS (the bright, noisy water) with the electric shock, and the taste component (tasty water) with the radiation. They were unable to associate sights and sounds with radiation, nor did they learn to avoid the sweet taste after it had been paired with an electric shock. Garcia's interpretation of the results was that not all stimuli can be associated with each other. Some stimuli—ones that belong together—are easily associated. Taste and sickness are easily paired, he argued, because rats

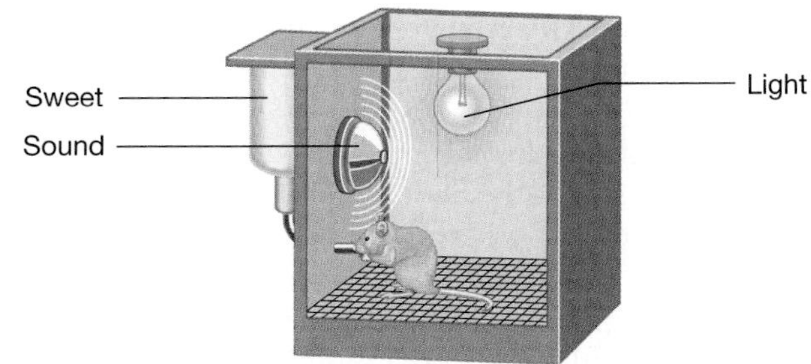

All rats drink bright, noisy, tasty water (the CS).

Half receive mild electric shock (a US).

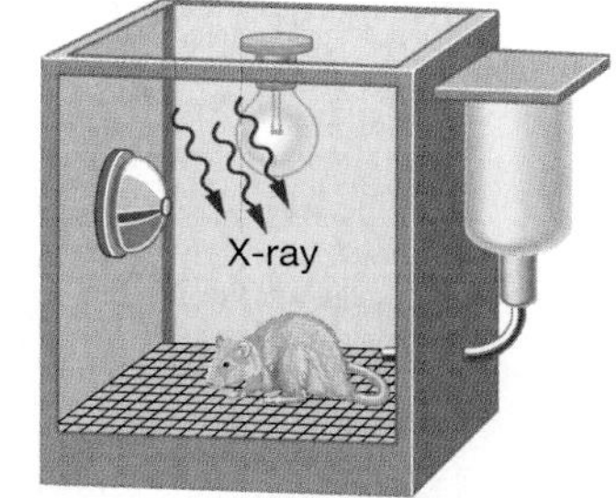

Half receive X-rays (a US).

Rats that had the shock-US avoided the bright, noisy components of the CS and drank the sweetened water.

Rats that had the X-ray-US avoided the sweetened water, ignored the bright, noisy components of the CS, and drank the water.

Figure 6.12 **John Garcia's bright, noisy, tasty water experiment.** Some stimuli are more easily associated than others. Rats in Garcia's experiment associated brightness and noise with an electric shock (bottom left) and sweetness with radiation (bottom right).
Source: From LEARNING AND BEHAVIOR 3rd ed. by Lewis Barker. Copyright © 2001 by Pearson Education, Inc. Reprinted by permission.

have brains that have evolved to associate flavors with the consequences of eating. Likewise, the sights and sounds of predators are more likely to be conditioned with pain cues than with sickness.

This view that some learning situations are primed to be learned quickly has been expressed as a theory of *preparedness* by Paul Rozin of the University of Pennsylvania:

> What an organism learns in the laboratory or in his natural habitat is the result not only of the contingencies which he faces and has faced in his past but also of the contingencies which his species faced before him—its evolutionary history and genetic outcome. (Rozin & Kalat, 1971)

The concept of preparedness, in turn, can be interpreted in terms of the distal (genetic) and proximal (learned) causes of behavior. The distal causes of a rat's feeding behavior include foraging strategies and other species-specific behavioral tendencies, such as neophobia when confronted with unfamiliar foods. Even hungry rats will approach new foods cautiously: they sniff, retreat, approach, sniff and nibble (taste), and retreat. The brain organization underlying this innate wariness toward new foods is likely to be the (distal) basis for the rat's ability to form flavor-illness associations in only one trial—the trial being a proximal cause of its feeding behavior.

Brain organization influences behavior in unexpected ways. Recall that Skinner's research strategy was to investigate how animals learned "arbitrary behaviors." He assumed that both lever pressing in rats and key pecking in pigeons were "uncontaminated" by distal causes of behavior. Surely the posture and positioning of the neck muscles in pigeons were unrelated to their eating and drinking, he thought—but look closely at the photographs below.

As they show, a pigeon that has been reinforced with food (top row) will peck differently at a key than a pigeon that has been reinforced with water (bottom row). Water reinforcement produces an opened-mouth pecking response, whereas food reinforcement produces a closed-mouth posture that pigeons use in eating grain (Jenkins & Moore, 1973). In this instance, the operant is not as arbitrary as Skinner had thought. A pigeon is innately programmed to peck at seeds and sip at water. Structures in the pigeon's brain are activated by visual stimuli related to these activities.

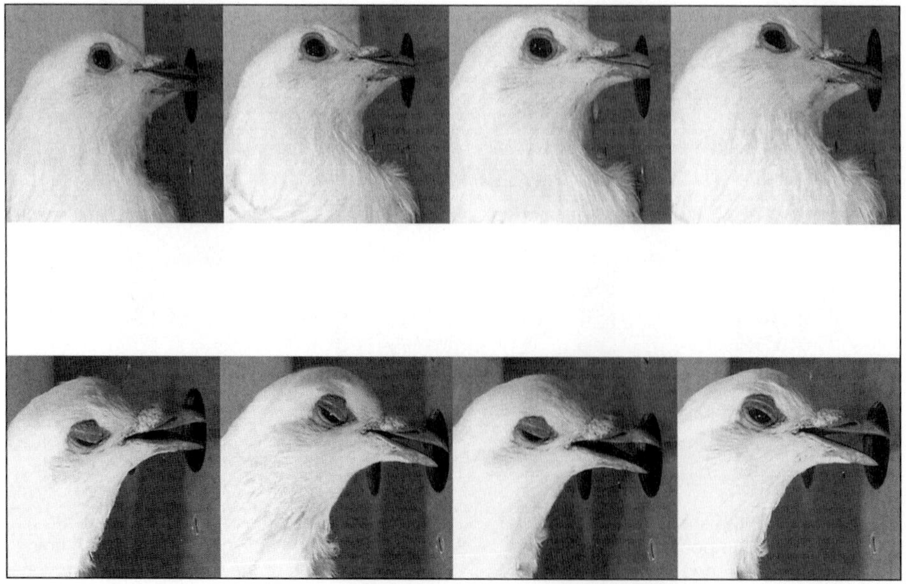

Pigeons will peck at keys with open beaks if they are reinforced with water (lower row) and with closed beaks if they are reinforced with food (upper row). This subtle difference in their response is innately determined.

INTERIM SUMMARY

1. In training animals for circus acts, the Brelands noted a failure of the law of effect. They found that pigs and raccoons would delay the food-reinforced response of dropping coins, and instead "wash" and "root" at the coins. The Brelands explained the animals' behavior in terms of ***instinctive drift***.
2. Animals seem to form a mental representation of the shortest path to a destination, what Tolman called a ***cognitive map***.
3. ***Latent learning*** is the term Tolman used to account for the fact that rats would learn a maze while exploring it, even in the absence of food reinforcement. Hungry rats engage in innate ***foraging patterns*** when placed in a maze, and soon learn where food is not as well as where it is.
4. A number of animal learning experiments have demonstrated that some associations are more easily made than others. One-trial associations indicate that animals are evolutionarily predisposed to learn certain tasks that promote survival. This predisposition is called *preparedness*.
5. Rapid learning of taste associations is aided by innate feeding behaviors. Neophobia toward new foods is adaptive, in that it minimizes the danger of poisoning.
6. Garcia's "bright, noisy, tasty water" experiment showed that in rats, a flavor (CS) is easily associated with illness (US) but not with electric shock, and that visual and auditory CSs are easily associated with pain, but not with illness.
7. Contrary to B. F. Skinner's assertion that a pigeon's key peck is an arbitrary response, pigeons will peck differently at keys, depending on whether they are reinforced with food or water.

For Further Thought

1. Recognizing that rats and humans are both omnivorous mammals, would you expect that in addition to neophobia, each species has other feeding propensities in common? How do you think a human would perform on Garcia's bright, noisy, tasty water test?
2. Because of selective pressures, the human brain has been adapted to seek pleasure, avoid pain, and learn according to the law of effect. Do you think people are *prepared* to abuse drugs?

CONCEPTUAL LEARNING

In this chapter we have used relatively simple models of association formation—both classical and instrumental conditioning—to account for acquired behaviors in humans and other animals. We have seen that all can be classically conditioned. In later chapters we will see that insights attained through the application of such learning models are useful in understanding complex behaviors, including health practices, eating habits, and emotional behavior.

Nevertheless, this approach to learning is likely to have frustrated you when it was applied to human behavior. Surely, you may have thought, this is *not* the way in which concepts that define human nature are transferred from one generation to the next. Indeed, most humans believe there are *qualitative* differences between human behavior and the human mind, on the one hand, and nonhuman animal behavior and the animal mind on the other. Are human **cognitive processes**—perceiving, thinking, knowing, remembering, and so forth—qualitatively different from those of other animals? The answer is yes, because putting individual differences aside for the moment, we humans are the only animals who can think and express ideas through symbolic language.

cognitive processes The psychological processes of perceiving, thinking, knowing, remembering, and so forth.

Compare perceptual awareness and cognition, Chapter 9, p. 308 and development of cognitive processes, Chapter 11, p. 392

Yet we also know from a variety of experiments that animals can think, form concepts, and solve problems (Cook, 1993). That is what Tolman had in mind when he hypothesized that rats develop "cognitive maps" of the mazes they are learning. Pigeons can group objects into categories, though they cannot group them conceptually (Wright, 1997). In contrast, monkeys, chimpanzees, and humans can form concepts. (For purposes of comparison, we will describe human concept formation briefly here; the development of human cognitive processes will be discussed in more detail in Chapters 11 and 12.) Keep in mind, however, that both humans and other animals can learn through the simple processes of reinforcement and punishment.

Concept Formation in Primates

Humans and chimpanzees are genetically similar; hence, their brains are similarly organized. Can we expect the mind and behavior of chimps and monkeys to be more like those of humans than other animals? Let's begin with how they learn.

Imagine you are a Rhesus monkey in Harry Harlow's psychology lab at the University of Wisconsin. You are presented with two small toys, a red block and a thimble; you must choose one. You know that if you choose correctly, you will find a raisin in a food cup underneath the toy. You choose the red block, push it aside, and reach into the cup: no raisin. On the next trial, you see the same red block and thimble. Which will you choose this time? It wasn't under the red block last time, you think to yourself, so you try the thimble. Bingo! You retrieve the raisin and await the next trial. Harlow (1949) repeated this procedure, called a *learning set*, for six trials using the same two toys; then he introduced two new toys in a new learning set. A typical experiment involved hundreds of learning sets.

In successfully choosing the thimble and being reinforced for it, what did you learn? If you could think and talk like a human, you might say that you haven't learned anything, except that the thimble predicts food. How would your behavior change if two new toys were introduced? Harlow found that monkeys eventually learned a **win-stay, lose-shift strategy**, which they used to make correct choices about 75 percent of the time. In this strategy, animals continue the same behavior that produced reinforcement in the past (win-stay), but switch to a different behavior if they are not reinforced (lose-shift).

Once the monkeys had mastered this concept, they no longer needed six trials to learn the correct response to each new set of paired objects. In Harlow's terms, they had learned how to learn, and began to apply the general strategy of win-stay, lose-shift on the second trial. About 250 trials later, after learning to learn, Harlow's monkeys were about 98 percent accurate in their responses to each newly introduced pair of stimuli. Figure 6.13 shows that different animals learn this simple concept at different rates: some need more trials than others.

Monkeys, chimps, and pigeons have been taught other perceptual tasks, which Wright (1997) calls "configural patterns," that may or may not be conceptual. Wright suggests that skill in performing these tasks is necessary for an animal to master other tasks, such as sameness and oddity problems. The sameness problem requires an animal to remember and pick from novel pictures a previously presented picture or pattern. The oddity problem requires that given an array of three stimuli, two of which are the same, the animal must select the "odd" stimulus.

win-stay, lose-shift strategy (Harlow) A strategy in which an animal continues to make a response that is reinforced (win-stay) but switches to a different response when not reinforced (lose-shift).

No matter how they solve sameness and oddity problems, nonhuman animals require thousands of training trials to do it. To the extent that they learn concepts, both Pavlovian and instrumental conditioning can account for their performance (Petri & Mishkin, 1994). But before we humans stick up our noses at our primate cousins, we should acknowledge that many kinds of learning do not come easily to us, either. For example, in English, learning the letters of the

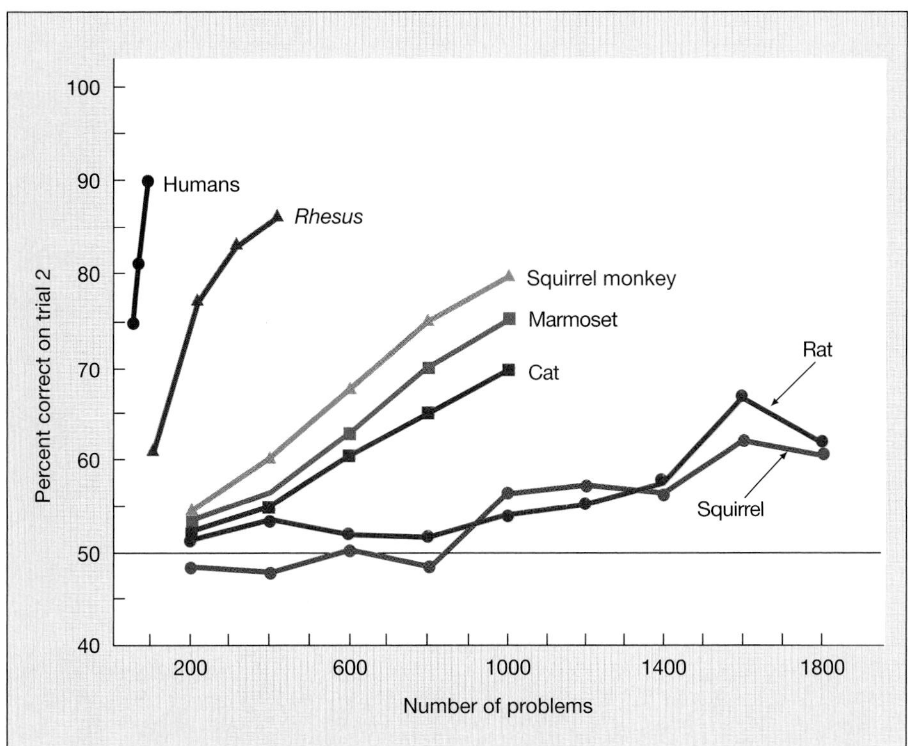

Figure 6.13 Learning the win-stay, lose-shift strategy. On a two-choice task, animals eventually learned to stay with their first choice if they were reinforced, and to shift to the alternative response if they were not reinforced. Humans and monkeys learn this strategy more quickly than other animals.

alphabet requires 52 sight-sound associations (both uppercase and lowercase). As we have seen, classical conditioning provides the best explanation of how such associations are formed. The sight of the letter becomes associated both with its sound and with the stimulus cues controlling the tongue and lips, which make the sound. The fact is, learning to make these 52 sight-sound associations requires hundreds or thousands of trials over many hundreds of hours. By 6 years of age, many children still have not learned their alphabet.

From Reflexes to Literacy

In Chapter 3 we learned that genes are the source of the distal (distant) determinants of an animal's behavior. In this chapter we have focused on the development of memes, the proximal (immediate) determinants of behavior. Figure 6.14 summarizes the relationship between the two. Behavioral complexity is plotted on one axis and environmental complexity on the other. As the figure shows, reflexes, the simplest innate behaviors, can be elicited by relatively simple environmental stimuli. Likewise, the distally determined processes of habituation and sensitization, which require no special training, are controlled by relatively simple environmental stimuli; most animals can easily express these nonassociative learning processes.

Genes and environment, Chapter 3, p. 84

More complex environments are required for skill learning and conceptual learning. Hence, animals whose behavior has been reinforced or punished in unique ways will manifest individual differences in learning. Literacy requires an extremely complex environment, the effects of which take years to fully develop. This increased behavioral complexity comes primarily from the environment; nothing in the human genotype specifically supports music composition, novel writing, or other memes characteristic of civilization. Rather, these uniquely human tasks require a highly structured cultural environment that shapes the brain and behavior throughout a lifetime.

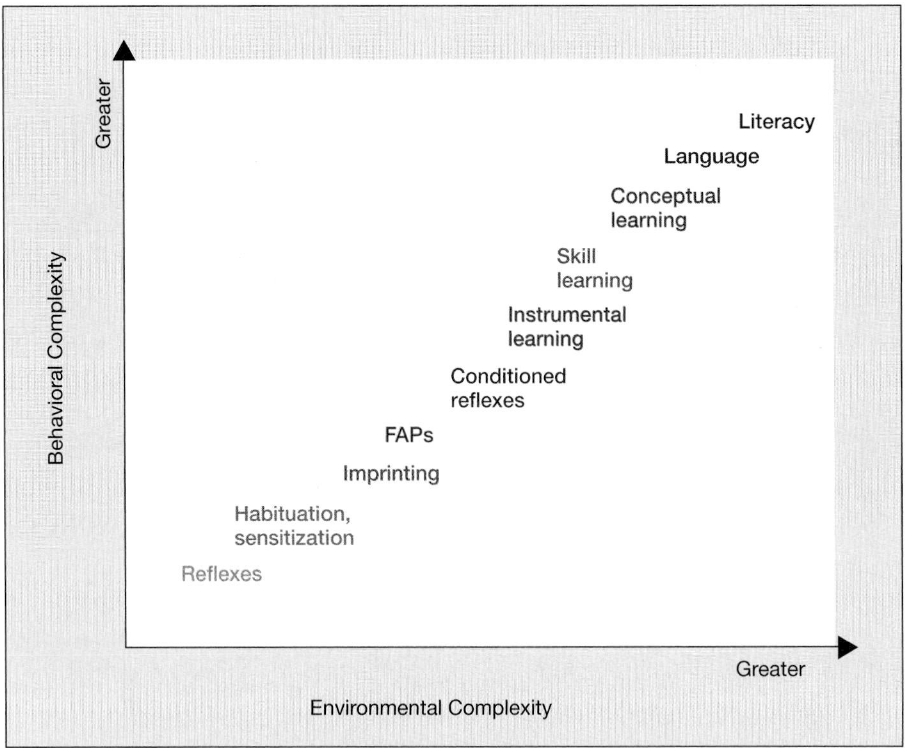

Figure 6.14 Role of the environment in determining behavior. Reflexes are simple innate behaviors that are tied to simple environmental stimuli. Complex behaviors like language depend on a complex environment.

INTERIM SUMMARY

1. Human *cognitive processes*—perceiving, thinking, knowing, remembering, and so forth—can be compared to those of other animals by studying how nonhuman animals learn complex tasks.
2. Given a two-choice task, a variety of animals (including children, pigeons, and rats) can learn a *win-stay, lose-shift strategy*. By *learning to learn*, Harlow's monkeys showed that they could successfully use such a learned rule to solve novel problems.
3. Human and nonhuman animals can learn simple concepts and form general rules to solve problems such as *sameness* and *oddity* tasks. Nonhumans require thousands of training trials to learn simple concepts.
4. Behavior has both distal and proximal determinants. The more complex the behavior, such as conceptual learning or literacy, the more complex the environment required to learn the behavior.

For Further Thought

1. In your own experience, is rule learning difficult? Can you verbalize the rules you have memorized in algebra or trigonometry? Were your aha experiences attained by trial and error or by insight? (After reading this chapter, do you suspect that these terms are not mutually exclusive?)

CONCLUDING THOUGHTS

Animal behavior is accounted for by the interaction of nature, or heredity, and nurture, or the environment. Research in the psychological sciences continues to uncover ways in which human genes and memes interact to yield the behaviors that differentiate humans from other animals. Each species' behavior reflects both its evolutionary history and its environmental learning. Animals exhibit innate reflexive behaviors in relatively uncomplicated environments. In contrast, humans are less dependent on innate reflexive behaviors and more dependent on complex, environmentally determined behaviors.

In addition to reflexes, all vertebrates exhibit the basic processes of habituation and sensitization, as well as a plasticity that underlies more complex learned behaviors. Classical conditioning and instrumental learning are two forms of learning characterized by the ability to make new associations. In responding to their environments, animals learn that some events signal other events. A CS that signals a US provides an animal with useful information about the environment. Learning to predict environmental outcomes is an adaptive skill.

B. F. Skinner, an environmental determinist, proposed that animal behavior is best accounted for by learning. In his view, behavior can come under the control of stimuli that signal the consequences of a response—that is, whether or not it will be reinforced or punished. A response that produces pleasure is adaptive and will be selected over a response that produces pain. No wonder that positive reinforcement and punishment shape and guide our responses.

Human behavior seems to be guided more by memes than by reflexes. This learning process takes a long time and depends on a highly structured environment that conditions emotional responses and guides food selection. Children learn the meaning and signaling value of words through their association with the environment. Words quickly become the secondary reinforcers and punishers that shape and guide human behavior.

Some environments support language usage, concept formation, and the development of literacy better than others. Even in the best of environments, learning a culture's memes can take decades. The plasticity of learned behavior—its variation with the environment—differentiates one human from another, and humans from other animals.

KEY TERMS

annoyer *206*
associative process *190*
avoidance learning *214*
behavior *186*
behavioral control *211*
classical conditioning *191*
cognitive map *217*
cognitive processes *221*
conditioned compensatory response *202*
conditioned emotional response *198*
conditioned response (CR) *192*
conditioned stimulus (CS) *192*
conditioned taste aversion *201*
continous reinforcement *208*
differential reinforcement of high rates (DRH) *210*
differential reinforcement of low rates (DRL) *210*
discrimination *195*
discriminative stimulus (S^d) *212*
escape *214*
extinction *193, 210*
fixed interval (FI) schedule *209*
fixed ratio (FR) schedule *208*
foraging pattern *218*
habituation *193*
higher-order conditioning *194*
instinctive drift *217*
instrumental learning *205*
instrumental response *204*
latent learning *218*
law of effect *206*
learning *186*
meme *187*
negative reinforcement *214*
negative discriminative stimulus (S^{Δ}) *212*
observational learning *215*
operant *206*
operant conditioning *207*
orienting reflex *191*
partial reinforcement *208*
partial reinforcement effect (PRE) *210*
positive reinforcement *207*
positive reinforcer *207*
punishment *212*
reflex *190*
satisfier *206*
schedule of reinforcement *207*
second-signal system *199*
secondary reinforcer *207*
sensitization *193*
shaping *207*
spontaneous recovery *193*
stimulus control *212*
stimulus generalization *195*
unconditioned response (UR) *191*
unconditioned stimulus (US) *191*
variable interval (VI) schedule *209*
variable ratio (VR) schedule *209*
win-stay, lose-shift strategy *222*

7

Sensation

Paul Cezanne (1839–1906), French, "Une Baignade." Christie's Images / SuperStock.

Introduction to the Senses
The Senses as Evolved Adaptations
Psychophysics
Psychophysical Methods
Signal Detection Theory
The Two-Point Limen
Subliminal Perception
A Five-Stage Model of Sensory Systems
Interim Summary
For Further Thought

Seeing
Structure of the Eye
Seeing at the Level of the Retina
Visual Nerve Pathways
Nonseeing Functions of the Eye
Dark Adaptation
Color Vision
Color Blindness
Interim Summary
For Further Thought

Hearing
Structure of the Ear
Place Theory and the Traveling Wave
The Sensation of Loudness
Hearing Loss and Deafness
Central Auditory Processes
Interim Summary
For Further Thought

Tasting and Smelling: The Intimate Senses
What We Taste
How We Taste
Why and How We Smell
Interim Summary
For Further Thought

The Skin Senses: Touch, Pressure, Temperature, and Pain
The Human Skin
The Sense of Pain
Interim Summary
For Further Thought

Concluding Thoughts

Like other animals, most humans see, hear, taste, and smell; seek the touch of physical contact; and dislike the pain caused by the sting of a bee. We take these senses for granted; only after encountering someone who is deaf or blind might we reflect on what it would be like not to see or not to hear.

Imagine eating at your favorite restaurant. You hear, see, feel, taste, and smell the inviting environment all at once. In Oliver Sacks's (1990) words, usually without being conscious of it, we experience a consensus of the senses. By that Sacks means that all our senses work together to give us a unified impression of the physical world.

Yet examining the senses individually is also instructive. What could be more adaptive than the sense of pain, which keeps people from engaging in behaviors that could cause tissue damage or possibly death? Likewise, the person who sees an oncoming car and hears "Watch out!" is more likely to respond adaptively, to survive and reproduce. The sense of smell and words that describe smells, conveyed through the sense of hearing, also communicate information with adaptive consequences. Consider the following description of some of the things humans smell:

> In eighteenth-century France . . . there reigned in the cities a stench barely conceivable to us modern men and women. The streets stank of manure, the courtyards of urine, the stairwells stank of moldering wood and rat droppings, the kitchens of cabbage and mutton fat; the unaired parlors stank of stale dust, the bedrooms of greasy sheets, damp featherbeds, and the pungently sweet aroma of chamber pots. . . . People stank of sweat and unwashed clothes . . . even the king himself stank, stank like a rank lion, and the queen like an old goat, summer and winter. (Süskind, 1986, pp. 3–4)

These words make us uncomfortable, because they trigger the negative emotion of disgust, and disgust motivates avoidance behavior. Whether in 18th-century France or in 21st-century New York, courtyards and stairwells that reek of urine and rat droppings adaptively signal BEWARE: THIS PLACE IS UNHEALTHY.

Likewise, odors that are fresh, clean, and fragrant, and words that describe such odors, are associated with good foods and healthy people. Humans are adaptively attracted to, and often engage in reproductive behaviors with, healthy people. Listen, for example, to Plutarch's description of 20-year-old Alexander the Great, who lived in Macedonia in 330 B.C.E.:

> He was fair and of a light color, passing into ruddiness in his face and upon his breast. Aristoxenus in his Memoirs tells us that a most agreeable odor exhaled from his skin, and that his breath and body all over was so fragrant as to perfume the clothes which he wore. . . . (Bernard & Hodges, 1958, p. 11)

We can infer that Alexander the Great did not suffer from decaying teeth or illnesses that produced disagreeable body odors, and that unlike the kings and queens of 18th-century France, he kept himself clean instead of covering his stench with artificial perfumes. Undoubtedly other humans were attracted to Alexander the Great.

In this chapter, on sensation, and the next, on perception, we'll consider the senses in detail. We'll see that the way in which an adult perceives the environment is far more complicated than the simple processes through which a newborn senses the world. The very way in which we use the word *see*, in fact, illustrates the difference between sensing and perceiving. People who wear corrective lenses, for example, see more clearly with them than without. This use of the word *see* is different from "I see how that's done." The first has to do with the mechanics of vision (sensation); the second, with understanding (perception), which occurs when we interpret sensations. Both wearing corrective lenses and understanding through observation are highly adaptive.

We'll begin this chapter by considering the distal causes of sensing—why we see, hear, and otherwise sense the world. Then we'll examine some principles, theories, and methods that can be applied to all five senses. Finally, we'll take a detailed look at how we see, hear, taste, and smell, and how we feel touch, pressure, temperature, and pain.

INTRODUCTION TO THE SENSES

Because a knowledge of evolution is helpful in understanding the human senses, we will begin by briefly considering the distal causes of our senses of vision, audition, olfaction, and taste, as well as the several skin senses. Then we will survey the principles and methods scientists use in investigating the senses. Before moving on to a detailed description of each of the senses, we will examine a five-stage model that can be applied to all of them.

LINK
Proximal and distal determinants of behavior, Chapter 3, p. 70

The Senses as Evolved Adaptations

To begin, the senses are essential to adaptive reflexes, such as the spitting reflex in reaction to bitter-tasting substances, the rooting reflex seen in infants when they are touched around the mouth, and the startle reflex in response to an unexpected sound. Thus the receptors for seeing, hearing, smelling, tasting, and touching are concentrated on the head end of most animals, which encounters the environment first. Likewise, the skin on the face, lips, and tongue is more sensitive than skin in most other areas of the body.

Sensing Tastes and Smells. Consider that the earliest animals evolved in a liquid chemical environment called the sea, where their sensitivity to chemicals facilitated their feeding and reproduction. Bacteria, worms, insects, and vertebrates all developed sophisticated chemical receptors, some for sensing chemicals inside the body and others for detecting chemicals on the outside. With time, the outer chemical sensors took on one of two different functions: they either *smelled* the chemicals given off by plants and animals or *tasted* the chemicals on objects they touched. By the time vertebrates evolved, these two types of receptors had evolved into full-blown sensory systems, similar in many respects to vision and hearing.

Sensing Light. Throughout this long evolutionary period, the sun's energy bathed the seas, lakes, and land on the earth's surface. Plants were sensitive to the sun's energy, and eventually harnessed it through a process called *photosynthesis*. Likewise, primitive animals evolved cells containing pigments called photochemicals, which responded whenever light fell on them. Following many millions of years of mutation and natural selection, some animals evolved the photochemical rhodopsin, the basis of human sight. (Rhodopsin will be discussed in more detail in the next section.)

Richard Dawkins (1996) has proposed that in addition to providing the energy for all life, over the course of millions of years the sun has encouraged the evolution of an accurate "remote guidance technology"—visual systems capable of sensing the environment at a distance, in ways that enhance survival. Hence, many different forms of eyes have evolved to detect form, color, and movement.

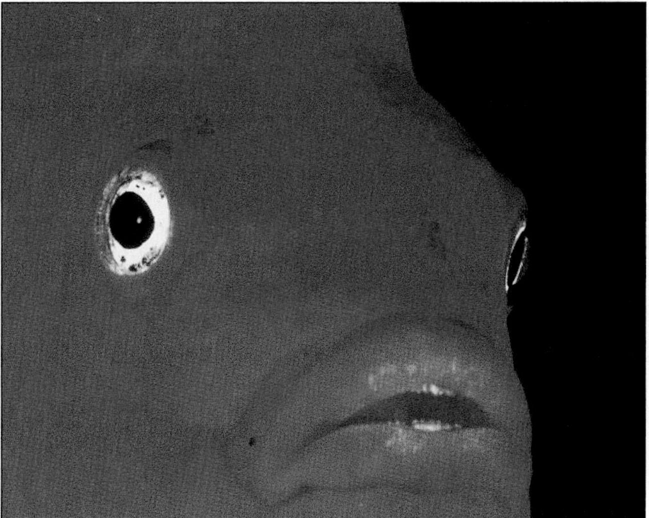

To adapt to their environment, animals have evolved various types of eyes: (a) the compound eye of a Robber Fly and (b) the camera-type eye of a garibaldi fish (*Hypsypops ribicundus*).

The photographs on page 229 show a sampling of them, from the simple light and movement detectors called compound eyes (photo a) to the camera-like eyes that are more like those of humans (photo b). These variations in eye type provide an answer to the question Why do we see? Eyes are adaptations that promote the perception of form, color, and movement, and ultimately the precise *visual acuity* (ability to discriminate one object or part of an object from another) afforded by primate visual systems.

Sensing Sounds. All vertebrates hear sounds. Fish don't have ears, but they have a sensory system that detects vibrations in water; it evolved to sense airborne sounds in amphibians, reptiles, birds, and mammals. The sounds mammals can hear seem to be critical to the environmental niches they occupy (Masterton, 1992). For example, mice and bats are sensitive to ultrasound emissions, which are beyond a human's range of hearing. Mice pups emit sounds that precisely match their mother's hearing range, allowing them to signal mother when they wander from the nest. Bats emit sounds that bounce off objects and return, allowing them to *echolocate* within their immediate environment (Griffin, 1959).

In general terms, hearing serves three main adaptive functions for all animals: (1) to identify *what* is making a sound; (2) to identify *where* a sound is coming from; and (3) to allow *conspecific communication* (communication with members of the same species). In daylight, seeing and hearing, sometimes referred to as the distance senses, combine to give an animal information about what is moving where. The whats may be potential mates, offspring, predators, or prey animals. But in the dark, there is only hearing. Through the long nights, hearing is the first line of defense against potentially dangerous moving objects that lie beyond the range of smell. (What *was* that sound, and did it come from in front of or behind me?) When communication is necessary, sounds can be heard and made in the dark.

Sensing Touch, Warmth, and Pain. The skin senses, especially touch and warmth receptors that help to locate and identify nearby objects, are also adaptive. Touch enables skilled movements, such as eating and drinking (chewing and swallowing), talking, walking, running, and swimming, each of which requires sophisticated sensory-motor programs. And while humans didn't evolve receptors on their lips in order to play a trumpet, or receptors on their fingers and thumbs to put a backspin on a free throw, their presence makes such skilled human behaviors possible.

Sensorimotor integration in the brain, Chapter 4, p. 126

Pain is arguably the most adaptive sense, because it motivates animals to behave in a way that prevents or alleviates it. Humans born with an inability to experience pain do not thrive. One such person, the daughter of a physician, was studied until her death at the age of 29 (Baxter & Olszewski, 1960). Her tongue was deformed from having repeatedly bitten it; because she could not sense situations that caused bruises and burns, she never learned to avoid them. At age 22, during a neurological examination, this young woman was accidentally burned with water that was hot enough to cause blistering, but she reported no pain. The fact that her heart rate, blood pressure, and breathing did not change showed that she was not faking the absence of pain. In other tests, her skin senses proved normal, including her ability to localize touch and discriminate between warm and cold water. Although she could tell when water was hot, she felt no pain when it burned her.

A person who can sense that water is hot but cannot experience pain raises a number of questions. Do we know how touch, warmth, and pain—indeed, all the senses—are related? Are there important individual differences in what people can sense, and if so, are those differences due primarily to genes or culture? To answer these questions, we must turn to the relationship between sensation and perception. Formally defined, **sensation** is the raw experience of a stimulus, such as light or sound. Light activates receptors in the eye, producing the sensation of sight; chemicals activate receptors on the tongue, producing the sensation of taste. **Perception** refers to the active organization and interpretation of the visual, auditory, taste, and smell sensations animals experience. The subjective nature of perception is philosophically unsettling, raising questions about whether any two individuals, or two different species, see and taste the world in exactly the same way. In the next sections we will see how scientists have grappled with the question of whether sensation is absolute or relative.

Psychophysics

In the history of psychology, few individuals were as peculiar as Gustav Fechner (1801–1887). In 1839, Fechner, a promising 38-year-old professor of physics at the University of Leipzig, Germany, took the first of several abrupt turns in his career. Fechner apparently became neurotic by "overworking," then injured his eyes by staring at the sun through colored glasses while conducting research on negative afterimages. Severely depressed, he resigned his professorship and went into seclusion. After several years of eating a bizarre diet and not speaking, he inexplicably made a rapid recovery and began to write. In 1851 he published a book titled *Zend-Avesta*—roughly translated, *A Revelation of the Word* (Boring, 1929). A mystical tract about the unity of humans, gods, and a conscious nature, Fechner's book contained the philosophical underpinnings of a new science called **psychophysics**, the study of how humans and animals respond to sensory stimuli. Years before, a colleague of Fechner's at Leipzig, Ernst Weber (1795–1878), had conducted some experiments that suggested a mathematical relationship between the physical characteristics of an object and the way humans sensed it. Fechner considered psychophysics to be an "exact" theory of how humans and nature are related. Historians consider the publication of Fechner's next book, *Elemente der Psychophysik* (1860/1966), one of the founding events in experimental psychology. What was his mysterious theory of psychophysics?

Just Noticeable Differences. Weber had asked human subjects to lift two similar weights and judge the difference in their weight. Could he measure the **just noticeable difference (jnd)** that made one feel heavier than the other, he wondered? Weber was looking for a **difference threshold**, the minimal amount of change in a stimulus that humans could detect. He found that the answer to his question depended on the size of the weights he used. A jnd, he reasoned, must be equal to a constant (k) times the intensity (I) of the stimulus:

$$\text{jnd} = kI$$

This relationship, now known as **Weber's law**, simply indicates that a sensation is proportional to the intensity of the stimulus. For example, if each of two weights weighs only a few ounces, the just noticeable difference between their weight would be measured in fractions of an *ounce*. But if the two weights each weighed a few pounds, the jnd between them would be measured in fractions of a *pound*. Weber's law is often expressed as $\Delta I/I = k$, or "The ratio of the change in the intensity of a stimulus (ΔI) to the initial intensity (I) is equal to a constant (k)." The constant k is referred to as *Weber's fraction*.

In a series of experiments, Weber discovered that the constant k varied depending on which sensory modality he measured. There was a different k for

sensation The raw experience of a sensory stimulus, such as light or sound.

perception The interpretation of sensory information according to expectations and prior learning.

psychophysics The mathematical relationship of sensory intensity to the magnitude of a physical stimulus.

just noticeable difference (jnd) The minimal amount of sensory change in a stimulus that a person can detect.

Weber's law The statement that a sensation is proportional to the intensity (I) of the stimulus times a constant, k.

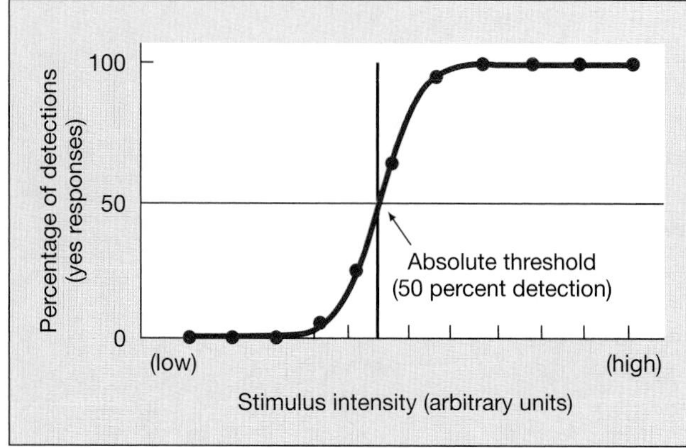

Figure 7.1 **Determining an absolute threshold.** This graph shows the percentage of correct detections of a stimulus as a function of the intensity of the stimulus. It is the outcome of many trials in which a weak stimulus was presented to a subject, who was asked whether it was detectable. The absolute threshold for a stimulus is calculated as the intensity at which a stimulus is detected 50 percent of the time.

light intensities, for odor concentrations, and so forth. The law held in every modality, though. For example, in very dim light, even a small increase in light intensity is noticeable, but in very bright light, a great increase in light intensity is necessary before the difference becomes noticeable.

These demonstrations of a mathematical relationship between sensation and the physical world meant something different to Fechner than they did to Weber. Fechner reasoned that jnds were psychological measurements that could be used to measure the psyche in the same the way that a yardstick is used to measure distance. Perhaps he could use jnds to measure how a person's consciousness was related to nature's consciousness—for surely, to be so orderly, nature must also be conscious? Psychophysics would then become a form of universal measurement. Fechner assumed that every jnd (a psychological unit) was equivalent, just as every inch on a yardstick is equivalent. Therefore jnds could be added and subtracted like any other measurement.

The Absolute Threshold. Fechner reasoned further that in comparing a subject's reaction to weak stimuli, he was measuring the subject's threshold of sensitivity, or *absolute threshold*. The **absolute threshold** is defined as the minimal amount of stimulation that a subject can detect on half the trials (and cannot detect on the other half). The calculation of an absolute threshold is illustrated in Figure 7.1. Although Fechner's dream of measuring consciousness has been only partially realized, the methods of sensory measurement he developed have been widely applied. Let's look at some other methods scientists use.

Psychophysical Methods

Audiologists measure hearing sensitivity using a combination of methods. To measure the absolute threshold, for example, they sounded a tone below the threshold for hearing (see Figure 7.1). Then, using the ascending **method of limits**, they gradually increase the volume until the subject reports just barely detecting the sound. This procedure is repeated several times. Finally, they compute the average value of the volume at which the person reports hearing the tone and establish it as the absolute threshold for hearing. The procedure is reversed in the descending method of limits, in which an audible tone is reduced in intensity on successive trials until the subject can no longer hear it.

The ascending method of limits may yield somewhat different results than the descending method of limits, for two reasons. With the ascending method, a person's attention may wander during the times when a sound cannot be heard, causing the person to miss an audible stimulus. This type of inaccuracy will result in a threshold that is too high. With the descending method, the subject may anticipate when the next stimulus should be presented and report hearing a stimulus that is actually below threshold. This method, then, may yield an absolute threshold that is too low.

To correct for the effects of attention and expectation, scientists developed the **method of constant stimuli**. What is "constant" is that on successive trials, stimuli above and below the threshold are equally likely to be presented. The subject cannot predict what will happen next. This method, then, helps both to maintain a subject's attention and to reduce expectations about the next stimulus.

absolute threshold The minimal amount of stimulation that a subject can detect on half the trials.

method of limits A psychophysical method of establishing a sensory threshold value by increasing or decreasing the intensity of a stimulus until a subject can detect it 50 percent of the time.

method of constant stimuli A psychophysical method in which a threshold value is reached by presenting stimuli in a random order.

In the 1930s, the psychologist S. S. Stevens of Harvard University asked subjects to do some strange tasks, such as "Adjust the brightness of this light until it matches the loudness of the following tone." Stevens called this type of task *cross-modal matching*. Although the idea may seem odd, the fact is, human subjects can accomplish such tasks as if they know exactly what they are doing.

In another experiment, Stevens asked subjects to estimate the intensity of a tone by assigning it a number, typically from 1 to 100. He found that subjects could apply this **method of magnitude estimation** to a wide range of stimuli. Moreover, like Fechner, Stevens found that the differences subjects reported between two loud sounds were proportionately greater than the differences they reported between two soft sounds; and that the differences they reported between two bright lights were proportionately greater than the differences they reported between two dim lights. After repeatedly comparing the perceived magnitude of a sensation with the stimulus intensity, Stevens described the relationship as a mathematical power function (Stevens, 1936, 1962). He later found that this function varied greatly across sensory systems. Figure 7.2 shows two power functions, one for the relationship of perceived pain to stimulus intensity and the other for perceived brightness.

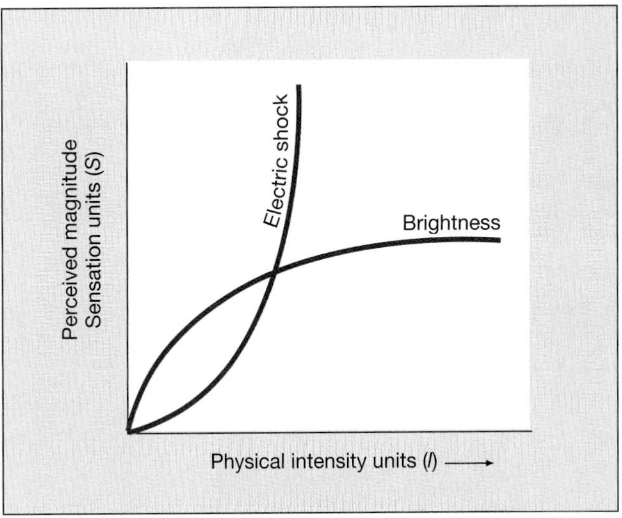

Figure 7.2 Stevens's power law. Plotting the perceived magnitude, or intensity, of a stimulus (vertical axis) against its physical intensity (horizontal axis) yields a mathematical function described as a power function. Here, the perceived magnitude of an electric shock increases sharply with only slight increases in the intensity of the shock, whereas the perceived brightness of a light increases more slowly as the light intensity increases.

Signal Detection Theory

Somatosensory cortex, Chapter 4, p. 123

It should come as no surprise that there are individual differences in sensory thresholds, and that the same person may respond differently from one test to another. For example, I am likely to be more motivated in having my hearing tested to correct a hearing loss than I am in participating in a hearing experiment. Certainly when one is tired or irritated, responses to a testing situation will differ from when one is rested. Practice effects, motivation, alertness, and expectations all combine to influence one's performance on a sensory detection task.

Signal detection theory is a mathematical theory that takes a subject's response bias into account (Green & Swets, 1966). Figure 7.3 shows a decision matrix in which both an event (a sensory signal) and a response to it may or may not occur. Two events can happen when a signal occurs: a person can report it, a judgment called a *hit*, or fail to report it, a judgment called a *miss*. If an event does not occur, but the subject reports that it did, the judgment is called a *false alarm* (or false positive). If a subject correctly reports that a stimulus did not occur, the judgment is called a *correct rejection*.

Experiments have demonstrated that a subject's response bias to such a task changes under different motivating conditions. That is, a person will make more or fewer hits, and more or fewer false alarms, depending on the consequences of the decision. If, for example, you earned $1 for each correct identification of a stimulus, and paid no penalty for false alarms, your response bias would be lenient, and you would likely report (guess) the presence of even a subthreshold stimulus. But if you were penalized $2 for false alarms, your response bias would change. You might even make some misses to decrease your false alarm rate. In other words, even such seemingly basic processes of sensation as determining the minimal amount of detectable physical energy are better understood as complicated perceptual processes involving motivation and expectation. Signal detection theory separates the sensory process from the decision process in these tasks.

method of magnitude estimation A psychophysical method in which subjects use numbers to describe the perceived intensity of a stimulus.

signal detection theory Proposal that the detection of stimuli involves decision processes as well as sensory processes.

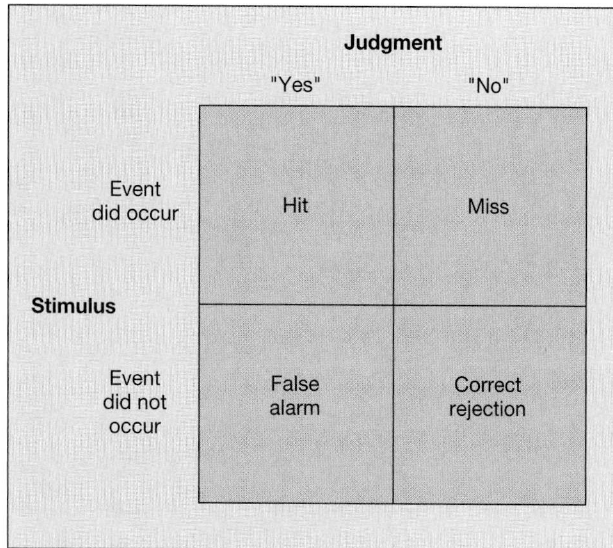

Judgment
"Yes"
"No"
Event did occur
Hit
Miss
Stimulus
Event did not occur
False alarm
Correct rejection

Figure 7.3 Signal detection matrix. In reporting the presence or absence of an event that may or may not have occurred, four outcomes are possible: a hit, a miss, a false alarm, or a correct rejection.

The Two-Point Limen

In Chapter 4 we learned that the somatosensory cortex is organized in a way that reflects different degrees of sensitivity to touch on the body's surface. The skin on the face and hands is more sensitive than skin in other places because it contains more receptors whose nerves synapse on larger numbers of cortical neurons. An easy way to demonstrate this is to measure what is called a *two-point limen* on yourself or another person. To begin, simply take a compass (the kind used for drawing circles on paper) and move the steel point and pencil point close together. Carefully place the two points simultaneously on the skin's surface in various parts of the body—a finger, stomach, nose, and so forth. Can you feel both points, or are they sufficiently close together that you feel only a single point of stimulation? Now increase the distance between the two points until you can distinguish two separate sensations. This distance is the two-point limen. Measuring the two-point limen all over the body shows differences in sensitivity that correlate well with the sensory homunculus shown on page 123 (Weinstein, 1968). On the fingers, thumb, and lips the two-point limen is only a millimeter or so, whereas in the middle of the back, it may be as wide as 10 millimeters.

Subliminal Perception

Subliminal perception refers to the detection of stimuli below the absolute threshold, or below the threshold of conscious awareness. The evidence on this phenomenon falls into one of two categories: the claims of promoters and advertisers and the findings of science. Fifty years ago, the news media began publishing reports that to boost snack sales, advertisers were subjecting movie audiences to rapidly flashed, consciously imperceptible slogans such as EAT POPCORN (Pratkanis, 1992). The idea was that advertisers could influence the unconscious mind in this way. Years of research have not supported it, however.

Interestingly enough, laboratory research has been successful in demonstrating that subliminal perception exists. Imagine that while you are watching TV, the word BREAD is presented for a fraction of a second—so rapidly that you cannot read the word, but can detect a "flash." If the word BREAD were presented for a few fractions of a second longer, you could see the word. The meaning of the event, then, becomes clear only with longer presentation times. Yet even a brief flash can be shown to affect your behavior; it apparently *primes* the memory for related words. For instance, subjects who are unaware of the target word BREAD can more readily see flashed words such as BUTTER in an array of distracter words (Marcel, 1983; see also Bornstein & Pittman, 1992).

LINK ▶ Subliminal perception with priming, Chapter 10, p. 360

This strange phenomenon isn't restricted to words that are flashed on a computer screen. In a clever study, Krosnick and his colleagues (1992) flashed emotion-laden pictures of a dead body or a basketful of kittens just prior to showing subjects various portraits. The researchers then asked the subjects to apply positive or negative labels to the portraits. Subjects applied more negative labels to a portrait after unconsciously viewing a dead body; the picture of kittens had the opposite effect (Krosnick, Betz, Jussim, & Lynn, 1992). That an emotion-laden image, seen either consciously or unconsciously, can affect the perception of another image means that perceptual processes such as expectations are involved. Subliminal perception cannot be explained solely by reference to visual receptors and the optic nerve.

subliminal perception Perception of a stimulus below its absolute threshold.

We have seen that the concept of psychophysics—the relationship between a physical stimulus and sensory intensity—can be applied to the very different senses of seeing, hearing, touching, tasting, and smelling. To organize the similarities and differences across these senses, let's examine a general model of sensory systems.

A Five-Stage Model of Sensory Systems

Sensory systems can be characterized by a five-stage model in which each system must have

1. An adequate stimulus from the outside world
2. Receptors that are adapted to a particular stimulus
3. Nerve pathways that connect the receptors with the brain
4. Places of synapse and integration at destination points in the brain
5. Sensing and perceiving, a psychological experience

In this analysis of sensory systems, an adequate stimulus (stage 1) is one to which a particular receptor is "tuned" (adapted). A receptor (stage 2) is an evolved adaptation of the nervous system that is sensitive to energy (light, sound, chemicals) in the environment. Because each sensory receptor has evolved so that it is sensitive only to certain features in the environment, an adequate stimulus perfectly "fits" its receptor. For example, we'll see that the receptors called *rods* and *cones* in the retina of the eye are sensitive to different aspects of light energy: rods are sensitive in very dim light, and cones are activated by brighter light. Other energy forms provide an adequate stimulus for other types of receptors.

Receptors are the beginning parts of nerves (stage 3), which travel to specific parts of the brain. For example, the process of seeing requires nerve pathways that connect the retina to the brain. Nerve pathways typically synapse at various places in the brain (stage 4) before arriving at their destination points. The psychological experiences of sensing and perceiving (stage 5) result from the integration of incoming impulses at sensory destination points with impulses in other areas of the brain. (How brain activity produces the experiences of seeing, hearing, and so forth, is unknown; hence the mind-body problem.)

Mind-body problem, Chapter 1, p. 5

Table 7.1 summarizes the sensory systems that produce perceptions. The first four stages in this analysis—*stimuli, receptors, nerve pathways,* and *destination points in the brain*—apply to the sensory systems in other animals as well as humans. What other animals may sense or perceive in stage 5, when sensory nerve activity occurs in their brains, is unknown.

Table 7.1 Sensory Systems

SENSE	STIMULUS	RECEPTOR	NERVES	PART OF BRAIN	SENSATION/PERCEPTION
Vision	Light waves	Rods and cones in retina	Optic nerve	Thalamus, occipital lobe	Brightness, color, motion, patterns, figures, faces
Hearing	Sound waves	Hair cells on the basilar membrane	Auditory nerve	Thalamus, temporal lobe	Noise, tones, language, music
Taste	Chemicals	Taste buds on tongue	Glossopharyngeal nerve	Medulla, somatosensory cortex	Tastes (sweet, sour, salty, bitter)
Smell	Chemicals (volatile)	Hair cells on the olfactory epithelium	Olfactory nerve	Olfactory bulb	Odors (flowery, musky, pheromones, foods
Skin senses	External contact	Nerve endings in skin (free nerve endings, Pacinian corpuscles)	Sensory nerves from skin, facial nerve	Thalamus, somatosensory cortex	Touch, warmth, cold, pain, contact comfort

INTERIM SUMMARY

1. Over millions of years receptors evolved specific sensitivities to features of the environment. Taste buds evolved a sensitivity to chemicals; rods and cones, a sensitivity to light energy; hair cells, a sensitivity to vibrations; and the skin senses, a sensitivity to contact, warmth, and pain. All these adaptations enhanced an animal's fitness.
2. Historically, the term ***sensation*** has been used to describe the simple effects of seeing light, hearing sound, and other sensory experiences. ***Perception*** is the term used to describe the attachment of meaning to the sensory experience.
3. ***Psychophysics*** is the study of the mathematical relationship between the senses (psychology) and the physical world, as described by Fechner.
4. Weber defined a ***just noticeable difference (jnd)*** as the minimal amount of change in a stimulus that a person can detect. ***Weber's law*** states that a jnd = kI (a constant k times the intensity of the stimulus). Put more simply, the intensity of a sensory experience is proportional to the intensity of the stimulus.
5. The ***absolute threshold*** is defined as the minimal intensity of a stimulus that a subject can detect on half the experimental trials.
6. A person's threshold for hearing can be measured using either the ascending and descending ***method of limits*** or the ***method of constant stimuli.***
7. Loudness can be related to stimulus intensity using the ***method of magnitude estimation.***
8. ***Signal detection theory*** is a mathematical theory that takes a subject's response bias into account in the measurement of sensory thresholds.
9. The threshold for discriminating between two separate points contacting the skin is called a *two-point limen.* This threshold is lower in sensitive body areas, such as the face and lips, than in less-sensitive areas, such as the middle of the back, and is related to the size of the corresponding area in the somatosensory cortex.
10. ***Subliminal perception*** has been demonstrated by subjects who report not seeing a briefly presented word, but then behave in a way that reflects unconscious awareness of the word. Subliminal perception can affect the conscious perception of other images.
11. Sensory systems can be described by a five-stage model that begins with the detection of an *adequate stimulus* by a particular *receptor. Nerve pathways* connect the receptor to specific places of synapse in the brain, producing a unique *perception.*

For Further Thought

1. Would extraterrestrials be likely to see us in the same way we would see them? Why or why not?
2. Humans no longer swing through trees. Can you explain why good vision is still an important selection factor in human evolution?
3. Why do monkeys see the world more like we do than our pet dogs and cats do?

SEEING

Humans can talk about what they see, so we know that most normally sighted people see about the same thing when they open their eyes. Through clever testing of other animals, we know that some share certain features of our visual world. But other animals do not see as we do—even those with eyes that seem similar to ours. Each animal lives in its own unique sensory world. For example, as your cat approaches you (and your image grows larger on its retina), the clothes you are wearing might appear to change color. For cats, small objects like cherries are gray, but larger objects like apples appear to be red! To understand why, we must examine the human visual apparatus in more detail, then compare it to that of other animals.

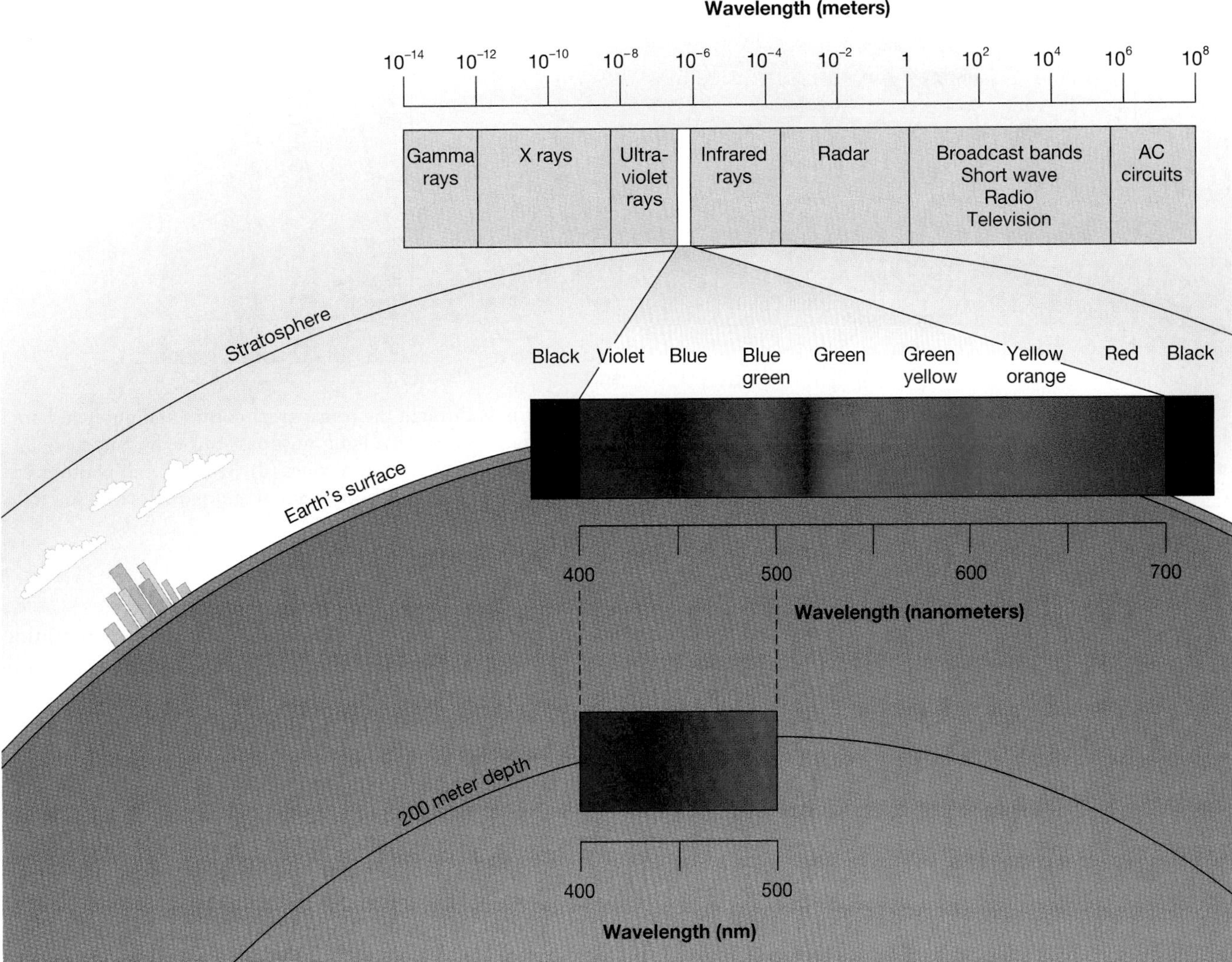

Figure 7.4 The electromagnetic spectrum. The sun's radiations vary in both power and wavelength. The shorter wavelengths, such as gamma rays (upper left), have more penetrating power than the longer broadcast bands. Because the stratosphere blocks or reflects 80 percent of the sun's electromagnetic energy, only a restricted range of wavelengths, called the visible spectrum, actually strikes the Earth's surface. Shorter wavelengths (400 to 500 nm) are more powerful and can penetrate to depths of about 200 meters. *Note:* The distances from the stratosphere to the Earth's surface, and from the Earth's surface to a depth of 200 meters, are *not* proportional.

Structure of the Eye

Because photochemicals—as well as eyes and visual systems—evolved in response to the sun's energy, a remarkable correspondence exists between biology and nature. Figure 7.4 shows the sun's electromagnetic spectrum, only a small portion of which (about 1/70th) impacts the Earth's surface in the form of visible light. Visible light—also called the **visible spectrum**—consists of a range of wavelengths of approximately 400 to 700 nanometers (nm)—a length equal to just billionths of a meter. English-speaking humans have learned to label the sensation produced by a 440 nm light "blue," and the sensation produced by a 650 nm light "red." We cannot see wavelengths outside the 400 to 700 nm range, though we can detect infrared radiation as it strikes the surface of our bodies, warming and sometimes burning us. And though we cannot see X rays, we can measure their effect when they pass through us. (Bones block some X rays, so that fewer of them are

visible spectrum The portion of the electromagnetic spectrum between about 400 to 700 nanometers.

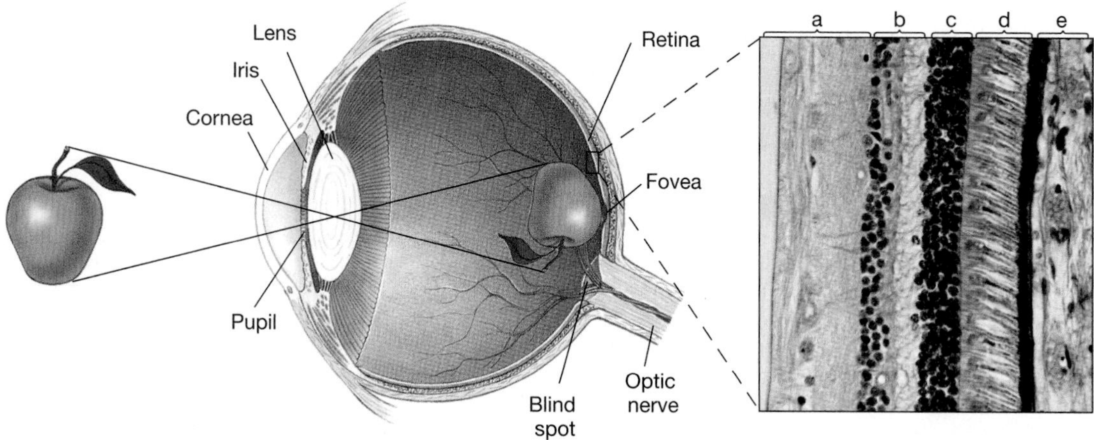

Figure 7.5 **The human eye and retina.** Light rays reflected off an object pass through the transparent cornea and pupil and are focused by the lens onto the fovea of the retina. The right-hand side of this figure shows that light must pass through many neurons—including ganglion cells (b) and other retinal cells (c)—before being absorbed by rods and cones (d). There are no photoreceptors in the blind spot, where the axons of the ganglion cells (a) leave the eyeball to form the optic nerve. Light particles that fail to strike a rod or cone are absorbed by epithelial cells in the back of the eyeball (e) (see also Figure 7.6).

absorbed by the sensitive chemicals on an X ray film.) Like these penetrating X rays, the shorter wavelengths have the most energy. "Blue" wavelengths, for example, have more energy than the longer "red" wavelengths; for this reason (as we will see), fewer of them are necessary to elicit a sensation.

What we see is directly connected to *how* we see, because our visual apparatus was specially designed to capture light reflected from our immediate world. Figure 7.5 shows how the camera-like human eye works. Light rays (the stimulus) are reflected off the image of an apple into the clear outer surface of the eye (the *cornea*). They pass through the *pupil* and are focused by a *lens* (which reverses the image) onto the *fovea* of the **retina**, a multilayered structure on the inner surface of the eye. The process of seeing begins in the retina, in photoreceptors called rods and cones.

Within the five-layered retina, light particles strike the bottom-most (fifth) layer, which contains the rod and cone photoreceptors (see the photograph on page 239). **Rods** are dim-light photoreceptors that contain the photopigment rhodopsin; **cones** are bright-light photoreceptors that contain one of three different photopigments. Cones are located primarily in the fovea and are activated by the relatively high light intensities of daylight. Rods, located primarily in the periphery of the retina, are activated by the relatively low light intensities of early dawn, late dusk, and moonlight. Hence, humans and many other animals have what is called a *duplex retina,* in which rods that do not function during daylight and cones that do not function in low-level illumination act as two separate visual systems.

When light strikes the rods and cones and activates photochemicals, it converts the sun's electromagnetic energy into electrochemical energy through a process called **transduction**. Rods and cones, and indeed all the cells in the retina, are neurons—an extension of the brain residing in the periphery of the body. Thus the brain's neurons do not sense the outside world directly; photic energy must first be transduced into electrical potentials before the nervous system can process it.

retina A multilayered structure on the inner surface of the eye.

rods Dim-light receptors in the retina that contain the photopigment rhodopsin.

cones Bright-light receptors in the retina that contain one of three different photopigments.

transduction The conversion of energy from one type to another.

Seeing at the Level of the Retina

Photographs are made when light strikes and activates particles of silver bromide on camera film. The more silver bromide particles per mm^2 of film, the better the image. We might assume, then, that the tightly packed foveal cones are responsible for human visual acuity, but that is only partially true. The information carried by the optic nerve does not faithfully mimic the pattern of light that lands on the rods and cones. True, rods and cones initiate the visual process by generating the first nerve signals. But the *ganglion cell* layer of the retina integrates information that comes from rods, cones, and other neurons in the retina, and sends it on to the brain. In each sensory system, the sensory nerves *encode* information from the environment in a way that preserves its essential features.

Figure 7.6 shows how the retina processes information from the rods and cones. Recall that the rods and cones are at the very back of the retina. Other neurons, called *bipolar cells, horizontal cells,* and *amacrine cells,* intervene between the rods and cones and the ganglion cells in front. Let's analyze what happens when light of different wavelengths reflects off the apple in Figure 7.5. Processing begins with transduction in rods and cones, which synapse directly onto the bipolar cells. The bipolar cells, in turn, synapse directly onto the **ganglion cells**, whose axons gather together and exit the eye through the blind spot (see Figure 7.5).

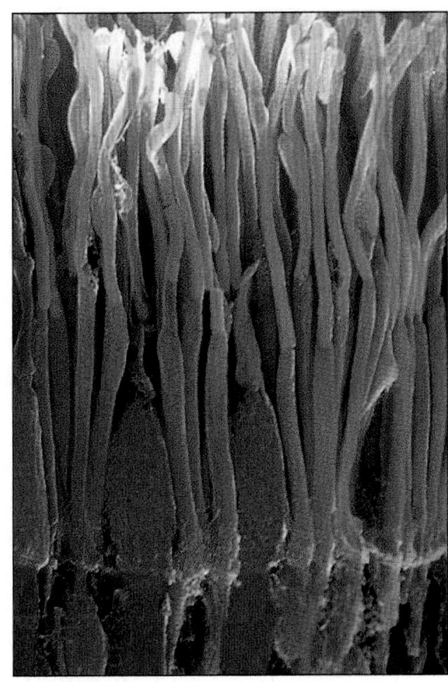

Rods and cones are found at the receptor-cell layer of the retina. The rods are cylinder shaped; the cones are squatter and more rounded.

Some bipolar cells receive input from a single cone and synapse directly onto a ganglion cell. (The two cones at the left side of Figure 7.6 fit this pattern.) Such cone-bipolar-ganglion-cell paths are found in the densely packed all-cone fovea. Toward the periphery of the retina, the pattern changes; there a bipolar cell may serve more than one rod (and more than one cone), and may project to more than one ganglion cell (see the right side of Figure 7.6).

In the far periphery of the retina, horizontal cells provide lateral connections to bipolar cells. This arrangement is similar to the array of interconnected satellite dishes used in radioastronomy to measure extremely low levels of illumination from the most remote stars. In the human eye, bipolar cells that are connected to rod receptors through horizontal cells are more likely to detect an occasional photon that hits a rod, and to pass that information on to the brain through a ganglion cell.

Visual Nerve Pathways

We have seen how an adequate stimulus is transduced by receptors and modified by synapses prior to arriving at a ganglion cell, which carries the resulting electrochemical impulse in the optic nerve. The optic nerve carries coded information regarding color, movement, and light intensity. Light intensity is coded by the rate of nerve firing; the higher the intensity of light falling on the retina, the faster the nerve fires (see Figure 7.7).

The *optic nerve pathway* runs from the eyes to two destination points in the brain, the **lateral geniculate nucleus** (**LGN**) in the thalamus and the **striate cortex** in the occipital lobe (see Figure 7.8). (You may want to revisit Figure 4.5, on page 112, for a better view of the thalamus.) Another name for the striate cortex is the *primary visual cortex*. This portion of the visual system was described in reference to the split-brain procedure (see Figure 4.18 on page 134).

Visual fields and striate cortex in split-brain procedure, Chapter 4, p. 134

Note in Figure 7.8 that the optic nerve fibers from the left and right halves of each eye form a point-to-point retinotopic projection on both the LGN and the striate cortex. That is, the picture on the retina is mapped onto the LGN and striate cortex in a way that preserves the relative position of each part of the picture. Because a large portion of the visual field of each eye is represented in the striate cortex in each hemisphere, most of a person's total visual field can be seen with one eye closed.

Where does "seeing" begin? Obviously, we need eyes to see, but if we had only eyes, we would be blind. Seeing requires the integrity of the entire system shown in Figure 7.8—an intact retina, a functional LGN, and a striate cortex. This system is sometimes referred to as the *conscious visual pathway,* because these and other

ganglion cells (retina) The fifth layer of cells in the retina, whose axons form the optic nerve.

lateral geniculate nucleus (LGN) A portion of the thalamus that receives impulses from the retina through the optic nerve.

striate cortex The primary visual cortex in the occipital lobe.

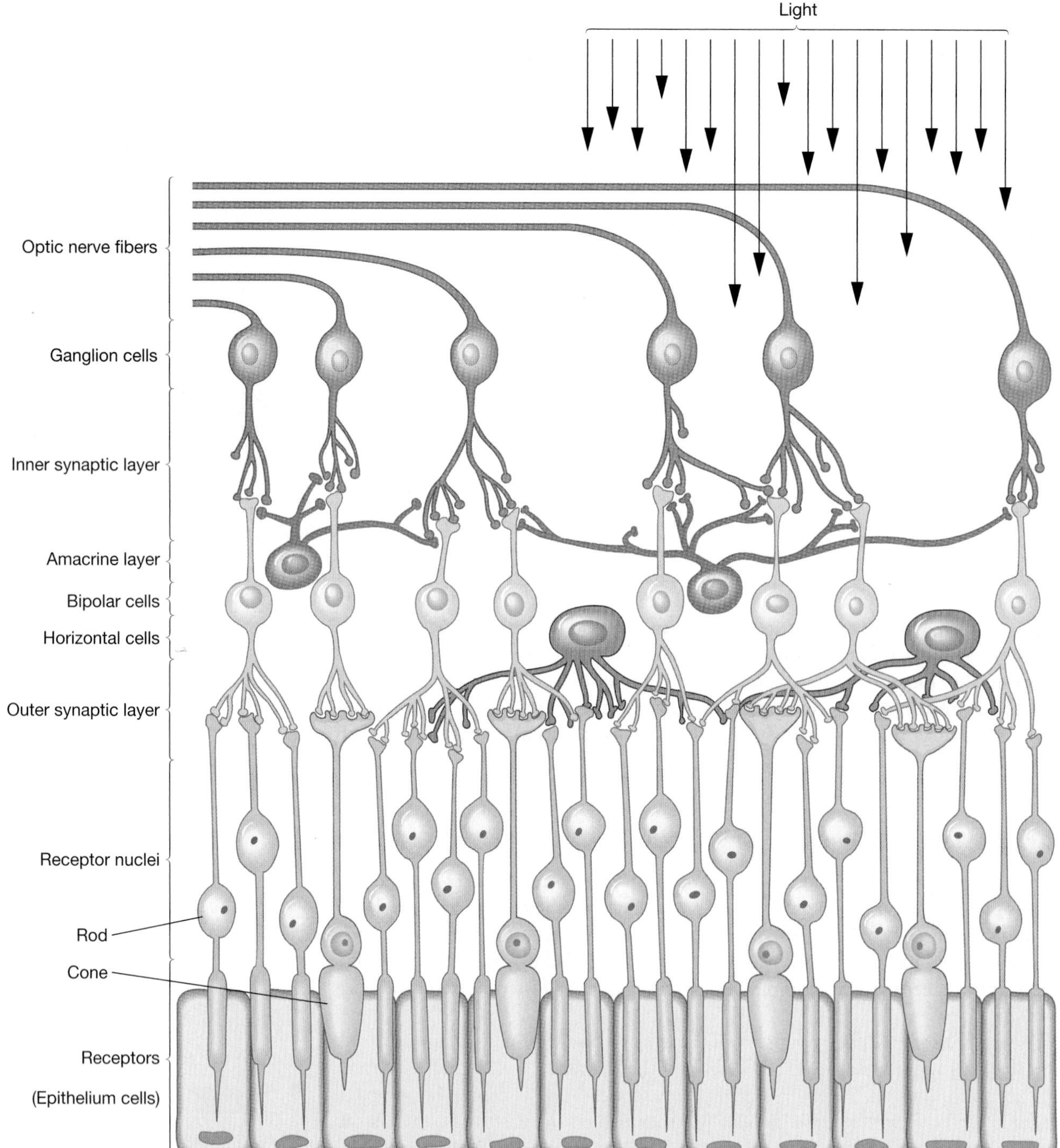

Figure 7.6 **The five-layer retina.** Electrical impulses from rods and cones travel through the retina along different paths. Each of the two cones on the left side of this schematic drawing connects directly to a separate bipolar cell and a separate ganglion cell. In contrast, two cones on the right side of the drawing synapse on a common bipolar cell; a horizontal cell complicates the contacts. Still another route can be seen at the far right, where four different rods connect to a single bipolar cell. *Source:* Modified from Lindsay & Norman, 1977, p. 71.

parts of the brain mediate consciousness. Even though this pathway determines *what we see,* not all the pathways in the visual system are involved in seeing.

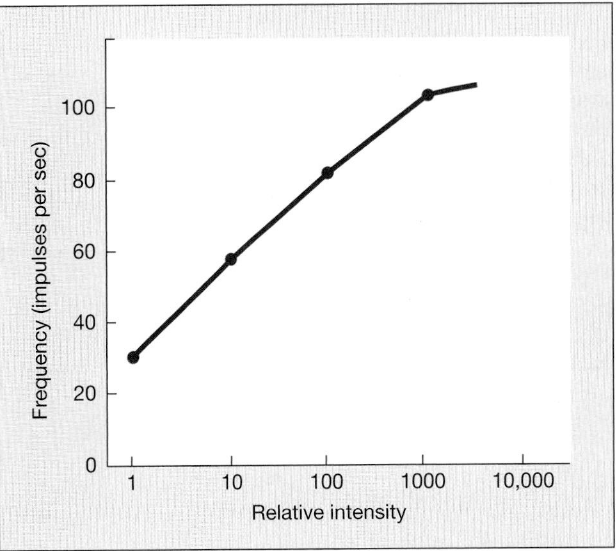

Figure 7.7 The coding of light intensity. The rate at which the optic nerve fires (vertical axis) is proportional to the intensity of light falling on the retina (horizontal axis).
Source: From "Light and Dark Adaptation of Single Photoreceptor Elements in the Eye of the Limulus" by H. K. Hartline and C. H. Graham, *Journal of Cellular and Comparative Physiology*, (1932), vol. 30, pp. 225–232. © 1932 by John Wiley & Sons. Reprinted by permission.

Nonseeing Functions of the Eye

Are humans aware of everything they see? You may think so, but in fact we are *not* conscious of all the information that is carried from the retina to the brain. Most retinal fibers arrive at the LGN through the optic nerve, carrying conscious visual information that allows us to see. But eight sets of ganglion cell fibers from each eye project to nonconscious parts of the brain (Weiskrantz, 1997). We will briefly describe two of these noncortical pathways. Their functions reflect our evolutionary history, reminding us that sunlight affected us long before we could see images with a camera-type eye.

Paying Attention. The largest noncortical visual pathway consists of nerves from approximately 150,000 non-image-forming ganglion cells in the retina. These fibers, which constitute about one-tenth of the optic nerve, project to the superior colliculus, a part of the brainstem just under the cerebellum. What do they accomplish? All of us have experienced the reflexive movement caused by a fast-moving object entering our peripheral visual field. ("Duck!") How do the muscles controlling the neck, head, and eyes know precisely where to turn to focus the moving object on the tiny fovea? The *superior colliculus* causes the head to orient itself to a new stimulus, acting as a kind of servomechanism (Moschovakis & Highstein, 1994).

The superior colliculus does more than cause reflexive movements. Think about what you were expected to do when your fifth-grade teacher admonished you to pay attention or focus on what you were doing. To "pay attention" means to turn your head and focus on a particular visual image. Most skilled movements, such as working on a computer, playing a Liszt concerto, or learning to drive a car, require attention and a highly practiced hand-eye coordination—both of which involve unconscious as well as conscious processes. The conscious visual pathway runs from the retina to the LGN to the striate cortex. The unconscious processes are mediated by a midbrain pathway to the superior colliculus. The cortical system processes *what we see;* the subcortical system processes *where we look.*

Cortical and subcortical pathways, Chapter 4, p. 122

Paying attention, of course, is not restricted to seeing: blind as well as sighted individuals pay attention "auditorially" as well as visually. In addition, after we learn highly skilled behaviors, we rely less on visual searching and more on automatic movements. That is, skilled typists, musicians, skiers, and drivers rely less on visual cues than novices. Nevertheless, humans do rely on vision, both conscious and unconscious, for most of their highly skilled movements.

Automatic movement, Chapter 4, p. 119

Seeing Under Different Lighting Conditions. Another nonconscious visual pathway adjusts—without our awareness—how we see under different lighting conditions. Modern cameras have computers that sense the amount of available light and adjust the lens opening accordingly. In humans, how does the eye know what size the pupil should be? The answer is that the eye and brain work together in a manner similar to that of a modern camera. Some retinal fibers do not go to the LGN, but instead project to an area of the midbrain called the pretectum. There these fibers stimulate motor neurons that project to the eye's iris, which contains a muscle that controls the size of the pupil (see Figure 7.5). The more constricted the pupil, the less light is admitted to the eye, and vice

Figure 7.8 Projection of the optic nerve to the LGN. The two optic nerves, one from each eye, partially cross at the optic chiasma before synapsing at the lateral geniculate nucleus (LGN). The point-to-point representation of an image from the retina to the LGN to the striate cortex is called a retinotopic projection. *Source:* From HUMAN INFORMATION PROCESSING: An Introduction to Psychology by Peter H. Lindsay and Donald A. Norman. Copyright © 1972 by Harcourt, Inc. Reproduced by permission of the publisher.

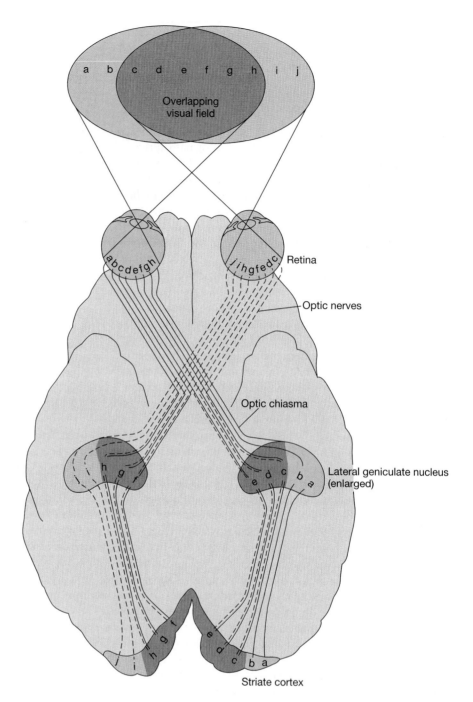

versa. In both sighted and blind people, intense light causes a high rate of firing in the retinal ganglion cells, increased motor nerve activity in the pretectal area, and greater constriction of the iris, which reduces the amount of light impinging on the retina. Light regulation is a marvelous example of a homeostatic mechanism that works unconsciously through a system of negative feedback.

Dark Adaptation

Visual attention and reticular formation, Chapter 4, p. 122

The retina appears to be designed to see under a variety of conditions. The cone-packed fovea allows us to see colorful features in the environment during the day with good visual acuity, and the rods gather light and detect movement under low-level illumination. Having been blinded for a minute or two after walking from a

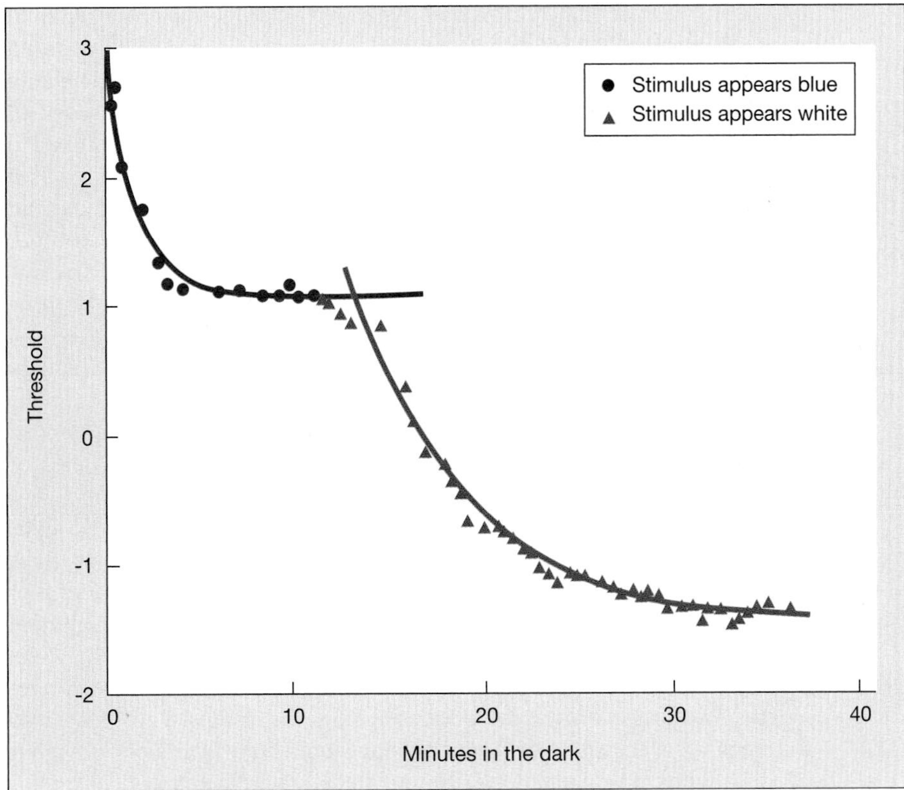

Figure 7.9 The dark adaptation function. This graph shows the results of an experiment in which a male subject was shown a blue light at an intensity that he could just see. Over a 10-minute period, his eyes became sensitive to decreasing intensities of the light, as shown by the circles plotted on the graph. After about 12 to 14 minutes, the subject could see the dim blue light only as a white light—his cones had quit functioning, but his rods could still detect the light (triangles). The longer the subject remained in the dark, the more sensitive the rods became. The crossover between the two visual systems is called the rod-cone break.
Source: Hecht, Schlaer, & Pirenne, 1942.

bright area into a darkened theater, you know firsthand that you are not always sensitive to very dim light. Testing the absolute threshold for light, then, requires that a test subject must first become adapted to the dark before being shown a dim light.

The results of a classic test of dark adaptation are shown in Figure 7.9, which summarizes much of what is known about the roles of rods and cones in vision (Hecht, Schlaer, & Pirenne, 1942). The curve, called a **dark adaptation** function, shows the intensity of a briefly flashed light that a subject could see as a function of how long the subject sat in the dark. Early in the test, the subject could see only a very bright light, much as a person who enters a dark theater sees only bright lights. As the subject's eyes adapted to the dark over the first 10 minutes, he could detect dimmer and dimmer intensities of the light. Then, after 12 to 14 minutes in the dark, something quite remarkable happened. When presented with an even dimmer blue light, the subject could see it, but could no longer tell that it was blue. At that point, indicated by the change from circles to triangles in Figure 7.9, the subject responded by saying "white" instead of "blue." Over the next 15 minutes or so, the subject became even more sensitive to the fading light.

This famous study by Hecht and his colleagues demonstrated that cones (which allow for color vision) are sensitive to dim light, but work best at higher intensities. In very dim light, the cones quit working and the rods (which detect light but not color) become functional. The crossover from the cone-mediated vision to rod-mediated vision is called the **rod-cone break**. In other words, humans have two visual systems, one for bright light and the other for dim light.

dark adaptation An increase in visual sensitivity as a result of time spent in the dark.

rod-cone break During dark adaptation, the point at which the rods become increasingly sensitive to dim light.

Color Vision

Objects that are covered with different pigments reflect light differently, and we see those differences as color. Two competing theories have been proposed to explain this phenomenon. The trichromatic (three-color) theory of color vision is based on the fact that the human eye contains three different types of photochemicals. The English scientist Thomas Young in 1802 proposed an early form of trichromatic theory and the German scientist Hermann von Helmholtz modified it in 1852. The *Young-Helmholtz theory of color vision* was based on experiments demonstrating that all colors can be represented by mixing just three pigments: blue, green, and red (see Figure 7.10). Neither Young nor Helmholtz knew that the retina would one day be found to contain photochemicals with absorption spectra that matched these three primary colors. As it is now formulated, the **trichromatic theory** states that three-color vision is mediated by three cone types, each maximally sensitive to one of three wavelengths of light.

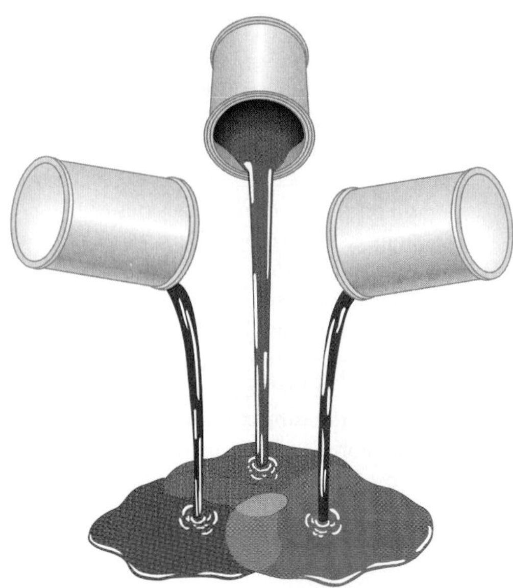

Figure 7.10 Subtractive color mixing. Mixed together in various proportions, red, green, and blue paints can make all colors—here, gray. (Compare the results of mixing the colored lights shown in the photograph on page 245.)

But the mixing of pigments to produce different colors, called *subtractive color mixing*, is not the same as mixing light from the sun. The color changes that come from subtractive color mixing are important in color photography, color printing, and fabric dying, but the process of getting brown by mixing green and yellow pigments is totally different from the way the eye functions. The eye sees the colors of reflected light, which mix in a different way from pigments. The photograph on page 245 reveals the surprising results of **additive color mixing**, the mixing of long (red), medium (green), and short (blue) wavelengths on a reflective surface like a theater screen. Note that the intersection of two wavelengths generates a new color, whereas the intersection of all three wavelengths produces white. In fact, adjusting the intensity of just two different wavelengths of light will produce white light. Pairs of lights that produce white when added together are called **complementary colors.**

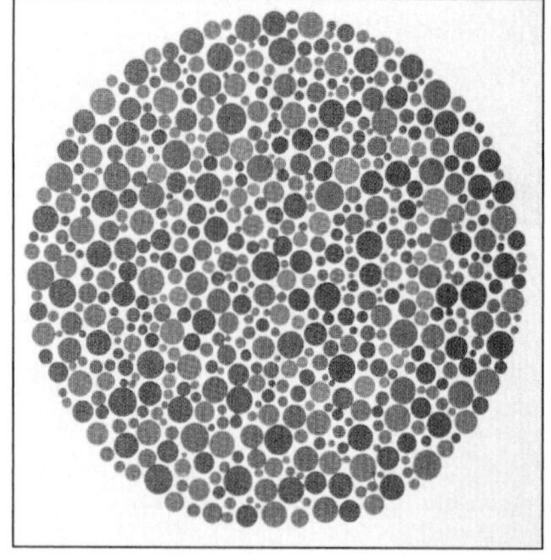

Can you see the colored pattern in this picture, known as the Ishihara color-blindness test? A red-green dichromat will not see the number 29.

trichromatic theory The theory that color vision is mediated by three cone pigments, each maximally sensitive to one of three wavelengths.

additive color mixing The mixing of two or more colors of light to create different color.

complementary colors Pairs of lights that when added together produce white.

Color Blindness

People who are commonly referred to as "color blind" can typically see color, but they do not share the rich, trichromatic sight of other primates. Most colorblind people lack one of the three cone pigments, and for that reason are called *dichromats* (meaning that they have only two color pigments instead of three). Most dichromats can see the yellow-blue portions of the spectrum, but they confuse the red and green wavelengths because of a defective red or green photo-pigment. Dichromatism is a genetic defect that is linked to the x chromosome; it is found in about 8 percent of all males in the United States (Piantanida, 1988). An even rarer form of color blindness, also genetically determined, involves the confusion of blue and yellow, probably due to a defective blue photopigment. The photograph on this page shows the familiar Ishihara test for color blindness.

What does confusing red with green really mean? The question brings us back to the difficulty of knowing what individuals experience when they see color. The photographs on page 245 yield some insight into this mystery. When asked to reproduce the scene in the left-hand panel, a red-green dichromat both reversed and invented colors (center panel). He most definitely was *not* able to match the colors on his palette with the colors in the painting. Obviously, the red-green dichromat sees something *other* than either red or green; otherwise, he would see green and confuse red only, or see red and confuse green only! We'll return to this matter later.

Individuals who cannot see *any* color are extremely rare. They are called *monochromats*, and what they see depends on the nature of their deficiency. People who were born without cones in their foveae (or whose foveal cones lack the three pigments) must rely on scotopic vision. They are sometimes called *rod monochromats*. Recall that the rods function only in dim light, and for peripheral vision only. These monochromats, then, do not see well: they typically wear bottle-bottom corrective lenses, dislike daylight, and function best at night.

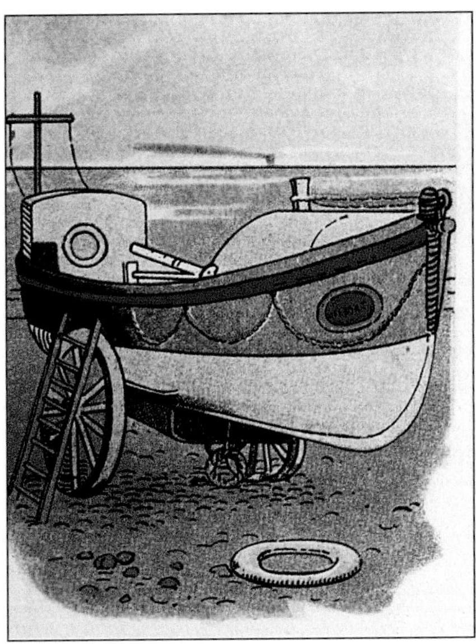
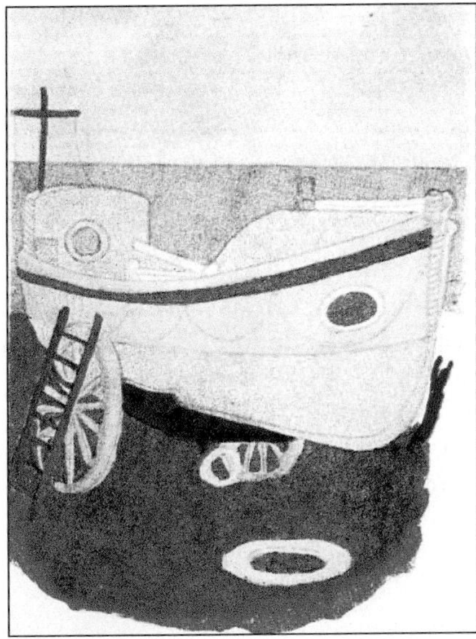

A painting by a normal trichromat (left), as repainted by a red-green dichromat (center) and a monochromat with a functioning fovea (right).

Opponent-Process Theory. Unfortunately, trichromatic theory does not explain all aspects of color perception. For example, why do some dichromats confuse reds and greens if one or the other photopigment is intact? And why do others confuse yellows and blues? Why not confuse a red with a blue, or a yellow with a green? In 1874, a German physiologist, Ewald Hering, proposed a theory that explains these and other puzzles better than trichromatic color theory. Hering was interested in accounting for the complementary colors described earlier. Why, he wondered, when one wavelength of light is gradually added to its complement, does the process seem to dilute both lights? Hering's **opponent-process theory** states that colors are perceived in red-green and blue-yellow pairs, which he called *opponents*. Actually, Hering's model presumed the existence of three rather than two opponent pairs, the third pair being white-black. According to his theory, when these pairs of wavelengths are sensed together, they cancel each other out and produce white. A red light, for example, would oppose (inhibit) green, and vice versa. Yellow and blue would also work as opponents, producing white, a colorless light.

In additive color mixing, colored lights of different wavelengths are mixed to form new colors. All colors can be produced by varying the intensity of two or three lights.

The phenomenon of *negative afterimages* (also called *complementary afterimages*) provides a dramatic test of Hering's theory. Read the instructions accompanying the photograph on page 246 and then view the image. Why do the complementary colors green, black, and yellow form a red, white, and blue flag in the afterimage? One hypothesis is that the colors of the afterimage are related to prior learning—that they activate the visual memory of a familiar image. But a test of this hypothesis using unfamiliar images reveals the same phenomenon of color reversal, so that is not the answer. Another hypothesis is that staring at the image for 30 seconds in some way "fatigues" or inactivates some photoreceptors, allowing others to produce the afterimage. But this argument doesn't sound right, either, because there are no black, white, or yellow receptors in the fovea.

opponent-process theory Hering's theory that all colors are sensed in red-green, blue-yellow, and white-black opposing pairs, so that when they are sensed together, they produce white.

Color-Opponent Cells. As Figure 7.6 shows, photoreceptors connect to the ganglion cells in a variety of ways. As it turns out, many of the ganglion cells, called *color-opponent cells*, do connect pairs of color receptors. They receive inputs from red-green and blue-yellow pairs, and activate neurons in the LGN in a way that preserves those opponent pairs (DeValois, Abramov, &

If you stare at the center of this flag for 30 to 40 seconds, its image will begin to shimmer and glow. Now shift your eyes to the adjacent white area. What you see can be explained by the way the retina processes color pairs.

Jacobs, 1966; Jameson & Hurvich, 1989). Some LGN cells, for example, are inhibited by green wavelengths and excited by red ones. Others are excited by blue and inhibited by yellow. When you gaze at the flag image on this page, you are inhibiting one type of ganglion cell (green), which tends to hyperactivate the other (red). In sum, red and green wavelengths and blue and yellow wavelengths seem to work in opponent pairs at the level of the ganglion cells and LGN. Color-opponent cells in the retina activate one color of a pair after being exposed to the other.

Psychological tests of color perception and a knowledge of its physiological underpinnings support Hering's opponent-process theory. His theory complements rather than contradicts trichromatic theory. In the same way that we understand light in terms of both particles (photons) and waves (because different observations require both theories), we understand color in terms of both trichromatic and opponent-process theory.

INTERIM SUMMARY

1. Most of the sun's energy does not penetrate the stratosphere. The portion that does includes the wavelengths between about 300 and 1,100 nm. The ***visible spectrum*** contains wavelengths of about 400 to 700 nm.
2. Humans have a camera-type eye that allows reflected light to pass through an adjustable pupil and be focused by an adjustable lens on the fovea of the ***retina.***
3. Light particles that strike the ***rod*** and ***cone*** photoreceptors initiate nerve activity through a process called ***transduction.***
4. Rods are found in great numbers in the periphery of the retina, whereas cones are concentrated in the fovea. The tightly packed foveal cones allow color vision with great acuity in bright light; the rods function only in dim light.
5. The rod and cone receptors synapse onto bipolar cells, which in turn synapse onto ***ganglion cells.*** Amacrine and horizontal cells modify the synapses between receptors and ganglion cells.
6. Axons of the ganglion cells leave the retina at the *blind spot* and project retinotopically to the brain, first to the ***lateral geniculate nucleus (LGN)*** and then to the ***striate cortex***, in the occipital lobe.
7. The LGN-to-striate-cortex route is a *conscious visual pathway*. A separate *midbrain pathway* to the colliculus allows for the unconscious detection of stimuli. Several nonvisual optic nerve connections bypass the LGN.
8. Optic nerve connections to the midbrain provide a negative feedback system that controls the size of the pupil under different lighting conditions. This connection also allows for both reflexive and voluntary head and eye movements.
9. Nerve signals from the retina to the LGN command attention and moderate the visual information that is sent to the cortex.
10. With the passage of time, both rods and cones become more sensitive to dim light. The curve that describes the eye's changing sensitivity to light is called the ***dark adaptation*** function.
11. The ***rod-cone break*** occurs after about 12 minutes in the dark, when the cones can no longer detect color and the rods become sensitive to low-intensity light.
12. The ***trichromatic*** (*Young-Helmholtz*) ***theory*** of color vision was originally based on color-mixing experiments with three different wavelengths of light.
13. Two wavelengths of light mixed together will produce a third color, a phenomenon known as ***additive color mixing.***
14. Two wavelengths of light that create the color white when mixed together are called ***complementary colors.***
15. Most color-blind individuals are *dichromats*; they confuse red with green, or more rarely, blue with yellow. A *monochromat* sees no color at all.
16. According to the ***opponent-process theory*** of color vision, ganglion cells in the retina and the LGN in the brain process color in complementary pairs of red-green, white-black, and blue-yellow. When one color is active, it inhibits the perception of the other.
17. *Negative afterimages* are caused by *color-opponent cells,* which activate one color of a complementary pair after exposure to the other.

For Further Thought

1. Why is visual acuity poor in peripheral vision?
2. In some cities in Mexico, traffic signals have green lights at the top and red at the bottom. Why would this arrangement present a problem for a dichromat who learned to drive in the United States?

HEARING

What makes a sound that can be heard? Sounds have their origin in the movement of air or water, which causes vibrations. The stimulus is a wave of compressed air called a *sound wave*. For example, vibrating vocal cords are the source of an auditory stimulus. By contrast with the complex frequencies of voices, the pure tone of a tuning fork generates a simple sinusoidal wave (see Figure 7.11).

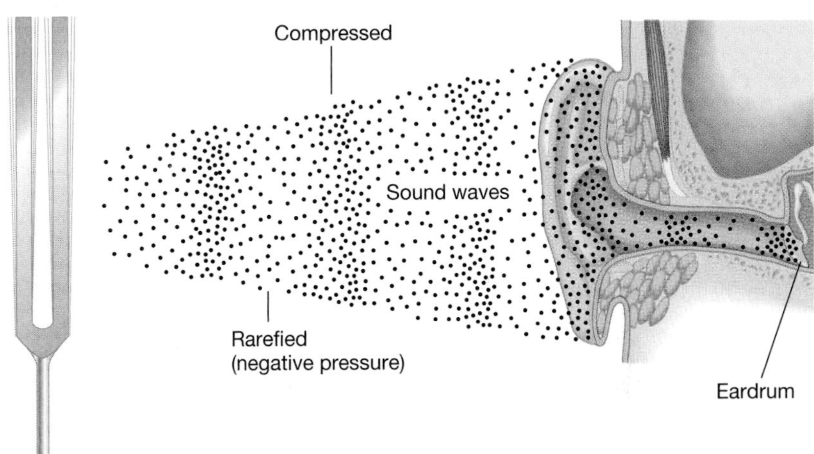

Figure 7.11 The mechanics of sound. A vibrating tuning fork sends molecules of air into a wavelike motion. The sinusoidal wave that results is formed by alternately compressed (close together) and rarefied (far apart) air molecules. This pattern of compressed and rarefied air is preserved as it enters the ear.

Unlike light, which can be described as both particles and waves, sounds are waves of air that vary in their **amplitude** (intensity, or vertical size of the wave) and **frequency** (number of waves, or cycles, per second, measured horizontally; see Figure 7.12). Amplitude is perceived as loudness, whereas frequency is perceived as pitch. Waveforms can also be simple or complex; the perception of their relative complexity is called *timbre*. The unit of measure of amplitude is a decibel (dB); that of frequency, the Hertz (Hz). A whispered "shush" produces a low-amplitude, complex waveform that is dominated by relatively low frequencies. Shrill screams are composed of high-amplitude high frequencies. Tables 7.2a and 7.2b show the amplitudes and frequencies of some common sounds.

Sound, loudness, and *pitch* are psychological terms. A tree falling in the proverbial forest generates a waveform that varies in amplitude and frequency, but is called a sound only if it is heard. Humans can hear sound intensities ranging from that of the softest wind to the most deafening explosions. Personal preferences in

Table 7.2a Amplitudes (Intensity) of Common Sounds

SOUND	INTENSITY (DB)
Absolute threshold at 1,000 Hz	0
Rustling leaves, soft whisper	20–30
Quiet residential community	40
Average speaking voice	60–80
Loud music, heavy traffic	80–100
Shouting	100
Lightning strike, highly amplified rock band	120–140
Pain threshold	130–150
Spacecraft launch at 150 feet	180

Sources: Lindsay & Norman, 1972, p. 224; Schiffman, 2000, p. 324.

amplitude The intensity or size of a waveform, measured vertically.

frequency The number of waves, or cycles, per second of a waveform, measured horizontally.

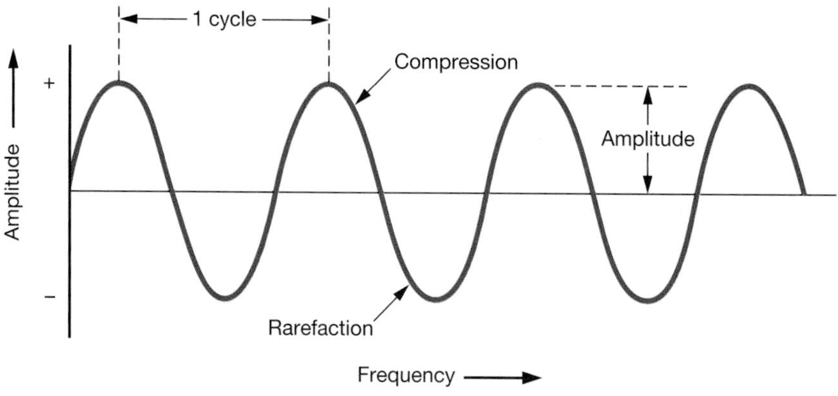

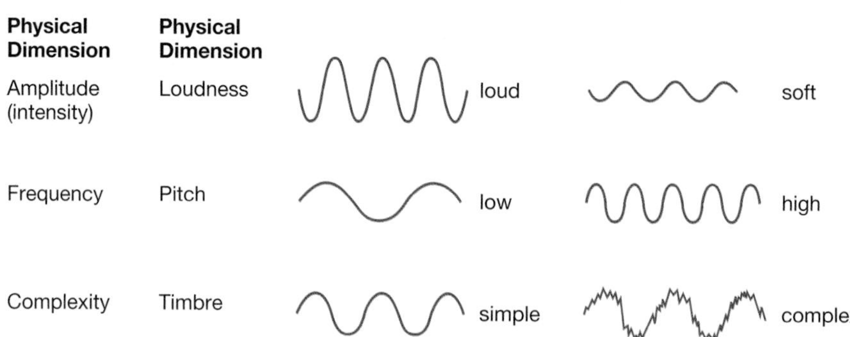

Figure 7.12 Characteristics of sound waves. Sounds can vary in their amplitude, frequency, and complexity. High-amplitude sounds (measured vertically) are perceived as loud; high-frequency sounds (measured horizontally) are perceived as high-pitched. Complex sounds vary in timbre.

sound intensities—which are quite different from the ability to hear sounds—range from absolute quiet to high-amplitude rock music. The range of intensities humans can hear is similar: from approximately zero to 150 to 180 decibels.

Though humans can hear a range of frequencies from about 20 to 20,000 Hz, most sounds they are interested in lie well between those extremes. A convenient scale of the familiar sounds made by a piano illustrates this point. As Table 7.2b indicates, the lowest note (frequency) on a piano is 27.4 Hz; the highest is 4,214 Hz (Geldard, 1972). These are not pure sounds, however; some overtones

Table 7.2b Frequencies (Pitch) of Common Sounds

SOUND	FREQUENCY (HZ)
Lowest note on the piano	27.4
Middle C on the piano	261.6
Human speech sounds: *b, d, j, n, m, th*	200–400
Standard tuning pitch (A above middle C)	440
Upper range of a soprano	1,000
Human speech sounds: *b, d, h, k, p, sh*	1,600–3,200
Highest note on the piano	4,214
Harmonics (overtones) of musical instruments	10,000–12,000
Limit of hearing for older people	12,000 or less
Limit of hearing for younger people	18,000–20,000

Sources: Lindsay & Norman, 1972, p. 224; Schiffman, 2000, p. 324; Geldard, 1972, p. 161.

produced by musical instruments extend to 12,000 Hz. To give another example, most human speech ranges from about 200 to 5,000 Hz. As we will see, even after the inevitable loss of high-frequency hearing in middle age—a condition called *presbycusis,* from the Greek for "old man hearing"—humans can still hear the frequencies comprising speech and music.

Structure of the Ear

Figure 7.13 shows the outer, middle, and inner parts of the human ear. Sound waves first strike the pinna, or visible outer ear. Unlike the pinna in some other mammals, such as dogs and cats, the human pinna isn't connected to muscles that allow it to move and focus on the source of a sound. People whose hearing is impaired, however, can reposition their heads in order to hear better. When properly

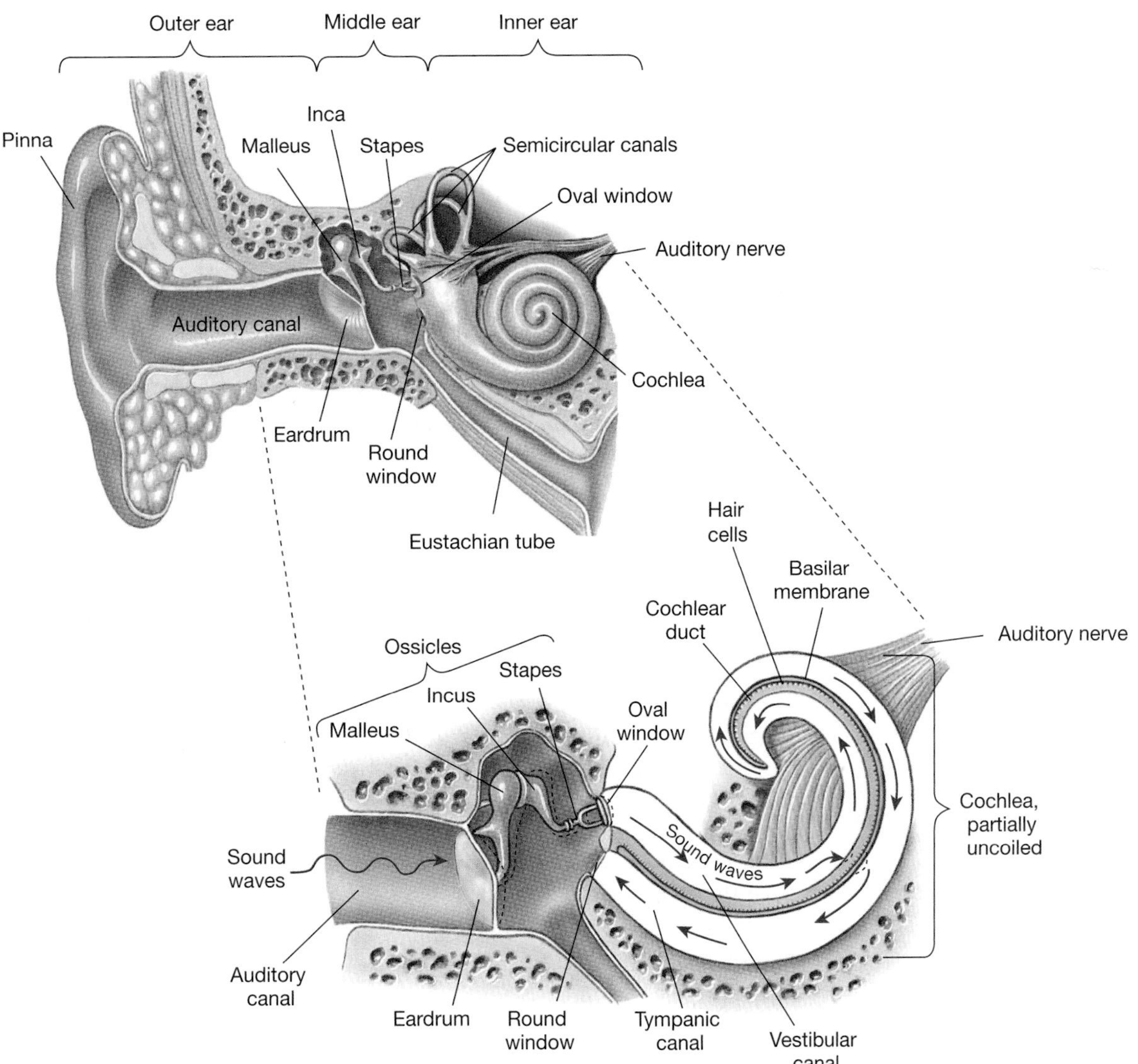

Figure 7.13 The human ear. The human ear is divided into three parts: the outer, middle, and inner ear. Each plays a different part in the conversion of sound waves into nerve impulses. The outer ear helps to localize and amplify selected frequencies. The vibrations of the tympanic membrane (the eardrum) move the malleus, incus, and stapes (the ossicles) in a way that faithfully mimics the characteristics of waveforms. The ossicles further amplify the waveform and set the fluids in the cochlea in motion. There, mechanical energy is transduced to nerve impulses by hair cells on the basilar membrane. The resulting action potentials reflect the characteristics of the original waveform.

aligned, the ear's shape slightly enhances the amplitude of wavelengths between 1,500 and 7,000 Hz, rendering weak sounds more audible (Gulick, Gescheider, & Frisina, 1989).

The Outer Ear. Sound waves continue into the *auditory canal,* which ends at a structure called the **tympanic membrane**, or eardrum. (*Tympanic* is Greek for "drum.") The tympanic membrane, which divides the outer from the middle ear, is protected from dirt and small foreign objects by hairs and wax secreted by glands in the ear canal. Sound waves hit the tympanic membrane, causing it to move in a way that preserves the waves' characteristics.

The Middle Ear. The middle ear is comprised of a chain of three small bones called *ossicles,* which vibrate, or oscillate, with the tympanic membrane. The ossicles further amplify the waveform, setting in motion fluids in the snail-like **cochlea,** or inner ear. The first of the three bones, the **malleus,** is connected to the eardrum and moves with it. The second is called the **incus,** and the third the **stapes.** (You may have been taught to call these bones the hammer, anvil, and stirrup. The acronym MIS is a good way to remember their formal names.) The stapes, in turn, is connected to the fluid-filled cochlea at the **oval window.**

Under Helmholtz's microscope, these three bones appeared to be a system of levers connected to the oval window. Helmholtz thought the overall effect was to amplify the pressure of airborne sounds, to better transmit them through a fluid medium. Without these structures, he reasoned, the cochlear fluid would impede further transmission of sounds. Scientists who came after Helmholtz have found that the lever action of these tiny bones does indeed increase the mechanical advantage of airborne waves. The pressure of airborne sound waves hitting the large surface of the tympanic membrane increases about 17-fold before reaching the comparatively tiny stapes at the oval window. If you have ever been stepped on by a person wearing high heels, you have experienced pressure distributed over a very small area. Thus the amplified airborne waveform is faithfully transmitted to and through fluid in the cochlea.

Though the *semicircular canals* have nothing to do with hearing, they are located in the inner ear, as Figure 7.13 shows. All vertebrates have a similar anatomical structure, which helps them to maintain a sense of balance. Part of the *vestibular system,* the semicircular canals are fluid-filled tubes that contain small rocklike particles called *otoliths.* Moving the head from front to back and side to side causes the otoliths to collide. Through negative feedback, neurons attached to the canals respond less when the head is upright and stationary and more when it moves, helping to correct an animal's balance.

Transduction in vision and hearing, Chapter 7, p. 238

The English language suggests that balance is a sense. For instance, we say that walking a tightrope requires "a keen sense of balance." Identifying an adequate stimulus for this "sense," however, presents a problem. Unlike the other senses, this sense is experienced primarily in its absence (being off balance, or dizziness) rather than through its presence. Neural information regarding a lack of balance travels over a portion of a cranial nerve to the thalamus and medulla. These structures accomplish the postural adjustments necessary to maintain one's equilibrium.

The Inner Ear. Mechanical energy in the form of sound waves moves the muscles and bones in the middle ear. The transduction of this energy into nerve activity occurs in the cochlea. Figure 7.14 is a schematic diagram of a partially uncoiled cochlea. When the stapes vibrates against the oval window, the waveform is carried through the fluid in the *vestibular canal,* on the inner side of the cochlea. This displaced fluid then continues into the *tympanic canal,* on the outer side of the cochlea. At the end of the tympanic canal, the fluid pushes outward against the *round window.* The energy that began with the displacement of fluid

tympanic membrane A membrane (the eardrum) that separates the outer ear from the middle ear.

cochlea A coiled, fluid-filled tube in the inner ear that contains the receptors for hearing.

malleus The ossicle attached to the eardrum.

incus The middle ossicle in the middle ear.

stapes The ossicle in the middle ear that is connected to the oval window.

oval window A membrane that connects the stapes in the middle ear with the vestibular canal in the inner ear.

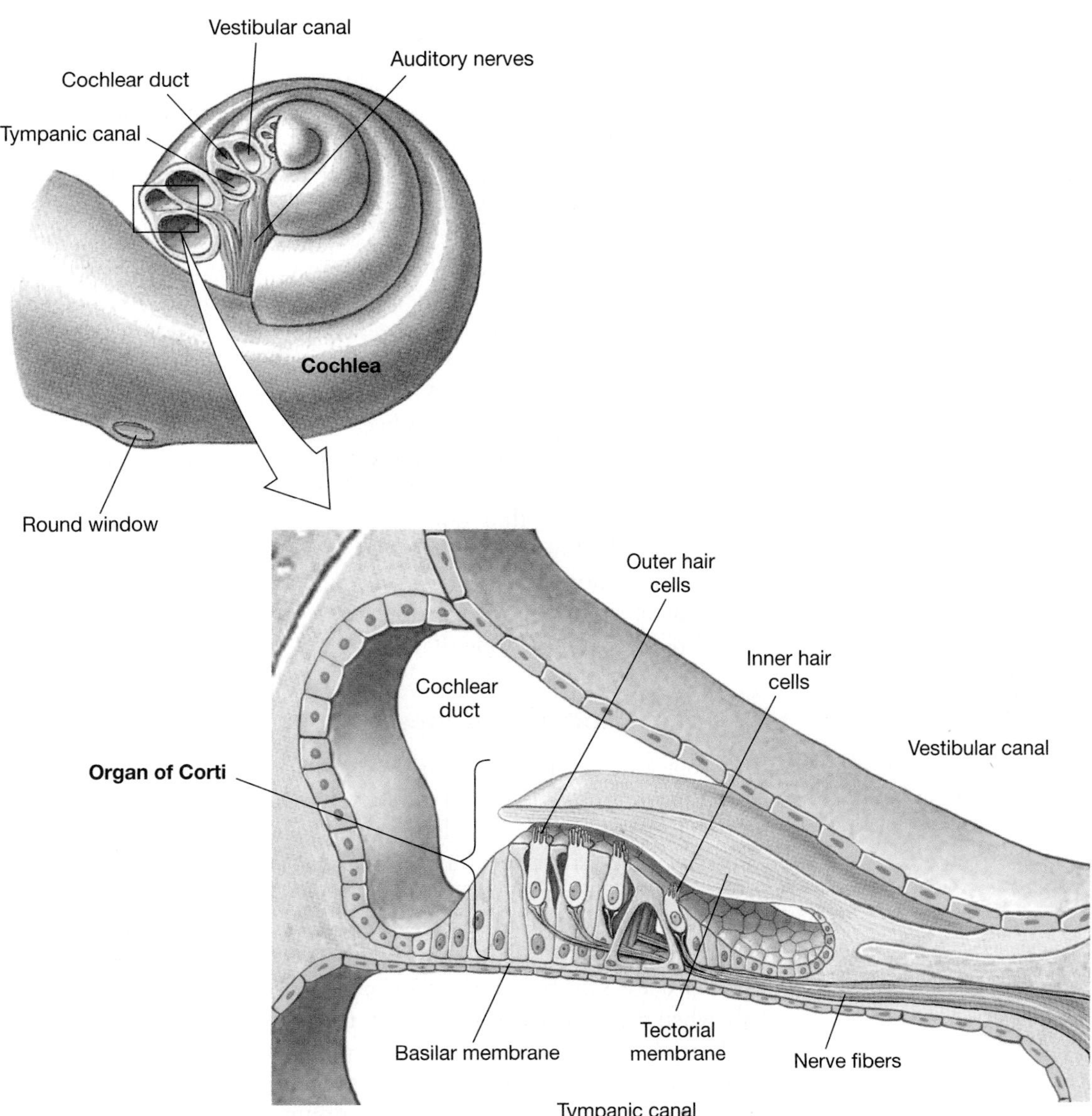

Figure 7.14 Anatomy of the cochlea. The fluid-filled chambers of the cochlea and details of the organ of Corti are shown here in cross-section. In the tympanic canal, vibrating fluid causes the basilar membrane to flex, bending the hair cells and causing them to generate electrical potentials. Although the cochlea looks like a snail, in actuality it is merely a hollow portion of the skull containing membranes and fluids. You can feel it as the bulge in the skull behind your ear. *Source:* From HUMAN INFORMATION PROCESSING: An Introduction to Psychology by Peter H. Lindsay and Donald A. Norman. Copyright © 1972 by Harcourt, Inc. Reproduced by permission of the publisher.

at the oval window dissipates at the round window. Since the fluid-filled system is a closed one, the bulges made by the waves hitting the round window match the vibrations that started the waves at the oval window.

We must look carefully at the microstructure of the cochlea to see how transduction occurs. Figure 7.14 shows a cross-section of the vestibular and tympanic canals. We are interested primarily in two structures, the *organ of Corti* and the **basilar membrane**. Note that **hair cells** in the organ of Corti stretch between the basilar membrane and the *tectorial membrane*. When fluid courses through the cochlea, the basilar membrane vibrates, stretching and bending the hair cells. This temporary change in the position of the hair cells generates excitatory postsynaptic potentials, or EPSPs. These EPSPs, in turn, generate action potentials in adjacent bipolar cells (called *spiral ganglion cells*), whose axons become the auditory nerve.

basilar membrane A membrane in the cochlea that contains the hair cells.

hair cells The receptors for hearing, located on the basilar membrane.

Place Theory and the Traveling Wave

Precisely how, given the cochlea's anatomy, is the frequency, or pitch, of a tone encoded? This question is analogous to the question of how color is encoded. According to the **place theory**, the frequency of a sound is encoded by the stimulation of a particular place on the basilar membrane. The idea is that each place on the basilar membrane vibrates maximally to a given frequency. Beginning at the oval window, the fluid vibrates all the way to the round window, setting up a wavelike movement of the basilar membrane. Figure 7.15 shows the form this **traveling wave** takes, as envisioned by the Nobel laureate Georg von Békésy, who was recognized in 1961 for his 25 years of innovative work on the hydrodynamics of the inner ear (Békésy, 1963).

The basilar membrane is like a coiled, flattened spring; it vibrates maximally at different places along its length because it is narrow and thin near its beginning (at the oval window) and broad and thick at the end. The lower part of Figure 7.15 shows schematically that the higher frequencies (bottom) cause maximum displacement on the thin portion of the membrane at the beginning of the cochlea, and the lower frequencies (top) cause maximum displacement near the end. The fluid along the basilar membrane is constantly in motion, and the peak amplitude of a particular place along the membrane is always shifting, depending on the frequency of the tone that causes the fluid displacement.

The Sensation of Loudness

If the place theory is correct—that the place of maximal stimulation along the basilar membrane gives rise to the sensation of pitch—then how do we hear loudness and softness? Three mechanisms, all related to the traveling wave, combine to produce the sensation of amplitude. As you might expect, higher amplitudes move the basilar membrane a greater distance, causing a larger wave. This larger wave bends the outer hair cells more, generating larger EPSPs, which cause a more rapid rate of discharge in the auditory nerve. Second, the inner hair cells, which are less sensitive to the movement of the basilar membrane, are activated only when the auditory stimulus is 50 to 60 decibels above the absolute threshold for hearing. Their EPSPs also cause more auditory nerves to fire. Finally, the greater size of the traveling wave causes more hair cells to fire near the peak of the wave. During the ear's normal functioning, then, the number of hair cells that are discharging, their rate of discharge, and their position on the basilar membrane combine to allow us to hear loud and soft tones of various frequencies.

One theory of why older people lose their high-frequency hearing is that after a lifetime of vibration, the hair cells on the thin portion of the basilar membrane, which are less protected than those on the thick portion, become disabled. Indeed, as we will see in the next section, at rock-band amplitudes, large numbers of hair cells can become dysfunctional after just a few hours. With repeated exposure to high-amplitude sounds, hair cells in young as well as old listeners can die.

EPSPs can be recorded from individual neurons in the auditory nerve. Each neuron produces what is called a *tuning curve:* it responds maximally to one frequency, less well to similar frequencies, and least well to frequencies farthest from its preferred frequency (Kiang, Watanbe, Thomas, & Clark, 1962). The action potentials of individual neurons preserve the coding of frequency and amplitude information as the impulse ascends through the auditory nerve to the brain.

place theory The theory that the frequency of sound is coded through the stimulation of a particular place on the basilar membrane.

traveling wave The pattern of vibration in the cochlear fluid, which varies as a function of the amplitude and frequency of an airborne sound.

Hearing Loss and Deafness

About 30 million Americans have impaired hearing, including a third of those age 65 to 74, and half those age 85 and older. These numbers suggest that almost inevitably, hearing loss accompanies the aging process. Fortunately, modern

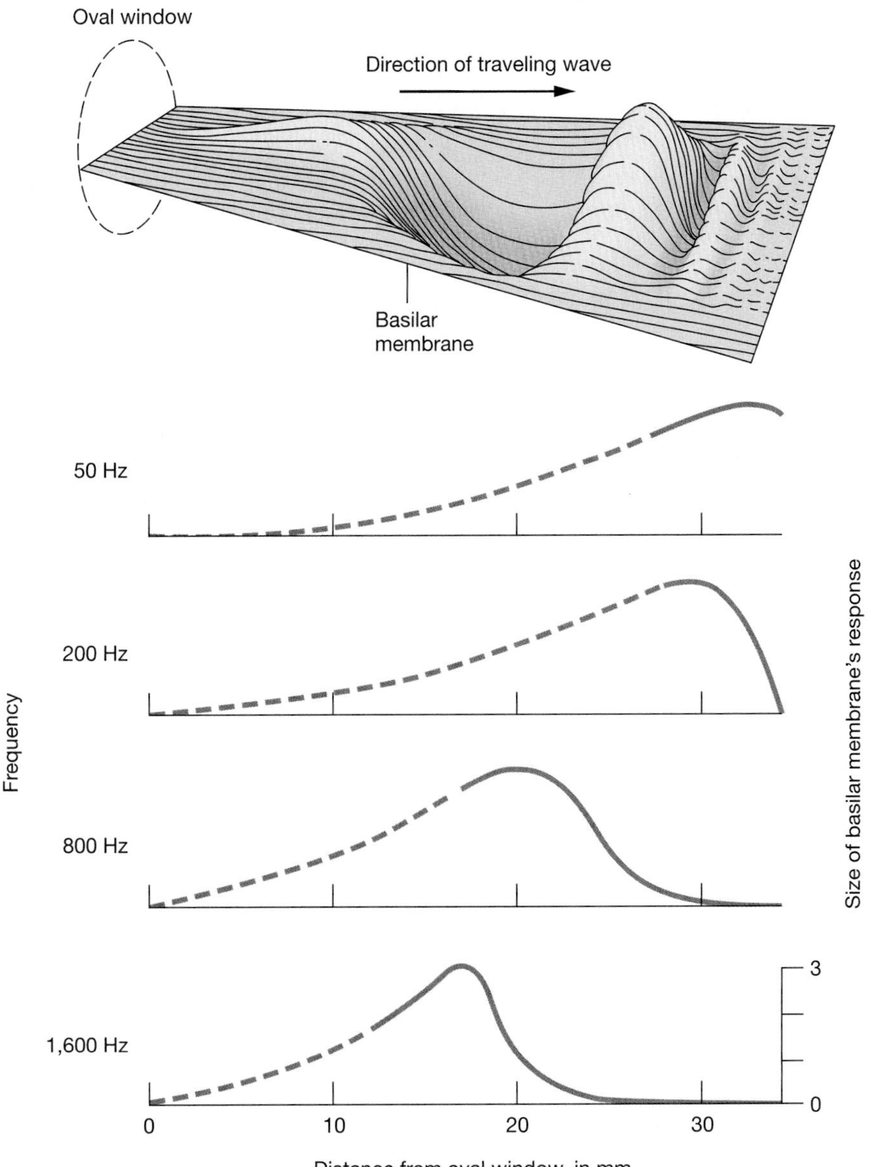

Figure 7.15 **A wave traveling through the cochlea.** Different frequencies of sounds stimulate the basilar membrane at different places along its length, providing support for the place theory of hearing. For example, at 20 mm from the oval window, the basilar membrane responds maximally to 800 Hz. (The range of frequencies from 50 Hz to 1600 Hz corresponds to the keys on a piano, from the low end to the middle.) *Source:* From "Hearing Theories and Complex Sounds" by G. von Békésy, *Journal of the Acoustical Society of America,* vol. 35, (1963), pp. 588–601. Copyright © 1963 by Acoustical Society of America. Reprinted by permission.

technology in the form of *cochlear implants* and other computer-assisted hearing aids can reduce the problems of the hearing impaired.

Blindness can occur in three ways: through retinal damage, optic nerve damage, and damage to the midbrain or cortical structures. Deafness can also be divided into three categories: *conductive, sensorineural,* and *central hearing loss* (Gulick et al., 1989).

Conductive Hearing Loss. Damage to the outer or middle ear produces **conductive hearing loss**, of which there are three types. A small lesion or tear in the eardrum, caused by an impact or an extremely loud noise such as an

conductive hearing loss Deafness due to outer or middle ear damage.

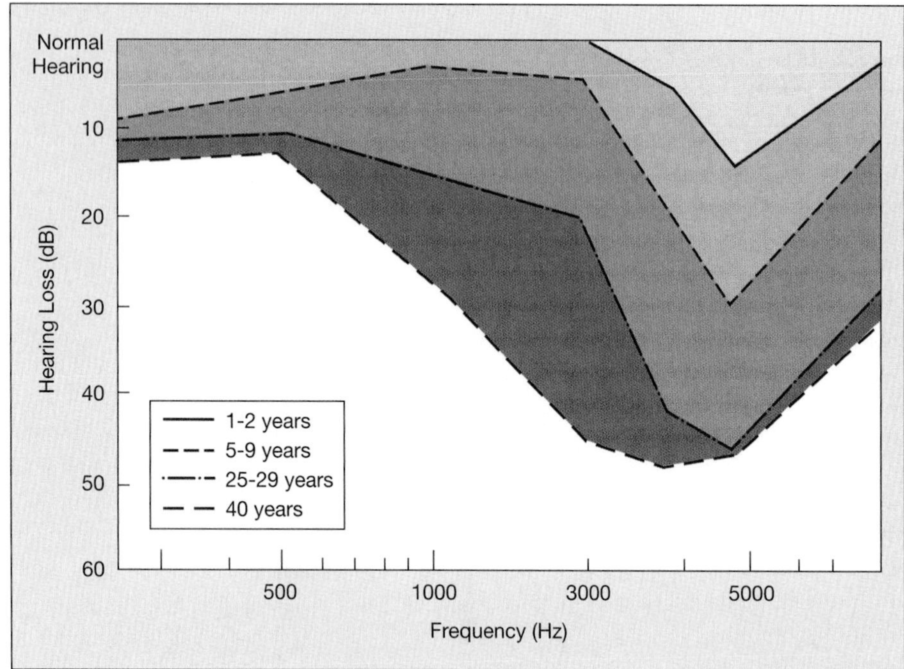

Figure 7.16 The relationship between noise and deafness. This graph shows the progression of hearing loss caused by long-term employment in a noisy jute-weaving factory. Note that high frequencies (light pink curve) are lost first after only 1or 2 years of exposure. With increased exposure (the darker shades of pink), hearing loss widens to include lower sound frequencies. After 40 years of exposure to the noise (red), hearing is lost over a broad range of frequencies. Data from Taylor, Pearson, Mair, & Burns, 1965. *Source:* From "Study of Noise and Hearing in Jute Weaving" by W. Taylor, et al., *Journal of the Acoustical Society of America,* vol. 38, (1965), pp. 113–120. Copyright © 1965 by Acoustical Society of America. Reprinted by permission.

explosion, can interfere with the conduction of vibrations to the ossicles. Small tears are self-healing, so the resulting hearing loss is temporary. However, if the eardrum is destroyed to the point that it will not heal or cannot be surgically repaired, a person will effectively be deaf in that ear. Another type of conductive hearing loss results from the build-up of calcium deposits on the ossicles, or damage to the tendons that connect them, so that they no longer pivot effectively. In this case, airborne sounds are not effectively conducted to the cochlea. This form of deafness can be corrected surgically.

The most common form of conduction hearing loss is due to infection of the middle ear, called *otitis media.* Middle-ear infections often result from blockage of the Eustachian tubes, which prevents the equalization of pressure in the middle ear, essential to the airborne transmission of sound waves. Otitis media may also cause fluid accumulation, tissue damage, and adhesions in the middle ear. The auditory nerve has only a short distance (~1/8 inch) to travel before it enters the brain stem and synapses there. One implication of the proximity of the middle and inner ear to the brain is that left untreated, the ear infections to which small children in particular are susceptible may result in meningitis, an infection of the tissue covering the brain.

Sensorineural Hearing Loss. **Sensorineural hearing loss** is caused by damage to the cochlea. Its most common form is presbycusis, which occurs beginning at age 50 in most men and age 60 in most women. Whether this type of loss is due to excessive noise, long-term drug use, normal aging, and/or disease, most elderly individuals suffer a degeneration of the hair cells and nerve fibers in the cochlea.

The most profitable way to think about noise, cochlear damage, and hearing loss is in terms of patterns of exposure to high sound intensities over time. Hearing loss following several hours of exposure to highly amplified music will typically be recovered within 24 hours. But rock musicians who are exposed to amplified music in 4-hour practice sets and performances over a period of several years will sustain permanent hearing loss, no matter what their age. Working in any noisy environment over a long period will produce hearing loss. As Figure 7.16 shows, working 8 hours per day in a noisy factory for only 1or 2 years can cause permanent hearing loss.

sensorineural hearing loss Deafness due to damage to the cochlea.

Table 7.3 provides some guidelines for protecting your ears from this type of damage. Note that there is no safe exposure time for the most highly amplified rock music. You may not want to go to a rock concert wearing the over-the-ear muffs airport personnel wear to protect their hearing, but cheap in-the-ear protectors are effective and unobtrusive. Ignoring this advice will not doom you to a life lived in silence. Continuing advances in hearing aids, including cochlear implants, are allowing people with damaged hair cells to hear well enough to understand speech.

Table 7.3 Noise and Hearing Loss

Exposure to very intense sounds (such as 115 dB) for only a few minutes each day produces permanent hearing loss.

DURATION PER DAY (HOURS)	SOUND LEVELS (AVERAGE DB)
8	90
6	92
4	95
3	97
2	100
1.5	102
1	105
0.5	110
0.25 or less	115

Source: From FUNDAMENTALS OF HEARING: An Introduction, Second Edition by W. A. Yost and D. W. Nielsen. Copyright © 1985 by Academic Press. Reproduced by permission of the publisher.

Central Hearing Loss. Cortical brain damage resulting from lesions and tumors produces the third type of impaired hearing, called **central hearing loss.** The location of the damage determines what is lost. For example, Wernicke's area, in the temporal lobe, receives nerve fibers from the primary auditory cortex. A person who has suffered damage to Wernicke's area can hear sounds and words, but cannot make sense of them (see Chapter 12). As with vision, the meaning of sounds is learned over a lifetime; this learned information, which depends on an intact hearing system, is mediated cortically. One way to assess the role of hearing in learning (and of learning in hearing) is to study children who were born deaf.

Central hearing loss and Wernicke's aphasia, Chapter 12, p. 418

Congenital Deafness. Children who were born with middle or inner ear damage may never hear. How would you compare their social and psychological worlds with the world of the congenitally blind? Unarguably, both conditions are devastating. One might argue that a blind child is more dependent on others than a deaf child. Others might counter that language development is more seriously impaired in the deaf, and since language is a defining characteristic of human beings, the deaf are worse off than the blind.

The fact is, the ability to hear is connected with important psychological developments that are seemingly unrelated to hearing, such as the ability to think. But while not being able to speak severely constrains the development of communication, and of types of thinking that depend on audiovisual learning, early intervention and special training in sign language can overcome many of the psychological problems of the deaf. We will discuss sign language in Chapter 12, because sign language is a language, not a primitive mode of communication.

Sign language, Chapter 12, p. 430

Central Auditory Processes

To this point we have followed an adequate stimulus (a particular frequency and intensity of sound) to a place of transduction through specific receptors (hair cells lying on a particular section of the basilar membrane). The auditory nerve then initiates the nerve and brain activity associated with hearing. Figure 7.17 shows the ascending nerve pathways that carry the information to various brain structures. This network of auditory pathways eventually reaches brain structures near those of the visual pathway. Both senses project to portions of the thalamus, the colliculus, and the cortex (Masterton, 1992). There are differences as well as similarities between the two systems, however. All the auditory nerve fibers first enter the brainstem, where they synapse in the *cochlear nucleus* and *superior olive* before ascending to the midbrain. The auditory receptors, then, take a more circuitous route to the thalamus and the midbrain than the visual receptors.

What do these pathways tell us about hearing? First, the auditory nerve tells the brain the location of a sound in the environment. We have seen this process before. For example, Pavlov's dog made a reflexive orienting response

central hearing loss Hearing loss that results from lesions and tumors in the brain.

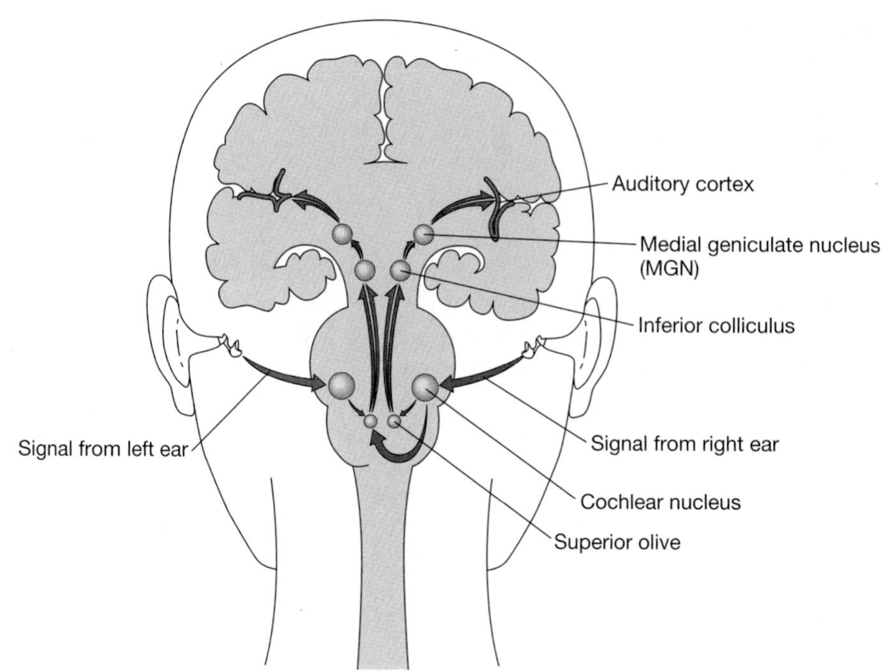

Figure 7.17 Ascending auditory nerve pathways. The auditory nerve synapses first in the cochlear nucleus of the brainstem and an adjacent area called the superior olive. Its fibers then ascend over a major auditory nerve pathway to the inferior colliculus in the midbrain. Next, the auditory pathway projects to the medial geniculate nucleus (MGN) of the thalamus, and then to the primary auditory cortex in the temporal lobe. Note that the brainstem receives input from both ears; this binaural information is preserved as it ascends through the brain. *Source:* From HUMAN INFORMATION PROCESSING: An Introduction to Psychology by Peter H. Lindsay and Donald A. Norman. Copyright © 1972 by Harcourt, Inc. Reproduced by permission of the publisher.

to the sound of a bell. One of the main functions of hearing, then—locating the source of a sound—is accomplished by auditory centers in the brainstem and midbrain.

Figure 7.18 shows how we locate a sound in space. Note that a sound that is coming from the left will reach the left ear sooner than the right ear. This slight difference in the processing time of nerve impulses from the left and right ears helps to identify the location of the sound source. The hearer can then look in the direction of the source to identify it.

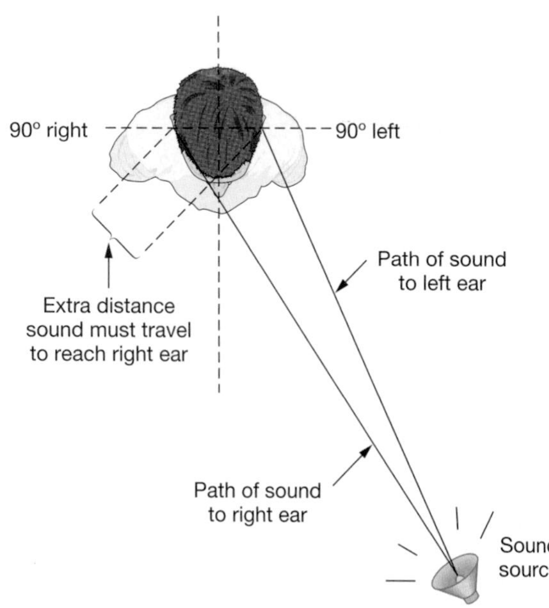

Figure 7.18 Locating the source of a sound. A sound coming from the hearer's left arrives at the left ear sooner than at the right ear, allowing the hearer to locate the source of the sound. Other sound-localizing cues include subtle differences in both the intensity and frequency of the sound waves entering the right ear, due to the shadow of the head in the sound field.

From the midbrain, the auditory pathway projects next to the *medial geniculate nucleus (MGN)* of the thalamus. This part of the brain is immediately adjacent to the LGN, which mediates seeing. The nerve fibers connecting the LGN with the MGN provide the basis for a learned association between what we see and what we hear. This learned coordination helps to account for the disconcerting feeling we have when, in a badly dubbed foreign film, we continue to hear a character's voice after her lips have stopped moving. Because of the way our neural pathways are connected, we have learned to expect a correspondence between what we see and what we hear.

Nerve fibers that extend from the hair cells on the basilar membrane project *tonotopically* to the midbrain and the primary auditory cortex. For example, brain cells that respond best to 450 Hz lie adjacent to cells that respond best to 440 and 460 Hz. The result is a tonotopic map that corresponds to the physical features of the sound stimulus.

Eventually, auditory information arrives at the primary auditory cortex (and the secondary auditory cortex, not shown) in the temporal lobe. There the most interesting part of the story begins, because at this level the role of hearing in language, music, and consciousness unfolds, as we'll learn in the next chapter.

INTERIM SUMMARY

1. Audition and vision are considered *distance senses*, because they are concerned with the detection and location of objects away from the body's surface. Hearing also plays a role in *conspecific communication*.
2. The adequate stimulus for human hearing is a wave of compressed air, called a *sound wave*, that can vary in ***amplitude***, ***frequency***, and complexity. Amplitude (measured in dB) is perceived psychologically as *loudness*, frequency (measured in dB) as *pitch*, and complexity as *timbre*.
3. Humans with excellent hearing are sensitive to a range of frequencies from about 20 to 20,000 Hz. Speech frequencies range from about 500 to 4,000 Hz.
4. The ear can be divided into the outer, middle, and inner ear. Sound waves traveling through the outer ear strike the ***tympanic membrane***, or eardrum, which pushes against three small bones, or *ossicles*, in the middle ear.
5. The ossicles, called the ***malleus***, ***incus***, and ***stapes***, amplify the compressed air, and transmit its vibrations to the ***oval window***, setting the fluids in the ***cochlea***, on the other side of the window, into motion.
6. In the inner ear, a ***traveling wave*** moves along the ***basilar membrane*** that runs the length of the cochlea. In the fluid-filled *organ of Corti*, ***hair cells*** that stretch between the basilar membrane and the *tectorial membrane* vibrate with the wave.
7. The hair cells are receptors that transduce mechanical into electrochemical energy. Their EPSPs cause the bipolar cells to generate action potentials that are coded for pitch.
8. According to the ***place theory***, frequency is coded by the movement of hair cells at various places along the length of the basilar membrane.
9. Information about the frequency and location of a sound is transmitted over the auditory nerve to tonotopically organized areas in the midbrain and the *primary auditory cortex*.
10. Deafness can be caused by *conductive*, *sensorineural*, or *central hearing loss*.
11. ***Conductive hearing loss*** most often results from *otitis media*, an infection of the middle ear; from a small lesion in the eardrum; or from malfunctioning ossicles.
12. Presbycusis, a form of ***sensorineural hearing loss*** common in older adults, is caused by damage to the cochlea. Prolonged exposure to intense sounds at any age can cause permanent sensorineural damage.
13. Damage to Wernicke's area, in the temporal lobe, may result in ***central hearing loss***, an inability to attach meaning to what is heard.
14. Congenital deafness can have a profound effect on a person's psychological development.

For Further Thought

1. Why are sounds neither generated nor heard in deep space?
2. Standard hearing aids are designed to improve hearing by amplifying sound at all frequencies. Why might users not appreciate this feature of a standard hearing aid?
3. Our nearest common ancestor with chimpanzees, a creature that lived 7 million years ago, probably heard about the same frequencies of sound as we do. (This statement is an inference based on the fact that chimpanzees' hearing is similar to humans' hearing.) Given this assumption, which part of the human hearing system differs from that of chimpanzees, and presumably from that of our common ancestor?

TASTING AND SMELLING: THE INTIMATE SENSES

The evolution of the two systems of smell and taste reflect the most basic of selective pressures, the need to be sensitive to foods and to avoid prey, and for those animals that reproduce sexually, the need to court and mate. For this reason taste and smell can be considered "intimate senses." We like or dislike tastes and smells; seldom are we neutral. In fact, within several hours of their birth, infants actively like or dislike certain tastes, though they are relatively indifferent to what they see and hear. While such early preferences are innate, most smells acquire their emotional and motivational power through learning, as we'll see in the next chapter.

What We Taste

Mothers taste dozens of different baby foods before putting them into baby's mouth. Students taste colas, spicy burritos, lipstick, and hundreds of other flavors. These foods and liquids are actually chemicals, to which our taste receptors have become attuned. The cultures into which we are born guide our emotional and affective responses to them. No matter what the culture, however, all humans recognize four basic tastes.

What is surprising is how simple the human sense of taste is compared to the sense of smell. For example, scientists who have dissolved hundreds of chemicals in distilled water, squirted the solutions onto the tongues of humans and other animals, and measured their responses electrophysiologically tell us that humans recognize only four basic tastes: *sweet, sour, salty,* and *bitter*. Why the discrepancy between these four basic tastes and the huge number of tastes we seem to experience? There is no good answer to this question (Bartoshuk, 1991). Part of the answer is that we seldom experience taste separately from smell. In fact, we often use imprecise words to describe their relative contributions. For example, apples and potatoes can be described similarly in taste terms, even though they are differentiated by smell. Thus, a really bad head cold that blocks the sense of smell can make discriminating between a raw potato and a raw apple difficult. While an apple may be described simply in terms of its sweetness or sourness, its appleness is primarily an olfactory sensation. Foods are perhaps best described by their flavor, a term that combines both taste and smell.

With special training, humans can learn to compare the flavors of different varieties of wines. Each wine may contain as many as 700 chemical compounds.

In comparison with hearing and seeing, our perception and labeling of tastes and smells is crude. A typical person's judgment of the flavor of a food is an emotional one, usually either "good" or "bad." That is, people tend to react affectively first, and then if asked, to say that a flavor is more or less sweet, more or less salty, and so forth (Capaldi & Powley, 1990).

Unlike the experience of seeing and hearing, taste relates to the actual properties of the source: Something may taste "like a banana" or smell "like dirty gym socks." With training, humans can make highly accurate taste judgments. For example, about 500 different chemicals contribute to the flavor of chocolate, and up to 700 chemical compounds to the flavor of red wine. Professional tasters can usually pinpoint the predominant chemicals.

How We Taste

The chemicals we taste defy easy categorization. A sweet taste, for example, can be elicited by chemically different compounds. Saccharin is not sucrose is not aspartame; none of the three contains a common physical compound that is the essence of sweetness. So how do we taste sweetness?

Taste receptors are found in **taste buds** on the tongue (see Figure 7.19). Each of the different types of taste buds contains about 50 receptor cells, which can't be seen because they are buried within a pore in the center of the bud. The taste buds are buried, too. Stick out your tongue and look in the mirror. You will see little red *fungiform papillae* on the front of your tongue, *foliate papillae* on the back, and a chevron of *circumvallate papillae* at the very back. These papillae contain taste buds, as does the soft palate.

taste buds Structures on the tongue that contain taste receptors.

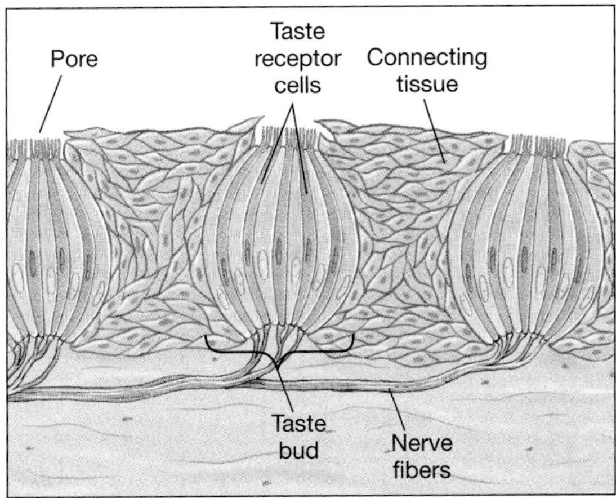

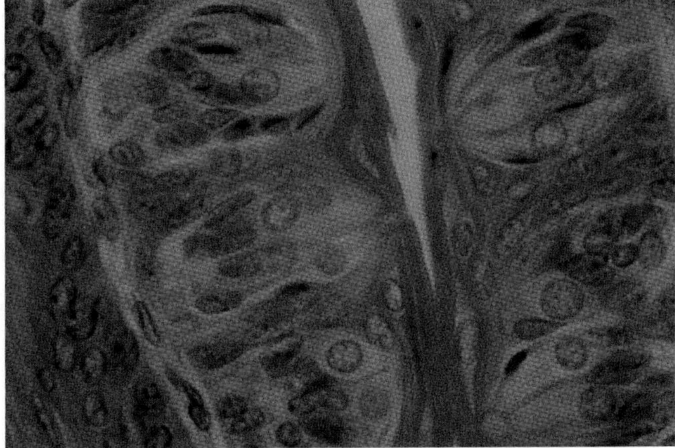

Figure 7.19 **Taste buds on the tongue.** The taste receptor cells in a taste bud are arranged around a pore. When chemicals dissolved in saliva enter the pore, they stimulate the taste receptor cells. Taste nerves then carry the resulting information to the brainstem.

Within each bud, the membranes of the receptor cells are bathed in a range of chemicals dissolved in saliva. These dissolved chemicals wear down the membranes of the taste receptors (and the smell receptors), so that they must eventually be replaced by cells in an underlying tissue layer. This regeneration of receptor cells is similar to the neurogenesis found in parts of the brain.

LINK
Neurogenesis, Chapter 4, p. 129

EPSPs from the receptor cells generate action potentials in the taste nerves. The intensity of a taste is coded by how fast these nerves fire, much as light intensity is coded in the optic nerve. Although any of a number of chemicals can excite a taste receptor, each part of the human tongue best senses one of the four basic tastes (see Figure 7.20). The circumvallate and soft-palate papillae are most sensitive to bitter tastes; the front part of the tongue, to sweet tastes; and the sides, to salty and sour tastes. You can easily demonstrate this by dipping a Q-tip® into a sugar solution and placing it carefully on the back of your tongue. You won't taste the sugar unless you "retrieve it" with the tip of your tongue. Neither will you taste a bitter solution on the front of your tongue. A bitter detector at the opening of the esophagus causes reflexive gagging, adaptively protecting animals from toxins that have a bitter taste.

The axons of sensory nerves in the tongue form part of three cranial nerves. These cranial nerves enter the brainstem and synapse at the *solitary nucleus,* before ascending to the thalamus (see Figure 7.20) and the tongue area of the *somatosensory cortex* (see also Figure 4.17). This rather simple organization allows the taste system to accomplish a singular goal, detecting the difference between edible and inedible foods.

Taste and somatosensory cortex, Chapter 4, p. 123

Why and How We Smell

Although humans can detect only four basic tastes, they can smell literally thousands of volatile chemicals in the environment. They are particularly sensitive to the glandular secretions of plants and animals, meant to help in finding food and mates. One type of secretion, which produces an airborne olfactant that affects another animal's behavior, especially its reproductive behavior, is called a **pheromone** (Keverne, 1987). Because smells acquire meaning through experience, we will discuss what humans smell further in the next chapter, on perception.

pheromone A chemical secretion that communicates information from one animal to another.

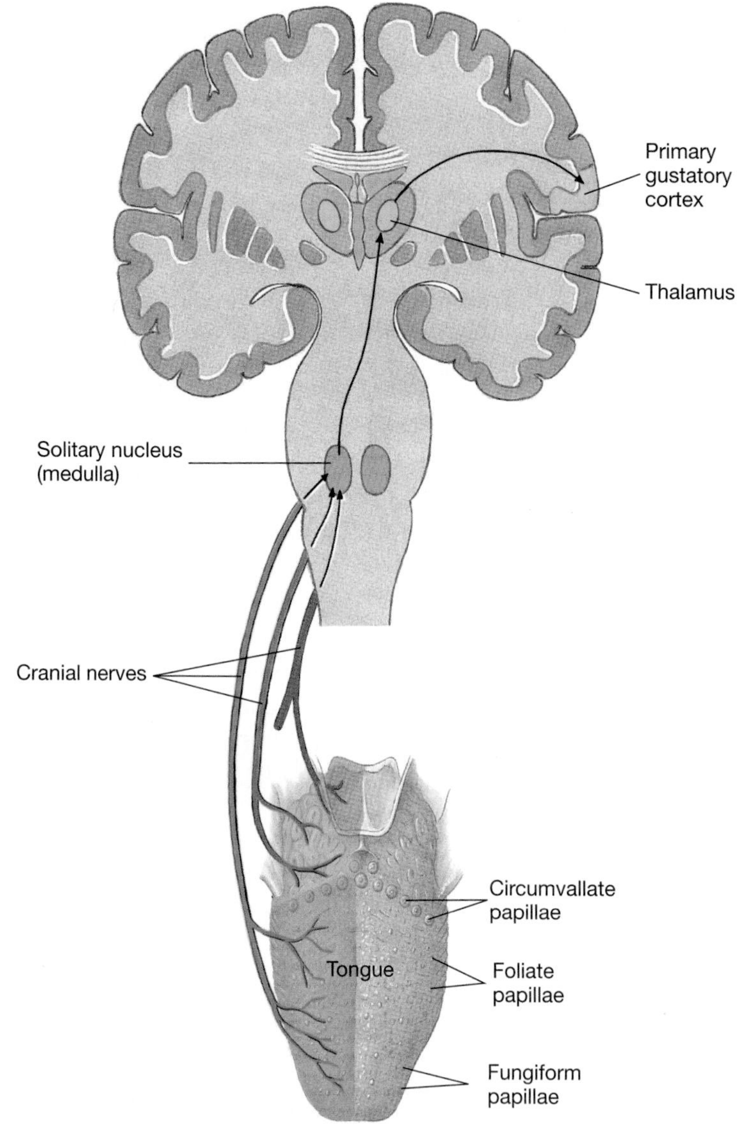

Figure 7.20 Tasting with the tongue and the brain. Receptors in papillae on the tongue are sensitive to taste. Information from these papillae is carried over three cranial nerves to the solitary nucleus in the medulla. From there, it travels to the thalamus and primary gustatory cortex.

As Figure 7.21 shows, the coiled dendrites of the olfactory receptor dangle in a mucous-filled nasal passage called the *olfactory mucosa*. Olfactants that are breathed in quickly dissolve in the olfactory mucosa, where they initiate EPSPs in about 5 million olfactory neurons. The axons of these neurons penetrate the skull through small openings and synapse in the **olfactory bulb**. The speed with which these nerves fire indicates the intensity of a smell; the higher their discharge rate, the more concentrated the olfactant.

Two types of cell in the olfactory bulb project further into the brain, along different routes. One set of nerve fibers provides a conscious sense of smell, to which we can apply verbal labels; another influences our unconscious behavior. As Figure 7.21 shows, the conscious route synapses first in the *pyriform cortex*, then in the thalamus and the cortex. Using this part of the brain, you may associate an individual's fragrance with his or her voice and appearance. Under some circumstances, a smell may bring back the memory of a particular occasion with astonishing clarity, as described by Marcel Proust in *Remembrance of Things Past*. The unconscious route, not shown in the figure, projects to the brainstem, hippocampus, and hypothalamus.

olfactory bulb The part of the brain that synapses with the smell receptors through the olfactory nerve.

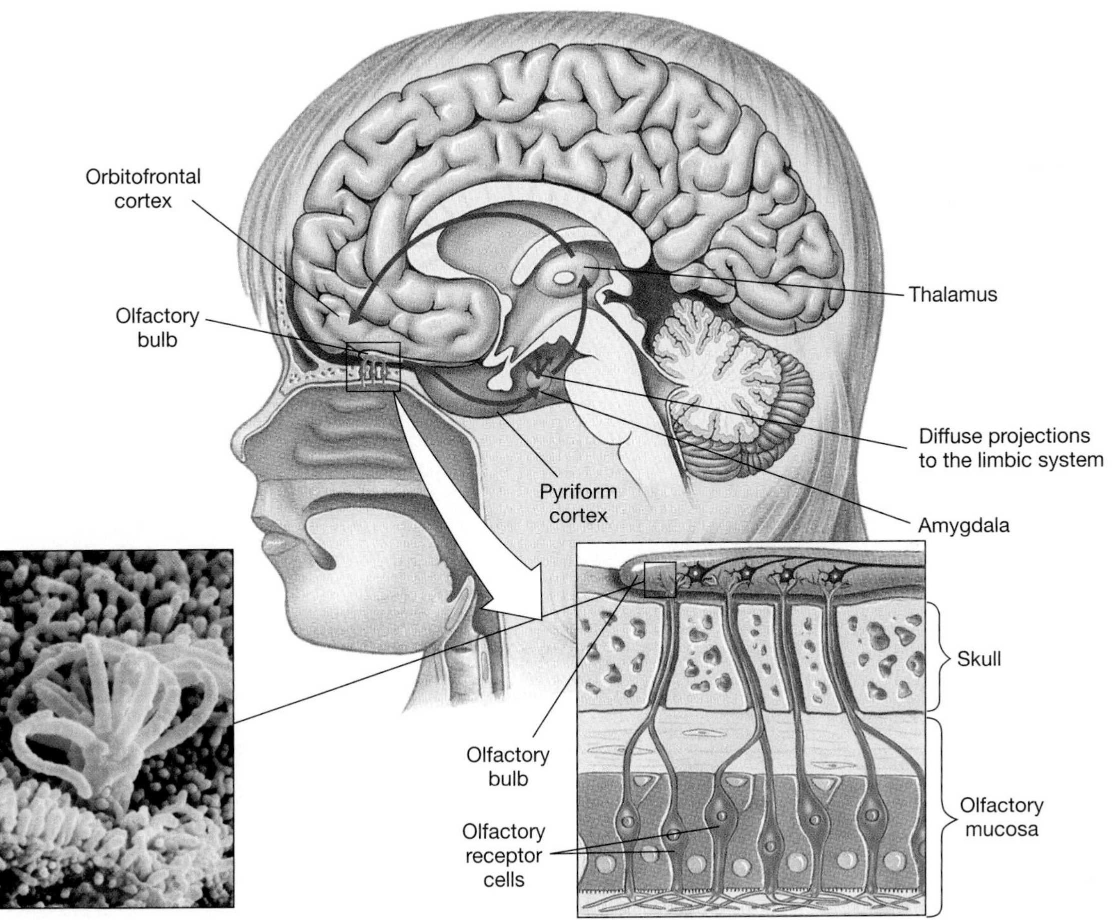

Figure 7.21 Smelling with the nose and brain. The dendrites of olfactory receptor cells (one is shown in the inset) are stimulated by olfactants dissolved in the olfactory mucosa, the lining of the nasal passage (inset). The axons of these receptor cells pass through small openings in the skull and synapse in the olfactory bulb. Nerves from the olfactory bulb then synapse with neurons in the amygdala, the pyriform cortex, the thalamus, and the orbitofrontal cortex. *Photo Source:* E. Morrison & R. Costanzo.

Another structure not shown in Figure 7.21 is a small pit in the nasal passage called the *vomeronasal organ*. In many other animals, olfactory receptors in the vomeronasal organ are sensitive to sexual smells; nerves carrying such information project directly to the amygdala. The function of the vomeronasal organ in humans is controversial, but it is likely involved in sexual attraction. This organ and its pathway to the amygdala, as well as the olfactory path to the hypothalamus, provide the mechanism for the smell-related sexual behavior of humans and other animals.

INTERIM SUMMARY

1. Smell and taste are psychologically intimate chemical senses that play an important role in the identification of food and the communication of information to other animals.
2. Animals sense chemicals in their environment using their taste and smell receptors. Humans are sensitive to four basic tastes: *sweet, sour, salty,* and *bitter*.
3. Most foods are better described by their flavor (a term that combines both taste and smell) than by their taste.

4. ***Taste buds,*** found by the hundreds in papillae on the front, back, and sides of the tongue, are the taste receptors for chemical stimuli.
5. The human olfactory receptors, nerves, and brain have evolved a sensitivity to many different types of chemicals, including the glandular secretions of other plants and animals.
6. A ***pheromone*** is an airborne molecule of animal odor that is detected by, and affects the behavior of, another animal. Pheromones seem to be especially influential in animals' reproductive behavior.
7. Chemicals are detected when they are breathed in through the nose and contact the olfactory receptors' dendrites in the *olfactory mucosa.*
8. Olfactory information follows at least two routes to the brain: a conscious pathway from the ***olfactory bulb*** to the pyriform cortex, the thalamus, and the cortex, and an unconscious pathway to the hypothalamus.

For Further Thought

1. Recall that the term *sensation* refers to simple sensory impressions, whereas *perception* refers to the understanding and meaning of what is sensed. Given that humans are not emotionally neutral about tastes and smells, is the distinction between sensation and perception meaningful with regard to the chemical senses?
2. On the surface, the term *chemistry,* a scientific term, seems an odd word to use in describing couple's romantic feelings, as in the phrase "the right chemistry" or "a strong chemical attraction." Can you think of other ways in which the English language ties the chemical senses of smell and taste to sexual behavior?

THE SKIN SENSES: TOUCH, PRESSURE, TEMPERATURE, AND PAIN

Like the nose and mouth, the skin is a sensuous organ that tells us much about our external environment. In this section we'll discuss the skin and many of its parts. Together, the skin senses are sometimes referred to as the body senses, the somatosenses, or the *cutaneous senses.* The receptors, nerves, and brain that serve these sensory systems produce a variety of experiences, including touch (such as a pinch or caress), pressure (from light to intense), temperature (from just right to too hot or too cold), itching and tickling, and vibration. Pleasure and pain can also originate in the skin.

The Human Skin

The human skin is the largest sensory organ in the body (see Figure 7.22). Although it is only about 0.5 millimeters thick (except on the soles, where it may be 4.0 millimeters), it is about 1.8 square meters in area and weighs about 9 pounds. Skin serves as the defining boundary, both physical and psychological, between a person and the outside world. Not only does it house receptors that give pleasure when rubbed and bathed, it is a remarkable protective barrier against an uncaring environment. On contact, it protects against teeth, thorns, tears, and toxins, and sometimes against the harmful rays of the sun. It sweats and shivers. Its hairs and glands attract other animals. Figure 7.23 shows a diagram of the skin in cross-section.

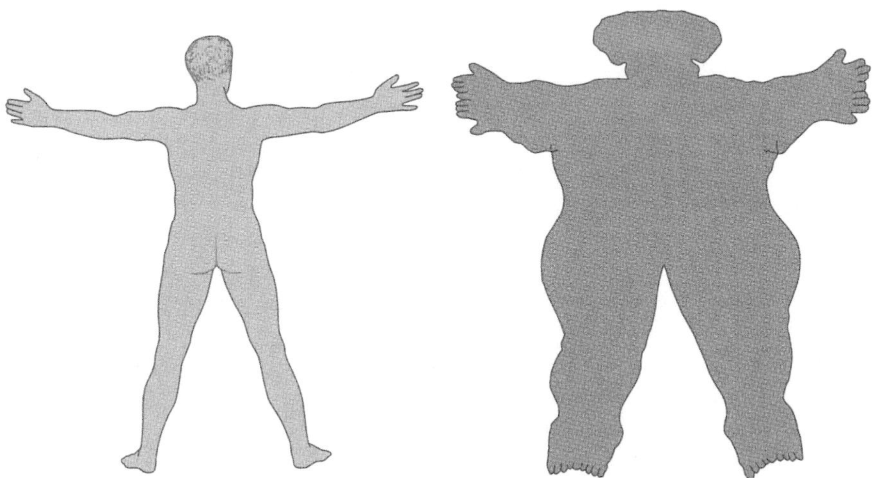

Figure 7.22 A human, skinned. The skin of an adult is a huge 1.8-square-meter sensory surface that weighs about 9 pounds. *Source:* Montagna, 1965, pp. 58–59.

Among the skin's most distinguishing features are hair follicles, each wrapped beneath the skin's surface (called the *epidermis*) with a receptor. When the hair is displaced slightly, such as when a flea crawls through it, the receptor produces EPSPs. One of the main functions of the skin senses, then, is similar to that of seeing and hearing: to detect potentially dangerous objects.

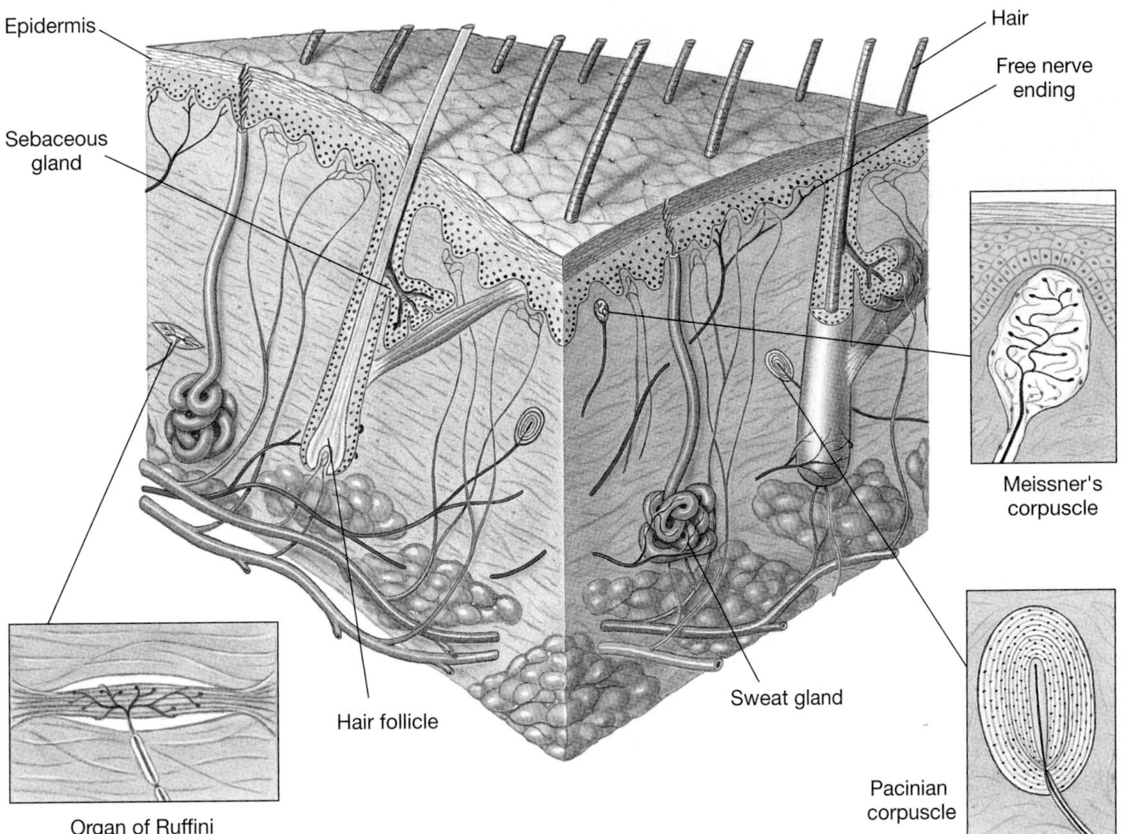

Figure 7.23 A cross-section of human skin. This composite diagram illustrates the variety of receptors, glands, hair follicles, and other tissues in the skin. The receptors shown here include free nerve endings, Meissner's corpuscle, a Pacinian corpuscle, and an Organ of Ruffini.

Figure 7.23 shows other specialized receptors distributed in the skin. Nerves with undistinguished-looking dendrites, called ***free nerve endings***, are now considered the most likely receptors for touch, temperature, and pain. Their patterns of firing may distinguish different types of sensory information. Another receptor type shown in Figure 7.23 is the *Pacinian corpuscle,* a "deep pressure" receptor with a distinctively rounded, onion-layered structure. These receptors serve a wide skin area, and react rapidly with a burst of action potentials to sudden changes in skin pressure. Other structurally identifiable receptors, Meissner's corpuscle and the Organ of Ruffini, respond slowly to gradual changes in skin pressure. Scientists have not yet identified a receptor for temperature, but they suspect free nerve endings may play a role.

On the whole, the skin adapts rapidly to stimulation. Within a second or so of putting on clothes, for example, we don't feel them. To describe an object by feel we must repeatedly run our fingers over its surface, forcing the rapidly adapting receptors to continue to discharge. (The nerve pathways for the skin senses are described on pages 122 of Chapter 4.)

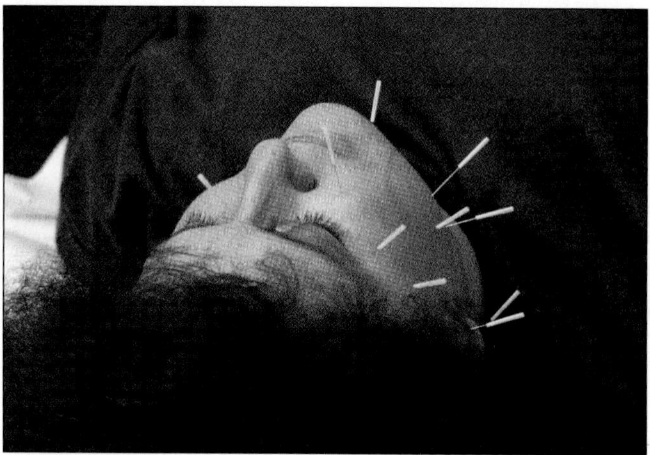

Acupuncture is an ancient Chinese treatment that has proven to be an effective pain reliever in both humans and non-human animals.

The Sense of Pain

Pain is an enigma. Unlike the other senses, the psychological experience of pain can occur without a physical stimulus. For example, telling a child that a hypodermic injection will be very painful produces a different result than suggesting that it won't hurt much. Pain can be localized to specific places in the body, or it can be a diffuse, otherworldly experience. Intense sounds, bright lights, very high and very low temperatures, and crushing pressure on the skin can all cause pain.

It is interesting that scientists focus on the sense of pain rather than the sense of pleasure, because we also get pleasure from the senses: music as opposed to loud noise; beauty as opposed to bright lights; a soft rather than a hurting touch; warm and cozy temperatures on a cold day, and cool temperatures on a hot day. Under most conditions, the normal functioning of eyes, ears, and skin is neutral—neither painful nor pleasurable.

How We Sense Pain. Identifying an adequate stimulus for pain is difficult, for several reasons. First is the great variety of pain-inducing stimuli, including intense pressure, warmth, cold, and so on. These stimuli, which can cause tissue damage, excite the free nerve endings shown in Figure 7.23, whose fibers synapse in the brainstem, medulla, and somatosensory cortex, near the same areas as the touch fibers.

Control of pain by hypnosis, Chapter 9, p. 328

Where is pain processed in the brain? This question continues to intrigue neuroscientists. Compared to vision, audition, taste, smell, and touch, pain appears to be organized subcortically. Removing part of the cortex will not relieve pain, nor will electrically stimulating part of the cortex produce pain. What is intriguing, however, is that expectation and prior learning *do* influence the perception of pain. In fact, as we will see in Chapter 9, pain can be partially blocked by hypnosis. Massage, holding your breath and grimacing, biting down on a stick, and acupuncture (see the photograph on this page) also help.

free nerve ending A skin receptor with an undifferentiated dendrite, involved in the senses of touch, temperature, and pain.

gate-control theory Melzack's theory that nerve impulses from the brain activate gates in the spinal cord, effectively blocking pain.

Factors That Influence the Perception of Pain. One explanation of how we experience pain, and how cognition, emotion, and physical stimulation can influence the perception of pain, is the **gate-control theory**, first proposed by the psychologist Ronald Melzack and the biologist David Wall (1982). According to this theory, nerve activity *from the brain to the spinal cord* activates "gates" in the spinal cord, which block pain signals. Specifically, the activity of larger nerves, such as the nerves that carry touch information from massaged areas around a wound, can block the action of smaller nerves.

More recent theorizing about how impulses from the brain to the spinal cord can influence pain focuses on an area in the upper part of the medulla called the *periaquaductal gray* ("around the aqueduct," or ventricle). Stimulating the periaquaductal gray (PAG) with an electrical current provides sufficient analgesia to perform surgery on a rat (Reynolds, 1969). The PAG neurons and their projection to the spinal cord apparently block pain by releasing endorphins, neurochemicals associated with pain and pleasure (see Chapter 4). The chemical structure of endorphins is similar to that of morphine, which occupies the same receptor sites in the PAG and is also highly effective in relieving pain. (For further discussion of the role of drugs and placebos in the control of pain, see Chapter 17.)

The PAG, drugs, and placebos, in Chapter 18, p. 630

One mystifying type of pain is experienced by amputees. Most people who have an arm or leg amputated report that they continue to "feel" the part that is missing, a phenomenon called **phantom limb** (Melzack, 1992). A phantom limb has the same perceived shape as its real counterpart, and seems to move, stretch, and function normally. More than half of all amputees report severe pain in their phantom limbs, which cannot be successfully treated with drugs or surgery.

Why would a person feel a limb that doesn't exist? First, many of the nerve endings for touch and pain remain in the stump following an amputation. These nerves can continue to stimulate other neurons in the spinal cord, as well as ascending neurons in the somatosensory strip, on the cortex. Severing these nerves, however, provides only temporary relief from the pain of phantom limb, which returns in a few months. Since under normal conditions, the neurons in the somatosensory strip allow us to sense our extremities, their continued functioning after an amputation likely serves as the basis for a phantom limb. Over months to years the phenomenon usually subsides, and the phantom limb reportedly "shrinks." The neurons that serve the missing part of the body probably reorganize themselves and assume other functions, allowing the phantom limb to disappear (Pons et al., 1991; Ramachandran, 1993). How the cortex reorganizes itself is now being studied using fMRI techniques (Moore et al., 2000).

phantom limb The perception that an amputated limb still exists.

INTERIM SUMMARY

1. The human skin is the largest sensory organ in the body; it also provides a protective barrier against the environment. The skin contains hair follicles, glands, and skin sense receptors.
2. The *skin senses* (or *cutaneous senses*) include touch, pressure, temperature, and pain.
3. The most common receptors in the skin are ***free nerve endings***, which serve the senses of touch, temperature, and pain. *Pacinian corpuscles* are onion-shaped, "deep pressure" receptors that are sensitive to sudden changes in pressure on the skin.
4. Pain differs from other senses in several ways. Most important, there is no specific area of the cortex devoted to the processing of pain. In large measure, prior learning and expectation determine the perception of pain.
5. The perception of pain is influenced by both brain and spinal cord mechanisms. According to the ***gate-control theory***, impulses from the brain to the spinal cord can block pain.
6. Neurochemicals in the *periaquaductal gray (PAG)*, such as endorphins, are associated with pain.
7. Amputees report feeling arms and legs that no longer exist, a phenomenon called ***phantom limb***. Over time the feeling disappears, but some amputees continue to experience severe pain.

For Further Thought

1. In Western cultures, with numerous exceptions, males seem to handle painful events differently from females. Support the argument that these differences are more likely due to culture than to the physiology of pain.
2. What does the expression "no pain, no gain" mean? Can you discuss it using the concept of negative feedback?

CONCLUDING THOUGHTS

Animals have evolved receptors and brains that allow them to adaptively sense their environment. The conscious perceptions of seeing, hearing, tasting, smelling, touching, and feeling pain begin in specialized receptors, each of which is sensitive to a particular aspect of the environment. Under normal conditions, we use our eyes to view nature and fine art, our ears to listen to conversations and enjoy music, and our tongues and noses to savor the chemicals in *haute cuisine* and exotic perfumes. The various receptors for the senses are connected by nerves to certain areas in the brain. Acting together, these systems produce a seamless "consensus of the senses." In addition, unequivocal evidence now exists for the *unconscious* perception of sights, sounds, and smells.

Had the sun's rays not penetrated the Earth's atmosphere for more than 3 billion years, animals living on the Earth's surface would not have evolved a sensitivity to the wavelengths that make up the visible spectrum. Humans have since evolved a complicated retina and brain, including visual pathways that allow them to see shapes, movement, and color with great acuity.

Humans evolved ears and the ability to hear in order to detect the location and form of objects in their environment. Moving objects set up vibrations in the air, to which the ear is exquisitely sensitive. Related nerves and parts of the brain allow them to perceive and understand these stimuli. Although humans are sensitive to a wide range of sounds, like other animals, they are most sensitive to sounds made by their own species. The social and psychological effects of losing one's hearing highlight the important role of this sense in human consciousness.

Humans evolved chemical receptors both outside and inside the body to locate nutrients and potential mates. The four basic tastes of sweet, sour, salty, and bitter help to identify sources of calories and essential nutrients, as well as toxins harmful to the body. Together, the taste and smell of food are perceived as flavor. Humans do not eat reflexively; rather, they learn to prefer the foods of their own culture. Their olfactory system affords also them a conscious sensitivity to the glandular secretions of other plants and animals. Although we cannot detect pheromones at a conscious level, they are nevertheless intimately involved in sexual attraction and reproduction.

The skin is the largest sensory surface. A variety of evolved receptors in the skin, their nerves, and parts of the brain allow us to sense temperature and objects that touch us and to experience pain. Pain often indicates tissue damage, motivating a person to respond adaptively in ways that relieve it.

Together, seeing, hearing, tasting, smelling, touching, and feeling pain all merge to define our conscious perception of the world, the topic of the next chapter.

KEY TERMS

absolute threshold *232*
additive color mixing *244*
amplitude *247*
basilar membrane *251*
central hearing loss *255*
cochlea *250*
complementary colors *244*
conductive hearing loss *253*
cones *238*
dark adaptation *243*
free nerve endings *264*
frequency *247*
ganglion cells *239*
gate-control theory *264*
hair cells *251*
incus *250*
just noticeable difference (jnd) *231*
lateral geniculate nucleus (LGN) *239*
malleus *250*
method of constant stimuli *232*
method of limits *232*
method of magnitude estimation *233*
olfactory bulb *260*
opponent-process theory *245*
oval window *250*
perception *231*
phantom limb *265*
pheromone *259*
place theory *252*
psychophysics *231*
retina *238*
rod-cone break *243*
rods *238*
sensation *231*
sensorineural hearing loss *254*
signal detection theory *233*
stapes *250*
striate cortex *239*
subliminal perception *234*
taste buds *258*
transduction *238*
traveling wave *252*
trichromatic theory *244*
tympanic membrane *250*
visible spectrum *237*
Weber's law *231*

8

Perception

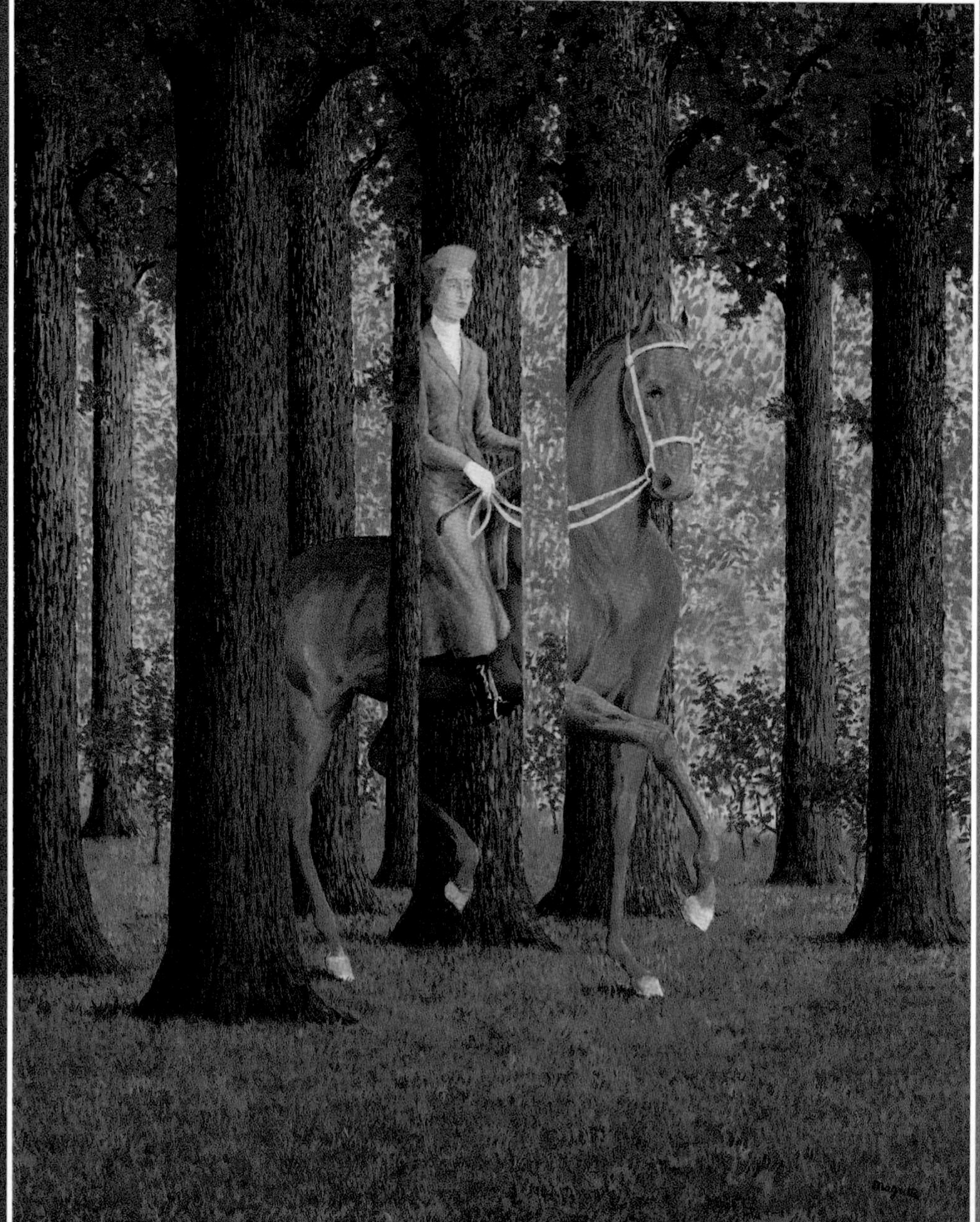

Rene Magritte "The Blank Signature" 1965, oil on canvas, .813 × .651 (32 × 25 5/8); framed .984 × .825 × .044 (38 3/4 × 32 1/2 × 1 3/4). Collection of Mr. and Mrs. Paul Mellon. Photograph © 2001 Board of Trustees, National Gallery of Art, Washington, D.C. © 2002 C. Hersovici, Brussels/Artists Rights Society (ARS), New York.

Perception of Shapes, Edges, and Movement
Bottom-Up and Top-Down Processes
Receptive Fields and Feature Detectors
Cortical Processing of Features
Interim Summary
For Further Thought

Depth Perception, Perceptual Constancies, and Illusions
Depth Perception
Perceptual Constancies
Illusions and Ambiguous Figures
Interim Summary
For Further Thought

Conscious and Unconscious Processes in Perception
The Phenomenon of Blindsight
Seeing with the Whole Brain
Seeing Versus Awareness
The Mind-Body Problem Again
Interim Summary
For Further Thought

Perception of the Whole
Apparent Movement and the Phi Phenomenon
Principles of Perceptual Organization
Interim Summary
For Further Thought

Perception of Sound, Taste, Smell, and Touch
The Perception of Meaningful Sounds
The Perception of Odors and Tastes
The Perception of Touch
Integration Across the Senses
Interim Summary
For Further Thought

Concluding Thoughts

Sensory and perceptual processes are not as simply divided as the analysis in Chapter 7 suggested. Consider a patient, Dr. P., who had experienced some problems with his eyes for several years. After being diagnosed with diabetes, he finally had his eyes examined; the ophthalmologist, amazed by what he discovered, referred him to the British neurologist Oliver Sacks. The fact was, Dr. P.'s eyes were fine; he sensed the world in a normal manner. However, he had perceptual difficulties that sometimes caused him to misinterpret what he saw. In Dr. P.'s words, "I occasionally make mistakes" (Sacks, 1987, p. 9).

From a brief interview and examination of the patient, Sacks learned that Dr. P was a singer and music teacher of some renown. He was physically sound, a charming conversationalist, and apparently mentally intact. Sacks instructed Dr. P. to dress and left the room. On returning several minutes later, puzzled why Dr. P. hadn't put on one of his shoes, the neurologist asked if he could help, and the following exchange ensued:

> "Help what? Help whom?"
> "Help you put on your shoe."
> "Ach," he said, "I had forgotten the shoe," adding, sotto voce, "The shoe? The shoe?" He seemed baffled.
> "Your shoe," I repeated. "Perhaps you'd put it on."
> He continued to look downwards, though not at the shoe, with an intense but misplaced concentration. Finally his gaze settled on his foot: "That is my shoe, yes?"
> Did I mis-hear? Did he mis-see?

"My eyes," he explained, and put a hand to his foot. "This is my shoe, no?"
"No, it is not. That is your foot. There is your shoe."
"Ah! I thought that was my foot."
Was he joking? Was he mad? Was he blind? If this was one of his "strange mistakes," it was the strangest mistake I had ever come across. (Sacks, 1987, p. 10).

The story of Dr. P. dramatically illustrates the fact that there is nothing simple about seeing; the same may be said for hearing, tasting, and touching. Not surprisingly, the perception of each of these senses is accomplished in succinct parts of the brain; yet even within a sense, such as vision, damage to one part of the brain can leave some types of vision intact while devastating others. For example, Dr. P. could see and discriminate among complex shapes; in a deck of cards, he could accurately name the jacks, queens, and kings. But he could not recognize and identify pictures of his family, friends, or even himself. Similarly, he could pick out the details in a scene, such as a landscape, but could not identify it as a landscape. When Sacks gave him a red rose and asked him what it was, he responded:

"About six inches in length. A convoluted red form with a linear green attachment."
"Yes . . . and what do you think it is, Dr. P.?"
"Not easy to say." He seemed perplexed. . . . "I think this could be an inflorescence or flower."
"Could be? Smell it."
He again looked somewhat puzzled, then smelled it.
"Beautiful!" he exclaimed. "An early rose. What a heavenly smell." (Sacks, 1987, p. 14)

On another occasion, Sacks gave Dr. P. a leather glove. The patient described it as "a continuous surface . . . infolded on itself . . . with five outpouchings," but had no idea what it was or what it was for. In describing this test, Sacks remarked that

no child would have the power to see and speak of "a continuous surface . . . infolded on itself," but any child, any infant, would immediately know a glove as a glove, see it as familiar, as going with a hand. Dr. P. didn't. He saw nothing as familiar. Visually, he was lost in a world of lifeless abstractions . . . he did not have a real visual world. (Sacks, 1987, pp. 14–15)

We humans take for granted the adaptiveness of our inherited sensory systems. But as Dr. P.'s case shows, perception is a complicated and delicate process that can become quite maladaptive as a result of brain damage. In this chapter we will examine visual perception in detail—how we attach meaning to the images of shapes, edges, and movement that fall on our retinas. Then we'll discuss how culture influences what we hear, especially language and music. The chapter concludes with a discussion of the perception of taste, smell, and touch and their adaptive significance.

PERCEPTION OF SHAPES, EDGES, AND MOVEMENT

Seeing is sensing. ("Can you see the rainbow?")

Seeing is understanding. ("I see!")

Seeing is believing. ("I saw it with my own two eyes.")

The psychological experience of seeing is qualitatively different from the senses of hearing, smelling, tasting, touching, balancing, and feeling pain and pleasure. Seeing is more than the color picture that appears to sighted people when they open their eyes in a lighted environment. Its psychological dimensions include sensing, believing, understanding, and the *insight* of self-reflection. Seeing is the *image* in *imagination*, the *light* in en*light*enment, and in this chapter, the *focus* of our attention. In short, an intimate connection exists between seeing and human consciousness.

Figure 8.1 What do you see? At first glance, these white, gray, and black rectangles form a simple visual pattern on the receptors in your eyes. With further processing in your human visual system, the pattern may become a complex image.

Bottom-Up and Top-Down Processes

Chapter 7 described the human visual process and probed its adaptive significance—why we see. Here we will consider more complex processes of vision, including what we see and how we know what we see. For convenience, we can think of the sensory process as a kind of **bottom-up process.** Receptors in the retina, for instance, provide information about details such as color, shape, and movement. By contrast, perception is a **top-down process,** in which an object is perceived at once as a whole. For example, Figure 8.1 can be seen as a pattern made of light and dark blocks (bottom-up process), but its visual image is *understood* through a top-down process. Cultural history in the form of questions such as *Do you see a face?* or *Who was the tenth President of the United States?* may aid your perception of the figure. (If you're still having trouble perceiving a famous face, either view the picture from across the room or hold it at a normal reading distance and squint.) In actuality, the distinction between sensing and perceiving is more complicated than this explanation suggests; indeed, sometimes it is arbitrary. The subjective nature of perception is philosophically unsettling: we can't be sure that any two individuals—even those who share the same culture—see the world in exactly the same way.

Though shape, color, size, and orientation all help humans and other animals to recognize objects, shape plays the most prominent role. A chair can vary in color and size, but its shape allows us to categorize it as a chair in the same way that the shape in Figure 8.1 defines a face. Learning is involved in object recognition; although a person from a different culture might perceive the face in Figure 8.1, he or she would not likely recognize it as Lincoln. Members of our culture *perceive* Lincoln's face after *sensing* its patterns of white, gray, and black. In the next section, we'll discuss the way in which higher cortical functions allow Lincoln's portrait to emerge from the image's details. But we'll begin with how the brain detects the details of physical features such as shape and movement.

Method of introspection, Chapter 1, p. 19

Psychophysics, Chapter 7, p. 231

bottom-up process An analysis of the action of feature detectors in a sensory experience.

top-down process An analysis of the effects of expectation and prior learning on a sensory experience.

Receptive Fields and Feature Detectors

The introspective method of bringing subjects into a laboratory and asking them what they see, hear, smell, and taste has contributed a great deal to our knowledge of sensation and perception. Because nonhuman animals can't talk, scientists have modified Fechner's psychophysical methods to provide answers about their sensory worlds.

Feature Detection in Frogs. A report titled "What the frog's eye tells the frog's brain," published by Lettvin, Maturana, McCulloch, and Pitts (1959), provided the model for interdisciplinary research on visual perception. Each scientist on Lettvin's team at the Massachusetts Institute of Technology had a research specialty—in evolutionary theory, frog anatomy, frog physiology, or frog behavior—which led to their collaboration. Together, they agreed on an experimental procedure. They brought a frog into the lab, anesthetized it, and positioned recording electrodes in the axons of the ganglion cells coursing from the frog's retina into its brain. Next, they showed the unconscious frog objects by dangling them in various portions of its *visual field* (everything the stationary eye can see). Then they measured the action potentials generated in ganglion cells in the frog's retina in response to the visual stimulation.

The researchers found that each ganglion cell had a specific **receptive field**—a portion of the visual field to which the cell responded when it was visually stimulated. After recording from a number of frog retinas, Lettvin and his colleagues concluded that the ganglion cells were **feature detectors** that were sensitive to particular visual features, such as shapes, edges, and movement. Some ganglion cells, for example, responded to the *edges* of objects that *moved* through their receptive field. Others responded best to a small object that either came into their receptive field and stopped or simply moved through it. The point is that the ganglion cells were not just detecting light and dark areas in the frog's visual field; rather, they were "seeing" specific features of objects in the visual field.

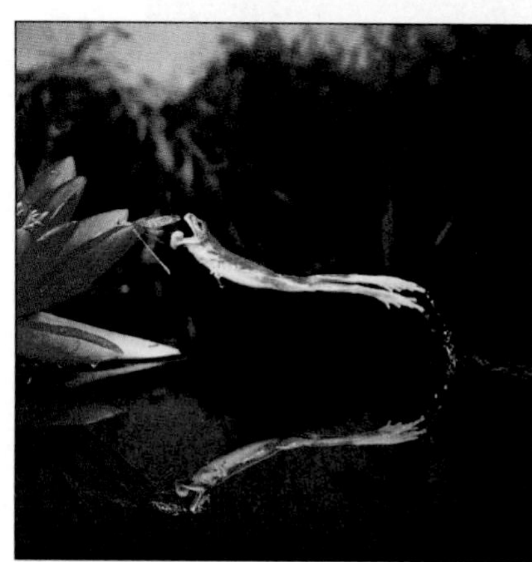

Frogs are reflexive feeders. The movement of tiny objects (such as bugs) across its visual field elicits a tongue flick.

These findings undermined the notion that the retina is involved in sensation, whereas the brain is responsible for perception. Rather, seeing begins in the retina. Furthermore, the organization of the frog's retina suggests that it is designed to see best that part of its environment that is most relevant to its survival. As frog-collecting youngsters throughout history have discovered, frogs don't eat dead flies. Unlike mammals and birds, they do not actively search for food by moving the head and eyes. Rather, a frog assumes a stationary position, with its eyes open. A small moving object that crosses its receptive field elicits a reflexive tongue-flick. *Ribet.* Other feature detectors provide information about the shadows of large objects that move into the frog's visual field and stop. Rather than a tongue flick, the large shadow may elicit a defensive movement. *Plop.*

Feature Detection in Mammals. Similar electrophysiological experiments on cats and monkeys have led to the discovery of what appears to be a common pattern of retinal organization for feature detection in mammals. Figure 8.2 illustrates the feature-detection system in cats and monkeys. In these and other mammals, the ganglion cells in the retina receive input in the form of concentric circles from groups of receptors and bipolar cells.

As Figure 8.2 indicates, a small spot of light landing on one portion of the retina will excite some ganglion cells to fire, but will inhibit others. With careful probing, early experimenters discovered the concentric-circle organization of this pattern (Kuffler, 1953). Small spots of light will summate within the center of the receptive field of an **on-center cell** (see Figure 8.2a). Likewise, a ring of light will maximally stimulate the **off-center cell** (see Figure 8.2b). Light that falls in the *off* areas of both types of cells inhibits firing. Finally, light that totally covers both concentric circles causes very little firing in either type of cell. Instead, it cancels out the separate on- and off-center properties of the ganglion cells.

None of the foregoing, however, tells us anything about the features humans see in their visual world: seldom (if ever) do small spots of white light, or small spots of a particular wavelength, fall on restricted portions of our retinas. How do on-center and off-center receptive fields combine to form complex features of movement, color, and form, such as the image of a jumping green frog, in the visual cortex? The answer to this question begins with cats and monkeys.

receptive field The portion of the visual field to which a cell in the nervous system responds when visually stimulated.

feature detector A visual neuron that is sensitive to a particular visual feature, such as a shape, edges, or movement.

on-center cells Ganglion cells with concentric-circle receptive fields that are excitatory and inhibitory when light falls inside and outside, respectively.

off-center cells Ganglion cells with concentric-circle receptive fields that are inhibitory and excitatory when light falls inside and outside, respectively.

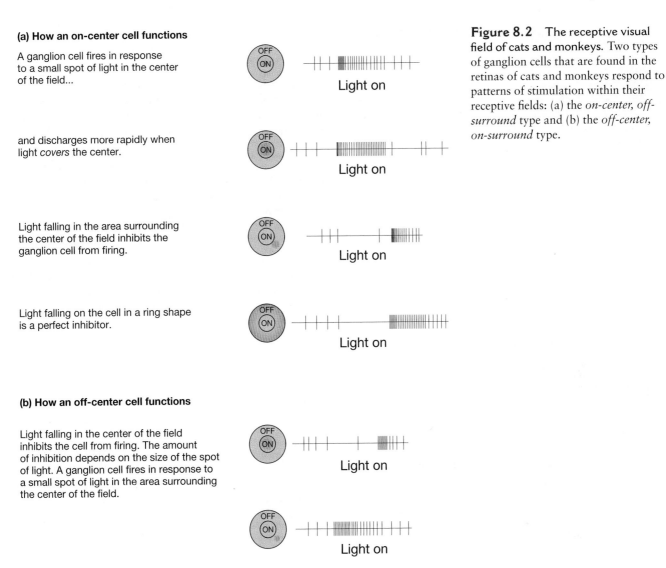

(a) How an on-center cell functions

A ganglion cell fires in response to a small spot of light in the center of the field...

and discharges more rapidly when light *covers* the center.

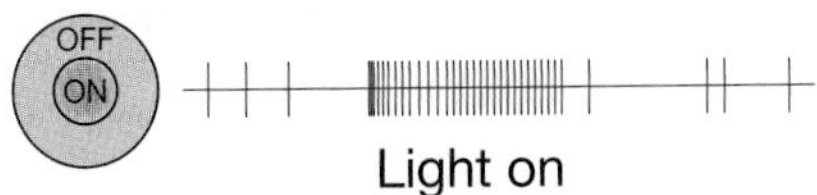

Light falling in the area surrounding the center of the field inhibits the ganglion cell from firing.

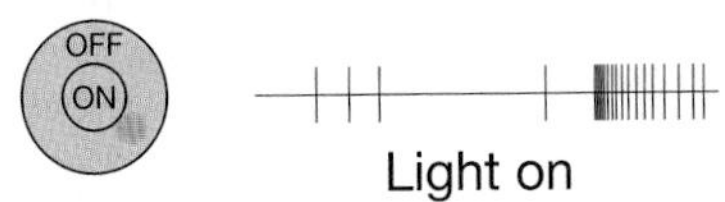

Light falling on the cell in a ring shape is a perfect inhibitor.

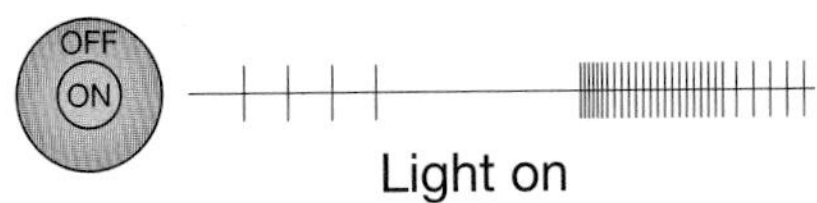

(b) How an off-center cell functions

Light falling in the center of the field inhibits the cell from firing. The amount of inhibition depends on the size of the spot of light. A ganglion cell fires in response to a small spot of light in the area surrounding the center of the field.

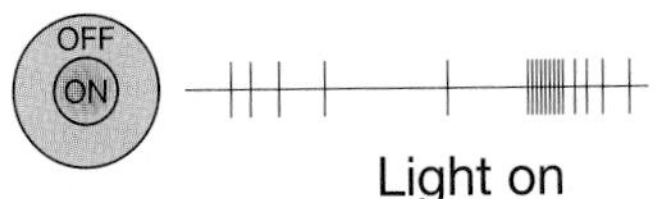

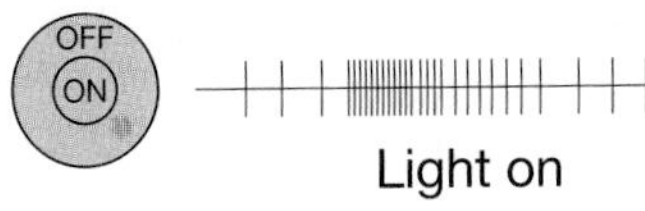

Figure 8.2 The receptive visual field of cats and monkeys. Two types of ganglion cells that are found in the retinas of cats and monkeys respond to patterns of stimulation within their receptive fields: (a) the *on-center, off-surround* type and (b) the *off-center, on-surround* type.

Cortical Processing of Features

Research on cortical processing has been dominated by the more than 35-year-long collaboration of David Hubel and Torsten Wiesel at the Johns Hopkins University hospital. Recently Dr. Hubel described the role that chance played in their investigations. In the early 1950s they were attempting to record the electrical activity of a neuron (cell #3004) in the visual cortex of a cat. They tried stimulating this cell in two ways: by shining a tiny spot of light onto the retina (looking for an on-center field) or bathing in light all but a tiny "black" spot on the retina (looking for an off-center field). Despite hours of searching for the right stimulus, however, they were unsuccessful. Finally the cell responded:

> It seemed that what the cell wanted in order to respond was the faint shadow of the edge of the glass as it crossed a particular part of the animal's retina. After working with that one cell for 9 hours, we finally concluded that the shadow only worked over a restricted range of orientations: when the orientation was right, the cell would respond with a roar of impulses. (David Hubel, quoted in Bear, Conners, & Paradiso, 1996, p. 260)

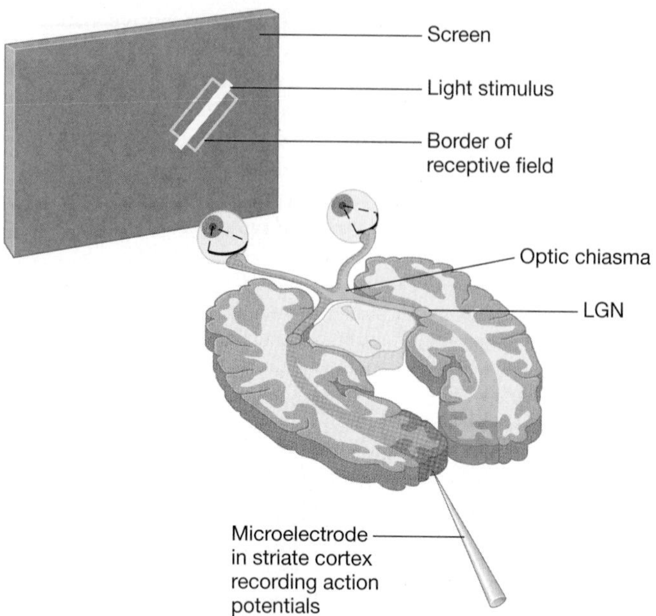

Figure 8.3 **Visual processing in the brain.** A microelectrode can record the feature-detecting properties of cells in a monkey's striate cortex. When an object is shown to a particular part of the monkey's visual field, the action potentials of a cell in the striate cortex increase. *Source:* From NEUROSCIENCE: Exploring the Brain by M. F. Bear, B. W. Connors & M. A. Paradiso. Copyright © 1996. Reprinted by permission of Lippincott Williams & Wilkins.

Subsequently, this Nobel-prize winning research team discovered a variety of *edge detectors* and other feature-detecting cells in the visual cortex of both cats (Hubel & Wiesel, 1962) and monkeys (Hubel & Wiesel, 1977). Figure 8.3 demonstrates the methodology they used to stimulate an animal's eyes and record the reaction of brain cells in the striate cortex. Because of Hubel and Wiesel's work, we have an excellent understanding of what the human eye tells the human brain. But the question remains: How do on- and off-center cells in the retina become edge detectors in the striate cortex?

Figure 8.3 shows a diagonal bar being detected by cells in the striate cortex. The edges of the image—in this case, the edges that define the diagonal bar—stimulate cells in the retina: off-center cells if the edge is dark, or on-center cells if the edge is light. The output of the ganglion cells that are sensitive to these features is then projected to the LGN and the striate cortex. Thus, pattern recognition in mammals is based on (a) stimulation of the on- and off-center cells that detect the edge of the bar and (b) transmission of their output to the LGN and the striate cortex, where (c) neuron firing initiates visual perception of the diagonal bar.

Over time, Hubel and Wiesel investigated the feature-detection capabilities of thousands of cells in various layers of the striate cortex (see Figure 8.4). They found that each layer contains neurons with different feature-detection properties, and that serve different parts of the retina. For example, cell #3004 (just described) was maximally sensitive to the position and orientation of edges (lines) in a strictly defined portion of its receptive field. Such cells are now called **simple cells.** Located in layer IV (see Figure 8.4), cell #3004 had a receptive field that was most sensitive to a dark edge or a slit of light of a particular orientation. Other simple cells are sensitive to the direction of movement across their receptive fields. An edge moving from top to bottom of the receptive field, for

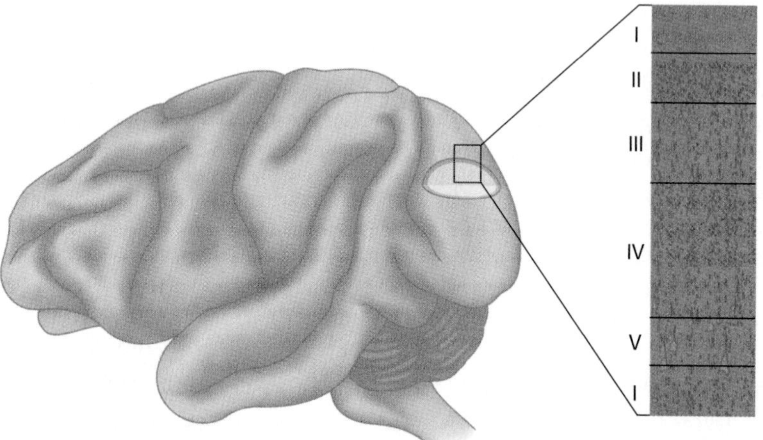

Figure 8.4 **Layers of the striate cortex.** The striate, or visual, cortex, is a thin (2 millimeters, or one-twelfth of an inch), multilayered structure. Neuroscientists have designated each cell layer with Roman numerals and letters. Cells with feature-detecting properties are found primarily in layers III and IV. *Source:* From NEUROSCIENCE: Exploring the Brain by M. F. Bear, B. W. Connors, & M. A. Paradiso. Copyright © 1996. Reprinted by permission of Lippincott Williams & Wilkins.

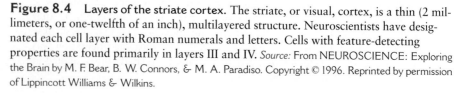

simple cell A neuron in the striate cortex that is maximally sensitive to the position and orientation of edges (lines) in the receptive field.

example, might generate a nerve impulse, but the same stimulus moving from bottom to top might not. Some simple cells, then, seem to analyze an object's motion.

Hubel and Wiesel labeled other cortical neurons **complex cells**, because they were more difficult to analyze than simple cells. A simple cell has a fairly small receptive field; it might respond to any number of edges, but only within a few degrees of orientation. A complex cell, in contrast, has a larger receptive field and will respond to an exactly oriented angle even when it is presented at several places within the field. Some complex cells are also more sensitive than simple cells to the wavelength of the image in their receptive fields. Finally, some complex cells are binocular; that is, they respond to the same image detected simultaneously by both eyes.

INTERIM SUMMARY

1. The sensory process of vision can best be understood as a ***bottom-up process*** attributable to retinal receptors that provide information about color, shape, and movement. The perceptual processes of vision derive from a ***top-down process*** in which other parts of the brain allow an object to be perceived as a whole.
2. Ganglion cells in the retina and neurons in the LGN are both called ***feature detectors,*** because their ***receptive fields*** are sensitive to certain patterns of stimulation on the retina. Some of the features they detect include size, movement, angle of orientation, and position on the retina.
3. In cats, monkeys, and humans, physical features are detected by ***on-center*** and ***off-center cells.*** Named for their concentric-circle organization, these cells are either excited or inhibited when a light shines on their center.
4. The multilayered striate cortex receives retinotopic projections from the LGN. Researchers Hubel and Wiesel demonstrated that ***simple cells*** in the striate cortex respond to edges and angles of orientation, providing the basis for pattern recognition in mammals.
5. ***Complex cells*** have larger receptive fields than simple cells. They are sensitive to particular wavelengths and can process input from both eyes simultaneously.

For Further Thought

1. Are you bothered by the fact that vision can be studied by showing pictures to unconscious animals and recording the response of neurons in their retinas and brains? Does this methodology address bottom-up or top-down processing?
2. Recall the research of Konrad Lorenz, whose newly hatched goslings followed the first thing they saw moving (page 90). Lorenz thought that such fixed action patterns were triggered by sign stimuli. Can you relate Lorenz's concept of an innate releasing mechanism (a brain mechanism that is sensitive to a sign stimulus) to the idea that some animals are born with functional feature detectors?

Feature detectors with innate releasing mechanisms, Chapter 3, p. 90

DEPTH PERCEPTION, PERCEPTUAL CONSTANCIES, AND ILLUSIONS

Pattern recognition, as important as it is, cannot account for the richness of our visual experience. Images land on our two-dimensional retinas, yet our normal visual experience is of depth as well as height and breadth. Certainly we do not see the photograph of a human face as a flat, two-dimensional image; nor when comparing a wallet-sized photo with an 8 × 10 do we perceive the smaller one as a child and the larger one as an adult. Rather, we adjust the sizes to fit our expectations, a phenomenon called a perceptual constancy. Perception, then, is true to

complex cell A neuron in the striate cortex that is sensitive to the position and orientation of edges (or lines) *anywhere* within the receptive field.

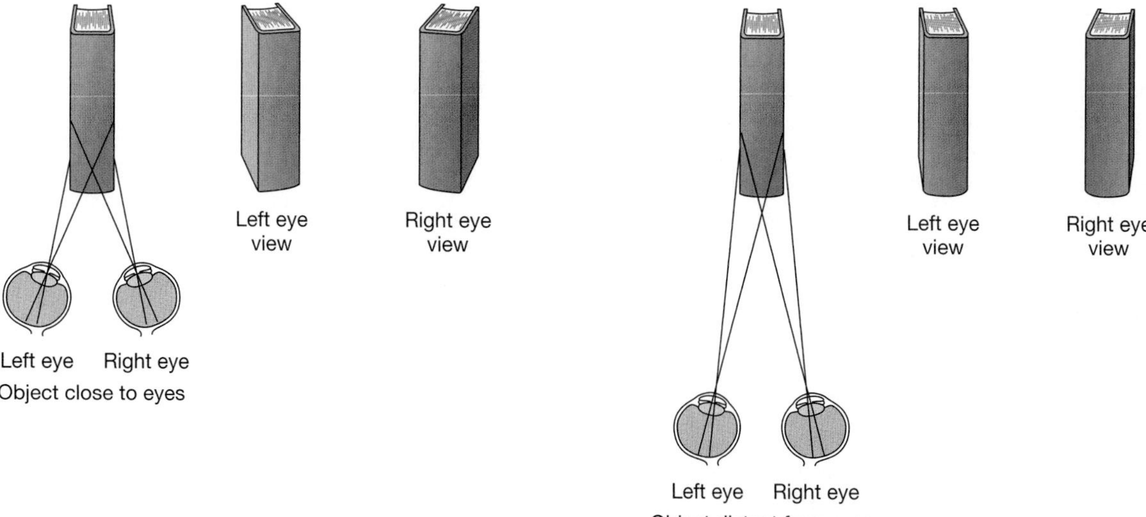

Figure 8.5 Depth perception and retinal disparity cues. The angle of light reflecting off nearby objects (left) is greater than the angle of light reflecting off far-away objects (right). Thus, a three-dimensional object appears noticeably different when viewed from different distances. *Source:* After Gray, p. 310.

the world, not to the image on our retinas. And yet our eyes *can* play tricks on us, so that the study of illusions helps us to better understand normal perceptual processes.

Depth Perception

Depth perception arises from a combination of cues, which when added together, create the illusion of three dimensions. For convenience, we can divide these cues into binocular cues, which involve both eyes, and monocular cues, which depend on just one eye. There are several types of each.

Binocular Cue of Retinal Disparity. As a child, you may have discovered the slightly different views of the world you see through each eye. If you hold a finger upright 5 or 6 inches in front of your eyes and close first one eye and then the other, you'll see that the finger appears to move from one side to the other. That's because the retina in each eye views the finger from a slightly different angle. This difference in the view from each eye, which arises from the distance between the two retinas, is called **retinal disparity**.

You can demonstrate retinal disparity in another way by holding the tips of both index fingers together 5 or 6 inches in front of your eyes. Now look past your fingers and focus across the room. The two slightly disparate views will produce a "third finger" between the other two. If you slowly pull your fingers apart, the third finger will float between them. Retinal disparity decreases as distance increases; it is not a useful cue when focusing on far distant objects.

Retinal disparity provides an important depth cue. The angle of light reflecting off a nearby object is different from the angle of light reflecting off a far-away object. Figure 8.5 shows how the two different angles can serve as a depth cue. When impulses from the ganglion cells of each retina travel through the LGN to the striate cortex and beyond, the two slightly different images merge. The physiological (and psychological) fusion of the two images produces the perception of depth.

retinal disparity The difference in the view from each of two eyes, which provides a binocular cue for depth perception.

The monocular depth cues of interposition, relative size, and linear perspective add to the illusion of depth in this two-dimensional photo of the interior of the Crystal Palace, London.

Georges Seurat's, (French, 1859–1891) *A Sunday Afternoon on the Island of La Grande Jatte-1884,* 1884–86. Oil on canvas, 207.6 × 308 cm. Helen Birch Bartlett Memorial Collection, 1926.224. Photograph © 2001 The Art Institute of Chicago. All Rights Reserved.

Binocular Cue of Convergence. Another binocular depth cue has to do with the position of your eye muscles. Your two eyes provide different sensations when you focus on a nearby object compared to a far-away object. (You can demonstrate this phenomenon by noticing the discomfort you feel when you cross your eyes.) The inward turning of the eyes to focus on nearby objects is called **convergence.** Like retinal disparity cues, convergence cues are greatest for nearby objects, because the eyes turn in the most when focusing on them. We are not normally aware of either cue; both promote depth perception at an unconscious level.

Monocular Cues of Interposition, Relative Size, and Linear Perspective. Monocular depth cues work in conjunction with binocular cues, but their effects do not depend on seeing with two eyes. Interposition is a cue to the relative depth of two or more objects. For example, in viewing the photograph of the interior of the old Crystal Palace in London (above, left), you receive the one-eyed cue that the fountain is slightly farther away than the people in the foreground, because the people partially obscure the fountain. That is, the people are interposed between you (the viewer) and the fountain.

Several monocular cues can work together, as the photograph of the Crystal Palace demonstrates. An object casts a smaller image on the retina when viewed at a distance then when seen close up. The *relative size* of an image on the retina, then, is a monocular depth cue. In the picture of the Crystal Palace, note that the human figures in the foreground are larger than the human figures in the background. The picture also shows the overhead glass ceiling (with the larger panes of glass in the front) converging toward a "disappearing point" in the distance. The use of converging lines to represent depth, or **linear perspective,** is another monocular cue.

convergence A binocular depth cue that results when the eyes turn inward to see nearby objects.

linear perspective A scene containing converging lines, which provides a monocular cue for depth perception.

Monocular Cues of Relative Clarity and Texture Gradient. Within the past thousand years or so, painters have learned to use other monocular cues to convey depth on a two-dimensional surface. Georges Seurat's *A Sunday Afternoon on the Island of La Grande Jatte* (above, right) illustrates two such cues, relative clarity and texture gradient. Note that the figures in the foreground are sharper than those in the background. Because visual acuity decreases with distance, Seurat painted progressively fewer details in the trees, people, and shadows in the background. Note too that in comparison to the woman in red (at the focal point in the center of the painting), the colors of the background are less brilliant. Through the *relative clarity* of details, the painter created the illusion of depth.

Seurat's painting is an example of a style of painting called *pointilism*, in which dots of light, color, and texture are used to convey form and depth. Pointilists construct images in the same way that they are seen: the discrete dots (points) of color that they paint are analogous to the individual photons of light that stimulate the cones and rods. Together, the dots combine to create a *texture gradient* such that the objects nearest the viewer are sharper than those at a distance. The overall effect conveys depth.

Monocular Cue of Relative Motion. Another monocular cue, *relative motion*, uses the speed at which images move across the retina as a distance cue. For example, the image of a ball that has just been hit by a batter zooms across the visual fields of nearby infielders, but moves more slowly across the visual field of an outfielder. Relative motion, then, can be used to judge distance. The viewer need not remain stationary to use this depth cue. If you see that the image of the car traveling in front of you is getting larger, it doesn't matter whether it is slowing down or you are speeding up. You use the cue of relative motion to respond appropriately and step on the brake.

Table 8.1 summarizes the binocular and monocular depth cues. Pick out an object within your field of vision and see how many of the cues you can use to describe why you are seeing the object "in depth."

Perceptual Constancies

Recall that the size of the image of a baseball on an outfielder's retina changes as the ball comes closer, and that the outfielder can use that cue to estimate the ball's distance. Likewise, a driver can use the image of a car on the retina to estimate the car's distance. Although these retinal cues help us to estimate depth, at the same time they pose a challenge to our perception of size.

Size Constancy. Look again at Seurat's painting (page 277); notice the child dressed in white (next to the woman with the red umbrella). The child casts a larger image on your retina than the adults in the background, yet you do

Table 8.1 Depth Cues

BINOCULAR CUES	
Retinal disparity	The slightly different images from each eye combine to create a three-dimensional view.
Convergence	The eyes must turn in more to see close objects than distant objects, producing an unconscious muscular sensation.
MONOCULAR CUES	
Interposition	Objects "in front" obscure the view of objects behind.
Relative size	Nearby objects cast a larger image on the retina than distant objects.
Linear perspective	Lines converging on an artificial horizon convey distance.
Relative clarity	Nearby objects appear clearer than distant objects.
Texture gradient	Detailed textures convey the appearance of closeness; hazy textures, the appearance of distance.
Relative motion	Nearby objects seem to move more quickly than distant objects.

not interpret their images as *large child* and *small adults*. Rather, your perception of the size of an object remains constant no matter what the image's size. **Size constancy** is the tendency to see same-sized figures despite changes in retinal size. That is, when distance varies, changes in retinal size do not produce changes in perceived size. Size constancy is one example of what are known as the *perceptual constancies*. Let's look at some others.

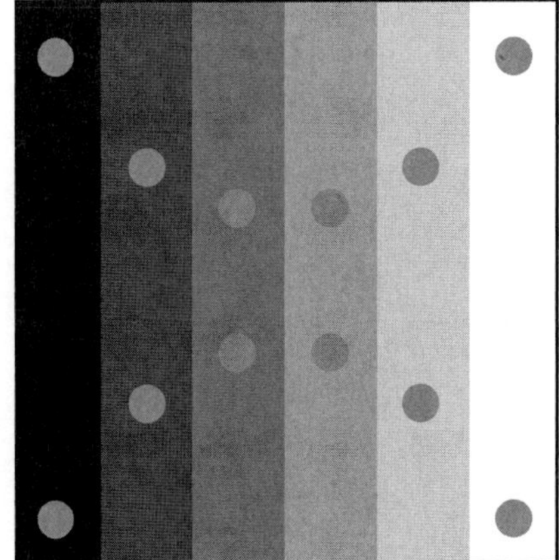

Figure 8.6a Brightness Contrast. These gray circles are identical but appear differently against lighter and darker backgrounds.

Shape Constancy. The tendency to see an object as being of the same shape despite a change in its retinal image, called **shape constancy**, is another example of a perceptual constancy. Look again at the books in Figure 8.5. No matter what image lands on the retina, a book remains rectangular in appearance. Another example of shape constancy is the door near where you are studying. Unless you are standing *exactly* in front of it, the image that lands on your retina will not be a perfect rectangle. A swinging door creates a variety of trapezoidal images on your retina, but you still interpret the door as being rectangular.

Lightness Constancy. Books and doors have brightness and color as well as size and shape. **Lightness constancy** refers to the tendency to see an object as being the same color, even under varying light intensities. In dim light as well as very bright light, a yellow book looks yellow, and a blue book looks blue.

You can demonstrate lightness constancy by looking at Seurat's painting first in the bright light of a reading lamp, and then in relative darkness. Although you may be struck by the differences in the brightness of its colors under these two conditions, you can probably imagine that if you were viewing this painting outside, as the sun was setting, the change in its appearance would not be dramatic or even noticeable. One way to think about lightness constancy, then, is to think of the "lightness" of an object—say, a painting or a book—in terms of its relationship to the lightness of objects around it. As the general illumination dims, both the book and the objects making up its background reflect less light. The ratio of figure light to background light remains constant. Lightness constancy occurs because of a change in illumination over the entire retina.

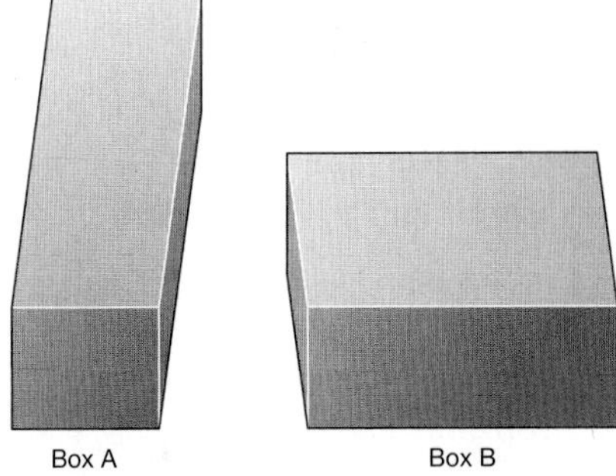

Figure 8.6b A shape illusion. Two identical surfaces appear to be different in shape when different details are added, suggesting that they are box tops being viewed from different angles. Misleading depth perception cues cause this illusion.

Brightness Contrast. A difference in illumination over parts of the retina can produce some surprising results. Figure 8.6a demonstrates **brightness contrast,** in which two objects are perceived to differ in brightness because of their contrast with their backgrounds. In this figure, identical gray circles appear to differ in color due to their vastly different backgrounds. At the retinal level, inhibitory processes in the adjacent receptors enhance the edges of the circles. These enhanced edges are the features that mislead us into thinking that the circles are different shades of gray (Shapley, 1986). This perceptual error, then, can be attributed to bottom-up processing.

When racing down a busy street on your bicycle, how do you make sense of the fleeting images that whisk across your retinas? Unlike a cat's view, which changes color when the size of the image on the retina increases or decreases, the human's visual world is remarkably constant. Colors, sizes, shapes, and lightness appear to be roughly the same even when they are not. Taken together, size, shape, and lightness constancy seem to reflect top-down processing. You interpret the images you see in terms of learned expectancies derived from previous bike rides.

size constancy The tendency to see a figure as being the same size, despite changes in its retinal size.

shape constancy The tendency to see a form as unchanging, despite changes in its retinal image.

lightness constancy The tendency to see an object as being the same, even under varying light intensities.

brightness contrast The perception of a difference in brightness reflected from two different areas of the visual field.

Illusions and Ambiguous Figures

Figure 8.6 shows two figures that together violate shape constancy. Because of past experience in viewing a variety of boxes from a limitless number of angles, we have developed expectations about size, even when size cues are absent. In

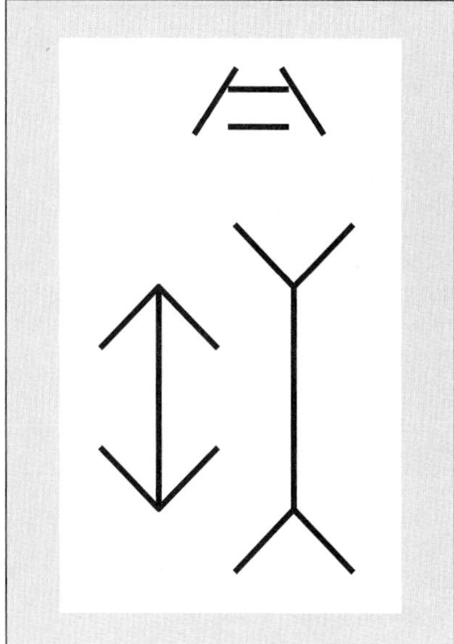

Figure 8.7 Two depth illusions. In both these drawings, two identical lines appear to differ in length. In the Ponzo illusion (top), a linear perspective depth cue suggests that the line on top is longer than the one on the bottom. In the Mueller-Lyer illusion (bottom), the line on the right appears longer than the one on the left, again because of depth cues.

Figure 8.6b, misleading depth cues cause us to perceive the "tops" of each box to be of different sizes, yet they are identical in surface area. (Recall a sentence from the opening of this chapter, "Seeing is believing." I have measured these two tops on more than one occasion and still can't see—or believe—that they are the same size!)

An **illusion** is a false perception that can arise for several reasons—for example, when information from the striate feature detectors (bottom-up processing) conflicts with a cognitive expectation (top-down processing). The gray circles in the Figure 8.6a appear to differ in color because of retinal mechanisms. But retinal feature detectors do not cause the box illusion in Figure 8.6b. Apparently, we unconsciously infer that the two tops are different in shape because of the near absence of a depth cue when the left box is viewed almost from overhead.

The Ponzo Illusion. Figure 8.7 (top) shows the classic *Ponzo illusion;* the photograph on this page, a real-life application of it. In this illusion, two horizontal lines appear to be of unequal length, even though they are actually the same length. The top line appears to be longer than the bottom one because the converging lines on either side of it provide a linear perspective depth cue suggesting that the top of the figure is further away than the bottom. Making the horizontal lines vertical destroys the illusion (Schiffman & Thompson, 1978).

The pickup truck parked on the railroad tracks creates a similar illusion. In this photo, the bottom railroad tie is obviously closer to the viewer than the top one. From experience, we know that the lengths of the pickup truck and the railroad ties are fixed by size constancy. Yet when asked to match the apparent length of the truck with the length of one of the railroad ties, most people pick the fourth tie from the bottom. In this example, linear perspective depth perception cues interact with size constancy cues to create a very powerful illusion.

The Mueller-Lyer Illusion. In the *Mueller-Lyer illusion* (Figure 8.7, bottom), two vertical lines appear to be of different lengths. Once again, however, they are the same length. As in the Ponzo illusion, though each casts the same size

Which railroad tie is the same length as the pickup truck? Answer: Although the fourth railroad tie from the bottom may appear to match the length of the truck, all are, of course, the same length.

illusion A false perception.

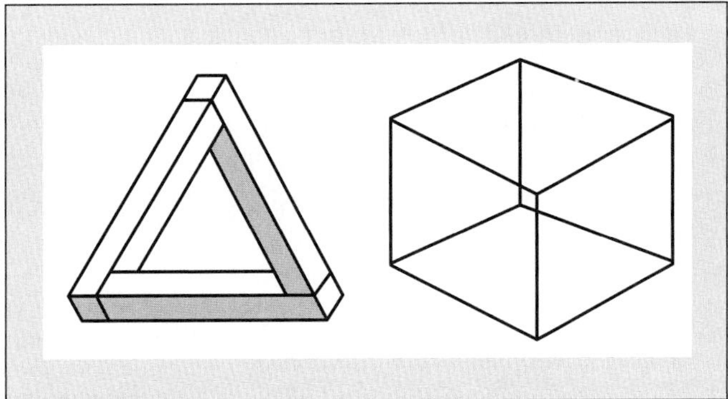

Figure 8.8 Visually ambiguous figures. The triangle on the left is not as simple as it appears to be. The corners are accurately drawn, but the rules whereby a surface is enclosed have been violated. The drawing on the right, called a Necker cube, represents a three-dimensional object. But not enough information has been provided for the viewer to determine the perspective from which the cube is drawn.

image on the retina, because of distance cues one appears to be longer than the other. Note that the building in the photograph on this page has the same shape as the lines in the figure. Experience with the angles produced by the corners of buildings may explain why you do not perceive the building's walls to be of different heights at different corners.

Experience with the depth of buildings may help to explain why this real-life version of the Mueller-Lyer illusion does not confuse us.

Ambiguous Figures. Consider next the triangular drawing displayed on the left side of Figure 8.8. Surely this simple structure could easily be perceived by the activity of a few edge detectors in the striate cortex? But look more closely: the figure is an illusion, known as an *impossible figure*. Here a conflict exists between information coming from the striate feature detectors and our cognitive expectations. Because of prior experience, we tend to make perceptual *hypotheses* about the images that fall on our retinas (Day, 1984). One way to think about these cognitive expectations is to consider that a normal triangle has conditioned stimulus (CS) properties that signal other learned associations.

The drawing on the right side of Figure 8.8 is called a *Necker cube*. If you stare at this hollow cube long enough, you will see it from two different perspectives. The Necker cube is a perceptually ambiguous figure whose meaning or pattern changes even though the input sensed by the edge detectors in the striate cortex presumably does not. The firing of neurons in the striate cortex yields only relatively simple sensory information, but your hypothesis that the image is just another hollow cube in one or another position is a perception based on your life experience.

To give another example, the retinal image of an injured Dalmatian may appear the same to different people, but it means something different to the dog's owner, to the veterinarian who treats the dog, and to the person who inadvertently injured the dog. The signal value of the dog (the conditioned stimulus) is different for each of these people, because of their different experiences with it. Bottom-up processing may be the same for each person, but top-down processing is different.

LINK

Perception as learned associations, Chapter 6, p. 190

INTERIM SUMMARY

1. Both *binocular* and *monocular* cues mediate *depth perception*. Binocular depth cues include ***retinal disparity*** and ***convergence***.
2. Monocular depth cues in perception include *interposition, relative size,* ***linear perspective,*** *relative clarity, texture gradient,* and *relative motion*.

3. ***Size, shape,*** and ***lightness constancies*** occur when we perceive known objects as being of the same size, shape, or lightness, even though their retinal images change at different viewing angles and under different lighting conditions. All are examples of *perceptual constancies.*
4. ***Brightness contrast*** is the perception of a difference in brightness between two objects because of their contrast with different backgrounds. Brightness contrast results from bottom-up processing.
5. ***Illusions*** are false perceptions. Two classic illusions, the *Ponzo illusion* and the *Mueller-Lyer illusion,* occur in part because of misinterpreted depth cues.

For Further Thought

1. How many of the depth perception cues in Table 8.1 are learned and how many are innate? Can you make the argument that the redundancy of depth perception cues reflects the demands of the primate's ecological niche?
2. Are illusions maladaptive?

CONSCIOUS AND UNCONSCIOUS PROCESSES IN PERCEPTION

Seeing is believing and understanding as well as the sensing of images that land on our retinas. From the past several decades of research, an intriguing story has emerged of a brain that can see both consciously and unconsciously. One example of unconscious seeing, subliminal perception, was described in the last chapter. This section connects the process of perception to attention, and to conscious and unconscious mental processes. Here we'll gain further insight into Dr. P., the patient whose visual problems caused him to confuse his foot with his shoe.

The Phenomenon of Blindsight

During surgery at the National Hospital in London in 1973, a 33-year-old Englishman had a large portion of his striate cortex removed. Known to researchers by his initials, D.B., he has since become famous because of what he sees but says he can't see. At age 14, D.B. suffered from visual problems and migraine headaches caused by malformed blood vessels in the right side of his occipital lobe—that is, in his striate cortex (see Figure 8.3). In removing the blood vessels and brain tissue that caused the problems, surgeons effectively destroyed the destination points of the LGN fibers serving the left temporal field of both eyes. As a result of the surgery, D.B. is now partially blind. Figure 8.9 shows the results of two vision tests he took, one conducted 8 months after the operation and the other about 4 years later.

At first, D.B. had a severe *hemianopia*: he could see only the right visual fields in each eye, and was effectively blind on the left side. Further testing by Larry Weiskrantz, an experimental psychologist at Oxford, and his colleagues revealed that D.B. could in fact detect images that were projected onto his left field of vision. However, D.B. repeatedly denied that he could see them. For example, if a stick in a horizontal or vertical position was shown to his blind field, he would say he couldn't see it. But when the experimenter asked D.B. to guess

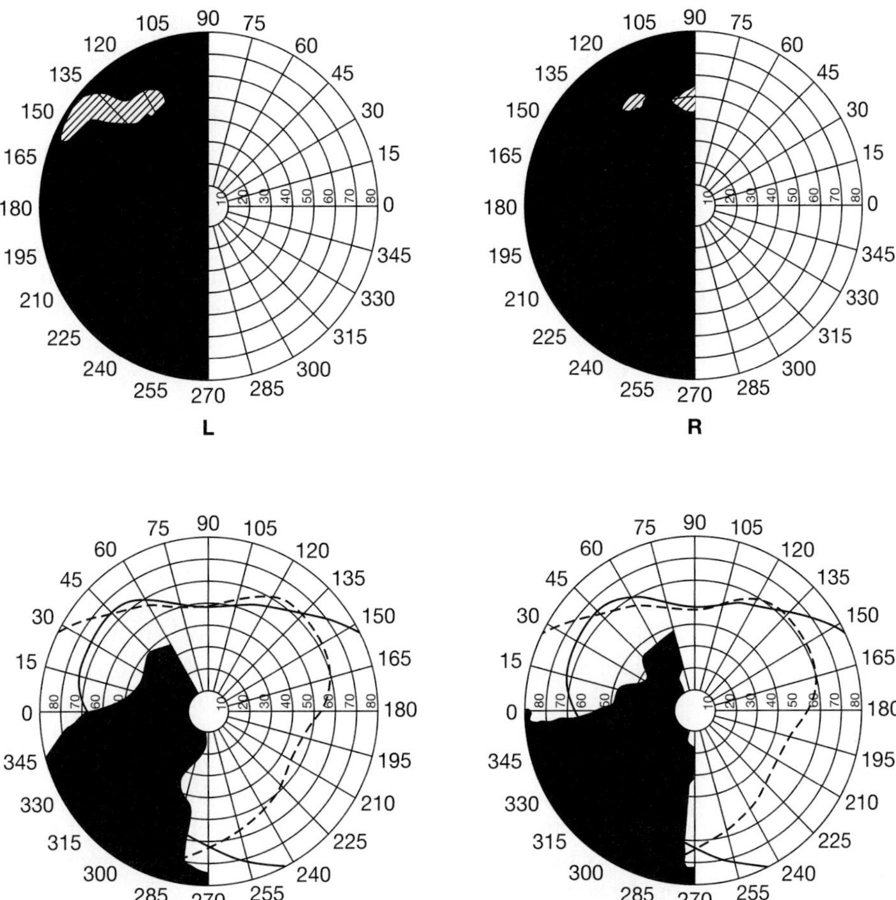

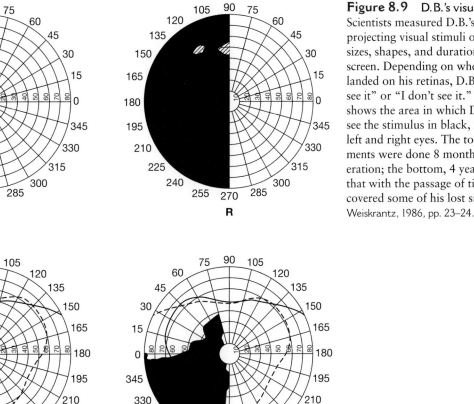

Figure 8.9 D.B.'s visual fields. Scientists measured D.B.'s vision by projecting visual stimuli of varying sizes, shapes, and durations onto a screen. Depending on where the image landed on his retinas, D.B. reported "I see it" or "I don't see it." This figure shows the area in which D.B. could *not* see the stimulus in black, for both the left and right eyes. The top measurements were done 8 months after the operation; the bottom, 4 years after. Note that with the passage of time, D.B. recovered some of his lost sight. *Source:* Weiskrantz, 1986, pp. 23–24.

whether the stick was in a vertical or horizontal position, D.B. seldom made an error. When Weiskrantz informed D.B. that he could detect the difference between the horizontal and the vertical stick, D.B. expressed surprise.

Weiskrantz and his colleagues called this phenomenon of seeing without conscious awareness **blindsight.** Blindsight has been studied under laboratory conditions in another patient, G.Y., who also had striate cortex damage. Figure 8.10 reveals the dissociation between G.Y.'s visual awareness of a moving spot of light and his performance in detecting it in a forced-choice test. Like D.B., this subject performed consistently and with great accuracy on a vision test in which he reported seeing nothing.

The Role of the Striate Cortex. Recall the visual aberrations of split-brain subjects, described in Chapter 4 (see page 133). Split-brain subjects showed a reduced awareness of images that were briefly flashed in the temporal portions of their right visual fields (the part that projects to the area of the visual cortex, which was removed from D.B.'s brain). Because language is located primarily in the left hemisphere of the brain, split-brain subjects could not describe what they were seeing in their right visual fields. Thus, a nude picture flashed to the nonverbal right hemisphere provoked chuckling (indicating both detection and recognition), though the subject denied seeing anything. Like the split-brain subjects, D.B. and G.Y. were unable to comment on *what* they saw, but indicated nonverbally that they did see *something*. The difference, then, is that with the striate cortex intact, the split-brain subjects consciously saw the nude, whereas with the

blindsight Seeing without awareness.

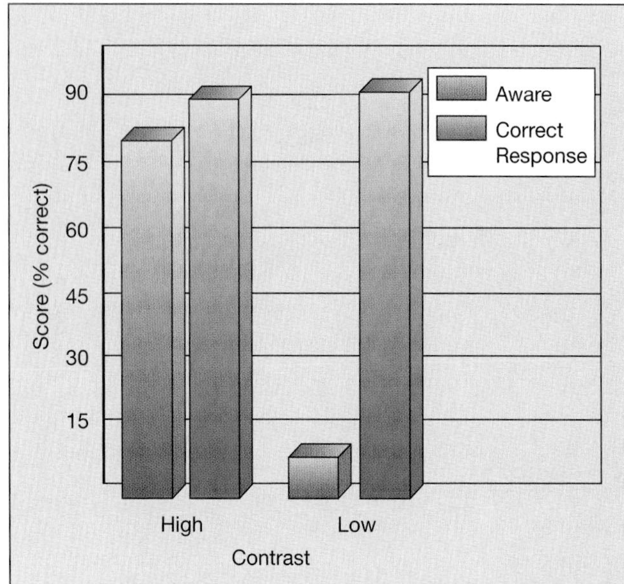

Figure 8.10 Blindsight in a blind subject. A blind subject called G.Y. was forced to guess whether a spot of light moved horizontally across his field of vision and to indicate whether he was aware of it. When the contrast between the spot of light and its background was high, G.Y. detected "something" (though not the normal sensation of sight) and correctly specified the direction of its movement. When the contrast between the spot and its background was low, G.Y. was unaware of its presence, but continued to report the direction of its movement accurately. *Source:* Adapted from Weiskrantz, Barbur, & Sahraie, 1995.

striate cortex removed, D.B. and G.Y. unconsciously saw the stick and moving spot of light. From these findings we can conclude that the striate cortex is responsible for conscious seeing (Weiskrantz, 1986, 1997; Weiskrantz, Barbur, & Sahraie, 1995). Subsequent work with several other patients with a damaged striate cortex, also using the forced-choice technique, has demonstrated an ability to detect the direction of a moving stimulus in the blind visual field (Azzopardi & Cowey, 2001). The question shifts, then, to understanding what parts of the brain are responsible for unconscious perception, such as blindsight, subliminal perception, and other examples of seeing without awareness.

Blindsight in Normally Sighted Subjects. That emotion and other unconscious factors can influence visual perception raises the possibility that normally sighted individuals might exhibit blindsight. After all, no one thought of asking what blind people could see until researchers asked them to guess! In another clever experiment conducted at Cal Tech in 1995, F. Christopher Kolb and Jochen Braun used subliminal techniques and blindsight methodology to test normally sighted subjects. Each subject viewed a computer screen on which randomly moving dots gave the appearance of one transparent surface sliding over the other (see Figure 8.11). This one-directional movement masked a movement in the opposite direction (shown in the upper left quadrant in Figure 8.11), which could be positioned in one of four areas on the screen.

On each trial, subjects guessed in which of the four quadrants the opposite motion appeared and rated their confidence in their choices. Under some conditions, different rates of movement would make the opposite motion of the target image "pop-out" more easily. On those occasions, subjects could consciously see the moving figure against the background. The researchers found that even when subjects reported not being able to see the target stimulus, they could guess its correct location about 75 percent of the time (Kolb & Braun, 1995). As with D.B., they documented a nearly complete dissociation between the subjects' performance (good) and their conscious visual perception (lacking) over a broad range of stimulus conditions.

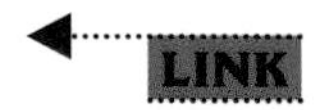

Seeing in blindsight and split-brain subjects, Chapter 4, p. 133

Perception and emotion, Chapter 5, p. 171

Seeing with the Whole Brain

The subjects who experienced subliminal perception and blindsight in Kolb and Braun's experiments were *not* brain damaged. Their ability to see unconsciously must have been mediated by parts of the brain other than the striate cortex. No fewer than eight separate nerve tracts connect the retina to the nonconscious parts of the brain. Researchers now know that some of these—the 150,000 fibers that project to the superior colliculus, in particular—are responsible for unconscious seeing. Let's look briefly at some others.

Parallel Processing of Visual Information. Research on blindsight and subliminal perception has opened up an entirely new way to think about what we see. Scientists now understand that seeing involves the integration of separate visual systems located in separate parts of the brain, each of which contributes to the overall picture. Indeed, as much as *40 percent of the entire cerebral cortex* is devoted to seeing—an indication of the relative importance of sight in natural selection.

Another part of the brain that contributes to seeing is the **extrastriate cortex**, the vision-related cortical material located near the striate cortex. Damage to the extrastriate cortex produces an incredible array of visual deficits. From the study of these clinical defects, as well as from hundreds of experiments on monkeys, a picture of how we normally see has emerged. This story is filled with complexities, because seeing is accomplished by the integration of both conscious and unconscious *parallel visual pathways*.

For instance, the integration of form, depth, motion, and color into a meaningful visual pattern is accomplished through independent visual pathways from the retina to the LGN, the striate cortex, and the extrastriate cortex, and from there to the temporal and parietal lobes. Figure 8.12 is a simplified representation of these pathways. In general, two main types of information from the retina, where the image is and what it is, are processed simultaneously and in parallel. Stage 1 is the visual stimulus in the physical world (see the figure). In stages 2, 3, and 4, ganglion cells from the rods and cones in the retina carry information through the LGN to the striate cortex, the first cortical area for processing vision. Further processing is accomplished in

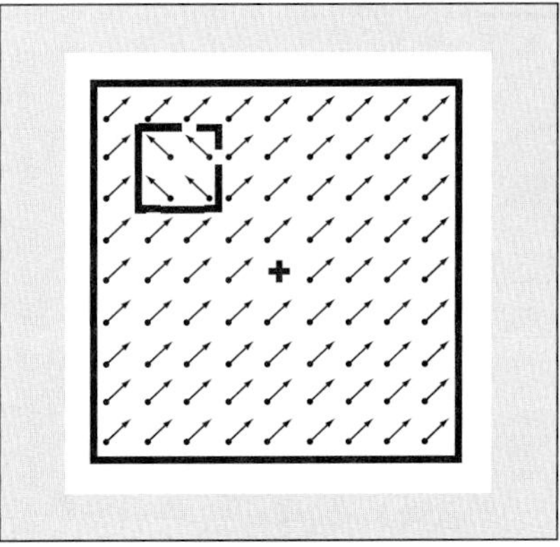

Figure 8.11 Blindsight in sighted subjects. Sighted subjects were asked to view a computer screen with a moving visual display and to guess in which quadrant a reverse movement appeared (see the arrows in the box at the upper left). Though the subjects could not consciously see the reverse movement, they could guess its direction with a high degree of accuracy. *Source:* "Blindsight in Normal Observers" by F. C. Kolb and J. Braun in *Nature*, Volume 377, (1995), pp. 336-338. Copyright © 1995. Reprinted by permission of *Nature*.

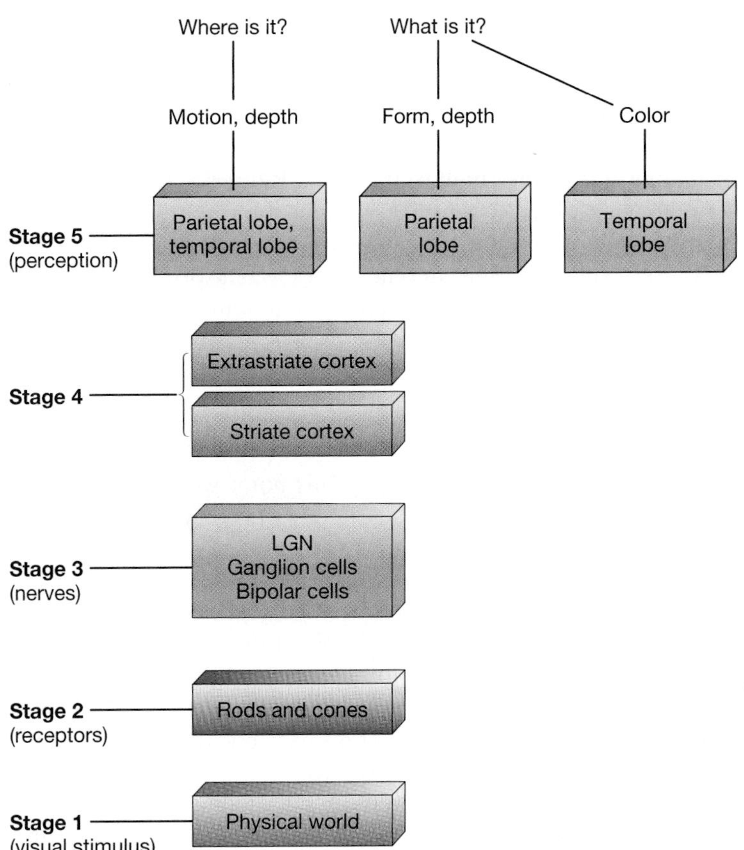

Figure 8.12 The five stages of seeing. In stage 1 of seeing, a visual stimulus originates in the physical world. In stage 2, the rods and cones in the retina transduce the stimulus into nervous energy. Independent nerve pathways (stage 3) connect these receptors to the striate and extrastriate cortex (stage 4), resulting in a perception of the world in the parietal and temporal lobes (stage 5). *Source:* From ESSENTIALS OF NEURAL SCIENCE AND BEHAVIOR by E. R. Kandel, J. H. Schwartz, and T. M. Jessell. Copyright © 1995. Reprinted by permission of The McGraw-Hill Companies.

extrastriate cortex A vision-related area of the cortex located around the striate cortex.

the extrastriate cortex. Vision researchers think they have identified four different modules in the extrastriate cortex that process color, form, movement, and combinations of those features.

How do researchers know what each of these areas of the brain contributes to the visual experience? Three different methodologies have helped them to map these areas: MRI and PET scans, studies of feature detection in monkeys, and clinical observations of humans who have suffered cerebral-vascular accidents. To illustrate, we will examine the cases of several individuals with unusual visual problems. Some suffered damage to the extrastriate cortex; others, damage to the temporal lobe.

Damage to the Extrastriate Cortex. The first case concerns a person who sustained brain damage after having an automobile accident. This man complained of visual problems that within a short time left him completely color blind (Sacks, 1995). He could still see form, motion, and depth, and he understood and could talk about what he could see. An artist, he painted the watercolor rendering of the boat on page 245 (right-hand panel) after losing his color vision. The question is, what part of his brain accounted for his deficit? Neurologists who studied this patient concluded that he had suffered restricted damage to a discrete area in the extrastriate cortex. What was striking in this case was the complete absence of color vision in a human who had intact cones, retinal ganglion cells, LGN, striate cortex, and most of the extrastriate cortex, as well as functioning temporal and parietal lobes!

Neurologists and vision researchers have studied another person who could see everything except moving objects (Zihl, Cramon, & Mai, 1983). She sought medical help when she could no longer see cars moving along the street or people moving from one side of the room to the other. Rather, a visual target would appear first in one place, then in another, without the smooth movement that normally connects such an action. Each visual event, no doubt, was a frightening surprise. Even pouring the right amount of tea was a problem, because the tea appeared to be stationary between pot and cup. Researchers believe that another part of the extrastriate cortex was likely to have been damaged in this patient; recordings from this same brain area in monkeys indicate that neurons there respond to movement.

Damage to the Temporal Lobe. To this point we have discussed the role of both the striate and the extrastriate cortex in seeing. Stage 5 in Figure 8.12 indicates that neurons in both the temporal and parietal lobes are also involved in seeing. What are their roles? In his book *The Man Who Mistook His Wife for a Hat*, the neurologist Oliver Sacks described a patient who had suffered a stroke in a portion of his temporal lobe. The book's title comes from an incident in which the patient, an otherwise mentally competent professional, tried to retrieve his hat from a coatrack near where his wife was standing. Missing his target, he attempted to lift his wife's head instead of his hat. Yes, this was Dr. P., the patient you were introduced to in the opening vignette.

The part of the brain that allowed Dr. P. to attach meaning to what he was seeing—his temporal lobe—had been damaged, resulting in incredibly debilitating visual confusions called **visual agnosias**. Each object this patient looked at had become disconnected from its meaning. Perhaps because hats go on top of heads, he confused a head with a hat, and because shoes go on feet, he confused a foot with a shoe. At any rate, he literally was not aware that heads and hats are different objects. The temporal lobes, then, are one source of top-down processing. A visual agnosia is an example of a so-called *disconnection*

visual agnosia A visual disability that is characterized by seeing without knowing the meaning of what is seen.

syndrome, in which visual objects are seen perfectly but have lost their meaning. These syndromes occur following damage to the temporal and parietal cortex.

Prosopagnosia is another visual agnosia in which a patient cannot recognize faces. It occurs sufficiently often that researchers suspect that a specific visual area in the temporal lobe is devoted to face detection. Oddly, these patients can correctly identify eyes and ears and noses (because the brain areas subserving them are intact), but cannot remember or recognize even familiar faces. As one patient explained: "I cannot recognize people in photographs, not even myself. At the club I saw someone strange staring at me and asked the steward who it was. I'd been looking at myself in a mirror" (Pallis, 1955, p. 27). We can conclude that to see and to understand what we see requires the integration of neural pathways that connect the occipital, temporal, and parietal lobes.

Seeing Versus Awareness

Conscious seeing obviously contributes to and largely determines the worldviews of sighted people. As Oliver Sacks (1995) has observed, conscious seeing allows sighted people to live in space as well as time, whereas the blind are restricted to living in time only. But how does unconscious seeing come into play? Perhaps the unconscious gets involved only when conscious seeing is no longer possible, or when emotion clouds normal consciousness, as in subliminal perception experiments. However, numerous demonstrations have shown the intrusion of unconscious seeing into normal conscious vision. An anecdotal demonstration and an experiment with words and colors will illustrate.

Many people who drive automobiles have experienced the eerie phenomenon of "waking up" and realizing that they have little conscious recollection of seeing the road for several miles. (Have I *really* passed other cars and not even seen them? I hope I obeyed the traffic signals I didn't see.) Ordinary, "normal" people, then, sometimes see and move without awareness, an experience that occurs when unconscious seeing intrudes into conscious seeing.

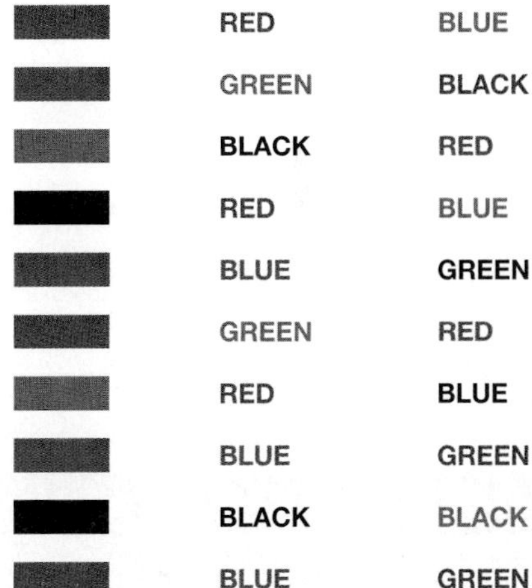

Figure 8.13 The Stroop effect. Ask a friend to name the ink colors in each column of this figure. Taking longer to name the ink colors in the right-hand column than those in the left is called the Stroop effect.

Consider also the work in the 1930s of J. Ridley Stroop, who demonstrated that language influences what we see, and that what we see influences our use of language. Stroop asked subjects to name the ink colors of the printed words for colors, a task they found difficult when the ink colors did not match the words (see Figure 8.13). For example, when the word RED was written in green ink, Stroop's subjects took longer to read it than when it was written in red ink (Stroop, 1935). Even well-practiced adults find it difficult to report the ink color rather than the color the letters spell. These results are now known as the **Stroop effect**.

What creates the difficulty in this task? Each of us has been through tens of millions of trials in reading words, but far fewer trials in applying names to colors. That is, the task of detecting the features that define words has become an unconscious process, but the Stroop task requires that we focus consciously on the individual characteristics of printed words—the color of the letters—a task in which we have had no practice. In Stroop's experiments, conscious seeing intrudes on the unconscious mechanics of reading. With practice, then, the visual perception of reading words—and driving a car—begin to occur at an unconscious level.

Stroop effect The tendency of the words that denote colors to interfere with the naming of the ink colors in which the words are printed.

What happens when the link between seeing and knowing is broken? If a person is blind, the "seeing" part of the link isn't there. Better than 95 percent of the blind people in the world cannot see because of damage to the retina or optic nerve. With special training, however, blind people can learn to function independently, to "know" the world and get along in it. But the sighted individual who

Connected images and association formation, Chapter 1, p. 14

suddenly can no longer see tea pouring, nor recognize hats or faces, cannot function independently. The very integrity of our perception of the world depends on the predictability of movement, form, size, and color; when those are lost, so is the person.

People who suffer from Alzheimer's disease demonstrate all too well how the loss of both conscious and unconscious seeing affects "knowing." These individuals suffer from visual and motor memory losses when the neurons that support those functions die. Forgetfulness and distractibility in early-onset Alzheimer's eventually give way in the later stages of the illness to a complete inability to recognize oneself and others. When seeing is no longer believing, as is the case for people who cannot see motion, recognize familiar faces, or connect what they see with what they know, the integrity of the personality is shattered, and lifelong patterns of independent living are lost.

The Mind-Body Problem Again

The plight of Alzheimer's patients underscores the connection between perception and personality in intact humans. Indeed, visual experience and the consciousness it affords lies at the heart of the mind-body problem. For all our knowledge of the *how* of seeing and the *what* of seeing, no one yet knows just how they are connected. No one knows how the psychological experience of seeing is generated by physiology, nor even if framing the question in that way is meaningful. Adding to this quandary what is now known about *unconscious* visual processes, we have yet another layer of mystery—a mind-body formulation in which the mind can be either conscious or unconscious!

INTERIM SUMMARY

1. Both conscious and unconscious processes affect what we see.
2. Subjects who report not seeing a briefly presented word, but who then behave in a way that reflects their unconscious awareness of the word, are demonstrating subliminal perception.
3. Briefly presented emotional pictures (of which subjects are unaware) can affect the conscious perception of another image.
4. Though individuals who have had some portion of their striate cortex removed report being blind, they are nevertheless able to detect objects in their field of vision when forced to guess. This unconscious ability is called ***blindsight.***
5. An intact striate cortex is necessary for conscious seeing.
6. Blindsight has been demonstrated in normally sighted individuals, who under certain conditions can correctly "guess" the direction of a moving pattern even though they cannot consciously see it.
7. The ability to see form, color, motion, and so forth, either consciously or unconsciously, is mediated by parallel processing of visual information that is carried through separate tracts to the striate and ***extrastriate cortex***, the superior colliculus, and the temporal and parietal lobes.
8. ***Visual agnosia*** is a type of *disconnection syndrome* in which words and objects lose their meaning. In one case of visual agnosia, a man mistook his wife for a hat. The inability to recognize faces, called prosopagnosia, is another type of visual agnosia.
9. The ***Stroop effect*** illustrates the difficulty of shifting one's attention from reading, which requires a partially nonconscious visual focus on language, to color detection, which requires conscious perception of colors.
10. With practice, the perceptual aspects of reading and driving can become automatic (unconscious). Conditioning with visual CSs can also occur unconsciously.
11. The integrity of the personality of a sighted person depends on an intact visual nervous system. The neuronal loss seen in Alzheimer's disease demonstrates that people *understand* by successfully perceiving, integrating, and labeling the form, size, and color of moving objects.

For Further Thought

1. Humans have a part of the brain that can see and remember individual faces, another part that can read and understand books, and yet other parts that coordinate the fingers, eyes, and ears in playing a musical instrument. Can you supply evolutionary arguments for any or all of these abilities?
2. Children who are just beginning to read do not show as strong a Stroop effect as adults (Gibson, 1971). Could the reason for these differences have something to do with the fact that adults are more practiced readers?
3. Women, we learned in Chapter 5, are better able than men to detect another person's emotional state by "reading" subtle facial cues. Is this ability an example of subliminal perception?
4. An athlete trains and runs races wearing his glasses, because (he says) they help him to focus on his running. In your experience, does blurred vision prevent you from concentrating?
5. Why do you think the English language reflects a connection between vision and states of concentration and attention? Or would you rather not *focus* on this question?

PERCEPTION OF THE WHOLE

Despite the clever and painstaking experiments conducted by Hubel, Wiesel, and other vision researchers, our understanding of the bottom-up processing of shape, movement, and color remains primitive. Humans do see meaningful images of objects, patterns, and movement in a three-dimensional world, and when needed, an incredible richness of detail in isolated objects. How do we build those images from simple sensations of light and dark, edges, and patches of color? The answer, according to Gestalt psychologists, is that we don't. Rather, we use top-down processing to perceive the world in a meaningful way.

Gestalt psychology is based on a different premise from the one underlying most 20th-century psychological research. As we saw in Chapter 1, many of the first psychologists took their methods and ideas from physiological research. But Gestalt psychologists argued that perception does not grow from its component parts, but from the experience as a whole. To a Gestalt psychologist, perceiving is qualitatively more complicated than sensing: we see wholes, not parts. When we look at a frog, our perception is based on the frog's *frogness*. Furthermore, a Gestalt psychologist would argue, *our existing cognitive knowledge of frogness* helps us to organize the sensory details of green color, small size, round body, and angular legs into something more meaningful. Gestalt psychologists have wondered whether innate principles govern how people organize details in the visual field into "whole" figures. For example, how do people perceive complex figures such as the one in the photograph on page 290?

The German word *Gestalt*, meaning "whole" or "form," refers specifically to a whole pattern—one that is so unified, it cannot be divided into component parts. In the words of the Gestalt psychologist Max Wertheimer (1880–1943), *the whole is greater than the sum of its parts.* A common example of a Gestalt is a melody that (a) cannot be meaningfully analyzed as a sequence of notes, and (b) is recognizable as the same melody, even if it is played using different notes (by changing the key) or different instruments (such as a mouth harp or violin). The melody is a Gestalt: it organizes the notes, not vice versa.

People can often perceive complex figures even when the available sensory information is minimal. Turn this book upside down and look for a pattern. Do you see the image of a dog? Could you have been primed for this perception by the discussion of the injured dog on page 281?

In the photograph above, the Gestalt organizes the patches of dark and white, meaningless by themselves, into a meaningful whole, a Dalmatian dog. As this example shows, prior experience can influence a Gestalt. Indeed, until you were informed that the ambiguous figure was a dog, you might not have noticed the pattern. In later chapters you'll see that because language influences both how you perceive and think, the description of a wounded Dalmatian on page 281 may have primed your memory for this image. The same pattern could also have emerged when the word *dog* (or more specifically, *Dalmatian*) signaled the idea of dog. Again, the word *dog* serves as a conditioned stimulus that cues your expectations. These top-down processes help you to perceive the dog.

Perception and implicit memory, Chapter 10, p. 360

Perception and language and thought, Chapter 12, p. 440

Three German researchers defined and dominated Gestalt psychology. Along with Max Wertheimer, Kurt Koffka (1886–1941) and Wolfgang Kohler (1887–1967) conducted research on a wide range of topics, including the perception of negative afterimages, apparent movement, figure-ground relationships, and other principles of perceptual organization. Let's look at some of their discoveries.

Apparent Movement and the Phi Phenomenon

In the early 1900s, no TV, cinema, or neon sign illustrated Wertheimer's theory that rapidly moving lights give the illusion of movement (hence, *apparent* movement). He demonstrated the phenomenon in his laboratory by rapidly alternating the projected images of a vertical and a diagonal slit of light (Fancher, 1990). When displayed at intervals of one-fifth of a second, the two lights appeared to be two separate images. When Wertheimer reduced the interval separating the images to less than one-hundredth of a second, they appeared to be two stationary images. (A stationary image on TV is achieved in the same way.) At intervals of approximately one-twentieth of a second, however, the two lights appeared to be one moving image. Wertheimer called this apparent movement of a stationary light source the **phi phenomenon**.

phi phenomenon The apparent movement of a stationary light source.

For Wertheimer, the phenomenon of apparent movement demonstrated that the perception of movement was independent of, and could not be analyzed through, the sensory components that produced it. Rather, he reasoned, move-

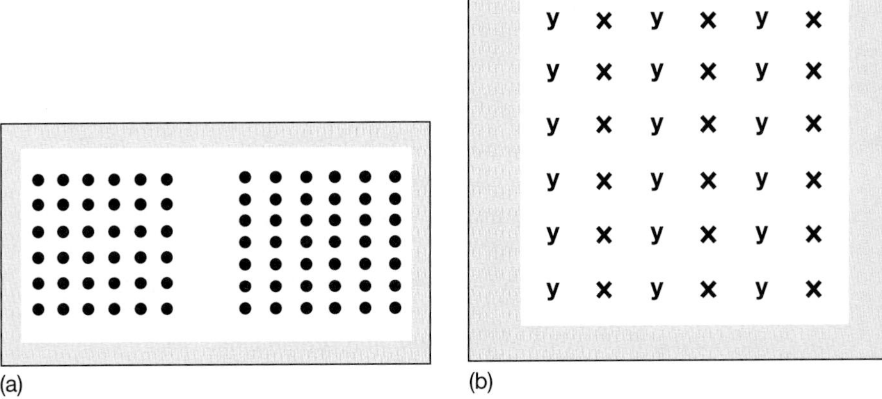

(a) (b)

Figure 8.14 Grouping by proximity and similarity. (a) You perceive the dot pattern on the right as six vertical columns because the seven black dots in each column are closer together (more proximate) than the six dots in each horizontal row. Cover the left-hand pattern and stare at the right one for 10 to15 seconds. Now shift your gaze to the pattern on the left. The appearance of horizontal rows can be attributed to the adaptation of vertical detectors in the LGN and striate cortex. (b) This figure contains six evenly spaced columns and rows. You see six columns because the brain groups the Xs and Ys according to their similarity. *Source:* From SIGHT AND MIND: An Introduction to Visual Perception by Lloyd Kaufman. © 1974 by Oxford University Press, Inc. Used by permission of Oxford University Press, Inc.

ment was an independent phenomenon. Apparent movement is explained differently today. We now know that the movement of images across the retina stimulates feature detectors, whose output is analyzed by cortical neurons. Wertheimer's interpretation of the phi phenomenon is interesting, though, because it illustrates the Gestalt interpretation of perception. Let's look at some other Gestalt theories that have stood the test of time.

Principles of Perceptual Organization

Both Wertheimer and Koffka believed that the innate properties of the human nervous system compel us to group sensory elements according to certain *principles of perceptual organization.* These principles include proximity and similarity; continuity; good form; common movement; and figure-ground relationship.

Grouping by Proximity and Similarity. Figure 8.14 demonstrates two ways in which the grouping of parts can organize our perceptions. First, parts of images that appear close together (in proximity) are usually seen as belonging together. Figure 8.14a, for example, shows two similar dot patterns, yet we see columns on the right but not on the left. In the right-hand figure, the dots are closer together vertically than they are horizontally, so we perceive them as columns. The words you are reading are another example of grouping by proximity. Words are perceived as distinct elements because in the continuous stream of letters that make up a line of type, the letters *within* words are closer together than the letters *between* words.

Figure 8.14b demonstrates the principle of grouping by similarity. You see columns rather than rows because the Xs and Ys form two separate groups. Because all the parts are the same distance from one another, grouping by similarity takes precedence over grouping by proximity.

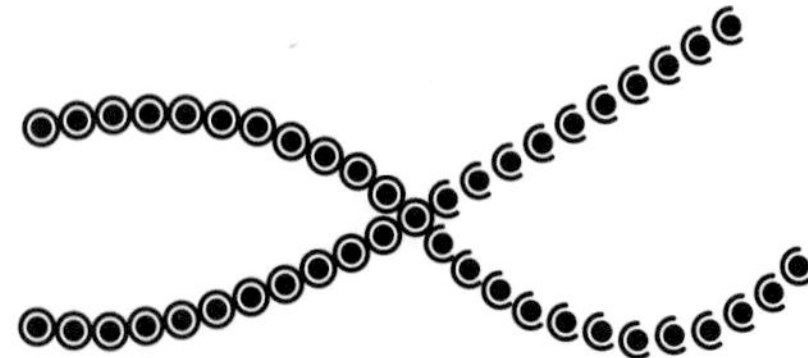

Figure 8.15 The Gestalt principle of continuity. Despite the difference between the parts on the left and right side of this pattern, you see two continuous lines crossing. Here, the principle of continuity overrides grouping by similarity.

The Gestalt Principle of Continuity. Figure 8.15 can be seen in two ways: (1) as a pattern of partially encircled elements on the right and completely encircled elements on the left, or (2) as two crossing lines. Since the pattern forms two continuous lines crossing as if in a cursive *X* , grouping by continuity overrides grouping by similarity of parts.

The Gestalt Principle of Pragnanz (Good Figure). Figure 8.16a illustrates *closure,* one aspect of the principle of good figure. Focusing on the incompleteness of the circle, the brain tends to mentally (visually) complete it. Another aspect of the principle of good figure is symmetry. If a figure is not drawn perfectly, the brain notices the imperfections, because they violate the Gestalt principle of good figure (or *pragnanz*). According to this principle, incompleteness, flaws, and imperfections disturb our visual system, as the overlarge dot in Figure 8.16b illustrates.

Why do humans prefer symmetry over asymmetry? One possibility is that the brain is designed to see straight edges (due to its columnar organization); processing asymmetrical figures requires more synapses. Another possibility is that language creates expectations that are independent of visual experience. We'll explore this intriguing possibility more fully in the next section.

The Principle of Common Movement. The left-hand photograph on page 000 illustrates another Gestalt principle, that of common movement. According to this principle, an object can be detected by the movement of its common elements. In the movie *Predator*, the transparent monster achieved form only through its subtle movement cues.

Figure-Ground Relationships. Gestalt principles of perceptual organization are not mutually exclusive. In some visual scenes, several principles apply. How do we decide which elements belong together—which form the figures and which the background? The right-hand photograph on page 293 illustrates a **figure-ground relationship** in which the perceived distinction of the figure from its background is especially striking. This vase-face picture is a *reversible figure.* Most people see it as a vase against a dark background; only when they are cued to reverse the figure do they notice the two dark faces looking at each other.

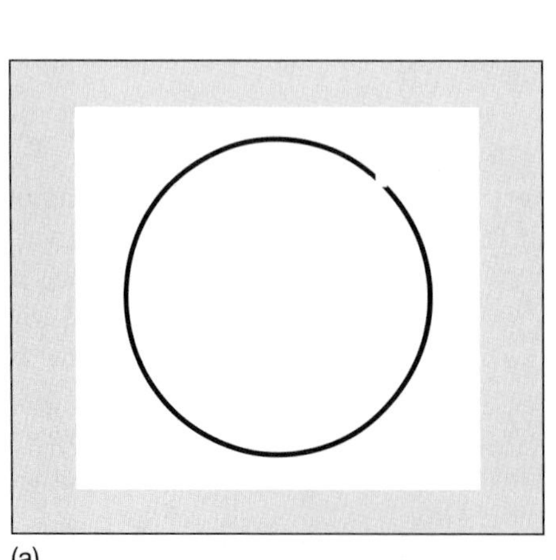

(a)

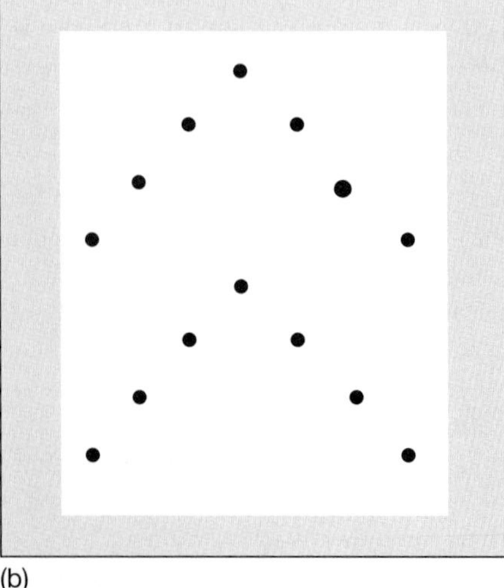

(b)

Figure 8.16 The Gestalt principle of pragnanz (good figure). (a) Your brain tends to close the gap in this drawing, completing a perfect circle. (b) Your brain prefers symmetry over asymmetry. An element that is out of place, such as the overlarge dot on the right, disturbs our visual system.

figure-ground relationship The perceived distinction between an object (figure) and its background.

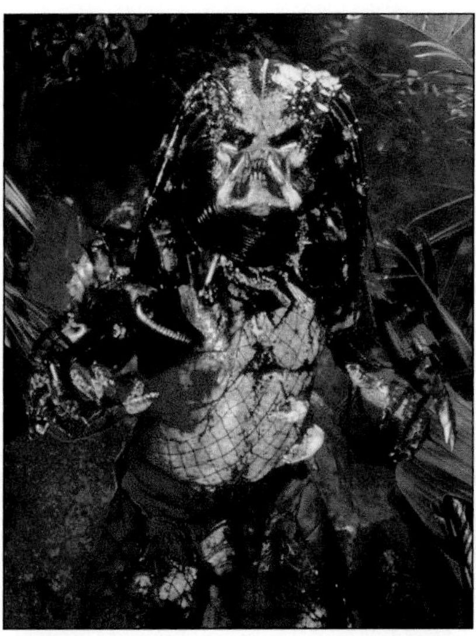

Because the monster in the movie *Predator* was perfectly camouflaged against the jungle background, it could be seen only when it moved.

Do you recognize the two high-profile individuals from Great Britain in the reversal of the figure-ground relationship in this photograph? Answer: Queen Elizabeth (right) and Prince Philip.

When that happens, the vase becomes the background. Every picture, figure, and word in this text is an example of a figure against a white background. Can you use the idea of figure-ground relationship to describe the Necker cube, the reversible image in Figure 8.8 (page 281)?

INTERIM SUMMARY

1. Humans see colors, shapes, and patterns through both bottom-up processes (the analysis of component parts) and top-down processes (the application of organizing principles).
2. The word *Gestalt* means "whole" or "form." Gestalt psychologists studied how the mind imposes order on raw sensations to perceive phenomena such as movement, shape, and depth. Their principles of perceptual organization are based on top-down processing.
3. The ***phi phenomenon*** describes the apparent movement of stationary lights when flashed on and off at certain time intervals.
4. The Gestalt *principles of perceptual organization* include the principles of *proximity, similarity, continuity, closure, good figure,* and *common movement.*
5. A ***figure-ground relationship*** is the perceived distinction between an object and its background. This relationship is illustrated by *reversible figures* such as the vase-face illusion.

For Further Thought

1. Would Gestalt psychologists be surprised to learn that individuals who are recovering their sight after being blind from birth are bothered by imperfections in what they see?
2. If you were primed and successfully picked out the Dalmatian in the photo on page 290, when did you become aware of it?

PERCEPTION OF SOUND, TASTE, SMELL, AND TOUCH

For several reasons, this chapter's focus has been visual perception. We know more about visual perception than auditory, chemical, or somatosensory perception, perhaps because it dominates the consciousness of most sighted people. Or sight may dominate human consciousness simply because more of the brain is devoted to visual perception than to auditory, chemical, or somatosensory perception. By way of comparison, rats and dogs sense the world primarily through olfaction, and to a lesser extent through seeing and hearing.

Gestalt psychologists recognized that a melody, played in different keys and by different instruments, is an identifiable whole that is not easily analyzed with respect to specific sound frequencies. Similarly, neither fine wines nor lowly hamburgers are easily analyzed in terms of their four basic tastes and countless chemical odors. Wines and hamburgers have a meaning, an essence, of their own. In this concluding section we'll look at what sounds, smells, tastes, and touches mean to us.

The Perception of Meaningful Sounds

In the preceding section we learned that the sense of sight affords us a level of consciousness unattainable by blinded humans. The same is true of the sense of hearing: life without conversations, gentle breezes and noisy streams, and the refrain of our favorite music would be incomplete and socially isolating. Hearing the sounds of our environment is as much a part of the fabric of living as what we see, smell, touch, and taste.

Language and temporal lobe organization, Chapter 12, p. 418

The role of the hippocampus in memory formation, Chapter 10, p. 374

Animals have evolved the ability not just to locate and assign meaning to sounds, but also to interpret audible patterns of communication. Indeed, as we will see in Chapter 12, parts of the left temporal lobe in humans—Wernicke's area—have evolved a special sensitivity to the meaningful sounds of spoken language. We'll see in Chapter 10 that another brain structure in the left temporal lobe, the hippocampus, allows us to learn and remember the sounds of language differently from other sounds. There is no doubt that the psychology of hearing is dominated by language, an idea to which we will return later.

Besides language, music fills a large part of human consciousness. Music—sound arranged into patterns that are pleasing to hear—was made in the earliest ages of human prehistory, as evidenced by the existence of 50,000-year-old flutes. Both music and language are examples of top-down processing. Both connect the intellect with emotion, expressing feelings as well as ideas. And both serve a wide assortment of social and psychological functions. Based on the organization of the brain, some researchers have hypothesized that music may have evolved even *earlier than language* (Lynch, 1996).

The sounds of music have wide-ranging effects on human behavior. Cross-culturally, music has motivational and emotional effects: it can energize or soothe, make us laugh or cry. It can also enhance concentration, strengthen learning and memory, stimulate digestion, stir passion and movement, increase the release of endorphins, and help to organize neurons. For most people, the general effect of listening to music while studying is distracting (see page 349), but some people use music to enhance their focus while studying (Crawford & Strapp, 1994). Music has been shown to relieve stress in patients awaiting surgery (Miluk-Kolasa, Matejek, & Stupnicki, 1996) and to reduce some of the symptoms of depressed patients (Hanser & Thompson, 1994).

One of the first clues to the way in which we perceive music was reported several centuries ago in a patient with a damaged left hemisphere which had resulted in speech loss and paralysis of the right side of the body. However, "[he could] sing certain hymns, which he had learned before he became ill, as clearly and distinctly as any healthy person." (Springer & Deutsch, 1998, p. 18) Since then, various aspects of music perception have been found to depend on an intact *right* hemisphere (Joseph, 1988). The composer Ravel, for example, lost his language abilities following a stroke, and afterward could not label musical notes, read or write music, or play the piano. However, some of his other musical skills remained intact: he recognized melodies, was critical of imperfections in the way music was played, and maintained the ability to tell whether a piano was in tune (Justine, 1993). Still, the picture is far from clear. In nonmusicians, the perception of complex, unfamiliar melodies is centered largely in the *left* hemisphere (LaBarba, Kingsberg, & Martin, 1992), and both hemispheres are involved in singing and perceiving music.

The Perception of Odors and Tastes

In Chapter 7 we learned that different parts of the brain are involved in the conscious and unconscious detection of smells. The conscious brain allows you to attach meaning to what you smell; hence, the aroma of pizza predicts one eating experience; the smell of hamburger, another. Cultures are defined in part by their foods, and the perception of their tastes depends on a lifetime of experience.

A person may not be aware of all the factors that influence food preferences, however. For many years, nonhuman animal research suggested that taste and smell preferences can begin to develop in utero (Mistretta & Bradley, 1977). In a recent study, half the members of a group of pregnant women ate anise and half did not (Schaal, 2000). Shortly after birth, all their infants were exposed to the odor of anise to see whether they showed an attraction or aversion to the smell. Those infants born to mothers who had eaten anise turned toward the smell, while those whose mothers had not eaten anise either ignored it or turned away from the odor. We can conclude, then, that top-down processes influence the conscious perception of smell.

But what about unconscious smells? Let's begin by exploring the adaptive significance of smell. Did you know:

- That in women, nasal congestion often occurs during the menstrual cycle and the third trimester of pregnancy?
- That men and women who are *anosmic* (lacking in the sense of smell) often have both underdeveloped olfactory bulbs *and* underdeveloped gonads?
- That the smell of the urine of a strange male rat will cause pregnant female rats to abort their litters?
- That the smell of the urine of a dominant male primate can cause a reduction in the testosterone levels of mature males of the same species?

Smell, Pheromones, and Reproduction. The fact that neurons in the olfactory bulb are derived from the same embryological tissue as neurons in the hypothalamus helps to explain the connections between smell, endocrinology, and reproduction. You may recall from our study of seeing and hearing that cells in the hypothalamus and other subcortical areas have an unconscious influence on our behavior. A clever study by Martha McClintock (1971) showed that smell does indeed affect our physiology and behavior at an unconscious level. McClintock began by monitoring the menstrual cycles of women living in the same dormitory. Some of the rooms had a common air supply with the main hallway; others did not. She found that the women who breathed common air—including, presumably, the smells of other women—tended to menstruate at the same time more often than those who did not, even though many women in the

The sebaceous and apocrine glands are concentrated in specific areas of the body. Their secretions play a role in sexual attraction.
Source: From Stoddart (1990).

study were conscious only of their own cycles. More than likely, the women who shared a common air supply detected one another's sexual secretions unconsciously, through smell.

We learned earlier about pheromones, chemical secretions that influence other animals' behavior, especially their reproductive behavior. Thus the pheromones in a male rat's urine can cause the abortion of a female rat's pups; the pheromones of dominant male monkeys can influence the endocrinology of other male monkeys. How might human pheromones have caused the menstrual synchrony McClintock observed in female dorm residents?

The photograph shows the sites of scent production in the human body. The axillae (armpits) contain large numbers of apocrine glands, which exude the steroid *androstenone,* a demonstrated pheromone in many animals. Androstenone can influence the breeding patterns of the musk deer; perfumers use the scent in the manufacture of fragrances.

In a follow-up to McClintock's research, scientists tested the hypothesis that androstenone was influencing the menstrual cycles of the women who breathed common air. They made an extract of androstenone by collecting the axillary secretions of a female volunteer, mixing them with alcohol, and soaking cotton strips in the solution (Russell, 1976; Russell, Switz, Thompson, 1980). Female volunteers wore these small strips under their noses three times a week for several months, and members of a control group wore strips that had not been soaked in the secretions. Figure 8.17 shows the results. During the 4 months of the experiment, the menstrual cycles of the females wearing the pheromone-soaked strips gradually shifted and became synchronized with the cycle of the source female.

Women who sleep with men, or who wear a patch treated with male axillary secretions, have more regular menstrual cycles (Cutler, Preti, Krieger, Huggins, & Garcia, 1986). Male pheromones also affect women's fertility. Cutler and colleagues found that women who sleep regularly with men ovulate during 90 percent of their menstrual periods, whereas women who are celibate or who rarely sleep with men ovulate during only 50 percent of their periods (Cutler, Preti, Huggins, Erickson, & Garcia, 1985).

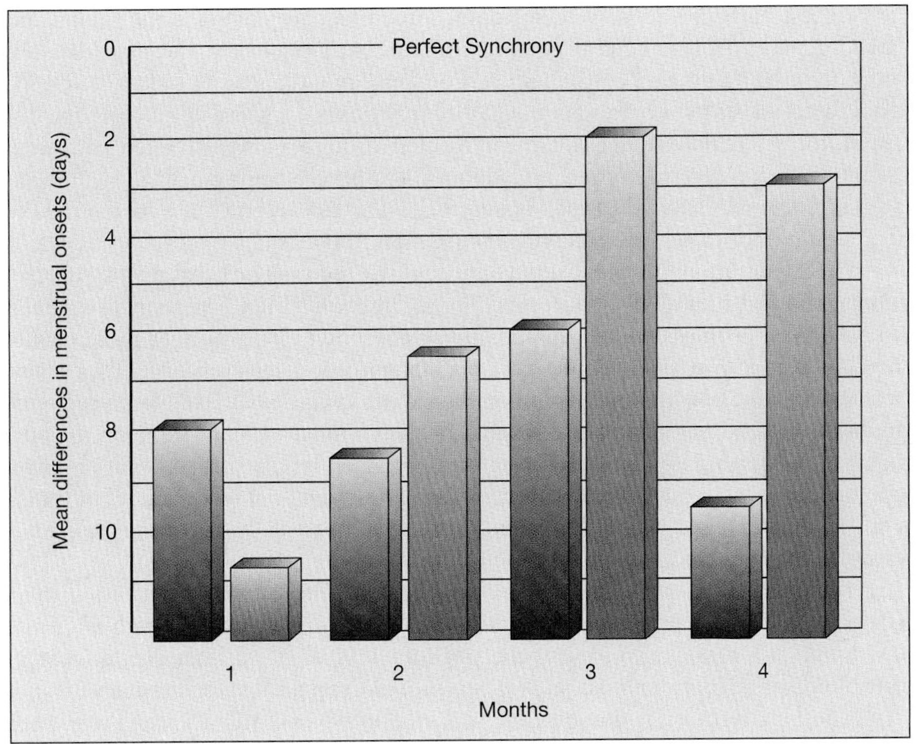

Figure 8.17 The effect of pheromones on the human menstrual cycle. An extract made from the apocrine gland secretions of a donor female synchronized the menstrual cycles of target females (green) who volunteered to wear a scented patch on their upper lip three days a week over a period of several months. A control group (blue) of females who unknowingly wore a scent pad without the pheromone did not show the same effect. *Source:* From "Olfactory Influences on the Human Menstrual Cycle" by M. J. Russell, G. M. Switz, & K. Thomson, *Pharmacology, Biochemistry & Behavior,* vol. 13 (1980), pp. 737–738. Copyright © 1980 by Elsevier Science. Reprinted by permission.

Pheromones and Sexual Attraction. That the smell of androstenone influences ovulation and the menstrual cycle raises the possibility that androstenone might enhance a male's sexual attractiveness. To the extent that this pheromone can be consciously smelled, however, most women find it unattractive. Thus, perfumers who use musk, a similar smell, usually mask its "goaty" smell with floral, woody, or spicy smells. Still, the sebaceous and apocrine glands secrete many other chemicals, so some other secretion might increase a male's or female's sexual attractiveness.

One clue to the existence of a sexual attractant comes from an unlikely source. The Swiss researcher Claus Wedekind and his colleagues began to wonder why some couples who shared a particular genetic pattern had more difficulty than others in starting families. Why, if a pregnancy occurred, was it less likely to go to term? And if it did go to term, why was the newborn more likely than others to be sickly and underweight? Genetic testing of these couples revealed that they shared a common section of DNA that coded for the *major histocompatibility complex*, or MHC. In other words, like first cousins Charles Darwin and his wife, Emma, these couples shared too many gene sites at which the deleterious effects of recessive genes could be expressed.

Factors involved in sexual attractiveness, Chapter 15, p. 529

But Wedekind thought there might be more to the problem than a bad genetic match. Research with mice had shown that female mice used pheromones to select mates with *nonmatching* MHC profiles. That is, mice with different MHC profiles smelled different, presumably because their apocrine secretions included a chemical related to their MHC. Thus, through adaptive smell-based choices, the female mice were able to mate with those males most likely to produce viable offspring. Wedekind reasoned that human females might also use pheromonal information to select males with nonmatching MHC profiles. Perhaps the couples who were having reproductive problems were having pheromonal problems.

MHC complex with inbreeding, Chapter 3, p. 78

Recessive genes, Chapter 3, p. 77

To test his hypothesis, Wedekind and his colleagues collected the smells and MHC genetic profiles of college-aged volunteers. They asked the men to sleep alone for two nights in a cotton t-shirt. For those two days they could not smoke, drink alcohol, eat spicy foods, or have sex; they could wash without soap, but could not use deodorant or colognes. Women volunteers then smelled and rated each t-shirt in response to three questions: How "sexy" is the smell? How "pleasant" is the smell? How "intense" is the smell? The researchers then correlated the women's psychological ratings with their genetic data.

The main finding of this study confirmed the data on rats: by a 2 to 1 factor, women tended to rate as "more sexy" and "more pleasant" the smells of men whose MHC profiles differed the most from their own. Interestingly, these results suggest that few males (in theory, none) smell good to everyone. That these women had already used smell to pick their dates could be inferred from their description of the sexiest t-shirt smells as those most similar to their current boyfriends' or past lovers'. That their sense of smell reflected their MHC profiles could be inferred from other data: the women described the t-shirt odors of males with closely matched MHC profiles as smelling "like dad" or "like my brother"—pleasant, but not sexy.

The women in this study consciously smelled men's t-shirts and rated their odors. Could they have arrived at the same ratings even if they couldn't smell anything, in a manner similar to the phenomenon of blindsight? Recall that in one blindsight experiment, subjects with normal eyesight detected movement in a visual test pattern, even though they reported not being able to see it (see page 285). In fact, scientists have demonstrated the unconscious detection of smells. Some students who were participating in a smell study were about to be excluded because they were unable to smell the test stimulus, androstenone. But an insightful researcher connected them to a skin-conductance device that measured their emotional arousal. As in the blindsight studies, some subjects showed changes in skin conductance when they sniffed the odor of androstenone, though they reported they did not smell anything (Van Toller, Kirk-Smith, Wood, Lombard, & Dodd, 1983).

Instinctive Versus Cultural Responses to Smell. The intimate senses of taste and smell affect human behavior in important ways. Smell shapes human consciousness by triggering memories of places we have been, foods we have eaten, and people we have known. At an unconscious level certain smells, including pheromones, influence our endocrine, immune, and reproductive systems, as well as our relationships with other people. These chemical senses are highly adaptive, then; but does that mean that they guide our behavior instinctively? The answer is that they do, but only in broad ways.

Let's take an example that the evolutionary psychologists Leda Cosmides and John Tooby have used to show that specific brain structures evolved to keep humans from being attracted to and eating feces (Cosmides & Tooby, 1997). Because feces may contain substances that can cause sickness when consumed, Cosmides & Tooby argue, they constitute a selective pressure. Those individuals who eat feces will sicken and die more often than others, leaving fewer offspring; those who do not do so will be healthier and have more children. In all cultures today, humans express a highly adaptive disgust in response to feces.

There are problems with this analysis, however. If disgust toward feces is part of our evolutionary heritage, and a unique part of human nature, we might expect to see small children exhibit the response. But much to the dismay of new parents, small children (and other primates) play with their feces, put them in their mouths, and do other disgusting things with them! In fact, as we will see in Chapter 14, Sigmund Freud's theory of psychosexual development posits that up

LINK
Child's attraction to odors and psychosexual development, Chapter 14, p. 501

to the age of 5, children's sexuality is focused on feces, fecal odor, and intestinal gas. Children are often attracted to, rather than disgusted by, feces.

In a variety of ways, parents teach children what is and is not appropriate to put in their mouths. For example, they show children how to dispose of feces (in culture-specific ways) rather than ingest them. In fact, cultural wisdom plays a large role in determining what smells good or bad. In Dawkin's (1976) terms, this is *meme* rather than *gene* knowledge. With patience, you can even teach your child that bitter coffee tastes good and that fetid Limburger cheese smells exquisite. Yet some odors do seem to elicit species-specific disgust responses. A close friend, for example, tells me that as a very young child, she smelled a dead cow and retched without having to be told that putrid smells were bad. Subjecting infants to putrid smells in a laboratory, however, does not elicit a disgust response.

Teaching disgust responses and memes, Chapter 3, p. 188

Conditioning and learning associations with smells, Chapter 6, p. 200

There seems little doubt that human smell receptors, nerves, and brains are hardwired to sense the odors of other humans, at both a conscious and an unconscious level. But culture also plays a large role in how individuals respond to sexual odors. As we will see in Chapter 15, patterns of courting and sexual behavior can be highly variable and are learned within cultures.

The Perception of Touch

We saw in Chapter 7 that the two-point limen method revealed a correspondence between skin sensitivity and the distribution of touch receptors. In what way does skin sensitivity affect human behavior? In part, the skin senses are involved in adaptive reflexes. Examples include the rooting reflex, seen when an infant is touched around the mouth, and the eye-blink reflex, seen when receptors on and around the cornea are touched. But touch plays a much greater role in human behavior than these simple reflexes suggest.

Infant's rooting reflex, Chapter 6, p. 191

Eye-blink reflex, Chapter 6, p. 191

Grooming and Contact Comfort. Touch also includes touching and being touched. The primate heritage of humans is never more evident than in observations of how they touch each other. Most mammals (dogs, cats, rats, sheep, cows, and horses) groom each other by licking, which is for the most part a behavior that mothers direct toward their offspring. In contrast, adult primates spend inordinate amounts of time using their fingers and tongues to groom themselves and each other. Though it is normally conspecific, this behavior can occur across species as well. For example, we cuddle our house pets and they lick us back. To take another example, a chimpanzee friend of mine used to hold my arm with one hand and pick through my hairs with her large forefinger and tongue. She would visually inspect the skin by gently blowing on the hairs to move them. She picked at any imperfections such as a spot, mole, or scab. (Did they resemble insects, lice, and fleas, which chimpanzees pick from each other?) She would then offer her arm, or turn her back to me, to elicit reciprocal grooming. What is the function of this behavior, other than to remove an occasional bug?

Harry Harlow of the University of Wisconsin uncovered several possible answers to this question while investigating the role of mother-infant pair bonding in Rhesus monkeys. Recall that in his research, he allowed infant monkeys to choose between two "surrogate mothers," one a wire frame with a nursing bottle attached, and the other a terry-cloth-covered wire frame without a bottle. When the infants clung to the nonnutritive terry-cloth mother almost exclusively, he speculated that primates had a biological need for *contact comfort*. In related research, Harlow (1969) found that "social contact" during infancy—smelling, seeing, hearing, and touching—influenced brain development and adult social behavior in highly adaptive ways. Those monkeys who lacked a

Contact comfort and attachment, Chapter 11, p. 405

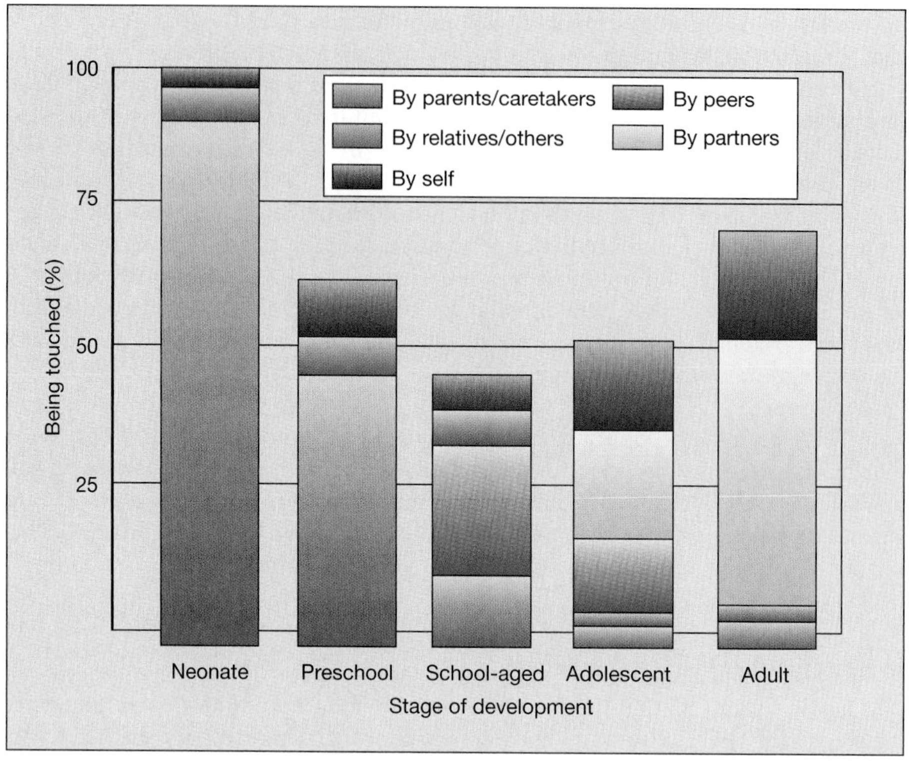

Figure 8.18 **Touching and being touched throughout the life span.** How often people are touched, and by whom, varies with their stage of life. Infants are touched the most; preschool and school-aged children, adolescents, and adults, less often. Infants and preschoolers are touched most often by their parents; adults, by their partners. Data are from the United States. *Source:* Modified from McAnarney, 1984.

physical relationship with their mothers or with same-age peers exhibited maladaptive social behavior, including abnormal courting, mating, and mothering. Touching, then, is one basis for developing adaptive social behavior.

Who Gets Touched? To varying degrees, humans are like other primates in the way they touch their children and each other. Touching and being touched feels good to us. It is human nature to touch, stroke, and groom; adults who do not engage in this behavior likely learned *not* to as children. Elizabeth McAnarney has investigated the developmental sequence of touching and of being touched in the United States. As Figure 8.18 shows, newborns are touched the most, and parents do most of the touching. In contrast, the typical adolescent is touched less than half as much as a newborn, and sadly, only rarely by a parent; peers and partners do most of the touching at this time. People also touch themselves more during adolescence than at any other time in their lives (McAnarney, 1984).

In other parts of this text we will see that physical contact promotes the attachment of infant and caretaker (Chapter 11) and helps to define courting and mating (Chapter 15). Touching and being touched is also good for our health. For example, handling (touching and massaging) promotes more rapid weight gain and greater neurological development in both infant rats (Meany, Aitken, Van Berkel, Bhatnagar, & Sapolsky, 1988) and prematurely born humans (Field et al., 1986). Finally, both young and old humans can lower their blood pressure merely by touching a pet dog (Vormbrock & Grossberg, 1988). Not surprisingly, being petted also lowers the dog's blood pressure.

LINK ▶
Touching and health psychology, Chapter 16, p. 533

For the skin senses, then, the Gestalt psychologists are right in insisting that touch is more than an understanding of which receptors underlay certain spots of skins and in knowing that the two-point limen is different on the lips and knees. The perception of touch, exemplified by such human behaviors as grooming and hair washing, is best understood as the integration of information from touch and temperature receptors, which above all produces health and pleasure in both mind and body. Brain mechanisms underlying these adaptive behaviors are not well understood.

Integration Across the Senses

That touching and being touched is beneficial to one's health speaks volumes about mind-body integration. An apple, for instance, is red, sweet, crunchy, and pleasurable all at the same time. Two recently reported lines of research show some surprising effects of these sensory interactions. Macaluso, Frith, and Drive (2000) have demonstrated that a sudden touch on the hand boosts an experimental subject's ability to respond to briefly flashed lights. The part of the brain that is active during this demonstration, the visual cortex, was once thought to be involved only in seeing. The researchers suggest that nerve fibers carrying touch information project to the parietal lobe and then to the visual cortex, mediating the integration of touch and vision.

Sensory association areas in parietal lobe, Chapter 4, p. 126

Another example of how one type of sensory information can affect another is a newly discovered illusion. When a single flash of light in the periphery of the eye is accompanied by two beeps, it is perceived as two flashes (Shams, Kamitani, & Shimojo, 2000). Such eye-ear interactions are so frequent, we take them for granted. Recall that the inferior and superior colliculus, at the base of the brain, receive fibers from both the eyes and ears, and are involved in the coordination of head movements to locate the source of sounds. In fact, visual perception is enhanced by this orienting response (McDonald, Teder-Salejarvi, & Hillyard, 2000). The unknown brain areas involved in the two-beep illusion may also be responsible for the fact that we are better able to understand a person's speech when we can see their lips moving. Both sight-touch and sight-sound integration provide evidence that humans experience *a consensus of the senses* (Sacks, 1990).

INTERIM SUMMARY

1. The perception of both language and music depends on one's culture.
2. Music has both motivational and emotional effects on human behavior.
3. The perception of taste and smell is determined through both bottom-up and top-down processes. These "intimate senses" evolved to detect foods and reproductive partners.
4. Pheromones unconsciously affect animals' behavior, especially their reproductive behavior.
5. Both male and female pheromones can affect a woman's menstrual cycle. Over time, the menstrual cycles of females who smelled the olfactants of a menstruating female became synchronized with her cycle. Smelling a male pheromone affects the timing of female menstrual cycles.
6. Pheromones appear to be involved in sexual attraction. For example, a male whose *major histocompatibility complex* (MHC) differs the most from that of a given female will smell "sexier" to that female.
7. Culture helps to determine behavior that is influenced by smell.
8. Mammals are social animals that touch themselves and each other. Social grooming may reflect the need for *contact comfort*, which is critical to the physical and social development of young primates.
9. Touching is the basis not only for adaptive social behavior, but also for neurological development and physical and emotional health.
10. Several lines of evidence show that the senses interact: both auditory beeps and touch can influence the perception of briefly flashed lights.

For Further Thought

1. What is the adaptive significance, if any, of the statement that "music can energize and soothe, can make us laugh and make us cry." (Do people who make music have more sexual opportunities than those who don't?)
2. What policies and procedures regarding infant handling would you want to know about before you enrolled your newborn in a day-care center? (Is it relevant that when a puppy is not petted, it behaves differently than other puppies as an adult?)
3. Why do you think adolescents touch themselves so much? Why do you think parents touch their adolescent children so infrequently?

CONCLUDING THOUGHTS

Perceptual processes add meaning to a human's sensitivity to light, sound, and the chemical environment. Culture and learning guide top-down processing, which allows us to perceive wholes rather than disconnected parts. That is, humans with intact brains see faces and shoes, participate in conversations and enjoy music, and select foods and mates, as opposed to merely sensing photons, vibrations, and chemicals. Gestalt psychologists were among the first to appreciate wholeness: their principles of perceptual organization include the grouping of images by proximity, similarity, continuity, common movement, and good form. Our eyes seem to want to see a figure against a background, and both monocular and binocular cues help us to see in depth.

A less obvious feature of the visual system is its nonconscious functioning. Despite the ever-changing images on our retinas, we enjoy the perceptual constancies of size, shape, lightness, and brightness. Our eyes adjust reflexively to different lighting conditions, and move in a highly coordinated way so as to focus on a particular image. Experiments with subliminal perception and blindsight suggest that nonconscious vision influences our everyday lives to a greater degree than we are aware.

Understanding how humans perceive continues to challenge psychologists and neuroscientists. The bottom-up and top-down processes of the five-stage model provide one way to think about vision. Experiments on subliminal perception and blindsight and brain-based studies of humans and other animals are other approaches. Throughout the brain, integrated neural pathways seem to allow us to see and understand what we see, to hear and understand what we hear. But a form of the mind-body problem persists: How do we consciously experience sight, sound, smell, touch, and taste from the action of neurons in receptors and the brain? How can similar neural events produce such different perceptions as a sunset, an aria, and the aromas of a five-course meal?

Among the most important survival tasks humans face is finding food and securing mates. One part of the brain has evolved to consciously smell and remember which objects are suitable to ingest and which are not. Another part of the brain appears to be sensitive to pheromones in ways that are not well understood. Pheromones can subconsciously influence a person's reproductive behavior.

The next task for researchers is to understand the many interactions among perceptual processes, which allow humans to seamlessly integrate their sensory experiences. Sounds (beeps) and touching influence what we see via brain pathways that are only now being discovered. Such perceptual integration should not be surprising. No one eats green meat, no matter how it smells, or drinks milk if someone says it isn't fresh. The perceptual and cognitive perspectives on human behavior will be developed further in the next two chapters, on consciousness and memory.

KEY TERMS

blindsight *283*
bottom-up process *271*
brightness contrast *279*
complex cells *275*
convergence *277*
extrastriate cortex *285*
feature detectors *272*
figure-ground relationship *292*
illusion *280*
lightness constancy *279*
linear perspective *277*
off-center cells *272*
on-center cells *272*
phi phenomenon *290*
receptive field *272*
retinal disparity *276*
shape constancy *279*
simple cells *274*
size constancy *279*
Stroop effect *287*
top-down process *271*
visual agnosia *286*

9

Consciousness

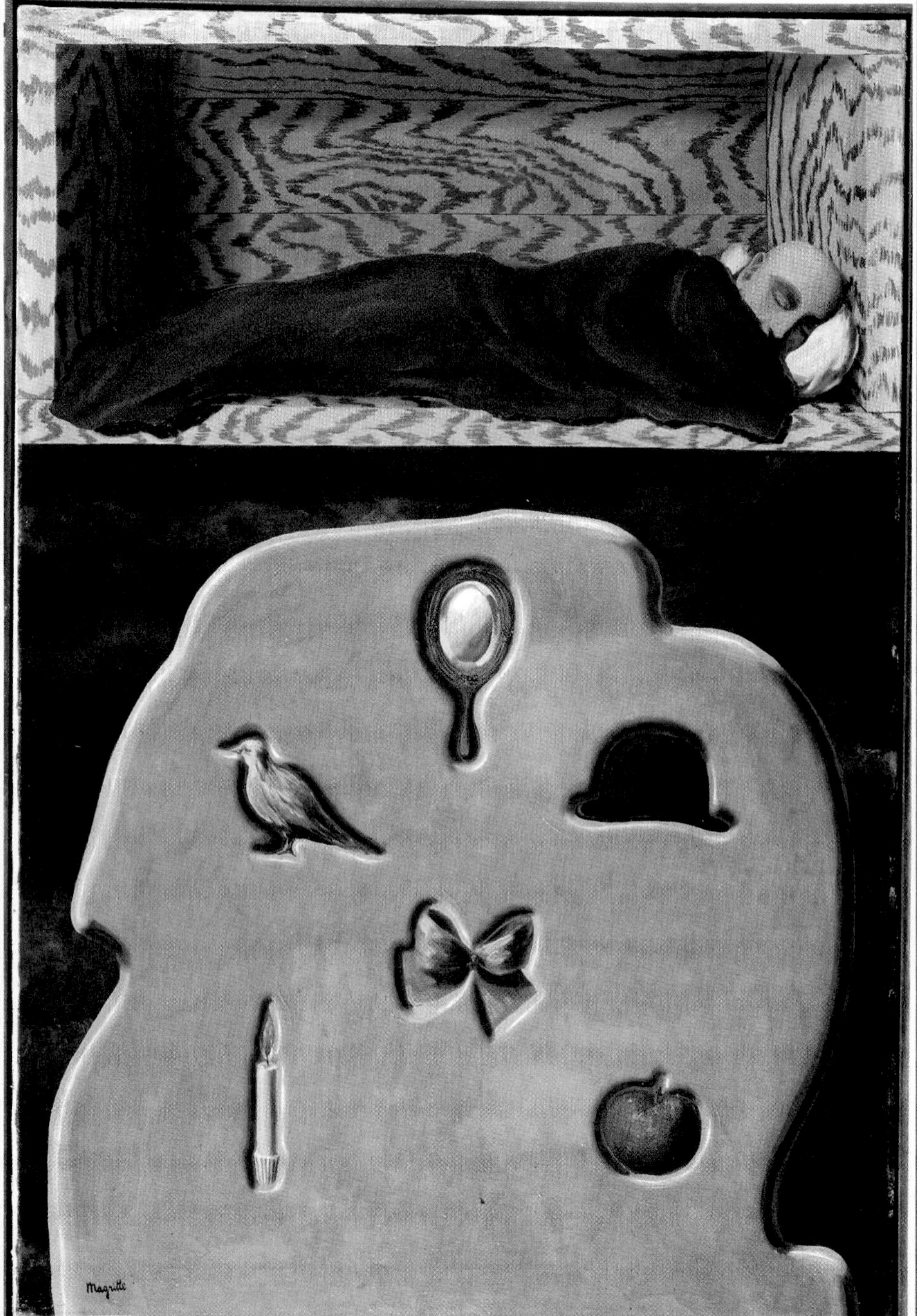

Rene Magritte (1898–1967) *The Reckless Sleeper* 1928. Tate Gallery, London / Art Resource, NY. © 2002C. Herscovici, Brussels / Artists Rights Society (ARS), New York.

The Many Meanings of Mind and Consciousness

Mind and Consciousness in the History of Psychology
Biological Bases of Consciousness
Contemporary Thinking About Mind and Consciousness
Interim Summary
For Further Thought

Resonating with the Sun and Moon: Biological Clocks

Circadian Rhythms
Biological Clocks
Free-Running Rhythms and Zeitgeibers
Disruption of Light-Dark Cycles
Lunar and Seasonal Rhythms
Interim Summary
For Further Thought

Sleep and Dreams

Why We Sleep
A Normal Night's Sleep
REM Sleep
The Effects of Sleep Deprivation
Insomnia
Dreams and Dreaming
Interim Summary
For Further Thought

Alterations of the Waking State: Daydreams, Hypnotism, and Meditation

Daydreaming
Hypnosis
Meditation to Achieve an Altered State of Consciousness
Interim Summary
For Further Thought

Drug-Induced Alterations of Consciousness

Why Humans Use Drugs
Depressants: Alcohol and Barbiturates
Antianxiety Drugs
Stimulants, Legal and Illegal
Antidepressants
Narcotics: Heroin and Morphine
Hallucinogens: Marijuana and LSD
Drug Tolerance
Drug Dependence and Drug Addiction
Drugs and Society
Interim Summary
For Further Thought

Concluding Thoughts

Several decades ago I attended a workshop sponsored by the American Society for Clinical Hypnosis, an association that licenses physicians, psychologists, and counselors to use hypnosis in anesthesia and psychotherapy. The leaders included an obstetrician-gynecologist, a dentist, and a licensed clinical psychologist. As a well-trained experimental psychologist, I was highly skeptical of hypnosis as a special state of consciousness, but curious. Like others, I became a willing subject and student of hypnosis.

During one session in which the hypnotist was demonstrating an induction procedure with me as his subject, I inadvertently banged my elbow against the arm of a chair, and the pain brought me out of my trance. When asked about it, I explained that I had hurt my elbow playing racquetball, that a physician had informed me that the pain and swelling were caused by an accumulation of fluid on my elbow, and that the fluid would dissipate after a few months. Until then, he had told me, my elbow would be swollen, sore, and tender whenever I moved it. The hypnotist suggested that I treat the elbow with hypnotherapy by thinking about "making it warm" while in a trance state, and visualizing the movement of fluid away from my elbow. Think *no pain*, *no swelling*, he told me; *think healing thoughts*.

I felt foolish. My belief in the scientific method collided with something I didn't understand, something that smacked of quackery—no, *defined* quackery. Nevertheless, with nothing to lose, I became a willing, suggestible subject, and for the remainder of the day,

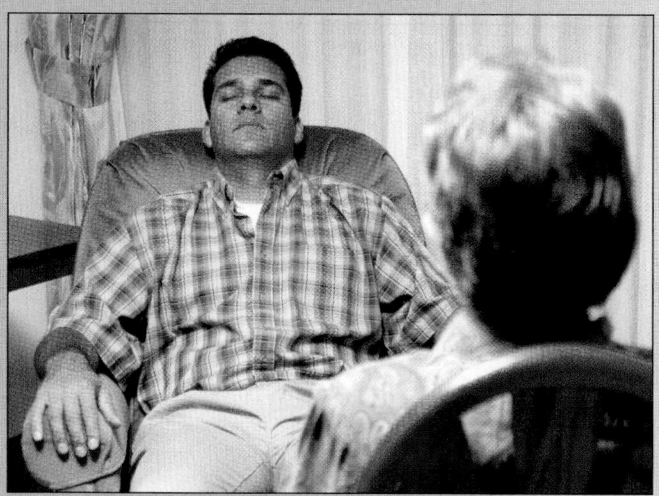

A client in a hypnotic state is susceptible to suggestions.

being easily hypnotized, I entered a trance state whenever anyone else was induced. And I concentrated on thinking healing thoughts.

The next morning, I awoke symptom free—no swelling, no pain, either on movement or to the touch. The hypnotist was not surprised. "Moving water around in the body is pretty easy," he opined. "Wait 'til you see the videotape of one of my patients, who underwent general surgery without anesthesia." Later, as I watched the tape, and observed others as they ignored painful stimuli under hypnosis, it occurred to me that while I might not understand how hypnosis alters consciousness, my first-hand experiences had given me a greater appreciation of altered states.

Whatever form consciousness takes in humans, most psychologists would agree that it is an adaptive outcome of evolutionary processes. Conscious animals are better able to sense information from the environment, and to plan and respond intelligently, than nonconscious animals. In this chapter we'll see that parts of the human brain have evolved to permit our self-awareness, as well as our awareness that other humans are conscious. And because our brains and the brains of other animals evolved over millions of years of sunrises and sunsets, our "normal" consciousness fluctuates in regular sleep-wake cycles. We'll explore why we dream and why we daydream. Finally, we'll confront some of the mysteries of consciousness, including the unconscious mind, drug-altered states, and hypnosis.

THE MANY MEANINGS OF MIND AND CONSCIOUSNESS

Consciousness, like *learning* and *memory,* is a psychological term that everyone recognizes. Standard dictionaries define **consciousness** as the quality or state of being aware. Other terms, such as *mind, thought, learning,* and *memory,* are related to consciousness. At various points in the history of psychology, different thinkers have used these terms in different ways.

Mind and Consciousness in the History of Psychology

To the psychologists who have studied consciousness, the word is a deceptively simple term for several different psychological states. William James, for example, wrote of a state of normal consciousness that he distinguished from other states:

> Our normal waking consciousness is but one special type of consciousness, whilst all about it, parted from it by the filmiest of screens, there lie potential forms of consciousness entirely different. No account of the universe in its totality can be final which leaves these other forms of consciousness quite disregarded. (James, 1902, pp. 307–08).

consciousness The quality or state of being aware.

James (1890) also referred to the "stream of consciousness" a person experiences while sitting quietly and reflecting, the mind flitting here and there, back to the past and into the future. As you read this passage, for example, your stream of consciousness moves from the beginning of the sentence to the very words you are focusing on now and then to the period at the end of the sentence. In raising this matter of the fleeting nature of conscious awareness, James anticipated our current understanding of short-term memory and working memory (see Chapter 10).

LINK
Stream of consciousness and short-term memory, Chapter 10, p. 350

Sigmund Freud, a contemporary of James, developed some very different ideas about consciousness. We will study Freud's personality theory in depth in Chapter 14, but briefly mention his concept of the unconscious here. In developing what is now called the psychoanalytical approach to the structure of personality, Freud was struck by how little insight his patients had into their emotional problems. He reasoned that the conscious mind must have difficulty accessing and understanding the workings of the *unconscious mind*. In Freud's original use of the term, which was integral to his personality theory, the **unconscious mind** was the repository of socially unacceptable thoughts and feelings. In modern usage, the term refers to information processing and brain functioning of which we are unaware, or nonconscious, as in the following description: "various nonconscious mental systems perform the lion's share of the self-regulatory burden," including "an automatic effect of perception on action, automatic goal pursuit, and a continual automatic evaluation of one's experience" (Bargh & Chartrand, 1999, p. 462).

Other researchers, contemporaries of Freud and James, held conflicting views of consciousness. In Russia, Ivan Pavlov concentrated on the physiology of the mind in his conditioning experiments. In the United States, John B. Watson, expressing his frustration with philosophical arguments about mind and consciousness, and his disdain for Wilhelm Wundt's structuralist approach (see Chapter 1), focused exclusively on behavior. Watson declared:

> The time seems to have come when psychology must discard all reference to consciousness; when it need no longer delude itself into thinking that it is making mental states the object of observation. . . . I believe we can write a [behavioral] psychology . . . and never use the terms consciousness, mental states, mind, content . . . and the like. (Watson, 1919, p. 9)

In the middle of the 20th century, Watson's influence on the direction of psychology was substantial. Only in the last two or three decades have the terms *mind* and *consciousness* (and even the *unconscious*) reentered discussions of scientific psychology. In the 1970s, textbooks again began to define psychology as "the study of the mind" as well as "the study of behavior."

Watson and behaviorism, Chapter 6, p. 198

Biological Bases of Consciousness

One line of thinking about human consciousness is that it is an *emergent property* of the interactions of billions of neurons in a large brain (Humphrey, 1992). (An emergent property is the unforeseen result of the synthesis of individual elements.) In this view, the kind of consciousness an animal experiences depends on both the size and the organization of its brain. The level of consciousness of a great ape, for example, presumably exceeds that of a snail because of the nature, size, and complexity of the ape's receptors, nerves, and brain. Questions about animal consciousness remain largely unanswered, however (Wasserman, 1993).

Brain organization and DNA, Chapter 3, p. 83

A simple experiment tests the notion that humans enjoy a consciousness, or awareness of self, that differs from that of most other animals (Gallup, 1970). During the course of examining the common chimpanzee (*Pan troglodyte*), a researcher drew a circle around its eye. Some time later, he gave the chimp a mirror. The chimp looked at its reflection, and just as a human might, seemed to notice the change in its appearance, and curiously explored the eye makeup with its fingers. The researcher's interpretation of the chimp's behavior was that in recognizing itself the chimp had revealed a *concept of self*, or an understanding of its own existence, as distinct from

unconscious mind Information processing and brain functioning of which a person is unaware; in Freudian theory, the repository of unacceptable thoughts and feelings.

"Wait! Wait! Listen to me! ... We don't *have* to be just sheep!"

Gary Larson has made a career out of wondering about the mental life of animals. The Far Side (R) by Gary Larson © 1982 FarWorks, Inc. All Rights Reserved. Used with permission. Dist. by Creators Syndicate.

that of other animals. Other research has shown that the right hemisphere (Keenan, Nelson, O'Connor, & Pascual-Leone, 2001), together with the associative cortex in the left hemisphere (Kircher et al., 2001), underlies a human's ability to recognize the self in photographs.

After confronting animals other than humans and chimpanzees with their reflections and observing what they do (or typically do *not* do) in response, researchers have concluded that most other animals lack self-awareness. Monkeys and birds, for example, will respond to their reflection as if it were another animal: Monkeys make threatening gestures by exposing their fangs, and birds court their reflections. In contrast, at age one humans begin to recognize themselves in a mirror. Just because an animal does not *appear* to recognize itself in a mirror, however, does not mean that it is not self-aware. As Nicholas Humphrey has stated most eloquently, "The fact that we cannot see the other side of the moon . . . does not mean it is not there, and likewise, the fact we cannot confirm in conversation that dogs are conscious does not mean that they are not" (Humphrey, 1992, p. 209).

Humans may enjoy aspects of consciousness unlike those of other animals. Language, for example, likely makes for a uniquely human form of consciousness (Bickerton, 2000). And only humans may have a *theory of mind*, or the ability to empathize with another person's experiences. Even some humans, such as autistic people (Baron-Cohen, Leslie, & Frith, 1985) and people with damaged forebrains (Channon & Channon, 2000), have difficulty comprehending another person's perspective, being sympathetic, or understanding humor and deceit.

Researchers have studied theory of mind in the laboratory by asking subjects with forebrain damage to solve problems by "reading" (that is, taking cues from) experimenters while their brain activity is monitored using the fMRI procedure. In one study, two experimenters gave correct or incorrect information about where a ball was hidden in a cup (Stuss, Gallup, & Alexander, 2001). Subjects who had a theory of mind could take another person's visual perspective and determine whether the experimenter's answers were honest or deceitful, but those with damage to localized areas within the frontal lobes had great difficulty with this task. In another study, researchers discovered that *mirror neurons* in a monkey's frontal cortex fire both during the performance of a task and while the monkey watches another subject perform the task (Galesse & Goldman, 1998). Such studies demonstrate that the consciousness underlying a theory of mind is related to biochemical changes in specific areas of the brain. Researchers advise caution, however: "there will never be an area of the brain that 'secretes consciousness' or any other mental state. We potentially remove the mystery by knowing the relevant brain mechanisms, but we are only at the very beginning of this quest for understanding" (Weiskrantz, 2001).

Contemporary Thinking About Mind and Consciousness

Today, mind and consciousness are defined in physiological and evolutionary terms as well as behavioral terms. Consider representative book titles from the 1990s: *The Conscious Mind: In Search of a Fundamental Theory* (Chalmers,

1997); *The Adapted Mind: Evolutionary Psychology and the Generation of Culture* (Barkow, Cosmides, & Tooby, 1992); *How the Mind Works* (Pinker, 1997); *Consciousness Lost and Found* (Weiskrantz, 1997); and *The Biology of Mind: Origins and Structures of Mind, Brain, and Consciousness* (Bownds, 1999). In addition to a renewed interest in consciousness per se, most psychologists continue to study specific aspects of mind and consciousness, such as perceiving, learning, thinking and speaking, paying attention and forming memories, acting intelligently or abnormally, and so forth. Relative to the more general terms of *mind* and *consciousness*, these terms can be operationally defined, and hence studied scientifically from the evolutionary, physiological, and behavioral perspectives. (These topics, of course, are reflected in chapter titles in this textbook.)

INTERIM SUMMARY

1. ***Consciousness*** is defined as the quality or state of being aware.
2. William James distinguished between "waking consciousness" and other forms of consciousness. He also described "a stream of consciousness," a psychological process that connects the immediate past to the present moment.
3. Sigmund Freud proposed the existence of an ***unconscious mind***, the repository of unacceptable thoughts and feelings. Today, the term *unconscious* (or nonconscious) is used to refer to information processing and brain functioning that takes place outside of a person's awareness.
4. During most of the 20th century, psychologists moved from philosophical speculation to scientific inquiry. They defined and studied specific aspects of consciousness, such as perception, learning, thinking, and memory.
5. Consciousness has evolved with the brain. To the extent that we share a similar brain organization with other animals, we likely share similar levels of consciousness.
6. Most present-day psychologists assume that consciousness is an emergent property of biochemical changes in the brain.
7. Focal areas in the frontal lobes allow humans to have a *theory of mind*, or the ability to take another person's perspective. A monkey's *mirror neurons* fire when it performs a task and when it observes another animal performing the task.

For Further Thought

1. Is William James's term *ordinary consciousness* a useful one? Do all people share the same ordinary consciousness?
2. John B. Watson would have objected to the following italicized terms:

   "That boy has a *mind* of his own."

   "I wasn't *aware* of that."

   (On a basketball court) "I've never seen her make so many baskets. She was *unconscious* out there."

   Despite Watson's objections, do you think these terms are useful?
3. Is your pet dog or cat conscious? Defend your answer.

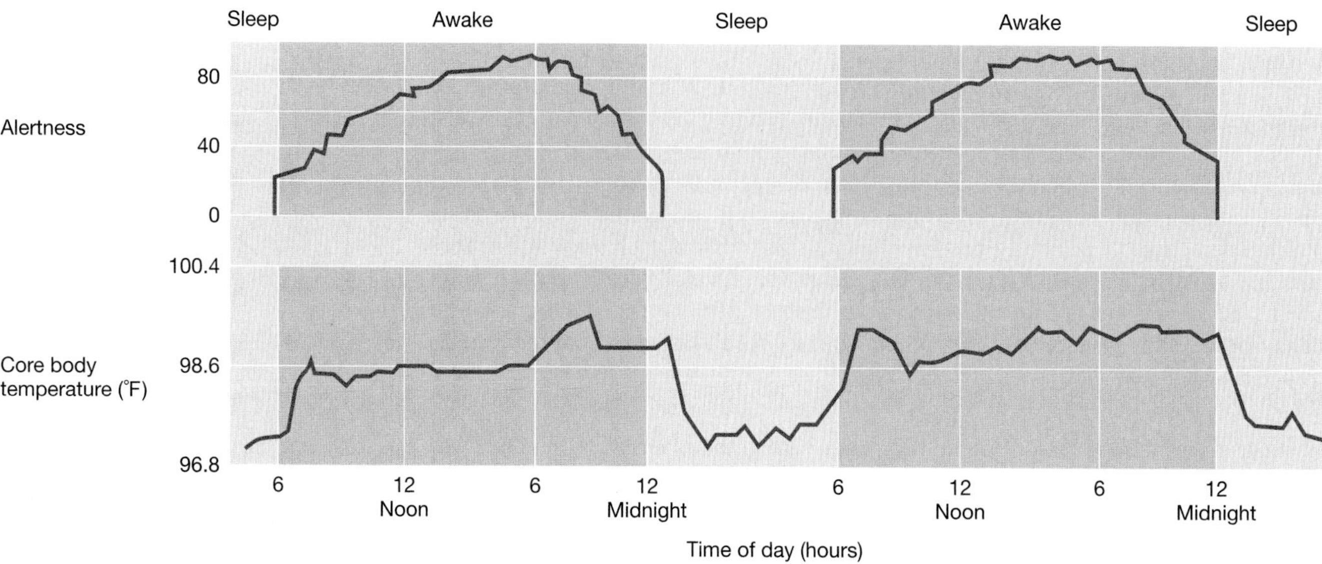

Figure 9.1 Circadian rhythms in temperature and alertness. Alertness (top) varies over a 24-hour period, from a complete lack of alertness (during sleep) to a peak during the late afternoon and early evening hours. In the two complete cycles (48 hours) shown here, body temperature (bottom) drops precipitously during sleep, then rises and remains steady throughout most of the day.

RESONATING WITH THE SUN AND MOON: BIOLOGICAL CLOCKS

In Chapter 7 we learned that photoreceptors in our eyes connect to various subcortical and cortical areas of the brain. This sensory system allows us to consciously see images when light from the sun reflects off objects on the Earth's surface. We evolved our receptors, nerves, and brain on a rotating planet that is periodically bathed with sunlight and moonlight. The Earth's yearly traverse around the sun also produces changing seasons. In this section we will examine evidence that humans have evolved a sensitivity to day and night and the progression of the seasons as well as to the reflected wavelengths we see as visual images.

Circadian Rhythms

Humans and other animals experience **circadian rhythms**, or cyclic changes in consciousness (such as sleep-wake cycles), physiology (such as body temperature), and behavior (such as activity level), over a 24-hour period. (The term *circadian* comes from the Latin *circa*, for "about," and *dies*, for "day.") Such rhythms attest to an animal's adaptation to a particular environmental niche. Some prey animals—bats, cats, moths, owls, and rats, for example—feed exclusively at night and remain inactive during the day, presumably because this behavior pattern gives them a selective advantage. Others—primates, bees, and cows, for instance—are more active during daylight hours. Interestingly, all modern mammals derive from nocturnal ancestors (Foster, 1993).

circadian rhythm Cyclic changes in consciousness (such as sleeping and waking), physiology (such as body temperature), and behavior (such as activity level) that are experienced over a 24-hour period.

Humans commonly experience daily alterations in their consciousness, behavior, and physiology. Basal metabolism and body temperature, for example, are at their low points a few hours before sunrise; we reach for the covers. No wonder, then, that humans tend to be more alert and active in midafternoon than in the early morning. The psychologist Jurgen Aschoff and his colleagues at Max Plank Institute in Germany have demonstrated a relationship between body temperature and alertness (Aschoff & Wever, 1981). As Figure 9.1 shows, warmer bodies are associated with higher levels of alertness than cooler bodies. The major alteration in consciousness, of course, occurs during sleep. All animals experience periodic cycles of sleep and wakefulness or alertness. Later in this chapter we will see that sleep may be seen as a type of consciousness or unconsciousness, depending on whether a person is dreaming.

Circadian rhythms are often described in terms of an animal's activity level. In the laboratory, for example, activity level is measured when an animal's movement breaks a photocell beam. Figure 9.2 shows an activity record for a flying squirrel from midnight to midnight over a 65-day period (Gould, 1982). This squirrel lived under two different lighting conditions: For the first 17 days it lived in constant darkness; thereafter it experienced alternating periods of light and darkness each day. The red line on day 1 indicate that the squirrel was most active between 8 A.M. and 4 P.M. Note that over days 1 through 17, its activity peaked a little sooner each day, so that after a couple of weeks its activity cycle was beginning around 5 A.M.

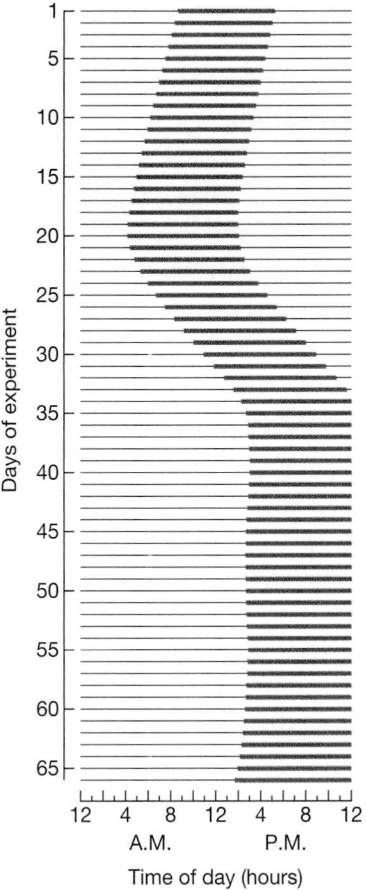

Figure 9.2 Circadian rhythms in activity level. This activity record for a flying squirrel shows that while it lived in constant darkness (days 1 through 17), its activity level peaked a little earlier each day, shifting its pattern of activity leftward. On days 21 through 61, an alternative light-dark schedule synchronized the squirrel's activity: it was most active when the light was on.
Source: From ETHOLOGY: The Mechanisms and Evolution of Behavior by James L. Gould. Copyright © 1982 by James L. Gould. Used by permission of W. W. Norton & Company, Inc.

Biological Clocks

Besides circadian rhythms, all plants and animals have **biological clocks**—cells that function as timekeepers, cycling on a solar, lunar, or seasonal basis. The existence of biological clocks is reflected in an animal's activity patterns, which differ not just during day and night, but from season to season. Because life evolved under conditions of cycling light, we might expect a biological clock that responds to the sun to keep proper time. But the experiment with flying squirrels showed that if squirrels are deprived of light cues, their internal clocks will speed up. (The effect is the same as a wristwatch that gains a few minutes each day.) This result provides evidence for the existence of a timing function that comes from *within* the animal. For this reason, an animal's biological clock is said to be *endogenous* (cued from within).

Location of Biological Clocks. If biological clocks are endogenous, where are they located? In humans, neurons in the hypothalamus—specifically, in the *suprachiasmatic nucleus*, or *SCN*—function as the main biological clock. The SCN is located near the parts of the hypothalamus that monitor body temperature and control eating and drinking (see Figure 5.6 on page 000). It is stimulated by impulses from nonvisual fibers in the retina that indicate the presence or absence of light. Such information helps the hypothalamus to regulate temperature and other physiological functions in the body's cells, glands, and other organ systems.

Nonvisual fibers in the retina, Chapter 7, p. 241

A variety of evidence suggests that animals have more than one biological clock. For example, cells in the golden hamster's retinal tissue have been found to regulate production of the hormone melatonin in a circadian rhythm that is independent of the rhythm generated by the hamster's SCN (Toscini & Menaker, 1995). These retinal cells are not ordinary rods and cones. Blind mole rats that do not have rods and cones and do not respond to flashes of bright light still have circadian rhythms based on lighting conditions (deJong and others, 1990). In fact, timekeeping may be an as-yet-unmeasured function of most cells. A single neuron from the nervous system of *Apysia* (the marine snail used in conditioning experiments in Chapter 6) will continue to respond rhythmically to a light-dark cycle even after it has been removed from the organism (Strumwasser, 1965).

Resetting the Biological Clock. Each animal's main biological clock is set to circadian time, meaning that its period is about a day long. Biological clocks vary from nocturnal animals to diurnal animals, as well as from individual to individual within a species (Carpenter & Grossberg, 1984). In the same way that animals can be shown to have endogenous rhythms by putting them in *constant*

biological clock Cells that function as endogenous timekeepers, cycling on solar or lunar time.

Even without eyes, a blind mole rat can have its biological clock reset by light.

darkness or constant light, their sensitivity to exogenous cues (cues from the *outside* world) can be shown by *alternating* periods of light with periods of darkness. In the flying squirrel experiment, when daily light-dark cycles were restored (see Figure 9.2), the squirrel's activity pattern shifted and began to cycle over a period *longer* than 24 hours. From days 17 to 33, the squirrel's activity began a few minutes later each day, shifting the pattern of dark lines rightward.

After about 2 weeks, researchers noticed an interesting effect. From days 34 to 61, the squirrel's activity pattern began and ended at the same time each day, making the record of its activity perfectly straight. Aided by the cycles of light and dark in the laboratory, the animal's biological clock was keeping perfect time. Its circadian rhythms had become *entrained* to the light-dark cycle in which it lived.

Free-Running Rhythms and Zeitgeibers

What an interesting way to keep time! In response to the Earth's rotation around the sun, flying squirrels, humans, and even plants have evolved endogenous timing devices that cycle at about 24 hours, tying their activity levels to the sunlight (or in nocturnal animals, to its absence). Under normal circumstances, these natural cycles change only slowly throughout the seasons. As the days slowly grow longer and the nights shorter in spring and summer, animals' activity cycles remain synchronized. As best we know, there have been no abrupt shifts in these seasonal patterns for millions of years.

In a natural setting, sunlight provides the external cues that synchronize an animal's biological clock. In the same way that the pacemaker cells in the heart are influenced by the vagus nerve (see page 115), the SCN's clock can be speeded up (or slowed down) by information from the retinal nerves. For this reason, early researchers called the light from the sun a *zeitgeiber*, German for "time-giver." A **zeitgeiber** is a stimulus, usually daylight, that entrains or ties an animal's biological clock to the Earth's rotational period, preventing its activity cycle from *free-running*, or cycling independently of light cues.

By manipulating light and dark in the laboratory, researchers can induce free-running in laboratory animals. If an animal is kept in total darkness, retinal neurons cannot signal the animal's biological clock in the SCN. The clock will begin to free-run, shifting the animal's daily activity pattern. For example, during day 1 to 17 of the flying squirrel experiment, the activity pattern was slightly less than 24 hours, a schedule not seen under normal lighting conditions (see Figure 9.2).

Recall that a human's body temperature and alertness also cycle in circadian fashion (see Figure 9.1). Does the sun set the clock, regulating body temperature, or has the body evolved to respond to the morning sun's warmth as well as light? That is, does the sun's *warmth* act as a zeitgeiber? Laboratory studies have shown that warmth and light can act independently as zeitgeibers. For squirrels that are kept in laboratories at constant temperatures, light is the zeitgeiber, as shown in Figure 9.2. But for animals that are kept in constant light or darkness, in a laboratory where the *temperature* cycles every 24 hours, temperature is the zeitgeiber. That is, the animals' activity cycle becomes synchronized to changes in temperature.

Can we conclude from this analysis that the sun causes the human body temperature to cycle through both its warmth and its light? The answer is no. In another experiment, researchers allowed a human's circadian rhythm to free-run by removing day-night cues (Eible-Eibesfeldt, 1975). Their subject, who lived deep in a cave, developed a body temperature cycle that differed from his sleep cycle. As Figure 9.3 shows, in the absence of light-dark cues, this subject went to sleep a little later each day. Over the same 17-day period, his body temperature cycle did not change significantly. Body temperature, we must conclude, responds to a different internal clock, one that cannot easily be shifted.

zeitgeiber A stimulus (usually daylight) that entrains a biological clock to the Earth's rotation, preventing an animal's activity cycle from free-running. (German for "time giver.")

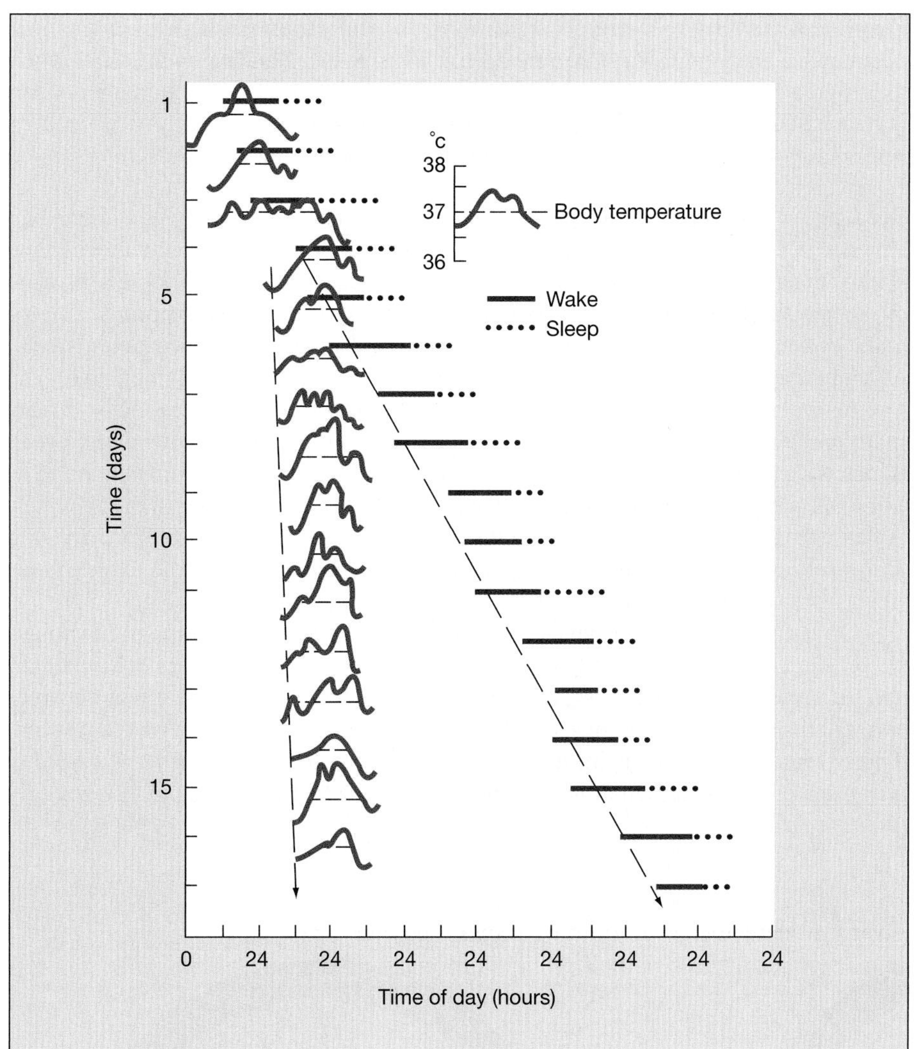

Figure 9.3 Circadian rhythm in a cave. Researchers measured the activity level and temperature of a volunteer who lived in a cave, isolated from all time cues, for 17 days. Over the first 4 days, the subject's temperature shifted and then stabilized; after that his high and low temperatures occurred at about the same time each day. In contrast, his activity cycle continued to begin a little later each day. *Source:* From Eible-Eibesfeldt, 1975, p. 438.

One last example will show the importance of zeitgeibers, and how much a free-running circadian rhythm can disrupt a person's life. A 28-year-old blind man who suffered periodically from sleep disturbances, depression, and fatigue, was found to be free-running on a cycle of 24.9 rather than 24 hours (Miles, Raynal, & Wilson, 1979). His overlong biological clock meant that about every 13 days, his sleep pattern, body temperature, and alertness were completely out of synchrony with the sun. His body was preparing to sleep at the same time everyone else's was preparing to face the day. Like the subject in the cave, he lacked or was insensitive to the zeitgeibers that keep most people from free-running.

Disruption of Light-Dark Cycles

Free-running circadian rhythms typically cycle at 24.5 to 25 hours (the pattern seen in Figure 9.3, and on days 18 to 34 in Figure 9.2). Thus humans (and most diurnal animals) have a natural rhythm that is half an hour to an hour *longer* than a day. This longer free-running rhythm helps to explain the unpleasant effects of disruptions to our entrained rhythms, such as those produced by the transition to daylight savings time.

Daylight Savings Time. Transitions to and from daylight savings time occur twice each year. Most people adjust better when "falling back" than when "springing forward," because they gain an hour, and the normal human rhythm is closer to 25 than to 24 hours. When they "spring forward," the day is only 23 hours long—more than an hour shorter than the body's natural rhythm.

Jet Lag. Another example of the unpleasant effects of the disruption of circadian rhythms is jet lag. When a human travels rapidly from one time zone to another, the body's circadian rhythms must shift from the light-dark cycle of the home time zone to the light-dark cycle of the destination time zone. The resulting disruption of sleep-wake cycles, alertness, and other physiological and psychological variables is typically greater than that produced by the shift to and from daylight savings time.

As we might expect, the amount of jet lag we experience depends on how many time zones we cross. Less obvious is the importance of the direction in which we travel: most people experience greater jet lag traveling from west to east. For example, a person who is flying from Dallas to London crosses six time zones. A flight that leaves Dallas at 4 P.M. takes about 8 hours to get to London, arriving at approximately 6 A.M. local time. The problem is, according to the traveler's biological clock, the flight arrives at midnight (see the inner clock in Figure 9.4).

Obviously, the traveler will want to sleep for the next few hours, even though he or she may need to conduct business the same day. Travelers who remain awake, conduct their business, and take a return flight that evening will be tired, but will disrupt their biological clocks less than they would if they stayed a week. Those who do not return immediately are advised to get through the first day without sleeping and then adjust to the local time schedule. Doing so is especially

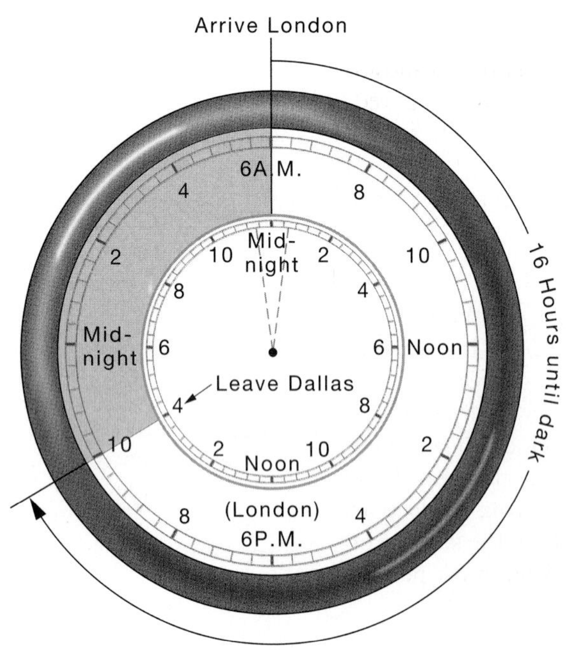

Figure 9.4 **Jet lag: West to east.** A person who flies from Dallas to London travels for 8 hours, crossing six time zones in the process. The journey causes a 6-hour shift in the traveler's entrained light-dark cycle. Taking off from Dallas at 4 P.M. (inner circle), the traveler arrives in London, where the local time is 6 A.M. (outer circle). This discrepancy between the traveler's biological clock and the time in the local time zone causes jet lag. To confound the problem, the traveler must get through 16 hours of daylight before the sun sets and it is time to sleep.

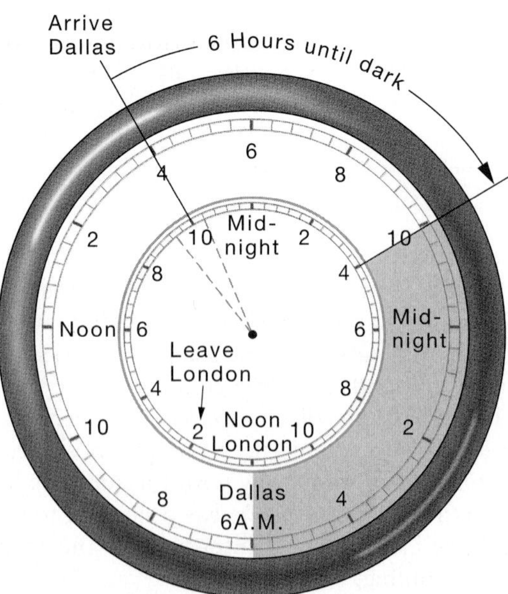

Figure 9.5 **Jet lag: East to west.** The Dallas-to-London flight is easier for most people than the London-to-Dallas flight. The 8-hour flight leaves London at 2 P.M. (inner circle), arriving in Dallas (outer circle) at 4 P.M. The traveler, still entrained to London time, feels as if it is midnight, but only 6 hours remain until sunset.

difficult in the summer, when London receives 16 hours of daylight. To delay sleep until the sun goes down, a traveler must stay awake 30 or more hours.

For most people, the return flight from London to Dallas is easier. A flight that leaves London at 2 P.M. arrives in Dallas about 4 P.M. (see Figure 9.5). According to the traveler's biological clock, the time is about 10 P.M., and again the tendency is to want to go to sleep. In general, people shift their biological clocks more quickly when traveling east to west. In one study, the average person took 30 to 40 minutes to fall asleep after flying from west to east; on east-to-west trips, the time was less than 20 minutes (Nicholson et al., 1986). Even though the duration of the flight is the same, so that the traveler has been awake about the same number of hours (and should therefore be equally tired), the number of daylight hours remaining on arrival differs. Arriving in Dallas, the traveler has only 6 hours of daylight to endure before darkness. Unfortunately, the biological clock will insist on waking the traveler up at 2 A.M.! Staying up longer helps to speed the shift back to local time.

Taking a moderate dose of melatonin in the afternoon can minimize the symptoms of jet lag. One of the functions of the SCN cells is to signal the pineal gland to increase or decrease the production and secretion of melatonin, a hormone. The increased release of melatonin around 8 to 10 P.M. each evening causes sleepiness several hours later (Haimov & Lavie, 1996). Eastbound travelers, then, can shift their sleep-wake cycles a couple of hours by taking melatonin in the late afternoon (several hours early), wearing an eyeshade to cut out the light, and refraining from eating, drinking, or smoking. The idea is to go to sleep early and awake the next morning in the new time zone.

Individual differences in the east-versus-west phenomenon are worth noting. A friend of mine who travels to Europe with students each summer claims to experience more jet lag on returning home (flying west) than on arriving in London (flying east). His reasoning is that the excitement of beginning a trip (and anticipating the fast pace of sightseeing in Europe) overrides his jet lag.

Can excitement override the disruption caused by jet lag? Figure 9.6 shows one line of evidence that does *not* support this hypothesis. Researchers compared the win-loss records of visiting major-league baseball teams to see if the teams would win the same number of games whether they flew east or west. While the excitement factor should have been about equal in both cases, the teams lost more games after flying east than after flying west (Recht, Lew, & Schwartz, 1995). These performance data support subjective reports of a greater west-to-east disruption.

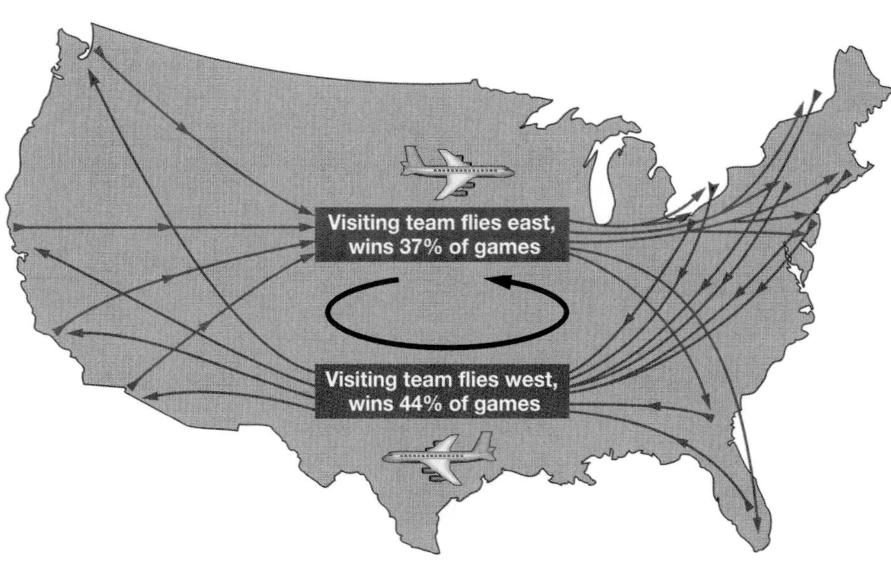

Figure 9.6 The effect of jet lag on visiting baseball teams. Visiting teams that fly east to compete in a major-league baseball game win only 37 percent of the time, whereas visiting teams that fly west win 44 percent of the time.

An estimated 30 to 50 percent of young people are chronically sleep deprived.

Sleep Deprivation. If the effects of disrupted circadian rhythms were restricted to those people who occasionally cross time zones, we wouldn't be discussing them in detail. The fact is, modern lifestyles in and of themselves tend to disrupt our biological clocks. As any student who has pulled an all-nighter knows, getting through the next day is a problem, as is getting back on schedule Monday morning following a weekend of partying. The disruption of normal sleeping patterns alters a person's attention span, alertness, and performance. But why? Is the problem caused by disruption of the circadian rhythm, a loss of sleep, or both?

To answer this question, let's analyze the typical student's sleeping pattern. Both high school and college students get less than 8 hours of sleep each night. In one study, 152 male and female college students averaged 6.9 hours of sleep on school nights, while 125 others averaged 6.5 hours *plus* 1.3 hours of napping. Men and women did not differ in their napping, but the differences in total sleep time between nappers and nonnappers was significant (Barker, 1977).

These deficits in sleep time are compounded by changes in circadian rhythms. College students' schedules vary from semester to semester, and their days and nights are filled with diverse activities. Electric lighting allows students to work after the sun sets, and lights, temperature changes, clocks, and other zeitgeibers help many to keep a more or less regular schedule 5 days a week. On weekends, chronically sleep-deprived students try to balance sleep with other activities, including recreation. By staying up late and sleeping late, they allow their biological clocks to free-run at about 24.50 to 24.75 hours. From late Friday to early Sunday, their biological clocks can shift as much as 2 hours (Moore-Ede, Czeisler, & Richardson, 1983). On Monday morning, the alarm clock may indicate 7:30 A.M., but the student's biological clock says it is 5:30. Both sleep deprivation and the disruption of circadian rhythms, then, account for blue Mondays and the all-nighter phenomenon.

Shift Work. Like students, people who work the night shift desynchronize their biological clocks. Shift workers may labor for months or even years on a reverse light-dark cycle, sleeping during the day and attempting to function at night. They are more prone to fatigue and accident than day workers. Lack of sleep, for instance, contributed to the human error that caused the disastrous nuclear accidents at Chernobyl and Three Mile Island, both of which occurred around 4:00 A.M. (Coleman, 1986). People who work at night and sleep during the day are also more susceptible than others to psychological and physical problems, including cardiovascular disease, ulcers, hypertension, and insomnia (Moore-Ede et al., 1983).

Because our complicated society continues to demand that shift workers and others function around the clock, researchers have tried to identify those variables that most affect human performance during the night. In one study, researchers monitored two groups of young men who worked at night and slept during the day (Czeisler et al., 1990). The idea was to see how long they would take to become entrained to a light-dark reversal after working at a daytime job. The treatment group worked under bright lights and slept in a dark room during the day; the control group worked and slept in ordinary room light. Researchers found that the treatment group adjusted more quickly than the control group to the shift in their circadian rhythms. Within about 4 days they had returned to their normal performance levels, aided by brighter lights. The control group did not entrain to the new rhythm as quickly.

Two lessons can be drawn from this research. First, a college student or shift worker who must work through the night will be more alert and will perform better in a well-lighted environment. Turn *all* the lights on! Second, napping during the day can further disrupt already disturbed circadian rhythms. And as we will see in the next section, the sleep a nap provides differs in quality from nighttime sleep. Humans evolved to function optimally during daylight hours and to sleep through the night. Altering these patterns incurs both physical and psychological costs.

Lunar and Seasonal Rhythms

The sun is both the driving source of circadian rhythms and the most important zeitgeiber. But what about the other natural source of illumination for our planet, the moon? Do humans respond to lunar rhythms? Long the source of speculation, lunar effects on human behavior are not as easily measured as the sun's. (If humans were a form of marine life whose eating habits and reproduction patterns depended on the tides, our species' evolution *would* be tied more directly to the moon's phases.) For reasons that remain unclear, female menstrual cycles likely reflect the moon's prehistoric influence on animal fertility (Jongbloet, 1983).

The seasons, of course, arise from the yearly orbit of the Earth around the sun. There are many examples of animal behavior that reflect seasonal changes. Migration patterns are cued by seasonal zeitgeibers, including changes in both temperature and the length of the day. Likewise, many animals hibernate, or otherwise reduce their activity in winter, and then increase their activity as daylight and temperature increase each spring (Nelson, Badura, & Goldman, 1990). Humans, too, are affected by these solar cycles, as the following examples show.

Seasonal Affective Disorder. During the winter months, too little light, especially in the far northern climes, has been linked to a form of depression called *seasonal affective disorder*, or *SAD*. Therapy for SAD is simple: increasing the amount of light a person receives each day produces the same effects as an earlier sunrise and a later sunset. Specifically, beginning the day in a special room illuminated with high-intensity lights delays the production of melatonin, while extending the day in the same way increases levels of the neurotransmitter serotonin, which reduces both fatigue and depression (Nelson et al., 1990). Here is another example of how light activates and energizes human performance by altering the brain's biochemical balance.

Season of Birth. In many species, sexual behavior has a seasonal rhythm. Male rhesus monkeys experience a seasonal increase in testosterone, which along with cues from females' menstrual cycles produces a breeding and a birthing season (Gordon, Bernstein, & Rose, 1978). Because human females are "concealed ovulators," human sexual behavior is less explicitly tied to menstrual cycles than the estrous-driven sexual behavior of other primates. But some controversial research seems to show a relationship between the season of birth and human disorders such as schizophrenia. Evidence gathered by many different researchers indicates that more schizophrenics are born in the winter and spring months than in the summer and fall months (Franzek & Beckmann, 1996). Other epidemiological studies have suggested that the season in which a person is born can predispose a person to multiple sclerosis (Wiberg & Templer, 1994) and alcoholism (Modestin, Ammann, & Wurmie, 1995).

None of these studies indicates a connection between the signs of the zodiac and mental illness. Rather, environmental factors such as cold temperatures (and lack of sunlight?) in the northern parts of the northern hemisphere, and perhaps greater susceptibility to viral agents during that time, may affect pregnant women during critical periods of the fetus's brain development. This research will be interesting to follow in coming years.

In sum, in modern societies, most humans do not show extreme seasonal shifts in behavior. This finding may reflect the civilizing effects of climate-controlled housing. Spring fever, however, remains unexplained.

INTERIM SUMMARY

1. Plants and animals have evolved a sensitivity to the periods of natural light and dark that we call day and night. As a result, animals experience ***circadian rhythms***—sleep and body temperature cycles that vary systematically over a period of approximately 24 hours.
2. Activity records of laboratory animals that live in constant light or dark have led to the discovery of an endogenous ***biological clock***. In the absence of light and dark cues, sleep and wake cycles and temperature fall out of phase, occurring either earlier (in constant darkness) or later (in constant lightness) each day. Cycling without reference to light and dark cues is called *free-running*.
3. An animal's main biological clock is located in the self-paced activity of neurons in the *suprachiasmatic nucleus (SCN)* of the hypothalamus. Other cells in the body also have timing functions.
4. The rising and setting of the sun provides the external cues that reset and synchronize the human biological clock. If left to free-run, the human biological clock will reset to a cycle of about 24.5 to 25 hours.
5. Light is the most important ***zeitgeiber*** that entrains an animal's biological clock to the Earth's rotation, preventing it from free-running. Temperature change is another zeitgeiber.
6. Both daylight savings time and *jet lag*, caused by rapid travel from one time zone to another, disrupt circadian rhythms, producing fatigue, decreased alertness, and altered sleep-wake cycles.
7. Most people experience greater jet lag traveling from west to east than from east to west.
8. Melatonin is a hormone that is released on a circadian cycle. Its level peaks in the evening, contributing to sleepiness several hours later.
9. One result of civilized life is that many people continue their activities into the nighttime hours, and as a result, suffer chronic sleep deprivation. Sleeping-in on weekends tends to shift the human biological clock by as much as 2 hours, making Monday mornings difficult.
10. Shift workers who attempt to function on a reversed light-dark cycle disrupt their biological clocks, subjecting themselves to chronic fatigue, raising their accident rates, and increasing their susceptibility to cardiovascular disease, ulcers, hypertension, and insomnia.
11. *Seasonal affective disorder (SAD)* can be attributed to the dearth of sunlight during winter months. Artificial lighting reduces the depressive symptoms of SAD by decreasing the amount of melatonin and increasing the amount of serotonin produced in the brain.
12. Humans born in the winter and spring are at greater risk than others for schizophrenia. Research suggests that other disorders, such as multiple sclerosis and alcoholism, may be correlated with the season of birth.

For Further Thought

1. Circadian rhythms were once called *diurnal*, or daily, rhythms. Why do you think researchers began to use the term *circadian* instead?
2. What therapy would you suggest for the blind man who experienced periodical sleep disturbances because of his free-running circadian rhythms?
3. Is there such a thing as spring fever? If so, how might it be adaptive?
4. A person whose zodiac sign is Taurus was probably conceived in August. What might that fact—and the latitude of the person's birthplace—have to do with the determinants of the individual's personality?

SLEEP AND DREAMS

Though scientists have discovered much about the electrophysiological and biochemical nature of sleep and dreams, their function remains elusive. While we can easily understand the need for sleep in humans and other animals, we can only speculate about the purpose of dreams. Yet an analysis of the function of dreams is especially critical to an understanding of the human mind, for dreams are a form of consciousness that influences our waking behavior. Let's begin this section by looking at the relationship between sleep and the light-dark cycles that determine our circadian rhythms. We will see that sleep has a rhythm of its own, of which dreaming is an integral part.

Why We Sleep

In humans, sleeping is associated with the night. But the amount of sleep humans average each day isn't tied to darkness. In London, for example, the amount of darkness varies from 8 to 16 hours per day, depending on the season. Around the world, the amount of day and night people experience varies with both season and latitude. Eight hours of sleep per night corresponds to the length of summer nights in northern climes. During the 16 hours of darkness in the winter months, however, humans continue to sleep for about 8 hours a day. Sleep, then, is only loosely tied to darkness.

Compared to other animals, humans sleep a moderate amount of time (see Figure 9.7). One striking fact is that while the length of the night is the same for all animals in a given location and season, the length of their sleep is not. Likewise, there is no simple relationship between the length of the night and the length of an animal's sleep. Why is there so much variability in sleep time among animals? Why, in fact, do they sleep?

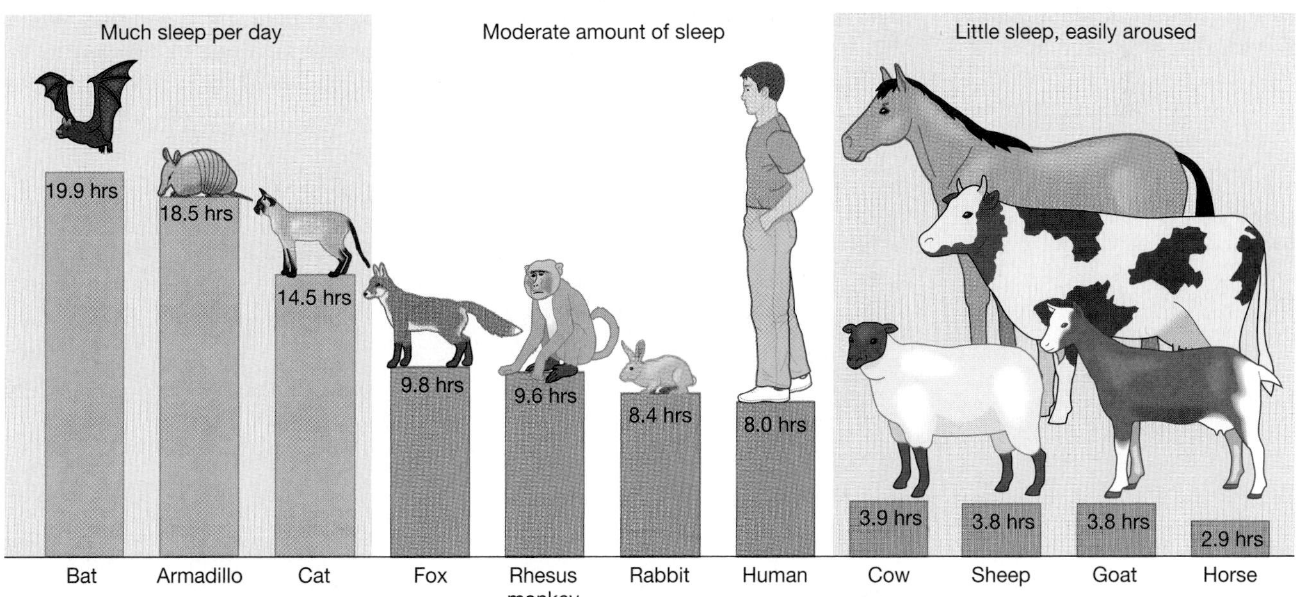

Figure 9.7 Sleeping time in various animals. Different animals sleep for different amounts of time, even in the same latitudes and seasons. In general, predators (left) sleep more than prey animals (right). Animals that are secure in their sleep, such as the armored armadillo and burrowing rodents, also tend to sleep longer than prey animals. This relationship is not perfect, however, as the mixed group of moderate sleepers (middle) attests. Other variables that affect the amount of time an animal sleeps include the need to conserve energy and the time of day (day or night). *Source:* From BIOLOGICAL PSYCHOLOGY 6th ed. by J. Kalat. Copyright © 1998. Reprinted by permission of Brooks/Cole, an imprint of The Wadsworth Group, a division of Thomas Learning. Fax 800 730-2215.

Two tentative explanations for why animals sleep are the conservation of energy that results from inactivity and the relative safety of "hiding" in the dark. As Figure 9.1 shows, body temperature decreases during sleep, because of a reduction in metabolic activity. Because primates and many other animals depend on their vision to find food, and are thus relatively inefficient at hunting in darkness, they may rest to conserve their energy at night (Berger & Phillips, 1995). Being inactive at night also minimizes an animal's movement, and therefore the probability of being discovered by predators. In contrast, animals such as bats, which occupy a high-protein nocturnal feeding niche, escape predators by hiding in the safety of dark caves during daylight, sleeping there for close to 20 hours per day. Taken together, these findings suggest that sleep has evolved differently in predators and prey animals, influenced by the need for light to find food and the need to conserve energy.

A Normal Night's Sleep

We have seen that humans sleep about 8 hours each day, no matter when the sun goes down. Researchers have discovered this fact by observing human subjects in a sleep laboratory, where temperature and lighting can be controlled, brain activity can be monitored, and other aspects of sleeping behavior can be measured.

To monitor the brain's activity during sleep, scientists attach electrodes to the surface of a subject's scalp and connect them to a computer that produces an **electroencephalogram (EEG)**, a record of the voltage changes in a particular part of the brain. The EEG shows both the amplitude and frequency of the brain waves (see Figure 9.8). In addition, researchers attach two separate electrodes, one on the forehead and the other on the skin just outside the eye, to measure the electrical potentials of the muscles that move the eyes. In some sleep studies, scientists also attach electrodes to representative muscles throughout the body to measure how muscle tone changes during sleep.

To understand sleep patterns, researchers first record a subject's brain activity while awake and alert. The top left portion of Figure 9.9 shows that William James's "normal waking consciousness" is characterized not by one but by two different types of brain wave, called *beta* and *alpha waves*. Beta waves are a low-

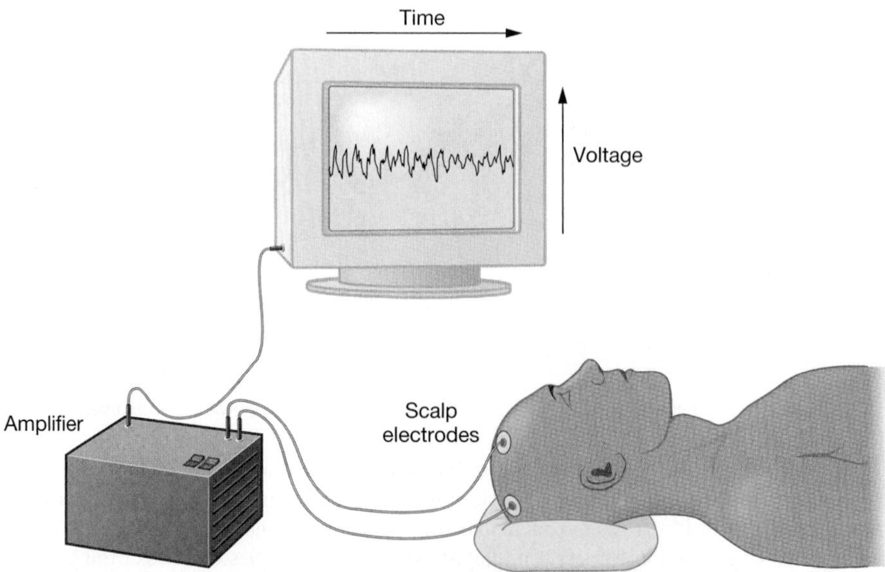

Figure 9.8 Recording an EEG. In an EEG, tiny voltage changes in the brain are captured by electrodes, amplified, and displayed visually on computer screens.

electroencephalogram (EEG) A visual record of voltage changes in the brain.

amplitude, high-frequency wave form that is observed only when a person is wide awake and alert. Alpha waves are also low in amplitude, but they are of lower frequency—that is, they are slower than beta waves. This pattern of electrical activity is seen when a person is awake but drowsy, with the eyes closed and the mind wandering. Merely opening one's eyes blocks the alpha waves. Visual experience, then, plays a pivotal role in maintaining consciousness.

Graphically, what does a typical night's sleep look like? The description is surprisingly similar from night to night and individual to individual. Figure 9.9 shows the overall pattern of sleep during a typical night. When a person first falls asleep, the alpha and beta patterns that accompany waking consciousness change to what is called stage 1 sleep, which is characterized by irregular, low-voltage *theta* waves. During the first hour of sleep, stage 1 progresses to stage 2, followed by stages 3 and 4. These later stages are also defined by their distinctive waveforms: stage 2, for instance, is characterized by sleep spindles and K complexes (see Figure 9.9). More important, the sleeper's heart rate and breathing slow down in each successive stage, and the waveform increases in amplitude and becomes more regular. Together, the high-amplitude *delta* waves that characterize stages 3 and 4 are known as *slow-wave sleep*.

REM Sleep

Figure 9.9 shows that a sleeper reaches slow-wave sleep after about an hour. During this time the muscles relax, and researchers have a difficult time awakening the subject. Half an hour later, another major change occurs: the sleep pattern

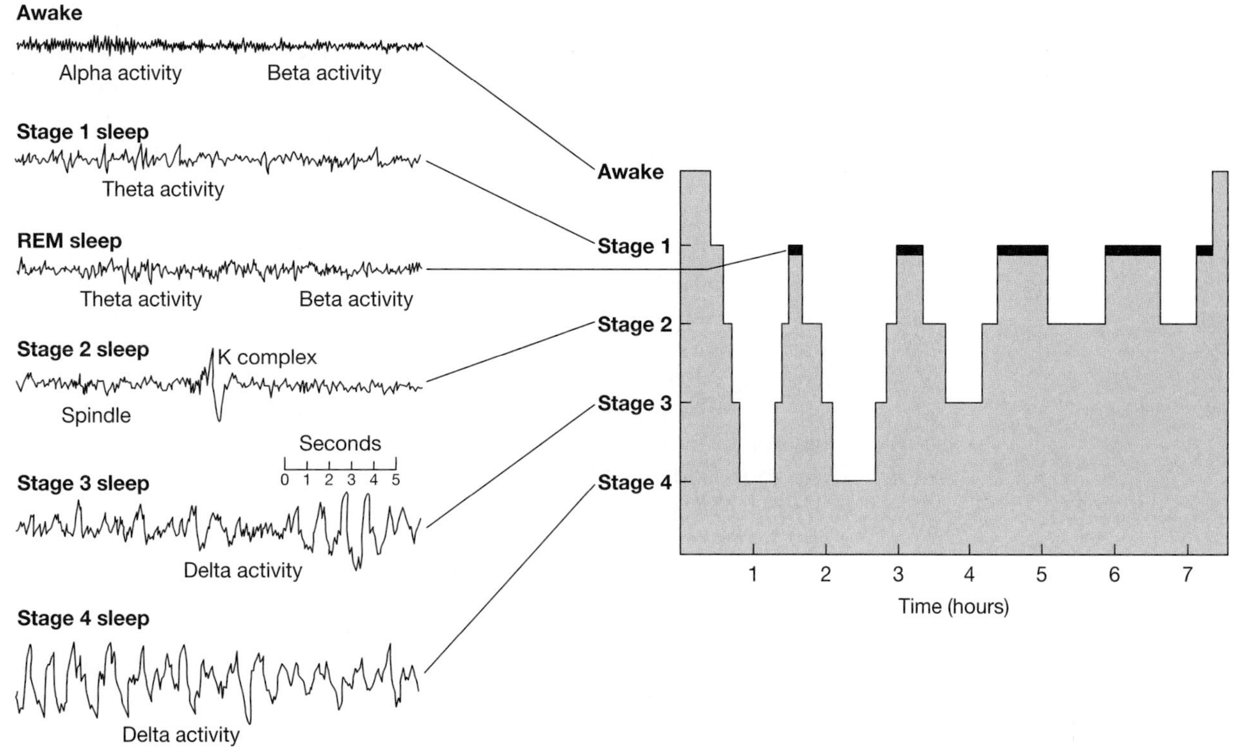

Figure 9.9 **Record of a good night's sleep.** During an average night's sleep, a typical person cycles through stages 1 through 4 and back several times, producing the sawtooth pattern shown here. Each sleep stage is defined by unique brain wave patterns. Note that REM sleep first appears about 90 minutes after sleep begins and recurs at approximately 90-minute intervals, each time for a progressively longer period. This record shows four complete REM episodes (dreams) and a fifth that was interrupted when the sleeper awoke. *Sources:* Adapted from Horne, 1988, and from Hartman, 1967.

A human subject in a sleep laboratory, wired for the night.

rapidly reverses itself, and the sleeper enters another stage, called *paradoxical sleep*, or **REM sleep**. The term *paradoxical* refers to the fact that the EEG for this stage resembles that of a person who is wide awake—that is, it shows beta activity. In actuality, however, the sleeper is in a deep sleep. A measure of muscle activity during this stage shows that it is at its lowest level of the night.

REM Cycles During Sleep. The REM stage (so-called because it is characterized by rapid eye movements) is the stage in which storylike dreams occur. Heart rate increases, and breathing becomes irregular, accented by short gasps. REM sleep is not the only sleep stage in which dreams occur, as early researchers reported (Dement, 1978). With improved EEG monitoring of subjects sleeping under relatively normal conditions at home, researchers have found that 83 percent of the time, subjects who are awakened from REM sleep recall storylike dreams. Fifty-four percent of sleepers who are awakened during non-REM stages report briefer, less elaborate nonnarrative dreams (Stickgold, Pace-Schott, & Hobson, 1994).

The cyclic changes between slow-wave sleep and REM sleep continue throughout the night. REM periods occur about every hour and a half; each new dream lasts a little longer than the last. As the night wears on, sleepers experience less slow-wave sleep (stages 3 and 4) and more REM sleep (see Figure 9.9). On an average night, a sleeper spends 1.5 to 2 hours dreaming. The following night the process begins anew, so that after a month's time a person has experienced 125 to 150 dreams. Few of them are remembered; sleepers who are awakened and asked for a dream report as little as 8 minutes after the end of a REM stage have no memory of their dreams. The dream sleepers do recall is typically the one that occurs just prior to awakening in the morning (Kelley, 1991).

As we noted earlier, muscle activity is inhibited during dreaming, which prevents potentially dangerous bodily movements. Sleepwalkers, then, are not acting out their dreams; rather, they are usually in stage 3 or 4, when the muscles are not inhibited. The exception to the general paralysis that accompanies REM sleep is that males typically have erections. But only rarely when they are awakened during REM sleep do sleepers report feeling sexually aroused or having dreams with sexual content.

The Need for REM Sleep. Over a lifetime, the cycle of waking states to non-REM and REM sleep varies, exhibiting different patterns at different ages. Figure 9.10 shows sleep patterns from birth through old age. Newborns spend about 8 hours a day in REM sleep and another 8 hours in non-REM. Interestingly, babies who are born prematurely spend even more time in REM sleep—up to 65 percent of their sleep time. Humans sleep less and less over the course of their lives, averaging only about 4 to 5 hours a night after age 70. Throughout a lifetime, however, a relatively constant fraction of sleep is taken up by dreams. Sleeping during the day also varies with age. Newborn infants take frequent naps, and young children nap once a day. Adults who keep relatively regular schedules tend to go without naps, but elderly adults often return to napping (Kelley, 1991).

Figure 9.7 compares the amount of sleep different animals get each night. What do we know about REM sleep in animals? Of the mammals that have been investigated, only the spiny anteater, arguably the most primitive of all mammals, does *not* enter REM periods when sleeping. Birds (but probably not fish, amphibians, or reptiles) also experience REM and non-REM sleep cycles. Whether animals dream during their REM periods is at present an unanswerable question. We can observe the rapid eye movements beneath the closed lids of both human infants and puppies, but without verbal reports from them, there is no way to know what their mental experiences are like.

REM sleep A stage of sleep that is characterized by storylike dreams and **r**apid **e**ye **m**ovements.

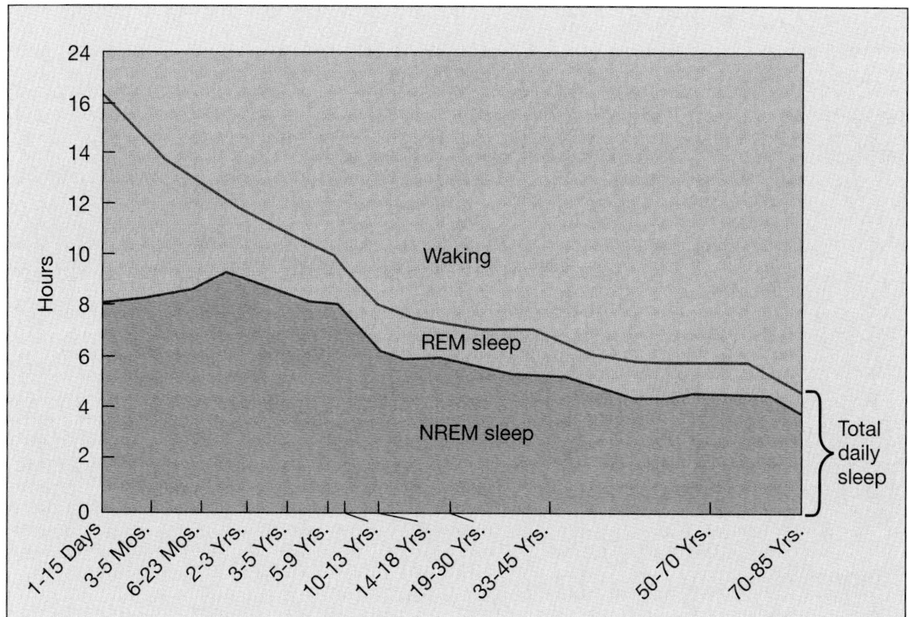

Figure 9.10 Sleep patterns over a lifetime. Infants and children sleep more, and spend more time in REM sleep, than older people. Throughout adulthood, time spent in REM sleep remains a fairly constant fraction of the sleep cycle. *Source:* From "Ontogenetic Development of the Human Sleep-Dream Cycle" by H. P. Roffwarg, J. N. Muzio and W. C. Dement, *Science*, vol. 152, (1966), pp. 604–619. Copyright © 1966 by American Association for the Advancement of Science. Reprinted by permission.

The Effects of Sleep Deprivation

Each of us has experienced the overwhelming desire to sleep after staying awake too long. Seeking sleep can be added to the list of primary drives discussed in Chapter 5. We seek sleep just as we seek food when we are hungry and water when we are thirsty.

Sleep and primary drive, Chapter 5, p. 155

Chronically tired, drowsy college students are part of a teenage subculture that routinely gets insufficient sleep. According to one estimate, teenagers in the United States are getting about 2 hours less sleep than their counterparts did in the early 1900s (Holden, 1993). What are the effects of such chronic sleep deprivation? Not surprisingly, sleep researchers who have studied sleep-deprived volunteers under laboratory conditions have reported deteriorating performance on tasks that require subjects to pay attention. Whether an individual is studying or driving, the primary effect of sleep deprivation is a tendency to "nod off"—a loss of focus and attention that normally accompanies entry into stage 1 sleep. The nuclear plant accidents mentioned earlier were likely caused by lapses of attention—dozing off—in shift workers with disturbed circadian rhythms, as they fought the need to sleep.

The question of why sleep deprivation has these effects can be reframed in terms of REM deprivation. Although evolutionary answers to this question focus on the need to stay safe in the dark and conserve energy, studies in which subjects are selectively deprived of REM or non-REM sleep provide a different answer. William Dement (1978) tested the effects of REM deprivation in several males by watching sleepers' EEGs and awakening them just as a REM episode started. After following this procedure for several nights, Dement found that he needed to interrupt subjects more frequently to keep them from going into a REM episode. When these REM-deprived subjects were finally allowed to sleep uninterrupted, they entered REM sleep early and spent much more time than usual in the REM stage. This phenomenon, called *REM rebound,* suggests that humans have a specific need for REM sleep. Compared to a control group of subjects who were awakened equally often, but not during REM episodes, REM-deprived subjects were irritable, anxious, and less able to concentrate the next day.

In another study, REM-sleep-deprived subjects were unable to remember perceptual training they had undergone the preceding day (Karni, Tanne, Rubenstein, Askenasy, & Sagi, 1994). Significantly, recent brain research on rats has suggested that REM sleep may help in *memory consolidation*. As the rats learned a circular maze, researchers recorded unique patterns of brain activity in the hippocampus. Later, the rats exhibited precisely the same brain patterns in the same area during REM sleep. Perhaps their daily activities are encoded and stored as memories during REM sleep (Kenway & Wilson, 2001).

Yet other sleep studies have shown that selectively depriving subjects of slow-wave sleep (stages 3 and 4) also produces a rebound effect. When allowed to sleep uninterrupted, subjects compensated for lost slow-wave sleep by entering the stage sooner and staying in it longer. Apparently two drive states need to be met—the need for REM and the need for slow-wave sleep—though the nature of those drives remains unknown. Observations of REM and slow-wave rebound effects suggest that sleep has some kind of *restorative* function, but what exactly is restored is unclear. Certainly, after going to bed dog-tired, most people feel restored by a good night's sleep. Physically active people who experience weariness and muscle soreness after work or heavy exercise find that sleep is far more effective than pain relievers in restoring their sense of well-being.

One-third of adults report moderate to severe insomnia.

Insomnia

At one time or another, most people have been tired but unable to sleep. Perhaps there are presents to be opened the next day or a trip to be planned, or perhaps you simply can't stop thinking of the date you just had. On these occasions, saying that you have insomnia would not be correct. **Insomnia** refers to chronic problems in getting to sleep or staying asleep. Although a sleeping problem that occurs a few times each year is merely annoying, insomnia is a debilitating disorder that produces chronic fatigue, depression, and a compromised immune system (Bootzin, Manber, Perlis, Salvio, & Wyatt, 1993). Approximately one-third of the adult population reports moderate to severe insomnia; older people are most affected.

Insomniacs give many reasons for their condition, including anxiety, stress, depression, and pain, but why these complaints manifest themselves in a sleep disorder in some people rather than others is not known. Nor is there a universal treatment for insomnia. Sedatives are effective and have been used for decades; because they are highly addictive, however, they have caused as many problems as they have solved (Mendelson, 1993). To remain effective, sedatives must be taken in progressively higher doses, which can cause debilitating side effects. Withdrawal from sedatives can be dangerous.

If you are experiencing sleep problems, the following advice may help you:

- *Get tired during the day.* A regular program of daily exercise may be the trick to becoming physically tired.
- *Get regular.* Eat, work, and be active during the day; sleep at night. Do not confuse "going to sleep" cues with "studying" cues: Sleep in one place and study in another.
- *Restrict stimulants before bedtime.* Coffee, nicotine, and the caffeine in soft drinks will tend to keep you awake.
- *Clear your mind.* Read a novel or listen to soothing music for 10 or 20 minutes to clear your mind of personal problems. Turn out the lights only when heavy eyelids begin to interfere with your reading. Sweet dreams.

insomnia A chronic sleep disorder in which a person experiences difficulty getting to sleep or staying asleep.

Dreams and Dreaming

Research seems to indicate that most people dream every night of their lives. Dreaming is an altered form of consciousness in which the sighted dreamer sees and the blind dreamer hears events in an alter-world. This special form of mental activity may play a significant role in determining the course of events during normal waking consciousness. Dreams of victory can compel and motivate superior performance or provide inspiration to the perplexed, as in Shakespeare's *Hamlet*. Let's look at some theories of why we dream.

Freudian Theory. The first psychologist to attempt to explain the function of dreams was Sigmund Freud, whose analysis of the primal nature of dreams is both fascinating and untestable. As Freud noted in his book *The Interpretation of Dreams* (1900), people often do things in their dreams that they wouldn't do in normal life. Because dreams are a less-inhibited form of consciousness, Freud suggested, they are often symbolic of repressed thoughts and desires. Freud thought that dreams have both a *manifest content* (their story line) and a *latent content* (their disguised meaning). Two functions of dreams, according to Freud, are *wish fulfillment* and the maintenance of the integrity of waking consciousness through harmless dissipation of repressed thoughts and emotions. (A fuller discussion of the role of dreams in Freudian theory will be presented in Chapter 14.)

Dreams and Freud's psychoanalytic theory, Chapter 14, p. 498

The Activation-Synthesis Hypothesis. Dr. J. Allan Hobson of the Harvard Medical School recently described dreaming in this way:

> Dreaming is characterized by formal visual imagery (akin to hallucination), by inconstancy of time, place, and person (akin to disorientation), by a scenario-like knitting together of disparate elements (akin to confabulation), and by an inability to recall (akin to amnesia). Taken together, these four dream features are similar to the delirium of organic brain disease. (Hobson, 1997, p. 128)

Organic brain disease will be described in Chapter 18. Hobson's point is that dreaming produces a type of consciousness that, were it experienced in a normal waking state, would be deemed pathological.

Based on his research, Hobson has proposed a brain-based theory of dreaming called the *activation-synthesis hypothesis* (Hobson, 1988). The idea is that dreams are experienced consciously because the brain is physiologically active during the REM state, and many areas that are involved in waking consciousness are activated. One difference between the two states is that the sensory experiences (seeing, hearing, and so forth) that focus and direct waking consciousness are missing from REM sleep, so that dreams are not tied to reality. Without an anchor in sensory experience, dreams assume a phantasmagorical nature (Hobson, 1988). The activation-synthesis hypothesis helps to account for many commonly experienced dreams, such as running without getting anywhere and falling without hitting the ground.

More recent neuroimaging research indicates that different parts of the brain are active during REM and non-REM sleep states. As you might guess from an analysis of some of your own dreams, the parts of the frontal lobe that are involved in logical planning and thinking are deactivated during REM sleep, and the brainstem and limbic structures involved in emotion are activated (Hobson, Stickgold, & Pace-Schott, 1998).

The activation-synthesis hypothesis is quite different from Freudian theory. Freud saw dreaming as a therapeutic, even homeostatic, function that maintains the integrity of the personality during waking hours. Hobson sees dreaming as a side effect of running only part of the machinery underlying normal consciousness—that is, as an altered, less-rational form of consciousness. There may be some truth to both theories. Even though dreams are not tied to reality because the senses have been disengaged, memories do intrude and direct them, albeit nonlogically. You may have noticed that if you interrupt the writing of a term paper by going to sleep, you are likely to dream about writing a term paper. Likewise, children often dream they are urinating shortly before urinating in their sleep. The unconscious brain may direct these dreams in a way that reflects reality. (Another possibility is that the reality of writing a paper or urinating may direct the dreams.) In both cases, the dreams are meaningful, reflecting the operation of discrete parts of the brain. Dreams may be weird, but they are seldom uninterpretable to the dreamer.

Dreams as Problem Solving. Another theory of dreams, proposed by Rosalind Cartwright, is that they allow people the opportunity to work through their problems. Because dreams need not be logical, the dreamer can entertain more potential solutions to a problem than those wide awake (Cartwright, 1977; Cartwright & Lamberg, 1992). Anecdotal support for Cartwright's view comes from a common experience: when faced with a tough decision, we may decide to "sleep on it." Another source of support for this theory can be seen in descriptions of problem solving by famous scientists who achieved new insights into their research after a period of dreaming or daydreaming. And then there are those rats who seem to dream of how to solve a maze. . . .

INTERIM SUMMARY

1. Compared to other animals, humans sleep a moderate amount of time—about 8 hours in a 24-hour period. Although most humans sleep at night, there is no simple relationship between the length of darkness and the length of a sleep period.
2. Evolutionary explanations for why periods of activity alternate with periods of inactivity include both the need to conserve energy and the need to hide from predators.
3. An **electroencephalogram** (EEG) is a record of electrical changes in the brain. Microvoltages of varying amplitude and frequency help to define several different stages of sleep.
4. Normal waking consciousness is defined by low-amplitude, high-frequency waveforms when the eyes are open. The first four stages of sleep are characterized by high-amplitude slow waves, deep breathing, reduced heart rate, and difficulty in awakening.
5. An hour and a half after going to sleep, a person typically enters *paradoxical sleep*, or ***REM sleep.*** REM is an acronym for *rapid eye movement,* which occurs during paradoxical sleep. Though brain wave activity during this stage indicates that a person is awake, she or he is actually in the deepest stage of sleep. If awakened, the person will usually report dreaming.
6. Over a night's sleep, a person has 4 or 5 dreams totaling about 1.5 to 2 hours worth of sleep time. A person who is not allowed to dream for several days will exhibit REM rebound, a tendency to spend more time than usual in a dream state. Subjects who are deprived of slow-wave sleep also compensate by spending more time in slow-wave sleep.
7. Most birds and mammals experience both REM and non-REM sleep cycles. Human newborns spend 8 hours a day in REM. The brain may consolidate memories during REM.
8. ***Insomnia*** refers to chronic problems in getting to sleep or in staying asleep.
9. Freud thought that dreams reflected the working of the unconscious mind. According to Hobson's *activation-synthesis hypothesis*, dreams occur because the brain is physiologically active during sleep. Cartwright's theory is that dreams allow people an opportunity to work through their problems.

For Further Thought

1. What evidence can you bring to bear on the false assertion that the brain is less active during sleep than during waking hours?
2. Freud thought that many people could not remember their dreams because they represented a psychological threat. What might be an alternative explanation for an inability to remember one's dreams? (Hint: What happens when you ask a dreamer to recall a dream 5 or 10 minutes after it ends?)

3. The sound of a ringing telephone or dripping water can be incorporated into an ongoing dream. Does this evidence support the activation-synthesis hypothesis?
4. How might regular sleeping habits, including 1.5 to 2 hours of REM sleep each night, help a student to get good grades?

ALTERATIONS OF THE WAKING STATE: DAYDREAMS, HYPNOTISM, AND MEDITATION

Recall William James's (1902) assertion that separate from our normal waking consciousness, "there lie potential forms of consciousness entirely different." In the next two sections we will discuss some of these other forms of consciousness. A partial list might include daydreaming, focused attention, hypnosis, prayer or meditation, delirium, and drug-induced altered states.

Daydreaming

Everyone has experienced a wandering mind. (*Something—what was it?—that the prof said triggered my memory of the phone call, which brought to mind the friend who has a car like mine—I need to get that tire changed so I can get to work—or should I study instead? I should have studied for the test last night . . . but last night was so special.*) Such extraneous thoughts and *daydreams* often interrupt our attention.

Different from normal waking consciousness, **daydreams** are waking fantasies that divert attention from an ongoing task; they may be reveries of the past or wishful thinking about the future. Daydreams are common from childhood through old age (Singer, 1975). Although everyone daydreams, individuals differ in both the content and frequency of their daydreams.

In one study, for example, researchers asked how well two groups of people could attend to a 40-minute vigilance task. Subjects were asked to monitor a screen and report when a stimulus array changed—a task similar to an air-traffic controller's job. Researchers designated the two groups type A or type B, depending on how subjects had scored on tests of stress and time urgency. (Type A and type B personalities will be discussed in Chapter 16.) As predicted, members of the type A group stayed on task better and missed fewer signals. They also had fewer "mind-wanderings"; as the 40-minute interval wore on, members of the type B group began to daydream much more frequently (Perry & Laurie, 1992).

Daydreaming as a Source of Inattention. One estimate of the extent of mind-wandering is mind-boggling. At two universities, students of introductory psychology were interrupted in the classroom by confederates of researchers and asked what they had been thinking about in the last 5 minutes (Cameron & Biber, 1973). Forty-eight percent of 541 males and 33 percent of 629 females reported that they had had or were having a sexual fantasy. In another study, researchers found no gender difference in the frequency of "sexual, aggressive, and heroic daydreams" (Gold & Gold, 1982). In a third, researchers reported that females' daydreams were more likely than males' daydreams to involve problem solving and to be oriented to the future. Males in that study were more likely than females to report that their daydreams did not interfere with other tasks (Goldstein & Baskin, 1988). Although these studies suggest that men and women may daydream about different subjects, there were no reported gender differences in time spent daydreaming.

daydream A reverie or waking fantasy based on wishes or fears.

The distinction between paying attention and daydreaming may be a false one, however. Introspective evidence suggests that one can be more or less attentive without engaging in a daydream, and that reveries can easily be distinguished from meditation or from the mindlessness of an afternoon walk on a perfect day. In the next chapter we will use the terms *attention* and *focus* to describe a narrowing of consciousness. The process is something like searching a vast space with a flashlight and looking only where the light shines. Picking out a single voice at a noisy party is a practical example of this type of consciousness.

LINK

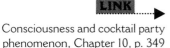

Consciousness and cocktail party phenomenon, Chapter 10, p. 349

Consciousness as visual consciousness, Chapter 8, p. 282

Attention is directed by specific parts of the brain. Chapter 7 described visual and auditory attention in terms of both "conscious" pathways in the brain including subcortical brain structures that coordinate head turning so as to focus on the source of a sound (see page 241). Conscious, voluntary efforts to attend to a particular stimulus seem to arise in the frontal lobe. Less voluntary types of attention seem to be directed from within rather than driven by sensory cues.

Daydreaming as a Source of Creativity and Imagination. Daydreaming is a type of consciousness that is probably undervalued: it may play a role in creativity, including mathematical and scientific breakthroughs. Some of the insights that led to Albert Einstein's concept of relativity, for example, arose from visual images the great thinker experienced while daydreaming (Kosslyn, 1987). More research is needed on this fascinating topic.

Recognizing these alterations of consciousness in small children is easy. Indeed, children blend fantasy with reality to such a degree that if an adult expressed their level of consciousness, it would be labeled pathological. A kindergartner's attention flits like a flashlight from the picture on the wall to Juanita's new dress to the teacher's whispered "shush." In fact, children (and psychotics) sometimes act as if they can't tell the difference between their sensory experiences and the voices and memories inside their heads (Jaynes, 1973). Children (but not adults) can have imaginary friends.

Basic to a child's maturation is the training of attentional processes throughout childhood. By college age, some but not all students can pay attention to classroom activities for 50 minutes at a time, with minimal flights of fancy. However, given the results of Cameron and Biber's study (1973) of daydreaming, we can estimate that at any given point, approximately 25 percent of the students in a college class will not be paying attention. At this age, attentional lapses may be considered normal. Such individual differences in the richness of imagination make our lives interesting and meaningful.

Hypnosis

As a child, I saw a demonstration of hypnosis that has haunted me ever since. The television program I was watching was broadcast live. A guest was introduced as a hypnotist, and another guest as his "subject." The hypnotist asked the subject to close his eyes and proceeded to hypnotize him. Then the hypnotist showed the audience a piece of chalk, and after telling the subject "Now I'm going to burn you with a lighted cigarette," he placed the chalk on the subject's forearm. The subject jerked his arm away.

"Did it hurt?" the hypnotist asked.

"Yes, it did," the subject mumbled.

The camera focused on the subject's arm, which within a few minutes developed a cigarette-sized blister. (This demonstration has been replicated in the laboratory by Spanos & Chaves, 1989.)

Hypnosis is a procedure that induces a temporary, trancelike state in which a person is more suggestible than usual. A Scottish physician named James Braid coined the term. An early proponent of hypnosis, he likened the hypnotic state to sleep (*Hypnos* was the Greek god of sleep). The only resemblance between hypnosis and sleep, however, is that the eyes are closed and behavior is arguably under less-than-normal voluntary control.

Hypnosis became a topic of general interest in 18th-century Europe, as interest in science and scientific explanations for natural phenomena increased. There an Austrian physician, Franz Mesmer (1734–1815), began public demonstrations of what became known as *mesmerism.* In a routine that involved magnets, a variety of mechanical contraptions, and a "laying on of hands," Mesmer claimed to effect an alleged "animal magnetism." In all likelihood, Mesmer's influence over his subjects came from his voice and manner rather than his contraptions, however. His legacy survives in the modern-day term *mesmerized.*

Today, hypnotism enjoys a dual status in Western culture. The stage variety of hypnosis is an easy target for those who are frustrated because the phenomenon is difficult to study scientifically, as well as for those who believe there is no such thing as a hypnotic state. But researchers seem to agree that whatever hypnosis is, it can be understood as a state of consciousness (Barber, 1979; Spanos, 1986).

Public demonstrations of "animal magnetism" captured the public's imagination in 18th-century Europe.

Hypnotic States in Animals. Because hypnotic states are found cross-culturally in a variety of guises, they are likely to have been part of human consciousness for as long as humans have existed. Is the same true of other animals—can they be hypnotized? Several lines of evidence suggest that in addition to sleep, some animals may experience altered states of consciousness similar to hypnosis. Prey animals that have been attacked, for example, often appear to be in a state of paralysis and shock: they become passive, their eyes glaze over, and they appear not to respond to pain. In the laboratory, all the vertebrates exhibit a phenomenon called *tonic immobility* (Prestrude, 1977). When mammals, birds, reptiles, amphibians, and fish are confined, held, and rhythmically stroked, their eyes glaze over and their bodies become rigid and immobile.

You may have noticed a similar phenomenon while rhythmically stroking your pet or being massaged yourself. A dog's, cat's, or lover's eyes will lose focus, quiver, and close, and the body exhibits something like tonic immobility. This property of the nervous system is ancient; all vertebrates exhibit some form of this behavior. Its adaptive value may be related to species-specific defense reactions (SSDRs)—for instance, freezing instead of fleeing when confronted by a threatening situation (Gallup & Rager, 1996). Tonic immobility has also been related to a condition called catatonia, which is seen in a rare form of schizophrenia (Gallup & Maser, 1977). Catatonic patients may remain immobile in an awkward, rigid posture for hours at a time.

Tonic immobility and touching, Chapter 8, p. 300

Tonic immobility and SSDRs, Chapter 3, p. 91

What Happens During Hypnosis? Hypnosis starts as a social relationship between two people. The hypnotist's (or hypnotherapist's) role is that of a guide, and the patient's that of a directed traveler. Techniques vary, but most presume a relationship of trust and agreed-upon goals for the treatment. As the patient sits or reclines in a comfortable chair in a room with reduced lightning, the hypnotherapist begins a procedure called *progressive relaxation,* instructing the patient to focus on the sensations in groups of muscles, beginning with the toes. After telling the patient to consciously relax the toes, the therapist then suggests, in a cadenced voice, that the relaxation will spread passively up the legs and into the torso. In doing so the hypnotist induces a calm, peaceful state in the subject, whose mind is preoccupied with the task of voluntarily relaxing the muscles. Popular misconceptions to the contrary, the object of hypnosis is to focus one's attention rather than suspend control of one's mind.

hypnosis A procedure that induces a temporary, trancelike state in which a person is more suggestible than usual.

Physiologically, some changes occur during hypnosis: the EEG of a hypnotized person is different from that of a person who is not hypnotized. Individuals who are easily hypnotized tend to display brain patterns associated with imagery; those who are not easily hypnotized, to display patterns associated with cognitive activity (Ray, 1997). Measures of neurochemistry and cerebral blood flow support the idea that reduced responsiveness to pain during hypnosis is accomplished by active inhibition of attention in the frontal cortex, thalamic, and subcortical systems (Crawford, Knebel, & Vendemia, 1998). Some evidence suggests that the right hemisphere is more active than the left during hypnosis (Gruzelier, 1998), but other evidence points to control of hypnotic phenomena by the left hemisphere (Jasiukaitis, Nouriani, Hugdahl, & Spiegel, 1997). In sum, a unique type of brain activity underlies the trancelike states some individuals experience.

LINK
Hypnotherapy as psychotherapy, Chapter 18, p. 620

Therapeutic Uses of Hypnosis. Hundreds, perhaps thousands, of psychotherapists, dentists, and increasingly, physicians use hypnosis as both as a medium for behavioral change (Gibson & Heap, 1991; Kirsch, Capafons, Cardena-Buelna, & Amigo, 1999) and an anesthetic (Crawford et al., 1998). Highly suggestible subjects—perhaps as many as 10 percent of the population—can undergo dental and surgical procedures using only hypnosis as anesthesia. A higher percentage of children make excellent hypnotic subjects, perhaps because of their suggestibility and active fantasy lives. Years ago I observed my 12-year-old daughter being hypnotized by a dentist just prior to being stuck with a hypodermic syringe in the tissue above her front teeth. She made no response, and when questioned later said that while she vaguely remembered someone "messing around" in her mouth, she had experienced no pain.

The degree to which humans can gain access to parts of their brain that are normally beyond control in a waking state is remarkable. We have seen, for example, that a hypnotized subject's brain can be directed to produce a blister in a particular place on the body. In another case, a patient who had a caesarean section under hypnosis, but without other anesthesia, reported no pain. Amazingly, she demonstrated voluntary control over vasoconstriction and vasodilation by bleeding alternately from one side of the incision and then the other. After much training, she accomplished these feats through self-hypnosis.

Theories of Hypnosis. How can a hypnotized subject become focused, and after concentrating on the hypnotist's instructions, form a blister? The psychologists John Kihlstrom and Nick Spanos and his colleagues see hypnosis as a social interaction between two people, in which one agrees to allow the other to influence his or her perception, memory, and voluntary action (Kihlstrom, 1985; Spanos & Burgess, 1994; Gwynn & Spanos, 1996). With further training, a person can learn self-hypnosis, reliance on an inner voice to direct the hypnotic state.

Ernest Hilgard, Nick Spanos, and others have examined evidence that hypnosis produces a *dissociation* in consciousness (Hilgard, 1973; Lynn & Rhue, 1994; Spanos & Burgess, 1994). **Dissociation** refers to the separation, or isolation, of specific mental processes such as memory or consciousness from the integrated personality (Spiegel & Cardena, 1991). In this analysis, the responses of a hypnotized person's autonomic nervous system to painful stimuli do not differ from those of nonhypnotized subjects. Hypnotized subjects merely respond less emotionally than others and behave as if they do not feel pain. Hilgard postulates that one part of the hypnotized person's consciousness is aware of the pain and can speak about it, but another part of the person's consciousness does not experience the pain. He calls the aware part the **hidden observer**.

dissociation The separation or isolation of mental processes, such as memory or consciousness, from the integrated personality

hidden observer (Hilgard) A part of consciousness that is aware of another part of consciousness.

More recent formulations call into question the existence of a hidden observer. Spanos and his colleagues have suggested that the dissociative behavior of a hypnotized person is a rule-governed social construction. In their interpretation, a hypnotized person's behavior and thoughts are "created, legitimated, maintained, and altered" through social interaction with the hypnotist or therapist (Spanos & Burgess, 1994). (This argument can be extended to people with multiple personality disorders; see Chapter 17.) In other words, hypnotized subjects learn to respond in the ways they do.

Dissociation and depersonalization disorder, Chapter 17, p. 592

Hilgard's concept of the hidden observer is one of the more contentious aspects of research on hypnosis. For example, my 12-year-old daughter had no memory (hence, no hidden observer) of having a hypodermic needle plunged into her upper gum. Researchers agree that a dissociation or splitting of consciousness does occur, often during long drives or repetitive tasks. In such cases, the overlearned automaticity of the task leaves part of one's consciousness free to think, fantasize, and carry on a conversation. Just as most people *can* walk and chew gum at the same time, a hypnotized person may experience two different states of consciousness at the same time.

Meditation to Achieve an Altered State of Consciousness

Another type of altered consciousness is achieved through meditation. Meditation is usually undertaken to reduce or eliminate "mind chatter," the runaway thoughts and fantasies that accompany life in the fast lane (Kabat-Zinn, 1993). The religious exercises of the Eastern religions (Buddhism and Taoism, for example) have as a realizable goal the absence of consciousness, or the mind as a blank slate. Meditation allows its practitioners to achieve this goal, and in the process to voluntarily reduce their basal metabolism by reducing their heart and respiration rates and their oxygen consumption. Some Yoga masters can reduce their basal metabolism as much as 40 percent for over an hour (Wallace & Benson, 1972). Meditation, hypnosis, daydreams—all produce an altered state of consciousness.

INTERIM SUMMARY

1. In adult humans, consciousness varies from moment to moment between attentiveness and a wandering of the mind. Attention involves a narrowing of consciousness in order to focus on a particular aspect of the environment.
2. ***Daydreams*** are waking fantasies. Researchers have found that men and women daydream for about the same amount of time each day, but disagree on the existence of gender differences in the reported content of daydreams.
3. The imagination displayed by children (and to a lesser extent, adults) is a conscious state that blends fantasy with reality.
4. ***Hypnosis*** is a trancelike state in which a person is more suggestible than usual and agrees to allow a hypnotist to influence his or her perception, memory, and voluntary behavior.
5. Humans and other animals, if held and rhythmically stroked, will enter a state of *tonic immobility* in which their bodies become rigid and immobile.
6. A hypnotist typically begins an *induction* procedure by asking the subject to relax the toes. Using a technique called *progressive relaxation,* the hypnotist then suggests that the relaxed feeling will spread up the legs and into the torso.
7. The EEG, neurochemistry, and cerebral blood flow of a hypnotized person differ from those of a nonhypnotized person. The brain of a person in a hypnotic state is characterized by an inhibitory process in frontal cortex and other changes in the thalamus and subcortical systems.
8. Psychotherapists use hypnosis to produce behavioral change; dentists and physicians use it as an anesthetic.
9. Hypnosis may produce ***dissociation,*** or a splitting of consciousness. Dissociation can be seen in skilled behaviors that have become automatic, such as driving, which allow a person to act consciously and unconsciously at the same time.
10. Ernest Hilgard proposed that part of a hypnotized person's consciousness is aware of and can comment on other aspects of the person's consciousness. He called the aware part the ***hidden observer.***

11. Other researchers dispute the existence of a hidden observer, and stress that learning—that is, learning to follow a hypnotist's or therapist's instructions—plays a role in hypnosis.

12. Meditation is a practice whose goal is to achieve a level of consciousness that reduces or eliminates normal thoughts and fantasies.

For Further Thought

1. A person who is awakened from a dream and asked how long the dream has lasted can usually give an accurate estimate. However, people who have been under anesthesia or taken hallucinogenic drugs cannot accurately estimate the passage of time. Does this finding constitute evidence that dreams are more like waking consciousness than drug-induced states?
2. Einstein and the theory of relativity aside, have *you* ever come up with an interesting idea while daydreaming?
3. Have you ever experienced a trancelike state?
4. Do you think you yourself can be hypnotized? Why or why not? Is your answer to question 3 related to your answer to this question?
5. Given what you have learned about the effects of light on activity levels, why do you suppose a hypnotherapist reduces the lighting in a room and requests the subject to close his or her eyes before inducing a trance?

DRUG-INDUCED ALTERATIONS OF CONSCIOUSNESS

A person who is asked to free-associate on the subject of altered states of consciousness is likely to respond with "drugs" before mentioning sleep, daydreams, hypnosis, or meditation. Drugs are so pervasive, and their effects so well known, that large numbers of people throughout the world use them on a daily basis.

Not all drugs affect consciousness. Like a vitamin pill, a drug called allopurinol, which helps to regulate the metabolic processes related to gout, does not have an immediately perceptible effect, and therefore does not alter consciousness. Those drugs that *do* affect consciousness are called *psychoactive* drugs. To the extent that a nonprescription pain reliever such as aspirin reduces pain, it may be considered a psychoactive drug. Coffee, tea, alcoholic beverages, tobacco, and pain relievers are among the most common examples of psychoactive drugs in use today.

Why Humans Use Drugs

Why do so many people voluntarily use drugs? Is there something wrong with James's waking state of consciousness—something that can easily be corrected by drugs? We know that most small children (and many adults) like to alter their waking state by holding their breath or spinning around long enough to become dizzy, lose their balance, and fall down. In this respect, amusement parks can be thought of as chemical-free environments that are designed to alter human consciousness. (Is sensation seeking on a roller coaster the modern-day equivalent of swinging rapidly through the branches of high trees?)

If humans voluntarily alter their consciousness to achieve a pleasurable state, they also take drugs to reduce or alleviate pain—that is, to achieve a *normal* state of consciousness. Both these hedonistic tendencies—seeking pleasure and avoiding pain—have evolved to increase our fitness. Unfortunately, they cause many people to abuse drugs as well. Psychoactive drugs act directly on ancient brain mechanisms that control emotion and behavior, bypassing adaptive information-processing systems. Although alcohol, amphetamines, and cocaine can produce elation and euphoria, from an evolutionary perspective, they falsely signal states of mind that normally enhance fitness (Nesse & Berridge, 1997). Because false euphoria can deprive an individual of useful information, drug abuse is inherently maladaptive.

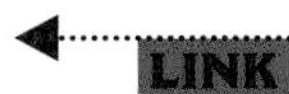

Adaptive characteristics of brain structures, Chapter 4, p. 107

Consider another evolutionary scenario, however. Alcohol in particular has disinhibiting properties that facilitate social interactions. Men and women who drink alcohol together tend to dance, to flirt, and to make love. It may be that those individuals whose genes provide the recipe for brains that "like" alcohol make more copies of themselves (through sexual reproduction) at a greater rate than individuals whose brains (and therefore behavior) are less sensitive to alcohol's disinhibiting effects.

Humans are not the only animals to voluntarily alter their consciousness by taking drugs. Outside the laboratory, chimpanzees have been observed to eat fermented fruit and become intoxicated—and to return the next day for more. Inside the laboratory, animals will as readily press a lever to receive pleasure-producing drugs as they will to receive food or ESB. Drugs may stimulate brain sites that have evolved to give humans and other animals pleasure for other, more adaptive reasons.

Pleasure centers in the brain, Chapter 2, p. 47

The natural environment contains many drugs that speed up, slow down, or otherwise alter consciousness. In addition to these natural plant compounds, humans have learned to design chemical compounds that mimic the effects of natural compounds (see Table 9.1). Let's look at some of these drugs and their effects.

Depressants: Alcohol and Barbiturates

Depressants alter waking consciousness by depressing it, or slowing it down. Table 9.1 lists two categories of depressants, alcohol (one form of which, ethanol, is found in beer, wine, and spirits) and barbiturates (such as Seconal). The overall effect of these drugs is to induce relaxation and reduce physical activity. Primarily because barbiturates are dangerous to use (unintentional fatal overdoses were once common), they are not often prescribed today, though they still are abused. Alcohol is the most used and abused drug in the world.

Like other drugs, alcohol has a number of effects, depending on the dosage. Its immediate effect is pleasurable: alcohol stimulates the release of dopamine, a neurotransmitter that causes pleasure. (Dopamine can also be released by other drugs, such as cocaine, and by electrical stimulation of the brain, the ingestion of tasty food, or the experience of reading a good book.) The pleasure a person derives from imbibing alcohol has been described as a rush of euphoria. Figure 9.11 shows some of the progressive effects of increasing dosages of alcohol or any other depressant. Low doses tend to produce relaxation, a lessening of anxiety, and disinhibition (less inhibited behavior). Higher doses can produce sedation or even a loss of consciousness. Too many Seconal pills, a fifth of vodka, or a combination of the two can cause coma or death.

Recall from Chapter 4 that the neurotransmitter GABA has an inhibitory effect on brain functioning. Alcohol alters consciousness in part by activating GABA receptors, which increase the inhibitory effect. In particular, alcohol depresses neural activity in the frontal cortex, which normally inhibits behavior. After imbibing moderate doses of alcohol, a person may exhibit heightened sexuality, aggressiveness, or playfulness. Somewhat higher doses produce slower sensory-motor

Effect of damage to frontal cortex in Phineas Gage, Chapter 4, p. 105

Table 9.1 How Drugs Affect Consciousness

DRUG CLASSIFICATION	COMMON NAME	SPECIFIC EFFECT	MAIN EFFECT
Depressants	**Depressants Alter Consciousness by Slowing Down the User**		
Alcohol	Beer, wine, spirits	Mellow, buzz, mild euphoria	Relaxation
Barbiturates (tranquilizers)	Nembutal, Seconal	Mellow, mild sedation	
Antianxiety Drugs	**Antianxiety Drugs Alter Consciousness by Reducing Anxiety**		
Benzodiazepines	Valium, Ativan	Calming, reduce anxiety	Anxiety reduction
Second-generation anxiolytic	BuSpar	Calming, reduce anxiety	
Antiepileptic drugs	Tegretol, Xanax	Calming, reduce anxiety	
Stimulants	**Stimulants Alter Consciousness by Speeding-up the User**		
Amphetamines	Methamphetamine, speed, Ritalin, Dexedrine	Stimulate, rush, increased alertness	Stimulation, excitement
Cocaine	Cocaine, crack	Stimulate, rush, elation	
Nicotine	Tobacco	Stimulate, rush, increased alertness	
Caffeine	Coffee, tea	Stimulate, increased alertness	
Antidepressants	**Antidepressants Alter Consiousness by Relieving Depression and by Normalizing Mood**		
Tricyclics	Imipramine, Elavil	Relieve depression, uplift	Relieve depression, normalize mood
SSRIs	Prozac, Effexor, Zoloft	Relieve depression, uplift	
Narcotics	**Narcotics Alter Consiousness by Inducing Euphoria**		
Opiates	Morphine, heroin	Mellow, stuporous, euphoria	Euphoria
Psychedelics and Hallucinogens	**Psychedelics Distort Consciousness by Altering Perception**		
	Marijuana, hashish, LSD	Altered time and sensory perception	Distort consciousness, alter perception

reaction times, disordered thought, slurred speech, poorer-than-normal judgment, and poor coordination. At high doses alcohol becomes extremely dangerous: sleepiness, unconsciousness, coma, and death can occur quickly.

As with most drugs, alcohol's tragic effects on human behavior and society are due less to moderate use than to overuse, which reduces an individual's self-awareness (Hull & Bond, 1986). Blood alcohol levels of 0.1 to 0.2 percent can affect judgment, so that the user underestimates the drug's deleterious effects. One result is a high alcohol-related accident rate, the single greatest cause of death in Americans between ages 20 and 30. Each year, more people die from overuse of alcohol than from all illegal drugs combined (Siegel, 1990).

Antianxiety Drugs

As their name implies, antianxiety drugs (also called anxiolytics) alter consciousness by acting on the brain in a way that reduces anxiety. The benzodiazepines—Librium, Valium, and Ativan—were among the earliest of these drugs. Because antianxiety drugs were safer and less addictive than barbiturates, they all but replaced them in the treatment of stress-related anxiety (Julien, 1995). By 1989 anxiolytics were the fourth most frequently prescribed class of drugs.

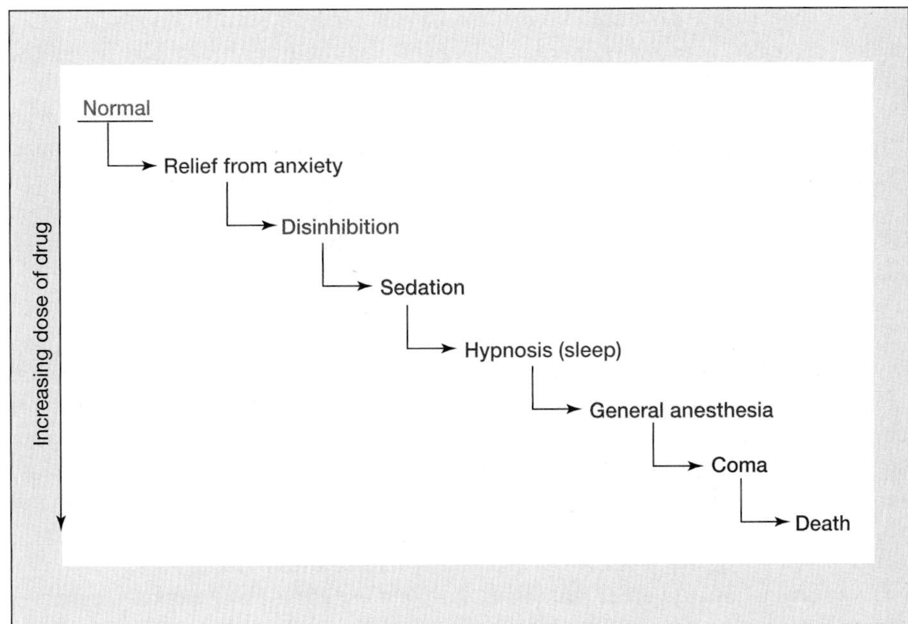

Figure 9.11 The effects of increasing doses of a depressant. As the dose of a depressant increases, consciousness changes from a normal waking state to mellow relaxation, sedation, and then sleep. Overdoses of many drugs—not just depressants—can lead to coma and death. *Source:* From A PRIMER OF DRUG ACTION, Seventh Edition by Robert M. Julien. Copyright © 2001, 1998, 1995, 1992, 1988, 1985, 1981, 1978, 1975 by W. H. Freeman and Company. Reprinted by permission.

Today, physicians prescribe newer, so-called second-generation anxiolytics, such as BuSpar, as well as drugs developed for other purposes, but which also reduce anxiety (Tegretol and Xanax). All have side effects: sleep disorders and lethargy are common. When used together with alcohol, anxiolytics can produce sedation, confusion, disorientation, and a host of other disorders. These drugs are habit forming and can interfere with normal learning and memory processes.

Stimulants, Legal and Illegal

Stimulants such as amphetamine, cocaine, nicotine, and caffeine energize and excite users (see Table 9.1). Thus a popular name for methamphetamine is *speed*. Caffeine is a mild stimulant, but if taken in high doses it can make a person feel nervous and jittery.

Stimulants are sometimes referred to as sympathomimetics, because their action mimics the sympathetic nervous system. Recall that the primary neurotransmitter of the sympathetic nervous system, epinephrine, is involved in arousal (see Chapter 4). When you say that a near miss in an automobile "got your adrenaline going," you are using the common term for epinephrine. Under sympathetic activation, then, a person is more alert, stimulated, and emotionally aroused. Let's look more closely at several types of stimulants.

Amphetamines. The stimulant *d-amphetamine* was first manufactured in 1887, and its effects on the CNS first documented in 1927. The chemists who made these discoveries were looking for a cheap way to manufacture a drug called *ephedrine,* whose medicinal properties had been known in China for over 5,000 years. Doctors prescribed d-amphetamine for asthma, and the military used it to enhance soldiers' performance. By the early 1970s, fully 10 percent of all Americans over the age of 14 used amphetamine as a legal, prescribed drug, at the rate of 10 billion tablets per year, or 50 tablets per person (McKim, 1991).

Today, both d-amphetamine (Dexedrine) and methamphetamine are known primarily as drugs of abuse whose use can cause brain damage. Easily procured on the black market, amphetamines are often used recreationally for the "rush" of excitement they produce. One form of methamphetamine, known as *ICE*, *crank*, or *crystal*, can be smoked. Those who use the drug habitually develop a tolerance to it and must take increasingly large doses.

Amphetamines are dopamine-potentiating agents. High doses may lead to an "amphetamine psychosis"—severe paranoid hallucinations that are associated with aggressive, destructive behavior. Ironically, chronic use at high dosages can cause permanent damage to the neurons that make dopamine and serotonin. These permanent changes in brain function may be expressed as lifelong sleep disturbances, sexual dysfunction, depression, poor memory, loss of coordination, and even schizophrenia (Julien, 1995).

Ritalin. Ritalin is a prescription stimulant that alters consciousness somewhat differently from amphetamines. For several decades it has been prescribed for children with attention-deficit disorder. In these children, the drug has the opposite of its usual effect: it calms them, allowing them to focus better on their class work. Adults with attention-deficit disorder report that the drug both stimulates them and helps them to focus (pay attention) and think more clearly. Many students who use Ritalin report improved study habits and better grades.

Unfortunately, like other stimulants, habitual use of Ritalin leads to tolerance—the need for higher doses to produce the same effect (see page 202). Users often find that higher doses have the same exhilarating properties as other stimulants, that the drug can become addictive, and that discontinuing its use has aversive side effects.

Cocaine. Cocaine is a stimulant found in a plant that is used for medicinal (and probably recreational) purposes in Peru and Bolivia. Chewing the leaves of a coca plant to slowly release its juice produces a pleasant effect, allowing users to overcome fatigue while working. Processing the plant produces a much more concentrated and potent form of the extract, cocaine. Either in powder form or in *rocks*, cocaine can be taken by sniffing (*snorting*) or smoking (*tooting*).

Reuptake mechanism, Chapter 4, p. 144

Cocaine's primary effect is to block the reuptake of dopamine, allowing the neurotransmitter to remain longer in the reward and pleasure centers near the hypothalamus. In concentrated form it produces a highly pleasurable rush of exhilaration that some people describe in sexual terms. People who take cocaine feel euphoric, powerful, and talkative. Tolerance to the drug develops rapidly; higher doses are associated with increasingly unpredictable, schizophrenia-like behavior.

Nicotine. Like caffeine, so many people have used nicotine over such long periods that its effects are usually considered much less powerful and dangerous than those of amphetamines or cocaine. Because it is smoked in the form of standardized cigarettes, its effects can be better regulated than those of illegal stimulants. Nevertheless, nicotine is a more addictive drug than either cocaine or amphetamine.

Nicotine produces its pleasurable effect by releasing epinephrine from various sites in the body, causing CNS arousal and the release of an endogenous opiate, beta-endorphin. Because nicotine also stimulates acetylcholine and dopamine receptors, tolerance to the drug develops rapidly. It is also addictive, as hundreds of thousands of smokers who have tried to quit will attest. Most smokers dose themselves at high rates on a daily basis. Depending on the dosage level, withdrawal may occur between doses, even in the middle of the night.

Sympathetic nervous system, Chapter 4, p. 115

Nicotine may be classified as a stimulant, but most smokers say that it relaxes them, much as alcohol does. Nicotine does increase heart rate and blood pressure, as would be expected with stimulation of the sympathetic nervous system, but it also stimulates dopamine receptors, much as alcohol does. These two drugs show *cross-tolerance effects,* meaning that physical dependence on one can be satisfied by taking the other. Cross-tolerance may explain why so many heavy alcohol users smoke, and vice versa (Collins, Wilkins, Siobe, Cao, & Bullock, 1996). Between cigarettes, regular smokers are in an agitated state of withdrawal, and alcohol "relaxes" them.

The long-term health effects of nicotine are due primarily to other products in cigarette smoke, which lead to higher levels of heart disease and cancer. Unlike alcohol, the other legal drug millions of people use, nicotine appears to enhance both motor performance and the ability to perform intellectual tasks. Nicotine increases both the speed and efficiency of information processing by enhancing alertness and focusing attention; on monotonous tasks, it decreases daydreaming (Wesnes & Warburton, 1983).

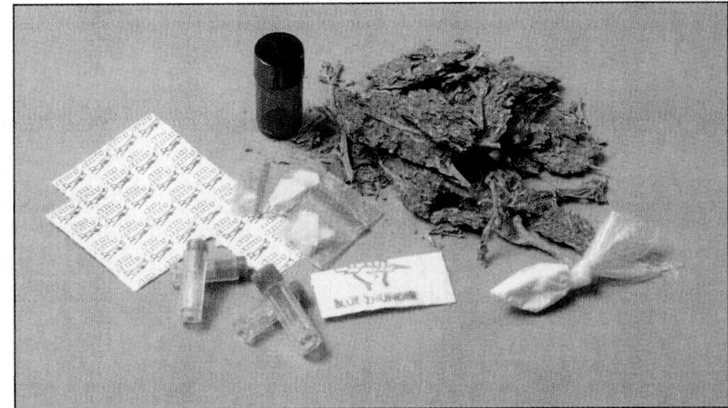

Humans are attracted to a variety of consciousness-altering drugs.

Caffeine. Caffeine is a naturally occurring chemical called a xanthine that is found in many plants, the most common of which are used to make coffee, tea, and chocolate. Effective doses of caffeine range from 50 mg (a moderate dose) to 200 mg (a relatively high dose). The amount of caffeine in a cup of coffee can range from 50 to 150 mg; in tea, from 25 to 50 mg; in chocolate, from 5 mg (milk chocolate) to 35 (bittersweet chocolate). Coca-Cola has about 45 mg of caffeine; Excedrin, 65 mg; No-Doz, 100 mg; and Vivarin, 200 mg.

Studies have shown that caffeine enhances alertness and increases physical performance. It has no effect on intellectual performance, unless it is used to overcome fatigue and sleepiness, which detract from performance. Caffeine can produce moderate to high insomnia, as students who study all night have discovered. Though people who use caffeine regularly do not experience these effects to the same extent as others, heavy users sometimes feel grumpy or even ill until they have had their first cup of coffee in the morning.

Antidepressants

Antidepressants alter consciousness by correcting an imbalance in existing neurotransmitters. In doing so, they elevate a person's mood, alleviating a state of depression. Two examples of this class of drugs are Elavil (a tricyclic antidepressant, so called because of its chemical structure) and Prozac, a *selective serotonin reuptake inhibitor* (SSRI). An SSRI works by blocking the reuptake of the neurotransmitter serotonin, allowing it to act longer during synaptic transmission.

Stimulants and depressants alter normal waking consciousness, whereas antidepressants return a depressed person to a normal waking state. Antidepressants, that is, are taken for the express purpose of *correcting* an altered consciousness. In the short time in which antidepressants have been in existence, many millions of people have used them to correct deficiencies in their brain chemistry, which they may have inherited at birth, developed as a result of life's vicissitudes, or both.

Narcotics: Heroin and Morphine

No one knows why plants and animals evolved some chemical properties in common. One example, described on page 000, is the glutamate receptor that is found both in the brains of vertebrates (where it is sensitive to neurotransmitters) and in plants (where it may be involved in communication). An even more intriguing example is that of a flower—the poppy—which contains chemicals that fit perfectly with so-called opiate receptors in the human brain (Pert & Snyder, 1973). Heroin and morphine, two common opiates, are extracted from the poppy's seedpod. The brain receptors that are sensitive to these chemicals are found in the limbic system, near the hypothalamus. Stimulation of these

Glutamate receptors, Chapter 4, p. 143

receptor sites by opiates produces analgesia—a reduced perception of pain—and euphoria. Opiates are highly addictive; users crave their effects and actively seek them out.

Researchers have identified chemicals called *endogenous opioids* in vertebrate brains. (Here, *endogenous* means "made from within.") One of these chemicals, called endorphin (a contraction of the term *endogenous morphine*), has a structure that is similar to that of morphine. The effects of endorphin are similar to the effects of morphine: its release in the brain produces a pleasurable state of consciousness.

Hallucinogens: Marijuana and LSD

Unlike stimulants and depressants, marijuana and LSD are *hallucinogens*, substances that alter consciousness by distorting a person's sensory experiences (see Table 9.1). Marijuana is a plant; LSD (*d-lysergic acid diethylamide*) is a chemical compound first concocted by Albert Hoffman in 1938. A person who takes either drug may experience the perceptual distortion of a sensation, or even a hallucination—a sensory experience that has no physical reality. For example, a wall might seem to vibrate, melt, or change color. Perceptual distortions might include an altered perception of the passage of time, the feeling of being lost in a familiar place, or an inability to recognize one's reflection in a mirror. Because hallucinogens create intensified sensory experiences and perceptual distortions, they are also referred to as *psychedelics*.

Marijuana and LSD produce not only a variety of perceptual effects, but also emotional changes ranging from mellowness to a relaxed stupor and euphoria, and finally despair and paranoia. Unlike the predictable reduction in anxiety that is associated with alcohol use, the effects of psychedelic drugs like marijuana and LSD are not always the same. One effect seems to be the opposite of tolerance: First-time users can be exposed to large quantities of the drug with little noticeable effects, but on subsequent exposures, very small quantities can produce hallucinations. The unpredictability of the drug's effect can be disturbing: the feeling of being hopelessly lost in a familiar shopping mall could seem funny, or it could be incredibly frightening.

Although researchers have identified a cannabinoid receptor for THC, the active ingredient in marijuana (Smith, 1995), the effects of hallucinogens on the brain remain a mystery. Habitual use is likely due to psychological rather than physical dependence. Marijuana causes vasodilatation of the blood vessels in the eyes, which make it useful in the treatment of glaucoma (a condition characterized by high blood pressure within the eye). It also acts as an anti-emetic, relieving nausea and vomiting, and as an anticonvulsant. When sick people smoke marijuana, they tend to laugh—and as we will see in Chapter 16, laughing is good for one's health. For these and other reasons, the question of whether marijuana should be classified as a medicine or a recreational drug, and what penalty if any should be imposed on its recreational use, continues to challenge government officials who regulate drug use.

Drug Tolerance

Tolerance in Chapter 6, p. 202

tolerance A reduction in the intensity of a drug's effect, requiring a larger dose to achieve the same effect.

With repeated use of alcohol or drugs, a user can develop a *tolerance* for them. **Tolerance** is defined in two related ways: (1) as a reduction in the intensity of a drug's effect following repeated exposure, and (2) as the need for a larger dose to achieve the same effect following repeated exposure. There are two types of tolerance, pharmacological and behavioral.

Pharmacological tolerance varies from drug to drug. One type of pharmacological tolerance occurs when the liver increases its production of an enzyme called *alcohol dehydrogenase,* which metabolizes alcohol. An increased level of this enzyme reduces the amount of the drug that reaches receptor sites in the brain. Another type of pharmacological tolerance occurs when the receptive sites on neurons in the brain change in ways that reduce alcohol's effect on them.

Animals also develop *behavioral tolerance* to cope with the effect of drugs on perception and movement. Given enough trials in a drugged state, for example, rats under the influence of alcohol can learn to maintain their balance while traversing a narrow ledge, despite the drug's effects (Wenger, Tiffany, Bombardier, Nicholls, & Woods, 1981). Demonstrations of tolerance to nondrug stimuli suggest the existence of a general tolerance mechanism. For example, behavioral tolerance may develop to a variety of physical circumstances, including heat, cold, electric shock, exercise, and even brain lesions. Like pharmacological tolerance, behavioral tolerance can be interpreted as an adaptive homeostatic adjustment that reduces the deleterious effects of a drug. Such adjustments are often overwhelmed by the increasingly larger doses of a drug users take to overcome tolerance, however.

Drug Dependence and Drug Addiction

With time, heavy users of drugs and alcohol become dangerously habituated to the substances. Some researchers have proposed that in susceptible individuals, alcohol and other drugs hypersensitize specific neural systems (Berridge & Robinson, 1995; Robinson & Berridge, 1993). In turn, these brain systems set in motion motivational processes best described as cravings. Addicts needn't be conscious of a craving, which may be distinguished from the pleasurable effects of a drug. This theory helps to explain the fact that addicts often continue to take drugs that no longer give them pleasure.

Continued use of alcohol, morphine, heroin, and Seconal can lead to *drug dependence*. **Physical dependence** occurs when the user takes a drug to avoid experiencing withdrawal symptoms. Withdrawal can be nasty, including flu-like symptoms such as fever and chills, vomiting and diarrhea, and body aches. Since taking more of the drug reduces these symptoms, physical dependence can be seen as a homeostatic feedback loop involving behavioral regulation, in which the drug-taking behavior is reinforced by relief from sickness.

Reinforcement, Chapter 6, p. 207

Not all drug taking is motivated by the relief of withdrawal symptoms, however. Depressants can cause **psychological dependence**, which is best defined as an intense emotional craving for the drug. Physical and psychological dependence are not mutually exclusive, however. The mechanisms that underlie human-drug interactions are complex and not well understood.

Over the long term, drug dependence and addiction can have serious consequences. A chronic drug abuser is much more likely than others to experience poor health, impaired memory, ruptured social relationships, diminished earning capacity, and an early death. These devastating effects are in part the direct result of brain damage. A growing body of research indicates that alcohol and drugs change the way neurons function in both the developing brains of young people and the damaged brains of chronic abusers.

Drugs and Society

In 1777, Frederick the Great of Prussia made the following comment about a new drug his subjects were experimenting with:

> It is disgusting to notice the increase in the quantity of coffee used by my subjects, and the amount of money that goes out of the country as a consequence. Everybody is using coffee; this must be prevented. His Majesty was brought up on beer, and so were both his ancestors and officers. Many battles have been fought and won by soldiers nourished on beer, and the King does not believe that coffee-drinking soldiers can be relied upon to endure hardships in case of another war. (cited in Vallee, 1998, p. 57)

As Frederick's now humorous pronouncement shows, what is and is not considered a legal drug has more to do with politics than with pharmacology. How does a

physical dependence The need to take a drug to avoid withdrawal symptoms.

psychological dependence An intense emotional craving for a drug.

Every culture in the world uses both "legal" and "illegal" drugs.

person who drinks alcohol to relax or smokes a cigarette for the rush differ from one who asks a physician to prescribe an SSRI for depression? Isn't all drug use an attempt to alter consciousness in a way that brings pleasure, relief from pain, or enhanced performance? Today, this philosophical question has become an important one as more and more people, including children, take powerful, mind-altering prescription drugs or use alcohol and nicotine legally, while at the same time others are imprisoned for using or selling illegal street drugs. Caffeine, nicotine, and alcohol are distributed by legitimate multi-billion-dollar industries; should we be surprised that people also want to use marijuana and speed?

This question brings us back to why people use drugs to distort their normal waking state. Again, there are no simple answers. To say that drug use is a response to the harsh demands of civilization on a brain that evolved to meet the needs of a hunter-gatherer society would be incorrect. The use of alcohol, caffeine, and all other drugs made from plants predates recorded history; these and other naturally occurring drugs likely were used in hunter-gatherer cultures long before cities existed (McKim, 1991). Over the past 100,000 years, human beings have probably used drugs voluntarily and routinely to alter their normal waking state and will likely continue to do so in the future.

INTERIM SUMMARY

1. Psychoactive drugs act directly on ancient brain mechanisms that control emotion and behavior.
2. Other than to obtain pleasure or relief from pain, the reasons why so many humans and other animals voluntarily alter their consciousness remain a mystery.
3. Alcohol, amphetamine, and cocaine use is inherently maladaptive, because such drugs falsely signal states of mind that normally enhance fitness.
4. In low doses, *depressants* such as alcohol and barbiturates provide relaxation and pleasure; they also impair judgment and motor coordination. In high doses, depressants produce sedation and sleep, and ultimately coma and death.
5. Antianxiety drugs include benzodiazepines, such as Valium, and other anxiolytics, such as BuSpar, Tegretol, and Xanax. These drugs help the user to relax, reducing stress-related anxiety.
6. Stimulants such as amphetamine, cocaine, nicotine, Ritalin, and caffeine alter waking consciousness by speeding it up. Amphetamine, cocaine, nicotine, and Ritalin all have a high potential for abuse because they produce an intensely pleasurable rush. Tolerance to these drugs builds rapidly and craving may become intense with habitual use.
7. Nicotine and alcohol show cross-tolerance effects. That is, alcohol helps to relieve the withdrawal symptoms produced by nicotine, and vice versa.
8. Antidepressants are a class of drugs that includes SSRIs (selective serotonin reuptake inhibitors), such as Prozac. These prescription drugs help severely depressed patients to normalize their mood.
9. Narcotics, such as morphine and heroin, alter consciousness by depressing it, or slowing it down. They produce a pleasing state of euphoria, but they are highly addictive.
10. *Hallucinogens* like marijuana and LSD alter consciousness by distorting perception. These drugs can produce unpredictable emotional changes ranging from mellowness and a relaxed stupor to euphoria, despair, and paranoia.
11. Long-term use of alcohol or other drugs may hypersensitize the neural system in susceptible individuals, producing a craving for the substance.
12. *Tolerance* following habitual drug use is defined in two ways: as a reduction in the intensity of a drug's effect and as the need for a progressively larger dose to achieve the same effect.
13. ***Physical dependence*** occurs when a user takes a drug to avoid experiencing withdrawal symptoms. ***Psychological dependence*** is characterized by an intense emotional craving for a drug.
14. In the United States, the determination of which drugs should be legal and which should be illegal is too often made on political rather than pharmacological grounds.

For Further Thought

1. An eminent researcher once wrote that there is nothing wrong with sugar, other than the fact that because it tastes good, people tend to overuse it, causing health problems. Could you make the same argument for some drugs? If so, which ones?
2. Do you agree with the statement that politics rather than pharmacology is the determining factor in deciding which drugs should be legal?
3. Assume you are a factory owner who employs unskilled laborers. If you are concerned only with the bottom line—how much money you will make—why might you encourage your employees to smoke, but prohibit them from using alcohol and marijuana?

CONCLUDING THOUGHTS

"Understanding consciousness" is still a good answer to the question "What is psychology about?" A century's worth of research has expanded rather than answered our questions about the nature of human consciousness.

Humans and other animals evolved on an earth that is periodically bathed in light and darkness. This fact explains the most basic features of consciousness—the underlying patterns of activity and quiescence. Humans tend to be alert during the day and to sleep at night, but within this major cycle there are smaller ones: periods of daydreaming versus activity during waking hours, and periods of dreaming versus nondreaming during sleep. Though the functions of dreams and daydreams are largely unknown, they are defining aspects of human consciousness.

Light-dark cycles are so pervasive that even single living cells show evidence of periodicity. Life throbs. Its pulse is set not just by the sun, but by cycles of the moon and the earth's yearly orbit around the sun. These cycles are reflected both in physiological phenomena, such as the human menstrual cycle, and in behavior, such as avian migration patterns. Humans also have an endogenous biological clock that can be disrupted by rapid travel across time zones. To recover from jet lag, the traveler must synchronize this internal clock with the sun.

Human consciousness can be defined in terms of alertness and self-awareness. Mirror studies suggest that humans exhibit more self-awareness than any other animal, except perhaps the chimpanzee. Other measures of self-awareness, especially those afforded by language and creativity, put humans in a class by themselves. The complexities of human consciousness parallel the evolution of the larger and more complicated human brain.

Over the past century, interdisciplinary scientific methods have shown that many parts of the brain function independently of, and unknown to, our conscious awareness. Responding to the absence of light, neurons in the hypothalamus prompt the pineal gland to secrete melatonin, inducing sleepiness and altering consciousness. The presence of light increases the production of serotonin, which reduces fatigue and depression. Yet neurological research reminds us that awareness is not something secreted by the brain, and that understanding the brain's biochemistry will not answer philosophical questions about the human mind.

Dreams and daydreams are altered states of consciousness that inspire and mystify us, nourishing our scientific and artistic creativity. Meditation and hypnosis are other forms of consciousness that differ from a normal waking state. The reasons why humans voluntarily engage in behavior that alters their consciousness, including drug taking, may never be fully established. Some people may take drugs to increase their performance, others to experience pleasure or escape from reality. The urge to do so is probably prehistoric. Fully understanding such alterations in consciousness may be a logical impossibility, because we are part of the system we are trying to understand.

KEY TERMS

biological clock *311*
circadian rhythms *310*
consciousness *306*
daydreams *327*
dissociation *330*
electroencephalogram (EEG) *320*
hidden observer *330*
hypnosis *329*
insomnia *324*
physical dependence *339*
psychological dependence *339*
REM sleep *322*
tolerance *338*
unconscious mind *307*
zeitgeiber *312*

10

Memory

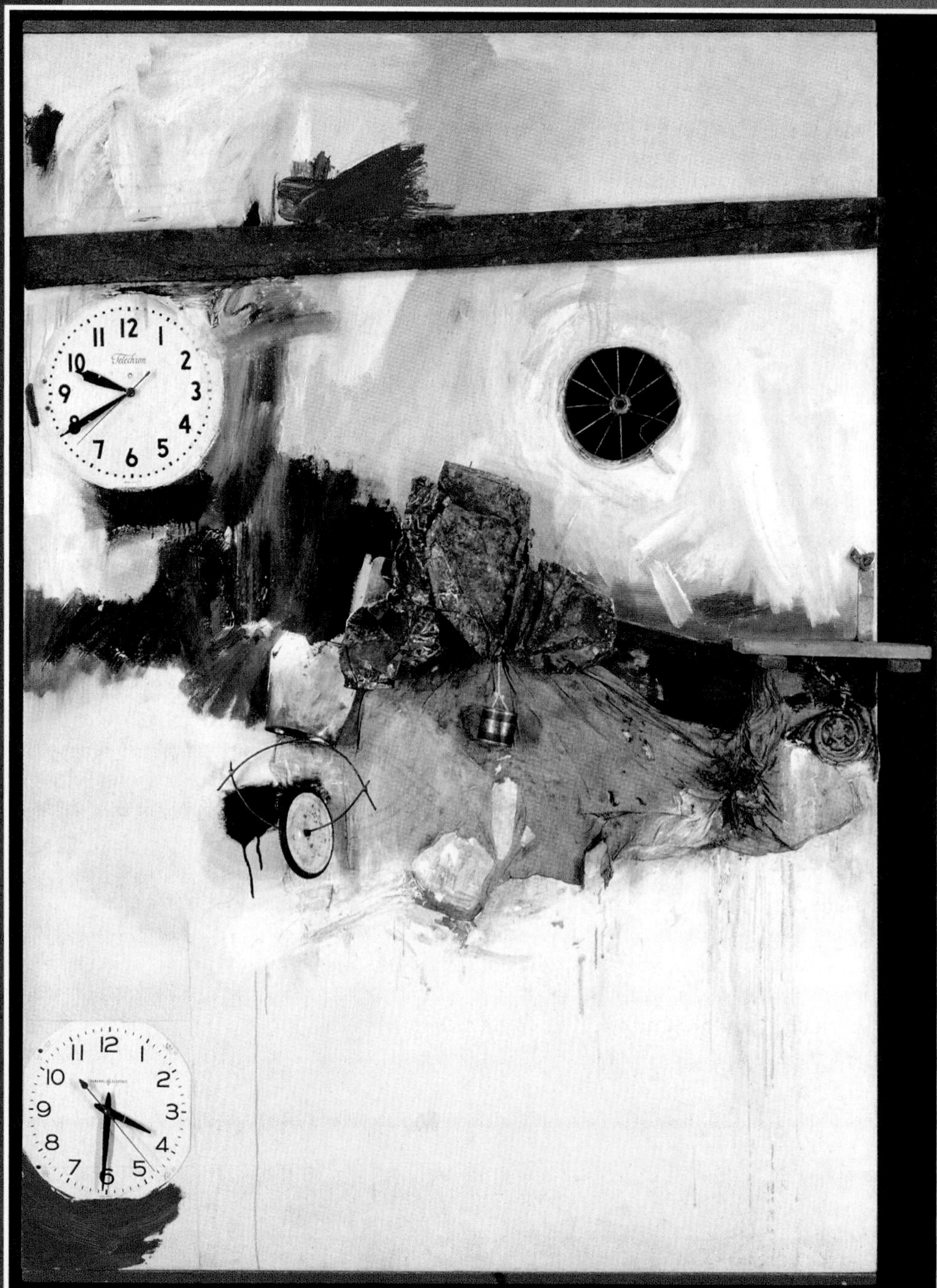

The Evolution of Memory
The Adaptive Significance of Memory
The Evolution of Multiple Memory Systems
Interim Summary
For Further Thought

The Information-Processing Approach to Memory
Sensory Memory
Selective Attention to Information
Short-Term (Working) Memory
Long-Term Memory
Interim Summary
For Further Thought

Encoding and Short-Term Memory
The Recency Effect
The Phonological Loop
The Primacy Effect
The Process of Encoding
The Levels-of-Processing Hypothesis
Interim Summary
For Further Thought

The Enigma of Long-Term Memory
Implicit and Explicit Memories
Schemas
The Effect of Leading Questions
Remembering Versus Knowing
Interim Summary
For Further Thought

Memory for Movement, Events, and Words
Procedural Memory
Declarative Memory
Interim Summary
For Further Thought

Memorizing, Forgetting, and Improving Memory
Theories of Forgetting
Explanations for Exceptional Memory
The Process of Retrieval from Memory
Interim Summary
For Further Thought

Memory in Normal Versus Damaged Brains
The Case of H. M.
Alzheimer's Disease
Interim Summary
For Further Thought

Concluding Thoughts

Wayne Wickelgren, a psychologist, recounts the following story of his introduction to a brain-damaged patient known as N. A.:

> "I was introduced to N. A. in a small coffee room in the Psychology Department at MIT. N. A. heard my name and he said, 'Wickelgren, that's a German name isn't it?' I said 'no.' 'Irish?' 'No.' 'Scandinavian?' 'Yes, it's Scandinavian.'"

After more chit-chat, Wickelgren left the room to make a phone call. On his return a few minutes later, there wasn't a glimmer of recognition in N. A.'s eyes. The psychologist reintroduced himself, to which N. A. replied:

> "'Wickelgren, that's a German name isn't it?' 'No.' 'Irish?' 'No.' 'Scandinavian?' 'Yes, it's Scandinavian.'" (Lindsay & Norman, 1977, p. 310)

Most of us have suffered the inconvenience or embarrassment of forgetting a phone number, a name, or a special occasion, but we take for granted the ability to remember where we are, what we are doing, and what we were doing just minutes ago. This aspect of memory—paying attention and connecting the immediate past with plans for the future—is highly adaptive, allowing us to learn from experience. Without it, we would not cope well with the demands of daily life. For example, we wouldn't trust N. A. to look after a small infant, to leave the house on an errand, or to fry bacon unassisted. Indeed, a person like N. A. must depend on someone else for personal care and other needs.

No aspect of human consciousness is more intriguing, or so poorly understood, as memory. Formally defined, **memory** refers to those psychological processes that both store and retrieve previously experienced sensory impressions, such as words and images. Memories connect the past with the present and future, and in doing so, help to define a person's sense of self. N. A., you might surmise from this story, seems to be stuck in a perpetual present. He can search his existing memory for names and make plausible guesses about their origin, but he apparently cannot add new memories. Shortly after Wickelgren left the room, N. A. had no memory of having met him.

In everyday language, the term *memory* is often used as a noun to mean an *engram*, or trace, of an event, as in "I have a memory of having met you before." The verb form is also used, as in "I *memorized* the capitals of the European countries." Yet another usage suggests that memory is a place, as in "It's somewhere in my memory." But as N. A.'s case shows, memory is much more than that: it is a defining aspect of consciousness—who I am, what I've been, and how I'll know if and when I achieve my goals. Throughout my lifetime I've been frustrated by what I've forgotten, and as I age I share the common fear of losing my memory. In this sense, memory is intertwined with mind and personality. The study of memory is important because it is a basic characteristic of the human mind.

In this chapter we'll look at the adaptive nature of both remembering and forgetting. We'll see that humans evolved multiple memory systems to cope with their environment. We'll study memory in terms of encoding and information processing, make distinctions between memory recall and memory reconstruction, and consider false memories, unconscious memories, photographic memory, and exceptional memory. And we'll apply what we learn about remembering and forgetting to the task of studying, putting research on this topic to practical use.

THE EVOLUTION OF MEMORY

Memory is present in some form or another in all animals. The stored recipes inherent in genes can be considered memories that help to determine the anatomy, physiology, and behavior of animals. Recall that each genotype carries a limited amount of information. Insects with tiny brains live more reflexively than larger-brained (and longer-lived) mammals. They occupy a relatively small ecological niche, have a short life span, and seem to live quite simply, "in the moment." Similarly, reflexes can be thought of as genetically determined "memories" of sensory-motor connections. But reflexes and instincts are inadequate for larger-brained animals, which survive by adaptively learning from their environment. The memory capacity of a species, then, is related to the amount of information it must learn and retain during a lifetime.

Genotypic differences, Chapter 3, p. 70

The Adaptive Significance of Memory

Learning and memory are related, in that *learning is the process by which we acquire memories*. The question of whether memory systems evolved differently in different species can be addressed by comparing the anatomy and brain function of different species, as well as through laboratory analyses of memory processes. Some learned behavior, you may recall, is highly prepared and takes

memory The psychological processes involved in storing and retrieving previously experienced sensory impressions, such as words and images.

but a few trials to learn. For instance, learning which foods, when eaten, will make you nauseous is a highly prepared form of learning; so is the knowledge that a hot, glowing orange object will burn you if you touch it. Most mammals have sufficient amounts of hippocampus, cerebellum, and associative cortex to rapidly learn and easily remember such simple associations.

Brain size and psychological complexity, Chapter 4, p. 107

Memory with memes, Chapter 6, p. 187

Other types of learning require many trials. Humans complement their genetically predisposed behavior by learning memes, the accumulated cultural wisdom that is stored in memory and then transferred to the next generation. For example, humans who learned by accident that plants will grow better if the soil is enriched with animal waste products can store that information in memory and transmit it to another person. The ability to store memes in memory is adaptive. Over time, individuals who could do so had more offspring, and they helped those offspring commit to memory memes that enhanced *their* fitness. One answer to the question of why human memory evolved as it has, then, is that humans require a large-capacity memory system to store memes.

Humans can store many facts in long-term memory.

The Evolution of Multiple Memory Systems

The various demands of memory include remembering in the short term—that is, being conscious—as well as the ability to access and update information that has been stored away for the long term. To meet these varied needs, humans have evolved multiple memory systems with capabilities that extend beyond simple storage capacity (Sherry & Schacter, 1987).

The advantage of multiple memory systems is apparent in the way humans solve problems. For example, humans, rats, and chimpanzees can form cognitive maps of food sources within a three-dimensional area. When hungry, each of these species can locate the food source, but humans have infinitely more alternatives than other animals. Their multiple memory systems allow them to talk about and direct others to the right locations; to draw a map of the locations; and to find other locations by referring to compass points. From past experience, humans can identify those places where food and water *should* be located, given the time of year and a knowledge of climate patterns. Obviously, these memory-based responses can provide a selective advantage to those who use them effectively.

Not all memories and memes are adaptive, however. The human memory is full of meaningless jingles, fantasies, and disconnected thoughts that do not contribute to fitness in any obvious way. Some memories may actually *detract* from fitness. For instance, inaccurate or **false memories**—memories of events that never happened—could be maladaptive. If the food you stashed for use in times of famine turns out *not* to be where you remembered it was, the consequences could be severe. False memories are to true memories as hallucinations are to true visual images. Both give unreal accounts of the world, and as such, both present problems for evolutionists.

Are false memories unusual, or do they occur frequently? In the 1990s, when under hypnosis, hundreds of psychotherapy patients began to remember long-forgotten details of sexual abuse by family members, this question became one of general interest. Respected memory experts, such as the University of Washington's Elizabeth Loftus, have urged caution in interpreting such "recovered" memories of early childhood. Loftus's research on eyewitness testimony, discussed later in this chapter, indicates that verbal suggestion can alter the memories of even nonhypnotized subjects (Loftus, 1979). She and others have reasoned that given the state of heightened suggestibility a patient experiences

false memories Memories of events that never happened.

during hypnosis, a therapist could inadvertently cue false memories (Loftus, 1997). Research shows that people are often overconfident about the accuracy of their memories, and that they frequently misjudge or misremember information they have learned (Spanos, 1996). According to a panel of memory experts from the United States and England, "there is no reliable means of distinguishing a true memory from an illusory one other than by external confirmation" (False Memory Syndrome Foundation, 1998).

In sum, human memory systems seem to have evolved because they enhanced fitness. But memory isn't perfect, and false memories can affect a person's psychological well-being, social relationships, and even fitness.

INTERIM SUMMARY

1. ***Memory*** refers to psychological processes that store and retrieve previously experienced sensory impressions, such as words and images.
2. The processes of learning and memory are related.
3. An animal's memory requirements vary according to its ecological niche, depending in part on how much of the animal's behavior is governed by reflexes.
4. The human's high-capacity memory system is adaptive in that it allows humans to commit to memory memes that enhance fitness, and to pass those memes on to the next generation.
5. Language, and the thinking that language supports, requires a memory system that functions differently from that of other animals.
6. Memory is adaptive, but memories may or may not contribute directly to fitness.
7. To some degree, most humans suffer from inaccurate memories and ***false memories*** (memories of events that never happened), which can compromise an individual's fitness.
8. In general, people are overly confident about the accuracy of their memories. The only way to discriminate between a true memory and a false one is by verifiable empirical evidence.

For Further Thought

1. Computers come with both ROM (read-only memory) and RAM (random-access memory). ROM, like reflexes, has very specific functions; RAM, like general-process learning, can be used for a variety of purposes. Why do computers and humans have both types of memory?
2. In Chapter 12 we will see that individual differences in vocabulary range from about 15,000 or so words to over 100,000 words. Can you construct a scenario in which genes interact with a particular environment to produce individual differences in the memory systems that support language and literacy?

information-processing model of memory A framework for describing how different memory systems sense, rehearse, encode, store, and ultimately retrieve information.

sensory memory A brief representation of what is being sensed—for example, a visual afterimage.

THE INFORMATION-PROCESSING APPROACH TO MEMORY

The fact that memory is defined in various ways suggests that it involves distinct processes in different parts of the brain. Figure 10.1 shows a diagram of the **information-processing model of memory** (Atkinson & Shiffrin, 1971), which posits a three-part memory system. The first part, **sensory memory**, is a fleeting

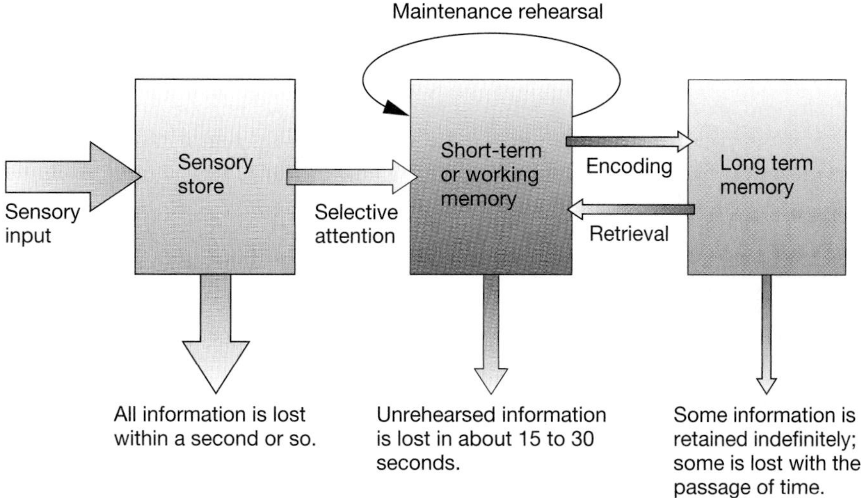
Maintenance rehearsal
Sensory input
Sensory store
Selective attention
Short-term or working memory
Encoding
Retrieval
Long term memory
All information is lost within a second or so.
Unrehearsed information is lost in about 15 to 30 seconds.
Some information is retained indefinitely; some is lost with the passage of time.

Figure 10.1 The information-processing model of memory. Memory may be thought of as a three-stage process, in which information in each stage lasts longer than in the preceding one. Only by paying attention can a person move information from the sensory store to short-term, or working, memory. From there, information is encoded into long-term memory through a variety of processes, including maintenance rehearsal. Long-term memories can be retrieved for further processing in working memory. *Source:* After Atkinson & Shiffrin, 1971.

representation of what is being sensed. The second part, called **short-term memory (STM)**, is a limited-capacity temporary store that lasts from 15 to 30 seconds. (The term *store* refers to a hypothetical storage place.) The third part, an unlimited memory store that can hold information indefinitely, is called **long-term memory (LTM).**

The process shown in Figure 10.1 suggests the interrelatedness of sensing, learning, and memory. Sensory memory begins when receptors initiate seeing, hearing, smelling, and so forth. From the barrage of incoming sensory information, the brain's attentional processes select some information for further processing in short-term memory. With **rehearsal**, or the conscious repetition of material in short-term memory, some of this information may continue to be processed, and eventually enter into long-term memory; but most of it is lost.

The words *short-term* underscore the limited nature of information processing in this intermediate memory system. When the emphasis is on the conscious properties of information processing, researchers prefer to use the term *working memory*. **Working memory** can be thought of as the process of integrating the current contents of consciousness with long-term memory. Working memory not only allows information to enter long-term memory, but also brings information back from long-term memory, a process called **retrieval.** In short, it mediates the cognitive tasks of learning, reasoning, and comprehending (Baddeley, 1998). Let's take a closer look at the information-processing model of memory, beginning with the first memory store, sensory memory.

short-term memory (STM) A temporary memory store of limited capacity that lasts about 15 to 30 seconds.

long-term memory (LTM) A memory store of unlimited capacity that can hold information indefinitely.

rehearsal The conscious repetition of material in short-term memory.

working memory The process of holding incoming information in consciousness and retrieving and manipulating information from long-term memory, enabling cognitive tasks such as learning and thinking.

retrieval The process through which working memory brings a stored memory into consciousness.

Sensory Memory

Sensory memory results from bottom-up processing of visual, auditory, tactile, and other kinds of sensory information. The only reason this information is considered to be a memory store is that it persists for a fraction of a second (for information that is seen) to a few seconds (for information that is heard). If you have ever created patterns by waving a sparkler on a dark night, you have experienced the brief visual afterimages that make up sensory memory. When we attend to information in sensory memory, short-term memory processing begins.

Fortunately, if it is not attended to, the information that enters sensory memory is lost. Imagine what is happening as you read this paragraph: information from hundreds of thousands of cells in your eyes, ears, tongue, and nose, as well as touch, temperature, and pain receptors all over your body, is converging in your brain. If the effects of all these inputs were to persist beyond a second or so, your sensory memory would quickly be overwhelmed. However, because the information is rapidly lost, you can direct your attention to what is happening now, rather than to minutes-old information. Thus the sensory impression of the words you were reading at the beginning of this sentence is gone by the time you reach its end. But if you have been paying attention, and have been rehearsing the information you read (see Figure 10.1), you will likely retain the information, even though the visual images of the letters and the sounds of the words you read silently have faded from your sensory memory.

Estimates of how long sensory information persists come from a variety of experiments. In one classic experiment, the psychologist George Sperling measured the duration of a visual image, which he called an *icon* (see Figure 10.2). Sperling projected three rows of four letters each onto a screen for one-twentieth of a second—too brief a time for subjects to read them normally. But by "viewing" a visual afterimage of the icon, subjects could report 3 or 4 of the 12 letters correctly. Sperling estimated that their *iconic memory* of the image lasted about one-third to a one-half second.

Sperling was concerned that his method handicapped subjects, however, because their afterimage faded during the few seconds they took to deliver their verbal reports. So he modified the procedure by asking subjects to report the letters from only one of the three rows, signaled by a high-, medium-, or low-pitched tone sounded immediately after the display of all three rows. (Subjects did not know which line they would be asked to read until they were cued.) Sperling found that when cued, most subjects got all four letters on the line. From these data he reasoned that subjects could see the entire display of 12 letters only briefly, before it faded. He concluded that people can see more than they can process, and that *attention* determines which information they do process (Sperling, 1960).

Selective Attention to Information

More recent research on attention has complicated our understanding of sensory memory. For example, Johnston, McCann, and Remington (1995) conducted letter identification studies in which they presented stimuli successively, within a few milliseconds of each other. Subjects had to respond to the second stimulus while their attention was taken up by the first. These researchers reported evidence for two types of attentional processes, one of which they called *input attention* and the other, *central attention*. Does this finding mean that you *can* watch TV and study at the same time? The answer is no, but it does indicate that attention (central attention) can be rapidly diverted by a second stimulus (input attention). You *can* hear a knock on the door, even though you are thoroughly engrossed in a novel.

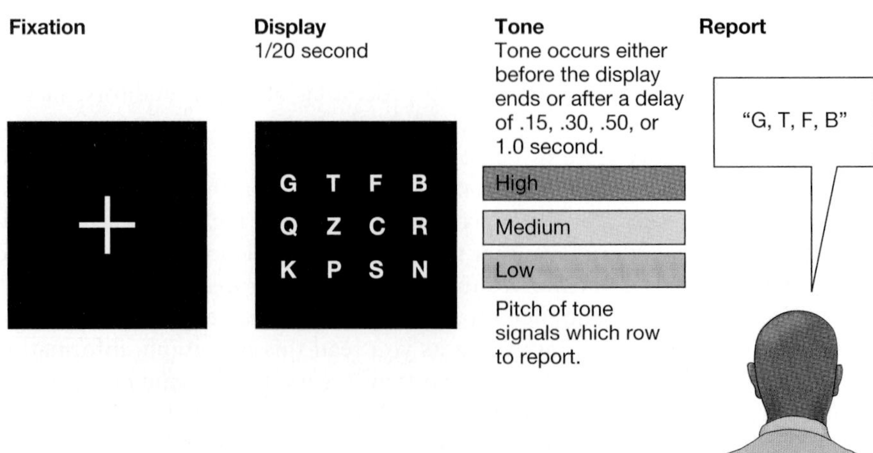

Figure 10.2 **Measuring the duration of sensory memory.** Subjects first stare at a cross on a screen, which is followed by a display of three rows of four letters each that lasts for one-twentieth of a second. After a delay, a tone cues the subject to repeat one of the three rows. *Source:* From "The Information Available in Brief Visual Presentation" by G. Sperling, *Psychological Monographs*, 74, Whole No. 498, (1960). Published by American Psychological Assn.

Another line of research suggests that attention is similar to a flashlight shining in a dark room: whatever it falls on is attended to (Broadbent, 1982). In one experiment, while a subject was focusing on a letter presented in one part of the visual field, researchers briefly flashed other letters in another part (Kramer & Hahn, 1995). They found that subjects could divide their attention in a way that allowed them to attend to letters in both areas. But the time intervals separating the two displays were mere fractions of a second. No one has yet demonstrated that subjects can maintain two separate trains of thought for even a few seconds.

Conversing at a noisy party requires selective attention.

The ability to divide one's attention varies from one individual to another. By rapidly (and effortlessly) shifting their attention, most people can drive a car, listen to music, and hold a conversation, all at the same time. They can do so because different parts of the brain can function relatively independently. Just how well a person can divide his or her attention depends on the amount of conscious effort required by each task (Damos, 1992). An oncoming car that is going too fast will capture a driver's attention even in the midst of an intense conversation. But lacking that kind of emergency, how do we know which incoming information should receive our attention?

The process of moving information from the sensory store to short-term memory is called **selective attention.** Selective attention is a focusing of consciousness that is accomplished by excluding all but the selected information (Neisser, 1967). Even though the research evidence on selective attention is thin, everyday examples abound. For example, some students manage to study in noisy, visually distracting environments. (A room with the television on is a noisy, visually distracting environment.) Others find that they can focus their attention better by studying in a quiet place, with few sensory distractions. In both cases, students are selecting the information they attend to.

A common example of selective attention is the **cocktail party phenomenon**—the ability to pick out and selectively hear one voice among many. In fact, the cocktail party phenomenon tells researchers quite a lot about selective attention, including the surprising finding that other sounds are *not* totally blocked. You may think you're not listening to anyone else, for example, but you are likely to shift your attention abruptly if you overhear someone say your name or the name of your significant other. The words seem to cut right through the din.

Psychologists have studied the cocktail party phenomenon in the laboratory, where they can better control the variables that influence selective attention. In one experiment, a researcher played different sounds into subjects' left and right ears using headphones (see Figure 10.3), and asked them to *shadow*, or repeat aloud, one message or the other (Cherry, 1953). Later in this **dichotic listening task**, the researcher asked subjects to recall what they had shadowed, and whether they could remember anything from the message that was played into the other ear. He found that subjects could recall the shadowed material fairly well, but not the unshadowed message, unless it contained a familiar name or sexually explicit language (Nielson & Sarason, 1981). Laboratory study of the cocktail party phenomenon, then, replicated most people's experience when attending to a signal in a noisy environment. But researchers also obtained some unexpected results. For example, due to the pitch and volume of the message in the unshadowed ear, subjects could surmise whether the voice they heard was

selective attention The process of attending to information that results in the encoding of short-term memories.

cocktail party phenomenon The ability to listen selectively to one particular voice among many simultaneous conversations.

dichotic listening task A procedure in which subjects hear two messages in different ears and then report on what they remember hearing.

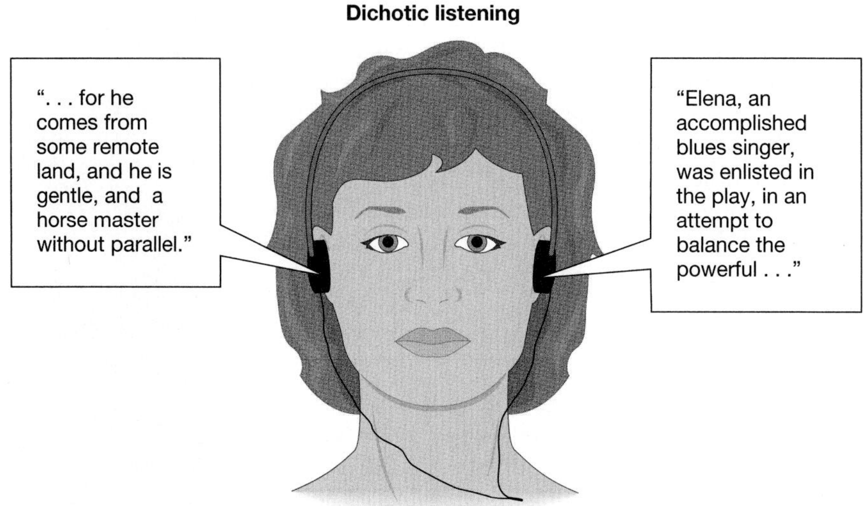

Dichotic listening
"... for he comes from some remote land, and he is gentle, and a horse master without parallel."
"Elena, an accomplished blues singer, was enlisted in the play, in an attempt to balance the powerful ..."

Figure 10.3 Dichotic listening. A person can pay attention to only one of two different messages played into the ears. In dichotic listening, a subject shadows, or repeats back, the message in one ear. (In this figure, the subject is shadowing the message on the left.) Typically, subjects can detect the physical characteristics of sounds presented to the other ear, but not their meaning.

male or female. The sensory store, then, accomplishes bottom-up processing of the physical characteristics of stimuli rather than top-down processing of the meaning of a message (Cherry, 1953; see also Broadbent, 1958).

Short-Term (Working) Memory

Top-down processes, including selective attention, determine what sensory information enters short-term memory. That is fortunate, for short-term memory has its limitations. In a paper titled *The Magical Number Seven, Plus or Minus Two,* George Miller of Harvard University pointed out the limits of the average person's *memory span* (Miller, 1956). Miller found that most people can hold just 5 to 9 items at a time in short-term memory. In a *digit-span test*, in which a subject repeats back a list of numbers read aloud at a rate of one item per second, subjects with certain types of brain damage may be able to repeat only 1or 2 items, while those with exceptional memory may be able to repeat as many as a dozen. Most people can handle lists of 5 to 9 items. One result of these limits is that 5-digit ZIP codes and 7-digit telephone numbers do not present a problem for most people, but 9-digit ZIP codes, 10-digit phone numbers, and 16-digit credit card numbers do.

The common experience of looking up a telephone number highlights the limited capacity of short-term memory. By first reading and then repeating a number (that is, rehearsing the 7 digits), most people can hold a number in memory long enough to finish dialing it. Rehearsal keeps the number active in short-term memory. But if the rehearsal is interrupted (because the doorbell rings, or someone interrupts), the caller may not remember the number long enough to complete the call. To reintroduce the number into short-term memory, one must look it up again. Adding an area code brings the digit count to 10; even while paying attention, a caller may not remember all the digits.

chunking The process of reorganizing material so as to admit more units, or bits, of information into short-term memory.

Chunking. If the area code is familiar, different rules apply. Short-term memory is not strictly limited to 5 to 9 items. If it were, you wouldn't be able to remember the first part of this 17 word sentence. Miller found that subjects could expand the limited capacity of short-term memory by a top-down process he called *chunking*. **Chunking** is the process of reorganizing material into meaningful units. For example, letters can be *chunked* as words, words can be chunked as phrases, and phrases can be chunked sentences.

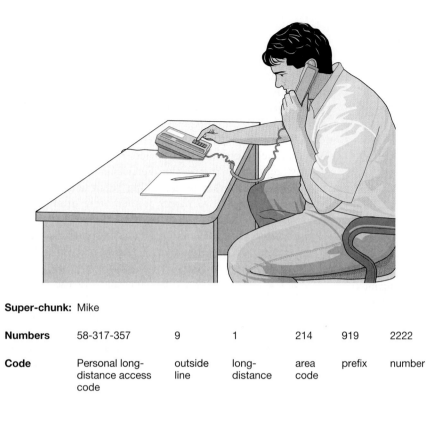

Super-chunk:	Mike					
Numbers	58-317-357	9	1	214	919	2222
Code	Personal long-distance access code	outside line	long-distance	area code	prefix	number

Figure 10.4 Chunking a 20-digit telephone number. Breaking down a 20-digit telephone number into six chunks helps in memorizing it.

Figure 10.4 shows how telephone numbers are chunked in terms of area codes and prefixes. Let's say I want to call my friend Mike, who lives in a different city. I may need to dial six chunks of numbers from my office, including an access code, a long-distance code, and so forth. After many rehearsals, these six chunks may collapse into a single chunk that I can bring into STM from LTM. Furthermore, my motor memories (stored in the cerebellum) allow me to rapidly and efficiently hit the appropriate buttons on the phone. As this example demonstrates, a memory may exist in several forms. After dozens of trials of dialing Mike, I may be asked to write the phone number, only to find that I don't "know" it in words. But given a phone pad, I can hit the numbers with my finger and record them as I do. (We'll discuss nonverbal motor memories in another section.)

Mnemonics. Chunking is an example of a **mnemonic** (a memory aid) that expands the amount of information one can process in a given period. With laboratory training, this memory aid can increase one's digit span quite remarkably. Steve Faloon was an average college student who could remember about 7 digits when he began 18 months of training in the laboratory of Anders Ericsson and his colleagues (Ericsson et al., 1980; Ericsson, 1985). Using a top-down mnemonic in which he related digits to previously memorized track times in running events, Faloon was eventually able to recall lists of up to 80 digits. In one portion of a list, for example, the sequence of digits might be 3–5–9–4, a series Faloon might recognize as Roger Bannister's record time of 3 minutes, 59.4 seconds (Bannister was the first to break the 4-minute mile). Do such experiments demonstrate that short-term memory can be improved by training? Not exactly. Though Faloon's digit span increased, when researchers introduced random *letters*, it dropped back to 7 ± 2. His chunking ability was specific to the mnemonic he was using.

mnemonic A memory aid that increases the amount of information a person can remember.

As Figure 10.1 indicates, short-term memory is restricted by time as well as by the number of items it can hold. The memory for information that enters STM persists considerably longer than the input in sensory memory, but as the

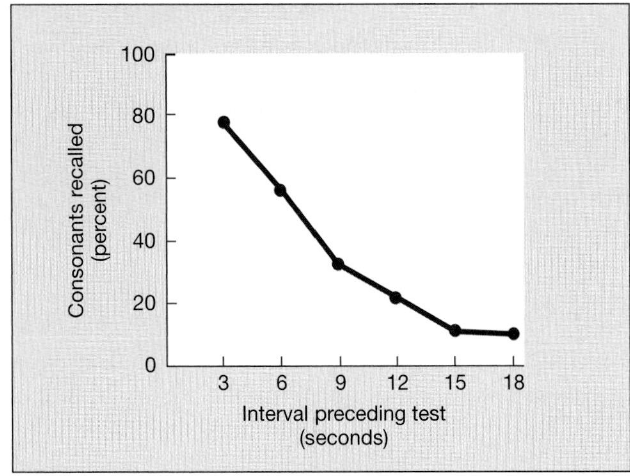

Figure 10.5 The duration of short-term memory. Three to 18 seconds after hearing three consonants and being unable to rehearse them, subjects were asked to recall them. As the time interval between hearing and recall increased, the percentage of consonants the subjects recalled decreased. *Source:* From Peterson & Peterson , 1959.

telephone example suggests, its duration is still quite restricted, especially if its rehearsal is interrupted. In a classic study, psychologists Lloyd and Margaret Peterson (1959) monitored what happens to information in short-term memory if it is not rehearsed. Their procedure was simple: they read subjects an unpronounceable sequence of three letters, such as "MBD" or "PJQ," and asked them to repeat the letters after varying time intervals (the longest was 18 seconds). While subjects could hold the letter sequences in mind by silently repeating them, the Petersons deliberately interrupted their rehearsal by assigning them a *distracter task*, counting *backward by threes* immediately after they were given the three-letter sequence. For example, after hearing "PJQ," subjects would be instructed to remember the three letters while counting backward by threes from 788 ("785, 782, 779 . . .").

After a short interval the Petersons told the subjects to stop counting and asked them to report the three-letter sequence. Figure 10.5 shows the percentage of the letter sequences subjects recalled after being distracted for varying intervals. If their rehearsal was interrupted for 15 seconds, their recall was close to zero. The duration of short-term memory, the Petersons reasoned, must be about 15 seconds.

The fact that short-term memory lasts only seconds has important practical implications. When you study and watch TV at the same time, you alternate between two streams of consciousness. Each time you switch from one to the other, you lose your ability to maintain continuity of thought in your short-term

Figure 10.6 Long-term memory for Spanish. Researchers measured how much Spanish people retained years after they had studied the language. Surprisingly, people who had taken several semesters of high-school Spanish retained 40 percent of what they had learned, even after 50 years. *Source:* From "Semantic Memory Context in Permastore: Fifty Years of Memory for Spanish Learned in School" by H. P. Bahrick, *Journal of Experimental Psychology: General*, (1984), vol. 113, pp. 1–29. Copyright © 1984 by the American Psychological Association. Reprinted by permission.

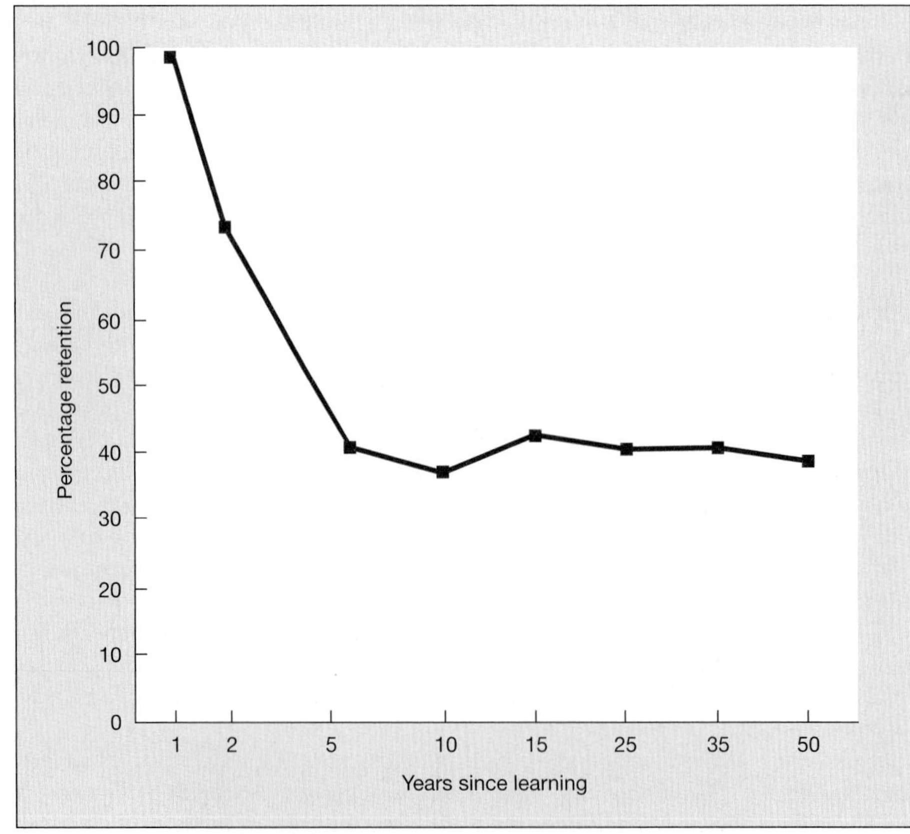

memory. As we saw earlier, we can successfully divide our attention only if neither of the tasks we are attending to requires much conscious effort (Damos, 1992). Certainly, TV viewing requires less effort than studying, but in all likelihood, neither the material you are studying nor the images on your TV will persist long enough to enter your long-term memory.

Long-Term Memory

We have seen that sensory memory lasts for fractions of a second to a few seconds at most, and that without rehearsal, short-term memory lasts only about 15 seconds. Most common uses of the term *memory*, however, refer to information that is long lasting. As Figure 10.1 indicated, long-term memory can be thought of as the relatively permanent repository of events experienced over a lifetime. These memories persist despite the fact that years may go by without their rehearsal. And unlike the limited capacity of short-term memory, long-term memory capacity seems to be unlimited.

A sight, a sound, or even a smell can trigger recall of a long-term memory. Harry Bahrick (1984) has demonstrated the capacity of long-term memory by asking people what they remembered of the foreign language they studied in high school. While their first response was usually "very little," Bahrick found that even if people had not used their high-school Spanish for many years, they could remember a surprising amount of it (see Figure 10.6).

INTERIM SUMMARY

1. According to the ***information-processing model of memory,*** human memory has three components: a brief ***sensory memory;*** a ***short-term memory (STM)*** lasting about 15 seconds; and an unlimited ***long-term memory (LTM).***
2. ***Rehearsal,*** or the conscious repetition of material in short-term memory, helps in retaining information.
3. ***Working memory*** is a conscious process characterized by the learning of new information and the ***retrieval*** of existing information from long-term memory. Working memory is similar to short-term memory.
4. Sperling (1960) measured the duration of sensory memory by briefly presenting an icon, or visual image, to subjects and asking them to report what they saw. He estimated the duration of sensory memory to be about one-third to one-half second.
5. The ability to pay attention to one voice in a noisy environment has been called the ***cocktail party phenomenon.*** In the laboratory, researchers use ***dichotic listening tasks*** to study the process of ***selective attention***—how information gets from the sensory store to short-term memory.
6. In his classic article *The Magical Number Seven, Plus or Minus Two,* George Miller proposed that short-term memory capacity is limited to between five and nine bits of information. ***Chunking*** increases short-term memory capacity.
7. A ***mnemonic*** is a memory aid that increases the amount of information a person can remember.
8. The capacity of long-term memory is unlimited; some information may persist for a lifetime.

For Further Thought

1. Melodies are excellent mnemonic devices. For example, many of us learned our ABCs by memorizing the alphabet song. Can you use association theory (see Chapter 6) to account for the effectiveness of mnemonic devices?

2. In what ways is the brief duration of sensory memory and short-term memory adaptive?
3. You are intently reading a magazine or book when someone asks you a question. You respond, "What did you say?" but before the person repeats the question, you "hear" it in your mind and answer it. What does this common experience tell us about central attention and input attention, and the duration of short-term memory?

ENCODING AND SHORT-TERM MEMORY

Everyday experience does not suggest the existence of three distinct memory systems. Rather, memory seems unitary. But the three-part model of memory is useful, because it helps us to understand aspects of memory that we otherwise would not. Let's use the concept of short-term, or working, memory to examine some interesting experimental findings.

The Recency Effect

In a now-classic experiment (Murdock, 1962), a researcher asked college students to remember as many words as they could from a series of common words read aloud to them. After hearing 20 words at a rate of about one per second, the students tried to recall the words in any order, a method known as **free recall.** Figure 10.7 shows the percentage of words they remembered as a function of the position of the words on the list. The U-shaped curve reveals that subjects recalled more words from the beginning and end of the list than from the middle, a phenomenon known as the **serial position effect.**

Psychologists agree that the serial position effect reflects the operation of both short-term memory and long-term memory. After hearing a list, most subjects will write down the last few items they heard (which are still in short-term memory), followed by the first few items they heard. The right-hand part of the U-shaped curve in Figure 10.7 shows that they remember the words at the end of a list better than words in the middle, called the **recency effect.** How do psychologists know that the recency effect is due to short-term memory? One way to test this hypothesis is to introduce a brief delay between the end of the list and the signal to recall the items. Glanzer and Cunitz (1966) did such an experiment and found that delaying recall by as little as 10 seconds completely eliminated the recency effect. That is, subjects remembered the last few items on the list no better than the items in the middle.

free recall A test of memory in which the items to be remembered can be recalled in any order.

serial position effect The tendency for items at the beginning and end of a list to be remembered better than those in the middle.

recency effect The tendency for items at the end of a list to be remembered better than items in the middle.

phonological loop A part of working memory that allows a person to remember speech sounds for a brief period.

The Phonological Loop

To explain the recency effect, Allan Baddeley of the University of Bristol has postulated a *phonological storage process*—that is, a process for remembering sounds for just a second or two (Baddeley, 1998). By hearing a word and silently repeating it, we can maintain it in what Baddeley calls a **phonological loop** in working memory.

In one series of experiments, Baddeley and his colleagues used a variation on the dichotic listening method. They were interested in determining what *type* of information would interfere with what was being attended to. Other researchers had demonstrated that subjects could pick out their names and sexually explicit language from the background noise they heard. Baddeley and his colleagues found that both words and *nonsense syllables* interfered with subjects' ability to attend to a verbal message. (A nonsense syllable is a three letter "word" that has no meaning—usually two consonants separated by a vowel, such as *ZEM* or *CIJ*.) Subjects could tune out pulsed noise, but vocal music, and to a much lesser extent, instrumental music (both classical and modern), interfered with their attention to visually presented information (Salamé & Baddeley, 1987, 1989). There are some individual differences in response to music: Crawford & Strapp (1994) identified a few students who were less sensitive than others to noise, were highly capable of focusing their attention, and preferred studying with music. However, all subjects were distracted by speech sounds, called *phonemes*. Apparently only nonspeech sounds can be kept out of the phonological loop.

Baddeley and his colleagues also found that the short-term memory for words is determined by the number of syllables in the phonological loop. For example, monosyllabic words like *bird*, *train*, and *house* are likely to be remembered if they are the last three items on a list, but *caterpillar*, *individual*, and *revolution*, which contain a total of 13 syllables, are less likely to be recalled. Not just recall, but reading speed is directly related to the number of syllables in a word (see Figure 10.8).

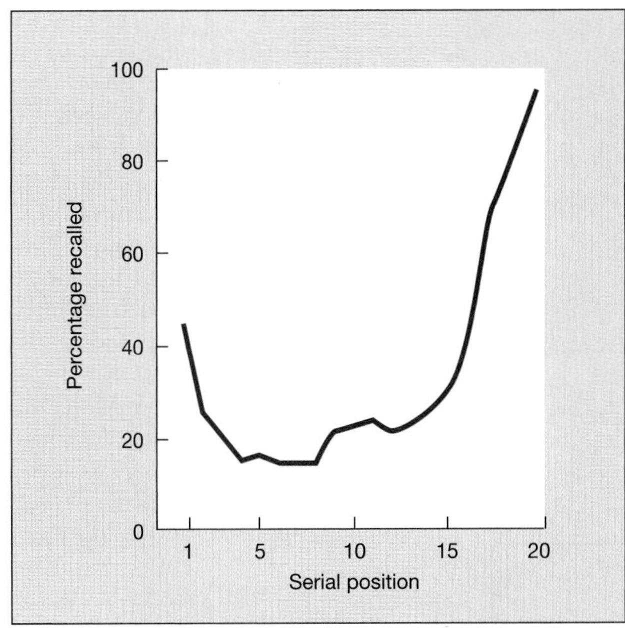

Figure 10.7 **The serial position effect.** After hearing a list of 20 words, subjects immediately wrote down as many as they could remember, in any order. With few exceptions, they remembered more words from the beginning and end of the list than from the middle, producing this u-shaped function.

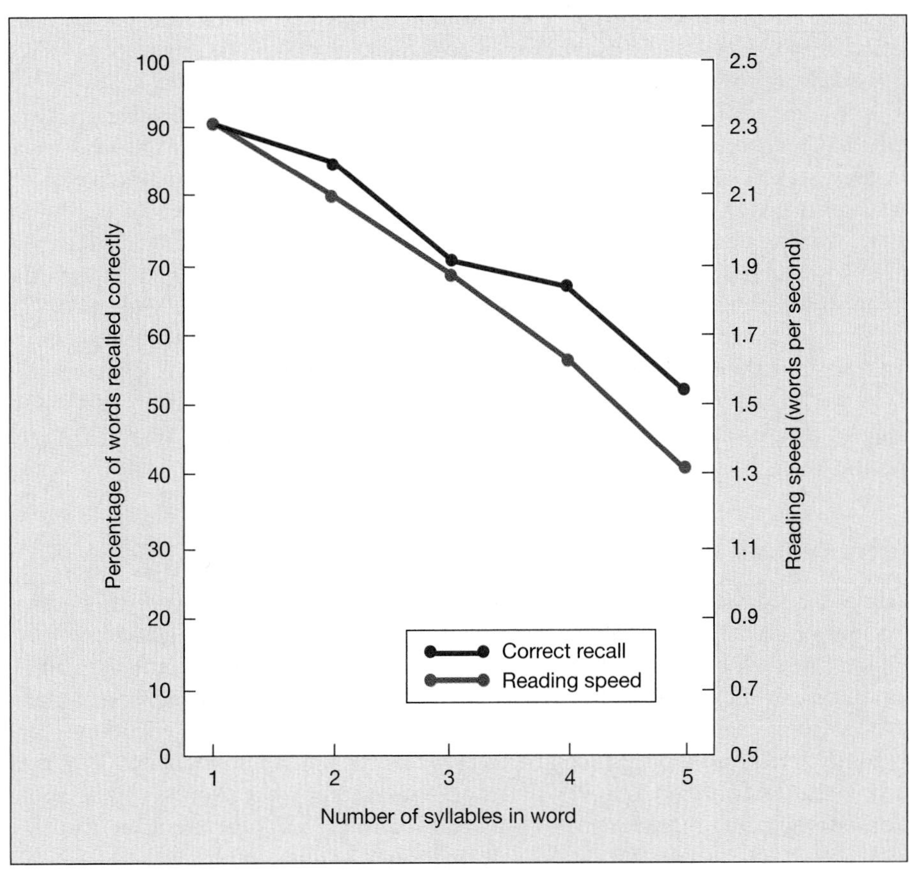

Figure 10.8 **Word length, reading speed, and recall.** Polysyllabic words are read at a slower rate than shorter words, and recalled less often in tests of memory. In one experiment, subjects read one-syllable words (*x*-axis) at a rate of about 2 per second (*y*-axis), but four-syllable words at about half that rate. Likewise, they recalled 90 percent of the one-syllable words (*y*-axis), but less than 50 percent of the four-syllable words. *Sources:* From "Word Length and the Structure of Short-Term Memory" by A. D. Baddeley, et al. in *Journal of Verbal Learning and Verbal Behavior*, Vol. 14, (1975), pp. 575–589. Copyright © 1975 by the American Psychological Association. Reprinted by permission.

The fact that sounds can be held in short-term memory for only a limited period helps to explain individual differences in reading and learning. People who read slowly do not put as much information into their phonological loops as people who read more quickly. As a result, they process information more slowly. Even fast readers may slow down to increase their comprehension. On encountering a difficult passage, skilled readers are likely to stop and reread it, increasing the amount of time the words are kept in their phonological loop. After they have had time to understand the passage, they resume their normal reading speed.

The limits of the phonological loop also explain variations in the speed of processing in different languages. A clear relationship exists between memory span and the speed with which the numbers 1 through 10 can be articulated in different languages (Naveh-Benjamin & Ayres, 1986). In those languages with polysyllabic words for numbers, such as Arabic and Welsh, subjects can hold fewer digits in memory than in English (in which only the number 7 has two syllables). Beyond 1 through 10, Chinese numbers have even fewer syllables than English numbers. As a result, Chinese speakers articulate numbers more quickly, and hold more of them in the phonological loop, than English speakers. In one study, researchers found that English-speaking students took twice as long as Chinese students to articulate multiplication tables. In fact, the correlation between memory span and grades on mathematics tests is .38, a relationship that is likely due to limitations in the phonological loop (Hoosain & Salili, 1988).

The Primacy Effect

The phonological loop accounts for the recency effect, but it does not explain why a higher percentage of items is recalled from the beginning of a list. Better recall of the first items on a list compared with the middle items is known as the **primacy effect** (see Figure 10.7). Psychologists have speculated that the primacy effect may be caused by **maintenance rehearsal**, or the silent repetition of each item as it is processed.

Say, for example, that the first three items on a list are *coach, blue,* and *elephant*. You hear the word *coach*, and silently repeat it to yourself. The next word is *blue*, so you silently say *coach, blue*. Next is *elephant,* so your maintenance rehearsal is *coach, blue, elephant*. At the end of about 20 seconds (for a 20-item list), you may have repeated *coach, blue*, and *elephant* many times. In fact, the number of rehearsal trials of the first items on a list is highly correlated with the number of words a subject can remember during free recall (Rundus, 1971). Maintenance rehearsal, then, is one way to get a word from short-term memory to long-term memory. This process may sound familiar because it is similar to the way we learn foreign-language vocabulary (see Chapter 6). The more trials during which the word *bueno* is associated with *good*, the less likely the student is to forget it.

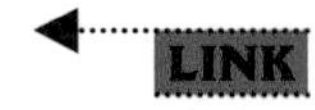

Maintenance rehearsal and associative processes, Chapter 6, p. 190

primacy effect The tendency for items at the beginning of a list to be remembered better than items in the middle.

maintenance rehearsal The act of holding information in short-term memory by silently repeating each item as it is presented.

encoding The transfer of information from short-term to long-term memory.

storage The process of retaining information in long-term memory.

The Process of Encoding

Maintenance rehearsal doesn't always get information from short-term memory to long-term memory. Despite the repetition of information, many people form inaccurate memories of spellings, vocabulary definitions, phone numbers, names, and book or movie titles. To successfully get information from short-term memory to long-term memory, students must use a process called **encoding**: consciously attending to particular features of the information. Encoding may transform information in a way that makes its **storage**—the process of adding information to long-term memory—more probable. Without attention to detail and some kind of transformation, information may not be encoded.

Without a doubt, for instance, you have seen the image of a penny many hundreds of times. Can you pick out the correct drawing of a penny from the 15 versions shown in Figure 10.9? Most people cannot (Nickerson & Adams, 1979), probably because they have failed to pay attention to its features. You may know the size, color, and weight of a penny, but you probably have not inspected each and every one of its features. From an adaptive perspective, you can recognize enough features to discriminate among different coins, which is all you need to do to use them. If your job required you to handle different currencies, or catch counterfeiters, you would soon enough learn to discriminate and commit to long-term memory the specific features of coins and bills.

Figure 10.9 **Which is the real penny?** Unless you have an exceedingly good memory for detail, you probably will *not* be able identify the real penny in this group of 15 slightly different versions. (The first on top left is correct.) *Source:* From Nickerson & Adams, 1979.

With specific instructions, a person can engage in what has been called *intentional encoding*. For example, you could use a mnemonic device to learn the items on a list or examine a penny in detail so as to recognize a counterfeit. But much of what people encounter, and later remember imperfectly, is the result of *incidental*, or *automatic, encoding*. Consider the following questions:

1. In the house (or apartment) where you last lived, when you entered the front door, was the doorknob on the left or the right side? (Lindsay & Norman, 1977).
2. How many times did you drive your car (or ride your bicycle) last week?

The answers to both these questions would have been encoded incidentally, as is most information having to do with time and place (Hasher & Zacks, 1984). Studying, in contrast, is *effortful*, or *intentional*, *encoding*. Which raises the question: Why does *effort* increase the amount of information that enters long-term memory?

The Levels-of-Processing Hypothesis

According to Craik and Lockhart's (1972) *levels-of-processing hypothesis*, information in long-term memory may be encoded at a shallow or deep level. Shallow processing is equivalent to incidental encoding; deep processing requires effort. Consider an experiment by Craik and Tulving (1975), in which subjects were first shown a long list of unrelated words, then divided into three groups and asked different questions. Group 1 was asked about the *case* of a word (whether it was written in uppercase or lowercase); group 2, whether the word *rhymed* with another word; and group 3, whether the word could be used in a specific sentence. One word on the list, for example, was *dog*. The questions posed to subjects in groups 1, 2, and 3, respectively, were:

1. *yes* or *no*, is this word written in uppercase letters? (DOG)
2. *yes* or *no*, does it rhyme with *log*?
3. *yes* or *no*, does it fit in the sentence "The ___ was in its kennel"?

These three conditions required subjects to engage in three different **levels of processing**, from shallow to deep. Obviously, using a word in a sentence takes more effort than noticing whether the word is written in uppercase or lowercase letters.

levels of processing The levels, either shallow or deep, at which information is encoded in long-term memory.

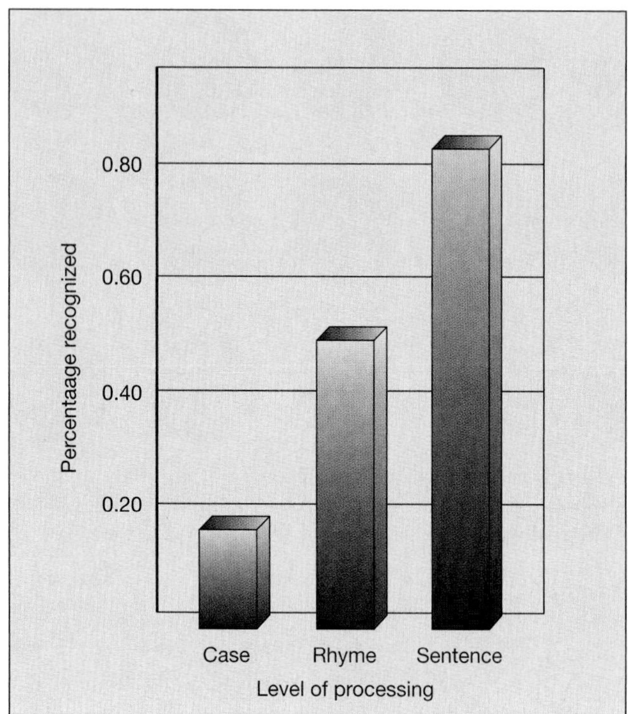

Figure 10.10 **Deep processing enhances memory.** Subjects who rehearsed words in terms of their physical characteristics (lowercase or uppercase letters) did not remember them well. Subjects who rehearsed them in the form of rhymes or used them in sentences remembered them better.
Source: Graph from "Depth of Processing and retention of Words in Episodic Memory" by F. I. M. Craik & E. Tulving, *Journal of Experimental Psychology, General*, 104, pp. 268–294 © 1975 by APA.

Figure 10.10 shows the results of this experiment. When presented with the long list of words again, and asked if they recognized them, subjects who had processed the list most deeply (those in group 3) recalled the most items. These subjects had engaged in **elaborative rehearsal,** in which they associated the words to be learned with other information (the sentences into which they put the words). Subjects in group 2 recognized an intermediate number of words, and subjects in group 1 recognized the fewest. This finding is reminiscent of the research on penny recognition. Just as people don't study pennies, most of us wouldn't pay much attention to whether the words on a list were in uppercase or lowercase letters.

Do you suffer the common problem of immediately forgetting the name of a person to whom you have just been introduced? Using elaborative rehearsal can help you to overcome this problem (see Figure 10.11). Try associating the name with other things you know about the person, including a mutual friend, the person's home town, and so forth. With elaboration, you are more likely to recall the name a few minutes or even a few months later.

Figure 10.11 **How to remember names.** If you are introduced to a person and want to remember her name, use elaborative rehearsal. Unless you associate the name with other facts you know about the person, you are likely to forget it.

elaborative rehearsal The strategy of associating a target stimulus with other information at the time of encoding.

INTERIM SUMMARY

1. In some experiments on memory, subjects hear a list of items and are asked to recall them in any order, a method called *free recall.* Subjects recall more words from the beginning and end of the list than from the middle, a phenomenon called the *serial position effect.*
2. The tendency to remember more items from the end of a list is called the *recency effect.* Items at the end of a list are remembered better for as long as they remain in the *phonological loop,* a limited memory store for sounds.
3. Nonspeech sounds can be kept out of the phonological loop, but speech sounds compete for attention and interfere with a subject's ability to shadow language.
4. The duration of the short-term memory for words is determined by the number of syllables in the phonological loop.
5. The *primacy effect*—better recall for the first items on a list than for the middle items—is due to *maintenance rehearsal,* or the silent repetition of the items. Maintenance rehearsal is one way of acquiring long-term memories.
6. *Encoding* is accomplished through conscious attention to particular features of information, a process that enhances the *storage* of information in long-term memory. *Incidental,* or *automatic encoding* can occur as well as *intentional,* or *effortful, encoding.*
7. According to one hypothesis, encoding can occur at several *levels of processing,* from superficial to deep. Items that are deeply processed are encoded better than items that are processed superficially.
8. Deep processing can be accomplished through *elaborative rehearsal,* associating an item with other information.

For Further Thought

1. According to research on the phonological loop, why does vocal music interfere more than instrumental music with a person's ability to study? What characterizes those people who appear to be able to study in the midst of chaos?
2. The duration of the phonological loop is measured in seconds. Do you think that increasing the reading speed of children in the lower elementary grades is a worthwhile objective? Why or why not?
3. Like blindsight, incidental or automatic encoding occurs without conscious awareness. Do you suspect that the brain mechanisms involved in automatic encoding are different from those involved in effortful encoding?
4. Who is N. A.? Why have you remembered or forgotten his initials?

THE ENIGMA OF LONG-TERM MEMORY

Long-term memory is what most people mean when they speak of memory. Though we tend to take for granted our ability to remember things that are important to us, we sometimes discover that our memory is less than perfect. Can we trust long-term memory? Do we have memories of which we are unaware? Surprisingly, these questions are related.

Implicit and Explicit Memories

Can you retrieve from your long-term memory a discussion of the phenomenon of blindsight, covered in Chapter 8? Recall that subjects with blindsight denied seeing anything, yet behaved as if they could. A similar phenomenon has been discovered in research on visual and auditory memories. Can you

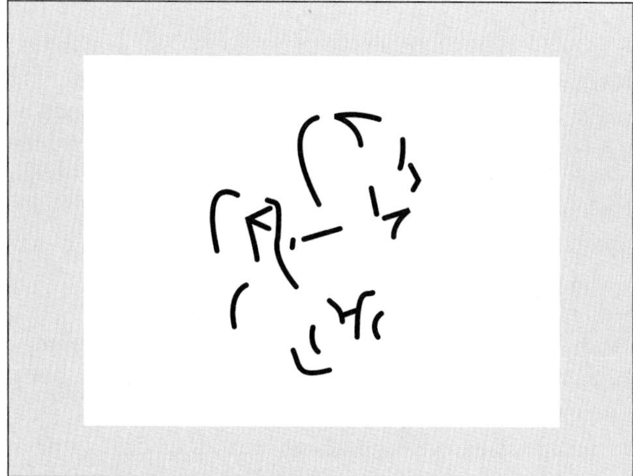

Figure 10.12 Can you recognize this picture? If you can't recognize this fragmented picture, read the top paragraph on this page. *Source:* "Developmental Studies of Visual Recognition of Incomplete Objects" by E. S. Gollin in *Perceptual and Motor Skills*, 1960, 11, pp. 289–298. Copyright © 1960 by Southern Universities Press. Used by permission.

identify the fragmented picture in Figure 10.12, for example? Probably not, though research has shown that if you had seen the word *baby buggy* the day before you read this, you would have been more likely to identify the picture, even if you could not recall having seen the word. The phenomenon of being influenced by the memory of a past experience, even though you have no conscious memory of it, is called **implicit memory** (Roediger & McDermott, 1993). An example of implicit memory is the common feeling known as déjà vu: I've been here/done this before, but I can't remember when.

Researchers have explored the intriguing world of implicit memory using a method called *priming*. In **priming**, subjects might view a target word such as a *baby buggy* in whole or in part. Seeing the word increases the probability that they will recall the word later (Schacter, 1996). Suppose, for example, that you carefully studied the following words:

assassin octopus avocado mystery sheriff climate

and then returned an hour later to be tested. If you were given a list containing these words, you would probably have little difficulty identifying them. But instead, you might be asked to complete the following sentence fragments:

ch _ _ mu _ _   o _ t _ _ us   _ og _ y _ _ _   _ v _ c _ do

If you were able to complete the words *octopus* and *avocado*, but not *chipmunk* and *bogeyman*, you have demonstrated the effects of priming. Now suppose that one week (rather than one hour) were to pass between priming and testing. Amazingly, while you would be likely to forget most of the primed words, you would still be able to complete most of the fragments (see Figure 10.13; Tulving, Schacter, & Stark, 1982). Like blindsight, priming works even when people have no recollection of ever having seen the target words.

That priming occurs independently of conscious memory allows us insight into other failures of memory (Schacter, 1996). All of us have had the experience of saying or writing an idea that we think is new, only to find that it isn't, or hearing an "original" idea from a friend that echoes something we said weeks earlier. Plagiarism, of course, is the explicit act of stealing another person's ideas. Inadvertent plagiarism, called *cryptomnesia*, is an example of implicit memory now being studied in the laboratory (Brown & Murphy, 1989; Marsh & Landau, 1995). Clearly, long-term memory contains information of which we are unaware. But how accurate is that information?

Memory as a perceptual process, Chapter 8, p. 271

implicit memory The unconscious memory of a past experience.

priming Presentation of a target memory, in whole or part, prior to its recall.

schema A personal interpretation of a sensory event that biases the memory of the event.

Schemas

Memory failures, and unconscious intrusion of implicit memories, are disconcerting. The integrity of one's personality is contingent on *veridical memories*—memories that are a more or less accurate record of past events. But is memory veridical? In 1932 Sir Frederick Bartlett challenged the idea that memory is a faithful reproduction of events. Instead, he proposed that memory is *reconstructive*. That is, people do not reliably remember past events as they actually happened, but as they perceived them to happen.

According to Bartlett, the memory a person recalls is biased by interpretations of sensory events made at the time the memories were being formed. He called such perceptions personal **schemas**. Bartlett used a simple research method to arrive at this conclusion. He read an Indian legend called *War of the Ghosts* to subjects; later, he asked them to recall the story. Bartlett found that subjects remembered the story based on the way they had interpreted it (encoded it) during the reading. They *reconstructed* it by introducing distortions and changes based on what they thought had "probably" occurred. On subsequent retellings, they changed the story again.

At some point in your life, you might have played a game similar to Bartlett's experiment. One person reads a short, simple "story" with several details to another person; the second person repeats the story to a third, and so on until the story has been transmitted 8 to10 times. Then the last person repeats aloud what she or he has heard. Without fail, the story has been distorted, often to the point of becoming unrecognizable.

Bartlett did not restrict his investigation of memory to stories. The drawings below show the results of another experiment, in which he asked a person to study a stylized drawing of an owl, and some time later asked him reproduce it from memory. A second subject studied the first subject's drawing and produced a second reproduction. The process continued through 10 subjects. By the 10th drawing, the owl had been transformed into a cat.

If personal schemas influence our memories, can we trust them? Elizabeth Loftus of the University of Washington

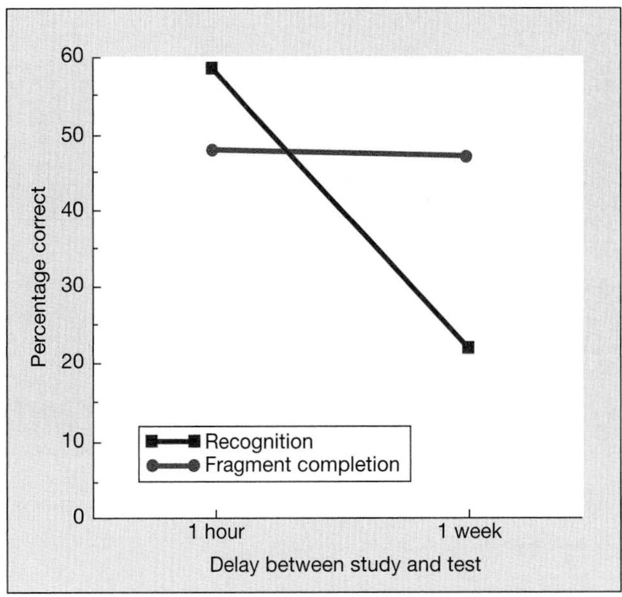

Figure 10.13 Implicit memories last longer than explicit memories. Subjects forgot a list of words they learned after a week, but their performance on a sentence completion task was relatively unchanged. Subjects often do not remember the words that prime their responses, suggesting that implicit (unconscious) memories last longer than explicit (conscious) memories.

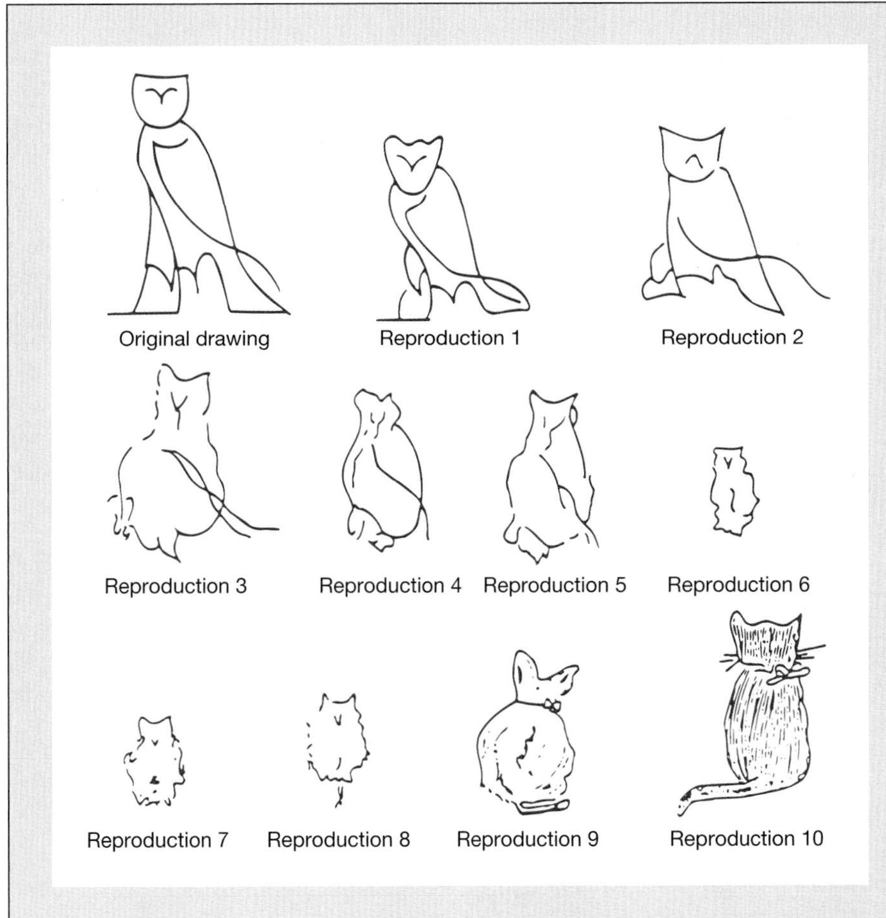

A series of ten subjects viewed and later redrew an image from memory. By the tenth redrawing, the original drawing of an owl had been transformed into a cat through a series of encoding distortions.

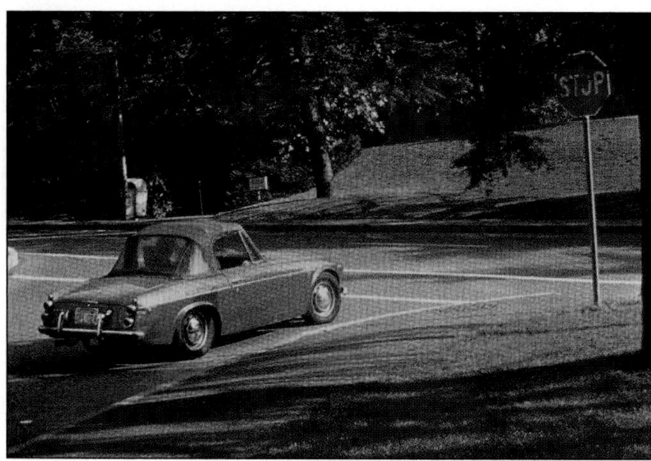

Which view is correct? Subjects viewed one of these scenes in a series of photos showing the events leading up to an accident. When asked later which of the nearly identical scenes they saw, their recollections were influenced by verbal instructions that confirmed or disconfirmed the photo's content.

LINK
Seeing and believing, Chapter 8, p. 271

thinks not. Loftus studied the visual memories of experimental subjects and found that they were influenced not just by schemas, but by the questions they were asked at the time of recall.

The Effect of Leading Questions

The two photographs above are slides from a laboratory experiment Loftus, Miller, and Burns (1978) conducted, showing events leading up to an automobile's collision with a pedestrian. Half the subjects saw the slide on the left, with a stop sign, and half saw the one on the right, with a yield sign. Later, Loftus asked the subjects one of two questions: *Did you see the* stop *sign*? or *Did you see the* yield *sign*? Only 41 percent of the subjects who were given the wrong information were able to pick out the slide they actually did see. This finding means that about 60 percent of the subjects had formed false memories. But if subjects were asked to identify the sign they *had* seen, their memories were more accurate: about 75 percent picked the slide they had actually been shown.

As time passed, subjects' memories were influenced even more by the leading questions researchers asked. These findings suggest that after sensory details fade, false memories can easily be created. Because subjects' recall was strongly influenced by the leading questions, this research is relevant to the value of *eyewitness testimony* (Loftus, 1979). Based on these findings Loftus is extremely skeptical that memories recovered from early childhood can be accurate (Loftus, 1997).

Other research on eyewitness testimony (Loftus & Palmer, 1974) shows that even small differences in the choice of words can influence a person's perception. Subjects first viewed a videotape of two automobiles colliding. Then each was asked one of five different versions of the question *How fast was the car going when it* ________ *with the other?* The subjects' speed estimates varied with the verb used in the question, as follows:

VERB USED	SPEED (MPH)
contacted	32
hit	34
bumped	38
collided	39
smashed	41

What is striking about this example is that all subjects viewed the same collision, yet they "saw" it differently. (No wonder that the home team sees a very different game from the visiting team!) When asked if the accident involved broken glass (it did not), subjects were more likely to say *yes* if they had been told that the cars *smashed* rather than *hit* each other. Likewise, in a drama that could be played out in your local courtroom, when Loftus asked subjects *Did you see the broken headlight*, they were more likely to answer yes than when she asked *Did you see a broken headlight*? This, of course, is why judges regularly admonish lawyers not to lead the witness.

Remembering Versus Knowing

How much do you trust your own memory for details? Think back to a recent conversation with a friend. You *know* the conversation occurred, but you are unlikely to *remember* the precise words that were said. Likewise, I *know* that I've been to hundreds of basketball games over the years, but I *remember* few of the details. Tulving (1985) thinks that this distinction between *remembering* and *knowing* is an important organizing feature of memory. Knowing, as opposed to remembering, is experienced as a "feeling." (Consider the phrase "I know in my heart.") That a state of knowing is experienced emotionally suggests that it arises in the limbic system, which includes both cortical and subcortical structures. Loftus's research tells us that what we see is in part determined by what we know, and what we know is in part determined by what we see. Remembering and knowing are distinct but intertwined.

INTERIM SUMMARY

1. Memories can be explicit (conscious) or implicit (unconscious). The effect of being influenced by a past experience, even though one has no explicit memory of it, is called ***implicit memory***.
2. In studies of implicit memory, a word or concept is presented to a subject before testing, a process called ***priming***.
3. Inadvertent plagiarism, also known as *cryptomnesia*, is an example of how implicit memory can affect behavior.
4. The notion that memory is reproductive in content has been refuted by research that indicates that memory is *reconstructive*. People's personal ***schemas***, or interpretations of events made at the time memories are formed, tend to distort or change what they remember.
5. Loftus's research on *eyewitness testimony* has demonstrated that memory is susceptible to misinformation and leading questions.
6. Remembering is not the same as knowing. We can know that events have occurred without being able to remember the details.

For Further Thought

1. An implicit memory is a memory of a past experience of which you are not conscious. How do implicit memories differ from false memories?
2. Have you recently experienced déjà vu? If so, can you recall the event that elicited the state?
3. Can Bartlett's theory that memory is reconstructive help to explain how rumors get started?

4. Grammatically speaking, *the* is a definite article and *a* is an indefinite article. *The* refers to a specific event or item, whereas *a* refers to a class of events or items. For testing purposes, should you remember that Elizabeth Loftus is *a* memory researcher, or that Elizabeth Loftus is *the* memory researcher who studied eyewitness testimony?
5. Which is more adaptive, a memory system that keeps a person from acting until every last detail has been checked for accuracy, or one that allows a person to act without verification? Do people act more often based on what they know or on what they remember?

MEMORY FOR MOVEMENT, EVENTS, AND WORDS

We have seen that long-term memories are reconstructive rather than reproductive—that their encoding can easily be influenced by personal schemas. But humans learn and transmit an incredible number of memes over their lifetime, so they must have memory systems that store their knowledge of people, places, activities, and language. Let's look at some theories of how different types of memory might be organized.

The psychologist Endel Tulving systematized long-term memory based on the different functions it serves in humans and other animals (Tulving, 1985, 1993). Tulving divided long-term memory into two separate systems: *procedural memory* and *declarative memory*. The first, procedural memory, is an unconscious system; the second, declarative memory, is a conscious memory system. Let's look at each in turn.

Procedural Memory

From an evolutionary perspective, the oldest, most basic memory system is the **procedural memory** for skilled performance that results from reinforced practice. This memory system is adaptive, because it allows animals to cope effectively with their environment. The nonassociative learning, conditioned responses, and instrumentally learned behaviors discussed in Chapter 6 make up this memory system.

Procedural memory with instrumental and conditioned responses, Chapter 6, p. 204

One example of procedural memory is remembering how you got to school from the house where you grew up. Instrumentally learned behaviors would include using a remote and balancing on a bicycle. Once learned, these memories are relatively permanent. (I recall hearing as a child the adage "You never forget how to swim or how to ride a bicycle.") Although such learned skills can be brought into consciousness, for the most part they are unconscious. They are mediated at the subcortical level, allowing one to carry on a conversation while jogging with a friend.

procedural memory The memory for skilled performance that results from reinforced practice.

declarative memory The conscious memory for facts and words and for personal events and episodes.

Declarative Memory

Conscious memories for facts and words, as well as for events and episodes of personal significance, make up **declarative memory**. As we will see, these memories seem to be mediated by cortical rather than subcortical brain structures. Tulving separated declarative memory into two main categories, *semantic* and *episodic memory* (see Figure 10.14). Earlier we discussed the difference between

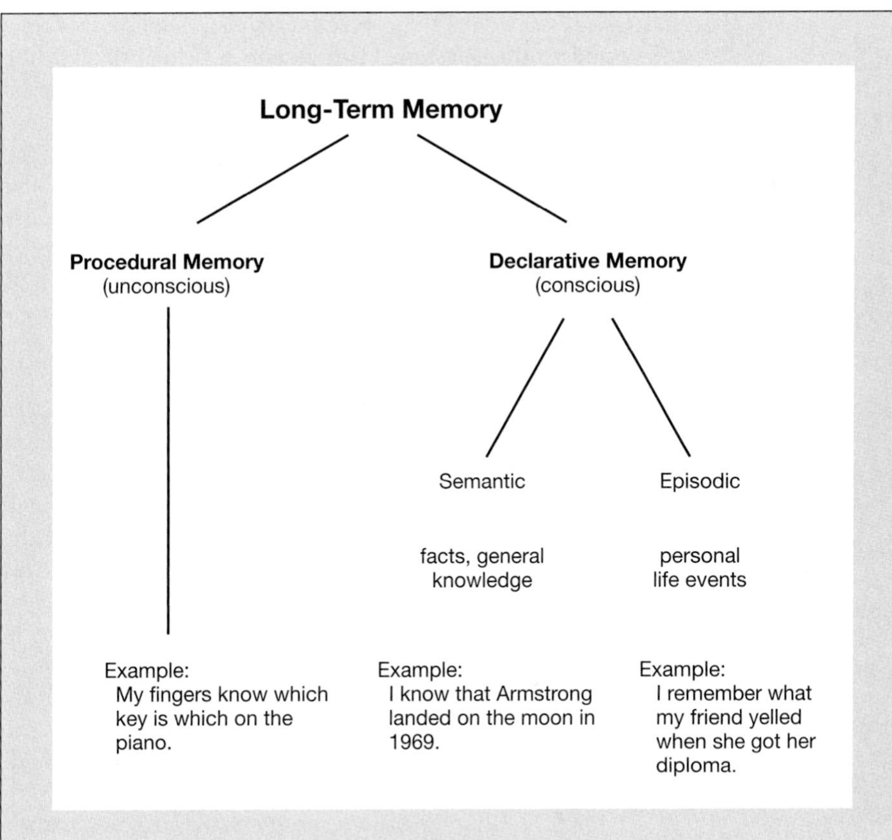
Long-Term Memory
Procedural Memory
(unconscious)
Declarative Memory
(conscious)
Semantic
Episodic
facts, general knowledge
personal life events
Example:
My fingers know which key is which on the piano.
Example:
I know that Armstrong landed on the moon in 1969.
Example:
I remember what my friend yelled when she got her diploma.

Figure 10.14 Tulving's multiple memory systems. According to Tulving (1985), human memory can be divided into several different memory systems.

knowing and remembering. Semantic memory can be thought of as a person's general store of knowledge. Episodic memory, in contrast, is made up of a person's most intimate memories. A great deal is now known about these conscious memory systems.

Semantic Memory. **Semantic memory** consists of an organism's learned knowledge about how to recognize and respond appropriately to particular features of the environment, including language. In Baddeley's (1998, p. 252) words, "the semantic system is part of the processes that have evolved for seeing, hearing, and acting." Whereas procedural memory controls muscle movement, semantic memory is representational. Procedural memory allows a skier to negotiate a ski slope by making muscle adjustments that affect her speed and attack. Semantic memory helps the skier to recognize that a particular slope is a more difficult one than others.

Procedure memory allows you to make unconscious muscle adjustments in skilled activities.

Semantic memory is more complicated in humans than in other animals, because humans use language to make connections with the world. A human's semantic memory contains both a lexicon and the rules for language usage, as well as the memory for sights and sounds. Given that most readers can recognize between 50,000 to 100,000 words, semantic memory must be enormous, yet we seem to use it effortlessly. For example, a person who is asked a question usually knows immediately whether the information exists in memory (Lindsay & Norman, 1977). How do we know what we *don't* know without doing an exhaustive memory search?

semantic memory The memory for particular features of the environment, including language.

One model of how words might be organized in long-term memory posits the existence of categories and levels (Collins & Quillian, 1969). Researchers measured subjects' reaction times (in fractions of a second) in answering simple

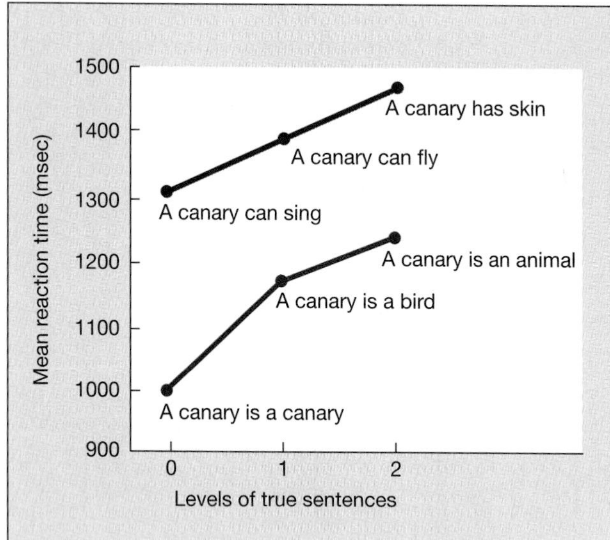

Figure 10.15 Hierarchical memory. Subjects took a fraction of a second longer to respond to the question "Does a canary have skin?" than to the question "Can a canary sing?" They also took less time to respond to the question "Is a canary a bird?" than to the question "Is a canary an animal?" (1,200 milliseconds equals 1.2 seconds.) *Source:* From "Retrieval Time from Semantic Memory", *Journal of Verbal Learning and Verbal Behavior*, Vol. 8, (1969), pp. 240–247. Copyright © 1969 by Academic Press, Inc. Reprinted by permission.

questions. Figure 10.15 shows subjects took slightly less time to respond to the question "Is a canary a bird?" than to the question "Is a canary an animal?" The researchers surmised that the second question required a longer memory search than the first. If the desired information wasn't located at the first level of organization, the search proceeded to the next level (see Figure 10.16). Searching more levels would require more time. Researchers accounted for their results, then, by proposing that words were arranged in a logical hierarchy, as shown in the figure.

One problem with this model of semantic memory is that few of the 50,000 or so commonly used English words are organized in this way. Another is that while most people are aware that canaries sing and are yellow, they probably have never considered whether a shark has feathers (Conrad, 1972). A different way of putting this is that the words *yellow* and *canary* are associated much more frequently than the words *canary* and *animal*, or *shark* and *feathers*. To test this hypothesis, one researcher made up lists of words that varied in organizational level, like those in Figure 10.16, but not in their frequency of association. Under these conditions, differences in retrieval time vanished. Search times, then, have more to do with the frequency of association of words than with the hierarchical structure of memory (Conrad, 1972). These findings raise the strong possibility that the simple laws of learning set forth in Chapter 6 underlie the structure of semantic memory. The more frequently words are associated, the deeper their processing, and the more quickly they become available during a memory search.

Frequency of association and learning, Chapter 6, p. 207

Episodic Memory. Remembering an episode in one's life is different from recalling general knowledge. Knowing, for example, that a shark has teeth is a semantic memory, one that is very different from remembering the toothache that sent you to the dentist last week. Tulving referred to an individual's personal memories, with their attendant meanings and emotions, as **episodic memory**.

Though semantic and episodic memory are separate, they interact. For example, when you learned to drive, you received verbal instruction on the location of the brakes and how to apply them. These instructions are part of your *semantic memory*. In contrast, your personal memory of the events that occurred the first time you got behind the wheel—how you cautiously stepped on the accelerator and then oversteered coming out of a turn—are part of your *episodic memory*. Although we share our language and environment with other people, our episodic memories are highly individual. Tulving's categorization of semantic and episodic memory is as much a theory of personal consciousness as it is of memory.

Rightly or wrongly, we tend to have more confidence in the accuracy of episodic memory than of semantic memory. You may have doubts about how much you will remember from reading this chapter (semantic memory), but you are likely to be quite confident about your ability to recall events in your life, even after many years. Such *autobiographical memories* are best thought of as a subset of episodic memory. They provide humans with a sense of continuity—a personal consciousness that extends from several years after birth through senescence (Rubin, 1996).

episodic memory An individual's memory for personal events and life episodes.

What makes a life event memorable? Pavlov and other researchers found that novel, unique events are learned more readily and form longer-lasting memories than familiar events. In fact, animal learning research has consistently shown that

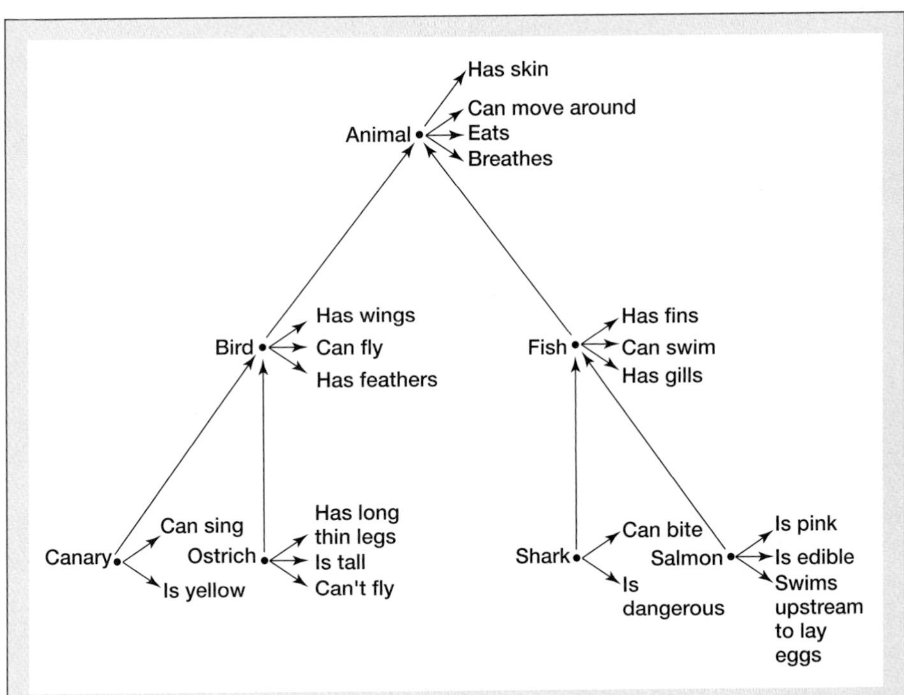

Figure 10.16 The mental lexicon: Words in categories. In Collins and Quillian's (1969) model of semantic memory, each word is a *node* in a memory network that is organized hierarchically. In answering questions about animals, subjects took more time to search for answers involving two or more nodes (A canary can fly) than to search for answers found at a single node (A canary can sing.) *Source:* From "Retrieval Time from Semantic Memory", *Journal of Verbal Learning and Verbal Behavior*, Vol. 8, (1969), pp. 240–247, Copyright © 1969 by Academic Press, Inc. Reprinted by permission.

traumatic events can lead to one-trial learning. One hypothesis, then, might be that when extraordinary events contain strong emotional components, people form indelible images, which are often called **flashbulb memories.**

Memory and one-trial learning, Chapter 6, p. 201

To test this hypothesis, researchers asked people about their personal memories of national tragedies—for example, what they were doing or wearing when they heard about the assassination of President John F. Kennedy in 1963 (Brown & Kulik, 1977). Other researchers did similar studies following the explosion of the space shuttle *Challenger* in 1986 (McCloskey, Wible, & Cohen, 1988) and Operation Desert Storm in 1991 (Weaver, 1993). How accurate were subjects' flashbulb memories of these events? Without documentation against which subjects' memories could be verified, researchers had no way of knowing whether their personal memories matched the actual event. McCloskey and his colleagues solved this problem by distributing a questionnaire to subjects a few days after the explosion of the *Challenger*, and then again about 9 months later. He found that subjects' memory for the explosion was good but not perfect—certainly not photographic, as implied by the term *flashbulb memory*. In another study (Neisser & Harsh, 1992), researchers found that one out of every four subjects *incorrectly* recalled the memories they had reported 3 years earlier. When confronted with their original handwritten reports, subjects insisted that their recollections of the event were accurate.

Humans form flashbulb memories of dramatic events, such as the outpouring of sympathy following the death of Princess Diana.

Given these findings, are so-called flashbulb memories truly different from other types of memories? A fortuitous experiment by Charles Weaver at Baylor University suggested that flashbulb memories are quite ordinary. As a class exercise, Weaver instructed his students to intentionally remember the details surrounding their next chance encounter with a roommate or friend, telling them they would be asked to report these details later. By coincidence, Operation Desert

flashbulb memories Memories of extraordinary events that contain strong emotional components.

Storm (the U.S. bombing of Iraq in 1991) began that night, giving students an opportunity to form a flashbulb memory of the event. A year later, Weaver assessed the students' memories for both the ordinary and extraordinary events of the day and found no differences in accuracy. Even so, students expressed more confidence in their flashbulb memories. Weaver concluded that flashbulb memories are unique only to the extent that people believe in their accuracy.

INTERIM SUMMARY

1. Tulving proposed the existence of two separate long-term memory systems, ***procedural memory*** and ***declarative memory***.
2. Procedural memory is the more basic of the two memory systems. Learned skills are stored in and retrieved from procedural memory, often unconsciously.
3. Declarative memory contains general knowledge; it is subdivided into ***semantic memory*** and ***episodic memory***.
4. Semantic memory includes the rules for using language and for acting adaptively based on learned associations. It represents a person's knowledge of the world, as opposed to personal memories.
5. Both hierarchical and associative models have been proposed to account for the way words are organized in semantic memory.
6. Episodic memory is the personal memory of specific events or episodes in a person's lifetime. It is characterized by *remembering* rather than *knowing*.
7. Studies of autobiographical memory and so-called ***flashbulb memories*** indicate that episodic memory is reconstructed rather than reproduced.
8. Flashbulb memories are no more accurate than normal memories, but people place more confidence in them.

For Further Thought

1. An implicit memory is an unconscious memory of a past experience. How do implicit memories differ from false memories?
2. Think of an incident—perhaps a birthday party—that happened when you were 10 years old. Can you separate what you know about the event from what you remember?
3. Do you have a personal flashbulb memory? If so, do you agree with researchers who have found that flashbulb memories are neither more nor less accurate that other memories?

MEMORIZING, FORGETTING, AND IMPROVING MEMORY

Had this chapter been organized chronologically, we would already have discussed the first experiments on memory, conducted by Hermann Ebbinghaus (1850–1909). The consonant-vowel-consonant nonsense syllable was Ebbinghaus's invention, as was list learning as a procedure for creating memories in the laboratory. Ebbinghaus was also the first researcher to study forgetting.

Ebbinghaus was his own subject. For 5 years, at the same time each day, he committed lists of nonsense syllables to memory. Following varying intervals, he attempted to recall them. Ebbinghaus was as interested in the amount of time he took to memorize lists with total accuracy as he was in testing his subsequent

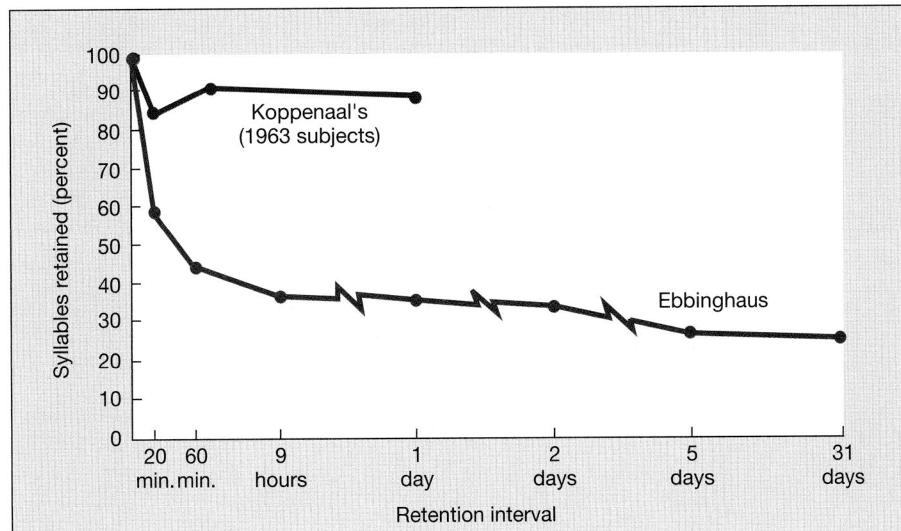

Figure 10.17 The forgetting function. Ebbinghaus (1885) forgot many more nonsense syllables than college students who were tested under similar conditions (Koppenaal, 1963). The thousands of lists Ebbinghaus had learned previously interfered with his recall.

recall. He found that *overlearning* a list (repeatedly rehearsing it after he had learned it completely) produced both a longer retention period and greater time *savings* when he attempted to relearn the list months later (Ebbinghaus, 1885/1913).

Ebbinghaus was meticulous in following his experimental procedure. He first learned a list containing 13 nonsense syllables until he could recite them in order, perfectly. (Note that this *serial learning* procedure differs from the method of free recall, described earlier.) Then he waited for a period ranging from an hour to several days before testing himself to see how many nonsense syllables he had forgotten. This task completed, he learned another list, waited a different amount of time, measured his retention, and so forth. As the curve in Figure 10.17 shows, Ebbinghaus forgot over half the items on each list within an hour. After that initial drop, he forgot very little, even after 24 hours.

The upper curve in Figure 10.17 shows the results when undergraduate students replicated Ebbinghaus's procedure decades later. The students had much better memory than Ebbinghaus, retaining between 80 and 90 percent of the nonsense syllables they learned, even after a 24-hour delay (Koppenaal, 1963). How can we explain such different results? The answer lies in two main theories of forgetting: *decay theory* and *interference theory.*

Theories of Forgetting

According to the **decay theory** of forgetting, learning results in "traces," or changes in the brain, that dissipate (decay) over time. In contrast, **interference theory** emphasizes the interference of old memories with both the encoding and retrieval of new memories. Ebbinghaus's dismal performance compared to undergraduate students is accounted for better by interference theory. Because he had learned hundreds of lists of nonsense syllables by the time he obtained the results in Figure 10.17, he experienced a great deal of interference in his attempt learn and remember a new list. This type of interference is called **proactive interference.** Because Koppenaal's subjects had not learned thousands of other nonsense syllables, their encoding and recall were much better.

A second kind of interference, called *retroactive interference*, may also have hindered Ebbinghaus's learning. **Retroactive interference** occurs when the learning of new material interferes with the recall of old material. When Ebbinghaus memorized several lists during a work session, a new list may have begun to interfere with his recall of the old ones. Some of the forgetting Ebbinghaus suffered, then,

decay theory The theory that forgetting is caused by the dissipation (or decay) of a hypothetical brain trace over time.

interference theory The theory that existing memories interfere with the encoding and retrieval of memories.

proactive interference Interference in the learning of new information caused by existing memories.

retroactive interference Interference in the retrieval of old memories caused by newly learned information.

Table 10.1 Effective Study Habits

1. Be disciplined: Study at the same time and place each day.
2. Be focused: Study with a purpose. Scan the material you're about to read so you will have some idea what it is about and how it is organized. Intentionally, as an act of will, try to learn or memorize what you are reading. Concentrate on the task at hand because you know you will be tested on it. Ask yourself questions as you go along. Look for key terms and other information you are likely to be tested on.
3. Spend sufficient time on each task: An important predictor of how much you will remember at test time is the total amount of *time on task* you have spent studying *effectively*.
4. Distribute your study time: Spreading out your studying is better than trying to do it all at once. Even though total time on task is important, distributed study increases the amount of material learned per unit of time. Review the material one last time before the exam.

might well have been an encoding problem (retroactive interference) rather than a retrieval problem (proactive interference). As a legendary professor of ichthyology reported, "Every time I learn a student's name, I forget a fish!"

Should students be concerned about interference effects when they are studying? Probably not; most of the research on retroactive (McGeoch & McDonald, 1931) and proactive interference (Tulving & Psotka, 1971) has been done using lists of unrelated words and nonsense syllables rather than meaningful material. As long as you distribute your study time, your semantic memory for history should not interfere with your memory for psychology. If you review the material immediately before taking an examination, neither retroactive nor proactive interference should trouble you. (For a list of effective study habits gleaned from Ebbinghaus's research, see Table 10.1.)

Explanations for Exceptional Memory

What would having a perfect memory be like? No more dreary note taking, you might think; no searching through notes to jog your memory before finals. Yet research suggests that a perfect memory is no blessing. For three decades, a Russian neurologist (Luria, 1968) studied an individual with an exceptional memory, named Shereshevski. Known in the research as "S," he enjoyed *eidetic imagery*, better known as *photographic memory* (Haber & Haber, 1964). For example, he could look at a table of numbers arranged randomly in rows and columns for a couple of minutes. Later he could read the table backward, diagonally, or any other way by calling up his mental picture of the table. He could also "record" multimedia memories containing words and their images, sounds, and smells. S was not pleased with his memory, however, because when he tried to forget something, he couldn't. In desperation, he began to write down what he wanted to forget and then burn the paper on which it was written. Luria found S to be a dull, superficial person who had difficulty following normal conversations—not a surprising discovery, given the fact that the relationship between memory and intelligence is not a simple one.

LINK
Memory and intelligence, Chapter 13, p. 455

What can people with a normal memory learn from S? The answer is, not much. If S were alive today, researchers would probably want to look at a PET scan or fMRI to see how his brain functioned during encoding and retrieval. We do know that he encoded information much faster than most people, and retrieved it not just faster, but probably in a very different way.

Most people have some of S's ability, however. Remember the last time you tried to find a passage you had read in a textbook? As you flipped through the pages, you *knew* the material you were looking for would be found on the lower part of a right-hand page. You had learned its location *implicitly*, as you were attempting to encode the meaning of the words. That is, the position of the words on the page provided the *context* for what you were reading, a context you encoded implicitly. You may even have been able to use the location of the passage on the page as a retrieval cue for when and where you were when you read the material. The photographic memory S had was a profound exaggeration of these relatively normal abilities.

To some extent, photographic memory can be learned. Chess experts can remember the placement of chess pieces far better than beginners, for instance. In one study, expert and novice players studied the position of pieces on a chessboard for about 5 seconds, about 20 moves into a game. Afterward, the expert players could recall the position of about 90 percent of the pieces; novices could place only about 40 percent (deGroot, 1965). But when asked to recall the position of pieces placed randomly, experts did no better than novices. A chess player's expertise, then, derives in part from learning to recognize patterns, presumably by chunking pieces that continually appear together. According to one estimate, a chess master may hold in memory as many as 50,000 chunks, or memorized pictures, of chess pieces on the board (Simon & Gilmartin, 1973).

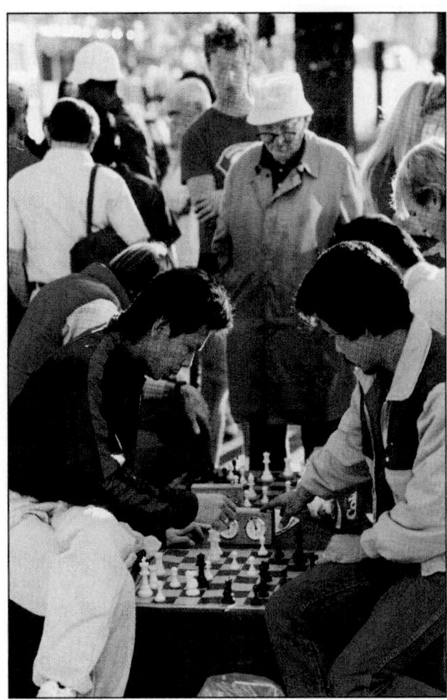

Chess masters can store and remember many more configurations of chess pieces on a chessboard than amateur players can.

The Process of Retrieval from Memory

Most of the demands we place on memory have little to do with recalling nonsense syllables or recognizing chess patterns. A more common example of memory failure occurs when we can't come up with a familiar name or word. For example, in describing a scene in a movie featuring a well-known star, the mind goes blank: "What *was* her name—you know, the one who was in—(another blank)." Or in answering an exam question about nonsense syllables, "Who *was* that guy with the funny name . . . Herman House? Webbing . . . Ebson . . . EBBINGHAUS!"

At one time or another, each of us has experienced this *tip-of-the-tongue phenomenon*, a state of mind in which a word one is trying to remember seems right on the brink of consciousness. One can guess with a fair degree of accuracy the first letter of the word, how many syllables it has (Brown & McNeil, 1966), and even its meaning and associated facts (Reason & Mycielska, 1982). Not knowing the name of that person with the three-syllable name beginning with the letter E, who had something to do with nonsense syllables, is a good example. In such situations, retrieval cues can help to bring the forgotten word to mind.

Retrieval Cues and Context Effects. Perhaps your memory has failed you when you tried to match a celebrity's name with his face, to remember the new surname of a friend who has recently married, or to recall the distinction between two types of learning on a psychology test. Bits of information called *retrieval cues* can help to jog your memory for these facts. Mnemonic devices such as rhymes and songs are retrieval cues. The context in which a memory was formed can also serve as a powerful retrieval cue. You may not remember much about your years in elementary school, for example, but returning there would likely bring back memories of that time and place. The enhanced retrieval of memories when the original context is restored, called a *context effect*, is best understood in terms of matching encoding cues with retrieval cues. Because context cues are encoded when a memory is formed, they are said to have *encoding specificity* (Tulving & Thompson, 1973).

Context effects have been studied in a variety of ways. In an impressive experiment on memory formation in deep-sea divers, subjects learned word lists both on land and 15 feet underwater. They were then asked to retrieve the lists in

Table 10.2 Remembering in Context

Subjects who encoded and retrieved lists in the same environment performed better than those who encoded a list in one context and retrieved it in another.

	RETRIEVED ON LAND	RETRIEVED UNDERWATER
ENCODED ON LAND	better performance	worse performance
ENCODED UNDERWATER	worse performance	better performance

both places. Table 10.2 shows the basic design and outcome of this experiment. The lists learned underwater were recalled better underwater, and the lists learned on land were recalled better on land (Godden & Baddeley, 1975). Reinstating the context cues that were present during encoding enhances the retrieval process.

Context effects have been seen in both semantic (list learning) and episodic memory (the school playground), but the most powerful context effects are seen in procedural memory. Though you may not be able to recall a long-distance phone number verbally, your fingers on the keypad can remember it. Likewise, even after many years, your body knows how to maintain its balance on a bike. Recall the experiment in which rats were made morphine tolerant in one environment, but lost their tolerance when tested in another environment (Siegel, 1977; see p. 202). Context effects, then, can be seen in all the memory systems.

Context effects on memory and on conditioned tolerance, Chapter 6, p. 202

Do the experimental findings on the underwater context apply to learning in the classroom? Context effects have proven difficult to demonstrate in the classroom. In one experiment, students who studied in one room and were tested in another showed little effect on their learning (Fernandez & Glenberg, 1985). Context effects may be less important in classroom learning than in learning lists of nonsense syllables. Nonetheless, studying at the same time and place each day remains good advice.

State-Dependency Effects. One reason the experiment on divers produced different results from the experiment on classroom learning may be that the divers experienced different emotions on land and underwater. They were likely to have been more anxious underwater, and as every test taker knows, anxiety can affect one's performance on a test. Because emotions determine an organism's physiological and psychological state at the time of encoding and retrieval, this effect is often called a *state-dependency effect.*

Effects of marijuana on memory, Chapter 9, p. 338

We saw in Chapter 9 that marijuana affects perception, emotion, and physiology. One researcher (Eich, 1980) has studied state-dependency effects on learning under the influence of marijuana. His approach was similar to the one in the study of divers: subjects encoded and retrieved lists of words while straight or stoned. Obviously, they performed better straight. Yet this study supported the existence of a state-dependency effect. Subjects who encoded lists under the influence of marijuana recalled them better under the influence. To reiterate: Eich did *not* find that marijuana enhances memory.

Mood, too, can affect one's memory. A depressed person, for example, retrieves negative thoughts and memories more frequently than positive thoughts and memories; a happy person does the opposite (Gilligan & Bower, 1984). The tendency to remember information that matches one's current mood is called *mood-congruent recall* (Blaney, 1986). In everyday life, family celebrations can put us in a mood to recall happy memories of past celebrations. Hearing and laughing at a joke can raise the memory of other jokes. And hearing a favorite passage of music can act as a powerful retrieval cue, opening a flood of memories of the past. Music—melodies in particular—provides a rich structure for retrieving information (Wallace, 1994).

Mood-congruent recall has implications for both the etiology and treatment of depression, as we'll see in Chapter 18. Significantly, the recovered memories that are supposedly recalled in therapy sessions are seldom happy memories. Both severe clinical depression and Alzheimer's disease have serious effects on memory, likely due to biochemical and structural changes they cause in the brain.

INTERIM SUMMARY

1. Ebbinghaus's forgetting function showed a rapid initial drop, followed by a leveling off over hours and days.
2. According to the ***decay theory*** of forgetting, memories cause changes in the brain that dissipate with the passage of time. In contrast, ***interference theories*** suggest that existing memories interfere with the encoding and retrieval of a new memory (***proactive interference***) and that learning new memories can interfere with the retrieval of old memories (***retroactive interference***).
3. *Eidetic imagery* (or *photographic memory*) is the ability to look at a picture and encode an accurate mental representation of its details. Luria's subject S showed unusual eidetic imagery, but had difficulty forgetting unwanted memories.
4. An expert chess player can encode as many as 50,000 chunks (memorized pictures) of the position of chess pieces on a chessboard.
5. The *tip-of-the-tongue phenomenon* is an anxious state of mind that precedes a (usually successful) memory retrieval.
6. *Retrieval cues* help people to solve problems and answer questions by using available bits of information, including mnemonics, rhymes, and songs, to direct memory searches.
7. *Context effects* on memory can occur when retrieval cues match encoding cues. *Encoding specificity* refers to context cues encoded during memory formation.
8. A *state-dependency effect* on memory can occur when a subject's physiological or psychological state at the time of retrieval matches the state at the time of encoding.
9. People tend to remember information they encoded in a mood that matches their mood at the time of recall, a phenomenon called *mood-congruent recall*.

For Further Thought

1. Identify the built-in retrieval cues in a fill-in-the-blank test format. Why is a fill-in-the-blank test easier than other test formats?
2. Should the environment in which you take tests be the same as the environment in which you study? If a person studies for a test with the TV on, will that person's test performance suffer because a TV is not on during the test?
3. Children in Japanese schools study fewer subjects than children of the same age in the United States, and they cover fewer topics in mathematics. Yet Japanese children perform better than U.S. children on math tests, at every grade level. Can you use time on task, retroactive and proactive interference, and exceptional memory to help account for these differences?
4. "Smile and you'll be happier." People who intentionally try to put themselves in a good mood often find they do feel better for the effort. Do you think smiling acts as a retrieval cue for happy memories? If so, does it provide evidence for mood-congruent recall?

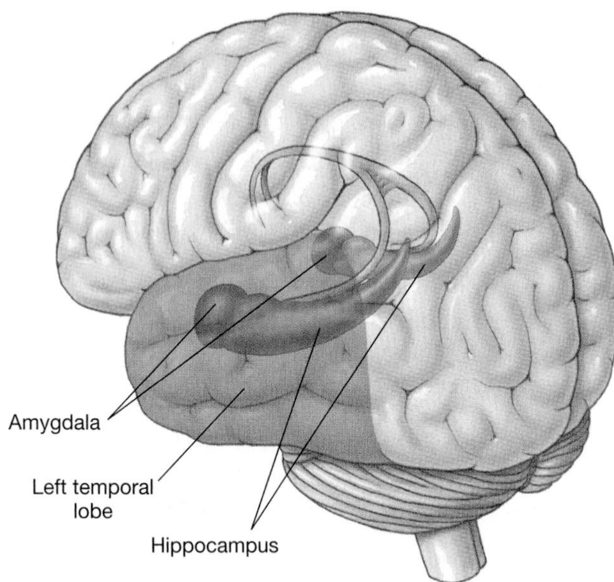

Figure 10.18 Brain areas involved in the formation of memory. The hippocampus and amygdala are bilateral structures located within the left (green) and right temporal lobes. These structures, together with some surrounding tissue, are the basis for working memory—the process of encoding information into long-term memory.

MEMORY IN NORMAL VERSUS DAMAGED BRAINS

Ebbinghaus's research defined the *behavioral* study of memory and forgetting over the past century. The *biological* study of memory has been greatly aided by a person known only as H. M., an unwitting, if gracious, research subject since his brain surgery in 1953. For nearly 50 years, Dr. Brenda Milner of the Montreal Neurological Institute and other psychologists and neuroscientists have studied H. M.'s memory problems (Milner, 1970; Milner, Corkin, & Teuber, 1968). They are similar to those of N. A., whose intriguing difficulties were described at the beginning of this chapter. These and other patients have spawned a great deal of brain research on memory mechanisms in laboratory animals, as well.

The Case of H. M.

When H. M. was 27, surgeons removed a large portion of the underside of the temporal lobe on each side of his brain, in an attempt to control his epileptic seizures. Following H. M.'s brain surgery, about two-thirds of his hippocampus, the amygdala, and some of the cortex in his temporal lobes had been removed. Figure 10.18 shows a schematic drawing of the hippocampus and amygdala. Buried deep within the temporal lobe, these structures are responsible in part for memory.

Epilepsy and cutting the corpus callosum, Chapter 4, p. 133

Although H. M.'s seizures stopped, and his perceptual processes, personality, and intelligence remained much the same, the large lesions in his brain caused severe memory problems. Since the surgery, amnesia has prevented him from living an independent life. H. M. lost his memory for a few years preceding the surgery, a phenomenon called **retrograde amnesia**. Brain injuries often result in the loss of recently formed long-term memories. But in addition, H. M. experienced a profound **anterograde amnesia**: like N. A., he cannot form any new memories. Though he *can* memorize materials, as soon as his attention is distracted, he forgets them. He will read a magazine, but if someone interrupts him to talk with him for a while, he will return to the beginning of the article, because he does not remember what he has just read.

Observations of H. M., N. A., and other people with damaged brains support Tulving's proposed memory systems (see also Squire, 1987, 1992). Recall that procedural memory depends on nonconscious pathways in subcortical structures, including the cerebellum. H. M.'s cerebellum and subcortical structures are intact; he can form procedural memories, but with difficulty. For example, 8 years after moving to a new house, he could find his way from room to room, but when he attempted to give directions to a person who was driving him home, he ended up at his old residence (Milner et al., 1968). Figure 10.19 shows the results of a formal test of H. M.'s procedural memory: his performance on this relatively difficult *mirror drawing task* improved over three consecutive days (Blakemore, 1977). Clearly, H. M.'s procedural memory is relatively intact.

retrograde amnesia The loss of memory for events that preceded a brain injury.

anterograde amnesia The inability to form new memories following an injury to the brain.

For the most part, H. M.'s deficits are restricted to his declarative memory, which requires an intact amygdala and hippocampus—the parts of H. M.'s brain that were severely damaged. His deficits include problems in learning new facts and adding to his general store of knowledge (semantic memory). H. M. is incapable of forming new memories of even the most personal life events, such as what he did on his birthday. When shown a picture of a person's face and then distracted for as little as 2 minutes, he cannot remember the face. Likewise, he cannot remember a simple series of numbers or nonsense syllables after a short delay. (Recall that N. A. could not remember Wayne Wickelgren's face, nor his name, after just a few minutes; it is safe to assume that N. A. suffered damage to the same brain areas as H. M.)

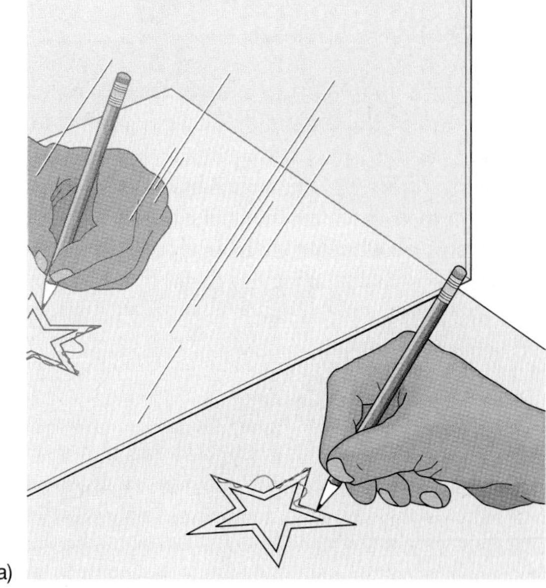

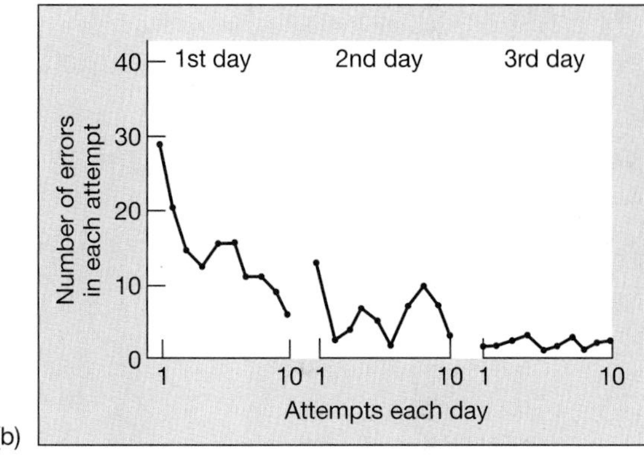

Figure 10.19 Keeping between the lines. In a mirror drawing task (top), the subject attempts to trace a line between the inner and outer diagrams of a star by watching a reflection of the task in a mirror (which reverses the movement of the pen). In consecutive attempts over three days (bottom), H. M. made fewer errors on each trial. *Source:* From MECHANICS OF THE MIND by Colin Blakemore. Copyright © 1977. Reprinted by permission of Cambridge University Press.

Alzheimer's Disease

Memory has been characterized as adaptive, in that the ability to remember what one has learned enhances the probability of survival and reproduction. Although a good memory allows a person to live independently, memory problems like H. M.'s are so disabling, they prevent independent living. Severe memory disorders are not just disabling, but dangerous.

Alzheimer's disease is an example of a life-threatening memory disorder. The most common form of dementia, it causes an overall degeneration of consciousness (Wurtman, 1985) in approximately 5 percent of people aged 65 and over and 10 percent of those aged 80 and older. The most obvious symptom of this disease is the progressive loss of memory. Because most people have occasional problems remembering lists, names, and telephone numbers, aging individuals (including your author) often fear that their memory lapses are signaling an early stage of the disease. Most age-related problems are simply failures to recall specific items stored in memory, however.

Over time, the symptoms of Alzheimer's become increasingly serious, and problems with semantic memory become more obvious. A victim may not remember that the eating utensil with which one eats soup is called a spoon, or that the person she lives with is her spouse. Because recognition, not just recall, is affected, the consequences can be dire.

Alzheimer's disease causes a number of changes in the brain that ultimately lead to death. People with Alzheimer's may lack adequate amounts of the neurotransmitters acetylcholine (Albert & Moss, 1992) and glutamate (Baudry & Davis, 1992). Those areas of the brain involved in procedural memory remain intact the longest, because the brain stem and cerebellum are spared in the midstages of the disease (Kolb & Whishaw, 1996). In advanced stages of the disease, however, Alzheimer's patients may become incontinent. Autobiographical memory can be lost in the intermediate to late stages, when patients may not even recognize their own reflections. Caretakers must keep an eye on such patients, who can easily become lost and who may talk nonsensically. Walking is mediated by brainstem structures that are spared in the midstages of Alzheimer's, but knowing where one is depends on an intact cerebral cortex. As more of the cerebral cortex becomes dysfunctional, patients become progressively more helpless, even bedridden (Khachaturian & Blass, 1992). At postmortem, their brains show a marked shrinkage of the cerebral cortex, as well as nonneuronal growths among the neurons (called *neurofibrillary tangles*) and scar tissue caused by the degeneration of neurons (called *amyloid plaques*). Scar tissue is particularly evident in the declarative memory structures, the amygdala, and hippocampus (O'Banion, Coleman, & Callahan, 1994).

INTERIM SUMMARY

1. About a half-century ago, surgeons removed a large portion of the underside of the temporal lobe on either side of the brain of a patient known as H. M. The study of H. M. following his surgery has helped psychologists and neurologists to better understand the brain's memory processes.
2. H. M. suffered some ***retrograde amnesia,*** or loss of memory for events that preceded his surgery. His primary memory disorder, however, is an inability to form new memories, a condition known as ***anterograde amnesia.***
3. The study of H. M. supports the theory that humans have two memory systems, one for declarative memory (conscious, explicit semantic and episodic memories) and the other for procedural memory (unconscious, implicit memories formed through nonassociative learning, associative skill learning, and conditioning).
4. The hippocampus, amygdala, and some of the cortex of the temporal lobe support declarative memory. Because H. M. lacks this brain tissue, he cannot form new declarative memories.
5. H. M. can learn procedural memory tasks, such as the mirror-reversed drawing of figures.
6. The brain changes that characterize *Alzheimer's disease* provide more evidence for the brain's role in memory formation. Alzheimer's disease is characterized by intellectual deterioration and the progressive loss of memory.
7. Alzheimer's patients suffer from changes in the level of neurotransmitters, the loss of neurons, and the growth of scar tissue. The declarative memory system suffers the most during the early and middle stages of the disease, which are characterized by changes in the amygdala, hippocampus, and cerebral cortex. Ultimately, procedural memory is lost, leading to helplessness and death.

For Further Thought

1. Over time, the human brain has evolved a newer cerebral cortex that covers the more primitive brainstem. Why do you think humans have two separate memory systems, one for declarative memory and the other for procedural memory?
2. An elderly relative has suffered a stroke that caused damage to the language area on the surface of the left temporal lobe. Will he still be able to recognize you and remember your last visit? Why or why not?

CONCLUDING THOUGHTS

Humans have evolved brains that allow them to learn, remember, and transmit memes that enhance fitness to the next generation. But humans also encode and recall inaccurate memories that have the potential to be maladaptive.

Humans share with other animals a procedural memory: unconscious, implicit memories that are formed through conditioning and associative skill learning. They may also share with other animals some aspects of declarative memory: conscious, explicit episodic memories. Declarative memories of facts and life events comprise an individual's consciousness. Semantic memory, a part of declarative memory that is unique to humans, contains tens of thousands of words and rules for how to use them. Semantic memory enables humans to share their episodic memories; its contents are arguably the most important memes.

Human memory systems can be understood in terms of information management: sensing, encoding, storing, and retrieving information via sensory memory, short-term memory, and long-term memory. Moving information from sensory memory to short-term, or working, memory requires selective attention, which ensures that information will be processed further. Working memory is normally limited to 7 ± 2 items, but its capacity can be increased by a process called chunking. Elaborative rehearsal of the information in working memory helps to encode it into long-term memory.

Memories can be unconscious as well as conscious. Humans are normally unaware of their procedural memories, which are encoded and stored in subcortical structures. Evidence from priming experiments suggests the existence of an implicit memory system—a part of semantic memory that operates apart from conscious awareness. Unconscious memories can influence the way new memories are encoded. Inaccuracies in memory may be caused by unconscious influences on the encoding process, such as the choice of words used to describe the speed of an auto. The existence of implicit memories supports Bartlett's theory that memory is reconstructive rather than reproductive. People encode and retrieve memories based not on what actually happened, but on their personal schemas.

An intact memory system determines the nature of a person's consciousness. In contrast to the procedural memory for *how* we live, declarative memory stores *what* we know. Declarative memories are encoded by the hippocampus and amygdala and stored in the cerebral cortex. Damage to H. M.'s hippocampus and amygdala interferes with his encoding of new declarative memories, causing anterograde amnesia. In contrast, Alzheimer's disease causes retrograde amnesia, in which old declarative memories are lost as the cerebral cortex deteriorates. In young and old alike, the loss of memory produces a disintegration of consciousness and a loss of self-sufficiency.

KEY TERMS

anterograde amnesia *374*
chunking *350*
cocktail party phenomenon *349*
decay theory *369*
declarative memory *364*
dichotic listening task *349*
elaborative rehearsal *358*
encoding *356*
episodic memory *366*
false memories *345*
flashbulb memories *367*
free recall *354*
implicit memory *360*
information-processing model of memory *346*
interference theory *369*
levels of processing *357*
long-term memory *347*
maintenance rehearsal *356*
memory *344*
mnemonic *351*
phonological loop *354*
primacy effect *356*
priming *360*
proactive interference *369*
procedural memory *364*
recency effect *354*
rehearsal *347*
retrieval *347*
retroactive interference *369*
retrograde amnesia *374*
schema *360*
selective attention *349*
semantic memory *365*
sensory memory *346*
serial position effect *354*
short-term memory *347*
storage *356*
working memory *347*

11

Human Development

Pablo Picasso *Girl Before a Mirror*. Boisgeloup, March 1932. Oil on canvas, 64 × 51 1/4 in. (162.3 × 130.2 cm). The Museum of Modern Art, New York. Gift of Mrs. Simon Guggenheim.

Conception and Prenatal Development
Prenatal Physical Development
Fetal Mind and Behavior
Interim Summary
For Further Thought

Birth and Early Childhood Development
Continuous Versus Stagelike Development
Perceptual Development
Interim Summary
For Further Thought

Cognitive Development Throughout the Life Span
Piaget's Stage Theory of Cognitive Development
Challenges to Piaget's Theory
Vygotsky's Sociocultural Theory of Cognitive Development
Cognition and Memory Throughout the Life Span
Kohlberg's Stage Theory of Moral Development
Interim Summary
For Further Thought

Psychosocial Development Throughout the Life Span
Infancy: Attachment and Temperament
Early Childhood
Adolescence and Adulthood
Bereavement: The Loss of Attachment
Interim Summary
For Further Thought

Concluding Thoughts

When families gather, they share their histories and life passages. Some of my best memories of my mother are her stories of her early childhood. She grew up in an environment that was foreign to me: life on a farm in rural Nebraska, without electricity or indoor plumbing. In the 1920s, her brothers and sisters were born at home, with no physician attending. She struggled to learn to read and write English at a German-speaking elementary school, then taught her parents.

My mother's story continued with her courtship and marriage to my father, and the birth of my brother and me. Next came stories of my parents' life work—their hopes and aspirations, disappointments and illnesses. The overriding theme of these tales was their continuous adaptation to changing times and changing environments, as they lived through the Great Depression, the Second World War, and the decline of the family farm. Such are the experiences that lead, in part, to our individual differences.

Formally defined, **human development** is the lifelong process of physical, cognitive, and social development. As we learned in Chapter 3, this process begins when a sperm successfully fertilizes an egg. What happens thereafter is the subject of this chapter: the predictable and unpredictable ways in which humans change throughout a lifetime. What is predictable, all else being equal, is birth, physical and psychological growth, sometimes reproduction, and always death.

Much of human development has been characterized as a biological unfolding. Each human's genes provide the instructions for the development of bones and muscles, brains and immune systems. They guide physical and psychological growth through infancy, childhood, adolescence, and adulthood. Yet human development unfolds only within the context of a specific environment. Thus our personal histories, our memories, and our stories become part of the fabric of our lives just as surely as our genes.

Genes and memes, Chapter 6, p. 187

Nature and nurture, Chapter 3, p. 85

In this chapter we will see how, through growth and experience, infants develop from defenseless animals into perceptive and thoughtful children, adolescents, and adults. We will follow the process of social and emotional development from the early *attachment* of infant and mother to the emotional changes adults experience when a loved one dies. These processes are, of course, highly adaptive. Let's begin at the beginning, with conception and the ensuing physical development that results in birth.

CONCEPTION AND PRENATAL DEVELOPMENT

Life begins when a sperm fertilizes an egg, and the new cell, called a zygote, begins to divide (see page 78). The zygote contains 23 chromosomes—strands of DNA—from each parent, which combine to make a human with 46 chromosomes. Each DNA molecule contains genes that will control many of the processes of the developing zygote, and eventually, the lifelong development of the organism.

Prenatal Physical Development

For convenience, the 9-month human gestational period is divided into three main stages: the *germinal stage* (conception to 2 weeks), the *embryonic stage* (3 to 9 weeks), and the *fetal stage* (9th week to birth). About one week after conception, the human embryo begins a weeklong process of implanting itself in the uterine wall. For reasons that are poorly understood, only about 20 percent of all fertilized eggs are successfully implanted (Wilcox et al., 1988). Once the egg has been implanted, the placenta forms, securing a source of nutrients and a method of waste disposal for the growing embryo. At about 3 weeks, when the embryo is about one-sixth of an inch in length, the rapidly developing heart tissue begins to beat. The photographs below show a human embryo at 6 weeks (left) and later as a fetus, at 4 months (right).

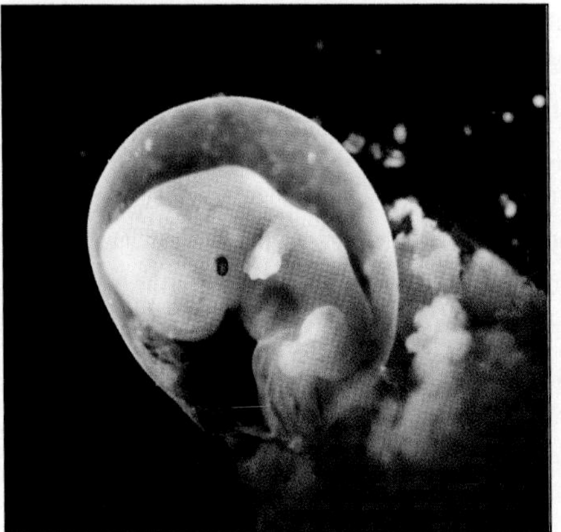

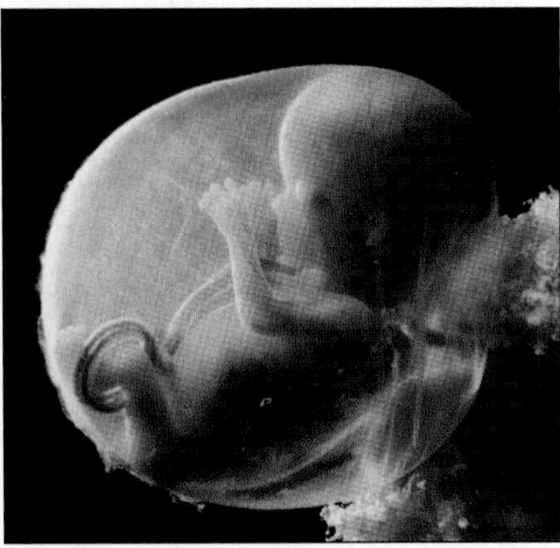

A 6-week-old human embryo (left) and a 4-month-old fetus (right). Note the red heart in the fetus. The embryo is only about 2 to 4 inches long, but is recognizably human.

human development The lifelong process of physical, cognitive, and social growth and development.

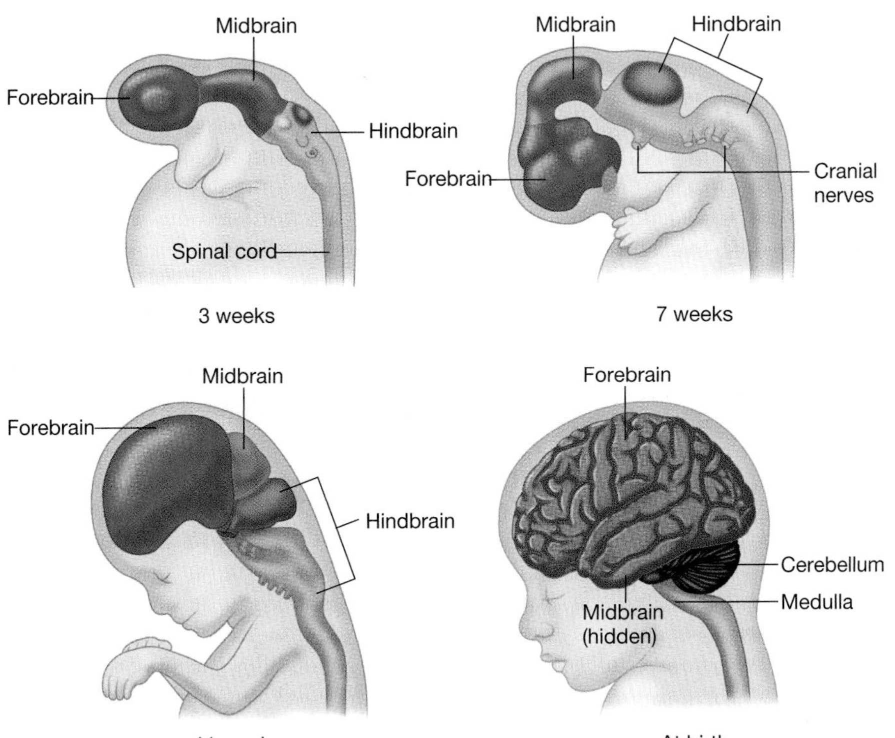

Figure 11.1 Prenatal development of the human brain. The forebrain, midbrain, and hindbrain take shape as early as 3 weeks after conception (compare Figure 4.2). By about 11 weeks, the cerebral hemispheres have assumed their familiar shape. At 7 months (not shown), the cerebral cortex begins to fold, increasing its surface area. At birth, the external landmarks that divide the brain into four lobes are identifiable (compare Figure 4.2).

Prenatal Brain Development. As Figure 11.1 shows, the prenatal brain develops rapidly, generating about a quarter of a million new neurons *each minute* during the third trimester. At birth, the brain contains about 100 billion neurons (Cowan, 1979) and is 60 percent of its eventual adult size. This large brain is contained in a large head: in a 2-month-old fetus, the ratio of head size to height is about 1:2. In fact, a baby's characteristic features are due in part to its large head and relatively small body. At birth the ratio of head size to height is 1:4, compared with 1:6 in an adult (see Figure 11.2). After birth the brain continues to grow more rapidly than the rest of the body, doubling in size by age 2.

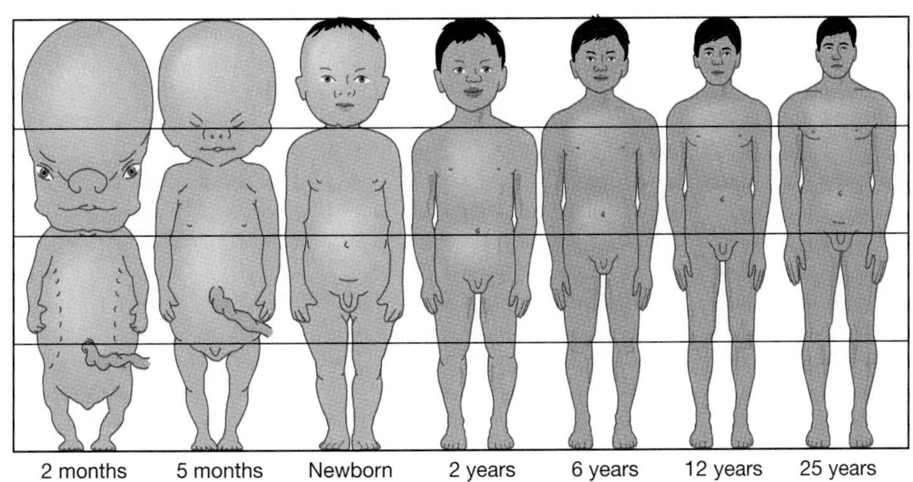

Figure 11.2 Changes in body proportions, prenatal stage through young adulthood. Half the body area of a 2-month-old fetus is devoted to the head and brain. At birth, the head measures one-fourth the body's length, giving the infant its characteristic baby look.

The study of the brain's growth and development has led to the surprising finding that the developing brain makes far more neurons than necessary. Apparently as many as 50 percent of neurons die during fetal development (Hockfield & Kalb, 1993; Kalil, 1989). Why does the brain make "extra" neurons, and what determines which neurons live and which die? No one knows for sure. One way to characterize the pruning process is in Darwinian terms: neurons that are used survive, while those that are not used die (Pinel, 1997). This process is similar to neurogenesis, which occurs throughout the life of the brain.

Neurogenesis, Chapter 4, p. 129

Animals that are raised in complicated environments, for example, have more neurons than others of their species, and the dendrites of those neurons are better developed (Rosensweig, Krech, Bennett, & Diamond, 1967). During the first few months of a human's life, the number of connections (synapses) between neurons increases twentyfold. Which neurons get connected to one another depends in large measure on the environment the child is experiencing. An axon grows by securing a *nerve growth factor (NGF)* from a target neuron. NGF promotes an axon's survival over other axons that do not receive it. The brain's early development, then, is influenced not only by genetic recipes, but also by environmental influences. Throughout a lifetime, brain growth and development follow a "use it or lose it" principle. From birth to death, the environment continuously shapes the physical structure of the brain (Nelson, 1999).

Prenatal Brain Injury. The fetal brain's genetic recipe leads to normal growth and development, but only in an adequate environment. For optimal gene expression, the brain must receive balanced nutrition, including sufficient amounts of protein and trace nutrients, an absence of harmful chemicals, and a supportive physical, educational, emotional, and cognitive environment (Brown, 1999). Malnutrition can do much more harm to the fetal brain than it does to a fully developed brain (Levitsky & Strupp, 1995), affecting mental development into childhood (Ricciuti, 1993). In addition, as many as 200 genetic mutations can cause brain damage and mental retardation (Thapar, Gottesman, Owen, O'Donovan, & McGuffin, 1994). The brain is most vulnerable during the rapid growth of the embryonic period (Shatz, 1992).

Table 11.1 Common Teratogens and Their Effects

Alcohol	Fetal alcohol syndrome (FAS) may result from excessive alcohol intake during embryonic and/or fetal development. Even moderate drinking is associated with decreased attention span, motor development, and IQ.
Tobacco	Low birth weight, miscarriage, and premature birth are associated with smoking during pregnancy, including passive smoking.
Cocaine	Low birth weight and attentional difficulties are associated with cocaine (in combination with other drug use) during pregnancy.
Lead	Birth defects, premature birth, and abnormal responses to sensory stimuli may result from lead exposure in utero.
Marijuana	Premature birth and abnormal responses to sensory stimuli are associated with heavy marijuana use during pregnancy.
Narcotics	Premature birth and the addiction of the newborn are associated with maternal addiction to heroin.
Maternal illness	A variety of developmental problems may affect fetuses whose mothers are ill with AIDS, cholera, genital herpes, mumps, measles, radiation sickness, smallpox, syphilis, and other disorders.

Given the vulnerability of the fetus, should pregnant women be concerned about what they eat? Interestingly, they are more sensitive than others about their diets, but not because of a conscious decision. Margie Profet, a biologist in Seattle, has proposed that *morning sickness* serves to restrict a pregnant woman's diet. Her research indicates that healthy pregnant women are put off by foods with strong odors and flavors, which are often associated with plant toxins and the fungal and bacterial decomposition of meat, fish, and poultry products (Flaxman & Sherman, 2000; Profet, 1992). This dislike for the smells and tastes of potentially harmful foods during early pregnancy is highly adaptive. Profet has shown that pregnant women who do not experience morning sickness (and who presumably eat normally, exposing the fetus to more toxins) are more prone than others to miscarry. More research will likely be done on the relationship between food preferences and fetal development.

In addition to the usual hazards, the developing brain is threatened by even more harmful substances called *teratogens* (from the Greek word for *monster*), which can seriously impair brain growth and development. Common teratogens—lead, alcohol, cocaine, and the other chemicals shown in Table 11.1—can cause irreversible damage to the embryonic and fetal brain. We saw in Chapter 9, for instance, that because alcohol interferes with the normal processes of synaptic transmission, drinking beer, wine, or spirits alters consciousness, causing inebriation. These biochemical effects are usually reversible, but not always. A woman who drinks alcohol while she is pregnant may cause permanent brain damage to her developing fetus.

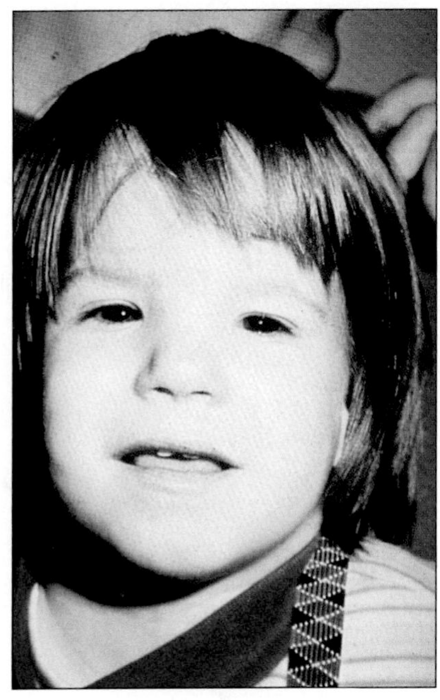

The face of fetal alcohol syndrome.

Fetal alcohol syndrome (FAS) is a clinical condition seen in the children of mothers who drank alcohol during pregnancy. It is characterized by hyperactivity, mental retardation, heart defects, a lack of alertness, and problems with movement. FAS children have characteristic facial features (see the photograph on this page). Scientists do not know whether there is a critical period during which alcohol causes these devastating effects. Studies have shown that the ingestion of even moderate amounts of alcohol—three beers a day—during pregnancy is associated with slightly lower IQ and shorter attention span after birth (Hunt, Streissguth, Kerr, & Carmichael-Olson, 1995). The safe thing to do is not to drink *any* alcohol while pregnant.

Other recreational drugs can have similar adverse effects. Pregnant women who smoke cocaine bear smaller babies who seem to show less interest in what is going on around them (Lewis & Bendersky, 1995). These women are typically polydrug users, however, so their fetuses are exposed to many potentially harmful agents. In addition to cocaine, they often drink alcohol, smoke cigarettes, and use other recreational drugs. In the laboratory, rat pups that have been exposed to cocaine develop learning deficits (Heyser, Spear, & Spear, 1993), but we cannot conclude from such studies that cocaine has a teratogenic effect in humans.

Is tobacco harmful to the developing fetus? Recently a relationship has been found between fetal development and smoking during pregnancy. When the mother smokes, her baby is more likely than others to be born underweight and premature. Women who smoke also suffer more miscarriages than other women (Neiberg, Marks, McLaren, & Remongton, 1985). As Table 11.1 shows, maternal illnesses and environmental hazards, such as radiation and lead exposure, can also have a serious effect on the fetus.

fetal alcohol syndrome (FAS) A clinical condition seen in the children of mothers who drank alcohol during pregnancy; characterized by hyperactivity, mental retardation, heart defects, a lack of alertness, and problems with movement.

Fetal Mind and Behavior

Fathers are observers rather than participants during fetal development. Lacking the mother's intimate connection with the fetus, the father may wonder "what it feels like" to hold another organism inside oneself. Perhaps this parental desire to make contact with the unborn child has raised questions

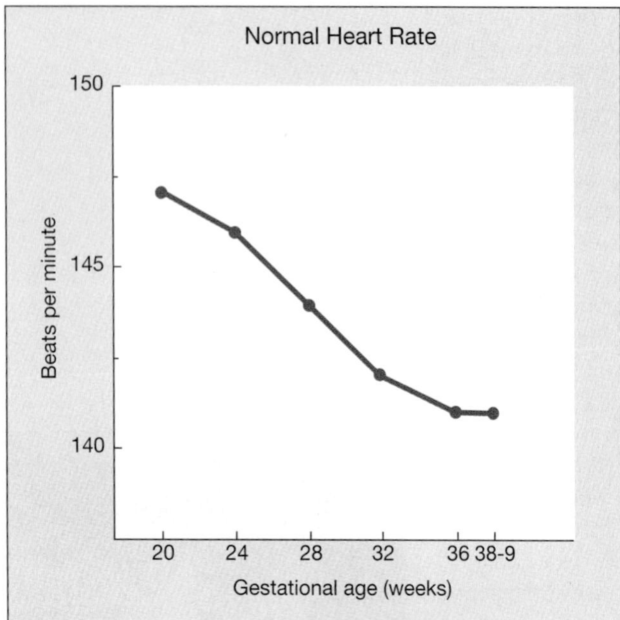

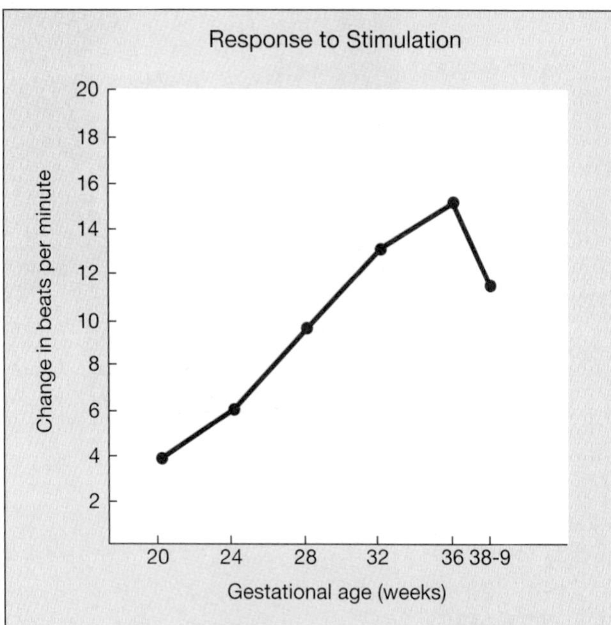

Figure 11.3 Fetal response to vibration. As the fetus grows, its heart rate decreases slightly (top). But in the same way that an unexpected touch on the shoulder increases your heart rate, a vibrator placed on the mother's abdomen increases a fetus's heart rate. The change in heart rate is linear until a couple of weeks before birth (bottom). *Source:* From "Cross-Cultural Patterns of Attachment: A Meta-Analysis of the Strange Situation" by M. H. van Ijzendoorn and P. M. Kroonenberg, *Child Development*, 59, (1988), pp. 147–156. Copyright © 1988 by Society for Research in Child Development. Reprinted by permission.

about what the fetus experiences of the outside world. Figure 11.1 showed the rapid brain development that begins shortly after conception. Do any of the fetus's senses function, we might wonder?

This question is important, because we know that once a child is born, a large source of her or his experience with the environment is sensory driven. In fact, we now know that hearing, tasting, movement, and learning are part of prenatal behavior (Smotherman & Robinson, 1990, 1996). Figure 11.3 shows the average change in heart rate when a fetus is briefly stimulated with a vibrator. Sensing the stimulation, the fetal nervous system responds with a faster heart rate as early as 20 weeks after conception. Responsiveness increases until 36 weeks after conception (DiPietro, Hodgson, Costigan, Hilton, & Johnson, 1996).

The human fetus is also highly likely to be sensitive to its chemical environment, including the taste of its mother's amniotic fluid. Bob Bradley (1972) has shown that 8 weeks after conception, the fetus has taste buds; 14 weeks after conception they appear to be structurally intact, and presumably are functioning. Scientists have recorded electrical potentials from taste nerves in fetal sheep (Bradley & Mistretta, 1973). Because all mammals swallow amniotic fluid, their ability to control ingestion based on taste may begin prior to birth (Lipsitt & Behl, 1990). The olfactory system is also functional before birth (Pedersen, Greer, & Shepard, 1988). We saw in Chapter 8 that food preferences are determined in part by genetically based preferences for some tastes and smells. This research raises the possibility that an infant's food preferences may be affected as well by what the mother eats during pregnancy (Smotherman & Robinson, 1996).

We know, then, that the fetus responds to touch (vibration) and taste, but is it aware of the sounds of the outside world? Certainly a fetus has the necessary auditory apparatus. Even if not yet structurally intact, the auditory system (outer, middle, and inner ear, and the cochlear nucleus in the brainstem) is functional during the last month or so of gestation. Experiments suggest not only that a fetus might be sensitive to sounds outside the uterine wall, but also that its brain is well enough developed to remember such experiences.

In one study, 16 women in the last 6 weeks of pregnancy read aloud from a child's storybook twice each day, using a particular rate of speed and a characteristic intonation. Three days after birth, each child was exposed to recordings of these distinctive passages under laboratory conditions. The dependent variable in this experiment was a measure of the rate of sucking on a pacifier, which in turn controlled what the newborn heard over earphones. Faster sucking speeded up the recording of the mother's voice reading the story; slower sucking slowed down the recording. Researchers found that 13 of 16 infants sucked at a rate that matched the rate of their mother's voice before birth (DeCasper & Spence, 1986). A late-term fetus, then, can both hear and remember speech patterns.

Auditory apparatus and hearing, Chapter 7, p. 250

If singing calms and gives pleasure to the mother-to-be, the effect on the fetus is likely to be the same. However, the long-term effects, if any, of listening to music *in utero* are unknown. The experiment just described, on the memory for speech patterns in newborns, produced a measure of procedural memory (that is, remembering *that* something occurred) rather than declarative memory (that is, remembering *what* occurred). But it would be interesting to assess the fate of those procedural memories by retesting the infants in later childhood and adulthood, perhaps by using a priming technique (see Chapter 10).

Declarative and procedural memories, Chapter 10, p. 364

Anecdotally, I am aware that some expectant mothers begin to read to their late-term fetus on a daily basis. Their intent is to begin the attachment process by exposing the fetus to the basic sounds and patterns of their native language. These mothers fully expect the fetus to develop procedural memories for the sounds and patterns of language. Although their expectations may sound far-fetched, a recent experiment supports them. Researchers enabled newborns to choose what they heard over headphones by adjusting their rate of sucking on a pacifier. They found that infants who had heard Spanish *in utero* were more likely to choose Spanish over English, and vice versa (Fifer & Moon, 1995). These researchers reported that fetuses could hear and remember the reader's voice characteristics as well as the specific sounds of one language or another.

The long-term effects of reading to a fetus are unknown, but at the very least the practice is likely to contribute to mother-infant attachment; it may also sensitize the developing brain to language. Research has shown that throughout childhood, daily readings have a positive effect on the development of a child's reading ability (Snow, Burns, & Griffin, 1998).

INTERIM SUMMARY

1. ***Human development*** is the lifelong process of physical, cognitive, and social growth and development.
2. The 38-week human gestational period is divided into a *germinal stage* (conception to 2 weeks), an *embryonic stage* (3 to 9 weeks), and a *fetal stage* (9th week to birth).
3. The human brain develops rapidly; at birth it contains about 100 billion neurons. Large numbers of neurons that are not used die in the first years of life. Those that are used develop thousands of synaptic connections in response to the presence of a *nerve growth factor (NGF)*.
4. Mental retardation may be caused by genetic or environmental factors, or both. Normal brain growth requires an adequate supply of essential nutrients and an absence of harmful chemicals.
5. Morning sickness may be an evolutionary adaptation that minimizes the fetus's exposure to food-related toxins and bacteria.
6. Maternal use of alcohol, cocaine, or tobacco, or exposure to tobacco smoke, lead, or other *teratogens*, can harm the developing fetus.
7. ***Fetal alcohol syndrome (FAS)*** occurs in the offspring of women who drink excessive amounts of alcohol during pregnancy. Even moderate use of alcohol during pregnancy puts an unborn child at risk of lowered intelligence and behavioral problems.
8. Women who smoke during pregnancy tend to have more miscarriages, more premature babies, and more underweight babies than women who don't smoke.
9. The fetus responds to auditory and touch stimuli outside the uterus, and to the chemical constituents of the mother's amniotic fluid. Newborns both remember and choose to listen to the language they heard before birth.

For Further Thought

1. A woman with irregular menstrual periods may be unaware that she is pregnant for several months. To what risks might she unknowingly expose her fetus?
2. Pregnant females have been characterized as "conservative" eaters who only rarely crave a specific food item, such as pickles. Even more rarely do they display *pica*, a craving for non-foods such as clay. Why might conservative food choices and occasional cravings be adaptive for a pregnant female?
3. Can you think of some reasons why mom (and dad?) might benefit as well as the fetus if one or both parents were to sing or read aloud on a daily basis during late pregnancy?

BIRTH AND EARLY CHILDHOOD DEVELOPMENT

The birth of a child is a time of unsurpassed joy and excitement for most parents. New parents often awaken their baby in the middle of night, to reassure themselves that the child is alive, I suspect, and confirm its reality. Their focus on maintaining the well-being of their newborn is highly adaptive, for without their intense and prolonged efforts, a newborn baby would not survive through childhood.

Most new parents wonder how well their child is progressing relative to other children of the same age. That is, parents expect that their children can be compared to some standard of *normative development.* Although normative standards do exist, they allow for *individual differences* in development. In this section we will examine both normative development and individual differences.

Figure 11.4 shows the development of an average child's motor skills, an example of normative development. It allows parents to compare the time at which an individual child begins to sit, crawl, and walk with the time at which other children accomplish those behaviors. Even though children may vary in their rate of development—beginning to stand by holding onto something as early as 5 months or as late as 10 months, for example—the sequence of sitting, crawling, and walking seldom varies. My niece gave birth to fraternal twins, most of whose physical and psychological characteristics were similar in their first year of life. But one began to crawl at 7 months of age, whereas the other was content to sit and watch his brother for the next 3 months. Mom anguished over this "slow" development until she understood the lesson of Figure 11.4. Any age within the range of ages indicated by the bars is standard, or "normative." Nevertheless, she was relieved when at about one year of age, both twins began to walk.

Continuous Versus Stagelike Development

What are we to make of the *rate* of development, if anything? Psychologists use two models of development, one continuous and the other stagelike. *Continuous development* is characterized by an almost imperceptible, incrementally slow growth, like the continuous physical growth of a chicken (see Figure 11.5, top). Stagelike development, in contrast, is characterized by a series of discrete, qualitatively different phases, such as the development of a butterfly (see Figure 11.5, bottom).

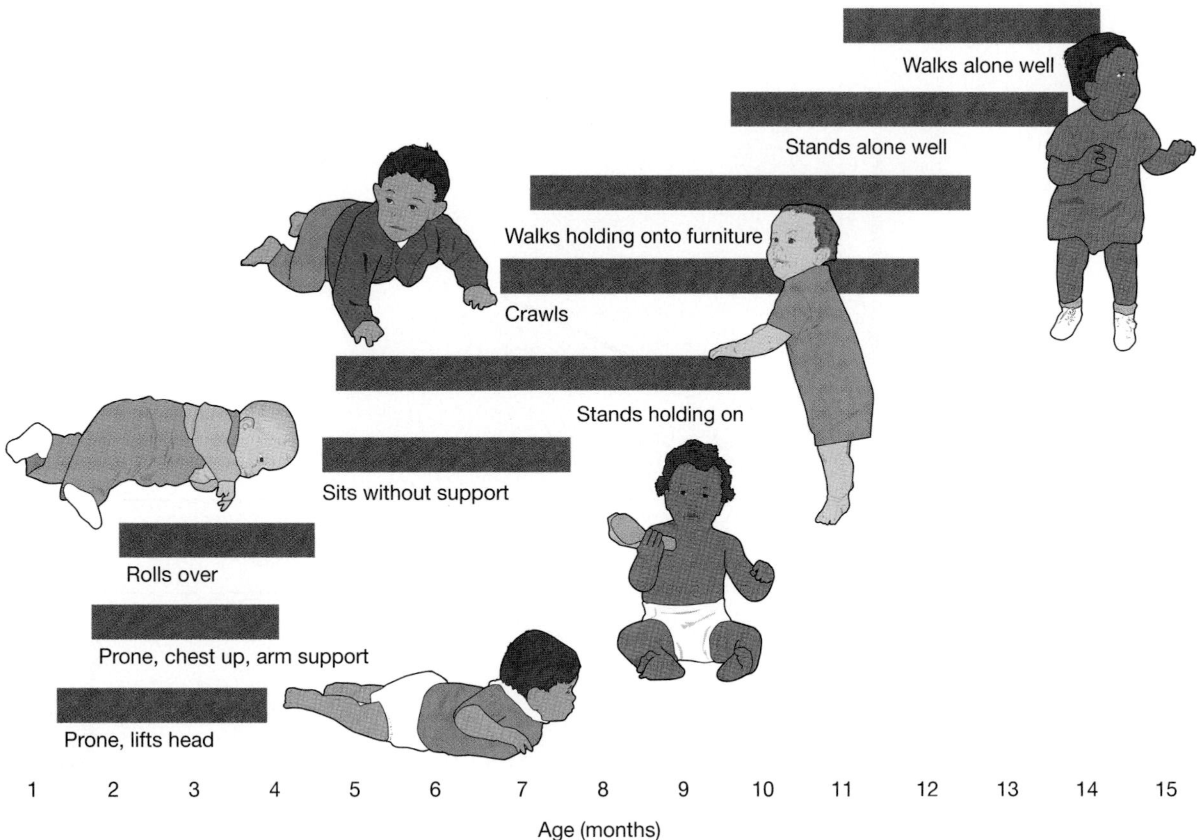

Figure 11.4 Motor development, birth through 15 months. Motor skills develop in about the same sequence from one child to the next, but the age at which an individual begins to sit without support or to stand alone may vary by several months. *Source:* From Frankenburg, Dodds, Archer, Shapiro, & Bresnick, 1992.

In talking about the development of a small child, parents often refer to stages, as in the comment "She's just going through a stage." Stage theory implies that development is discrete, and that a child passes milestones along the way. In contrast, the statement "He's growing like a weed" implies continuous development. In continuous development, growth from 2′ 8″ to 2′ 9″ is assumed to be no different than growth from 3′ 8″ to 3′ 9″.

The reality of human development is that it supports both theories. Many aspects of human physical and behavioral development are stagelike. As Figure 11.4 shows, stagelike changes occur in the first year of life in the development of motor skills: crawling is different from standing, and standing is different from walking. Indeed, the metamorphosis of a human being from a single cell into an adult is no less remarkable than that of a caterpillar into a butterfly. Other aspects of physical development, such as growth in height, appear to be continuous (see Figure 11.6). Daily measurement of a child's growth reveals a much different picture, however. From birth to 21 months, some infants show no growth in height for a week, then grow as much as half an inch a day (Lapml, Veldhuis, & Johnson, 1992). We'll return to the question of stage versus continuous development throughout this chapter.

Perceptual Development

We have seen that unborn fetuses can taste, respond to touch, hear, and remember as newborns what they heard before birth. As we saw in Chapter 7 (p. 258), newborns also express adaptive taste and smell preferences only a few hours after

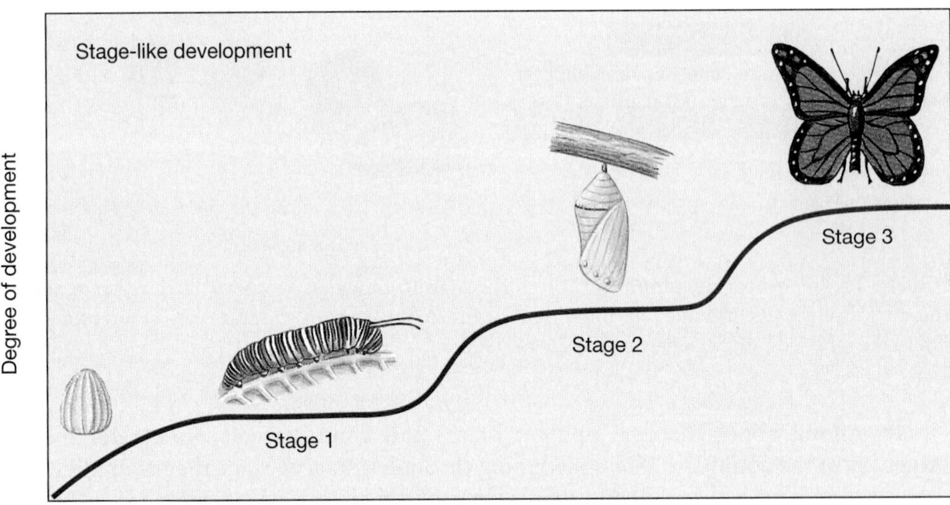

Figure 11.5 **Stagelike versus continuous development.** Physical and mental development can be thought of in terms of gradual, continuous growth (top) or stagelike growth (bottom). Evidence supports both ways of viewing human development.

birth. Human infants can locate and orient to a mother's breast by smell (Russell, 1976), and they prefer their mothers' smell (and the smell of other lactating females) to the smell of nonlactating females (Porter, Makin, Davis, & Christensen, 1992). How do the infant's perceptions develop over time?

Hearing. In Chapter 8 we discussed an infant's ability to localize sounds and hear language. Not surprisingly, both skills appear early in life. The ability to localize the direction of sounds appears in the first few months and increases dramatically over the next year and a half (Hillier, Hewitt, & Morrongiello, 1992). Using the same rate-of-sucking method described earlier, researchers have determined that infants are more sensitive to high-pitched than to low-pitched sounds (Aslin, 1989), and they are especially sensitive to the human voice. Infants who are just one week old can distinguish mother's voice from another woman's (Spence & DeCasper, 1987); within a couple of months, they can discriminate between similar speech sounds, such as *tuh* and *duh*. At about 5 months of age,

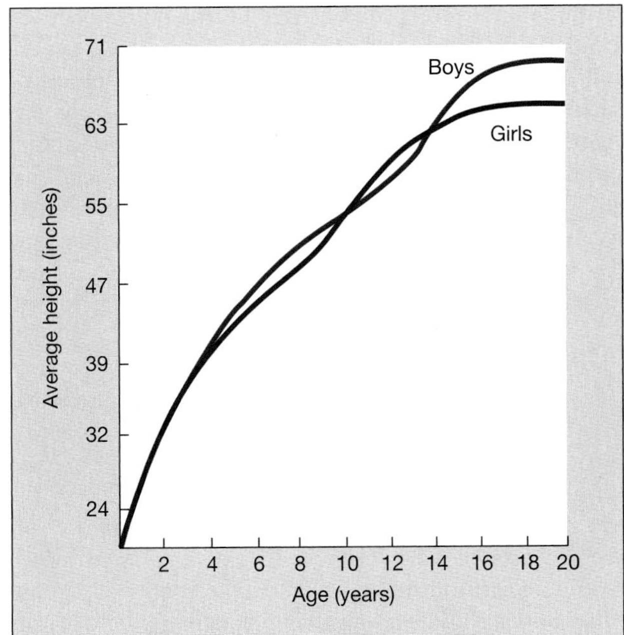

Figure 11.6 Growth, birth through early adulthood. These familiar curves represent the average growth of many humans, measured periodically. *Source:* After Malina, 1975.

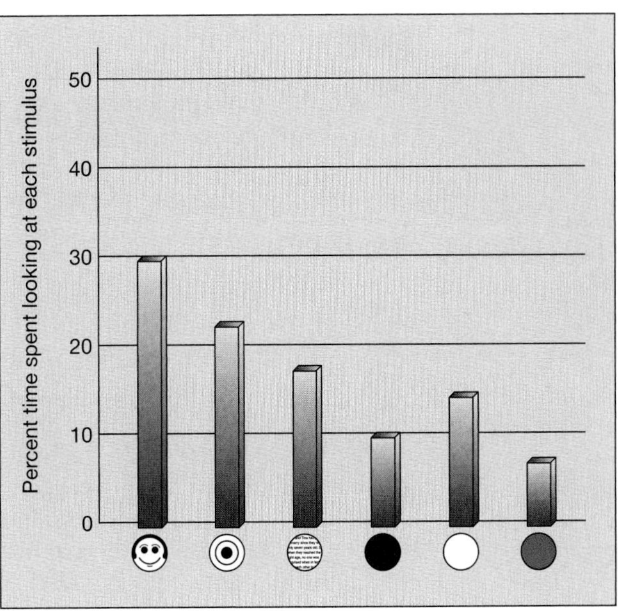

Figure 11.7 Visual preferences in newborns. Newborn infants spend more time looking at cartoonlike faces than at a variety of other objects that vary in color and pattern. *Source:* After Fantz, 1961.

infants respond differently to their own names than to ones that sound similar (Mandel, Juscyzk, & Pisoni, 1995). Laboratory research with 8-month-olds has demonstrated that infants have a remarkable ability to pick out meaningful combinations of sound from amidst a continuous sound stream (Aslin, Saffran, & Newport, 1998). Their sensitivity to speech sounds provides a foundation for the development of language skills.

Vision. Only in the last half century have researchers learned what infants can see. Most parents know that newborns don't see very well—certainly they appear to have difficulty focusing—but that their eyesight gradually improves with age. Infant visual acuity *has* been found to be poor—about 20/600, which means that they can see up close only what a normally sighted person can barely see at 600 feet (Courage & Adams, 1990). Infant visual acuity is poor for several reasons: Neither the cones around the fovea (Abramov et al., 1982) nor the eye muscles that control the lens (Banks, 1980) are fully developed at birth. Yet even prior to the development of the cortical pathways that enable a person to see moving targets well, such stimuli will capture an infant's attention and elicit eye movements (Braddick, Atkinson, & Hood, 1996). A variety of evidence leads to the conclusion that 6-month-old infants see the world much as adults do (Johnson, 1997). By 6 months, the infant's visual acuity has improved to 20/100; it is 20/20 (normal) by the age of 2 years (Courage & Adams, 1990).

What do infants do with their ability to see? Interestingly, Robert Fantz (1961) has demonstrated that newborn infants have viewing *preferences* by measuring the amount of time that 2- to 5-day-old infants gazed at six different objects (see Figure 11.7). He found they preferred to look at cartoon of a human face rather than at a bull's-eye, newsprint, or red, white, or yellow circles. And no wonder, for infants only a few hours old are excellent at facial recognition. An infant probably distinguishes mother's face from others (Walton, Bower, & Bower, 1992) by forming a prototype of her distinguishing features during less than a minute's exposure (Walton & Bower, 1993).

Locke's *tabula rasa,* Chapter 1, p. 14

These findings bear on three questions posed earlier in this book: Is an infant born a blank slate (a *tabula rasa* in John Locke's terms) on which experience writes? Is the infant's consciousness best characterized as a "bloomin' buzzin' confusion," in William James's terms? Or is the infant's mind *innately organized* so as to make sense of its earliest experiences? In fact, the infant's brain *must* be innately organized for the newborn to prefer viewing facial features to nonfacial features. In that sense, the infant's brain is similar to a goose's brain, which is organized to respond in a meaningful way to the first moving object it sees (page 90). Newborn infants' preference for mom's smell over another female's provides additional evidence for an evolutionarily prepared brain.

Although sucking on a nipple is an involuntary reflex, the ability to visually track a moving object is a voluntary act. You may recall that a part of the brain called the *superior colliculus* initiates head turning in order to locate a visual image on the fovea of the retina. The infant's ability to fixate on and track a moving target improves steadily over the first 6 months of life (Hainline, 1993), indicating that the visual and motor connections that coordinate these activities have developed. Very early in life, sensory and motor skills appear together in stagelike fashion, to complement each other and supplement involuntary reflexes. Both brain development and experience with the environment allow the infant to visually explore the world and begin to move around in it.

Long before an infant begins to crawl, it may exhibit other movements that fascinate and entertain parents. The photographs below show an infant imitating the facial movements of an adult. This ability to imitate develops within a few days to a few weeks after birth (Meltzoff & Moore, 1989). The infant's incredible responsiveness to the human face seems to indicate the existence of

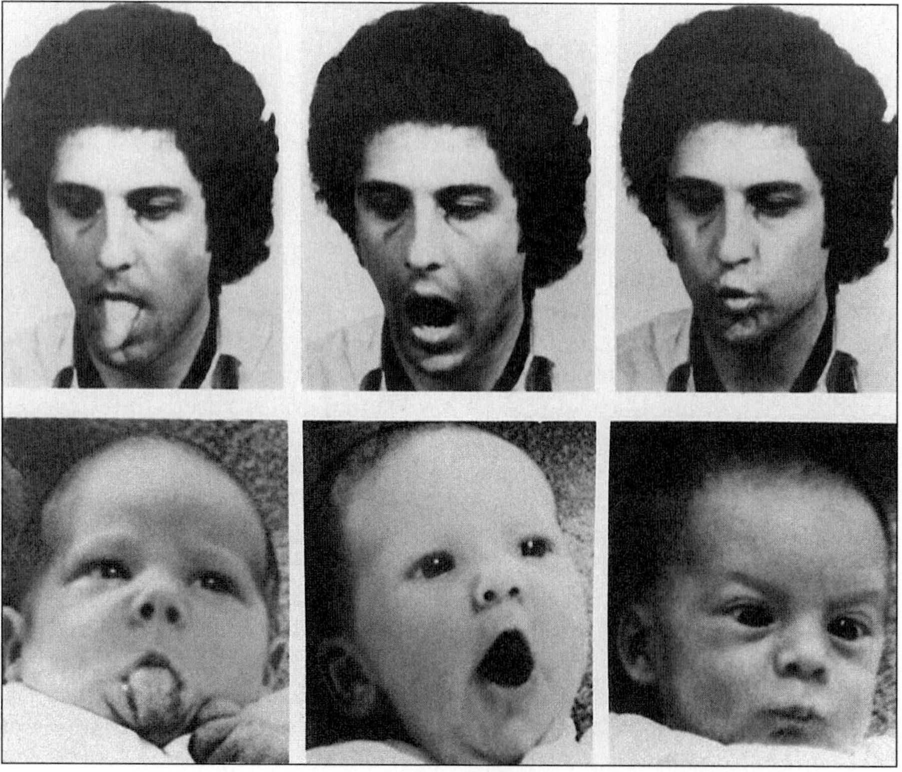

Infants often imitate adult facial movements. Here 2- to 3-week-old infants respond by sticking out a tongue, making an "O" with the mouth, and pursing the lips. Reprinted from: A. N. Meltzoff & M. K. Moore (1977). "Imitation of facial and manual gestures by human neonates." Science, "198", 75–78. Copyright American Association for the Advancement of Science.

innate motor programs, similar to motor reflexes but different in that the adult's facial expression does not invariably elicit the same response. Sometimes an infant will turn its head when an adult sticks out a tongue; at other times it will stick its tongue out in response to an adult's head movement. The adaptive significance of this imitative behavior, if any, is unknown.

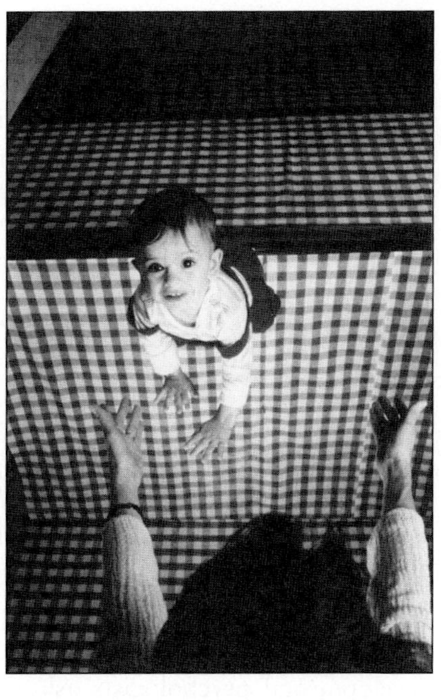

This child's ability to perceive depth is indicated by her hesitancy to crawl off the so-called visual cliff, from the "shallow surface" of the tabletop onto the "deep" surface of transparent glass.

The crawling infant soon begins to develop depth perception. Eleanor Gibson and Richard Walk (1960) used a *visual cliff* apparatus to study this ability (see photograph). They covered a table with a checked tablecloth and a piece of transparent glass that extended past the edge of the table. A baby would readily crawl onto the tabletop, they found, but would express fear as the surface appeared to drop off. They concluded that the crawling infant could perceive the depth of the space below the glass. Additional research has shown that as early as 2 to 3 months after birth, infants become sensitive to binocular depth cues; by 6 months their depth perception is much improved (Banks & Salapatek, 1983).

Depth perception, Chapter 8, p. 276

Subsequent research has complicated these initial conclusions, however. New crawlers will continue onto the glass, apparently unaware of the "depth." The infant's avoidance behavior appears after 6 to 8 weeks of crawling (Bertenthal, Campos, & Kermoian, 1994). Not surprisingly, infants with more crawling experience show the most fear of depth. The codevelopment of crawling and visual processing helps to structure brain development by strengthening certain synaptic connections in the cortex (Fox, Calkins, & Bell, 1994). Indeed, some researchers believe that crawling and other exploratory experiences play an underappreciated role in the developmental process (Bertenthal et al., 1994).

INTERIM SUMMARY

1. An individual child's development may be compared with *normative patterns of development*—the average age at which children begin to sit, crawl, walk, and talk.
2. Physical maturation and psychological development can be characterized as both *stagelike* and *continuous*.
3. A child's perceptual systems begin to function *in utero* and continue to develop for several years after birth. The child responds to taste before responding to touch, hearing, or seeing.
4. What a newborn senses can be determined by measuring its rate of sucking on an artificial nipple. A one-week-old infant can identify its mother by her smell and voice.
5. Infants can detect an object's movement before its form. Their visual acuity is poor for several months, because neurons in the retina and brain are not fully developed.
6. Human brains are innately organized to prefer viewing faces rather than other equally complex patterns. Within a few weeks, an infant prefers mother's face to other female faces. Infants just a few days old will sometimes imitate the faces an adult makes.
7. Using a *visual cliff* apparatus, researchers have determined that 2- to 3-month-old infants are sensitive to binocular depth cues.

For Further Thought

1. How did your own development compare to the normative developmental patterns for sitting, crawling, walking, and talking? Can you identify genetic or environmental influences that might have accounted for any idiosyncrasies in your development?
2. Why do babies put everything they can grab into their mouths?
3. Can you make a case that *bipedalism*—walking upright on two legs—is an innately organized motor skill?

COGNITIVE DEVELOPMENT THROUGHOUT THE LIFE SPAN

Parents look into baby's dark eyes and wonder, "What is she thinking?" Is she *aware* that she doesn't like the strained apples she spits out, or is her rejection merely a reflexive response to their sour flavor? These are the kinds of questions developmental psychologists ask about an infant's **cognitive development**, the way in which a child's thinking about the world changes with maturity. As babies grow and their behavior becomes more complex, the questions researchers ask about their cognitive development become more sophisticated.

The most influential researcher in child development, the Swiss psychologist Jean Piaget (1896–1980), observed children of all ages for over 60 years. Early in his career Piaget headed a child development institute. His writings, and those of his collaborators, were voluminous. In over 40 books and numerous articles, Piaget spelled out his understanding of how children thought about the world (Piaget, 1932; Piaget & Inhelder, 1956, 1969). From observations of their behavior—of how they interacted with their environment at different ages and solved or failed to solve problems—Piaget formulated a stage theory of child cognitive development.

Piaget's Stage Theory of Cognitive Development

Nativism, Chapter 1, p. 15

Schemas, Chapter 10, p. 360

In assuming that children around the world developed in about the same way, Piaget was a nativist. He assumed that children went through predictable stages—more or less unvarying patterns of basic biological and behavioral sequences. These stages, he thought, reflected a genetic unfolding.

Central to Piaget's thinking was the idea that children are not reflexive machines. Rather, they exhibit an active curiosity about their environment. Indeed, children's curiosity is as innate as the capacity to see and hear. As their sensory and motor systems develop, they form *schemas*—mental representations—of their environment. Piaget thought that a child's schemas changed with each new encounter with the world. A child would actively try to integrate new information into an existing schema through a process he called **assimilation.** But if new information could not be assimilated, the child would change to a new schema through a process called **accommodation.**

Piaget proposed that a child's schema developed in four main stages (see Table 11.2), each characterized by a sequential unfolding of mind and behavior. He referred to the four stages as the *sensorimotor, preoperational, concrete operational,* and *formal operational stages.*

cognitive development The way in which a child's thinking about the world changes with maturity and experience.

assimilation (Piaget) The process of integrating new information into an existing schema.

accommodation (Piaget) The process of modifying an existing schema.

sensorimotor stage Piaget's first stage of cognitive development, from 2 to 7 years of age, characterized by sensing and moving through the environment.

The Sensorimotor Stage. Piaget called the first of the major developmental periods, from birth through about 2 years of age, the *sensorimotor stage.* In the **sensorimotor stage,** before infants and toddlers develop language and begin

Table 11.2 Piaget's Four Stages of Cognitive Development

Approximate Age	Stage	Child's Major Characteristics
Birth–2 years	Sensorimotor	Explores with the senses and moves through the environment. Develops the concept of object permanence.
2–6 years	Preoperational	Begins to use symbols. Is egocentric. Does not conserve volume or number.
7–12 years	Concrete operational	Begins to think logically; conserves volume and number. Performs mathematical operations. Can take the perspective of another person.
12 years–adult	Formal operational	Is capable of thinking hypothetically. Is capable of hypothesis testing.

to think, they learn about and understand their environment through their senses and movement. We have seen that infants rapidly develop the senses of seeing, hearing, and touching to complement their innate abilities of taste and smell. Their first movements are reflexive responses, but within months they are crawling up steps and grasping and drinking from a cup—instrumental responses through which they operate on the environment. There is much to be learned by grasping, pulling, hitting, and sucking objects that look, sound, smell, and taste a certain way. The brain's sensory-motor organization, described in Chapter 4, provides the basis for Piaget's sensorimotor stage.

Reflexive movements and instrumental responses, Chapter 6, p. 204

The senses of taste and smell, as well as the sucking reflex, are well developed at birth. Perhaps that is why young infants appear to learn about the shape and texture of an object by sucking on it (Gibson & Walker, 1984). Infants only a few days old can learn about an object's shape or dimension either visually or orally, and then recognize the object with the other sense, a phenomenon called *cross-modal* transfer (Kaye & Bower, 1994). In one experiment, an infant controlled the image it saw by the rate at which it sucked on a pacifier. When it was shown pacifiers of different shapes, the infant preferred to gaze at the same shape as the one in its mouth (Kaye & Bower, 1994). During the next few months of life (Rochat, 1989), more of the senses become involved in cross-modal transfer, presumably because such input guides brain development.

Peek-a-boo! In play a child both anticipates and imitates his grandmother.

A major step in the development of a child's grasp of reality is the concept of **object permanence,** or the understanding that objects continue to exist even when they are out of sight. Before the development of object permanence, a child equates seeing with reality. Piaget demonstrated the concept of object permanence by hiding objects from the children he studied. After hiding a toy behind a pillow, for example, he noted that a young infant would not search for the toy. At this stage the infant's behavior could be characterized in terms of "out of sight, out of mind." By about 8 months of age, however, an infant will push the pillow aside and reach for the toy. At this stage, the child begins to play "peek-a-boo" and other social games, evidence of a shared understanding of reality between parent and child.

object permanence The understanding that objects continue to exist, even when they are out of sight.

The Preoperational Stage. Remembering that a toy was hidden behind a pillow a few seconds ago is evidence that a child has begun to develop mental images in short-term memory. In a more developed form, these mental images

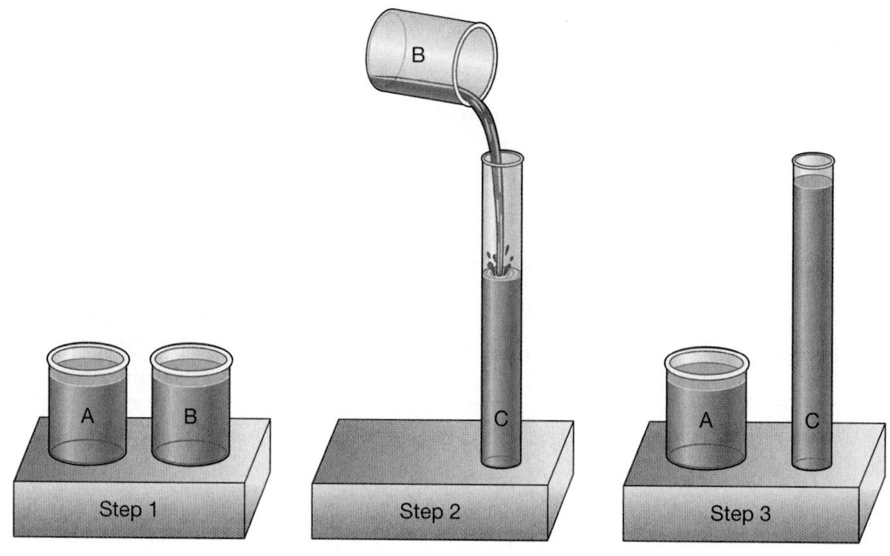

Figure 11.8 Conservation of volume. Even young children will recognize that beakers A and B (left) contain the same amount of fluid. But when beaker B's contents are poured into Beaker C (middle) only children who understand the conservation of volume will report that beakers A and C contain the same amount of fluid (right). Younger children in the preoperational stage will report that beaker C contains more fluid than beaker A.

will become the basis for symbolic thinking, the major accomplishment of Piaget's **preoperational stage** of cognitive development. The preoperational stage runs roughly from ages 2 to 6. Although it is characterized by rapid growth in symbolic representation, the child's thinking in this stage is not necessarily logical. The development of language (discussed in Chapter 12), which begins in the latter part of the sensorimotor stage, continues throughout the preoperational stage.

To better appreciate the strides in thinking that a child makes during this period, consider the way in which a child *cannot* think. In Piaget's classic experiments in preoperational cognitive development, he presented thought problems to children of different ages. He found that older but not younger children could understand that some aspects of physical objects remain the same despite changes in their appearance, a concept known as **conservation.** For example, a young child may think that pouring a fixed amount of fluid from a small glass to a larger glass increases the amount of fluid (see Figure 11.8). When the child understands that the volume of fluid remains the same no matter what the container looks like, he or she has reached the concrete operational stage.

Other examples of conservation are shown in Figure 11.9. *Conservation of mass* is the understanding that changing the shape of an object does not change its mass. Changing the shape of a ball of clay by rolling it into a snakelike form presents a problem for a child who is unable to *conserve mass. Conservation of number* is the understanding that physically rearranging items does not change their number. For a child who is unable to *conserve number,* making a row of items longer seems to increase the number of items.

According to Piaget, the preoperational stage is characterized by three types of thought processes: *centration, irreversibility,* and *egocentrism*. Together, these thought processes interfere with a child's ability to conserve volume, mass, and number. *Centration* refers to a tendency to focus on one aspect of an operation to the exclusion of others. For example, in Figure 11.8, a child might focus on the height of the fluid in beaker C rather than on the amount. Height is a two-dimensional measure, while volume (amount) is three-dimensional—a more difficult concept. Focusing on the simpler concept, height, precludes solving the problem, which requires attention to amount. Likewise, focusing exclusively on the length of the row of apples in Figure 11.9 interferes with attention to the number of items in the row.

preoperational stage Piaget's second stage of cognitive development, from birth to 2 years, characterized by the rapid growth of symbolic thinking.

conservation (Piaget) The understanding that certain attributes of a physical object (such as volume, number, and mass) do not change, despite changes in the object's appearance.

	Conservation Tasks	Approximate Age of Mastery
	Conservation of Number	6–7
	Child agrees that both rows have the same number of objects. The child who says that the lengthened row has the same number of objects is able to conserve number.	
	Conservation of Mass	7–8
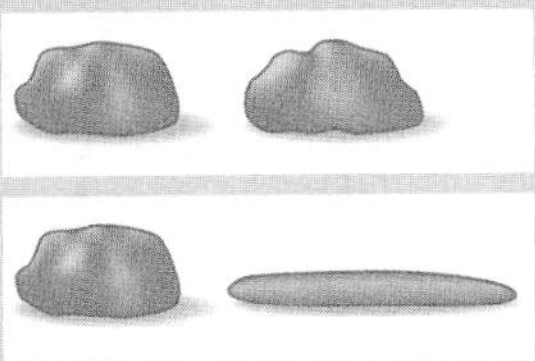	Child agrees that clay balls are equal. The child who says that the ball rolled into a snake still contains the same amount of clay is able to conserve mass.	
	Conservation of Length	7–8
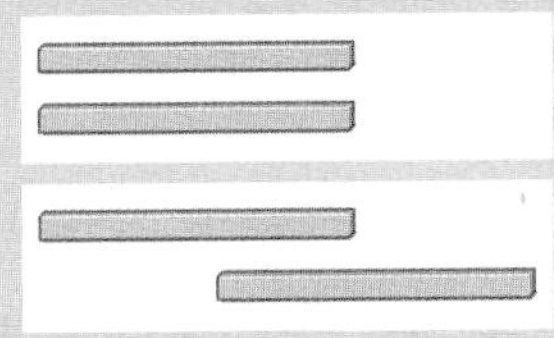	Child agrees that two sticks that are equally aligned are equal in length. The child who says that the nonaligned sticks are still of equal length is able to conserve length.	
	Conservation of Area	8–9
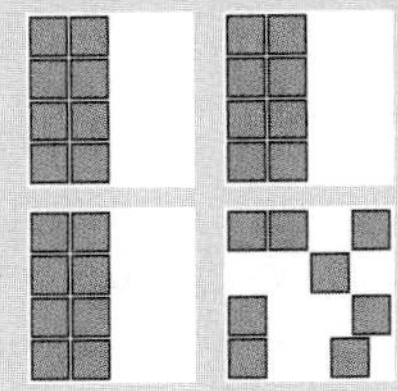	Child agrees that blocks cover equal areas, and leave uncovered equal areas. The child who says that the disrupted pattern of blocks still leaves uncovered areas equal to those on the left is able to conserve area.	

Figure 11.9 Other examples of conservation. Besides the conservation of volume, children eventually develop an understanding of the conservation of number, mass, length, and area. Conservation of area is the last concept to develop, during the concrete operations stage.

Irreversibility refers to an inability to reverse an operation. For example, a preoperational child cannot recognize that the volume of liquid in beaker C, which seems to have increased, must be the same when poured back into beaker B. Likewise, the preoperational child cannot mentally reverse a ball of clay that has been rolled into the shape of a snake. *Egocentrism* refers to the difficulty a young child has in seeing the world from another's person's perspective. A preoperational child literally cannot imagine, even if shown, what the world looks like from a few feet off the ground. That another person might really like the taste of spinach is inconceivable to the child. Egocentrism can persist into late childhood, and remains a problem even for some adults.

The Concrete Operational Stage. At about 7 years of age, children enter what Piaget called the **concrete operational stage,** which is characterized by the growth of logical reasoning. At this point children begin to demonstrate an understanding of the conservation of volume, mass, and number. Before this stage, children cannot mentally undo what they have seen done; but now, increasingly, their

concrete operational stage Piaget's third stage of cognitive development, from about 7 to 12 years, characterized by the development of logical reasoning.

reasoning shows the property of reversibility. At this stage, children can make and follow a plan. For example, they can classify and sort a group of objects based on color and size. If asked to arrange a group of items from smallest to largest, they can do so in an orderly way. (This emerging ability likely reflects the growth and development of the cerebral cortex, in the frontal and parietal lobes.) By age 7 and 8, a child can demonstrate a reasoning ability called *transitive inference*. After observing that stick A is larger than stick B, for example, and in another pairing, that stick B is larger than stick C, a 7- or 8-year-old can infer verbally that stick A is larger than stick C without comparing them visually (Chapman & Lindenberger, 1988).

Only by the ages of 11 or 12, however, does language develop sufficiently to support the ability to reason abstractly. The 7- or 8-year-old can do the stick problem after seeing the sticks, but cannot solve the problem in purely verbal form, such as "*Tracy is taller than Juan, and Juan is taller than Garret; is Tracy taller than Garret?*" Perhaps the ability to reason abstractly depends on the development of a longer processing loop in short-term memory, which would allow a thinker to hold in mind at one time all the elements needed to solve the problem.

LINK
Phonological loop and working memory, Chapter 10, p. 354

During the concrete operational stage, children become less egocentric. For example, they begin to do *mental rotations*, recognizing that their own left and right sides are not the same as someone else's left and right (Roberts & Aman, 1993). Figuratively speaking, they can put themselves in someone else's shoes and see the world from another's perspective. In addition, children of this age begin to form *cognitive maps* of their surroundings. For example, a 10-year-old child who is standing at point A can explain how to get to point B, as well as how to get from point B to point C (Plumert, Pick, Marks, Kintsch, & Wegesin, 1994).

The Formal Operational Stage. The last of Piaget's stages, the **formal operational stage** (from about 12 years to adulthood), is characterized by the ability to think hypothetically (abstractly) and to engage in hypothesis testing. In this stage, children and adults can arrive at general rules that allow them to make predictions about the world. For example, were you to ask a 10-year-old child which is faster, a plane or a train, the child would likely answer a plane. If you then asked why planes can travel faster than trains, you might get an assortment of answers, including some at the level of concrete operations. The child might say that planes go faster than trains because they have larger engines, which is logical. If you persisted, however, and asked why planes with the same-size engines as trains go faster than trains, the child might be stumped. Indeed, an adult might be stumped, for the level of formal operations is the great divide in cognitive development. From about age 12 to adulthood, some individuals begin to engage in formal operations; others may never do so.

In the formal operational stage, a person uses all the tools of logic, including deductive and inductive reasoning. Deductive reasoning is reasoning from a general proposition to a specific instance. For example, given the general proposition that larger engines allow vehicles to travel faster, a plane with a larger engine than a train must travel faster than a train. Inductive reasoning is reasoning from specific instances to a general proposition. For example, air travel differs from land travel in terms of the amount of friction a vehicle encounters in air and on land. There is a general rule regarding the amount of force that is necessary to overcome friction. So given the same size force, airplanes that experience little friction will travel faster than trains that experience a lot of friction.

formal operational stage Piaget's fourth stage of cognitive development, from 12 years to adulthood, characterized by the ability to think hypothetically (abstractly) and engage in hypothesis testing.

Formal operations are characterized by a form of problem solving, sometimes called hypothetico-deductive reasoning, that resembles the scientific method. According to Piaget, by 12 years of age a human is capable of generating hypotheses to solve problems. At this stage, concrete operations—reasoning about things that can be seen and held—are replaced by formal operations—the use of words, symbols, and rules of logic to solve abstract verbal problems (Inhelder & Piaget, 1958).

Challenges to Piaget's Theory

Was Piaget right? Do all children progress through these four stages of cognitive development? Though most psychologists agree that Piaget defined many of the important issues in child development (Brainerd, 1996; Flavell, 1996), some point to methodological deficiencies in his work, or find the range of questions he asked about development to be restricted (Gelman & Kit-Fong, 1996). John Flavell, a psychologist at Stanford University, has studied what children think about, and at what age they develop each type of conscious activity (Flavell, 1993). When, for example, do children develop a theory of mind? When do they become aware that they think, and that other people think? In one study of 3- and 4-year-olds, Flavell showed a child a trick box that appeared to be empty, but when reopened contained money. Turning to a cohort, he asked how that had happened. The cohort replied, "That's a hard question. Hmm. Give me a minute." While the cohort was looking pensive, Flavell asked the child, "What is she doing right now?" Some of the 3-year-olds and all the 4-year-olds replied, "She's thinking" (Flavell, 1993). In contrast, Piaget thought that this type of sophisticated thinking was synonymous with language development and would first appear in 6- or 7-year-old children.

Jean Piaget's developmental theories were influenced by observations of his own children.

One criticism of Piaget's theory is that the stages emerge only gradually, often after years (Gross, 1985). Such a finding violates the whole notion of stage theory and tends to support theories of continuous development. Another criticism is that Piaget's developmental schema do not account well for marked individual differences among same-age children. In particular, a child's learning and use of language play a small role in Piaget's theory (Gelman, 1997). Furthermore, the theory is not well integrated with the behavioral neurosciences: The underlying brain changes that are responsible for Piaget's observed developmental changes are only beginning to be investigated.

Perhaps the question raised most often about Piaget's theory concerns the effect of the environment on the timing of these stages. For example, will a child who stares passively at a television during most of her waking hours develop at the same rate as a child who is stimulated to think? Both the environment and the way in which caretakers reinforce or extinguish a child's exploratory behavior likely affect brain and behavior development more than Piaget proposed. Although behaviorists acknowledge that the environment can be more or less important at some stages, particularly critical periods, they think that brain and behavioral development are continuously influenced by the environment, past and present.

Cross-cultural research can help to isolate the relative contributions of biology and environment to the emergence of new behaviors (Greenfield, 1994). For example, in cultures that promote conservation and other logical processes at home and in the classroom, the four stages emerge earlier than Piaget reported (Light & Perrett-Clermont, 1989). In addition, unschooled children who live in agrarian cultures may be delayed a few years in their development (Fahrmeier, 1978). Ironically, cross-cultural research supports the behaviorist's position on child development as much as it does Piaget's nativism.

Vygotsky's Sociocultural Theory of Cognitive Development

The Russian psychologist Lev Semenovich Vygotsky (1896–1934) has proposed a formidable alternative to Piaget's stage theory. Vygotsky's *sociocultural theory* focuses on the beliefs and educational values of the social group in which a child is raised (Vygotsky, 1934/1986). Recall that Piaget emphasized children's natural curiosity and schema formation rather than their environment. In contrast, Vygotsky argues that adults play a major role in a child's cognitive development.

Specifically, a child's advancement depends more on the use of language to communicate with parents and other elders than on a natural progression through biologically based stages. Vygotsky's theory of early ontogenetic development, then, emphasizes the passing on of memes from parent to child through language.

LINK
Language development, Chapter 12, p. 426

Early language is particularly important in Vygotsky's theory. Small children often talk to themselves, a behavior Vygotsky interpreted as a form of self-direction. As the child grows older, these early, vocalized "self-talks" become the child's internal voice, or *private speech*. Children who use private speech during problem solving have been found to be more successful than those who do not (Berk, 1997). Vygotsky thinks that private speech underlies all cognitive processes, including attention and planning. His theories have been put to practical use in classrooms that emphasize *assisted discovery,* a process in which teachers help to elicit a child's own thinking through explanations, demonstrations, and careful questioning.

Because Vygotsky emphasizes the role of both language and a supportive environment in a child's cognitive development, his view may be described as a *cognitive-behavioral* approach. For instance, teachers who use assisted discovery to help a child solve problems *reinforce* the child's thought processes and problem-solving behavior. Unlike stage theories of cognitive development, in the cognitive-behavioral approach, development is seen as incremental and cumulative.

Cognition and Memory Throughout the Life Span

Another approach to cognitive development is to determine what children remember, and what they have forgotten, of their past. General memory processes were the subject of Chapter 10. Here we will consider how memory changes over a lifetime.

Memory in Infants and Children. Sigmund Freud was one of the first psychologists to write about *infantile amnesia*—the fact that most humans remember nothing of their first few years of life. One explanation for infantile amnesia (also called childhood amnesia) is that early in life, the frontal lobes of the brain have not developed sufficiently to allow memories to be encoded (Wheeler, Struss, & Tulving, 1997). If this theory is true, the rate of brain development must vary widely. Most of us cannot remember anything before the age of 2, but some people are amnesic until the age of 8. The average age of first memory is 3½ (Pillemer, Picariello, & Pruett, 1994).

Autobiographical memory, Chapter 10, p. 366

Katherine Nelson, a psychologist at City University of New York, has focused on children's autobiographical memories in her research (Nelson, 1993). She and her colleagues want to identify the conditions that lead to memory formation. To remember an event, a child must apparently reexperience much of the original context; in simple terms, the child must have a second trial to remember the event. (For life-threatening events, a single trial may produce a permanent memory.) With the development of language, a child can experience second and third trials through verbal descriptions of the event. Caregivers play an important role in cueing the rehearsal of early memories, which may have adaptive significance.

With colleagues, Carolyn Rovee-Collier of Rutgers University is testing the proposition that young infants are unable to form memories. Rovee-Collier has developed procedures for measuring the *duration* of a newly formed memory in infants aged 2 to 18 months. Taking advantage of the fact that young infants will kick a mobile to move it, she has tested infants' recognition of a mobile after various delays. She found that 3-month-olds remembered (and hence, immediately kicked) the mobile after a one-week delay, and 6-month-olds remembered it after a 2-week delay. In fact, using a button that moves a model train, Rovee-Collier (1999) has shown that 18-month-old infants can remember events for as long as 3 months (see Figure 11.10).

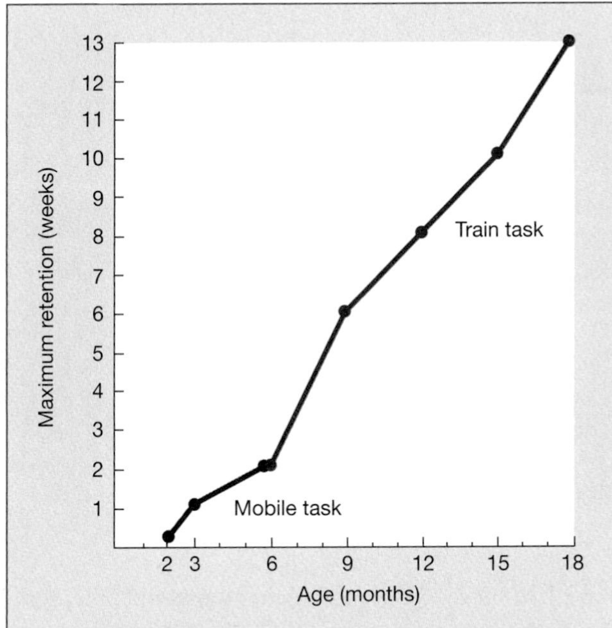

Figure 11.10 The development of infant memories. Infants who had learned to move a mobile by kicking it (red circles) or to make a train move by pressing a button (blue circles) could remember the experience. The older they were when they learned the task, the longer they could remember it. *Source:* From "The Development of Infant Memory" by C. Rovee-Collier in *Current Directions in Psychological Science,* (1999), vol. 8, pp. 80–85. © by the American Psychological Society. Reprinted by permission of Blackwell Publishers.

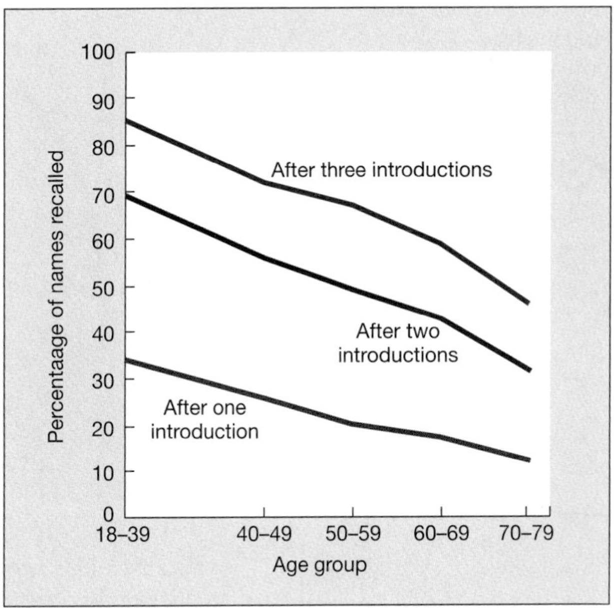

Figure 11.11 Memory for names as a function of age. The ability to remember a new name declines with age. Rehearsal (three introductions compared to just a single introduction) greatly aids name recall in the young but not the old.

Memory in Adults. As a general rule, memory abilities change with age. With few exceptions, older people tend to think their memories are not as good as when they were younger, and some laboratory tests support their suspicions. For example, older people seem not to remember the names of new acquaintances as well as young people. In one study of over 1,200 subjects of different ages, people introduced themselves on videotape, mentioning their names and some personal information. Later, subjects reviewed the videotapes and were asked to provide the names of the people on screen. Figure 11.11 shows what we all have experienced: most of us are unlikely to recall someone's name after just one introduction. After two or three trials, however, 70 percent of younger people but just 30 percent of older people can recall a person's name (Crook & West, 1990). This research suggests that older people have trouble learning new material, a short-term memory problem.

Researchers have used a variety of methods to study long-term memory in the elderly. The study of a person's autobiographical memories was described in Chapter 10 (see page 366). In another study, researchers asked subjects who had graduated from high school 35 to 50 years earlier to identify photos of their classmates (Bahrick, Bahrick, & Wittlinger, 1975). Subjects were able to do so with an accuracy of 70 percent or higher, surprising even themselves. But in another study, subjects' ability to recall words, given common definitions, showed a steady decline after age 60—more so among males than among females (Schaie, 1980). Using somewhat different methods, other researchers have reported similar results (Craik & Jacoby, 1996). Indeed, a consistent finding of memory studies is that in the elderly, recall is impaired more than recognition. For example, the elderly are more likely to recognize a TV program as a rerun than to recall the story line of a particular episode.

Long-term memory, Chapter 10, p. 347

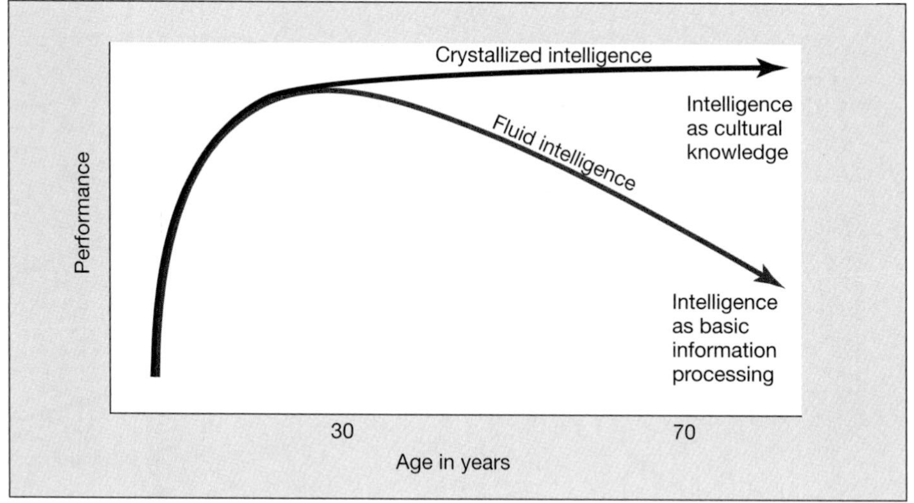

Figure 11.12 Fluid and crystallized intelligence as a function of age. Crystallized intelligence (social judgment, vocabulary, and general information) is relatively unaffected by age, but fluid intelligence (basic memory capacity and speed of information processing) begins to decline after age 30.

Because older people have had more experiences than younger people, some of their memory problems can be construed as the result of interference during recall (Kausler, 1994). Older people simply have more to remember than younger people, and their excess memories may get in the way, confusing them and reducing their recall of specific memories. One way to reduce such confusion is to use external aids (reminders). In fact, far more of the elderly use memory prompts than young people (Loewen, Shaw, & Craik, 1990). Relying on sticky notes is an adaptive behavior!

LINK Alzheimer's disease, Chapter 17, p. 592

Cognitive Changes in Old Age. Other than memory changes, the continuing development of a person's cognitive abilities—language, thinking, and intelligent behavior—is discussed in detail in the next two chapters. Here we will note some general trends in cognitive changes in the elderly, other than those caused by injury or disease, such as stroke or Alzheimer's disease. The most consistent research finding is one of selective cognitive change, rather than the progressive deterioration of all physical and mental abilities. For example, intelligence may be separated into two broad categories, *fluid* and *crystal intelligence* (see Figure 11.12). **Fluid intelligence** includes basic information processing, which involves short-term memory capacity, as well as the ability to see patterns and relationships in ambiguous test stimuli. **Crystallized intelligence** is a measure of language use, social and cultural conventions, and general information. As Figure 11.12 shows, advancing age affects fluid intelligence more than crystallized intelligence. Even with more time to perform a task and more rehearsal trials, the elderly can't handle as much information or multitask as well as younger people. But in general, their cultural knowledge and use of language are unimpaired well into old age.

fluid intelligence The ability to process information and see patterns and relationships in ambiguous test stimuli.

crystallized intelligence A knowledge of general information, including how language is used and the social conventions of culture.

Kohlberg's Stage Theory of Moral Development

In his writings on cognitive development, Piaget (1932) also addressed how children develop a sense of morality. Following Piaget's lead, Lawrence Kohlberg (1969, 1984) devised a unique experimental method to investigate how children and adults distinguish between right and wrong. Kohlberg had researchers read stories about ethical dilemmas to children, adolescents, and adults, and ask them to analyze and resolve the dilemmas. The best-known example of this research is the "Heinz dilemma," a story set in 19th-century Europe, which may be simplified as follows:

> A woman was near death from cancer and needed one particular drug to cure her. The village druggist had the drug, but it cost far more than the sick woman's husband, Heinz, could afford. Desperate, Heinz broke into the pharmacy and stole the drug for his wife. Should Heinz have stolen the drug? Why or why not?

Rather than assuming there were right and wrong answers to these questions, Kohlberg examined the type of reasoning subjects used to answer the dilemmas. The following arguments for and against stealing the drug illustrate his interest in the reasoning process rather than the decision itself:

> (*In favor of stealing the drug*) "If you let your wife die, you will get in trouble. You'll be blamed for not spending the money to help her and there'll be an investigation of you and the druggist for your wife's death." (Kohlberg, 1969, p. 381)
>
> (*Opposed to stealing the drug*) "You shouldn't steal the drug because you'll be caught and sent to jail if you do. If you do get away, your conscience would bother you thinking how the police would catch up with you any minute." (Kohlberg, 1969, p. 381)

As Kohlberg pointed out, these reasons for behaving morally—fear of authority and the avoidance of punishment—are limited ways of understanding the dilemma.

Kohlberg divided subjects' responses into six different categories representing different moral stages (see Table 11.3). For comparison, Piaget's cognitive stages are included in the same table. Kohlberg's research suggests that certain cognitive processes must be in place before a person is capable of higher-order moral reasoning. For example, Kohlberg's first stage, the punishment and obedience orientation, parallels Piaget's preoperational level, when children cannot hold two separate views at the same time (for example, water in a tall glass is "more," and therefore can't be the same amount as water in a short glass). The ability to understand Heinz's predicament in only one way, then, reflects preconventional thinking.

In Kohlberg's second stage, called the *instrumental purpose orientation* (see Table 11.3), subjects' responses emphasize the belief that moral decisions should be based on personal needs. That is, Heinz should steal the drug if he really loves his wife. Not until Kohlberg's fourth stage, the *social-order orientation*, do some adolescents and adults begin to describe morality in terms of a duty to uphold the laws. This stage requires the abstract thinking that characterizes Piaget's formal operational stage. The development of moral reasoning is slow; most people do not move beyond the fourth stage (Walker & Taylor, 1991). At the two "highest" levels in Table 11.3, morality is defined in terms of abstract principles and values that presumably apply to all societies.

Table 11.3 Kohlberg's Six Stages of Moral Development

Kohlberg's Moral Stage	Basic Moral Principle	Piaget's Cognitive Stage
Punishment and obedience orientation	Fear of authority and avoidance of punishment	Preoperational, concrete operational
Instrumental purpose orientation	Satisfying personal needs	Concrete operational
Good-boy, good-girl orientation	Maintaining the affection and approval of friends and relatives	Early formal operational
Social-order orientation	Upholding laws and rules for their own sake	Formal operational
Social contract orientation	Changing laws to protect individual rights and the needs of the majority	
Universal ethical principle orientation	Abstract universal principles that are valid for all humanity	

An example of moral reasoning that fits the *universal ethical principle orientation*, Kohlberg's highest moral stage, illustrates the advanced nature of logical reasoning required in this stage:

> If Heinz does not do everything he can to save his wife, then he is putting some value higher than the value of life. It doesn't make sense to put respect for property above respect for life itself. (People) could live together without private property at all. Respect for human life and personality is absolute, and, accordingly, (people) have a mutual duty to save one another from dying. (Rest, 1979, p. 37)

Again, Kohlberg's interest was in the moral reasoning process, rather than whether an argument was right or wrong—in this case, whether an absolute universal ethical principle actually exists. The point of his work is that moral reasoning progresses through stages, maturing with age as one's thinking ability develops from the concrete to the abstract.

INTERIM SUMMARY

1. ***Cognitive development*** concerns how and when humans begin to think about the world.
2. Piaget studied how children interacted with their environment and solved problems. He formulated a stage theory of cognitive development, according to which children proceed through a genetically based biological and behavioral sequence.
3. Piaget proposed that children formed *schemas,* or mental representations of the world. They then integrate new information into those schemas through a process called ***assimilation,*** or change the schemas through a process called ***accommodation***.
4. Piaget proposed that humans progress through four developmental stages: the ***sensorimotor, preoperational, concrete operational,*** and ***formal operational stages.***
5. In the *sensorimotor stage* (birth to 2 years), children learn about the environment through their senses and through movement, first by sucking and tasting objects and eventually through coordinated seeing and touching. They also learn the concept of ***object permanence***—the fact that objects continue to exist even when they are out of sight.
6. During the *preoperational stage* (2 to 6 years), children learn language and become capable of other symbolic mental representations.
7. During the *concrete operational stage* (7 to 12 years), children begin to engage in logical reasoning. They demonstrate an understanding of the ***conservation*** of volume, mass, and number, in part by not becoming fixed on just one solution to a problem (*centration*). In this stage, children can mentally undo what they have seen done (*reversibility*) and take another person's perspective (in other words, they overcome *egocentrism*).
8. During Piaget's final stage, designated the *formal operational stage* (age 12 to adult), humans can learn to think hypothetically (abstractly) and engage in hypothesis testing, but only in an environment that supports such cognitive development.
9. Piaget's theory of cognitive development has not yet been supported by research in the emerging field of behavioral neuroscience. Cross-cultural research suggests that the environment plays a greater role in cognitive development than Piaget's theory indicates.
10. Vygotsky's *sociocultural theory* emphasizes the effect of a child's early environment, particularly parents' language, beliefs, and educational values, on the child's cognitive development. As early as 18 months of age, children develop *private speech,* an inner language that guides their cognitive development.
11. Vygotsky's theory is an example of a *cognitive-behavioral* approach to development, which emphasizes the reinforcement and punishment a child encounters in the home and the classroom. The practice of using *assisted discovery* to help a child solve problems is based on Vygotsky's theory.
12. Older people have trouble learning new material, such as names, probably because of a problem with short-term memory. Their recall from long-term memory is more impaired than their recognition, likely because of interference from other memories.

13. The cognitive changes that accompany aging include a decrease in ***fluid intelligence,*** or the speed of basic information processing and the capacity of short-term memory. ***Crystallized intelligence,*** which includes language use and general information, is not much affected by age.

14. Kohlberg divided moral development from childhood through adulthood into six stages: the punishment and obedience orientation; the instrumental purpose orientation; the good-boy, good-girl orientation; the social-order orientation; the social contract orientation; and the universal ethical principle orientation.

For Further Thought

1. Are Piaget's concepts of assimilation and accommodation similar to the concepts of generalization and discrimination discussed in Chapter 6?
2. We will encounter Piaget's concept of centration in Chapter 12, in the context of problem solving and *lateral thinking*. Adults often *centrate* in their thinking, failing to solve a problem because they focus too narrowly on it, ignoring "the big picture." Do you think centration is inherent in a cognitive stage that is eventually outgrown; that it depends on specific environmental experiences; or both?
3. What is your first memory, and why do you think you remember it? Is it likely that your memory for the event was reconstructed (see Chapter 10)?
4. Figure 11.11 indicates that compared with the young, older people aren't as efficient at remembering new names. Can you make a case that the older subjects in this study may not have been as motivated as the younger ones to learn the names of the strangers whom they viewed on videotape in an experimental setting?
5. Kohlberg was more interested in the development of moral reasoning than in establishing the truth of a particular moral viewpoint. Do *absolute universal ethical principles* exist?

PSYCHOSOCIAL DEVELOPMENT THROUGHOUT THE LIFE SPAN

The process of socialization—learning to live and interact meaningfully with others—begins in infancy and lasts longer in humans than in any other animal. The importance of this period of socialization cannot be overemphasized. Not having adequate human caretakers can have devastating effects. In Chapter 5 we read about the children Amala and Kamala, who were raised by wolves; and in Chapter 12 we will learn about Genie, a severely neglected child who was raised in a closet. Not only were Genie's language abilities permanently impaired; she failed to develop normal social interactions (Curtiss, 1977). The specifics of an adequate environment for socialization are still unknown, however.

Feral children, Chapter 5, p. 171

The story of "Genie," Chapter 12, p. 431

To organize our study of human social development, we will use the psychologist Erik Erikson's (1968) schema of *psychosocial stages* (see Table 11.4). Erikson described eight stages, from infancy through adulthood, all couched in oppositional terms: trust versus mistrust, autonomy versus shame and doubt, initiative versus guilt, competency versus inferiority, identity versus role confusion, intimacy versus isolation, generativity versus stagnation, and integrity versus

Table 11.4 Erikson's Stages of Psychosocial Development

LIFE STAGE	ERIKSON'S PSYCHOSOCIAL STAGE	DESCRIPTION
Infancy	Trust versus mistrust	Infants develop positive (or negative) expectations based on their experiences.
Toddler	Autonomy versus shame and doubt	Toddlers initiate voluntary behavior and exhibit independent behavior and self-control, or fail to do so.
Preschool and primary grades	Initiative versus guilt	A child develops a conscience and assumes responsibility for her or his own behavior, or experiences guilt at becoming independent.
Late childhood	Competency versus inferiority	A child develops cognitive, social, and physical skills, or fails to and feels inferior to peers.
Adolescence	Identity versus role confusion	The adolescent seeks to answer the question "Who am I?" by trying on various roles.
Young adulthood (*20s–early 40s*)	Intimacy versus isolation	The young adult asks, "Should I be safe in my solitude, or should I trust and become intimate with another person?"
Midlife (*40s–early 60s*)	Generativity versus stagnation	The midlife adult asks, "Am I achieving my life goals, or am I 'just going through the motions'?"
Later years (*late 60s to death*)	Integrity versus despair	The elderly adult asks, "What does it all mean? Was my life a success or a failure?"

despair. He proposed that a person develops as a social being by encountering and resolving the eight *identity crises* represented in these stages. By *identity,* Erikson meant a person's self-perception—who one is. An identity crisis, then, can be thought of as a psychosocial crossroad; its resolution—that is, the direction taken at the crossroad—becomes a major determinant of a person's psychosocial development.

The first stage, *trust versus mistrust,* is best resolved by the successful emotional attachment of a very young child to a caretaker. Such an attachment is critical to the development of any further socialization, for it produces hopeful expectations that can generalize to other people throughout one's lifetime. For example, infants who are fed and changed regularly develop the expectation that their caretakers can be trusted to respond to their discomfort. Unfortunately, the opposite is also true; a child who is not well cared for can become mistrustful of both the caretaker and others. This process is so important, we will describe it in detail.

Infancy: Attachment and Temperament

Cross-culturally, babies, puppies, and kittens elicit the same adoring reaction from most adults. Why do photos of infants and small animals prompt involuntary "aahhs" and "oohs"? Such feelings, and the fact that most societies have laws specifically protecting the young and defenseless, likely have sociobiological origins. The recognition that our offspring need our attention and protection seems to be innate.

In the mammalian world, suckling mothers do most of the feeding and grooming of the young, and provide most of their social contact. Even among primates, most fathers exhibit curiosity, but little direct social contact. In this respect, the caregiving behavior of many human fathers is the exception to the rule of quite strict gender roles in neonatal care. Of all animals, human fathers spend the most time securing food for and feeding their young (Alexander, Hoogland, Howard, Noonan, & Sherman, 1979). Recent studies have shown that a father's love and affection play a significant role in the development of a child's emotional and behavioral well-being (Rohner, 1998). Hence, in humans, both mothers and fathers typically develop a strong emotional attachment to their offspring.

Formally defined, **attachment** is a strong and enduring emotional bond between two people. People who are attached to each other are happy when they are together and miserable when they are separated. Developmental psychologists study the attachment of infants to their caregivers by measuring their responses as they interact. Attachment begins with awe—the sense of marvel and wonder parents feel about the new person who has come into their life. It deepens as the child grows, spending countless hours in parents' loving care. Emotional attachment can be seen in parents' affection and sensitivity to every aspect of the infant's behavior. Even the changing of a diaper may be welcomed as an opportunity to bond with the new baby.

Attachment and secondary reinforcement, Chapter 6, p. 207

Through secondary reinforcement, the attachment of a child to parents is extended to many other aspects of life. Mama is the *feel good* of our earliest experiences: of warmth, food in the stomach, familiar smells and tastes, and physical contact. Parents, both the people and the ideas they represent, soothe our fears and protect us from the dark, from nightmares and the unknown. Our lifelong quest for self-understanding begins with our efforts to cope when they are not there. Throughout a lifetime, through good times and bad, each experience with a parent deepens this increasingly complex attachment.

The psychologist John Bowlby assumed that the attachment process is instinctive. But is it? We can begin to answer this question by asking whether the clinging and nursing behavior of infant primates, and the nurturing behavior of adult primates, is instinctive. Normally, all primates, including humans, engage in these behaviors, which suggests that they are evolutionarily prepared adaptive behaviors. However, these behaviors also depend on a supportive environment—that is, on proximal as well as distal determinants.

For example, Harry and Margaret Harlow (1962) of the University of Wisconsin demonstrated that in the absence of a real mother, monkeys will cling to a terry-cloth-covered artificial mother in preference to a wire-frame mother that provides milk. The Harlows proposed that monkeys—indeed, all primates—have a primary need for *contact comfort,* or the satisfaction of holding and being held; merely being fed is not sufficient for attachment. Furthermore, the Harlows thought that contact comfort promoted *pair bonding,* which essentially is the same as the process Bowlby called attachment. For these instinctive behaviors to occur, however, the environment must be supportive. Recall from Chapter 3 that an infant monkey's failure to attach to its mother had consequences that extended into adulthood. As adults, *motherless mothers* failed to attach to their offspring. The Harlows' work has been replicated and extended in other monkeys (Champoux, Byrne, DeLizio, & Suomi, 1992). In sum, normally reared monkeys form attachments to their infants, but monkeys reared without mothers are deficient in mothering skills, and their offspring are adversely affected—a serious cross-generational defect. Thus, the presence of a nurturing mother is a critical component of child rearing.

Contact comfort and pair bonding, Chapter 3, p. 93

John Bowlby based his theory of attachment on comparative studies like the Harlows', as well as on evolutionary theory and the ethology of Konrad Lorenz. Bowlby thought that in humans, both infant and mother brought to their early interactions instinctive behaviors that provided the basis for their attachment (Bowlby, 1982). Depending on whether they are securely or insecurely attached, children perceive their world and respond to other people differently (Belsky, Spritz, & Crnic, 1996). Let's take a closer look at Bowlby's theory.

Bowlby divided the attachment process into four stages: the *preattachment* phase (birth to 6 weeks), the *attachment-in-the-making* phase (6 weeks to 6 to 8 months), *"clear-cut" attachment* (6 to 8 months to about 18 months), and

attachment A strong and enduring emotional bond between a caretaker and child.

reciprocal attachment (18 months to 2 years and beyond). In the preattachment phase, a hungry, crying infant elicits instinctive behavior from the caretaker. The warmth, nursing, and comforting afforded by the mother or other caretaker calms the infant. Even though infants in this stage can identify mom—can recognize her smell and voice—they do not object to being held and cared for by other caretakers. In turn, the mother receives pleasure both from nursing and from contact with a warm body. Both mother and infant, then, bring innate behaviors to their interaction, and ideally, both receive pleasure. To the extent that they do, their interaction is reinforced and is likely to continue.

In the attachment-in-the-making phase, the caretaker's affection continues to grow, and the infant begins to respond differently to the familiar caretaker than to a strange caretaker. To the delight of other adults (especially grandparents), however, babies will still respond to anyone who will hold, comfort, and feed them. The start of the clear-cut attachment phase is signaled by the infant's development of *separation anxiety.* When the primary caretaker leaves, the infant or small child feels abandoned; distraught, the infant will cry inconsolably. In the final phase of reciprocal attachment, the child's growing command of language lends some predictability to the caretaker's presence. That is, the child's developing cognitive structures help to define the attachment process. Both the clear-cut and reciprocal attachment stages are characterized by an intensity of focus between child and caretaker. During the entire attachment process, infant and parent exhibit highly adaptive behavior that is clearly designed to promote the offspring's survival.

Secure Versus Insecure Attachment. Attachment has been studied in the laboratory using a procedure developed by Mary Ainsworth, called the **strange situation test** (Ainsworth, Blehar, Waters, & Wall, 1978). In this method, an infant is placed in an unfamiliar room, and either the caregiver or a stranger comes and goes for brief periods. The child's responses to these comings and goings are videotaped and scored in terms of the security of the attachment.

An infant is considered to be securely attached if the caregiver's presence is sufficient to motivate the child to explore the room, using the caregiver as a kind of home base. Cross-culturally, about two of every three children show a secure attachment (Colin, 1996). An insecure attachment is shown by clinging or rejecting behavior. For example, a child may cling to the mother and refuse to explore the new environment. Or when the mother leaves and then returns, the child may become angry and push her away, exhibiting a so-called *resistant attachment.* Another form of insecure attachment is seen in babies who are unresponsive to the mother when they enter a strange situation and express no emotion when she leaves. When the mother returns, the child still may not respond to her. This form of insecure attachment is called an *avoidant attachment.*

Not surprisingly, the way in which caretakers relate to their children affects their behavior in the strange situation. Those parents who are sensitive and responsive, who talk and play with their infants, are more likely than others to have a secure child (Ainsworth, 1993; Isabella, 1993). Indeed, some researchers have argued that the strange situation test is valid only for children from stable families, who have been raised to respond appropriately in the situation (Lamb, 1985). If so, we might expect to find cultural differences in the way children respond to the strange situation test.

strange situation test A procedure used to study attachment, in which an infant is placed in a novel environment and is observed reacting to it in the presence and then absence of a caregiver.

Cross-Cultural Differences in Attachment. As Figure 11.13 shows, babies from Germany, Japan, and the United States react differently to the strange situation test. Compared to children in the United States, fewer Japanese babies show an avoidant attachment, while substantially more German babies do (van IJzendoorn & Kroonenberg, 1988). Does their behavior reflect cultural differences or genetic predispositions? One interpretation of the avoidant attachment often seen in German babies is that German parents reinforce their children for exhibiting independent behavior (Grossman, Grossman, Spangler, Suess, & Unzner, 1985), perhaps by allowing clinging behaviors to extinguish, or by withholding physical contact in response to clinging. Figure 11.13 also shows that more Japanese babies than German or American babies display a resistant attachment. Because Japanese mothers typically do not leave their babies in unfamiliar surroundings, these babies become very upset when they are placed in a strange situation. One lesson of Figure 11.13 is that different cultures have different expectations of their offspring, and reinforce and punish children so as to encourage the expected behavior. We should not be surprised when their children behave as they do.

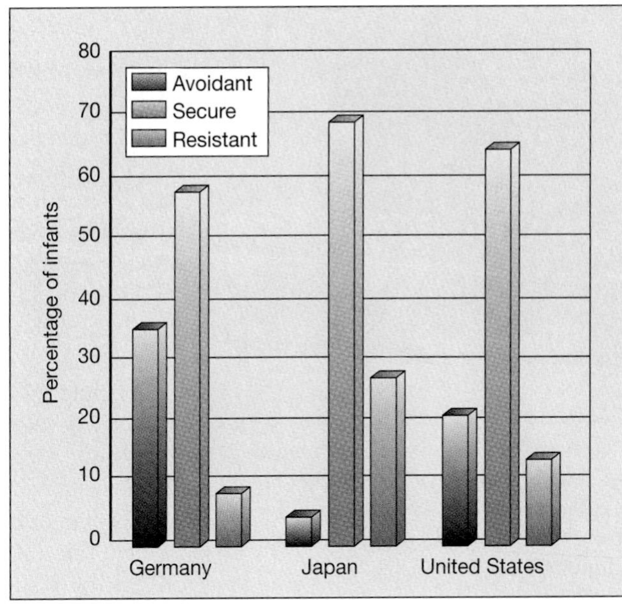

Figure 11.13 **Cross-cultural responses to the strange situation test.** The majority of babies from Japan, Germany, and the United States are securely attached to their mothers. In comparison with American children, however, Japanese babies show more resistant attachment, and German babies show more avoidant attachment. *Source:* Modified from van Ijzendoorn & Kroonenberg, 1988.

Temperament. We have seen that cultural differences influence a child's developmental processes. Could genetic differences influence a child's response to different environments? In particular, might a child's innate temperament influence both how that child interacts with caretakers and how he or she responds to the strange situation test? **Temperament**, which is defined as a trait that is characterized by the quality and intensity of an individual's emotional reactions, is a stable, though not immutable, aspect of personality. According to some researchers, temperament "modulate(s) the expression of activity, reactivity, emotionality, and sociability" (Goldsmith et al., 1987). The biological basis of temperament is apparent in infancy and is a measurable feature of adult personality (Kagan, 1994).

Earlier (page 89) we saw that studies of fearfulness in cocker spaniels and basenji hounds indicate that the trait is likely due to a single-gene effect (Scott & Fuller, 1965). Researchers have also studied shyness in human beings, through assessments of sociability in monozygotic and dyzygotic twins, cross-cultural comparisons, and behavioral and physiological measures. They have discovered that sociability scores are more similar in monozygotic than in dyzygotic twins (Bouchard, Lykken, McGue, Segal, & Tellegen, 1990; Plomin, 1994). In addition, for reasons that are not understood, shyness is related to certain physical traits: People with thin faces, blue eyes, and hay fever tend to be shy (Arcus & Kagan, 1995). Yet culture is also important in the expression of personality traits. Japanese and Chinese infants are calmer, and recover more quickly when stressed (Kagan et al., 1994), than Western infants. Asian cultures value and reinforce calm behavior starting at birth. Both distal and proximal causes, then, probably account for cross-cultural differences in personality traits.

LINK
Temperament in dogs, Chapter 3, p. 89

The relationship between shyness and physiology is not clear-cut. In the strange situation test, shy children showed the physiological changes associated with crying—pupillary dilation, increased heart rate, and muscle tension (Kagan & Snidman, 1991, 1992). And 18-month-old children who showed pronounced fearfulness and insecure attachment in the strange situation test had higher levels of cortisol (a hormone associated with stress) than other children (Gunnar, Tout, de Haan, & Pierce, 1997). These differences in cortisol levels did not persist in follow-up studies that began 2 months later, however. The long-term physiological consequences of shyness, if any, are unknown.

temperament A trait that is characterized by the quality and intensity of an individual's emotional reactions.

The brains and cognitive development of children who have been allowed to explore complex environments differ from those of children raised in less-stimulating environments.

Early Childhood

When toddlers begin to actively explore their environment, they enter the second stage of psychosocial development, *autonomy versus shame and doubt* (see Table 11.4). In their early social interactions with caretakers, they learn that their behavior produces outcomes that may be reinforced, punished, or ignored. From these interactions, a child develops certain expectations. Erickson proposed that in this stage, parental praise for early exploration and manipulation of the environment produces feelings of self-worth and autonomy in the child. For example, a child may take apart and crumple an old newspaper. The parent's response can either affirm the child's behavior or make the child feel she or he has done something wrong—a reaction that produces shame and self-doubt.

As children approach puberty, they go through two more stages in their psychosocial development. As Table 11.4 shows, the best outcome of the initiative-versus-guilt identity crisis is that a child develops a conscience and begins to assume responsibility for his or her own behavior. A child who *resists* expectations of independent behavior may experience guilt and anxiety. Again, the social environment the child encounters is the determining factor. A mother or father may tie a 6-year-old's shoes to save time, or because child-tied shoes too often come undone. Their behavior may foster feelings of inadequacy and incompetency in the child, as well as guilt in the presence of peers who can tie their own shoes.

In most cultures around the world, the psychosocial development of children from age 5 through puberty is heavily influenced by their school performance. Getting good grades, making friends, and developing musical or athletic skills all contribute to a child's sense of competency, and the appropriate resolution of the competency-versus-inferiority identity crisis. The child who is not competent at these tasks may develop feelings of inferiority. Again, a supportive social environment that encourages performance at the highest level of a person's ability—one that reinforces age-appropriate behaviors—helps a child to successfully resolve the crisis.

Reinforcement and social learning theory, Chapter 6, p. 215

Because cultures differ in the way they socialize children, however, a successful resolution in Western culture may not be seen as such in a non-Western culture. For example, cultures differ in the extent to which they value *individualism* as opposed to *collectivism* (Hofstede, 1983; Triandis, 1995). Those cultures that value individualism stress self-reliance, independence, and autonomy, whereas those that value *inter*dependence stress collective success, cooperation, and social harmony. In heavily industrialized countries such as the United States, Canada, and Western Europe, most people tend to rank high on scales of individualism. Chinese and Native Americans, members of collective cultures, tend to rank high on scales of interdependence. In one study, for instance, American students were found more likely than others to describe themselves by reference to their personal traits, whereas Chinese students were more likely to refer to their group affiliations (Trafimow et al., 1991).

One implication of these cultural differences is that success in school can be motivated in two different ways. Children may be reinforced for their individual class ranking—how they stack up against the competition—or for bringing honor to the group (both other students and the family).

Adolescence and Adulthood

Puberty lasts from the preteens to the college years, making adolescent socialization a long and varied process. Erikson (1968) saw adolescence as a time of psychological turmoil, because both societal demands and life choices become more complicated during this stage. A child must not only begin to assume an adult role, but also choose from a multitude of role models. Parents who fail to practice what they preach during this stage present a confusing role model ("My parents drink; why shouldn't I?"). Often, the adolescent's response is to try out different identities.

Erikson called this developmental dilemma the crisis of *identity versus role confusion*. Research shows that in this stage, "parents matter less than you think and peers matter more" (Harris, 1998). For that reason, adolescents may explore their identity by smoking cigarettes and drinking alcohol (Paikoff & Brooks-Gunn, 1991).

An adolescent's search for identity need not lead to conflict with parents; in fact, conflict is the exception rather than the rule. To a remarkable degree, factors that contribute to adolescents' identity, such as their religious, political, and social views, reflect the views of their parents. The choice of continuing to live at home or away, of going to college or getting a job, also helps to determine a person's identity. Eventually, a young person's identity becomes stable. Not surprisingly, college seniors report a clearer sense of identity than first-year college students (Waterman, 1988).

In early adulthood, adolescence merges (often indistinguishably) into Erikson's sixth stage, *intimacy versus isolation*. In this stage, the crisis is a conflict between the need for intimacy with others and the need to be alone. Intimacy is often expressed through friendship, dating, and sexual behavior, discussed in detail in Chapter 15. And yet adult development doesn't end with marriage or a long-term relationship. All too quickly, 30-something turns into the less-than-glamorous ages of 40, 50, and then 60. During this long period, some people experience a midlife crisis that Erikson called *generativity versus stagnation*. "Is my job (or marriage) a meaningful one," they ask themselves, "or am I just going through the motions?"

Interestingly, research has *not* supported the widespread existence of a midlife crisis, which has become a common theme of popular magazines and television shows. In one study, for example, researchers looked for signs of dissatisfaction with family life, work, and social relationships. They found no significant increase in turmoil and emotional instability in people of middle age, compared with those in their mid-thirties (McCrae & Costa, 1990).

The sense of mortality begins to loom large in old age, and with it, nagging doubts about life's meaning. In this stage, questions about the worth of one's life work are replaced with questions about the worth of life itself. In Erikson's terms (see Table 11.4), this final crisis is one of *personal integrity versus despair*. Rather than thinking "I play a meaningful role in my family and the community," some elders may conclude bitterly, "I've done my bit. Let someone else do it; I no longer care." Illness and the death of loved ones contribute to despair in later life. As those around them begin to die, the aged are confronted more and more with their own mortality.

Bereavement: The Loss of Attachment

Just as attachment helps to define the human condition, so does *bereavement*—the loss of an attachment through the death of a child, a parent, or another loved one. In fact, the loss of a child or parent is often the worst experience of a lifetime (Stillion, 1995). Like attachment, the grieving process that accompanies bereavement is part of human nature. Cross-culturally, everyone experiences both attachment and bereavement.

Although the cultural forms of bereavement differ, they generally include three distinct psychological processes, or stages of grieving: *avoidance, confrontation,* and *accommodation* (Bowlby, 1980; Rando, 1995). Avoidance is characterized by a disbelief, profound sadness, and incomprehension that may last for a few hours or in some, a few weeks. In the confrontation stage, the bereaved person confronts the reality of the loved one's absence. This stage is characterized by feelings of helplessness, anger, frustration, and abandonment; by a preoccupation with memories of the deceased; and by reduced concentration, loss of appetite, and sleep disturbance. Over time, confrontation leads to the final stage, accommodation. The reality of life without the deceased becomes familiar, and the grieving person slowly resumes a normal life.

INTERIM SUMMARY

1. Although human fathers are more involved with their young than males of other species, around the world, mothers tend to have more contact than fathers with their infants and children.
2. Erik Erikson's eight *psychosocial stages* provide a framework for understanding the development of a person's *identity,* or perception of self. Each stage is characterized as an *identity crisis,* the resolution of which determines the person's psychosocial development.
3. Successful ***attachment***—a strong and enduring emotional bond between parent and child—leads to the development of *trust* and hopeful expectations that can generalize to other individuals.
4. A caregiver who feeds, protects, and provides *contact comfort* to an infant promotes *pair bonding* (another name for attachment). In monkeys and probably humans, pair bonding is related to the infant's adult development.
5. John Bowlby's four phases of attachment include the *preattachment* phase (birth to 6 weeks), the *attachment-in-the-making* phase (6 weeks to 6 to 8 months), *clear-cut attachment* (6 to 8 months to about 18 months), and *reciprocal attachment* (18 months to 2 years and beyond).
6. In Ainsworth's ***strange situation test,*** a child is placed in an unfamiliar room, and researchers note the child's response to the mother's presence and absence. A child who explores the room confidently in mom's presence is thought to exhibit a *secure attachment.*
7. Insecure attachment has two forms, *resistant attachment* (the child becomes angry when the mother returns after leaving the strange situation) and *avoidant attachment* (the child expresses no emotion when the mother leaves and returns).
8. In industrialized countries, most children show a secure attachment. But German children exhibit more avoidant attachment, and Japanese children, more resistant attachment, than others, probably because of their caretakers' cultural expectations.
9. ***Temperament*** refers to the quality and intensity of a person's innate emotional reactions to others.
10. According to Erikson's theory of psychosocial development, toddlers resolve the identity crisis of *autonomy versus shame* through interactions with their caregivers. By promoting children's feelings of independence and self-worth, caretakers then help them to resolve the initiative-versus-guilt and competency-versus-inferiority identity crises.
11. Adolescence is a time of psychological turmoil that Erikson characterizes as a crisis of *identity versus role confusion.* Adolescents often adopt religious, political, and social views that are similar to their parents' views.
12. The intimacy-versus-isolation crisis young adults face is characterized by the conflict between the need to be alone with the need for human closeness.
13. From their mid-30s to mid-50s, most people report that they are satisfied with their jobs, families, and social relationships. According to Erikson, they should be experiencing the crisis of *generativity versus stagnation.*
14. The last stage of psychosocial development, *integrity versus despair,* typically includes bereavement over the death of a loved one. People of all cultures experience the three stages of grieving: *avoidance, confrontation,* and *accommodation.*

For Further Thought

1. Do you think that insecure attachments are due more to the infant's or the caregiver's behavior?
2. According to Erikson, what happens to a child who experiences no personal success in the classroom, athletics, the performing arts, and so forth? What are the implications for the design of curricular and extracurricular activities in elementary schools?
3. Given all the confusion, rebellion, and searching that occur during the teen years, why do you think most young people adopt the religious, political, and social values of their parents?
4. Waterman's (1988) research on identity crises in college students suggested that seniors had resolved their issues better than first-year students. Do you think he would have found the same results for those of the same age who did not attend college?
5. Few would argue with the viewpoint that attachment is adaptive. What about bereavement?

CONCLUDING THOUGHTS

Throughout the human life cycle, genes and environment interact to guide human behavior in adaptive ways. Children learn to look before crossing the street; to count, read, and write; and to observe basic rules of social behavior. Young adults mature, become self-sufficient, and begin to look for a mate. Such adaptive behavior promotes fitness and the continuation of the life cycle through the creation of more offspring.

One of the more remarkable facts of nature—and nurture—is that human beings begin their existence as a single cell, yet ultimately achieve an almost unimaginable physical and psychological complexity. The human genotype contains recipes for brain and behavior development; the environment adds the ingredients and does the cooking. The recipes may be faulty, as happens with a mutated gene, in which case the developing human may not turn out as well as hoped. The environment may be faulty, as in the case of fetal exposure to alcohol or other teratogens; again, the developing human may have problems. But if all goes well, over a 38-week period, a single cell will divide, grow, and develop, culminating in the birth of a normal child.

The mind begins to develop while the child is still a fetus. The sense organs develop, as do their connections to the brain. The motor systems develop, causing reflexive arm and leg movements. With this basic sensory-motor apparatus in place, the fetus begins to react to its surroundings. It swallows amniotic fluid, detects vibrations through the mother's stomach, and hears the outside world well enough to recognize different voices.

A newborn's mind reflects both an innate brain organization and responsivity to its new environment. The newborn sees forms and is especially sensitive to the visual characteristics of the human face. Newborns mimic what they see, cry when they are hungry, and suckle and swallow when they are stimulated by the smell, temperature, and tactile properties of a nipple.

According to Piaget, childhood cognitive development unfolds in four stages. By seeing, touching, grasping, and moving, a very young child forms a basic impression of the world. With further development, the child learns that objects exist even when they cannot be seen and begins to solve simple thought problems. Yet the very young child cannot take another person's perspective or conserve volume, mass, or number when the appearance of an object changes. These cognitive abilities, and the ability to think logically, appear in later childhood. Finally, with a boost from caretakers in a supportive environment, the adolescent child develops abstract thinking and conceptual abilities. Moral reasoning unfolds in a similar manner, beginning with a concern for "not getting into trouble" and culminating after many years, in some individuals, in abstract thinking about universal ethical principles. Near the end of life, some changes in memory and thinking occur. Older adults do not learn new names quickly and may need to rely on memory aids, but they retain language and cultural information well.

Erikson proposed that from infancy through adulthood, people experience eight identity crises during eight psychosocial stages. Social and emotional development begin with the infant's attachment to a caretaker, the first stage in the process of socialization. Whether an infant develops a secure or avoidant attachment depends on both its temperament and the goals and cultural expectations of its caretakers. During subsequent development, children's identities reflect varying degrees of autonomy, personal initiative, independence, and self-worth, again as a function both of the child's temperament and of the caretakers' child-rearing practices.

Adolescent social development is characterized by a search for personal identity, which is influenced by the value systems and behaviors of both peers and parents. Most people learn the values and social beliefs of their parents, which typically reflect the dominant cultural beliefs and practices. During adolescence and early adulthood, socialization typically includes the development of a sexual identity, attraction to others, courtship, reproduction, and the care of offspring. According to Erikson, older adults face a midlife crisis based on a conflict between generativity and stagnation, yet most such adults report satisfaction with their families, social relationships, and careers. Those who are approaching the end of the life cycle face the crisis of maintaining integrity in the face of despair. This stage typically includes bereavement, a universal response to the death of a loved one. Bereavement has three stages: *avoidance, confrontation,* and *accommodation*. That humans eventually resume a more or less normal life after the loss of a loved one is testimony to the strength of the human spirit and an intuitive understanding of the meaning of the life cycle.

KEY TERMS

accommodation *392*
assimilation *392*
attachment *405*
cognitive development *392*
concrete operational stage *395*
conservation *394*
crystallized intelligence *400*
fetal alcohol syndrome (FAS) *383*
fluid intelligence *400*
formal operational stage *396*
human development *380*
object permanence *393*
preoperational stage *394*
sensorimotor stage *392*
strange situation test *406*
temperament *407*

12 Language and Thought

Phillip Taaffe (b. 1955) *Passionale per Circulum Anni* 1993–1994, mixed media on canvas, sight: 137 1/4 × 116 in. (348.6 × 294.6 cm). Purchase, with funds from the Painting and Sculpture Committee and the Ruth and Seymour M. Klein Foundation, with additional funding from Sandra and Gerald Fineberg and Linda and Harry Macklowe. 94.68. Photograph copyright © 1997: Whitney Museum of American Art, New York.

The Origins and Nature of Human Language

Why Language Evolved
Brain Organization, Handedness, and Language
Language Areas in the Human Brain
Brain Damage and Language Loss: The Aphasias
Interim Summary
For Further Thought

Communication and the Question of Animal "Language"

Animal Communication
Communicating with Porpoises and Dolphins
Connecting with Chimpanzees and Gorillas
Talking with Alex, the Parrot
Human and Animal Language Compared
Interim Summary
For Further Thought

How Children Acquire Language

First Sounds: Crying
Cooing, Babbling, and Pointing
First Words
Parental Encouragement of Language Acquisition
The Growth of Vocabulary and Appearance of Grammar
A Critical Period for Language Acquisition?
Interim Summary
For Further Thought

Thinking Without Language

Thinking in Nonspeaking Humans and Nonhuman Animals
Problem Solving
Generating Solutions to Problems
Means-End Analyses
Insight
Interim Summary
For Further Thought

Thinking with Language

The Influence of Language on Perception and Thought
The Linguistic Relativity Hypothesis
The Effect of Mental Set on Problem Solving
Types of Thinking
Word Problems
Interim Summary
For Further Thought

Concluding Thoughts

First words are among the great pleasures a child bestows on parents. As the father of four children, I breathed a sigh of relief each time these words appeared, like clockwork, between 9 and 12 months of age. The appearance of language is a sign of a healthy child who will likely continue to develop normally.

At 17 months of age, my daughter Jane's 16-word vocabulary included the word *pup-pee.* I had been counting her words every few months, but at 17 months, the growth of her vocabulary was so rapid that I gave up counting. Together we turned the pages of her picture books, and she responded "pup-pee" to any picture of a cow, horse, dog, or even, for a while, an elephant. Apparently, all brown, fuzzy animals—and some others—fit under her umbrella term *puppy*.

Soon Jane learned to distinguish a rhinoceros from an elephant. As she rapidly acquired words over the next few months, she began to correctly apply the word *dog* to both real dogs and pictures of dogs. *Puppy* became a word that was restricted to small, young dogs with certain "cute" characteristics. A year or so later, *puppy* became a word in a sentence: "I want a puppy." After another year, blending logic, emotion, and charm, Jane was using many words and gestures to convince her parents that in addition to the kitty she had, she simply *had* to have a pony. Her sophisticated use of language revealed a keen mind filled with many thoughts. Like others, she was adaptively learning to use language to her own advantage.

Language is a form of communication. Though many animals communicate with each other, humans seem to be the only ones with brains that are uniquely organized to communicate intentions and ideas related to the past, the present, and the future. The adaptive advantages of speech to a species are quite obvious: With language, a child can tell a parent about a headache or ask for a snack; a student can answer a history professor's question, and one president can try to convince another that missiles must be removed from Cuba. Given its unique role in human behavior and culture, most educated people consider language to be the distinctive, defining characteristic of *Homo sapiens.* Language makes humans the highly social animals they are, allowing them to share their perceptual and emotional experiences with others—parents and children, teachers and customers, friends, even presidents.

In this chapter we'll compare human communication with animal communication and identify the brain structures that support language in humans. We'll consider in detail how language develops and how it is related to thinking. In the process we'll discover that language is not synonymous with thinking. Even before Jane said the word *puppy,* she responded to words in a way that indicated that she was aware of their meaning—that she was thinking. In the last two sections we'll examine the differences between thinking with language and thinking without it.

THE ORIGINS AND NATURE OF HUMAN LANGUAGE

Human language has been described both as a biological adaptation and as a cultural invention. Based on an analysis of animal communication systems and on comparative brain studies, the psychologist Steven Pinker has described language as a human instinct (Pinker, 1994), a biologically based adaptation that is similar in many respects to other animals' communication systems. From Pinker's nativist perspective, then, language is a genetically predisposed behavior with a long evolutionary history. But while humans communicate with one another like other animals, using pheromones and visual displays—so-called body language—their principle method of communication is spoken language. In this respect, language can be thought of as *Homo sapiens'* most important meme, the very basis of human culture.

Communication by pheromone, Chapter 7, p. 259

The word *language* comes from the Latin word *lingua,* meaning "tongue." One's native tongue is the language of one's birth. Around the world, humans speak an estimated 5,000 to 7,000 languages, about 4,000 to 5,000 of them classified as indigenous languages, which linguists have grouped into about a dozen families, called *parent languages*. The largest family of languages is Indo-European. Sanskrit, Gaelic, Farsi, Latin, Greek, and English are all Indo-European languages, descended from the same original language over the past seven thousand years. All Indo-European languages have the same structure, based on common parts of speech and similar inflections, or changes in pitch and tone of voice.

Languages are dynamic; the English language is changing as we speak. Twenty years ago the phrase *world wide web (WWW)* did not exist. Thirty generations from now, our spoken English will likely be as foreign to our descendents as Medieval English sounds to us now. The dynamic nature of language is adaptive, allowing humans to respond to rapid cultural changes. Let's look at some theories of how and why human language evolved.

Why Language Evolved

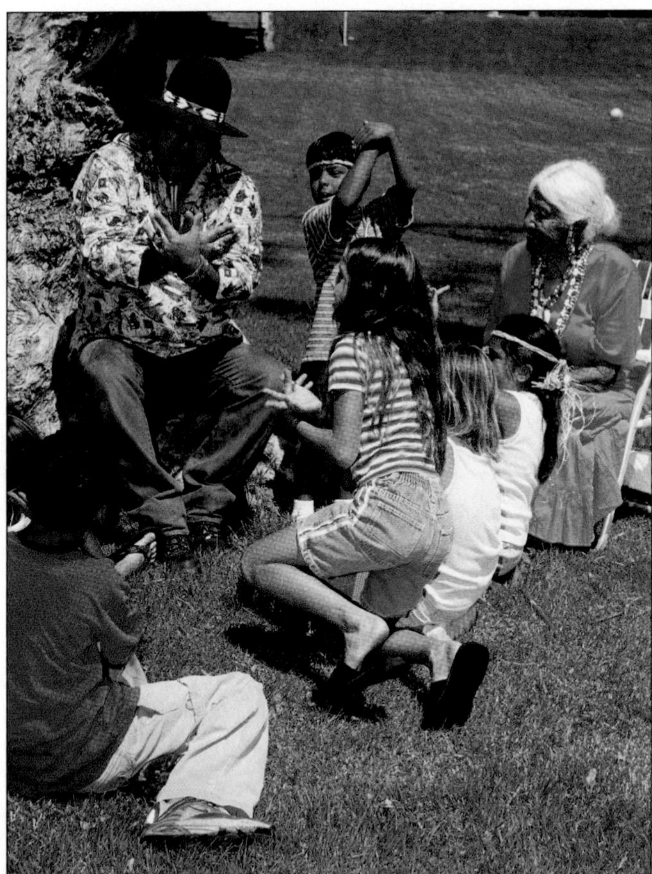

One function of language is to help people form social groups. Humans have transmitted their cultural memes through the spoken word for 100,000 to 200,000 years.

In the movie *Quest for Fire,* primitive hominids were characterized as having limited language capabilities. In one- and two-word utterances, these 500,000-year-old almost-humans named objects and signaled their actions and intentions. Although the movie was fictional, its characterization of early humans agreed with the tenets of evolutionary psychology. Because language does not fossilize, we have no record of its origins. Yet even in the absence of spoken evidence, scientists assume that human language evolved, presumably from simple to complex forms.

According to the theory of natural selection, language evolved because it afforded those individuals who used it a selective advantage over those who didn't. One scenario is that language was a social adaptation that solved the problem of cooperative communication (Knight, 2000). The generation of "sounds with meaning" would have furthered the learning of cultural memes such as food sources, food preparation, habitat management, the use of natural medicines, and features of local geography (Studdert-Kennedy, Hurford, & Knight, 2000). According to this hypothesis, language would have aided migration and group hunting and facilitated tool making. Such information would have been passed down the generations through songs, stories, tools, and art forms.

A slightly different hypothesis is that language evolved because it was an efficient way to organize groups (Dunbar, 1993). That is, language served a primarily social function. In this view, when hunter-gatherer bands of 30 to 50 (usually related) protohumans organized into tribes of 500 to 2,500 individuals, their survival was enhanced. According to this hypothesis, brain size, group size, and language evolved together, beginning about 250,000 years ago. At first, language supported social exchanges, beginning with mutual grooming and vocalizations and progressing to gossip. Symbolic language would not have appeared until about 40,000 to 50,000 years ago (Broadfield, Holloway, Mowbray, Silvers, & Marquez, 2001; Dunbar, 1993). Thus, the problem solving and intricate grammar that characterizes modern language can be thought of as a by-product of social activity (Fouts, 1991). Indeed, most people today talk primarily about social relationships; even among students, few spend much time talking about abstract ideas (Dunbar, 1993).

A third theory of the evolution of language stresses a three-stage cognitive transformation, from prelanguage through protolanguage and speech to reading and writing (Donald, 1993). According to this view, the prelanguage stage involved two skills that only humans can accomplish, *mimesis,* and *voluntary retrievability*. Mimesis is the skilled, rhythmic movement that comes about through practice, as in dancing. Voluntary retrievability is the basis for conscious control over muscles and memories (Donald, 1993). In this stage, *Homo erectus* began to make tools, which may be evidence of "a mind that sees in advance." That is, given a rock, *Homo erectus* could imagine it having a sharp edge that could be used to cut another object, and through trial and error, could learn the motor skills needed to produce the imagined tool.

The second stage, protolanguage to speech, was characterized by *lexical invention,* a process in which sounds acquired specific meanings. In this stage, protohumans discovered they had vocal cords and a brain that provided a fast, portable "phonological apparatus." *Homo erectus,* who lived 1.8 million years ago, was likely capable of memorizing one- and two-word utterances and applying them in appropriate situations. *Homo sapiens* had about 50,000 years to refine this language invention. In fact, language-enhanced consciousness may have provided a selective advantage to *Homo sapiens,* enabling them to displace *Homo Neanderthal.* Certainly, enhanced consciousness would have given these humans a better understanding of their world and improved their ability to solve problems related to survival and reproduction (Donald, 1993).

The third stage, reading and writing, occurred over the last 10,000 years. This new form of language allowed for external memory *storage* (writing) and *retrieval* (reading) of useful information. However, reading and writing may have come at a cost. Many millions of cortical neurons may have evolved for other uses, such as learning and remembering the appearance of thousands of plants and animals, predicting seasonal changes, and remembering migration patterns, to name but a few selective pressures. Many of those neurons may have been coopted to support the demands of literacy.

Brain Organization, Handedness, and Language

As Sue Savage-Rumbaugh, a researcher who works with primates, has pointed out, language *receptivity* precedes language *productivity* in humans as well as chimpanzees. In the course of evolution, she suggests, receptivity likely preceded productivity. Her analysis is consistent within the evolution of different parts of the brain, which today fit together to form a kind of mosaic. That is, some parts of the brain seem to have evolved to receive sensory signals and others to cause movement (Rachlin, 1995; Wilkins & Wakefield, 1995). Somehow, language emerged from this *mosaic organization* (McArthur, 1995). Our nonhuman ancestors made vibrating sounds by pushing air past a tongue and lips that had evolved for other reasons.

In an attempt to probe the origins of human language, researchers have compared the organization of the human brain—especially the left hemisphere—with the brains of other living primates. Peter MacNeilage of the University of Texas at Austin, among others, has investigated the relationship of handedness and language (MacNeilage, 1991). Why, he asks, does the left hemisphere (which controls the right hand) also contain the brain areas that are specialized for speech? MacNeilage studied the brains and behavior of tree shrews, living descendants of the most primitive primates. He found that the right hemisphere of these animals' brains is specialized for postural control—holding onto a limb with the left hand, for example. MacNeilage speculated that this ancient adaptation freed the left hemisphere for the production of communicative gestures, such as pointing.

Referential pointing, or the extension of the right hand and finger(s) to indicate an object in the environment, is considered a form of nonverbal communication in both humans (Butterworth & Morissette, 1996; Harris, Barlow-Brown, & Chasin, 1995) and nonhumans (Hewes, 1992; Leavens, Hopkins, & Bard, 1996). A left hemisphere that supported communication through pointing and gesturing with the right hand could have provided the basis for productive and receptive language. Researchers have found a brain area in monkeys that is similar to the speech production area in the human brain (Arbib & Rizzolatti, 1996). In the monkey's brain, this area links the sensation of seeing an object with the motor skill of grasping the object with the right hand. Nearby *mirror neurons* in the frontal cortex fire both during the performance of a task and while the monkey (Gallese & Goldman, 1998) or human (Buccino, Gallese, & Rizzolatti, 2001) watches someone else perform the same task.

referential pointing Extension of the right hand and index finger to call attention to an object in the environment.

Two and a half million years ago, our ancestors' brains had evolved sufficiently to allow them to use tools. A case can be made that the left hemisphere of the brain, which is involved in tool making and language production and reception, was already specialized by that time (Ambrose, 2001; Bradshaw, 1991). For example, the planum temporale, part of the temporal lobe that includes the receptive language areas in humans (see Figure 12.1), is larger in the left than in the right hemisphere. Recently, scientists reported that in both the chimpanzee's brain (Gannon, Holloway, Broadfield, & Braun, 1998) and a reconstructed brain from a 400,000-year-old (pre-*Homo sapiens*) cranium (Broadfield et al., 2001), the planum temporale is larger in the left hemisphere than in the right.

Our common ancestor with chimps lived about 7 million years ago, suggesting that for millions of years humans have had brain areas that would support some form of protolanguage. Cortical neurons in the planum temporale develop rapidly during the first 2 years of human life, allowing a child to point, manipulate objects, use tools, and begin to speak (Greenfield, 1991).

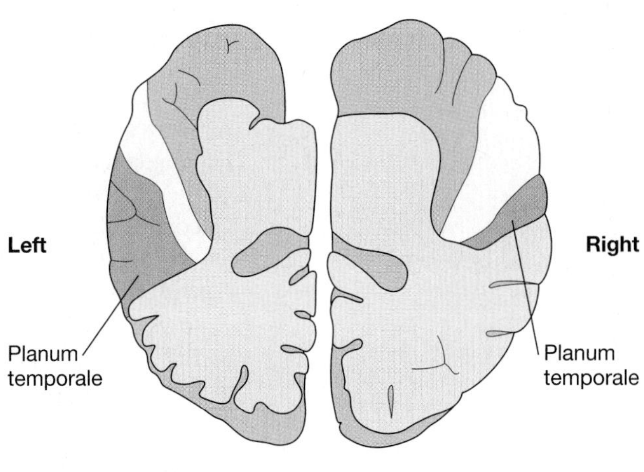

Figure 12.1 **The planum temporale.** In both chimpanzees and humans, the planum temporale is larger in the left than in the right hemisphere. This diagram shows a cross-section about midway from the top of the human brain.

Language Areas in the Human Brain

We saw in Chapter 4 that the human brain is *lateralized,* meaning that the left and right cerebral hemispheres have different functions. Split-brain investigations, wada tests, and other evidence have demonstrated that in about 99 percent of all right-handed people, primary language abilities—both speaking and understanding language—are located in the left hemisphere. Figure 12.2 shows the language areas that have been found in the human brain. *Wernicke's area,* named

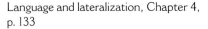

Language and lateralization, Chapter 4, p. 133

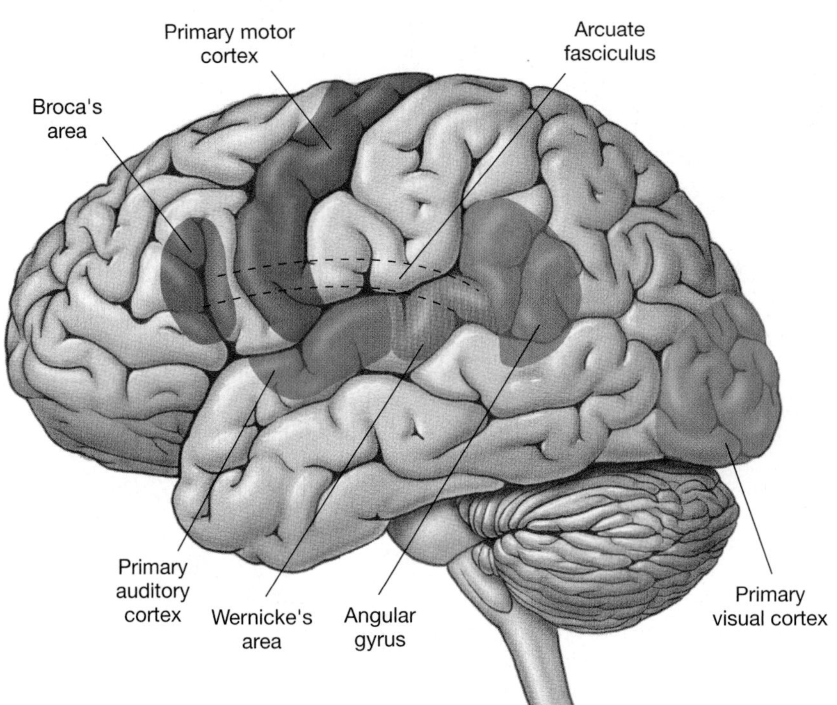

Figure 12.2 **Language areas of the brain.** This diagram shows the left hemisphere, where the language centers are located in most humans. Language involves both the primary auditory and visual cortex (for hearing and reading) and the primary motor cortex (for moving the lips and tongue). Wernicke's area, in the primary auditory cortex, is involved in understanding the language one hears; Broca's area, near the primary motor cortex, is involved in spoken language. These two areas are connected by the arcuate fasciculus. The angular gyrus, located near the visual cortex, is necessary for reading language. *Source:* Pinel, p. 426.

after the researcher who discovered that this area of the brain was damaged in patients with specific language disabilities, is located in the planum temporale in the left temporal lobe, adjacent to the primary auditory cortex. **Wernicke's area** allows humans to attach meaning to what they hear; it is the center of receptive language.

Broca's area is found in the left frontal lobe, adjacent to the primary motor cortex. **Broca's area** is involved in speaking. A hidden bundle of nerves called the *arcuate fasciculus* connects the language comprehension area (Wernicke's area) with the language production area (Broca's area). An intact arcuate fasciculus allows a person to easily and reliably connect language that is heard and read with the ability to talk about it. Damage to the parietal lobe, through which the arcuate fasciculus courses, causes a *conduction aphasia,* or the inability to repeat what one has just heard.

Other brain structures in the left hemisphere support the connection of visual symbols with language. For example, the visual cortex allows a person to see printed words. As Figure 12.2 shows, the *angular gyrus* connects the primary visual cortex with Wernicke's area. The angular gyrus is a visual area that is specialized for associating visual symbols with their meaning. It allows humans to translate and attach meaning to printed words. A person who has sustained damage to the angular gyrus can see and understand spoken language, but cannot make sense out of what he or she reads.

Brain Damage and Language Loss: The Aphasias

Language and brain damage, Chapter 4, p. 127

Among the most tragic kinds of brain damage are those that produce **aphasia,** the partial or complete loss of language abilities. We have seen that a conduction aphasia results from injury to the arcuate fasciculus, and that a person with a damaged angular gyrus can see but cannot read. Two other types of injury to the left hemisphere can also result in aphasia. People who have sustained an injury to Wernicke's area suffer from *Wernicke's aphasia.* Though they can hear sounds

This picture was shown to aphasia patients. People with Broca's aphasia had trouble generating phrases and sentences with which to describe the action in the picture. People with Wernicke's aphasia could generate words, but could not explain what was going on.

Wernicke's area The area in the left temporal lobe that is involved in understanding spoken and written language.

Broca's area The portion of the left frontal lobe that is involved in speaking.

aphasia A partial or complete loss of language abilities following brain damage.

and speak, they cannot use language in a meaningful way. Conversely, people who have sustained damage to Broca's area can understand language, but have difficulty producing fluent language, a disorder called *Broca's aphasia.* In Chapter 4 we learned that Phineas Gage suffered brain damage to the frontal lobes from a tamping rod. Had this accident damaged Broca's area, Gage would have had difficulty generating language and speaking in a meaningful way. Because Gage's ability to communicate through language was spared, we know that neither Wernicke's area nor Broca's area was damaged.

To better understand and remember these two different types of aphasia, read aloud the following descriptions given by two different brain-injured patients in response to a picture shown to them (see the picture on the preceding page). Which patient do you think had suffered damage to Wernicke's area, and which damage to Broca's area?

> **Patient 1:** "Well this is . . . mother is away here working her work out o' here to get her better, but when she's looking, the two boys look in the other part. One their small tile into her time here. She's working another time because she's getting to. So two boys work together and one is sneaking' around here, making his work an' his further *funnas* his time he had." (pp. 81–82, Goodlass & Kaplan, 1983)

> **Patient 2:** "Cookie jar . . . fall over . . . chair . . . water . . . empty." (Goodglass & Kaplan, 1983, p. 76)

The first patient, number 1, exhibited Wernicke's aphasia, whereas the second suffered from Broca's aphasia. The first patient could generate words, but could not describe the action shown in the picture. This type of language has been called a *word salad;* it sounds relatively normal but is incomprehensible. The second patient had difficulty generating the syntactically correct phrases and sentences found in normal language.

INTERIM SUMMARY

1. Though the evolution of language is lost in prehistory, it presumably increased human fitness by facilitating the transmission of memes about foods, local habitats, and essential information from one generation to the next.
2. According to one theory, the evolution of language promoted social organization and social harmony. Language began with social exchanges between individuals, then progressed to gossip and later symbolic language.
3. According to another view, language was one stage in the three-stage development of a distinctively human mind. The process began with mimesis, followed by speaking and then by reading and writing.
4. The brain's language areas evolved from a *mosaic organization* of preexisting brain structures. Some brain structures are sensitive to sounds; others control the motor systems involved in the movement of fingers, hands, lips, and tongue.
5. The common ancestor of primates likely had a left hemisphere that evolved to communicate through **referential pointing**—use of the right hand to grab, gesture, and point.
6. In both humans and chimpanzees, the left temporal lobe contains a larger planum temporale than the right temporal lobe. The left planum temporale is involved in tool use and language.
7. The left temporal lobe contains ***Wernicke's area***, a brain part that is involved in hearing and understanding spoken language.
8. The left frontal lobe includes ***Broca's area***, which is involved in generating spoken language.
9. The *arcuate fasciculus* connects the language comprehension area (Wernicke's area) with the language production area (Broca's area).
10. The *angular gyrus* connects the visual brain with the language reception area, allowing a person to read words.

11. Damage to the language areas of the brain produces a condition called **aphasia**—the partial or complete loss of language abilities.
12. A person with *Broca's aphasia* can understand language, but has difficulty producing fluent language. A person with *Wernicke's aphasia* can hear but cannot understand words.

For Further Thought

1. Why do *you* think language evolved?
2. Why do you think humans spend so much time gossiping?
3. A person who had been diagnosed as having Wernicke's aphasia was shown the photo on page 418, but could not describe in words what he saw. What part of the brain other than Wernicke's area might have been damaged?
4. Do you agree with Dunbar (1993) that most human language concerns social relationships? Think of people you know who may differ in this regard. Can you think of any substantive differences in the way males and females use language?
5. Can you think of exceptions to Donald's (1993) assertion that humans are the only animals that consciously practice to improve their performance of a skilled act?

COMMUNICATION AND THE QUESTION OF ANIMAL "LANGUAGE"

Birds sing and snakes hiss, but are they talking? Scientists who study these issues often distinguish between animal *communication* and animal *language*. Many animals, including humans, communicate with *conspecifics*, or members of the same species. **Animal communication** typically involves both the production and reception of signals that are meaningful only to conspecifics (Bradbury & Vehrencamp, 1998). Such signals include pheromones and visual displays as well as vocalizations. Even though these communications are modifiable by experience, they are considered reflexive; that is, they are elicited by specific stimuli in the environment. For example, some snakes hiss reflexively when a warm, moving object enters their territory.

But are these signals *language*, "a body of words, and systems for their use, common to a people of the same community" (Random House Dictionary, 1979)? Such a definition restricts the use of the term *language* to humans. Compared to nonhuman animal communication, human language is less reflexive and more intentional. Put another way, humans are thought to be conscious of what they are talking about, whereas animals are thought to be restricted to stimulus-response sequences. We will keep these issues in mind as we compare communications among various species.

Because language is a species-specific behavior, researchers have looked for evidence of *protolanguage*—the precursors of human language—in other animals with large, well-developed brains. The existence of protolanguage may bear on the origins of human language. In this section we will examine a few examples of how some other species communicate. Then we will look at the successes and failures of researchers who have tried to teach rudimentary language to a few animals of different species.

animal communication The production and reception of signals that typically are meaningful only to members of the same species.

Animal Communication

Animals send signals to and receive signals from their conspecifics because those behaviors are adaptive (Alcock, 1998). For example, we saw in Chapter 3 that genetically determined brain areas and hormones mediate birdsong, and that male birds who sing in particular ways can attract and impregnate females (Nottebohm, 1991; Ball & Hulse, 1998). In turn, female birds have evolved brain areas that make them responsive to the male birds' song. Let's look at another example of adaptive communication in birds.

Squawking Ravens. Not all birdcalls serve courtship purposes. Raven mobs have been observed to squawk loudly when they consume the carcass of a dead animal. Their squawking attracts others to the feast, reducing each bird's portion.

The evolutionary biologist Bernd Heinrich has spent years trying to understand the reason for this behavior. Through careful observation and testing, Heinrich determined that only some ravens squawk, and only some of the time. If a male-female pair of ravens share exclusive rights to the territory on which they find a carcass, they will *not* trumpet their find. Instead, they will keep quiet and enjoy large portions. However, if a single raven from outside their territory chances upon the carcass, it will call loudly, attracting other ravens. This gathering of large numbers of ravens diverts the attack of the territorial male-female pair against the intruder (Alcock, 1998). Raven squawking is not a reflexive response to a food stimulus, then; it does or does not occur, depending on which bird finds the food and under what conditions.

A similar analysis has been used to explain monkey calls that communicate the discovery of food (Cain, Addington, & Windfelder, 1995). This form of communication is best understood, then, as an adaptation that increases the fitness of those species that use it. Frogs, flies, ants, bees, red deer, kangaroo rats, monkeys, and all other animals who communicate with conspecifics enjoy similar benefits (Alcock, 1998).

Vervet monkeys make three different types of alarm calls in response to three different types of predator.

Vervet Monkeys. Another intriguing example of animal communication is some clever research on vervet monkeys, first reported by Seyfarth, Cheney, and Marler (1980). In the presence of predators, vervet monkeys can make three different alarm calls. One of the calls causes the monkeys to look upward (for predatory eagles); another, to look around on the ground (for pythons); and yet another, to take to the trees (to escape leopards). The researchers recorded these calls and played them back from carefully hidden speakers, to observe the monkey's reactions. Infant vervet monkeys vocalized the alarm calls imperfectly at first, but improved with age and experience (Cheney & Seyfarth, 1992).

How should we interpret the vervet monkeys' alarm calls? Are they *words*? To think of them as words would suggest that a monkey *intends* to warn others. An alternative way to think about alarm calls is that the sight of a predator may function as a sign-releasing stimulus, triggering a fixed action pattern. In this example, the FAP would consist of a unique vocalization.

Alarm calls as a FAP, Chapter 3, p. 90

The philosopher Dan Dennett (1983) argued the case for intentionality in vervet monkey calls, and in some other instances of animal communication. He cited an observation by Seyfarth and his colleagues: A vervet monkey, alone and out of the hearing range of other monkeys, saw a leopard. Instead of vocalizing an alarm call, the monkey silently climbed to safety. Dennett concluded from this observation that the vervets' alarm call is not reflexive, but an intentional warning. Not all behavioral scientists who study animal communication agree with Dennett's analysis, however. They would like to see evidence of intentionality other than innate vocalizations—for example, shaking a branch, pointing, or throwing something in response to an intruder. Intentional or not, the vervet monkeys' behavior shows that primates other than humans can adaptively use vocalized signals to communicate with one another.

Although humans share many features of their brain organization with other primates, the fact is, humans speak and other large-brained animals do not. Obviously, if animals could talk, we could ask them about their intentions, as well as other aspects of their experience. Seyfarth and his colleagues' research strategy was to eavesdrop on vervet monkeys within their ecological niche, analyze their responses, and interpret what they meant. A different research strategy is to try to teach animals an artificial language. During the past century researchers have tried to develop simplified, symbolic languages for use with different species. Let's look at some of the results, beginning with porpoises and dolphins.

Communicating with Porpoises and Dolphins

Porpoises and dolphins vocalize among themselves in their natural habitats. Because of their abilities, and their apparent eagerness to interact and communicate with humans (Lilly, 1961), a number of dolphins have been subjected to intensive symbolic language training. If you have ever had the good fortune of watching a dolphin perform, you have probably wondered how it was trained to respond to a series of verbal and hand signals by fetching a red ball and shooting it toward a basket on one side of the pool.

Researchers are divided on the question of whether porpoises respond to language, or whether communication between humans and porpoises is merely an elaborate conditioned response. Herman, Richards, and Wolz (1984) thought that their trained bottlenose dolphin, named Ake, had a "tacit knowledge of syntactic rules" that allowed it to comprehend three- to five-word "sentences." In Ake's training, each sentence had three essential components—an *object, action,* and *agent*—all hand-signaled in sequence. In the example just given, the object was *the basket on the right-hand side of the pool,* the action was *fetch,* and the agent was *red ball.* Both the color of the agent and the position of the object (right or left) were modifiers that required Ake to select from alternatives. The researchers who worked with Ake thought that the sentence components were "words," and that "dolphins are sensitive to the semantic and syntactic features of the sentences we construct in those languages, because their responses co-vary with variations in those features" (Herman, 1989, p. 46).

While acknowledging the complexity of the tasks Ake has learned, other researchers have challenged this analysis. A different research team replicated Herman's studies using the same techniques with dolphins and sea lions, but came to a different conclusion (Schusterman & Gisner, 1988, 1989). In their view, the animal's response was a *conditional sequential discrimination* involving three categories of signs and two rules:

> 1. **If** an OBJECT is designated by one, two, or three signs (one OBJECT sign and one or two modifiers), **then** perform the designated ACTION to that object.
>
> 2. **If** two OBJECTS are designated (again, using one, two, or three signs) and the ACTION is *FETCH*, **then** take the second designated object to the first. (Schusterman & Gisner, 1988, p. 346)

In other words, the dolphins learned conditioned responses rather than understanding language as humans do.

Learning conditioned responses, Chapter 6, p. 192

Which analysis is correct? Are these animals using language or making conditioned responses? The more parsimonious analysis (Schusterman's) runs the risk of underemphasizing a complexity of thought that may in fact accompany the dolphin's performance. As usual, however, the more parsimonious account is probably closer to the truth. The dolphins required many hundreds of trials, using both classical and operant conditioning techniques, to learn their trained behaviors. From a conditioning perspective, nothing emerged from this communication system that was not put into it.

One problem with concluding that dolphins don't use language, however, is that they were removed from their ecological niche in these experiments. Inquisitive by nature in the ocean, in captivity they are asked to accomplish the unnatural task of communicating on human terms. Given the primitive language components human researchers provided them, there is no way that the dolphins *could* use language as humans do. We'll return to this general criticism of animal language studies in a later section. Clearly, dolphins are capable of learning rules. The "If x, then y" rule is similar to the *win-stay, lose-shift* response strategy that the Harlows' monkeys learned (see Chapter 6).

Learning about rules and concepts, Chapter 6, p. 222

Connecting with Chimpanzees and Gorillas

Winthrop and Luella Kellogg were among the earliest researchers in the 20th century to attempt to break the communication barrier with chimpanzees. In their book *The Ape and the Child,* the Kelloggs described their 9-month experiment of raising an infant chimp named Gua with their 10-month-old child, Donald (Kellogg & Kellogg, 1933). The Kelloggs wanted to see whether a chimp would display humanlike behavior if it were raised in a human environment. Their hypothesis was that a chimp's brain was similar to humans', and that if the chimp experienced human language during a critical period, it might talk. Unfortunately, Gua not only remained mute, but also seemed to have had a retarding effect on Donald's language acquisition (Benjamin & Bruce, 1982). Mrs. Kellogg stopped the experiment when Donald persisted in making chimp sounds! Similar efforts to teach a chimpanzee named Viki to talk proved equally ineffective, although a home-produced film shows Viki attempting to articulate *mama, cup,* and several other simple words (Hayes, 1951).

The Kelloggs raised a chimpanzee named Gua (shown here at 16 months) with their son, Donald (18 months), to provide the chimp with an environment conducive to language development.

Washoe, Nim, Koko, and Sign Language. Though their work was fascinating, the Kelloggs' and Hayes' failure to teach chimps to speak may be more of a methodological problem than a statement about chimpanzees' capacity for language. The common chimp (*Pan troglodyte*) rarely makes humanlike sounds, so we shouldn't expect it to speak. Allen and Beatrice Gardner attempted to solve this problem by training a chimpanzee named Washoe to sign with *American Sign Language (ASL)*. Using both food and praise as reinforcers, they reportedly taught Washoe well over 100 signed words (Gardner & Gardner, 1969). Also using ASL, Herb Terrace (1979) trained *Nim Chimpsky* (named after Noam Chomsky, a noted language researcher we'll meet later) to make hand gestures. However, contrary to the Gardners' conclusions about Washoe's language capabilities, Terrace (1979) was struck more by the differences between humans' and chimps' language usage, pointing out that chimps require many trials to learn even the simplest of words. In addition, the size of Nim's vocabulary (the number of signs) increased at a painstakingly slow pace, requiring intensive effort on the experimenters' part. Nim seldom made hand gestures spontaneously, without prompting from the experimenter.

Similar criticism has been made of the language skills of a lowland gorilla named Koko following ASL training by Patterson and Linden (1981). Koko learned several hundred hand gestures, but even after thousands of training trials did not always use them correctly. Terrace's assessment of both Nim's and Koko's skills was that they reacted to signals with conditioned responses rather than language. Indeed, Pinker (1994) has questioned whether nonhuman sign language is ever generative. Human signing *is* a true language, but chimpanzees and gorillas, he wrote, only mimic the hand gestures, without truly communicating (Pinker, 1994). The absence of the spontaneous generation of language has become a major issue in these studies.

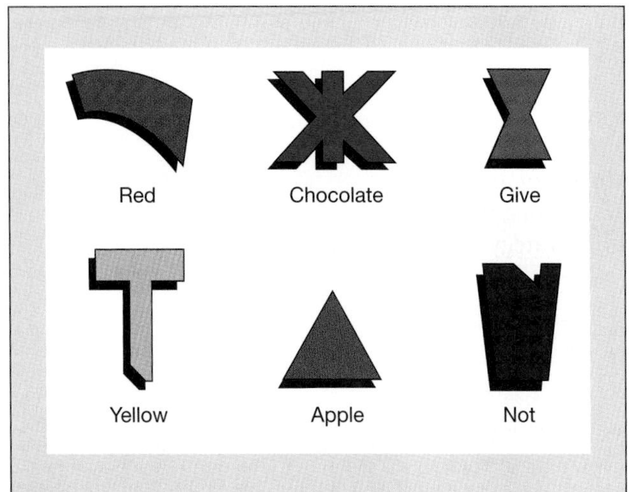

Figure 12.3 Sara's symbols. The Premacks trained a chimp named Sara to associate artificial symbols such as these, called *lexigrams*, with agent, object, and action words. Sara then learned to arrange the lexigrams in sequences that signaled requests.

Sara, Lana, and Lexigrams. In the 1970s, two different research groups used food reinforcement to train chimps to associate artificial symbols with actions and objects. In one study, a chimp named Sara was taught to first "read" and then physically arrange a three-token sequence of magnetized plastic symbols. After several years of training, Sara had a functional vocabulary of about 130 words; she eventually learned to use the *agent-action-object* format to create unique "sentences" that had never been reinforced (Premack & Premack, 1972).

Sometime later, Duane Rumbaugh and colleagues built a computer interface to train a chimp named Lana (Rumbaugh & Gill, 1976, Rumbaugh, 1977). Lana interacted with her trainers by pushing keys illuminated with geometric symbols called lexigrams. Each lexigram symbolized an object, agent, action, or other grammatical element. If Lana produced a correct sequence of lexigrams, she received food reinforcement. Figure 12.3 shows several of the lexigrams used in Rumbaugh's research.

Sherman and Austin: Combined Methods. During the 1980s, researchers at the Language Research Center in Georgia developed a more sophisticated computer interface. Sue Savage-Rumbaugh and her colleagues trained two chimps, Sherman and Austin, to communicate using a combination of lexigrams, ASL, and real-world objects (Savage-Rumbaugh, McDonald, Sevcik, Hopkins, & Rubert, 1986). The researchers found that Sherman and Austin could sort and categorize both objects and lexigrams on the first trial of a blind test. They could also carry out commands without seeing an object (for example, they could go into another room and retrieve an object on request). Finally, the chimps could make statements (arrange lexigrams) about future actions and engage in cooperative behavior (such as food sharing) after using their "language" to solve a problem together (Savage-Rumbaugh, 1987).

Carl Sagan (1977) once admonished human researchers not to indulge in *speciesism*, or the tendency to take a human-centered approach to the study of other animals. Judging animal communication by human standards may well be unrealistic (King, 1994). An analogy would be to take a young child into a laboratory, give her a saxophone, and assess how well she "uses language" by measuring which notes she plays on certain occasions, whether she plays the instrument spontaneously, and whether she tries to get other children to play it. Under these conditions, the child's "language abilities" would likely be found wanting.

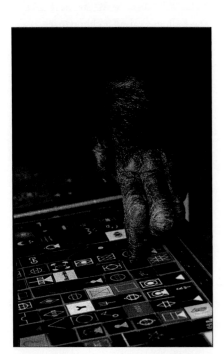

Chimps have learned to communicate with humans through a touch-activated keyboard. Each symbol, or lexigram, stands for an object, agent, or action.

Kanzi: Real Speech? And yet, chimpanzees and humans are closely related primates, with quite similar brain organization. We saw in Chapter 3 that the pygmy chimpanzee (*Pan paniscus*, also known as the *bonobo*) shares more genes with humans than does the common chimpanzee (see Figure 3.9, page 81). As an infant, a pygmy chimp named Kanzi watched his mother, Matata, learn lexigrams (Savage-Rumbaugh et al., 1993). A year or so later, without prodding, Kanzi began to show interest in the lexigrams. With no formal training, he quickly learned to respond to the keyboard symbols. At no time did Kanzi receive food rewards for his behavior. Rather, his behavior is better characterized as the kind of imitation and modeling that children engage in (Bandura, 1971).

Without formal training, Kanzi learned more language than any other chimpanzee. And though his accent is still thick, he seems to have learned a bit of

English. At one point his receptive and generative language skills were comparable to those of a 2-year-old child (Savage-Rumbaugh et al., 1993). In a test of 660 human-chimp interactions (compared with a like number of human-child interactions), Kanzi was found to *understand* more spoken English than a child. Language production was a different matter, however; the human 2-year-old's spoken language was decidedly better than Kanzi's. Although both species of chimpanzees are said to lack the mouth and tongue construction necessary to form consonants, Savage-Rumbaugh and her colleagues are convinced that Kanzi engages in intentional vocalizing, "answering, disagreeing, or expressing emotion" vocally. Kanzi has spoken and used appropriately the English words *bunny, good, groom, sweet potato,* and *tomato,* as well as words that "sound like" *lettuce, orange drink, raisins,* and *carrot.* Although most of these words refer to food, he also vocalizes words that sound like *yes, there, knife, snake, hot, oil, paint, get it,* and others (Savage-Rumbaugh et al., 1993).

What can we conclude from this study? Savage-Rumbaugh emphasizes the empowering role of a culture that is geared to training language skills in humans: "When an ape can, simply by virtue of human rearing, begin to comprehend human speech, the power of culture learning looms very large indeed" (Savage-Rumbaugh et al., 1986, p. 231). Kanzi's language skills, then, are best interpreted as the result of proximal (local) causes as well as distal (distant, or genetic) causes.

Proximal and distal causation of behavior, Chapter 3, p. 70

Talking with Alex, the Parrot

Like Kanzi, an African grey parrot named Alex has acquired a considerable vocabulary by observing and listening to his human trainers (Pepperberg, 1991, 1994). Irene Pepperberg began training Alex in the 1970s to do what parrots are known for—namely, to parrot whatever was said to him. Though we take for granted what parrots do, it is no small feat. According to Pepperberg (1999), Alex talks, alternates between listening and making sounds, and as a child does, "plays" with sounds. He also counts (and adds) objects that are presented him, and correctly identifies shapes and colors with about 80 percent accuracy.

Alex learned to talk by modeling after human trainers. In his presence, the trainers carried on extended conversations about the color, number, and shape of objects they presented to him. Two other grey parrots, trained using audiotapes rather than human trainers, failed to develop Alex's abilities. These findings convinced Pepperberg and McLaughlin (1996) that social interactions, including eye contact and paying attention, are as essential to language learning in parrots as they are in humans.

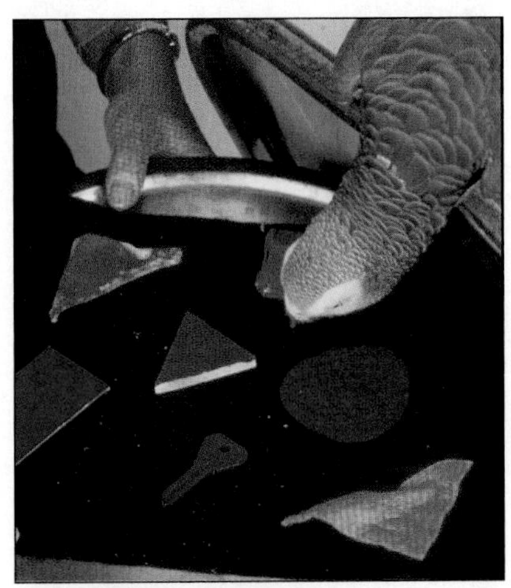

Alex, an African grey parrot, has been trained to count and to identify colors and shapes. Here he responds to the question "What toy is blue and triangular?"

Human and Animal Language Compared

Human language shares some features with other animal communication. Like other animals, humans communicate through pheromones and visual displays as well as vocalizations. In humans, however, language is a window to the mind. Psychologists who have studied nonhuman language are in general agreement that no such window has been opened into the mind of another species. We do not know, to paraphrase Dennett (1983, p. 344), what dolphins or chimpanzees *know,* what they *want,* what they *understand,* or what they *mean.* Nor do other animals share with humans those aspects of language that make us "uniquely human" (Lieberman, 1991). What other animal speaks a language that incorporates confabulation, irony, metaphor, and storytelling?

INTERIM SUMMARY

1. **Animal communication** can be distinguished from language. Most animal communication involves a sender and a receiver, and can be thought of in terms of innately determined fixed action patterns.
2. One question raised by the study of animal communication concerns *intentionality*. Vervet monkeys alert one another to the presence of predators; their vocalizations can be thought of either as involuntary, reflexive behaviors or as voluntary, intentional acts.
3. Dolphins can learn to perform relatively complex acts in response to artificial signals. These behaviors are best thought of in terms of conditioned responses and the application of learned rules rather than an acted-out grammar.
4. The common chimpanzee (*Pan troglodyte*) does not vocalize words, but can be trained to respond to humans through gesturing (Washoe, Nim) and the manipulation of plastic tokens (Sara) or lexigrams (Lana, Sherman, and Austin). These chimps can engage in meaningful language-like behaviors with their human caretakers.
5. Kanzi, a pygmy chimpanzee (*Pan paniscus*), has exhibited humanlike language abilities. Kanzi's speech comprehension and vocalizations are qualitatively different from those of the common chimpanzee. Nevertheless, relative to a human child, the pygmy chimpanzee's language abilities are meager.
6. By interacting with trainers who paid attention to and praised him for correct responses, Alex, an African grey parrot, learned to correctly identify colors and shapes by name.

For Further Thought

1. My dog, Sadie, barks when someone comes near the house. Is her barking best thought of as a reflexive response, or is she sending a signal to the humans she lives with? To answer this question, what would you want to know about Sadie's behavior when no one is home?
2. Do you agree with Dennett's (1983) assessment that because chimpanzees lack language, humans will never be able to understand what they *know*, *want*, *understand*, or *mean*?
3. Kanzi managed to learn some human language. What does his achievement say about the plasticity of the bonobo brain?

HOW CHILDREN ACQUIRE LANGUAGE

Children acquire language rapidly, progressing from a few words to whole sentences in just a few years. Do they learn to put words together by trial and error, or as the linguist Noam Chomsky thinks, do they acquire language through an innate, species-specific language acquisition mechanism (Chomsky, 1980)? According to Chomsky, language development does not resemble learning at all. Indeed, scientists might coax a chimpanzee to combine lexigrams into an *object, action, agent* "sentence," but such a process has nothing to do with how a child learns to speak. Behaviorally oriented theorists disagree with Chomsky, however. Keeping in mind these two viewpoints, let's examine the process of language acquisition, beginning with a baby's first sounds.

First Sounds: Crying

The first sounds human infants make are distress cries. Their crying is adaptive, alerting caregivers to the need to alleviate hunger, pain, changes in temperature, and other discomforts. Crying can be characterized as a species-specific behavior, a particular pattern of both sound production (by the species' offspring) and sound reception (by the parents). In fact, crying meets all the criteria of a fixed action pattern (see Chapter 3). That is, it is stereotyped, occurring in about the same way in most members of the species. Once begun, the behavior is difficult to disrupt, and must run its course. As with other FAPs, a crying bout is usually followed by a latent period. Also like other FAPs, the behavior appears early in life and does not need to be learned.

Like other behaviors, crying can be reinforced, so that older, more experienced infants may begin to cry *instrumentally.* That is, a child who is consistently reinforced for crying will begin to cry more frequently. Within and between cultures, caregivers adopt various strategies for dealing with instrumental crying. If, after a feeding and a diaper change, an infant continues to cry, parents might decide to let him or her "cry it out." By failing to respond to the crying, they are in effect withholding their affection as a form of punishment. Theoretically, then, the frequency of an infant's vocalizations can be manipulated through reinforcement and punishment.

Cooing, Babbling, and Pointing

A baby begins to coo and babble a few months after birth (Kaplan & Kaplan, 1970). Because deaf infants cry, coo, and babble just like other infants, there is general agreement that these vocalizations are innate.

Humans who speak different languages make between 11 (Polynesian) and 141 (Khoisan) distinct sounds, each called a phoneme (Pinker, 1994). English speakers make about 40 phonemic sounds, corresponding roughly to the 26 letters of the alphabet plus diphthongs. For example, a child who babbles "da" is combining two phonemes, the *d* sound and the *a* ("ah" sound). There is some controversy about whether the smallest unit of sound people actually *hear* is a phoneme; often the sounds that follow a phoneme influence the way it is heard (Ganong, 1980). But researchers agree that the sound "pa" (as in Grandpa) is composed of two phonemes, a "puh" sound (as in *put*) and an "ah" sound. The problem is that human speech is continuous, so the sounds run together. (For this reason, most of us quickly become discouraged in trying to distinguish separate words in an unfamiliar foreign language.) To extract meaning from spoken sounds, listeners must perform a top-down analysis, taking advantage of prior learning about the sounds of a language. In a process that is not understood, infants acquire the ability to perform a top-down analysis of speech sounds within the first year of life.

The *morphemes* in words are easier to analyze. A morpheme is the smallest meaningful unit into which words can be divided; "pa" is one example (Pinker, 1994). Figure 12.4 shows how morphemes can be combined with other morphemes to make up words.

After infants coo and babble, but before they begin to speak words, they communicate by pointing. On average, girls point earlier than boys, and both sexes point much more frequently with the right hand than the left (Butterworth & Morissette, 1996). When pointing, an infant often looks to the caretaker to make sure that the pointer and the object being pointed at are noticed. Earlier we wondered whether nonhuman animals *intend* to communicate; in human children, there is no doubt. Referential pointing is the first instance of communication that involves intentionality, evidencing an awareness of self as distinct from others (Franco & Butterworth, 1996).

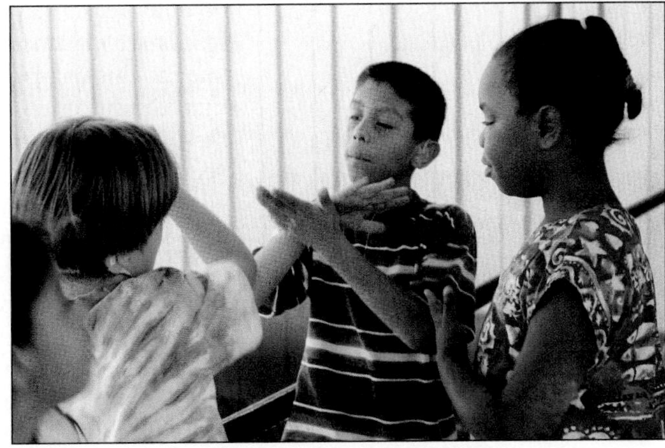
Deaf children use their hands and fingers to communicate through signs.

WORDS	The	cats	ate	the	playdough
MORPHEMES	The	cat s	ate	the	play dough
PHONEMES	ðə	c ae t s	e t	ðə	pley d o

Figure 12.4 **Phonemes, morphemes, and words.** Language is formed from meaningless sounds, called phonemes, which can be combined into meaningful syllables, called morphemes, and words.

Pointing with the right hand is evidence of the ongoing lateralization of a child's brain. In most people, language develops in the left hemisphere, the same one that controls the right hand. Hemispheric specialization occurs even in deaf children who do not develop vocal language. In these children, the language areas of the left hemisphere organize the use of hand signals, a language known as *signing*. Signing is one example of the progressive development of communicative language that begins with pointing.

First Words

Infants may vary by several months in the age at which they speak their first word, but at about 10 to 12 months, a child both understands and begins to speak the language he or she has been hearing. A child's first words are usually the names of objects (such as *mama* and *milk*) and actions (such as *get* and *go*). Infants may not express phonemes in the same way their caretakers do, but their sounds are close enough to be recognized and reinforced (Risley, 1977).

Adults judge the meaning of these single words by the context in which they are delivered. For example, sitting in a high chair and reaching for her cup, a child might say "wa-wa"—short for "I'm thirsty; I want some water." Later, "wa-wa" might be playfully splashed (and drunk) during an evening bath. For obvious reasons, this period is known as the **one-word utterance stage.** First words are evidence that a child is thinking (an argument that will be developed later in this chapter), and the growth of the child's thinking can be linked with the acquisition of new words (Gopnik & Meltzoff, 1986). But where do these first words come from? Although the process is unknown, several theories have been advanced.

Nativism, Chapter 1, p. 15

We have seen that for Noam Chomsky, a child's first words reflect the operation of an innate **language acquisition device (LAD)**, a brain-based structure that is responsible for the comprehension and production of speech (Chomsky, 1965, 1975). According to Chomsky, the LAD provides the basis for infants' listening, babbling, and first words. From his nativist perspective, the infant's task is to "map" each new word onto this innate cognitive structure (Levine & Carey, 1982). For example, an infant associates the word *mama* with a preverbal concept of mama. Interestingly enough, Chomsky does not see the LAD as the necessary outcome of natural selection, even though he conceptualizes it as an innate capacity.

one-word utterance stage The first words spoken in any language, typically the names of objects in the environment, such as "mama" and "milk," or of actions, such as "get" and "go."

language acquisition device (LAD) (Chomsky) A species-specific brain mechanism that allows a child to acquire language rapidly.

Chomsky's position is countered by behaviorists, who stress the role of the environment (Stemmer, 1990; Moerk, 1990). B. F. Skinner (1957), for example, thought that first words, like babbling sounds, are best described as operant responses. Skinner was less concerned about where in the brain the sounds originated than in how they could be manipulated. Once emitted, he proposed, the sounds could be shaped through reinforcement. Parents who smiled, comforted, and made their own endearing sounds would reinforce an infant's babbling and cooing. Eventually, the parent's words would acquire secondary reinforcing properties.

In the behaviorist's view, not all sounds that an infant makes are reinforced. Those sounds that are closest to the sounds of the parent's language are reinforced; phonemes that are *not* part of the native language are *not* reinforced, and soon extinguish. Children also learn to use cooing sounds and words instrumentally. That is, they make sounds that have been reinforced in the past, in the same way that a rat presses a lever for food. The way in which sounds and words are reinforced (or extinguished, or punished) influences their frequency of usage (Risley, 1977).

Words as operant responses that are reinforced, Chapter 6, p. 200

Behaviorists reject the notion that a child *maps* words for objects in the environment onto an innate cognitive structure (Stemmer, 1989, 1990). Skinner believed that stimulus generalization and discrimination could explain the learning of words. For example, a child making its first sounds might say "da-da" in reference to both *daddy* and the *dog*—an example of stimulus generalization. (The words *dad* and *dog* share a phoneme and other sound characteristics.) There is no need to postulate an innate cognitive mechanism to explain the process. Later, through stimulus discrimination, the word *da-da* becomes associated exclusively with "daddy," and *dog* with "dog." In this analysis of language acquisition, stimulus generalization and discrimination enable a child to know, label, and remember sight-sound associations (Stemmer, 1989).

Another theory advanced by behaviorists is that children tend to imitate what they hear, and that a child's first words are a result of *generalized imitation* (Baer & Sherman, 1964; Poulson & Kymissis, 1990). When a child makes sounds that are similar to what he or she hears, those sounds are maintained by reinforcement. In this analysis, imitation is an innate behavior, which combined with reinforcement, produces a child's first word in the language to which the child is exposed.

By 6 months, hearing babies begin to respond differently to the sounds they hear regularly, compared with the sounds of another language (Kuhl, William, Lacerda, Stephens, & Lindblom, 1992). Once a child learns the phonemes of the native language, she or he is soon unable to hear certain phonemes that are distinctive to other languages. By 12 months, children vocalize "intonal patterns" that resemble the sounds of the caregiver's language (Weir, 1966; Werker & Tees, 1984). An infant who does not hear the phonemic distinctions that are characteristic of a particular language cannot mimic those sounds as an adult speaker. A common example is the Chinese speaker who learns English as a second language. Because in infancy, this person did not hear English "Rs" (as distinguished from "Ls"), as an adult the person cannot hear the difference between the two sounds. As a result, many Chinese speakers use these sounds interchangeably. Adult English speakers who learn Chinese, of course, mispronounce certain phonemes common to the Chinese language, for the same reason.

Parental Encouragement of Language Acquisition

child-directed speech A simplified form of speech that caretakers use with a child (sometimes called *motherese*).

Most caregivers interact with infants by replying to their endearing sounds. This behavior likely has a genetic basis. For example, most caretakers simplify the language they speak to a toddler (Furrow, Nelson, & Benedict, 1979). This **child-directed speech**, sometimes called *motherese*, holds the child's attention better than adult-directed language (Kaplan, Goldstein, Huckeby, & Penneton-Cooper, 1995). Slower and higher pitched than adult language, clearly paced and pronounced, child-directed speech contains few abstract words and is spoken with exaggerated intonations. Presumably, motherese enables the child to understand what is being communicated. However, children also hear a lot of adult-directed language, and as every parent knows, preverbal children can understand more than they can say. The child's understanding, or receptive language, is better at the one- and two-word utterance stage than is her or his speaking ability, or productive language.

Environmental differences can produce differences in language development. Deaf children, who occupy a soundless environment, do not hear their caretaker's vocalizations. After the babbling stage they stop making sounds altogether. Deaf children who see sign language during this time, however, will develop the ability to communicate by signing (Meier, 1991).

Language-impoverished environments may also affect language acquisition. Parents who do not talk to their infants provide less modeling of the target language. In addition, parents who provide less reinforcement for their infant's babbling and early vocalizations (by not paying attention to them) will affect the child's language development. With some noted exceptions, language *will* develop in children who are exposed to moderately impoverished language environments. But the enormous individual differences that are seen in adult language behavior likely have their origins at least in part in early social interactions between infant and caregiver.

The Growth of Vocabulary and Appearance of Grammar

The growth of language is very rapid. By 18 months, the average child speaks about 30 words, but the next few years bring a virtual word explosion. By age 2, a child has approximately 250 words (Woodward, Markman, & Fitzsimmons, 1994); by age 6, several thousand words of receptive vocabulary (Medin & Ross, 1990). Children also acquire their parents' grammar and speech patterns (if not their working vocabulary) by about age 3 1/2.

How does a child acquire grammar—the rules for how words are used? One of the simplest grammatical forms, called *telegraphic speech,* appears cross-culturally from 18 to 36 months. **Telegraphic speech** consists of simple noun-verb sentences that observe the grammatical conventions of the parent language (Bloom, 1970). For example, a child of English-speaking parents will say "get cookie," not "cookie get." Chomsky considered this simple form of grammar innate, but behaviorists stress the role of imitation and experience with the environment. For example, during this time children get a lot of practice using language; they even speak (and hear themselves speak) when no one is around. A conservative estimate is that during the first 5 years of life, children spend 10,000 hours "practicing speaking" (Anderson, 1990).

In his earliest writings, Chomsky was struck by the appearance of this two-word utterance stage in cultures around the world. He proposed a theory of **universal grammar**: that humans have an innate, species-specific language ability that allows them to speak in a grammatically correct manner. In no meaningful way, he reasoned, could *learning* account for the appearance of grammatically patterned communication by 18 months; the environment must trigger and shape some genetically based program (Chomsky, 1980). In the same way that acorns do not learn to be oak trees, but simply grow into oaks, language unfolds in growing children (Pateman, 1985).

Several researchers tested Chomsky's assertions by recording the verbal interactions of middle-class parents (primarily mothers) with their children (Brown & Hanlon, 1970). In their huge database of findings, these researchers found

telegraphic speech A stage of language development, appearing at about 18 to 36 months, in which children begin to string two words together in a grammatically meaningful way.

universal grammar (Chomsky) The theory that humans have an innately determined species-specific language ability that allows them to speak in a grammatically correct manner.

instances in which middle-class parents did *not* consistently reinforce a child's correct grammar. For example, a toddler whose mother was brushing her hair observed, "Her curl my hair," and was immediately reinforced by mom, who said, "That's right, darling." On another occasion, the same child, in referring to a television program, made the grammatically correct comment, "Walt Disney comes on Tuesday." The parent responded, "No it doesn't, it comes on Thursday." Brown and his colleagues concluded that the parent was reinforcing "truth value"—that is, the semantic meaning of an utterance rather than its grammar. Their research supported Chomsky's nativist view.

However, researchers who reexamined and rescored Brown and Hanlon's (1970) huge database reached different conclusions (Moerk, 1990). Most instances of grammatically incorrect statements, they found, *were* corrected by parents. These child-parent exchanges are better understood within a social reinforcement framework (Bandura, 1971). For example, when a child spoke incorrectly, the parent would respond by modeling the correct usage. In response, the child would imitate the parent and be reinforced by the parent's acceptance of the corrected grammar (Moerk, 1990; Stemmer, 1990). Exchanges of this type are more numerous than those involving a discrete reinforcer or punisher. The conclusion of these studies is that many caretakers *do* take an active role in guiding language development.

A Critical Period for Language Acquisition?

The best evidence for Chomsky's nativist theory is that humans, and humans alone, have a brain that specifically supports the learning of a first language (Rasmussen & Milner, 1977). In addition, several studies support the idea that there is a critical period for acquiring both spoken language (Johnson & Newport, 1989; Hurford, 1991) and sign language (Mayberry & Eichen, 1991). Older children and young adults who attempt to learn a second language find the experience so different from learning their first that they have difficulty even comparing the two experiences. The second language is encoded in a different memory system from the first language (Jiang & Forster, 2001), in a different part of the brain (Kim, Relkin, Lee, & Hirsch, 1997).

The effects of brain injury and impoverished environments also support the idea that there is a critical period for language acquisition. People who lose their language ability before puberty, as a result of damage to the left hemisphere, can relearn it more easily than people in puberty (or older) with equivalent brain damage and language loss. But people who do not experience language in early childhood cannot learn it later in life (Curtiss, 1977; Candland, 1993). Presumably, failure to exercise the neurons responsible for language is a form of irreversible brain damage. One such case was "Genie," a neglected child who was raised in a closet until early puberty (Curtiss, 1977). Despite Herculean efforts by psychologists at UCLA and elsewhere, Genie could not learn to use language, except in very primitive fashion. Her comments, such as "Applesauce buy store" and "Genie have Momma have baby grow up" (Pinker, 1994, p. 292) show the crippling effects of failure to hear normal language in early childhood.

Other well-documented cases of "wild children" raised without language include Peter (found in Germany in 1724), Victor (found in France in 1799), and Kamala and Amala (found in India in 1920). Candland (1993) recounts their stories in a highly readable book. The severe language problems these children experienced, despite language training, likely stemmed from deprivation-induced deficiencies of neurons in their language areas. Because they did not need language in their environments, their brains adapted to other demands.

Kamala and Amala, Chapter 5, p. 171

Neural development in enriched environments, Chapter 4, p.128

A critical period for language acquisition does exist, then. Given minimal language environments, most children about 6 years of age and under can readily learn to speak. Between age 6 and puberty, however, the brain appears to lose its plasticity for language. Beyond puberty, language that is lost to brain injury can rarely be recovered. In sum, the human capacity for language is present only in early childhood and can be expressed only in environments that support language. Clearly, language acquisition is determined by the interaction of biology, behavior, and culture.

INTERIM SUMMARY

1. Crying is the first vocalized communication pattern in humans. Crying can be thought of both as an innate FAP and as an instrumental behavior that can be reinforced or punished.
2. Cooing and babbling occur at an age when infants begin to hear and discriminate among the 40 to 50 distinct sounds, or phonemes, of their parents' language. Simple phonemes can be combined to form a morpheme, a meaningful sound.
3. Cross-culturally, a child's first words occur at about one year of age, through a process that has yet to be explained.
4. Chomsky proposed an innate mechanism called a ***language acquisition device (LAD)*** to account for a child's first words. Behaviorists counter that children imitate what they hear.
5. Cross-culturally, children learn how to talk without formal instruction. Their early ***one-word utterances*** merge into ***telegraphic speech*** during the second year of life.
6. To account for cross-cultural similarities in language acquisition, Chomsky proposed a ***universal grammar,*** an innate language program that unfolds during a critical period of development.
7. Behaviorists emphasize the role of the environment in shaping language acquisition and usage through the processes of reinforcement and punishment.
8. The role of the environment can be clearly seen in children's production of and receptivity to phonemes, in their associative learning of words, in their parents' ***child-directed speech,*** and in the study of neglected and feral children.
9. Across the population, the range of spoken language and language comprehension is wide. Individual differences are better accounted for by reference to the environment rather than to an innate language mechanism.

For Further Thought

1. What would John Locke have thought about innate, preverbal cognitive structures?
2. What significance, if any, do you attach to the finding that like human infants, the pigmy chimpanzee Kanzi had far greater receptive than productive language capabilities?
3. Chomsky's *LAD* and the behaviorist's construct of *imitation* both depend on hypothetical brain structures. What is the difference, if any, between the two theories?

THINKING WITHOUT LANGUAGE

Thinking is a term that refers to images, ideas, or conceptions held in the mind. It is inextricably intertwined with other psychological constructs, such as consciousness, memory, and to a great extent in humans, language. Most definitions suggest that to think, a person or other animal must be conscious. Beyond that, the analytical and explanatory power psychologists and other scientists bring to bear on the nature of human thinking may never produce adequate understanding. Logically, the functioning human brain may not be fully able to understand itself. And realistically, at this point in the science, psychologists don't even understand how the brains of less complicated animals "think."

Though thinking doesn't depend on language, we must use language to describe it. We will begin with what scientists know about thinking in nonhuman animals and preverbal children. In the last section of this chapter we'll look at what language adds to the thought process.

Thinking in Nonspeaking Humans and Nonhuman Animals

The idea that nonhuman animals can think was raised in Chapter 6, where we saw that animals are capable of learning rules, strategies, and concepts—evidence of simple thinking. Many laboratory studies of humans and other animals support the idea that language is *not* essential to complex cognitive skills (Weiskrantz, 1988). For example, severely aphasic patients can achieve high scores on Raven's Matrices, intelligence tests that do not involve language (Kertesz, 1988; Newcombe, 1987). And preverbal infants "can sometimes apprehend the unity, the boundaries, the persistence, and the identity of objects," signs of a conceptual knowledge of the world (Spelke, 1988, p. 180). Thinking, then, is not restricted to speaking adults and can be dissociated from language.

Nonverbal tests of intelligence, Chapter 13, p. 455

But human thinking is influenced by uniquely human activities. No other animal composes music, writes it down, builds the instruments on which to play it, or invests the time and effort necessary to offer a virtuoso performance. (Nor would any animal other than a human attend the performance.) Likewise, no other animal's behavior approaches human accomplishments in the arts, home construction, mathematics, cooking, athletics, science, or technology. So we can agree with Dennett's (1995) conclusion that humans are the only animals to use language, and that language makes us smarter, because it allows us to think both differently from and better than other animals.

Problem Solving

One way to describe thinking is in terms of problem solving (Newell & Simon, 1972), which usually involves answering questions or achieving a goal. Problem solving can involve language, as in answering questions such as "Where did I leave my keys *this* time?" For a pigeon or chimpanzee, the unverbalized question may require determining how to obtain food reinforcement. Learning a win-stay, lose-shift strategy, for example, requires a monkey to remember what happened the last time it selected a particular response. Although the monkey can solve problems, we can't ask it how, what, or if it was thinking.

Retrieving the answer to a question from memory is different from solving a problem. If we know the answer, there is no problem to be solved. When memory fails, however, we must define what the problem is, generate possible solutions, and decide how to solve it. Most of the mental activity we call thinking takes place rapidly, and not always systematically. Whether nonhuman animals share similar mental activity in similar situations is unknown.

Mental Images. One approach to solving a problem such as "Where *did* I leave my keys?" is to generate *mental images* of recent activities. In my mind's eye, can I see myself putting my keys on the desk? No. I remember parking the car in the South Parking Lot, because I was early enough to get my favorite spot. I remember locking the car door . . . Maybe they're in my pocket. I wore my overcoat today, so that's probably where they are.

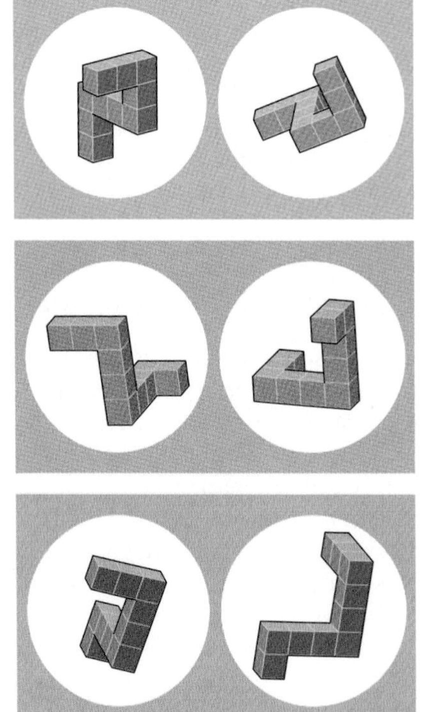

Figure 12.5 Are these objects identical? In this task, the problem is to determine whether the two objects in each pair are identical. Solving the problem requires a person to mentally rotate one object to align it with the other.

Mental images such as these are formed from stored memories. Remembering where car keys are located involves the selective retrieval of stored visual memories and their use in solving a specific problem. To give another example, suppose you decide to cook an Italian meal for a friend. Preparing a meal is a form of problem solving that involves the retrieval of motor sequences, as well as the memory of the sights, smells, textures, and tastes of certain foods. A basic knowledge of physics and chemistry helps in making decisions on timing and temperature. As with other types of skilled performance, this kind of thinking involves movement more than language, because it is usually learned by imitation of another's behavior.

As we will see in the next chapter, people differ in their ability to form mental images. Figure 12.5 shows three pairs of objects similar to those found on IQ tests; the problem is to decide whether the objects in each pair are identical. To solve the problem, a person must mentally rotate one of the two objects to see if it matches the other (Shepard & Cooper, 1982). The further out of alignment the objects are, the longer the time subjects need to solve the problem. During such tasks, the visual areas in the brain become more active (Isha & Sagi, 1995).

Mental Models. Solving problems by forming mental images may be one of the simplest forms of thinking. Many nonhuman animals form cognitive maps. In the delayed match-to-sample problem discussed in Chapter 6, animals memorized the image of an object and later retrieved it from memory. A more challenging task involves forming a *mental model* of events rather than a mental image. Figure 12.6 shows the mental models a person might generate about the likely outcomes of two simple physics experiments (McCloskey & Kuhl, 1983). Subjects (including physics students) do not always perform well on these tasks. Many fail to accurately predict the marble's path as it emerges from a coiled tube (McCloskey & Kuhl, 1983), or the angle of the plane of water in the inclined glass (Hecht & Proffitt, 1995).

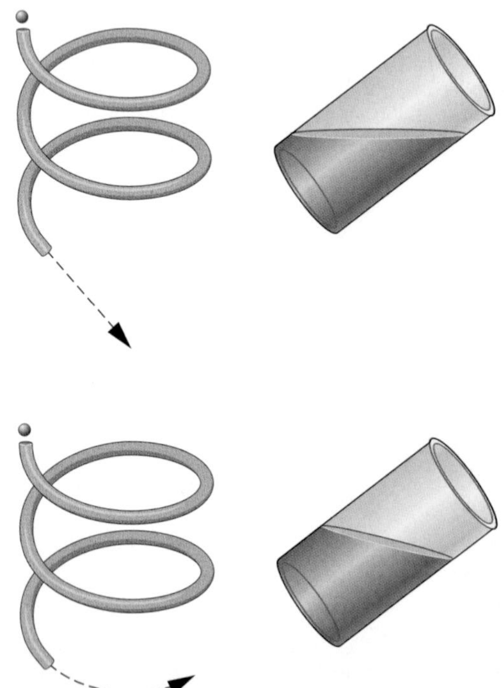

Figure 12.6 Which pictures are correct? Subjects were asked to make mental models of the likely path of a marble dropped through a coiled tube and the likely angle of water in a tilted glass. The solutions on the top are correct.

That humans do not easily solve such problems is evidence that their mental models are not always accurate. One implication of this finding is that much of our knowledge of the physical world is learned (or mislearned) rather than intuited. As Piaget's experiments on the conservation of volume and mass showed (see Chapter 11), both age and experience were necessary for children to understand basic principles of physics.

Cognitive Maps. When you try to determine the fastest (or safest, or easiest) way to cross town, your thinking will involve a variety of problem-solving measures. One is to make a mental map (or *cognitive map*) of where you are relative to where you want to be, and plot the appropriate course in your mind's eye. Rats and chimpanzees can readily form cognitive maps of their terrain, so this kind of thinking does not necessarily involve language. For instance, by age 3 the chimpanzee Kanzi had learned the locations of food stashed on a 55-acre forest and could point them out on a photograph or identify them by lexigram. He could even guide researchers to locations 30 minutes away (Savage-Rumbaugh et al., 1986). This behavior, which confirms previous reports of chimpanzees' foraging abilities (Menzel, 1978), shows a high degree of planning and intentionality (Savage-Rumbaugh, 1987).

Forming a cognitive map is more difficult than forming a simple mental image. First, the fastest, safest, or easiest route across town may not be the most *direct* route. One must first define the problem (the fastest, safest, or easiest way), then generate possible solutions (make a mental model), and finally decide how to solve the problem (Davidson & Sternberg, 1984). Compared to the 50 percent chance of deciding correctly whether a marble emerging from a coil will or will not spiral, this process has more room for error. For example, successful modeling of the problem would incorporate information about the time of day, weather, street conditions, traffic flow, speed limit, construction delays, and so forth. If the person is taking a subway instead of walking or driving, the pertinent information would include the status of the underground system, ease of transfer, crime rates, and so forth. Finally, forming memories for spatial relations involves the right hemisphere of the brain, while adding language to the problem-solving task involves the left hemisphere and frontal lobes.

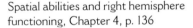

Spatial abilities and right hemisphere functioning, Chapter 4, p. 136

Generating Solutions to Problems

A mental model is a "best guess" based on past experience and available evidence. Most such "best guesses" are based on previous *trial-and-error* experiences. People learn about the features of their environment much as other animals do. For example, rats learn mazes by investigating blind alleys (errors); on subsequent trials, they remember the consequences of wrong turns. **Trial-and-error learning**, then, can be described as learning from one's mistakes.

Thorndike's *law of effect* states that animals tend to repeat behaviors that are reinforced and discontinue those that aren't. But because humans can think about (imagine or visualize) the probable consequences of their actions, they can engage in **vicarious trial-and-error learning**. For example, I can imagine what the traffic will be like at quitting time on the highway that passes by the factory; I don't have to learn by experiencing it. Therefore, I can solve the problem of getting across town by taking an alternate route. Likewise, imagining the consequences of provoking an armed psychopath is adaptive: Some things we absolutely do *not* want to learn by trial and error.

Thorndike's law of effect, Chapter 6, p. 206

Heuristics. In Chapter 6 we saw that given hundreds of trial-and-error learning experiences, monkeys can learn a win-stay, lose-shift strategy. Specifically, when confronted with a succession of identical problems in which one of two stimuli consistently predicts a food reward, a monkey learns to solve the problem. It does so by picking the *same* object it was rewarded for on the previous trial, or by picking the *other* object if it was not rewarded on the previous trial. Another way of expressing this strategy is to say that the monkey is applying a heuristic, or a simple rule—in this case, a win-stay, lose-shift rule.

Win-stay, lose-shift heuristic, Chapter 6, p. 222

Using a simple rule, or heuristic, to solve a problem is more effective than trial-and-error learning (Greeno & Simon, 1988). Lacking language, the monkey cannot repeat to itself "win-stay, lose-shift"; nevertheless, its behavior indicates that it is applying this simple heuristic. The rule that vehicles traveling at or below the speed limit should use the right-hand lane is another heuristic, which when followed, solves the problem inherent in cars traveling together at different speeds. One final example: children learning to write the letters of the alphabet often confuse (and therefore interchange) the letter *b* with the letter *d*. One way

trial-and-error learning Learning from the consequences of one's actions.

vicarious trial-and-error learning Learning by imagining the probable consequences of one's actions.

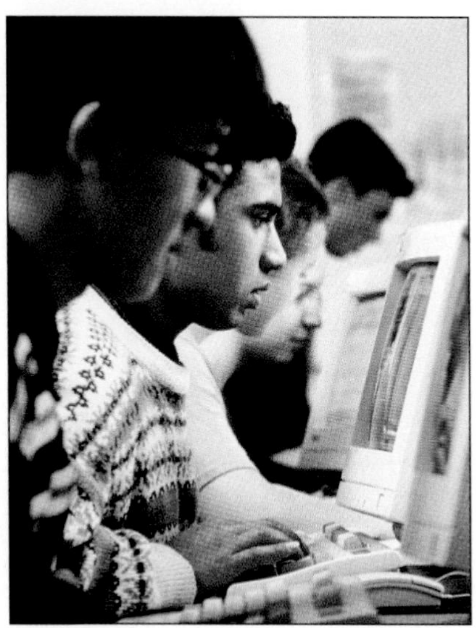

Heuristics such as category labels, dates, file sizes, and icons help people to manage the information in their personal computers.

to help is to point out to the child that the word *bed* not only contains *both* letters, but looks like a bed. The ascender of the letter *b* makes the headboard, and the ascender of the *d* makes the footboard. In applying this heuristic, the child becomes sensitive to the distinguishing features of the two letters. In comparison with this simple rule, trial-and-error learning of the difference between *b* and *d* is often inefficient and frustrating.

Algorithms. An **algorithm** is a problem-solving strategy that involves the systematic and exhaustive exploration of all possible alternatives. For example, one way to solve the problem of determining the fastest way to get from point *a* to point *b* is to systematically try all possible routes. Using this algorithm, you don't have to *think* about what you're doing; rather, you merely keep track of the routes you have covered and those yet to be tried. Given enough time and trials, this "brute force" procedure is guaranteed to arrive at a best answer. To give another example, suppose you haven't used the combination lock on your locker for a while, and you can't remember the entire number sequence. If you do remember that part of the combination is 05 - 4 -, you might decide to try all the numbers from 1 to 50 in the third position. This exhaustive strategy is sure to work.

Heuristics and algorithms are often used in combination to solve problems. For example, if you remember that one of the numbers in the last position is a 3, you can use a heuristic to modify the 1 to 50 algorithm, trying every combination in the series 03, 13, 23, 33, and 43. If that doesn't work, you can try every combination in the series 30, 31, 32, 33, and 34. If one of the numbers was a three, this algorithm is guaranteed to be both successful and efficient.

Or suppose you are trying to locate a term paper you wrote last year, which is stored on your hard drive in a folder called CLASSWORK. Your problem is that you don't remember the file name, and that folder has over 100 files. You could adopt a search strategy that combines the two heuristics Date of file (you remember writing the paper sometime in March or April) and Size of file (it was a long paper). Your algorithm? Open every large file stored during those two months.

Means-End Analyses

Heuristics and algorithms can solve only certain types of problems. For example, the simple heuristic of eating smaller portions may help you to solve the problem of how to lose a few pounds. But maintaining an optimal height/weight ratio over a lifetime typically requires some goal setting and *means-end analyses*. A **means-end analysis** is a heuristic in which a current state is compared with a goal state, and changes are made to reduce the difference between the two states (Newell & Simon, 1972). For example, the ideal weight of a person who is 5'3" tall is between 118 to 135 pounds. The problem facing a person of this height who weighs *150* pounds is either to grow taller or to lose weight. For an adult, the long-term solution to this problem involves forming many subgoals to control weight. Those subgoals might include daily exercise, eating smaller portions or fewer meals, eliminating snacks, weighing oneself frequently, and so forth. Pursuing these subgoals in a systematic fashion is the means a person can use to meet the overall end goal of controlling body weight. In this example, the end goal may be to lose 20 pounds. Consistently meeting subgoals that allow one to lose a pound each week (another subgoal) will solve this problem in 20 weeks.

algorithm An exhaustive, systematic problem-solving strategy that is guaranteed to produce the correct answer.

means-end analysis Comparison of a current state with a goal state to determine changes that will reduce the differences between the two states.

The setting and meeting of subgoals can be thought of as breaking a large problem down into smaller, more manageable parts. Consider another example, the *Tower of Hanoi* puzzle (see Figure 12.7). The goal is to move the three rings on peg A to peg C without placing a larger ring on a smaller one, and by moving only the top ring on a peg. If you are not familiar with this problem, you may want to try to solve it before reading further. If you have trouble solving the problem, Kotovsky and others (1985) suggest dividing the problem into subgoals. *Let the first subgoal be to get ring 3 to peg C,* a process accomplished in 4 steps: 1—>C; 2—>B; 1—>B; 3—>C. *Let the second subgoal be to get ring 2 to peg C,* which can be accomplished in 2 steps: 1—>A; 2—>C. At this point, you are one step away from getting ring 1 to peg C and completing the task. Besides helping to solve the problem, successfully accomplishing the subgoals serves another function. In meeting each subgoal, you know that you are not merely repeating the same incorrect strategy try after try, a tactic commonly known as *spinning your wheels.*

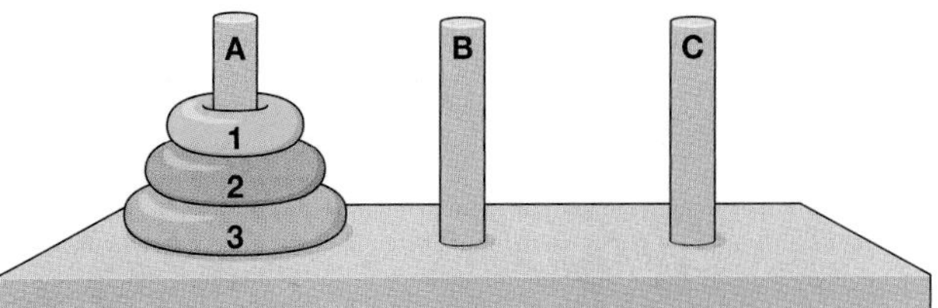

Figure 12.7 The Tower of Hanoi puzzle. Can you move the stacked rings from peg A to peg C by moving the rings one at a time, and never placing a large ring over a smaller one?

Insight

Everyone has had the experience of being stumped by a problem—at the point of giving up—and suddenly arriving at the answer, or after sleeping on a problem, coming up with an unexpected solution. An **insight** is a sudden, unexpected solution to a problem, or a strategy that leads to a solution. The Gestalt psychologist Köhler (1925) wrote that his ape, Sultan, solved problems in this way. In one case, Sultan could not reach some bananas that had been suspended from the ceiling. He stacked some boxes together and climbed onto them to reach the bananas. On another occasion, Sultan supposedly had the insight that fastening two sticks together would make a stick long enough to knock down the bananas.

Although insight may or may not involve trial and error, it does depend on prior learning, including imitation and modeling. For example, Sultan may have observed a caretaker stacking some boxes, or fitting two sticks together, prior to spotting the out-of-reach bananas. The distinction between insight and prior learning is an important one, for some psychologists believe that insight can be

insight A sudden, unexpected solution or strategy for solving a problem.

A chimp named Sultan had an insight that he could reach a bunch of bananas by stacking some boxes on top of one another and standing on them. An unknown chimpanzee demonstrates the process.

Figure 12.8 Duncker's candle problem. Given the materials shown here—a candle, a book of matches, and a box of thumbtacks—how would you attach the candle to the wall?

Figure 12.9 The string problem. Even by standing on the table with both hands fully outstretched, this man could not reach the two strings suspended from the ceiling. Given a book of matches, a screwdriver, and a few pieces of cotton, how could he tie the two strings together?

explained by normal learning processes (Epstein, Kirshnit, Lanza, & Rubin, 1984; Langley, Simon, Bradshaw, & Zytkow, 1986). Perhaps Sultan's insight was in *applying* skills he had previously seen and learned to a new problem.

The psychologists Janet Davidson and Robert Sternberg think that insight is best characterized as a three-stage process (Davidson & Sternberg, 1984). When faced with a problem, a person or other animal must first determine the important variables. (For Sultan, the bananas being out of reach was an important variable, as was the presence of the boxes.) Second, the learner must consider previous information and alternative solutions. (Sultan may have climbed on both boxes and trees, and he certainly knew that bananas were good to eat.) Finally, the learner must combine this information in a unique way.

To arrive at their three-stage model of insight, Davidson and Sternberg (1984) analyzed gifted children's thinking. They concluded that the creative part of insight is taking what is given to solve a problem and combining those familiar elements in a new way. Figure 12.8 shows the elements of *Duncker's candle problem*: Given a candle, a box of thumbtacks, and a book of matches, how can you mount a lighted candle to the wall? This problem is considered difficult to solve because the familiar elements cannot easily be recombined. (When you are through trying to solve this problem, turn to Figure 12.10, on p. 439 for the solution.)

Failure to solve this problem is evidence of **functional fixedness**, a mental set that hinders the discovery of unique solutions to problems. Functional fixedness stems from rigid (overlearned) thinking about rules, including the normal functions of objects such as tools. In this sense, functional fixedness can be thought of as a form of memory interference. Examples of problem solving that are *not* hampered by functional fixedness are typically seen as clever solutions. Recently, for example, I saw a person spray painting several large rubber mats that he had clipped to battery cables thrown over a limb, which allowed him to spray the mats from different angles. To give another example, a student once told me that a broken lightbulb can be safely removed by cutting a potato in half, pushing it into the edge of the bulb, and twisting. (I might add, for safety's sake, that the light switch must first be placed in the off position.) In these examples, the battery cables and potato were used in unique ways, outside their normal range of function. Likewise, in Duncker's candle problem, "seeing" that the box containing the thumbtacks could also function as a platform for the candle allows the insightful recombining of old elements.

functional fixedness A mental set involving rigid thinking about the functions of objects, which hinders the discovery of unique solutions to problems.

Can one overcome functional fixedness? That is, does knowing that familiar knowledge can interfere with problem solving help people to solve problems? Consider the *string problem* posed in Figure 12.9. Which of the elements will help to solve this problem, and which are misleading? Can you recombine these familiar elements to solve the problem? Take a few minutes to consider it before turning to Figure 12.11 (p. 439).

INTERIM SUMMARY

1. Thinking is a cognitive activity that involves both consciousness and memory. Thinking without language has been demonstrated in many species, including humans.
2. Some problem solving involves nonverbal thought. Nonhuman animals can be trained to solve problems by applying rules that lead to positive reinforcement.
3. One form of problem solving is thinking by forming a *mental image*. In the mind's eye, a person imagines (remembers) objects, events, and situations, and uses those images to solve problems.
4. Another form of thinking involves mentally *manipulating images*, such as mentally rotating the image of a three-dimensional object and comparing its position with that of a static image.
5. Thinking can reflect learned experience, from which we form *mental models* of how the world works. Many people have difficulty thinking about and successfully predicting the outcomes of physical events.
6. Humans and other animals make *cognitive maps* of their relative position in the environment and use those maps to solve problems of spatial relationships.
7. Solutions to problems may involve ***trial-and-error learning*** (learning from one's mistakes) and ***vicarious trial-and-error learning*** (imagining the consequences of an action).
8. A *heuristic* is a simple rule that is used to solve a problem. An ***algorithm*** is a systematic, exhaustive problem-solving strategy that is guaranteed to produce a correct solution.
9. A ***means-end analysis*** is a heuristic in which a current state is compared with a goal state, and changes are made to reduce the difference between the two states.
10. ***Insight*** is a sudden, unexpected solution or a strategy that leads to a solution to a problem. Insight depends on prior learning experience.
11. ***Functional fixedness*** is a mental set that hinders the discovery of solutions to problems.

For Further Thought

1. Referring to Figure 12.6, why do you think humans are prone to "coyote physics" (named after the impossible events depicted in Roadrunner® cartoons)?
2. In Chapter 9 we learned that daydreams involve future plans as well as fantasies and memories. In what way is vicarious trial-and-error learning related to daydreams? Why do you think this type of thinking evolved?

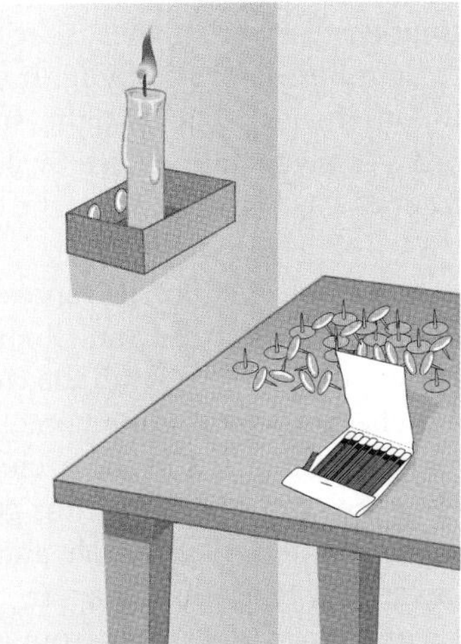

Figure 12.10 Solution to Duncker's candle problem. The box that contains the thumbtacks, if tacked to the wall, can be used as a platform for the candle.

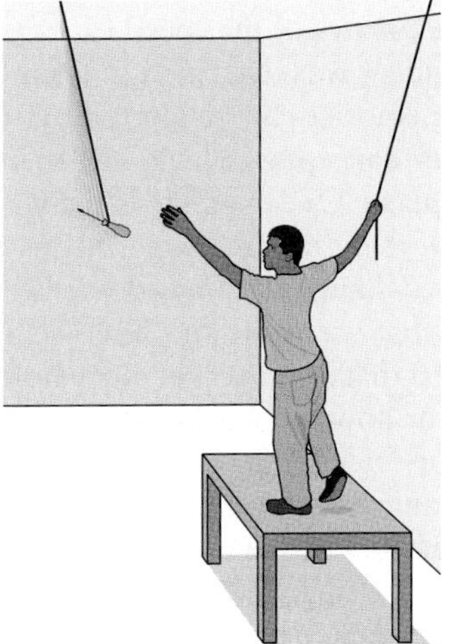

Figure 12.11 Solution to the string problem. To solve this problem, tie the screwdriver to the string and stand on the table. Then swing the screwdriver away from you, grab the other string, and catch the screwdriver when it comes back to you. While holding onto the other string, untie the screwdriver, then tie the two strings together.

3. In Chapter 9 we also learned that one function of dreams may be to "practice" what was learned earlier in the day. When faced with a problem to be solved, why might "I'll sleep on it" be a good strategy?
4. Are there lessons to be learned from the difficulties people have in *mental imaging* and *mental rotation,* which might apply to "seeing things from someone else's point of view"?
5. Is the rule "*i* before *e* except after *c*, or when sounded as *a* as in *neighbor* or *weigh*" a heuristic or an algorithm?
6. What is the role of persistence in problem solving? Do you think a child could be trained to become more insightful if teachers and parents reinforced persistence? HINT: Having an insight, and successful problem solving in general, are positively reinforcing events.

THINKING WITH LANGUAGE

If you see a person smiling or laughing and no one else is around, chances are that person is thinking of something funny. He may have just heard a joke or had a phone conversation and is mentally recalling the experience. Such private conversations and remembrances often guide our social interactions.

One of the most important functions of language is to connect the thinking of one human being with another. A professor who asks a student to solve a math problem or conjugate a verb, for example, assumes that the student will think in words and symbols to come up with the answer. The words in our head determine much of what we think about, including our silent problem solving. But speaking, listening, writing, and reading are primarily social enterprises.

The Influence of Language on Perception and Thought

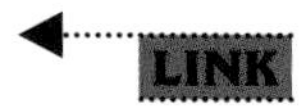

Misleading language influences perception and memory, Chapter 10, p. 362

Thinking in words is not divorced from thinking in images. Recall that in Elizabeth Loftus's (1979) research on eyewitness testimony, the way in which a question was posed could influence a person's perceptions. Specifically, witnesses' estimates of the speed of a car at the time it hit another car were higher if the accident was described in terms of *smashing* rather than *hitting* or *bumping*. If our memories can be altered by words, then certainly other aspects of thought, such as concepts—which are themselves merely words—can be influenced by language. One example is the way in which the concept of God is affected by the use of the pronoun *he* or *she*.

Language and semantic memory, Chapter 10, p. 365

Language also provides an important basis for knowledge: words represent what we know and how we know it (Kintsch, 1974, 1998). Recall from Chapter 10 that *semantic memory* holds both a lexicon (a mental dictionary) and the rules for how the words in that lexicon are used. In that chapter we examined one line of evidence suggesting that long-term memory may be organized in hierarchical language-based categories. (*Is a canary a bird?*) But the seemingly effortless generation of speech and the automaticity of skilled reading defy such simple analysis. Using visual sensory and perceptual processes to read this chapter, for example, your eye movements effortlessly move from left to right, and from line to line (Schiffman, 1972). But if you come upon a statement that doesn't seem to make sense, you get some insight into this mysterious process. You stop, reread the sentence until you understand it, and then resume your normal reading speed (Ericsson & Simon, 1993). People seem to read and understand effortlessly unless and until they lose their train of thought. In other words, reading often seems to *be* thinking. One question, then, is the extent to which language *determines* the way we think.

The Linguistic Relativity Hypothesis

According to the **linguistic relativity hypothesis,** differences in language are responsible for differences in the way people think. Also known as the Sapir-Whorf hypothesis (after its two vocal proponents, Edwin Sapir and Benjamin Whorf), the linguistic relativity hypothesis can be applied at both the cultural and the individual level. Let's look first at the role of language in culture.

Whorf (1956) proposed that words, and the way we use them, shape our conception of the world. For example, Native Americans living in the Northwest can discriminate among dozens of wild mushrooms, whereas a person who lacks their experience would tend to generalize all of them as mushrooms. In this example, both the names for mushrooms and experience with them allow Native Americans to form multiple concepts of these plants—as food, poison, drugs, and so forth.

The most widely known example of the Sapir-Whorf hypothesis concerns the number of words Inuits have for snow. Inuits were once mistakenly thought to have more words than other groups for the varieties of snow (sleet, slush, ice, and so forth). Whorf argued, therefore, that Inuits have more concepts of snow. But in fact they have no more words for snow and ice than other peoples who live in northern climes (Martin, 1986; Pullum, 1991). The language of a culture does not necessarily force differences in concepts, then, as the linguistic relativity hypothesis suggests.

Another way to think about the linguistic relativity hypothesis is in terms of individual differences. No matter how many words for snow Inuits or Colorado natives have, most of us would trust their knowledge of winter weather more than the knowledge of a native Floridian. The same is as true for the person who has spent a lifetime gathering mushrooms for a meal or teaching algebra to college-bound students. Individual experience is what counts. In Chapter 10 we saw that chess experts differ from novices in that they recognize more patterns in the placement of chess pieces on the board (deGroot, 1965). But *expert knowledge* can also be defined in terms of the language or unique vocabularies of specially trained individuals. Physicians, historians, plumbers, and attorneys all have their own specialized language, or *jargon,* for thinking about and solving their domain-specific problems. Because of their specialized language and the concepts it represents, experts think differently from other people and are more effective in their domains.

In fact, language use helps to define all sorts of individual differences. Merely by listening to those around us, we can hear these differences. Some people have more to say than others, and more words to express their ideas with. Estimates of vocabulary size range from a few thousand words in some individuals to tens of thousands in others. Not surprisingly, verbal intelligence is related to language expertise. IQ tests sample not only how many words a person knows, but also how that person uses words to solve problems. As we'll see in the next two chapters, individuals vary considerably in their verbal abilities, in their measured IQ scores, and in their personalities. In part, these differences are due to differences in language-related thinking.

Finally, Kanzi's thought processes are severely limited because he has only a few words to think with. He makes no inquiries about what humans are thinking, because he hasn't got the words with which to think about the existence of other minds. At the individual level, then, both for chimps and for humans, differences in language capabilities determine differences in thinking.

linguistic relativity hypothesis (Sapir and Whorf) The theory that differences in language are responsible for differences in the way people think.

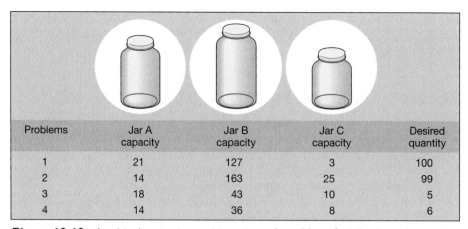

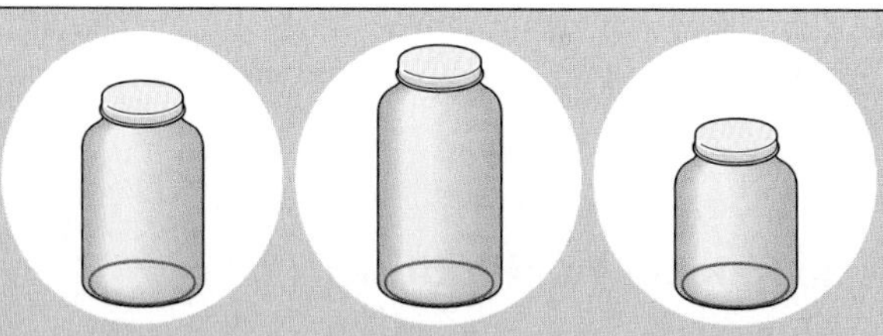

Problems	Jar A capacity	Jar B capacity	Jar C capacity	Desired quantity
1	21	127	3	100
2	14	163	25	99
3	18	43	10	5
4	14	36	8	6

Figure 12.12 Luchins' water jar problem. In each problem, find the desired quantity (column 5) by filling and emptying some combination of the jars A, B, and C. (See below for the solution.)

The Effect of Mental Set on Problem Solving

Figure 12.12 poses a problem of a different type from the others. Although both the banana and crate problem and Duncker's candle problem can be solved without language, Luchins' water jar experiment requires both language and mathematical manipulation (Luchins, 1942). Figure 12.12 shows three water jars of different capacity. The idea is to combine the water in the three different jars so as to obtain a specified quantity of water (see column 5). For example, in problem 1, to arrive at 100 cups of water you would fill jar B to capacity (127 cups), then pour 21 cups from jar B into jar A, leaving 106 cups in jar B (127 – 21 = 106). Next, you would fill jar C from jar B, dump it, and fill it again. The amount of water remaining in jar B would then be 100 cups (106 – 3 – 3 = 100).

You may want to take a few minutes to solve problems 2 though 4. If you have difficulty with problem 4, you can attribute it to the expectations, or **mental set**, you formed in doing the first three problems. That is, problems 1 through 3 are all solved in a similar manner. Because problem 4 looks like problems 1 through 3, most people try to solve it the same way. In Luchins' original experiment, students solved 10 similar problems before being shown a different one.

A mental set forms when a particular behavior is consistently reinforced. Under many circumstances, mental sets are desirable, but not always. Being reinforced for pounding nails with a hammer can instill the mental set that *hammers are for pounding nails*—a mental set related to functional fixedness. Thus you may never discover that you can also use a hammer as a lever. From an educational point of view, students should be exposed to a variety of problems, whether they involve mathematics or home repair. Extensive repetition of just one type of problem encourages the stereotypical thinking characteristic of functional fixedness.

Types of consciousness and thinking, Chapter 9, p. 306

mental set Expectations formed from repeated reinforced trials.

Types of Thinking

Earlier in this chapter, we recognized that the musician, mathematician, athlete, and scientist all have unique ways of viewing and expressing reality. Each thinks about the world differently, and because of those differences, each approaches problem solving differently. For example, rational thinking may be required to solve problems in mathematics, but not to perform music or run a race. Let's look at several different types of thinking.

Deductive Reasoning. If A is equal to B, and B is equal to C, then A is equal to C. This familiar statement is a general rule about the concept of equality. In **deductive reasoning,** a general rule such as this one is applied to particular circumstances. For instance, if the value of $1 equals the value of 10 dimes, and that in turn equals the value of 100 pennies, we can deduce that $1 and 100 pennies have the same value.

Although we seldom use the formal term, deductive reasoning governs much of our thinking. However, formal deductive reasoning must be learned, and some people are better at it than others (Johnson-Laird, 1985). Consider the following:

All college students like pizza.

Bill Smith likes pizza.

Therefore, Bill Smith is a college student.

This group of sentences is called a *syllogism.* The first sentence is called a *major premise,* the second a *minor premise,* and the last a *conclusion.* In this example, the conclusion is false, because the major premise leaves open the possibility that some noncollege students may also like pizza—and Bill Smith may be one of them.

Now consider this syllogism:

Most athletes scored high on the standardized test.

Jake is an athlete.

Therefore, Jake scored high on the standardized test.

The conclusion to this syllogism is also false, because Jake could be among those athletes who did not score high on the test. If you knew Bill or Jake, you might stop before jumping to the wrong conclusion. The tendency to look for evidence that verifies our own preconceptions is called **confirmation bias.** To guard against confirmation bias, a logician would attempt to *disconfirm* rather than confirm the conclusions of these syllogisms (Wason, 1968; Johnson-Laird & Wason, 1977).

Inductive Reasoning. Although scientists often use deductive reasoning to test their hypotheses, they also use imagery, mental modeling, and other types of thinking (Krueger, 1976). For example, Albert Einstein visualized his mathematical theory of relativity in terms of the relative movement of passing trains. Another type of logical thinking scientists use is called **inductive reasoning,** or reasoning from particular instances to a general rule. For instance, I may notice that the hot-water faucet is on the left-hand side of the sink in my house, your house, and other places. If so, I may form the general rule that the hot-water faucet is always on the left. Children use the same process to acquire basic concepts. For instance, children who have encountered specific instances of the phrase "less than" and "more than" learn the general concepts of less and more.

The experimental psychologist Doug Gillan has demonstrated that chimpanzees can be trained to use the same type of reasoning without language (Gillan, 1981, 1983). Gillan presented a chimp pairs of containers, each with a different cover and a different amount of food. The chimp's task was to learn that one of the containers in each pair always had more food than the other, and that the color of the cover signaled which had more. For example, in a green versus blue pair, the green-colored top always covered more food than the blue-colored top; in a red versus green pair, the red top always covered more than the green. After extensive training, Gillan presented a problem the chimp had never before seen: in a red versus blue pair, which container has more food? Chimps consistently chose red over blue—evidence of inductive reasoning. The chimps' ability resembles the inductive reasoning abilities of children in learning the *greater than* rule.

deductive reasoning A type of rational thinking in which specific instances are inferred from a general rule or principle.

confirmation bias The tendency to look for evidence that verifies one's preconceptions.

inductive reasoning A type of rational thinking in which particular instances are used to form a general rule.

Both inductive and deductive reasoning are examples of rational thinking. Knowing rules and being able to derive rules from specific instances, however, does not guarantee either rational thinking or rational behavior. For example, everyone knows that drinking impairs one's driving ability, and that impaired driving is a factor in automobile accidents. Logically, then, people who think rationally should not drink. But large numbers of people who would not describe themselves as irrational thinkers do drink and drive. In part, this maladaptive behavior is due to disruption of the brain activity that underlies rational thinking.

Word Problems

Are you ready to solve a word problem? Try this one:

> Susan drives her car from Boston to New York City at an average speed of 50 mph. Twenty minutes after she leaves, Allan leaves New York City and starts for Boston at 60 mph. Both take the same 220-mile route between the two cities. Which car is closest to Boston when they meet? (Sternberg, 1986, p. 215)

Depending on what kind of thinker you are, your past experiences with word problems, and your performance on other problems presented in this chapter, you may think you recognize this kind of problem. However, let me suggest a different mental set. This is not a math problem at all: the quantification is designed to mislead you into thinking that some sort of calculation is required. Focus your attention instead on the last sentence of the problem, and try again. Is one car closer to Boston when they meet? (See Figure 12.13.)

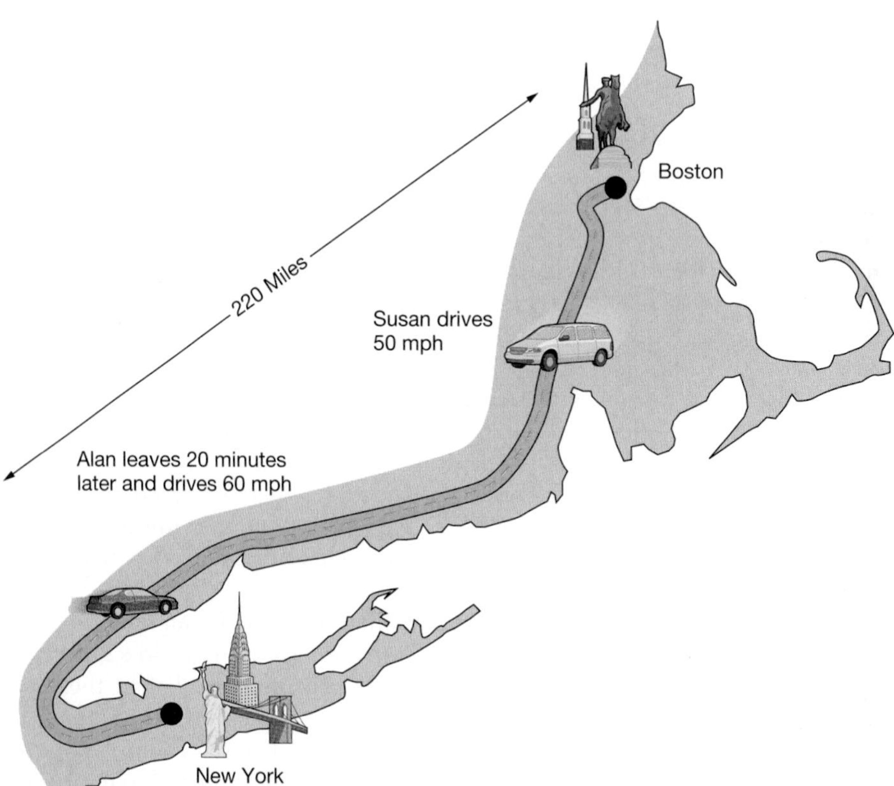

Figure 12.13 **Visualizing a word problem.** Making a sketch of a word problem often helps in its solution. (See discussion, this page and next.)

Word problems can be difficult for many different reasons. To solve them, a person must be a critically perceptive reader (and listener) who focuses first on framing the question (determining the important variables and discarding irrelevant information). Once the question has been framed, one can try to recall similar problems one has encountered in the past. In fact, a major difficulty students have in solving word problems is recognizing that problem A is similar to problem B, and that both can be solved using similar reasoning (Weaver & Kintsch, 1992). The successful solution of a word problem requires the consideration of alternative methods and all relevant information (Davidson & Sternberg, 1984).

The way in which a problem is expressed has a huge effect on its solution. For example, researchers asked different groups of first-graders to solve one of these two versions of a math problem (Hudson, 1983):

Version A Joe has 8 sticks.
He has 5 more sticks than Tom has.
How many sticks does Tom have?

Version B There are 8 birds and 5 worms.
How many birds did not get a worm?

Even though the arithmetic is identical, only 39 percent of the first-graders solved version A, compared with 79 percent for version B (Hudson, 1983).

Finally, different word problems are solved in different ways. Some can be solved verbally; others must be solved mathematically, by applying the rules for setting up equations and manipulating numbers spatially (using a graph, for example), or in yet other ways (Halpern, 1989). Word problems are probably difficult because of their many different conceptual components, which are mediated by different brain areas and must be integrated in the solution. Fortunately, problems such as where two cars that are traveling at different speeds will meet occur infrequently in day-to-day problem solving. (They'll both be the same distance from Boston when they meet.)

INTERIM SUMMARY

1. Thinking with language is reflected in the social actions of speaking and listening.
2. Language influences our perceptions and thoughts, allowing us to make connections with the world and providing one basis for our knowledge.
3. Unless it is interrupted by a question about meaning, skilled reading *is* effortless thought.
4. According to the ***linguistic relativity*** hypothesis (also known as the Sapir-Whorf hypothesis), the words we use determine the way in which we think.
5. Experts have unique vocabularies with which to express their specialized knowledge. Language plays a role both in the way a person thinks and in verbal intelligence.
6. People who encounter the same type of problem repeatedly develop a ***mental set*** that can interfere with the solution of other problems.
7. Rational thinking includes both ***deductive*** and ***inductive reasoning.*** In deductive reasoning, a general rule is used to make inferences about specific instances. In inductive reasoning, particular instances are used to form a general rule.
8. Looking for evidence that verifies one's preconceptions, while ignoring contradictory evidence, is called a ***confirmation bias.***
9. The successful solution of word problems requires a careful reading and framing of the question, as well as the determination of what information is and is not relevant. The process also requires the recall of analogous problems and the methods of reasoning used to solve them.
10. Word problems are difficult because their solution requires a combination of verbal, mathematical, and spatial reasoning.

WEB ACTIVITY

For Further Thought

1. A person's thinking may be inferred from his or her behavior. Analyze the statement "I can see by your eyes that you don't understand what I'm saying." What does the statement "I hear what you're saying" mean?
2. Most math books are divided into chapters, each of which ends with a set of similar problems. Can you think of one good reason for this study strategy and one bad reason?
3. Your child is attending a local elementary school with an innovative curriculum that is supposed to build extensive vocabularies. Some parents and teachers think the teacher's time could be better spent on other activities. Can you use the Sapir-Whorf hypothesis to support the curriculum?
4. What is the point of the key term definitions in the margins of this text? Why might you consider studying the end-of-text glossary in preparing for a comprehensive final exam?

CONCLUDING THOUGHTS

Thinking and the use of language are cognitive activities that require the conscious integration of perception and memory. Presumably, humans evolved language, problem solving, and thinking because those abilities allowed them to share perceptual and emotional experiences, which increased their fitness by promoting social organization and harmony. Language is a critical stage in the development of human consciousness, and the most important means for transmitting memes from one generation to the next.

Historically, psychologists believed that language and thinking separated humans from other animals. However, many animals think: they solve problems, form cognitive maps, and communicate intentionally with other members of their species. The brains of humans, chimpanzees, and other complicated animals are organized in a way that allows them to attend to and vocalize sounds, to point, to make tools, and to think ahead. Yet language abilities make humans unique.

How children learn language is a matter of intense debate. Nativists such as Noam Chomsky stress genetic programs, including a proposed language acquisition device (LAD) and a universal grammar that unfolds during a critical period of development. Behaviorists acknowledge the cortical basis for language, but emphasize the role of the environment in shaping language acquisition and usage through modeling and reinforcement. While humans have a genetic capacity for speech, they require a supportive environment in which to express it. The importance of culture in language development is overwhelming. Environment determines a speaker's native tongue, vocabulary, and the emotional meaning of words. The absence of cultural support has a devastating impact on language development, as can be seen in cases of neglected and feral children.

Thinking can be demonstrated in the ability to form and manipulate mental images and mental models of how the world works. Humans have insights, learn from their mistakes (trial-and-error learning), and can imagine the consequences of an action (vicarious trial-and-error learning). They use heuristics, algorithms, means-end analyses, and deductive and inductive reasoning to solve problems. All these forms of thinking are adaptive. Humans also use language to think, and the way in which they think is heavily influenced by language. Logical analyses and rational thinking depend on a thorough knowledge of the meaning of words. We will see in the next chapter that individual differences in intelligence are also related to language.

KEY TERMS

algorithm *436*
animal communication *420*
aphasia *418*
Broca's area *418*
child-directed speech *429*
confirmation bias *443*
deductive reasoning *443*
functional fixedness *438*
inductive reasoning *443*
insight *437*
language acquisition device (LAD) *428*
linguistic relativity hypothesis *441*
means-end analysis *436*
mental set *442*
one-word utterance stage *428*
referential pointing *416*
telegraphic speech *430*
trial-and-error learning *435*
universal grammar *430*
vicarious trial-and-error-learning *435*
Wernicke's area *418*

13

Intelligence

Sigmund Walter Hampel *Allegory of Genius of Beethoven*. Beethoven House, Vienna, Austria / ET Archive, London / SuperStock

A Brief History of Intelligence Testing
The Pioneering Work of Francis Galton
Alfred Binet's Program of Intelligence Testing
Spearman's Concept of General Intelligence (g)
The Stanford-Binet Intelligence Test
The Army Alpha and Beta Tests
The Wechsler Intelligence Tests
Interim Summary
For Further Thought

IQ and Alternative Theories of Intelligence
The Meaning of an IQ Score
The Validity of IQ Tests
The Construct of Intelligence
Alternatives to IQ Tests
Gardner's Theory of Multiple Intelligences
Sternberg's Triarchic Theory of Intelligence
Interim Summary
For Further Thought

The Bell Curve Wars: The Sources of Intelligence
Genes and Cognitive Abilities
Effect of the Environment on Intelligence
Interaction of Genes and Environment
Passive Versus Dynamic Exposure
Equal Environments and Opportunities, and Unequal Outcomes
The Flynn Effect
Biological Bases of Intelligence
Interim Summary
For Further Thought

The Bell Curve Wars: Intelligence and Culture
Ethnic Differences in IQ
Educational Implications of Ethnic Differences
Real-World Consequences of Differences in IQ
Interim Summary
For Further Thought

Concluding Thoughts

In the following letter, published in the *APA Monitor* (June, 1989), the psychologist John Garcia described his personal experience with intelligence tests:

> In 1925 I flunked the third grade and had to repeat it. Mom said I flunked because I hung out with Grandpa talking Spanish, but what did Mom know? Interpreting the graph (of the growth of average intelligence test scores between 1918–1989) I estimated my IQ in 1925 was 78. No wonder I flunked!
>
> In 1983 when I got into the National Academy of Sciences my estimated IQ was only 97; I hope I don't get kicked out!
>
> In the *American Psychologist* in 1981 I wrote how IQ was completely cooked up by statistical finagling, but now I am convinced I got lots of late-blooming smart genes from Grandpa.
>
> By the year 2000 my IQ will rise to about 105, then I may be able to figure out exactly how ephemeral IQ is causally linked to durable genes; and exactly why, a few years back, college admission scores like SAT were falling while IQ was rising.

Yes, this is the same John Garcia who did the bright, noisy, tasty water experiment described in Chapter 6. His derisive letter points out many of the contradictions inherent in our understanding of intelligence. A bright, articulate member of the National Academy of Sciences, Garcia has difficulty reconciling his academic and life success (high) with his alleged score on a common intelligence test (average). Furthermore, he challenges proponents of intelligence testing to explain how, despite the fact that the human genetic endowment hasn't changed substantially over the past 100,000 years, a person's intelligence score can rise over a lifetime.

Students of all ages take aptitude tests.

Few subjects in psychology are as interesting or as controversial as the study of intelligence. Humans see, hear, and sleep in about the same way, but individual differences in intelligence are marked. What is more, they have a significant effect on people's personal lives. Differences in higher-level cognitive abilities affect people's social interactions, incomes, and educational and career opportunities, as well as the policies educators follow in the schools they and their children attend.

The study of intelligence also brings to the forefront a conflict within the field of psychology. Fundamentally, it is a conflict between psychologists' scientific goals and their ethical obligations to society. Even if psychologists can agree on what intelligence is and how to measure it—and that is by no means assured—the question remains: How should psychologists, educators, and employers use intelligence testing? Too often, people who score low on such tests end up among society's have-nots. How many "late bloomers" like John Garcia are overlooked because they fail to shine on an IQ test?

Not surprisingly, questions about intelligence have often been framed in terms of nature and nurture, two themes that have run throughout this text. Does a person do well in school because he or she is intelligent to begin with, or do schooling and home environment make a person smart? If intelligence is inherited, then it is like all the other psychological constructs we have encountered so far: It evolved because it enhanced the species' fitness. But if intelligence results from the combined efforts of parents, teachers, and a supportive culture, then its expression is more an example of current adaptiveness. We will see that this characteristic is adaptive in both senses of the word. In fact, researchers agree that intelligence is one of the most adaptive of all human characteristics.

In this chapter we will discuss theories of intelligence in some detail. We will begin with a brief history of the development of intelligence tests. Then we will consider the question of whether there is one kind of intelligence or many. We will examine the evidence for both genetic and cultural contributions to intelligence. Later in the chapter we will return to Garcia's conundrum and try to explain why intelligence scores have been rising in recent decades. Finally, we will confront the thorny question of the ethics of intelligence testing.

A BRIEF HISTORY OF INTELLIGENCE TESTING

Ironically, given its central importance in psychology, interest in intelligence is relatively recent. The term does not appear in William James's (1890) *Principles of Psychology,* and was mentioned in only a few psychology books before 1927 (Spearman, 1927). In part, the concept of intelligence has proved controversial because of a lack of agreement on its definition. The word *intelligence* (from the Latin for "to choose between") predates by thousands of years the attempts of both early and present-day psychologists to conceptualize and measure intelligence. Nonscientific definitions and synonyms are important, in that they portend many theories of intelligence that psychologists have since proposed. Over the centuries, the intelligent have been described as *bright,* as having *a natural quickness of understanding,* while those who are less than intelligent have been described as *dull* or *slow*. Other terms used to describe intelligent people are *astute, clever, alert, apt, discerning, shrewd, sharp,* and *smart*. From these basic definitions emerge two points: that individuals differ in intelligence, and that having more intelligence than others is good, while having less is not so good. Intelligence, then, is a defining aspect of one's personality.

Beginning with Francis Galton's work in the 1860s (about which more will be said shortly), several generations of researchers have attempted to measure individual differences in intelligence, but have achieved little consensus. More than a century after Galton, a survey of a dozen or more theorists revealed that they continued to define intelligence in different ways (Sternberg & Detterman, 1986). More recently, in an article entitled "Intelligence: Knowns and Unknowns," a panel of psychologists attempted to summarize what was known about intelligence and address some of the controversy surrounding the concept (Neisser et al., 1996). In doing so, they proposed that an intelligent person could adapt effectively to the environment, learn from experience, overcome obstacles by thinking, engage in various forms of reasoning, and understand complex ideas. To be useful, however, each of the reasonable-sounding abilities in this definition would need to be operationally defined. How *would* psychologists go about measuring the ability to adapt to the environment or to learn from experience?

To gain a better appreciation of the difficulties involved in the scientific study of intelligence, let's start at the beginning, with Francis Galton's work.

The Pioneering Work of Francis Galton

The first intelligence test, a collection of nonlanguage performance tests, was given in the 19th century. The theory, methods, and intended use of the test Francis Galton (1822–1911) developed were similar to those of today's IQ tests in one important respect: they contained the seeds of current controversies over intelligence testing. In many other respects, Galton's test differed from modern intelligence tests.

Galton was Charles Darwin's younger cousin. Much impressed with Darwin's theory of evolution, he wondered whether it could be applied to intelligence. In *Hereditary Genius,* published in 1869, Galton observed that statistically, eminent British men were more likely to be genetically related to other eminent men than would be expected simply by chance. (He did not develop the same argument for women, who for most of the 19th century were not allowed access to higher education or positions of authority. Perhaps because of his place in this culture, Galton thought *a priori* that women were generally less intelligent than men.) Galton theorized that these differences in intelligence had evolved through natural selection.

Galton's Methods. Galton had examined the family trees of famous judges, statesmen, military commanders, writers, scientists, poets, and musicians (Fancher, 1990). He found that any two of these men were four times more likely to enjoy a close genetic relationship (such as father-son) than a second-degree relationship (such as grandfather-grandson). Moreover, second-degree relationships were also four times more frequent than third-degree relationships (to great-grandparents, cousins, and so forth). Galton concluded that intelligence was an inherited trait.

Later, in related research, Galton (1874) sent self-questionnaires to scientists in the Royal Society and asked them what they thought had contributed most to their successful careers. In their responses many acknowledged the role of class privilege, education, and the motivating factor of prestige. The results of the survey forced Galton to acknowledge that culture as well as genes contributed to eminence. To describe the two general influences on intelligence he coined the expression, *nature and nurture*.

In later work, Galton (1888) collected data from the general population in a laboratory in London. He measured head size (to estimate brain size), reaction times, seeing and hearing abilities, and so forth. Again he found these measures to be normally distributed across the general population. That is, the distribution of each of these abilities throughout the population as a whole was described by a bell-shaped curve (see Figure 2.6, page 53).

During this period in England, scientists were breeding plants and animals for a variety of physical and behavioral characteristics. Galton's work was motivated in part by his desire to promote *eugenics,* a program for improving the overall intelligence of the human species. Only those individuals who scored highest on his intelligence tests, he believed, should be allowed to breed (Fancher, 1990).

Psychological abilities are normally distributed, Chapter 2, p. 52

Galton's Legacy. Despite his sexist views and his controversial beliefs about the uses of intelligence tests, Galton made a number of lasting contributions to the study of intelligence. He was the first scientist to measure and statistically analyze psychological variables related to intelligence. We may not agree with Galton's analysis of the sources of eminence, or with his hypothesis that head size and reaction time were related to intelligence. But he was the first scientist to discover that psychological variables were normally distributed, in the same way as physical variables. Furthermore, Galton's acknowledgment of the dual influence of nature and nurture persists to the present, though genetic analyses and studies of twins have replaced his analysis of family trees. Galton rightly guessed that differences in brain structure are related to intelligence. Some current scientists agree with his proposal that brain size is another important variable in intelligence, as we'll see later. Current research supports his idea that differences in reaction time (quickness) are correlated with intelligence.

Galton was a modern scientist, in the sense that he valued the objective study of natural phenomena and believed that even something as intimate as intelligence could and should be studied objectively. However, as a member of England's elite upper class, he was oblivious to the consequences of the value judgments inherent in his scientific pronouncements. From his position of inherited privilege and superior intelligence, he looked down and passed judgment on the relative worth of those who were less privileged and intelligent. In naming the bell-shaped curve a "normal curve," he suggested to later generations that *normal* meant *mediocre* (Hacking, 1996). Certainly he and other eminent white British males considered themselves better in every respect than commoners. His advocacy of eugenics crossed the line between science (observation and understanding) and public policy (interpreting and acting on scientific knowledge). We'll return to these issues in the last section of this chapter.

Alfred Binet is credited with developing the first modern intelligence test, similar to those in use today.

Alfred Binet's Program of Intelligence Testing

In the mid-1800s, the government of France embarked on the universal education of French children. By the end of the century, French educators had become interested in the problem of how to educate "subnormal" children. At that time there was no way to measure and compare children's intelligence. Alfred Binet (1857–1911) accepted the challenge of developing a national test to identify children of marginal intellectual competence.

Binet, like Galton, was independently wealthy. From 1894 until his death 17 years later he directed the laboratory for the study of physiological psychology at the Sorbonne, the premiere university of France. Based on his laboratory research and the careful observation of his two young daughters, Binet (1903) published *The Experimental Study of Intelligence*. Like Galton, he believed that intelligence varied widely among individuals and was positively related to brain size.

In 1905, in collaboration with a colleague named Theodore Simon, Binet developed and administered a 31-item national test for French children. The Binet-Simon test began with performance abilities that all but the most profoundly retarded children could complete, such practical matters as unwrapping and eating a piece of candy and complying with gestures or spoken requests. More difficult items, such as telling the difference between paper and cardboard and memorizing a simple phrase, could easily be accomplished by normal 6-year-olds. The last items were intended to identify children with superior intelligence. For example, only a few children could construct a sentence containing the three words *Paris, river,* and *fortune* (Fancher, 1990).

Revisions of the test in 1908 and 1911 established "normal" third grade and sixth grade intellectual levels. Children were tested on five items at each grade level, covering short-term and long-term memory tests for math, vocabulary, reasoning ability, general knowledge, and even mental imagery. To solve a time problem, Binet asked children to mentally rotate the hands of a clock. In the 1911 version, a child's score was reported as the number of items that were answered correctly at each grade level. For example, if an 8-year-old child in the third grade got all of the second grade items correct (+ 2.0 points), 4 out of 5 of the third grade items (+ 0.8), and 2 out of 5 of the fourth grade items (+ 0.4), the child's intellectual level was reported as 3.2 (that is, 2.0 + 0.8 + 0.4 = 3.2). A third grader working at a level of 3.2 was considered to be slightly above average.

Even more than Galton, Binet emphasized the fact that individuals differed in intelligence. He added the idea of developmental differences in intelligence that could be quantified in terms of age. That is, people differ predictably in their intellectual levels throughout their childhood years. Binet was also struck by qualitative differences in intelligence. When his two daughters were teenagers, he gave them a leaf from a tree and asked them to write about it. One of his daughters described it as a scientist might, and the other one wrote about it as a romanticized symbol of the life cycle (Fancher, 1990). Binet concluded that people can express their intelligence in different ways.

Spearman's Concept of General Intelligence (*g*)

Even after testing the mental abilities of hundreds of adults and children, Binet remained skeptical of efforts to quantify mental abilities. He thought that individual intelligence was too varied to be reduced to a few numbers. Such was not the case with his contemporary in England, Charles Spearman (1863–1945). Spearman was impressed with the fact that different measures of intelligence were correlated. For example, children who scored high on certain measures of sensory acuity tended to score high on a rating of "cleverness in school" (Hergenhahn, 1992). Spearman (1904) proposed that different tests of intelligence all measured a common ability, which he named **general intelligence** (*g*). Ironically, the measures of visual and auditory acuity that Galton and Spearman considered indicators of intelligence do *not* correlate with currently accepted measures of intelligence. Nevertheless, Spearman's proposal of a general intellectual capability, *g*, remains a central issue in contemporary theories of intelligence (Deary, 2001; Jensen, 1998).

general intelligence (*g*) A common intellectual ability inferred from the correlation of scores for specific abilities on intelligence tests.

The Stanford-Binet Intelligence Test

In 1916, Lewis Terman of Stanford University modified the Binet test slightly because California children's results did not match French children. In California, 5-year-olds were more advanced than French children, but by age 12, Californians had fallen behind. Terman revised the items, simplified the scoring, and standardized the test on a large sample of American students. Eventually it became known as the **Stanford-Binet** test, and is today one of the most widely used of all intelligence tests in the United States.

Terman saw the usefulness of a single score for all age levels. He designated the score a child made on the test as a "mental age." For example, if an 8-year-old's score was an average score for that age group, he set it arbitrarily at "8." Then he divided the child's mental age by the child's chronological age, and multiplied the result by 100 to get rid of the decimals. He called the resulting ratio an **intelligence quotient (IQ)**:

$$\text{Intelligence Quotient, or IQ} = \frac{\text{mental age}}{\text{chronological age}} \times 100$$

In this example, an average 8-year-old with a score of 8 would have an IQ of 100. But what if the 8-year-old performed at a higher or lower level? Let's say the child was 8 1/2 years old and had scored at the 9-year, 3-month-old level. Doing the math, we find an above-average score:

$$\text{IQ} = \frac{9.25}{8.5} = 1.09 \times 100 = 109$$

One last example: Let's say you are 20 years old and score at the average level for a 20-year-old. Your IQ on the Stanford-Binet test would be $20/20 \times 100 = 100$. But, suppose that at age 20 you know all that you are ever going to know in your lifetime. If you take the same test when you're 40 years old and make exactly the same score, your IQ will be:

$$20/40 \times 100 = 50$$

Obviously, the computational method had to be changed if the Stanford-Binet test was to be administered to adults. Adult scores are now compared to the scores of other adults. If an adult's score is average compared to those of all other adult test takers, his or her IQ is set at 100.

The Army Alpha and Beta Tests

Intelligence testing of children proved both useful and popular. When World War I began, it brought an immediate need for an adult version. In 1917, Terman and a colleague, Robert Yerkes, convinced the United States Army that intelligence testing could aid in the placement of the large number of inductees and in the appointment of officers. Yerkes was made a major, and for the next 2 years oversaw the testing of 1.75 million servicemen.

The army developed two different tests. The Army Alpha was developed for those inductees who could read, and the Army Beta, for the 40 percent of inductees who were either illiterate or spoke a foreign language. The validity of these tests, and their usefulness to the army, are both open to question (Hergenhahn, 1992). Their significance lies in their demonstration that the large-scale psychological testing of groups was feasible. They also set the stage for the use of psychological testing for purposes other than general intellectual assessment and school placement.

Stanford-Binet A commonly used standardized intelligence test that yields an IQ score.

intelligence quotient (IQ) A single number that represents a child's intelligence, computed by dividing the child's mental age by the child's chronological age and multiplying the result by 100.

The large-scale intellectual assessment of adults began in 1917 when soldiers were inducted into the U.S. Army for service in World War I.

Today, all branches of the military use sophisticated psychological tests to select pilots, officers, and other specialized personnel. More than one million people take the Armed Services Vocational Aptitude Battery (ASVAB) each year, as well as over 9,000 skill classification tests (Murphy & Davidshofer, 1998). The use of group testing has spread to institutions of higher learning. Many colleges select the most promising students based on their performance on the Scholastic Assessment Test (SAT) or the American College Test (ACT). In addition, the GRE, LSAT, and MCAT are used to predict who will perform the best in academic, legal, and medical programs. Later in this chapter we'll look at the relationship between these standardized tests and intelligence tests.

The Wechsler Intelligence Tests

To fill a need for an adult equivalent of the Stanford-Binet test, David Wechsler (1958) developed the first individual IQ test for adults. Today, the revised **Wechsler Adult Intelligence Scale (WAIS-III)** is the most widely administered test of people ages 16 to 74 (Wechsler, 1997). Its success led to the development and revision of the *Wechsler Intelligence Scale for Children (WISC-III)* for people ages 6 to 16 (Wechsler, 1991). The *Wechsler Preschool and Primary Scales of Intelligence-Revised (WPPSI-R)* is given to children from ages 4 to 6½.

As with the Stanford-Binet, a licensed psychologist or counselor administers the WAIS-III one-on-one. The timed tests are given in the same way to each person so that the results can be compared across individuals. Individual testing offers subjects the advantage of undivided time and attention to the task at hand. But testing a large number of people in this way is time consuming, and the professionals' time is expensive.

Like the revised version of the Stanford-Binet, the WAIS-III contains a variety of test items; for simplicity they are often divided into verbal and performance categories (see Figure 13.1). The verbal subtests cover general information, comprehension, math, similarities, digit span, and vocabulary. The performance subtests include picture completion, block design, object assembly, and picture arrangement. The items that are answered correctly on each subtest are added together, and the two scores are combined to yield a total score. The result is an IQ score that is interpreted in the same way as the Stanford-Binet. The subtests of the WAIS-III will be discussed further in the next section.

Wechsler Adult Intelligence Scale (WAIS-III) A commonly used intelligence test whose combined verbal and performance subtest scores yield an IQ score.

Verbal Subtest

1 *Information*: "What is the capital of the United States?"
2 *Comprehension*: "What does 'A stitch in time saves 9' mean?"
3 *Arithmetic*: "If 3 candy bars cost 25 cents, how much will 18 candy bars cost?"
4 *Similarities*: "How are peanut butter and jelly alike?"
5 *Digit Span*: Repeating a series of numbers forward and backward.
6 *Vocabulary*: "What does canal mean?"

Performance Subtest

Picture Completion

What is missing from this picture?

Block Design Use the separate blocks on the right to make the patterns on the left.

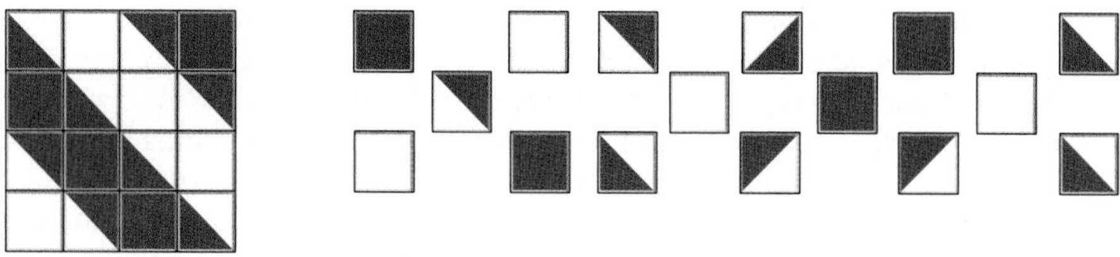

Object Assembly When put together, these parts make a familiar figure. Please put them together as quickly as you can.

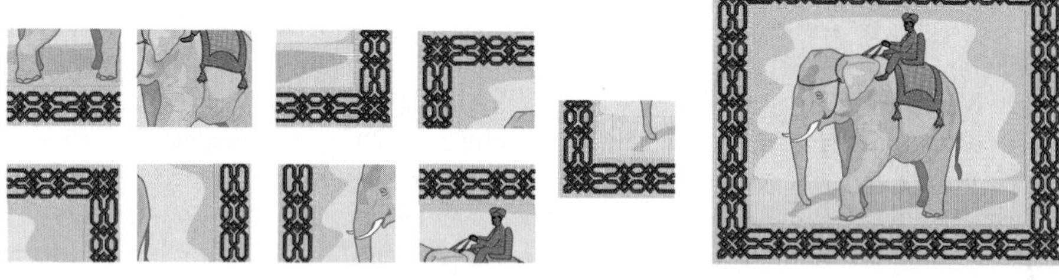

Picture Arrangement Arrange these pictures so that they tell a story.

Figure 13.1 Sample Questions from the *Wechsler Adult Intelligence Scale (WAIS-III).* The following items are similar but not identical to actual test items on the WAIS-III. *Source:*

INTERIM SUMMARY

1. Historically, intelligence is a term that has been used to mean *a natural quickness of understanding*. Psychologists define intelligence as an adaptive capacity to learn from experience, to solve problems, to think rationally, and to understand complex ideas.
2. The history of intelligence testing reveals a focus on individual differences and disagreements about how intelligence should be defined.
3. Francis Galton's (1822–1911) first intelligence test included measurements of head size, reaction times, and visual and auditory acuity. Though Galton eventually modified his position to acknowledge that both "nature and nurture" contributed to a person's intellectual endowment, he assumed that intelligence was inherited. His major contributions include innovations in the measurement and statistical analysis of psychological variables, and the demonstration that those variables are normally distributed.
4. Alfred Binet (1857–1911) developed the first tests to measure and compare the intelligence of children. In doing so he found that each child's schoolwork could be related to grade-level norms. Binet's test items were "modern" in that they included subtests of mathematical ability, vocabulary, reasoning ability, general knowledge, and mental imagery.
5. Charles Spearman (1863–1945) found that individual subtests of intelligence were correlated, and concluded that there is a ***general intelligence (g)*** factor.
6. Lewis Terman modified Binet's test for use with schoolchildren in the United States. A child's or adult's score on the ***Stanford-Binet*** intelligence test is reported as an ***intelligence quotient (IQ)***.
7. Group intelligence testing was first undertaken in the United States Army during World War I. Robert Yerkes developed two different tests, the *Army Alpha* (for readers of English), and the *Army Beta* (for those who couldn't read English, or who spoke a foreign language). Modern versions of group-administered aptitude tests include the ASVAB, SAT, GRE, and others.
8. David Wechsler's ***Wechsler Adult Intelligence Scale (WAIS-III)*** is composed of verbal and performance subtests whose scores are combined to yield an IQ value similar to the Stanford-Binet's.

For Further Thought

1. Given the historical definition of intelligence, and those that psychologists now use (see item 1 in the Interim Summary), which definition do you think best suits the individuals you consider to be intelligent?
2. What problems are inherent in any eugenics program?
3. Binet thought that his two daughters were equally intelligent, but in two different ways. Does this approach to intelligence make sense to you? Because Binet preferred to think of intelligence as a collection of abilities, he was leery of reducing intelligence to a number. Do you agree?
4. In his stage theory of development (see Chapter 11), Piaget proposed that children become more intelligent as they mature. Likewise, Binet found that older schoolchildren could answer more difficult questions than younger ones. Can you think of any differences between these two positions?

IQ AND ALTERNATIVE THEORIES OF INTELLIGENCE

The development and extended use of intelligence testing during the past century has kept psychologists focused on the general nature of intelligence. Not everyone agrees that current intelligence tests are valid—that is, that they truly measure intelligence. And not everyone accepts the dictum that "intelligence is what intelligence tests measure." In this section we will examine the premises on which intelligence tests are based, then explore some alternative theories of intelligence that broaden the traditional definition.

The Meaning of an IQ Score

Test reliability and validity, Chapter 2, p. 60

As the use of IQ tests increased, questions naturally arose about their reliability and validity. After a great deal of research done over many years, experts have confirmed that the WAIS-III and the Stanford-Binet are high in both test-retest and in split-half reliability (see Chapter 2, page 000). For the most part, the questions concerning IQ tests have to do with their *validity*—what they actually measure. The question of validity will be addressed in the next section.

For present purposes, let's assume that intelligence can be operationally defined by the items on an IQ test. By administering IQ tests to thousands of subjects, scientists have developed *standardization norms* that allow individual scores to be compared to all other test takers' scores. For example, after standardization, the distribution of WAIS-III scores form a bell-shaped curve; everyone who takes the test is represented in the area underneath the bell curve (see Figure 13.2). Many people score near the average, and fewer people score very high and very low.

Recall that during the standardization process, the average IQ score is arbitrarily set at a value of 100, so that half the test takers score above 100, and the other half score below 100. The bell curve is then divided into standard deviations, or measures of variance on both sides of the mean score. During the standardization process, test makers adjust the difficulty of the items in order to change the proportions of items that test takers answer correctly. In the final version, one standard deviation from the mean score is equal to 15 IQ points.

Given the characteristics of a normal curve, 68 percent of test takers will have IQs between 85 and 115. Ninety-five percent of all test takers (± 2 standard deviations from the mean) will have IQs between 70 and 130. If you were to be tested tomorrow, your results would be compared to these standardization norms. One implication of this distribution of scores is that IQ is best thought of as a continuous variable rather than a dichotomous one. That is, rather than being characterized by dichotomous terms such as *bright* or *dull, intelligent* or *unintelligent,* an individual's intelligence score lies along a wide range, or continuum of scores.

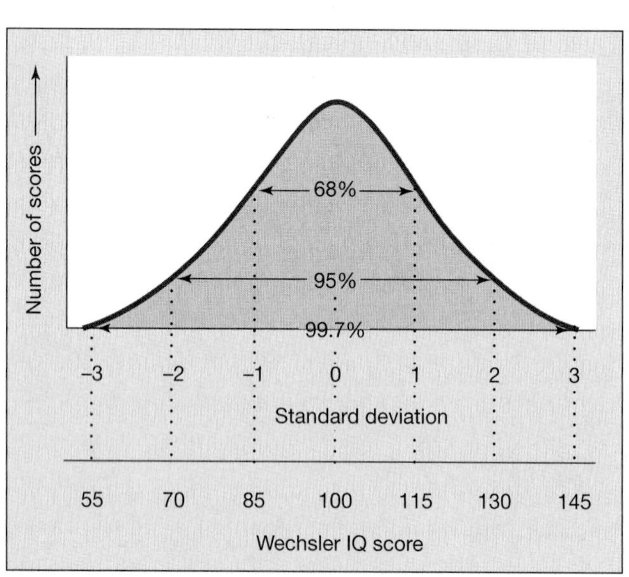

Figure 13.2 The Normal Distribution of IQ Scores. The scores of people who take an IQ test are normally distributed, forming a bell-shaped curve. The highest point of the curve, which represents an average score, is arbitrarily set at 100. As this figure shows, 68 percent of the test takers make scores between 85 and 115, or one standard deviation from the mean. Ninety five percent make scores between 70 and 130, two standard deviations from the mean. The standard deviation is a measure of variance on both sides of the mean score. Few people score very high or very low on the test, as shown by the left-hand and right-hand sides of the curve. Only a fraction of 1 percent of all individuals score above 145 and below 55.

The Validity of IQ Tests

The Stanford-Binet test assumes that intelligence is the ability to succeed in the classroom. From this perspective, a valid test is one that accurately reflects how well a student does schoolwork compared to peers, and predicts how well that student will perform in the future. Because these tests measure a variety of intellectual abilities commonly used in the classroom, the WISC and the Stanford-Binet are highly correlated (about .50) with grades. To earn a high IQ score, a child must do well on tests of language, reasoning, mathematics, spatial abilities, general information, and so forth. These portions of the IQ test are said to give it *content validity*. For example, the general information category contains questions on facts such as the boiling point of water. The more such information a person knows, the higher the score on that subtest. In fact, except for the vocabulary subtest, the general information subtest is the best predictor of a person's overall IQ. People considered intelligent and who score high on IQ tests have larger vocabularies and know more information than others.

Computing standard deviation, Appendix, p. 640

Conversely, a child who doesn't score well on IQ tests typically has problems mastering schoolwork. Some students know less general information than others, and over the years, they learn less. Thus, both the child and adult versions of these tests predict how well a person will perform in the upper grade levels and higher education. Within an educational framework, then, intelligence tests have a degree of *predictive validity*.

The Construct of Intelligence

Just because a test predicts how well a person will do in school, it is not necessarily a good test of general intelligence. To return to the question of how to define intelligence, most people would agree that a person may perform well in school without being especially astute, clever, alert, apt, discerning, or shrewd. Perhaps no intelligence test will ever satisfy a construct of intelligence that includes all those attributes! However, at a minimum, a test of intelligence should test the attributes listed in Table 13.1. Intelligent people should be able to process information rapidly, to solve complex problems that stump others, and to excel at many endeavors (as opposed to just one special skill).

Table 13.1 Three Basic Components That Make Up the Construct of Intelligence

1. The rapid processing, retrieval, and manipulation of information.
2. The ability to think abstractly and solve complex problems using reasoning and conprehension skills.
3. The ability to do a wide variety of tasks, as opposed to one specialized task.

Source: Adapted from Murphy & Davidshofer, 1998.

When applied to schoolwork, traditional IQ tests such as the Stanford-Binet do distinguish people according these three criteria. They also capture some of the elements most psychologists (and most people) think are related to intelligence. That is, an IQ test measures *g*, the general intelligence factor proposed by Spearman, as well as a fairly wide range of specific abilities. One proponent of the view that intelligence is due to a collection of specific abilities was Louis Thurstone (1938, 1947). Thurstone analyzed people's scores on dozens of different intelligence tests using a statistical method called **factor analysis** that measures the relationships among various tests to see what they have in common. This statistical procedure seeks to identify common factors that run through all the tests. Thurstone thought that Spearman had overemphasized *g*; through factor analysis, he identified seven *primary mental abilities,* including perceptual speed and six others found in WAIS-III subtests. His analyses stressed the relative independence of these seven abilities. If individuals differed in these dimensions, he argued, reducing the concept of intelligence to one variable, *g*, would obscure the differences.

Many researchers have been influenced by Thurstone's factor analytic techniques, and by how a person's specific abilities are related to *g*. Figure 13.3 shows a recent formulation, using both factor analysis and *equation modeling* methods, that relate *g* to 4 group factors, which in turn are related to the 13 subtests on the WAIS-III (Deary, 2001). The 4 group factors are verbal comprehension, perceptual organization, working memory, and processing speed.

factor analysis A statistical method for measuring the relationships among scores on various tests to determine what they have in common.

Alternatives to IQ Tests

Because some creative, productive people do not score highly on traditional IQ tests, psychologists have sought alternatives. All of us know people with modest IQs who are "street smart"—that is, who can organize and motivate others. In

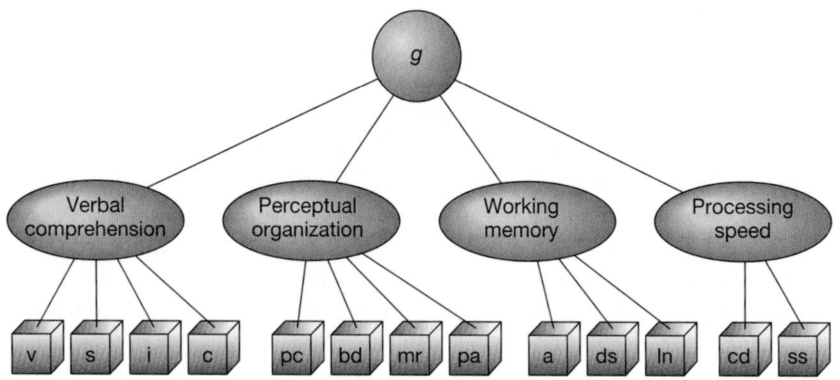

Figure 13.3 How Specific Abilities Are Related to *g*. Both factor analysis and structural equation modeling techniques reveal that a person who shows a specific ability on one of the WAIS-III subtests also tends to score well on other specific abilities. Here, the WAIS-III subtests (squares) are grouped as verbal comprehension, perceptual organization, working memory, and processing speed (ellipses), which together provide evidence of general intelligence (*g*) (circle). Abbreviations: v, vocabulary; s, similarities; i, information; c, comprehension; pc, picture completion; bd, block design; mr, matrix reasoning; pa, picture arrangement; a, arithmetic; ds, digit span; ln, letter-numbering sequencing; cd, digit-symbol coding; ss, symbol search. *Source:* From "Human Intelligence Differences: A Recent History" by I. J. Deary from *Current Trends in Cognitive Sciences,* (2001), vol. 5. pp. 127–130. Copyright © 2001 by Elsevier Science. Reprinted by permission.

one study, for example, researchers found no relationship between IQ and the ability to successfully handicap racehorses (Ceci & Liker, 1986). Successful handicappers must take into account such variables as the condition of the track, recent workout data, the jockeys' and horses' past won-loss records, which jockeys won on which horses, and so forth. People with high IQs who lack the experience of handicappers cannot successfully pick winners. Yet for the most part, successful handicappers do not score well on IQ tests even though most people would agree that they are astute, clever, alert, apt, discerning, shrewd, sharp, and smart at what they do.

The handicappers certainly satisfy points 1 and 2 in Table 13.1, but what about the third point? Before agreeing that their special ability amounts to general intelligence, some psychologists would like to know about other successes the handicappers have had—that is, about their *other* cognitive abilities. Psychologists with these concerns stress the importance of *g*. Other psychologists, however, think that the special abilities of handicappers is evidence that IQ defines intelligence too narrowly. Let's look at the theory of one such psychologist, Howard Gardner.

Gardner's Theory of Multiple Intelligences

Dissatisfied with what he perceived to be the mismatch between IQ and a person's actual abilities, the psychologist Howard Gardner (1983, 1993) has proposed a new term—intelligenc*es*—to describe individual differences. Table 13.2 lists Gardner's *seven* distinct kinds of intelligence: linguistic, logical-mathematical, spatial, musical, movement (or bodily kinesthetic), interpersonal, and intrapersonal. (Note that Gardner's intelligences are not the same as Thurstone's seven primary mental abilities.) Items 1 through 3 are familiar: there are subscales for language, math and logic, and spatial intelligence on both the WAIS-III and the Stanford-Binet test. Gardner added the abilities listed in Items 4 through 7. The first two of these, musical intelligence and movement intelligence,

Table 13.2 Gardner's Theory of Multiple Intelligences

1. *Linguistic intelligence* The skillful use of oral language as in storytelling, teaching, public speaking, and of written language as in poetry, prose, and journalism.
2. *Logical-mathematical intelligence* The ability to think quantitatively; to pose and solve mathematical problems; and to use logic and reason to solve problems in science, engineering, and related fields.
3. *Spatial intelligence* The ability to locate objects in three-dimensional space, to visualize them from multiple perspectives and orientations, and to pose and solve mazes using an internal compass (and a mental map).
4. *Musical intelligence* The ability to sing, play musical instruments, and compose music.
5. *Movement intelligence* The ability to dance and play competitive sports, and to skillfully control the fingers and arms in tasks such as in typing, playing a musical instrument, or performing surgery.
6. *Interpersonal intelligence* The ability to understand, motivate, and "read" other people in a way that facilitates social interactions. Social leaders such as teachers, city council persons, and chairpersons display a high degree of interpersonal intelligence.
7. *Intrapersonal intelligence* The ability to gain insight into one's thoughts and feelings, to understand the causes for and consequences of one's actions, and to apply that knowledge in decision making.

are sometimes referred to as a physical (as opposed to mental) intelligence. The last two, interpersonal and intrapersonal intelligence, can be thought of as social intelligence.

Physical Versus Mental Intelligence. While professional athletes and entertainers are paid enormous salaries for their *movement* and *musical abilities,* their talents are not usually considered signs of intelligence. The question, then, is how to define intelligence. Should the traditional definition of intelligence be redefined to include skilled performance?

Traditional IQ tests do include performance items, such as the block design subtest on the WAIS-III (see Figure 13.1). One difference between this WAIS-III subtest and musical and athletic performance is that block design is a *mental test,* whereas dancing and passing a soccer ball are *physical abilities*. That is, people who do well on block design tests tend to do well on other tests of mental ability, such as vocabulary and general information tests. In contrast, physical abilities do not correlate well with tests of mental ability. Rather, people vary in their special talents just as they vary in their mental ability. For most

Multiple Intelligences. The psychologist Howard Gardner believes that people exhibit intelligence in many different ways.

people, characterizing a clumsy person as "unintelligent" would be a misnomer. Nevertheless, Gardner's theory does recognize individual differences not captured in an IQ score.

Social Intelligence. Many psychologists see the concepts of interpersonal and intrapersonal intelligence, which contribute to a person's *social intelligence,* as important additions to the overall construct of intelligence. As Gordon Gallup—who developed a theory of the evolution of social intelligence (Gallup, 1998)—has pointed out, academic intelligence was *not* among the selection pressures that early hominids faced. That is, humans did not evolve to perform well on paper-and-pencil tests of academic ability. Rather, they evolved strategies for competing and cooperating, for leading and following one another. Those humans who were more successful than others in social situations involving gratitude, empathy, deception, grudge holding, and pretending left more offspring than those who were less successful in those situations. Certainly, individuals vary in these social attributes, none of which are measured by IQ tests.

LINK ▶ Intelligence and individual differences in personality, Chapter 14, p. 491

Thus, we should be leery of people who score well on IQ tests but fail miserably in other realms of life. Consider these comments by Ted Kaczynski, a person with an IQ of 170 who became a brilliant mathematician and professor:

> I often had fantasies of killing the kind of people whom I hated (e.g., government officials, police, computer scientists, behavioral scientists, the rowdy type of college students who left their piles of beer-cans in the Arboretum, etc., etc., etc.) and I had high hopes of eventually committing such crimes.
>
> . . . from the journals of the Unabomber, Ted Kaczynski (Government's Sentencing Memorandum, 1998)

Ted Kaczynski, better known as the Unabomber.

Despite his reasoned objections to the contrary, Kaczynski, better known as the Unabomber, was diagnosed with paranoid schizophrenia, that prevented him from interacting normally with others. Mental illness, like physical ability, is unrelated to IQ. In the next chapter we will consider some of the many dimensions of personality that are not related to traditional constructs of intelligence.

Sternberg's Triarchic Theory of Intelligence

Another theory that widens the concept of intelligence was proposed by Robert Sternberg of Yale University. According to his **triarchic theory of intelligence** (Sternberg, 1985), people's intelligence varies in three fundamental ways: *analytic, practical,* and *creative* (see Figure 13.4).

Analytic (Academic) Intelligence. By analytic (or academic) intelligence, Sternberg meant the type of problem-solving ability that is measured by IQ tests: The problems on IQ tests are clearly defined, contain all the information necessary to arrive at a solution, and typically can be solved by only one method. While some researchers think that such problems are of little practical interest (Neisser, 1976; Sternberg, 1985), they are similar in many respects to academic coursework. Interestingly, Sternberg himself didn't do well on these tests as a student. Being an intelligent person, he has since spent much of his career trying to understand why.

triarchic theory of intelligence Robert Sternberg's theory that intelligence is composed of three abilities: analytic, creative, and practical.

Practical Intelligence. Some people who do not do well on tests of academic intelligence *can* solve practical problems. Such problems differ from academic coursework in that they are typically poorly defined. Once the problem *is* recognized, it must often be reformulated before it can be solved. Reformulating the problem usually means seeking additional information, which requires

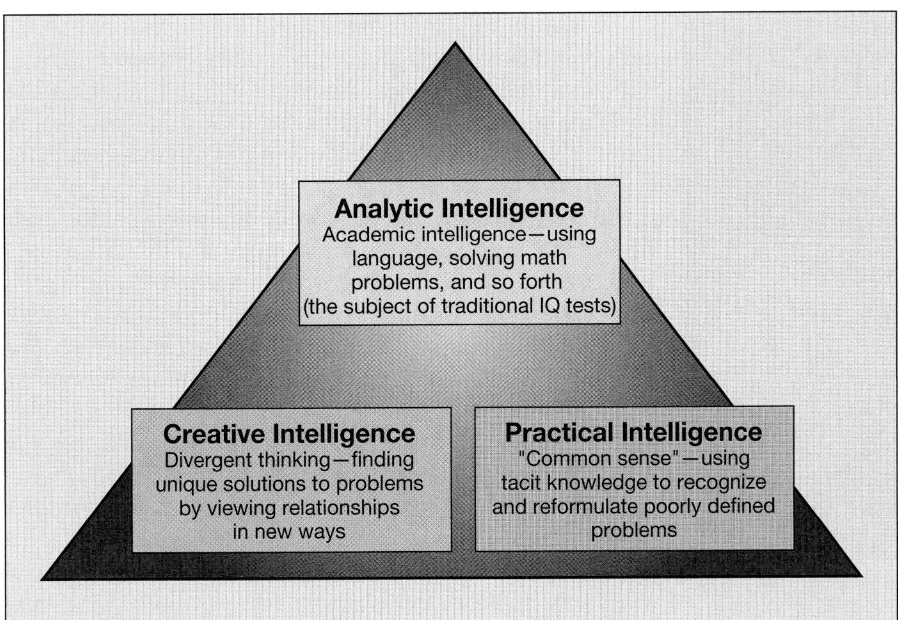

Figure 13.4 Sternberg's Triarchic Theory of Intelligence.

knowing what questions to ask and where to find the answers. When faced with such obstacles, a person with practical intelligence must be motivated to engage them using prior learning as an imperfect guide.

Practical intelligence is not the same as *common sense.* (Marvin Minsky, a neuroscientist at MIT, recently defined common sense as "knowing 30 or 50 million things about the world and having them represented so that when something happens, you can make analogies with other [things]" [Dreifus, 1998]). Consider the practical problems a college student might face over several years:

Common sense, Chapter 1, p. 10

> Tuition is due in a month. Have I exhausted my scholarship opportunities? Maybe I should take a semester off to work and get caught up financially. Or should I borrow from parents or the bank? I'd better call both—and talk to people in the student loan office—to see what my options are.
>
> Where will I live next year? I've got to have a quiet place to study, but where I am now is so convenient to campus. But if it's cheaper . . . hmmm.
>
> Grocery shopping is *definitely* cheaper than eating out, but it's such a pain and takes time. But eating out is fattening.
>
> I can make a better grade in Smith's class, but I'd learn more in Garcia's. . . . hmm.

Sternberg and others (1995) have proposed that people who can solve such practical problems to achieve their personal goals display an intellectual ability called *tacit knowledge* (action-oriented knowledge). A person who lacks the practical intelligence to solve such problems is not likely to be able to solve academic problems.

Recognizing that the business world rewards people who display practical knowledge, Sternberg and his collaborators have developed tests to measure managers' thinking potential. They include some typical workplace problems with a variety of solutions to be rank ordered. For example, should an otherwise highly competent employee who is always late for work (a) be fired; (b) be publicly reprimanded; (c) incur a financial penalty; (d) be approached privately about the matter; or (e) be ignored? Successfully solving this problem requires *social intelligence,* an aspect of practical intelligence that is lacking on tests of analytic intelligence. The results of such tests correlate well with job performance as rated by supervisors (Sternberg & Wagner, 1993; Sternberg et al., 1995).

Police must have practical intelligence to solve everyday problems.

Some psychologists have argued that practical intelligence is related to analytic intelligence, however (Jensen, 1993a, 1998; Herrnstein & Murray, 1994; Gottfredson, 1997b). In one study, IQ tests for people in 400 occupations ranging from unskilled manual laborers to graduate-level mathematics correlated both with the type of job a person had and with the person's job performance (Jensen, 1980). An analysis of thousands of reports found that general tests of mental ability correlate about .5 in predicting job performance (Schmidt & Hunter, 1998). In fact, IQ is correlated with achievement motivation, creativity, health and fitness, leadership, and social skills, among other variables (Brand, 1987). After analyzing many studies correlating intelligence scores with human performance, one researcher concluded that a person's IQ has "significance as a predictor of real-world academic, social, and occupational accomplishments" (Ceci, 1991 p. 721). Psychologists disagree, then, on the practical significance of *g*, the general intelligence factor. A reasonable answer to the question of which measure, practical intelligence or general intelligence, better predicts job performance is that they both do, and often are correlated. We'll return to the question of what *g* means for overall success in life in the last section of this chapter.

Creative Intelligence. The third element of Sternberg's theory of triarchic intelligence is creativity. Creative people are clever people who can do things most others can't, such as choreograph a dance. Their contributions change and enrich culture (Csikszentmihalyi, 1996). Creativity comes in many forms, including artistic endeavors (painting, design, sculpture, dance, music, and so forth), spoken and written language (poetry, essays, novels, and so forth), and practical inventions (tools, structures, vehicles, patented devices, and so forth). Creative people develop new insights into problems, often by combining familiar elements in a new way (Davidson & Sternberg, 1984). Not surprisingly, creative people have higher-than-average IQs.

Creativity and functional fixedness, Chapter 12, p. 438

The last chapter described how insight allows people to solve problems in creative ways, and how functional fixedness prevents creative problem solving. One component of Sternberg's creative intelligence is a type of thinking called *lateral thinking*, which is best understood in contrast with *vertical thinking* (de Bono, 1976, 1991). Vertical thinking is thinking that concentrates on information that is relevant and meaningful in problem solving. In contrast, lateral thinking is divergent: it welcomes the intrusion of irrelevant thoughts and looks for different ways to approach a problem. For example, a chemist once designed a glue that was too weak to permanently bind paper to another surface. It was useless, until someone in the 3M Company thought of Post-it® notes.

Where does creative intelligence come from? A strong argument can be made for genetic predisposition (Csikszentmihalyi, 1996), but certainly a supportive environment would nurture its survival and allow it to thrive. Educators who work with gifted children in England claim to have stimulated creative intelligence in them by presenting them with open-ended tasks and reinforcing lateral thinking (Kerry, 1987).

Sternberg's triarchic theory of intelligence—analytical, practical, and creative—can help us to understand Mark, a close acquaintance of mine. Mark suffered severe damage to his forebrain at age 8 after being hit by a car. His spoken language was unimpaired, but he was a horrible speller and his writing contained gross syntactical errors. His IQ score was well above normal only because of his performance and analytical subscale scores. As an adult, Mark showed a keen sense of humor and sly wit, both evidence of social intelligence. A computer programmer, he was hired to develop the software for a new operating system. His employers knew about his writing problems, but assured him that he need not worry: all the computers he would use had spell-checkers. Mark's creative software designs, though not adequately measured by traditional IQ tests, propelled him into a successful career.

INTERIM SUMMARY

1. Although IQ tests are reliable, not all psychologists agree that they are valid. The WISC and the Stanford-Binet test have *predictive validity* because to a certain extent, they predict performance in school from kindergarten through college. Both these tests have *content validity* because they cover language, reasoning, mathematics, spatial abilities, and general information—all of which are part of schoolwork.
2. IQ tests have been standardized by administering them to thousands of test takers. The distribution of scores forms a bell-shaped curve, the mean of which is set at 100, with a standard deviation of 15 points.
3. Most psychologists agree that intelligent people can process information rapidly, solve complex problems, and perform well at a variety of tasks.
4. Louis Thurstone used ***factor analysis,*** a statistical measure of factors common to a set of test items, to identify seven *primary mental abilities.* Other analyses suggest that IQ subtests can be grouped in terms of verbal comprehension, perceptual organization, working memory, and processing speed, all related to *g.*
5. Arguing that traditional IQ tests do not predict individuals' actual abilities, Howard Gardner proposed a theory of *multiple intelligences.* According to his theory, there are seven distinct kinds of intelligence: linguistic, logical-mathematical, spatial, musical, movement (bodily kinesthetic), interpersonal, and intrapersonal. Psychologists who disagree with Gardner's theory think that he confused skilled performance with traditionally defined intelligence.
6. A person can have a high IQ score and still be mentally impaired. By itself, IQ provides a useful but limited assessment of a person's intellectual and creative abilities.
7. According to Robert Sternberg's ***triarchic theory of intelligence,*** there are three types of intelligence: analytic, practical, and creative.
8. Sternberg considered practical intelligence (*tacit knowledge,* or "action-oriented knowledge") to be different from the analytic intelligence measured on IQ tests, but other psychologists argue that practical intelligence is related to analytical intelligence, and that IQ predicts real-world achievements.
9. *Creative intelligence* includes the ability to combine familiar elements in new ways. Creative people tend to have higher-than-normal IQs.
10. Creative solutions to problems often involve *lateral thinking*—looking for nonanalytic, often irrelevant thoughts that may lead to unorthodox solutions.

For Further Thought

1. Which of two different constructs of intelligence shown in Figure 13.3 do you think is more characteristic of your own intellectual abilities? Why?
2. Do you agree with Gardner that the plural term *intelligences* is a better one than the singular *intelligence*? Why or why not?
3. Natural selection is typically thought of in terms of competition and the survival of the fittest. Why might a person who promotes social harmony produce a lot of offspring?
4. Mark excelled in creative and social intelligence as well as analytical intelligence. Does his story support Sternberg's theory, the theory of *g*, or both?

THE BELL CURVE WARS: THE SOURCES OF INTELLIGENCE

Controversies about the nature of intelligence and about the nature (and fairness) of intelligence tests seemed to culminate in 1994 with the publication of *The Bell Curve,* written by the psychologist Richard Herrnstein and political scientist Charles Murray. Herrnstein and Murray's (1994) core theses were that IQ is more a product of genetics than of education and family environment; that there are racial and ethnic differences in IQ; and that IQ predicts a person's economic and social success. Their book was assailed by some as "social Darwinism"—a 19th-century view that society will always have a permanently poor, genetically inferior underclass (Gould, 1994). Many others attacked it as representative of all that was wrong with intelligence testing. Critics challenged the validity of IQ tests and genetic theories of intelligence, the heavy emphasis on *g*, the lack of a cultural perspective, the widespread theoretical differences on the nature of intelligence, and even the integrity of the psychologists who study IQ (Fraser, 1995; Jacoby & Glauberman, 1995).

Two separate groups of researchers responded to the attacks on *The Bell Curve.* To counter the charge of widespread theoretical differences, a group of 52 scientists signed a statement of 25 "facts" representing a mainstream academic understanding of intelligence (Gottfredson, 1997a). At about the same time, the American Psychological Association appointed an independent task force to reexamine what was known and unknown about intelligence (Neisser et al., 1996). While the members of this group could not agree about *all* the issues raised by *The Bell Curve,* their report has helped to make sense of the controversy. In this section and the next we will address the issues raised by *The Bell Curve.* We have already reviewed the evidence that IQ tests measure *g*, a general cognitive ability. Recognizing that not all psychologists agree on the importance of *g*, we also looked at alternative theories of intelligence. Here we will revisit the concept of *g*, and how genes and environment shape IQ. (In the concluding section of this chapter, we'll take a closer look at the relationship of intelligence and culture.)

Genes and Cognitive Abilities

Is intelligence really inherited, as Galton, Spearman, and other researchers proposed? Researchers have estimated the separate effects of genes and environment in the expression of intelligence by comparing monozygotic and dizygotic twins raised in the same environment with those raised in different environments (Plomin, 1990; Bouchard et al., 1990). Think of twin studies as experiments of nature (monozygotic and dizygotic twins) and experiments of nurture (raised in birth families or adoptive families). Genes and environment are correlated in birth families because the same parents provide both genes and environment. In adoptive families, the birth parents provide the genes and the adoptive parents provide the environment. These studies have shown that the correlation of the IQs of monozygotic twins raised in different environments (adoptive families) is very high, 0.72. By comparison, the correlation of the IQs of siblings raised in different environments is low, just over 0.20 (Bouchard & McGue, 1981). Monozygotic twins, of course, share 100 percent of their genes, whereas dizygotic twins and other siblings share 50 percent. Clearly, genes have a strong effect on IQ.

However, the outcomes of twin studies do not refer to individual members of the populations under study. In other words, conclusions about the relationship of genes to IQ cannot be applied to individuals.

The Heritability of Intelligence. The many twin studies undertaken over several decades have found that genes play a substantial role in intelligence. As Bouchard and McGue (1981, p. 1055) put it, "the higher the proportion of genes two family members have in common, the higher the average correlation between their IQs." Figure 13.5 summarizes the role of genes in measures of IQ. Estimates of heritability in the early years are about 0.4, in late adulthood, about 0.8. Another way of saying this is that as people grow older, environmental effects on intelligence become relatively unimportant (Plomin, Fulker, Corley, & DeFries, 1997; Petrill et al., 1998).

The decreasing role of environment in IQ is counterintuitive. A more reasonable hypothesis would be that the longer identical twins experience different environments, the more dissimilar they would become. That is, the cumulative effects of accidents, illness, social contacts, and so forth should be measurable in later life (Plomin & Petrill, 1997). As Figure 13.5 shows, however, the opposite occurs. One question that arises, then, is why the environment has so little effect on IQ in older adults. Does environment have little effect on other personality variables as well?

Let's take a closer look at a particular pair of twins, Harry and Larry Carothers, monozygotic twins living in Texas. Both are 6' 4" tall, have identically low cholesterol levels, and suffer migraines on hot summer days. They like exactly the same foods, and dislike recreational drugs, including alcohol. Harry and Larry describe themselves as life-long best friends who anticipate each other's thoughts, feelings, and responses in social situations. Their IQ scores are only a point or two apart.

Most of their lives Harry and Larry shared the same family, friends, classrooms, and athletic experiences. Both majored in secondary education and served in the ROTC. Following a brief separation in the military, they ended up in the same small town in Texas, double-dated together, and married college roommates. Each had two children within a few years of each other, and both chose the same parenting style. Both gained positions in upper-level management (in different companies) and employed a similar management style.

Speculating on how the two men's shared environment affected their development is perhaps too easy. After all, affiliating with a Southern Baptist church as they do (in different congregations) is not unusual for people living in the southwestern United States. Predictably, they describe themselves as moderately conservative in religion and politics, and they think similarly about such social issues as abortion, drug use, and so forth. (In fact, they say they adopted their parent's values.) But the southwestern culture is also permeated with male traditions such

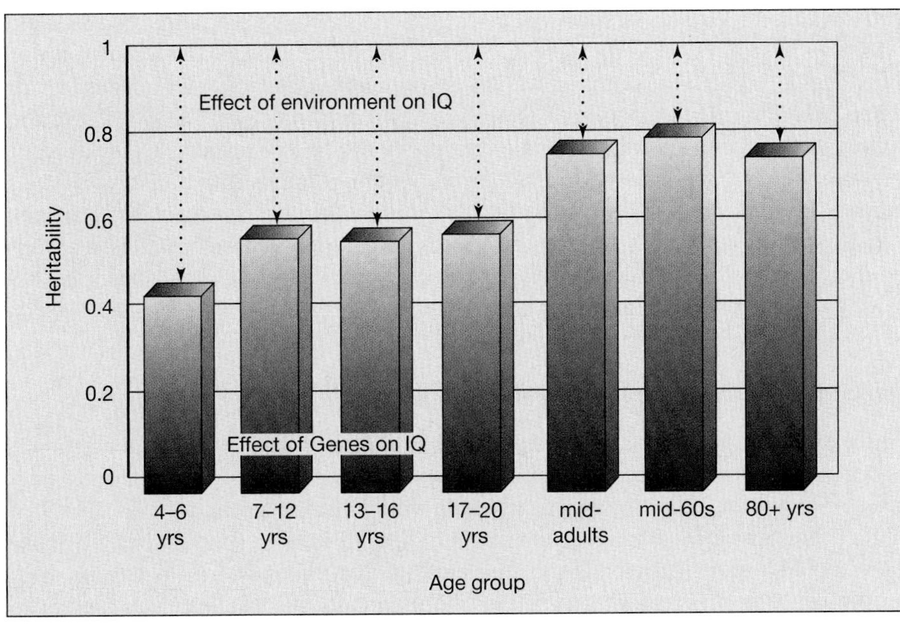

Figure 13.5 **The Heritability of Intelligence.** Genetic influences on intelligence increase as people grow older. In studies of monozygotic twins raised in different environments, tested at different ages, the effect of genes on IQ (called the heritability score) increased from just over 0.4 when twins first tested, to about 0.8 when tested in older adults. In other words, the effect of the environment on IQ is important in childhood, but becomes increasingly *unimportant* in adulthood. *Source:* After Plomin & Petrill, 1997; 80+ data from Petrill et al., 1998.

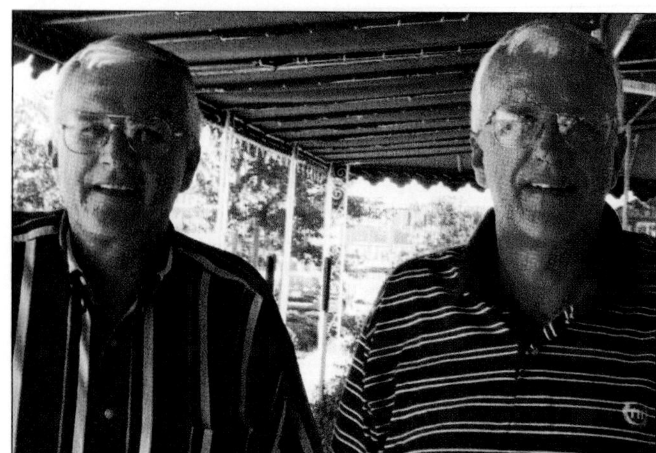

These two monozygotic twins share many remarkable similarities, including identical food preferences and cholesterol levels and almost identical IQ scores.

as hunting and fishing, and neither twin hunts or fishes. The two men prefer easy listening to the country music that pervades the region. They like musicals better than action-adventure movies, and regularly swap mystery-adventure novels. These twins seem to have developed the same preferences with a far greater frequency than would be expected by chance, then, even in a shared culture.

The Stability of Intelligence. Given the large role of genes and the lesser role of environment in IQ, an individual's IQ should not change appreciably over a lifetime. In fact, intelligence before one year of age correlates substantially (.41) with intelligence at ages 17 to 18 (Carroll, 1993; Moffitt, Caspi, Harkness, & Silva, 1993). Moreover, the IQs of first- and second-graders correlate .82 with their IQs at high school graduation (Jones & Bayley, 1941; Pinneau, 1961). In these comparisons, then, as well as results from twin studies, genetic endowment is a quite good predictor of IQ.

Effect of the Environment on Intelligence

Researchers have developed a number of ways to measure the effect of the environment on intelligence. For example, they have compared the IQ scores of both monozygotic and dizygotic twins raised in the same family to the scores of twins raised in different families. As Figure 13.5 shows, they have found that the scores of twins raised together are more highly correlated than the scores of those raised apart. From the results of these and other genetic studies, scientists have estimated that the effect of a *shared family environment* accounts for about 35 percent of the variance in children's IQ scores. In other words, supportive home environments enhance children's IQ scores slightly, and unsupportive environments lower them.

Another way to study the effects of the environment is to compare the scores of unrelated siblings raised together to those of related siblings. The IQs of these paired children with no genetic similarity can then be compared with the IQs of MZ and DZ twins, and with siblings who have been reared together. Table 13.3 shows that when researchers make these comparisons, they find the IQs of unrelated, same-age children are not well correlated—about .17 (Segal, 1997). By comparison, the correlation of pairs who share both genes and a family environment is .86 for monozygotic twins, .60 for dizygotic twins, and .48 for siblings. (Recall that monozygotic twins share 100 percent of their genes, while dizygotic twins and siblings share 50 percent of their genes.) Being raised in the same family, then, accounts for very *little* of the variability in IQ scores, while the closeness of the genetic relationship accounts for the similarities in IQ scores. The environment—especially for adults—is relatively unimportant.

Interaction of Genes and Environment

reaction range A range of possible IQ scores for a given person, representing the potential effect of the environment in which one is raised.

The interaction of genes and environments is captured in a concept called the **reaction range,** or the range of possible IQ scores a person might achieve given various environments. For example, a person with a genotype that yields an IQ of 100 in an "average" environment might score 90 in an impoverished environment or 110 in an enriched environment. In this example, the reaction range would be 20 points (from 90 to 110). The upper panel of Figure 13.6 illustrates

Table 13.3 The Role of the Environment in Intelligence

The effect of the environment on IQ can be estimated by comparing pairs of children of the same age, related and unrelated, raised together and raised apart. As these correlations indicate, the effect of the family environment on a child's intelligence is minimal. The correlation of the IQs of genetically unrelated people living together is .17, while that of monozygotic twins living in different families is .72.

	CORRELATION OF IQS	
	Children Raised Together	Children Raised Apart
Monozygotic twins (100% of genes shared)	.86	.72
Dizygotic twins (50% of genes shared)	.60	.33
Siblings (50% of genes shared)	.48	.24
Unrelated children (same age) (0% of genes ahared)	.17	.00

Source: Data from Segal, 1997, and from Plomin & Petrill, 1997.

the reaction range for three different seed types in a fertile and a barren field. In the barren field, the genotype "c" would be small compared to its height when planted in a fertile field, as well as small in relation to genotypes a and b when planted in a fertile field. The specific outcome of the interaction of genes and environment is called a *gene-by-environment interaction.* This concept can be applied to human and other animals' physical and psychological characteristics as well (lower panel).

The concept of a reaction range has limited usefulness, because there is no good way to measure a person's potential intelligence independently of IQ. One estimate of the reaction range for intelligence is 20 to 25 IQ points (Weinberg,

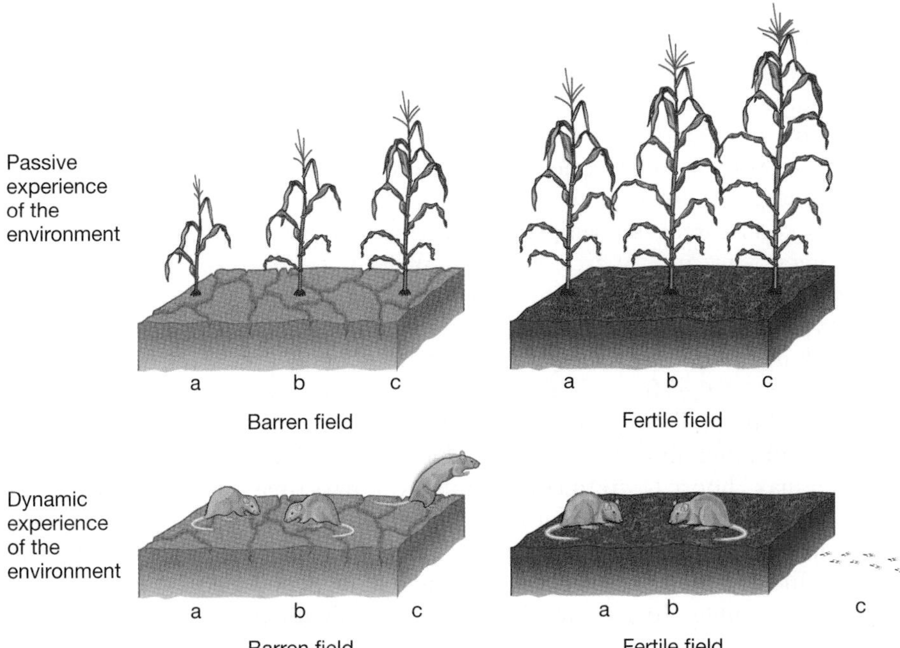

Figure 13.6 Passive versus Dynamic Experience of the Environment. The expression of a genotype in a passively experienced environment is demonstrated in the upper panel. Seeds with poor, medium, and excellent genotypes (a, b, and c, respectively) grow better, yet differently, in a fertile field; even the worst seed genotype (type a) does much better in the fertile field than the best seed genotype (type c) in the barren field. Animals with genotypes a, b, and c (lower panel) also thrive in the fertile field. Yet the animal with genotype c (for curious) actively changes its environment when it moves from a barren to a fertile environment. Its counterpart living in the fertile field also has left, having selected still another environment.

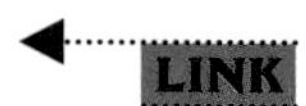

Genie, Amala, Kamala and critical period, Chapter 12, p. 431

1989), but it may not hold for all genotypes in a wide range of environments. Genie, the child raised in a closet, and Amala and Kamala, the children raised with wolves, would likely have had a much wider reaction range. The fact that people can change the environment in which they live (see lower panel, Figure 13.6), also limits the usefulness of the concept. Indeed, enhancing the environment invariably shifts IQ toward the positive end of the reaction range.

Passive Versus Dynamic Exposure

The finding that environment is relatively unimportant compared to genes in determining IQ is a puzzling one. I can imagine being raised by different parents in a different part of the world and as a result, becoming a very different individual. Such a view is reminiscent of John Locke's blank slate (*tabula rasa*) upon which experience writes. Today it is known as a *passive exposure theory of intelligence* (Rowe, 1997). From this perspective, intelligence becomes the sum total of a person's learning experiences, so that environments that offer more learning opportunities produce more intelligent people (see Figure 6.14).

Role of environment in complex behavior, Chapter 6, p. 224

A newer understanding of "the environment," however, challenges such thinking. In this view, individuals actively experience their environment. For example, a squirrel can bury a nut, or leap from limb to limb 100 feet above ground, in the process experiencing two different environments that differ in details from those experienced by other squirrels. In either case the environment does not act passively on the squirrels; rather, the environment the squirrels experience varies according to their selective behavior. Similarly, some investigators have suggested that humans also interact with and even create the environments in which they live (Plomin, DeFries, & Loehlin, 1977; Scarr & McCartney, 1983).

Even a child who might seem to be "trapped" in the home environment can act upon it. Consider, for example, the unexpected finding from monozygotic twin studies that vocabulary size is predicted better by genes than by the home environment. Again, this seems counterintuitive, in that "high" language environments are very different from those with little spoken or written language. One explanation for this finding is that children encounter huge numbers of words in most environments, but their exposure to those words is not passive. That is, while newspapers, books, and magazines may be available, children must pick them up and read them in order to be exposed to them. Apparently, like the active mouse, c, shown in the bottom panel of Figure 13.6, some people are more curious and are more motivated to read.

Vocabulary size and environment, Chapter 12, p. 441

To give another example, intelligent parents do little good if they are seldom available to a child. A child who manages to get help from dad or mom has a better learning environment than a brother or sister who fails to enlist a parent's help. But child-parent interactions can have unpredictable effects. Some parent-child interactions may, in fact, produce intellectual *differences* between parent and child (Loehlin et al., 1997). For example, overbearing parents may produce children who go out of their way to go their own way. Even with the same parents, each new child experiences a different environment.

This view of the effects of an interactive environment is not restricted to developing children. Through desire or ability people can place themselves in an environment different from the one in which they find themselves. For example, a person may choose to go to college and work part time rather than work full time and earn enough money for new car payments. In turn, the different environments that result from these choices can affect the other choices a person makes. One is likely to encounter more interesting people in a college environment, for example. To give another example, individual differences in ability might allow some students to excel, opening up a range of postgraduate or other career opportunities, along with the associated financial rewards. Students who do not excel would have more limited options, and nonstudents even fewer.

Equal Environments and Opportunities, and Unequal Outcomes

The view that individuals select the environments that affect them, rather than experience them passively, has some interesting implications. One is that equalizing people's opportunities does not necessarily produce equal results. Suppose that the same task—learning a multiplication table, for example—is presented to all the students in a classroom. Even if everyone practices memorizing the table for the same amount of time, not everyone will learn at the same rate, or learn as well as others. Individuals who vary in intellectual ability do not experience the "same environment"—the task, the repetition, the reward—in the same way.

In fact, there is no human talent for which practice alone is sufficient to develop the talent. Even if all members of a basketball team shoot 100 free throws a day, some players will be more skillful than others. Likewise, practice alone does not guarantee a smart student. Rather, biological differences in both athletic and intellectual ability help individuals to structure their environments so as to achieve different results. In Howard Gardner's words, ". . . those individuals who combine high psychometric intelligence in childhood with diligent practice in (and out of) school are more likely to become expert thinkers or scholars than those who can only practice (so called overachievers) or those who do not practice at all (so called underachievers)" (Gardner, 1995, p. 802).

The Flynn Effect

Recall that Rowe's (1997) passive exposure theory of intelligence predicts that environments that offer more learning opportunities produce more intelligent people. If this is so, people should be smarter now, in the space age, than during the horse-and-buggy era a century ago. In fact, James Flynn has found evidence of a steady rise in IQ worldwide, a phenomenon called the **Flynn Effect** (Flynn, 1984, 1987; Neisser, 1998). Specifically, IQ scores have been rising about 3 IQ points per decade during the last half-century. Flynn made his discovery by comparing the performances of different populations on the WAIS-III and Stanford-Binet tests as they were restandardized over the years. Recall that in standardizing IQ tests, researchers always set the mean score at 100 points. This practice masked the rise in scores until Flynn recognized what was happening, that on the average, test takers in the 1980s would have performed many points better had they taken the older version of the test.

How can entire nations be getting smarter? Certainly, the Flynn Effect argues against the effect of genes on intelligence: There has been no significant redistribution of genes in the world's population over the past half-century. Several environmental causes have been proposed. One is that daily life increased in complexity over the last few decades (Schooler, 1998; Williams, 1998). Relatively simple farm and factory jobs have been replaced by jobs requiring more mental effort. A cash economy has been replaced by a "moneyless" economy requiring more abstract thought and foresight, such as keeping checkbooks and credit cards in synchrony with paydays (Gottfredson, 1997b). Telephones and television, computers and the World Wide Web have increased the daily flow of information. From an early age, people now process more information for more hours. These increases in mental activity may continually rewire our brains in a way that enhances our intellectual abilities, a hypothesis bolstered by studies of neuron growth and of the effect of

Environmental complexity and brain organization, Chapter 4, p. 129

Flynn Effect The finding of a steady worldwide rise in IQ over the second half of the 20th century.

enriched environments on IQ. Certainly, John Garcia (the scientist who opened this chapter) experienced a challenging environment during his lifetime, one that was optimal for both brain growth and IQ enhancement.

Another possible explanation for the Flynn Effect is enhanced nutrition. In developing nations, nutritionally based increases in height have paralleled the gains in IQ (Lynn, 1990, 1998). Because larger people have larger brains, these nutritional gains may be producing smarter people. But as Flynn (1987) himself argued, rising scores on IQ tests may not be the same as gains in intelligence more broadly defined. In his view, no corresponding cultural gain has occurred as the result of the increased scores. His findings, then, raise questions about the relationship of IQ scores to the construct of intelligence.

LINK
Intelligence and brain size, Chapter 3, p. 107

Biological Bases of Intelligence

Genes affect intelligence primarily because they code the proteins that make up an individual's brain. While humans have a larger brain-to-body-size ratio than most other animals, brain organization rather than size is thought to account for individual differences in perception, memory, learning, intelligence, and so forth. (Some psychologists argue otherwise; see Lynn, 1993, and Rushton, 1995, for evidence that brain size does affect human intelligence.) For instance, we have seen evidence that the left hemisphere specializes in language and analytic abilities, while the right hemisphere specializes in spatial abilities. This organization conveniently mirrors the verbal and performance subtests on the WAIS-III (see Figure 13.1)

Lateralization of abilities in left and right hemispheres, Chapter 4, p. 136

Speed of Cortical Processing. Galton and Spearman thought that differences in processing speed reflected differences in intelligence. For example, children can learn simple rules such as a win-stay, lose-shift strategy more quickly than monkeys and other animals (see Figure 6.13 on page 223). Because children take only a few dozen rather than hundreds of trials to learn such rules, we can conclude that they are smarter than adult monkeys. The speed with which a person learns paired associates such as foreign language vocabulary words and their English language equivalents is another such measure of intelligence. When subjects are presented with such word pairs at a high speed (see Figure 13.7), people who score well on IQ tests learn more pairs than people who do not (Neisser et al., 1996). In the classroom and in the workplace, similar speed-of-processing criteria are used to categorize a person as "quick" or "slow."

Another measure of processing speed is the time subjects take to make simple judgments, called *inspection time* (IT). In this simple perceptual measure, two lines of the same or different lengths are flashed on a computer screen for a fraction of a second (see Figure 13.7). Some people need to see the image for a longer time than others to judge their relative length. Incredibly, this simple measure has been found to correlate with the performance subtests on the WAIS-III. The measured correlation between the two, –.55, is negative because people with the shortest inspection times have the highest IQs (Eysenck & Barrett, 1993). Quickness of visual perception apparently translates into quickness of intellect (see also Vernon, 1987).

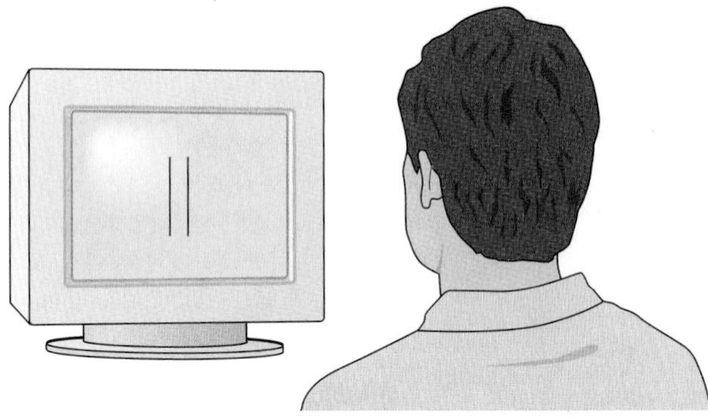

Figure 13.7 High IQ and Speed of Information Processing. Individuals differ in the speed with which they can process word pairs (top) and make judgments about the relative length of lines (bottom). They learn word pairs (paired associates) at nearly equal rates when the pairs are presented at a relaxed pace. However, when a list of word pairs is presented rapidly, people with higher IQs learn more word pairs than others. Likewise, people with higher IQs can make accurate judgments about the length of lines, even when the exposure time is minimal.

Yet another measure of processing speed that correlates with intelligence is physical reaction time in tasks involving discrimination and choice. For example, the time an individual takes to press a lever in response to several different stimulus conditions is highly correlated with intelligence—roughly –70 (Jensen, 1993b). Interestingly, this correlation holds only for a reaction time of about 1 second or so; if the complexity of a task becomes too great, the relationship of speed to IQ disappears.

Intelligence and short-term memory, Chapter 10, p. 356

Arthur Jensen, who has proposed that speed is a *g* factor, thinks of the results of experiments with reaction time in terms of working memory. The faster a person processes information, the more items are in working memory, and if successfully rehearsed, get stored in long-term memory (LTM). (A variant of this theory, Baddeley's phonological loop, was discussed in Chapter 10; see page 356.) Thus, an individual who processes information quickly acquires more knowledge and skills, retrieves information from LTM more efficiently, reasons better, and solves more complex problems than others (Jensen, 1993b). Although, as seen in Figure 13.3, the WAIS-III subtests for processing speed (digit-symbol coding and symbol search) can be grouped separately from those for working memory (arithmetic, digit span, and letter-numbering sequence), individual differences in the speed of processing syllables have been shown to correlate with performance on math tests (Baddley, 1998).

Intelligence and phonological loops, Chapter 10, p. 356

Why do humans differ in their speed of information processing? Some researchers point to differences in the way various components of the nervous system work (Eysenck, 1986; Jensen, 1993b). For example, Jensen notes several possible sources of differences in reaction time. One is the speed of information transmission, which he equates with the velocity of nerve conduction from the eyes' receptors to the visual areas in the brain (Reed & Jensen, 1992). He also hypothesizes that neuron's "activation thresholds," their resistance to distractibility, and the "rate of decay of neural traces" differ from one individual to the next (Jensen, 1993b). But these interesting ideas are only beginning to be investigated. In reality, very little is known about how differences in brain function are related to differences in intelligence.

Intrauterine Environment. We have seen that in general humans tend to experience their environments in an active rather than a passive way. However, passive exposure to certain chemicals before birth can affect a person's IQ. For example, mothers who drink excessive amounts of alcohol during pregnancy tend to have offspring with lower-than-normal IQs. Even a couple of drinks each day have been shown to produce children whose IQs at age 4 are five points below those of control subjects (Streissgguth, Barr, Sampson, Darby, & Martin, 1989).

Intelligence and fetal alcohol syndrome, Chapter 11, p. 383

More subtle intrauterine effects can be seen in twin studies. Monozygotic twins gestate in separate or shared *chorions* (the sacks containing amniotic fluid; see Figure 13.8). Hence, each twin has either a separate or a shared placenta. A number of experiments have shown that monozygotic twins who share a chorion differ *more* in physical size and on some behavioral measures than monozygotic twins who do not (Phelps, Davis, & Schartz, 1997). However, other studies (Gutknect, Spitz, & Carlier, 1999) have shown that twins who share the same chorion are more similar than others in their scores on some WISC-R subtests, as well as on a measure of personality.

While monozygotic twins who shared a chorion have the same genes, surprisingly, some elements of their intrauterine environment differ. In a shared chorion, the blood supply from the shared placenta is uneven: Each twin receives a different amount of blood. In comparison, twins who each have their own placenta receive more equal amounts of blood. Such differences could contribute to the disparities found in monozygotic twins. Why might twins who share the same

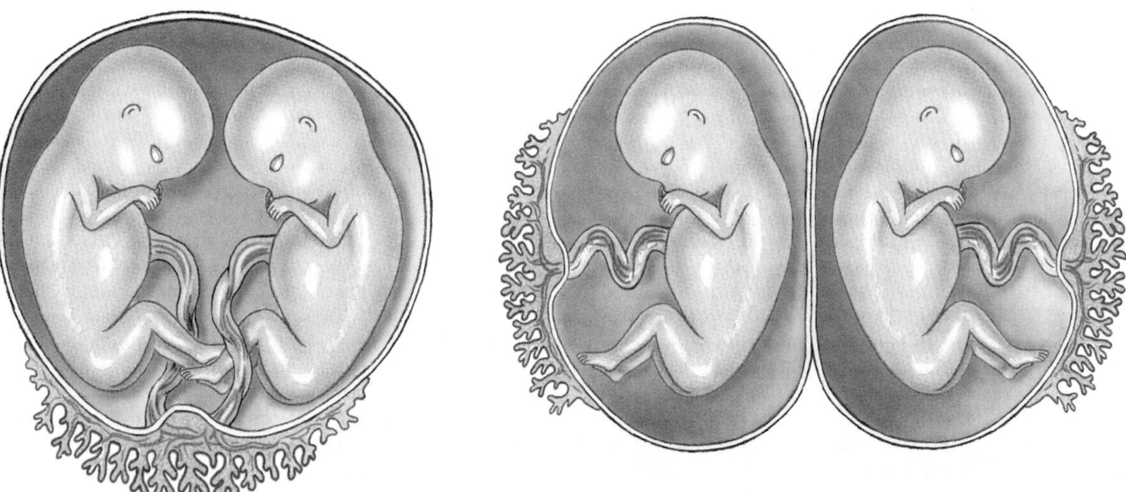

Figure 13.8 Early Environmental Differences. Before birth, twins either share a single chorion (left) or develop in separate chorions (right). Twins who develop in the same chorion share a common blood supply. Under most circumstances, they share more hormones, viruses, and so forth than twins who develop in separate chorions. These environmental similarities may account for the fact that monozygotic twins who share a single chorion score more closely on some intellectual and personality measures than monozygotic twins who develop in separate chorions. *Source:* From Phelps et al., 1997.

chorion be more *similar* on certain of their psychological measures? The evidence is unclear, but one reason may be that they share more of the same intrachorion chemicals than twins in separate chorions.

Harry and Larry Carothers' mother recalls that her twins shared the same placenta and that they varied in their birthweight by about one pound. But as adults their similarities are overwhelming, as we might predict from the fact that their genotypes are identical. We can surmise that the two shared a chorion and thus a similar environment even before birth.

INTERIM SUMMARY

1. Psychologists and other academicians disagree about the validity of IQ tests, the uses of IQ testing, and the relative roles of genes and the environment in intelligence.
2. In the 1990s Herrnstein and Murray's *The Bell Curve* became the focal point of the controversy over IQ testing. These authors proposed that IQ is more a product of genetics than environment; that intelligence varies as a function of race and ethnicity; and that people's economic and social success are tied directly to their IQ.
3. By comparing the IQ scores of monozygotic twins who shared a family environment with those who were separated at birth, scientists can compute a *heritability* score for intelligence. Genes account for about .4 of the variance of IQ in children and as much as .8 in late adulthood.
4. Among unrelated children raised in the same family, the correlation of IQ is only .17, which suggests that the role of the environment in IQ is minimal. However, genes account for only about half the variance in the IQ of identical twins raised apart, which suggests a large role for the environment.
5. Individuals can experience the environment either passively or actively. Different people experience the same environment differently, so equal opportunity does not guarantee equal outcomes in different individuals.
6. The gene-by-environment interaction in the expression of intelligence produces a ***reaction range*** of an estimated 20 to 25 IQ points.

7. Equal amounts of practice do not guarantee equal achievement among individuals. Some individuals, called *overachievers,* work hard but lack intellectual ability. Others, called *underachievers,* are smart but do not practice.
8. Worldwide, there has been a steady rise in IQ of about 3 points per decade, a phenomenon called the ***Flynn Effect.*** Several environmental theories have been proposed to account for this increase, including an increase in the complexity of life that may cause corresponding changes in the brain, and enhanced nutrition, which increases brain size.
9. The verbal/analytical and performance subscales of the WAIS-III reflect the functioning of the left and right cerebral hemispheres.
10. People with high IQs need fewer trials than others to learn conceptual tasks, can learn more word pairs at high rates of speed, have faster reaction times when faced with complex choices, and require less *inspection time* to form perceptual judgments.
11. Speed of information processing is related to IQ; smart people encode to and retrieve information from LTM quickly and effectively.
12. Nerve conduction velocity is higher in people with high IQs, but the essential differences in brain functioning among people with different IQs are unknown.
13. The intrauterine environment has been shown to affect adult IQ scores. Monozygotic twins who share a chorion are more similar than monozygotic twins who developed in separate chorions.

For Further Thought

1. We all know someone who always seems to understand the *first* time a teacher ran through a difficult problem. But we also know people who excel in the long run, even though they aren't first to come up with an answer. Can you think of an evolutionary trade-off between speed (impulsivity) and reflective thoroughness?
2. Given individual differences in the speed of thinking, can you explain why there might be fewer not-so-fast thinkers than fast thinkers?
3. Are there more overachievers than underachievers among your close friends? Do you know some people for whom this kind of judgment is hard to make?
4. If I were to be cloned, because of an age difference, I would become a grandfather to my monozygotic twin. Would my IQ be more similar to that of my natural twin than to my cloned twin? Why or why not?
5. James Flynn argues that the Flynn Effect has more to do with IQ tests themselves than with actual intelligence, since it has produced no corresponding gains in our cultural institutions. Do you agree?
6. Do you think younger people are more environmentally conscious than older people? If so, are younger people more intelligent?

THE BELL CURVE WARS: INTELLIGENCE AND CULTURE

In *The Bell Curve,* Herrnstein and Murray candidly described individual differences in intellectual abilities, and the often-adverse effects of IQ testing on people's lives. For example, they reminded readers that individual differences in IQ mean that some schoolchildren are placed in advanced classes, some in regular classes, and others in special education classes. Based on IQ and related achievement and aptitude tests, some students are accepted into the nation's best colleges and universities; others are passed over. In turn, the best graduates of those schools receive most of the top jobs in medicine, law, government, education, business, and the military. Intelligence testing is controversial, then, because the results tend to determine one's niche in society. Add to these considerations the fact that the mean IQs of African Americans, Hispanic Americans, Asian Americans, and whites differ, and intelligence testing becomes a divisive matter for an entire culture.

Ethnic Differences in IQ

The focus on individual differences in this chapter here shifts to questions of ethnic differences. Kottak (1994) defines race in social and ethnic as well as biological terms, and argues that *ethnicity* is more descriptive than *race*. The human genome project has revealed that about 85 percent of all human variation occurs between individuals of the same population, and less than 10 percent of the variation occurs between Africans, Asians, and Europeans. For our purposes, then, an ethnic group is one whose members share certain beliefs, values, habits, customs, norms, and, typically, some genes. The question is, are there ethnic differences in intelligence, and, if so, where do they come from?

These are not easy questions to answer. Critics of *The Bell Curve* charged that the authors oversimplified the relationship between IQ and ethnicity. Explaining ethnic differences on the basis of *g*, some suggested, is like defining consciousness solely in terms of visual experience. Just as there are other aspects of consciousness besides vision, other factors besides *g* affect children's school performance, including their beliefs, values, habits, customs, norms, as well as genetic kinship.

Consider the ethnic differences in achievement shown in Figure 13.9. In the late 1990s, fewer than half the African American and Hispanic American students in Texas graduated from high school, and less than 10 percent graduated from college. In contrast, 70 to 80 percent of Asian Americans and whites gradu-

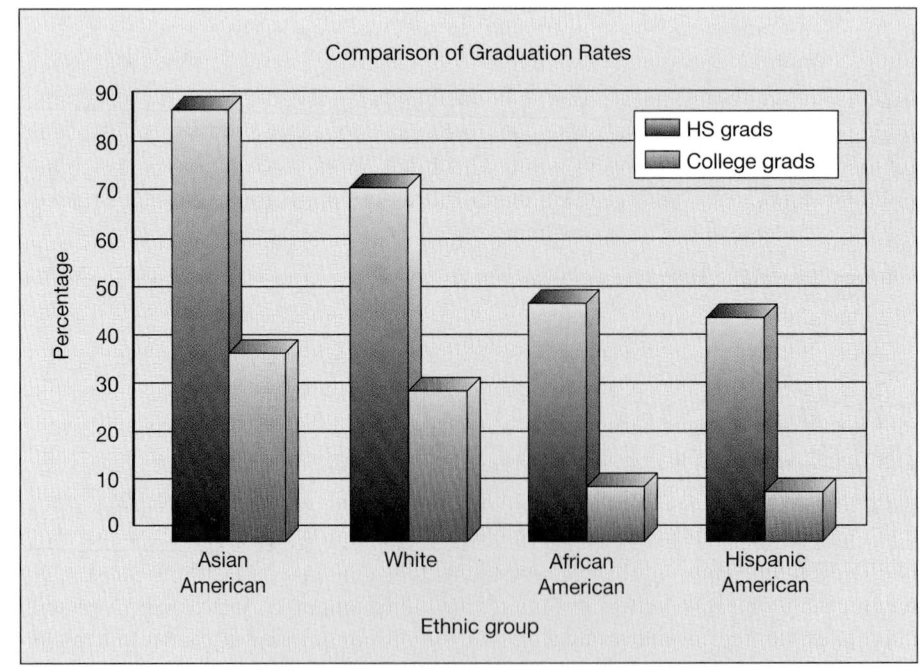

Figure 13.9 Ethnic Differences in Graduation Rates, Texas, 1996. This graph shows the percentage of students from different ethnic groups who graduated from high schools in Texas in 1996, as well as the percentage of students from each group who earned college degrees. These percentages obscure the fact that Texas has more white students than African American and Hispanic American students, and a relatively small population of Asian Americans. However, they are representative of national trends.

ated from high school, and 25 to 35 percent graduated from college. (In California, 20 percent of white adults, 40 percent of Asian adults, and about 5 percent of African American and Latino adults hold college degrees [Kaplan, 1998].)

What accounts for these differences? The authors of *The Bell Curve* asserted that they reflect genetic influences in the distribution of general intelligence, *g*. That is, since *g* is determined more by genes than by environment, and is positively correlated with success in school, in large measure *g* determines the differences in graduation rates seen in Figure 13.9. Critics of *The Bell Curve* countered that there is no evidence linking IQ to a particular genotype, and that the social environment of these ethnic groups better accounts for differences in school performance and IQ.

IQ does vary from one ethnic group to another. The combined results of several studies have yielded a mean IQ for Asian Americans of 104, followed by 100 for whites, about 93 for Hispanic Americans, and about 85 for African Americans. But while the mean IQs for these groups differ, significant portions of the bell-shaped curve for each group overlap; that is, within an ethnic group, high, medium, and low scorers overlap with the other ethnic groups.

The simple answer to the question of what determines differences in educational achievement is that *g* alone does not determine grades and graduation rates. Many factors contribute to grades and graduation rates, of which *g* is an important one. The correlation between IQ and grades is about .50, between IQ and number of years of schooling, 0.55. While these correlations are high, they account for only 25 to 30 percent of the variance between the two variables. (A rough estimate of variance can be computed by squaring the correlation of two variables.) In addition to intellectual ability, success in school likely depends on personal characteristics such as persistence, study habits, and interest in the subject matter (Neisser et al., 1996). Cultural attitudes toward schoolwork are also important. Chinese and Japanese parents, for example, require their children to study mathematics for more hours each week than American parents (Stevenson & Stigler, 1992).

In part because they proposed that ethnic differences in school performance could be attributed to *g*, Herrnstein and Murray (1994) were broadly criticized for promulgating racist views. However, the report of the APA's commission acknowledged the role of genes in IQ, but also recognized that differences in IQ are only one among many variables that produce the ethnic differences in educational achievement (Neisser et al., 1996). Yet, the question of what causes differences in IQ remains. For several decades, anthropologists, sociologists, and psychologists have addressed this question. They have suggested that racial discrimination, socioeconomic factors, and other cultural differences may account for differences in school performance. Specifically:

1. Irrespective of ethnicity, the children of poor people do not do as well as the children of the rich on IQ tests or in their schoolwork.
2. IQ tests that are given in English place bilingual Hispanic American students at a disadvantage, especially if Spanish is their native tongue. Likewise, the various dialects of "Black English" may impair African Americans' performance on IQ tests that are conducted in Standard English.
3. Different ethnic groups have different opinions of the worth of education. One theorist has suggested that many African Americans have been profoundly alienated from mainstream society because of racial discrimination (Serpell & Boykin, 1994). As a consequence, many blacks reject outright the coursework and testing methods of schools representing the dominant white culture.

All in all, no one knows for sure why ethnic differences exist in both school performance and IQ. In the words of the psychologist Linda Gottfredson,

> All societies are characterized by wide disparities in intelligence, or IQ "bell curves." [Such individual differences are] an enduring feature of human populations. Research on intelligence has always asked *why do these differences exist* and . . . *what are their effects*? Accumulated research has . . . shattered enough presumptions on all sides of past debates to suggest that no one, neither liberals nor conservatives, neither hereditarians nor environmentalists, have been on the right track in answering these questions. (Gottfredson, 1997a, p. 1)

Educational Implications of Ethnic Differences

Despite the significance of cultural differences, IQ is important to both classroom performance and educational policy. Recall that Binet developed the first IQ test to identify students who were unlikely to learn the standard school curriculum. Currently, many schools use an IQ of about 70, plus other performance variables, as a cutoff score for mainstream schooling. That is, most students with IQs of 70 or below cannot master the basic skills expected at each grade level, so they are placed in special education courses. As Figure 13.2 shows, an IQ of 70 is two standard deviations below the mean; about 2.5 percent of the population falls into this area under the bell curve. But when the same standard is applied to African American students, whose mean IQ is one standard deviation below the mean for whites, about 16 percent of their population falls below the cutoff point. Such a policy puts far more African Americans (and, to a lesser extent, Hispanic Americans) into special education classes. Fewer of these students graduate from high school, contributing to the ethnic disparities in graduation rates seen in Figure 13.9.

What is the minimum IQ that allows students to master the basic skills at each grade level? Because the United States does not have a national curriculum, this question is difficult to answer. However, the state of Texas has used grade-level standardized achievement tests since 1992, and students must achieve a minimum score to graduate from high school. Using data from these tests, it can be estimated that most students with IQs of about 80 or above can pass grade-level achievement tests. This means that roughly 9 out of 10 of the white students, and 6 out of 10 African American students can pass these tests. (Note that educators in Texas do *not* use IQ scores to determine who will graduate from high school. Rather, performance on the state's achievement test can be predicted by IQ.)

Real-World Consequences of Differences in IQ

IQ scores and school achievement are correlated with income. However, scholars do not understand the nature of the relationship. Schooling may increase intelligence and income, or being rich may increase the availability of schooling, and hence intelligence. Conversely, intelligence may increase both the number of years spent in school, which in turn increases income (Ceci & Williams, 1997). In this final section we'll look at evidence supporting the notion that IQ is the most important piece of this puzzle (Jensen, 1980; Herrnstein & Murray, 1994; Gottfredson, 1997b; Gordon, 1997). The real-world consequences of IQ can be staggering. Studies show that IQ affects one's health and safety, employment, and opportunity for success in life.

Health and Safety. Some people make more errors of judgment than others, and some scientists believe that IQ plays a key role. As the sociologist Robert Gordon puts it, "To error is human. . . . There is good reason, however, for supposing that the probabilities of making a mistake in any given situation, independent of experience, vary from individual to individual according to IQ, or . . . any good test of *g*" (Gordon, 1997, p. 203).

What is the evidence for such a statement? Let's first consider a common activity, driving a car. Several studies have shown a relationship between IQ, judgment, and the rate of automobile accidents (Iskant & Joliet, 1968; O'Toole, 1990). For example, the mortality rate among male drivers whose IQ is under 85 is 2.85 times greater than it is for males whose IQ is 100 (O'Toole, 1990). What isn't known is whether people with higher-than-average IQ scores make even safer drivers.

IQ is also inversely related to risk-taking behavior and the kind of poor judgment that produces juvenile delinquency, crime, and HIV infection (Gordon, 1997). Individuals of low IQ tend to form networks or gangs with other people of low IQ. These groups tend to reinforce their member's bad judgment. Choosing an ill-advised sex partner or needle sharer, for example, means that a person "accepts the judgments concerning lifestyle, partners, and precautionary practices as well as the sexual choices available throughout that person's network of partners . . . [thus] the collective intelligence of the network . . . figures in the outcome of every individual decision" (Gordon, 1997, p. 243). People of low IQ are also less healthy, poorer, more closely associated with a dysfunctional family (more of whom include unwed mothers), and more often incarcerated than people of average and above-average intelligence (Herrnstein & Murray, 1994; Gordon, 1997).

Finally, IQ may be related to longevity. One study in Scotland correlated IQ scores measured at 11 years of age with how long these individuals lived (up to age 76), and found a modest positive relationship (Whalley & Deary, 2001). These researchers also pointed out the confound that people scoring higher on IQ tests tend to be wealthier, which could also account for the increased longevity.

Employment. The nation's schools are not the only institutions that use intelligence tests. As we have seen, the military uses intelligence and aptitude tests to screen and place its recruits. The minimum IQ required by the United States military is about 85 for the Army, 88 for the Air Force and Marines, and 91 for the Navy. These cutoffs are based on decades of experience with hundreds of thousands of recruits who have taken the Armed Forces Qualifying Test (AFQT). The military has found that individuals with low scores on this test (which are equivalent to low IQs) do not do well in even the most basic training programs. They are limited in what they can learn no matter how long they remain in a training program (Gottfredson, 1997b).

Similarly, many civilian employers use the 50-item Wonderlic Personnel Test (WPT) to screen job applicants. Like AFQT scores, WPT scores are normally distributed and correlate highly with scores on the WAIS-III (see Gottfredson, 1997b). Even without factoring in social and personality variables, WPT scores predict job performance very well. Table 13.4 shows that certain representative occupations demand higher WPT scores than others. While the range of scores (and IQs) needed at each occupational level can vary by 15 to 20 IQ points, a minimum score is necessary to function at each (Gottfredson, 1997b).

Both the AFQT and the WPT have what is called *criterion validity*: they are valid for a particular criterion, in this case, on-the-job performance. Recall that traditional IQ tests have been criticized for predicting school performance only, and none too well at that. These tests show that measures of general intellectual ability (*g*) can fulfill the criterion of fitting people to jobs. *G*-loaded tests are most useful for predicting on-the-job performance in highly complex occupations

Table 13.4 The Relationship Between Occupation and IQ

Successful performance in certain occupations is correlated with scores on the Wonderlic Personnel Test (WPT) and on IQ tests. This table shows the estimated minimum IQ scores for certain representative occupations.

Occupation	WPT Score	Minimum IQ	Percentile (General Population)
Lawyer Research analyst Advertising manager	30	120	91st
Accountant/teacher Nurse Sales rep	25	112	81st
Cashier Meter reader Bank teller	20	100	50th
Custodian Material handler	15	90	25th
?	10	80	10th

(Hunter, 1986). They do *not* measure social or creative intelligence—yet is there a better definition of practical intelligence than how well one performs in a given occupation?

Life's Chances. Intellectual abilities, then, have real-world consequences. Linda Gottfredson (1997b, p. 79) argues that intelligence has a "surprisingly pervasive importance in the lives of individuals." She further suggests that "intelligence . . . operating over a lifetime like a consistent bias—a thumb on the scale of life—that enhances or depresses the individual's odds of success . . . in virtually all of life's endeavors" (1997a, p. 7).

Figure 13.10 summarizes the effect of intellectual ability on the lives people live. Gottfredson describes the life chances of people in the bottom 5 percent of the IQ distribution as "high risk." (In the United States this segment of the population includes 13.5 million individuals.) Because the training potential of these people is low, requiring slow, simplified instruction from an ever-present supervisor, they are apt to be chronically unemployed. People in the next 20 percent of

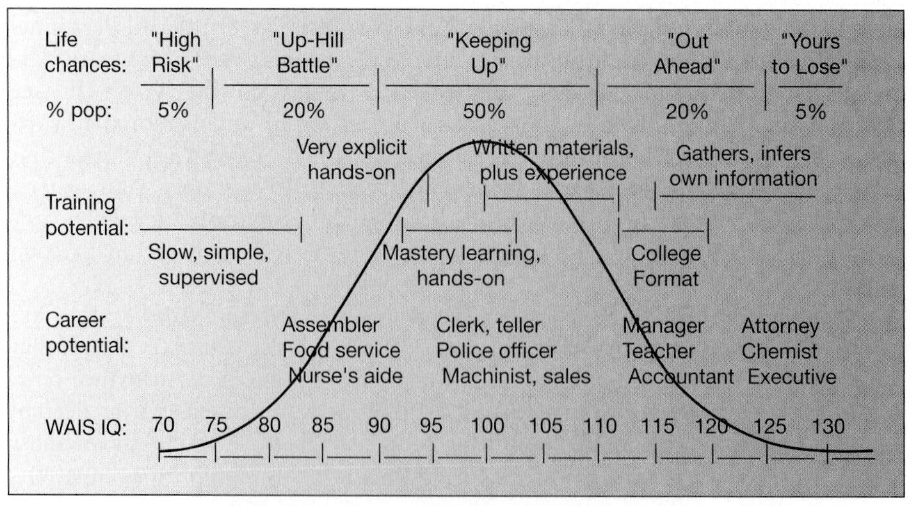

Figure 13.10 The Relationship Between Intelligence and Life Success. Differences in IQ are correlated with profound differences in learning ability, career options, and the chances of succeeding in life. *Source:* From "Why g Matters: The Complexity of Everyday Life" by L. S. Gottfredson in *Intelligence,* (1997), vol. 24, pp. 13–23. Published by Ablex Publishing Corp.

the population (54 million individuals) face an up-hill battle in meeting life's challenges. Capable of working only on assembly lines and in fast-food restaurants, they will be chronically poor throughout their lives. The majority of the nation's populace—people in the middle 50 percent of the bell curve, with IQs of about 90 to 110—must work hard at "keeping up." The fortunate top 25 percent of the population (about 67 million people) make up the professional class. They hold most of the college degrees, can function well without supervision, and can afford to maintain their financial stability not just in the present but in the future as well. These people pay most of the taxes that provide structure and order for society. Finally, people in the top 5 percent, with IQs of about 128 and above, can handle large amounts of information and choose almost any occupation. While succeeding in life at any level requires effort, for this group, success comes relatively easy. For these reasons, intelligence may be the most adaptive of all human characteristics.

INTERIM SUMMARY

1. Intelligence is a controversial concept because it describes value-laden abilities that vary widely in a population. It has become a focal point for the nature-nurture controversy, for the inheritance of intellectual abilities, for the social implications of racial and ethnic differences, and for the role of psychology in addressing public-policy issues.
2. Individual differences in intelligence are normally distributed in the general population and in ethnically defined populations.
3. Ethnic groups differ in their high school and college graduation rates and their performance on IQ tests. The mean differences in IQ among groups are substantial, amounting to one full standard deviation. However, high and low IQ scores can be found in all ethnic groups.
4. Behavioral scientists disagree on the causes of ethnic differences in school performance and in scores on IQ tests. Some emphasize genetic influences on intelligence; others note that IQ accounts for only about 25 percent of the variance in school performance.
5. Performance on IQ tests is linked to school performance and income level.
6. Ethnic groups have distinctive beliefs, values, habits, customs, and norms that affect both their academic performance and their IQ scores.
7. Educators use IQ scores to help place students in special education programs (IQ < 70). They use IQ, achievement, and aptitude tests to set passing standards and admit students to institutions of higher education.
8. Effective performance of highly skilled tasks requires a high IQ. People with low IQs make more errors and suffer more accidents than people with high IQs.
9. Statistically, people with low IQs are poorer and less healthy than others. Their families are more dysfunctional than other families, and their poor judgment often results in juvenile delinquency, crime, incarceration, or HIV infection.
10. Employers use the WPT, and the military, the AFQT, to match people's needs and abilities with appropriate jobs. Individuals with scores equivalent to an IQ of 80 or below are highly restricted in employment potential. They benefit little from training and require constant direct supervision.
11. People who score highly on *g*-loaded tests typically choose more demanding occupations, for which they are compensated at above-average rates.
12. Intelligence affects all of life's endeavors. High intelligence increases the odds for a successful life; low intelligence diminishes them.

For Further Thought

1. Should psychologists continue to study aspects of mind and behavior—such as intelligence—that may produce racial discord and social unrest in society at large? Why or why not?

For Further Thought

2. Should we be discouraged that half of the population of the United States has an IQ less than 100? Why or why not?
3. Should AFQT scores in the military, and WPT scores in industry, play significant roles in job assignments? Why or why not?
4. Not everyone is in agreement that SAT scores should play a significant role in college admissions. What do you think?
5. Do the real-life consequences of intelligence in contemporary life have parallels in a hunter-gatherer society?

CONCLUDING THOUGHTS

All humans perceive the world, process information, and learn from experience in about the same way. Yet, intelligence varies markedly from one person to the next, from very low to very high. For this reason, the study of intelligence epitomizes psychologists' historical interest in individual differences.

Intelligence refers to the ability to solve problems, think rationally, and understand complex ideas. The study of intelligence is controversial because it concerns value-laden abilities that have wide-reaching consequences. People care deeply about intelligence testing because it places them in either the valued upper half or a less respected lower half of society.

Francis Galton developed the first intelligence test to test his hypothesis that inherent differences in intellectual endowment separated "men of eminence" from the common people. Alfred Binet developed the first intelligence test for children to identify those who needed special education programs. He found that the vast majority of children worked at an average level, and others worked above or below grade level.

The development and improvement of intelligence tests has paralleled the growth of psychometric testing. Our current understanding of the construct of intelligence comes in part from studies involving correlational methods and factor analysis. Charles Spearman used factor analysis to analyze the subtests that make up standard IQ tests. His discovery that these subtests correlated with each another led him to propose the existence of a general intelligence factor (*g*). In contrast, Louis Thurstone's statistical treatment of subtest scores led him to propose a theory of intelligence based on many separate abilities. Both views of intelligence have proponents today.

The translation of Binet's test for French schoolchildren into English led to the development of the widely used Stanford-Binet test. Administered individually to both children and adults, this test yields a score known as an intelligence quotient, or IQ. Another commonly used intelligence test for adults is David Wechsler's WAIS-III, composed of both verbal and performance scales that when combined yield an IQ score. Both tests are highly reliable, and both are thought to yield good estimates of *g*.

IQ tests have predictive validity with regard to schoolwork. That is, they predict school performance from kindergarten through college fairly well. IQ tests also have content validity: They test the language, reasoning, mathematics, spatial abilities, and general information required in both job-related tasks and schoolwork. Most people who take IQ tests make an average score, and only a few people score very high or very low. When plotted on a graph, the scores form a bell-shaped curve. The mean of such a distribution of IQ scores has been set at 100, with a standard deviation of 15 points.

Unhappy with the *g*-based construct of intelligence, Howard Gardner proposed a theory of *multiple intelligences*. To the basic concept of IQ Gardner added movement intelligence, social intelligence, and self-knowledge. One effect of his theory of multiple intelligences has been to broaden the range of individual differences that are of interest to psychologists. However, some psychologists think Gardner misapplied the term *intelligence* to dancing and athletic ability. The psychologist Robert Sternberg agrees with Gardner that the analytic abilities measured by IQ tests define intelligence too narrowly. His *triarchic theory of intelligence* includes analytic, practical, and creative abilities. Sternberg believes that people use practical intelligence rather than the type of thinking that is measured on an IQ test to solve real-life problems. In this he disagrees with other psychologists, who argue that a person's IQ does predict real-world abilities. Most psychologists agree that IQ tests do *not* do a good job of identifying the many ways in which people can be creative, excel in social situations, or solve problems through lateral thinking.

Both inherited and learned abilities contribute to differences in intelligence. By comparing the IQ scores of monozygotic twins with dizygotic twins and unrelated children of the same age, behavioral geneticists have estimated that the heritability of intelligence varies from about 0.4 in early childhood to 0.8 in late adulthood. Environment effects are important in early childhood, but become less important later in life. Shared environments and equal amounts of practice, however, do not produce the same results in all individuals. Differences in IQ are assumed to be brain based; some may be characterized in terms of cortical processing speed. For example, people with high IQs take fewer trials to learn conceptual tasks. They also process information, make complex choices, and form perceptual judgments more quickly than others.

Publication of *The Bell Curve* in 1994 was controversial because of its thesis that ethnic differences in IQ are due primarily to genetic influences. While performance on IQ tests is positively correlated with school success and income, separating cause from effect is difficult. Family structure and ethnic differences in beliefs, values, habits, customs, and norms may also affect academic performance, IQ, and career choices that determine income. The real-world consequences of differences in IQ are significant. Low IQs correlate with poor health, poverty, dysfunctional families, juvenile delinquency, crime, and incarceration. High IQs increase the odds for success in life in terms of health, educational opportunities, career options, and financial rewards.

KEY TERMS

factor analysis *459*
Flynn Effect *471*
general intelligence (*g*) *453*
intelligence quotient (IQ) *454*
reaction range *468*
Stanford-Binet *454*
triarchic theory of intelligence *462*
Wechsler Adult Intelligence Scale (WAIS-III) *455*

14

Personality

Andy Warhol (1928–1987) American, "Marilyns," Leo Castelli Gallery, New York City / SuperStock © 2002 Andy Warhol Foundation for the Visual Arts / Artists Rights Society (ARS), New York.

Personality: An Overview
The Adaptiveness of Personality
Theoretical Approaches to Personality

The Trait Approach
Greek Personality Types
Body Types and Personality
How Many Personality Types?
The Big Five Personality Factors
Genetics and Personality Types
Interim Summary
For Further Thought

Social-Learning and Social-Cognitive Approaches
Behavioral Conditioning of Personality
Cognition and Personality
The Interaction of Genes and Culture
Interim Summary
For Further Thought

The Psychodynamic Approach
Freud's Psychoanalytic Theory
The Structure of Personality
Anxiety and Defense Mechanisms
Sexual Energy and the Death Force
Psychosexual Development
The Evaluation of Freudian Theory
The Analytic Theory of Carl Jung
Alfred Adler's Self Psychology
Interim Summary
For Further Thought

Humanistic Approaches
Carl Rogers's Person-Centered Approach
Abraham Maslow's Theory of Self-Actualization
An Evaluation of Humanistic Personality Theories
Interim Summary
For Further Thought

Concluding Thoughts

In her autobiography, *Reason for Hope*, Jane Goodall (1999) reflected on her lifetime spent studying chimpanzees in Africa. In the process, she revealed much about her personality—what kind of person she is:

> People . . . are always asking where I find my energy. They also comment on how peaceful I seem. How can I be so peaceful? They ask. Do I meditate? Am I religious? Do I pray? Most of all they ask how I can be so optimistic in the face of so much environmental destruction and human suffering; in the face of overpopulation and overconsumption, pollution, deforestation, desertification, poverty, famine, cruelty, hatred, greed, violence, and war. Does she really believe what she says? they seem to be wondering. What does she really think, deep down? What is her philosophy of life? What is the secret ingredient for her optimism, her hope? (p. xvi)

The terms *person* and *personality* are derived from the Greek word *persona*, meaning "mask." That *personality*, a word referring to inner states such as optimism, should be derived from *mask*, a word more descriptive of outer appearances, is interesting. Obviously, the Greeks were aware that only occasionally do humans show what they really think and feel, "deep down."

Psychologists have struggled to understand personality, because for the most part, they are forced to rely on self-reports of what people feel and think. As we all know, people are not always objective in their self-descriptions; everyone has secrets. Is Goodall really energetic, peaceful, and optimistic, or is that the mask she wears? Ironically, her observations of chimpanzees reveal them to be the only other species besides humans that practices self-deception.

Jane Goodall with chimpanzees.

In part, Goodall's peacefulness and optimism in the face of famine, overpopulation, and deforestation may reflect her adaptation to her solitary way of life in the wild. Or Goodall may have been moved to spend a lifetime sitting quietly, watching chimpanzees, and reflecting on the meaning of life because of an innate tendency toward peacefulness and contemplation. Certain aspects of personality, then, may be adaptive in both the proximal and the distal sense.

Proximal and distal determinants of behavior, Chapter 3, p. 70

In this chapter we'll review various theories of personality beginning with the ideas of the ancient Greeks. We'll see that personality can be viewed in terms of both inherited traits and social learning. We'll examine Freud's psychoanalytic perspective and the humanistic view of personality development. And we will apply our understanding of brain function to this elusive concept. To paraphrase Jane Goodall, *What does one really think, deep down, behind the mask?*

PERSONALITY: AN OVERVIEW

Humans are unquestionably the most fascinating of all life forms. At one time or another, most of us have sat on a park bench or walked through a mall merely to watch others go about their lives. As people watchers, we marvel at the shapes, sizes, and behavior of those who stroll by. Based on what we see, hear, and intuit, we may try to guess what kind of people they are—*outgoing* or *introverted, vain* or *unself-conscious*. In a word, we attribute personality characteristics to them. But some wear impenetrable masks. Why do people differ so much in their personalities, and why do we care? As you might suspect, personality and our awareness of it is adaptive.

The Adaptiveness of Personality

Personality can be defined as the thoughts, feelings, desires, intentions, and behavioral tendencies that contribute to a person's individuality (Brody & Ehrlichman, 1998). Earlier chapters of this book were concerned with general features of human behavior—what motivates us, how we sense, perceive, learn, and remember. Personality is the study of how individuals differ. What is it that determines the essence of the person?

The novelist Lawrence Durrell observed in his novel *Justine* that people reveal only a portion of their personalities to others (Durrell, 1957), presenting different personas to different people. Depending on whether you are with a parent, a child, a best friend, a casual acquaintance, or a lover, your language may change, as well as your mood. To Durrell, personality was like a prism or jewel: people show different facets of their personality to different people, in the same way that a finely cut gemstone reflects light in different ways, depending on the angle at which it is held.

personality The thoughts, feelings, desires, intentions, and behavioral tendencies that contribute to one's individuality.

Perceiving and treating others as individuals is adaptive in that it promotes bonding and social adhesion. For example, because you know your two best friends will react differently to the same words, you are likely to approach each differently. One may appreciate your humor, while the other does not. One may accept a word of advice and the other scorn it. A knowledge of people's personalities permits you to predict their behavior, a highly adaptive skill. Will this person you love share a life with you, support you, and care for your children? Will this employee be trustworthy? *What is this person really like, deep down, behind the mask?*

Personality is like a cut gem: it appears to change when viewed from different angles.

Theoretical Approaches to Personality

Because personality encompasses so many aspects of an individual's mental and emotional life, theories of personality are wide ranging. In this chapter we will consider several theoretical approaches, some of which emphasize inborn traits and others social and cultural influences.

The Trait Approach. As the name implies, the *trait approach* is based on the idea that individuals can be described in terms of a limited number of relatively basic types or temperaments, called traits. Traits may have a genetic basis. For example, some dog breeds are known to have an aggressive or docile temperament; humans have similar genetic predispositions.

Genetic bases of temperament in dogs, Chapter 3, p. 89

The Social-Learning and Social-Cognitive Approaches. The *social-learning approach* stresses the role of environment and culture in shaping a person's behavior. According to this approach, the way we think about ourselves and interpret our social roles determines the kind of people we are. To understand why Jane Goodall chose to spend her life studying chimpanzees and writing about the human condition, then, a social-learning or social-cognitive psychologist would examine her early upbringing, school experiences, and so forth. Combining the trait approach with the social-learning and social-cognitive approaches allows psychologists to study how nature and nurture interact in the development of personality.

The Psychodynamic Approach. The *psychodynamic approach* to personality is probably the best known and one of the most influential perspectives in Western culture. Based on the seminal writings of Sigmund Freud, this approach to individual differences stresses the often-unpredictable interaction of conscious and unconscious mental processes. Novelists, playwrights, and even historians have joined psychologists in probing the sources of irrational thinking and unconscious motivation from the psychodynamic perspective.

Humanistic Approach. The *humanistic approach* to personality is an attempt to transcend the limitations of scientific determinism. Humanists stress the role of an individual's free will and self-esteem in the development of personality. Indeed, they ask people to see themselves as self-propelled actors rather than passive respondents to genetic and environmental forces.

The Biological Basis of Personality. As we saw in Chapter 13, comparisons of monozygotic and dizygotic twins have suggested that there is a genetic basis for intelligence. At relevant points in this chapter we'll examine evidence that other aspects of personality may also have a genetic basis. And we'll use our knowledge of brain processes—including the conscious and unconscious pathways for the senses, learning, and memory—to evaluate the trait, social learning, psychodynamic, and humanistic approaches to personality. Recall, for example, that Phineas Gage's personality changed after a steel rod damaged his frontal lobes, turning him from a conscientious, mild-mannered person into a foul-mouthed, undisciplined laggard.

Phineas Gage, Chapter 4, p. 105

Endomorphic
Relaxed, sociable,
affectionate,
good natured

Mesomorphic
Competitive, aggressive
energetic, athletic

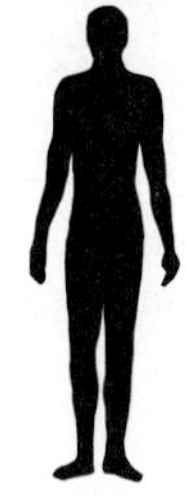

Ectomorphic
Intellectual, introverted
inhibited, self-conscious

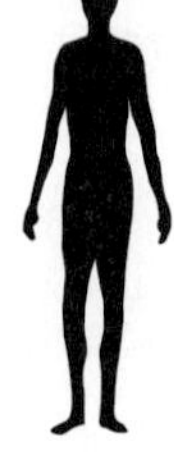

Figure 14.1 Sheldon's Body Types. William Sheldon thought that a person's body type determined his or her personality. Research has not supported his intriguing theory, however.

THE TRAIT APPROACH

We will begin by focusing on *traits,* or *types,* because they are what most people think of as personality. A **trait** is the tendency of an individual to act consistently in a characteristic way. For example, if a person is sad most of the time, then sadness would be one of that person's traits. Note that this definition is merely descriptive; it does not indicate why individuals have traits such as sadness, happiness, and anger. The concept of traits is an old one, dating back to the ancient Greeks. Although the Greeks' thinking did not have a scientific basis, it has influenced contemporary personality theorists.

Greek Personality Types

The Greeks gave us not only our word for personality, but also one of the earliest attempts to understand personality by reference to individual types. The Greek physician Hippocrates (~400 B.C.E.) postulated four personality types: *choleric* (angry and violent), *melancholic* (gloomy), *phlegmatic* (calm and passive), and *sanguine* (cheerful and active). Unaware either of the central importance of genes or of brain-behavior relationships, Hippocrates thought that these psychological differences among individuals were caused by physiological imbalances. For example, he thought an angry or violent person suffered from too much yellow bile and that cheerful people had an excess of blood. While Hippocrates was wrong about the physiological basis of personality traits, his four basic personality types are still with us.

Body Types and Personality

Like Hippocrates, some recent psychologists have tied personality types to physiological differences. According to William Sheldon's (1942) *somatotype* theory, personality is related to a person's body shape. Sheldon identified three primary body types: *endomorph, mesomorph,* and *ectomorph* (see Figure 14.1). An endomorph's body build is fat, round, and soft; a mesomorph's is muscular and strong. The ectomorph is thin, tall, and relatively fragile. Sheldon hypothesized that an individual's personality would correspond with her or his body type in "predictable" ways. For example, endomorphs would be highly social, relaxed, and easily amused. Mesomorphs, he believed, would be assertive, courageous, and energetic, while ectomorphs would be brainy, artistic, and introverted.

As you might imagine, there were problems with this simplified view of human behavior. Except for some obvious correlations—people with round body types tend to overeat, and people with muscular builds tend to be athletic—a person's body type does not predict his or her personality (Tucker, 1983). Personality, in fact, is far more complicated than either Hippocrates or Sheldon thought.

How Many Personality Types?

Individuals seem to differ in more than three or four major ways, but how many? The psychologists Gordon Allport and H. S. Odbert searched the dictionary for terms that describe individual differences and found over 18,000 descriptive adjectives (Allport & Odbert, 1936) reflecting observations made over hundreds of generations (Goldberg, 1982). Terms that describe the ways in which people think, feel, and act can be found in all languages (Dixon, 1977). But clearly, 18,000 traits is an unwieldy number. Two researchers, Raymond Cattell and Hans Eysenck tried to reduce that number to a more manageable one.

trait The tendency of an individual to act consistently in a characteristic way.

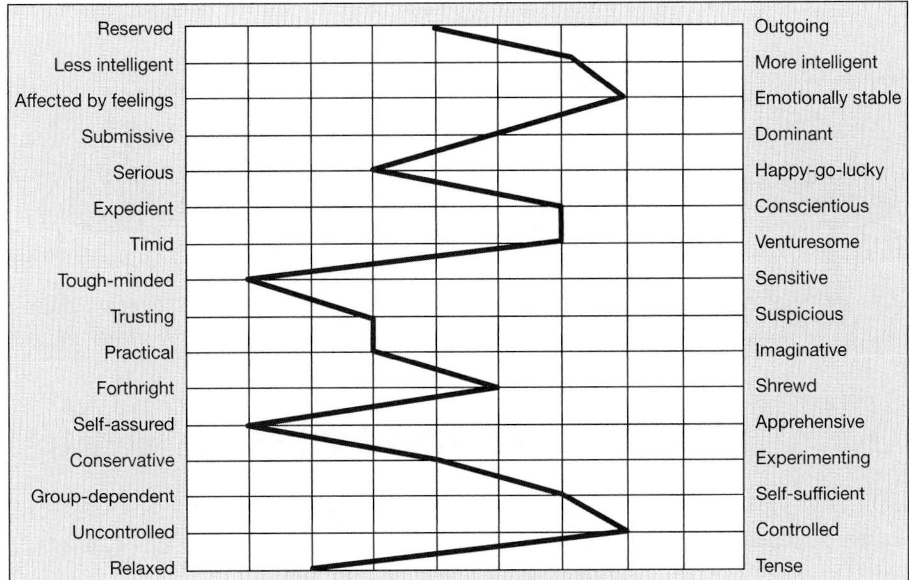

Figure 14.2 Cattell's 16PF Personality Profile. This score sheet from Raymond Cattell's 16PF personality test shows the 16 basic personality traits and their opposites. Individuals vary along a continuum between each pair of opposites; scores midway in the continuum are considered average. This score sheet shows the profile of a retired military pilot. Note that he scored above average in intelligence, emotional stability, tough-mindedness, self-assurance, and control.

Cattell's 16PF Personality Test. Raymond Cattell (1957, 1990) initially reduced Allport and Odbert's list to about 4,500, then eliminated synonyms and obscure terms to arrive at 171 trait names. Cattell and his colleagues tested numerous subjects for these traits and then used factor analysis to study the results (Cattell, 1957, 1990). (Recall that factor analysis is a statistical procedure in which test items that measure a common factor are clustered, or grouped together.)

Because Cattell found 16 basic personality factors, he called his test the 16PF personality test. This self-administered measure consists of a series of personal questions related to the personality factors, each of which has an opposite. For example, a person can be more or less *timid* along a dimension that varies from timid to venturesome, or more or less *self-assured* along a dimension that varies from self-assured to apprehensive (see Figure 14.2). Cattell found that each subject had a fairly unique profile; Figure 14.2, for example, is the profile of a retired military pilot.

Eysenck's Personality Theory. Hans Eysenck (1953, 1990) extended the concept of traits by developing them into personality types. As Figure 14.3 shows, Eysenck began with an individual's specific responses, which he grouped into habits. From groups of habits he formed traits, and from trait clusters he built personality types. Eysenck defined a **type** as the highest level of organization of the personality. His research suggested that there are relatively few basic personality types. Later researchers who have built on Eysenck's methods have settled on five.

The Big Five Personality Factors

The terms *trait* and *type* are biological terms that suggest that personality is heritable. We will examine the evidence for a genetic basis of personality in the following section; here we take a more descriptive approach—that is, one that doesn't address the *origin* of personality. In general, personality researchers have assumed that traits and types are relatively stable over time, and that they are displayed consistently from one situation to the next. To the extent that

type The highest level of organization of the personality.

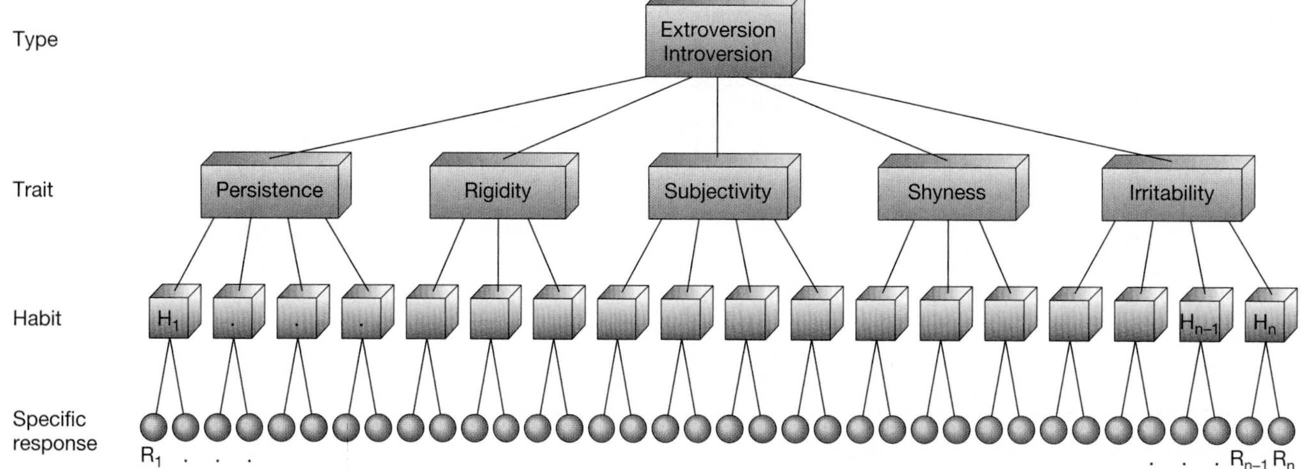

Figure 14.3 Eysenck's Personality Type. According to Eysenck's hierarchical analysis of personality, a person's habits form that person's traits, which together make up his or her personality type. For example, preferring to be alone and not answering the telephone are the habits of a person with the *trait* of shyness. A shy person who is also persistent, rigid, subjective, and irritable displays an introverted personality *type*.

these assumptions are true, the way you behaved in a variety of situations when you were 10 years old was predictive of your behavior into your twenties and thirties—indeed, into your old age (McCrae & Costa, 1994, 1997).

Researchers use paper-and-pencil tests to measure a subject's personality factors. On a 5-point scale, subjects indicate the extent to which they *strongly agree, agree,* are *neutral, disagree,* or *strongly disagree* with a couple of hundred test items. For example, "I often dislike the people I'm forced to work with," "I get mad easily," "I'm generally a happy person," and "People consider me a workaholic." Researchers then subject their results to factor analysis, looking for patterns in their responses.

Most researchers now agree that there are five basic personality factors, known as the **big five personality factors** (Goldberg, 1993; John, 1990, McCrae & Costa, 1990, 1997; Norman, 1963). Those five dimensions, considered the main, or *superset factors,* of personality, are extraversion, agreeableness, conscientiousness, emotional stability (neuroticism), and openness to experience (intellect) (see Table 14.1). Individual personalities differ in the way these factors are combined and the strength with which they are displayed.

Comparing the terms in Table 14.1 with Eysenck's hierarchical analysis of personality in Figure 14.3 reveals how factor analysis is used. Each of the big five superset factors is comprised of a number of *subset factors* that tend to cluster together when an individual's responses to a personality measure are analyzed. For example, the terms listed under *agreeableness* include softhearted, trusting, generous, and good natured, because subjects tend to respond in similar ways to test items on those traits. In other words, a softhearted person tends also to be trusting, generous, and good natured. Likewise, someone who is lazy tends also to be disorganized and is often late for appointments. Of the thousands of adjectives with which humans can be described, then, just five are needed to describe an individual quite accurately (Goldberg, 1993; John, 1990).

big five personality factors The basic five personality factors found consistently in factor-analytic studies of the personality: extroversion, agreeableness, conscientiousness, emotional stability (neuroticism), and intellect (openness to experience).

We saw in an earlier chapter that sensory psychologists have identified "four basic tastes" and a limited number of categories of smell. In reality, we experience a multitude of flavors, each comprised of distinctive combinations of taste and smell. Attempts to characterize personality through factor analysis also suffer from oversimplification. As Goldberg (1993) has pointed out, the intention of those psychologists who have proposed the big five personality factors is not to

Table 14.1 The Big Five Personality Factors

I. Extraversion	IV. Emotional stability (neuroticism)
Reserved–affectionate	Calm–worrying
Loner–joiner	Even-tempered–temperamental
Quiet–talkative	Self-satisfied–self-pitying
Passive–active	Comfortable–self-conscious
Sober–fun loving	Unemotional–emotional
Unfeeling–passionate	Hardy–vulnerable
II. Agreeableness	**V. Openness to experience (intellect)**
Ruthless–soft-hearted	Down-to-earth–imaginative
Suspicious–trusting	Uncreative–creative
Stingy–generous	Conventional–original
Antagonistic–acquiescent	Prefer routine–prefer variety
Critical–lenient	Uncurious–curious
Irritable–good natured	Conservative–liberal
III. Conscientiousness	
Negligent–conscientious	
Lazy–hardworking	
Disorganized–well organized	
Late–punctual	
Aimless–ambitious	
Quitting–persevering	

Source: Adapted from PERSONALITY IN ADULTHOOD by R. R. McCrae & P. T. Costa. © 1990. Reprinted by permission of The Guilford Press.

"reduce the rich tapestry of personality" to five measured quantities. Rather, it is to provide a scientific framework with which to "organize the myriad individual differences that characterize humankind" (p. 27).

Cattell and Eysenck developed their theories of personality independently from the concept of intelligence, as measured by IQ tests. But note that the descriptors under Openness to Experience (Intellect) in Table 14.1 include *imaginative, creative, original, prefers variety, curious,* and *liberal.* Certainly a case can be made that people with high IQs tend to be more imaginative and curious than others, because IQ is positively (but weakly) correlated with openness (McCrae & Costa, 1997). But just as IQ researchers have struggled to define intelligence using verbal, quantitative, and reasoning subscales, personality researchers have fumbled for a term that includes being liberal (rather than conservative), preferring variety, and shunning the conventional (see Table 14.1). Failing to find a single term that encompasses all aspects of this trait, they have settled on *openness to experience.*

Intelligence and creativity, Chapter 13, p. 464

Genetics and Personality Types

Eysenck thought personality was determined more by genes than by environmental factors. Recall from Chapter 13 the story of Harry and Larry, identical twins with similar IQ scores, careers, management styles, beliefs, and values. These men's genetic makeup, in interaction with their similar environments, produced their closeness. To what extent can a person's genetic makeup influence his or her personality?

Heritability of the Big Five Factors. Because traits and types are relatively stable over time, the fact that the heritabilities of the big five factors vary from 0.30 to 0.60 should not be surprising (Tellegen et al., 1988; Zuckerman, 1998). Recall from Chapter 3 that a high heritability score (i.e., one approaching 1.0) means that a trait is largely determined by genetic and

Heritability, Chapter 3, p. 88

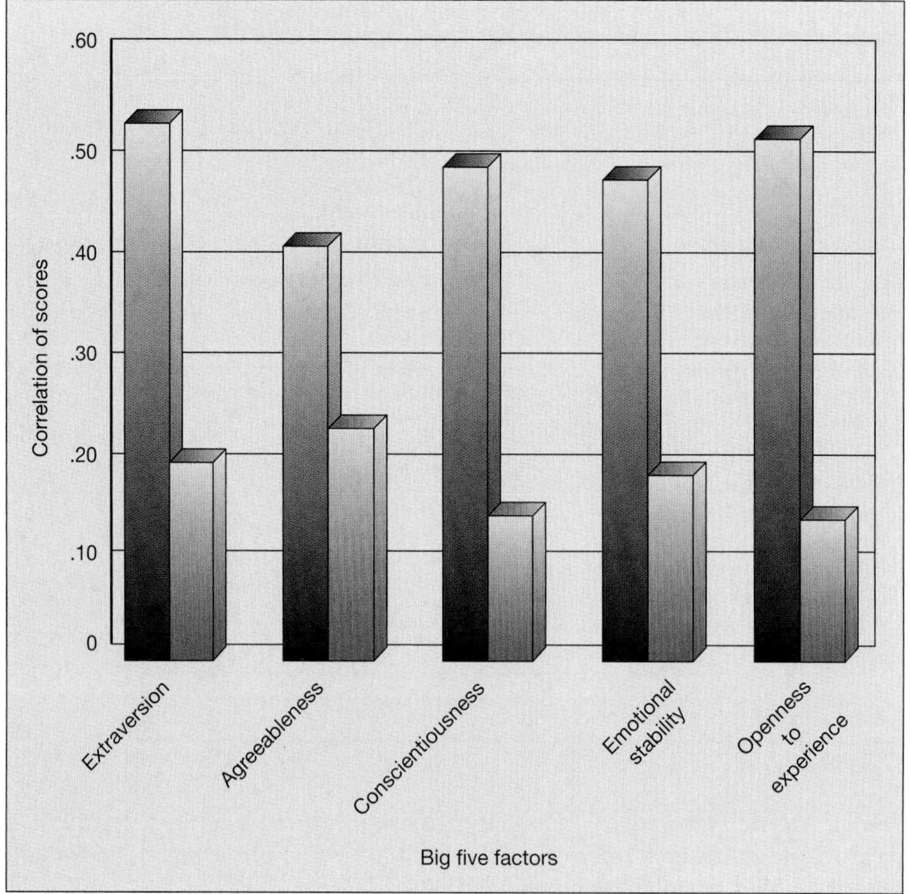

Figure 14.4 Personalities of Identical and Fraternal Twins. This graph shows the degree to which identical and fraternal twins differ in their expression of the big five personality factors. The scores of identical twins (blue) have a correlation of approximately 50 percent, while those of fraternal twins (green) have a correlation of only about 15 to 20 percent. *Source:* from GENES AND ENVIRONMENT IN PERSONALITY DEVELOPMENT by J. C. Loehlin. © 1992. Reprinted by permission of Sage Publications, Inc.

physiological variables. Scores near zero indicate that a trait is determined primarily by the environment. Thus, identical twins would share more of those traits with high heritability scores than would fraternal twins or unrelated people. (That is, the personality score of one identical twin would be more highly correlated with the other identical twin's score than would the scores of two fraternal twins.) As Figure 14.4 shows, the scores of identical twins on the big five personality factors are indeed more highly correlated than the scores of fraternal twins.

Culture Does Not Change the Big Five Factors. Even if about half of the variability in human personality is due to inheritance, as these data suggest, (Bouchard, 1994), the environment constrains the expression of those inherited tendencies. For example, a person may have a genotype that is expressed as "unemotional" in a normal range of environments. But should that person be born into a chaotic, violent environment, that person may become highly emotional. If the big five factors are in part genetically determined, then the effects of culture on their expression should be less important than the effects of genes. This proposition has been tested in a number of ways. In Chapter 13, for example, we saw that when identical twins were raised in different environments, they nevertheless showed a marked similarity in measured IQ. Another line of evidence comes from cross-cultural research. Researchers tested large, representative samples of German, Portuguese, Hebrew, Chinese, Korean, and Japanese subjects using translated versions of their personality tests. When they analyzed the results, the same big five factors emerged (McCrae & Costa, 1997).

INTERIM SUMMARY

1. ***Personality*** is defined as an individual's thoughts, feelings, desires, intentions, and behavioral tendencies.
2. Personality has been studied through the trait approach, the social-learning and social-cognitive approaches, the psychodynamic approach, and the humanistic approach.
3. A ***trait*** is the tendency of an individual to act in a consistent and characteristic way.
4. The Greek philosophers identified four classic personality types: *choleric, melancholic, phlegmatic,* and *sanguine.*
5. Research does *not* support the notion that one's personality corresponds to one's body type, or, *somatotype.*
6. Raymond Cattell's *16PF Personality Test* is a commonly administered paper-and-pencil test containing questions related to 16 basic personality factors derived using factor analysis.
7. The highest level of organization of personality, a personality ***type,*** includes several characteristic traits. Across cultures, the ***big five personality factors,*** or types, are extraversion, agreeableness, conscientiousness, emotional stability (neuroticism), and openness to experience (intellect).
8. Heritability scores for the big five factors vary from 0.30 to 0.60. But an individual's personality depends on the environment in which his or her genetic tendencies are expressed.

For Further Thought

1. Is it trivial that muscular athletes (Sheldon's mesomorphs) are often aggressive and highly competitive? Can you think of a nature-nurture interaction that might underlie this relationship?
2. Depending on the theorist, humans may have 18,000, 171, 16, or 5 personality factors. In your experience with other people, what is a reasonable number of ways in which they may vary?
3. Is your best friend an extrovert or an introvert? Turn to Table 14.1 (page 491) to see how many of the subset terms (reserved–affectionate, loner–joiner, and so forth) apply to this big five factor. Would a personality theorist see your friend the same way you do, or do you see certain aspects of your friend's personality that others don't?

THE SOCIAL-LEARNING AND SOCIAL-COGNITIVE APPROACHES

Why are you the way you are? Most humans who entertain this question will quickly point to their early childhood experiences, especially the role of parents and other significant people. Listen again to Jane Goodall (1999):

> Through the years I have encountered people and been involved in events that have had huge impact, knocked off rough corners, lifted me to the heights of joy, plunged me into the depth of sorrow and anguish, taught me to laugh, especially at myself—in other words, my life experiences and the people with whom I share them have been my teachers. (p. 2)

Goodall is advocating what is known as a *social-learning approach* to personality. Social-learning theorists stress the many ways that childhood experiences leave permanent marks on an adult's personality.

Behavioral Conditioning of Personality

John B. Watson, Chapter 1, p. 22; B. F. Skinner and Albert Bandura, Chapter 6, pp. 206, 215

Social-learning theory is built on behaviorism, which stressed conditioning of a person's behavior. Recall John B. Watson's belief that were he able to control the reinforcers and punishers in a child's early environment, he could raise that child to become either a doctor or a thief (Watson, 1924). Watson's position is tempered by more recent evidence of genetically predisposed personality factors. For example, the behaviorist B. F. Skinner held that the environment into which a person is born conditions that person's personality as well as behavior (Skinner, 1971). Social-learning theorists think that much of this kind of learning is due to modeling. Perhaps innately, children model what they see and hear, a process Albert Bandura called observational learning (Bandura, 1971). Interestingly, most of the research on modeling has been concerned with the effects of poor role models.

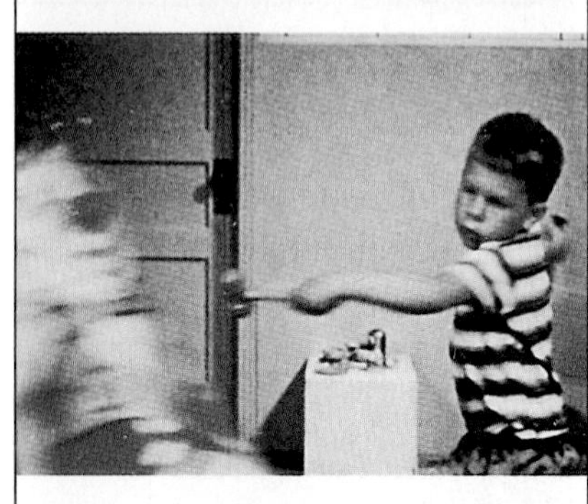

Children who watched an adult strike an inflated rubber doll readily modeled her aggressive behavior (Bandura & Walters, 1963).

Consider the big five personality factor of agreeableness (see Table 14.1). Can a person become more ruthless, irritable, and antagonistic by modeling after a violent role model? In a classic study (Bandura, Ross, & Ross, 1963), researchers allowed 4-year-old boys and girls to watch a short film in which one boy beat up another and got away with it. Another group of children saw a similar scene in which the boy was punished for his violent behavior. After viewing one or the other film, the researchers observed the children at play and rated the number of instances of aggressive behavior they displayed. Bandura and his colleagues reported that the children who saw the film in which the boy's aggressive behavior went unpunished exhibited more aggression than children in the other group. In related research (see the photographs on this page), children modeled their behavior after an adult whom they observed striking a large doll (Bandura & Walters, 1963). The effect of watching violence on television on the expression of violent behavior is discussed in the next chapter.

Cognition and Personality

In Chapter 10 we saw that based on past experiences, individuals develop schemas that guide their interpretation of their environment. One way to think about schemas is as cognitive representations of behavior. Some psychologists think that cognitive schemas may influence an individual's personality.

Note that one of the big five personality factors is conscientiousness (see Table 14.1), and that conscientious people tend to be well organized, punctual, and ambitious. Does *thinking* about being well organized, punctual, and ambitious help to determine this major personality factor? Consider the high school student whose personal goal is to become a lawyer. Assuming that lawyers are conscientious, this student's career schema may encourage her to become punctual and well organized. Even when she is tired, this student may persevere rather than quit (see the subfactors under conscientiousness in Table 14.1). It seems reasonable that having a career goal, and developing a schema to achieve that career goal, would influence the expression of a personality characteristic such as conscientiousness (Srull & Wyer, 1994).

Schemas, Chapter 10, p. 360

This scenario may be a classic instance of putting the cart before the horse, however. An alternative way of thinking about cause and effect is that the genetically predisposed trait of conscientiousness may help to determine the student's schema, rather than vice versa. Many personality traits interact to determine a person's choices and behavior. An individual with an inherent predisposition toward conscientiousness, who is also low on *neuroticism* (that is, who tends to be calm, self-satisfied, unemotional, and hardy) and high on *openness to experience* (that is, imaginative, creative, and curious) may be attracted to the study of law and related subjects, such as political science.

The Interaction of Genes and Culture

Memes, Chapter 6, p. 187

We have seen that together, genes and culture determine one's personality. The term *culture* covers a wide variety of child-rearing practices, including those of parents and peers, schools and churches, as well as the mores presented in music and movies, books and magazines. These cultural influences allow individuals to express themselves in unique ways. Who among us has not wondered what life would have been like had we been born in the suburbs or the inner city, met a significant someone else, or been raised in a different religion? Even allowing for the effect of genes, the possibilities seem endless.

Parents and other early child-care providers are important in that they frame the environment in which a child develops. On the surface, this simple assertion seems so obviously true that to argue otherwise is sure to capture people's attention. That is precisely what happened when Judith Rich Harris published a book titled *The Nurture Assumption: Why children turn out the way they do; Parents matter less than you think and peers matter more* (Harris, 1998). Although Harris is a professional writer rather than a psychologist, she cited over 700 research reports to support her contention that children's peers affect their behavior—specifically, their ability to form relationships, their sense of self-worth, and their personalities, including their intelligence—more than their parents.

Judith Harris thinks that a teen's peer group has more influence than parents.

Harris was inspired to write her book because her two daughters—one her birth child, the other adopted—turned out quite differently, despite the same rich home environment. She can be considered a trait theorist, in that she argues for the pervasive role of genetics in determining behavior. Her thinking is similar to that of behavioral geneticists, such as Steven Pinker (1994), who think the environment has a minimal influence on children's personality.

No psychologist would deny that peers are a major determinant of a child's development. Yet in arguing against the importance of parental influence, Harris oversimplifies the gene-environment interaction. A child's innate temperament can elicit (and thereby control) a parent's response to that child. In this critical sense, a child's temperament is determining the environment rather than reacting passively to it. Despite Harris's claims to the contrary, she *did not* provide the same environment to her two daughters. And while studies of identical twins raised in different environments (that is, by different parents) show that they grow more alike in old age (see Figure 13.5, page 468), these studies also show that environment contributes to differences in IQ. An estimated 30 to 60 percent of the variance in identical twins' IQ scores is due to gene-environment interactions.

Compare passive and dynamic effects of environment, Chapter 13, p. 469

Research by psychologists such as Jerome Kagan (see Chapter 10) indicates that the kind of parents children have does in fact have a significant influence on their development. Shyness, for example, can be partially overcome by a parent through careful shaping of the child's behavior. Children who become more outgoing because of their parents' efforts will in turn influence and be influenced by their peers, due as much to their parents' actions as their own genetic propensities. Moreover, parents influence their children's environment by choosing the neighborhoods in which they will live and the schools they will attend. In this regard, they have a direct hand in determining their children's peers. Harris's (1998) thesis, though it has the ring of truth, underestimates the pervasive role of culture in the expression of genetic tendencies.

INTERIM SUMMARY

1. Behaviorists such as John B. Watson and B. F. Skinner proposed that personality as well as behavior is conditioned by environmental reinforcement and punishment.
2. Albert Bandura proposed that children have an innate tendency to model what they see and hear, a process he called observational learning. Real-life models are more influential than the models children see on TV.
3. Cognitive schemas influence the expression of the big five personality factors. In turn, innate personality characteristics affect the environment a person encounters.
4. The expression of a child's innate personality characteristics is determined in part by the environment parents and other caretakers provide. Children also have an effect on their environment.

For Further Thought

1. Figure 14.2 suggests that a person's score on a measure of extraversion, emotional stability, agreeableness, conscientiousness, and openness to experience is genetically predisposed. Can you use the same figure to argue the importance of the environment in the expression of the big five personality factors?
2. People seldom model the violence they see on TV in real life. Can you explain why?
3. Do you agree with Harris's (1998) conclusion that "parents matter less than you think and peers matter more" in determining a child's behavior? Why or why not?

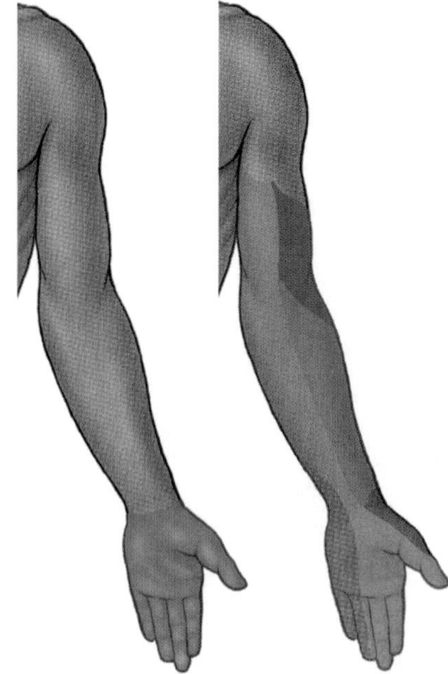

Figure 14.5 Glove Anesthesia. The arm on the right shows the distribution of sensory nerves in the arm and hand. A patient with a glove anesthesia reported no sensation in the area of the hand that would normally be covered by a glove (left). Charcot diagnosed this abnormal pattern of insensitivity as a "conversion disorder."

THE PSYCHODYNAMIC APPROACH

Unlike the trait and social-learning theories of personality, which were developed by many researchers, the origins of the psychodynamic perspective on personality can be traced to one person, Sigmund Freud. Even though Freud's work is arguably unscientific, we will discuss it in detail for historical and other reasons. Freud was less concerned with pursuing science than he was with unraveling the mysteries of human nature. His work bridges the gap between the informal theories of classicists, novelists, philosophers, and theologians and the more precise findings of quantitative psychologists. Because of his pervasive influence on contemporary culture, *Time* magazine recognized him as one of the most influential "scientists/thinkers" of the 20th century.

Freud was born to a middle-class Jewish family in Vienna 3 years before Charles Darwin published his *Origin of Species* (1859) in England. An excellent student, he earned a medical degree by the age of 25 and began a practice specializing in the emerging science of neurology. After a few years Freud moved to Paris to study with the renowned neurologist Jean Charcot. Some of Charcot's patients were displaying what were called *conversion disorders*—physical disorders such as paralysis for which there was no obvious physical explanation. One patient, for instance, could not move a hand or feel a pinprick on a finger of that hand. Figure 14.5 illustrates the problem, called *glove anesthesia*. Since the area in which the patient reported no feeling is innervated by several different nerves, there is no physiological reason why the patient would not feel a pinprick.

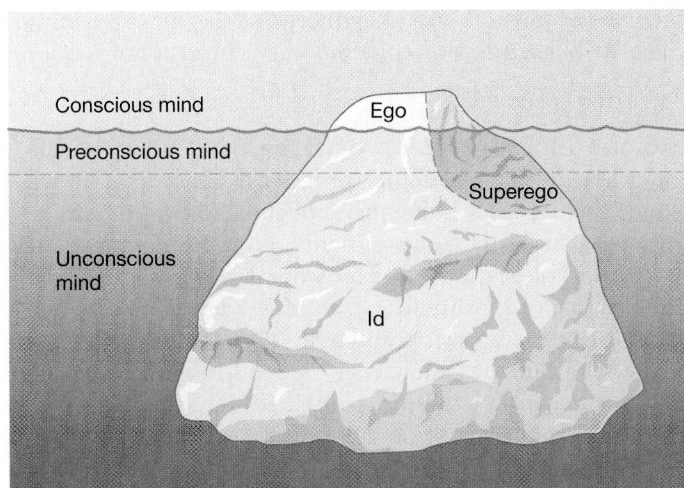

Figure 14.6 Freud's Conception of the Personality. Freud believed that humans are motivated more by hidden, unconscious processes than by conscious thoughts and emotions. According to his theory, the ego (the conscious part of the mind) operates according to the reality principle. At an unconscious level, the superego (our moral values) is in conflict with the id, the largely unconscious source of motivation that operates according to the pleasure principle.

To Freud's and the world's amazement, when Charcot hypnotized these patients, they often expressed different symptoms and were sometimes cured of their ailments. Freud's lifelong interest became clear: he would investigate the powers of the mind from a neurological perspective. Like Darwin, Freud had no one to emulate. Because of his creative insights, humans would forever think differently about themselves.

Freud's Psychoanalytic Theory

When he returned to Vienna, Freud began to see patients with "nervous problems," including anxiety, panic, irrational fears, obsessive disorders, and sexual problems. Freud's treatment method, which he termed *psychoanalysis,* did not involve hypnosis. Rather, he talked with patients as they reclined on a chaise lounge, questioning them and listening carefully to their answers. In short, Freud invented talk therapy, about which more will be said in Chapter 18 on treatment. He also "tested" his insights through self-analysis and by comparing his findings with those of other analysts.

Based on what his patients had to say (and what they were reluctant to say), Freud developed his *psychoanalytic theory* of personality (Freud, 1901/1960, 1924, 1940/1949). His main contribution was his development of the idea of unconscious, which is often represented as the larger, submerged portion of an iceberg (see Figure 14.6), representing his belief that unconscious processes are more important than conscious ones. According to Freud, the **unconscious** is comprised of memories and desires that influence one's behavior without one's awareness. Freud believed these unconscious processes often conflicted both with conscious processes and with the **preconscious**—the normal memories one can readily access from long-term memory. The resolution of this conflict was one of

Conscious and unconscious processes, Chapter 9, p. 307

Long-term and working memory, Chapter 10, p. 307

unconscious (Freud) Memories and desires that influence one's behavior without one's awareness.

preconscious (Freud) Memories that can be readily accessed from long-term memory.

the goals of his psychoanalytic method. Freud's concept of the conscious mind, the ego, or self, can also be likened to our contemporary construct of working memory.

Freudian Slips and the Interpretation of Dreams. What evidence did Freud have for the existence of unconscious processes? He found two windows to the unconscious: one a person's memories of the past and the other a person's dreams. In listening carefully to his patients, Freud sometimes noted what he considered to be suspicious lapses of memory. A patient might temporarily forget a familiar name or repeatedly fail to mail a letter, meet a deadline, or arrive on time for a therapy appointment. Freud interpreted such memory failures as a sign of an unconscious wish to avoid something. For example, a patient might repeatedly be late for therapy because Freud was probing the patient's unconscious sources of anxiety. From these experiences, Freud developed a theory of *unconscious motivation*—that is, that behavior is often motivated by mental processes of which we are unaware.

Psychoanalysis, Chapter 18, p. 614

On other occasions, Freud heard patients make strange errors in their speech—so-called slips of the tongue, or *Freudian slips*. For example, a student once told me that while writing a term paper with her boyfriend, she mistakenly typed *lover* instead of *lower*. Freudian thought these unintentional errors had a hidden meaning. He also analyzed humor, because he thought the hidden meanings, word plays, and double entendres in jokes reflected unconscious motivations (Jones, 1955).

One of Freud's most enduring contributions to Western culture was his analysis of dreams (1900/1950). Dreams, he reasoned, had both *manifest* and *latent content*. For example, in a dream in which a train enters a tunnel, the manifest content would be the train entering the tunnel. Freud thought that the latent content, or symbolic meaning, of this dream was a wish for sexual intercourse (the train being a symbol of the male sex organ and the tunnel of the female). Dreams, then, were a way for the unconscious mind to communicate its intentions. In Freud's words (1900/1950):

"Good morning, beheaded—uh, I mean beloved."

> . . . there are no guileless dreams . . . whatever one dreams is either plainly recognizable as being psychically significant, or it is distorted and can be judged correctly only after complete interpretation, when it proves after all to be of psychic significance. The dream never concerns itself with trifles; we do not allow sleep to be disturbed by trivialities . . . (p. 86)

Id and biological motivation, Chapter 5, p. 155

The Structure of Personality

To Freud, the personality was always in a state of conflict. He coined three terms, the *ego, id,* and *superego,* to represent the conflict between conscious and unconscious thoughts (see Figure 14.6). The **id** represents basic biological drives and impulses—the need to eat and drink, have sex, and so forth—which are governed by what Freud called the *pleasure principle*. Unhampered, the id demands *immediate* gratification. (I want it now!) The **ego** or the personality's conscious interface with the world, keeps the id in check. (I'll have to wait a few minutes.) The **superego**—that part of the personality that knows right from wrong—provides the moral standard the ego attempts to achieve. The superego is our conscience, or in Freud's term, our *ego ideal,* learned during childhood. (You can't always have what you want.)

id (Freud) Unconscious biological drives and impulses that operate according to the *pleasure principle*.

ego (Freud) The personality's conscious interface with the world.

superego (Freud) The conscience; the part of the personality that knows right from wrong and provides the moral standard the ego attempts to achieve.

Table 14.2 Freudian Defense Mechanisms

DEFENSE MECHANISM	DEFINITION	EXAMPLE
Rationalization	The reinterpretation of unacceptable thoughts in a less anxiety-provoking way	You think, "If he wasn't so busy, he would have called me as he promised."
Repression	The removal of unacceptable thoughts or emotions to the unconscious	You forget instances of childhood abuse.
Denial	A form of repression in which guilt-inducing thoughts are placed in the unconscious	You refuse to believe evidence that shows that cigarette smoking is a health risk.
Projection	The act of attributing (or projecting) unacceptable personal thoughts or emotions to others	You feel guilty about not liking a person, so you think instead that the person doesn't like you.
Reaction formation	The process of turning a forbidden impulse into its opposite	You can't stand kids, so you open a day-care center.
Regression	A reversion to an earlier stage of development	You resort to name-calling during an emotional argument.
Sublimation	The channeling of repressed sexual urges into acceptable activities	You become absorbed in creative writing, painting, performing, and other activities.

In Freud's theory, the ego and id represent the conscious and unconscious mind, respectively. The id's *primary-process thinking* (irrational and fanciful) must be reconciled with the ego's *secondary-process thinking* (logical and problem solving). Both these aspects of personality are hedonistic; the ego seeks pleasure just as the id does, but within cultural constraints. Once a child has learned the rules of culture (by age 3 to 5), the *superego* forms. As Figure 14.6 indicates, even though the superego operates primarily at an unconscious level, the ego can become conscious of it, as well as of the id. According to Freud, the id and the superego are perpetually at odds with each other. ("I want it now." "No, it's against the rules.")

There is a tendency to think of the id, ego, and superego as three little people playing out a psychological melodrama. To Freud, however, these three elements of the personality represented alternative response patterns. Because the ego mediates between the conflicting demands of biological motivations and the cultural constraints, it is the key element of the personality.

Anxiety and Defense Mechanisms

According to Freudian theory, conflict among the ego, id, and superego creates a state of emotional distress called **anxiety**. Freud saw anxiety as a normal consequence of civilization. To cope with anxiety, the ego employs a variety of **defense mechanisms**, or strategies for resolving conflicts between the id and superego. Table 14.2 lists some of the defense mechanisms Freud identified.

Defense mechanisms operate unconsciously. Were they conscious, they would merely contribute to the anxiety they are meant to deal with. Consider, for example, the runner who always finishes second. Suppose one of the values embodied in this runner's superego is that second place is second rate. Coming in second, then, causes the runner anxiety. The runner's ego may reduce this anxiety through a defense mechanism called **rationalization** the process of reinterpreting unacceptable thoughts in more acceptable terms. For example, the runner could reason that running is less important than schoolwork. (*If I didn't have to study so hard to get my As and Bs, I could spend more time training.*)

A rationalization does not need to be realistic or logical to relieve anxiety. The runner in question, for example, may not be talented enough to win races, but the rationalization that schoolwork is more important allows him or her to get through each day without achieving the ego ideal. Defense mechanisms are

anxiety (Freud) A state of emotional distress caused by the ego's need to resolve the conflicting motivational states of the id and superego.

defense mechanisms (Freud) The ego's strategies for resolving conflicts between the id and superego, including rationalization, repression, and denial.

rationalization (Freud) A defense mechanism in which unacceptable thoughts are reinterpreted in less distressing terms.

face-saving psychological devices—the little white lies we tell ourselves that allow us to continue to meet tomorrow's challenges imperfectly, but adequately. Their adaptive value should be obvious.

Denial is another defense mechanism (see Table 14.2) in which a person deals with anxiety by avoiding too careful an examination of his or her thought process. For example, smokers who fail to recognize the long-term consequences of their habit are engaging in denial. One of my favorite stories concerns a client who was referred to a counselor as part of a court order. Convicted of driving while intoxicated, for the third time, he had been sentenced to serve a 6-month jail term. When the counselor asked how long he had had a drinking problem, the client replied, "I don't have a drinking problem." In Freud's terms, denial is a form of **repression**, in which guilt-inducing thoughts are actively forced out of consciousness.

Sexual Energy and the Death Force

Freud developed his theory of the way in which the id, ego, and superego interact over many years, as he listened to patients describe their problems. Eventually he came to believe that two fundamental drives, a life force and a death force, underlay all human behavior. Freud believed that the life force, Eros, manifested itself as a sex drive or sexual energy, called the *libido*, which energizes all human behavior. For example, the libido could be *sublimated* into artistic expression, athleticism, or the pursuit of a career (see Table 14.2). According to Freud, the life force is biological in origin. We might wonder how Darwin's ideas may have affected Freud's thinking; certainly the libido can be related to the "motives" of self-replicating DNA molecules (see page 96).

The "motives" of DNA, Chapter 3, p. 96

Late in his life, when the rise of the Nazis threatened Freud's homeland and the lives of all Jews, Freud, ill with cancer, took refuge in London. There he speculated about the death drive he had first proposed two decades earlier (Freud, 1920). The aggression and death that was rampaging through Europe seemed to him clear evidence of the "destructive instinct" he called *Thanatos*. But in his lifetime he wrote far less about the death force than the life force. Indeed, he based his theory of psychosexual development on the libido.

Psychosexual Development

Freud arrived at his theory of *psychosexual development* by asking his adult patients questions about their childhood and attempting to reconstruct their personality development. Ironically, though most of his patients were female, he focused mainly on male personality development. Table 14.3 summarizes the stages of human psychosexual development according to Freud's theory. Freud thought that a newborn's sexual energy, or libido, could be properly or improperly focused during the first stage, which he called the *oral stage*. During this stage he supposed the focus of the libido to be the pleasure an infant experienced while nursing. Depending on the mother's expectations and cultural rules, a child could either progress from the oral stage to the second stage, called the anal stage, or become *fixated* at the oral stage. Freud blamed **fixation**—failure to progress to the next stage of development—on the ego's unsuccessful resolution of the conflicting demands of id and superego.

denial (Freud) A defense mechanism that is a type of repression, in which a person avoids guilt-inducing thoughts by forcing them into the unconscious.

repression (Freud) A defense mechanism that involves suppressing unacceptable thoughts or emotions by relegating them to the unconscious.

fixation (Freud) Failure to progress to the next stage of psychosexual development due to an unsuccessful resolution of the conflicting demands of the id and superego.

Fixation at the Oral Stage. As Table 14.3 indicates, Freud thought that fixation at the oral stage produced an adult personality with an "oral character." Much as in infancy, adults with an oral character would tend to be passive and dependent. On the other hand, the child's ego might use the defense mechanism of reaction formation (see Table 14.2) to quell the anxiety caused by weaning

Table 14.3 Freud's Stages of Psychosexual Development

Stage	Age	Erotic Focus	Interface with Environment	Consequences	
				Fixation	"Oral character" (passive, dependent)
Oral	1	Stimulation of mouth (sucking, biting, chewing)	Weaning	Reaction formation	Opposite of dependent (active, tough)
				Fixation	Disorderly
Anal	2–3	Stimulation of bowels during defecation	Initiation of toilet training	Reaction formation	"Anal character" (obsessively compulsive, stingy, obstinate)
Phallic	3–5	Stimulation of genitals/infantile masturbation	Interactions with mother and father	Development of oedipal complex (male)	• Sexual desire for mother • Hostility toward father • Formation of superego
				Development of electra complex (female)	• Sexual desire for father • Hostility toward mother • Formation of superego
Latency	6–13	Sexuality repressed			
Genital	puberty–adult	Stimulation of genitals; sexual intimacy	Courting/heterosexual interactions	Development of sexual desire, both erotic love and love of family	

(the id desires to nurse; the superego expresses the need to be weaned). In that case, the child would become active and tough. But what happens in cultures in which children are nursed for several years? Later we'll see that Freud's theory doesn't explain cultural variability very well.

The Anal Character. A child who has passed through the oral stage enters the *anal stage,* in which the libido focuses on the pleasure experienced during defecation. The ego's task in this stage is to negotiate the anxiety produced during toilet training. (The superego's rules concerning appropriate times and places conflict with the id's desire to urinate and defecate *right now.*) Freud theorized that the unsuccessful resolution of this anxiety would result in an adult who was fixated at the anal stage (see Table 14.3). Such an adult might be expected to be a disorderly person. More likely, however (because it arouses less anxiety), the ego's defense mechanism of reaction formation would produce the classic "anal character"—stingy, miserly, obstinate, and obsessed with the order and cleanliness. Because of Freud's theory, Western culture has become sensitized to the issues of the optimal age and conditions surrounding both toilet training and weaning.

The anxiety produced by the oral and anal stages of a child's development culminated in a third stage, the *phallic stage.* Freud thought that the erotic focus of the libido in 3- to 5-year-olds was their genitalia, and that this stage was characterized by masturbation. Even in our relatively open 21st-century culture, many people are reluctant to recognize overt sexuality in prepubescent children. (In case you're wondering, 3- to 5-year-old children do masturbate, both males and females.)

The Oedipal Complex. Freud's thinking about the third stage of psychosexual development resulted in some of his most creative (and controversial) theorizing. In this stage he focused on males—hence the name "phallic" stage, from the Greek word, *phallos,* meaning penis. Male children, Freud proposed, developed an *oedipal complex* in this stage. Like the mythological character Oedipus, who killed his father and married his mother, young males develop a sexual desire for their mother and reject their fathers, whom they view as competitors for mom's love and affection. This process, Freud argued, was a normal and necessary part of heterosexual development. A sexual attachment to the mother at this early stage would facilitate a similar, more appropriate sexual attachment to a same-aged female during adulthood. To resolve the anxiety resulting from the child's hostile feelings toward the father, the child would come to identify with (and love) the father. In this way, as Freud put it, the "child is the father to the man."

The Electra Complex. If Freud's theory of the psychosexual development of males was controversial, his ideas about the development of females earned him the disdain of otherwise admiring theorists, and the wrath of women in general. Freud proposed that females experienced an *Electra complex* (after the Greek myth of Electra, who convinced her brother to kill their mother). In this counterpart to the oedipal complex, a female child forms a psychological attachment to her father and becomes hostile toward her mother. Freud went on to speculate that young girls feel more unworthy compared to boys, would actually prefer to be boys, and in fact, envies boys' penises. Their *penis envy* causes them to blame their mother because she too does not have a penis (and is probably the reason the child does not have a penis). Only by repressing these troubling thoughts about mother does the female child eventually come to identify with her.

Latency and the Genital Stages. Following the phallic stage, Freud postulated, preadolescent children entered a *latency stage* in which their libido did not attach to other persons; indeed, their sexuality is repressed. Then at puberty, a child enters the *genital stage* of development, becomes aware of his or her emerging sexuality, and begins to notice potential sexual partners of the same age. In courting a member of the opposite sex, the child becomes an adult, capable of sexual desire, erotic love, and eventually a parent's love of family.

Freud believed that the appropriate resolution of anxiety during childhood psychosexual development allowed the adult to function effectively in coping with the kind of anxiety adults experience. However, unresolved childhood anxiety (such as occurs in fixation) could lead to *identity crises* in adulthood. In the next section we will evaluate Freud's theory and his contributions to the study of personality.

The Evaluation of Freudian Theory

Like all seminal thinkers, Freud provoked controversy among both admirers and detractors. With the passage of time and the accumulation of scientific research on human behavior, some aspects of Freud's theory have been supported, while doubt has been cast on others. Here we will consider current thinking on Freud's theory, as well as why, like Charles Darwin, Freud will likely be remembered well into the 21st century.

Psychosexual development with stage theories, Chapter 11, p. 386, learning theory, Chapter 6, p. 186

Accepted Aspects of the Theory. A recognized hallmark of Freudian theory is the notion that an adult's personality development begins in infancy. Few present-day psychologists would disagree with this assertion. In fact, Freud's developmental theory foreshadowed Jean Piaget's stage theory of cognitive development, as well as John B. Watson's belief that 11-month-old Little Albert could be conditioned in a way that would shape his adult behavior.

Freud's assertion that infants have an innate sexual nature, and that they experience both anxiety and passion, forever changed the way we think about our offspring. But then, Freud saw a pervasive sexual motivation in humans of all ages. In this respect he anticipated the ethologists' understanding of consummatory behaviors, instinctive courting, mating, and care of offspring; Dawkins' selfish gene; and the evolutionary psychologists' argument that human anatomy, physiology, and behavior are elaborate adaptations whose purpose is to enhance fitness. Should we be surprised, then, that sexual themes play a dominant role in our arts, literature, advertising, fashion, and media? Freud wouldn't be.

Consummatory behaviors and evolutionary psychology, Chapter 3, p. 89

Freud's genius was most evident in his recognition of unconscious motivation and the role of defense mechanisms. As we saw in Chapter 10, recent laboratory studies of *priming* have demonstrated that a person need not be conscious of a memory for it to affect that person's conscious awareness. The phenomena of subliminal perception and blindsight also show that humans can experience events without being aware of them. How often, when queried, have you heard yourself or someone else say, "I have no idea why I did that," or "I don't know what motivated me to say that"? In part because of Freud, we now accept the reality of our impulsive, irrational behavior, our slips of the tongue, and our unconscious motivations. Likewise, when we do not meet with success in all life's tasks, unconscious defense mechanisms allow us to carry on.

Priming, Chapter 10 p. 360, and subliminal perception, Chapter 7, p. 234

Questionable Aspects of the Theory. Carl Jung found it ironic that despite Freud's interest in anthropology, he did not appreciate the extent to which his thinking was rooted in Viennese culture. The sexually repressed Victorian culture of turn-of-the-century Vienna brought Freud mostly female patients of the middle- and upper-class, from whom he attempted to construct a cross-cultural theory of personality. Such women likely had different issues from those of working-class women living then or now, either in Vienna or Detroit.

Equally suspect is Freud's theory of psychosexual development. Learning theory and empirical observations have supported the notion that childhood events can influence the adult, and that cross-culturally, children aged 1 to 3 show a fascination with urination and defecation. But the idea that suckling and defecating are sexual acts mediated by sexual energy remains controversial. The theory that infants and small children can develop long-lasting oedipal and Electra complexes because of their failure to negotiate the phallic stage is even more farfetched. Even after many decades of research, no support has been found for this assertion. (See Ellenberger, 1970, and Sulloway, 1979, for critical discussions of Freud's place in psychology.) Freud's personality structures have not been related to neurotransmitters or specific areas of the brain. So while evidence supports the existence of infantile sexuality, most psychologists and laypeople think the concept of penis envy—to take but one example—should be discarded.

Finally, as Jung pointed out, Freud underemphasized the fact that adults are motivated by diverse goals. Indeed, his theory of human motivation appears narrow compared with a more balanced evolutionary understanding of human motivation, which allows for kin selection, cooperation, altruism, and the different sexual agendas of males and females (Kriegman, 1988). His unconscionable denigration of women has not stood the test of time. Even given his idea that the libido can be sublimated, Freud underestimated the role of acquired motivation in human behavior.

Sociobiology, Chapter 3, p. 95

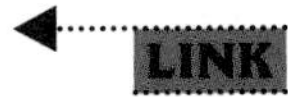

Acquired motivation, Chapter 5, p. 155

Why Freud Will Likely Be Remembered. Freud was one of the few grand theorizers in psychology. (Everything concerning the human mind interested him: count the number of ← links in this section.) Nearly 100 years of hindsight suggests that the human psyche is far more complicated than even he imagined, however. A strict determinist, Freud believed that every thought, statement, and dream was influenced by prior events; nothing occurred by chance, and one's own motives were suspect. While contemporary psychologists take a broader view of personality, Freud's wide-ranging, analytic mind opened up many avenues of thought that scientists are still exploring today.

Freud was also among the first to address the adverse consequences of living in an increasingly civilized world. Our evolutionary history of living and working with small bands of relatives did not prepare us to cope with either an industrial or an information age. In his classic book *Civilization and Its Discontents* (1930/1961), Freud wrote that anxiety is the inevitable byproduct of an innately selfish id constrained by schedules, rules, mortgages, and commitments. From his vantage point, all of us live lives of quiet desperation.

Finally, Freud's psychoanalytic theory was picked up and eventually modified by a noted group of professionals called *neo-Freudians*. A partial listing includes Carl Jung, Alfred Adler, Freud's daughter Anna Freud, Karen Horney (1937, 1950), Harry Stack Sullivan (1953), and Erik Erikson. Erikson's work was discussed in Chapter 11. In the following sections we will discuss the work of two other members of this group, Jung and Adler.

Eric Erikson, the development of identity, Chapter 11, p. 403

The Analytic Theory of Carl Jung

Carl Jung, a young colleague of Freud who hailed his genius, was heavily influenced by Freud's publications. Jung first wrote a letter to "the master" in 1906; over the course of the next few years, their correspondence mushroomed (McGuire, 1974). In his letters Jung began to question and challenge certain aspects of Freud's theory, particularly the libido and infantile sexuality. His disagreement with Freud on these questions eventually led Jung to develop his own version of Freudian theory. In calling his version *analytic psychology*, Jung both acknowledged and distanced himself from Freud's psychoanalytic theory. Today, he is best known for his concepts of archetypes and the collective unconscious.

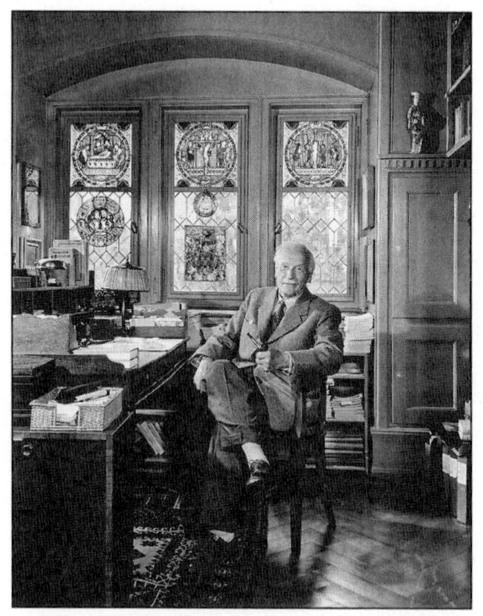

Carl Jung is considered a "mystical" psychologist because of his theory of archetypes and the collective unconscious.

The Collective Unconscious. Instead of sexual energy, Jung proposed that a universal "life force" with a more general kind of psychological energy underlay human motivation. He retained Freud's idea of the unconscious as a source of conflict and motivation, expanding it to address his anthropological interests. Both Freud and Jung derived some of their ideas from cross-cultural studies. Jung, for instance, interpreted similarities among different cultures as evidence that the unconscious was instinctual. All humans, he believed, shared a **collective unconscious** (Jung, 1936/1968), a knowledge of universal ideas and symbols that was passed genetically from parent to offspring. To support his view, Jung noted that all cultures have similar ideas of God, mother, earth, birth, and gender, and many use similar symbols to represent those ideas in legends and literature. Jung called these universal ideas *archetypes*.

Archetypes. Jung believed that both the ego ("the self") and archetypal thoughts influenced people's dreams and creative efforts. Neither Freud nor Jung fit the archetype of a scientist; Jung was more of a mystic. In his writing he developed the idea that mystery, spirituality, and religious thinking were an important part of each adult personality, and that each human possesses a universal archetype of God (Jung, 1933). As evidence, he cited the findings of anthropologists who reported cross-cultural similarities in myths, symbols, and deity worship. Today, Jung's thinking exerts enormous influence outside of psychology, especially in religion, literature, and other forms of artistic expression.

collective unconscious (Jung) A knowledge of archetypes and universal symbols that is passed genetically from parent to offspring.

Alfred Adler's Self Psychology

Early in his career, Freud and his followers formed the Vienna Psychoanalytic Society. As Jung and others went their own way, the society fractured. One renegade that Freud personally denounced was Alfred Adler.

Like other neo-Freudians, Adler opposed the centrality of sex in Freud's theory. He proposed instead that humans were motivated by their *striving for superiority*. Throughout childhood, Adler reasoned, children were weak and inferior; only by successfully overcoming life's obstacles could they become competent. Until a person achieved personal mastery over the environment, then, she or he would suffer from *feelings of inferiority*. Thus one's prime motivation in life is to achieve higher status, not to resolve sexual conflict. Adler's approach became known as *self psychology*.

In addition to the notion of an *inferiority complex,* Adler coined the term for the process through which people strive to overcome inferiority, *compensation*. A short male, for example, may attempt to compensate for his relative lack of height by developing some special expertise to set himself apart from taller counterparts. For the same reason, such a person might drive a powerful car or develop an interest in weaponry.

INTERIM SUMMARY

1. In the late 1800s, the young Viennese physician Sigmund Freud observed patients with *conversion disorders* such as a "glove anesthesia," and became interested in studying the mind.
2. Freud treated patients who complained of "nervous problems" such as anxiety, by a method he called *psychoanalysis*. On the basis of his talks with patients, he developed a *psychoanalytic theory* of the personality.
3. Freud divided the mind into three parts: the conscious, the ***preconscious,*** and the ***unconscious***.
4. According to Freudian theory, *Freudian slips* (mistakes of speech that reveal hidden wishes) and *dream analysis* can reveal *unconscious motivations*. Freud called the simple description of a dream its *manifest content,* and an analysis of the dream's symbolic meaning (typically a need for wish fulfillment) its *latent content*.
5. Freud thought that the personality had a three-part structure: the ***id*** (an unconscious biological drive that operates according to the *pleasure principle*); the ***ego*** (the conscious self, which operates according to the *reality principle*); and the ***superego*** (a primarily unconscious conscience, which provides the *ego ideal*).
6. Freud believed that ***anxiety*** occurs when the id and superego come into conflict in the unconscious. The ego's function is to resolve differences between the id and superego by invoking ***defense mechanisms*** such as ***rationalization, denial,*** *projection, reaction formation, regression,* ***repression,*** and *sublimation*.
7. According to Freud, two fundamental drives underlay all human behavior, a life force called *Eros* and a death force called *Thanatos*. He thought the life force was comprised of sexual energy, which he called the *libido*.
8. In his theory of *psychosexual development,* Freud proposed that infants progress through five developmental stages: *oral, anal, phallic, latency*, and *genital*. At each stage the child might experience ***fixation,*** or problems in attaching the libido to a culturally appropriate object, producing an anxiety that could persist into adulthood.
9. In Freud's theory, if *infant sexuality* is not successfully resolved during the *phallic stage*, boys may develop an *oedipal complex* (sexual desire for the mother and hostility toward the father) and girls may develop an *Electra complex* (attachment to the father and hostility toward the mother).
10. Freud's personality theory is difficult to evaluate because of the breadth of the issues he addressed. His idea of unconscious motivation has received some support from contemporary studies of perception and memory. Little evidence exists, however, for much of his theory of infantile sexuality. Humans are both sexually motivated and beset by anxiety, but alternative sources of human motivation exist.

11. Psychoanalytically oriented psychologists who were influenced by Freud, called *neo-Freudians,* included Carl Jung and Alfred Adler. Jung's *analytic psychology* and Adler's *self psychology* differed with respect to the libido: Jung proposed a nonsexual *life force,* while Adler thought people were motivated primarily by the need to overcome *feelings of inferiority.*

12. Jung proposed that humans had a ***collective unconscious***—symbols and ideas that were passed from parents to offspring genetically. These ideas and legends of earth, mother, god, and so forth, which are expressed cross-culturally, he called *archetypes,* or universal symbols.

For Further Thought

1. A therapist might advise an anxious and sexually frustrated individual to throw himself into his work. What defense mechanism would the therapist be recommending?
2. In one of his books, Freud (1900/1950, pp. 247–248) related the dream of a young woman patient: *"I am walking in the street in summer; I am wearing a straw hat of a peculiar shape, the middle piece of which is bent upwards, while the side pieces hang downwards . . . one hangs lower than the other."* How might Freud interpret this dream?
3. Freudian and Jungian themes run through many of Woody Allen's movies, including *Annie Hall, Manhattan, Hannah and Her Sisters,* and *A Midsummer Night's Sex Comedy.* Can you identify sources of sexual guilt (the clash of id and superego) or the use of defense mechanisms in one or more of his films? What about Jungian symbols?
4. Freud proposed that anxiety is related to civilized behavior. What are some common features of vacations that might reduce anxiety?

HUMANISTIC APPROACHES

We have seen that Freud (and the neo-Freudians) proposed their theories of personality based on their experience with patients they were treating for nervous disorders. Freud believed that humans (and other animals) are motivated primarily by biological impulses (the id). Likewise, the researchers who developed the trait and the social-learning approaches, though they worked with nonclinical populations, took an objective, deterministic view of personality.

In contrast, humanistic psychologists developed their personality theories in the 1950s and 1960s, in opposition to the psychoanalytic and behavioral perspectives. They were described as *humanistic* because they believed other approaches to personality were dehumanizing. Little could be learned about a human, they asserted, if researchers focused on their physiology. While Freud and Skinner denied that humans had free will, humanists insisted on it. Rather than being restricted by their animal nature, humans could rise above it to create, grow, and seek out intellectual, emotional, and moral development. We will study the theories of two humanistic psychologists, Carl Rogers and Abraham Maslow.

Carl Rogers's Person-Centered Approach

Like Freud and Jung, Carl Rogers's (1951, 1959) humanistic theory grew out of his practice of psychotherapy (described in Chapter 18). Rogers developed a *person-centered* approach in which he listened carefully to patients but offered little advice. This therapeutic method reflected his belief that people have an innate "goodness," a *true self* that changes if they are insufficiently loved and nurtured, especially during childhood. When a person's true self becomes distorted in this way, Rogers believed, he or she presents a *false self* to the world. (Recall our discussion of persona—the masks we wear in confronting the world.)

For Rogers, a person's *self-concept* was the most important determinant of personality. A **self-concept** is comprised of one's beliefs about one's own basic nature and behavior. For this reason, Rogers' theory of personality is said to reflect a *phenomenological approach*: reality is what it is *perceived* to be, not necessarily what it is.

To remove the false self and project the true self, a person requires an environment of acceptance and respect, or what Rogers called *unconditional love*. By **unconditional love** Rogers meant a love that affirms and accepts another's behavior with no strings attached. For example, parents who offer their children unconditional love do not tie their love to their children's grades, to polite behavior, or to the absence of temper tantrums. In Rogers' view, parents who put conditions on their love ("Mommy will love you if you keep your room picked up"; "You'll go to hell if you don't say your prayers") promote anxiety and the development of a false self.

Carl Rogers's approach to personality emphasizes the importance of a person's perceptions.

In adulthood, the main source of anxiety is the discrepancy between a person's self-concept and the perception other people hold. To a person who thinks he is a talented writer with important things to say, for example, friends and editors who do not share the same view are sources of anxiety. Without a supportive environment, Rogers believed, such a person would adopt defense mechanisms similar to those proposed by Freud: denial, rationalization, and other ploys designed to reduce anxiety. The writer might rationalize his self-concept by thinking that he is ahead of his time and may not be appreciated until after his death. The self-concept is bolstered and anxiety reduced by this rationalization.

Abraham Maslow's Theory of Self-Actualization

Abraham Maslow thought that Freud painted too dark a picture of human nature. (Ironically, he described his own childhood as an unhappy one, and his childhood personality as lonely and isolated.) As we saw in Chapter 5, Maslow proposed a hierarchy of needs, in which he placed personal needs after the satisfaction of basic biological and security needs. In his therapy he aimed to promote the psychological growth of his adult patients. The angst patients felt was due less to unresolved childhood anxiety, he thought, than a quest to invest life with meaning. Humans, Maslow wrote, have a need for **self-actualization**—finding and fulfilling their potential (Maslow, 1954, 1968).

Maslow's need hierarchy, Chapter 5, p. 168

How do people determine their potential and go about achieving it? In his research Maslow attempted to define what constituted a "healthy personality." Interestingly, rather than examining the entire range of personalities, healthy to unhealthy, he focused on those he considered to be the most fulfilled, analyzing the personalities of historical characters (Thomas Jefferson and others), accomplished friends, and top students at Brandeis University, where he taught. He called those he considered the most healthy *self-actualized*. Table 14.4 contains a partial listing of the characteristics of self-actualized individuals.

self-concept The perception a person has of his or her own basic nature and typical behavior.

unconditional love Love that affirms and accepts another's behavior without condition.

self-actualization (Maslow) Finding and fulfilling one's potential.

An Evaluation of Humanistic Personality Theories

The trait and social-learning theories represent scientific, quantitative approaches to the study of the human personality. In contrast, psychoanalytic and humanistic psychologists avoided operational definitions, quantification, and integration with the other sciences (such as behavioral genetics and brain-based approaches).

Table 14.4 Maslow's Characteristics of Self-Actualized People (A Partial Listing)

- Is spontaneous and natural
- Has sense of humor
- Is capable of childlike delight at the ordinary
- Needs privacy, but feels connected to other humans
- Has a few good friends
- Is autonomous and independent in thought and action
- Knows right from wrong
- Is absorbed in a mission or cause (and perhaps a different one tomorrow)
- Has mystical experiences and seeks peak experiences

To those interested in building an integrative science of behavior, therefore, humanistic theories like Maslow's have little to offer.

Ironically, the humanistic approach permeates our popular culture. For example, most of us have had feelings of inferiority at some time in our lives. We readily understand the need for self-actualization, for the hope of *doing better in life* seems to motivate people of all classes.

From another point of view, the characteristics of the self-actualized person (see Table 14.4) may be seen as a representation of our culture's *ego ideal.* They describe the ideal personality—one we can all aspire to. Maslow's theory isn't testable, and little if any evidence supports it. Its contribution lies in the vision it presents: that scientific psychologists will one day be challenged to investigate the motivation, creativity, and behavioral characteristics of really interesting, "healthy" people. In this regard, Maslow's understanding of personality may have heuristic value. Humanistic personality theories may not be scientific, but they capture and portray the human condition well and aid in our self-understanding.

INTERIM SUMMARY

1. Humanistic psychologists developed their theories of personality in the 1950s and 1960s in the belief that the psychoanalytic and behavioral perspectives were dehumanizing.
2. Humanistic psychologists see the biological approach to human nature as too restrictive. They believe that humans have free will and actively seek to better themselves.
3. Carl Rogers developed a *person-centered* approach to therapy that emphasized the innate "goodness" of a person's *true self*. If people are unloved, they develop a *false self* that interferes with their self-development.
4. A person's ***self-concept*** is phenomenological, in that it reflects what a person *thinks* is true about himself or herself rather than what actually is true.
5. A person who accepts another's behavior and affirms that person "no matter what" is offering ***unconditional love.*** Children who are raised with unconditional love have the best opportunity for positive psychological growth and development.
6. Abraham Maslow proposed that humans were motivated by a hierarchy of needs. After their basic biological and security needs have been satisfied, they pursue their need for ***self-actualization***—for finding and fulfilling their potential.
7. Maslow's research led him to characterize self-actualized people as spontaneous and independent in thought and action. They have a need for privacy and confide in a few close friends. They can become absorbed in a mission or cause, and they seek out peak experiences.
8. Humanistic personality theories are not scientific. They are useful because they capture the human condition and facilitate self-understanding.

For Further Thought

1. Is there a danger in seeing oneself from a phenomenological perspective?
2. In what way does Freud's structure of personality conflict with Rogers's "true self"?
3. Do you extend unconditional love to a best friend? Might there be problems in extending unconditional love to a spouse, and expecting it in return?

CONCLUDING THOUGHTS

In studying brain-behavior relationships, perception, learning, and memory, scientists can do controlled quantitative experiments. But defining and studying personality scientifically has proven difficult. How ironic. The very things we want to know most—the basis for our thoughts, feelings, desires, intentions, and behavior—remain elusive.

In this chapter we have examined several theories of personality, including the trait, social-learning, biological, psychodynamic, and humanistic approaches. The first three approaches rely on the scientific method. Using quantitative techniques such as factor analysis to analyze the results of self-reports, psychologists have identified five basic personality factors. Those five factors, or personality traits, are extraversion, agreeableness, conscientiousness, emotional stability (neuroticism), and openness to experience (intellect). They have been found to have a genetic basis and can be measured cross-culturally.

The social-learning approach to the study of personality is scientific in that it stresses the lawful, predictable, and highly adaptable ways in which humans and other animals learn. For example, humans model their behavior after both real-life and media examples. They can use a personal schema to organize what they observe, or their observations can affect their personal schema. Reinforcement and punishment can also change people's behavior. Thus child rearing is highly influential in the development and expression of an individual's personality. Taken together, the trait (genetic) approach and the learning (environment) approach can explain much about personality development.

The psychoanalytic theories of Sigmund Freud have made him one of the most influential thinkers of the 20th century, and the most recognizable name in psychology. Freud was a determinist who believed that adult psychological development was rooted in childhood experiences, and that people are motivated by unconscious conflicts. His theories are for the most part untestable, and many of his ideas fanciful, if not downright wrong.

Like Freudian theory, the neo-Freudian and humanistic approaches to personality lie outside the realm of science. Jung's concept of the collective unconscious speaks to the psychological nature of all humans: mother, father, and God *are* universally recognized archetypes. He was almost alone among psychologists in addressing humanity's religious yearnings and fascination with ritual. Adler's notions of inferiority and compensation have become widely recognized and accepted by both laypeople and professionals.

In rejecting the scientific approach to personality, both Carl Rogers and Abraham Maslow struck a responsive chord. In Rogers's view, humans who are devoid of love—either of self or of others—are psychologically unhealthy, while humans who enjoy unconditional love thrive. Maslow stressed the potential of humans, when properly nourished, to achieve higher levels of psychological growth. Under the right conditions, he believed, a person can achieve self-actualization, or a state of fulfilled potential.

In sum, science blends with humanism in the study of personality, an exciting and wide-open field.

KEY TERMS

anxiety *499*
big five personality factors *490*
collective unconscious *504*
defense mechanisms *499*
denial *500*
ego *498*
fixation *500*
id *498*
personality *486*
preconscious *497*
rationalization *499*
repression *500*
self-actualization *507*
self-concept *507*
superego *498*
trait *488*
type *489*
unconditional love *507*
unconscious *497*

15

Social Psychology

Diana Ong (b. 1940) Chinese / USA *Mingling*. SuperStock.

Social Cognition: Processing Social Information
Attribution
Attitudes Change and Formation
Cognitive Dissonance
Interim Summary
For Further Thought

Social Influences on Behavior
Conformity
Obedience: Compliance With Authority
Group Influence on Personal Performance
Interim Summary
For Further Thought

Gender, Attraction, and Love
Gender and Sexual Orientation
Genes, Hormones, and Sexual Behavior
Attraction and Attractiveness
Attractive Faces
Friendship and Love
Interim Summary
For Further Thought

Social Relations
Prejudice and Stereotyping
Aggression
Interim Summary
For Further Thought

Concluding Thoughts

Poets, lovers, and even psychologists have written about love, a complex emotion that forms the basis for our deepest relationships. One kind of love, romantic love, begins with sexual attraction to one special person. The psychological state of being "in love" includes intense pleasure in the loved one's presence and a strong physical attraction. As the poet Robert Francis (American, born 1901) wrote:

> The eye is not more exquisitely designed
> For seeing than it is for being loved.
> The same lips curved to speak are curved to kiss.
> Even the workaday and practical arm
> Becomes all love for love's sake to the lover.
>
> If this is nature's thrift, love thrives on it.
> Love never asks the body different
> Or ever wants it less ambiguous,
> The eye being lovelier for what it sees,
> The arm for all it does, the lips for speaking.

Why do people fall in love? To begin, romantic love is adaptive. We saw in earlier chapters that reflexive emotions such as fear, anger, and disgust are necessary to our survival. In this poem, Francis suggests that the physical attraction lovers feel is compatible with other adaptations. Because romantic love is a complex emotion that involves sustained interactions with another person, its expression might be thought to vary from culture to culture. Yet it doesn't: in 90 percent of the cultures psychologists have studied, people report experiencing romantic love (Evans, 2001). We may suspect, then, that this kind of love serves an adaptive purpose in promoting mutual attraction between the sexes, and ultimately the reproduction of the species (Darwin, 1859/1962). While some aspects of romantic love may seem irrational, this strong emotion may be vital not just to attracting but to keeping a mate long enough to rear children (Evans, 2001).

To this point our focus has been on individual behavior—how a person develops, perceives, learns, thinks, and remembers. In contrast, social psychologists are concerned with the behavior of individuals in pairs and groups. According to one estimate, about two-thirds of a person's waking life is spent in the presence of other people (Larson & Bradney, 1988). Like other mammals, humans evolved as members of families and small groups, whose close companionship promoted their survival and reproduction. Thus our social relations are likely to have been honed by evolutionary processes. Our influence on one other not only is fundamental to the human condition, but also reflects genetic tendencies.

Evolutionary psychology and sociobiology, Chapter 3, p. 95

Certainly our present-day culture is vastly different from our ancestral past. Hence, our social relations differ from those of our ancestors (Cantor, 1990). In present-day social relations, managers influence workers, parents influence children, teachers influence students, and you influence your best friend. Many social psychologists think these *social interactions* can be either adaptive or maladaptive, promoting or undermining the kind of group harmony that makes civilized life possible.

In Chapter 11 we saw that the process of socialization begins with an attachment between caretaker and infant, and continues through late childhood and early adolescence. In this chapter we'll look more closely at the ways in which we form our attitudes, beliefs, friendships, and romantic attachments. We'll ask how we develop a gender identity and begin to assume gender roles. And we'll see how others influence our thoughts and behavior for good and for ill. Because each of us lives within a culture or subculture, we develop ethnic identities—and too often, prejudices—that reflect our membership in that culture. In short, we express our individualism within the boundaries established by groups.

SOCIAL COGNITION: PROCESSING SOCIAL INFORMATION

In April 1999, 17-year-old Dylan Klebold and 18-year-old Eric Harris shot and killed 12 classmates and a teacher before executing themselves in the library at Columbine High School in Littleton, Colorado. Unfortunately, this type of incident, though little understood, was not unheard of. For weeks, newspaper, magazine, and television reporters pored over every detail of the shooting in an attempt to explain how and why it had occurred. The diary of one of the shooters provided some evidence of his motivation for perpetrating the massacre. "We want to be different, we want to be strange and we don't want jocks or other people putting [us] down," he wrote. "We're going to punish you" (Hendren, 1999).

Attribution

Why did two students attempt to destroy their school and kill several classmates before turning their guns on themselves?

What are we to make of this crime? Psychologists and criminologists have great difficulty identifying (before the fact) the motivation of mass murderers, serial killers, and other aberrant personalities. But they have discovered quite a bit about how others account for such behavior, a process called *social perception*. Not everyone reacts in the same way. For example, a local county sheriff said of the Columbine massacre: "The bottom line . . . is they wanted to do as much damage as they could possibly do, and destroy as many children as they could and go out in flames" (Hendren, 1999). President Bill Clinton remarked, "They had the wrong reaction to the fact that they were dissed." "Everybody gets dissed sometime in life, even the President" (Seelye, 1999). Both these statements as well as the statement in the shooter's diary are **attributions,** inferences people make about the causes of their own behavior and the behavior of others.

Attribution Theory. **Attribution theory** is the study of how people perceive the causes of behavior (Heider, 1958; Kelley, 1973). Trying to make sense of another's behavior, a person typically makes one of two inferences: that the behavior was caused by the individual's personal thoughts (sometimes called *internal attributions*) or that it was provoked by someone else (*external attribution*). Internal attribution may be considered proactive; external attribution more reactive. In evaluating the behavior of the Columbine shooters, the sheriff attributed the behavior to a deliberate intention (internal attribution). The President attributed it to the provocation of being dissed by other students (external attribution). The shooters themselves suggested both types of motivation: an investment in being strange (internal) and a response to being put down by others (external). Thus, the internal attribution of behavior refers to a person's traits, abilities, and dispositions, while the external attribution of behavior refers to perceived environmental demands.

Environmental determinants of behavior, Chapter 6, p. 212

The psychologist Harold Kelley has proposed a model to account for the factors a person incorporates into an attribution (Kelley, 1973). This *covariation model* includes three types of information: *consistency, distinctiveness,* and *consensus*. For example, in applying Kelley's covariation model to the massacre at Columbine High, we might ask whether the incident was characteristic of these shooters' behavior—that is, was it *consistent* with their past behaviors, or was it *distinctive?* We might also ask whether other students engage in such behavior—that is, was there some social consensus? Depending on how these three factors covary, Kelley's theory predicts people attribute a behavior to either internal or external causes. Because the shooting was a rare, distinctive event that most students don't engage in, Kelley would predict that people would attribute it to external factors. Other researchers think Kelley's model is too simple to account for such complex behavior (Fiske & Taylor, 1991). A better use for Kelley's model would be to analyze the reaction of Sally's classmates to the news that she got the top grade in the class on a recent calculus test. They might determine that her behavior was not consistent but was distinctive (since she seldom got a high grade). Hence they would attribute her grade to external factors: she studied far more than usual, or got help from someone.

attribution An inference about the cause of one's own behavior and the behavior of others.

attribution theory A theory of how people perceive the causes of behavior.

The Fundamental Attribution Error. In a classic experiment (Jones & Harris, 1967), college students listened to a writer present a position paper on Fidel Castro's Cuba. Half the subjects were told the writer of the paper had been assigned to communicate a pro-Castro perspective (external attribution); the other half were told that the paper represented the writer's own views (internal attribution). At the time of the experiment, the students, like most people living in the United States, were anti-Castro; they took a negative view of anyone who supported Castro. While one might assume that being *assigned* the task of taking an unpopular position would absolve the writer of personal responsibility for the paper, that was not the audience's reaction. Students reacted negatively to the writer in both experimental conditions. This often-replicated phenomenon (Ross, 1977; Gilbert & Malone, 1995) has been called the **fundamental attribution error**, or the tendency to attribute the causes of another person's behavior to his or her personal character rather than the demands of the situation. Thus, you are more likely to consider the person who cut in front of you and took the parking space you wanted to be selfish rather than late for an appointment. Similarly, a professor who enforces the university attendance policy is thought of as "anal" rather than as someone who is fulfilling her contractual obligations.

But how fundamental is this human tendency? In general, people who live in Western cultures tend to be more individualistic than those who live in non-Western cultures, who are more concerned with fulfilling a group role (Hofstede, 1983). Individualism presupposes responsibility for one's own behavior. Not surprisingly, then, people from Western cultures are more likely than those from non-Western cultures to make the fundamental attribution error (Fletcher & Ward, 1988; Miller, 1984). Research subjects from India, for example, were asked to choose between attributions similar to the ones in the anti-Castro study. Researchers found they were more likely to explain people's behavior in terms of their social obligations, roles, and responsibilities (Fletcher & Ward, 1988). The reasons for these cultural tendencies are not easily explained; they may be due to cultural differences in child rearing. In Western cultures, for example, parents tend to teach their children that their personal choices and behavior determine the kind of life they will live.

The Self-Serving Bias. The assumption is, then, that individuals accept responsibility for their own behavior. But do they? We have seen that the fundamental attribution error overemphasizes personal accountability and minimizes the pressures of the situations people find themselves in. Most of us believe that prisons are full of bad people, for example, and that smokers with lung cancer brought the disease on themselves. These attributions help us to preserve our belief in a *just world*—one in which people generally get what they deserve; good behavior is rewarded and inappropriate behavior is punished (Lerner & Miller, 1978). When it comes to *self*-attribution, however, we tend to see ourselves as victims of circumstance. (The good things that happen to us, of course, are of our own making.) This tendency to attribute our own failures to situational factors and our own successes to personal factors is called the **self-serving bias** (Burger, 1986). The self-serving bias is more common in Western cultures than in others, such as the Japanese (Markus & Kitayama, 1991) and Chinese (Lee & Seligman, 1997). In Japan and China, a person who experiences success is typically more self-effacing than a Westerner would be.

Attribution theory has implications for the practice of law and social policy. For example, a juror who thinks that people commit crimes because they are bad will react differently from a juror who attributes bad behavior to a bad environment. A husband who attributes his wife's stinging remarks to her irritating personality rather than her 12-hour workday is more likely than another husband to consider divorce (Fincham & Bradbury, 1993). Is homelessness more a failure of

fundamental attribution error The tendency to attribute the causes of another person's behavior to personal dispositions rather than the demands of a situation.

self-serving bias The tendency to attribute one's failures to the situation and one's successes to personal factors.

Table 15.1 An ABC Analysis of Attitudes Toward the Death Penalty

	Affective Component (feelings, emotions)	"Murderers should suffer the same fate as their victims."
Attitude: Support Death Penalty	Behavioral Component (predispositions to act)	"I won't vote for a politician who doesn't support the death penalty."
	Cognitive Component (thoughts and beliefs)	"Killing criminals prevents them from hurting anyone else, and sets an example for all others."
	Affective Component (feelings, emotions)	"I don't want anyone's blood on my hands, even a criminal's."
Attitude: Against Death Penalty	Behavioral Component (predispositions to act)	"I'll demonstrate at the execution."
	Cognitive Component (thoughts and beliefs)	"The death penalty doesn't deter murderers, but a life sentence prevents them from hurting anyone else."

personal initiative, or the result of poverty and lack of education? Our attributions will determine our political response (see Zucker & Weiner, 1993, for a discussion of these issues).

Attitude Change and Formation

An attribution is a response to a specific situation or behavior; an attitude is a more general and lasting pattern of response. Consider the phrase, That person has an *attitude!* In this sense, an **attitude** is a person's general manner, or disposition, to respond favorably or unfavorably to a person or a situation (Chaiken & Stangor, 1987). Social psychologists who have studied attitudes see them as complex mixtures of three different components: affective, behavioral, and cognitive. This framework has come to be known as the ABC approach (Rajecki, 1990).

Consider Ghandi's attitude toward violence, for example. Ghandi believed passionately that nonviolence was a better approach than warfare to resolving serious conflict. His passion illustrates the affective component; the nonviolent marches and worker strikes he led illustrate the behavioral component; and his rational belief that living is better than dying demonstrates the cognitive component. Table 15.1 analyzes the pros and cons—and the ABCs—of attitudes toward the death penalty.

The Relationship Between Attitudes and Behavior. You may think people form attitudes by combining thoughts and emotions and then acting accordingly. A recent review of a large number of studies, however, shows that this is not the case (Krause, 1995): the average correlation between attitudes and behavior was just 0.38. Consider, for example, that two out of every three teenagers do not use condoms, even though they are aware that condoms prevent disease and pregnancy (Flora, Maibach, & Maccoby, 1989). Assuming they care about the risks involved, why the disparity between their thoughts and actions? Research shows that in general, attitudes do not predict specific behaviors, only general response patterns (Ajzen, 1991; Ajzen & Fishbein, 1980).

Attitudes not only fail to predict behavior, but also can actually be changed by behavior. We will see in a later section that student volunteers who assumed the roles of either a prisoner or a prison guard rapidly transformed both their behavior and attitudes accordingly (see page 000). Daryl Bem has proposed a theory of

attitude A person's manner or disposition to respond favorably or unfavorably to a person or situation.

self-perception to explain such effects (Bem, 1967). According to Bem's theory, a person first becomes aware of his or her behavior, and then forms an attitude based on that awareness. For example, "I don't get good grades in math (behavior); therefore I really don't like math (attitude)."

The Foot-in-the-Door Phenomenon. The brainwashing of American prisoners during the Korean war led to a good deal of research on role playing and attitude change. Chinese prison guards who ran the prison camps in Korea did not use torture and brutality to undermine the loyalty of U. S. soldiers. Rather, they relied on what is now called the **foot-in-the-door phenomenon**: getting a person to comply with a large request by starting out with smaller requests (Schein, 1956). For example, they rewarded prisoners for complying with simple requests to say and write innocuous statements. Later they asked them to participate in discussions favorable to communism and critical of capitalism. Finally, they coaxed the prisoners into uttering public confessions and self-criticisms. Some prisoners even renounced their citizenship at war's end.

Another common application of the foot-in-the-door phenomenon is courting behavior. A relationship may begin with flowers and hand holding, and over time progress to kissing and hugging. It may culminate in undressing, sexual exploration, and intercourse. These behavioral changes can be understood in part as an example of successive approximation. Recall the learning experiments in which researchers reinforced rats for simple behaviors (sniffing near a lever), and then for more complex behavior, such as lever pressing (see Chapter 6, page 207). But shaping alone cannot account for courting behavior or brainwashing prisoners of war. We'll return to this topic in a later section.

Shaping behaviors, Chapter 6, p. 207

Technique of Persuasive Communication. A friend of mine once observed "Someone's always selling something." Salespeople pitch their products on TV and the telephone; politicians want your vote; and parents, professors, and preachers try their best to influence your attitudes and behavior. The title of a recent book, *Age of Propaganda: The Everyday Use and Abuse of Persuasion,* suggests the ubiquity of attempts to influence people's attitudes (Pratkanis & Aronson, 1992).

The science of persuading consumers to buy particular products is rooted in psychology. Following a successful academic career, John B. Watson (the father of behaviorism) left Johns Hopkins University to take a sales position with a large advertising agency. There he began to apply the principles of conditioning to commercial advertising (Buckley, 1989). He found that bright-colored, highly repetitious advertisements featuring positive stimuli (such as attractive women) were more effective than others. Later, military researchers who had been studying political propaganda during World War II continued their research on *persuasive communication* at universities (Hovland, Lumsdaine, & Scheffield, 1949). These psychologists studied not just the characteristics of effective advertisements, but the entire process of persuasion from start to finish.

Rules for effective conditioning, Chapter 6, p. 207

Figure 15.1 shows how a communication gets from a source to a receiver (McGuire, 1985). The five basic components of persuasion are the *source,* the *message,* the *channel,* the *receiver,* and the *target behavior*. To increase the effectiveness of a message, the *source*—usually a speaker—should be attractive and credible (knowledgeable, believable), and hold a powerful position such as a government official or a doctor's degree (Chaiken, 1980). During the Gulf War, for example, U. S. Secretary of Defense Colin Powell briefed reporters daily on the conduct and results of the military engagement in Iraq. His message was effective, due in part to his presence: a tall attractive man, confident and knowledgeable, wearing a highly decorated uniform.

foot-in-the-door phenomenon
Greater compliance with large requests following compliance with small requests.

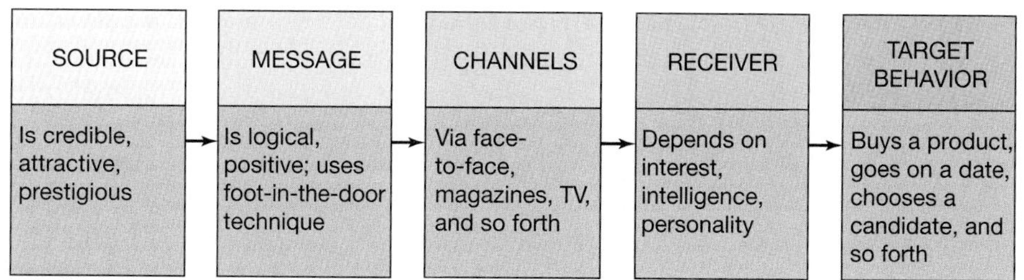

Figure 15.1 The Five Components of Persuasion. The five components of a persuasive message include the source of the message, the message, the channel (or medium) over which the message is delivered, the receiver of the message, and target behavior (the effect of the message).

To be effective, the *message* should be stated clearly and logically, in a positive manner. After President Reagan was hospitalized following an assassination attempt, Secretary of State Alexander Haig jumped in front of a camera and blurted out "I'm in charge." His too-lusty assumption of power did not have the reassuring effect he intended, because the actual succession of leadership runs from the President to the Vice-President (who was out of the country) to the Speaker of the House—not the Secretary of State. A more effective message would have been delivered by a calm and reassuring speaker who had the facts straight.

The *channel*, or method, used to deliver a message also affects its persuasiveness. Two days ago you may have said unkind words to a friend. What would be the best way for you to persuade your friend to forgive you—sending flowers, a card or a letter, making a phone call, or surprising the friend with a visit? Your past experience with the friend would tell you which channel is likely to be most effective.

Messages aren't received equally well by all people. The receiver's interests, intelligence, personality, and gender all affect the reception of a message. For example, most men ignore ads for feminine hygiene products. Jurors whose attention has wandered during a summation will not hear the same message as those who are attentive. And those who score low on IQ tests or who have low self-esteem will be more easily persuaded by messages an intelligent person might discount (Rhodes & Wood, 1992). One's mood can also be important in whether a message is persuasive or not. A person who is in a serious mood is more likely to hear, appreciate, and learn from a highly structured, logical lecture than someone who is in a light, exuberant mood (Petty, Schumann, Richman, & Strathman, 1993).

One of my history professors urged her students to adopt a cynical attitude in reading accounts of historical events. Her reasoning was that historians try to convince readers of their interpretation of the facts rather than merely present them. Discerning readers of history, then, receive messages cautiously and analyze them carefully. They might display a *disconfirmation bias,* subjecting ideas that conflict with their own to more scrutiny than ideas they agree with (Edwards & Smith, 1996).

To explain the effect of receiver characteristics on the persuasiveness of a message, Richard Petty and John Cacioppo proposed the existence of two separate communication routes, the central and the peripheral. The *central route* is the actual content of a message, a logical argument based on facts. The peripheral route is the packaging for the facts presented through the central route (Petty & Cacioppo, 1986). Everyone appreciates a speaker's attractive appearance and manner, the use of humor and other uplifting emotions. Whether a speaker is delivering a sermon in a crystal cathedral or an appeal to buy MyGuy® jeans, to be persuasive the messages must meet both the cognitive and the emotional needs of the intended audience (Snyder & DeBono, 1985).

Behavioral Change: The Ultimate Goal. The final goal of persuasion is a receiver who acts on the message and displays a *target behavior*. The life-insurance salesperson (politician, coach) has delivered her spiel; are you prepared to buy (vote, play)? Several factors determine whether a person will be persuaded to act on a message. The first is the *primacy effect:* of two competing messages, the first is more likely to be heard and acted on (Insko, 1964). Another factor is the use of *attitude inoculation:* pointing out weaknesses in the opposition's arguments, thereby "stealing their thunder" (McGuire, 1961). For example, a PC salesperson might claim "Macintosh computers are a little more user friendly, but there is more software for PCs." Presenting a weak argument before the opposition does tends to undermine the argument. Consider another example: One of my daughters once volunteered the message that her friends would all be attending the same party with her, and had agreed they would all be home by 1:00 A.M., "because some of their parents thought that a 2:00 A.M. curfew was too late." Would you be surprised to learn that her normal curfew was 12:30?

Cognitive Dissonance

People do not always hold consistent attitudes, nor act on them in consistent ways. Psychologists are interested in the white lies people tell themselves to resolve such inconsistencies. Many years ago, for example, I bought an old, relatively cheap convertible to run back and forth to work. Only a few months later it required engine work costing half again as much as the cost of the car. I had to decide whether to invest more money in the car or get rid of it, thereby losing my initial investment. I fixed the car, but found myself in a highly conflicted psychological state. I now realize that I was experiencing what social psychologists call *cognitive dissonance.*

Cognitive dissonance refers to an unpleasant psychological state caused by two conflicting, often contradictory thoughts (Festinger, 1957). My first thought was that my initial judgment was sound: the car was worth what I paid for it. My second thought was that the car might not be worth fixing, and perhaps my judgment had *not* been sound. According to Festinger's theory, such competing cognitions create an unpleasant psychological state, motivating people to resolve the conflict. Freud proposed that people did so by invoking a defense mechanism, such as repression or sublimation. Festinger simply said that people altered their thoughts to reduce the dissonance.

Freudian defense mechanism, Chapter 14, p. 499

To test this hypothesis, Festinger and Carlsmith (1959) first induced a state of cognitive dissonance in college students by paying them to tell a white lie to other students. Although the laboratory task they had just finished had been extremely boring, they were told to tell incoming subjects it was interesting. For this simple deception, half the subjects were paid about $3 (in today's dollars) while the other half were paid about $60. Which of the two groups of students do you think experienced more cognitive dissonance, the ones who were paid $3 to lie, or the ones who were paid $60?

In debriefing the subjects after the experiment, Festinger asked them how they *really* felt about the task. The ones who were paid $60 responded that the task was boring, but the subjects who were paid $3 said they had changed their minds: the task wasn't as boring as it first seemed to them. Festinger interpreted this result as follows: Subjects who were paid $60 experienced little cognitive dissonance because their thinking was not contradictory: the task was boring, but they were paid a nice sum of money to lie about it. Subjects who were paid $3, however, experienced considerable dissonance. The task was boring, and they had accepted a pittance to lie about it. To reduce their dissonance, Festinger reasoned, they changed their thinking about the task.

cognitive dissonance An unpleasant psychological state caused by two contradictory thoughts.

What did I do to reduce my cognitive dissonance concerning the value of my car? In retrospect, I did just what Festinger would have predicted. After retrieving the car from the repair shop, I washed and waxed it, and thought to myself that it really *was* worth the money I had invested in it. Dissonance reduced, my uneasiness vanished. Can we apply this theory to the brainwashed prisoners in Korea? We can surmise that even the slightest collaboration with the enemy would have aroused extreme cognitive dissonance in the prisoners. ("I should not cooperate with the enemy. I am cooperating with the enemy.) One way to reduce their dissonance would have been to change their initial thinking about the enemy. ("The enemy is not bad, therefore I can cooperate with them.")

INTERIM SUMMARY

1. Social psychology is the study of how an individual's behavior is influenced by his or her social interactions.
2. People make inferences about what motivates their own and others' behavior. Social psychologists study these *social perceptions* by analyzing the statements, or ***attributions,*** people make to explain behavior.
3. According to ***attribution theory,*** people explain behavior in terms of both *internal attributions*—one's personal characteristics—and *external attributions*—environmental demands on behavior.
4. Kelley's covariation model states that people attribute the causes of behavior as a function of three factors: whether the person's behavior was (1) *consistent* with or (2) *distinctive* from a person's past behaviors, and the social factor, (3) *consensus,* on how unique the behavior is relative to other humans.
5. The ***fundamental attribution error*** is the tendency to attribute other people's behavior to their personal characteristics rather than the demands of the situation.
6. People who live in individualistic Western cultures are more likely than people from other cultures to make the fundamental attribution error and to have a ***self-serving bias*** (attributing their own failures to situational factors and their successes to personal factors).
7. An ***attitude*** is a person's general manner, or disposition to respond favorably or unfavorably to a person or situation. According to the ABC approach, attitudes have three basic yet interactive components: affective, behavioral, and cognitive.
8. The way in which a person behaves is only loosely tied to that person's attitudes. Attitudes determine general response patterns rather than specific behaviors, which are tied more closely to environmental contingencies.
9. A behavior such as role playing can affect a person's attitudes in the same way that attitudes can affect behavior. According to *self-perception* theory, as people become aware of their behavior, their awareness helps to form their attitudes.
10. The ***foot-in-the-door phenomenon*** describes how a person gets someone to comply with a big request by starting out with a small one. This technique is similar to shaping behavior through successive approximation.
11. The five components of a persuasive message are the source, the message, the channel, the receiver, and the target behavior. Messages are persuasive when their source is credible, powerful, and attractive; when they are stated clearly and logically through a medium that is appropriate to the situation; and when the receiver is attentive and intelligent and has high self-esteem.
12. In a persuasive argument the *central route* (cognitive) is logical and factual; the *peripheral route* (emotional) is the packaging of the argument—the sender's appearance, social status, and so forth.
13. Of two competing messages, the first one heard is the more persuasive (the *primacy effect).* An opposing argument can be effectively countered by *attitude inoculation*—pointing out weaknesses in the opposition's arguments.
14. ***Cognitive dissonance*** is an unpleasant psychological state caused by two contradictory thoughts about the same event. People usually reduce the dissonance by altering their thoughts and behavior.

For Further Thought

1. How is the external attribution of behavior similar to B. F. Skinner's theory of environmental determinism?
2. In the story about the Columbine High massacre, did the sheriff make the fundamental attribution error? Did President Clinton?
3. The James-Lange theory of emotion (Chapter 5, p. 179) suggests we don't run because we fear a bear, rather, we run first, and the fear grows out of the running behavior. Can you compare this theory of emotion with a theory relating behavior to attitude formation?
4. Consider an elementary school curriculum "the message." How would you advise a school district on ways to improve students' behavioral responses to the message?
5. Can you think of a personal example of having experienced cognitive dissonance? How did you resolve it?

SOCIAL INFLUENCES ON BEHAVIOR

Most of us are influenced by the people around us to accept group standards, or *norms*. We tend to mimic each other's hairstyles, language patterns, and dress. In other words, we care what others think about us. Why do the self-professed rugged individualists of Western culture conform so often to group standards?

Suppose you have been selected to sit on a jury considering the guilt or innocence of a murder suspect. You are instructed by the judge to evaluate the evidence on your own and make up your own mind. After having listened to all the

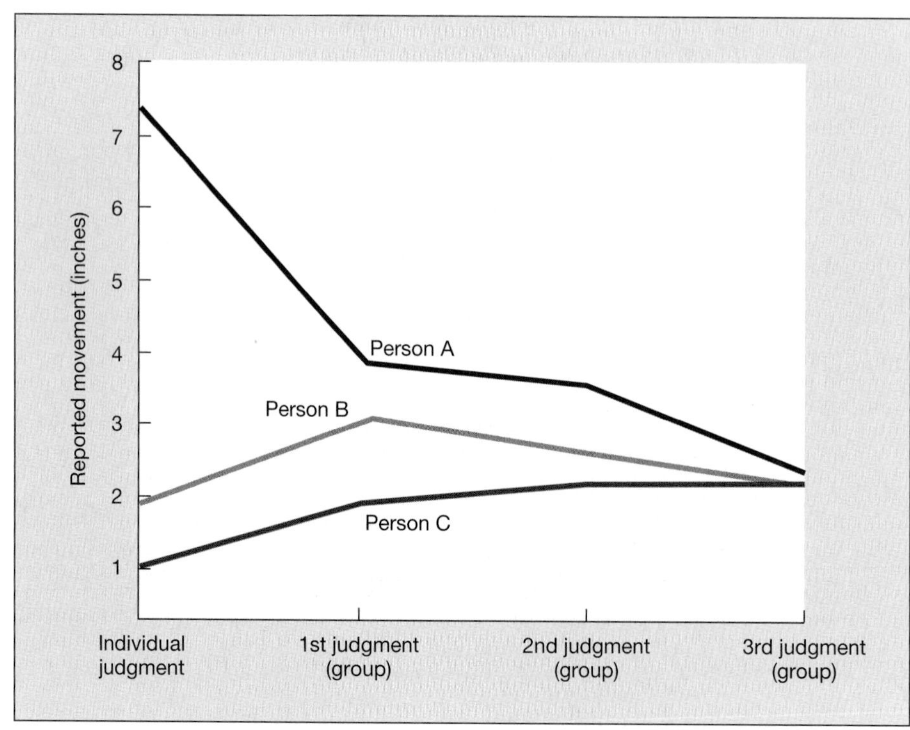

Figure 15.2 Social Influences on Apparent Movement. Three people who viewed a stationary light suspended in a darkened room reported that it appeared to move. When tested alone, person A reported an apparent movement of about 7 inches, person B reported a movement of 2 inches, and person C reported movement of 1 inch. During three shared sessions, person A was influenced by the other subjects' judgment. By the third session, all agreed that the light had moved just over 2 inches.

evidence, you conclude that the accused is innocent. But when the jury begins to deliberate, you begin doubting your own judgment and, finding you hold a minority opinion, feel isolated. How are you likely to vote?

Conformity

Psychologists have studied group pressure on individual behavior for many decades. One classic study (Sherif, 1936) took advantage of what is called the phi phenomenon: For unknown reasons, when a tiny light is viewed from a distance in a pitch-black room, it appears to move. Some individuals report that it moves as much as a foot, while others report minimal movement. The experimenter first asked individuals how much the light appeared to move, then asked them to make the same judgments in groups of three. Figure 15.2 shows the results: Over three sessions, the subjects' length estimates converged, suggesting that in ambiguous situations, individuals conform relatively quickly to a group standard.

1 2 3
Standard line Comparison lines

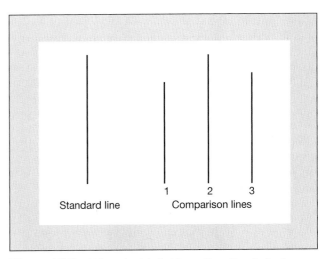

Figure 15.3 What Asch's Subjects Saw. Psychologist Solomon Asch showed these lines to a group of subjects, some of whom were confederates who deliberately lied about what they saw.

Another classic study showed that individuals are susceptible to group standards even when the task is less ambiguous (Asch, 1955). In this experiment, Solomon Asch showed the lines in Figure 15.3 to seven people, three of whom appear in the photograph below. The person in the middle (number 6) has just listened to six people before him state that line 3 was similar in length to the standard line—an obvious error. Bewildered, he peers intently at the lines, trying to see what the others say they are seeing. The confederates must have been quite convincing, because one out of every three subjects in this experiment did not believe their own eyes, and agreed instead that line 3 matched the length of the standard line.

Before jumping to the conclusion these results are outdated—that contemporary college students would be more independent than Asch's students—consider that the results of this experiment have been replicated (Larsen, 1990) and extended to other cognitive tasks (Schneider & Watkins, 1996). For instance, watching TV with other people has been shown to influence people's behavior. In

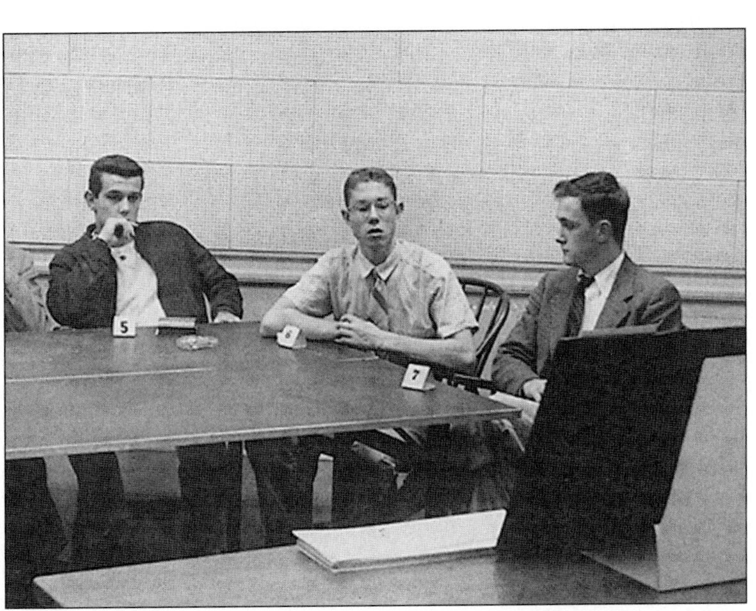

Perplexed, subject number 6 peers at the lines shown in Figure 15.3. Confederates number 5 and 7 have already lied, stating that the length of comparison line 3 is the same as the standard line. About one-third of the subjects in this experiment agreed with the confederates' lies. Seeing is believing, but when the group decides otherwise, sometimes we can convince ourselves to see it their way.
Photo William Vandivert and Scientific American. From "Opinions and Social Pressure" by Solomon E. Asch, November 1955.

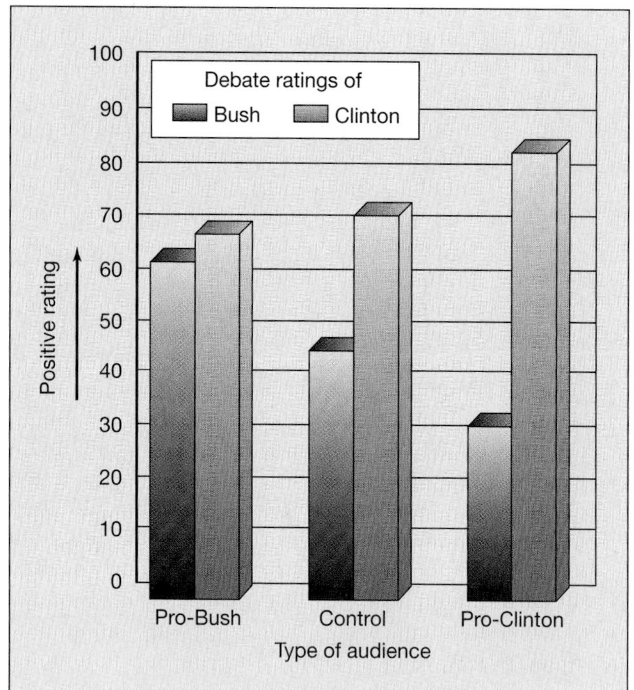

Figure 15.4 Social Influences in the Bush–Clinton Debate. Confederates cheering for George Bush and booing Bill Clinton (left bars) during a televised debate in 1992 influenced an audience's rating of how Bush performed, in comparison with a control condition. Similarly, confederates cheering for Clinton and booing Bush (right bars) influenced another audience's reactions to Clinton.

one study three groups of 30 students each viewed a televised presidential debate between George Bush and Bill Clinton (Fein, Goethals, Kassin, & Cross, 1993). Confederates in one group cheered Bill Clinton and booed George Bush, and in another group booed Clinton and cheered for Bush. A control group contained no confederates. Figure 15.4 shows the results of the debate for the three groups: booing Clinton, and cheering for Bush increased Bush's popularity, while cheering for Clinton and booing Bush increased Clinton's popularity.

All these studies indicate that under certain conditions, some people's judgment can be swayed by the group's opinion. Furthermore, in ambiguous situations such as jury rooms, people tend to adopt a group standard. If eleven jurors favor a guilty verdict, the social pressure on the lone twelfth juror will be great. But what if at least one other person agrees with that juror? Asch (1956) found that the presence of even one confederate who reported a line length correctly markedly reduced subjects' tendency to conform to the group standard. In general, however, the results of these studies are consistent. The power of the group is compelling.

Obedience: Compliance With Authority

Whether in a jury room, a church, or a battlefield, the social influences of the group are an important determinant of individual behavior. Groups typically have leaders, so conformity often takes the form of *obedience,* or compliance with authority. During World War II, Nazi authorities ordered soldiers to collect European Jews in concentration camps and carry out their genocide. Most complied; only a few resisted. The willingness to "follow orders" is not restricted to times of war. When the religious leader Jim Jones convinced 912 people to commit suicide in 1972, mothers and fathers obeyed him, but only after making sure their children had first drunk poisoned Kool-Aide. Why would these people maladaptively comply with such heartless instructions?

Milgram's Classic Obedience Studies. Stanley Milgram, unable to understand how soldiers could willingly inflict atrocities on innocent people, designed an experiment that would allow subjects to inflict pain on strangers under the guise of "following orders." His findings continue to shock and dismay psychology students (Milgram, 1963, 1974).

Milgram recruited subjects through newspaper ads and paid them to participate in his study, which was ostensibly about the role of punishment in a paired-associate learning task. Subjects were told that some of them were to be assigned as "teachers" and others as "learners." A white-coated experimenter told "teachers" to administer electric shock to the "learners" when they made errors (see the photograph on next page). For each mistake, teachers were instructed to increase the shock level by 15 volts. The learners—who remained out of sight of the teachers—were Milgram's confederates; they made deliberate errors and reacted to the shocks, which were faked, by grunting, screaming, and, at the higher shock levels, pleading with the teacher to stop. When the learner's cries became shrill, the experimenter assured the teacher that the learner was overreacting and told the teacher to continue with the experiment.

Milgram found that two out of every three teachers continued to shock the learners even at the highest voltage levels. One teacher continued to administer

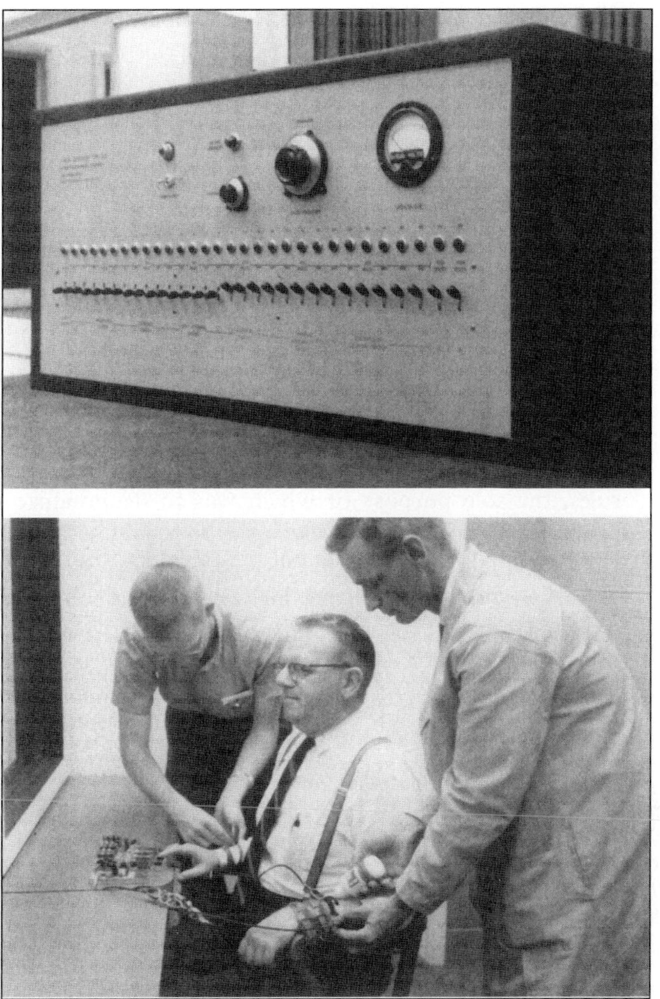

The fake shock-control device (top) used in Stanley Milgram's experiments had switches that supposedly allowed a *teacher* to administer shocks up to 450 volts to a *learner* when ordered to do so by the experimenter. A teacher witnessed a learner being strapped to a chair (bottom) prior to a session. Copyright 1955 by Stanley Milgram. From the film OBEDIENCE, distributed by Penn State Media Sales.

shocks long after a learner had screamed to stop, because he had a heart condition, and then fell ominously silent. Many of the teachers expressed dismay with their task, but obediently continued when they were told to do so.

In subsequent experiments, Milgram tested whether obedience to orders diminish if the teacher could see the learner. About 30 percent of the teachers continued to administer the shocks even when they could see the painful results.

The subjects in these experiments justified their actions in terms of following orders. The experimenter, they explained, was in charge, acted as if he knew what he was doing, and assumed responsibility when asked if the experiment should continue. (The parallel with obedience to the "chain of command" in organizations is clear.) Still, they felt dehumanized by the experience.

Explaining how ordinary people could allow themselves to administer 450 volts of shock to "slow learners" is difficult. Milgram thought that the "process" of the experiment gradually became more important than the participant's roles. The slow elevation of the shock levels allowed the teachers to become accustomed to the procedures, and to be reinforced for complying with the experimenter's increasing demands. Once the teachers complied with the demand to administer the first shock, the experimenter had his foot in the door. Nevertheless, the finding that obedience to authority can overcome personal misgivings about harmful behavior is disconcerting. Milgram's findings have been replicated cross-culturally among office workers in the Netherlands (Meeus & Raaijmakers, 1986).

Zimbardo's Prison Study. In Milgram's study of obedience, subjects accepted the authority of the person in charge and complied with his unethical demands. The phrase "just following orders" is often heard in groups, especially hierarchically organized groups. About 10 years after Milgram's research, psychologist Philip Zimbardo studied the role of authority in groups at Stanford University. Zimbardo assigned college students different roles in a mock prison. Some of the paid volunteers (who had been screened for emotional stability) were assigned the role of prisoners serving a 2-week sentence. Others became their guards whose only instructions were to *maintain law and order* (Zimbardo, Haney, & Banks, 1973). To say that both prisoners and guards got into their roles would be an understatement. On the second day, the prisoners, wearing prison garb and locked into cells, revolted. The guards met them with force, threatening them with clubs and spraying them with fire extinguishers.

Over the course of the next week, relations between prisoners and guards deteriorated further. The guards used degrading language and created unnecessary rules, the sole purpose of which was to dehumanize the prisoners. Zimbardo ended the experiment a week earlier than planned, because he found the unforeseen personality changes subjects experienced to be frightening. He concluded that the lessons learned from his research were all too clear. Given power within a group setting, even well-meaning, well-adjusted people will abuse their positions of authority. Even though Westerners conform less to group standards than non-Westerners (Bond & Smith, 1994), research consistently shows that people from many cultures abuse positions of power in hierarchically organized groups.

Table 15.2 Home Advantage in Sports

Sport	Games Studied	Home Team Winning Percentage
Baseball	23,034	53.5
Football	2,592	57.3
Ice hockey	4,322	61.1
Basketball	13,596	64.4
Soccer	37,702	69.0

Source: Adapted from "The Home Advantage in Sports Competition: A Literature Review" by K. S. Courneya & A. V. Carron in *Journal of Sport & Exercise Physiology.* (1992), vol 14 pp. 13–27. Copyright © 1992. Reprinted by permission of Human Kinetics.

Group Influence on Personal Performance

We have seen that a person's behavior is highly influenced by the demands of a group, as well as by perceived roles within the group. Most of the examples we have studied have been negative: people tend to misperceive simple stimuli, conform in response to group pressure, and act badly when authorized to do so. Yet under certain conditions individuals will perform better as part of a group.

Social Facilitation. **Social facilitation** simply means than an individual performs better in the presence of others. As Table 15.2 shows, for example, on average, athletes perform better at home events, with supportive groups of fans, than at away events. (Note, however, the home field advantage is less important for baseball than for basketball and soccer.) Why does the presence of other people change one's behavior? The social psychologist Robert Zajonc reasoned that social facilitation occurs because individuals are aroused by the group (Zajonc, 1965), a finding supported by other researchers (Geen & Gange, 1983). The relationship of performance to arousal is not a simple one, however. Only optimal levels of arousal increase a person's performance: too little and too much arousal ("choking") are associated with underperformance.

Another factor that determines the way in which arousal affects social facilitation is the task itself. Relatively easy, overlearned tasks are more easily facilitated by groups than are difficult tasks (Zajonc, 1965). For example, an enthusiastic audience will facilitate a runner's performance during a race, but can hinder a golfer's 6-foot pressure putt. Running is easier than golfing, so it is more likely to be socially facilitated. To give another example, when expert and amateur pool players performed alone and then in front of an audience, the experts improved but the amateurs' performance suffered (Michaels, Bloomel, Brocato, Linkous, & Rowe, 1982). Returning to Table 15.2, hitting a curveball is arguably more difficult than the open-field play in soccer, making it less susceptible to social facilitation.

social facilitation The enhancement of an individual's performance due to the presence of others.

Social Loafing. As anyone who has worked on a group project can attest, the presence of other people doesn't guarantee arousal and enhanced performance; some people are prepared to let others do the work. Two factors contribute to the reduced productivity of individuals in groups, efficiency and reduced effort. The reduction in efficiency is due to impaired coordination and cooperation; dividing work into subtasks and putting a finished project together is often more difficult than working alone. But cooperation and coordination aren't the whole story: individuals often do not put out as much effort when working in groups as they do when working alone, a phenomenon called **social loafing** (Latané, Williams, & Harkins, 1979). Social loafing has been demonstrated in a variety of tasks, including brainstorming for new ideas, solving mazes, editing newspapers, and athletic competition (Karau & Williams, 1993; Shepperd, 1993). People are less likely to loaf when everyone in the group values and demands one another's effort (Sheppard & Taylor, 1999). And not surprisingly, social loafing is less prominent in collectivist cultures (Karau & Williams, 1993, 1995).

The Bystander Effect. A group can influence the extent to which one individual will help another. When a researcher's confederate convincingly feigned an illness in an experimental situation, about 4 out of 5 individuals responded to her plea for help (Darley & Latané, 1968). However, if two people heard the cry for help, the ratio of subjects who responded dropped to 3 out of 5. When groups of four heard the distress call, fewer than 1 out of 3 offered to help. These paradoxical findings illustrate the **bystander effect**: a person is more likely to offer help to a stranger when alone than when accompanied by others. This phenomenon has been replicated in both emergency and everyday situations, such as changing a flat tire or picking up dropped objects (Latané & Nida, 1981).

The bystander effect is typically explained in terms of *diffusion of responsibility*. The person who thinks he or she is the only one able to come to another's aid is more likely to respond than one who recognizes that others can (and should) share the responsibility. Other contributing factors include concerns about personal safety and convenience. For example, a person is less likely to stop to help a stranger on a dark road than in a mall.

social loafing The tendency of a person to exert less effort in a group task compared to an individual task.

bystander effect The greater willingness of a lone individual to offer help to a stranger compared to that of a group.

INTERIM SUMMARY

1. Research on conformity—the power of the group to shape individual behavior—shows that most individuals can be swayed by group pressure. The presence of one dissenter affords considerable protection against group pressure, however.
2. Leaders and authority figures often demand obedience (compliance with authority) from others, even when compliance would be unethical. Milgram's research indicates that most people will follow the directions of an authority figure.
3. People will assume assigned roles in a group and alter their behavior to fit those roles. Zimbardo's prison study demonstrated that normal individuals will abuse power that has been arbitrarily assigned to them and will become fearful and anxious in the assigned role of prisoner.
4. *Social facilitation* is the enhancement of an individual's performance in the presence of others. This effect is likely caused by arousal. Simple tasks are more likely than complex behaviors to be socially facilitated.
5. Individuals often work more effectively alone than in groups, a phenomenon called *social loafing.*
6. A person who is alone is more likely than a member of a group to help someone in need, a phenomenon called the *bystander effect.*

For Further Thought

1. Why do you think the presence of another person with similar views affords protection against group pressure? Is this effect an example of social facilitation?
2. When is "following orders" adaptive in an evolutionary sense? When is it not?
3. How would you respond if you were made a jailer in Zimbardo's prison experiment? Are you sure?

GENDER, ATTRACTION, AND LOVE

Beginning with physical and emotional contact with caretakers, a person's social identity emerges over a lifetime, including one's attitudes, beliefs, gender identity, sexuality, friendships, and love. For most people there are no more important issues in life. We begin with gender and sexual orientation.

Gender and Sexual Orientation

During development, people take on *gender identity* and assume *gender roles* within a culture. In this section we will describe the meaning of gender and what is known about the genetic and cultural bases for sexual relationships and sexual orientation.

Gender Roles. **Gender roles** are culturally determined sex-appropriate behaviors for females and males. Boys and girls learn what is expected from them by observing how their parents behave and listening to what their parents tell them; by observing others around them; and by observing how their environments have been structured for them. For example, mothers and fathers play differently with boys than they do with girls. Fathers are more likely to engage in physical play with sons than with daughters, and mothers are less physical than men with children of both sexes (Lindsay, Mize, & Pettit, 1997). Parents also inculcate gender roles through gender-specific behavioral modeling and by differential patterns of reinforcement and punishment. Gender roles can also be influenced by environments that may or may not be structured by team sports, dance lessons, and other sources of gender influence.

As a culture changes, gender roles change with it. Girls born in the United States in the first part of the 19th century were usually given dolls to play with; they watched as father left in the morning and returned home in the evening, and modeled themselves after their homemaker mothers. Similarly, young women in the 1950s learned that to be feminine they should "act like a lady," attract and marry an eligible man, and be prepared to stay home and raise a family. During that time television played a role in the development of gender roles, portraying women mainly as wives and mothers (Long & Simon, 1974). Time and circumstance eventually changed these gender roles as women entered the work force in large numbers. By the late 1980s, 80 percent of Americans approved of career women, even if they were married (Niemi, Mueller, & Smith, 1989).

gender roles Culturally determined appropriate behaviors for females and males.

A culture may change its ideas about gender roles, but a number of cross-cultural and other types of studies provide evidence for biologically determined gender roles. For example, cross-culturally, boys and girls tend to play differently. By age 3, boys are engaging in "play fighting," including wrestling and hitting, three to six times more frequently than girls of the same age (Geary, 1999). During this developmental stage, cross-culturally girls play at "parenting." (In a later section we'll consider evidence that genetically determined hormones are involved in these differences.) From an evolutionary perspective, these different play behaviors may be interpreted as adaptive preparation for adult lifestyles (Keeley, 1996; Geary, 1999).

In another study, researchers asked men and women from 25 different cultures to assign descriptive adjectives to one or the other sex (Williams & Best, 1982). As Table 15.3 shows, the results indicate that men and women consistently see each other as behaving in gender-specific ways. In all 25 cultures, respondents described men as adventurous, dominant, and forceful, and women as sentimental and submissive.

These findings raise a number of questions. One wonders, for instance, how many respondents did *not* assign adjectives such as *clear thinking* to males and *attractive* to females. Certainly one would expect to find sex differences in assigning these adjectives: women, for example, might be more likely to assign the adjective *attractive* to males and the adjective *clear thinking* to females. Another question concerns the impact of cultural change on gender roles. We have seen that in the United States, attitudes toward women who work outside the home changed as the nation moved from a predominantly rural culture to an urban and suburban culture. Are women from Western countries more likely than others to assign "male" adjectives such as active, adventurous, rational, and self-confident to females, and if so, will the gender typing of adjectives change as cultures change? Finally, cultures vary along many dimensions, such as educational, governmental, and economic. How do these factors influence the way men and women perceive each other?

Genes, Hormones, and Sexual Behavior

Recall that according to Erikson's theory of development, sexuality is the central focus of intimacy-versus-isolation stage (see Chapter 11). During this stage, young people's sexual activity leads to the birth of the next generation.

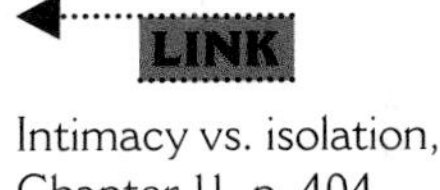

Intimacy vs. isolation, Chapter 11, p. 404

Table 15.3 Gender-typed Adjectives

Men and women from 25 cultures were asked to associate the following adjectives with females or males. The results revealed a great deal of agreement across cultures.

"Male" Adjectives	Number of Cultures	"Female" Adjectives	Number of Cultures
active	23	affectionate	24
adventurous	25	attractive	23
aggressive	24	dependent	23
coarse	21	emotional	23
courageous	23	fearful	23
cruel	21	gentle	21
dominant	25	sensitive	24
egotistical	21	sentimental	25
forceful	25	sexy	22
hardhearted	21	submissive	25
lazy	21	weak	23
rational	20		
self-confident	21		
unemotional	23		
wise	23		

Source: From MEASURING SEX STEREOTYPES: A Thirty–Nation Study by J. E. Williams & D. L. Best. Copyright © 1982. Reprinted by permission of Sage Publications, Inc.

A human's sexuality is determined by the combined influence of genetic processes, hormones, and culture. The genetic mechanisms that result in the creation of a new human were discussed in Chapter 3. Most people who carry an XX form of the 23rd chromosome become biological females, while those who carry the XY form become biological males. Genes that code for tissues and enzymes interact with the environment to produce behavior, and behavior, in turn, influences tissues, enzymes, and gene expression. (Taking certain drugs and the effects of an eating disorder are examples of behavior influencing one's physiology.) A person's sexual nature, then, depends very much on the environment in which it developed and in which it is expressed.

John Money and his colleagues at Johns Hopkins University, among other researchers, have described how events that occur in a zygote contribute to an individual's sexual nature (Breedlove, 1994; Money & Ehrhardt, 1972). The *organizational effects* of the hormones testosterone and estrogen affect both the developing genitalia and the parts of the brain that control sexuality and sexual behavior. In most individuals, the results are anatomically correct males and females whose sexual behavior falls within well-described norms. But many other possibilities exist. In females, too much testosterone at certain stages of fetal development can produce an *androgenital syndrome.* At birth, such females may have an enlarged clitoris; later in life they may manifest "tomboyishness," show little interest in women's clothes and makeup, and fail to model maternal behaviors, such as playing with dolls. Males who are exposed to less androgen and more estrogen than normal may also develop abnormal genitalia. As boys, they may seem "sissy-like" and may show little interest in men's attire and in modeling paternal behavior (Ehrhardt & Meyer-Bahlberg, 1981).

Hormones also have *activational effects* that influence sexual behavior over a lifetime. Figure 15.5 shows what happens to the behavior of a castrated male (who produces no testosterone) when testosterone is artificially introduced to and then taken away from his body. As the figure shows, the presence of testosterone influences a man's thinking about sex as well as his sexual behaviors. But since behavior also influences hormones, human sexual behavior is highly influenced by the environment and culture in which a child develops—for example, the fashions, magazines, and movies a child sees as well as parental attitudes toward sex.

Sexual Orientation. Courting practices, including sexual exploration, are accompanied by some of the most profound emotions a person can experience, such as passionate love and the struggle with commitment. Young people may feel an almost overwhelming sexual urgency, yet they may prefer their own company to the command performances required by committed social relationships. The conflict is even greater if a young person is unsure of his or her sexual orientation.

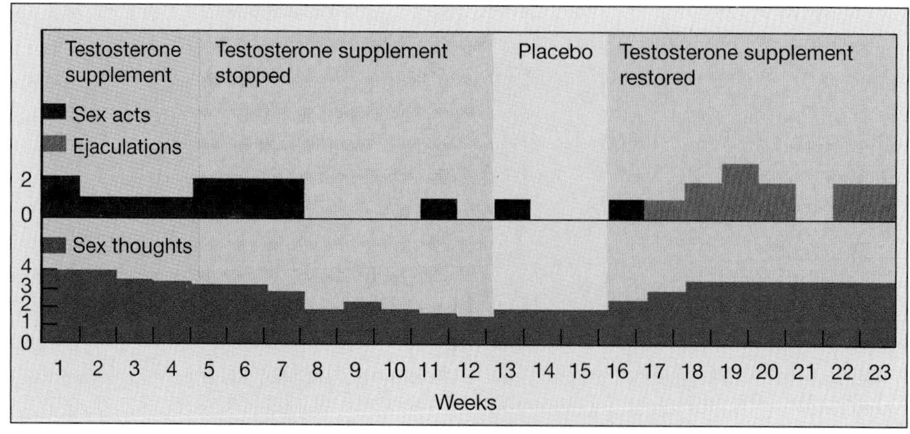

Figure 15.5 Testosterone Increases Sexual Thoughts and Behaviors. A testosterone supplement administered to a castrated male increased how often he thought about sex and engaged in sexual behaviors, compared with withdrawal of testosterone or when he received a placebo.

A person's **sexual orientation** is that person's sexual attraction to and preference for others of the same or opposite sex. Throughout the world, heterosexuality is the norm (Bullough, 1990). Given most people's heterosexuality, how can we explain homosexuality and bisexuality (attraction to both sexes)? At present there are no simple answers to this question. On the surface homosexuality would appear to be a genetic dead end. That is, were the estimated 3 or 4 percent of males, and 1 percent of females in the United States (National Center for Health Statistics, 1995) to engage in sexual practices that produced no offspring, their genes would disappear from the gene pool after only a few generations. However, homosexuality has been present from the earliest recorded history, and occurs in other species as well (Money, 1987). Whether genetic patterns predispose a person to become homosexual is not known. We do know that at different times and places—during the Golden Age of Greece, for example—homosexual behavior has been more common, more open, and socially acceptable than it is now (Adams, 1985).

Homosexuality has existed in all cultures from the earliest human records.

In part because of negative cultural experiences, homosexuals may experience emotional stress or become confused about their sexual orientation. Many struggle with a conflict between their emotional experience (a same-sex orientation) and their cognitive experience (a desire to conform to heterosexual norms). In Freudian terms, some resolve this conflict by suppressing or otherwise denying their feelings, or even by establishing a sexual relationship with the opposite sex (a reaction formation). Some of these heterosexual relationships may produce offspring—contributions to the human gene pool that predispose an individual to develop a homosexual orientation.

For many homosexuals, the end result of this identity crisis, only after much pain and self-recrimination, is an acceptance of their homosexual orientation. Their homosexual behavior can take several forms, ranging from celibacy to a long-lasting stable relationship with one person to promiscuity. Here there are gender differences in homosexual behavior: women are more likely than men to establish an extended relationship with one partner; men are more likely to be promiscuous (Peplau, 1982). Note, however, that heterosexuals exhibit the same gender differences in showing these three behavior patterns: the sexual behavior of a celibate heterosexual is identical to a celibate homosexual, and heterosexual men engage in more premarital and marital sex with more different partners than do heterosexual women (Janus & Janus, 1993). Promiscuous individuals of both orientations may have dozens of sexual encounters each week and dozens of sexual partners each month; but for their preference for one sex over the other, their sexual appetites and behavior are similar. And among those homosexuals and heterosexuals who form stable relationships, the primary difference we see is the preference for a same-sex or opposite-sex partner. According to John Money, part of the problem with the labels *homosexuality* and *heterosexuality* is that the terms do not adequately describe the myriad patterns of sexual behavior seen among humans (Money, 1987).

Attraction and Attractiveness

To what extent does physical appearance affect social relationships—for example, among parents, with a friend, a child, a lover, or a significant other? To begin, people who are physically attractive have better social relationships than those who are not. Research has shown that teachers tend to see physically attractive children as smarter and less likely to be troublemakers than other children. On the playground, attractive children are more sought after as friends than are less attractive peers. As adults, attractive people get the nod over others in a job interview (Hatfield & Spretcher, 1986). A review of research on this "stereotype" showed that attractive people are even thought to be happier and more successful than others (Eagly, Ashmore, Makhijani, & Kennedy, 1991).

sexual orientation The sexual attraction to and preference for others of the same or opposite sex.

Not surprisingly, then, a person's physical attractiveness is related to sexual attraction. In his book *The Descent of Man, and Selection in Relation to Sex* (1871/1981), Charles Darwin proposed a theory of *sexual selection* based on the physical characteristics of the opposite sex. The ornate plumage of male birds and the coloration in some mammals, Darwin reasoned, served to attract mates, contributing to the perpetuation of the species through sexual reproduction. Similarly, humans of different cultures paint their faces, pierce or embed objects in their bodies, wear high-heeled shoes or go barefoot, style their hair, or shave it off. One might reasonably conclude that the perception of beauty and physical attractiveness depends on culture. Yet laboratory experiments show that irrespective of age, sex, or skin color, human infants will look at attractive faces longer than less attractive ones (Langlois, Ritter, Roggman, & Vaughn, 1991). This finding suggests that humans are born with a biased visual system that supports an innate preference for beauty, similar to infants' innate preference for sweet tastes, warm fluids, and contact comfort. In this section we will explore the variables that make one person more attractive than another, and the evidence regarding an innate versus learned basis for such preferences.

LINK
Visual development, Chapter 9, p. 389

Gender Differences in Attraction. As we learned in Chapter 3, sociobiologists and evolutionary psychologists think that sexual behavior is influenced by more than another person's physical attractiveness. That is, females and males have unique sexual agendas that reflect a biological urge to propagate their genes (Cunningham, Druen, & Barbee, 1997; Farrell, 1986). What is the evidence for this theory?

Evolutionary psychology and sociobiology, Chapter 3, p. 95

Cross-culturally, males prefer females who are young and physically attractive (Buss, 1996; Buss & Schmidt, 1993; Cunningham, 1986) and who have smooth facial skin texture (Fink, Grammer, & Thornhill, 2001). The evolutionary psychologist David Buss and others speculate that attractiveness and youth are predictors of good health; thus males are drawn to physically attractive women both consciously and unconsciously because a healthy woman will produce more viable offspring than an unhealthy woman.

Is there an ideal female body type to which men are attracted? Devandra Singh and his colleagues at the University of Texas at Austin have studied this question and obtained results that may surprise you. Singh reports that cross-culturally, men are not as obsessed with female breasts and buttocks as the mass media might suggest. Rather, they are most attracted to a low waist-to-hip ratio, optimally 5:9 (Singh, 1993; Singh & Luis, 1995; Singh & Young, 1995). Like Buss and many other researchers, Singh believes that such signs of youth and health are optimal for child bearing.

Should females be attracted to young, handsome males with an optimal shoulder-to-waist ratio, then? Actually, a male's physical looks are less important to a female than a female's are to a male. Cross-culturally, women seek mates who are capable of promoting the survival and well-being of her offspring—men with high social status, financial resources, ambition, and energy (Buss, 1996). Figure 15.6 illustrates how the different sexual agendas of women and men differ.

A classic study by Russell Clark and Elaine Hatfield conducted at Florida State University supported this gender difference in sexual agendas. The researchers trained confederates to approach students of the opposite sex who were sitting alone. (The confederates were rated as "slightly unattractive" to "moderately attractive," and the student they approached "moderately attractive" to "very attractive.") Using the come-on line "I have been noticing you around campus. I find you to be very attractive," the confederates then asked one of three questions: "Would you go out with me tonight?" "Would you come over to my apartment tonight?" or

SWF attractive, seeking SWM, bright, well-to-do, w/ sense of humor.

SWM, ~~seeking Playboy-type blonde~~ 120 IQ, $$$, loves kids.

Figure 15.6 Classified Ads

"Would you go to bed with me tonight?" The results were not surprising; 69 percent of males agreed to go to a female's apartment, and 75 percent said they would go to bed with her. In contrast, only 6 percent of females said they would go to a male confederate's apartment, and none said they would go to bed with him (Clark & Hatfield, 1989). These pre-AIDS data were collected in the late 1970s and early 1980s. A follow-up study confirmed the results (Clark, 1990), even though males were reminded that they could contract AIDS from a single casual sexual contact.

Some research suggests that people will tell an outright lie, such as exaggerating financial resources, to attract a date. In one study, researchers asked men and women to rate how willing they would be to lie to get a date. They found a positive correlation (0.53) between the importance women placed on certain qualities in a date and the men's willingness to lie in order to match those qualities (Rowatt, Cunningham, Rowatt, Druen, & Miles, 1999). The psychologist Wade Rowatt has proposed that deception may have evolved as a selection strategy. In another study, researchers set up a mock dating service in which undergraduates reviewed the profiles of two prospective dates (Rowatt, Cunningham, & Druen, 1998). Each profile included a yearbook-type photograph, a personality description, and a list of qualities the person's ideal date would have. After reviewing the two profiles, each participant rated his or her own physical attractiveness and described his or her personal characteristics. The researchers defined deception as a discrepancy between a person's self-presentation to the two different prospective dates. They found that both men and women conformed to the expectations of the dates they desired. They also estimated their own attractiveness differently, depending on which date they thought would be reading the profile. The research supports the not-surprising idea that males and females often have selfish motives in dating.

Selfish genes, Chapter 3, p. 96

Attractive Faces

For both males and females, sexual interest is influenced by a host of factors that are unrelated to physical attractiveness, including personality, values, and affection (Symons, 1979). Yet, it has long been known we generally prefer people with attractive faces (Walster, Aronson, Abrahams, & Rottman, 1966). There are some general rules that predict faces we find attractive, including physical similarity, familiarity, and an "average face."

In general, people tend to be attracted to others whose looks resemble their own. They socialize with people of similar age, race, height, and socioeconomic status, all of which are determinants of a person's looks (Byrne, 1971). The face most people see daily is their own, and people tend to think that their own mirror images are more attractive than what others see (Mita, Dermer, & Knight, 1977). These findings have led Feingold (1990) to propose that people tend to choose partners of near equal attractiveness, a theory called the *matching hypothesis*.

Furthermore, just as the repeated sampling of novel foods and music increases the preference for these foods and music, repeated exposure to a face produces a *familiarity effect,* increasing the preference for that face (Bornstein, 1989). You may be able to think of someone who at first seemed unattractive to you, but through repeated exposure became familiar and attractive. Perhaps we prefer other faces that look like our own, and a mirror image over a photo image of ourselves, because these looks are familiar to us. Surprisingly, people with average features are perceived to be the *most* attractive (see photographs, next page). Judith Langlois and Lori Roggman showed photographs of faces and computer-altered versions of those same faces to college students, and asked them to rate their attractiveness (Langlois & Roggman, 1990; Langlois, Roggman, & Musselman, 1994). Subjects rated the faces with average-shaped noses, eyes,

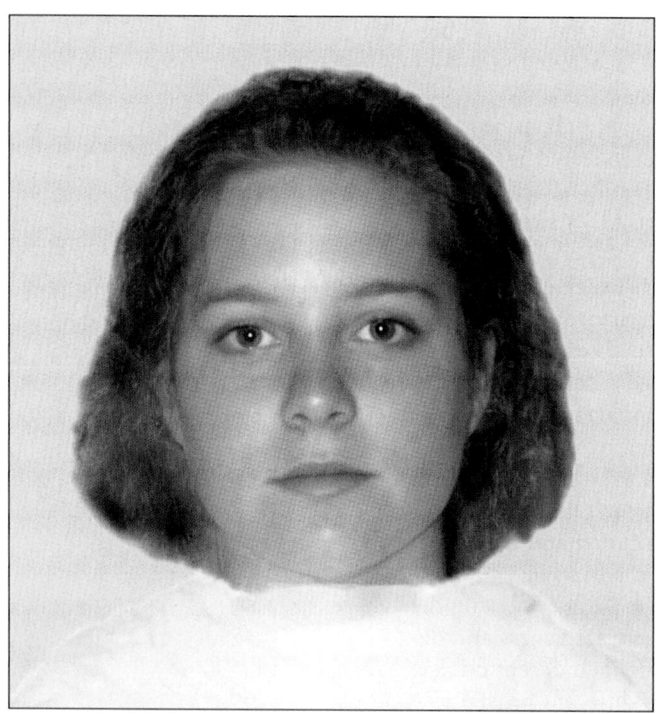

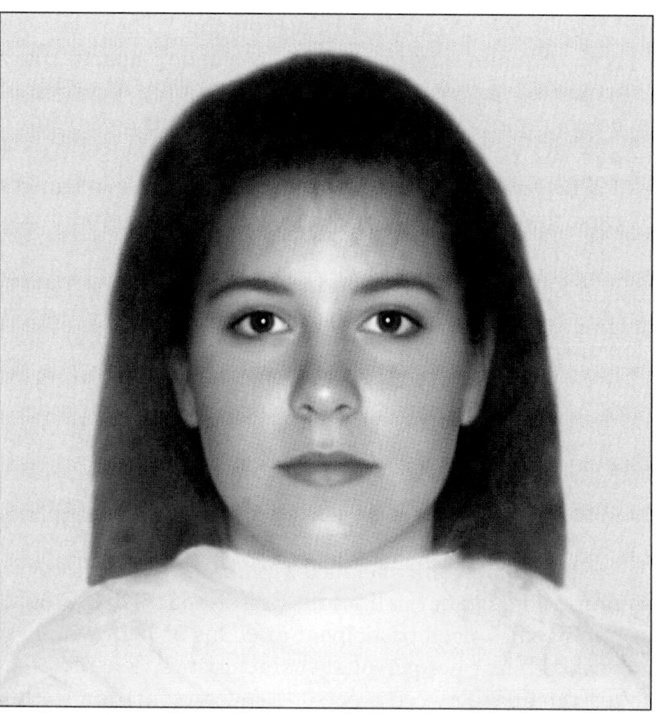

Computer programs modify extreme shapes of noses, lips, eyes, and other facial features by averaging them, producing faces most people consider attractive.

Gestalt psychology, Chapter 8, p. 289

chins, and other features as the most attractive. In fact, people prefer faces that approach perfect symmetry as well as faces with computer-generated average features (Rhodes, Proffitt, Grady, & Sumich, 1998; Rhodes, Sumich, & Byatt, 1999). Perhaps as suggested by Gestalt psychologists, the human brain innately perceives facial "good form" or "good figure" in which average equals good. From an evolutionary perspective, symmetrical faces may reflect both health and "genetic quality" (Rhodes et al., 1998).

Friendship and Love

Researchers are just beginning to explore attraction, friendship, and love from adolescence through late adulthood (Fehr, 1996; Hendrick & Hendrick, 1993; Sternberg, 1986). A friend is one for whom a person feels affection and attachment. No two friends are alike; a sister, neighbor, or someone 40 years older or younger can be a best friend. Some researchers suggest gender difference in same-sex friendships. For example, women's friendships tend to be "face-to-face" talking relationships, while men's friendships are more often "side by side," activity-centered relationships (Wright, 1982; Duck & Wright, 1993). But other researchers think gender differences in friendship have been exaggerated (Walker, 1994).

Passionate Versus Companionate Love. The intense feelings one person can have for another make the study of friendship and love difficult. Just as lust is not the same as romantic love, the love of a parent for a child is not the same as love for a family pet. In particular, psychologists distinguish between *companionate love* and *passionate love* (Bersheid, 1988; Walster & Bersheid, 1974). Passionate love involves intense emotions and sexual attraction, and companionate love is what most people would call friendship. In many relationships, the two overlap.

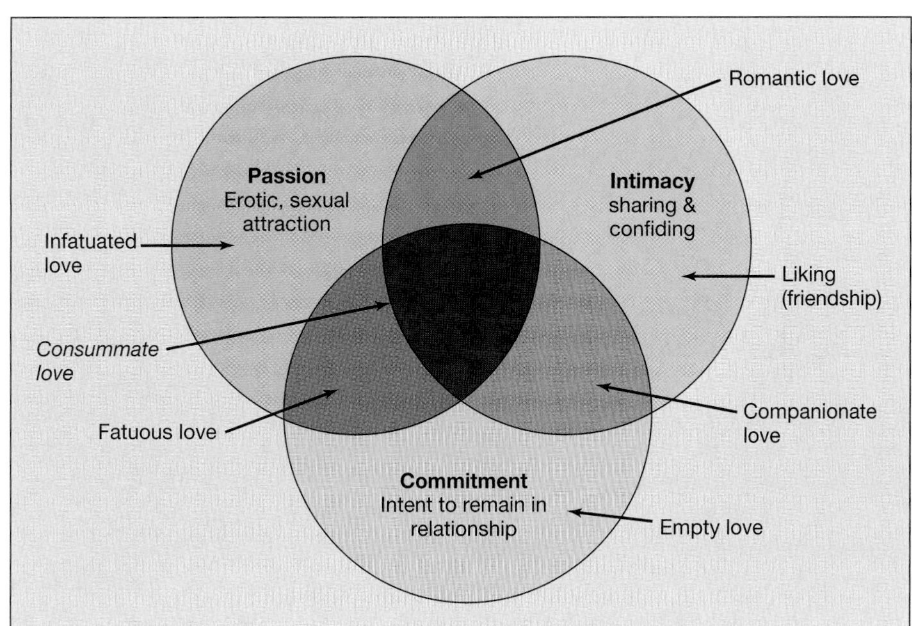

Figure 15.7 Sternberg's Triarchic Theory of Love.

Sternberg's Triarchic Theory of Love. Sternberg's (1986) *triarchic theory of love* captures some of the complexities of friendship and love. According to this theory, successful, long-lasting relationships between couples are characterized by passion, intimacy, and commitment (see Figure 15.7). As Figure 15.8 shows, a relationship endures on the strength of increased intimacy (sharing and emotional closeness) and commitment (surviving bad times), both of which may be thought of as components of companionate love. While some research supports Sternberg's triarchic theory (Aron & Westbay, 1996; Evans, 2001), nevertheless, some couples experience both passionate and companionate love throughout a lifetime.

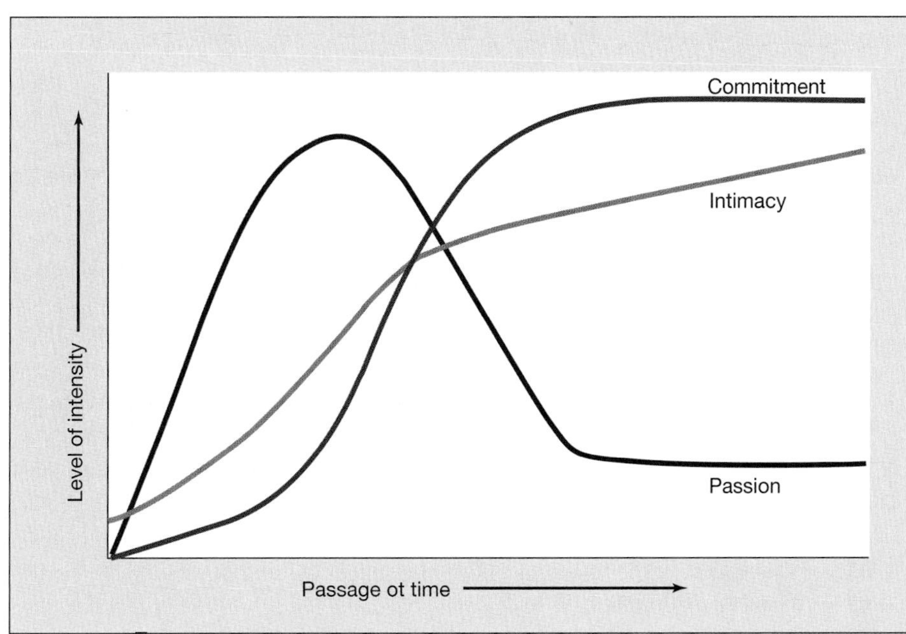

Figure 15.8 Love Changes Over Time. Sternberg proposes that passion, intimacy, and commitment are different aspects of a long-lasting relationship. Passion typically peaks during the early stages of a relationship, while intimacy and commitment grow slowly and can endure for a lifetime.

Given the complexity of marriage, defining a "successful" marriage is difficult to do. Certainly, many marriages endure despite unhappiness on the part of one or both partners. But because commitment and intimacy increases slowly, marriages that are based on passion alone tend to be short-lived. In fact, of all marriages that end in divorce, most fail within the first year or two.

INTERIM SUMMARY

1. An individual's normative development depends on socialization by other humans.
2. People learn their ***gender role*** identities—culturally determined, sex-appropriate behaviors—in childhood. Cultures that foster individualism tend to reinforce a different set of roles from cultures that stress cooperation.
3. A person's *sexual identity* (male or female) is determined by genetic processes and hormones such as testosterone and estrogen. At puberty, hormones can have *activational effects* on sexual behavior. The environment one experiences within a culture also influences human sexual behavior.
4. ***Sexual orientation*** is a person's sexual attraction to and preference for others of the same (homosexual) or opposite (heterosexual) sex.
5. Homosexuality has existed in all cultures from the earliest human records. Male homosexuals tend to be more promiscuous than female homosexuals, who tend to form stable relationships. In general, except for same-sex partner, homosexual sexual patterns resemble those of heterosexuals.
6. A person who is physically attractive has better social relationships than one who is not attractive. Teachers, friends, and employers prefer to associate with, and think more highly of, attractive people.
7. Infants look at attractive faces longer than at less attractive faces, suggesting that there is a biological basis for an appreciation of human attractiveness.
8. Cross-culturally, males prefer females who are young, physically attractive, and have a waist-to-hip ratio of 5:9. Evolutionary psychologists think such factors are predictive of good health and an ability to produce healthy offspring.
9. Cross-culturally, women seek men with high social status, adequate financial resources, and ambition. Evolutionary psychologists think such factors indicate an ability to provide for her offspring.
10. Males are more responsive to offers of casual sex than women and engage in premarital sex with more different partners. Both sexes practice deception during courtship.
11. People tend to prefer similar, familiar, and average facial features. Most of us prefer to socialize with others of similar age, race, height, and socioeconomic status.
12. Psychologists distinguish between friends (*companionate love*) and lovers (*passionate love*). Passionate love, or romantic love, is characterized by intense emotions and feelings of sexual attraction.
13. According to Sternberg's *triarchic theory of love*, enduring love is characterized by passion, intimacy, and commitment. In a long-term relationship such as a marriage, passion often diminishes quickly, whereas intimacy and commitment gradually increase.

For Further Thought

1. Make one list each for your grandmother, grandfather, mother, father, and self. Fill out each list using the adjectives in Table 15.3. Can you see gender roles changing across the generations?
2. Both Plato and Immanuel Kant proposed the existence of universal concepts of form and beauty. How do you think they would respond to research showing that infants and adults prefer to view beautiful faces?
3. What general rules governing attractiveness help to explain why parents find their own children more attractive than others do?
4. Female chimpanzees have been observed initiating sexual encounters. Do you think the dance between the sexes has changed much during the last 200,000 years?

5. Why do you think most people have only one or at most two best friends?
6. From your observations, do you think male-male friendships are different from female-female friendships? How so?
7. Do you know any middle-aged people who are still passionate about a spouse or significant other? If so, what do you think contributes to the persistence of their passion?

SOCIAL RELATIONS

Psychologists study social relations such as forming groups, cooperation, stereotyping, aggression, and so forth. In Chapter 3 we saw that altruistic and cooperative behaviors are typically extended to those in a group—usually kin. There we discussed the tendencies to form cooperative social relationships, and to treat kin preferentially, in terms of the distal determinants of behavior. In this chapter we will consider both distal and proximal (cultural) determinants of social relationships.

Proximal and distal determinants of behavior, Chapter 3, p. 70

Prejudice and Stereotyping

When O. J. Simpson's "not guilty" verdict was announced on TV, the facial expressions in this audience reflected deep racial divisions.

As the photograph on this page shows, Americans tend to be racially divided in their attitudes. For weeks during 1995, O. J. Simpson's murder trial received international news coverage. Simpson, an African American and sports icon, stood accused of killing his attractive, blonde wife. Though everyone watched the same trial, blacks and whites reached different conclusions about the verdict and the jury's fairness. Figure 15.9 shows how sharply opinion divided along racial lines; by and large, blacks were satisfied with the judicial process and outcome, while whites mistrusted both.

At the root of such differences in opinion is **prejudice**, the tendency to evaluate others negatively simply because they are members of a certain group. Stating that women don't have the ability to hold high elected office, for example, shows a prejudice against women. Prejudice is often based on a **stereotype**, an attitude or belief about a person's gender, race, or ethnicity rather than their thoughts or behavior. The idea that African Americans are more likely than whites to be good athletes is a stereotype.

Priming and implicit memory, Chapter 10, p. 360

Stereotypical thinking often occurs unconsciously. In a clever research design reported by Wittenbrink and colleagues, researchers primed subjects by briefly flashing the words *black* and *white* on a screen before asking them to respond to target words, which were either positive or negative adjectives (Wittenbrink, Judd, & Park, 1997). Subjects' reaction times differed depending on whether they were primed with the word *black* or *white*: they responded faster to positive traits when primed with the word *white*, and to negative traits when primed with the word *black* (see Table 15.4). The subjects then filled out rating scales to indicate their level of prejudice. Not surprisingly, those who expressed racial prejudice more openly showed the greatest priming effects.

prejudice Evaluating other people negatively because they are members of a certain group.

stereotype An attitude or belief based on a person's gender, race, or ethnicity rather than on an individual's thoughts or behavior.

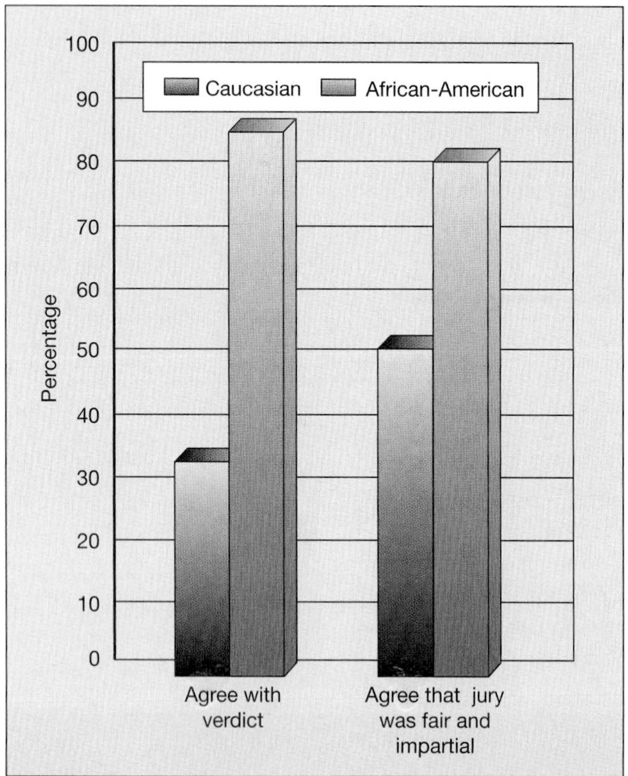

Figure 15.9 Racial Attitudes Toward the O. J. Simpson Verdict. In 1995, roughly 33 percent of white Americans and 85 percent of African Americans agreed with the verdict in the O. J. Simpson trials. A racial divide was also evident in public opinion of the jury. Eighty percent of African Americans thought the jury fair and impartial; only 50 percent of white Americans agreed. *Source:* "White vs. blacks," in *Newsweek* November 16, 1995. Copyright © 1995 by Newsweek, Inc. All rights reserved. Used by permission.

Because prejudices and stereotypes reflect the way individuals view themselves in relation to others, they are embedded in group affiliations. Around the world humans form *in-groups* to differentiate themselves from *out-groups*. All sophomores are an in-group, so are gang members, jocks, geeks, and freaks. Some anthropologists and evolutionary psychologists believe that the tendency to identify with one group rather than another is rooted in the ancient practice of kin banding together in tribes (in-groups), as well as in gender differences. This tribal tendency is similar to the organization of other primates and reflects humans' long history of living in groups of 25 to 30 people. Those who do not belong to an easily identified group are *strangers*, and most humans, including infants, are prejudiced against strangers (see page 406).

One of my favorite examples of a stereotype is based on a description of eating habits among Ethiopians (Simoons, 1982). Southern but not northern Ethiopians eat a banana-like plant called *ensete*. Northerners belittle southerners as "lowly ensete eaters." This stereotype could be founded in ancient kin groups. Not surprisingly, researchers have demonstrated that people tend to overestimate the similarity of members of their in-group, and underestimate the diversity of members of out-groups (Bothwell, Brigham, & Malpass, 1989; Ostrom & Sedikides, 1992). People of European descent, for example, discriminate facial features among whites better than facial features of other ethnic groups.

Whereas alliances and group loyalties are as adaptive today as they were in the small-group cultures of our ancestors, humans have a great propensity toward positive *in-group bias* and negative out-group stereotypes that in no way is based on kinship or kin recognition (Whitely, 1999). Fierce rivalries exist among high schools, among colleges,

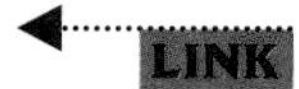

Strange situation test, Chapter 11, p. 406

Table 15.4 Assessing Racial Stereotypes Using a Priming Task

Researchers asked subjects who had been primed with the briefly flashed words, *white* or *black* to categorize these adjectives as positive or negative. White subjects who had been primed with the word *black* took longer to identify positive traits than when primed with *white*; the situation was reversed for African American subjects. Findings are evidence of unconscious racial stereotypes.

	Positive Traits	Negative Traits
Stereotypic of African Americans	Playful	Ignorant
	Sensitive	Poor
	Humorous	Dishonest
	Charming	Complaining
	Fashionable	Violent
Stereotypic of white Americans	Intelligent	Boastful
	Organized	Exploitative
	Competitive	Stubborn
	Successful	Materialistic
	Independent	Stuffy

Note: To test for implicit racial stereotypes, researchers used positive and negative trait terms that have typically been associated with white and African Americans.
Source: Wittenbrink et al., 1997.

and between gangs of unrelated individuals. Clearly prejudices and stereotyping are culturally determined and are transmitted to children through a social-learning process (Ashmore & DelBoca, 1976).

Though evidence suggests that negative racial stereotyping has been subsiding in the United States (Gaertner et al., 1999), some researchers believe that both racism (Dovidio & Gaertner, 1999) and sexism (Swim, Aikin, Hall, & Hunter, 1995) may only have become subtler. That is, whites may continue to hold negative stereotypes about African Americans, but may be more careful in expressing them. Men may continue to think a woman's place is in the home, but may no longer say so openly. And while a man might acknowledge another man's homosexuality, and even vote for him, he may not want him teaching children in a classroom. Because prejudices are highly personal and emotional, and are often reinforced by other members of an in-group, they are highly resistant to change. Think of the last time you laughed at an ethnic joke that a member of your in-group told you.

And yet because prejudices are learned, one can hope for even more substantial change than has occurred in the preceding century. Cultures are comprised of people, and the collective behavior of those people can change a culture. Most of us would agree that religious, racial, and gender prejudice is mean-spirited and diverts energy from more positive behavior. As a people, we should strive to recognize our differences, work to dispel our prejudices, and aim to raise our children in such a way that nonprejudice becomes the cultural norm. Anything less would be maladaptive.

Social learning processes, Chapter 6, p. 215, and Chapter 11, p. 397

Aggression

Whereas friendship, love, and kinship are largely adaptive, positive, and constructive in social influences, *aggression* is by definition a destructive force. Psychologists define **aggression** as physical or verbal behavior that is intended to harm another person. Aggression takes many forms, from domestic arguments to road rage to war. Recall that Freud became so disillusioned with the atrocities leading to World War II that he postulated the existence of a death force, Thanatos, one as inherent in the human condition as Eros, the life force. Today, psychologists would express this concept in terms of genetically predisposed (distally determined) aggressive impulses. But others argue that aggressive behavior is better understood as a cultural phenomenon. On the whole, for example, the U.S. culture is more violent than others that resemble it: one is 80 percent less likely to be murdered while living in Canada or Australia than in the United States (United Nations, 1997). In this section we will review evidence supporting the sociobiological and evolutionary view that genes interact with culture to produce unique instances of aggressive behavior.

Freud's Thanatos, Chapter 14, p. 500

Let's take the example of defending one's territory. Many different species claim an area within their ecological niche as their own. Presumably they are genetically predisposed to do so. As we saw in Chapter 3, ethologists like Konrad Lorenz (1966) have identified many behaviors, including aggression, that allow animals to gather and keep the resources necessary for survival, mating, reproducing, and caring for offspring. Finding, taking, and holding a territory provides the stage on which this life cycle is played out.

Instinctive behaviors, Chapter 3, p. 70

Because much animal aggression is centered on mating, the idea that natural selection predisposes animals toward aggressive behaviors is easily predicted. Male and female animals compete for mates, and patterns of sexual behavior help us understand various forms of aggressive behavior. In many different species of birds, for example, both males and females attempt to restrict sexual access to their mates by defending their territory. After the birth of offspring, many birds and mammals defend their territory (a nest, or a den) against predators. Social animals, including wolves, chimps, and humans, cooperate to guard extensive feeding areas.

Sexual patterns of behavior, Chapter 3, p. 98

aggression Physical or verbal behavior intended to harm another person.

"And now, Randy, by use of song, the male sparrow will stake out his territory ... an instinct common in the lower animals."

Such territories are not always defended with physical aggression. Many species engage in *territorial signaling*—singing birds, howling wolves, and chest-beating chimpanzees are familiar examples. Wolves and neighborhood dogs and cats use scent marking to stakeout their territory (Bradbury & Vehrencamp, 1998). Besides sounds and scent, animals may use visual displays (see the picture on page 000). Darwin postulated that threat gestures and snarling were adaptive behaviors that signaled anger. The point of territorial signaling is to *prevent,* not provoke, physically aggressive behavior (Alcock, 1998). Being injured as a result of provoking physical aggression is maladaptive. However, territorial signaling does not always work, so fighting does occur. Animals usually succeed in defending their territory, typically by fighting more viciously than intruders.

Which of these biology lessons from "other" animals in nature apply to humans living in modern cultures? Here psychologists disagree. Evolutionary psychologists think they do, and suggest that humans are territorial for the same reasons as other animals (Barkow, Cosmides, & Tooby, 1992). A saber-rattling human is engaging in territorial signaling. Most men and women of child-rearing age, they point out, attempt to restrict their mate's sexual activities, using territorial signaling and emotional displays. Both jealousy and aggression during courtship and mating are seen in arguments (territorial signaling) and physical fighting (when signaling fails). Men in many cultures and subcultures continue to think of wives as property—part of the territory they defend. Because our uniquely human behavior patterns evolved tens of thousands of years ago, problems can arise when "stone-age minds" predispose emotional behaviors at variance with contemporary culture (Barkow et al., 1992).

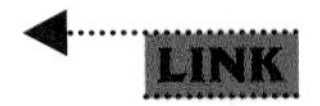

Aggressive behavior and emotion, Chapter 5, p. 172

Genes, Gender, Hormones, and Aggression. Before considering sociocultural theories of aggressive behavior, let's look at other biological evidence. Twin studies (Miles & Carey, 1997; Rowe, Almeida, & Jacobson, 1999) and the existence of gender differences (Buss & Perry, 1992; Loeber & Hay, 1997) support the idea that genes predispose a person toward aggressive behavior. Comparison studies of identical twins reared together and apart show a genetic effect on aggression (one that is considerably smaller than the effect on intelligence, however). And, as we all know from early childhood, boys' play (which includes wrestling and fighting) is more physically aggressive than girls' play. From his observations of young boys, David Geary (1999) has proposed that their play patterns reflect an evolved adaptation that prepares them for hunting and primitive warfare. Both the predisposition for this type of behavior and the play behavior itself may shape the male brain in ways that allow them to perform better than females on spatial tasks (Silverman & Phillips, 1998).

Brain plasticity, Chapter 4, p. 129

Finally, the presence of the male hormone testosterone is related to aggression. Laboratory experiments with mice and monkeys have shown that castration both lowers testosterone levels and reduces aggressive behavior. Conversely, the administration of testosterone to castrated animals and normal animals increases aggressive behavior. Furthermore, males who have been imprisoned for violent crimes, and who are more violent than others while imprisoned, have higher testosterone levels than less violent prisoners (Dabbs, Carr, Frady, & Riad, 1995).

The Environment and Aggression. Some people respond aggressively when things aren't going their way. A bad exam grade or a foul odor may elicit a curse, for example. According to a classic theory called the **frustration-aggression hypothesis**, aggression is a predictable response to frustration (Dollard, Doob, Miller, Mowrer, & Sears, 1939). This theory has been used to explain such disparate phenomena as road rage, acting out in response to pain, and rioting during a heat wave. By itself, however, the theory is not predictive of individual behavior. Many people experience daily frustrations, but few people behave aggressively in response to traffic jams.

Starting in the 1960s, Los Angeles, Miami, and other large cities in the United States periodically suffered violent rioting during the hot summer months. As Figure 15.10 shows, the correlation between heat and violence is a worldwide phenomenon. Presumably, hot weather makes people uncomfortable, and some of them behave more aggressively as a result. The relationship between heat and violence is confounded by the wide gap between the rich and poor and by single-parent families. For example, high crime rates in Houston, Texas, and the riots in Los Angeles and Miami occurred in economically poorer neighborhoods where homes and businesses were not always air-conditioned and where many single-parent families lived (Anderson & Anderson, 1984; Triandis, 1994). Heat, then, is only one variable—perhaps a minor one—among myriad factors that cause frustration and produce aggressive behavior. For this reason, as Figure 2.1 on page 36 indicates, predicting social behavior is problematic. (That is why social psychology is considered a "soft" science.)

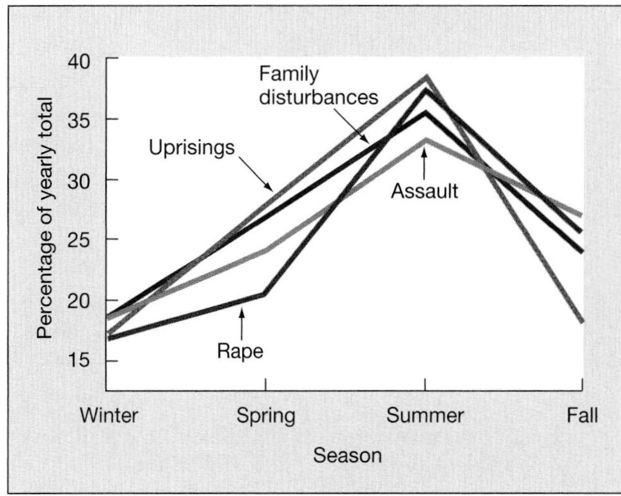

Figure 15.10 Relationship Between Heat and Violence. Higher percentages of family disturbances, rapes and other assaults, and even government coups occur more often in the summer than during other seasons, presumably because of hotter temperatures.

Hard and soft sciences, Chapter 2, p. 36

In covering the Columbine shootings, reporters noted the shooters' viewings of the movie *Natural Born Killers,* and their attraction to violent video games, suggesting that these behaviors might help to explain the tragedy. Do people actually become violent by watching violence on television or playing violent video games? This question is not easy to answer for the same reason we cannot conclude that heat causes violence. There is some correlational evidence as well as some experimental evidence to support a connection between observed violence and violent behavior, however. As we learned in Chapter 6, children model the behavior of others through observational learning (Bandura, 1971). Indeed, in his original studies, Bandura reported that children who saw a video of other children punching an inflated stand-up toy (a "Bobo doll") were more likely than others to behave in the same way when given the opportunity (see the photo on page 494). In a follow-up to Bandura's studies, children who viewed "Mighty Morphin Power Rangers" later imitated these characters' karate kicks and mimicked their violent acts during play sessions with peers (Boyatzis, Matillo, & Nesbitt, 1995).

Social-learning processes, Chapter 14, p. 494

But could watching a violent television program provoke real rather than play violence? Several investigators have reported short-term effects of television violence. Both young children (Singer & Singer, 1986) and adolescents (Wood et al., 1991) behaved more aggressively immediately after watching a violent TV program. The causes of their immediate change in behavior were probably multifactorial, including heightened arousal (which likely reduces behavioral inhibition) and desensitization from repeated viewings (Gunter & McAleer, 1990). Another study seemed to show that children who have emotional problems are harmed more than others by TV violence (Gadow & Sprafkin, 1993).

In general, however, research results have been equivocal, suggesting to some psychologists that TV violence may cause less harm than they first suspected (see McGuire, 1986, for a review). Children who have not been exposed to violent TV programs nevertheless exhibit play patterns similar to those who have. And not all

frustration-aggression hypothesis The proposal that aggression is more likely to occur when a person becomes frustrated.

children respond the same way to TV violence; more aggressive children may seek it out. Perhaps more disturbing are findings demonstrating that repeatedly viewing TV and movie violence desensitizes people to real-world violence. In one experiment, males who viewed violent movies over a 3-day period became more indifferent to shooting, stabbing, and sexual violence against women, as revealed by their expressions of sympathy for victims and their ratings of the severity of the injuries they had viewed (Mullin & Linz, 1995). Children especially may not have developed the cognitive structures needed to separate fantasy from reality.

If the effects of viewing TV violence are weak, viewing real-life violence, whether it be a drive-by shooting or domestic abuse, has an unequivocally adverse effect on children's behavior (Gunter & McAleer, 1990). Young boys who witness men physically and psychologically abusing women over many years are more likely than others to engage in similar behavior as adults. And young girls who observe such interactions tend to learn that physical and psychological abuse is "normal." Fortunately, not all role models are negative. The example of a good role model, and appropriate reinforcement of good behavior, can have an equally long-lasting effect on a child's behavior.

INTERIM SUMMARY

1. ***Prejudice*** is viewing others negatively simply because they are members of a certain group.
2. A ***stereotype*** is an attitude or belief that is based on people's gender, race, or ethnicity rather than on their thoughts or behavior. Prejudices and stereotypes are culture-specific beliefs and attitudes that are transmitted to children during their socialization.
3. Humans tend to form *in-groups* to differentiate themselves from *out-groups.*
4. People tend to develop positive *in-group biases* and negative out-group stereotypes.
5. ***Aggression*** is physical or verbal behavior that is intended to harm another person.
6. Many animals engage in *territorial signaling* to defend their territory for mating, reproductive, and feeding purposes. Territorial signaling is adaptive because it prevents potentially destructive aggressive behavior.
7. Both twin studies and differences in the way boys and girls play indicate a strong biological foundation for aggressive behavior.
8. People with higher levels of testosterone are more aggressive than those with lower levels.
9. According to the ***frustration-aggression hypothesis***, a person is more likely to become aggressive when frustrated.
10. Heat, poor economic conditions, single-parent households, and TV violence are all associated with increases in violent behavior.

For Further Thought

1. Using the principles of social psychology you have learned in this chapter, explain why I think my prejudices are less egregious than yours.
2. Which provides a better explanation for positive *in-group biases* and negative out-group stereotypes—distal or proximal causes of behavior?
3. Is an engagement or wedding ring an example of territorial signaling? Can you think of other examples?
4. What predictions might we make about the effects of global warming on social behavior?
5. Should children be prevented from watching the 70 percent of all TV programs that include violent content?

CONCLUDING THOUGHTS

In this chapter we have examined both distal and proximal influences on social interactions, the most complex of all human behaviors. People interact with each other in countless ways; perhaps in an attempt to make interactions with others more predictable, they make inferences (attributions) about other people's motives. In doing so, they too often make the fundamental attribution error—attributing someone else's behavior to personal inadequacies rather than the demands of a difficult situation. At the same time they are lenient with themselves, bragging about their successes and blaming their shortcomings on others—a tendency called the self-serving bias. Even in highly individualistic Western cultures, people tend to conform to group standards, yield to group pressure, and given the authority, abuse their power over others. On the positive side, humans form alliances, cooperate with others, and conform to group standards, contributing to the social order in the process.

Environment and learning determine people's attitudes—both how they are formed and how they are changed. Persuasive messages can change a person's attitude both directly, through the central route, and indirectly, through the peripheral route. The first message a person hears tends to be the most persuasive, a phenomenon called the primacy effect. Persuading a person to comply with a small request often helps convince the person to comply with a large request, a ploy called the foot-in-the-door technique. Behavior is not always consistent with a person's professed attitudes. To resolve the cognitive dissonance caused by contradictory thoughts, people may alter both their thoughts and their behavior.

The socialization process begins with attachment following birth and continues throughout a lifetime. Girls and boys learn gender roles appropriate to the culture in which they are born. During adolescence, social interactions are highly influenced by one's emerging sexuality. Sexual behavior and a person's sexual orientation are determined by the interaction of genetic processes, physiology, and culture. Physical attractiveness influences one's interactions with others. More attractive people have a better social life and enjoy more privileges than less attractive people.

Friendships are the most common of human interactions and are qualitatively different from the relationship between lovers. Romantic love may lead to marriage, but lasting marriages and long-term commitments are characterized more by friendship and intimacy than by passion.

Humans also form and hold destructive attitudes. Most are prejudiced and harbor stereotypes regarding gender, race, religion, ethnicity, and other means of differentiating in-groups from out-groups. While such attitudes may have been adaptive at some point in human evolution, they present a problem in a globalized, multicultural world. Like other animals, humans defend their territory, sometimes aggressively. Such behavior is adaptive and has both distal and proximal determinants. Males tend to be more aggressive than females, in part because of their higher testosterone levels. Life's frustrations can also lead to aggressive behavior: Environmental variables such as heat and poverty are correlated with increases in violence.

Few would argue with the statement that romantic love is adaptive, and few would disagree that the excessive violence expressed in Western culture is maladaptive. Men's aggressiveness against women is neither justified by their higher testosterone levels nor adequately explained by distal influences. Rather, inappropriate aggression and other maladaptive behaviors are failures in the transmission of memes that make civilized behavior possible.

KEY TERMS

aggression *537*
attitude *515*
attributions *513*
attribution theory *513*
bystander effect *525*
cognitive dissonance *518*
foot-in-the-door phenomenon *516*
frustration-aggression hypothesis *539*
fundamental attribution error *514*
gender roles *526*
prejudice *535*
self-serving bias *514*
sexual orientation *529*
social facilitation *524*
social loafing *525*
stereotype *535*

16

Health Psychology

Cultural Understandings of Health
Cross-Cultural Concepts of Health
Cross-Cultural Systems of Medicine
Interim Summary
For Further Thought

Evolutionary and Ecological Perspectives on Health
Why We Become Ill
Research on Behavioral Causes of Illness
Behavioral Causes of Heart Disease
Interim Summary
For Further Thought

Psychosomatic Disorders and Stress
Psychosomatic Disorders
Stress
Interim Summary
For Further Thought

Psychoneuroimmunology
Integrating Mind and Body
Functions of the Immune System
Conditioning of the Immune System
Medical Implications of Conditioning Experiments
Personality and the Immune System
Interim Summary
For Further Thought

Concluding Thoughts

Many years ago, when I was a senior in college, I was surprised when my best friend told me that his girlfriend was pregnant. During the next few months she became absolutely radiant. I left town before she had her baby; months later, I received a letter from my friend. "She was never really pregnant," he wrote. "It was a false pregnancy, or something like that." Apparently she had gone into labor, but after arriving at the hospital, found she had no baby to deliver.

False pregnancy, now called *pseudopregnancy*, was first described centuries ago (Cohen, 1982). It is currently defined as a condition in which a female shows signs of pregnancy, but is not really pregnant (*Tabor's Cyclopedic Medical Dictionary*, 1997). To a remarkable degree, the bodily changes of pseudopregnancy mimic those of a real pregnancy. The menstrual period stops, the breasts swell, and the woman gains weight. Often morning sickness and *pica*—an appetite for unusual foods—develop. Fluid accumulates in the abdomen, and the apparent mother-to-be may even experience sensations of fetal movement. Early pregnancy tests or physicians' diagnoses may reveal that these cases are not true pregnancies, but sometimes even the physician is fooled.

Some women continue to experience pseudopregnancy for 9 months, then enter labor "on time." Much as in a real delivery, initial slight contractions are followed by deepening, periodic contractions. The cervix begins to dilate, and the "water breaks." At the hospital, however, doctors cannot detect a fetal heartbeat. And then, climactically, comes the nonevent, creating confusion, embarrassment, and bewilderment all around. Childless, the woman responds with anger, denial, and grief.

Later in this chapter we will consider some possible causes, both physical and psychological, of pseudopregnancy. Is this condition a health issue? How this question is answered depends on one's definition of health. In contemporary Western culture, a woman who is in labor typically goes to a hospital to be delivered by a physician. But many millions of babies are borne each year by women who do not go to hospitals. Pseudopregnancy aside, having a baby may or may not be considered a medical condition.

Health psychology is the study of the relationship between one's lifestyle, thoughts, and emotions and one's physical health. As such, it is an interface between psychology and medicine (Baum, Newman, Weinman, West, & McManus, 1997; Matarazzo, 1994). Some health psychologists treat patients; others use epidemiological methods to study wellness and illness. Health psychology is closely related to the interdisciplinary field of **behavioral medicine**, which unites physicians, biomedical scientists, and behavioral scientists who study the behavioral components of chronic diseases, such as heart and lung disease (Schwartz & Weiss, 1978). The ultimate goal of behavioral medicine is to prevent or reverse disease by changing people's behavior.

We'll begin this chapter on health psychology by comparing the concepts of health and medicine in different cultures. Both good health, which is adaptive, and poor health, which is maladaptive, can be understood in terms of nature and nurture. Evolutionary processes have pitted humans and microorganisms, such as bacteria and viruses, against one another—though in some cases, we'll learn, bacteria are beneficial to humans. Evolved behaviors such as eating, sleeping, and exercising also influence a person's health, either for good or ill. Similarly, the environment can be conducive to physical and mental health (moderate temperatures, clean air and water, and pleasant people) or a source of stress (extreme temperatures, filthy living conditions, and rude, inconsiderate people). Given this perspective, illness and wellness are best understood in terms of the integration of biological, psychological, and sociocultural factors. An understanding of health as the integration of the immune system with behavior, mind, and culture should emerge.

CULTURAL UNDERSTANDINGS OF HEALTH

"¡Hola! ¿Como esta usted?"

"Hello. How are you?"

"здрáвствуйте!"

health psychology An interface between psychology and medicine, concerned with the relationship between one's lifestyle, thoughts, and emotions and one's physical health.

behavioral medicine An interdisciplinary field that unites physicians, biomedical scientists, and behavioral scientists.

Around the world, people greet each other in similar ways. (The Russian greeting, pronounced *draws-twitch-uh*, means *both hello* and *How are you*?) A friend or acquaintance who asks *How's it going*? is usually inquiring about more than your physical health. *How's it goin'?* might refer to your new job, a relationship, a recent bout of flu, your diet, an upcoming exam, or a host of other activities. Biology (genes and physiology), psychology (thoughts, emotions, and behaviors), and sociocultural factors (cultural beliefs, social support systems, access to clean water and health care, and so forth) are all important determinants of one's health and well-being.

Our personal health and that of others is never far from our consciousness. Indeed, when people are asked about its importance, they rank health higher than any other personal value (Rokeach, 1973). Ironically, we are seldom conscious of our health when we are free of pain or healthy. Only when we catch the flu, step on the scale, or grow depressed about a relationship do we become aware of our state of health.

Worldwide, health or its absence is a major concern of every person, from the cradle to the grave. Yet different cultures define health differently and address health concerns in different ways. Let's take a look at a few of those perspectives and the systems of medicine associated with them.

Cross-Cultural Concepts of Health

Throughout history, the term *health* has been defined in many ways, as Table 16.1 indicates. Yet from the beginning of recorded history, people have recognized that health involves the mind as well as the body. Early Greeks and Romans, for example, defined a healthy person—an ideal person—as *mens sana in corpore sano*—a sound mind in a sound body. In many cultures, health also involves a person's relationships with others. For thousands of years, according to the *I Ching* (Legge, 1964), the Chinese have understood health as a state of harmony with oneself and one's family, friends, and culture. Healthy people reflect and contribute to the harmony of the cosmos.

Descartes's mind-body dualism, Chapter 1, p. 6

Within an individual, the Chinese believe, harmonic balance is achieved when *yin* (the male principle) and *yang* (the female principle) are in a state of equilibrium. The energy of yin and yang, which they call *chi*, is thought to flow in channels throughout the body. In traditional Chinese medicine, both physical and

Table 16.1 Cultural Conceptions of Health, Prehistory to the Present

CULTURE	TIME PERIOD	HEALTH
Prehistoric	~10,000 BCE	Endangered by spirits that can enter the body (hypothesized)
India	from 3000 BCE	Results from the practice of *Ayurveda*, living in harmony by integrating physical healing, diet, herbs, and massage (Fabrego & Manning, 1979)
Babylonians & Assyrians	1800–700 BCE	Endangered by the gods, who send illness as a punishment
Ancient Hebrews	1000–3000 BCE	A gift from God, but illness is a punishment from God
Ancient Greeks	500 BCE	A holistic unity of body and spirit
China	from 1100 BCE	A function of patterns of *chi* energy seeking harmony and balance of yin and yang (Legge, 1964)
Roman Empire	~500 BCE–~350 AD	*Mens sana in corpore sano* (A sound mind in a sound body)
Galen in Rome	200 AD	The absence of pathogens, such as bad air or body fluids, that cause disease
Early Christians	to 600 AD	Suffering and illness are signs that one is chosen by God
Rene Descartes	1600	A condition of the mechanical body, which is separate from the mind
Central Mexico (Ladinos)	pre-1800s	*Consistencia*, the integration of biological, psychological, social, and physical variables (Collinge, 1996)
Native Americans	pre-1800s	Being in harmony with nature, and in union with the universal spirit or divine force that embraces all (Patton, 1999)
Vichow in Germany	late 1800s	Endangered by microscopic organisms that invade cells, producing disease
Sigmund Freud	late 1800s	A physical condition influenced by emotions and the mind
World Health Organization	1948	A state of complete physical, mental, and social well-being and not merely the absence of disease or infirmity

Source: Modified from Table 1.2, p. 10 from HEALTH PSYCHOLOGY: An Introduction to Behavior and Health, 4th ed. by L. Brannon & J. Feist. Copyright © 2000 Reprinted with permission of Brooks / Cole, an imprint of the Wadsworth Group, a division of Thompson Learning, Fax 800-730-2215

Table 16.2 The Biomedical and Biopsychosocial Models Compared

BIOMEDICAL MODEL	BIOPSYCHOSOCIAL MODEL
Good health = healthy body	Good health = healthy mind, healthy body, healthy social integration
Treatment: focused, physician centered	Treatment: diffuse, community centered
Goal: absence of disease	Goal: absence of disease
Method: treat symptoms of disease *Example: treat high blood pressure that results from obesity with drugs*	Method: treat causes of disease *Example: treat obesity through counseling, goal setting, education, and behavioral intervention*
Patient's role: passive subject of drug treatment and surgery	Patient's role: promote wellness through lifetime; education in schools, home, and community

psychological disorders are thought to be due to an imbalance in the flow of chi. This view provides the historical justification for the practice of placing needles on the body's surface to redirect the flow of chi, now known as acupuncture.

Table 16.1 lists some other cultural conceptions of health. Rene Descartes's conception of health as a purely physical property continues to influence contemporary Western medicine. But note the World Health Organization's definition of **health** as a state of complete physical, mental, and social well-being, not merely the absence of disease or infirmity. According to the World Health Organization, a healthy person has an adequate job and housing as well as physical integrity and psychological well-being. In fact, people's physical and mental health *are* affected by poverty and disenfranchisement. Worldwide, poor people have more morbidity (sickness) and higher mortality (death rates) than others.

This all-encompassing concept of health is an expression of the beliefs of many contemporary cultures. For example, the definitions of health espoused by the native peoples of Mexico, India, and the United States are not dissimilar (see Table 16.1). All stress the integration and harmony of body, mind, and culture.

Native-American healers promote the harmony of mind, body, and culture.

Cross-Cultural Systems of Medicine

The medical practices common to different cultures are many and varied. To alter the flow of *chi,* the traditional Chinese practitioner may use herbal and dietary prescriptions, poultices, acupuncture, acupressure (applying the finger and thumb at specific body points), and moxabustion (burning a dried herb at a specific body point) (Williams, 1996). The traditional Mexican healer may prescribe foods and herbs for physical and psychological problems, alcohol to neutralize excess emotion, and "talk therapy" to reestablish harmonious social relationships (Fabrega & Manning, 1979). In India, the Ayruvedic healer will seek to discover what has gone awry in the integration of mind, body, and culture, resulting in illness. Treatment may include herbs, ritual diets, touching and massage, and changes in sleeping and toilet habits (Collinge, 1996). Native American healers may suggest using plants with hallucinogenic properties as a way for the ailing and the healthy alike to seek unity with nature. By convention, some of these non-Western treatments are categorized as forms of *alternative medicine*, or *complementary medicine*.

In modern Western medicine, physicians generally rely on drugs such as antibiotics, surgery, and other procedures designed to correct physical ailments. In the **biomedical model**, poor health is as the result of pathogens (germs or viruses) or physical malfunction. Recently, however, physicians have begun to recognize the influence of psychological and social factors on health.

health (World Health Organization) A state of complete physical, mental, and social well-being, not merely the absence of disease or infirmity.

biomedical model A model of health care that emphasizes the use of drugs, surgery, and other procedures designed to correct physical ailments.

biopsychosocial model A model of health care that emphasizes the effect of behaviors, thoughts, feelings, and culture on a person's physical health.

In the **biopsychosocial model**, health problems are thought to be the result not just of microorganisms and failed physiology, but of an individual's behaviors, thoughts, feelings, and social relationships. The primary mode of treatment in the biopsychosocial model is the prevention of disease through education. (Table 16.2 contrasts the two models.)

The Western practitioner who endorses the biopsychosocial model typically does *not* use alternative, or complementary, techniques. Instead, a Western physician may refer a person who complains of sleep difficulties, depression, or drug abuse to a *psychotherapist* (discussed in Chapter 18, Treatment). Implicit in this diagnosis and referral is the notion that bodily ailments are separate from mental problems, a position, we'll see throughout this chapter, that is no longer tenable.

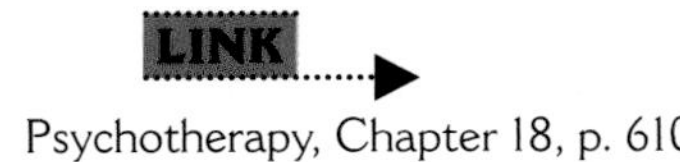

Psychotherapy, Chapter 18, p. 610

INTERIM SUMMARY

1. *Health psychology* is the study of how people's thoughts, emotions, behaviors, and lifestyles affect their physical health. Health psychologists use epidemiological methods to measure the relationship of one's behavior to one's health.
2. *Behavioral medicine* is an interdisciplinary field that integrates research efforts and treatment methods of physicians, biomedical scientists, and behavioral scientists.
3. Most people rate their health higher than any other personal value.
4. Throughout recorded history, cultures have defined health in many different ways.
5. Most definitions of health encompass the well-being of the mind, the body, and one's relations with others and with nature.
6. The World Health Organization defines *health* as a state of complete physical, mental, and social well-being, not merely the absence of disease or infirmity.
7. In this society, non-Western medicine is typically characterized as *alternative* or *complementary* medicine.
8. In the *biomedical model* of medicine, physicians treat physical illness, which they believe is caused by pathogens and physical malfunctions, by relying on drugs such as antibiotics, and surgery.
9. Besides microorganisms, physicians who subscribe to the *biopsychosocial model* emphasize the role of people's behaviors, thoughts, feelings, and social surroundings in causing and curing illness. The primary mode of treatment in this model is preventative, through education.

For Further Thought

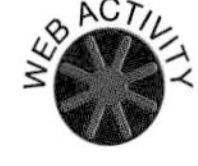

1. What do you think will happen to the biomedical model of medicine as a result of immigration to the United States? Have you personally experienced any cultural changes in health care?
2. Discuss the proposition that the World Health Organization's definition of health is as much political as it is medical.
3. Assume that physical health can be separated from mental health. From the perspective of inclusive fitness, is one more important than the other?
4. Can any nation afford to take a biopsychosocial approach to health? Can any nation afford *not* to?
5. Traditionally, Western physicians have been trained to diagnose and treat physical disorders. Should people *other* than physicians have a say in the health-care system?

EVOLUTIONARY AND ECOLOGICAL PERSPECTIVES ON HEALTH

Many of us, while suffering through a bout of the stomach flu, have found ourselves wondering "Why am I sick?" or simply "Why me?" Sickness, like pain, is a personal event with motivating properties. (*Somebody, please, do something.*) Weak, we become dependent and may seek attention from others.

Illness has many causes, from pathogens to genetic makeup and maladaptive behavioral patterns. In this section we'll examine these causes, with an emphasis on the behavioral components of illness. Then we'll apply what we have learned to a major health problem, heart disease.

Why We Become Ill

The history of Western medicine has been characterized by a search for the causes of infectious disease and effective treatments for it. The success of this enterprise can be inferred from a comparison of Figure 16.1 and Figure 16.2. Figure 16.1 shows the illnesses from which most people died at the beginning of the 20th century; Figure 16.2 shows the leading causes of death at the end of the 20th century. Notice that the leading cause of death, heart disease, did not change. But by 1996 (see Figure 16.2), the threat of infectious diseases—flu, tuberculosis, typhoid fever, diphtheria, and bacterial infections such as gastritis and colitis—had greatly diminished.

Microorganisms. In 1900, about 15 out of every 100 babies born in the United States died before their first birthday. At present, the infant mortality rate is just under 1 percent and falling. The average life span of Americans is now 75 years, compared to about 50 years at the beginning of the last century. To a large extent, these improvements in public health stem from reductions in infectious diseases.

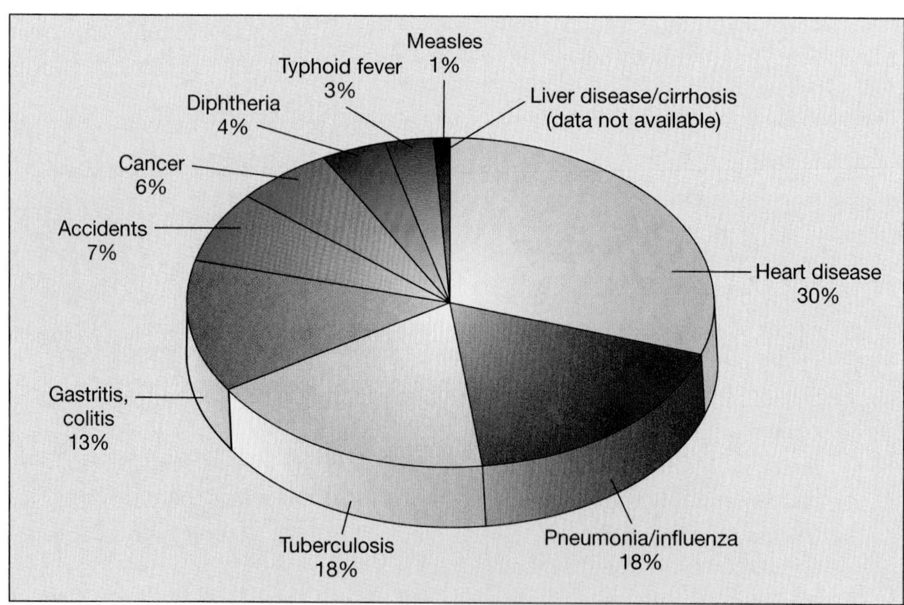

Figure 16.1 The Top 10 Causes of Death in 1900. A century ago, most people died of heart disease and infectious diseases such as pneumonia, influenza, and tuberculosis.
Source: Brannon & Feist, 1997, p. 5.

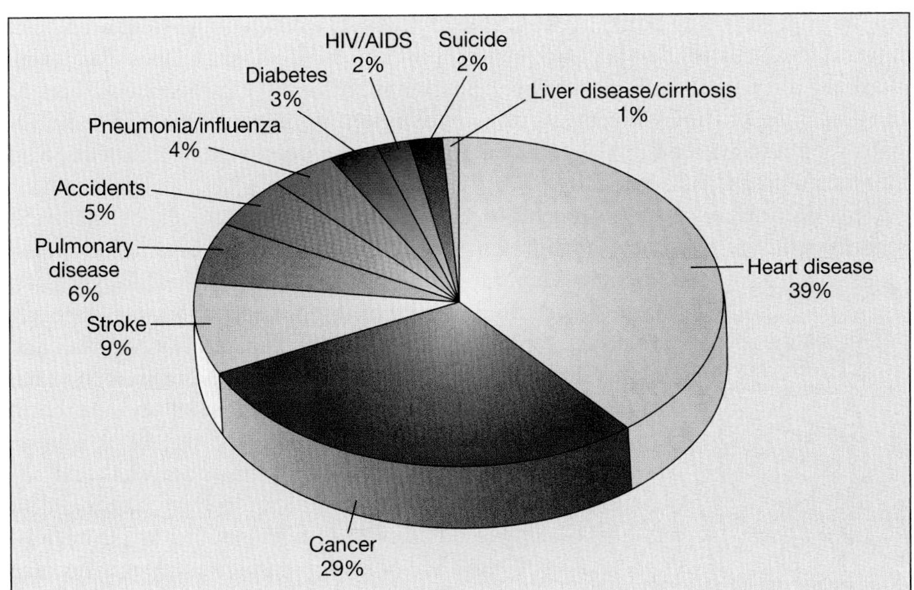

Figure 16.2 The Current Top 10 Causes of Death (in 1996). Heart disease, cancer, and stroke currently account for more than three-fourths of all deaths in the United States. *Source:* National Vital Statistics Reports, 1996.

Infectious diseases are caused by other life forms, primarily bacteria and viruses, which have evolved by natural selection (Ewald, 1980). Successful pathogens are those that have overcome selective pressures and reproduced more than their less efficient counterparts. When they invade the human body, these successful life forms threaten the lives of their hosts. One way to think about the relationship of humans and the microorganisms that cause illness, then, is in terms of survival of the fittest (Nesse & Williams, 1994). Each wants to live at the expense of the other. Unfortunately, antibiotics that are designed to kill bacteria can act as a selective pressure that hastens the evolution of drug-resistant bacteria (Gold & Moellering, 1996; Moellering, 1998).

During the 20th century, Western medicine made great progress in controlling tuberculosis bacillus, flu viruses, and other microbial life forms. Interestingly enough, most of that progress probably did *not* result from the development of antibiotics and immunizations. Rather, improvements in health over the past century are better attributed to public health measures such as sanitation and purification of the water supply (Knowles, 1977). Let's look at the evidence.

The picture on the right is a cartoonist's impression of London's water supply in the 19th century. One of the world's first medical epidemiologists, who lived in London during this period, traced the high death rate from cholera in various parts of the city to their contaminated water pumps. In the city or the country, water must be kept free of human and other animal fecal material to be safe for drinking. The cholera virus, for example, is transmitted from one human to another human via contaminated water (Knowles, 1977; Nesse & Williams, 1994). Even today, securing an adequate supply of drinking water is a problem in many areas. In Mexico City, tourists and wealthy Mexicans drink bottled water because parts of the water supply are contaminated with fecal material containing *V. Cholerae*. In a recent study, 10 percent of the city's population reported chronic diarrhea, and deaths from cholera are not uncommon there (Downs, Cifuentes-Garcia, & Suffet, 1999).

A DROP OF LONDON WATER.

The use of soap is another public health measure that has contributed to the decline in infectious disease. Soap and water has antiseptic properties, much like an alcohol swab. Recall the description of life in 18th-century Paris, in which the

The smells of 18th-century France, Chapter 7, p. 227

common person was born, lived, and died without ever bathing. When unclean fingers touched food, they frequently contaminated it with fecal material. Washing dirty food with clean water eliminates this source of disease. When, at the beginning of the 20th century, physicians began to routinely wash their hands with soap and water before performing surgery, the percentage of patients who survived increased dramatically.

Significantly, the development of effective antibiotics and other high-tech medical practices *followed* advances in public health, such as disinfected water, and contributed far less to improvements in health (Knowles, 1977). Figure 16.3 shows cases of measles, scarlet fever, tuberculosis, typhoid, pneumonia, influenza, diphtheria, and poliomyelitis from 1900 to about 1970. Note that for each disease, high-tech medicine provided a small benefit compared to advances achieved through the use of soap and water. Since 1970, public health measures, antiviral and antibacterial research, and public education have continued to diminish the impact of microbes on human health. Ironically, in parts of the United States, water supplies have now become contaminated with the byproducts of disinfectants. Today, public health officials must balance the need to control microbial pathogens with the need to reduce levels of cancer-causing byproducts of the disinfectants (Boorman et al., 1999).

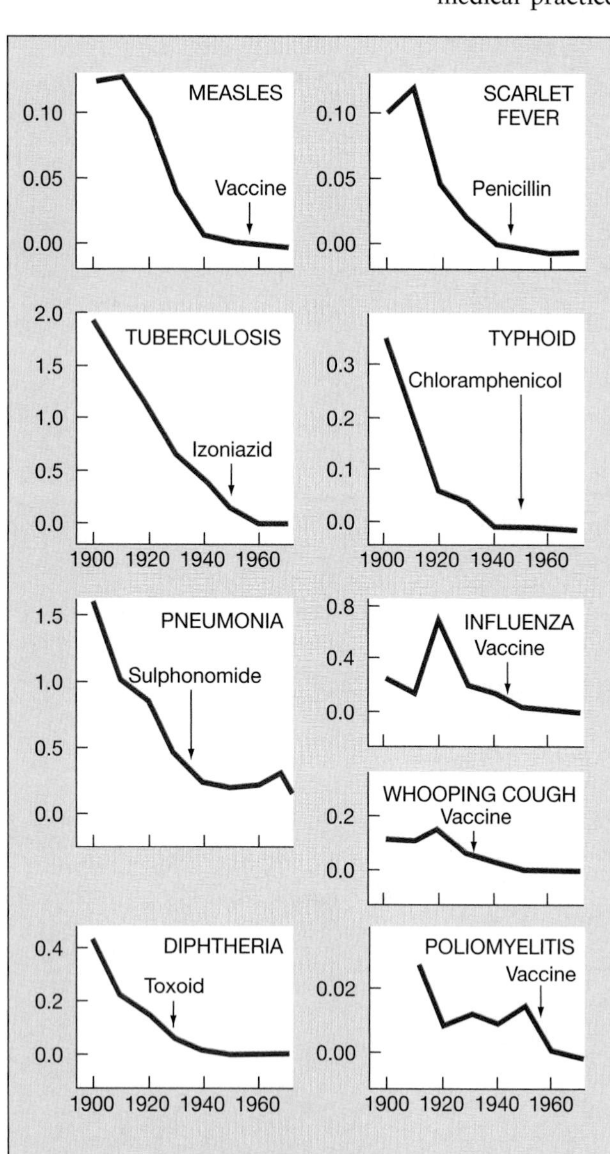

Figure 16.3 Public Health Measures Versus High-Tech Medicine. From 1900 to 1970, the death rate from eight infectious diseases diminished markedly. Most of these reductions came from improvements in public health—mainly clean water—rather than from drug interventions such as antibiotics and vaccines. (The arrows indicate the introduction of specific drug treatments.) *Source:* Graphs from "The Questionable Contribution of Medical Measure to the Decline of Mortality in the US in the Twentieth Century" in *Millbank Memorial Fund Quarterly–Health and Society,* (1977), 55, pp. 405–428. Copyright © 1977 by Blackwell Publishers. Reprinted by permission.

Genetic Causes. On the surface, human susceptibility to microbial disease does not seem like an evolutionary success story. Because suffering seems maladaptive, we wonder why evolutionary processes didn't prepare us to live healthier lives. Two scientists who study disease from an evolutionary perspective frame the question in this way:

> Why, in a body of such exquisite design, are there a thousand flaws and frailties that make us vulnerable to disease? If evolution by natural selection can shape sophisticated mechanisms such as the eye, heart, and brain, why hasn't it shaped ways to prevent nearsightedness, heart attacks, and Alzheimer's disease? (Nesse & Williams, 1994, p. 3)

These are daunting questions, and Darwinian answers are controversial (Berlim & Abeche, 2001; Nesse & Williams, 1994). Darwinian theorists suggest that the diseases to which we are susceptible have evolutionary, and hence genetic, causes. Such thinking is already familiar to us. For example, we encountered in Chapter 7 the proposal that pain is adaptive, because it motivates us to change what we are doing. Likewise, some scientists have argued that fever is adaptive, because a higher body temperature provides a less optimal breeding ground for bacteria. Because bacteria thrive in warm, moist tropical climes, the people who live there would benefit most from such a mechanism. In fact, researchers recently found that the genes involved in the fever response are more prevalent in populations of tropical ancestry than in populations from temperate regions (Le Souef, Goldblatt, & Lynch, 2000).

Serious infectious diseases likely developed through the coevolution of microbes with humans and other animals. When humans domesticated animals about 10 thousand years ago, they began living in close proximity with them, which facilitated the transmission of the microbes these animals carried (Diamond, 1999). A number of those microbes are responsible for the infectious diseases that periodically sweep through densely populated areas. Measles, tuberculosis, and smallpox, for example, are likely caused by microorganisms that were originally carried by cattle, while flu probably comes from microbes carried by pigs and ducks (Diamond, 1999).

In some cases, genes actually cause disease. A Darwinian explanation for this apparent oxymoron is that such genes must also provide some kind of selective advantage. In other words, one genetically based disease may offer protection against another, more deadly condition. Genes that have more than one effect are called *pleiotropic* genes.

Hemoglobin and sickle-cell anemia, Chapter 3, p. 83

A classic example of a genetically caused disease is sickle-cell anemia. As described in Chapter 3 (see page 83), sickle-cell anemia is a disorder that impedes the pick-up and release of oxygen by the hemoglobin molecules in red blood cells. But while sickled red blood cells (so-called because of their crescent shape) cause illness, they also provide protection against malaria during childhood. Because children with sickled cells survive malaria long enough to reproduce, they pass the defective gene on to the next generation. (This thinking follows the insight of J. B. S. Haldane, who in 1942 was among the first to realize that there would be no selection against genes whose effects occurred *after* an animal had reproduced.) In contrast, children who *don't* have sickled cells die more often of malaria, before they have had a chance to reproduce. The genes that code for sickled cells remain in the gene pool, then, even though they are deadly. Another example of pleiotropic genes are those that promote calcium metabolism, allowing broken bones to heal more quickly, while at the same time promoting calcium deposits in the arteries ("hardening of the arteries") (Nesse & Williams, 1994).

Behavioral Causes. Some diseases occur because we stress our bodies; we can think of these as ecological diseases. For example, the stress put on the eyeballs due to excessive reading and other "close work," and the stress put on the heart by a fatty diet and lack of exercise, are ecologically induced maladies. Dental caries (due to excessive sugar consumption) and tennis elbow are other common examples. Note that a person's behavior is an integral part of these maladies. Although such behaviors are not transmitted from one generation to the next by genes, they can be passed on as memes. Figure 16.2 shows the major killers of people living in the United States today. Note that so-called *lifestyle variables*, as opposed to disease-causing microorganisms, are now heavily implicated in early mortality. Behaviors that contribute to early mortality (often referred to as *noncommunicable disorders*) include smoking, which can cause cancer and cardiovascular disease; overeating and lack of exercise, which produce obesity and cardiovascular disease; and excessive consumption of alcohol, which impairs both driving ability and the normal functioning of the heart and liver.

The role of memes in behavior, Chapter 6, p. 187

While young people die from different causes than older people, they too suffer from maladaptive behaviors. Figure 16.4 shows the top 10 causes of death for young Americans between the ages of 15 and 24. Car accidents alone are responsible for about 38 percent of all deaths. In half of these fatalities, driving after drinking excessive amounts of alcohol was a factor (Hunt, 1993). Alcohol acts on the amygdala, reducing sensory-motor functioning and the ability to judge spatial relationships and monitor speed (Mathews, Best, White, Vandergriff, & Simson, 1996). Emotional problems and impaired judgment also contribute to accidents, as well as to homicide and suicide. Together, these three causes are responsible for 76 percent of all deaths among young people.

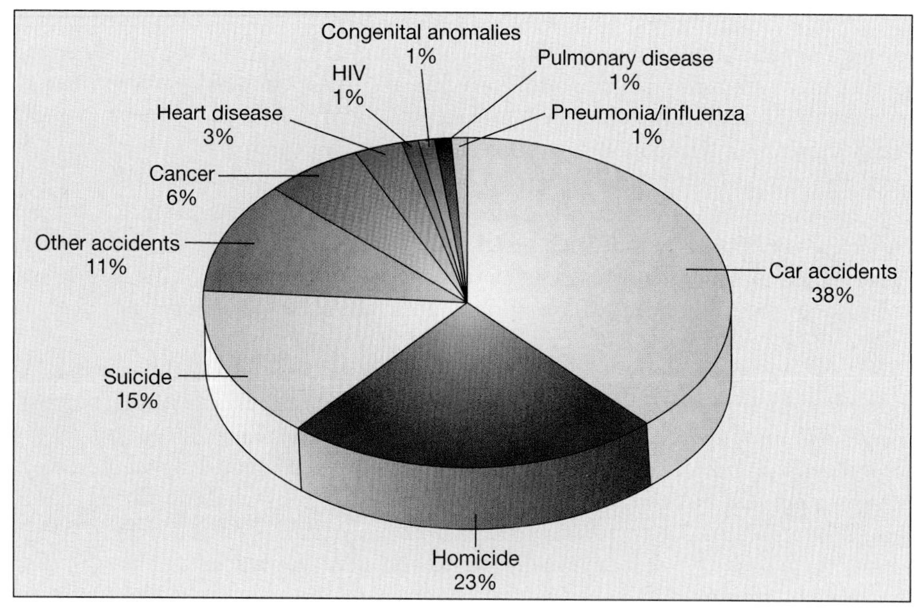

Figure 16.4 Top 10 Causes of Death in the United States, Ages 15 to 24. In the United States, young people die from accidents, homicide, and suicide. *Source:* National Vital Statistics Reports, 1996.

Research on Behavioral Causes of Illness

Epidemiological methods, Chapter 2, p. 53

To investigate the role of behavior in illness, health psychologists generally use epidemiological methods. Recall from Chapter 2 that in epidemiological research, correlational techniques are used to establish relationships between behavior and health. Using this method, researchers can identify certain factors that put one's health at risk. A number of studies have provided data to account for the major causes of death in the 1990s, shown in Figure 16.2. They have implicated lifestyle factors in both morbidity and mortality.

The Role of Lifestyle Factors. One example of a large-scale, ongoing investigation of the role of health habits in both morbidity and mortality is the Alameda County Study. Beginning in 1965, about 7,000 subjects over the age of 20 responded to detailed questionnaires about their health habits (Belloc & Breslow, 1972). They were asked initially about their disabilities and illnesses, as well as seven basic health practices, only one of which, smoking, was thought to be correlated with poor health at the time:

1. Do you get 7–8 hours of sleep daily?
2. Do you eat breakfast every day?
3. Do you rarely snack between meals?
4. Do you drink alcohol moderately or not at all?
5. Do you smoke cigarettes?
6. Do you exercise regularly?
7. Do you maintain your weight within an acceptable range?

The first results of this study were published several years later. After controlling for degrees of initial illness, researchers discovered that fewer of the people who practiced six of the seven habits had died compared with those who practiced three or less (Belloc, 1973). In fact, health habits turned out to be a better predictor of mortality than income level.

In a follow-up study conducted 9 years later, researchers asked some additional questions to clarify the role of behavior in health (Berkman & Breslow, 1983). They found that eating breakfast and snacking between meals were unrelated to

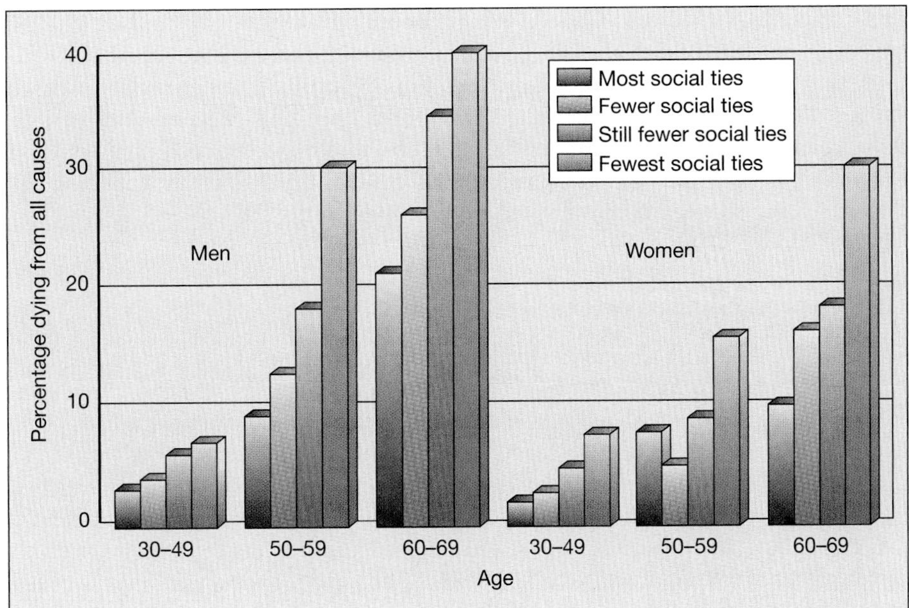

Figure 16.5 Social Connections and Life Expectancy. From age 50 to 70, both men and women remain healthier if they belong to a social network of family and friends. Men who have few social ties are more likely to die than women with few social ties.

mortality; sleep time and obesity were only weakly related. Three noncommunicable disorders *were* correlated with death, however: smoking, excessive drinking, and lack of exercise.

Working with a subset of the original participants, investigators identified those individuals whose health had changed for better or for worse in the intervening years. After computing the correlations between those health changes and individual lifestyles, they found that moderate exercise improves health; that people who smoke have more health problems than nonsmokers; that both too little and *too much* sleep is associated with poorer health; and that people who are either 30 percent overweight or 10 percent underweight are less healthy than those of moderate weight (Camacho & Wiley, 1983; Wiley & Camacho, 1980). Surprisingly, moderate drinking—one or two drinks daily—was associated with lower morbidity and mortality rates than total abstinence. This finding has been replicated for both men (Rimm et al., 1991) and women (Fuchs et al., 1995). On the basis of this evidence, some physicians now advise those who suffer from heart disease, as well as those who desire to prevent it, to imbibe one or two drinks per day.

Social Isolation and Mortality. One highly intriguing finding that emerged from the Alameda County study concerns the effect of social isolation. As Figure 16.5 shows, participants who did not have supportive networks of family and friends died at a rate 2.5 times greater than those who did. The effect of social isolation was more fatal for men than for women (Berkman & Syme, 1979). A follow-up study done in Finland showed an even larger gender effect: isolation had no effect on women's mortality, but it raised men's risk of early death 1.5 to 2.0 times (Kaplan et al., 1988). One researcher has suggested that women typically have larger social networks than men, and more intimate friendships, which may help them to cope with isolation (Argyle, 1999). For whatever reason, women seem to do better than men at living alone.

Gender differences aside, why does social isolation raise the risk of early death? One possibility is that men and women with few social ties may not be touched very often. Touch is important in traditional Chinese and Ayurvedic medicine. It is also important in the processes of childhood attachment and contact comfort, and later in courting and mating. Studies have shown that touching

Role of touch in attachment, contact comfort, Chapter 11, p. 405

and massaging a prematurely born infant encourages weight gain and neurological development (Field et al., 1986). In fact, touching and being touched likely affects brain development throughout life. Certainly touch is beneficial to other species. Petting a dog, for example, lowers both its blood pressure and the petter's (Vormbrock & Grossberg, 1988). Touching and being touched, then, is good for one's physical, mental, and sociocultural health. Unfortunately, touching decreases as social contacts diminish among the elderly.

Role of touch in adaptive social behavior, Chapter 3, p. 93

Behavioral Causes of Heart Disease

Together, the Alameda County Study and another epidemiological study named the Framingham Heart Study (Dawber, 1980) uncovered the lifestyle factors that contribute to heart disease. All over the world, a higher percentage of people die of cardiovascular disease (CVD, or heart disease) than from any other cause. In industrialized countries, heart disease claims one of every two lives, killing nearly a million people each year in the United States alone (American Heart Association, 1999). Because these statistics are based on the causes of death written on death certificates, the source of almost all epidemiological data, they mask the role of behavioral factors in mortality. "Heart failure" is commonly assigned as a general cause of death. "Obesity" does not usually appear on a death certificate, even if a person's death could logically be attributed to being grossly overweight.

The main categories of cardiovascular disease are coronary heart disease (CHD, or heart attacks), hypertension (high blood pressure), rheumatic fever (an infectious disease), and cerebrovascular disease (stroke). Risk factors for CVD include a family history of heart disease, physiological conditions such as hypertension and blocked arteries, and lifestyle factors such as drinking, smoking, overeating, and lack of exercise. With some exceptions, heart disease occurs in middle age for men and old age for both men and women. Its severity is determined by the interaction of poorly understood genetic factors and lifestyle.

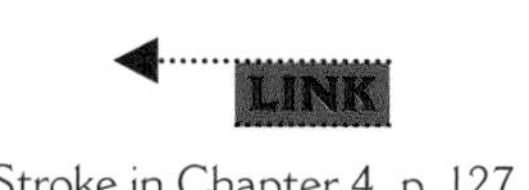

Stroke in Chapter 4, p. 127

Heart disease is related to hyperlipidemia, an unhealthy condition in which lipids (fats) are found in high numbers in the bloodstream. There are two basic types of lipids, low-density lipid-protein structures (LDL) and high-density lipoproteins (HDL). Both LDL and HDL carry cholesterol, a substance used to form cell membranes and hormones. High levels of LDL can build up plaque on the inner surfaces of the arteries. In contrast, high levels of HDL do not cause plaque. For this reason, HDL is sometimes referred to as "good cholesterol" and LDL as "bad cholesterol."

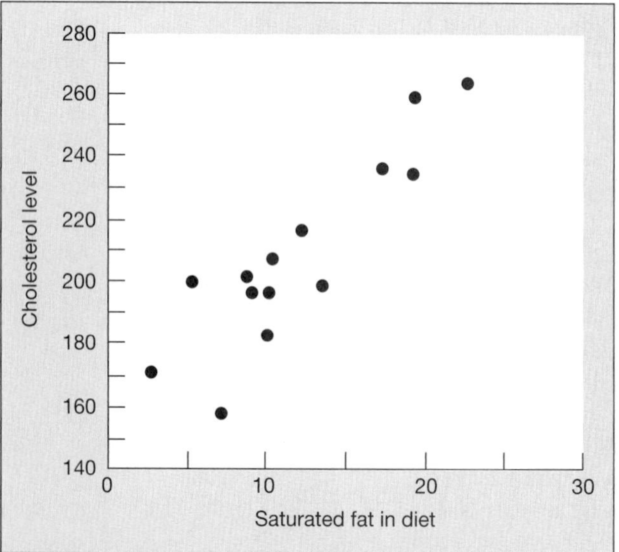

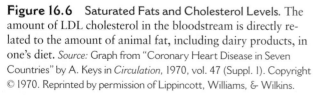

Figure 16.6 Saturated Fats and Cholesterol Levels. The amount of LDL cholesterol in the bloodstream is directly related to the amount of animal fat, including dairy products, in one's diet. *Source:* Graph from "Coronary Heart Disease in Seven Countries" by A. Keys in *Circulation,* 1970, vol. 47 (Suppl. 1). Copyright © 1970. Reprinted by permission of Lippincott, Williams, & Wilkins.

Arterial plaque can have two major effects. First, it narrows the arteries, raising a person's blood pressure (hypertension). Second, if the plaque grows large enough it can block the passage of blood through an artery, interrupting the flow of oxygen to the heart, brain, or other organs. Cells die when they are deprived of oxygen. If enough heart cells die, a person may suffer a myocardial infarction (MI), better known as a heart attack. In the brain, dying cells can cause a stroke.

Moderate exercise and moderate alcohol intake (one to two drinks daily) increase levels of good cholesterol (HDL). Among adults, alcohol alone provides a 30 to 50 percent reduction in heart disease (Gaziano et al., 1993). Lack of exercise and the consumption of excessive amounts of cholesterol, found in animal fats and dairy products, will increase bad cholesterol (LDL) levels (see Figure 16.6). Smoking has been found to decrease levels of good cholesterol (American Heart Association, 1999). All these and other problems are related to obesity, which raises blood pressure as much as three times the normal level. Obesity can also lead to congestive heart failure, primarily because of changes in the muscles of the ventricular walls. A postmortem on 22 patients with severe obesity found fatal heart damage in all of them (Duflou et al., 1995).

Obesity. Obesity is the condition of being overweight. There is no agreed-upon operational definition of obesity, but Table 16.3 shows a portion of the body mass index (BMI), which provides a general guide to obesity based on height and weight. For example, someone who is 5 feet 4 inches tall (64 inches) and weighs 145 pounds would have a BMI of 25 and an obesity grade of 1. BMIs of 25–29, 30–39, and 40 and above correspond to grades 1, 2, and 3 obesity, respectively. Lower BMIs are associated with better-than-normal health (19–20 is considered optimal); higher BMIs with sickness and a shorter-than-normal lifetime.

No one knows for sure why some people become obese; it mainly occurs in individuals who are genetically predisposed to gain weight, and who combine unhealthy eating with a sedentary way of life (WHO, 1999). Simply put, when the intake of energy exceeds the expenditure of energy, the excess is stored in adipose tissue, in the form of body fat. Because people who live in developed countries consume more calories and expend less energy, they tend to be more obese than people from third-world countries. Up to 40 percent of African American women in the United States, for example, are grade 2 obese, compared with only 12 percent of Congolese women (American Heart Association, 1999). About 20 percent of Europeans and white Americans between the ages of 20 and 60 are grade 2 obese.

The genetic mechanisms involved in obesity are largely unknown, but most likely the effects are polygenic. In Chapter 3, we saw how the *Ob* gene causes

Table 16.3 Body Mass Index (BMI) Calculation

HEIGHT (INCHES)	BODY WEIGHT (LBS.)			
58	96	119	143	191
59	99	124	148	198
60	102	128	153	204
61	106	132	158	211
62	109	136	164	218
63	113	141	169	225
64	116	145	174	232
65	120	150	180	240
66	124	155	186	247
67	127	159	191	255
68	131	164	197	262
69	135	169	203	270
70	139	174	207	278
71	143	179	215	286
72	147	184	221	294
73	151	189	227	302
74	155	194	233	311
75	160	200	240	319
76	164	205	246	328
Body Mass Index (BMI) (kg/m2)	20	25	30	40

To compute your body mass index (BMI), find your height (in inches) in the left-hand column, then read across the four columns to the right to find the number closest to your weight. Your BMI is the number beneath that column. (This table includes only BMIs of 20, 25, 30, and 40; for the complete table, see http://www.niddk.nih.gov/health/nutrit/pubs/table.htm.)

Source: Adapted from "Obesity: Part 1: Pathogenesis" by G. Bray & D. S. Gray in *Western Journal of Medicine*. (1988), vol. 149, pp. 429–441.

Ob genes, Chapter 3, p. 87

Hypothalamic control of eating and drinking, Chapter 4, p. 163

Homeostasis and set point, Chapter 5, p. 152

Taste receptors, Chapter 8, p. 258

mice to overeat when the food supply is plentiful. In a study of identical and fraternal twins (Stunkard, Harris, Pederson, & McLearn, 1990), the BMIs of identical twins had a correlation of greater than 0.70, while the BMIs of fraternal twins correlate 0.25 to 0.30.

Throughout human history, overeating was probably adaptive. Genes responsible for overeating and for converting excess calories to fat during times of plenty would have been favored by natural selection, because individuals who could live off their own fat during times of famine would have survived others. The evidence for this view can be seen in receptors sensitive to sweet and fat; in neural mechanisms that allow for pleasure in eating; in mechanisms for insulin regulation; in the ventromedial nucleus of the hypothalamus, which is involved in food regulation; and in the existence of a *set point*—a genetically determined point of stability in one's body weight. All these features of the human body have been discussed in previous chapters.

A preoccupation with obesity can cause other health concerns, including anorexia nervosa and bulimia, discussed in the next two chapters. Here we will restrict our discussion to those individuals who have reached grade 2 obesity, and who can achieve more optimal health and live longer if they lose weight. As most of us know, losing weight is one thing; keeping it off is another. That is, one's set point can be raised seemingly without effort, but lowering it is vexing (Keesey & Powley, 1986). Temporary dieting doesn't work; repeated attempts to lose weight may lead to *weight cycling*, which in itself may be associated with adverse health consequences. Other than surgery (Matts et al., 1995), permanent changes in dietary patterns and exercise are the only way to lose weight for good.

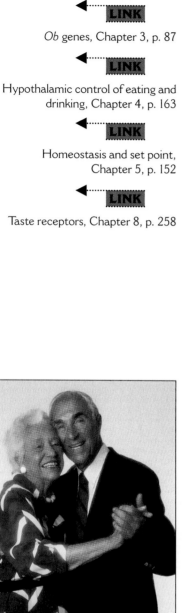

The pleasure of dancing combines intimacy, therapeutic touch, and low-level exercise.

Lack of Exercise. An important contribution to obesity is lack of exercise. People become overweight not just because they eat too much but because they exercise too little. Hunter-gathers are not obese. Perhaps in response to the lack of energy expenditure in modern life, about 7 of every 10 adults in the United States take part in some type of physical recreation (Siegel, Brackbill, & Heath, 1995).

Of the many different types of exercise, only one contributes to cardiorespiratory health. Contrary to common belief, the beneficial effect of **aerobic exercise**—physical activity that increases oxygen consumption for an extended period—is *not* the burnoff of excess calories. Aerobic exercise *does* require calories, but 60 to 75 percent of the caloric expenditure occurs after a run or step-dancing session. In the period immediately after aerobic exercise, the basal metabolism rate—the amount of energy required to maintain the body at rest—increases greatly. The exercise itself consumes about 15 to 30 percent of the total caloric expenditure, while the extended cool-down period consumes 60 to 75 percent (Poehlman, 1989). To get the maximum benefit, the heart rate must be elevated for 12 to 30 minutes—an effect that can be achieved by running 3 miles a day 3 times a week (Cooper 1968, 1985).

Table 16.4 shows the number of METs—the amount of oxygen used per kilogram of body weight per minute—associated with different kinds of exercise. Slow dancing requires 2.9 METs; jogging a 10-minute mile for several miles requires 10.2 METs. The more vigorous the exercise, the higher the MET value and the amount of energy expended.

The benefits of exercise are well worth it. Middle-aged men who exercise aerobically and work to maintain their physical fitness have about one-third the likelihood of suffering a fatal heart attack as other men, whether they live in Norway (Sandivk et al., 1993) or Dallas (Blair et al., 1995). Part of the reason has to do with body weight. Sedentary men who watch a lot of TV are 50 percent more likely to be overweight than men who engage in more active behaviors. Snacking is far easier to do while watching TV than while jogging

aerobic exercise Physical activity that increases oxygen consumption for an extended period.

Table 16.4 Estimated Energy Requirements of Various Activities

MILD EXERCISE	(METs)*	MODERATE EXERCISE	(METs)	VIGOROUS EXERCISE	(METs)
Playing piano	2.3	Cycling (leisurely)	3.5	Playing badminton	5.5
Walking	2.3	Playing drums	3.8	Dancing (fast)	5.5
Playing billiards	2.4	Doing calisthenics	4.0	Cycling (moderately)	5.7
Dancing (slow)	2.9	Swimming (slow)	4.5	Climbing hills	6.9
				Jogging (10-min mile)	10.2

*1 MET = resting metabolism oxygen uptake (= 3.5mL · kg^{-1} · min^{-1} oxygen uptake). Values are expressed as milliliters per kilogram per minute.
Source: Adapted from American Heart Association, 1999, Table 10, Exercise Standards. Copyright © 1999. Reprinted by permission of Lippincott, Williams, & Wilkins.

(Ching et al., 1996). Those who exercise aerobically also have increased HDL and reduced LDL levels, both factors in reduced heart disease (Slyper, 1994). People who exercise regularly also report feeling better. Finally, let's not forget the mouse research that shows that exercise enhances neurogenesis—neuron regeneration and growth.

Neurogenesis, Chapter 4, p. 129

INTERIM SUMMARY

1. Infectious diseases such as flu, tuberculosis, typhoid fever, and diphtheria caused most deaths in 1900, but relatively few deaths by the end of the 20th century.
2. In the late 1990s, heart disease, cancer, and stroke accounted for about 80 percent of the deaths in the United States.
3. Bacteria and viruses are life forms that use humans and other animals as hosts. Antibiotics provide a selective pressure that hastens the evolution of bacteria.
4. Long before the introduction of antibiotics and vaccines, clean water, soap, and other low-tech ecological measures helped to control infectious diseases.
5. Some pain and sickness is adaptive because it motivates a person to change unhealthy habits.
6. Although genes transmit some illness and disease, a person's behavior also plays a role in illness and pain. Lifestyles that promote both illness and wellness can be transmitted to the next generation through memes.
7. Sickle-cell anemia is an example of a disease transmitted genetically. It remains in the gene pool because it provides a selective advantage against malaria during childhood.
8. Smoking, overeating, underexercising, and chronic, excessive drinking are lifestyles that contribute to an early death.
9. Cardiovascular disease (CVD) includes heart attacks (CHD), rheumatic fever, and cerebrovascular disease (stroke). In industrialized countries, heart disease is responsible for half of all deaths.
10. Hyperlipidemia, or high levels of lipids in the bloodstream, is a major contributor to heart disease. High levels of so-called bad cholesterol, or low-density lipid-protein (LDL), are particularly associated with heart disease. High-density lipoproteins (HDL), sometimes called good cholesterol, protect against heart disease.
11. Smoking and eating a diet that is high in animal fats increases LDL levels. Reduced intake of fats, moderate consumption of alcohol, and exercise decrease LDL and increase HDL levels.
12. Obesity elevates blood pressure and damages heart muscles. Obesity can be measured by computing the body mass index, or BMI.

13. High BMIs—grade 2 obesity and above—are correlated with heart disease and increased risk for other noncommunicable diseases.
14. Obesity is caused by many factors, including a genetic predisposition to gain weight. Such a predisposition is adaptive during times of famine, but not in underactive adults overeating high-calorie foods.
15. *Aerobic exercise* contributes to cardio-respiratory health. The energy expenditure during and after exercise helps to balance the energy intake from eating.
16. Caloric expenditure is measured in terms of oxygen utilization during exercise (METS). Different activities have different exercise values. Both climbing and jogging have high exercise value.
17. Moderate exercise reduces the risk of heart attack.

For Further Thought

1. Is the water you drink on a daily basis safe? Are you sure?
2. Why is cleanliness next to godliness?
3. Are nonhuman animals clean, even though they don't use soap?
4. Would the world be a better place if fruits and grains didn't ferment?
5. Even though moderate alcohol use (one or two drinks daily) is correlated with increases in HDL (good cholesterol) levels and with a 30 to 50 percent reduction in heart disease, some health researchers (Kaplan, Strawbridge, Cohen, & Hungerford, 1996) advise doctors against prescribing it. They argue that the potential for alcohol abuse is greater than the benefits of moderate use. Do you agree?
6. Conduct a cost-benefit analysis of situating a parking facility as close as possible to the building it serves.

PSYCHOSOMATIC DISORDERS AND STRESS

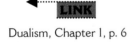

Dualism, Chapter 1, p. 6

The use of dualistic language in discussion of health is difficult to escape. Consider, for example, the existence of a National Institute of Mental Health (NIMH) within the National Institutes of Health (NIH). Although a depressed person may have physical maladies, mental disorders seem qualitatively different from physical disorders. And what about behavior? Is it mental, physical, or both? Psychosomatic disorders suggest there is a strong mind-body connection.

Glove anesthesia and hysteria, Chapter 14, p. 496

Somatoform disorders, Chapter 17, p. 589

psychosomatic disorder A disorder in which thoughts and emotions (the *psyche*) have an adverse effect on the body (the *soma*).

Psychosomatic Disorders

That the mind and body interact is well established. Blushing in response to a dirty joke (body reacting to mind) is one example. The idea that the mind can actually cause a bodily disorder is a part of many traditional belief systems (see Table 16.1). Psychologists have long recognized the mind's power over the body, and the disorders it can cause. A **psychosomatic disorder** is one in which a person's thoughts and emotions (the *psyche*) adversely affect the body (the *soma*). Charcot's glove anesthesia (discussed in Chapter 14, on page 496) is one example of a psychosomatic disorder. As we'll see in the next chapter, psychologically induced physical illnesses are now called *psychophysiological* disorders. Let's consider two disorders: one, pseudopregnancy, whose status as a psychophysiological disorder is unclear, and another, voodoo deaths, that is clearly psychophysiological.

Pseudopregnancy. Why some women experience pseudopregnancy is not known. Although psychological factors—emotions and belief systems—have been implicated (Cohen, 1982; Persinger, 1996), no single psychological pattern characterizes the women who experience this disorder (Miller, 1993). Pseudopregnancy may instead be the aftermath of an early spontaneous abortion, of which a woman is unaware. Only about 20 percent of all women who become pregnant carry the fetus to term. The other 80 percent experience the physiological changes associated with the early stages of pregnancy before they miscarry. Pseudopregnancy may be the result of a physiological process initiated by fertilization but interrupted by an unsuccessful implantation.

This explanation suggests that pseudopregnancy may be relatively normal. In fact, it is common in house pets. Female cats and dogs frequently swell and begin nesting in preparation for a new litter. Scientists have studied the hormonal changes that occur in laboratory mice and rats made pseudopregnant by cervical stimulation (DeFeo, 1966; Terkel, 1988). The evidence from these nonhuman animal experiments suggests that a woman's emotions and beliefs may play a role in whether she becomes pregnant and remains so, with or without a fetus. So if pregnancies, spontaneous abortions, and births are normal, perhaps pseudopregnancy should be thought of not as a disorder but as a statistically unusual natural event.

Voodoo Deaths. Ironically, one of the fathers of Western medicine, Walter B. Cannon, was one of the first people to recognize the importance of psychosomatic disorders (Cannon, 1942). Cannon described the phenomenon of voodoo deaths, in which a person's belief system can lead to an early and unexpected demise. This extreme example of the mind's effect on the body was later investigated in the laboratory by the Johns Hopkins psychobiologist Curt Richter (1957). In an article titled "On the phenomenon of sudden death in animals and man," Richter reported that rats that were placed in a "hopeless" situation unexpectedly died an untimely death. He cited these observations made by an anthropologist in the 1920s:

> A Brazilian Indian condemned and sentenced by a so-called medicine man is helpless against his own emotional response to this pronouncement—and dies within hours. In Africa a young Negro unknowingly eats the inviolably banned wild hen. On discovery of his "crime" he trembles, is overcome by fear and dies in twenty-four hours. In New Zealand a Maori woman eats fruit that she only later learns has come from a taboo place. Her chief has been profaned. By noon the next day she is dead. (Richter, 1957, p. 191)

Stress

Besides causing psychophysiological disorders, psychological stress is a major contributor to chronic illnesses. The term *stress* has been defined in many ways, sometimes with reference to *events* or to a person's *appraisal* of those events, and sometimes with reference to the relationship between events and their appraisal (Lazarus & Folkman, 1984). We will define **stress** as the perception that environmental elements or events may overwhelm one's ability to deal with them.

The General Adaptation Syndrome. Hans Selye, a physician at McGill University, coined the term *stress*. Selye was searching for common physiological responses among patients (and research animals) who had suffered different kinds of physical injury. When he exposed lab rats to heat or cold, X rays, mild electric shock, and other aversive events, he observed similar physiological patterns (Selye, 1956, 1973). The same was true of his clinical subjects: Whether they were recovering from injuries, illness, anesthesia, or surgery, they presented

stress The perception that events are beyond one's ability to deal with them.

Hans Selye

with the same general physiological responses. Selye labeled the injurious stimuli *stressors*, and the response to them, *stress*.

Selye found that the stress response had three stages: *alarm*, *resistance*, and *exhaustion*. He called this three-stage pattern the **general adaptation syndrome**. In the first stage, alarm, the sympathetic nervous system reacts to the stressor—for example, engine noise at an airport—by increasing the flow of ACTH (adrenocorticotropic hormone). ACTH prompts the adrenal gland to produce the hormone adrenaline, which prepares the body for *fight or flight*; it also triggers the secretion of corticosteroids (including cortisol), which mobilize the body by increasing its access to energy stores. This alarm response is adaptive, because it motivates the person to act in response to the stressful situation—for example, by wearing earplugs to dampen the sound of noisy engines.

The second stage of the general adaptation syndrome, resistance, occurs only in response to repeated exposure to a stressor. Were the engine noise to persist, the body would begin to adjust to it homeostatically. The sympathetic response would be counteracted by parasympathetic activity, though the adrenaline level would remain higher than normal. Behaviorally, the person might temporarily adjust to the noise, but would become sensitized to further events. In the final stage, exhaustion, unrelieved stress compromises cellular and immune responses, depleting the person's energy. Tissue damage may result.

Sympathetic nervous system, Chapter 4, p. 116

Psychological Scales for Measuring Stress. Psychologists think that the general adaptation syndrome evolved in response to drought, famine, flood, and unrelenting heat—severe, long-lasting physiological stressors. Although humans are still vulnerable to such events, we suffer from chronic stress as well—finding enough money to pay the bills or meeting unreasonable deadlines, for example. Not everyone reacts the same way to these stressors. A ringing telephone may be an opportunity to some and an annoyance to others. And though a misplaced wallet is a nuisance to everyone, its perceived severity and significance might differ from one individual to the next.

Thomas Holmes and Richard Rahe were among the first researchers to attempt to measure how psychological stress affects physical health. They began by asking thousands of tuberculosis patients to describe their lives a few years before their illness. The researchers found that patients had had both good and bad experiences. To explain these results, they hypothesized that *change per se was stressful* (Holmes & Rahe, 1967). Both getting married and getting divorced would be stressful, for instance. Likewise, the arrival of a new baby would be stressful to the mother and father, because of the lifestyle changes it would require. They eventually developed the Holmes-Rahe Social Readjustment Rating Scale (see Table 16.5), which ranks typical life events in terms of their level of stress.

As Table 16.5 shows, Holmes and Rahe assigned numerical values to 43 life events, arbitrarily designating the death of a spouse as the most stressful (100 points). To investigate the relationship between stress and illness, the researchers asked subjects to check off those events they had experienced in the preceding year. Holmes and Rahe then added the values associated with those items and paired the scores with presence or absence of physiological symptoms. Finally, they computed the correlation between the numerical scores and the signs of physiological illness. Using the Social Readjustment Rating Scale, many different

general adaptation syndrome (Selye) A three-stage stress response that progresses from *alarm* to *resistance* and finally, *exhaustion*.

researchers have found that psychological stress occurs at higher-than-chance levels prior to physical illness (Creed, 1993; Derogatis & Coons, 1993; Gruen, 1993).

Some researchers have pointed out that most of the events on the Holmes-Rahe scale are negative. Thus, negative life events (rather than both positive and negative events) were responsible for most of the stress Holmes and Rahe measured (Turner & Wheaton, 1995). Other researchers, such as David Watson and James Pennebaker, have suggested that stress is caused by frustration and other negative emotions, not by an event itself (Watson & Pennebaker, 1989).

In any case, studies of poor people show that negative events such as drug addiction and homelessness markedly increase stress levels. Forty-seven percent of poor, substance-abusing mothers experience severe stress, compared with only 3.3 percent of poor mothers who do not abuse drugs (Kelley, 1998). Homeless mothers have much higher levels of stress and depression than low-income mothers who have housing (Banyard & Graham-Bermann, 1998). In one study, researchers found that homeless people had suffered a mean of 9.1 stressful events in their lives before becoming homeless (Munoz, Vazquez, Bermejo, & Vazquez, 1999). Subjects attributed their misfortune to economic problems, a breakdown of social ties, and mental illness.

Most people experience stress on the job, though some jobs are more stressful than others. Oncology nurses, for example, lose many patients to cancer. They often leave their jobs after only a few years, complaining of burnout (Butterworth, Carson, Jeacock, White, & Clements, 1999; Florio, Donnelly, & Zevon, 1998). Relations with physicians, organizational factors, ethical concerns, constant exposure to suffering, and the need to deal with death and dying are the most stressful aspects of their job. Some of these stressors can be remedied through hospital reorganization and sensitivity training for physicians, but most are inherent in the work. In other jobs, sources of stress may include the thought that one's work has little meaning.

Another source of stress is the daily hassles people must deal with. Paul Kohn, Richard Lazarus, and their colleagues gave a hundred middle-aged people a list of 117 irritants and asked them to identify the most annoying ones

Table 16.5 Holmes-Rahe Social Readjustment Rating Scale

Event	Rating
Death of a spouse	100
Divorce	73
Marital separation	65
Jail term	63
Death of a close family member	63
Personal injury or illness	53
Marriage	50
Fired at work	47
Marital reconciliation	45
Retirement	45
Change in health of family member	44
Pregnancy	40
Sex difficulties	39
Gain of a new family member	39
Business readjustment	39
Change in financial state	38
Death of a close friend	37
Change to a different line of work	36
Change in number of arguments with spouse	35
Mortgage or loan for major purchase (home, etc.)	31
Foreclosure of mortgage or loan	30
Change in responsibilities at work	29
Son or daughter leaving home	29
Trouble with in-laws	29
Outstanding personal achievement	28
Spouse begins or stops work	26
Begin or end school	26
Change in living conditions	25
Revision of personal habits	24
Trouble with boss	23
Change in work hours or conditions	20
Change in residence	20
Change in school	20
Change in recreation	19
Change in church activities	19
Change in social activities	18
Mortgage or loan for lesser purchase (car, TV, etc.)	17
Change in sleeping habits	16
Change in number of family get-togethers	15
Change in eating habits	15
Vacation	13
Christmas	12
Minor violations of the law	11

Source: From "The Social Readjustment Scale" by T. H. Holmes & R. H. Rahe in *Journal of Psychosomatic Research*, vol. 11, (1967), pp. 213–218. Copyright © 1967 by Elsevier Science. Reprinted by permission.

DILBERT reprinted by permission of United Feature Syndicate, Inc.

Table 16.6 Ten Most Frequently Checked Hassles

Rank of Item	Percentage of Times Checked
1. Concerns about weight	52.4
2. Health of a family member	48.1
3. Rising prices of common goods	43.7
4. Home maintenance	42.8
5. Too much to do	38.6
6. Misplacing or losing things	38.1
7. Yardwork/outside home maintenance	38.1
8. Property investment, or taxes	37.6
9. Crime	37.1
10. Physical appearance	35.9

Source: Modified from Kanner et al., 1981.

and weight them from 1 to 3. Table 16.6 lists the top ten items on the resulting *Hassle Scale* (Kanner, Coyne, Schaefer, & Lazarus, 1981). Making ends meet, concern for self and others, and time pressure are among life's most common hassles. How useful is the hassle scale? Lazarus (1984) and Kanner and others (1981) compared the Hassle Scale with the Holmes-Rahe Social Readjustment Rating Scale and found little correlation between them. They also found that the Hassle Scale predicted future illness better than the Holmes-Rahe scale.

Another scale, developed along the same lines as the Hassle Scale, measures the stress that young people experience. The Inventory of College Students' Recent Life Experiences (ICSRLE) is considered a reliable and valid measure of students' psychological stress (Kohn, Lafreniere, & Gurevich, 1990), and has some predictive validity regarding physical and psychological illness (Kohn & Gurevich, 1993). More research is necessary to increase the reliability and validity of these measures, however (Brannon & Feist, 2000).

The fundamental attribution error, Chapter 15, p. 514

Despite the fact that daily hassles are a common experience, people perceive and react to them in different ways. For example, when another driver cuts you off in traffic, you may become frustrated, cursing under your breath at the person's rudeness. Physiologically, your eyes may dilate and your breathing rate increase due to a surge of adrenaline. Or you may remain calm, your blood pressure and breathing unchanged. The way in which humans respond to stressors is a result of both innate and learned tendencies, individual differences in personality being among the innate ones.

Little Albert and learned emotional behavior, Chapter 6, p. 199

A Model for Learned Stress. John B. Watson's classical conditioning of 11-month-old Little Albert provides one model for the way in which people come to respond to stress. Albert's unconditioned response (UR) to a loud noise (the unconditioned stimulus, or US) was a startle reflex. After several pairings of the sight of a white rat (the CS) with the US, Albert learned a conditioned emotional response to the rat; on seeing it he cried and tried to escape. Although Watson and Rayner (1920) didn't measure the activity in Albert's sympathetic nervous system, we can assume that both his adrenaline and cortisol levels were high during these episodes. Without extinction, this learned response would likely have persisted, so that a white rat might have become a unique stressor in Albert's life. Other individuals likely would not perceive the rat in this way, and therefore would not have the same emotional and physiological responses.

Let's consider another laboratory example of how learning can adversely affect one's health—a *shuttle-avoidance task*, in which a dog learns to jump from one side of a two-sided compartment to the other, to escape a mild electric shock that is delivered through the floor. Dogs quickly learn that if they jump constantly from side to side, they can successfully avoid the shocks. Presumably, this task is stressful, such that the sight of the box produces an emotional response in the dogs.

Bruce Overmier and Martin Seligman used the shuttle-avoidance task to investigate the effects of intense stressors—in this case, both the anticipation and the pain of an electric shock. They confined a trained animal to one side of the box and administered an intense electric shock (Overmier & Seligman, 1967; Seligman & Maier, 1967). Because the barrier that separated the two compartments was high, the animal could not jump to the other side to escape the shock. The animal, however, did not take the opportunity; instead it lay on the floor and whined. Overmier and Seligman called the animal's failure to engage in self-preserving behavior following intensely aversive experiences **learned helplessness**.

learned helplessness The failure to initiate self-preserving behavior following exposure to intensely aversive events.

The concept of learned helplessness can be applied to humans who have experienced highly stressful life events. Seligman (1975) identified *motivational, cognitive,* and *emotional* consequences of learned helplessness in humans. Just as a dog that has learned to be helpless will not move to avoid an electric shock, a human might not get out of bed for several days (a motivational deficit). A cognitive interpretation, such as "Responding is futile" may accompany this behavior. This perception that a painful event is inescapable may be among the most stressful of all life events. Finally, people who perceive themselves as helpless experience emotional distress.

Since his initial experiments, Seligman (1990) has reinterpreted the concept of learned helplessness in humans. He no longer subscribes to a conditioning model; rather, he thinks that people make cognitive assessment of whether they have control and act accordingly. (*"If I can't do anything about it, there's no sense in responding."*) But Seligman's revised view is not inconsistent with the conditioning model.

Not all people who have been subjected to uncontrollable events suffer from learned helplessness (Buchwald, Coyne, & Cole, 1978; Maier & Jackson, 1979). Some individuals continue to live relatively normal lives even after having discovered they have a terminal illness and have only months to live. Others' lives may be highly disrupted by painful events. For example, withdrawal from class, not studying, and depression are common responses in college students who fail a first test, then study hard for the second one and fail it, too. Despite these individual differences in behavior, learned helplessness theory does fit the response patterns of many people. Taken together, the classical conditioning of negative emotional responses in dogs and humans helps to explain why some individuals perceive certain events as stressful, and others don't.

Illness in Response to Stress. How can we account for individual differences in the physiological response to stressors? Both nature and nurture are implicated. According to the **diathesis-stress model**, genetic predispositions and/or biochemical imbalances predispose individuals to specific illnesses when they are stressed (Gatchel, 1993). (*Diathesis* means "predisposition.") For example, the same stressors may cause stomach problems in an individual whose stomach is the weakest link, and asthma in another whose respiratory system is vulnerable. Although the diathesis-stress model is commonly accepted, a more comprehensive version awaits a better understanding of the role of genes in health.

Maslow's *need hierarchy*, Chapter 5, p. 168, and *self-actualization*, Chapter 14, p. 507

Some people seem almost immune to stress. I once remarked to a friend of 20 years that I could not recall ever seeing him sick. His response was, "I don't have time to get sick." Suzanne (Kobasa) Oullette has studied such individuals. She began by administering the Holmes-Rahe scale (see Table 16.5) to middle-aged executives, and then monitored their health for the next 3 years (Kobasa, 1979). Oullette identified some managers who were high-stress/low-illness, and others who were high-stress/high-illness. By comparing the two groups, she identified what she called a **hardy personality**: an individual who is committed to self, has an internal locus of control, and perceives events as challenges rather than stressors. Let's examine the attributes of the hardy personality more carefully.

In what way is hardiness connected to being "committed to self"? Oullette draws on the thinking of humanistic psychologists such as Abraham Maslow in describing an optimistic, "together" person for whom life has meaning and is worth living. For such people, each new day is full of surprises and challenges. Over time, in Maslow's terms, such a person can become self-actualized. The alternative is to feel powerless, to see oneself as a victim of circumstance (Oullette, 1993).

The second characteristic of hardiness, an *internal locus of control*, is based on Julian Rotter's (1996, 1990) work. According to Rotter, the **locus of control** is a person's perception of what controls his or her actions and destiny. It can vary

diathesis-stress model The theory that genetic predispositions and/or biochemical imbalances make stressed individuals vulnerable to specific illnesses.

hardy personality A high-stress/low-illness individual who is committed to self, has an internal locus of control, and perceives events as challenges rather than stressors.

locus of control The perception of who or what controls one's actions and destiny, oneself (internal locus) or chance events (external locus).

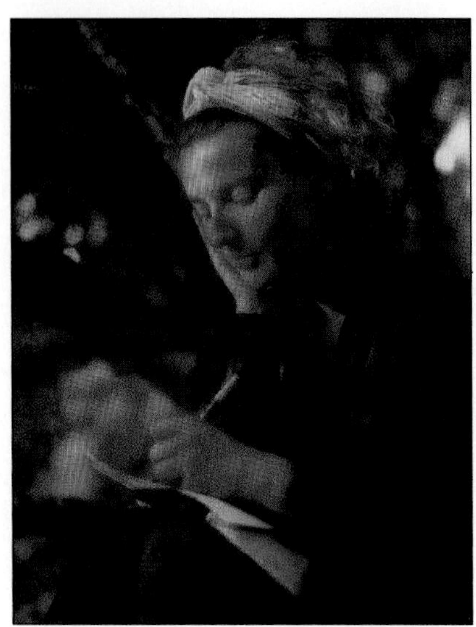

Writing in a diary helps a person make sense of one's life and has the beneficial side effect of strengthening one's immune system.

from a perception of being in personal control (an internal locus of control) to the perception of being controlled by chance events and outside forces (an external locus of control). Since Rotter's work, many subsequent studies have shown that people with an internal locus of control develop fewer psychological disorders, such as depression (Benassi, Sweeney, & Dufour, 1988) and suicidal thoughts (Burger, 1984), than others. In general, those who have an internal locus of control also exercise, do not smoke, and take more responsibility for their health than those with an external locus of control (Marshall, 1991).

Finally, individuals with a hardy personality enjoy the challenges that life affords. They relish events such as the Ironman competition in Hawaii, which tests the limits of a person's physical and psychological endurance. (Participants swim 2.5 miles in the open sea, ride a bicycle for 112 miles, and then run a 26-mile marathon.) Few people accept such challenges, which most of us would find incredibly stressful. At a more mundane level, some individuals find little joy in a stress-filled 40-hour workweek. Yet a hardy personality may perceive the same job as highly rewarding.

Having a hardy, high-stress personality pays off in terms of good health. Kobasa, Maddi, and Kahn (1982) found that "hardy" executives who lived highly stressful lives were sick less often than less-hardy executives. Follow-up research on this intuitively reasonable notion has yielded mixed results, however. Neither female secretaries (Schmied & Lawler, 1986) nor female college students (Ganellen & Blaney, 1984) showed the same results. Moreover, a review of research on the connection between hardiness and physical health did not support the theory (Funk, 1992). Rather, some components of a hardy personality seem to be more important to health than others. The locus-of-control concept *does* seem related to psychological well-being, but the "life as a challenge" attitude does not seem connected to physical health.

Coping With Stress. What do you do when life becomes overwhelming? Some people sleep; others eat (often too much), drink alcohol, smoke, cry, go for a run, watch television, write in a diary, meditate or pray, call someone, or withdraw from others. All these behaviors are attempts to cope with stress. **Coping** is a response that is aimed at reducing or better tolerating the perceived stress in our lives.

Ideally, coping is adaptive; that is, it is effective in reducing stress, optimizing health, and increasing fitness (Aldwin & Brustrom, 1997). The pervasive use of alcohol in many cultures, for example, may reflect its effectiveness as a stress reducer (Peyser, 1993). Other researchers have suggested that *eating* reduces stress (Grunberg & Straub, 1992). However, excessive eating and drinking may actually *increase* stress and precipitate illnesses such as alcoholism and obesity. At least one researcher has argued that there is no good evidence that people eat excessively in response to stress. Research on eating disorders such as obesity, anorexia, and bulimia has not established a stress-eating connection (Troop, 1998).

Effects of alcohol and nicotine, Chapter 9, p. 333

Other coping methods have already been mentioned in this and previous chapters: touching and being touched, drug use, progressive relaxation and hypnosis, meditation, and psychological defense mechanisms. Psychotherapeutic methods will be discussed in detail in Chapter 18; here we will review Freudian defense mechanisms to see how they are related to anxiety and what is called constructive coping. Freud saw anxiety in terms of the ego's attempt to resolve internal conflicts between personal demands (the id) and social demands (the superego). Compare this definition of anxiety with the concept of stress—the perception of being overwhelmed by, rather than in control of, life events. Can any person who is experiencing stress *not* feel anxious?

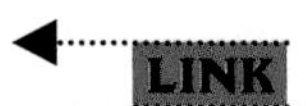

Freudian defense mechanisms, Chapter 14, p. 499

coping Responses that are intended to reduce or better tolerate the perceived stress of events.

Freud's defense mechanisms (see Table 14.2 on page 499) are often used to handle stress. Consider the mechanism of denial, an example of an *avoidance* coping style. Denial doesn't remove a stressor from a person's life. What about fantasy and intellectualizing? These might prove more useful. Consider a person who leaves a salaried position to start a new business. Financially stressed, he might see himself as an independent entrepreneur (intellectualizing) who will eventually become rich and famous (fantasy). These defense mechanisms (plus denial that he may have taken an ill-advised step) may give him the illusion of being in control, reducing his stress. As we have seen, people who have an internal locus of control are healthier than those who perceive themselves as being controlled by others.

Taking control does seem to be beneficial to one's health and self-esteem. In a classic study (Langer & Rodin, 1976), researchers assessed the health of nursing-home residents who were encouraged to take control of their day-to-day living. Their health was found to be significantly better than that of a matched control group of residents one floor removed, who were told to depend on the nursing staff. The illusion of control likely has a direct effect on the immune system. In a study of the effect of the stress of electric shock on the immune system, rats that had an opportunity to escape being shocked showed no ill effects, but those that could not escape suffered a compromised immune system (Laudenslager, Ryan, Drugan, Hyson, & Maier, 1983). The *perception* of the stressor, not the stressor alone, produced these changes in the immune function.

Shelley Taylor and Jonathon Brown (1988, 1994) have studied the effectiveness of fantasy and an illusion of control as coping responses. *Positive illusions*, they found, can be useful in dealing with stress. Thinking your coworkers respect the fact that you provoked the boss would be an example of a positive illusion. Maintaining such an illusion is easy, because as we learned in Chapter 15, people have a self-serving bias—a readiness to perceive themselves favorably. Another example of a self-serving bias that may reduce stress is the finding that university students think their SAT scores underestimate how much they really know (Shepperd, 1993). In general, we all have a Lake Wobegon willingness to see ourselves as "above average," no matter whom we are being compared with.

Self-serving bias, Chapter 15, p. 514

INTERIM SUMMARY

1. In ***psychosomatic disorder***, one's thoughts and emotions have an adverse effect on one's physical health. Examples include glove anesthesia and voodoo death.
2. ***Stress*** is the perception that events are beyond one's control.
3. Hans Selye proposed a three-stage model of the body's response to repeated stress, which he called the ***general adaptation syndrome***. The three stages—alarm, resistance, and exhaustion—involve both short- and long-term adjustments in the autonomic nervous system.
4. The Holmes-Rahe Social Readjustment Rating Scale measures the stress levels of both positive and negative life events. People who score high on this scale experience illness at higher-than-chance levels.
5. Aversive life events—poverty, drugs, homelessness, and stressful jobs—produce negative emotions that affect a person's physical health.
6. The *Hassle Scale* measures the stress caused by life's daily annoyances. High scores on this scale predict poor health.
7. John B. Watson classically conditioned an 11-month-old boy known as Little Albert to fear the appearance of a white rat. Specific stressors, then, can be learned.
8. ***Learned helplessness*** is the failure to initiate self-preserving behavior following an intensely aversive event. Learned helplessness has *motivational, cognitive*, and *emotional* consequences.
9. According to the ***diathesis-stress model***, people are genetically predisposed to develop specific illnesses in response to stress.
10. Some people are more stress resistant than others. The ***hardy personality*** is characterized as a high-stress/low-illness individual who is committed to self, has an internal locus of control, and perceives events as challenges rather than stressors.

11. An individual's ***locus of control*** can be *internal* (a perception of being in control) or *external* (a perception of being controlled by chance events and outside forces). People who have an internal locus of control handle stress better and have fewer health problems.
12. ***Coping*** is a response that is aimed at reducing or better tolerating the perceived stress of life events. Not all coping responses are adaptive.
13. Freudian defense mechanisms, such as denial, intellectualization, and fantasy, can be thought of as coping responses. Because some defense mechanisms offer the illusion of being in control, they can serve as effective coping responses.
14. Illusions are facilitated by the self-serving bias—a readiness to perceive ourselves in favorable terms.

For Further Thought

1. Seligman (1990) now thinks that learned helplessness is better understood in cognitive terms, as a response to the unpredictability of life, rather than in terms of emotional conditioning. Could it be both?
2. Is a person's locus of control learned?
3. Drinking alcohol in response to stress may eventually become a stressor. Can you think of any other examples in which a coping mechanism becomes a stressor?
4. How do you cope with stress? Do you respond differently to different stressors?

PSYCHONEUROIMMUNOLOGY

We began this chapter by examining cross-cultural conceptions of health, all of which are based on the interconnection of body, mind, and sociocultural context. In industrialized countries, most contemporary medical practitioners would agree with this biopsychosocial model of health. Interest in this model has produced the interdisciplinary field of **psychoneuroimmunology**, the study of how the mind (*psyche*), brain (*neuro*), immune system, and behavior are interconnected (Ader, Cohen, & Felton, 1991; Pelletier & Herzing, 1988). Figure 16.7 is a rough model of the psychoneuroimmunological approach to health, in which the central nervous system (CNS), autonomic nervous system (ANS), neuroendocrine system, and immune system function as an interactive whole, communicating with each other via neurotransmitters and hormones (Hall, McGillis, Spangelo, & Goldstein, 1985; Phillips & Evans, 1995). A working assumption of this model is that a person's thoughts, memories, and beliefs depend on and interact with that person's physiology. For our present purposes, this means that the way a person thinks and feels (the actions of the person's CNS) can alter the way the person's immune system functions. Likewise, the culture in which one lives can alter one's thoughts and feelings, and ultimately one's immune system.

psychoneuroimmunology The study of how the mind, brain, immune system, and behavior are interconnected.

Integrating Mind and Body

Robert Ader was among the first to demonstrate the connection between the mind and immune system, in groundbreaking laboratory research at the University of Rochester School of Medicine (Ader, 1993). Recognized by the

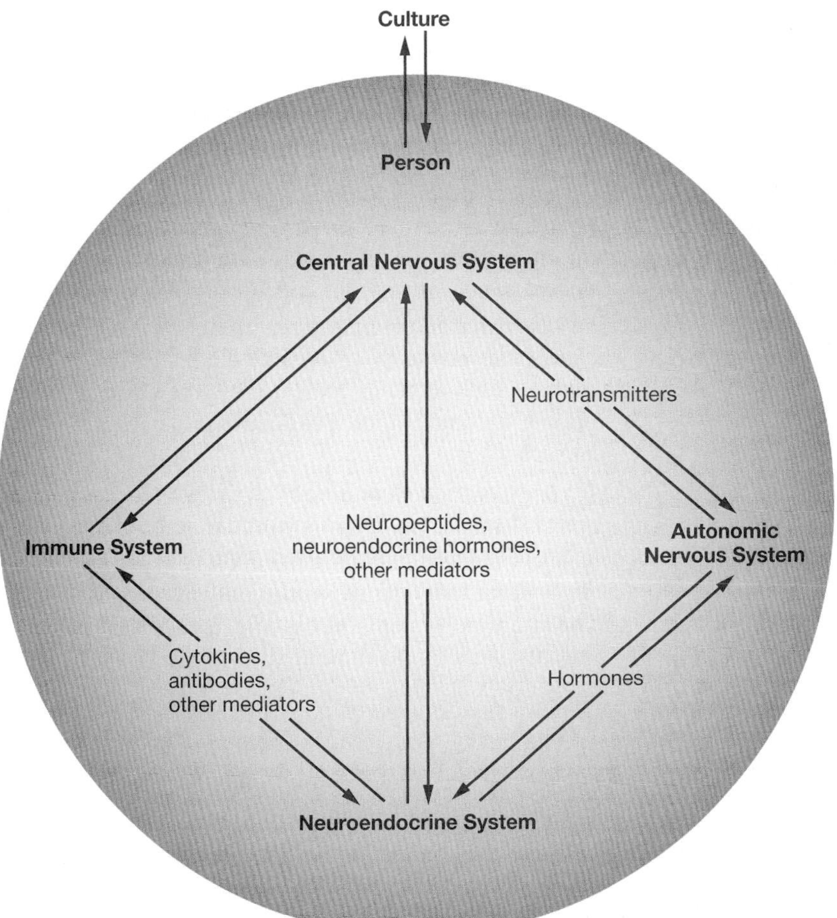

Figure 16.7 The Psychoneuroimmunological Model of Health. In the human body, four physiological systems—central nervous system, autonomic nervous system, neuroendocrine system, and immune system—communicate with each other via chemical messengers such as neurotransmitters and hormones. Thus the body and mind are intimately connected. A person's health is also affected by cultural influences.

National Institutes of Health, research in psychoneuroimmunology has been advancing despite the complexity of the undertaking (Kelley, 2001; Schleifer, 1999). To start our investigation of mind-body interactions, we'll begin with the immune system, whose integrity is the single best predictor of a person's overall health and well-being.

Functions of the Immune System

The *immune system* has two primary functions. One, called *immunosurveillance*, is to recognize and defend against foreign substances such as infectious organisms, which can damage tissues and organs. Immunosurveillance can be thought of as *innate immunity*. The other function, called *acquired immunity*, is to form antibodies and sensitized lymphocytes (white blood cells) in response to the introduction of foreign substances (Elgert, 1996). These antibodies and lymphocytes remember what they have encountered before, and lie ready and waiting to combat the next intrusion of a foreign substance.

These functions of the immune system can be thought of in philosophical terms, as the means by which the body recognizes and distinguishes "self" from "non-self" (Benjamini & Leskowitz, 1991). For example, a transplanted kidney is non-self—a fact that makes its rejection by the immune system highly predictable.

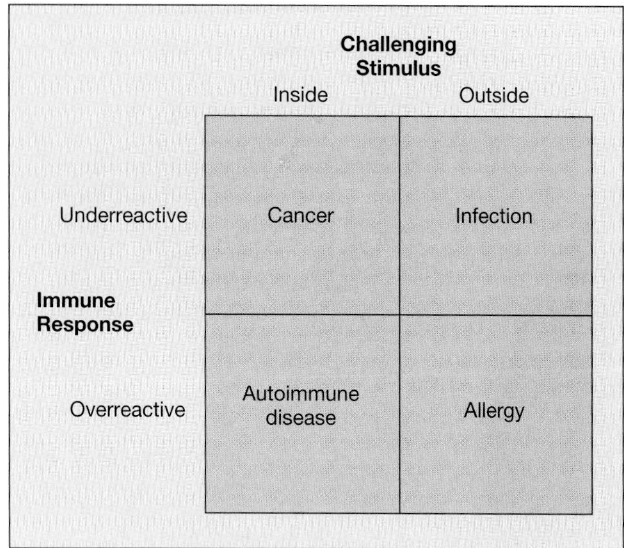

Challenging Stimulus
Inside
Outside
Underreactive
Cancer
Infection
Immune Response
Overreactive
Autoimmune disease
Allergy

Figure 16.8 Responses of the Immune System to Challenging Stimuli. The immune system responds to challenges from both inside and outside the body. Ideally, the system identifies and eliminates foreign substances from the body, but not always. Underreaction produces one type of disease; overreaction, another.

The immune system responds to challenges to the self from both the outside and the inside (see Figure 16.8). Most of the time it functions smoothly, eliminating sources of disease. But occasionally it malfunctions, resulting in disease of one type of another. For example (Locke, 1985):

1. An *underreaction* to an *outside* challenge results in *infection*. Either because of overwhelming numbers of bacteria or viruses, or because of immunosuppression, the system cannot mount an appropriate response.
2. An *overreaction* to an *outside* challenge results in an *allergy*. In response to an outside challenge in the form of *antigens* such as cedar pollen, the system forms excessive numbers of antibodies, producing an exaggerated physical reaction.
3. An *overreaction* to an *inside* challenge results in *autoimmune disease*. Failing to recognize part of the body as self, the immune system attempts to reject it.
4. An *underreaction* to an *inside* challenge results in *cancer*. The immune system mistakenly recognizes a tumor as self, and fails to mobilize against it.

Conditioning of the Immune System

The functioning of the immune system is too complex to be covered in full here. This discussion will be limited to the connection between the immune system and the brain. Some fascinating experiments have shown that the immune response can be conditioned—that is, triggered by learning. We'll start with *T lymphocytes*, immune system cells that bind directly to the membranes of invading cells, such as bacteria or transplant cells. Present from birth, these T cells release enzymes that attack the invading cells.

Classical conditioning, Chapter 6, p. 189

Conditioned Immunosuppression. Robert Ader's insight into how the central nervous system could affect the immune system was to demonstrate that he could manipulate the number of T cells in rats through simple conditioning (Ader, 1985). Ader injected rats with a drug called Cytoxan, the unconditioned stimulus in his experiments. (Cytoxan is commonly used to suppress the immune system in cancer patients.) The next day he recorded a reduced T-lymphocyte count, which he interpreted as an unconditioned response to the drug.

In the next step in his experiment, Ader conditioned some of the rats by allowing them to drink a saccharin solution (the conditioned stimulus) just before he injected them with Cytoxan (the US). He gave the others saccharin and Cytoxan on different days, so they would not associate the two stimuli. After several conditioning trials (one per day), Ader tested his hypothesis: he compared the number of T cells in both groups as they drank the saccharin. He found that the conditioned rats had lower T-cell counts: the mere taste of saccharin, a CNS-mediated event, had suppressed their immune systems, he reasoned.

Presumably the taste of saccharin (it could have been any other flavor) became associated with the drug, so that the immune system responded to the taste in the same way as to the drug. This reduction of T lymphocytes following a classical conditioning procedure is called *conditioned immunosuppression*. The likely mechanism for conditioning the immune system is the CNS nerve fibers that serve the immune system cells (Felten, 1993; Maier & Watkins, 1999).

Robert Ader's experiments are important because they demonstrate that parts of the immune system can be tricked into functioning in the absence of foreign stimuli. We should not be surprised by these findings. In Chapter 6 we learned that a dog's salivary response can be brought under the control of an arbitrary stimulus, such as a bell. But conditioned changes in salivation affect only the preliminary stages of digestion. The integrity of the immune system is vitally important to the optimal functioning of all the body's physiological systems. In showing that the immune system can be conditioned, Ader and others revealed a mechanism through which a person's underlying thoughts and feelings can affect that person's health (Ader, Weiner, & Baum, 1988).

Conditioned Allergies. Millions of people suffer from a baffling condition called asthma. From infants to the very old, from every walk of life, they have one thing in common: difficulty in breathing. Asthma attacks can occur under a variety of conditions, presumably for different reasons; sometimes they are fatal. In a given individual the same amount of external stimulus—cedar pollen, for example—does not always produce the same response. Asthma, then, is not a simple reflex.

Asthma is an allergic reaction to external stimuli called *allergens*, which activate the immune system. It is caused by *reagins*, sensitizing antibodies that trigger an allergic response by attaching antibodies to cells throughout the body, disrupting their functioning. If a sufficient number of cells are damaged in this *anaphylactic* reaction, death can ensue. The allergen-reagin reaction can be understood as an unconditioned reflex. Can it be classically conditioned, as in conditioned immunosuppression?

Because guinea pigs have especially sensitive airways, they are good subjects for asthma research. Justesen and his colleagues (1970) injected the animals with a foreign protein, egg albumin. Acting as a US, the albumin caused the guinea pigs' immune systems to make sensitizing antibodies (reagins). On subsequent trials, the researchers noted an allergen-reagin reaction in the bronchioles of the guinea pigs' lungs. There, mast cells released a *slow-reacting substance of anaphylaxis*, causing spasms in the bronchial smooth muscle. After just one sensitizing treatment, the guinea pigs died unless a vasodilator (in this case, a drug called Isuprel) was administered immediately. Their breathing difficulties can be considered an unconditioned response (UR) to the allergen.

After making their lab subjects asthmatic, Justesen and his colleagues classically conditioned them. They sprayed egg albumin (the US) into a chamber, disrupting the guinea pigs' breathing (the UR). The hissing sound of the spray soon became the conditioned stimulus (CS) that predicted the delivery of the allergen, airborne egg albumin. After each trial, the researchers administered Isuprel to the guinea pigs to return their breathing to baseline levels. After 6 to 12 trials, the guinea pigs displayed a conditioned disruption of their breathing following the sound of the spray alone. That is, the hissing sound became a CS, one that was capable of provoking an asthma attack.

Similar experiments have been done with humans. In a design similar to the guinea pig study, two different allergic individuals were exposed to allergens while using a breathing apparatus. After several trials, the use of the breathing apparatus alone produced an allergic reaction (Booth & Ashbridge, 1992). In fact, the clinical literature on asthma treatment contains numerous reports of conditioned asthma. One patient who was allergic to the smell of roses developed an allergic reaction to an artificial rose (reported by Gauci, Husband, & King, 1992). Apparently the visual features of the rose acted as a CS, so that the sights of the plastic rose alone produced a conditioned allergic response.

In another study of 30 healthy female college students, researchers induced breathing changes by asking the subjects to perform a stressful arithmetic problem. While the students performed the task, the researchers projected a colored light (a conditioned stimulus) onto a screen in front of them. After a number of trials, compared to controls, the color alone produced changes in both the subjects' respiration rate and their respiratory resistance (Miller & Kotses, 1995).

Medical Implications of Conditioning Experiments

Conditioned immunosuppression experiments have shown how the immune system can contribute to conditioned, or psychosomatic, disorders. Can the immune system's functioning be *enhanced* through conditioning? Several lines of evidence suggest that it can be.

The Placebo Effect. For centuries, physicians in all cultures have been aware of the **placebo effect**, a beneficial outcome of treatment that is unrelated to specific causal properties of the treatment (Harrington, 1997; Shapiro, 1971). For example, part of the effect of a drug treatment is due to the drug's pharmacological properties, but part is due merely to the experience of being treated. A review of research on the placebo effect found that physicians underestimate its importance: It can account for more than 33 percent of a given treatment effect (Turner, Deyo, Loeser, Von Korff, & Forrdyce, 1994).

All placebo effects are due to prior learning. One way to think about the placebo effect is as a conditioned response: the conditioned stimulus properties of a pill (its color and shape) become associated with the unconditioned stimulus properties of the drug itself. In the laboratory and the clinic, the symbols of medical treatment—pills, injections, lab coats—come to exert real physiological effects, regardless of what the pills contain or who wears the coat. Following many trials with medicines that cause various effects, a sugar pill can become a placebo (from the Latin word meaning "*I will please*") that mimics those effects. Likewise, the expectations and conditioned emotional responses that subjects developed in prior conditioning trials or treatments will affect the next treatment. Patients' expectations, then, can affect the course of their treatment (Harrington, 1997).

Second-signal conditioning of words, Chapter 6, p. 200

In one experiment, for example, researchers conditioned relief from allergic rhinitis (hay fever) in asthma sufferers (Gauci et al., 1992). They divided the subjects into three groups, each of which received one of three CSs: water, a "medicine" (actually an inert soft drink), or nothing. Immediately after the treatment, they challenged each subject with an allergen (the US). Two days later they repeated the treatment, this time administering the CSs but not the allergen. Compared to the other two groups, those subjects who received the "medicine" treatment showed diminished mast-cell activity—a classic placebo effect.

The Nocebo Effect. The apparent ease with which immune system responses can be conditioned helps to explain the *nocebo effect*, the opposite of the placebo effect. In a **nocebo effect**, sickness or pain results from negative expectations, despite the absence of a physical factor (Turner et al., 1994). Sometimes the expectation of pain (you may recall from your playground years) rather than the painful stimulus itself determines how painful it is. In laboratory research, subjects who think they are going to receive a painful electric shock (but do not) often gave false reports of pain (Hahn, 1997).

placebo effect A beneficial outcome of a treatment that cannot be related to specific causal properties of the treatment.

nocebo effect Sickness or pain resulting from negative expectations.

Another example of the nocebo effect occurs when people's expectations help to determine their psychological and physiological responses to a drug. In a classic study, researchers Stanley Schacter and Jerome Singer misled some of their subjects about the effects of certain drugs or placebos, and gave other subjects the correct information. Then they injected the subjects with either epinephrine or a placebo, and both groups were told they might experience a racing pulse and become somewhat agitated. The control group experienced the symptoms exactly as described. Subjects administered the epinephrine were told they wouldn't experience any signs . . . and they didn't (Schacter & Singer, 1962). This procedure has been replicated with a different drug, *carisoprodol* (Flaten, Simonsen, & Olsen, 1999). One interesting finding was that subjects' blood serum levels of the drug differed under the two different sets of instructions.

Personality and the Immune System

Do happy people have stronger immune systems than depressed people? There is growing evidence that they do, and that other personality characteristics affect immune function as well. Both perceived stress and immunosuppression during test taking have been found to vary with students' personality profiles (Jemmott et al., 1990). In one study, researchers found that the level of subjects' natural killer (NK) cells was correlated with their self-reports of positive and negative moods (Valdimarsdottir & Bovbjerg, 1997). Specifically, they found lower levels of NK cells in women with chronically negative moods. In another study, 21 acutely depressed but otherwise physically healthy young adults showed decreased levels of natural killer cells and increased levels of lymphocytes compared to a control group (Schleifer, Keller, & Bartlett, 1999). Lowered immune responses have also been found in people who score high on a test for neuroticism (Marsland, Cohen, Rabin, & Manuck, 2001).

Conversely, certain types of therapy can strengthen the immune system. Merely expressing oneself in writing, for example, increases immune functioning. James Pennebaker randomly assigned students to write about either their deepest thoughts and feelings or superficial topics, for four consecutive days (20 minutes each day). He found that they became relaxed while writing in their journals, and over time showed improved physical health, better immune function, and even better sleeping (Pennebaker, 1997). For the last few years, researchers have been exploring this effect more closely. One of the main benefits of journal keeping is that it helps people to come to terms with upsetting experiences and provides an efficient way to organize their emotions. Confession, then, may be good for both the body and the soul.

Norman Cousins is sometimes credited with having forced physicians to confront the limitations of the biomedical model (Cousins, 1979). When told by physicians in the mid-1960s that he had an incurable disease, one that he would die from, he refused to accept their prognosis. Working with a physician/friend who supported him, he embarked on a course of alternative medicine that included (among other things) high doses of both vitamin C and laughter. Cousins checked himself into a hotel, rented reels of Candid Camera films and other comedies, and proceeded to laugh himself silly. His illness went into remission, and he lived for another 20 years. Cousins' account was published in both medical journals and a popular paperback version (Cousins, 1979).

Laughter is an effective stress reducer.

Scientific studies have confirmed that laughter and a sense of humor are effective stress reducers, ones that have a direct effect on immune system function (Lefcourt & Thomas, 1998). In one study, researchers took saliva samples from 160 college students before and after they watched humorous or nonhumorous films (McClelland & Cheriff, 1997). They found that subjects' immune cell levels (salivary immunoglobulin A, S-IgA) increased significantly in response to humorous films. Those subjects with a strong sense of humor (measured independently) experienced major gains in S-IgA, putting them at lower risk for infection. These results, and those of studies showing that negative emotions and depression *suppress* the immune system (Breznitz et al., 1998), suggest that people who can look on the bright side have a significant health advantage.

INTERIM SUMMARY

1. The CNS, ANS, neuroendocrine, and immune systems function as an interactive whole. ***Psychoneuroimmunology*** is the study of connections among the mind, brain, immune system, and behavior.
2. The primary functions of the *immune system* are *immunosurveillance*—recognizing and defending against foreign substances—and *acquired immunity*—defending against foreign substances by forming antibodies.
3. An immune response can be underreactive, or immunosuppressed, as in illness; or overreactive, as in allergy and asthma.
4. After being paired with an immunosuppressant, a taste by itself can reduce the level of T cells in the immune system. Research demonstrating such *conditioned immunosuppression* shows that CNS activity, which underlies thoughts and feelings, can have a direct effect on the immune system.
5. Asthma has been classically conditioned. In both guinea pigs and humans, conditioned sounds and colors, respectively, can precipitate breathing difficulties.
6. A ***placebo effect*** is a beneficial outcome of a treatment that is not related to the treatment itself, but to conditioned stimuli associated with the treatment.
7. The opposite of the placebo effect is the **nocebo effect**, which occurs when sickness or pain results from negative expectations.
8. People who keep journals show improved physical health and better immune functioning.
9. Personality differences, mood, laughter, and a sense of humor can affect immune functioning.

For Further Thought

1. What is *self* in identical twins? Why can the liver of one identical twin be transplanted to the other without being rejected?
2. Three treatment groups are necessary to test the effects of a new drug: a drug group, a placebo group, and a no-treatment group. Why? Are there any ethical concerns inherent in such a research design?
3. Consider the phenomenon of voodoo deaths. Could you kill a guinea pig with the sound of a sprayer?
4. Suppose you trained an asthmatic guinea pig to associate a distinctive sound (clicks, for example) with the administration of a vasodilator (and hence, recovery from breathing difficulties). After training, would the clicks alone relieve the guinea pig's asthma attack? If so, would you consider the clicks a placebo?
5. What effect do you think prayer, meditation, yoga, self-hypnosis, or other "mindful awareness" activities might have on your immune system?
6. Both men and women look for a sense of humor in a potential marriage partner (Feingold, 1992). Can you make a case for the adaptive significance of choosing a mate with a sense of humor?

CONCLUDING THOUGHTS

Humans have evolved a physiology that is as self-corrective as it is self-reproductive. As evidenced by their immune systems, humans have genes that promote self-healing. They have also developed systems of medicine—memes that allow them to treat those whose immune systems have become compromised.

People become sick for a number of reasons. They compete with bacteria and viruses whose ecological niche is the human body. They seem to have inherited a predisposition toward some sicknesses because the associated genes offer a selective advantage against more deadly disorders. Humans also pollute their water, causing epidemics through water-borne infectious agents. Last but not least, humans become sick because they overindulge themselves. They consume too many calories, especially from animal fat; drink too much alcohol; smoke cigarettes; and abuse other drugs. Most of these activities can be accomplished while sitting on a couch.

In the past century, the rapid growth of the chemical and physical sciences supported a biomedical model of health. But advances against infectious disease have not been followed by similar reductions in other types of disease, such as heart disease and cancer. In industrialized Western nations, today, lifestyle factors rather than infectious diseases cause about 80 percent of premature deaths. We are faced now with having to relearn old health lessons: namely, that one's health is determined by psychological and sociocultural factors as well as by physiology. The biopsychosocial model, the basis for health psychology and behavioral medicine, emphasizes the importance of behavior, thoughts, feelings, and cultural considerations in understanding and preventing illness and early death.

The processes through which psychological and other lifestyle variables affect people's health can be investigated within a mind-body framework. Psychosomatic disorders can be analyzed as a learned response to psychological stress. For reasons that are not well understood, the mind can cause changes in the autonomic nervous system, the neuroendocrine system, and the immune system, resulting in voodoo deaths and stress-induced immunosuppression. Mind and behavior can also enhance health and well-being through exercise, laughter, and journal keeping.

Although life events such as drug addiction and homelessness are universally aversive, individuals differ in their perception of these stressors. Those with an internal locus of control cope better with stress, and have fewer adverse health consequences as a result of stress, than others. The self-serving bias helps to insulate people from life's unpleasant realities.

Psychoneuroimmunology is the study of the interconnectedness of the mind, brain, and immune system with behavior. It is proving to be one of the most effective ways of implementing a biopsychosocial health perspective. Studies that show how psychological events can affect the immune system are important because immune functioning is the single best predictor of a person's overall health. We now know that psychological variables such as conditioned stimuli, the pressure of studying, positive and negative affect, depression, and humor can weaken or strengthen the immune system. The power of these variables can be seen in the placebo effect, an important part of medicine's curative powers, and nocebo effect, in which negative expectations compromise a treatment's effectiveness. For centuries an accepted truth in most of the world's cultures, the biopsychosocial unity of health is now being verified by scientific research.

KEY TERMS

aerobic exercise *556*
behavioral medicine *544*
biomedical model *546*
biopsychosocial model *547*
coping *564*
diathesis-stress model *563*
general adaptation syndrome *560*
hardy personality *563*
health *546*
health psychology *544*
learned helplessness *562*
locus of control *563*
nocebo effect *570*
placebo effect *570*
psychoneuroimmunology *566*
psychosomatic disorder *558*
stress *559*

17

Abnormal Psychology

Ed Paschke (b. 1939), American. "Nervosa." Private Collection / Ed Paschke / SuperStock.

Perspectives on Abnormal Behavior
What Is Abnormal Behavior?
A Case in Point: Jeremy
The Prevalence of Mental Disorders
Interim Summary
For Further Thought

Categorization of Psychological Disorders
The Medical Versus the Psychological Model
Organic Versus Functional Disorders
Standardization of Diagnostic Terms
Using the *DSM-IV*
Interim Summary
For Further Thought

Anxiety Disorders
Phobic Disorder
Generalized Anxiety Disorder
Panic Disorder
Obsessive-Compulsive Disorder
Interim Summary
For Further Thought

Somatoform Disorders
Hypochondriasis
Somatization Disorders
Conversion Disorders
Interim Summary
For Further Thought

Dissociative Disorders
Dissociative Fugue States
Dissociative Amnesia
Depersonalization Disorder
Dissociative Identity Disorder
Interim Summary
For Further Thought

Mood Disorders
Bipolar and Unipolar Disorders
Depression
The Adaptiveness of Mood Disorders
Interim Summary
For Further Thought

Schizophrenia
Symptoms of Schizophrenia
Types of Schizophrenia
Causes of Schizophrenia
Interim Summary
For Further Thought

Personality Disorders
Categories of Personality Disorders
Borderline Personality Disorder
Antisocial Personality Disorder
Interim Summary
For Further Thought

Concluding Thoughts

Although George's mood alternated between depression and periods of intense, high-energy behavior, his school years were relatively normal. Strikingly handsome, he was a C student, liked sports, and didn't attract much attention—until an incident on an overnight trip. The police report mentioned cocaine and a destroyed hotel room. According to his friends, George had "just flipped out."

Following an unsuccessful first semester in college, George took a job as a stockboy in a supermarket, then abruptly quit and moved to Lake Tahoe to become a ski instructor. He did odd jobs, skied, fell in love, and planned to get married. But the relationship failed, as did his plans to become a ski instructor.

Back in Southern California, George worked at night and spent his days at the beach, surfing. Then, imagining that he would become a world-class surfer in Hawaii, he impulsively quit his job. Unfortunately, he was better at spending money than surfing, and soon exceeded the limit on his credit cards. His parents offered to pay off his debt on the condition he quit surfing, get a job, and see a psychotherapist.

George complied, and was diagnosed with bipolar disorder. The psychiatrist prescribed lithium, a chemical that regulated the oscillations in his mood and dampened his grandiose, unrealistic schemes, allowing him to study and obtain a realtor's license. But George didn't like the way the lithium made him feel, so he quit taking it. He began to work long hours, and over the next year entered into some ill-advised real estate deals. Forced to sell some unrentable apartments at a loss, he fell back on this parent's support.

Without the stabilizing influence of lithium, George's life didn't improve. He announced plans to become a professional boxer (by calling several people at 3:00 A.M.), trained intensely for several months, then quit after losing just one amateur fight. He lost a truck-driving job after being arrested for driving while intoxicated. Now in his thirties, he lives alone on a remote desert property he purchased but couldn't sell. He says that women find him too intense and has few social relationships with anyone outside his family.

Larson
© 1985 FarWorks, Inc. All Rights Reserved/Dist. by Creators Syndicate

How Nature says, "Do not touch."

At different times in our lives, many of us have had doubts about the soundness of our mental health. In a study in the early 1970s, 20 percent of respondents answered "yes" to the question *Have you ever felt you were having a nervous breakdown?* (U.S. Department of Health, Education, and Welfare, 1971). And yet most of the time, most of us think that we are normal. We are fascinated by others, whom, like George, we consider abnormal. In fact, George has a **psychological disorder,** a condition in which a person's thoughts, feelings, and behavior are so dysfunctional they interfere with daily living.

Not all dysfunctional behavior is abnormal. Grieving for a recently deceased loved one, for example, is dysfunctional in the sense that one's thoughts, feelings, and behavior interfere with one's usual activities. But grief is a normal reaction to loss. Similarly, not all abnormal behavior is dysfunctional. For most people, beating another person senseless is quite dysfunctional, but not for a boxer who makes millions of dollars engaging in the behavior. Culturally defined behaviors such as boxing are neither abnormal nor dysfunctional. (Even among boxers, however, biting off an opponent's ear *is* considered abnormal and dysfunctional.)

In this chapter we'll begin by considering what it means to be normal, and what constitutes a mental disorder. The Far Side cartoon suggests that psychological disorders have reproductive consequences. Though abnormal behavior may seem synonymous with "bad genes," hence maladaptation, we'll address the relative roles of inheritance of disorders as well as their various cultural expressions. Finally we'll see how mental disorders are categorized and understood from a brain-behavioral perspective.

PERSPECTIVES ON ABNORMAL BEHAVIOR

Abnormal psychology is the study of both abnormal behavior and psychological disorders. Behavior that is abnormal is neither simple to characterize nor easy to define. Sometimes it is simply unusual; it may reflect cultural mores. In this section, we'll consider just what makes a behavior abnormal, then we'll apply the concept of abnormal behavior to Jeremy, a young boy who is having difficulty in school.

What Is Abnormal Behavior?

A common way to think about abnormal behavior is that it is atypical. In this view, normal behavior is defined by the normal curve, in which 95 percent of all people lie within 2 standard deviations of the mean. That leaves 2.5 percent of the population at the extremes. In terms of cognitive functioning, for example, a small minority of people are either geniuses, or mentally retarded. But although referring to the normal curve is a good way to think about *normal* behavior, it is too simplistic an approach to use in studying psychological disorders.

Normal curve, Chapter 2, p. 53

Abnormal behavior is often, but not always, maladaptive. George's abnormal behavior resulted in personal distress, impaired functioning, and hardship on his family and friends. Consider the behavior of nudists, however. Their behavior is unusual, as well as culturally unacceptable: most people are inclined to think that going around naked is abnormal and weird. Yet nudists do not suffer personal distress or impaired functioning, nor is nudism otherwise maladaptive. How do psychologists decide what behavior, or set of behaviors, constitutes a psychological disorder?

The example of nudism illustrates an important distinction between abnormal behavior and psychological disorders: Abnormal behavior is defined by culture, and psychological disorders, within Western culture at least, are defined by psychologists and psychiatrists. In other cultures mental illness is categorized differently than in our own (Kleinman, 1988; Leff, 1988). The latter sections of this chapter are concerned with how psychologists and psychiatrists in the United States and Canada have defined psychological disorders. Still, there is considerable controversy over how psychological disorders are presently construed. Not everyone agrees that a given set of behaviors should be labeled a "mental disorder." To illustrate how psychologists go about determining the existence of a disorder and the ethics of treating, or attempting to correct, a disorder, let's look at the experience of a young boy called Jeremy.

A Case in Point: Jeremy

Eight-year-old Jeremy W. was in trouble in the classroom: he made too much noise, didn't follow directions, didn't do assigned work, and was disrespectful to his teacher (from Oltmanns & Emery, 1998). These behaviors didn't cause Jeremy personal distress; he rather enjoyed being noisy and disruptive. But in the culture into which he had been born, Jeremy's behavior was unacceptable. His teacher and school counselor advised Jeremy's parents to seek help from a psychologist.

Jeremy's problem is a familiar one that most psychologists would diagnosis as **attention-deficit/hyperactivity disorder (ADHD)**, a behavior problem characterized by inattention, overactivity, and impulsivity. ADHD is usually diagnosed in school-aged children, mostly male; about 8 million children, or 15 percent of the school-aged population in the United States, have been diagnosed with the disorder (Panksepp, 1998). Certainly Jeremy had some of the signs of ADHD, as indicated

psychological disorder A condition in which a person's thoughts, feelings, and behavior interfere with normal psychosocial functioning.

attention-deficit/hyperactivity disorder (ADHD) A behavior problem characterized by inattention, overactivity, and impulsivity.

Figure 17.1 A Teacher Rating Scale for ADHD. A hypothetical rating for Jeremy on the *Brief Conners Teacher Rating Scale for Attention-Deficit/Hyperactivity Disorder.* A score greater than 15 is used to diagnose and label ADHD. *Source:* From "A Teacher Rating Scale for Use with Drug Studies with Children" by C. K. Conners in *American Journal of Psychiatry,* (1969), vol. 126, pp. 864–888. Copyright © 1969 by the American Psychiatric Assn. Reprinted by Permission.

Observation	Degree of Activity			
CLASSROOM BEHAVIOR	**(0) Not At All**	**(1) Just a Little**	**(2) Pretty Much**	**(3) Very Much**
Constantly fidgeting			✓	
Demands must be met immediately—easily frustrated		✓		
Restless or overactive			✓	
Excitable, impulsive			✓	
Inattentive, easily distracted			✓	
Fails to finish things he starts—short attention span			✓	
Cries often and easily	✓			
Disturbs other children			✓	
Mood changes quickly and drastically		✓		
Temper outbursts; explosive and unpredictable behavior		✓		

by the checklist his teacher completed (see Figure 17.1.) On this behavioral scale, Jeremy scored a 15, making an ADHD diagnosis a real possibility. However, the psychologist who saw Jeremy hesitated to diagnose the disorder. Jeremy's IQ was 108, yet he was performing below grade level. Perhaps the primary cause of his classroom behavior was a **learning disorder,** defined as a discrepancy between a person's academic achievement and intellectual ability.

Jeremy's mother recognized that his failure to perform at grade level would be a problem throughout his school years, especially during adolescence. Surprisingly, Jeremy's father disagreed. He hadn't liked school either, and thought his son would be fine as an adult. And so another diagnosis presented itself. Perhaps Jeremy's behavior was his 8-year-old way of "being like dad," or a response to the marital problems his parents had been experiencing. To investigate this possibility, the psychologist talked with Jeremy to determine what *he* thought might be the problem.

learning disorder A disorder characterized by a discrepancy between one's academic achievement and one's intellectual ability.

What can we learn from this case history? First, the people with whom Jeremy interacted, not Jeremy himself, sought treatment for his behavior. In the eyes of others, Jeremy had disrupted his classroom, violating the norms of society. This point needs to be emphasized. When you and I observe someone—say a homeless person exhibiting some types of mental illness, the tendency is to feel sorry for or want to help the person. The underlying assumption is that the person is unhappy and would rather be "normal." However, some of the mentally ill are *not* unhappy and do not "suffer" from their disorders.

Nor is all abnormal behavior disruptive to society. People who take their clothes off in a nudist colony do not present a problem to society. People who take their clothes off in the middle of a busy intersection do, however. Depending on the social context, the same behavior may be considered either unusual (nudism) or abnormal *and* troublesome (indecent exposure).

The impact of social expectations is especially relevant to children diagnosed with attention-deficit/hyperactivity disorder. Jaak Panksepp (1998) has suggested that the increasing numbers of children who are diagnosed with ADHD (approaching 15 percent of all male children) is more a reflection of changing social expectations than of an increase in the frequency of this neurological condition. Humans are primates who evolved to engage in rough-and-tumble play during their developmental years, Panksepp argues. Being required to sit quietly for hours is unnatural for children, especially males, who in a less-restricted environment would be engaging in spontaneous play. Another researcher has suggested that the impulsiveness seen in hyperactive children would be useful in the hunter-gatherer society our ancestors lived in. That is, individuals with short, rapidly shifting attention may have been the best hunters (Hartmann, 1996). What is a liability in a highly structured classroom, then, might be an asset in another environment.

Typically, psychiatrists prescribe the stimulant Ritalin for children who are diagnosed with ADHD because it acts paradoxically to depress their motor behavior (see Table 9.1, page 334). Panksepp (1998) proposes instead that longer play periods be substituted for drug therapy. His argument is bolstered by the acknowledged benefits of play, which include enhanced brain growth and social development.

Let's hear it for longer recesses.

Psychotherapy using drugs, Chapter 18, p. 630

Environnmental complexity and brain organization, Chapter 4, p. 128

The Prevalence of Mental Disorders

The total number of people who have been diagnosed with mental disorders is impressive—about one of every five people living in the United States (Neugebauer, Dohrenwend, & Dohrenwend, 1980). If those with chemical dependencies are included, the figure increases to about 1 out of every 3 Americans (Regier & Kaelber, 1995). The seriousness of the problem is reflected in suicide statistics: each year, about 3 million Americans kill themselves. (In 1996, suicide was the third leading cause of death among ages 15–24.)

Some researchers have questioned the prevalence of mental illness. Thomas Szasz (1974, 1990) thinks that estimates of the number of the "afflicted" are grossly exaggerated because of errors in diagnosis and problems with a model that "medicalizes" mental disorders. Still, the amount of money Americans spend on mental health problems seems to indicate that it is a real problem. The bill, including the cost of lost productivity at work, was estimated at $148 billion dollars in 1990.

INTERIM SUMMARY

1. Abnormal psychology is concerned with atypical behavior that may or may not be dysfunctional. Cultures define what is and is not normal, and psychologists define and diagnose psychological disorders.
2. A *psychological disorder* is a condition in which a person's thoughts, feelings, and behavior are considered dysfunctional.

3. *Attention-deficit/hyperactivity disorder (ADHD)* is a childhood behavior problem characterized by inattention, overactivity, and impulsivity.
4. A *learning disorder* is defined as a discrepancy between a person's intellectual ability and academic achievement.
5. An abnormal behavior may be considered unusual, troublesome, or both, depending in part on its social context. Typically, someone else instigates the treatment of a person's abnormal or problematic behavior. The impulsiveness of a hyperactive child may be beneficial in other environments, and increased opportunities to play may be preferable to drug therapy.
6. Arguably, about one out of every five people in the United States has a mental disorder; millions more have chemical dependencies.

For Further Thought

1. Might some individuals be attracted to the human character in the Far Side cartoon on page 576? Might such attraction account for the persistence of some forms of abnormality in the gene pool?
2. Think of the most abnormal person you know. Does this person have any strengths that you lack?
3. The homeless, who often suffer from schizophrenia, lead lives filled with pain and fear. Yet many of them prefer to live on the streets rather than in locked hospital wards. Under what conditions should society assume authority and control over these people?
4. In his book *Civilization and Its Discontents*, Sigmund Freud (1930) proposed that curtailing the pleasure-seeking id is the inevitable cost of civilization. How does this statement apply to Jeremy?
5. When chemical dependencies are included, an estimated one out of every three people in the United States has a mental disorder. This raises the question of whether abnormal behavior is becoming the norm. If and when it does, will it no longer be considered abnormal?

CATEGORIZATION OF PSYCHOLOGICAL DISORDERS

Throughout most of human history, abnormal behavior has been poorly understood, if not completely misunderstood. In the 18th and 19th centuries, however, the growth of scientific understanding and the emergence of humanism laid the foundation for contemporary thinking about mental disorders. Today, these two approaches are reflected in the medical and psychological models of mental illness.

The Medical Versus the Psychological Model

medical model (of mental disorders) The theory that disordered thoughts and behavior result from a diseased or otherwise malfunctioning brain.

In the late 1700s, after inaugurating profound changes in the hospital care of the mentally ill, Benjamin Rush (1745–1813) wrote a book titled *Medical Inquiries and Observations on the Diseases of the Mind*. From his and others' efforts arose what is now called the **medical model** of mental illness, which holds that disordered thoughts and behavior are the result of a diseased or otherwise malfunctioning brain. The implication of this model was that mental disorders should be treated in a similar fashion to physical disorders. Today, medical doctors who are interested in treating mental illness specialize in *psychiatry*, and routinely treat their patients by prescribing medicine.

At about the same time that Rush developed the medical model, Philippe Pinel (1745–1826) began his campaign to improve the treatment of the mentally ill in French *insane asylums*. The movement to treat people with mental disorders in a more humane fashion soon spread to the United States. In contrast to the medical model, so-called *moral therapy* assumed that insanity and abnormal behavior were the result of severe psychological and social stress. The influence of moral therapy is present today in the ***psychological model,*** which assumes that psychological problems are caused and maintained by a person's past and present life experiences. Inherent in this view of mental illness is the idea that treatment should above all else be understanding, compassionate, and humane.

LINK
Insane asylums, Chapter 18, p. 611

Organic Versus Functional Disorders

These two historical conceptions of mental disorders underlie a basic distinction in terminology that is still with us today. Mental disorders that are clearly caused by brain dysfunction are called *organic mental disorders,* whereas mental disorders *not* so clearly linked to the brain are called *functional mental disorders.* An historic example of an organic mental disorder is *general paresis,* the outcome of untreated syphilis, in which the brain's neurons die. Progressive paralysis and confused, disorganized thinking are the result. At autopsy, the shrinkage of the lobes of the brain due to massive neuron death is clearly visible (see Figure 17.2). By contrast, in a functional mental disorder such as depression, the brain appears to be normal.

Recent findings in the neurosciences, however, have clouded this distinction between *organic* and *functional* disorders. In terms of receptors, neurotransmitters, and neurochemical pathways, functional and organic disorders have a demonstrable physical basis. Although the brain of a person who is suffering from depression may appear to be normal, its chemical balance is not.

Implicit in the distinction between organic and functional disorders is the notion that some mental disorders are more severe than others. Sigmund Freud made this distinction in differentiating between a *psychosis* and a *neurosis*. A **psychosis** is a severe mental disorder characterized by disorganized thought and a loss of contact with reality: general paresis would be one example. **Neurosis** is the Freudian term for a functional disorder, which Freud thought of as impaired personal and social functioning resulting from anxiety. Prior to the development of modern medication, a person with a psychosis was more often than not institutionalized, while people with neurosis were able to function (usually in less than an optimal fashion) in their homes, workplaces, and relationships. While these rudimentary distinctions were helpful, practitioners needed more detailed guidelines for the diagnosis of mental disorders. In time, a movement to standardize diagnostic terms arose.

Freud and neurosis, Chapter 14, p. 496

Standardization of Diagnostic Terms

The task of diagnosis is more difficult than one might imagine. Think of a hypothetical continuum that ranges from normal to abnormal. Only a small percentage of people exhibit severe disorders that everyone would agree on; the remaining diagnoses are judgment calls.

Moreover, just as people with normal personalities, motivation, and behavior can be studied from various theoretical perspectives, so can people with mental disorders. Because clinical psychologists are often trained within a particular theoretical perspective, they carry with them selective biases and expectations about how people should behave. One result is that prior to the standardization of mental diagnoses, different psychologists would diagnose the same individual using different terms (Adams & Cassidy, 1993; Garfield, 1993).

psychological model (of mental disorders) A theory of mental illness that an individual's past and present life experiences cause and maintain a psychological disorder.

psychosis A severe mental disorder characterized by disorganized thought and a loss of contact with reality.

neurosis (Freud) Impaired personal and social functioning due to anxiety.

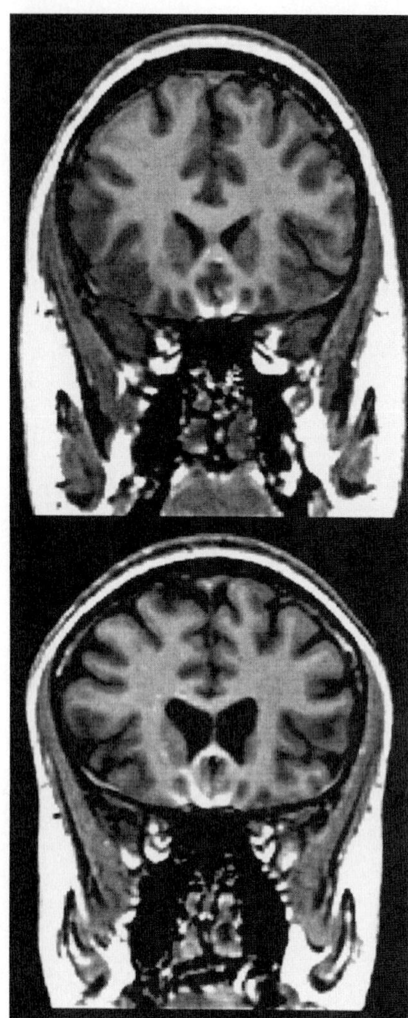

Figure 17.2 Organic Brain Damage. In many types of organic brain damage (bottom photo), the cortical lobes shrink (compare with normal brain, top photo). The MRI of the damaged brain also shows the increased size of the ventricles (black holes in middle of brain).

In the early 1950s, psychologists and psychiatrists recognized the need to standardize the diagnoses of mental disorders by creating the *Diagnostic and Statistical Manual of Mental Disorders (DSM)*. Published by the American Psychiatric Association, its revised form, the *DSM-IV*, published in 1994, recognizes over 200 different forms of mental disorder, arranged in 17 categories that may vary along one or more dimensions.

The *DSM-IV* represents the accumulated wisdom and experience of psychologists and psychiatrists for the past several decades. Often, the way in which a disorder is described and categorized reflects a committee decision that not everyone agrees with. In years to come, diagnoses will undoubtedly change, and categories shift, to reflect a new consensus on specific disorders. Nevertheless, most psychologists and psychiatrists would agree that their current understanding of abnormal behavior is far advanced over the general thinking in 1900. *DSM-IV* has improved the diagnosis of mental illness, but has not eliminated the need for complex analysis and careful judgment.

Using the *DSM-IV*

An overview of *DSM-IV* illustrates its complexity (see Table 17.1). The five axes represent five different ways of characterizing a disorder. When a case is brought to a psychologist's or psychiatrist's attention, it is diagnosed along one or more of these axes; thorough evaluation would include all five.

Axis I, *Clinical Syndromes,* organizes the most serious mental disorders in nine different categories: diseases of infancy, childhood, or adolescence (such as ADHD); organic mental disorders (such as dementia); substance-related disorders (such as alcoholism); schizophrenia; mood disorders (such as depression); anxiety disorders (such as panic); somatoform disorders (such as hypochondriasis); dissociative disorders (such as amnesia); and sexual and gender disorders. Axis I disorders are cyclic in nature; people who suffer from them have periods of *remission* in which they are symptom free.

Axis II lists chronic mental disorders, called *Personality Disorders*. Although people with personality disorders often behave maladaptively throughout a lifetime, they can function on a job and in other social settings. Their functioning is not as impaired as that of people with Axis I disorders during periods in which their cyclical disorders are expressed.

Axis III, *General Medical Conditions,* allows a practitioner to record physical symptoms that might accompany and interact with a patient's mental disorder. Axis IV, *Psychosocial and Environmental Problems,* usually includes a case history based on a structured interview. Environmental conditions that may affect both the diagnosis and treatment of a patient's disorder are recorded here. For example, a recent divorce would be noted on this axis.

Axis V, the *Global Assessment of Functioning (GAF) Scale,* is a 100-point scale that indicates the severity of a patient's impairment. The lower the point value, the more serious the impairment. A score of about 50 might indicate *serious* symptoms or impairment in social, occupational, or school functioning. With improvement in behavior, a score of about 60 might represent *moderate* symptoms or impairment in social, occupational, or school functioning.

Figure 17.3 shows an evaluation of a patient diagnosed with a bipolar disorder (commonly known as manic depression). Like George, this 35-year-old male presented with a history of intense mood swings, from high-energy euphoria to gloomy hopelessness. He had cycled between these extremes for many years. The social consequences of the disorder were that the patient dropped out of college and could not keep a job. His excessive use of alcohol had resulted in one citation for driving under the influence. At the time of the

Table 17.1 The Five Axes of the DSM-IV

Axis I Clinical Syndromes

Clinical syndromes are divided into nine categories: **disorders of infancy, childhood, or adolescence** (ADHD, autism, mental retardation, for example); **organic mental disorders** (delirium, dementia, memory loss); **substance-related disorders** (alcohol and cocaine abuse); **schizophrenia and other psychotic disorders; mood disorders**(depression, bipolar disorder); **anxiety disorders** (panic disorder); **somatoform disorders** (hypochondriasis); **dissociative disorders** (dissociative amnesia); **sexual and gender disorders.**

Axis II Personality Disorders

Long-standing, maladaptive personality traits that cause personal and social stress (avoidant personality, borderline personality, and antisocial personality).

Axis III General Medical Conditions

Physical disorders, including hyperthyroidism, diabetes, arthritis, and so on.

Axis IV Psychosocial and Environmental Problems

Environmental conditions that may influence, precipitate, or aggravate a mental disorder (divorce, death in the family).

Axis V Global Assessment of Functioning Scale

A scale ranging from 1 to 100, in which low scores indicate a tendency to hurt oneself or others; middle scores, moderate impairment in social and occupational settings; and high scores, high-level functioning.

Source: Adapted from *Diagnostic and Statistical Manual of Mental Disorders*, 4th ed., 1994, American Psychiatric Association.

interview the patient had been employed for 10 weeks and was not drinking. The therapist set his global assessment of functioning at 55, between *serious impairment (50)* and *moderate difficulty in functioning (60)*. This diagnosis, as we'll see in the next chapter, provides the justification for some type of therapy, including drug therapy.

In the following sections we will turn to the diagnosis and etiology (causes) of an important subset of the disorders found in *DSM-IV*. We will cover the most common disorders in our culture, namely anxiety disorders, somatoform disorders, dissociative disorders, mood disorders, schizophrenic disorders (all Axis I), and personality disorders (Axis II).

Axis I	Mood Disorder—bipolar disorder Alcohol abuse
Axis II	None
Axis III	Physical health good; occasional kidney stones
Axis IV	Difficulty in social relationships, including dating; difficulty keeping job; recent ticket for driving under the influence of alcohol, driver's license suspended for 2 months; lives alone in rural area
Axis V	Current global assessment of functioning (GAF): 55

Figure 17.3 Diagnostic Evaluation of a 33-Year-Old Male.

INTERIM SUMMARY

1. The growth of both humanistic and scientific thinking in the 18th and 19th centuries laid the foundation for contemporary thinking about mental illness.
2. According to the ***medical model,*** mental illness results from a diseased or damaged brain and should be treated like a physical disorder.
3. According to the ***psychological model,*** mental illness is caused by an individual's past and present life experiences. Disabling environments can both cause and maintain dysfunctional behavior.
4. *Organic mental disorders* are caused by known brain dysfunctions. Historically, mental illnesses that lacked a known basis in the brain were called *functional mental disorders*. Today, both functional and organic disorders are presumed to have a physical basis.
5. A ***psychosis*** is a severe mental disorder that is characterized by disorganized thinking and loss of contact with reality. A ***neurosis*** is a less severe disorder characterized by impaired functioning due to anxiety. Today, these Freudian terms have been largely replaced by more descriptive diagnostic categories.
6. In the 1950s, psychologists and psychiatrists classified and standardized diagnoses of mental disorders in the *Diagnostic and Statistical Manual of Mental Disorders (DSM)*. The most recent revision is the DSM-IV.
7. The *DSM-IV* characterizes mental disorders along five axes. Axis 1 (Clinical Syndromes) represents common cyclical disorders; Axis II (Personality Disorders) represents common chronic disorders; Axis III (General Medical Condition) describes the patient's general medical condition; and Axis IV (Psychosocial and Environmental Problems) denotes the patient's social environment. Axis V (Global Assessment of Functioning) quantifies the patient's overall functioning.

For Further Thought

1. The medical and psychological approaches to mental illness seem reminiscent of both mind-body and nature-nurture distinctions. How do they differ?
2. What are the advantages, and disadvantages, of having a diagnostic manual such as the *DSM-IV*?

ANXIETY DISORDERS

More Americans experience *anxiety disorders* than any other kind of psychological disorder (see Figure 17.4). One study found that 17 percent of the adult population of the United States had one type of anxiety disorder in any given year (Kessler et al., 1994). **Anxiety disorders** are characterized by persistent feelings of apprehension. Four types of anxiety disorders have been identified: phobic disorder, generalized anxiety disorder, panic disorder, and obsessive-compulsive disorder.

Phobic Disorder

A **phobic disorder** is characterized by a persistent, inappropriate fear of a specific object or situation. Figure 17.5 shows the prevalence of phobias reported in one mental health survey (Eaton, Dryman, & Weissman, 1991). The most common *simple phobias* are a paralyzing fear of snakes, insects, and other small, moving life forms, followed by a fear of heights, water, and storms. Many people also have *social phobias* (speaking in public, intense shyness) and *agoraphobia* (fear of open spaces and crowds).

Genes play a role in predisposing a person to phobic disorders. The study of identical twins has shown that if one twin has an anxiety disorder, the other has a 1 in 3 likelihood of sharing it compared with a 15 percent likelihood for two

anxiety disorder A mental disorder characterized by persistent feelings of apprehension.

phobic disorder An anxiety disorder characterized by a persistent, inappropriate fear of an object or situation.

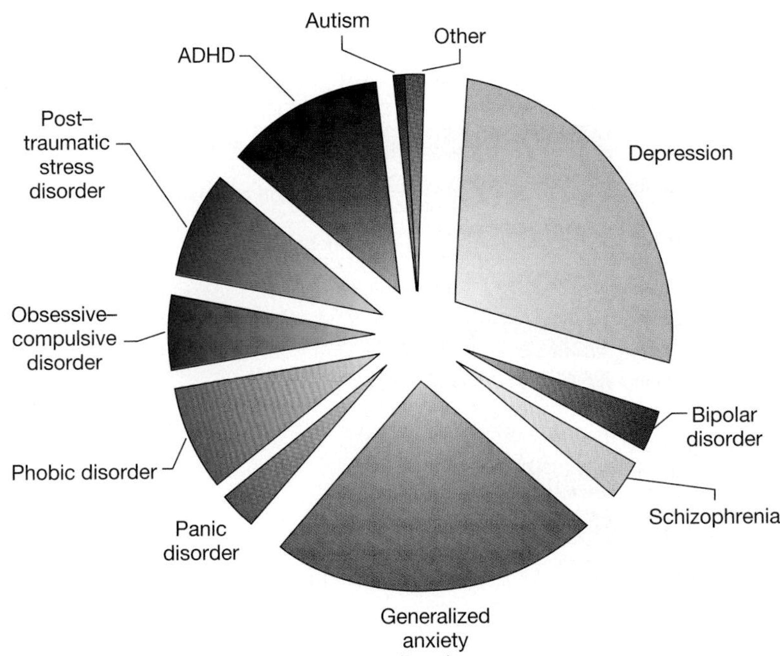

Figure 17.4 The Frequency of Major Mental Disorders in the United States. As a group, anxiety disorders (generalized anxiety disorders, panic disorder, phobic disorder, obsessive-compulsive disorder, and post-traumatic stress disorder) are the most common form of mental illness in the United States. Depression is the most common single disorder. *Source:* National Institutes of Mental Health, 1999.

dizygotic twins. Indeed, many phobias are exaggerations of an adaptive anxiety about environmental threats. There is good reason to be somewhat anxious about encounters with animals, heights, water, and storms.

A phobia can be exaggerated, or acquired, in one of two ways: by observing another person's reactions to a phobic object or through aversive conditioning. Parents who scream and jump onto chairs to escape mice, for example, or who are fearful in waist-deep water, are modeling phobic responses for their children. Recall, too, how 11-month-old Little Albert learned to fear a white rat after its appearance had been paired with loud, clanging noise. The noise produced anxiety and fear in Albert that was transferred to the white rat through classical conditioning.

Observational learning and conditioned fear response, Chapter 6, p. 215

Recall Paul Rozin's argument that animals are evolutionarily *prepared* to associate certain stimuli—that is, that some stimuli are more easily conditioned than others. Phobias often involve stimulus objects that are easily conditioned and are therefore highly memorable (McNally, 1987). Indeed, the most prevalent phobias involve Rozin's "prepared" stimuli, such as heights, water, and storms—all of which are potentially harmful. Just one conditioning trial involving an insect (CS) and its sting (US), or a broken arm after falling out of tree, can focus a person's anxiety on insects or heights.

Prepared learning, contextual cues, Chapter 6, p. 218

Generalized Anxiety Disorder

A **generalized anxiety disorder** is characterized by a persistent, inappropriate anxiety with no one apparent cause. This nonspecific "free-floating anxiety" is essentially Freud's notion of neurotic anxiety. Life is full of schedules that must be met and responsibilities that must be fulfilled (*Get flu shots, remember to floss, check your punctuation*). The result is anxiety (*All this worrying makes me feel dizzy*).

Stress, stressors, and anxiety, Chapter 16, p. 559

generalized anxiety disorder A mental disorder that is characterized by a persistent, inappropriate anxiety for which there is no apparent cause.

We can assume that a person with generalized anxiety disorder begins with a genetic tendency to overreact to life's subtle stressors. Indeed, the children of parents who have panic disorder are at higher risk than others for anxiety disorders (Biederman et al., 2001). Over many years a child may observe the panic, anxiety,

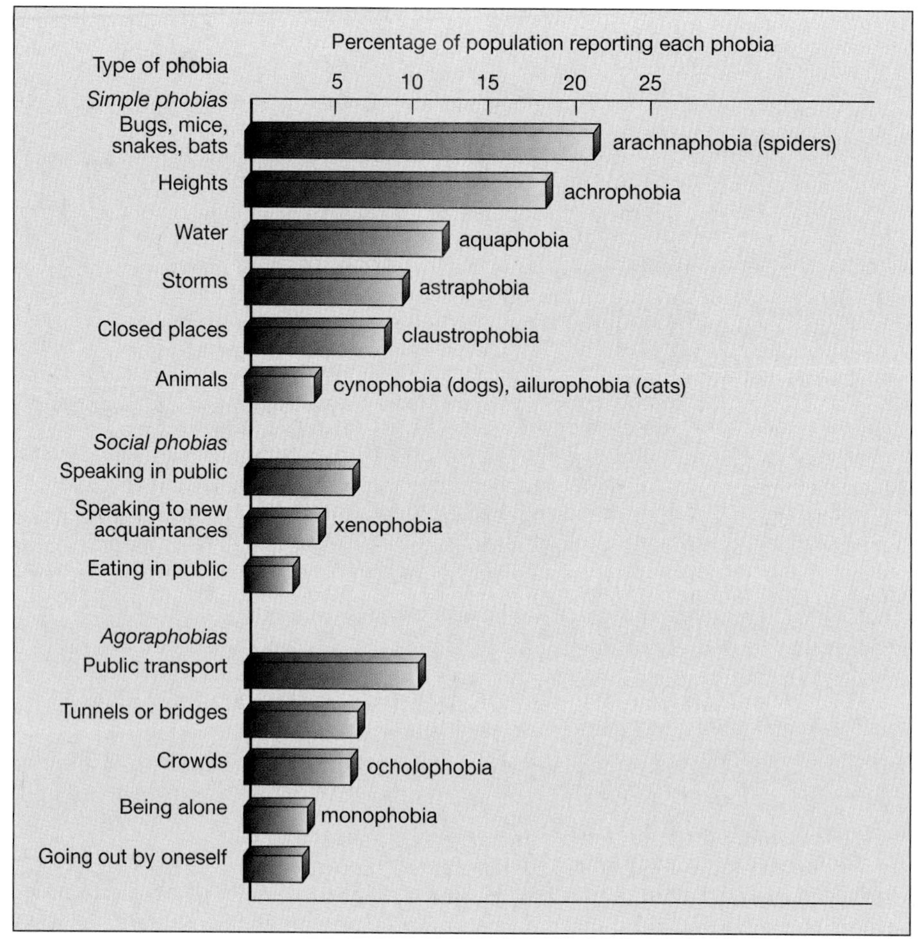

Figure 17.5 The Prevalence of Various Types of Phobias. *Source:* Modified from Eaton, Dryman, & Weissman, 1991.

and dismay of a parent who talks about, avoids, and finally goes *to see the dentist*. When this child experiences toothache as an adult, or sees a physician for an annual check-up, generalized anxiety may result.

Imagine a situation in which a small child is routinely punished by being grounded in her room, which happens to be painted blue. Unconsciously, the color of the room becomes paired with unhappiness and anxiety. Now, fast-forward 10 to 20 years. In adulthood, entering a blue room might produce a conditioned anxiety response in this individual. Unaware that her conditioned response was controlled by the color, she would develop a free-floating anxiety rather than a phobic response to blue rooms.

One explanation for generalized anxiety, then, is that although early childhood conditioning has been forgotten, conditioned stimuli continue to evoke the anxiety. In genetically predisposed people, many such stimuli could inadvertently elicit generalized anxiety in a variety of situations (Gantt, 1953). In this disorder, the stimulus is less memorable and perhaps less easily conditioned than the prepared stimuli that elicit phobias.

panic disorder A disorder characterized by recurring rushes of paralyzing anxiety that may last for several minutes.

Panic Disorder

A **panic disorder** is characterized by recurring rushes of paralyzing anxiety. In a panic attack, lasting about 15 minutes, sympathetic arousal makes the heart race, producing dizziness, disorientation, and difficulty in breathing (Taylor et al.,

1986). About 50 percent of those who experience panic attacks also become dissociative and depersonalized to the point of feeling they are going crazy or about to die. Most panic disorders occur in females (Rapee & Barlow, 1993).

The following case history illustrates some of the symptoms of a panic attack. May, a 21-year-old college student smoked marijuana for the first time on spring break in a Mexican border town. Some time later she began to feel anxious, fearful, and paranoid. She couldn't breathe, became dizzy, and experienced disorientation and loss of control. Her frightened friends took her to an emergency room where she spent the night, calmed with a sedative. Over the next several weeks, May continued to have panic attacks, and finally sought help. A combination of drug therapy and "talk therapy" lasting several months allowed her to "control" her panic disorder.

But, why, you might be wondering, would May's behavior be diagnosed as a panic disorder rather than an idiosyncratic response to marijuana? This is a good question, because marijuana and other drugs have been known to induce panic attacks in people who are genetically susceptible to them (Barlow, 1988; Gorman, Liebowitz, Fyer, & Stein, 1989). However, friends who smoked marijuana with her did not experience the same symptoms, and her symptoms persisted for weeks following her one-time use. Finally, she responded to therapy in the same way as others who are treated for panic disorder.

In this incident, May's panic attack was likely triggered by smoking marijuana in unfamiliar surroundings. In other individuals the trigger might be a traumatic event such as a car accident, or a miscarriage, or conditioned stimulus associated with such events. An increased awareness of subtle changes in breathing and heart rate can also elicit memories of past events, triggering a panic attack (Schmidt & Trakowski, 1997). Even thoughts can act as conditioned stimuli. People who suffer from asthma, for example, and have experienced the feeling of suffocation, are likely to trigger a panic attack simply by thinking about the experience.

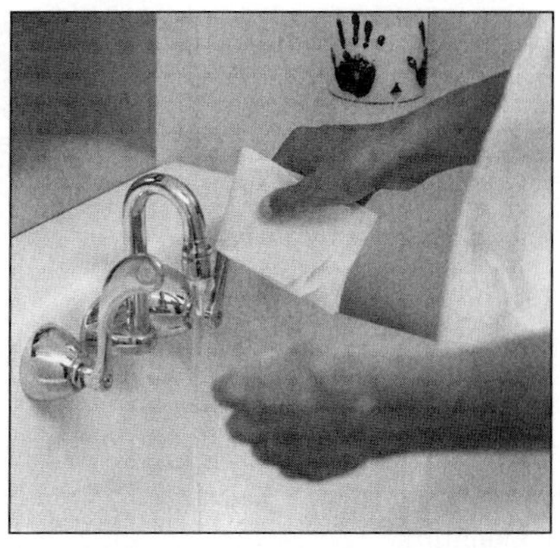

People with obsessive-compulsive disorders may use hand-washing rituals to deal with obsessive thoughts about cleanliness.

Obsessive-Compulsive Disorder

A degree of order in one's life is normal, but too much can be disabling. Consider a middle-aged man called Carl who schedules every activity in his life to the minute, including the exact time at which he plans to initiate love making, and the expected ending time. He is orderly to a fault in maintaining his apartment and his clothing. After wearing a suit, he methodically leaves a coin or two in a trouser pocket. The next time he wears those trousers, he shifts the change to the other pocket. When asked why he does so, Carl responds that one pocket will not wear out faster than the other, so that the suit will last longer.

Obsessive-compulsive disorders (OCD) are characterized by persistent, uncontrollable thoughts (obsessions) and ritualized behaviors (compulsions). Carl was obsessed with order and ritual, including the precise timing of his activities, and an unusual fixation on the rate at which his pants pockets wore out. Rituals of scheduling his day to the last minute and leaving a coin in one pocket helped him to manage the anxiety that constantly hung over him.

Table 17.2 lists the most typical obsessions and compulsions displayed by patients diagnosed with OCD. Research by Jenicke, Baer, and Minichiello (1986) indicates that individuals with OCD typically have more than one obsession and follow multiple rituals. Like Carl, about one-third express an overwhelming need for symmetry and order in their lives.

obsessive-compulsive disorder (OCD) A disorder characterized by obsessions (persistent, uncontrollable, worrisome thoughts) and compulsions (ritualized behaviors triggered by obsessions).

Carl and many others like him live highly productive lives, never missing appointments or tax deadlines. Carl always knows where his keys are, because he is always checking to make sure they are in the appropriate pocket. (Checking

Table 17.2 Common Obsessive Thoughts and Compulsions

Obsessive Thoughts	Percentage of Sample of OCD Patients
Dirt, germs, contamination	55
Aggressive impulses	50
Need for symmetry	37
Bodily concerns	35
Forbidden sexual impulses	32
Compulsive Rituals	
Checking (confirming)	79
Washing	58
Counting	21

Source: From Jenicke, Baer, & Minichiello, 1986.

and rechecking is a ritual many people with OCD perform; see Table 17.2.) After several failed marriages, he eventually found a mate who not only can fit into his highly scheduled life, but also finds satisfaction and security in doing so. The behavior of other people diagnosed with OCD, however, is highly maladaptive. The psychiatrist Judith Rapoport (1989) described a young boy obsessed with dirt and germs who scrubbed his hands raw from repetitive washing, and a woman so obsessed with the symmetry of her eyebrows that she plucked all the hairs on both sides trying to keep them even. Both individuals were so anxious to satisfy their compulsions that their disorder interfered with day-to-day functioning.

Compulsive thoughts are the most common symptom in an estimated 4 million patients diagnosed with OCD. Patients can't get certain thoughts such as "my spouse is cheating on me" out of their heads. The obsession occupies every waking moment, incapacitating the person at work and in social relationships. As we'll see in the next chapter, both antidepressant drugs and talk therapy directed at "thought stopping" have proven effective in helping OCD patients manage their symptoms.

INTERIM SUMMARY

1. People who experience *anxiety disorders* have persistent feelings of apprehension. The four types of anxiety disorders are phobic disorder, generalized anxiety disorder, panic disorder, and obsessive-compulsive disorder.
2. A *phobic disorder* is characterized by a persistent, inappropriate fear of a specific object or situation. A phobia can be simple (fear of snakes) or more complex, such as *agoraphobia* (fear of open spaces and of crowds).
3. Genes can predispose a person to become anxious.
4. In some individuals the adaptive human tendency to be anxious and fearful in certain situations can become a maladaptive disorder through observational learning or classical conditioning. Some stimuli may elicit more anxiety than others because humans are evolutionarily prepared to respond to them.
5. A *generalized anxiety disorder* is characterized by a persistent, inappropriate "free-floating" anxiety for which there is no apparent cause. One explanation for free-floating anxiety is that adults have forgotten early childhood aversive conditioning experiences, but the conditioned stimuli continue to evoke the anxious response.
6. A *panic disorder* is characterized by an overwhelming, disabling anxiety that may last for several minutes. A person with this disorder may become dizzy and disoriented, dissociative and depersonalized.
7. A panic attack can be triggered by drugs and other aversive situations, including one's thoughts and emotions. Panic attacks are more prevalent among females than males.
8. An *obsessive-compulsive disorder (OCD)* is characterized by persistent, uncontrollable thoughts (obsessions) and rituals (compulsions). Common obsessions include an uncontrollable need for order and runaway, repetitive thoughts. Common rituals include compulsive hand-washing, counting, and repetitious checking.

For Further Thought

1. Is a fear of snakes inappropriate for those who live in "snake country"? When does a fear of snakes constitute "a phobia"?
2. After falling from a horse, a person may be admonished to get back on it and ride ASAP. Is this good advice? Why?

3. In Chapter 7 we learned that in 18th-century France humans often lived their whole lives without ever having a bath. Were these people to construct the criteria for an obsessive-compulsive disorder, might they include "washes hair daily"? What does your answer to this question say about the *DSM-IV*?

SOMATOFORM DISORDERS

In Chapter 16 we saw that people's beliefs can influence their physical health, contributing to psychosomatic disorders from ulcers and asthma to voodoo deaths and false pregnancies. In the *DSM-IV* the term *somatoform disorder* refers to a particular subset of psychosomatic disorders.

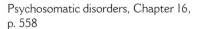

Psychosomatic disorders, Chapter 16, p. 558

Formally defined, a ***somatoform disorder*** is one in which a person experiences bodily symptoms that are due solely to psychological causes. People who have been diagnosed with a somatoform disorder report symptoms that seem to others, including physicians, to be imaginary and trivial and *entirely* psychological in origin. By contrast, ulcers and high blood pressure produce identifiable tissue damage.

Is the pain experienced by a person with a somatoform disorder imaginary, then? This question puzzles physicians and psychologists alike. All pain is experienced psychologically, though not all people perceive the same injury, or physical ailment, in the same way. Thus, people with a somatoform disorder are likely reporting pain they are actually experiencing. In phantom limb, for example, an amputee reports pain in a body part that is missing. The pain is not imaginary.

Pain, phantom limb, Chapter 7, p. 265

We will discuss three forms of somatoform disorders: hypochondriasis, somatization disorders, and conversion disorders.

Hypochondriasis

Soon after his father died, Charles Darwin, 40 years old, began to complain of nausea, vomiting, boils, headaches, sleeplessness, giddiness, and flatulence (Brown, 1995). For much of the rest of his life he kept a health diary in which he recorded how poorly he felt several times each day. Today Darwin would be diagnosed with **hypochondriasis,** a disorder in which a person becomes preoccupied with health and worries constantly about becoming ill.

The *hypochondriac* is a common character in novels and movies. A defining characteristic of this disorder is an unwillingness to be satisfied with the medical treatment one receives. Overly sensitive to subtle changes in their bodies, hypochondriacs live in constant fear that their head cold will become pneumonia, and a stomachache or headache portends a more serious ailment. No matter how many physicians they consult, none can help. These patients often remark that physicians cannot identify the rare form of disease that is troubling them.

Hypochondriasis is likely an exaggeration of an adaptive tendency both to monitor and maintain one's health. From an evolutionary perspective, hypochondriasis is more adaptive than its opposite, the denial of pain and illness. We don't encounter many people who maladaptively ignore pain (Strauss, Spitzer, and Muskin, 1990); congenital insensitivity to pain leads to earlier-than-normal death and a reduced likelihood of reproducing. In most people learning plays a role in the denial of pain: a child who is punished for expressing pain will be less likely to report it as an adult.

Genetic predispositions aside, we can hypothesize that people who have been diagnosed with hypochondriasis were conditioned as children to be sensitive to pain and to seek attention for the slightest illness. A caretaker who responds with

somatoform disorder A mental disorder in which a person experiences bodily symptoms that are solely due to psychological causes.

hypochondriasis A disorder in which a person is excessively preoccupied with health and worries constantly about becoming ill.

kindness, attention, and love to such requests for attention would reinforce the behavior, increasing its occurrence. Janet Brown (1995) has proposed that that is exactly what happened to Charles Darwin. No doubt he was ill, but his lifelong wife and caretaker, Emma, reinforced his illnesses. Her role in tending to his needs allowed her access to an otherwise private man who preferred to keep to himself. Darwin may have manufactured symptoms and, seeking attention, managed to control the amount of time he spent with her.

Somatization Disorders

A **somatization disorder** is characterized by a history of multiple physical complaints made over a period of several years. This diagnosis specifies the onset of symptoms before the age of 30 to eliminate the complaints of the elderly who also report multiple symptoms. The meaning of "multiple" physical complaints is rigidly defined: From specific lists of disorders, a patient must report four pain symptoms, two gastrointestinal symptoms, one sexual symptom, and one "pseudoneurologic" symptom such as blurred vision, hallucinations, balance problems, breathing difficulties, paralysis, or a similar complaint for which there is no organic basis. Pain symptoms must be felt in at least four different sites, including the head, abdomen, back, joints, extremities, chest, and rectum, as well as during sexual intercourse, menstruation, or urination.

Conversion Disorders

Freud's "glove anesthesia," Chapter 14, p. 496

Blindsight, Chapter 7, p. 283

somatization disorder A somatoform disorder characterized by a history of multiple physical complaints extending over a period of several years.

conversion disorder A temporary loss of a bodily function with no discernable physical cause.

A **conversion disorder** is the temporary loss of a bodily function with no discernable physical cause. Freud's interest in psychological disorders was piqued by one of Charcot's patients who had a "glove anesthesia" (see Figure 14.6, page 496). In this example of a conversion disorder, the reported symptom, a lack of sensation in the hand, did not match the underlying nerves for touch and pain. Hence, there was no physical basis for the disorder.

A more common occurrence, also not well understood, has been called *psychic blindness*. Though the visual system is apparently intact, a person with this type of conversion disorder acts as if blind. (This condition differs from that of blindsight, in which a person reports being blind, but in reality can "see" objects. Blindsight, but not psychic blindness, involves organic damage to the visual cortex.) Other types of conversion disorder include paralysis, deafness, and epilepsy. Conversion disorders are rare in contemporary Western culture; both their type and frequency of occurrence seem to be culturally dependent (Micale, 1995). How the brain produces a conversion disorder, or *any* somatoform disorder, is not yet understood.

INTERIM SUMMARY

1. A person who experiences bodily symptoms that are due solely to psychological causes suffers from some type of *somatoform disorder.*
2. Somatoform disorders—hypochondriasis, somatization disorders, and conversion disorders—are specific examples of psychosomatic disorders.
3. Even in the absence of objective evidence of tissue damage, the pain a person reports is real.
4. *Hypochondriasis* is a disorder in which a person becomes overly concerned with his or her health and worries constantly about becoming ill. This condition is thought to be an exaggeration of an evolved tendency to self-monitor for signs of illness.

5. A *somatization disorder* is characterized by a history of multiple physical complaints beginning before age 30 and extending over a period of several years. *DSM-IV* specifies that the patient must report four pain symptoms, two gastrointestinal symptoms, one sexual symptom, and one "pseudoneurologic" symptom.

6. A *conversion disorder* is the temporary loss of a bodily function for which there is no discernable physical cause. The frequency and type of conversion disorder people report varies from one culture to the next.

For Further Thought

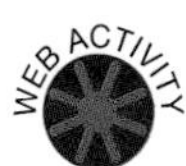

1. People who have been diagnosed with a conversion disorder and somatization disorder are often oddly detached and unconcerned in reporting their symptoms, displaying what the French call *la belle indifference*. Why do you think these people's behavior differs so markedly from that of hypochondriasis?
2. What are the advantages and disadvantages of ignoring the complaints of people with somatoform disorders? From a learning and conditioning perspective, what effect should ignoring someone's complaints have on the complaining behavior?

DISSOCIATIVE DISORDERS

We have seen that dissociation is common to a variety of mental disorders. Even though people who have been diagnosed with schizophrenia and other mental problems exhibit dissociative behavior, *dissociative disorders* are a separate category in *DSM-IV*. We will look at four subtypes in this category: *dissociative fugue, dissociative amnesia, depersonalization disorder,* and *dissociative identity disorder* (Spiegel & Cardena, 1991).

Dissociative Fugue States

A **dissociative fugue** is a disorder that is characterized by loss of memory for a period of time. Often, people with this disorder abruptly disappear from their normal surroundings, travel to a new place, and cannot remember who they are or what they are doing there. A fugue (a word that means "flight," as in *fugitive*) often occurs following a traumatic event. The person is aware of traveling, often for vague reasons. With time, disassociative fugue typically disappears. People begin to piece together (associate) their memories of the lost period, though most never fully recover all their lost memories. The subject of novels and movies, this rare condition presents problems for memory theorists because of the selectivity of the memory loss: general knowledge is retained, but autobiographical (personal) memories of a particular time period are lost. Although the stark dissociation from normal consciousness and the lack of memory for past events cannot be explained in terms of conscious processes (Wegner, 1994), attributing it to the unconscious (escape, denial, or repression) does not explain its occurrence either (Loftus & Klinger, 1992).

Autobiographical memory, Chapter 10, p. 366

dissociative fugue A mental disorder characterized by an abrupt disappearance from one's normal surroundings, travel to unfamiliar surroundings, and an inability to remember details of one's personal identity.

dissociative amnesia A disorder in which a person abruptly and inexplicably cannot recall large amounts of personal information.

Dissociative Amnesia

Dissociative amnesia is a disorder in which a person abruptly and inexplicably cannot recall large amounts of personal information. The *DSM-IV* specifies that this disorder is more problematic than the normal vagaries of memory, memory

Retrograde amnesia, Chapter 10, p. 374

loss following a head injury, or the progressive memory loss of Alzheimer's disease. Like a fugue, its sudden onset is often the result of trauma or a stressful life event. It typically involves a selective retrograde amnesia for prior events (Spiegel & Cardena, 1991). In Chapter 10 we learned that retrograde amnesia often results from a concussive blow to the head. In fugue and dissociative amnesia, the memory loss is considered to be *psychogenic*—that is, psychological in origin. That which can be remembered continues to provide the basis for one's personality; that which cannot be remembered constitutes the fragmentation, or dissociation, of personality.

Depersonalization Disorder

Have you ever had an experience in which you felt you were floating "outside" yourself, observing what you were doing or hearing yourself speak as if you were someone else? If so, you are in good company, for about half the population reports such experiences. Other common dissociative experiences include *déjà vu* (the feeling that what is happening now has happened before) and a waking consciousness that has a dreamlike quality. In his book *A Leg to Stand On,* the neurologist Oliver Sacks (1984) described the consequences of breaking a leg in a climbing accident, and what his insensate leg felt like weeks later. The leg and the pain were not part of his being, Sacks wrote; rather, they belonged to someone else. For him, the healing process meant reintegrating his leg into his being.

In a **depersonalization disorder,** the common dissociative experience is greatly magnified; a person has severe, persistent feelings of being detached from oneself. This disorder is accompanied by acute fear and personal distress. Because it can be relatively brief in duration, it does not involve memory loss and is often triggered by a new experience, such as a first-time drug use. Not all psychologists agree that this experience should be considered a dissociative disorder (Spiegel & Cardena, 1991). Indeed, a careful comparison of the symptoms May reported after smoking marijuana (that resulted in the diagnosis of panic disorder), shows they are not unlike the symptoms of depersonalization disorder.

Dissociative Identity Disorder

The final disorder to be discussed in this category, *dissociative identity disorder,* is so incredible that not all psychologists recognize its occurrence or its nature. A person with **dissociative identity disorder (DID)** has two or more distinct personalities. That is, the personality has fragmented, or split in two (or more) separate identities. At different times, one or the other personality is "in control" and may or may not be aware of the "other" personality.

Prior to *DSM-IV,* this disorder was called *multiple personality disorder*. The term has become popularized, and the idea of multiple identities became pervasive in Western culture, primarily because of the book (Thigpen & Cleckley, 1957) and movie *The Three Faces of Eve*. (*Sybil* is a more recent movie about the same subject.) Chris Sizemore, the person on whom *The Three Faces of Eve* was based, claimed that each of her identities was "so different that their tones of voice . . . appetites, tastes in clothes, handwritings, skills, and IQs were all different . . . and totally separate from the personality I was born with" (Sizemore, 1989, p. 9).

Numerous questions have been raised about this disorder, however. Mersky (1992) points out that it is rare to nonexistent in Europe and Japan. Have American psychologists invented a new disorder? If so, they have been successful: one review of DID cases included 843 patients (Ross, Joshi, & Currie, 1990). The large majority of these cases (88 percent) were women who reported experiencing sexual, physical, or emotional abuse as a child. They saw their alternate personalities as an outlet or escape from a damaged "main" personality (Ross, 1997).

depersonalization disorder A mental disorder characterized by severe, persistent feelings of being detached from oneself.

dissociative identity disorder (DID) (multiple personality disorder) A disorder in which a person presents with two or more distinct personalities.

Nicholas Spanos and his colleagues, also skeptical of the existence of DID, conducted studies in which they asked college students to role-play various personalities while hypnotized (Spanos, Weekes, & Betrand, 1985). The researchers suggested to subjects that an "alter" personality would keep certain information communicated to them hidden "behind walls. " On posthypnotic command, subjects were to allow the other personality to reveal the information, of which their "real" personality would be unaware. Seventy to eighty percent of the hypnotized subjects (and 30 percent of the nonhypnotized) subjects were able to do so.

Spanos (1996) and other researchers (Orne, Dinges, & Orne, 1984) concluded that patients who have been diagnosed with dissociative identity disorder are role playing. That is, in interaction with their therapists, they are generating alternate personalities that would not otherwise have existed. Their conclusion is similar to that of researchers who have studied alleged repressed memories (Spanos, 1996). Why large numbers of women report such complete splits in their personality is unknown. Demonstrating that most people with intact personalities can convincingly role play does not explain why a subset of women would also report such splits. In the next chapter, on psychotherapy, we'll return to Spanos's suggestion that therapists may be inadvertently maintaining this and other disorders.

False memories, Chapter 10, p. 345

INTERIM SUMMARY

1. The four subtypes of dissociative disorders are dissociative fugue, dissociative amnesia, depersonalization disorder, and dissociative identity disorder (DID).
2. A ***dissociative fugue*** is a disorder characterized by a sudden loss of memories for past events and personal identity and a flight from familiar surroundings.
3. ***Dissociative amnesia*** is a disorder in which a person suddenly cannot recall large amounts of autobiographical information, causing a fragmentation, or dissociation of personality.
4. Someone with a ***depersonalization disorder*** has severe feelings of detachment accompanied by acute fear and personal distress. This disorder resembles panic disorder.
5. A ***dissociative identity disorder (DID)***, formerly called *multiple personality disorder*, is characterized by a person seeming to have two or more distinct personalities. Some research suggests DID results from conscious role playing, reinforced by therapists.

For Further Thought

1. Imagine waking up in strange surroundings with little idea of who you are. Would you prefer antidepressant or antianxiety medication?
2. For half an hour my spouse had been jogging up and down some relatively steep trails. At one point she remarked that on one of them, she felt as if she was "floating uphill." Is such an event, a "runner's high," an example of a depersonalization disorder? Why or why not?

MOOD DISORDERS

We have been discussing thought disorders, some of which, like depersonalization disorder, may have emotional components. In contrast, a **mood disorder** is one that involves a sustained, pervasive emotion that interferes with normal functioning. Millions of Americans suffer from mood disorders, making them sad, angry, disgusted, or madly euphoric (see Figure 17.4).

mood disorder A mental disorder characterized by sustained, pervasive emotions that interfere with normal functioning.

Bipolar and Unipolar Disorders

The *DSM-IV* distinguishes between *bipolar* and *unipolar* mood disorders. Earlier, you met two individuals with bipolar disorders, George, and the patient described in Figure 17.3. **Bipolar disorders** involve drastic mood swings, from major depressive episode to either a *manic* or *hypomanic* episode. A *manic* episode is characterized by high energy, inflated self-esteem and grandiosity, a reduced need for sleep, and racing thoughts. A *hypomanic* episode is similar but lacks the intensity or severity of a manic episode. For example, a person with high energy and a reduced need for sleep, but not the flight of ideas characteristic of people with mania would be diagnosed as hypomanic.

A *unipolar disorder* is a noncycling disorder, either mania (rarely) or clinical depression, defined by one or more *major depressive episodes,* and the absence of a manic episode. **Depression** is characterized by despair and a pervasive sadness sometimes called *dysphoria*. From the outside you can see the negative affect of depression in faces and body language, and you can hear it in voices. From the inside, depression has been described as a deep, black hole into which no light can penetrate. The Pulitzer Prize winning author William Styron, who suffered from depression, described it as "despair beyond despair." Chronic depression that does not approach the severity of a major depressive episode is called a *dysthymic disorder*. More patients suffer from dysthymic disorders than from major depressive episodes.

Depression

Because normal people experience depression, the *DSM-IV* criteria distinguish it from *clinical depression*. Table 17.3 shows the five ways in which clinical depression differs from less severe forms. Both the intensity (severity) and quality of clinical depression differ from sadness. The disorder need not be precipitated by a loss to which sadness would be the normal response. It is also accompanied by thoughts and somatic complaints that are not associated with sadness. Finally, clinical depression tends to be cyclic in nature. A person may have a history of depression, but seldom a history of sadness. Clinical depression is not the same as seasonal affective disorder (SAD) that is triggered by too little light in the winter months (see Chapter 9).

The *DSM-IV* provides strict criteria for the diagnosis of unipolar depression. From a list of nine criteria, a patient must display five symptoms during the same 2-week period, one of them being either a depressed mood or "loss of interest or pleasure." Symptoms include feeling sad or empty, a diminished interest in most activities, weight loss and appetite disturbance, insomnia or sleep disturbance, fatigue (low energy), feelings of worthlessness, a diminished ability to concentrate, and recurrent thoughts of death or suicide.

Depression occurs cross-culturally, and its incidence seems to be increasing. Twice as many women as men are diagnosed with the disorder (Culbertson,

Table 17.3 Distinguishing Features of Clinical Depression

Intensity	Pervasive, impairs social and occupational functions
Precipitants	Not necessarily precipitated by an incident, or emotion may be grossly out of proportion to an incident
Quality	Qualitatively different from normal sadness
Associated symptoms	A cluster of signs and symptoms, including thoughts and bodily processes
History	Recurring episodes

Source: Modified from Whybrow, Akiskal, & McKinney, 1984.

bipolar disorders A mood disorder characterized by drastic mood swings, from major depressive episodes to either *manic* or *hypomanic* episodes.

depression A chronic mood disorder characterized by despair and a pervasive sadness.

1997), in part because twice as many women seek treatment. An estimated 12 percent of American males and 21 percent of American females will have a major depressive episode at some time in their lives (Kessler et al., 1994); half of them will experience a recurrence (Winoker, Coryell, Keller, Endicott, & Akisall, 1993). The average duration of a major depressive episode is several weeks.

The specific factors underlying depression are not known, but good evidence exists for the influence of both genes and environment. There is a 50 percent chance that if one identical twin has the disorder, the other will, compared to 20 percent for fraternal twins (McGuffin, Katz, Watkins, & Rutherford, 1996). Genetic differences in neurotransmitter levels probably account for differences in susceptibility. In general, people who have too much serotonin exhibit manic (or hypomanic) tendencies; those who have too little serotonin, depressive symptoms. In one study researchers used positron-emission tomography (PET) to measure dopamine, serotonin, and norepinephrine levels in 16 patients suffering from bipolar disorder. They found a 30 percent higher-than-normal density (Zubieta et al., 2000). As we'll see in the next chapter, drugs that elevate serotonin levels provide an effective treatment for depression.

What about environmental factors? The sadness, anxiety, and irritability that are symptomatic of depression create a positive-feedback environment. A depressed person exudes negativity in social interactions; in turn, people respond to them negatively, adding to their negative emotions. A vicious cycle ensues in which other people's rejection of them confirm the depressed person's feelings of self-worthlessness. One result is that depressed people tend to isolate themselves from others, giving up activities that could bring them joy. In a word, depressed people tend to perpetuate an environment that maintains their depressive thoughts and behavior.

Depression occurs cross-culturally, in twice as many women as men.

Neurotransmitter serotonin, Chapter 4, p. 143, and Chapter 9, p. 337

Suicide. Depression is often accompanied by anger that can be turned inward. If not reversed, self-punishment and self-blame can lead to thoughts of suicide. The threat of suicide is not an idle one: as many as 15 percent of people diagnosed with a history of major depressive episodes eventually kill themselves (National Institutes of Mental Health, 1999). Three times as many women as men attempt suicide, but men are three to four times more likely to succeed. As Figure 16.4 (page 552) shows, suicide is one of the leading causes of death among young people.

Suicide as leading cause of death, Chapter 16, p. 552

Table 17.4 lists 10 facts about suicide (Shneidman, 1966). One common misconception is that suicide is a pointless act. From the perspective of the person

Table 17.4 Ten Facts About Suicide

1. Suicide is seldom pointless or random; rather, it is viewed as a solution to life's unsolvable problems.
2. In the eyes of the person contemplating suicide, the goal is to become permanently unconscious.
3. Suicide relieves everything, even joy.
4. Frustration with unmet expectations is a common stressor that precipitates suicide.
5. Hopelessness and helplessness are the most common emotions accompanying suicide.
6. People who commit suicide tend to be ambivalent about it.
7. People who commit suicide do so as a last resort, believing they have few alternatives.
8. Common to all suicides is the desire to escape.
9. People communicate their intentions to commit suicide by talking about it.
10. Life-long escape strategies often precede an act of suicide.

Source: Modified from "Ten Facts About Suicide" from "Some Essentials for Suicide and Some Implications for Responses" by E. S. Schneidman in SUICIDE ed. by A. Roy. Copyright © 1966. Reprinted by permission of Lippincott, Williams, & Wilkins.

committing the act, suicide may be the only solution to otherwise unsolvable problems. Another myth is that people who make suicide plans keep them secret. The truth is, most people who are planning to commit suicide talk about it with family and friends. While they are ambivalent about committing suicide, their motivation is "to escape," and they typically have used other escape strategies throughout their lives.

The Adaptiveness of Mood Disorders

Depression may be linked to the human propensity to become sad. Why do some genetic combinations, when expressed in certain environments, have such disastrous consequences? One suggestion is that cross-culturally, sadness often accompanies a loss of "reproductive resources" (Nesse & Williams, 1994). The idea is that there are reproductive consequences of failed social relationships (including breaking-up and divorce), the death or estrangement of supportive family and friends, a loss of money, and so forth. A somewhat different evolutionary argument is that sadness and depression may be *adaptive* in signaling the need to change whatever isn't working (Beck, 1999). In the same way that pleasure reinforces some behavioral tendencies, sadness punishes other behavior, helping to define our adaptive, hedonistic tendencies. From this perspective, depression may actually *increase* people's ability to cope and survive by causing them to withdraw from situations that may result in danger, loss, bodily damage, or wasted effort (Nesse, 2000).

Hedonism and the law of effect, Chapter 6, p. 206

Another answer to the question, *Why are there mood disorders?* begins with a recognition of the desirability of genetic variation. One tenet of evolutionary theory is that some individuals prove to be better matches for the environment into which they were born than others. In the same way that retinal cones evolved to better exploit information provided by different wavelengths of light, could some forms of mental illness reflect an overall adaptive brain design?

Consider the link between mental illness and creativity. Figure 17.6 shows the results of a study of 1,005 successful (and famous) people (Ludwig, 1995). Notice the high correlation between mental illness and careers in the arts. Although it would be incorrect to infer that one must be mad to have a successful career in the arts, the connection between mental disorders and artistry is inescapable. A more direct link has been established between creativity and bipolar disorder, which has an even stronger genetic component than depression or anxiety disorders. The chance of the other twin developing bipolar disorder if one identical twin does is about 70 percent (Blehar, Weissman, Gershon, & Hirschfield, 1988). Moreover, a segment of the 18th chromosome has been identified for this disorder (MacKinnon, Jamison, & DePaulo, 1997). Several studies have shown that first-degree relatives (parents and children) of creative people with bipolar disorder display more creativity and more mental illness than the first-degree relatives of a representative control group (Andreasen, 1987; Coryell, Endicott, Keller, Andreasen, 1989). A review of the historical and empirical findings on the link between creativity and

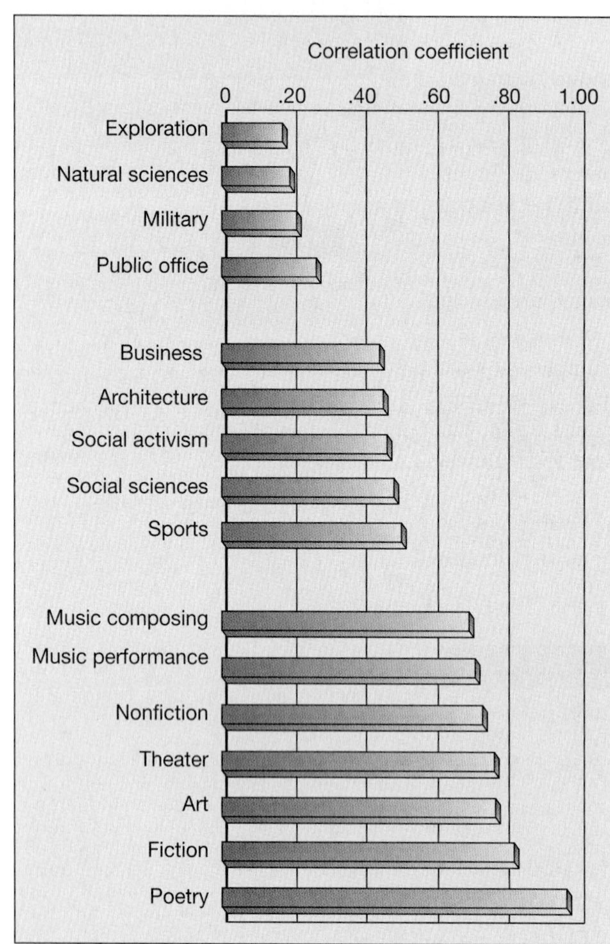

Figure 17.6 Mental Illness and Creativity. In highly talented and famous people, the likelihood of suffering at least one incident of mental illness in a lifetime is correlated with occupation. Notice the high frequency of mental illness among prominent people in the arts. *Source:* From THE PRICE OF GREATNESS: Resolving the Creativity and Madness Controversy by A. M. Ludwig. Copyright © 1995. Reprinted by permission of The Guilford Press.

mental illness has led Nancy Andreasen (1987) to hypothesize that a genetically predisposed personality and cognitive style supports both.

Just as intelligence can be seen as an adaptive characteristic that aids survival, so can creativity. A mind that sees the world differently can come up with unique solutions to survival, often through lateral thinking. Creativity and imagination provide the same advantages. For unknown reasons, the same minds that exhibit creativity are also subject to extremes of mood that too often are maladaptive (Nettle, 2001). Nevertheless, culture derives benefit from these individuals, expediting the flow of both their genes and memes.

Van Gogh's creative paintings were likely influenced by his mental illness.

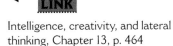

Intelligence, creativity, and lateral thinking, Chapter 13, p. 464

INTERIM SUMMARY

1. In a ***mood disorder,*** pervasive emotions interfere with normal functioning.
2. A ***bipolar disorder*** is defined by severe mood swings, from clinical depression to either *manic* or *hypomanic* episodes. A manic episode is characterized by high energy, inflated self-esteem and grandiosity, a reduced need for sleep, and racing thoughts. Hypomanic episodes are less severe.
3. A *unipolar disorder* is defined by one or more major depressive episodes and the absence of a manic episode. Chronic depression that does not include a major depressive episode is called a *dysthymic disorder*.
4. ***Depression*** is characterized by despair and a pervasive sadness. Clinical depression differs from sadness in terms of its intensity, quality, associated symptoms, history, and precipitants.
5. About 12 percent of American males and 21 percent of American females will experience a major depressive episode at some time in their lives.
6. Men are three to four times more successful in committing suicide than women, but three times as many women as men attempt suicide.
7. Some people may be genetically predisposed to mental illness, as evidenced by monozygotic twin studies. Sadness and depression may be adaptive in signaling the need for change.
8. Creativity and imagination are linked to mental illness, especially bipolar disorder.

For Further Thought

1. Do people have a right to end their own lives?
2. Can you think of some nongenetic reasons for the differences in the rates of depression among women and men?
3. Why do you think men are more successful than women in committing suicide?
4. What does slicing off one's ear have to do with being creative? Are all creative people eccentric to some extent?

SCHIZOPHRENIA

Schizophrenia is a disorder that is marked by disturbances in thought that may affect perception, emotions, and social processes. It is a fascinating if poorly understood mental disorder affecting over 2 million Americans, costing 35 to 40 billion dollars a year in the United States alone (Ettinger et al., 2001). In the following excerpt, a person who is suffering from schizophrenia responds to the question "Why do you think that people believe in God?":

> Uh, let's. I don't know why, let's see, balloon travel. He holds it up for you, the balloon. He don't let you fall out, your little legs sticking down through the clouds . . . legs sticking out. I don't know, looking down on the ground, heck, that'd make you so dizzy you just say and sleep you know, hold down and sleep there. I used to be sleep outdoors, you know, sleep out doors instead of going home. (Chapman & Chapman, 1973, p. 3)

Symptoms of Schizophrenia

The *DSM-IV* lists five major symptoms of schizophrenia: incoherent thinking, delusions, hallucinations, a deterioration of adaptive behavior, and a disturbance of affect. These symptoms must be noted over a 6-month period of progressive deterioration. As with other Axis I disorders, people with schizophrenia cycle in and out of their disorder, manifesting its major symptoms only during the active phases. Let's look more closely at the five major symptoms.

The first symptom of schizophrenia, *incoherent thinking*, can be seen in the excerpt. When asked an open-ended question about belief in God, this person's words revealed a characteristic thought disorder sometimes described as a "word salad." This patient's words are only loosely associated—clouds and balloons float; one can look down on the ground and sleep on the ground; and so forth. The patient cannot stay focused; ideas wander in a disconnected way. This symptom of the illness led the physician Eugen Bleuler in 1911 to coin the term *schizophrenia*. The root word *schizo* means split; Bleuler used the term to describe a schizophrenic's fragmented thinking, rather than a "split personality."

Another symptom of schizophrenia is **delusions**—false, unrealistic beliefs (Maher & Spitzer, 1993). Delusions of grandeur, or a false belief about one's identity, can also result from organic brain damage as in general paresis. For reasons that are not understood, schizophrenics often believe that they are some famous person, or that they have special powers that give them special knowledge (of gamma particles, intergalactic communication, and so forth). This symptom has been noted in many different cultures.

The third major symptom, **hallucinations**, are false perceptions. Individuals with schizophrenia often report hearing "voices" that others cannot hear. These auditory hallucinations are far more common than visual hallucinations. Cross-culturally, people who are schizophrenic describe the voices relating secret instructions and private information to people who are schizophrenic. For example, a former acquaintance of mine, "Bob," was convinced that the local cable company had installed a device on his television set that allowed his previous employers (in another state) both to track his whereabouts and to instruct him "what to do next."

Unfortunately, as is typically the case in people diagnosed with schizophrenia, the "voices" began to occupy more and more of Bob's time and energy. He couldn't sleep; he became convinced that his former employers had enlisted others in his new workplace to report on his every movement. His response was to withdraw from all social interactions and become wary of even the simplest job-related routines. Bob eventually lost his job and his marriage partner.

schizophrenia A disorder characterized by disturbances in thought that may affect perceptual, social, and emotional processes.

delusion A false, unrealistic belief.

hallucination A false perception that cannot be shared or verified.

What do you think Bob was like emotionally? You might imagine him as a wildly emotional person, but actually, he displayed a curious absence of emotion. The term an analyst might use to describe Bob would be *flattened affect*. A blank expression on his face, he would describe the "vibrations" coming through his TV cable in an unconcerned manner. However, people with schizophrenia can also display emotions that are out of synch with others, such as laughing at a funeral or crying for no apparent reason. Some people display specific sets of symptoms that constitute subtypes of the disorder.

People suffering from schizophrenia of the catatonic type may assume rigid postures for hours on end.

Types of Schizophrenia

The three most common forms of schizophrenia listed in the *DSM-IV* are *the disorganized type,* the *paranoid type,* and the *catatonic type.* Scientists are not sure whether these are different disorders or three variants of the same disorder (Gottesman, 1991). A gene that is associated with the catatonic type has been found on chromosome 22 (Meyer et al., 2001), but at present researchers have not compiled enough genetic or brain-based evidence to decide the issue.

The Disorganized Type. The word salad that opened this section is typical of the disorganized type of schizophrenia. Other symptoms include delusions and hallucinations, the content of which is not well organized. In fact, the lack of coherent thoughts is what differentiates this type of schizophrenia from the paranoid type.

The Paranoid Type. Some schizophrenics seem to think very clearly. Recall that "Bob" thought the cable company was keeping track of him and that others were part of the conspiracy. If asked, he could elaborate on the conspiracy in such a way that it might sound plausible. Two main themes characterize paranoid schizophrenic thinking: one, the most common, is that of being persecuted; the other is grandiose thinking. Auditory hallucinations are common, but not disorganized speech or behavior, or flat affect. (However, in relating their delusional scenarios, paranoid schizophrenics can become quite animated.)

The Catatonic Type. Schizophrenics of the catatonic type typically display symptoms of muscular rigidity; they may react to the sights and sounds around them. Their "rigidity" is waxy-like; should someone move a seemingly frozen limb to another position, for example, the catatonic schizophrenic will maintain the new position.

The three types are not as distinct as these textbook descriptions suggest. People with schizophrenic symptoms can change, so that over time the distinctions between subtypes become blurred (Kendler, Gruenberg, & Tsuang, 1985). For example, an organized type can become disorganized, and catatonic symptoms can appear and disappear. Finally, people with schizophrenic symptoms often go into remission. Although they typically maintain a flat or inappropriate affect, their behavior blends much better with that of "normal" people.

Causes of Schizophrenia

Researchers have evidence of genetic, physiological, and environmental causes of schizophrenia. We'll look at each in turn.

Genetic Factors. Evidence exists to suggest that people are genetically predisposed to exhibit schizophrenic behavior. Figure 17.7 shows the incidence of schizophrenia in the general population (about 1 percent) and in spouses of schizophrenics

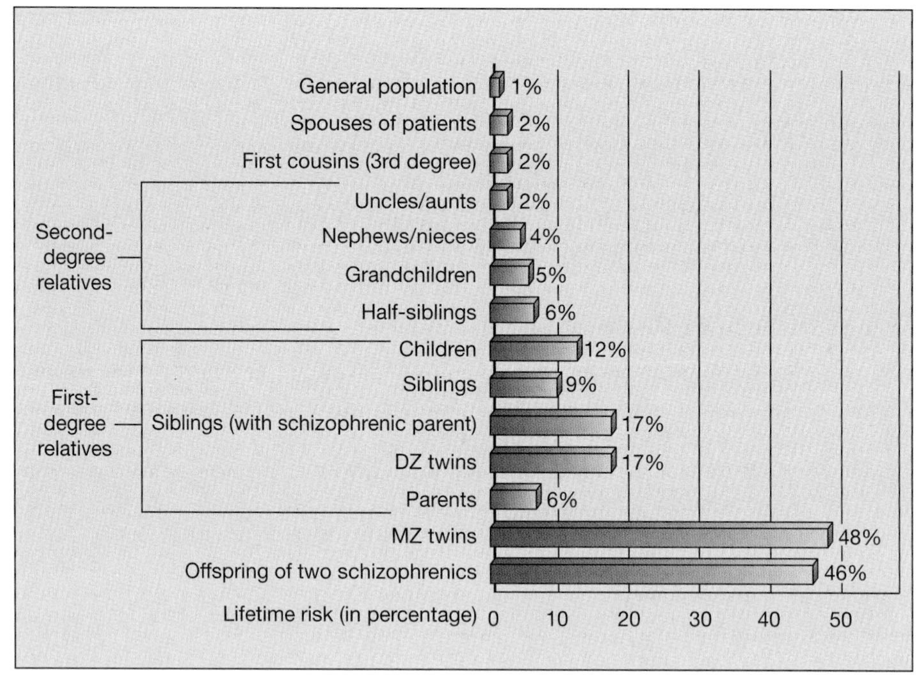

Figure 17.7 Incidence of Schizophrenia Among Related and Unrelated Individuals. *Source:* Graph from SCHIZOPHRENIA GENESIS: The Origins of Madness by I. I. Gottesman. Copyright © 1991.

(2 percent). As the figure shows, the more genes a person shares with a schizophrenic, the more likely that person is to have the illness (Gottesman, 1991; Kendler & Diehl, 1993). If your monozygotic twin is schizophrenic, for instance, you have about a 50 percent chance of also being schizophrenic.

Physiological Factors. Evidence at both the cellular and receptor level ties schizophrenia to brain functioning. On the cellular level, certain areas of the thalamus of schizophrenics are about 5 percent smaller than normal, which may underlie their sensory disturbances, such as hallucinations (Ettinger et al., 2001). At the receptor level, evidence has accumulated that schizophrenia stems from poor regulation of the neurotransmitter dopamine. Although dopamine receptors are found throughout the brain, current research has concentrated on such receptors in the prefrontal cortex of the frontal lobes (Knable & Weinberger, 1997; Lidow, Williams, & Goldman-Rakic, 1998).

LINK
Dopamine, Chapter 4, p. 143

The dopamine hypothesis evolved from attempts to understand how antipsychotic medications work (Creese, Burt, & Snyder, 1976) and from an increased understanding of the different types of dopamine receptors (Lidow et al., 1998). Specifically, drugs that block certain dopamine receptors tend to reduce hallucinations and other symptoms of schizophrenia. One common drug, amphetamine, acts on the same dopamine receptors; an overdose can cause too much dopamine release, producing schizophrenia-like symptoms called *amphetamine psychosis*.

Environmental Factors. No one knows why half the identical twins of schizophrenic patients do *not* themselves become schizophrenic. One interpretation of both the genetic evidence and the dopamine hypothesis is that given these biological conditions, certain types of environments—stressful ones?—are more likely than others to precipitate a schizophrenic episode. This view is based on the diathesis-stress model of acquired vulnerability, discussed in the preceding chapter (Fowles, 1992; Meehl, 1962, 1990). We might ask whether there are any known environmental triggers for schizophrenia? Does the fact that most schizophrenic disorders appear in adolescence or early adulthood mean that many years of a bad environment are necessary to develop this condition?

LINK
Diathesis-stress model, Chapter 16, p. 563

Researchers have gathered both sociocultural and psychological evidence on the environmental factors associated with the promotion and retention of schizophrenia. Schizophrenia has long been associated with low socioeconomic status; the question is whether relative poverty is a cause or a consequence of this debilitating disorder. There are no simple answers to this question. Some evidence supports the hypothesis that schizophrenia precedes and contributes negatively to a person's socioeconomic status (Dohrenwend et al., 1992), while other studies seem to show that living a life of relative poverty encourages the development of the disorder (Turner & Wagonfeld, 1967).

Researchers have also investigated the cognitive and emotional interactions of schizophrenic children and their families. Some research indicates that schizophrenics do not communicate clearly or effectively with their parents (Goldstein, 1987). Another line of research examined the psychological state of parents whose schizophrenic children returned home after being institutionalized (Brown, Birley, & Wing, 1972; Vaughn & Leff, 1976). In a series of experiments known as *EE* studies, researchers identified parents who expressed negative attitudes, hostility, and criticism toward their returning child. They called these parents an EE group (for "expressed emotion"). Family members of other schizophrenics who didn't express negative feelings were identified as a control group. Researchers found that during the first 9 months after schizophrenic patients returned home, those who entered EE homes had a 51 percent relapse rate, compared to a 13 percent relapse rate for the control group. (Hooley, 1986, reports that EE homes also produced a higher relapse rate for bipolar disorders.) As the diathesis-stress model would predict, social stressors may precipitate mental disorders.

While such studies do not constitute evidence that the family's emotional climate causes schizophrenia, it almost surely helps to maintain it, and possibly other disorders as well. In these studies, patients played an active role in generating their negative environments (Cook, Strachan, Goldstein, & Miklowitz, 1989; Goldstein, 1987). (See the discussion of passive versus active environments in Chapter 13.) Schizophrenic patients may elicit negativity by failing to respond to positive overtures, or by provoking negative interchanges. Indeed, they may interpret even a positive environment in negative ways, thereby perpetuating their illness (Rosenfarb, Goldstein, Mintz, & Nuechterlein, 1995).

Passive and active environments, Chapter 13, p. 469

INTERIM SUMMARY

1. ***Schizophrenia*** is diagnosed by grossly disorganized psychotic behavior over a 6-month period that typically (but not always) features delusions and hallucinations.
2. The five major symptoms of schizophrenia are incoherent thinking, delusions, hallucinations, deterioration of adaptive behavior, and disturbance of affect.
3. Rambling, disconnected speech, referred to as a *word salad,* is evidence of a schizophrenic's *incoherent thinking.*
4. Schizophrenics experience ***delusions***—false, unrealistic beliefs that often include delusions of grandeur—and ***hallucinations***—seeing and hearing things that others cannot.
5. Schizophrenics experience a *disturbance of affect* that may include both a curious absence of emotion and inappropriate emotions for a given situation.
6. Three common forms of schizophrenia are the *disorganized type,* the *paranoid type,* and the *catatonic type.* Whether these are three different disorders, or different expressions of the same disorder, is unknown.
7. The *disorganized type* of schizophrenia is characterized by incoherent thought patterns. The *paranoid schizophrenic* may think that he or she is being persecuted or may engage in grandiose thinking. The *catatonic type* displays symptoms of muscular rigidity accompanied by lack of responsiveness.

8. A schizophrenic's symptoms may change over the years, or may even disappear. Periods of remission are common.
9. Schizophrenia has a genetic basis: If one identical twin is schizophrenic, the other has a 50 percent chance of developing the disorder.
10. Schizophrenia has a neurophysiological basis. The *dopamine hypothesis* is based on the fact that schizophrenic symptoms diminish with drugs that block certain dopamine receptors, and that amphetamine stimulates dopamine receptors, producing schizophrenia-like symptoms (*amphetamine psychosis*).
11. Certain environmental factors seem to trigger schizophrenic symptoms, as predicted by the diathesis-stress model. *EE* ("expressed emotion") studies indicate that schizophrenic patients returning home from an institution have higher relapse rates than others when family members express negativity (hostility and criticism) toward them.

For Further Thought

1. What symptoms of schizophrenia could account for the fact that, historically, some cultures have revered and worshipped people with schizophrenia?
2. Cross-culturally, about 1 percent of the population is schizophrenic. Nesse and Williams (1994) have suggested that this relatively high percentage means that schizophrenic genes are being maintained in the population because they afford some kind of survival advantage. What "advantages" of schizophrenia might be selected for?

PERSONALITY DISORDERS

Personality disorders, characterized by long-term inflexible personality traits that cause personal distress and impaired social and workplace functioning, are Axis II disorders (see Table 17.5). Whereas Axis I disorders are cyclic, these Axis II disorders are chronic. Like Axis I disorders, these personality disorders disrupt people's lives—both the lives of those who experience them and the lives of others. Personality disorders can also be accompanied by anxiety and depression. They can last for a lifetime.

Categories of Personality Disorders

Table 17.5 lists the 10 personality disorders found in *DSM-IV*. Though some of the terms are used in the cyclic disorders as well, they do not have the same meaning. For example, a *paranoid personality disorder* (Axis II) is not the same as *paranoid schizophrenia* (Axis I). Neither are the *schizoid personality disorder* or the *schizotypal personality disorder* the same as schizophrenia. From reading the descriptions of the first three personality disorders listed in Table 17.5, however, you can see that they are reminiscent of certain behavioral characteristics of schizophrenia. These disorders lack the cyclic nature of schizophrenia, and, as we'll see in the next chapter, do not respond to the same medications.

personality disorder Any of a number of mental disorders characterized by inflexible personality traits that cause long-term personal distress and impaired social and workplace functioning.

A major problem with the *DSM-IV*'s categorization of personality disorders is that they overlap: a person who presents with a particular set of symptoms can be diagnosed with more than one disorder (Livesley, Schroeder, Jackson, & Jang, 1994; Oldham et al., 1995). For example, one study showed that over half of patients who had been diagnosed with a histrionic personality disorder (see Table 17.5)

Table 17.5 Listing of Axis II Personality Disorders

TYPE	PERSONALITY DISORDER	CHARACTERISTICS
	Paranoid	Distrust and suspicion
Odd, eccentric	Schizoid	Detachment from social relationships; restricted range of emotional expression
	Schizotypal	Acute discomfort in close relationships, cognitive or perceptual distortions; eccentricity
	Borderline	Impulsivity and instability in interpersonal relationships, self-concept, and emotion
Impulsive, dramatic	Antisocial	Disregard for and violation of the rights of others
	Histrionic	Excessive emotionality; attention seeking
	Narcissistic	Grandiosity, need for admiration; lack of empathy
	Avoidant	Social inhibition and avoidance, feelings of inadequacy; hypersensitivity to negative evaluation
Anxious, fearful	Dependent	Submissive, clinging behavior; excessive need to be taken care of
	Obsessive-compulsive	Preoccupation with orderliness, perfectionism, and need for control (fixed obsessions or compulsions need not be present, as in the anxiety disorder on Axis I)
Other	Personality disorder	Pervasive dysfunctional personality (not described by any other personality disorder)

Source: Adapted from "Listing of Axis II Personality Disorders" from *Diagnostic and Statistical Manual of Mental Disorders*, 4th ed., 1994, Text revision. Copyright © 2000 by American Psychiatric Association. Reprinted by permission.

could also be diagnosed as borderline personality disorder and narcissistic disorder (Morey, 1988). Overlapping categories undermine diagnostic consistency and complicate research into the etiology, prognosis, and treatment of personality disorders.

The schizophrenic-like personality disorders are characterized by *oddness and eccentricity*. Two other types have been identified: those that are characterized by impulsive and dramatic behavior, and those characterized by anxious and fearful behavior (Millon, 1981). The *impulsive and dramatic* type include borderline, antisocial, histrionic, and narcissistic personalities (see Table 17.5); the *anxious and fearful* type include avoidant, dependent, and obsessive-compulsive personalities.

Two of the most common personality disorders (and those most often represented in novels and films) are from the impulsive and dramatic category. One, borderline personality disorder, is more frequently diagnosed in females, while the other, antisocial personality disorder, is found more frequently in men.

Borderline Personality Disorder

A **borderline personality disorder** is characterized by a pervasive pattern of instability in self-image, mood, and social relationships. These people are insecure, impulsive, obnoxious, and desperate to be the center of everyone's attention, yet annoyingly difficult in social interactions. A person with a borderline personality disorder lacks a stable identity. Rapid mood shifts are common, for example, from intense anger (highly characteristic) to depression, and then to anxiety, all in an hour or two. Suicide threats are also common, perhaps because the borderline personality disorder is chronically bored and suffers from an "empty" feeling

borderline personality disorder A mental disorder characterized by a pervasive pattern of instability in self-image, mood, and social relationships.

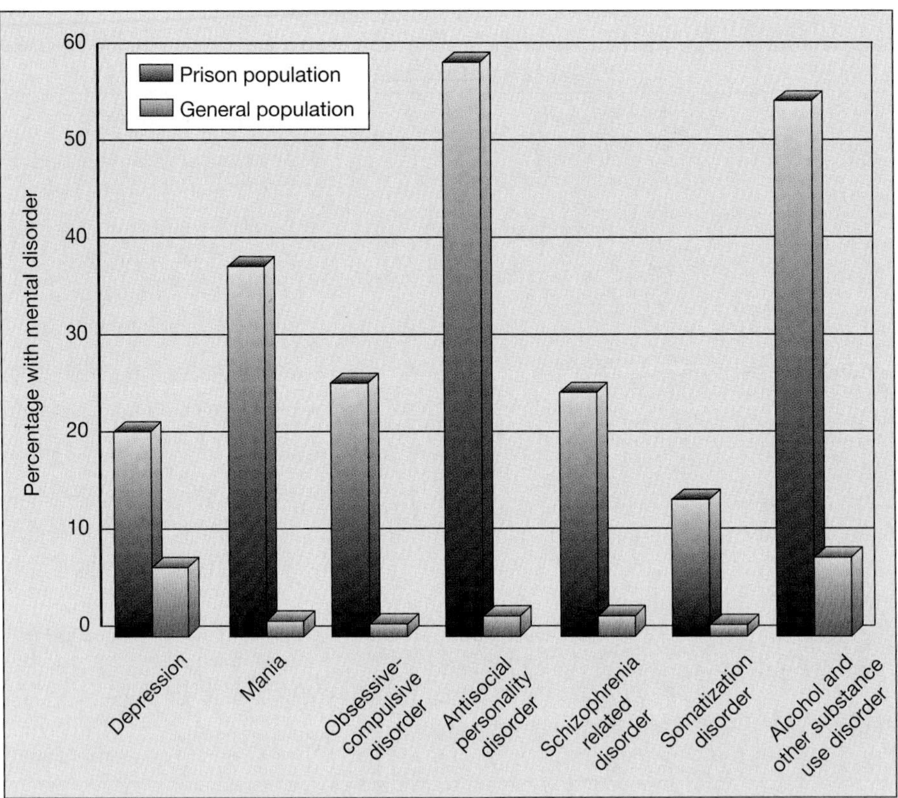

Figure 17.8 Mental Illness and Imprisonment. According to a study of 6,350 federal inmates, prisoners have significantly higher rates of mental illness than the general population. While more than half the prisoners had problems with drugs or alcohol abuse (compared to 7 percent of the general population), even more—58 percent—were diagnosed with antisocial personality disorders compared to 1 percent of the general population. *Source:* From "A Psychometric Study of Incarcerated Presidential Threateners" by E. I. McGeorge in *Criminal Justice & Behavior,* (1986), vol. 4, pp. 1–1169. Copyright © 1986. Reprinted by permission of Sage Publications, Inc.

(Krohn, 1980). This category of mental patients, two-thirds of whom are female, include about *20 percent* of all people with mental disorders—an estimated 3 to 5 percent of the general population (Frances & Widiger, 1986). There is some physiological evidence that people with this disorder have disturbances regulating serotonin (Hollander et al., 1994).

Antisocial Personality Disorder

antisocial personality disorder A mental disorder characterized by impulsive, manipulative, aggressive, and destructive behavior toward others.

Certain mental disorders, especially the **antisocial personality disorder,** are associated with criminal behavior. More common names for this disorder, which is characterized by impulsive, manipulative, aggressive, and destructive behavior toward others, are psychopathy and sociopathy. Of prisoners who have mental disorders, the highest percentage have been diagnosed with this disorder (see Figure 17.8). One interpretation of Figure 17.8 is that mentally ill people are more likely than others to engage in criminal behavior. Since those diagnosed with antisocial personality disorder represents only 2 percent in the general population (Robins, Tipp, & Przybeck, 1991), but 58 percent of the federal prisoners studied by MeGargee (1986), we can infer a strong relationship between this diagnosis and criminal behavior. Little wonder, then, that sociopaths are more commonly found in prisons than in psychiatric facilities (Vaillant & Perry, 1985).

In his book *Without Conscience: The Disturbing World of the Psychopaths Among Us,* R. D. Hare (1993) lists some of the attributes of the antisocial personality (see Table 17.6). Needless to say, these individuals, who wreak violence and destruction without remorse, are society's worst nightmare. Sociopaths combine charm and energy with a callous manipulation of those with whom they interact. They can be violent; laboratory studies reveal that when they are, their physiology remains icily calm (Blair, Jones, Clark, & Smith, 1997). From a Freudian perspective, the antisocial personality lacks a superego that distinguishes between right and wrong. As con artists, especially if they are intelligent, they often prey on the unsuspecting, including sexually responsive women, older people, and children (Lykken, 1995).

Psychologists don't know the origins of sociopathy. They do know that antisocial behaviors often emerge by the age of 15 and diminish after the age of 40 (Hare, 1993). Three times more men than women are diagnosed with this disorder (Robins et al., 1991). There is some evidence for a genetic predisposition for personality disorders in general (Nigg & Gold, 1994). In particular, male sociopaths are five times more likely than others, and female sociopaths ten times more likely than others, to have relatives with similarly diagnosis (Comer, 1992). Perhaps most distressing of all, no effective treatment has been found for this disorder (American Psychiatric Association, 1989).

Table 17.6 Characteristics of a Sociopath

Characteristics of a Sociopath
Glib and charming
Needs a great deal of stimulation
Pathologically untruthful
Cunning and manipulative
Remorseless, feels no guilt
Emotionally shallow
Callous and lacking in empathy
Parasitic
Poor behavioral control
Sexually promiscuous
Unconcerned with long-term goals
Irresponsible

Source: Table, "Characteristics of a Sociopath" from WITHOUT CONSCIENCE: The Disturbing World of the Psychopaths Among Us by Robert D. Hare. Copyright © 1998 by Robert D. Hare. Reprinted by permission of The Guilford Press.

INTERIM SUMMARY

1. ***Personality disorders*** are characterized by long-term, inflexible personality traits that cause personal distress and impair people's social and occupational functioning.
2. Unlike Axis I disorders, which are cyclic, personality disorders (Axis II) are chronic.
3. The *DSM-IV* lists ten personality disorders, many of which overlap. They may be grouped in three categories: *odd and eccentric* (paranoid, schizoid, and schizotypal personality); *impulsive and dramatic* (borderline, antisocial, histrionic, and narcissistic personality); and *anxious and fearful* (avoidant, dependent, and obsessive-compulsive personality.)
4. The ***borderline personality disorder*** is characterized by a pervasive pattern of instability in self-image, mood, and social relationships. Such people experience rapid mood shifts, from intense depression to anxiety, and feel chronically bored and "empty."
5. Three to five percent of the general population suffers from personality disorders.
6. The ***antisocial personality disorder*** is characterized by impulsive, manipulative, aggressive, and destructive behavior toward others. This behavior often leads to imprisonment rather than to treatment in mental health facilities.
7. Three times as many men as women are diagnosed with antisocial personality disorders. Because these people do not distinguish right from wrong and are remorselessly effective at charming and manipulating others, many become criminals.
8. No effective treatment has been found for people with antisocial personality disorder.

For Further Thought

1. How would you diagnose the character played by Glenn Close in the movie *Fatal Attraction*?

2. What would you do with a person who has been diagnosed with antisocial personality disorder, but who has yet to engage in criminal activity? Can you think of preventative "treatment"?
3. In the list of attributes of the antisocial personality (Table 17.6), which would be useful to a "good soldier" in warfare? Can you make the case that genetic selection has favored some of these attributes?

CONCLUDING THOUGHTS

Almost everyone, including psychologists, is fascinated with abnormal behavior. Each culture defines what is normal; in Western culture the study of psychopathology and the treatment of psychological disorders has been relegated to psychologists. As a result, people with psychological problems—an estimated 20 percent of all Americans—are routinely referred to psychologists by schools, families, the judicial system, and other social institutions.

The way in which psychologists view abnormal behavior reflects historical development in humanistic and scientific thinking that occurred during the past few centuries. Mental illness is currently framed within both a medical and a psychological model, both of which recognize the role of genetic predispositions in behavior. Psychologists distinguish between psychoses, severe disorders characterized by dissociation and a loss of contact with reality, and neuroses, less severe forms of mental illness caused by anxiety. Although some psychologists think that mental disorders are better understood as cultural rather than medical problems, all psychological disorders have a physical, or organic, basis; all are caused by a differently functioning brain.

Mental disorders are classified in the *Diagnostic and Statistical Manual of Mental Disorders (DSM)*, now in its fourth edition. The *DSM-IV* organizes mental disorders along five axes, the first two of which, Clinical Syndromes and Personality Disorders, list common mental disorders. Axis I, Clinical Syndromes, includes cyclic disorders; Axis II, chronic disorders. The first category in Axis I is anxiety disorders. People diagnosed with one of these common disorders experience irrational fears and feelings of apprehension. Anxiety disorders can take the form of phobias, generalized anxiety, panic attacks, and obsessive-compulsive disorder (OCD).

Somatoform disorders, another of the Axis I syndromes, are examples of mind-body or psychosomatic interactions. People with these disorders, including hypochondriasis, somatization disorders, and conversion disorders, experience pain and other somatic complaints in the absence of physical symptoms. Yet other Axis I disorders include dissociative disorders (dissociative fugue, dissociative amnesia, depersonalization disorder, dissociative identity disorder and mood disorders (clinical depression, dysthymia, and bipolar disorder). Depression is pervasive in our culture; one result is a high rate of suicide, especially among young people.

A serious Axis I disorder is schizophrenia, characterized by incoherent thinking, delusions, hallucinations, a deterioration of adaptive behavior, and a disturbance of affect. Schizophrenia may be expressed as one of three types: disorganized, paranoid, and catatonic. Many Axis I disorders have a genetic basis: if one of a twin pair is diagnosed with schizophrenia, the other twin has a 50 percent likelihood of expressing the same condition.

Personality disorders are chronic, long-term disorders that cause personal distress and impaired functioning in social relationships in 3 to 5 percent of the general population. These Axis II disorders include paranoid, schizoid, and schizotypal personality; borderline, antisocial, histrionic, and narcissistic personality; and avoidant, dependent, and obsessive-compulsive personality. Generally speaking, people with personality disorders do not do well in interpersonal relationships. Those with antisocial personality disorder, in particular, are a burden to the entire culture because often they engage in criminal behavior.

People with psychological disorders can be quite creative despite their suffering. So while most psychological disorders are considered maladaptive by the standards of Western civilization, the genes that predispose a person to so-called abnormal behavior may reflect distal adaptations. In the next chapter we will examine some of the treatment options available to those with mental disorders.

KEY TERMS

antisocial personality disorder *604*
anxiety disorder *584*
attention-deficit/hyperactivity disorder (ADHD) *577*
bipolar disorder *594*
borderline personality disorder *603*
conversion disorder *590*
delusion *598*
depersonalization disorder *592*
depression *594*
dissociative amnesia *591*
dissociative fugue *591*
dissociative identity disorder (DID) *592*
generalized anxiety disorder *585*
hallucination *598*
hypochondriasis *589*
learning disorder *578*
medical model *580*
mood disorder *593*
neurosis *581*
obsessive-compulsive disorder (OCD) *587*
panic disorder *586*
personality disorder *602*
phobic disorder *584*
psychological disorder *577*
psychological model *581*
psychosis *581*
schizophrenia *598*
somatization disorder *590*
somatoform disorder *589*

18 Treatment

History and Overview of Treatment
Treatment of Mental Illness in the 20th Century
The Mental Health Care System
Interim Summary
For Further Thought

The Psychoanalytic Perspective
Freudian Analysis
Other Analytical Therapies
Interim Summary
For Further Thought

Behavioral Therapies
Systematic Desensitization
Behavior Modification
Biofeedback Therapy
Interim Summary
For Further Thought

Insight Therapies
Cognitive Therapies
Humanistic Therapy
Cognitive-Behavioral Therapy
Group Therapy
Evaluating Insight Therapies
Interim Summary
For Further Thought

Medical Interventions
Psychosurgery: Revisiting Brain-Behavior Relationships
Electroconvulsive Shock Therapy
Drug Treatment
Interim Summary
For Further Thought

Concluding Thoughts

Roberta, a psychotherapist, was rescheduling all her patients' appointments because her daughter, who lived out of town, had given birth prematurely. In her private practice, Roberta counseled a variety of patients, including some with anxiety and panic disorders, others with sexual and gender-identity problems, and a few with personality disorders. Most were understanding, even congratulatory, about her need to reschedule, but one, let's call her Ann, became distraught and angry. In a phone call, Ann accused her therapist of being insensitive to her needs, indeed, putting pleasure ahead of patients' welfare. "You're like everyone else," she complained, "unfair, and always taking advantage of me." Couldn't Roberta make an exception, delay her travel a few hours, and see her that very day?

Knowing this patient well, Roberta asked a few simple questions and determined that Ann was not in crisis. Again, she attempted to reschedule Ann for the following week.

"No," Ann shouted angrily. "See me today, or I'll change therapists."

What did Roberta do? She didn't change her travel plans, and she refused to see Ann that day as Ann had demanded. A week later, following Roberta's return to her office, Ann telephoned. She tearfully apologized, requesting an appointment "when it's convenient—but please make it as soon as possible . . . today?"

You may have recognized Ann's borderline personality disorder, described in the previous chapter as a pervasive pattern of instability in self-image and social relationships.

The borderline patient is typically insecure, impulsive, and obnoxious, someone who in an hour or two may shift from intense anger to depression to anxiety. These clients are among the most difficult to treat.

Formally defined, **psychotherapy** is a general term for the use of psychological techniques and methods by a trained professional to treat people who are in need by changing their thoughts, emotions, and behavior. The number of treatment techniques and methods is large; Kazdin (1994) has counted over 400 forms of psychotherapy conducted by many different kinds of professionals. The treatment often follows the *DSM-IV* theoretical framework described Chapter 17.

In this chapter we'll focus on the theoretical training and practice of psychotherapists, who like Roberta provide services to people with psychological disorders. We'll begin with the historical background of contemporary practice and a brief overview of the mental health care system. Then we'll examine the various treatments, starting with psychoanalysis and including behavioral therapies and "talk" therapy. Finally, we'll see how drugs and other medical interventions have been integrated into psychotherapy.

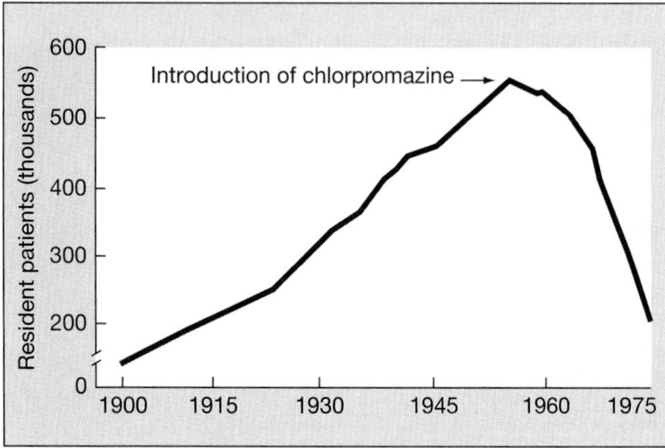

Figure 18.1 The Effect of Drug Treatment on Hospitalization for Mental Illness. The introduction of the antipsychotic drug chlorpromazine in 1956 made mental patients' symptoms more manageable, allowing them to leave hospitals.

HISTORY AND OVERVIEW OF TREATMENT

Mental illness has always been part of the human condition, though various cultures have dealt with it differently. In Western cultures, with the growth of large cities from the 17th to the 19th century, mentally ill patients began to be housed in special institutions for the insane. Large numbers of mentally ill were confined at Bethlehem Hospital in London, pronounced "Bedlam" by the locals. Patients had a roof over their heads and stablelike toilet facilities, but they were not well fed, and little attempt was made to protect them from one another's violence. Indeed, many patients "were chained to posts in dungeons, whipped, beaten, ridiculed, and fed only the coarsest of slops" (Reisman, 1976, p. 10). The scene, in short, was bedlam—a wild madhouse full of uproar and confusion (see the illustration on the next page).

Treatment of Mental Illness in the 20th Century

In the 19th century, pioneers such as Dorthea Dix succeeded in bettering the living conditions of those who were kept in "insane asylums." By the first part of the 20th century, over half a million Americans resided in private and governmental mental health care facilities. Although the conditions at these more modern institutions were better than at old Bedlam (no one was chained, sanitation was better, and caretakers were less abusive), patients continued to live quite miserable lives in open, public wards (see the photo, next page). Then, in 1956, physicians began to treat psychotics with *chlorpromazine,* a drug with properties that alleviated their symptoms. Within 20 years, the number of institutionalized people had dropped by several hundred thousand individuals (see Figure 18.1), and an important component of modern mental health care, the use of psychoactive drugs, had replaced the long-term incarceration of the mentally ill.

psychotherapy The use of psychological techniques and methods by a trained professional to change the thoughts, emotions, and behavior of a person in need.

The actual conditions in London's Bethlehem Hospital were even worse than this illustration suggests. The well-dressed ladies in the background were visiting the hospital much as we would visit a zoo. (By William Hogarth, 1697–1764).

Before the development of antipsychotic medications, psychotic patients were group-housed in open hospital bays.

This change in the way psychosis was treated accompanied a growing realization that those with lesser disorders—in Freudian terms, neurotic individuals—could and should be treated. As Figure 17.4 on page 585 shows, the anxiety disorders are the most prevalent of mental disorders. Two world wars in the first half of the 20th century produced many patients with anxiety disorders, including post-traumatic stress disorder. Following World War II, the U.S. government responded to veterans' needs by building a large number of Veterans Administration Hospitals to house those who had been physically and psychologically wounded, and by funding the training of large numbers of Ph.D. clinical psychologists to staff them. As a result, in the second half of the 20th century, research in clinical psychology flourished in the nation's universities, and a level of mental health care never before seen emerged in both the public and the private sectors.

The Mental Health Care System

In the United States today, the mental health care system includes many different types of providers, from a relatively few clinical psychologists and psychiatrists to large numbers of counselors and social workers. As Figure 18.2 shows, for every 100,000 Americans, there are 38 psychologists, school psychologists, and psychiatrists (combined), 36 social workers, and 35 counselors, including marriage and family therapists. Together, psychology and psychiatry account for only about 20 percent of all the mental health care workers represented in Figure 18.2 (Center for Mental Health Services, 1996). Mental health care is a growth industry: The number of all types of mental health care workers continues to grow faster than the general population.

In general terms, psychologists and psychiatrists are apt to see more patients with Axis I disorders, while counselors and social workers tend to see more people with "adjustment of living" problems. However, the reality is that all mental health care workers interact with all kinds of patients. Therapists differ both in how they are trained and licensed and in their work settings.

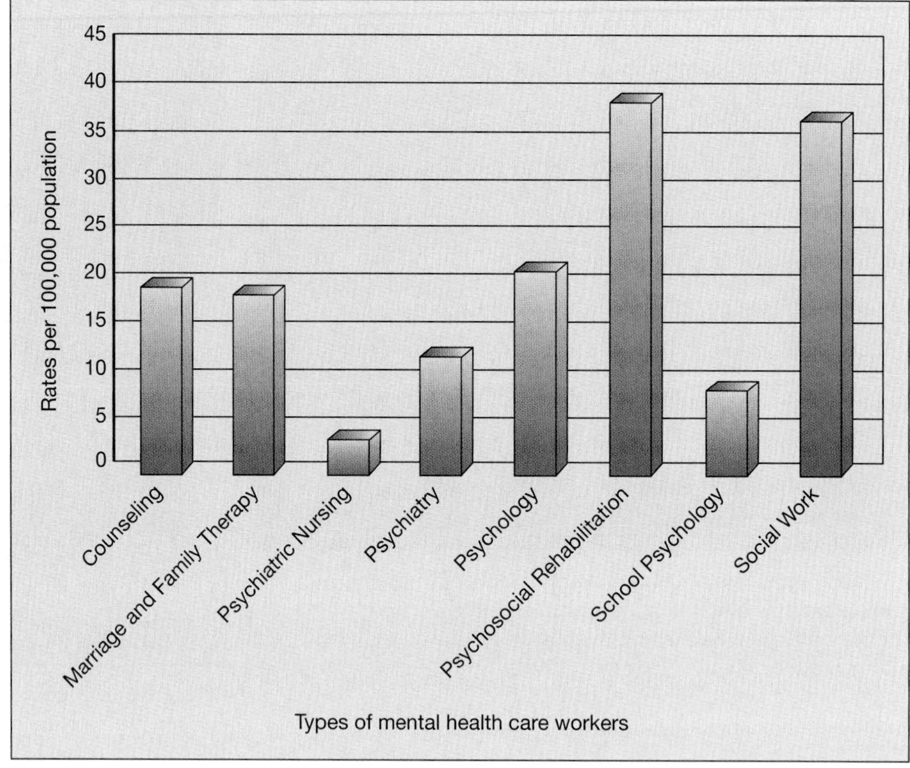

Figure 18.2 Who Does Psychotherapy? In the United States today, more counselors and social workers than psychologists and psychiatrists accomplish psychotherapy. The column labeled "Psychological Rehabilitation" represents people without training in psychology or sociology who occupy mental health care positions, typically in hospitals and government agencies. *Source:* Center for Mental Health Services. Mental Health, United States, 1996.

Psychologists and Psychiatrists. Clinical psychologists typically have one of three types of doctorate: a Ph.D. (Doctor of Philosophy in psychology), a Psy.D. (Doctor of Psychology), or an Ed.D. (Doctor of Education in psychology). By convention, the Ph.D. degree is a research degree; those who earn it are trained in the design, conduct, and analysis of experiments. Ph.D. psychologists typically divide their time among seeing patients, teaching, and doing research in university and research hospital settings. In contrast, psychologists with the Psy.D. degree have completed hands-on training programs in treating clients. They are more often found in private practice than in research. Psychologists with Ed.D.s are typically trained in Schools of Education and are more likely to become school counselors. About half of all psychologists with doctorates are employed in private practice (Center for Mental Health Services, 1996).

Psychiatrists are physicians with M.D.s and a specialty in psychology. They are most closely identified with the development of the *DSM-IV* and with the medical diagnoses and treatments of psychological disorders, primarily prescribing drugs. In comparison with other mental health care providers, psychiatrists are far less likely to use talk therapy (counseling) or be involved in marriage and family therapy or group therapy. Historically, they have been trained in psychoanalysis. Half of all psychiatrists can be found in private practice, and the remainder in hospitals (28 percent) and other settings (Center for Mental Health Services, 1996).

Counselors and Social Workers. The fastest-growing populations of mental health care workers are counselors and clinical social workers who work both in hospitals and in private practice. Increasingly, they treat clients in cooperation with psychiatrists, monitoring the effects of the psychiatric medications and providing counseling and talk therapy. In contrast to psychiatry, this workforce is comprised primarily of women. The majority of counselors and clinical social workers have master's degrees. Counselors work in schools (kindergarten through college) and a variety of social service agencies at the city, county, state, and federal level. Increasingly, master's level psychologists and social workers are seeing individuals, families, and groups in private practice.

Despite the differences in their backgrounds and training, all these therapists work with people in need. With the possible exception of psychiatrists, the similarities of their day-to-day interactions with clients tend to outweigh the differences.

INTERIM SUMMARY

1. With the growth of large cities in the 17th century, mentally ill patients began to be warehoused in institutions for the insane, aptly described as madhouses.
2. By the beginning of the 20th century humanistic social workers had improved the living conditions at institutions for the mentally ill. In the 1950s the drug *chlorpromazine* alleviated many psychotic symptoms, ushering in the modern era of mental health care.
3. There are about 400 different forms of ***psychotherapy***, or psychological techniques and methods used by trained professionals to help change the thoughts, emotions, and behavior of a person in need.
4. Psychotherapists include psychologists (Ph.D.s, Psy.D.s, and Ed.D.s) and psychiatrists (M.D.s), as well as social workers, counselors, and marriage and family therapists.
5. Psychiatrists (who developed the *DSM-IV*) tend to use medical diagnoses and drug treatments for psychological disorders. As a general rule, mental health care workers interact with each other and with all kinds of patients.

For Further Thought

1. People with psychological disorders occasionally engage in behaviors that are harmful to others. They also tend to behave in less predictable ways than "normal people." Which of these two characteristics do you think was the better reason why Bethlehem Hospital was established in 17th-century London?
2. Later in this chapter we will look at research on the relative effectiveness of drug treatment compared with talk therapy offered by psychologists. Which would you guess is more effective? Why? Are you prepared to be surprised?

THE PSYCHOANALYTIC PERSPECTIVE

The many theoretical perspectives that came together over the past 200 years to become modern psychology have been recounted throughout this text. In general, research psychologists have been more concerned with normal than with abnormal behavior, and with experimentation rather than psychotherapy. An early exception to this rule is the life and work of Sigmund Freud, who founded the psychoanalytic perspective on the human mind. We will begin with Freud because he helped to define the therapeutic process and because psychoanalytic therapy continues to be practiced in various forms even today (Eagle & Wolitzky, 1992).

Sigmund Freud, Chapter 14, p. 496

A recreation of Freud's Vienna study showing the couch his patients reclined on during psychoanalysis (Freud Museum, London).

Freudian Analysis

Freud's patients were primarily middle-class females who presented with symptoms of anxiety and depression. These early 20th-century-patients satisfied the same demographic variables as clients who seek help from psychologists today (Narrow, Regier, Rae, Manderscheid, & Locke, 1993). Few would have been found in a hospital like London's Bedlam. Like their modern counterparts, most of Freud's clients sought treatment not because they had a particular mental disorder (*psychosis*), but because they were anxious, discontented, fatigued, or "not well" (*neurotic*). Recall that Freud was a physician by training; his genius was in recognizing the psychological origins of his patient's physical complaints. According to current estimates, between 50 and 60 percent of patients who go to physicians with physical complaints would be better served, like Freud's patients, by psychological treatment (Brannon & Feist, 2000). Modern clients are also similar to Freud's patients in that they tend to be better educated—hence, more verbal than others—and can afford to pay for health care (Olfson & Pincus, 1996; Strupp, 1996).

Freud thought that most of his patients were experiencing unconscious anxiety caused by unresolved sexual conflicts from early childhood. He thought that during therapy, a patient's ego could slowly become conscious of such conflicts. By allowing his patients to talk openly and freely in a nonjudgmental environment, Freud helped his patients gain insight into the source of their anxiety. Thus the aim of **psychoanalysis** is to analyze childhood conflicts, determine how they affect a person in the present, alleviate the conflicts, and restore the patient to mental health. (The psychoanalytical method is sometimes referred to as the *analytical* method, process, or therapy.)

Defense mechanisms, Chapter 14, p. 499

To expedite this process, Freud developed the technique of **free association** in which the patient says whatever comes to mind, be it thoughts, images, or dreams. He found this process worked best if patients were relaxed, so he had them recline on a couch in a darkened room. The idea was to allow the unconscious to express itself. As we saw in Chapter 14, for example, Freud interpreted his patients' dreams in terms of both their manifest (conscious) and latent (unconscious) content. He analyzed his patients' slips-of-the-tongue in the same way, as intrusions of unconscious processes into consciousness.

In the early stages of therapy, Freud often encountered **resistance** in his patients—behavior that delayed the therapeutic process. To thwart the painful process of bringing sexual conflicts into consciousness, patients engaged defense mechanisms (see Table 14.2, page 499). The phenomenon of resistance is commonly seen in therapeutic settings today, regardless of the therapeutic method being used. Patients may express undue hostility toward the therapist, or "unintentionally" be late for or miss their appointments. Freud interpreted resistance as a sign that a person's therapy was "on schedule."

Another process Freud observed in psychoanalysis, also common in other forms of therapy, was the slow development of *transference*. In **transference**, patients redirect to the therapist emotions they had felt toward significant others in their childhood. Often these emotions take the form of intense love or hate. Because patients can easily become emotionally involved with their therapists, therapists must be aware of the phenomenon of *countertransference* (Kahn, 1997), in which the therapist projects emotions back onto the patient, often identifying with the patient's problems. Unfortunately for both, falling in love does not help the patient's mental health and may cost the therapist his or her career for violation of ethical guidelines.

psychoanalysis (Freud) A therapy involving the analysis of childhood conflicts to determine how they are presently affecting the client, and providing insight into alleviating the anxiety caused by these conflicts.

free association (Freud) An analytic technique in which the patient describes whatever comes to mind, including thoughts, images, and dreams.

resistance (Freud) In psychoanalysis, behaviors a patient engages in to delay the therapeutic process.

transference (Freud) In psychoanalysis, a process through which a patient redirects to the therapist emotions experienced with significant others in childhood.

Other Analytical Therapies

Freud's psychoanalytic approach influenced the development of other, related forms of psychoanalysis. The work of Carl Jung, Erik Erikson, and Alfred Adler, so-called neo-Freudians, has been discussed in other chapters. More recently, so-called *short-term psychodynamic therapies* have been shown to be effective with certain patients (Crits-Christoph, 1992; Strupp & Blackwood, 1985). These therapies focus on specific symptoms and complaints, limiting the duration of the treatment to a few months or a year at most. In contrast, Freud's open-ended psychoanalytic technique can last a lifetime for some patients. (Such patients, exemplified in Woody Allen films, are seeking the meaning of their lives in extended analytic conversations.) One consequence of limiting the duration of treatment is to make therapists more directive in keeping the patient's explorations of repressed emotion relevant to the problem at hand.

Carl Jung, Erik Erikson, Alfred Adler, Chapter 14, p. 504

INTERIM SUMMARY

1. Sigmund Freud developed the therapeutic process called the psychoanalytic approach, still used by some therapists today.
2. Freud's clients were verbal, educated, and, in his terms, *neurotic* rather than *psychotic*. Complaining of discontent or fatigue, they typically did not suffer from an acute mental disorder.
3. In ***psychoanalysis,*** Freud focused on helping his patients gain insight into childhood conflicts that served as sources of unconscious anxiety in their adult lives.
4. To access the unconscious, Freud used the technique of ***free association*** in which the relaxed patient says whatever thoughts, images, or dreams come to mind.
5. Freud's patients often exhibited ***resistance*** (behaviors that delayed the therapeutic process) and ***transference*** (redirection of their childhood emotions to the therapist).
6. The neo-Freudians Carl Jung, Erik Erikson, and Alfred Adler focused on patients' problems other than their childhood sexual conflicts. Today, many psychologists offer *short-term psychodynamic therapies* that are typically limited to the treatment of specific problems.

For Further Thought

1. Why might some HMOs and insurance companies be reluctant to pay for traditional psychoanalysis?
2. Why do you think free association often leads to insightful thinking, even in people who do not have psychological problems?
3. In the film *Prince of Tides,* Barbra Streisand played a psychiatrist who fell in love with her patient. Can you think of some reasons why patients and therapists might fall in love? Why do you think the state boards that are responsible for certifying psychologists, psychiatrists, and counselors have declared such patient-therapist relationships to be an ethical violation?

BEHAVIORAL THERAPIES

Not all psychologists agreed with Freud's views. Many saw neither the evidence for "intrapsychic conflict" nor the merits of basing a therapy on it. From the early 1900s, beginning with John B. Watson, to B. F. Skinner's experimental analysis of behavior in the middle of the century, behaviorism began to influence

Conditioning and learning, Chapter 6, p. 211

both the conception of mental health and its treatment. In particular, behaviorists suspected that many patients had acquired their psychological disorders through learning. Hence, a disorder could be unlearned through **behavioral therapy**, the treatment of a mental disorder through the application of basic principles of conditioning and learning (Skinner, Solomon, & Lindsley, 1953; Wolpe, Salter, & Reyna, 1964). Today, several forms of behavior therapy are practiced, including systematic desensitization, behavior modification, and biofeedback therapy.

Systematic Desensitization

Progressive relaxation, Chapter 9, p. 329

The debilitating fears people bring to the therapist's office can be thought of as classically conditioned responses. In the behavioral therapy called **systematic desensitization**, the principle of classical conditioning is used to reduce the fear associated with a phobia. Through progressive relaxation, a client is first trained to become aware of the bodily cues associated with relaxation. Then the client is trained step by step to relax in the presence of the fear-producing stimulus.

Figure 18.3 illustrates the procedure that is used in systematic desensitization—in this case to treat a snake phobia. In a series of steps, the client first looks at a picture of a snake from a distance (panel 1) and then in closer detail (panel 2). With time the client becomes less fearful in the presence of the picture and is exposed to a model of a wriggling rubber snake (panels 3 and 4). When fear of the rubber snake is extinguished, the client is exposed to a real snake (panels 5 through 7). In this process an imagined fear is replaced by a real fear. If the client overreacts to the real snake, the model is reintroduced and the procedure slowed down. Systematic desensitization is highly effective with phobic patients (Nietzel, Bernstein, & Milich, 1994), probably because it effectively reverses a learned fear response to the phobic object.

Behavior Modification

B. F. Skinner's operant conditioning and behavior control, Chapter 6, p. 212

B. F. Skinner's enduring contribution to psychology was his analysis of the control of human behavior through signaled reinforcement and punishment (Skinner, 1948, 1971). Although many consider his behavioral approach to be a too-restrictive view of human behavior, it can be used effectively to modify abnormal behavior. **Behavior modification** is a treatment in which a target behavior is modified through reinforcement and punishment. It has been used in mental hospitals to treat inappropriate behaviors by patients (Ayllon & Azrin, 1968), and in homes to change the behavior of juveniles who act out (Kazdin, 1982). Let's look at one example of behavior modification, aversion therapy.

behavioral therapy The treatment of a mental disorder through the application of basic principles of conditioning and learning.

systematic desensitization A behavioral therapy that is used to reduce the fear associated with a phobia.

behavior modification The modification of a target behavior through the application of the principles of reinforcement and punishment.

Aversion Therapy. Ruminative vomiting is a rare disorder in which a person regurgitates, chews, and reswallows food, producing what can be fatal malnutrition and starvation (Spiegler & Guevremont, 1998). Figure 18.4 shows the body weight of a 9-month-old infant whose ruminative vomiting had kept him hospitalized, near death. His pretreatment (baseline) body weight hovered around 15 pounds. To stop the life-threatening behavior, researchers administered brief, mild electric shocks to the infant's calf whenever he vomited. The treatment worked (Cunningham & Linscheid, 1976). As Figure 18.4 shows, the infant gained about 3 pounds during 2 weeks of aversion therapy. Six months later, the vomiting had stopped.

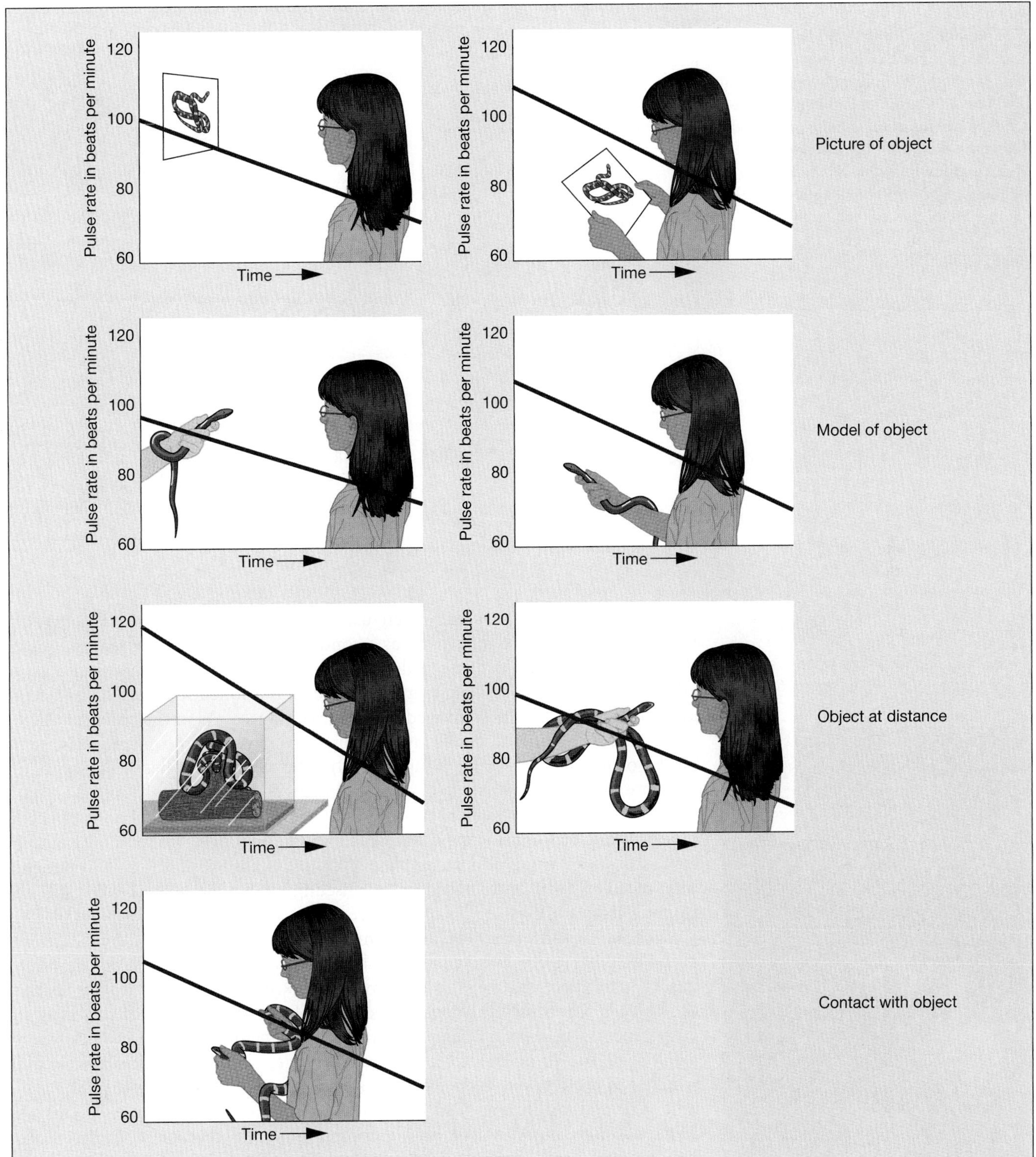

Figure 18.3 Systematic Desensitization to Snakes. In systematic desensitization, a client is slowly exposed to increasingly strong representations of a phobic object. In each stage, the client's pulse rate (dotted line) drops as the fear response is extinguished.

Figure 18.4 Effect of Aversion Therapy on an Infant's Body Weight. For 24 days, the baseline body weight of a 9-month-old infant hovered around 15 pounds because of ruminative vomiting. When aversion therapy was used to punish the vomiting, the infant quickly gained weight. *Source:* From "Elimination of Chronic Infant Ruminating by Electric Shock" by C. E. Cunningham & T. R. Linscheid in *Behavior Therapy,* (1976), vol. 7, pp. 231–234.

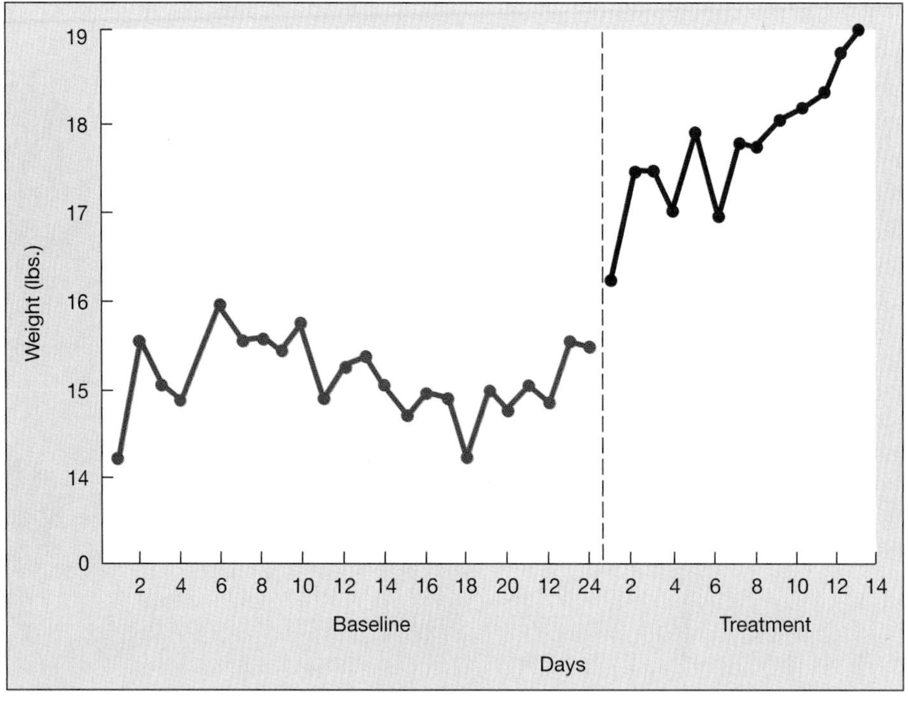

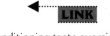

Conditioning taste aversions, Chapter 6, p. 200

Aversion therapy has also been used to treat alcoholism. As Figure 18.5 shows, the taste of alcohol can act as a conditioned stimulus for euphoria, one of the drug's effects. If a nausea-producing chemical (an unconditioned stimulus) is added to the alcohol, causing vomiting (an unconditioned response), the taste of alcohol can become a conditioned stimulus for nausea. As in the conditioning of other taste aversions, alcohol's taste becomes aversive, and people decrease their intake of it (Nathan, 1993; Wolpe, 1990). The same effect has been shown in similar experiments with rats (Lester, Nachman, & LeMagnen, 1970).

On the surface, aversion therapy may seem too simple to be an effective treatment for alcoholism, but it has been shown to reduce alcohol intake, and in some instances, bring about complete abstinence. In one study of 470 patients who received aversion therapy and counseling, about 60 percent were still abstaining from alcohol one year after treatment (Smith & Frawley, 1993). Two drawbacks keep aversion therapy from significantly reducing alcoholism, however. First, rats and people with a long history of alcohol require more conditioning trials to effect change, and their aversion extinguishes more rapidly (Barker & Johns, 1976; Rimmele, Howard, & Hilfrink, 1995). Second, this therapy requires the alcoholic's compliance in adding the chemical (commonly known as disulfiram, or Antabuse) to alcoholic beverages. The alcoholic's dilemma is whether to produce euphoria (within a self-destructive lifestyle) by drinking alcohol, or to add disulfiram, drink the alcoholic beverage, and become violently ill. Most alcoholics will not voluntarily comply with this therapeutic regimen. For this reason other pharmacological treatments, including antidepressants and antipsychotics, have been used to treat alcoholism (Gatch & Lal, 1998; see the last section of this chapter).

The taste of alcohol can be made aversive through classical conditioning.

Talk Therapy: A Behavioral Analysis. Ordinary therapeutic interactions can be analyzed in terms of behavior modification. That is, during conversations with a client, a therapist either models appropriate behavior or selectively reinforces, punishes, or extinguishes a client's inappropriate behavior. Consider, for example, a patient who presents with extreme shyness in social interactions.

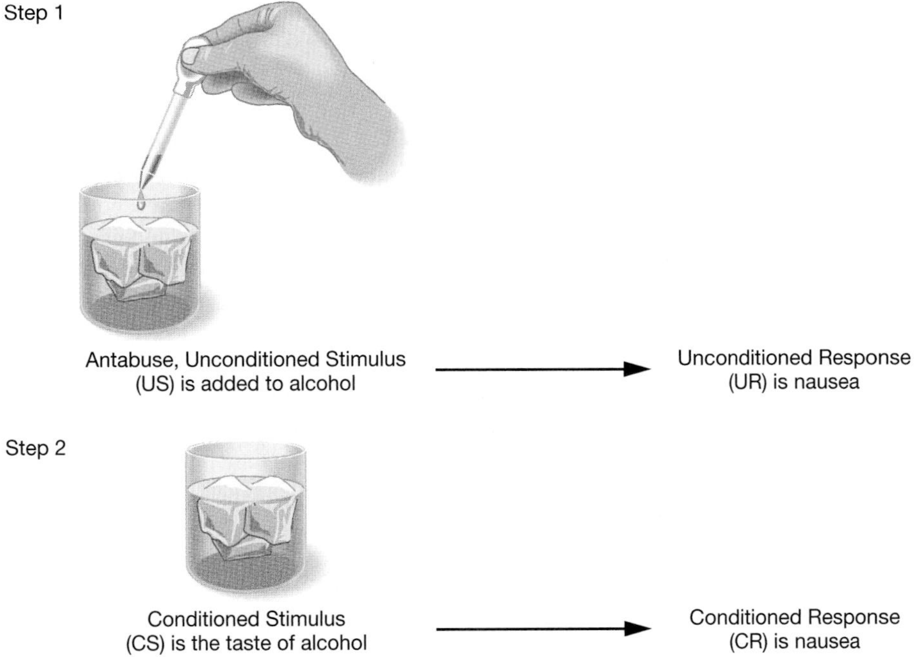

Figure 18.5 Conditioning an Aversion to Alcohol. When a drug such as Antabuse (the US) is added to alcohol (the CS) and imbibed, the unconditioned response is nausea. After several pairings of the CS and US (bottom), the CS alone (the taste of alcohol) produces a conditioned response of nausea.

To modify the client's behavior, the therapist would model socially appropriate interactions and ask the client to rehearse them. For example, the therapist might point out the client's lack of eye contact and too-soft speaking voice, responding "Good" or "That's better" (reinforcement) when the client modifies the behavior. In one form of this therapy, called *assertiveness training,* modeling and reinforcement are used to modify overly passive behavior. With training, clients learn to look after their self-interests better (Baggs & Spence, 1990).

Biofeedback Therapy

Psychosomatic disorders, in which psychological stress generates painful physical symptoms such as sore muscles and migraine headaches, can be treated through biofeedback. **Biofeedback** provides a client conscious information about the status of normally unconscious physiological systems. For example, in one type of biofeedback session, sensors attached to muscles on the head and neck and connected to an instrument that amplifies the muscles' electrical discharges, producing an *electromyogram*. In another type of biofeedback, called *thermal feedback,* sensors measure skin temperature; warm skin indicates relaxed muscles, and cold skin, tense muscles (Blanchard et al., 1990). Displaying the electrical activity of the muscles as a light or sound of varying intensity allows the client to "see" or "hear" changes in muscle tension as they occur. The tenser the muscles (or colder the skin), the brighter the light or louder the sound.

Once the client can hear or visualize the physiological response, the therapist instructs the client to "dim the light" or "dampen the sound." The results can be interesting. A colleague of mine reports that as a graduate student, he served as a subject in biofeedback research. With training, he was able to simultaneously reduce the temperature of one ear lobe and increase the temperature of the other. With practice the client can learn to use the same procedures outside of the therapeutic session.

biofeedback A behavioral therapy that provides clients with information about the status of normally unconscious physiological systems.

In conjunction with relaxation training, biofeedback therapy has reduced the frequency of clients' headaches by about half (Blanchard et al., 1990; Compas, Haaga, Keefe, Leitenberg, & Williams, 1998). However, a comparison of the results of biofeedback with the results of relaxation training or hypnosis alone showed no significant differences among them (Compas et al., 1998). Progressive relaxation training appears to be the common factor in both hypnosis and biofeedback; because relaxation training is less expensive and equally effective, it is the treatment of choice for many stress-related disorders, including migraine and tension headaches, low back pain, and hypertension (Brannon & Feist, 2000).

Progressive relaxation and hypnosis, Chapter 9, p. 329

Interestingly, most people can voluntarily change their body temperature without extensive training. You can convince yourself of this by a simple demonstration. Hold your hands out in front of you, palms up, and repeat to yourself the mantra, "my hands are hot and heavy" at 30 second intervals. Think about your hands becoming warmer. With a couple of minutes, they may become warm enough to turn pinkish in color. Now try making them cold.

INTERIM SUMMARY

1. Behaviorists see psychological disorders as learned behaviors that can be unlearned or relearned.
2. *Behavioral therapy* is the treatment of a mental disorder through the application of basic principles of conditioning and learning.
3. *Systematic desensitization* is a behavioral therapy used to reduce the fear associated with a phobia. Confronting a patient with a series of increasingly realistic models of a phobic stimulus and allowing the fear to extinguish at each stage slowly reduces the patient's fear.
4. *Behavior modification* is used to treat patients in mental hospitals as well as clients in need of *social-skills* and *assertiveness training*. The signaled reinforcement and punishment of operant conditioning are effective ways of modifying abnormal behavior.
5. Ruminative vomiting will diminish in frequency if it is punished by mild shock.
6. *Aversion therapy* is the treatment of a destructive behavior (such as alcohol abuse) by pairing the behavior with a punishing stimulus. For instance, a drug that produces nausea and vomiting is paired with alcohol to create a learned aversion to the taste of alcohol.
7. Chronically sore muscles, tension, and migraine headaches can be treated through ***biofeedback*** in which a computer displays information about the status of a client's physiological systems, allowing the client to gain voluntary control over them. Biofeedback has not been found to be more effective than relaxation therapy in reducing stress, however.

For Further Thought

1. Do you agree with behaviorally oriented psychologists that mental disorders are learned behaviors and can therefore be unlearned (or relearned)?
2. Imagine that you were sitting on an Institutional Review Board (IRB) whose purpose is to protect human subjects in research. What would you want to know before approving the use of electric shock on an infant for the purpose of controlling ruminative vomiting?
3. What kinds of behavior modification techniques do parents and teachers use?

INSIGHT THERAPIES

Behavioral therapies seem to be especially efficacious for phobias, drug dependence, and other behavioral disorders. But how are therapists to deal with a patient's private thoughts and emotions? Some psychologists find the behavioral approach too conceptually limited for the mental disorders many clients present with, such as obsessive-compulsive disorder. Some also find the psychoanalytic approach inappropriate. Few clients, after all, believe their anxiety or depression has anything to do with unresolved childhood sexual conflicts. Rather, they are anxious, fearful, or depressed in their day-to-day living. Perhaps therapists should simply assist such patients to become more insightful in solving their own problems.

From Freud to the present, different therapists have used different methods to help patients achieve self-understanding. Collectively these methods are known as insight therapies. We'll begin with cognitive therapies, then describe humanistic and cognitive-behavioral therapies.

Cognitive Therapies

Like psychoanalysis, **cognitive therapies** are a form of talk therapy designed to confront patients' irrational thoughts and emotions by challenging them to think more insightfully. In this section we'll consider the methods of Albert Ellis and Aaron Beck, both of whom were influential in the development of this approach.

Albert Ellis's Rational-Emotive Therapy. Albert Ellis began his practice as an analytically oriented therapist, but found he could achieve better results within a simpler approach. Most people with psychological disorders, he reasoned, feel bad and think irrationally. Negative events don't necessarily cause their unhappiness; rather, their *interpretation* (thoughts and beliefs) of these events influence their emotional responses. If he could get clients to think more clearly about the problems they were experiencing, Ellis reasoned, they would begin to feel better (Ellis, 1977, 1989). Recently Ellis (1999) revised his therapy to include a behavioral component, renaming it *rational-emotive behavioral therapy (REBT)*.

Consider a fictitious male client whose father had died and who had lost his job in the same month. One year later he was seeking therapy for depression and anxiety. In talking with the client, the cognitive therapist heard the patient express the belief "Life isn't fair; I shouldn't have been fired under those circumstances." Their conversation follows:

> Therapist: What circumstances are you referring to?
>
> Client: Being fired right after my dad died.
>
> Therapist: That your father died is unrelated to the fact you were fired from your job.
>
> Client: It's still unfair.
>
> Therapist: This has nothing to do with fairness. These two events are related only in your mind, and putting them together is irrational. What happened is unfortunate, but there is no conspiracy here. . . .

Notice how the therapist confronted the client's illogical, self-defeating thoughts. Rather than an exploration of unconscious motivation, rational-emotive behavioral therapy is aimed at instant intervention. The therapist forces the clients to deal with their ineffective coping styles and challenges them to think and behave differently.

cognitive therapies Talk therapies designed to confront clients' irrational thoughts and emotions by challenging them to think more insightfully.

Ellis (1999) reports difficulty in treating clients diagnosed with Axis II disorders, borderline personality disorder (BPD) in particular. These individuals are highly resistant to any kind of therapy, Ellis thinks, because they are severely dysfunctional in thoughts, feelings, and behavior. While drugs that raise serotonin levels are effective in treating some personality disorders, they are not very effective in treating borderline personality disorder (Ellis, 1999). Summarizing 50 years of experience in working with these clients, Ellis offered the following professional advice:

1. Try for real improvement, but expect limited gains.
2. Teach your clients specifically to accept themselves unconditionally (because in all likelihood they are not going to change much for the better, and self-hate is destructive).
3. Show clients that low frustration tolerance is self-defeating, and how to ameliorate it.
4. Psychoanalysis doesn't work. Use the methods of REBT to lessen dysfunctional thinking, feeling, and behavior.
5. Psychopharmacological treatment sometimes works in conjunction with REBT, but often does not.

Aaron Beck's Cognitive Therapy. Aaron Beck's cognitive therapy differs only slightly from Ellis's rational-emotive behavioral therapy (REBT). Beck describes the depressed person as one who presents with the *negative cognitive triad;* patients who see themselves as personally inadequate, social and occupational failures, and without hope (Beck, 1967, 1995). Like Ellis, Beck is interested in what the client *thinks* is wrong (that is, the client's perception of life events); therapy involves getting the client to restructure his or her thinking. However, Beck is less directive than Ellis, more inclined to allow clients to discover inconsistencies in their thoughts and behavior through patient questioning than point them out. In this sense, Ellis teaches clients to engage in an ongoing process of self-examination.

Writing in a diary, Chapter 16, p. 571

Beck also encourages clients to write about their experiences. The act of writing is therapeutic (see Chapter 16, p. 571), and the content can be analyzed during therapy sessions. In addition, Beck advises his clients to read self-help books espousing personal growth through cognitive therapy, a practice that enhances therapeutic outcomes (Jamison & Scogin, 1995). Finally, Beck helps clients to probe their life experiences for *self-fulfilling prophecies,* negative expectations that can influence one's actions in an adverse manner.

Consider a client who in her early twenties had had a hysterectomy and ever since had assumed long-term relationships were out of the question because she couldn't bear children. She withdrew from relationships before they got serious, making herself miserable in the process. To combat this self-fulfilling prophesy, her therapist suggested she conduct an anonymous poll of her male coworkers asking them what they would do if they found they were attracted to a woman who couldn't have children. Most said they would not care; some said they would break off the relationship, but others said they would continue it, because they didn't want children either (Craighead, Kazdin, & Mahoney, 1994, p. 96). The insight this patient gained from her less-than-scientific survey helped her to approach relationships in a less fearful way.

Positive self-fulfilling processes, in contrast, are adaptive, so developing them is a goal of Beck's therapy. For instance, viewing a marriage partner as someone who has certain strengths that enhance one's marriage and contribute to the family's well-being will allow forgiveness of some spousal mistakes. Even if somewhat unrealistic, viewing the world through rose-colored glasses enhances social and workplace relations and is psychologically healthier than being cynical and negative.

Humanistic Therapy

In the middle of the 20th century, humanistic psychologists rejected the scientific path that was becoming the mainstream of the discipline. In various ways, they were offended by what they considered the mechanistic view of human behavior taken by biologically oriented psychologists, including Freud and Skinner. In their view, mechanistic explanations both demeaned the human spirit and ignored individual goals and aspirations. Carl Rogers and Fritz Perls were among the most prominent of the humanistic therapists, who sought to affirm the self-worth of their patients.

Carl Rogers and humanistic psychology, Chapter 14, p. 506

Carl Rogers's Person-Centered Therapy. Carl Rogers, as we learned earlier, was a humanistic psychologist who thought that a person's self-appraisal was one of the most important determinants of personality. Healthy people are fulfilled people; they love and are loved unconditionally. In Rogers's view, people sought therapy because of problems with their self-concept. If the therapist arranged a supportive environment that bolstered a client's self-concept, Rogers thought, the client could regain a sense of self-affirmation. A Rogerian therapist is nonjudgmental and extends unconditional positive regard to clients, thereby affirming their self-worth. For this reason Rogers's therapy is called *person-centered*, or *client-centered, therapy* (Rogers, 1942, 1980).

For Rogers, the main source of a client's anxiety was the discrepancy between the self-concept and the opinion of others. Rogers thought clients needed time to explore this issue and discover for themselves how to personally grow and develop as a person. His main technique, called *nondirective therapy*, was to affirm (without reinforcing) whatever the client said, often in almost the same words as the client. Such paraphrasing acts as a mirror, allowing clients to hear what their thoughts sound like to others. Let's listen to a typical session in which a client-centered therapist is treating a depressed person (reported in Rogers, 1951, pp. 46–47):

> Client: I wish I'd never started this therapy. I was happy when I was living in my dream world. There I could be the kind of person I wanted. But now there is such a wide, wide gap—between my idea—and what I am . . .
>
> Therapist: It's really a tough struggle—digging into this like you are—and at times the shelter of your dream world looks more attractive and comfortable.
>
> Client: My dream world or suicide. . . . So I don't see why I should waste your time—coming in twice a week—I'm not worth it—What do you think?
>
> Therapist: It's up to you . . . it isn't wasting my time—I'd be glad to see you whenever you come—but it's how you feel about—if you don't want to come twice a week—or if you do want to come twice a week?—once a week? It's up to you.
>
> Client: You're not going to suggest that I come in oftener? You're not alarmed and think I ought to come in—every day—until I get out of this?
>
> Therapist: I believe you are able to make your own decision. I'll see you whenever you want to come.
>
> Client: (note of awe in her voice) I don't believe you are alarmed about—I see—I may be afraid of myself—but you aren't afraid of me.
>
> Therapist: You say you may be afraid of yourself—and are wondering why I don't seem to be afraid for you?
>
> Client: You have more confidence in me than I have. I'll see you next week—maybe.

When a physician sets a broken bone, it eventually heals, restoring full function to the individual. What heals as a result of client-centered therapy? Rogers (1951) proposed the following goals of humanistic therapy (Nietzel et al., 1994):

1. ***Increased awareness.*** As a result of therapy, a client should become more aware of self and of personal feelings (emotions) previously hidden (in the unconscious). ("*I can face my reality.*")
2. ***Increased self-acceptance.*** Clients should become less self-critical and more accepting of their limitations. ("*I'm basically a decent person who has a few warts—I'm working on them.*")
3. ***Increased interpersonal comfort.*** A client should become less defensive and more at ease in relationships with significant others. ("*I'm tired of games. I am who I am, and I'd like for us to be honest with each other.*")
4. ***Increased cognitive flexibility.*** Clients should become less rigid and better able to entertain life's complexities in a world that isn't all black and white.
5. ***Increased self-reliance.*** Clients should become less dependent on others for personal validation. Rather, their self-worth should come from an increased awareness of their personal strengths and from self-acceptance. ("*I'm going to study hard to pass this examination because it will make* me *feel good, not just because it will please my parents.*")
6. ***Increased overall functioning.*** A client should function better in social and occupational settings, with less tension, defensiveness, and stress. This improved behavior should continue even after the cessation of therapy. ("*I'm OK, you're OK.*")

Gestalt Therapy. Fritz Perls was a Gestalt psychologist who tried to accomplish what Carl Rogers set out to do using different methods. His basic premise, like Rogers's, was that by enhancing a client's awareness of self, he could promote both cognitive and emotional changes. Perls viewed "getting better" as the restoration of holistic functioning of the self, thus the name of his approach, Gestalt therapy (Perls, 1969, 1970).

Gestalt therapists differed from other cognitive therapists in that they viewed clients as people who were too comfortable with their "neurotic games." Therapy sessions were aimed at disavowing the patient's distorted perception of the world, often by bluntly confronting them with it. The idea was to keep the patient in the present—the "here and now"—and prevent them from making excuses for their behavior and for past problems. Let's listen to a session in which Perls responds to a patient's statement that the interview reminds her of when she was a little girl:

Therapist: Are you a little girl?

Client: Well, no, but it's the same feeling.

Therapist: Are you a little girl?

Client: "The feeling reminds me of it."

Therapist: (explosively) Are you a little girl!?

Client: (pause) No.

In this brief segment we can see one essential difference between Rogerian and Gestalt therapy: A Rogerian therapist patiently extends to the client unconditional positive self-regard through nondirective, reflective techniques. Here, Perls directly punishes a client for attempting to redirect her therapy to the past, rather than focusing on problems in the here and now. In Gestalt therapy, the client remains "on the hot seat" no matter how uncomfortable it may get (Perls, 1970).

Cognitive-Behavioral Therapy

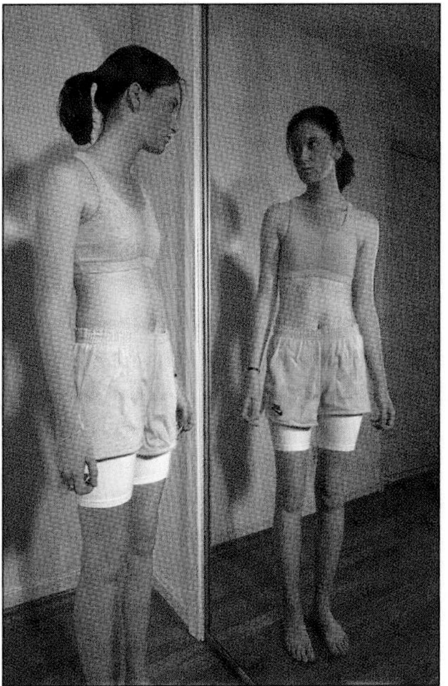

The causes of anorexia nervosa remain elusive.

Rather than subscribing to only one type of therapy, most therapists describe themselves as *eclectic,* both in their training and in the services they deliver. To be eclectic merely means that a therapist might mix approaches, depending on the client's personality and problems. Indeed, most therapists describe themselves as *cognitive-behavioral therapists.* They combine both talk and behavior therapies, and for some patients, may also include drug therapy in consultation with a psychiatrist (Craighead et al., 1994). The diversity of these cognitive-behavioral approaches can be seen in the treatment of eating disorders, anorexia nervosa and bulimia, and in panic disorder.

Treatment of Eating Disorders. Anorexia nervosa, first documented three centuries ago, is a common eating disorder occurring in as many as 1 to 2 percent of women, usually between the ages of 15 to 20 (Brannon & Feist, 2000). In extreme cases, starving women present with symptoms that include greatly reduced body weight and body fat, and amenorrhea (cessation of the menstrual cycle) (Hsu, 1990). Strangely, the anorexic holds the puzzling misperception of being overweight. The reasons why some women develop this disorder are unknown. However, one prominent psychotherapist has stated that without exception, every anorexic he had treated " . . . had come from a family with a disturbed dynamic" (D. Rudd, personal communication, October 15, 1999).

To better monitor the client's food intake, the treatment of anorexia nervosa is typically begun in a hospital setting. Using a behavioral approach, the therapist makes leaving the hospital contingent on the patient's weight gain. Since most people view the hospital as an aversive environment, escaping it acts as a negative reinforcer that maintains appropriate eating behavior. Once the patient gains a sufficient amount of weight, the therapist begins outpatient therapy using a cognitive approach. Cognitive therapy includes education about distorted body images and an investigation of the client's interpersonal problems (including family problems), which may be involved with the eating disorder. Though these procedures are generally successful in reestablishing and maintaining more normal eating habits, systematic studies of their effectiveness have not yet been published (Craighead et al., 1994). The behavioral component is essential in the treatment of *all* eating disorders.

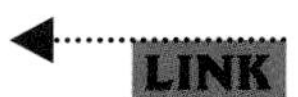

LINK

Negative reinforcement, Chapter 6, p. 214

Bulimia nervosa is another eating disorder characterized by binge eating followed by self-induced vomiting, laxatives, or other weight-control behaviors. The bulimic typically has obsessive thoughts about her body shape and/or weight, making her compulsive about what, how, and when to eat. Eating is followed by ritualistic behavior aimed at getting rid of the extra calories. Over time, this vicious cycle plays out with increasing frequency (Fairburn, 1988a).

Two types of cognitive-behavioral treatment may be used to treat bulimia The first, described by Fairburn (1984), has three stages. In stage 1, which lasts about 8 weeks, the patient attends twice-weekly educational sessions on the long-term health hazards of the disorder and the goals of treatment. Patients fulfill behavioral measures, such as eating three to four meals plus one to two snacks daily, keeping a food journal, and participating in weigh-ins. This intervention is usually successful in breaking the binge-purge cycle, allowing the client to enter stage 2 therapy. In the next 8 weeks , therapy is more cognitive: the therapist subjects the client's thoughts and beliefs about body size and the control of eating to rational scrutiny. To allow a transition to more normal (less predictable) eating habits, the client's rigidly prescribed eating patterns are relaxed. The last stage involves fewer visits to the therapist, allowing the client to develop insight and increased confidence in her ability to maintain healthy eating habits on her own.

A variation of this therapy focuses more on the vomiting than the bingeing. Vomiting acts as a reinforcer because it relieves the anxiety associated with binge eating. Therapy consists of a procedure called exposure and response prevention (ERP), in which the client is exposed to foods normally associated with vomiting, but is prevented from vomiting. Because the vomiting is not reinforced, this procedure eventually causes the response to extinguish. The bingeing behavior also decreases in frequency (Leitenberg, Gross, Peterson, & Rosen, 1984). Both forms of cognitive-behavioral therapy are successful in reducing bingeing and vomiting in about 60 to 90 percent of bulimic clients (Fairburn, 1988b).

Though both bulimia and anorexia nervosa respond well to the combination of behavioral therapy and cognitive therapy, cognitive therapy alone has not proven to be effective (Fairburn, 1984). Nor do patients with eating disorders improve over time without intervention. In a study that compared untreated bulimic anorexic control subjects with treated bulimic subjects, neither control group showed any improvement. (In studies of other disorders, about one-third show improvement merely with the passage of time.) Finally, some therapists combine antidepressants with cognitive-behavioral therapy in the treatment of anorexia nervosa.

Treatment of Panic Disorders. In Chapter 17 we learned panic disorder is an anxiety disorder that is characterized by recurrent panic attacks—episodes of intense fear—with dizziness, heart palpitations, and a fear of dying or "going crazy." In a carefully controlled study (Barlow, Craske, Cerny, Klosko, 1989), a cognitive-behavioral therapy called panic control treatment (PCT) was shown to be successful in alleviating panic attacks in 87 percent of clients. The therapy consists of "cognitive restructuring," exposure to the breathing cues associated with panic attacks, followed by the retraining of breathing. In controlled treatment sessions, the therapist trains patients to intentionally induce the breathing disruptions they normally experience during a panic attack. With the therapist's guidance, the patient experiences what "panic physiology" feels like and then learns to recover normal breathing patterns.

Consider the case of a woman who, while cleaning her swimming pool on a hot day, inadvertently breathed in chlorine gas, which caused nausea and hyperventilation for 10 to 15 minutes. This single conditioning experience scared her so badly that for many years, whenever she became "too hot" (the conditioned stimulus), she experienced breathing difficulties (the conditioned response). Because becoming too hot caused a panic attack, she began wearing short sleeves, bathing in cool water, and keeping her house temperature at 60°F year round. Her treatment involved education about what was happening to her both psychologically and physiologically during a panic attack, followed by exposure and response prevention procedures. On a warm day she kept the windows shut, bathed in warm water, and wore heavy clothing. Eventually she achieved insight into her fear response, and it extinguished. After just 11 sessions she no longer feared heat or hyperventilating (Craighead et al., 1994).

Group Therapy

In all the foregoing methods, the therapist treated one client at a time. In *group therapy,* one or two therapists work with groups ranging from 3 or 4 to 15 or 20 clients. Group therapy can be psychoanalytic, behavioral, cognitive, humanistic, or eclectic in approach. Humanist group therapy sessions, popular in the 1960s and 1970s, featured so-called *sensitivity training* sessions in which participants confronted one another with open, honest evaluations of their behavior. The object is to become more insightful into one's own behavior by listening to each other's thoughts and feelings. Bulimia has been successfully treated in groups of 3 to 4 clients (Craighead et al., 1994).

In another type of group therapy, individuals who present with the same symptoms are brought together for systematic desensitization training. One example is a program designed for people who are afraid of flying. After relaxation training and the experience of sitting in a stationary aircraft, members of the group fly together in an airplane. Confronting their fear with the support of others can be extremely helpful to phobic patients.

Alcoholics Anonymous (AA), begun in 1935, can be considered a form of group therapy although the organization operates outside the formal framework of psychotherapy. In AA meetings, one or more leaders (who are recovering alcoholics) bring other alcoholics together to help them gain insight into their disorder. The AA program combines cognitive therapy (education) with behavioral change (abstinence), social support, and spirituality (acknowledgment of a "higher power"). AA is popular. As many as 10 percent of Americans have participated in AA or a similar program (Room & Greenfield, 1993). Because it is structured to ensure the anonymity of its members, its effectiveness is difficult to assess. However, the program is generally acknowledged to have rehabilitated large numbers of recovering alcoholics (Emerick, 1987).

Many other groups exist outside of the framework of formal psychotherapy. Support groups for people with AIDS, battered women, gamblers, teen mothers, rape victims, weight watchers, smokers, and survivors of massacres and natural disasters are just a few examples. The American Psychological Association estimates that thousands of self-help groups serve tens of millions of people. To these groups can be added many more thousands of group exercise classes, martial arts instruction, cooking classes, scouting, organized sports, and church groups for sundry purposes, all of which claim a therapeutic value for their participants. There has been little systematic evaluation of the effectiveness of these groups (Christensen & Jacobson, 1994).

Evaluating Insight Therapies

Because some psychological disorders are more easily treated than others, assessing the general effectiveness of specific treatment methods is difficult. Research concerning the effectiveness of the insight therapies is mixed. As in any other profession, the therapeutic training and skills of therapists vary widely. Some studies suggest that any form of insight therapy is better than nontreatment (Barlow, 1995). Indeed, a meta-analysis of several hundred published studies showed a significant treatment effect compared with untreated control groups (Smith, Glass, & Miller, 1980). In addition, clients think the therapy they receive is effective (Seligman, 1995).

Yet questions abound concerning the effectiveness of psychotherapy, including the criteria that are used to evaluate the therapeutic outcome (Howard, Moras, Brill, Martinovich, & Lutz, 1996; Lambert & Hill, 1994). Who should be asked about the effectiveness of a treatment—clients, friends, relatives, employers, or therapists? Recognizing that psychologists and insurance agents have different goals (helping the patient versus controlling costs), what criteria should be used to judge a treatment's effectiveness? A cost-benefit analysis of the therapeutic gains over the course of insight therapy shows that most gains are made in the early sessions (Howard et al., 1996) (see Figure 18.6). This information is important to *both* psychologists and insurance companies.

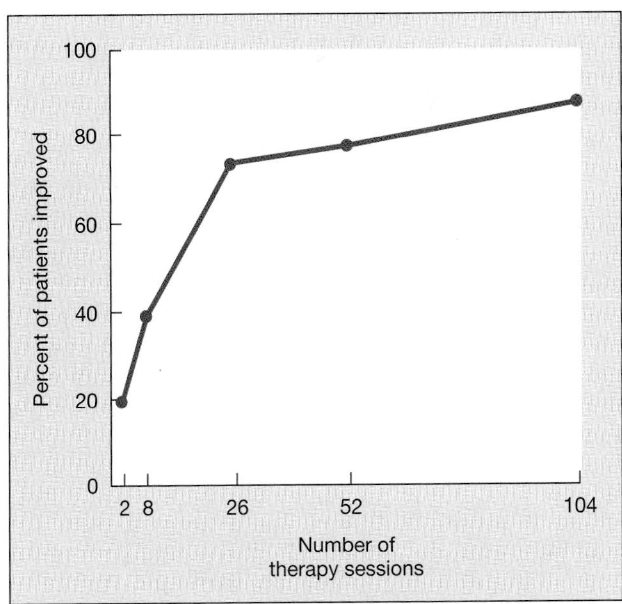

Figure 18.6 The Effectiveness of Short-Term versus Long-Term Therapy. In the first 10 to 20 therapy sessions, up to 75 percent of patients show improvement. Beyond 25 sessions (once a week for half a year) the chances of a client becoming better does not increase significantly. *Source:* Modified from Howard et al., 1996.

Two findings suggest that some forms of cognitive therapy are limited in their effectiveness. From an analysis of outcome studies done over many years, some researchers (such as Eysenck, 1993) have concluded that 30 to 40 percent of *untreated* clients also improve, making it difficult to show the effectiveness of different treatments. Others (such as Christensen & Jacobson, 1994) have pointed out that self-help groups do as much good as any particular kind of psychotherapy. Does the fact that clients *think* their therapy has been beneficial mean that it has been? Reinforcement theory would suggest that patients turn to therapists because the experience is a positive rather than an aversive one. But the fact that a therapeutic session can be reinforcing to a client (and a therapist) does not mean that it effects lasting behavioral change.

We have seen that cognitive-behavioral therapies are quite effective in treating diverse behavioral problems, from anxiety to eating disorders. In these therapies, both the cognitive and the behavioral components seem to contribute to the client's improvement. This consideration is important because more therapists identify their approach as cognitive-behavioral than those who take the cognitive or humanistic approach. Eclectic therapies that combine several different methods seem to be more effective than others. Before concluding whether insight therapies—especially cognitive-behavioral therapies—are effective, however, let's review the outcome of studies in which therapists added pharmacological interventions to other psychological methods.

INTERIM SUMMARY

1. In ***cognitive therapy*** (*talk therapy, insight therapy*), the therapist confronts a client's irrational thoughts and emotions and enjoins him or her to think and behave more insightfully.
2. Albert Ellis developed *rational-emotive therapy* (now *rational-emotive behavioral therapy*) based on the notion that clients who begin to think more clearly and rationally will begin to feel and behave better.
3. Aaron Beck's cognitive therapy is predicated on the theory that a *negative cognitive triad*—personal inadequacy, failed social relationships, and general hopelessness—underlies most of his client's problems. The goal of cognitive therapy is to reduce negative thoughts and encourage the growth of insightful thinking.
4. *Humanistic therapies,* such as Carl Rogers's person-centered therapy, emphasize the importance of a client's self-appraisal, individual goals, and aspirations in achieving psychological health. Rogerian therapists are nondirective and nonjudgmental; their aim is to extend unconditional positive regard to their clients.
5. For Rogers, the goals of cognitive therapy were increased awareness and self-acceptance, improved interpersonal relationships, and the enhancement of cognitive flexibility, self-reliance, and overall functioning.
6. The Gestalt psychologist Fritz Perls thought that mental illness resulted from a breakdown in holistic functioning of the self; the goal of therapy was to reverse the breakdown. In contrast with nondirective therapists, Gestalt therapists are blunt in confronting their clients about their irrational thoughts and behaviors.
7. *Cognitive-behavioral therapy* combines behavioral interventions with insight therapy in an attempt to change a client's behavior. Typically the therapist makes reinforcement contingent on behavioral change while subjecting the client's thoughts and beliefs to a rational analysis.
8. *Panic control treatment (PCT)* is a form of cognitive-behavioral therapy in which a client learns to recognize what "panic physiology" feels like, and then is trained to breathe normally when exposed to anxiety-provoking cues.
9. *Group therapy* is conducted with groups of clients with similar interests (battered women and weight watchers, for example). Alcoholics Anonymous is a form of group therapy combining education, social support, and spirituality with behavioral change to effect alcohol abstinence.
10. Most therapeutic gains are made in early rather than later psychotherapy sessions.
11. Despite the fact that 30 to 40 percent of *untreated* clients improve, cognitive therapy produces better results than nontreatment, and clients generally think they are improved. For selected disorders, cognitive-behavioral therapy produces better results than insight therapies alone.

For Further Thought

1. In the "therapy sessions" you conduct with your friends, do you talk more or listen more? What kind of therapy does your behavior most closely resemble?
2. Why do you think behavioral therapies are more effective in treating behavioral problems and cognitive therapies are relatively less effective in treating emotional and cognitive disorders?
3. Would you recommend group therapy for a person with a borderline personality disorder? Why or why not?

MEDICAL INTERVENTIONS

The middle part of the 20th century was a time of great innovation in the treatment of mental disorders. Treatment of schizophrenia by chlorpromazine was so effective it freed thousands of patients from insane asylums. At about the same time, surgeons began to experiment with an old treatment called psychosurgery.

Trephining, Chapter 1, p. 15

Split-brain preparation, Chapter 4, p. 132

Psychosurgery: Revisiting Brain-Behavior Relationships

Centuries ago, primitive healers had begun trephining holes in people's skulls to release evil spirits. In its modern form, *psychosurgery* is the surgical lesioning of the brain to alleviate psychological disorders. The methods and results of these experimental surgeries remain as controversial today as they were when they were performed several decades ago (Valenstein, 1986). In one procedure called a *lobotomy,* a hole was drilled in the skull over the frontal lobes. A sharp instrument was inserted into the brain and moved from side to side to effectively sever the frontal lobe connections to the rest of the brain. The fact that between 10,000 to 50,000 mentally ill patients were operated on in this manner over a relatively short period of time is eye-opening (National Commission for the Protection of Human Subjects in Biomedical and Behavioral Research, 1978). The surgery did alleviate much of the patients' mental anguish, making them more easily managed in an institutional setting. But they became apathetic and directionless, and lost the ability to think abstractly. Following this surgery they were unable to live independent lives outside a locked ward.

Some forms of experimental brain surgery are still performed, including small lesions in the cortex to treat depression and anxiety (Ballentine, Bouckoms, Thomas, & Giriunas, 1987), and the *split-brain procedure* described in Chapter 4 (Gazzaniga, 1998). At present, however, most medical interventions for mental illness are pharmacological. Before discussing psychopharmacology, let's look at one other type of medical treatment developed in the middle of the 20th century.

The historic use of electricity in quack medical cures.

Electroconvulsive Shock Therapy

When magnets and electricity first became available, they were used (usually by quacks) to treat all manner of physical ailments (Camp, 1973). It isn't surprising, then, by the 1950s electrical current was being passed through the brain to treat various mental disorders, a procedure called **electroconvulsive therapy** (ECT). Interestingly, such procedures can alleviate cases of severe depression that are not responsive to drugs; hence, they continue to be used today in limited fashion.

electroconvulsive therapy (ECT) The passage of an electrical current through the brain to treat severe depression.

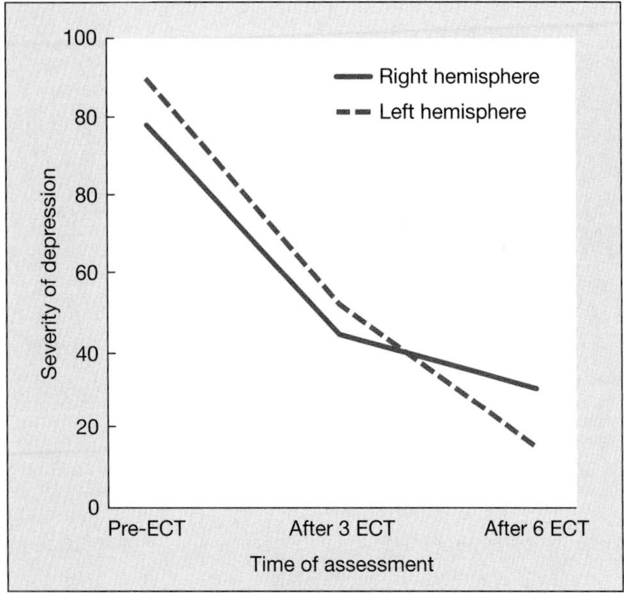

Figure 18.7 The Effects of Electroconvulsive Therapy. Three electroconvulsive shocks will significantly reduce depression from pretreatment levels (Pre-ECT), whether delivered to the right or left hemisphere. Additional treatments do not greatly reduce the severity of depression. *Source:* Modified from Abrams et al., 1989.

In Chapter 2 we learned that tiny pulses of electrical current delivered through electrodes buried deep within the brain mimic the normal functioning of neurons. Higher levels of electrical stimulation can simultaneously depolarize large numbers of neurons, causing seizures. In electroconvulsive therapy, physicians induce controlled seizures that have a lasting effect on the brain's functioning. Unfortunately, the earliest use of this treatment was in schizophrenics, who do not respond to the procedure. Today, ECT is used primarily to treat severe depression (see Figure 18.7), but not schizophrenia (Buchan, Johnson, McPherson, & Palmer, 1992). In one study, chronically depressed patients who received ECT in combination with antidepressant drugs showed fewer symptoms of depression than an antidepressant-only control group (Gagné, Furman, Carpenter, & Price, 2000). Ironically, ECT may work not by destroying damaged neurons, but by promoting neurogenesis, the formation of new brain cells. One study has reported that 2 to 4 weeks of chronically administered ECS in rats increased the number of their hippocampal neurons by 50 percent (Malberg, Eisch, Nestler, & Duman, 2000). ECT is safer now than it once was. Use of muscle relaxants and lower levels of electric current delivered to one side of the brain greatly lessens "side effects" of wrenched muscles, occasionally broken limbs, and severe memory loss (Abrams, Swartz, & Vedak, 1989).

Drug Treatment

LINK

Electrical stimulation of the brain (ESB), Chapter 2, p. 33

Brain seizures, Chapter 4, p. 133

Effects of drugs on consciousness, Table 9.1, p. 334

Neurogenesis, Chapter 4, p. 129

Humans have been self-administering psychoactive substances throughout recorded history. In Chapter 9 we saw that drinking beer, wine, and spirits can alleviate anxiety, reduce muscle pain, and relax muscles. Likewise, opium and its derivatives can induce euphoria. One reason people drink tea and coffee is for its stimulant properties (caffeine). Perhaps because these drugs are so readily available, and have been used to alter human consciousness for so long, they are seldom prescribed by psychiatrists for the treatment of mental disorders.

Table 18.1 outlines the use of plants containing psychoactive drugs from prehistory to the present. Modern pharmacology was born when the active ingredients in these plants were isolated and synthesized in laboratories. The term *pharmacology* comes from the Greek term *pharmakon,* meaning both medicine and poison. Its double meaning suggests ambivalence toward substances that can diminish pain, fight disease, and alter behavior, but which can also be abused and misused (Porter & Teich, 1995).

Psychopharmacology is the use of drugs by therapists to effect changes in a patient's mental state. In the previous chapter we saw that Ritalin, a stimulant, is often used to treat ADHD. Table 18.1 lists only a few of the psychoactive drugs in current use; a major part of the remaining discussion in this chapter will focus on them. We'll begin with chlorpromazine, which is used to treat psychosis.

Neurotransmitters and drugs bind to receptor sites of neurons, Chapter 4, p. 144

psychopharmacology A psychiatrist's use of drugs to effect changes in a patient's mental state.

Antipsychotic Drugs. Psychopharmacology came into being as new chemicals with psychoactive properties were being synthesized (see Table 18.1). One promising chemical, chlorpromazine, had calming properties and had been used in France to sedate patients before surgery. Would it calm the agitated state of a schizophrenic, psychiatrists wondered? The answer was yes; chlorpromazine not only sedated a patient, but reduced psychotic symptoms such as hallucinations (Grilly, 1989).

To understand why chlorpromazine is such an effective antipsychotic, we must return to our discussion of the etiology of schizophrenia in Chapter 17.

There we learned that the disorder may result from too much of the neurotransmitter dopamine at various sites throughout the brain. Chlorpromazine is a phenothiazine whose chemical structure is similar to dopamine, and so it can bind to dopamine receptors. Rather than not activating the receptors, it blocks the normal action of dopamine, reducing its effect. In fact, any drug that effectively blocks the dopamine receptor is an effective antipsychotic.

Chlorpromazine also produces side effects caused by reduced dopamine levels in other parts of the brain. Patients who are being treated with the drug may suffer motor disabilities such as *tardive dyskinesia*—involuntary movements of the tongue, mouth and jaw—and a shuffling gait. Newer antipsychotic drugs such as *clozapine* bind somewhat differently to the dopamine receptors, reducing the side effects associated with chlorpromazine.

Tobacco use among the Mayans.

Lithium. Lithium is an alkali metal appearing on the *Table of Periodic Elements*. It can be found in its salt form, as lithium chloride, in the Earth and dissolved in water. It looks and tastes like table salt (sodium chloride), so lithium chloride was used as a commercially available salt substitute until a number of people salted themselves to death. Its usefulness in the treatment of mania was discovered by an Australian psychiatrist in the 1940s, but it wasn't widely used during the next decade because psychiatrists considered it too toxic (Grilly, 1989). In a different form (lithium carbonate) this element is therapeutically effective in the treatment of bipolar disorder, but produces side effects indicative of its toxic nature, such as nausea, vomiting, diarrhea, and so forth. (You may

Table 18.1 The Use of Psychoactive Drugs, Prehistory to the Present

Time	Drug	Culture
Prehistoric	Herbs, mushrooms, alcohol from natural fermentation	
5000–3000 B.C.	Opium poppies	Mesopotamia, Egypt
2000 B.C. 1500 B.C.	Plant, mineral, and animal substances to treat ailments within mind/body framework; tea (brewed to release caffeine); marijuana (smoked)	Chinese and African cultures
	Hallucinogenic mushrooms and other herbs	Guatemala, native Americans
1000 B.C.	Coca leaf (chewed to release cocaine); tobacco (smoked to release nicotine); coffee (brewed to release caffeine)	South American natives
Medieval Europe	Various herbs to induce psychological changes; mandrake (scopalamine), belladonna (atropine):	Witch groups of central Europe
1805	morphine (isolated from opium to reduce pain, treat insanity)	
1826	bromine (used as sedative)	
1832	chloral (used as sleep-inducing agent)	
1857	cocaine (extracted from coca leaf to treat depression)	
1883	methylene blue, the first phenothiazine (used to treat mania and hallucinations)	
1884	cocaine (used to treat morphine addiction)	
1903	barbiturates introduced (used in sleep therapy)	
1927	amphetamine (used to treat narcolepsy, mild depression)	
1949	lithium (used to treat mania)	
1953	chlorpromazine (marketed as Thorazine, used to treat schizophrenia)	
1957	tricyclic antidepressants (imipramine, or Tofranil)	
1960s–1990s	antianxiety drugs (tranquilizers): benzodiazepines such as diazepam (Valium) and alprazolam (Xanax) antidepressants: selective serotonin reuptake inhibitors (SSRIs): fluoxetine (Prozac), Paxil, and Zoloft	

Sources: Ackerknecht, 1992; Camp, 1973; Goodman & Gilman, 1960; McKim, 1997; Porter & Teich, 1995.

remember George from Chapter 17 who wouldn't take lithium because it made him feel bad.) With time-release capsules, lithium can be maintained at a fairly constant blood level around the clock, minimizing its side effects.

Lithium controls a person's moods by preventing the wild oscillations between mania and depression that are characteristic of bipolar disorder. How it acts and what part of the brain it affects is not well understood. It seems to work by altering the balance of electrolytes in normal neurons, and by altering the functioning of many different types of neurotransmitters, including serotonin, norepinephrine, dopamine, acetylcholine, and GABA. For instance, it decreases the effects of norepinephrine and increases those of serotonin (McKim, 1997).

LINK
List of neurotransmitters, Table 4.3, p. 143

Antidepressant Drugs. For some people, the moderate use of ethanol (in beer, wine, and spirits) serves as a self-administered antidepressant drug. Ethanol use is correlated with clinical depression, however, so psychiatrists prefer to use other pharmacological interventions. Though lithium is effective in ameliorating the symptoms of bipolar disorder, typically it is not an effective treatment for unipolar depression. The search for effective antidepressants is ongoing. In 1957, psychiatrists began to treat people suffering from clinical depression with a drug developed for other reasons, monoamine oxidase (MAO) inhibitor. Used in treating tuberculosis patients, one of its side effects was that it enhanced their mood. MAO inhibitors indirectly increase the available amounts of dopamine, norepinephrine, and serotonin by inhibiting the production of an enzyme that destroys those neurotransmitters. Other first-generation antidepressant drugs included different kinds of MAO inhibitors, as well as another class of drugs called *tricyclic antidepressants,* such as imipramine (Tofranil) and Elavil. (Tricyclics have in common a molecular structure containing three rings; hence, tricyclics.) These drugs increase norepinephrine and serotonin levels indirectly by blocking their reuptake, allowing them to remain longer at postsynaptic sites.

Reuptake, deactivation of neurotransmitters at synapse, Figure 4.24, p. 144

The tricyclic antidepressants were developed as antipsychotics, a use for which they proved ineffective. Today, new versions of both MAO inhibitors and tricyclic antidepressants are effective and safe in the treatment of depression when used at the right doses (Kurtz, 1990). However, they produce side effects: constipation, dry mouth, dizziness, ringing in the ears, and significant blood pressure and cardiac effects. An important consideration in using these antidepressants is that an overdose can be fatal. Newer, so-called second-generation antidepressants minimize this danger.

Listing of psychologically active drugs, Table 9.1, p. 334

In Chapter 9 we discussed the consciousness-altering effects of the newer *selective serotonin reuptake inhibitors* (SSRIs), such as Prozac, Effexor, and Zoloft. As the name of this class of drugs implies, they allow serotonin to remain longer in the synaptic cleft by preventing its reuptake. The actual relationship, however, is more complex. People with elevated levels of serotonin do seem to be less depressed than those with low levels. But research indicates that a specific brain serotonin system is involved: Those who are depressed show reduced activity from the brainstem through the medial forebrain bundle to the forebrain. But the mechanism of action of SSRIs likely involves other changes in neurotransmitters, in so-called second messenger systems in the brain, as well as in biological rhythms, hormone levels, and the immune system (McKim, 1997). For example, research with rats has shown that following 2 to 4 weeks of treatment with several different types of antidepressants, increases of 20 to 40 percent of new brain cells (neurogenesis) can be seen in the hippocampus (Malberg et al., 2000).

After 2 to 3 weeks of taking SSRIs, many clients report feeling less depressed and more functional in social relationships and the workplace. Some report that for the first time in their lives, they know how nondepressed people feel. The side effects of SSRIs vary, but are generally less severe than those of MAO inhibitors or tricyclic antidepressants. Cognitive functioning is unchanged or improved.

The most common complaint is that males experience a loss of interest in sex and both sexes experience increased difficulty in achieving orgasm. One reason for these reduced side effects is that unlike the first generation-antidepressants, SSRIs leave the levels of the neurotransmitter norepinephrine, whose activity is responsible for many adverse physiological effects, unchanged. SSRIs have a wide margin of safety, making even intentional overdoses rare.

Antianxiety Drugs. The psychopharmacology revolution that brought relief to schizophrenics and people suffering from mood disorders also revolutionized the treatment of anxiety disorders, the most pervasive psychological complaints. Unfortunately, early interventions may have caused as many problems as they solved. For example, psychiatrists began prescribing barbiturates that reduce anxiety by depressing activity in the nervous system (see Table 9.1, p. 334). Barbiturates "tranquilize" by making a person drowsy and clumsy; they are highly addictive and have a low margin of safety at high doses. Far too many people have died after mixing depressant drugs, such as alcohol, with Seconal, a common barbiturate.

In the 1960s, the next generation of antianxiety drugs, called *benzodiazepines*, was introduced to minimize the problems inherent in barbiturate use. These tranquilizers included *chlordiazepoxide* (Librium) and *diazepam* (Valium); newer versions are *alprazolam* (Xanax) and *lorazepam* (Ativan). All relieve anxiety without producing the drowsiness of barbiturates, but their potential for abuse is greater, withdrawal from them is far riskier, and they tend to interact adversely with alcohol (McKim, 1997). Because Xanax and Ativan are addictive, psychiatrists are increasingly prescribing *antidepressants* rather than antianxiety drugs for anxiety. Antidepressants are proving to be just as effective, and as noted earlier, there is no potential for abuse with the SSRIs. One SSRI, *fluvoxamine*, has proven safe and effective in the treatment of social phobia, separation anxiety disorder, and generalized anxiety disorder in children aged 6 to 17 years (Walkup et al., 2001).

An Evaluation of Drugs and Treatments. Why should SSRIs—antidepressant medications—work on anxiety disorders? In part, their effectiveness may reflect the fact that many clients suffer from both anxiety *and* depression. But the simplest answer to this perplexing question is that neurotransmitters are interactive: a drug affecting one neurotransmitter affects others indirectly. Ironically, with the exception of a few drugs uniquely suited to treating a particular disorder—chlorpromazine for psychosis, lithium for manic depression—SSRIs are proving to be the most effective drugs in the pharmacologists' arsenal. SSRIs are effective in treating obsessive-compulsive disorder and panic disorder as well as depression and anxiety (Lickey & Gordon, 1991). And Zoloft has been shown effective in reducing the amount of ethanol consumed by stressed monkeys (Higley, Hasert, Suomi, & Linnoila, 1988); both it and other SSRIs are beneficial in helping recovering alcoholics abstain from alcohol.

Which is better, drug therapy, talk or behavioral therapy, or a combination of the two? This question is difficult to answer, because the type of disorder, type of therapist, and type of drugs differ alone and in combination. Consider Figure 18.8 that compares the outcomes of three types of therapy for panic disorder: cognitive-behavioral therapy (PCT), drug therapy, and relaxation therapy. Follow-up studies showed cognitive-behavioral therapy to be the most effective (Clark, Salkovskis, Hackmann, & Middleton, 1994), but all three approaches helped many patients to overcome a panic disorder for over a year.

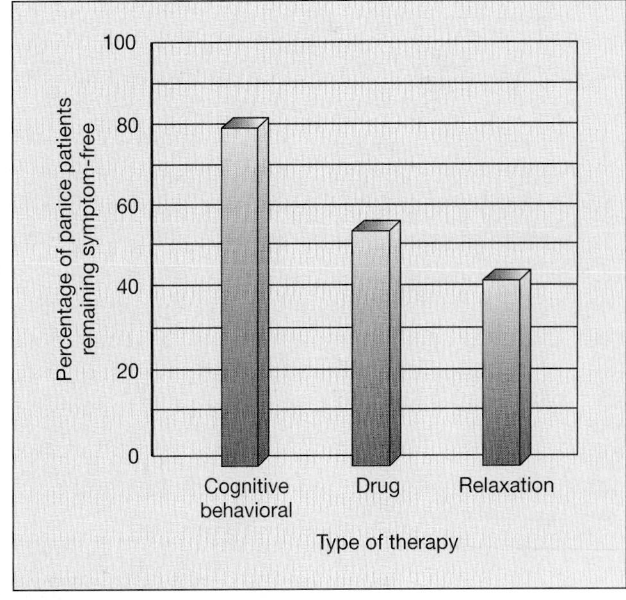

Figure 18.8 Three Treatment Outcomes for Panic Disorder. Drug therapy is not a cure-all. Compared to relaxation therapy, antianxiety drugs allow more patients with panic disorder to remain symptom-free a year after treatment. But cognitive-behavioral therapy is even more effective in treating the disorder. *Source:* Modified from Clark et al., 1994.

Cognitive-behavioral therapy alone is ineffective for patients with schizophrenia, bipolar disorder, depression, and borderline personality disorder. Though some psychologists (Scheff, 1999) consider the medical model inappropriate for the treatment of mental disorders, most now see the advantage of combining drug treatment with talk therapy in the treatment of many mental disorders. Increasingly patients with a wide variety of psychological disorders are receiving both pharmacological and cognitive-behavioral treatment. Because medications can be considerably cheaper than extended psychotherapy, mental health care often consists of a half-dozen or so psychotherapy sessions plus drugs—typically SSRIs—for anxiety and depression (Shulman, 1988). In this treatment model, psychiatrists prescribe the drugs and psychologists, counselors, or social workers do the psychotherapy. Ironically, though the scientific knowledge base of mental illness is now at its highest point, the delivery of services to the mentally ill is dictated by economic factors. Tens of millions of Americans who have no insurance receive minimal to no mental health care.

INTERIM SUMMARY

1. Biological treatments of mental illness include brain surgery, electroconvulsive therapy, and pharmacological interventions
2. ***Psychosurgery*** is the lesioning of the brain to treat psychological disorders. In a *lobotomy,* the connections between the frontal lobe and the rest of the brain are severed. Psychosurgery has all but been replaced by drug therapy.
3. In ***electroconvulsive therapy (ECT),*** electrical current is passed through the brain to treat severe depression. This treatment is effective when conducted over several sessions.
4. The first written records indicate that plants containing psychoactive drugs have been used for thousands of years to reduce pain, alleviate anxiety, and induce euphoria.
5. ***Psychopharmacology*** is the use of drugs by therapists to effect changes in a patient's mental state.
6. Chlorpromazine reduces psychotic symptoms such as hallucinations by blocking dopamine receptors. Since its introduction in 1956, chlorpromazine has enabled many schizophrenics to live outside an institutional setting.
7. Lithium is a toxic metal that effectively controls bipolar disorder in many individuals by preventing extreme oscillations between mania and depression. Its mode of action is unknown.
8. MAO inhibitors and tricyclic antidepressants are first-generation antidepressant drugs acting indirectly to increase dopamine, norepinephrine, and serotonin levels by inhibiting the production of an enzyme that destroys them, or by blocking their reuptake.
9. The *selective serotonin reuptake inhibitors* (SSRIs) Prozac, Effexor, and Zoloft are safe second-generation antidepressants with fewer physiological side effects than MAO inhibitors and tricyclic antidepressants.
10. Tranquilizing barbiturates are highly addictive anti-anxiety drugs that reduce anxiety but also make a person feel drowsy and clumsy. The *benzodiazepines* (Valium is one example) relieve anxiety without producing drowsiness, as do shorter acting tranquilizers such as Xanax. All these drugs are addictive.
11. SSRIs are now being prescribed for both anxiety and depression.
12. The effectiveness of a therapy—whether cognitive, behavioral, pharmacological, or an eclectic mix of these therapies—varies with the type of mental disorder being treated.

For Further Thought

1. What are the pros and cons of performing psychosurgery (a) to relieve intractable pain, in a child or in the elderly; (b) to relieve depression in people who do not respond to pharmacological intervention; and (c) to keep a psychopath from engaging in violent behavior?

2. Should a person relieve depression by taking an addictive drug?
3. Should society require homeless schizophrenics to take medicine to suppress their bizarre behavior?
4. Many HMOs and insurance companies pay physicians to treat patients with high blood pressure, but restrict payments to psychologists who treat obese patients. Discuss the pros and cons of this policy.

CONCLUDING THOUGHTS

A certain percentage of humans have always been mentally ill and have been treated differently because of it. Some had holes trephined in their skulls, while others were kept chained, out of sight. Only in the past two centuries did the mentally ill begin to be treated humanely, and, with the growth of science, be understood and treated effectively using biological and psychological methods. Today, a wide variety of professionally trained psychologists, psychiatrists, counselors, and social workers treat the mentally ill using hundreds of different therapeutic methods.

The proliferation of treatments in the 20th century reflected a growing understanding that the human brain can malfunction in many different ways. Schizophrenia, for example, is a major psychotic disorder that responds well to a specific chemical treatment—the drug chlorpromazine. The same drug has absolutely no effect on the thought processes of a neurotic patient, such as those Sigmund Freud treated. Freud's psychoanalytic method allowed some of his patients to gain insight into their problems, which reduced their anxiety, allowing them to live less troubled lives. Yet Freud's methods have absolutely no effect on psychotic or bipolar disorders. Effective psychotherapy, then, involves matching the mental disorder with the appropriate treatment.

Unlike schizophrenia, many mental disorders appear to be learned. Behavioral therapies have been developed to help patients unlearn fear responses (as in phobias) or correct inappropriate behavior through conditioning and learning. Depression and anxiety, the two most common disorders, are treated with cognitive, humanistic, or cognitive-behavioral therapy. In Albert Ellis's view, clients will begin to feel and behave better once they begin to think more clearly and rationally. For Aaron Beck, also a cognitive psychotherapist, the goal of therapy was to reduce the client's negative thinking and to replace it with insight. Carl Rogers thought that unhappy, negative people would change when they learned to love themselves; Rogers's therapy is loving, noncritical, and nondirective. Cognitive-behavioral therapists emphasize both behavioral change and insight into maladaptive behavior. All these psychotherapeutic techniques are effective to varying degrees. People who undergo therapy do better than those who do not, even after treatment is stopped.

Biological treatments of mental disorders include psychosurgery, electroconvulsive therapy, and pharmacological interventions. Psychosurgery has an ugly history and is performed today only under quite limited conditions. Early electroconvulsive therapy methods were equally unpalatable, but during the past several decades, when drugs for depression are ineffective, it is treated by passing an electric current through restricted parts of the brain.

Psychoactive drugs are the modern-day equivalent of plants with therapeutic properties. Some plants, when chewed, brewed, or smoked, reduce pain and anxiety, or induce euphoria, temporarily relieving the darkness of depression by altering consciousness. Psychopharmacology was born when scientists began to understand the psychoactive compounds in plants, and the many ways in which they affected receptor sites on neurons. Specific drug treatments now exist for both schizophrenia and bipolar disorder; new antianxiety and antidepressant medications are being developed for the tens of millions of people who need them. Many of these drugs are thought to work selectively on serotonin receptors, although the interaction of neurotransmitters suggests that any given drug will affect more than one neurotransmitter.

Someone once remarked that a culture should be judged according to how well it treats its criminals and the mentally ill. We are slowly making progress with both.

KEY TERMS

behavior modification *616*
behavioral therapy *616*
biofeedback *619*
cognitive therapies *621*
electroconvulsive therapy (ECT) *629*
free association *614*
psychoanalysis *614*
psychopharmacology *630*
psychotherapy *610*
resistance *614*
systematic desensitization *616*
transference *614*

Statistical Appendix

[Statistics are] the only tools by which an opening can be cut through the formidable thicket of difficulties that bars the path of those who pursue the Science of Man.

—*Sir Francis Galton*

This is a book about psychology, so why is there an appendix about statistics? As alluded to in the above quotation, statistics are invaluable tools that enable psychologists to make valid scientific conclusions concerning mind and behavior. Consequently, a thorough knowledge of statistics is one of the key skills necessary to understand, evaluate, and conduct research in psychology.

The goal of this appendix is to present you with an introduction to the use of statistics in psychology. If you select psychology as your major, you will likely take a subsequent course (or courses) that will provide you with specific training in statistics; for now, it is enough for you to be exposed to some of the major issues and topics that you will undoubtedly encounter in such a course. In Chapter 2, you learned about methodology in the behavioral sciences. As will (hopefully) become apparent, this appendix complements and extends the material presented in that chapter. You might therefore wish to briefly review Chapter 2 before proceeding further here. Although kept to a minimum, you will encounter a number of statistical formulas in this appendix. In my experience, many students experience an immediate aversive reaction to such formulas. However, these formulas are not intended to confuse matters, and they actually serve a useful purpose: they function to provide an efficient shortcut description for statistical procedures. Much in the way that a secretary may use shorthand to record a dictated memo, statisticians use formulas to record statistical procedures. These formulas require you to master some basic statistical notations (such as $\sum X$), but each formula will be explained in detail, so you will soon grasp this new language of statistics.

Statistics is a branch of mathematics that focuses on the collection, organization, and interpretation of numerical data. The study of statistics itself can be separated into two branches: *descriptive statistics* and *inferential statistics*. Descriptive statistics are used to organize and summarize *data* (the term that psychologists give to the numbers collected in an experiment). As implied in their name, inferential statistics are used to draw inferences (or conclusions) about data. Specifically, psychologists use inferential statistics to test *working hypotheses* (see Chapter 2, pp. 44, 48). We will first focus on descriptive statistics and then move on to consider inferential statistics.

DESCRIPTIVE STATISTICS

Think back to the study presented in Chapter 2 in which a researcher examined the amount of time students studied for a standardized math test and their subsequent scores on the test (see page 55). To provide an illustration of descriptive statistics, let us focus on the data of 10 students who participated in that study. Their data are depicted in Table A.1.

Imagine that a school principal asks the researcher how much time these students studied for the exam. If you were the researcher, how would you answer this question? One potential answer would be simply to list the amount of time that each of the 10 students studied for the test. With only 10 students (and therefore 10 scores), this solution might allow the principal to get a reasonable sense of the students' study time. However, imagine there were 100, or even 1,000, students in the study. (Remember, we are currently only focusing on 10 students to make the calculations manageable.) The principal would likely get a headache trying to keep track of the scores (and would most likely be none the wiser after the hearing them all)!

So, how else could you answer the principal's question? Perhaps it occurred to you to use some form of figure or table to summarize and organize the data. This would be an excellent approach. You may have heard the popular maxim "A picture is worth a thousand words." This maxim

Table A.1 Study Time and Test Scores

Student ID	Study Time (Hours)	Test Score (% Correct)
110	3	97
111	1.5	79
112	1	73
113	2	87
114	1.5	85
115	0	58
116	2.5	66
117	1.5	76
118	1	63
119	2	83

Table A.2 Frequency Table

STUDY TIME (HOURS)	NUMBER OF STUDENTS
3	1
2.5	1
2	2
1.5	3
1	2
0.5	0
0	1

is highly relevant to descriptive statistics, although it should perhaps be reworded as "A picture is worth a thousand numbers"! Accordingly, attention is now turned to consider ways of displaying data using graphical methods.

Graphical Display of Data

A relatively quick and simple way to display a set of scores is to use a *frequency table*. To form a frequency table, list all the possible scores in one column. Then, in a separate column, record the number of individuals who had each of the scores. Table A.2 depicts a frequency table for our data concerning students' study time. The possible study times are listed in the first column (from a minimum of 0 hours to a maximum of 3 hours, using 30-minute increments). The second column displays how many students studied for each of the study times. Be sure to check that you understand how the frequency table was derived from the original data shown in Table A.1. As you can see, this table provides a much more effective answer to the principal's question than simply listing all of the students' study times.

A slightly more elegant way to display data is to use a *histogram*. A histogram is a type of bar graph that shows the frequency of each possible score in a set of data. Psychologists typically refer to a set of data as a *distribution*. Since a histogram depicts the frequency of each score in the distribution, it can be thought of as representing a *frequency distribution*. To draw a histogram, plot the actual scores from your data on the horizontal axis of a graph. In our current example, these scores represent the number of hours of study. On the vertical axis, plot the number of times (that is, the frequency) that each score occurs in the data. A histogram of the students' study time in our example is shown in Figure A.1. As with the frequency table, check to ensure that this histogram corresponds with the original data shown in Table A.1.

Although a histogram provides an excellent means of displaying a frequency distribution, psychologists often prefer to examine a slightly different type of frequency distribution called a *frequency polygon*. Whereas the frequency of scores in a histogram is represented by the height of each bar, a frequency polygon displays frequency using a dot above each score. These dots are then joined to form a polygon (a multisided shape). A frequency polygon for our current example is shown in Figure A.2. A frequency polygon is often preferable to a histogram, since the pattern that is formed by the distribution is somewhat easier to view. In our example, this pattern shows that few students studied for either a relatively short time (less than 1 hour) or a relatively long time (more than 2 hours), and most students studied for a moderate time (1 to 2 hours).

Each of the three types of graphical display discussed above provides a picture of the pattern of a distribution. Although useful, each only provides us with a broad

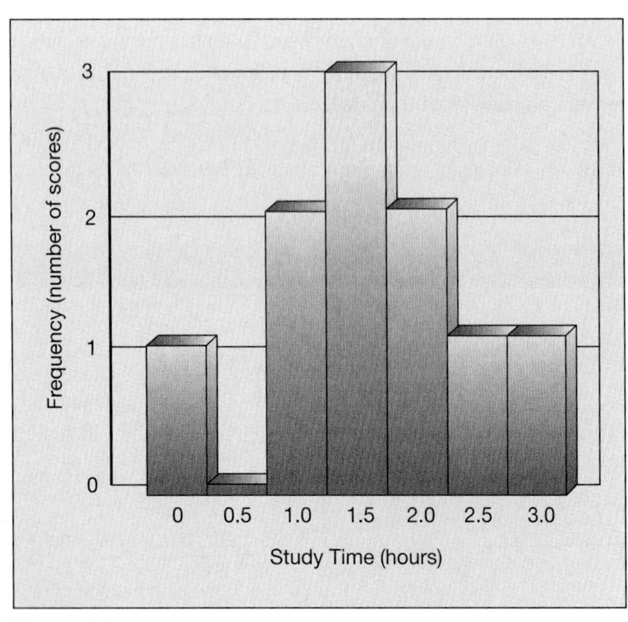

Figure A.1 A Histogram for Students' Study Time

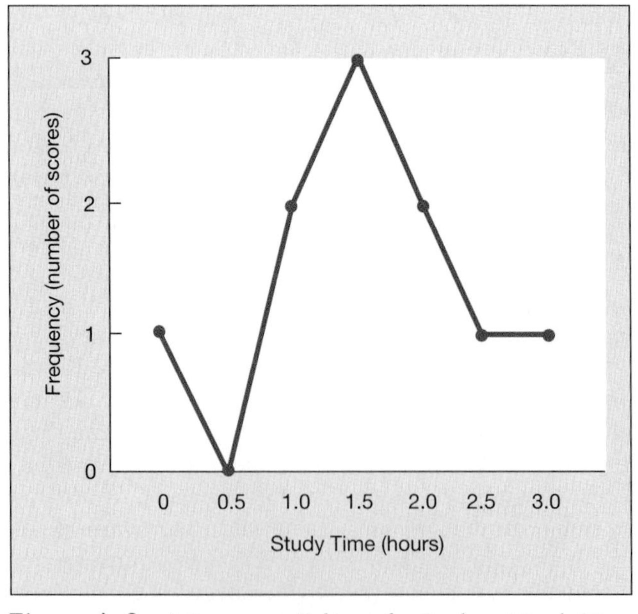

Figure A.2 A Frequency Polygon for Students' Study Time

overview of a distribution. To specify the characteristics of a distribution with more precision, we need to consider some basic statistical procedures. Two characteristics of a distribution are particularly important: *central tendency* and *variability* (or *spread*). We will discuss each in turn.

Measures of Central Tendency: The Mean, Median, and Mode

The middle point of a distribution provides us with a central focal point around which scores vary. Psychologists use three measures of central tendency: the *mean*, *median*, and *mode*.

Mean. The mean (sometimes called the *arithmetic mean*) is what you may already know as the *average* of a distribution. To calculate the mean score of a distribution, simply add up all of the scores and divide by the number of scores in the distribution. In our study of students' study time, adding up all the scores (3 + 1.5 + 1 + 2 + 1.5 + 0 + 2.5 + 1.5 + 1 +2) gives a total of 16. Dividing 16 by 10 (the number of scores in the distribution) gives a mean of 1.6 hours. This procedure of finding the mean by adding up all the score and dividing by the number of scores can be efficiently depicted as a statistical formula as follows: $M = \frac{\Sigma X}{N}$, where *M* refers to the mean, the Greek letter Σ (sigma) means "sum of" (or in other words, add up everything to the right), the term *X* refers to all the scores in the distribution (that is, it is used as a label for all the students' study times), and the term *N* refers to the number of scores in the distribution. So, to put all that in words again: to find the mean, add up all the scores in the distribution and divide by the number of scores in the distribution.

The mean is an excellent measure of central tendency, since it is calculated using every score in a distribution. If a score is altered in the distribution, the mean will inevitably change accordingly. The mean is the most commonly used measure of central tendency, and is used in many statistical procedures in psychology. However, as you will learn below, there are occasions when its value may not be an accurate representation of central tendency.

Mode. The mode captures a different aspect of central tendency by indicating the most frequent score(s) found in a distribution. The mode is 1.5 hours in our current example, since it appears most often (three times) in the distribution. The mode provides a sense of the most common score in a distribution, but it is a less sensitive measure than the mean, since its value may be unchanged despite (potentially major) alterations in the scores in the distribution.

Median. The median represents yet another aspect of central tendency by identifying the midpoint of the distribution; half of the scores lie below it, and half of the scores above it. To find the median, first arrange all of the scores in the distribution in increasing numerical order: 0, 1, 1, 1.5, 1.5, 1.5, 2, 2, 2.5, 3. Since there are 10 scores, the midpoint lies between the 5th and 6th scores (since that point has half of the scores below it and half above it). Therefore, to find the median we simply take the mean of these two scores. Both scores are 1.5, so the median study time is 1.5 hours. Had there been 11 scores in the distribution, the median score would have been the 6th score (since that score would have five scores below it and five scores about it).

The median is a particularly useful measure of central tendency when a distribution contains one or more extreme scores. Consider the following distribution: 1, 0, 1, 3, 2, 3, 39. The mean of this distribution is 7 (49 divided by 7). However, none of the scores is particularly close to that value, so here the mean does a poor job of describing the central tendency of the distribution. However, consider the median value of 2. The extreme score of 39 does not unduly influence the median, and its value of 2 does a better job than the mean of describing the central tendency of the distribution.

Remember, descriptive statistics are designed to summarize and organize distributions. Measures of central tendency do indeed serve that purpose, but they do not tell us the whole story. For example, the mean study time for our 10 students was 1.6 hours. Such a mean might reflect the fact that almost all students studied for 1 or 2 hours. However, a mean of 1.6 hours could also be obtained if most of the students studied for considerably less than 1 hour and a few students studied for 4 hours or more. The crucial point here is that measures of central tendency do not indicate how spread out the scores are in a distribution; psychologists refer to this spread of a distribution as *variability*. This point is made effectively by W. I. E. Gates, who describes a ". . . man who drowned crossing a stream with an average depth of 6 inches." The stream may have had a mean depth of 6 inches, but it may also have been 8 feet deep in parts! A knowledge of the variability of the depth of the stream may have alerted the man to the potential looming danger.

Measures of Variability: Range, Variance, and Standard Deviation

Range. The range is the simplest measure of variability. To find the range, subtract the lowest score in the distribution from the highest score. The range in our example is therefore 3 − 0 = 3 hours. The range does provide some sense of the variability of a distribution, but since it is only based on the two extreme scores, it is not an especially sensitive measure. Therefore, psychologists typically rely on two other measures to assess the variability of a distribution. These measures, the *variance* and *standard deviation*, assess the amount of variability (or spread) of scores around the mean of a distribution. If scores are spread a long way from the mean, the variance and standard deviation will be larger than if the scores are tightly grouped around the mean.

Variance and Standard Deviation. The variance and standard deviation are two closely related measures of variability. Both provide a measure of the average amount that each score varies from the mean. However, as you will notice when we go through the method of calculating the variance and standard deviation, the variance is measured in squared units. Since the standard deviation is measured in regular (that is, unsquared) units, the standard deviation is easier to understand.

The procedure for calculating the variance and standard deviation involves a number of steps.

Step 1: Calculate the mean of the distribution.

Step 2: Subtract the mean from each score. This gives you what is known as a *deviation score*: the distance between a score and the mean.

Step 3: Square each deviation score to create *squared deviation scores*.

Step 4: Add all the squared deviation scores to create the *sum of squared deviation scores*.

Step 5: Find the *variance* by dividing the sum of squared deviation scores by the total number of scores.

Step 6: Find the *standard deviation* by taking the square root of the variance.

The variance and standard deviation calculations for our example are shown in Table A.3. Use the above description and the steps and arrows marked on Table A.3 to track how the variance and standard deviation are calculated. As you will notice, the variance does indeed measure the average squared amount that each score varies from the mean: 0.64 squared hours for our example. Taking the square root of the variance ($\sqrt{.64} = 0.8$) gives us a measure of the average (unsquared) amount that each score varies from the mean: this is the standard deviation. As shown in Table A.3, each student's study time score varied by an average of 0.8 hours (or 48 minutes) from the mean study time of 1.6 hours (or 96 minutes). This provides us with an enhanced knowledge of the distribution, compared to simply knowing that the mean study time is 1.6 hours. In the next section, you will learn some useful applications of the standard deviation.

The Normal Distribution

In Chapter 2 (see p. 53), you encountered the *normal distribution* (or *normal curve*, sometimes also known as a *bell curve*). This distribution can be thought of as a *theoretical frequency distribution*. Figure A.3 shows a normal distribution. The normal distribution is symmetrical about its midpoint, which is the mean, mode, and median score. Since the median represents that point that has the same number of scores below it as above it, 50 percent of the

Table A.3 Calculations for Variance and Standard Deviation

	Step 1 →	Step 2 →	Step 3
STUDY TIME (HOURS)	MEAN STUDY TIME	DEVIATION SCORES	SQUARED DEVIATION SCORES
3	1.6	3 − 1.6 = 1.4	1.96
1.5	1.6	1.5 − 1.6 = −0.1	0.01
1	1.6	1 − 1.6 = −0.6	0.36
2	1.6	2 − 1.6 = 0.4	0.16
1.5	1.6	1.5 − 1.6 = −0.1	0.01
0	1.6	0 − 1.6 = −1.6	2.56
2.5	1.6	2.5 − 1.6 = 0.9	0.81
1.5	1.6	1.5 − 1.6 = −0.1	0.01
1	1.6	1 − 1.6 = −0.6	0.36
2	1.6	2 − 1.6 = 0.4	0.16
			Step 4: sum = 6.4

Step 5: **variance** = $\frac{\text{sum of squared deviation scores}}{\text{number of scores}} = \frac{6.4}{10} = 0.64$ squared hours

Step 6: **standard deviation** = $\sqrt{\text{variance}} = \sqrt{0.64} = 0.8$ hours

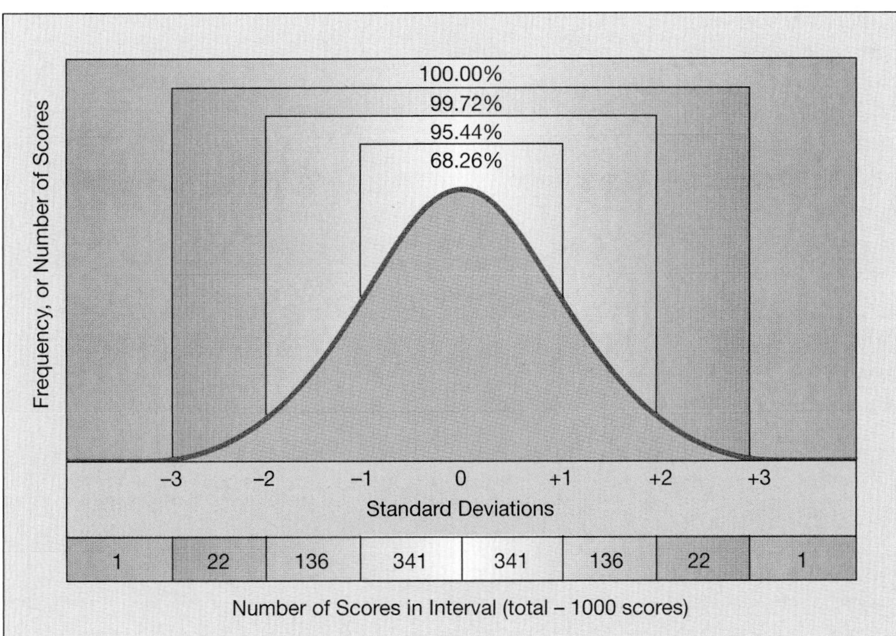

Figure A.3 A normal distribution. A normal curve (or normal distribution of scores) showing the mean (at "0 standard deviations") and the standard deviation of a population of 1,000 scores.

distribution lies below the midpoint and 50 percent lies above it.

To provide an illustration of how useful the normal distribution is, let us consider the scores on a midterm examination. It is not always true, but often such scores will conform approximately to a normal distribution, with a few students performing poorly on the exam, many students scoring somewhere close to the mean, and a few students obtaining very high scores. Imagine you get an 84 on a midterm exam. What is your initial reaction? Hopefully, before you decide whether you are happy or not, you will try to find out how your classmates did on the exam. If everybody else scored 90 or more, you might not be particularly satisfied with an 84. However, if everybody else scored less than 80, you will probably be very happy with an 84.

Another way of approaching this is to say that you are trying to locate your score on the distribution of scores for the whole class. In statistical terms, the way we do this is with standard deviations: specifically, the number of standard deviations you scored away from the mean. Imagine that the mean score on the midterm was 80, and the standard deviation was 4. Since you scored an 84, you can be said to have scored exactly one standard deviation above the mean. Look carefully at Figure A.3 and try to locate the exact point on the distribution corresponding to your midterm score of 84. You should be at the point that is exactly one standard deviation above the mean. If we assume that the distribution of midterm scores conformed to a normal distribution (also known as being *normally distributed*), 50 percent of the class will have scored below the midpoint. Note that Figure A.3 also depicts the percentage of scores that lie between scores that are one, two, and three standard deviations above and below the mean. Accordingly, 34.13 percent of the class will have scored from the midpoint to a score of one standard deviation above the mean (that is a score of 80 + 4 = **84**). Therefore, your score of 84 was as good as or better than 50 percent (all of the people scoring below the midpoint) + 34.13 percent (all of the people scoring from the midpoint to one standard deviation above the mean) = **84.13** percent of your classmates' scores.

What if you had scored an 88 on the midterm? Now you would have scored at two standard deviations above the mean (remember that each standard deviation = 4). You would therefore have scored as well as or better than 50 percent (all of the people scoring below the midpoint) + 34.13 percent (all of the people scoring from the midpoint to one standard deviation above the mean) + 13.59 percent (all of the people scoring from one to two standard deviations above the mean) = **97.72** percent of your classmates.

As shown above, linking the idea of standard deviations with the normal distribution allows you to determine exactly where a score lies on a particular distribution. When we carry out this procedure of identifying a score's distance from the mean in terms of standard deviations, this distance can be thought of as a special type of score: such scores are known as *Z scores*. To distinguish regular scores—such as a score out of 100 on a midterm exam, your weight in pounds, or your height in inches—from Z scores, regular scores are referred to as *raw scores*. To relate this to the above example, your score of 84 on the exam is a raw score. This raw score is one standard deviation (the value of which was 4) above the mean (which was 80) and therefore corresponds to a Z score of +1. If you had scored 76, you would have scored one standard deviation *below* the mean, which corresponds to a Z score of −1. The sign of the Z score denotes whether the score was above (a plus sign) or below (a negative mean) the mean. Therefore, the numbers listed on the horizontal axis of Figure A.3 (−3, −2, −1 . . . +2, +3) are Z scores (since they represent the number of standard deviations that a raw score was away from the mean). Note that the Z score of 0 denotes the mean of the distribution, since the mean is zero standard deviations away from the mean.

Transferring a Raw Score to a Z Score. It was very convenient that in our example the mean is 80, the standard deviation is 4, and a score of 84 lies one standard deviation above the mean, and is therefore associated with a Z score of +1. However, what are the Z scores associated with raw scores of 87 and 79? At this point, it becomes easier to use a simple formula to transfer the raw scores into Z scores (although note that you have already used that formula intuitively when determining that a raw score of 84 is associated with a Z score of +1).

Here is the formula: $Z = \frac{(X - M)}{\text{standard deviation}}$, where *X* is equal to the raw score and *M* is equal to the mean (as before). So, for the raw score of 87, $Z = \frac{(87 - 80)}{4} = +1.75$, and for the raw score of 79, $Z = \frac{(79 - 80)}{4} = -0.25$. This formula makes sense, since it first requires you (in the [X – M] part) to find out how far (in raw score units) your particular raw score is from the mean. Note that this creates a deviation score (see Step 2 of the calculations for the variance and standard deviation). The formula then requires you (by dividing by the standard deviation) to find out how many standard deviations that deviation score is from the mean. The result is a Z score that provides you with exact information concerning the score's location on the distribution. This information is itself of use, but it can also be of further use when we are interested in comparing the relationship between people's scores on two different variables. It is at this point that we move on to consider the topic of *correlation.*

Correlation

Quite often in psychology, researchers are interested in determining the relationship between two variables. For example, earlier we focused on a study concerning students' study time and their subsequent scores on a standardized mathematics test. The study time and math test scores for 10 students were shown in Table A.1. As shown in Chapter 2 (see page 55), these scores can be depicted using a *scatterplot.* A scatterplot for our example is shown in Figure A.4. Look at the scatterplot and see whether you can detect any kind of relationship (or *correlation*) between the two variables. Hopefully you noticed a general trend that as study time increases, so does math performance. As noted in Chapter 2 (see p. 56), such a relationship is referred to as a *positive correlation.* (If math performance actually decreased as study time increased, then this would be a *negative correlation.*) However, note that this trend we identified is not perfect, since one student studied for a relatively long time of 2.5 hours, but received a relatively low score of 66 on the test. The scatterplot therefore provides an excellent visual display of the relationship between the two variables, but we can specify this relationship more precisely by calculating a *correlation coefficient* between the two variables.

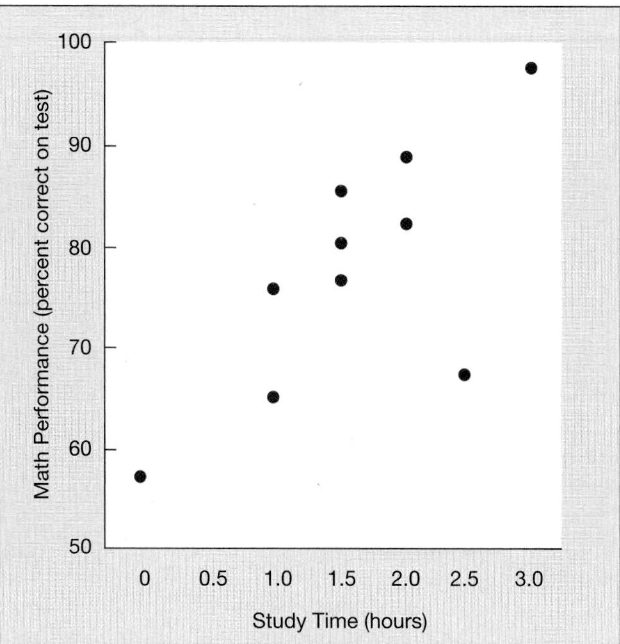

Figure A.4 A Scatterplot of Students' Study Time

A correlation coefficient can vary from –1.00 to +1.00. The sign of a correlation coefficient specifies the *direction* of the relationship between two variables: a negative correlation indicates that as scores on one variable increase, scores on the other variable tend to decrease; a positive correlation indicates that as scores on one variable increase, scores on the other variable tend to increase. The magnitude of a correlation coefficient (the actual value of the coefficient, ignoring its sign) indicates the *strength* of the relationship between the two variables. The maximum value (of –1.00 or +1.00) denotes a perfect (negative or positive) relationship. As the value decreases, this indicates a weaker and weaker relationship, down to a minimum of 0.00, indicating no relationship at all.

Let's next consider the calculations necessary to compute a correlation coefficient between students' study time and math test scores. As with the calculations for the variance and standard deviation, there are a number of steps to follow. To provide an easy distinction between the two variables, let us refer to the study time scores as *X* scores and the math test scores as *Y* scores (these arbitrary labels are commonly used in many statistical procedures).

Step 1: Using the formula described earlier, transfer all the raw X scores into Z scores, thereby creating Z_X scores (that is, Z scores for the X variable).

Step 2: Transfer all the raw Y scores into Z scores, creating Z_Y scores.

Step 3: Multiply each pair of Z_X and Z_Y scores to create Z_XZ_Y scores.

Table A.4 Calculations for Correlation Coefficient

Study Time (X scores)	Math Test Score (Y scores)	Step 1: Z_X Scores	Step 2: Z_Y Scores	Step 3: A_XZ_Y Scores
3	97	(3 – 1.6)/0.8 = 1.75	(97 – 76.7)/11.39 = 1.78	3.12
1.5	79	(1.5 – 1.6/0.8 = –0.13	(79 – 76.7)/11.39 = 0.20	–0.03
1	73	(1 – 1.6)/0.8 = –0.75	(73 – 76.7)/11.39 = –0.32	0.24
2	87	(2 – 1.6)/0.8 = 0.5	(87 – 76.7)/11.39 = 0.9	0.45
1.5	85	(1.5 – 1.6)/0.8 = –0.13	(85 – 76.7)/11.39 = 0.73	–0.09
0	58	(0 – 1.6)/0.8 = –2	(58 – 76.7)/11.39 = –1.64	3.28
2.5	66	(2.5 – 1.6)/0.8 = 1.13	(66 – 76.7)/11.39 = –0.94	–1.06
1.5	76	(1.5 – 1.6)/0.8 = –0.13	(76 – 76.7)/11.39 = –0.06	0.01
1	63	(1 – 1.6)/0.8 = –0.75	(63 – 76.7)/11.39 = –1.20	0.9
2	83	(2 – 1.6)/0.8 = 0.5	(83 – 76.7)/11.39 = 0.55	0.28
mean = 1.6 standard deviation = 0.8	mean = 76.7 standard deviation = 11.39			Step 4: sum = 7.1

Step 5: **correlation coefficient** = $\frac{\Sigma Z_X Z_Y}{N} = \frac{7.1}{10} = +0.71$

Step 4: Sum the $Z_X Z_Y$ scores.

Step 5: Divide the sum of the $Z_X Z_Y$ scores by the number of individuals (which is the same as the number of pairs of scores) to create the correlation coefficient.

The overall formula that summarizes these steps is: correlation coefficient = $\frac{\Sigma Z_X Z_Y}{N}$. The calculations associated with each of the above steps are shown in Table A.4. As shown in the table, the correlation coefficient between students' study time and math test scores is +0.71: a strong positive correlation. This allows the researcher to conclude that there is a strong relationship between a student's study time and his or her subsequent math test score. However, note that this does not allow the researcher to conclude that the amount of time spent studying exerts a direct *causal* effect on math test scores. (For further discussion of this issue, see page 57.)

INFERENTIAL STATISTICS

Until now, the focus has been on using descriptive statistics to summarize and organize data. However, psychologists often wish to extend their conclusions beyond the results of their experiment. In other words, they wish to make inferences that allow the results of the study to be generalized. For example, imagine that to help finance your college studies, you work as a server in a local restaurant (for some of you, this will require no imagination!). You soon learn from your fellow servers that there are a number of techniques you can use in an effort to boost the tips you receive from customers. One common technique is to draw a smiley face ☺ on each customer's check. As a curious person, you decide to investigate whether this particular technique does indeed increase tip size. Note that your goal in carrying out the experiment is to determine whether this technique will increase the tips you receive from all your future customers. In statistical terms, you can think of all these people as comprising a *population*. As noted in Chapter 2, a population is defined as a comprehensive set of individual scores. Of course, it wouldn't make sense to carry out the experiment with all these people. Therefore, you decide to conduct the experiment using all the customers you serve during a one-week period. These customers can be thought of as a *sample* (that is, a subset) of individuals from the larger population of your future customers.

You carry out the experiment as follows. For one week, just before you give the check to each customer, you toss a coin. If it lands on heads, you draw a smiley face on the check; if it lands on tails, you do not draw a smiley face. You then record the size of tip you get from each customer. After one week, you tabulate the results and note that the mean tip from people who had a smiley face on their check was \$5.63 and the mean tip from your other non-smiley-face customers was \$4.56. You might be happy to conclude immediately that the smiley face did indeed boost your tips. However, recall that your goal is to establish whether the smiley face will increase tips for your *future customers in general*. For example, imagine you repeat the study one month later and find that the mean tip for customers with a smiley face on their check is \$4.87 and the mean for the other customers is \$5.43. Would you now suddenly reverse your previous conclusion and instead decide that the smiley face lowered your tips? The crux of the matter is that you need to ascertain whether the results you obtained in your sample can be generalized to the larger population. The procedure for doing this is known as *hypothesis testing*.

Hypothesis Testing

The proposition that a smiley face will increase tips is referred to as the *working hypothesis*. This hypothesis is not itself explicitly tested. Instead, an alternate hypothesis is derived and tested. This *null hypothesis* says the exact opposite of the working hypothesis: drawing a smiley face will *not* increase the size of tip you receive. If this null hypothesis were true, this would mean that future customers seeing a smiley face would not tip more than customers not seeing a smiley face. However, even if this were true, one would not necessarily expect *identical* size tips from a sample of people, half of whom saw a smiley face and half of whom did not. That would be the same as expecting *exactly* 50 heads and 50 tails every time a coin is flipped 100 times.

Let us return to the scenario where those customers who saw the smiley face left a mean tip of $5.63 and the other customers left a mean tip of $4.56. In the light of the above discussion, the key question is as follows: if the null hypothesis is true (that is, a smiley face has no influence on tip size), how likely is it that we would obtain a mean tip size for the smiley-face customers $1.07 ($5.63 – $4.56) more than the mean tip size for the other customers? (Given the importance of the previous sentence, I recommend you read it to yourself slowly a couple of times.) If it is rather likely that we would obtain such a difference between the mean tip size if the null hypothesis were true, then our study does not allow us to reject the null hypothesis and we are left with evidence consistent with the notion that a smiley face does not influence tip size. Thus, the study would not provide evidence consistent with our proposed working hypothesis. However, if it is highly unlikely that we would obtain such a difference between the mean tip size if the null hypothesis were true, this allows us to reject the null hypothesis, thereby providing support for our *working hypothesis*. Our conclusion from the study would therefore be that a smiley face does indeed appear to increase tip size. [You may be interested to learn that a smiley face *can* increase tip size for female, but not male servers (Rind & Bordia, 1996).]

At this point, you may well be wondering how we determine the likelihood that we would obtain such a mean tip difference if the null hypothesis were true. To provide a short answer to this question, we use a specific *statistical test* (known as an *independent samples* t *test*) that tells us this likelihood. You may be relieved to know that the precise formulas and calculations associated with this test are beyond the scope of this appendix. However, you should note that understanding the logic of the test (as outlined above) is far more of a challenge than carrying out its mathematical calculations.

The logic of hypothesis testing may appear somewhat counterintuitive, but after rereading the above discussion a couple of times, you should gain an appreciation for its workings. The above experiment provides an example of one type of statistical test. This test provides a comparison of two means, each of which comes from a sample of separate individuals. The precise statistical test to be utilized in an experiment varies according to a number of factors, including the type of working hypothesis under test and the specific research design employed. However, the underlying logic of each test is the same as that described here.

This appendix has provided you with an introduction to the use of descriptive and inferential statistics and the basic logic of hypothesis testing. Although these topics were not discussed in great depth, your preliminary knowledge of them provides a solid foundation on which to build in future courses. It is hoped that you will take (and enjoy) such courses and will proceed to further understand and conduct statistics for psychology.

REFERENCE

Rind, B., & Bordia, P. (1996). Effect on restaurant tipping of male and female servers drawing a happy, smiling face on backs of customers' checks. *Journal of Applied Social Psychology, 29*, 139–144.

Glossary

absolute threshold The minimal amount of stimulation that a subject can detect on half the trials. p. 232

accommodation (Piaget) The process of modifying an existing schema. p. 392

acquired motivation Motives an individual learns during a lifetime. p. 155

action potential A nerve impulse; the firing or spiking of a neuron. p. 139

adaptation Any characteristic that improves the "fit" of a plant or animal with its environment, thereby increasing its chances of transmitting genes to the next generation. p. 71

additive color mixing The mixing of two or more colors of light to create different color. p. 244

aerobic exercise Physical activity that increases oxygen consumption for an extended period. p. 556

aggression Physical or verbal behavior intended to harm another person. p. 537

algorithm An exhaustive, systematic problem-solving strategy that is guaranteed to produce the correct answer. p. 436

all-or-none principle The rule that when the electrical change in a neuron exceeds a threshold voltage, an action potential must follow. p. 140

allele A particular form of a gene at a particular place on the chromosome. p. 77

alternate-form reliability A test is reliable if two forms of it give the same results. p. 61

altruism A behavior that helps another individual but may diminish one's survival or reproductive potential. p. 98

amplitude The intensity or size of a waveform, measured vertically. p. 247

animal communication The production and reception of signals that typically are meaningful only to members of the same species. p. 420

annoyer (Thorndike) An unpleasant stimulus. p. 206

antecedent condition The event that precedes and causes another event to occur. p. 37

anterograde amnesia The inability to form new memories following an injury to the brain. p. 374

anthropomorphism The attribution of human characteristics to animals. p. 92

antisocial personality disorder A mental disorder characterized by impulsive, manipulative, aggressive, and destructive behavior toward others. p. 604

anxiety (Freud) A state of emotional distress caused by the ego's need to resolve the conflicting motivational states of the id and superego. p. 499

anxiety disorder A mental disorder characterized by persistent feelings of apprehension. p. 584

aphasia A partial or complete loss of language abilities following brain damage. p. 418

appetitive behaviors Preliminary activities (such as searching) that precede and lead to consummatory behaviors. p. 89

artificial selection The deliberate selection of desired characteristics in plants and animals. p. 72

assimilation (Piaget) The process of integrating new information into an existing schema. p. 392

associationism The idea that learning, and the formation of complex ideas, is accomplished through the mental association of simpler ideas. p. 14

associative process The cognitive process that connects two stimuli, a stimulus and a response, or a response and a reinforcer. p. 190

attachment A strong and enduring emotional bond between a caretaker and child. p. 405

attention-deficit/hyperactivity disorder (ADHD) A behavior problem characterized by inattention, overactivity, and impulsivity. p. 577

attitude A person's manner or disposition to respond favorably or unfavorably to a person or situation. p. 515

attribution An inference about the cause of one's own behavior and the behavior of others. p. 513

attribution theory A theory of how people perceive the causes of behavior. p. 513

autonomic nervous system (ANS) The part of the peripheral nervous system that includes the parasympathetic division and the sympathetic division. p. 113

avoidance learning A procedure in which an instrumental response prevents an aversive stimulus. p. 214

axon The extension of a neuron over which an action potential is conducted. p. 117

basilar membrane A membrane in the cochlea that contains the hair cells. p. 251

behavior modification The modification of a target behavior through the application of the principles of reinforcement and punishment. p. 616

behavior The ways in which animals act or respond in an environment. p. 186

behavioral control The contingencies that determine the expression of a behavior through reinforcement and punishment. p. 211

behavioral genetics The study of how genes, interacting with environments, affect behavior. p. 86

behavioral medicine An interdisciplinary field that unites physicians, biomedical scientists, and behavioral scientists. p. 544

behavioral regulation Adaptive behaviors that help animals achieve a homeostatic state. p. 154

behavioral therapy The treatment of a mental disorder through the application of basic principles of conditioning and learning. p. 616

behaviorism The theory that the environment rather than genes is the primary determinant of both human and nonhuman animal behavior. p. 22

between-groups design An experimental design in which the effect of manipulating an independent variable (i.e., the treatment group) is compared to that of a control group. p. 45

big five personality factors The basic five personality factors found consistently in factor-analytic studies of the personality: extroversion, agreeableness, conscientiousness, emotional stability (neuroticism), and intellect (openness to experience). p. 490

biocultural evolution The process by which the selection, preparation, and consumption of particular types of food enhance the fitness of individuals in a culture. p. 161

biofeedback A behavioral therapy that provides clients with information about the status of normally unconscious physiological systems. p. 619

biological clock Cells that function as endogenous timekeepers, cycling on solar or lunar time. p. 311

biomedical model A model of health care that emphasizes the use of drugs, surgery, and other procedures designed to correct physical ailments. p. 546

biopsychosocial model A model of health care that emphasizes the effect of behaviors, thoughts, feelings, and culture on a person's physical health. p. 546

bipolar disorders A mood disorder characterized by drastic mood swings, from major depressive episodes to either *manic* or *hypomanic* episodes. p. 594

blindsight Seeing without awareness. p. 283

body of knowledge The written record of the outcomes of scientific investigations. p. 39

borderline personality disorder A mental disorder characterized by a pervasive pattern of instability in self-image, mood, and social relationships. p. 603

bottom-up process An analysis of the action of feature detectors in a sensory experience. p. 271

brainstem The entire brain except for the forebrain structures. p. 110

brightness contrast The perception of a difference in brightness reflected from two different areas of the visual field. p. 279

Broca's area The portion of the left frontal lobe that is involved in speaking. p. 418

bystander effect The greater willingness of a lone individual to offer help to a stranger compared to that of a group. p. 525

Cannon-Bard theory The theory that emotion results from subcortical brain activity, which causes both a physical response and an emotional experience. p. 179

case study An investigation of a single individual over time. p. 53

cell body The main part of a neuron, which contains the normal constituents of a living cell. p. 117

central hearing loss Hearing loss that results from lesions and tumors in the brain. p. 255

central nervous system (CNS) The part of the nervous system that includes the brain and spinal cord. p. 113

central sulcus The main fissure, or gap, that separates the frontal lobe from the parietal lobe. p. 124

cerebellum The large, walnut-shaped structure located at the intersection of the hindbrain and spinal cord. p. 110

cerebral cortex The thin layer of neocortex that covers the cerebral hemispheres. p. 108

cerebral hemispheres The two halves of the outer covering of the brain (the cerebrum). p. 108

child-directed speech A simplified form of speech that caretakers use with a child (sometimes called *motherese*). p. 429

chromosome A structure in the nucleus of a cell that carries genetic information in the form of a DNA molecule. p. 77

chunking The process of reorganizing material so as to admit more units, or bits, of information into short-term memory. p. 350

circadian rhythm Cyclic changes in consciousness (such as sleeping and waking), physiology (such as body temperature), and behavior (such as activity level) that are experienced over a 24-hour period. p. 310

classical conditioning A procedure in which a conditioned response results from the pairing of a conditioned stimulus with an unconditioned stimulus. (Also known as *Pavlovian conditioning*) p. 191

clinical psychology The branch of psychology that is concerned with the diagnosis and treatment of psychological disorders. p. 27

closed feeding system A feeding pattern characterized by reflexive responses to a narrow range of foods. p. 157

cochlea A coiled, fluid-filled tube in the inner ear that contains the receptors for hearing. p. 250

cocktail party phenomenon The ability to listen selectively to one particular voice among many simultaneous conversations. p. 349

cognitive development The way in which a child's thinking about the world changes with maturity and experience. p. 392

cognitive dissonance An unpleasant psychological state caused by two contradictory thoughts. p. 518

cognitive map (Tolman) A mental representation of the route or shortest path to a target destination. p. 217

cognitive processes The psychological processes of perceiving, thinking, knowing, remembering, and so forth. p. 221

cognitive therapies Talk therapies designed to confront clients' irrational thoughts and emotions by challenging them to think more insightfully. p. 621

collective unconscious (Jung) A knowledge of archetypes and universal symbols that is passed genetically from parent to offspring. p. 504

comparative psychology The study of the motivation and behavior of animals in order to identify similarities and differences among them. p. 92

complementary colors Pairs of lights that when added together produce white. p. 244

complex cell A neuron in the striate cortex that is sensitive to the position and orientation of edges (or lines) *anywhere* within the receptive field. p. 275

concrete operational stage Piaget's third stage of cognitive development, from about 7 to 12 years, characterized by the development of logical reasoning. p. 395

conditioned compensatory response (Siegel) A homeostatic response that counteracts a drug's effect after repeated exposures. p. 202

conditioned emotional response An emotional response (such as fear) that is triggered by a conditioned stimulus. p. 198

conditioned response (CR) (Pavlov) A reflexive response that is triggered by a conditioned stimulus. p. 192

conditioned stimulus (CS) (Pavlov) A stimulus (such as the sound of a bell) that can trigger a conditioned response (such as salivation). p. 192

conditioned taste aversion A conditioning procedure in which an animal drinks a flavored solution (the CS) and is then made sick by a toxin (the US). p. 201

conductive hearing loss Deafness due to outer or middle ear damage. p. 253

cones Bright-light receptors in the retina that contain one of three different photopigments. p. 238

confirmation bias The tendency to look for evidence that verifies one's preconceptions. p. 443

confounding variable An unknown or unidentified variable that causes an effect. p. 46

consciousness The quality or state of being aware. p. 306

conservation (Piaget) The understanding that certain attributes of a physical object (such as volume, number, and mass) do not change, despite changes in the object's appearance. p. 394

consummatory behaviors (Ethology) Innate "survival" behaviors such as copulating and eating. p. 89

continuity of species (Darwin) The theory tht all living organisms are adaptations of earlier life forms and are genetically related. p. 71

continuous reinforcement A procedure in which each response is followed by a reinforcer. p. 208

control group In an experiment, a comparison group exposed to all conditions of the treatment group except the independent variable. p. 45

convergence A binocular depth cue that results when the eyes turn inward to see nearby objects. p. 277

conversion disorder A temporary loss of a bodily function with no discernable physical cause. p. 590

coping Responses that are intended to reduce or better tolerate the perceived stress of events. p. 564

corpus callosum The broad band, or commissure, of fibers that connects the left and right hemispheres. p. 133

correlation coefficient A number that varies from +1.0 (a perfect, positive relationship between two variables) to 0.0 (the absence of a relationship), to −1.0 (a perfect, negative relationship between two variables). p. 56

corticalization An increase in the proportion of neocortex relative to other brain matter, a trend clearly seen in mammals. p. 108

cranial nerves Twelve pairs of nerves in the CNS that serve both sensory and motor functions. p. 110

criterion-related validity A test is valid if it correlates well with a separate, independent assessment of the construct being measured. p. 61

critical period (Ethology) A period when an animal is particularly sensitive to certain features in the environment. p. 89

crystallized intelligence A knowledge of general information, including how language is used and the social conventions of culture. p. 400

dark adaptation An increase in visual sensitivity as a result of time spent in the dark. p. 243

daydream A reverie or waking fantasy based on wishes or fears. p. 327

decay theory The theory that forgetting is caused by the dissipation (or decay) of a hypothetical brain trace over time. p. 369

declarative memory The conscious memory for facts and words and for personal events and episodes. p. 364

deductive reasoning A type of rational thinking in which specific instances are inferred from a general rule or principle. p. 443

defense mechanisms (Freud) The ego's strategies for resolving conflicts between the id and superego, including rationalization, repression, and denial. p. 499

delusion A false, unrealistic belief. p. 598

dendrites The receptive part of a neuron. p. 117

denial (Freud) A defense mechanism that is a type of repression, in which a person avoids guilt-inducing thoughts by forcing them into the unconscious. p. 500

deoxyribonucleic acid (DNA) A double-strand, helix-shaped structure containing genetic material. p. 77

dependent variable A response variable that changes as a function of the independent variable. p. 44

depersonalization disorder A mental disorder characterized by severe, persistent feelings of being detached from oneself. p. 592

depolarization A decrease in the membrane potential. p. 139

depression A chronic mood disorder characterized by despair and a pervasive sadness. p. 594

descriptive statistic Simple numerical descriptions of observations, such as the mean of a distribution of scores. p. 52

diathesis-stress model The theory that genetic predispositions and/or biochemical imbalances make stressed individuals vulnerable to specific illnesses. p. 563

dichotic listening task A procedure in which subjects hear two messages in different ears and then report on what they remember hearing. p. 349

dichotic listening test A test in which a subject is asked to repeat different numbers heard simultaneously in the left and right ear. p. 132

dichotomous traits A trait, such as color, tht occurs in one or another form, but never in combination. p. 75

differential reinforcement of high rates of response (DRH) A schedule of reinforcement that is designed to reinforce bursts of operant responses. p. 210

differential reinforcement of low rates of response (DRL) A schedule of reinforcement that is designed to reinforce pauses between operant responses. p. 210

discrimination The ability to perceive a difference between two stimuli. p. 195

discriminative stimulus (Sd) A signal that indicates when a response will be reinforced. p. 212

dissociation The separation or isolation of mental processes, such as memory or consciousness, from the integrated personality. p. 330

dissociative amnesia A disorder in which a person abruptly and inexplicably cannot recall large amounts of personal information. p. 591

dissociative fugue A mental disorder characterized by an abrupt disappearance from one's normal surroundings, travel to unfamiliar surroundings, and an inability to remember details of one's personal identity. p. 591

dissociative identity disorder (DID) (multiple personality disorder) A disorder in which a person presents with two or more distinct personalities. p. 592

distal causes Distant causes of behavior rooted in evolutionary and genetic determinants. p. 70

dominant allele (dominant gene) Of two alleles for the same trait, the one that is expressed in a heterozygote. p. 77

double-blind experiment An experiment in which neither the researcher nor the subjects are aware of the treatment condition. p. 57

drive reduction Motivation that is based on meeting or reducing needs and restoring homeostatic balance. p. 155

dualism The idea that the mind and body are distinct entities. p. 5

ecological niche The environmental habitat of an animal, including resources and interactions with other animals. p. 73

ego (Freud) The personality's conscious interface with the world. p. 498

elaborative rehearsal The strategy of associating a target stimulus with other information at the time of encoding. p. 358

electrical stimulation of the brain (ESB) An experimental technique in which electricity is passed through an electrode into the brain. p. 44

electroconvulsive therapy (ECT) The passage of an electrical current through the brain to treat severe depression. p. 629

electroencephalogram (EEG) A visual record of voltage changes in the brain. p. 320

emotion An affective psychological experience, such as anger, joy, or fear, that is accompanied by bodily arousal. p. 150

empiricism A method of obtaining knowledge by observation and experimentation. p. 14

encoding The transfer of information from short-term to long-term memory. p. 356

endocrine gland An organ that produces and releases hormones. p. 152

epidemiological research The use of correlation techniques to establish relationships between behavior and health. p. 58

episodic memory An individual's memory for personal events and life episodes. p. 366

escape A procedure in which an animal makes an instrumental response that terminates an aversive stimulus. p. 214

evolution Charles Darwin's theory that existing species of life on earth are the end result of a process of natural selection. p. 71

evolutionary psychology The study of human and animal minds and behavior from the perspective of evolutionary theory. p. 96

excitatory postsynaptic potential (EPSP) A local, graded excitatory potential that depolarizes a neuron's membrane. p. 139

experiment A test or trial to discover a cause-effect relationship. p. 34

experimental subject A human or other animal used in an experiment. p. 44

extinction *Classical conditioning:* a reduction in the conditioned response when the conditioned stimulus is presented without the unconditioned stimulus. p. 193

extinction *Instrumental conditioning:* a reduction in the rate of response when reinforcement is withheld. p. 210

extragenetic history Information in the form of cultural wisdom, including oral and written history, that is passed across generations. p. 85

extrastriate cortex A vision-related area of the cortex located around the striate cortex. p. 285

extrinsic motivation Motivation to meet the standards of others. p. 169

face validity The soundness of a test based on its surface appearance. p. 61

factor analysis A statistical method for measuring the relationships among scores on various tests to determine what they have in common. p. 459

false memories Memories of events that never happened. p. 345

feature detector A visual neuron that is sensitive to a particular visual feature, such as a shape, edges, or movement. p. 272

fetal alcohol syndrome (FAS) A clinical condition seen in the children of mothers who drank alcohol during pregnancy; characterized by hyperactivity, mental retardation, heart defects, a lack of alertness, and problems with movement. p. 383

figure-ground relationship The perceived distinction between an object (figure) and its background. p. 292

fitness The reproductive success of an individual relative to other individuals; the number of reproductively fertile copies an individual contributes to the next generation. p. 72

fixation (Freud) Failure to progress to the next stage of psychosexual development due to an unsuccessful resolution of the conflicting demands of the id and superego. p. 500

fixed action pattern (FAP) (Ethology) A programmed sequence of species-specific behaviors tht is triggered by a particular stimulus. p. 90

fixed interval (FI) schedule A schedule of reinforcement in which the first response made following a specified time interval is reinforced. p. 209

fixed ratio (FR) schedule A schedule of reinforcement in which a fixed number of responses must be made before a response is reinforced. p. 208

flashbulb memories Memories of extraordinary events that contain strong emotional components. p. 367

fluid intelligence The ability to process information and see patterns and relationships in ambiguous test stimuli. p. 400

Flynn Effect The finding of a steady worldwide rise in IQ over the second half of the 20th century. p. 471

foot-in-the-door phenomenon Greater compliance with large requests following compliance with small requests. p. 516

foraging pattern An innately determined food-searching behavior. p. 218

forebrain The front part of the brain, including the cerebrum, thalamus, hypothalamus, and other structures. p. 108

formal operational stage Piaget's fourth stage of cognitive development, from 12 years to adulthood, characterized by the ability to think hypothetically (abstractly) and engage in hypothesis testing. p. 396

free association (Freud) An analytic technique in which the patient describes whatever comes to mind, including thoughts, images, and dreams. p. 614

free nerve ending A skin receptor with an undifferentiated dendrite, involved in the senses of touch, temperature, and pain. p. 264

free recall A test of memory in which the items to be remembered can be recalled in any order. p. 354

frequency The number of waves, or cycles, per second of a waveform, measured horizontally. p. 247

frontal lobe The part of the cerebral cortex that is devoted to speech, planning, movement, association formation, and other psychological functions. p. 124
frustration-aggression hypothesis The proposal that aggression is more likely to occur when a person becomes frustrated. p. 539
functional fixedness A mental set involving rigid thinking about the functions of objects, which hinders the discovery of unique solutions to problems. p. 438
functional relationship An orderly relationship between a stimulus and response, or between two responses. p. 46
functionalism The study of the usefulness of consciousness and the utility and purposefulness of behavior. p. 20
fundamental attribution error The tendency to attribute the causes of another person's behavior to personal dispositions rather than the demands of a situation. p. 514

ganglion cells (retina) The fifth layer of cells in the retina, whose axons form the optic nerve. p. 239
gate-control theory Melzack's theory that nerve impulses from the brain activate gates in the spinal cord, effectively blocking pain. p. 264
gender roles Culturally determined appropriate behaviors for females and males. p. 526
gene The basic unit of heredity. p. 73
general adaptation syndrome (Selye) A three-stage stress response that progresses from *alarm* to *resistance* and finally, *exhaustion*. p. 560
general intelligence (g) A common intellectual ability inferred from the correlation of scores for specific abilities on intelligence tests. p. 453
generalized anxiety disorder A mental disorder that is characterized by a persistent, inappropriate anxiety for which there is no apparent cause. p. 585
genetics The study of patterns of heredity and variation in plants and animals. p. 75
genotype The genetic constitution of an individual organism. p. 77

habituation Decreased responsiveness to a repetitive stimulus. p. 193
hair cells The receptors for hearing, located on the basilar membrane. p. 251
hallucination A false perception that cannot be shared or verified. p. 598
hardy personality A high-stress/low-illness individual who is committed to self, has an internal locus of control, and perceives events as challenges rather than stressors. p. 563
health (World Health Organization) A state of complete physical, mental, and social well-being, not merely the absence of disease or infirmity. p. 546
health psychology An interface between psychology and medicine, concerned with the relationship between one's lifestyle, thoughts, and emotions and one's physical health. p. 544
hedonism The basic motivation of humans and other animals to seek pleasure and avoid pain. p. 150
heredity The genetic transmission of characteristics from one generation to the next. p. 75
heritability The relative influence of heredity in the expression of a trait. A heritability score varies between 0 and 1, with 1 meaning that a trait is largely determined by genetic and physiological variables and 0 meaning that it is primarily environmentally caused. p. 88
heterozygous Having two different alleles for a given trait, as in the form *Aa*. p. 77
heuristic Leading to or stimulating further research. p. 50
hidden observer (Hilgard) A part of consciousness that is aware of another part of consciousness. p. 330
higher-order conditioning (Pavlov) The process through which a conditioned stimulus acquires the properties of an unconditioned stimulus. p. 194
hindbrain The back part of the brain, including the cerebellum and medulla. p. 108
homeostasis The process in which the equilibrium of a physiological system is maintained through self-regulation. p. 152
homozygous Having the same allele for a given trait, as in the form *AA* or *aa*. p. 77
hormone A chemical such as a peptide, protein, or steroid that is produced by glands and released into the body. p. 152
human development The lifelong process of physical, cognitive, and social growth and development. p. 380
hyperpolarization An increase in the membrane potential. p. 140
hypnosis A procedure that induces a temporary, trancelike state in which a person is more suggestible than usual. p. 329
hypochondriasis A disorder in which a person is excessively preoccupied with health and worries constantly about becoming ill. p. 589
hypothalamus The part of the midbrain lying below the thalamus that controls biological functioning. p. 110
hypothesis A hunch, idea, or theory that is formally tested in an experiment. p. 43
hypovolemic thirst Thirst that results from an abnormally low blood volume. p. 155

id (Freud) Unconscious biological drives and impulses that operate according to the *pleasure principle*. p. 498
illusion A false perception. p. 280
implicit memory The unconscious memory of a past experience. p. 360
imprinting (Ethology) A highly adaptive innate behavioral process that involves the rapid development of a response to a specific stimulus at a particular stage of development. p. 89
incentive A goal or objective that motivates behavior. p. 155
inclusive fitness The fitness of an individual and related individuals (who carry many of the same genes). p. 97
incus The middle ossicle in the middle ear. p. 250
independent variable In an experiment, a variable that is manipulated to see its effect on the dependent variable. p. 44
individual differences The many ways in which individuals vary within a population. p. 52
inductive reasoning A type of rational thinking in which particular instances are used to form a general rule. p. 443
information-processing model of memory A framework for describing how different memory systems sense, rehearse, encode, store, and ultimately retrieve information. p. 346
inhibitory postsynaptic potential (IPSP) A local, graded excitatory potential that hyperpolarizes a neuron's membrane. p. 140
innate releasing mechanism (Ethology) A postulated neural mechanism tht triggers an innately organized motor program. p. 90

insight A sudden, unexpected solution or strategy for solving a problem. p. 437

insomnia A chronic sleep disorder in which a person experiences difficulty getting to sleep or staying asleep. p. 324

instinct Innately organized behavior. p. 70

instinctive drift (Breland) The theory that arbitrarily established responses erode (drift) in the face of more innate (instinctive) behavior. p. 217

instrumental learning The modification of a nonreflexive behavior using reinforcers and punishers. p. 205

instrumental response A voluntary, nonreflexive response that acts on the environment in a meaningful way. p. 204

intelligence quotient (IQ) A single number that represents a child's intelligence, computed by dividing the child's mental age by the child's chronological age and multiplying the result by 100. p. 454

interference theory The theory that existing memories interfere with the encoding and retrieval of memories. p. 369

intrinsic motivation Motivation to achieve self-satisfaction. p. 169

introspection The verbal reporting of one's conscious experience. p. 19

James-Lange theory The theory that emotion is the awareness of one's bodily response to a given stimulus. p. 179

just noticeable difference (jnd) The minimal amount of sensory change in a stimulus that a person can detect. p. 231

kin selection The theory that one promotes the well-being and inclusive fitness of a genetic relative because of shared genes. p. 97

Lamarckian evolution The theory that genetic changes can occur in populations through the inheritance of characteristics acquired during a lifetime. p. 73

language acquisition device (LAD) (Chomsky) A species-specific brain mechanism that allows a child to acquire language rapidly. p. 428

latent learning (Tolman) Learning that occurs in the absence of specific food rewards. p. 218

lateral fissure The main fissure that separates the temporal from the frontal lobe. p. 124

lateral geniculate nucleus (LGN) A portion of the thalamus that receives impulses from the retina through the optic nerve. p. 239

lateralization of function The differences in function between the left and right cerebral hemispheres. p. 131

law of effect (Thorndike) The rule that responses that are followed by "satisfiers" tend to be repeated, whereas responses that are followed by "annoyers" tend not to be repeated. p. 206

learned helplessness The failure to initiate self-preserving behavior following exposure to intensely aversive events. p. 562

learning A relatively permanent change in observable behavior that results from experience with an environment. p. 186

learning disorder A disorder characterized by a discrepancy between one's academic achievement and one's intellectual ability. p. 578

levels of processing The levels, either shallow or deep, at which information is encoded in long-term memory. p. 357

lightness constancy The tendency to see an object as being the same, even under varying light intensities. p. 279

linear perspective A scene containing converging lines, which provides a monocular cue for depth perception. p. 277

linguistic relativity hypothesis (Sapir and Whorf) The theory that differences in language are responsible for differences in the way people think. p. 441

locus of control The perception of who or what controls one's actions and destiny, oneself (internal locus) or chance events (external locus). p. 563

long-term memory (LTM) A memory store of unlimited capacity that can hold information indefinitely. p. 347

longitudinal fissure The main fissure or gap that separates the left and right cerebral hemispheres. p. 124

maintenance rehearsal The act of holding information in short-term memory by silently repeating each item as it is presented. p. 356

malleus The ossicle attached to the eardrum. p. 250

matched-groups design An experimental design in which subjects are assigned to groups so that a number of specified variables that might influence their performance are controlled. p. 58

mean The midpoint, or arithmetic average, of a population of scores. p. 52

means-end analysis Comparison of a current state with a goal state to determine changes that will reduce the differences between the two states. p. 436

medical model (of mental disorders) The theory that disordered thoughts and behavior result from a diseased or otherwise malfunctioning brain. p. 580

medulla The lower part of the brainstem, which connects with the spinal cord. p. 110

meiosis The process of cell division that produces sex cells (sperm and egg) containing one of each pair of chromosomes. p. 82

meme A cultural invention that is passed on from one generation to the next. p. 187

memory The psychological processes involved in storing and retrieving previously experienced sensory impressions, such as words and images. p. 344

mental set Expectations formed from repeated reinforced trials. p. 442

method of constant stimuli A psychophysical method in which a threshold value is reached by presenting stimuli in a random order. p. 232

method of limits A psychophysical method of establishing a sensory threshold value by increasing or decreasing the intensity of a stimulus until a subject can detect it 50 percent of the time. p. 232

method of magnitude estimation A psychophysical method in which subjects use numbers to describe the perceived intensity of a stimulus. p. 233

midbrain The middle part of the brain, including part of the reticular formation. p. 108

mind-body problem The question of the relationship between mind and body. p. 5

mnemonic A memory aid that increases the amount of information a person can remember. p. 351

modern synthesis The merging of Darwin's theory of evolution through natural selection with the science of genetics. p. 72
molar level In research, investigations of the behavior of whole, intact organisms. p. 37
molecular level In research, investigations of behavior at the physiological or biochemical level. p. 37
monism The idea that mind and body are different aspects of the same substance. p. 6
monogamy A mating pattern involving one female and one male. p. 98
mood disorder A mental disorder characterized by sustained, pervasive emotions that interfere with normal functioning. p. 593
Morgan's canon Morgan's (1894) admonition not to attribute complex psychological processes to nonhuman animals. p. 92
motivation The factors that cause an animal to behave. p. 150
mutation A permanent, random chemical change in DNA, usually detrimental to an individual's survival. p. 82
myelin The Schwann cells that form an outer covering on some axons. p. 118

nativism The idea that some kinds of perception and forms of thinking are innate. p. 15
natural selection (Darwin) The means by which organisms adapt to the environment and reproduce differentially. p. 72
nature-nurture issue The question of the relative effects on behavior of genes (nature) and environment (nurture). p. 7
need for achievement The motivation to accomplish a task quickly and effectively. p. 169
negative discriminative stimulus (SΔ) A stimulus that signals that a response will not be followed by reinforcement. p. 212
negative feedback A self-regulatory process in which movement away from a set point triggers a counteraction that moves the system back toward the set point. p. 153
negative reinforcement A process in which responses that prevent aversive events are learned, presumably because the absence of an aversive event is reinforcing. p. 214
neophobia Fear of something new; with regard to food, finickiness, or an innate tendency to cautiously approach, sniff, and taste a new food before ingesting it. p. 158
neuroendocrine system A network of neurons and glands that make and secrete hormones. p. 116
neuroethology The study of the relationship between the nervous system and consummatory behaviors. p. 94
neurogenesis The process of forming new neurons. p. 129
neurons Chemically sensitive cells in the nervous system that are responsible for nervous activity. p. 113
neurosis (Freud) Impaired personal and social functioning due to anxiety. p. 581
neurotransmitter One of a variety of chemicals that neurons secrete. p. 118
nocebo effect Sickness or pain resulting from negative expectations. p. 570
normal distribution A normal, or bell-shaped, curve representing the frequency of occurrence of scores for a given characteristic of a population. p. 52
null hypothesis A statement that no differences exist between two groups being compared in an experiment. p. 48
nutritional wisdom An innate predisposition to make adaptive food choices. p. 158

object permanence The understanding that objects continue to exist, even when they are out of sight. p. 393
observational learning Learning by watching others; imitation. p. 215
observer expectancy effects Observer bias—the tendency of an experimenter to make biased observations that would unduly support the working hypothesis. p. 57
obsessive-compulsive disorder (OCD) A disorder characterized by obsessions (persistent, uncontrollable, worrisome thoughts) and compulsions (ritualized behaviors triggered by obsessions). p. 587
occipital lobe The part of the cerebral cortex that contains the primary visual cortex and associative cortex, which are involved in seeing and visual consciousness. p. 124
off-center cells Ganglion cells with concentric-circle receptive fields that are inhibitory and excitatory when light falls inside and outside, respectively. p. 272
olfactory bulb The part of the brain that synapses with the smell receptors through the olfactory nerve. p. 260
omnivore's paradox The paradox that eating from a wide variety of food sources not only is nutritionally adaptive but also increases the risk of poisoning. p. 158
on-center cells Ganglion cells with concentric-circle receptive fields that are excitatory and inhibitory when light falls inside and outside, respectively. p. 272
one-word utterance stage The first words spoken in any language, typically the names of objects in the environment, such as "mama" and "milk," or of actions, such as "get" and "go." p. 428
ontogenetic history The history of an animal's entire development, from fertilization through death. p. 85
open feeding system A feeding pattern characterized by selection from a wide variety of food choices. p. 158
operant (Skinner) An instrumental response, such as a lever press, that effectively *operates* on the environment. p. 206
operant conditioning (Skinner) The process through which reinforcement strengthens (makes more probable) an operant response. p. 207
operational definition A definition of a concept in terms of how it is being measured. p. 44
opponent-process theory Hering's theory that all colors are sensed in red-green, blue-yellow, and white-black opposing pairs, so that when they are sensed together, they produce white. p. 245
orienting reflex (Pavlov) An instinctive response to a stimulus, such as turning the head to locate a sound source. p. 191
osmotic thirst Thirst that results from an above-optimal concentration of solutes in bodily fluids. p. 155
oval window A membrane that connects the stapes in the middle ear with the vestibular canal in the inner ear. p. 250
overjustification effect The loss of intrinsic motivation to perform a task that results from the addition of an extrinsic motivator. p. 169

pair bonding A strong and enduring affection that unites an infant with a parent. p. 93
panic disorder A disorder characterized by recurring rushes of paralyzing anxiety that may last for several minutes. p. 586
parasympathetic division The part of the autonomic nervous system that is involved in the functioning of a body at rest. p. 116

parietal lobe The part of the cerebral cortex that contains the somatosensory and associative cortex, which are involved in spatial perception and other psychological functions. p. 124

partial reinforcement A procedure in which *patterns* of responses (rather than single responses) are reinforced. p. 208

partial reinforcement effect (PRE) The tendency for responses that are being maintained on a partial reinforcement schedule to be highly resistant to extinction. p. 210

peer review The examination of an experimental finding by other scientists. p. 49

perception The interpretation of sensory information according to expectations and prior learning. p. 231

peripheral nervous system (PNS) The part of the nervous system that includes the somatic and autonomic nervous systems. p. 113

personality disorder Any of a number of mental disorders characterized by inflexible personality traits that cause long-term personal distress and impaired social and workplace functioning. p. 602

personality The thoughts, feelings, desires, intentions, and behavioral tendencies that contribute to one's individuality. p. 486

PET scan (positron-emission tomography) A method of visualizing actively functioning brain areas by measuring electrically charged particles. p. 132

phantom limb The perception that an amputated limb still exists. p. 265

phenotype The physical expression of features in an organism tht results from the interaction of its genotype with the environment. p. 77

pheromone A chemical secretion that communicates information from one animal to another. p. 259

phi phenomenon The apparent movement of a stationary light source. p. 290

phobic disorder An anxiety disorder characterized by a persistent, inappropriate fear of an object or situation. p. 584

phonological loop A part of working memory that allows a person to remember speech sounds for a brief period. p. 354

phylogenetic history The evolutionary history of a specific group of organisms. p. 85

physical dependence The need to take a drug to avoid withdrawal symptoms. p. 339

place theory The theory that the frequency of sound is coded through the stimulation of a particular place on the basilar membrane. p. 252

placebo effect A beneficial outcome of a treatment that cannot be related to specific causal properties of the treatment. p. 570

polyandry A mating pattern involving one female and more than one male. p. 98

polygandry (or promiscuity) A mating pattern comprised of more than one male and more than one female. p. 98

polygenic character A character that varies in a continous manner, presumable caused by the effects of many genes. p. 87

polygyny A mating pattern comprised of one male and more than one female. p. 98

population The complete set of individual scores of a particular characteristic. p. 54

positive reinforcement (Skinner) A process in which a reward such as food is used to reinforce an operant response. p. 207

positive reinforcer (Skinner) Any stimulus that follows an operant response and has the effect of increasing the rate of response. p. 207

preconscious (Freud) Memories that can be readily accessed from long-term memory. p. 497

prejudice Evaluating other people negatively because they are members of a certain group. p. 535

preoperational stage Piaget's second stage of cognitive development, from birth to 2 years, characterized by the rapid growth of symbolic thinking. p. 394

primacy effect The tendency for items at the beginning of a list to be remembered better than items in the middle. p. 356

primary motivation Instinctive or biologically motivated behavior. p. 155

priming Presentation of a target memory, in whole or part, prior to its recall. p. 360

proactive interference Interference in the learning of new information caused by existing memories. p. 369

probabilistic reasoning The idea that the causes of events may not be completely determined and may be specified only within a range of probabilities. p. 38

procedural memory The memory for skilled performance that results from reinforced practice. p. 364

programmatic research A succession of experiments each aimed at solving part of a larger problem. p. 39

proximal causes Causes of behavior that focus on immediate, local, psychological, and sociological determinants. p. 70

psychoanalysis (Freud) A therapy involving the analysis of childhood conflicts to determine how they are presently affecting the client, and providing insight into alleviating the anxiety caused by these conflicts. p. 614

psychological dependence An intense emotional craving for a drug. p. 339

psychological disorder A condition in which a person's thoughts, feelings, and behavior interfere with normal psychosocial functioning. p. 577

psychological model (of mental disorders) A theory of mental illness that an individual's past and present life experiences cause and maintain a psychological disorder. p. 581

psychology The scientific study of mind and behavior. p. 5

psychometrics Methods of measuring psychological processes. p. 60

psychoneuroimmunology The study of how the mind, brain, immune system, and behavior are interconnected. p. 566

psychopharmacology A psychiatrist's use of drugs to effect changes in a patient's mental state. p. 630

psychophysics The mathematical relationship of sensory intensity to the magnitude of a physical stimulus. p. 231

psychosis A severe mental disorder characterized by disorganized thought and a loss of contact with reality. p. 581

psychosomatic disorder A disorder in which thoughts and emotions (the *psyche*) have an adverse effect on the body (the *soma*). p. 558

psychosurgery Brain surgery performed with the object of changing a person's emotional behavior. p. 178

psychotherapy The use of psychological techniques and methods by a trained professional to change the thoughts, emotions, and behavior of a person in need. p. 610

punishment The process through which an aversive stimulus decreases the rate of the response to which it is applied. p. 212

rationalization (Freud) A defense mechanism in which unacceptable thoughts are reinterpreted in less distressing terms. p. 499

reaction range A range of possible IQ scores for a given person, representing the potential effect of the environment in which one is raised. p. 468

recency effect The tendency for items at the end of a list to be remembered better than items in the middle. p. 354

receptive field The portion of the visual field to which a cell in the nervous system responds when visually stimulated. p. 272

recessive allele (recessive gene) An unexpressed allele in a heterozygote, but is phenotypically expressed when homozygous. p. 77

recombination The process in which an organism emerges from meiosis with a combination of alleles different from that entering meiosis. p. 82

reductionism Explanation by reference to a more molecular level of analysis (such as physiology or biochemistry). p. 37

referential pointing Extension of the right hand and index finger to call attention to an object in the environment. p. 416

reflex An innate, involuntary response to a specific stimulus in the environment. p. 190

rehearsal The conscious repetition of material in short-term memory. p. 347

reliability The repeatability of an observation, experiment, or test score. p. 60

REM sleep A stage of sleep that is characterized by storylike dreams and rapid eye movements. p. 322

repression (Freud) A defense mechanism that involves suppressing unacceptable thoughts or emotions by relegating them to the unconscious. p. 500

resistance (Freud) In psychoanalysis, behaviors a patient engages in to delay the therapeutic process. p. 614

resting membrane potential The voltage across a neuron's membrane at rest, usually about –70 mV. p. 138

reticular formation A group of neurons extending from the hindbrain into the midbrain that serves to alert animals. p. 122

retina A multilayered structure on the inner surface of the eye. p. 238

retinal disparity The difference in the view from each of two eyes, which provides a binocular cue for depth perception. p. 276

retrieval The process through which working memory brings a stored memory into consciousness. p. 347

retroactive interference Interference in the retrieval of old memories caused by newly learned information. p. 369

retrograde amnesia The loss of memory for events that preceded a brain injury. p. 374

rod-cone break During dark adaptation, the point at which the rods become increasingly sensitive to dim light. p. 243

rods Dim-light receptors in the retina that contain the photopigment rhodopsin. p. 238

sample A subset of scores of a population. p. 54

satisfier (Thorndike) A pleasant stimulus. p. 206

scatterplot A distribution of data points that vary in two dimensions. p. 55

Schacter's emotional attribution theory The theory that emotion is experienced after a person appraises a stimulus and monitors the body's response. p. 180

schedule of reinforcement The pattern according to which responses are reinforced. p. 207

schema A personal interpretation of a sensory event that biases the memory of the event. p. 360

schizophrenia A disorder characterized by disturbances in thought that may affect perceptual, social, and emotional processes. p. 598

science Knowledge based on observation and experimentation and validated by other scientists. p. 34

scientific method A method of attaining knowledge based on observation and experimentation. p. 35

second-signal system (Pavlov) The way in which a word (the second signal) is attached to raw sensory input (the first signal). p. 199

secondary reinforcer A neutral stimulus that acquires reinforcing properties through the process of higher-order conditioning. p. 207

selective attention The process of attending to information that results in the encoding of short-term memories. p. 349

selective pressure Any feature of an environment that allows one phenotype to have reproductive advantage over another. p. 72

self-actualization (Maslow) Finding and fulfilling one's potential. p. 507

self-concept The perception a person has of his or her own basic nature and typical behavior. p. 507

self-report method A test (such as a paper-and-pencil test) that can be completed by an individual. p. 60

self-serving bias The tendency to attribute one's failures to the situation and one's successes to personal factors. p. 514

semantic memory The memory for particular features of the environment, including language. p. 365

sensation The raw experience of a sensory stimulus, such as light or sound. p. 231

sensitization Increased responsiveness following the presentation of a single stimulus. p. 193

sensorimotor stage Piaget's first stage of cognitive development, from 2 to 7 years of age, characterized by sensing and moving through the environment. p. 392

sensorineural hearing loss Deafness due to damage to the cochlea. p. 254

sensory memory A brief representation of what is being sensed—for example, a visual afterimage. p. 346

sensory-specific satiety Satiety that is experienced for the foods eaten during a meal, but not for other foods with different sensory properties. p. 160

serial position effect The tendency for items at the beginning and end of a list to be remembered better than those in the middle. p. 354

set point The point around which a system homeostatically regulates itself. p. 152

sexual orientation The sexual attraction to and preference for others of the same or opposite sex. p. 529

shape constancy The tendency to see a form as unchanging, despite changes in its retinal image. p. 279

shaping A procedure in which responses that approximate the target behavior are reinforced. p. 207

short-term memory (STM) A temporary memory store of limited capacity that lasts about 15 to 30 seconds. p. 347

sign stimulus (Ethology) A specific environmental stimulus that triggers innately organized behaviors. p. 90

signal detection theory Proposal that the detection of stimuli involves decision processes as well as sensory processes. p. 233
simple cell A neuron in the striate cortex that is maximally sensitive to the position and orientation of edges (lines) in the receptive field. p. 274
size constancy The tendency to see a figure as being the same size, despite changes in its retinal size. p. 279
social facilitation The enhancement of an individual's performance due to the presence of others. p. 524
social loafing The tendency of a person to exert less effort in a group task compared to an individual task. p. 525
sociobiology The study of the genetic determinants of social behavior. p. 96
somatic nervous system The part of the peripheral nervous system that includes the sensory and motor nerves. p. 113
somatization disorder A somatoform disorder characterized by a history of multiple physical complaints extending over a period of several years. p. 590
somatoform disorder A mental disorder in which a person experiences bodily symptoms that are solely due to psychological causes. p. 589
species A reproductively isolated breeding population. p. 70
species-specific behavior An adaptive, innate response pattern typical of a species. p. 85
species-specific defense reaction An innately organized hierarchy of defense behaviors elicited by signals indicating potential danger. p. 91
specific appetite An innate craving for salt or water. p. 155
spinal cord The part of the central nervous system that connects the brain with the lower body. p. 110
split-brain procedure Cutting the corpus callosum to disconnect the left and right cerebral hemispheres. p. 133
split-half reliability A test is reliable if the first half of the test gives the same result as the second half of the test. p. 61
spontaneous recovery (Pavlov) The reappearance of an extinguished response following a delay in the extinction process. p. 193
standard deviation A measure of variability around a mean within a population (see appendix). p. 52
standardized test A test that is administered using uniform procedures that generates scores that can be meaningfully compared to each other. p. 52
Stanford-Binet A commonly used standardized intelligence test that yields an IQ score. p. 454
stapes The ossicle in the middle ear that is connected to the oval window. p. 250
statistic A mathematical indicator that helps a researcher make decisions about experimental outcomes. p. 48
stereotype An attitude or belief based on a person's gender, race, or ethnicity rather than on an individual's thoughts or behavior. p. 535
stimulus control In discrimination training, the demonstration of a response in the presence of an S^d, but not in the presence of an S^{Δ}. p. 212
stimulus generalization The tendency to perceive stimuli that share common properties as being similar. p. 195
storage The process of retaining information in long-term memory. p. 356
strange situation test A procedure used to study attachment, in which an infant is placed in a novel environment and is observed reacting to it in the presence and then absence of a caregiver. p. 406
stress The perception that events are beyond one's ability to deal with them. p. 559
striate cortex The primary visual cortex in the occipital lobe. p. 239
Stroop effect The tendency of the words that denote colors to interfere with the naming of the ink colors in which the words are printed. p. 287
structuralism The study of consciousness in terms of its basic elements, combinations of those elements, and connections among those elements. p. 19
structured interview A formal interview procedure in which specified information is obtained. p. 60
subject expectancy effects A confounding variable; the expectations a subject brings to an experiment that can influence the outcome of the experiment. p. 58
subliminal perception Perception of a stimulus below its absolute threshold. p. 234
superego (Freud) The conscience; the part of the personality that knows right from wrong and provides the moral standard the ego attempts to achieve. p. 498
survey A measurement technique designed to find out about attitudes, aptitudes, and other behaviors. p. 53
sympathetic division The part of the autonomic nervous system that is involved in the functioning of the active body. p. 116
synapse The place where one neuron makes a chemical connection with another neuron. p. 118
systematic desensitization A behavioral therapy that is used to reduce the fear associated with a phobia. p. 616

taste buds Structures on the tongue that contain taste receptors. p. 258
telegraphic speech A stage of language development, appearing at about 18 to 36 months, in which children begin to string two words together in a grammatically meaningful way. p. 430
temperament A trait that is characterized by the quality and intensity of an individual's emotional reactions. p. 407
temporal lobe The part of the cerebral cortex that contains the primary auditory and associative cortex, which are involved in hearing and language. p. 124
test-retest reliability A test is reliable if it gives the same results each time it is taken. p. 61
thalamus A sensory-motor integrative center in the forebrain; in mammals, it connects the midbrain to the cerebrum. p. 108
tolerance A reduction in the intensity of a drug's effect, requiring a larger dose to achieve the same effect. p. 338
top-down process An analysis of the effects of expectation and prior learning on a sensory experience. p. 271
trait The tendency of an individual to act consistently in a characteristic way. p. 488
transduction The conversion of energy from one type to another. p. 238
transference (Freud) In psychoanalysis, a process through which a patient redirects to the therapist emotions experienced with significant others in childhood. p. 614
traveling wave The pattern of vibration in the cochlear fluid, which varies as a function of the amplitude and frequency of an airborne sound. p. 252

trial-and-error learning Learning from the consequences of one's actions. p. 435

triarchic theory of intelligence Robert Sternberg's theory that intelligence is composed of three abilities: analytic, creative, and practical. p. 462

trichromatic theory The theory that color vision is mediated by three cone pigments, each maximally sensitive to one of three wavelengths. p. 244

tympanic membrane A membrane (the eardrum) that separates the outer ear from the middle ear. p. 250

type The highest level of organization of the personality. p. 489

unconditional love Love that affirms and accepts another's behavior without condition. p. 507

unconditioned response (UR) (Pavlov) A reflexive response to an unconditioned stimulus (US). p. 191

unconditioned stimulus (US) (Pavlov) A stimulus that elicits an innate, involuntary, unconditioned response (UR). p. 191

unconscious (Freud) Memories and desires that influence one's behavior without one's awareness. p. 497

unconscious mind Information processing and brain functioning of which a person is unaware; in Freudian theory, the repository of unacceptable thoughts and feelings. p. 307

universal grammar (Chomsky) The theory that humans have an innately determined species-specific language ability that allows them to speak in a grammatically correct manner. p. 430

validation by consensus Support for the acceptance of an experimental finding by the agreement of other scientists who examine it. p. 49

validity The ability of a test to measure what it is designed to measure. p. 61

variable interval (VI) schedule A schedule of reinforcement in which the first response following a varying time interval is reinforced. p. 209

variable ratio (VR) schedule A schedule of reinforcement in which a varying number of responses must be made before a response is reinforced. p. 209

vicarious trial-and-error learning Learning by imagining the probable consequences of one's actions. p. 435

visible spectrum The portion of the electromagnetic spectrum between about 400 to 700 nanometers. p. 237

visual agnosia A visual disability that is characterized by seeing without knowing the meaning of what is seen. p. 286

Weber's law The statement that a sensation is proportional to the intensity (*I*) of the stimulus times a constant, *k*. p. 231

Wechsler Adult Intelligence Scale (WAIS-III) A commonly used intelligence test whose combined verbal and performance subtest scores yield an IQ score. p. 455

Wernicke's area The area in the left temporal lobe that is involved in understanding spoken and written language. p. 418

win-stay, lose-shift strategy (Harlow) A strategy in which an animal continues to make a response that is reinforced (win-stay) but switches to a different response when not reinforced (lose-shift). p. 222

within-subjects design The design of an experiment in which a pretreatment measure of the dependent variable is compared with a posttreatment measure in the same subjects. p. 45

working hypothesis A simple statement of what is expected to happen in an experiment. p. 44

working memory The process of holding incoming information in consciousness and retrieving and manipulating information from long-term memory, enabling cognitive tasks such as learning and thinking. p. 347

zeitgeiber A stimulus (usually daylight) that entrains a biological clock to the Earth's rotation, preventing an animal's activity cycle from free-running. (German for "time giver.") p. 312

zoomorphism The attribution of animal qualities to humans. p. 92

References

Abramov, I., Gordon, J., Hendrickson, A., Hainline, L., Dobson, V., & LaBossier, E. (1982). The retinal of the newborn human infant. *Science, 217*, 265–267.

Abrams, R., Swartz, C. M., & Vedak, C. (1989). Antidepressant effects of right versus left unilateral ECT and the lateralization theory of ECT action. *American Journal of Psychiatry, 146*, 1190–1192.

Ackerknecht, E. H. (1992). *A short history of medicine*. Baltimore: Johns Hopkins University Press.

Adams, B. D. (1985). Age, structure, and sexuality. *Journal of Homosexuality, 11*, 19–33.

Adams, H. E., & Cassidy, J. F. (1993). The classification of abnormal behavior: An overview. In P. B. Stuker & H. E. Adams (Eds.), *Comprehensive handbook of psychopathology* (2nd ed.). New York: Plenum.

Adcock, G. J., Dennis, E. S., Easteal, S., Guttley, G. A., Jermlin, L. S., Peacock, J. W., & Thorne, A. (2001). Mitochondrial DNA sequences in ancient Australians: Implications for modern human origins. *Proceedings of the National Academy of Sciences, USA, 98*, 537–542.

Ader, R. (1985). Conditioned taste aversions and immunopharmacology. *Annals of the New York Academy of Sciences, 443*, 293–307.

Ader, R., Cohen, N., & Felton, D. (1991). *Psychoneuroimmunology*. San Diego, CA: Academic Press.

Ader, R., Weiner, H., & Baum, A. (Eds.). (1988). *Experimental foundations of behavioral medicine: Conditioning approaches*. Hillsdale, NJ: Erlbaum.

Ainsworth, M. D. S. (1993). Attachment as related to mother-infant interaction. In C. Rovee-Collier & L. P. Lipsitt (Eds.), *Advances in infancy research* (Vol. 8). Norwood, NJ: Ablex.

Ainsworth, M. D. S., Blehar, M. C., Waters, E., & Wall, S. (1978). *Patterns of attachment*. Hillsdale, NJ: Erlbaum.

Ajzen, I. (1991). The theory of planned behavior. *Organizational Behavior and Human Decision Processes, 50*, 179–211.

Ajzen, I., & Fishbein, M. (1980). *Understanding attitudes and predicting behavior*. Englewood Cliffs, NJ: Prentice-Hall.

Albert, M. S., & Moss, M. B. (1992). The assessment of memory disorders in patients with Alzheimer's disease. In L. R. Squire & N. Butters (Eds.), *Neuropsychology of memory* (2nd ed.). New York: Guilford Press.

Alcock, J. (1998). *Animal behavior* (6th ed.), Sunderland, MA: Sinauer.

Aldwin, C. M., & Brustrom, J. (1997). Theories of coping with chronic stress: Illustrations from the health psychology and aging literatures. In B. H. Gottlieb (Ed.), Coping with chronic stress. New York, NY: Plenum Press.

Alexander, R. D., Hoogland, J. L., Howard, R. D., Noonan, K. M., & Sherman, P. W. (1979). In N. A. Chagnons & W. C. Irons (Eds.), *Evolutionary biology and human social behavior: An anthropological perspective*. North Scituate, MA: Duxbury Press.

Allen, A. (2001, February 13). Size doesn't matter. *Salon.com*. Available: http://www.salon.com/news/feature/2001/02/13/genome/index.html.

Allport, G., & Odbert, H. (1936). Trait-names: A psycho-lexical study. *Psychological Monographs, 47*. Reading, MA: Addison-Wesley.

Ambrose, S. H. (2001). Paleolithic technology and human evolution. *Science, 291*, 1748–1753.

American Heart Association. (1999). www.amhrt.org/statistics.

American Psychiatric Association. (1989). *Treatment of psychiatric disorders*. Washington, DC.

American Psychiatric Association. (1994). *Diagnostic and statistical manual of mental disorders* (4th ed.). Washington, DC.

American Psychological Association. (2000). http://research.apa.org.

American Psychological Society. (2000). http://www.psychologicalscience.org.

Anderson, A. K., Spencer, D. D., Fulbright, R. K., & Phelps, E. A. (2000). Contribution of the anteromedial temporal lobes to the evaluation of facial emotion. *Neuropsychology, 14*, 526–536.

Anderson, C. A., & Anderson, D. C. (1984). Ambient temperature and violent crime: Tests of the linear and curvilinear hypotheses. *Journal of Personality and Social Psychology, 46*, 91–97.

Anderson, C. D., Ferland, R. J., & Williams, M. D. (1992). Negative contrast associated with reinforcing stimulation of the brain. *Society for Neuroscience Abstracts, 18*, 874.

Anderson, J. R. (1990). *The adaptive character of thought*. Hillsdale, NJ: Erlbaum.

Andreasen, N. C. (1987). Creativity and mental illness: Prevalence rates in writers and their first-degree relatives. *American Journal of Psychiatry, 144*, 1288–1292.

Animal research enjoys wide support, poll says. (1998, December 4). *Chronicle of Higher Education*, p. A33.

Arbib, M. A., & Rizzolatti, G. (1996). Neural expectations: A possible evolutionary path from manual skills to language. *Communication and Cognition, 29*, 393–424.

Arcus, D., & Kagan, J. (1995). Temperament and craniofacial variation in the first two years. *Child Development, 66*, 1529–1540.

Argyle, M. (1999). Causes and correlates of happiness. In D. Kahneman, E. Diener, & N. Schwarz (Eds.), *Well-being: The foundations of hedonic psychology*. New York: Russell Sage Foundation.

Aron, A., & Westbay, L. (1996). Dimensions of the prototype of love. *Journal of Personality and Social Psychology, 60*, 52–63.

Asch, S. E. (1955). Opinions and social pressure. *Scientific American, 193*, 31–35.

Asch, S. E. (1956). Studies of independence and conformity: A minority of one against a unanimous majority. *Psychological Monographs 70*, (9, Whole No. 416).

Aschoff, J., & Wever, R. (1981). The circadian system of man. In J. Aschoff (Ed.), *Handbook of behavioral neurobiology: Vol. 4. Biological rhythms*. New York: Plenum.

Ashmore, R. D., & DelBoca, F. K. (1976). Psychological approaches to understanding intergroup conflicts. In P. A. Katz (Ed.), *Towards the elimination of racism*. Elmsford, NY: Pergamon Press.

Aslin, R. N. (1989). Discrimination of frequency transitions by human infants. *Journal of the Acoustical Society of America, 86*, 582–590.

Aslin, R. N., Saffran, J. R., & Newport, E. L. (1998). Computation of conditional probability statistics by 8-month-old infants. *Psychological Science, 9*, 321–324.

Atkinson, R. C., & Shiffrin, R. M. (1971). The control of short-term memory. *Scientific American, 225* (2), 82–90.

Averill, J. A. (1980). A constructionist view of emotion. In R. Plutchik & H. Kellerman (Eds.), *Emotion: Theory, research and experience: Vol. I. Theories of emotion*. New York: Academic Press.

Ayllon, T., & Azrin, N. (1968). *The token-economy: A motivational system for therapy and rehabilitation.* New York: Appleton-Century-Crofts.

Azzopardi, P., & Cowey, A. (2001). Motion discrimination in cortically blind patients. *Brain, 124,* 30–46.

Baddeley, A. (1998). *Working memory.* Needham Heights, MA: Allyn & Bacon.

Baddeley, A. D., Thompson, N., & Buchanan, M. (1975). Word length and the structure of short–term memory. *Journal of Verbal Learning and Verbal Behavior, 14,* 575–589.

Baer, D. M., & Sherman, J. A. (1964). Reinforcement control of generalized imitation in young children. *Journal of Experimental Child Psychology, 1,* 37–49.

Baggs, K., & Spence, S. H. (1990). Effectiveness of booster sessions in the maintenance and enhancement of treatment gains following assertion training. *Journal of Consulting and Clinical Psychology, 58,* 845–854.

Bahrick, H. P. (1984). Semantic memory content in permastore: Fifty years of memory for Spanish learning in school. *Journal of Experimental Psychology: General, 113,* 1–37.

Bahrick, H. P., Bahrick, P. O., & Wittlinger, R. P. (1975). Fifty years of memory for names and faces: A cross-sectional approach. *Journal of Experimental Psychology: General, 104,* 54–75.

Bahrick, H. P., & Phelps, E. (1987). Retention of Spanish vocabulary over eight years. *Journal of Experimental Psychology: General, 13,* 344–349.

Ball, G. F., & Hulse, S. H. (1998). Birdsong. *American Psychologist, 53,* 37–58.

Ballentine, H. T., Bouckoms, A. J., Thomas, E. K., & Giriunas, I. E. (1987). Treatment of psychiatric illness by stereotactic cingulotomy. *Biological Psychiatry, 22,* 807–820.

Band, M. R., Larson, J. H., Rebiez, M., Green, C. A., Heyen, D. W., Donovan, J., Windish, R., Steining, C., Mahyuddin, P., Womack, J. E., & Lewin, H. A. (2000). An ordered comparative map of the cattle and human genomes. *Genome Research, 10,* 1359–1368.

Bandura, A. (1971). *Social learning theory.* Englewood Cliffs, NJ: Prentice Hall.

Bandura, A., Ross, D., & Ross, S. (1963). Transmission of aggression through imitation of aggressive models. *Journal of Abnormal and Social Psychology, 66,* 3–11.

Bandura, A., & Walters, R. H. (1963). *Social learning and personality development.* New York: Holt, Rinehart, & Winston.

Banks, M. S. (1980). The development of visual accommodation during early infancy. *Child Development, 51,* 646–666.

Banks, M. S., & Salapatek, P. (1983). Infant visual perception. In M. M. Haith & J. J. Campos (Eds.), *Handbook of child psychology: Vol. 2. Infancy and developmental psychobiology* (4th ed., 435–571). New York: Wiley.

Banyard, V. L., & Graham-Bermann, S. A. (1998). Surviving poverty: Stress and coping in the lives of housed and homeless mothers. *American Journal of Orthopsychiatry, 68,* 479–489.

Barash, D. (1979). *The whisperings within: Evolution and the origin of human nature.* New York: Harper & Row.

Barash, D. (1982). *Sociobiology and behavior* (2nd ed.). New York: Elsevier.

Barber, T. X. (1979). Suggested ("hypnotic") behavior: The trance paradigm versus an alternative paradigm. In E. Fromm & R. E. Shor (Eds.), *Hypnosis: Developments in research and new perspectives.* New York: Aldine.

Bargh, J. A., & Chartrand, T. L. (1999). The unbearable automaticity of being. *American Psychologist, 54,* 462–479.

Barker, L. (1977). *Activity cycles and eating patterns of college students.* Unpublished manuscript.

Barker, L. M. (2001). *Learning and behavior: Theory and application* (3rd ed.). Upper Saddle River, NJ: Prentice Hall.

Barker, L. M., & Johns, T. (1976). Effect of ethanol preexposure on ethanol-induced conditioned taste aversion. *Journal of Studies on Alcohol, 39,* 39–46.

Barkow, J. H., Cosmides, L., & Tooby, J. (1992). *The adapted mind: Evolutionary psychology and the generation of culture.* New York: Oxford University Press.

Barlow, D. H. (1988). *Anxiety and its disorders.* New York: Guilford Press.

Barlow, D. H. (1995). Health care policy, psychotherapy research, and the future of psychotherapy. *American Psychologist, 50,* 965–974.

Barlow, D. H., Craske, M. G., Cerny, J. A., & Klosko, J. S. (1989). Behavioral treatment of panic disorder. *Behavior Therapy, 20,* 261–282.

Baron-Cohen, S., Leslie, A. M., & Frith, U. (1985). Does the autistic child have a "theory of mind"? *Cognition, 21,* 37–46.

Bartlett, F. C. (1932). *Remembering.* Cambridge: Cambridge University Press.

Bartoshuk, L. M. (1991). Taste, smell, and pleasure. In Robert C. Bolles (Ed.), *The hedonics of taste,* 15–28. Hillsdale, NJ: Erlbaum.

Baudry, M., & Davis, J. L. (1992). Neurotransmitter systems and memory. In L. R. Squire (Ed.), *Encyclopedia of learning and memory.* New York: Macmillan.

Baum, A., Newman, S., Weinman, J., West, R., & McManus, C. (Eds.). (1997). *Cambridge handbook of psychology, health, and medicine.* Cambridge, England: Cambridge University Press.

Baxter, D. W., & Olszewski, J. (1960). Congenital universal insensitivity to pain. *Brain, 83,* 381–393.

Bear, M. F., Conners, B. W., & Paradiso, M. A. (1996). *Neuroscience: Exploring the brain.* Baltimore: Williams & Wilkins.

Beck, A. (1967). *Cognitive therapy and the emotional disorders.* New York: International Universities Press.

Beck, A. (1995). *Cognitive therapy: Basics and beyond.* New York: Guilford Press.

Beck, A. T. (1967). *Depression: Clinical, experimental and theoretical aspects.* New York: Harper & Row.

Beck, A. T. (1999). Cognitive aspects of personality disorders and their relation to syndromal disorders: A psychoevolutionary approach. In C. R. Cloninger (Ed.), *Personality and psychopathology.* Washington, DC: American Psychiatric Press.

Békésy, G. von. (1963). Hearing theories and complex sounds. *Journal of the Acoustical Society of America, 35,* 588–601.

Belloc, N. (1973). Relationship of health practices and mortality. *Preventative Medicine, 2,* 67–81.

Belloc, N., & Breslow, L. (1972). Relationship of physical health status and health practices. *Preventative Medicine, 1,* 409–421.

Belsky, J., Spritz, B., & Crnic, K. (1996). Infant attachment security and affective-cognitive information processing at age 3. *Psychological Science, 7,* 111–114.

Bem, D. J. (1967). Self perception: An alternative interpretation of cognitive dissonance phenomena. *Psychological Review, 74,* 183–200.

Benassi, V. A., Sweeney, P. D., & Dufour, C. L. (1988). Is there a relationship between locus of control orientation and depression? *Journal of Abnormal Psychology, 97,* 357–367.

Benjamin, L. T., & Bruce, D. (1982). From bottle-fed chimp to bottlenose dolphin: A contemporary appraisal of Winthrop Kellogg. *The Psychological Record, 32,* 461–482.

Benjamini, W., & Leskowitz, S. (1991). *Immunology: A short course.* New York: Wiley-Liss.

Berger, R. J., & Phillips, N. H. (1995). Energy conservation and sleep. *Behavioural and Brain Research, 69,* 65–73.

Berk, L. E. (1997). *Child development* (4th ed.). Needham Heights, MA: Allyn & Bacon.

Berkman, L. F., & Breslow, L. (1983). *Health and ways of living: The Alameda County study.* New York: Oxford University Press.

Berkman, L. F., & Syme, S. L. (1979). Social networks, host resistance, and mortality: A nine-year follow-up study of Alameda County residents. *American Journal of Epidemiology, 109,* 186–204.

Berlim, M. T., & Abeche, A. M. (2001). Evolutionary Approach to Medicine. *Southern Medical Journal, 94*, 26–32.

Bernard, L., & Hodges, T. B. (1958). *Readings in European History.* New York: Macmillan.

Bernardis, L. L., & Bellinger, L. L. (1996). The lateral hypothalamic area revisited: Ingestive behavior. *Neuroscience and Biobehavioral Reviews, 20*, 189–287.

Berridge, K. C., & Robinson, T. E. (1995). The mind of an addicted brain: Neural sensitization of wanting versus liking. *Current Directions in Psychological Science, 4*, 71–76.

Bersheid, E. (1988). Some comments on love's anatomy: Or, whatever happened to old-fashioned lust? In R. J. Sternberg & M. L. Barnes (Eds.), *The psychology of love*. New Haven, CT: Yale University Press.

Bertenthal, B. I., Campos, J. J., & Kermoian, R. (1994). An epigenetic perspective on the development of self-produced locomotion and its consequences. *Current Directions in Psychological Science, 3*, 140–145.

Bickerton, D. (2000). *Language and human behavior*. Seattle: University of Washington Press.

Biederman, J., Faraone, S. V., Hirshfeld-Becker, D. R., Friedman, D., Robin, J. A., & Rosenbaum, J. F. (2001). Patterns of psychopathology and dysfunction in high-risk children of parents with panic disorder and major depression. *American Journal of Psychiatry, 158*, 49–57.

Binet, A. (1903). *The Experimental Study of Intelligence. (L'Étude expérimental de' Intelligence)* As cited in R. E. Fancher, (1990). *Pioneers of psychology* (2nd ed.). New York: Norton.

Blair, R. J. R., Jones, L., Clark, F., & Smith, M. (1997). The psychopathic individual: A lack of responsiveness to distress cues? *Psychophysiology, 34*, 192–198.

Blair, S. N., Kohl, H. W., Barlow, C. E., Paffenarger, R. S., Jr., Gibbons, L. W., & Macera, C. A. (1995). Changes in physical fitness and all-cause mortality: A prospective study of healthy and unhealthy men. *Journal of the American Medical Association, 273*, 1093–1098.

Blakemore, C. (1977). *Mechanics of the mind*. Cambridge: Cambridge University Press.

Blanchard, E. B., Appelbaum, K. A., Radniz, C. L., Morrill, B., Michultka, D., Kirsch, C., Guarnieri, P., Hillhouse, J., Evans, D. D., Jaccard, J., & Barron, K. D. (1990). A controlled evaluation of thermal biofeedback and thermal biofeedback combined with cognitive therapy in the treatment of vascular headache. *Journal of Consulting and Clinical Psychology, 58*, 216–224.

Blaney, P. H. (1986). Affect and memory: A review. Psychological Bulletin, 99, 229–246.

Blehar, M. C., Weissman, M. M., Gershon, E. S., & Hirschfeld, R. M. A. (1988). Family and genetic studies of affective disorders, *Archives of General Psychiatry, 45*, 289–292.

Bloom, L. (1970). *Language development: Form and function in emerging grammars*. Cambridge, MA: MIT Press.

Bogen, J. (1969). The other side of the brain, II: An appositional mind. *Bulletin of the Los Angeles Neurological Society, 34(3)*, 135–136.

Bolles, R. C. (1971). Species-specific defense reactions. In F. R. Brush (Ed.), *Aversive conditioning and learning*. New York: Academic Press.

Bond, R., & Smith, P. B. (1994). Culture and conformity: A meta-analysis of studies using Asch's (1952b, 1956) line judgment task. *Psychological Bulletin, 119*, 111–137.

Boorman, G. A., Dellarco, V., Dunnick, J. K., Chapin, R. E., Hunter, S., Hauchman, F., Gardner, H., Cox, M., & Sills R.C. (1999). Drinking water disinfection byproducts: Review and approach to toxicity evaluation. *Environmental Health Perspectives, 107*, 207–221.

Booth, D. (1991). Learned ingestive motivation and the pleasures of the palate. In R. C. Bolles (Ed.), *The hedonics of taste*, 29–58. Hillsdale, NJ: Lawrence Erlbaum.

Booth, R. J., & Ashbridge, K. R. (1992). Implications of psychoimmunology for models of the immune system. In A. J. Husband (Ed.), *Behavior and immunity.* London: CRC Press.

Bootzin, R. R., Manber, R., Perlis, M. L., Salvio, M. A., & Wyatt, J. K. (1993). Sleep disorders. In P. B. Sutker & H. E. Adams (Eds.), *Sleep mechanisms*. Berlin: Springer-Verlag.

Boring, E. G. (1929). *A history of experimental psychology.* New York: Century.

Bornstein, R. F. (1989). Exposure and affect: Overview and meta-analysis of research, 1968–1987. *Psychological Bulletin, 106*, 265–289.

Bornstein, R. F., & Pittman, T. S. (Eds.). (1992). *Perception without awareness: Cognitive, clinical, and social perspectives.* New York: Guilford Press.

Bothwell, R. K., Brigham, J. C., & Malpass, R. S. (1989). Cross-racial identification. *Personality and Social Psychology Bulletin, 15*, 19–25.

Bouchard, T. J., Jr. (1994). Genes, environment, and personality. *Science, 264*, 1700–1701.

Bouchard, T. J., Jr., Lykken, D. R., McGue, M., Segal, N. L., & Tellegen, A. (1990). Sources of human psychological differences: The Minnesota study of twins reared apart. *Science, 250*, 223–228.

Bouchard, T. J., Jr., & McGue, M. (1981). Familial studies of intelligence. *Science, 212*, 1055–1059.

Bower, J. M. (1996). Perhaps it's time to completely rethink cerebellar function. *Behavioral and Brain Sciences, 19*, 438–439, 503–527.

Bowers, D., Bauer, R. M., Coslett, H. B., & Heilman, K. M. (1985). Processing of face by patients with unilateral hemispheric lesions. I. Dissociations between judgments of facial affect and facial identity. *Brain Cognition, 4*, 258–272.

Bowlby, J. (1980). *Attachment and loss: Vol. 3. Loss: Sadness and depression.* New York: Basic Books.

Bowlby, J. (1982). *Attachment and loss: Vol. 1. Attachment* (2nd ed.). New York: Basic Books.

Bownds, M. D. (1999). *The biology of mind: Origins and structures of mind, brain, and consciousness.* Bethesda, MD: Fitzgerald Science Press.

Boyatzis, C. J., Matillo, G. M., & Nesbitt, K. M. (1995). Effects of the "Mighty Morphin Power Rangers" on children's aggression with peers. *Child Study Journal, 25*, 45–55.

Bradbury, J. W., & Vehrencamp, S. L. (1998). *Principles of animal communication.* Sunderland, MA: Sinauer.

Braddick, O. J., Atkinson, J., & Hood, B. (1996). Striate cortex, extrastriate cortex, and colliculus: Some new approaches. In F. Vital-Durand, J. Atkinson, & O. J. Braddick, (Eds.), *Infant vision.* Oxford: Oxford University Press.

Bradley, R. M. (1972). Development of the taste bud and gustatory papillae in human fetuses. In J. F. Bosma (Ed.), *The third symposium on oral sensation and perception: The mouth of the infant.* Springfield, IL: Thomas.

Bradley, R. M., & Mistretta, C. M. (1973). The gustatory sense in foetal sheep during the last third of gestation. *Journal of Physiology, 231*, 271–282.

Bradshaw, J. L. (1991). Animal asymmetry and human heredity: Dextrality, tool use, and language in evolution. *British Journal of Psychology, 82*, 39–59.

Bradshaw, J. L., & Nettleton, N. C. (1989). Lateral asymmetries in human evolution. *International Journal of Comparative Psychology, 3*, 37–71.

Brainerd, C. J. (1996). Piaget: A centennial celebration. *Psychological Science, 7*, 191–195.

Brand, C. (1987). The importance of general intelligence. In S. Modgil & C. Modgil (Eds.), *A. Jensen: Consensus and controversy.* New York: Falmer Press.

Brannon, L., & Feist, J. (2000). *Health psychology* (4th ed). Pacific Grove, CA: Brooks/Cole.

Bray, G., & Gray, D. S. (1988). Obesity. Part 1. Pathogenesis. *Western Journal of Medicine, 149*, 429–441.

Breedlove, S. M. (1994). Sexual differentiation of the human nervous system. *Annual Review of Psychology, 45*, 389–418.

Breland, K., & Breland, M. (1961). The misbehavior of organisms. *American Psychologist, 16*, 681–684.

Brennan, J. F. (1998). *History and systems of psychology* (5th ed.). Upper Saddle River, NJ: Prentice Hall.

Breznitz, S., Ben-Zur, H., Berzon, Y. W., David, W., Levitan, G., Tarcic, N., Lischinsky, S., Greenberg, A., Levi, N., & Zinder, O. (1998). Experimental induction and termination of acute psychological stress in human volunteers: Effects on immunological, neuroendocrine, cardiovascular, and psychological parameters. *Brain, Behavior and Immunity, 12*, 34–52.

Broadbent, D. E. (1958). *Perception and communication.* London: Pergamon Press.

Broadbent, D. E. (1982). Task combination and the selective intake of information. *Acta Psychologica, 50*, 253–290.

Broadfield, D. C., Holloway, R. L., Mowbray, K., Silvers, M. S., & Marquez, S. (2001). The endocast of Sambungmacan 3 (Sm 3): A new *Homo erectus* from Indonesia. *The Anatomical Record. 262*(4), 369–379.

Brody, N., & Ehrlichman, H. (1998). *Personality psychology: The science of individuality.* Upper Saddle River, NJ: Prentice Hall.

Brown, A. S., & Murphy, D. R. (1989). Cryptonesia: Delineating inadvertent plagiarism. *Journal of Experimental Psychology: Learning, Memory, and Cognition, 15*, 432–442.

Brown, B. (1999). Optimizing expression of the common human genome for child development. *Current Directions in Psychological Science, 8*, 37–41.

Brown, B. W., Birley, J. L. T., & Wing, J. K. (1972). Influence of family life on the course of schizophrenic disorders: A replication. *British Journal of Psychiatry, 121*, 241–258.

Brown, J. (1995). *Charles Darwin: Voyaging.* London: Pimlico.

Brown, R., & Hanlon, C. (1970). Derivational complexity and the order of acquisition of speech. In R. Brown (Ed.), *Psycholinguistics.* New York: Free Press.

Brown, R., & Kulik, J. (1977). Flashbulb memories. *Cognition, 5*, 73–79.

Brown, R., & McNeill, D. (1966). The "tip of the tongue" phenomenon. *Journal of Verbal Learning and Verbal Behavior, 5*, 325–337.

Buccino, R., Gallese, V., & Rizzolatti, G. (2001). Action observation activates premotor and parietal areas in a somatotopic manner: An fMRI study. *European Journal of Neuroscience, 13*, 400–404.

Buchan, H., Johnson, E., McPherson, K., & Palmer, R. L. (1992). Who benefits from electroconvulsive therapy? Combined results of the Leicester and Northwick Park trials. *British Journal of Psychiatry, 160*, 355–359.

Buchwald, A. M., Coyne, J. C., & Cole, C. S. (1978). A critical evaluation of the learned helplessness model of depression. *Journal of Abnormal Psychology, 87*, 180–193.

Buckley, K. W. (1989). *Mechanical man: John Broadus Watson and the beginnings of behaviorism.* New York: Guilford Press.

Bullough, V. (1990). The Kinsey scale in historical perspective. In D. P. McWhirter, S. A. Sanders, & J. M. Reinisch (Eds.), *Homosexuality/heterosexuality: Concepts of sexual orientation.* New York: Oxford University Press.

Burger, J. M. (1984). Desire for control, locus of control, and proneness to depression. *Journal of Personality, 52*, 71–89.

Burger, J. M. (1986). Temporal effects on attributions: Actor and observer differences. *Social Cognition, 4*, 377–387.

Buss, A. H., & Perry, M. (1992). The aggression questionnaire. *Journal of Personality and Social Psychology, 63*, 42–459.

Buss, D. (2000). The evolution of happiness. *American Psychologist, 55*, 15–23.

Buss, D. M. (1996). The evolutionary psychology of human social strategies. In E. T. Higgins & A W. Kruglanski (Eds.), *Social psychology: Handbook of basic principles.* New York: Guilford Press.

Buss, D. M., & Schmidt, D. P. (1993). Sexual strategies theory: An evolutionary perspective on human mating. *Psychological Review, 100*, 204–232.

Butterworth, G., & Morissette, P. (1996). Onset of pointing and the acquisition of language in infancy. *Journal of Reproductive and Infant Psychology, 14*, 219–231.

Butterworth, T., Carson, J., Jeacock, J., White, E., & Clements, A. (1999). Stress, coping, burnout and job satisfaction in British nurses: Findings from the Clinical Supervision Evaluation Project. *Stress Medicine, 15*, 27–33.

Byrne, D. (1971). *The attraction paradigm.* New York: Academic Press.

Cain, N. G., Addington, R. L., & Windfelder, T. L. (1995). Factors affecting the rates of food calls given by red-bellied tamarins. *Animal Behavior, 50*, 53–60.

Camacho, T. C., & Wiley, J. A. (1983). Health practices, social networks, and change in physical health. In L. F. Berkman & L. Breslow (Eds.), *Health and ways of living: The Alameda County Study.* New York: Oxford University Press.

Cameron, P., & Biber, H. (1973). Sexual thought throughout the lifespan. *Gerontologist, 13*, 144–177.

Camp, J. (1973). *Magic, myth, and medicine.* London: Priory Press.

Candland, D. K. (1993). *Feral children and clever animals.* New York: Oxford University Press.

Cannon, W. B. (1927). The James-Lange theory of emotions: A critical examination and an alternate theory. *American Journal of Psychology, 39*, 106–124.

Cannon, W. B. (1932). *Wisdom of the body.* New York: Norton.

Cannon, W. B. (1942). "Voodoo" death. *American Anthropologist, 44*, 169–182.

Cantor, N. (1990). Social psychology and sociobiology: What can we leave to evolution? *Motivation and Emotion, 14*, 245–254.

Capaldi, E. D., & Powley, T. L. (1990). *Taste, experience, and feeding.* Washington, DC: American Psychological Association.

Carpenter, G. A., & Grossberg, S. (1984). A neural theory of circadian rhythms: Aschoff's rule in diurnal and nocturnal mammals. *American Journal of Physiology, 247*, R1067–R1082.

Carroll, J. B. (1993). *Human cognitive abilities: A survey of factor-analytic studies.* New York: Cambridge University Press.

Carter, F. (1976). *The education of Little Tree.* Albuquerque: University of New Mexico Press.

Cartwright, R. (1977). *Nightlife: Explorations in dreaming.* Englewood Cliffs, NJ: Prentice Hall.

Cartwright, R., & Lamberg, L. (1992). *Crisis dreaming.* New York: HarperCollins.

Cattell, R. B. (1957). *Personality and motivation: Structure and measurement.* New York: Harcourt, Brace, and World.

Cattell, R. B. (1990). Advances in Cattellian personality theory. In L. Pervin (Ed.), *Handbook of personality: Theory and research.* New York: Guilford Press.

Ceci, S. J. (1991). How much does schooling influence general intelligence and its cognitive components: A reassessment of the evidence. *Developmental Psychology, 27*, 703.

Ceci, S. J., & Liker, J. (1986). Academic and nonacademic intelligence: An experimental separation. In R. J. Sternberg & R. K. Wagner (Eds.), *Practical intelligence: Nature and origins of competence in everyday life.* New York: Cambridge University Press.

Ceci, S. J., & Williams, W. M. (1997). Schooling, intelligence, and income. *American Psychologist, 52*, 1051–1058.

Center for Mental Health Services. Mental Health, United States (1996). R. W. Manderscheid & M. A., Sonnenchein (Eds.). Department of Health and Human Services Pub. No. (SMA) 96-3098. Washington, DC: Superintendents Office of Documents, U.S. Government Printing Office.

Chaiken, S. (1980). Heuristic versus systematic information processing and the use of source versus message cues in persuasion. *Journal of Personality and Social Psychology, 39*, 752–766.

Chaiken, S., & Stangor, C. (1987). Attitudes and attitude change. *Annual Review of Psychology, 38*, 575–630.

Chalmers, D. J. (1997). *The conscious mind: In search of a fundamental theory*. Oxford: Oxford University Press.

Champoux, M., Byrne, E., DeLizio, R., & Suomi, S. J. (1992). Motherless mothers revisited: Rhesus maternal behavior and rearing history. *Primates, 33*, 251–255.

Changeax, J. P. (1993, November). Chemical signaling in the brain. *Scientific American, 269*, 58–62.

Channon, S., & Channon, S. (2000). The effects of anterior lesions on performance of a story comprehension test: Left anterior impairment on a theory of mind-type task. *Neuropsychologia, 38*, 1006–1017.

Chapman, L. J., & Chapman, J. P. (1973). *Disordered thought in schizophrenia*. New York: Appleton-Century-Crofts.

Chapman, M., & Lindenberger, U. (1988). Functions, operations, and décalage in the development of transitivity. *Developmental Psychology, 24*, 542–551.

Cheney, D. L., & Seyfarth, R. M. (1992). Précis of *How monkeys see the world. Behavioral and Brain Sciences, 15*, 135–182.

Cherry, E. C. (1953). Some experiments on the recognition of speech, with one and with two ears. *Journal of the Acoustical Society of America, 25*, 975–979.

Ching, P. L. Y. H., Willett, W. C., Rimm, E. B., Colditz, G. A., Gortmaker, S. L., & Stampfer, M. J. (1996). Activity level and risk of overweight in male health professionals. *American Journal of Public Health, 86*, 25–30.

Chomsky, N. (1965). *Aspects of the theory of syntax*. Cambridge, MA: MIT Press.

Chomsky, N. (1975). *Reflections on language*. New York: Pantheon.

Chomsky, N. (1980). *Rules and representations*. New York: Columbia University Press.

Christensen, A., & Jacobson, N. S. (1994). Who (or what) can do psychotherapy: The status and challenge of nonprofessional therapies. *Psychological Science, 4*, 8–14.

Clark, D. M., Salkovskis, P. M., Hackmann, A., Middleton, H., & collaborator. (1994). A comparison of cognitive therapy, applied relaxation, and imipramine in the treatment of panic disorder. *British Journal of Psychiatry, 164*, 759–769.

Clark, R. D. III. (1990). The impact of AIDS on gender differences in willingness to engage in casual sex. *Journal of Applied Social Psychology, 20*, 771–782.

Clark, R. D. III, & Hatfield, E. (1989). Gender differences in receptivity to sexual offers. *Journal of Psychology & Human Sexuality, 21*, 39–55.

Cohen, L. M. (1982). A current perspective of pseudocyesis. *American Journal of Psychiatry, 139*, 1140–1144.

Coleman, R. M. (1986). *Wide awake at 3 a.m.* New York: W. H. Freeman.

Colin, V. L. (1996). *Human attachment*. Philadelphia: Temple University Press.

Collinge, W. (1996). *The American Holistic Health Association complete guide to alternative medicine*. New York: Warner Books.

Collins, A. C., Wilkins, L. H., Siobe, B. S., Cao, J., & Bullock, A. E. (1996). Long-term ethanol and nicotine treatment elicit tolerance to ethanol. *Alcoholism: Clinical and Experimental Research, 20*, 990–999.

Collins, A. M., & Quillian, M. R. (1969). Retrieval time from semantic memory. *Journal of Verbal Learning and Verbal Behavior, 8*, 240–247.

Comer, R. J. (1992). *Abnormal psychology*. New York: Freeman.

Compas, B. E., Haaga, D. A., Keefe, F. J., Leitenberg, H., & Williams, D. A. (1998). Sampling of empirically supported psychological treatments from health psychology: Smoking, chronic pain, cancer, and bulimia nervosa. *Journal of Consulting and Clinical Psychology, 66*, 89–112.

Conners, C. K. (1969). A teacher rating scale for use with drug studies with children. *American Journal of Psychiatry, 126*, 884–888.

Conrad, C. (1972). Cognitive economy in semantic memory. *Journal of Experimental Psychology, 92*, 149–154.

Cook, W. L., Strachan, A. M., Goldstein, M. J., & Miklowitz, D. J. (1989). Expressed emotion and reciprocal affective relationships in families of disturbed adolescents. *Family Process, 28*, 337–348.

Cooper, K. H. (1968). *Aerobics*. New York: Evans.

Cooper, K. H. (1985). *Running without fear: How to reduce the risks of heart attack and sudden death during aerobic exercise*. New York: Evans.

Coryell, W., Endicott, J., Keller, M., & Andreasen, N. (1989). Bipolar affective disorder and high achievement: A familial association. *American Journal of Psychiatry, 146*, 983–988.

Cosmides, L., & Tooby, J. (1997). *Evolutionary psychology: A primer [Online]*. Available: http://www.psych.ucsb.edu/research/cep/ [1999].

Courage, M. L., & Adams, R. J. (1990). Visual acuity assessment from birth to three years using the acuity card procedures: Cross-sectional and longitudinal samples. *Optometry and Vision Science, 67*, 713–718.

Courneya, K. S., & Carron, A. V. (1992). The home advantage in sports competitions: A literature review. *Journal of Sport and Exercise Psychology, 14*, 13–27.

Cousins, N. (1979). *Anatomy of an illness*. New York: Bantom Books.

Cowan, W. M. (1979). The development of the brain. *Scientific American, 241*, 112–133.

Craighead, L. W., Craighead, W. E., Kazdin, A. E., & Mahoney, M. J. (1994). *Cognitive and behavioral interventions: An empirical approach to mental health problems*. Boston: Allyn & Bacon.

Craik, F. I. M., & Jacoby, L. L. (1996). Aging and memory: Implications for skilled performance. In W. A. Rogers, A. D. Fisk, & N. Walker (Eds.), *Aging and skilled performance*. Mahwah, NJ: Erlbaum.

Craik, F. I. M., & Lockhart, R. S. (1972). Levels of processing: A framework for memory research. *Journal of Verbal Learning and Verbal Behavior, 11*, 671–684.

Craik, F. I. M., & Tulving, E. (1975). Depth of processing and retention of words in episodic memory. *Journal of Experimental Psychology: General, 104*, 268–294.

Crawford, H. J., Knebel, T., & Vendemia, J. M. (1998). The nature of hypnotic analgesia: Neurophysiological foundation and evidence. *Contemporary Hypnosis, 15*(1), 22–33.

Crawford, H. J., & Strapp, C. M. (1994). Effects of vocal and instrumental music on visuospatial and verbal performance as moderated by studying preference and personality. *Personality and Individual Differences, 16*, 237–245.

Creed, F. (1993). Stress and psychosomatic disorders. In L. Goldberger & S. Breznitz (Eds.), *Handbook of stress: Theoretical and clinical aspects* (2nd ed.). New York: Free Press.

Creese, I., Burt, D. R., & Snyder, S. H. (1976). Dopamine receptor binding predicts clinical and pharmacological potencies of antischizophrenic drugs. *Science, 192*, 481–483.

Critchley, H. D., & Rolls, E. (1996). Hunger and satiety modify the responses of olfactory and visual neurons in the primate orbitofrontal cortex. *Journal of Neurophysiology, 75*, 1673–1686.

Crits-Christoph, P. (1992). The efficacy of brief dynamic psychotherapy: A meta-analysis. *American Journal of Psychiatry, 149*, 151–158.

Crook, T. H., & West, R. L. (1990). Name recall preference across the life-span. *British Journal of Psychology, 81*, 335–340.

Csikszentmihalyi, M. (1996). *Creativity: Flow and the psychology of discovery and invention*. New York: HarperPerennial.

Culbertson, F. M. (1997). Depression and gender: An international review. *American Psychologist, 52*, 25–31.

Cunningham, C. E., & Linscheid, T. R. (1976). Elimination of chronic infant ruminating by electric shock. *Behavior Therapy, 7*, 231–234.

Cunningham, M. R. (1986). Measuring the physical in physical attractiveness: Quasi-experiments on the sociobiology of female facial beauty. *Journal of Personality and Social Psychology, 50*, 925–935.

Cunningham, M. R., Druen, P. B., & Barbee, A. P. (1997). Angels, mentors, and friends: Tradeoffs among evolutionary, social, and individual variables in physical appearance. In J. A. Simpson & D. T. Kenrick (Eds.), *Evolutionary social psychology*. Mahwah, NJ: Erlbaum.

Curtiss, S. (1977). *Genie: A psycholinguistic study of a modern-day "wild child."* New York: Academic Press.

Cutler, W. B., Preti, M., Huggins, G. R., Erickson, B., & Garcia, C.R. (1985). Sexual behavior frequency and biphasic ovulatory type menstrual cycles. *Physiology and Behavior, 34*, 805–810.

Cutler, W. B., Preti, M., Krieger, A., Huggins, G. R., Garcia, C.R., & Lawley, H. G. (1986). Human axillary secretions influence women's menstrual cycles: The role of donor extracts from men. *Hormones and Behavior, 20*, 463–473.

Czeisler, C. A., Johnson, M. P., Duffy, J. F., Brown, E. N., Ronda, J. M., & Kronauer, R. E. (1990). Exposure to bright light and darkness to treat physiologic maladaption to night work. *New England Journal of Medicine, 322*, 1253–1259.

Dabbs, J. M., Carr, T. S., Frady, R. L., & Riad, J. K. (1995). Testosterone, crime, and misbehavior among 692 male prison inmates. *Personality and Individual Differences, 18*, 627–633.

Daly, M., & Wilson, M. (1985). Child abuse and other risks of not living with both parents. *Ethology and Sociobiology, 6*, 197–210.

Damasio, A. (1994). *Descartes' error.* New York: Avon Books.

Damasio, A. (1999). *The feeling of what happens: Body and emotion in the making of consciousness.* New York: Harcourt Brace.

Damos, D. (1992). *Multiple task performance.* London: Taylor Francis.

Darley, J. M., & Latané, B. (1968). Bystander intervention in emergencies: Diffusion of responsibility. *Journal of Personality and Social Psychology, 8*, 377–383.

Darwin, C. (1962). *On the origin of species by means of natural selection.* New York: Collier Books. (Original work published 1859.)

Darwin, C. (1965). *The expression of emotions in man and animals.* Chicago: University of Chicago Press. (Original work published 1872.)

Davidson, J. E., & Sternberg, R. J. (1984). The role of insight in intellectual giftedness. *Gifted Child Quarterly, 28*, 58–64.

Davidson, R. J. (1992). Emotion and affective style: Hemispheric substrates. *Psychological Science, 3*, 39–43.

Davies, N. B. (1989). The dunnock: Cooperation and conflict among males and females in a variable mating system. In P. Stacey & W. Koenig (Eds.), *Cooperative breeding in birds*, 457–584. Cambridge: Cambridge University Press.

Davis, C. M. (1928). Self-selection of diet by newly weaned infants. *American Journal of Diseases of Children, 36*, 651–659.

Davis, C. M. (1939). The results of self-selection of diets by young children. *The Canadian Medical Association Journal, 41*, 257–261.

Dawber, T. R. (1980). *The Framingham study: The epidemiology of atherosclerotic disease.* Cambridge, MA: Harvard University Press.

Dawkins, R. (1976). *The selfish gene.* London: Oxford University Press.

Dawkins, R. (1996). *Climbing mount improbable.* London: Viking.

Day, R. H. (1984). The nature of perceptual illusions. *Interdisciplinary Science Reviews, 9*, 47–58.

de Bono, E. (1991a). *Teaching thinking.* London: Penguin Books. (Original work published 1976.)

de Bono, E. (1991b). Lateral and vertical thinking. In J. Henry (Ed.), *Creative management.* London: Sage Publications.

de Jong, W. W., Hendriks, W., Sanyal, S., & Nevo, E. (1990). The eye of the blind mole rat (Spalax ehrenbergi): Regressive evolution at the molecular level. In E. Nevo & O. A. Reig (Eds.), *Evolution of subterranean mammals at the organismal and molecular levels.* New York: Alan R. Liss.

Deary, I. J. (2001). Human intelligence differences: A recent history. *Trends in Cognitive Sciences, 5*, 127–130.

DeCasper, A. J., & Spence, M. J. (1986). Prenatal maternal speech influences newborns' perception of speech sounds. *Infant Behavior and Development, 9*, 133–150.

DeFeo, V. J. (1966). Vaginal-cervical vibration: A simple and effective method for the induction of pseudopregnancy in the rat. *Endocrinology, 79*, 440–442.

deGroot, A. D. (1965). *Thought and choice in chess.* The Hague: Mouton.

Dement, W. C. (1978). *Some must watch while some must sleep.* New York: Norton.

DeNeve, K. M. (1999). Happy as an extraverted clam? The role of personality for subjective well-being. *Current Directions in Psychological Science, 8*, 141–144.

Dennett, D. (1995). *Darwin's dangerous idea.* New York: Simon & Schuster.

Dennett, D. C. (1975). Why the law of effect will not go away. *Journal of the Theory of Social Behavior, 5*, 169–187.

Dennett, D. C. (1983). Intentional systems in cognitive ethology: The "Panglossian paradigm" defended. *The Behavioral and Brain Sciences, 6*, 343–355.

Derogatis, L. R., & Coons, H. L. (1993). Self-report measures of stress. In L. Goldberger & S. Breznitz (Eds.), *Handbook of stress: Theoretical and clinical aspects* (2nd ed.). New York: Free Press.

Descartes, R. (1637/1960). *Discourse on method and meditation* (L. J. Lafleuer, Ed. & Trans.). New York: Library of Liberal Arts. (As cited in R. E. Fancher, 1990, *Pioneers of psychology*, 2nd ed., New York: Norton.)

Dethier, V. (1962). *To know a fly.* San Francisco: Holden-Day.

DeValois, R. L., Abramov, I., & Jacobs, G. H. (1966). Analysis of response patterns of LGN cells. *Journal of the Optical Society of America, 56*, 966–977.

Dewsbury, D. A., & Rethlingshafer, D. A. (Eds.). (1973). *Comparative psychology: A modern survey.* New York: McGraw-Hill.

Diamond, J. (1992). *The third chimpanzee: The evolution and future of the human animal.* New York: HarperCollins.

Diamond, J. (1997). *Guns, germs, and steel: The fates of human societies.* New York: Norton.

Diamond, J. (1999). *Guns, germs, and steel: The fates of human societies.* New York: Norton.

Diener, E. (2000). Subjective well-being: The science of happiness and a proposal for a national index. *American Psychologist, 55*, 34–43.

Diener, E., Suh, E. M., Lucas, R. E., & Smith, H. L. (in press). Subjective well-being. *Psychological Bulletin.*

DiPietro, J. A., Hodgson, D. M., Costigan, K. A., Hilton, S. C., & Johnson, T. R. B. (1966). Fetal neurobehavioral development. *Child Development, 67*, 2553–2567.

Dixon, R. M. W. (1977). Where have all the adjectives gone? *Studies in Language, 1*, 19–80.

Dohrenwend, B. P., Levav, I., Shrout, P. E., S., Naveh, G., Link, B. G., Skodol, A. E., & Stueve, A. (1992). Socioeconomic status and psychiatric disorders: The causation-selection issue. *Science, 255*, 946–953.

Dollard, J., Doob, L. W., Miller, N. E., Mowrer, O. H., & Sears, R. R. (1939). *Frustration and aggression.* New Haven: Yale University Press.

Donald, M. (1993). Precis of origins of the modern mind: Three stages in the evolution of culture and cognition. *Behavioral and Brain Sciences, 16*, 737–791.

Dovidio, J. F., & Gaertner, S. L. (1999). Reducing prejudice: Combating intergroup biases. *Current Directions in Psychological Science, 8*, 101–105.

Downs, T. J. , Cifuentes-García, E., & Suffet, I. M. (1999). Risk screening for exposure to groundwater pollution in a wastewater irrigation district of the Mexico City region. *Environmental Health Perspectives, 107*, 553–561.

Dreifus, C. (1998, July 28). A conversation with Dr. Marvin Minsky. *The New York Times on the Web.* Available: http://search.nytimes.com:minsky

Duck, S., & Wright, P. H. (1993). Reexamining gender differences in same-sex friendships: A closer look at two kinds of data. *Sex Roles, 28*, 709–727.

Duflou, J., Virmani, R., Rabin, I., Burke, A., Farb, A., & Smialek, J. (1995). Sudden death as a result of heart disease in morbid obesity. *American Heart Journal, 130*, 306–313.

Dunbar, R. L. M. (1993). Coevolution of neocortical size, group size and language in humans. *Behavioral and Brain Sciences, 16*, 681–735.

Durrell, L. (1957). *Justine*. New York: Dutton.

Eagle, M. N., & Wolitzky, D. L. (1992). Psychoanalytic theories of psychotherapy. In D. K. Freedheim (Ed.), *History of psychotherapy: A century of change*. Washington, DC: American Psychological Association.

Eagly, A. H., Ashmore, R. D., Makhijani, M. G., & Kennedy, L. C. (1991). What is beautiful is good, but . . . : A meta-analytic review of research on the physical attractiveness stereotype. *Psychological Bulletin, 100*, 109–128.

Eaton, W. W., Dryman, A., & Weissman, M. M. (1991). Panic and phobia. In L. N. Robins & D. A. Regier (Eds.), *Psychiatric disorders in America: The epidemiologic catchment area study*. New York: Free Press.

Ebbinghaus, H. (1913). *Memory*. New York: Teachers College, Columbia University. (Original work published 1885.)

Edwards, K., & Smith, E. E. (1996). A disconfirmation bias in the evaluation of arguments. *Journal of Personality and Social Psychology, 71*, 5–24.

Ehrhardt, A. A., & Meyer-Bahlberg, H. F. L. (1981). Effects of prenatal sex hormones on gender-related behavior. *Science, 211*, 1312–1317.

Ehrlich, P. R. (2000). *Human natures: Genes, cultures, and the human prospect*. Washington, DC: Island Press.

Eibl-Eibesfeldt, I. (1970). *Ethology: The biology of behavior*. New York: Holt, Rinehart, & Winston.

Eibl-Eibesfeldt, I. (1975). *Ethology: The biology of behavior* (2nd ed.). New York: Holt, Rinehart, & Winston.

Eich, J. E. (1980). The cue-dependent nature of state-dependent learning. *Memory and Cognition, 8*, 157–173.

Ekman, P. (1993). Facial expression and emotion. *American Psychologist, 48*, 384–392.

Elgert, K. (1996). *Immunology, understanding the immune system*. New York: Wiley.

Ellenberger, H. (1970). *The discovery of the unconscious: The history and evolution of dynamic psychiatry*. New York: Basic Books.

Ellis, A. (1977). *Humanistic psychotherapy: The rational-emotive approach*. New York: Julian Press.

Ellis, A. (1989). Rational-emotive therapy. In R. J. Corsini & D. Wedding (Eds.), *Current psychotherapies*. Itasca, IL: F. E. Peacock.

Ellis, A. (1999). Treatment of borderline personality disorder with rational emotive behavioral therapy. In C. R. Cloninger (Ed.), *Personality and psychopathology*. Washington, DC: American Psychiatric Press.

Emerick, C. D. (1987). Alcoholics anonymous: Affiliation process and effectiveness as treatment. *Alcoholism: Clinical and Experimental Research, 11*, 416–423.

Epstein, R., Kirshnit, C. E., Lanza, R. P., & Rubin, L. C. (1984). Insight in the pigeon; Antecedents and determinants of an intelligent performance. *Nature, 308*, 61–62.

Ericsson, A. E. (1985). Memory skill. *Canadian Journal of Psychology, 39*, 188–231.

Ericsson, A. E., Chase, W. G., & Faloon, S. (1980). Acquisition of a memory skill. *Science, 208*, 1181–1182.

Ericsson, K. A., & Simon, H. A. (1993). *Protocol analysis: Verbal reports as data* (Rev. ed.). Cambridge, MA: MIT Press.

Erikson, E. (1968). *Identity: Youth and crisis*. New York: Norton.

Eriksson, P. S., Perfilieva, E., Bjork-Eriksson, T., Alborn, A. M., Nordborg, C., Peterson, D. A., & Gage, F. H. (1998). Neurogenesis in the adult human hippocampus. *Natural Medicine, 11*, 1313–1317.

Erlich, H. A., Bergstrom, R. F., Stoneking, M., & Gyllensten, U. (1996). HLA sequence polymorphism and the origin of humans. *Science, 274*, 1552–1553.

Erlich, P., & Erlich, A. (1981). *Extinction: The causes and consequences of the disappearance of species*. New York: Random House.

Ettinger, U., Chitnis, X. A., Kumari, V., Fannon, D. G., Sumich, A. L., O'Ceallaigh, S., Doku, V., & Sharm, T. (2001). Magnetic resonance imaging of the thalamus in first-episode psychosis. *American Journal of Psychiatry, 158*, 116–118.

Evans, D. (2001). *Emotion: The science of sentiment*. Oxford, UK: Oxford University Press.

Ewald, P. W. (1980). Evolutionary biology and the treatment of signs and symptoms of infectious disease. *Journal of Theoretical Biology, 86*, 169–176.

Eysenck, H. (1953). *The structure of human personality*. New York: Wiley.

Eysenck, H. (1990). Biological dimensions of personality. In L. Pervin (Ed.), *Handbook of personality: Theory and research*, 244–276. New York: Guilford Press.

Eysenck, H. J. (1986). Inspection time and intelligence: A historical introduction. *Personality and Individual Differences, 7*, 603–607.

Eysenck, H. J. (1993). Forty years on: The outcome problem in psychotherapy revisited. In T. R. Giles (Ed.), *Handbook of effective psychotherapy*. New York: Plenum Press.

Eysenck, H. J. & Barrett, P. T. (1993). Brain research related to giftedness. K. A. Heller & F. J. Moenks, (Eds). *International handbook of research and development of giftedness and talent*, 115–131. Elmsford, NY: Pergamon Press, Inc.

Fabrega, H., & Manning, P. K. (1979). An integrated theory of disease: Ladino-Mestizo views of disease in the Chiapas highlands. *Psychosomatic Medicine, 35*, 223–239.

Fahrmeier, E. D. (1978). The development of concrete operations among the Hausa. *Journal of Cross-Cultural Psychology, 9*, 23–44.

Fairburn, C. G. (1984). Cognitive behavioral treatment for bulimia. In D. M. Garner & P. E. Garfinkel (Eds.), *The handbook of psychotherapy for anorexia nervosa and bulimia*. New York: Guilford.

Fairburn, C. G. (1988a). The current status of the psychological treatments for bulimia nervosa. *Journal of Psychosomatic Research, 32*, 635–645.

Fairburn, C. G. (1988b). The uncertain status of the cognitive approach to bulimia nervosa. In K. M. Pirke, W. Vandereycken, & D. Ploog (Eds.), *The psychobiology of bulimia nervosa*. Berlin: Springer-Verlag.

Falconer, D. S. (1960). *Quantitative genetics*. New York: Ronald Press.

False Memory Syndrome Foundation, Professional and Scientific Advisory Board. (1998, July). *Statement by the Professional and Scientific Advisory Board*. Philadelphia, PA: Author. Available: http://www.msfonline.org/fmsf98.701.html.

Fancher, R. E. (1990). *Pioneers of psychology* (2nd ed.). New York: Norton.

Fantz, R. L. (1961). The origin of form perception. *Scientific American, 204*, 66–72.

Farrell, W. (1986). *Why men are the way they are*. New York: McGraw-Hill.

Fechner, G. (1966). *Elements of psychophysics* (H. E. Alder, Trans.). New York: Holt, Rinehart, & Winston. (Original work published 1860.)

Fehr, B. (1996). *Friendship processes*. Thousand Oaks, CA: Sage Publications.

Fein, S., Goethals, G. R., Kassin, S. M., & Cross, J. (1993, August). *Social influence and presidential debates*. Paper presented at the annual meeting of the American Psychological Association Toronto.

Feingold, A. (1990). Gender differences in the effects of physical attractiveness on romantic attraction: A comparison across five research paradigms. *Journal of Personality and Social Psychology, 59*, 981–993.

Feingold, A. (1992). Gender differences in mate selection preferences: A test of the parental investment model. *Psychological Bulletin, 112*, 125–139.

Felten, D. (1993). The brain and the immune system. In B. Moyers, (Ed.), *Healing and the mind*, 213–238. New York: Doubleday.

Fernandez, A., & Glenberg, A. M. (1985). Changing environmental context does not reliably affect memory. *Memory and Cognition, 13*, 333–345.

Festinger, L. (1957). *A theory of cognitive dissonance.* Stanford, CA: Stanford University Press.

Festinger, L., & Carlsmith, J. M. (1959). Cognitive consequences of forced compliance. *Journal of Abnormal and Social Psychology, 58,* 203–210.

Field, T. M., Schanberg, S. M., Scafidi, F., Bauer, C. R., Vega-Lahr, N., Garcia, R., Nystrom, J., & Kuhn, C. M. (1986). Tactile/kinesthetic stimulation effects on preterm neonates. *Pediatrics, 77,* 654–658.

Fifer, W. P., & Moon, C. M. (1995). The effect of fetal experience with sound. In J. Lecanuet, W. P. Fifer, N. A. Krasnegor, & W. P. Smotherman (Eds.), *Fetal development: A psychobiological perspective.* Mahwah, NJ: Erlbaum.

Fincham, F. D., & Bradbury, T. N. (1993). Marital satisfaction, depression, and attributions. A longitudinal analysis. *Journal of Personality and Social Psychology, 64,* 442–452.

Fink, B., Grammer, K., & Thornhill, R. (2001). Human (Homo sapiens) facial attractiveness in relation to skin texture and color. *Journal of Comparative Psychology, 115,* 92–99.

Fisher, J., & Hinde, R. A. (1949). The opening of milk bottles by birds. *British Birds, 42,* 347–358.

Fiske, S. T., & Taylor, S. E. (1991). *Social cognition.* New York: McGraw-Hill.

Flaten, M., Simonsen, T., & Olsen, H. (1999). Drug-related information generates placebo and nocebo responses that modify the drug response. *Psychosomatic Medicine, 61,* 250–255.

Flatz, G. (1987). Genetics of lactose digestion in humans. *Advances in Human Genetics, 16,* 1–77.

Flavell, J. H. (1993). Young children's understanding of thinking and consciousness. *Current Directions in Psychological Science, 2,* 43–46.

Flavell, J. H. (1996). Piaget's legacy. *Psychological Science, 7,* 200–203.

Flaxman, S. M., & Sherman, P. W. (2000). Morning sickness: A mechanism for protecting mother and embryo. *Quarterly Review of Biology, 75,* 113–148.

Fletcher, G., & Ward, C. (1988). Attribution theory and processes: A cross-cultural perspective. In M. Bond (Ed.), *The cross-cultural challenge to social psychology.* Beverly Hills, CA: Sage Publications.

Flora, J. A., Maibach, E. W., & Maccoby, N. (1989). The role of media across four levels of health promotion intervention. *Annual Review of Public Health, 10,* 181–201.

Florio, G. A., Donnelly, J. P., & Zevon, M. A. (1998). The structure of work-related stress and coping among oncology nurses in high-stress medical settings: A transactional analysis. *Journal of Occupational Health Psychology, 3,* 227–242.

Flynn, J. R. (1984). The mean IQ of Americans: Massive gains 1932 to 1978. *Psychological Bulletin, 101,* 171–191.

Flynn, J. R. (1987). Massive IQ gains in 14 nations: What IQ tests really measure. *Psychological Bulletin, 95,* 29–51.

Flynn, J. S. (1991). *Cocaine.* New York: Birch Lane Press.

Foster, R. G. (1993). Photoreceptors and circadian systems. *Current Directions, 2,* 34–39.

Fouts, R. S. (1991). Dirty bathwater, innateness, neonates, and the dating game. *Language and Communication, 11,* 41–43.

Fowles, D. C. (1992). Schizophrenia: Diathesis-stress revisited. *Annual Review of Psychology, 43,* 303–336.

Fox, N. A., Calkins, S. D., & Bell, M. A. (1994). Neural plasticity and development during the first two years of life: Evidence from cognitive and socioemotional domains of research. *Development and Psychopathology, 6,* 677–696.

Frances, A. J., & Widiger, T. (1986). The classification of personality disorders: An overview of problems and solutions. *Annual Review of Psychiatry, 5,* 240–257.

Franco, F., & Butterworth, G. (1996). Pointing and social awareness: Declaring and requestion in the second year. *Journal of Child Language, 23,* 307–336.

Frankenburg, W., Dodds, J., Archer, P., Shapiro, H., & Bresnick, B. (1992). The Denver II: A major revision and restandardization of the Denver Developmental Screening Test. *Pediatrics, 89,* 91–97.

Franzek, E., & Beckmann, H. (1996). Gene-environment interaction in schizophrenia: Season-of-birth effect reveals etiologically different subgroups. *Psychopathology, 29,* 14–26.

Fraser, S. (Ed.). (1995). *The Bell Curve wars: Race, intelligence, and the future of America.* New York: Basic Books.

Freud, S. (1920). *Beyond the pleasure principle. A study of the death instinct in human aggression* (J. Strachey, Trans.). New York: Bantam Books. (Reprinted in 1959)

Freud, S. (1924). *A general introduction to psychoanalysis.* New York: Boni & Liveright.

Freud, S. (1949). *An outline of psychoanalysis.* (James Strachey, Trans.). New York: Norton. (Original work published 1940.)

Freud, S. (1950). *The interpretation of dreams* (A. A. Brill, Trans.). New York: The Modern Library (Random House). (Original work published 1900.)

Freud, S. (1960). The psychopathology of everyday life. In J. Strachey (Ed.), *The standard edition of the complete psychological works of Sigmund Freud* (Vol. 6). London: Hogarth. (Original work published 1901.)

Freud, S. (1961). *Civilization and its discontents.* New York: Norton. (Original work published 1930.)

Freud, S. (1976). *The interpretation of dreams.* In J. Strachey (Trans. and Ed.), *The complete psychological works* (Vols. 4–5). New York: Norton. (Original work published 1900.)

Fuchs, C. S., Stampfer, M. J., Colditz, G. A., Giovannucci, E. L., Manson, J. E., Kawachi, I., Hunter, D. J., Hankinson, S. E., Hennekens, C. H., & Rosner, B. (1995). Alcohol consumption and mortality among women. *New England Journal of Medicine, 332,* 1245–1250.

Fuller, J. L., & Wimer, R. E. (1973). Neural, sensory, and motor functions. In D. A. Dewsbury & D. A. Rethlingshafer (Eds.), *Comparative psychology: A modern survey.* New York: McGraw-Hill.

Funk, S. C. (1992). Hardiness: A review of theory and research. *Health Psychology, 11,* 335–345.

Furrow, D., Nelson, K., & Benedict, H. (1979). Mothers' speech to children and syntactic development: Some simple relationships. *Journal of Child Language, 6,* 423–442.

Gadow, K., & Sprafkin, J. (1993). Television violence and children with emotional and behavioral disorders. *Journal of Emotional and Behavioral Disorders, 1,* 54–63.

Gaertner, S. L., Dovidio, J. F., Nier, J. A., Ward, C. M., & Banker, B. S. (1999). Across cultural divides: The value of a superordinate identity. In D. A. Prentice & D. T. Miller (Eds.), *Cultural divides: Understanding and overcoming group conflict.* New York: Russell Sage Foundation.

Gage, F. H. (1998). Stem cells of the central nervous system. *Current Opinion in Neurobiology, 8*(5), 671–676.

Gage, F. H. (2000). *Neurogenesis in the adult brain and spinal cord.* Presidential Symposium, 30th Annual Meeting of the Society for Neuroscience, New Orleans.

Gagné, G. C., Jr., Furman, M. J., Carpenter, L. L., & Price, L. H. (2000). Efficacy of continuation ECT and antidepressant drugs compared to long-term antidepressants alone in depressed patients. *American Journal of Psych Psychiatry, 157,* 1960–1965.

Gallese, V., & Goldman, A. (1998). Mirror neurons and the simulation theory of mind-reading. *Trends in Cognitive Sciences, 2,* 493.

Gallup, G. G. (1970). Chimpanzees: Self-recognition. *Science, l16,* 86–87.

Gallup, G. G. Jr. (1998). Self awareness and the evolution of social intelligence. *Behavioral Processes, 42,* 239–247.

Gallup, G. G. Jr., & Maser, J. D. (1977). Tonic immobility: Evolutionary underpinnings of human catalepsy and catatonia. In J. D. Maser & M.E.P. Seligman (Eds.), *Psychopathology: Experimental models.* San Francisco: Freeman.

Gallup, G. G. Jr., & Rager, D. R. (1996). Tonic immobility as a model of extreme stress of behavioral inhibition: Issues of methodology and measurement. In R. R. Sanberg, K. P. Ossenkopp, & M. Kavaliers (Eds.), *Motor activity and movement disorders: Research issues and applications.* Totowa, NJ: Humana Press.

Galton, F. (1888). Co-relations and their measurement, chiefly from anthropometric data. *Proceedings of the Royal Society, 45,* 135–145.

Galton, F. (1970). *English men of science: Their nature and nurture.* London: Frank Cass. (Original work published 1874.)

Galton, F. (1972). *Hereditary genius.* Gloucester, MA: Peter Smith. (Original work published 1869.)

Ganellen, R. J., & Blaney, P. H. (1984). Hardiness and social support as moderators of the effects of life stress. *Journal of Personality & Social Psychology, 47,* 156–163.

Gannon, P. J., Holloway, R. L., Broadfield, D. C., & Braun, A. R. (1998). Asymmetry of chimpanzee planum temporale: Humanlike pattern of Wernicke's brain language area homologue. *Science, 279,* 220–222.

Ganong, W. F. (1980). Phonetic categorization in auditory word perception. *Journal of Experimental Psychology: Human Perception and Performance. 6,* 110–125.

Gantt, W. H. (1953). Principles of nervous breakdown - schizokinesis and autokinesis. *Annals of the New York Academy of Medicine, 56,* 143–163.

Garcia, J., Kimeldorf, D. J., & Koelling, R. A. (1955). Conditioned aversion to saccharin resulting from exposure to gamma radiation. *Science, 122,* 157–158.

Garcia, J., & Koelling, R. A. (1966). Relation of cue to consequence in avoidance learning. *Psychonomic Science, 4,* 123–124.

Gardner, H. (1983). *Frames of mind: The theory of multiple intelligences.* New York: Basic Books.

Gardner, H. (1993). *Multiple intelligences: The theory in practice.* New York: Basic Books.

Gardner, H. (1995). Why would anyone become an expert? *American Psychologist, 50,* 802–803.

Gardner, R. A., & Gardner, B. I. (1969). Teaching sign language to a chimpanzee. *Science, 165,* 664–672.

Garfield, C. (1993). Methodological problems in clinical diagnosis. In P. B. Stuker & H. E. Adams (Eds.), *Comprehensive handbook of psychopathology* (2nd ed.) New York: Plenum.

Gatch, M. B., & Lal, H. (1998). Pharmacological treatment of alcoholism. *Progress in Neuro-Psychopharmacology and Biological Psychiatry, 22,* 917–944.

Gatchel, R. J. (1993). Psychophysiological disorders: Past and present perspectives. In R. J. Gatchel & E. B. Blanchard (Eds.), *Psychophysiological disorders: Research & clinical applications.* Washington, DC: American Psychological Association.

Gauci, M., Husband, A. J., & King, M. G. (1992). Conditioned allergic rhinitis: A model for central nervous system and immune system interaction in IgE-mediated allergic reactions. In A. J. Husband (Ed.), *Behavior and immunity.* London: CRC Press.

Gaziano, J. M., Buring, J. E., Breslow, J. L., Goldhaber, S. Z., Rosner, B., VanDenburgh, M., Willett, W., & Hennekens, C. H. (1993). Moderate alcohol intake, increased levels of high-density lipoprotein and its subfractions, and decreased risk of myocardial infarction. *New England Journal of Medicine, 329,* 1829–1834.

Gazzaniga, M. (1967). The split-brain in man. *Scientific American, 213,* 24–29.

Gazzaniga, M. (1970). *The bisected brain.* New York: Appleton-Century-Crofts.

Gazzaniga, M. (1998, July). The split brain revisited. *Scientific American, 274,* 51–55.

Geary, D. C. (1999). Evolution and developmental sex differences. *Current Directions in Psychological Science, 8,* 115–120.

Geen, R. G., & Gange, J. J. (1983). Social facilitation: Drive theory and beyond. In H. H. Blumberg, A. P. Hare, V. Kent, & M. Davies (Eds.), *Small groups and social interaction* (Vol. 1). New York: Wiley.

Geldard, F. A. (1972). *The human senses.* New York: Wiley.

Gelman, R. (1997). Constructing and using conceptual competence. *Current Directions in Psychological Science, 2,* 43–46.

Gelman, R., & Kit-Fong, R. (Eds.). (1996). *Perceptual and cognitive development: Handbook of perception and cognition* (2nd ed.). San Diego: Academic Press.

Gibson, E. J. (1971). Perceptual learning and the theory of word perception. *Cognitive Psychology, 2,* 351–358.

Gibson, E. J., & Walk, R. D. (1960). The "visual cliff." *Scientific American, 202,* 64–71.

Gibson, E. J., & Walker, A. S. (1984). Development of knowledge of visual-tactual affordances of substance. *Child Development, 55,* 453–461.

Gibson, H. B., & Heap, M. (1991). *Hypnosis in therapy.* Hillsdale, NJ: Erlbaum.

Gilbert, D. T., & Malone, P. W. (1995). The correspondence bias. *Psychological Bulletin, 117,* 21–38.

Gillan, D. J. (1981). Reasoning in the chimpanzee: II. Transitive inference. *Journal of Experimental Psychology: Animal Behavior Processes, 7,* 150–164.

Gillan, D. J. (1983). Inferences and the acquisition of knowledge by chimpanzees. In M. L. Commons, R. J. Herrnstein, & A. R. Wagner (Eds.), *Quantitative analyses of behavior. Vol. 4: Discrimination processes.* Cambridge, MA: Ballinger.

Gilligan, S. G., & Bower, G. H. (1984). Cognitive consequences of emotional arousal. In C. Izard, J. Kagan, & R. Zajonc (Eds.), *Emotions, cognition, and behavior.* New York: Cambridge University Press.

Glanzer, M., & Cunitz, A. R. (1966). Two storage mechanisms in free recall. *Journal of Verbal Learning and Verbal Behavior, 5,* 351–360.

Godden, D., & Baddeley, A. D. (1975). Context-dependent memory in two natural environments: On land and under water. *British Journal of Psychology, 66,* 325–331.

Gold, H. S., & Moellering, R. C. (1996). Antimicrobial-drug resistance. *The New England Journal of Medicine, 335*(19), 1445–1451.

Gold, R. J., & Gold, S. R. (1982). Sex differences in actual daydream content. *Journal of Mental Imagery, 6,* 109–112.

Goldberg, L. R. (1982). From ace to zombie: Some explorations in the language of personality. In C. Spielberger & J. N. Butcher (Eds.), *Advances in personality assessment* (Vol. 1,). Hillsdale, NJ: Erlbaum.

Goldberg, L. R. (1993). The structure of phenotypic personality traits. *American Psychologist, 48,* 26–34.

Goldsmith, H. H., Buss, A. H., Plomin, R., Rothbart, M., Klevjord, T. A., Chess, S., Hinde, R. A., & McCall, R. B. (1987). Roundtable: What is temperament? Four approaches. *Child Development, 58,* 505–529.

Goldstein, J., & Baskin, D. (1988). Sex differences in daydream behavior. *Journal of Mental Imagery, 12,* 83–90.

Goldstein, M. J. (1987). Family interaction patterns that antedate the onset of schizophrenia and related disorders: A further analysis of data from a longitudinal prospective study. In K. Hahlweg & M. J. Goldstein (Eds.), *Understanding major mental disorder: The contribution of family interaction research.* New York: Family Process Press.

Golin, E. S. (1960). Developmental studies of visual recognition of incomplete objects. *Perceptual and Motor Skills, 11,* 289–298.

Goodall, J. (1999). *Reason for hope: A spiritual journey.* New York: Warner Books.

Goodglass, H., & Kaplan, E. (1983). *The Boston diagnostic aphasia examination.* Philadelphia: Lea & Febiger.

Goodman, L. S., & Gilman, A. (1960). *The pharmacological basis of therapeutics* (2nd ed.). New York: Macmillan.

Goodwin, C. J. (1999). *A history of modern psychology.* New York: Wiley.

Gopnik, A., & Meltzoff, A. N. (1986). Relations between semantic and cognitive development in the one-word stage: The specificity hypothesis. *Child Development, 57,* 1040–1053.

Gordon, R. A. (1997). Everyday life as an intelligence test: Effects of intelligence and intelligence context. *Intelligence, 24,* 203–320.

Gordon, T. P., Bernstein, I. S., & Rose, R. M. (1978). Social and seasonal influences on testosterone secretion in the male rhesus monkey. *Physiology and Behavior, 21*, 623–627.

Gorman, J. M., Liebowitz, M. R., Fyer, A. J., & Stein, J. (1989). A neuroanatomical hypothesis for panic disorder. *American Journal of Psychiatry, 12*, 22–36.

Gottesman, I. I. (1991). *Schizophrenia genesis: The origins of madness*. New York: Freeman.

Gottfredson, L. S. (1997a). Editorial: Mainstream science on intelligence: An editorial with 52 signatories, history, and bibliography. *Intelligence, 24*, 1–23.

Gottfredson, L. S. (1997b). Why *g* matters: The complexity of everyday life. *Intelligence, 24*, 79–132.

Gould, J. L. (1982). *Ethology*. New York: Norton.

Gould, S. J. (1989). *Wonderful life: The burgess shale and the nature of history*. New York: Norton.

Gould, S. J. (1994, November 28). Curveball [Review of *The bell curve: Intelligence and class structure in American life*]. *New Yorker*, 139–149.

Government's Sentencing Memorandum. (1998). *United States of America vs. Theodore John Kaczynski* (CR. Ns. S-96-0259 GEB).

Green, D. M., & Swets, J. A. (1966). *Signal detection theory and psychophysics*. New York: Wiley.

Greenfield, P. M. (1991). Language, tools, and brain: The ontogeny and phylogeny of hierarchically organized sequential behavior. *Behavioral and Brain Sciences, 14*, 531–595.

Greenfield, P. M. (1994). Independence and interdependence as developmental scripts: Implications for theory, research, and practice. In P. M. Greenfield & R. R. Cocking (Eds.), *Cross-cultural roots of minority child development*. Hillsdale, NJ: Erlbaum.

Greeno, J. G., & Simon, H. A (1988). Problem solving and reasoning. In R. C. Atkinson, R. Herrnstein, G. Lindzey, & R. D. Luce (Eds.), *Steven's handbook of experimental psychology* (rev. ed.). New York: Wiley.

Griffin, D. (1959). *Echoes of bats and men*. Garden City, NY: Anchor Books/Doubleday.

Grilly, D. M. (1989). *Drugs and human behavior*. Boston: Allyn & Bacon.

Gross, T. F. (1985). *Cognitive development*. Monterey, CA: Brooks/Cole.

Grossmann, K., Grossmann, K. E., Spangler, G., Suess, G., & Unzner, L. (1985). Maternal sensitivity and newborns' orientation responses as related to quality of attachment in Northern Germany. In I. Bretherton & E. Waters (Eds.), *Growing points of attachment theory and research. Monographs of the Society for Research in Child Development, 50*, (1–2, Serial No. 209).

Gruen, R. J. (1993). Stress and depression: Toward the development of integrative models. In L. Goldberger & S. Breznitz (Eds.), *Handbook of stress: Theoretical and clinical aspects* (2nd ed.). New York: Free Press.

Grunberg, N. E., & Straub, R. O. (1992). The role of gender and taste class in the effects of stress on eating. *Health Psychology, 11*, 97–100.

Gruzelier, J. (1998). A working model of the neurophysiology of hypnosis: A review of evidence. *Contemporary Hypnosis, 15*(1), 3–21.

Gulick, W. L., Gescheider, G. A., & Frisina, R. D. (1989). *Hearing: Physiological acoustics, neural coding, and psychoacoustics*. New York: Oxford University Press.

Gunnar, M. R., Tout, K., de Haan, M., & Pierce, S. (1997). Temperament, social competence, and adrenocortical activity in preschoolers. *Developmental Psychobiology, 31*, 65–85.

Gunter, B., & McAleer, J. (1990). *Children and television: The one eyed monster*. London: Routledge.

Gutknect, L., Spitz, E., & Carlier, M. (1999). Long-term effect of placental type on anthropometrical and psychological traits among monozygotic twins: A follow up study. *Twin Research, 3*, 212–217.

Gwynn, M. I., & Spanos, N. P. (1996). Hypnotic responsiveness, nonhypnotic suggestibility, and responsiveness to social influence. In R. G. Kunzendorf, N. P. Spanos, & P. Nicholas (Eds.), *Hypnosis and imagination. Imagery and human development series*. Amityville, NY: Baywood Publishing.

Haber, R. N., & Haber, R. B. (1964). Eidetic imagery: 1. Frequency. *Perceptual and Motor Skills, 19*, 131–138.

Hacking, I. (1996). Normal people. In D. R. Olson & N. Torrance (Eds.), *Modes of thought: Explorations in culture and cognition*. Cambridge, UK: Cambridge University Press.

Hahn, R. A. (1997). The nocebo phenomenon: Scope and foundations. In A. Harrington (Ed.), *The placebo effect: An interdisciplinary exploration*. Cambridge, MA: Harvard University Press.

Haimov, I., & Lavie, P. (1996). Melatonin–A sophoric hormone. *Current Directions of Psychological Science*, 106–111.

Hainline, L. (1993). Conjugate eye movements of infants. In K. Simons (Ed.), *Early visual development: Normal and abnormal*. New York: Oxford University Press.

Hall, N., McGillis, J., Spangelo, B., & Goldstein, A. (1985). Evidence that thymosins and other biologic response modifiers can function as neuroactive immunotransmitters. *The Journal of Immunology, 135*, 535–539.

Halpern, D. F. (1989). *Thought and knowledge: An introduction to critical thinking* (2nd ed.). Hillsdale, NJ: Erlbaum.

Hamilton, W. D. (1964). The genetical evolution of social behavior. *Journal of Theoretical Biology, 7*, 1–52.

Hanser, S. B., & Thompson, L. W. (1994). Effects of a music therapy strategy on depressed older adults. *Journal of Gerontology, 49*, 265–269.

Hare, R. D. (1993). *Without conscience: The disturbing world of the psychopaths among us*. New York: Pocket Books.

Harker, L., & Keltner, D. (2001). Expressions of positive emotion in women's college yearbook pictures and their relationship to personality and life outcomes across adulthood. *Journal of Personality and Social Psychology, 80*, 112–124.

Harlow, H. F. (1949). The formation of learning sets. *Psychological Review, 56*, 51–65.

Harlow, H. F. (1969). Age-mate or peer affectional system. In D. S. Lehrman, R. H. Hinde, & E. Shaw (Eds.), *Advances in the study of behavior* (Vol. 2). New York: Academic Press.

Harlow, H. F., & Harlow, M. K. (1962). The effect of rearing conditions on behavior. *Bulletin of the Menninger Clinic, 26*, 213–224.

Harriman, A. E. (1955). The effect of a preoperative preference for sugar over salt upon compensatory salt selection by adrenalectomized rats. *Journal of Nutrition, 57*, 271–276.

Harrington, A. (Ed.). (1997). *The placebo effect: An interdisciplinary exploration*. Cambridge, MA: Harvard University Press.

Harris, J. R. (1998). *The nurture assumption: Why children turn out the way they do; Parents matter less than you think and peers matter more*. New York: Free Press.

Harris, M. (1974). *Cows, pigs, warts, & witches: The riddles of culture*. New York: Vintage Books.

Harris, M., Barlow-Brown, F., & Chasin, J. (1995). The emergence of referential understanding: Pointing and the comprehension of object names. *First Language, 15*, 19–34.

Hartel, C. (1999). (As quoted in B. Azar, 1996, Students need a broader outlook on career. *APA Monitor*. Available: http://www.apa.org/students/g-employ.html.)

Hartline, H. K., & Graham, C. H. (1932). Light and dark adaptation of single photoreceptor elements in the eye of Limulus. *Journal of Cellular and Comparative Physiology, 30*, 225–253.

Hartman, E. (1967). *The biology of dreaming*. Springfield, IL: Charles C. Thomas.

Hartmann, T. (1996). *Beyond ADD: Hunting for reasons in the past & present*. New York: Underwood Books.

Hasher, L., & Zacks, R. T. (1984). Automatic processing of fundamental information: The case of frequency. *American Psychologist, 39,* 1372–1388.

Hatfield, E., & Spretcher, S. (1986). *Mirror, mirror... The importance of looks in everyday life.* Albany: State University of New York Press.

Hayes, C. (1951). *The ape in our house.* New York: Harper & Row.

Heath, R. G. (1963). Electrical self-stimulation of the brain in man. *American Journal of Psychiatry, 120,* 571–577.

Hecht, H., & Proffitt, D. R. (1995). The price of expertise: Effects of experience on the water-level task. *Psychological Science, 6,* 90–95.

Hecht, S., Schlaer, S., & Pirenne, M. H. (1942). Energy, quanta, and vision. *Journal of General Physiology, 25,* 819–840.

Heider, F. (1958). *The psychology of interpersonal relations.* New York: Wiley.

Hendren, J. (1999, April 25). Boy's diary details plot, officials say. *Waco Tribune-Herald,* 1.

Hendrick, V., & Hendrick, S. (1993). *Romantic love.* Newbury Park, CA: Sage.

Hergenhahn, B. R. (1992). *An introduction to the history of psychology* (2nd ed.). Belmont, CA: Wadsworth.

Herman, L. M. (1989). In which procrustean bed does the sea lion sleep tonight? *Psychological Record, 39,* 19–50.

Herman, L. M., Richards, D. G., & Wolz, J. P. (1984). Comprehension of sentences by bottlenosed dolphins. *Cognition, 16,* 129–219.

Herrick, C. J. (1948). *The brain of the tiger salamander.* Chicago: University of Chicago Press.

Herrnstein, R. J., & Murray, C. (1994). *The bell curve: Intelligence and class struggle in American life.* New York: Free Press.

Hess, E. H., & Polt, J. M. (1960). Pupil size as related to interest value of visual stimuli. *Science, 132,* 149–150.

Hess, E. H., & Polt, J. M. (1964). Pupil size in relation to mental activity during simple problem solving. *Science, 140,* 1190–1192.

Hess, E. H. (1973). *Imprinting.* New York: van Nostrand.

Hetherington, M. M., & Rolls, B. J. (1997). Sensory-specific satiety: theoretical frameworks and central characteristics. In E. D. Capaldi (Ed.), *Why we eat what we eat: The psychology of eating.* Washington D.C.: American Psychiological Association.

Hewes, G. W. (1992). Primate communication and the gestural origin of language. *Current Anthropology, 33,* 65–84.

Heyser, C. J., Spear, N. E., & Spear, L. P. (1993). Effects of prenatal exposure to cocaine on conditional discrimination learning in adult rats. *Behavioral Neuroscience, 106,* 837–845.

Higley, J., Hasert, M., Suomi, S., & Linnoila, M. (1988). The serotonin reuptake inhibitor sertraline reduces excessive alcohol consumption in nonhuman primates: Effect of stress. *Neuropsychopharmacology, 18,* 431–442.

Hilgard, E. R. (1973). A neodissociation interpretation of pain reduction in hypnosis. *Psychological Review, 80,* 396–411.

Hillier, L., Hewitt, K. L., & Morrongiello, B. A. (1992). Infants' perceptions of illusions in sound localization: Reaching to sounds in the dark. *Journal of Experimental Child Psychology, 53,* 159–179.

Hobson, J. A. (1988). *The dreaming brain.* New York: Basic Books.

Hobson, J. A. (1997). Dreaming as delirium: A mental status analysis of our nightly madness. *Seminars in Neurology, 17*(2), 121–128.

Hobson J. A., Stickgold., R., & Pace-Schott, E. F. (1998). The neuropsychology of REM sleep dreaming. *Neuroreport, 9*(3), 1–14.

Hockfield, S., & Kalb, R. G. (1993). Activity dependent structural changes during neuronal development. *Current Opinion in Neurobiology, 3,* 87–92.

Hodos, W., & Campbell, C. B. G. (1969). Scala naturae: Why there is no theory in comparative psychology. *Psychological Review, 76,* 337–350.

Hoebel, B. G., & Hernandez, L. (1993). Basic neural mechanisms of feeding and weight regulation. In A. J. Stunkard & T. A. Wadden (Eds.), *Obesity: Theory and therapy* (2nd ed.). New York: Raven Press.

Hofstede, G. (1983). Dimensions of national cultures in fifty countries and three regions. In J. Deregowski, S. Dzuirawiec, & R. Annis (Eds.), *Explications in cross-cultural psychology.* Lisse: Swets and Zeitlinger.

Hogan, J. (1977). The ontogeny of food preferences in chicks and other animals. In L. M. Barker, M. R. Best, & M. Domjan (Eds.), *Learning mechanisms in food selection* 71–98. Waco, TX: Baylor University Press.

Holden, C. (1993). Wake-up call for sleep research. *Science, 259,* 305.

Hollander, E., Stein, D. J., DeCaria, C. M., Cohen, L., Saoud, J. B., Skodol, A. E., Kellman, D., Rosnick, L., & Oldham, J. M. (1994). Serotonergic sensitivity in borderline personality disorder: Preliminary findings. *American Journal of Psychiatry, 151,* 277–280.

Holmes, T. H., & Rahe, R. H. (1967). The Social Readjustment Rating Scale. *Journal of Psychosomatic Research, 11,* 213–218.

Hooley, J. M. (1986). Expressed emotion and depression: Interactions between patients and high- versus low-expressed emotion spouses. *Journal of Abnormal Psychology, 95,* 237–246.

Hoosain, R., & Salili, F. (1988). Language differences, working memory, and mathematical ability. In M. M. Gruneberg, P. E. Morris, & R. N. Sykes (Eds.), *Practical aspects of memory: Current research and issues, Vol. 2: Clinical and educational implications.* Chichester: Wiley.

Horne, J. A. (1988). *Why we sleep: The functions of sleep in humans and other mammals.* Oxford, England: Oxford University Press.

Horney, K. (1937). *The neurotic personality of our time.* New York: Norton.

Horney, K. (1950). *Neurosis and human growth: The struggle toward self-realization.* New York: Norton.

Hovland, C. I., Lumsdaine. A. A., & Scheffield, F. D. (1949). *Studies in social psychology in World War II. Vol. 3. Experiments in mass communication.* Princeton, NJ: Princeton University Press.

Howard, K. L., Moras, K., Brill, P. L., Martinovich, Z., & Lutz, W. (1996). Evaluation of psychotherapy: Efficacy, effectiveness, and patient progress. *American Psychologist, 51,* 1059–1064.

Hsieh, M. H., Lam, H. M., van de Loo, F. J., & Coruzzi, G. (1998). A PII-like protein in Arabidopsis: Putative role in nitrogen sensing. *Proceedings of the National Academy of Sciences, USA, 95*(23), 13965–13970.

Hsu, L. K. G. (1990). *Eating disorders.* New York: Guilford Press.

Hubel, D., & Wiesel, T. (1962). Receptive fields, binocular interaction and functional architecture in the cat's visual cortex. *Journal of Physiology (London), 160,* 106–154.

Hubel, D., & Wiesel, T. (1977). Functional architecture of the macaque monkey visual cortex (Ferrier lecture.) *Proceedings of the Royal Society of London, Series B, 198,* 1–59.

Hudson, T. (1983). Correspondences and numerical differences between disjoint sets. *Child Development, 54,* 84–90.

Hull, C. L. (1943). *Principles of behavior.* New York: Appleton.

Hull, J. G., & Bond, C. F., Jr. (1986). Social and behavioral consequences of alcohol consumption and expectancy: A meta-analysis. *Psychological Bulletin, 99,* 347–360.

Humphrey, N. (1992). *A history of the mind: Evolution and the birth of consciousness.* New York: HarperPerennial.

Hunt, E., Streissguth, A. P., Kerr, B., & Carmichael-Olson, H. (1995). Mothers' alcohol consumption during pregnancy: Effects on spatial-visual reasoning in 14-year-old children. *Psychological Science, 6,* 339–342.

Hunt, W. A. (1993). Neuroscience research: How has it contributed to our understanding of alcohol abuse and alcoholism? A review. *Alcoholism: Clinical and Experimental Research, 17,* 1055.

Hunter, J. E. (1986). Cognitive ability, cognitive aptitudes, job knowledge, and job performance. *Journal of Vocational Behavior, 29,* 340–362.

Hurford, J. R. (1991). The evolution of the critical period for language acquisition. *Cognition, 40,* 159–201.

Ingman, M., Kaessmann, H., Paabo, S., & Gyllensten, U. (2000). Mitochondrial genome variation and the origin of modern humans. *Nature, 408,* 708–713.

Inhelder, B., & Piaget, J. (1958). *The growth of logical thinking from childhood to adolescence: An essay on the construction of formal operational structures.* New York: Basic Books. (Original work published 1955.)

Insko, C. A. (1964). Primacy versus recency in persuasion as a function of the timing of arguments and measures. *Journal of Abnormal and Social Psychology, 69,* 381–391.

Isabella, R. A. (1993). Origins of attachment: Maternal interactive behavior across the first year. *Child Development, 64,* 605–621.

Isha, A., & Sagi, D. (1995). Common mechanisms of imagery and perception. *Science, 268,* 1772–1774.

Iskant, A. P., & Joliet, P. V. (1968). *Accidents and homicide.* Cambridge, MA: Harvard University Press.

Izard, C. E. (1984). Emotion-cognition relationships in human development. In C. E. Izard, J. Kagan, & R. B. Zajonc (Eds.), *Emotions, cognition and behavior.* Cambridge, England: Cambridge University Press.

Izard, C. E. (1991). *The psychology of emotions.* New York: Plenum.

Jacoby, R., & Glauberman, N. (Eds.). (1995). *The* Bell Curve *debate: History, documents, opinions.* New York: Times Books.

James, W. (1890). *The principles of psychology.* New York: Henry Holt.

James, W. (1902). *The varieties of religious experience.* New York: Longmans, Green.

Jameson, D., & Hurvich, L. M. (1989). Essay concerning color constancy. *Annual Review of Psychology, 40,* 1–22.

Jamison, C., & Scogin, R. (1995). The outcome of cognitive bibliotherapy with adults. *Journal of Consulting and Clinical Psychology, 63,* 644–650.

Jansen, A. S. P., Nguyen, X. V., Karpitskiy, V., Mettenleiter, T. C., & Loewy, A. D. (1995). Central command neurons of the sympathetic nervous system: Basis of the fight-or-flight response. *Science, 270,* 644–646.

Janus, S. S., & Janus, C. L. (1993). *The Janus report on sexual behavior.* New York: Wiley.

Jasiukaitis, P., Nouriani, B., Hugdahl, K., & Spiegel, D. (1997). Relateralizing hypnosis: Or, have we been barking up the wrong hemisphere? *International Journal of Clinical and Experimental Hypnosis, 45*(2), 158–177.

Jaynes, J. (1973). *The origins of consciousness in the breakdown of the bicameral mind.* Boston: Houghton Mifflin.

Jemmott, J. B. III, Hellman, C., McClelland, D. C., Locke, S. E., Kraus, L., Williams, R. M., & Valeri, C. R. (1990). Motivational syndromes associated with natural killer cell activity. *Journal of Behavioral Medicine, 13,* 53–73.

Jenicke, M. A., Baer, L., & Minichiello, W. E. (1986). *Obsessive-compulsive disorders: Theory and management.* Littleton, MA: PSG.

Jenkins, H. M., & Moore, B. R. (1973). The form of the autoshaped response with food or water reinforcers. *Journal of the Experimental Analysis of Behavior, 20,* 163–181.

Jensen, A. R. (1980). *Bias in mental testing.* New York: Free Press.

Jensen, A. R. (1993a). Test validity: *g* versus "tacit knowledge." *Current Directions in Psychological Science, 2,* 9–10.

Jensen, A. R. (1993b). Why is reaction time correlated with psychometric *g*? *Current Directions, 2,* 53–56.

Jensen, A. R. (1998). *The g factor: The science of mental ability.* Westport, CT: Praeger Publishers/Greenwood Publishing Group.

Jerison, H. J. (1973). *Evolution of the brain and intelligence.* New York: Academic Press.

Jiang, N., & Forster, K. I. (2001). Cross-language priming asymmetries in lexical decision and episodic recognition. *Journal of Memory and Language, 44,* 32–51.

John, O. P. (1990). The big five factor taxonomy: Dimensions of personality in the natural language and in questionnaires. In L. Pervin (Ed.), *Handbook of personality: Theory and research.* New York: Guilford Press.

Johnson, J. S., & Newport, E. L. (1989). Critical period effects in second language learning: The influence of maturational state on the acquisition of English as a second language. *Cognitive Psychology, 21,* 60–99.

Johnson, S. P. (1997). Young infant's perception of object unity: Implications for development of attentional and cognitive skills. *Current Directions in Psychological Science, 6,* 5–11.

Johnson-Laird, P. N. (1985). Deductive reasoning ability. In R. J. Sternberg (Ed.), *Human abilities: An information processing approach.* New York: Freeman.

Johnson-Laird, P. N., & Wason, P. (1977). *Thinking.* Cambridge, UK: Cambridge University Press.

Johnston, J. C., McCann, R. S., & Remington, R. W. (1995). Chronometric evidence for two types of attention. *Psychological Science, 6,* 365–369.

Jones, E. (1953). *The life and work of Sigmund Freud (Vol. 1).* New York: Basic Books.

Jones, E. (1955). *The life and work of Sigmund Freud (Vol. 2).* New York: Basic Books.

Jones, E. E., & Harris, V. A. (1967). The attribution of attitudes. *Journal of Experimental Social Psychology, 3,* 1–24.

Jones, H. E., & Bayley, N. (1941). The Berkeley growth study. *Child Development, 12,* 157–173.

Jongbloet, P. H. (1983). Menses and moon phases, ovulation and seasons, vitality and month of birth. *Developmental Medicine and Child Neurology, 25,* 527–531.

Joseph, R. (1988). The right cerebral hemisphere: Emotion, music, visual-spatial skills, body-image, dreams, and awareness. *Journal of Clinical Psychology, 44,* 630–673.

Julien, R. M. (1995). *A primer of drug action* (7th ed.). New York: Freeman.

Jung, C. G. (1933). *Modern man in search of a soul* (W. S. Dell & C. F. Baynes, Trans.). New York: Harcourt, Brace, & World.

Jung, C. G. (1968). *The archetypes and the collective unconscious* (R. F. C. Hull, Trans.). In H. Read, M. Fordham, & G. Adler (Eds.), *Collected works of C. G. Jung (Vol. 9, Pt. I).* Princeton, N.J: Princeton University Press. (Original work published 1936.)

Justesen, D. R., Braun, E. W., Garrison, R. G., & Pendleton, R. B. (1970). Pharmacological differentiation of allergic and classically conditioned asthma in the guinea pig. *Science, 170,* 864–866.

Justine, S. (1993). Music, the brain, and Ravel. *Trends in Neurosciences, 16,* 168–172.

Kabat-Zinn, J. (1993). Meditation. In B. Moyers (Ed.), *Healing and the mind* 115–144. New York: Doubleday.

Kagan, J. (1994). *Galen's prophesy: Temperament in human nature.* New York: Basic Books.

Kagan, J., Arcus, D., Snidman, N., Feng, W. Y., Hender, J., & Green, S. (1994). Reactivity in infants: A cross-national comparison. *Developmental Psychology, 30,* 342–345.

Kagan, J., & Snidman, N. (1991). Initial reactions to unfamiliarity. *Psychological Science, 1,* 40–44.

Kagan, J., & Snidman, N. (1992). Infant predictors of inhibited and uninhibited profiles. *Psychological Science, 2,* 40–44.

Kahn, M. (1997). *Between therapist and client: The new relationship.* New York: Freeman.

Kalat, J. (1997). *Biological psychology.* New York: Brooks-Cole.

Kalil, R. E. (1989, December). Synapse formation in the developing brain. *Scientific American, 261,* 76–85.

Kanner, A. D., Coyne, J. C., Schaefer, C., & Lazarus, R. S. (1981). Comparison of two modes of stress measurement: Daily hassles and uplifts versus major life events. *Journal of Behavioral Medicine, 4,* 14.

Kaplan, E. L., & Kaplan, G. A. (1970). The prelinguistic child. In J. Eliot (Ed.), *Human development and cognitive processes.* New York: Holt, Rinehart, & Winston.

Kaplan, G. A., Salonen, J. T., Cohen, R. D., Brand, R. J., Syme, S. L., & Puska, P. (1988). Social connections and mortality from all causes and from cardiovascular disease: Prospective evidence from eastern Finland. *American Journal of Epidemiology, 128,* 370–380.

Kaplan, G. A., Strawbridge, W. J., Cohen, R. D., & Hungerford, L. R. (1996). Natural history of leisure time physical activity and its correlates: Association with mortality from all causes and cardiovascular disease over 28 years. *American Journal of Epidemiology, 144,* 793–797.

Kaplan, P. S., Goldstein, M. H., Huckeby, E. R., & Panneton-Cooper, R. (1995). Habituation, sensitization, and infants' responses to motherese speech. *Developmental Psychobiology, 28,* 45–57.

Kaplan, R. D. (1998, August). Travels into America's future. *The Atlantic Monthly*, 37–61.

Karau, S. J., & Williams, K. D. (1993). Social loafing: A meta-analytic review and theoretical integration. *Journal of Personality and Social Psychology, 65,* 681–706.

Karau, S. J., & Williams, K. D. (1995). Social loafing: Research findings, implications, and future directions. *Current Directions in Psychological Science, 4,* 134–140.

Karni, A., Tanne, D., Rubenstein, B. S., Askenasy, J. J. M., & Sagi, D. (1994). Dependence on REM sleep of overnight improvement of a perceptual skill. *Science, 265,* 679.

Katz, S. (Ed.). (1975). *Biological anthropology: Selected readings from Scientific American.* San Francisco: Freeman.

Katz, S. (1982). Food, behavior, and biocultural evolution. In Barker, L. M. (Ed.), *The psychobiology of human food selection.* Westport, CT: AVI Publishing.

Kausler, D. H. (1994). *Learning and memory in normal aging.* San Diego, CA: Academic Press.

Kaye, K. L., & Bower, T. G. R. (1994). Learning and intermodal transfer of information in newborns. *Psychological Science, 5,* 286–288.

Kazdin, A. E. (1982). *Single-case research designs: Methods for clinical and applied settings.* New York: Oxford University Press.

Kazdin, A. E. (1994). Methodology, design, and evaluation in psychotherapy research. In A. Bergin & S. Garfield, (Eds.), *Handbook of psychotherapy and behavioral change* (4th ed.). New York: Wiley.

Keeley, L. H. (1996). *War before civilization: The myth of the peaceful savage.* New York: Oxford University Press.

Keenan, J. P., Nelson, A., O'Connor, M., & Pascual-Leone, A. (2001). Neurology: Self-recognition and the right hemisphere. *Nature, 409,* 305.

Keesey, R. E., & Powley, T. L. (1988). The regulation of body weight. *Annual Review of Psychology, 37,* 109–133.

Kelley, D. D. (1991). Sleep and dreams. In E. R. Kandel, J. H. Schwartz, & T. M. Jessel (Eds.), *Principles of neuroscience* (3rd ed.). New York: Elsevier.

Kelley, H. H. (1973). The process of causal attribution. *American Psychologist, 28,* 107–128.

Kelley, K. W. (2001). It's time for PsychoNeuroImmunology. *Brain, Behavior, and Immunity, 1,* 1–6.

Kelley, S. J. (1998). Stress and coping behaviors of substance-abusing mothers. *Journal of the Society of Pediatric Nurses, 3,* 103–110.

Kellogg, W. N., & Kellogg, L. A. (1933). *The ape and the child.* New York: Whittlesey House.

Kemperman, G., Kuhn, H. G., & Gage, F. H. (1998). Experience-induced neurogenesis in the senescent dentate gyrus. *Journal of Neuroscience, 18*(9), 3206–3212.

Kendler, K. S., & Diehl, S. R. (1993). The genetics of schizophrenia: A current, genetic-epidemiologic perspective. *Schizophrenia Bulletin, 19,* 261–285.

Kendler, K. S., Gruenberg, A. M., & Tsuang, M. T. (1985). Subtype stability in schizophrenia. *American Journal of Psychiatry, 142,* 827–832.

Kenway, L. K., & Wilson, M. A. (2001). Temporally structured replay of awake hippocampal ensemble activity during rapid eye movement sleep. *Neuron, 29,* 145–156.

Kerry, T. (1987). Primary topics and the able child. *Gifted Education International, 4,* 167–168.

Kertesz, A. (1988). Cognitive function in severe aphasia. In L. Weiskrantz (Ed.), *Thought without language.* Oxford, UK: Clarendon Press.

Kessler, R. C., McGonagle, K. A., Zhao, S., Nelson, C. B., Hughes, M., Eshleman, S., Wittchen, H. U., & Kendler, K. S. (1994). Lifetime and 12-month prevalence of DSM-IIIR psychiatric disorders in the United States. *Archives of General Psychiatry, 51,* 8–19.

Keverne, E. B. (1987). Pheromones. In G. Adelman (Ed.), *Encyclopedia of neuroscience* (Vol. 2, pp. 944–946). Boston: Birkhaüser.

Keys, A. (1970). Coronary heart disease in seven countries. *Circulation, 47*(Suppl. 1).

Khachaturian, D. S., & Blass, J. P. (1992). *Alzheimer's disease: New treatment strategies.* New York: Dekker.

Kiang, N. Y., Watanbe, S. T., Thomas, E. C., & Clark, L. F. (1962). Stimulus coding in the cat's auditory nerve. *Annals of Otology, Rhinology, and Laryngology, 71,* 1009–1025.

Kihlstrom, J. F. (1985). Hypnosis. *Annual Review of Psychology, 36,* 385–418.

Kim, K., Relkin, N., Lee, K. M., & Hirsch, J. (1997). Distinct cortical areas associated with native and second languages. *Nature, 388,* 171–174.

Kimura, D. (1964). Left-right differences in the perception of melodies. *Quarterly Journal of Experimental Psychology, 16,* 355–358.

Kimura, D. (1973). The asymmetry of the human brain. *Scientific American, 228,* 70–78.

King, B. J. (1994). Evolutionism, essentialism, and evolutionary perspective on language: Moving beyond the human standard. *Language and Communication, 14,* 1–13.

King, B. M., Smith, R. L., & Frohman, L. A. (1984). Hyperinsulinemia in rats with ventromedial hypothalamic lesions: Role of hyperphagia. *Behavioral Neuroscience, 98,* 152–155.

Kintsch, W. (1974). *The representation of meaning in memory.* Hillsdale, NJ: Erlbaum.

Kircher, T. T. J., Senior, C., Phillips, M. L., Rabe-Hesketh, S., Benson, P. J., Bullmore, E. T., Brammer, M., Simmons, A., Bartels, M., & David, A. S. (2001). Recognizing one's own face. *Cognition, 78,* B1–B15.

Kirk, R. W. (1995). *Experimental design: Procedures for the behavioral sciences* (3rd ed.). Belmont, CA: Brooks/Cole.

Kirsch, I., Capafons, A., Cardena-Buelna, E., & Amigo, S. (Eds.). (1999). *Clinical hypnosis and self-regulation: Cognitive-behavioral perspectives.* Washington, DC: American Psychological Association.

Kissin, B. (1986). *Conscious and unconscious programs in the brain.* New York: Plenum.

Kleinman, A. (1988). *Rethinking psychiatry: From cultural category to personal experience.* New York: Macmillan.

Knable, M. B., & Weinberger, D. R. (1997). Dopamine, the prefrontal cortex, and schizophrenia. *Journal of Psychopharmacology, 11,* 123–131.

Knight, C. (2000). The evolution of cooperative communication. In M. Studdert-Kennedy, J. R. Hurford, & C. Knight (Eds.), *The evolutionary emergence of language: Social function and the origins of linguistic form.* Cambridge, UK: Cambridge University Press.

Knowles, J. (1977). The responsibility of the individual. In J. Knowles (Ed.), *Doing better and feeling worse: Health in the United States* 1–7. New York: Norton.

Kobasa, S. C. O. (1979). Stressful life events, personality, and health: An inquiry into hardiness. *Journal of Personality and Social Psychology, 37*, 1–11.

Kobasa, S. C. O., Maddi, S. R., & Kahn, S. (1982). Hardiness and health: A prospective study. *Journal of Personality and Social Psychology, 42*, 168–177.

Koenigsberger, L. (1965). *Hermann von Helmholtz*. New York: Dover.

Kohlberg, L. (1969). Stage and sequence: The cognitive developmental approach to socialization. In D. A. Goslin (Ed.), *Handbook of socialization theory and research*. Chicago: Rand-McNally.

Kohlberg, L. (1984). *The psychology of moral development: Essays on moral development (Vol. II)*. San Francisco: Harper & Row.

Köhler, W. (1925). *The mentality of apes*. New York: Harcourt Brace.

Kohn, P. M., & Gurevich, M. (1993). The adequacy of the indirect method of measuring the primary appraisal of hassles-based stress. *Personality and Individual Differences, 14*, 679–684.

Kohn, P. M., Lafreniere, K., & Gurevich, M. (1990). The Inventory of College Students' Recent Life Experiences: A decontaminated hassles scale for a special population. *Journal of Behavioral Medicine, 13*, 619–630.

Kolb, B., & Whishaw, I. Q. (1996). *Fundamentals of human neuropsychology* (4th ed.). New York: Freeman.

Kolb, F. C., & Braun, J. (1995). Blindsight in normal observers. *Nature (London), 377*, 336–338.

Koppenaal, R. J. (1963). Time changes in the strengths of A-B, A-C lists: Spontaneous recovery? *Journal of Verbal Learning and Verbal Behavior, 2*, 310–319.

Kosslyn, S. M. (1987). Seeing and imagining in the cerebral hemispheres: A computational approach. *Psychological Review, 94*, 148–175.

Kotovsky, K., Hayes, J. R., & Simon, H. A. (1985). Why are some problems hard? Evidence from Tower of Hanoi. *Cognitive Psychology, 17*, 248–294.

Kottak, C. P. (1994). *Anthropology* (6th ed.). New York: McGraw-Hill.

Kramer, A. F., & Hahn, S. (1995). Splitting the beam: Distribution of attention over noncontiguous regions of the visual field. *Psychological Science, 6*, 381–386.

Krause, S. J. (1995). Attitudes and the prediction of behavior: A meta-analysis of the empirical literature. *Personality and Social Psychology Bulletin, 21*, 58–75.

Kriegman, D. (1988). Self psychology from the perspective of evolutionary biology: Toward a biological foundation for self psychology. In A. Goldberg (Ed.), *Progress in self psychology* (Vol. 3, pp. 253–274). Hillsdale, NJ: Analytic Press.

Krohn, A. (1980). Some clinical manifestations of structural defects in a borderline personality. *International Journal of Psychoanalytic Psychotherapy, 8*, 337–362.

Krosnick, J. A., Betz, A. L., Jussim, L. J., & Lynn, A. R. (1992). Subliminal conditioning of attitudes. *Personality and Social Psychology Bulletin, 18*, 152–162.

Krueger, T. H. (1976). *Visual imagery in problem solving and scientific creativity*. Derby, CT: Seal Press.

Kuffler, S. W. (1953). Discharge patterns and functional organization of mammalian retina. *Journal of Neurophysiology, 16*, 37–68.

Kuhl, P. K., William, K. A., Lacerda, F., Stephens, K., & Lindblom, B. (1992). Linguistic experiences alter phonetic perception in infants by 6 months of age. *Science, 255*, 606–608.

Kurtz, N. M. (1990). *Monoamine oxidase inhibiting drugs*. In J. D. Amsterdam (Ed.), *Pharmacotherapy of depression*. New York: Marcel Dekker.

LaBarba, R. C., Kingsberg, S. A., & Martin, P. K. (1992). Cerebral lateralization of unfamiliar music perception in nonmusicians. *Psychomusicology, 11*, 119–124.

Lamb, M. E. (1985). Security of infantile attachment as assessed in the "Strange Situation:" Its study and biological interpretation. *Annual Progress in Child Psychiatry and Child Development*, 53–114.

Lambert, M. J., & Hill, C. E. (1994). Assessing psychotherapy outcomes and processes. In A. E. Bergin & S. L. Garfield (Eds.), *Handbook of psychotherapy and behavior change* (4th ed.). New York: Wiley.

Langer, E. J., & Rodin, J. (1976). The effects of choice and enhanced personal responsibility for the aged: A field experiment in an institutional setting. *Journal of Personality and Social Psychology, 34*, 191–198.

Langley, P., Simon, H. A., Bradshaw, G. L., & Zytkow, J. M. (1986). *Scientific discovery: Computational explorations of the creative processes*. Cambridge, MA: MIT Press.

Langlois, J. H., Ritter, J. M., Roggman, L. A., & Vaughn, L. S. (1991). Facial diversity and infant preferences for attractive faces. *Developmental Psychology, 27*, 79–84.

Langlois, J. H., & Roggman, L. A. (1990). Attractive faces are only average. *Psychological Science, 1*, 115–121.

Langlois, J. H., Roggman, L. A., & Musselman, L. (1994). What is average and what is not average about attractive faces? *Psychological Science, 5*, 214–220.

Lapml, M., Veldhuis, J. D., & Johnson, M. L. (1992). Saltation and stasis: A model of human growth. *Science, 258*, 801–803.

Larsen, K. S. (1990). The Asch conformity experiment: Replication and transhistorical comparisons. *Journal of Social Behavior and Personality, 5*, 163–168.

Larson, R. W., & Bradney, N. (1988). Precious moments with family members and friends. In R. M. Milardo (Ed.), *Family and social networks*. Newbury Park, CA: Sage.

Latané, B., & Nida, S. A. (1981). Ten years of research on group size and helping. *Psychological Bulletin, 89*, 308–334.

Latanè B., Williams, K., & Harkins, S. (1979). Many hands make light the work: The causes and consequences of social loafing. *Journal of Personality and Social Psychology, 37*, 822–832.

Laudenslager, M. L., Ryan, S. M., Drugan, R. C., Hyson, R. L., & Maier, S. E. (1983). Coping and immunosuppression: Inescapable but not escapable shock suppresses lymphocyte proliferation. *Science, 221*, 568–570.

Lazarus, R. (1984). Puzzles in the study of daily hassles. *Journal of Behavioral Medicine, 7*, 735–789.

Lazarus, R., & Folkman, S. (1984). *Stress, appraisal, and coping*. New York: Springer.

Le Souef, P. N., Goldblatt, J., & Lynch, N. R. (2000). Evolutionary adaptation of inflammatory immune responses in human beings. *Lancet, 356*, 242–244.

Leavens, D. A., Hopkins, W. D., & Bard, K. A. (1996). Indexical and referential pointing in chimpanzees (Pan troglodytes). *Journal of Comparative Psychology, 110*, 346–353.

Lee, Y. T., & Seligman, M. E. P. (1997). Are Americans more optimistic than the Chinese? *Personality and Social Psychology Bulletin, 23*, 32–40.

Lefcourt, H. M., & Thomas, S. (1998). Humor and stress revisited. In W. Ruch (Ed.), *The sense of humor: Explorations of a personality characteristic*. Berlin, Germany: Walter De Gruyter.

Leff, J. (1988). *Psychiatry around the globe: A transcultural view*. (2nd ed.). London: Gaskell.

Legge, J. (Trans.). (1964). *I Ching: Book of Changes*. Secaucus, NJ: Citadel Press.

Leiner, H. C., Leiner, A. L., & Dow, R. S. (1993). Cognitive and language functions of the human cerebellum. *Trends in Neurosciences, 16*, 444–447.

Leitenberg, H., Gross, J., Peterson, J., & Rosen, J. C. (1984). Analysis of an anxiety model and the process of change during exposure plus response prevention treatment of bulimia nervosa. *Behavior Therapy, 15*, 3–20.

Lepper, M. R., Green, D., & Nisbett, R. E. (1973). Undermining children's intrinsic interest with extrinsic reward: A test of the "overjustification" hypothesis. *Journal of Personality and Social Psychology, 28*, 129–137.

Lerner, M. J., & Miller, D. T. (1978). Just world research and the attribution process: Looking back and ahead. *Psychological Bulletin, 85*, 1030–1051.

Lester, D., Nachman, M., & LeMagnen, J. (1970). Aversive conditioning by ethanol in the rat. *Quarterly Journal of Studies on Alcohol, 31*, 578–586.

Lettvin, J. Y., Maturana, H. R., McCulloch, W. S., & Pitts, W. H. (1959). What the frog's eye tells the frog's brain. *Proceedings of the IRE, 47*(11), 1940–1951.

Levine, S. C., & Carey, S. (1982). Up front: The acquisition of a concept and a word. *Journal of Child Language, 9*, 645–657.

Levitsky, D. A., & Strupp, B. J. (1995). Malnutrition and the brain: Changing concepts, changing concerns. *Journal of Nutrition, 125*(8 Suppl.), S2212–S2220.

Levy, J. (1969). Possible basis for the evolution of lateral specialization of the human brain. *Nature, 224*, 614–615.

Lewis, M., & Bendersky, M. (Eds.). (1995). *Mothers, babies, and cocaine: The role of toxins in development.* Mahwah, NJ: Erlbaum.

Lickey, M. E., & Gordon, B. (1991). *Medicine and mental illness.* New York: Freeman.

Lidow, M. S., Williams, G. V., & Goldman-Rakic, P. S. (1998). The cerebral cortex: A case for a common site of action of antipsychotics. *Trends in Pharmacological Science, 19*, 136–140.

Lieberman, P. (1991). *Uniquely human: The evolution of speech, thought, and selfless behavior.* Cambridge, MA: Harvard University Press.

Light, P., & Perrett-Clermont, A. N. (1989). Social context effects in learning and testing. In A. Gellatly, D. Rogers, & J. Sloboda (Eds.), *Cognition and social worlds.* Oxford: Clarendon Press.

Lilly, J. C. (1961). *Man and dolphin.* New York: Doubleday.

Lindsay, E. W., Mize, J., & Pettit, G. S. (1997). Differential play patterns of mothers and fathers of sons and daughters: Implications for children's gender role development. *Sex Roles, 37*, 643–650.

Lindsay, P. H., & Norman, D. A. (1972). *Human information processing: An introduction to psychology.* New York: Academic Press.

Lindsay, P. H., & Norman, D. A. (1977). *Human information processing: An introduction to psychology* (2nd ed.). New York: Academic Press.

Lipsitt, L. P., & Behl, G. (1990). Taste-mediated differences in the sucking behavior of human newborns. In E. D. Capaldi & T. L. Powley (Eds.), *Taste, experience, and feeding*, 75–93. Washington, DC: American Psychological Association.

Livesley, W. J., Schroeder, M. L., Jackson, D. N., & Jang, K. L. (1994). Categorical distinctions in the study of personality disorder: Implications for classification. *Journal of Abnormal Psychology, 103*, 6–17.

Livingstone, M. S. (2000). Is it warm? Is it real? Or just low spatial frequency? *Science, 290*, 1229.

Locke, S. (1985). *Foundations of psychoneuroimmunology.* New York: Aldine.

Loeber, R., & Hay, D. (1997). Key issues in the development of aggression and violence from childhood to early adulthood. *Annual Review of Psychology, 48*, 371–410.

Loehlin, J. C. (1992). *Genes and environment in personality development.* Newbury Park, CA: Sage.

Loehlin, J. C., Horn, J. M., & Willerman, L. (1997). Heredity, environment, and IQ in the Texas Adoption Project. In R. J. Sternberg & E. L. Grigorenko (Eds.), *Intelligence, heredity, and environment.* New York: Cambridge University Press.

Loewen, E. R., Shaw, R. J., & Craik, F. I. M. (1990). Age differences in components of metamemory. *Experimental Aging Research, 16*, 43–48.

Loftus, E. (1979). *Eyewitness testimony.* Cambridge, MA: Harvard University Press.

Loftus, E. (1997, September). Creating false memories. *Scientific American*, pp. 70–75.

Loftus, E., & Klinger, M. R. (1992). Is the unconscious smart or dumb. *American Psychologist, 47*, 761–765.

Loftus, E., & Palmer, J. C. (1974). Reconstruction of automobile destruction: An example of the interaction between language and memory. *Journal of Verbal Learning and Verbal Behavior, 13*, 585–589.

Loftus, E. F., Miller, D. G., & Burns, H. J. (1978). Semantic integration of verbal information into a visual memory. *Journal of Experimental Psychology, 4*, 19–31.

Long, M. L., & Simon, R. J. (1974). The roles and statuses of women on children and family TV programs. *Journalism Quarterly, 51*, 107–110.

Lorenz, K. (1966). *On aggression.* New York: Harcourt, Brace, & World.

Luchins, A. S. (1942). Mechanization in problem solving. *Psychological Monographs, 54* (6, Whole No. 248).

Ludwig, A. M. (1995). *The price of greatness: Resolving the creativity and madness controversy.* New York: Guilford Press.

Luria, A. R. (1968). *The mind of a mnemonist.* New York: Basic Books.

Lykken, D. (1995). *The antisocial personalities.* Mahwah, NJ: Erlbaum.

Lynch, M. P. (1996). And what of human musicality? *Behavioral and Brain Sciences, 19*, 796–798.

Lynn, R. (1990). The role of nutrition in secular increases in intelligence. *Personality and Individual Differences, 11*, 273–285.

Lynn, R. (1993). Further evidence for the existence of race and sex differences in cranial capacity. *Social Behavior and Personality, 21*, 89–92.

Lynn, R. (1998). In support of the nutrition theory. In U. Neisser, (Ed.), *The rising curve: Long-term gains in IQ and related measures*, 207–218. Washington, DC: American Psychological Association.

Lynn, S. J., & Rhue, J. W. (Eds.). (1994). *Dissociation: Clinical and theoretical perspectives.* New York: Guilford Press.

Macaluso, E., Frith, C., & Drive, J. (2000). Modulation of human visual cortex by crossmodal spatial attention. *Science, 286*, 1206–1208.

Mackenzie, S. A., Oltenacu, E. A. B., & Houpt, K. A. (1986). Canine behavioral genetics-A review. *Applied Animal Behavior Science*, 15, 365–393.

MacKinnon, D. F., Jamison, K. R., & DePaulo, J. R. (1997). Genetics of manic depressive illness. *Annual Review of Psychology, 20*, 355–373.

MacNeilage, P. F. (1991). The postural origins theory of neurobiological asymmetries in primates. In N. Krasnegor, D. Rumbaugh, M. Studdert-Kennedy, & R. Schiefelbusch (Eds.), *The biological foundations of language development.* Hillsdale, NJ: Erlbaum.

Maher, B. A., & Spitzer, M. (1993). Delusions. In P. B. Sutker & H. E. Adams (Eds.), *Comprehensive handbook of psychopathology* (2nd ed.). New York: Plenum.

Maier, S. F., & Jackson, R. L. (1979). Learned helplessness: All of us were right (and wrong): Inescapable shock has multiple effects. In G. H. Bower (Ed.), *The psychology of learning and motivation* (Vol. 13). New York: Academic Press.

Maier, S. F., & Watkins, L. R. (1999). Bidirectional communication between the brain and the immune system: Implications for behavior. *Animal Behaviour, 57*, 741–751.

Malberg, J. E., Eisch, A. J., Nestler, E. J., & Duman, R. S. (2000). Chronic antidepressant treatment increases neurogenesis in adult rat hippocampus. *The Journal of Neuroscience, 20*, 9104–9110.

Malina, R. M. (1975). *Growth and development: The first twenty years in man.* Minneapolis: Burgess Publishing.

Mandel, D. R., Juscyzk, P. W., & Pisoni, D. B. (1995). Infants' recognition of the sound patterns of their own names. *Psychological Science, 6*, 314–317.

Marcel, A. (1983). Conscious and unconscious perception: Experiments on visual masking and word recognition. *Cognitive Psychology, 15*, 197–237.

Markus, H. R., & Kitayama, S. (1991). Culture and the self: Implications for cognition, emotion, and motivation. *Psychological Review, 98*, 224–253.

Marler, P., & Peters, S. (1988). Sensitive periods for song acquisition from tape recordings and live tutors in the swamp sparrow, *melospiza georgiana*. *Ethology, 77,* 76–84.

Marsh, R. L., & Landau, J. D. (1995). Item availability in cryptomnesia: Assessing its role in two paradigms of unconscious plagiarism. *Journal of Experimental Psychology: Learning, Memory, and Cognition, 18,* 492–508.

Marshall, G. N. (1991). A multidimensional analysis of internal health locus of control beliefs: Separating the wheat from the chaff? *Journal of Personality and Social Psychology, 61,* 483–491.

Marsland, A. L., Cohen, S., Rabin, B. S., & Manuck, S. B. (2001). Associations between stress, trait negative affect, acute immune reactivity, and antibody response to hepatitis B injection in healthy young adults. *Health Psychology, 20,* 4.

Martin, L. (1986). Eskimo words for snow: A case study in the genesis and decay of an anthropological example. *American Psychologist, 88,* 418–423.

Maslow, A. H. (1954). *Motivation and personality.* New York: Harper & Row.

Maslow, A. H. (1968). *Toward a psychology of being.* New York: Van Nostrand.

Masterton, R. B. (1992). Role of the central auditory system in hearing: The new direction. *Trends in Neurosciences, 15,* 280–285.

Matarazzo, J. D. (1994). Health and behavior: The coming together of science and practice in psychology and medicine after a century of benign neglect. *Journal of Clinical Psychology in Medical Settings, 1,* 7–39.

Mathews, D. B., Best, P. J., White, A. M., Vandergriff, J. L., & Simson, P. E. (1996). Ethanol impairs spatial cognitive processing: New behavioral and electrophysiological findings. *Current Directions in Psychological Science, 5,* 111–115.

Matts, J. P., Buchwald, H., Fitch, L. L., Campos, C. T., Varco, R. L., Campbell, G. S., Pearce, M. B., Yellin, A. E., Smink, R. D., Jr., Sawin, H. S ., Jr., & Long, J. M. (1995). Subgroup analyses of the major clinical endpoints in the program on the surgical control of the hyperlipidemias (Posch): Overall mortality, atherosclerotic coronary heart disease (ACHD) mortality, and ACHD mortality or myocardial infarction. *Journal of Clinical Epidemiology, 48,* 389–405.

Mayberry, R. I., & Eichen, E. B. (1991). The long-lasting advantage of learning sign language in childhood: Another look at the critical period for language acquisition. *Journal of Memory and Language, 30,* 486–512.

Mayr, E. (1991). *One long argument: Charles Darwin and the genesis of modern evolutionary theory.* Cambridge, MA: Harvard University Press.

Mays, L. C. (1991). Exploring internal and external worlds: Reflections on being curious. *Psychoanalytic Study of the Child, 46,* 3–36.

McAnarney, E. R. (1984). Touching and adolescent sexuality. In C. C. Brown (Ed.), *The many facets of touch.* Pediatric Round Table: 10. The Johnson and Johnson Baby Products Company.

McArthur, D. (1995). Language: Mosaic or special faculty? *Sign-Language Studies, 86,* 37–44.

McClelland, D. C. (1985). How motives, skills and values determine what people do. *American Psychologist, 40,* 812–835.

McClelland, D. C., & Cheriff, A. D. (1997). The immunoenhancing effects of humor on secretory IgA and resistance to respiratory infections. *Psychology and Health, 12,* 329–344.

McClelland, D. C., & Koestner, R. (1992). The achievement motive. In C. P. Smith (Ed.), *Motivation and personality: Handbook of thematic content analysis.* New York: Cambridge University Press.

McClintock, M. K. (1971). Menstrual synchrony and suppression. *Nature, 229,* 244–245.

McCloskey, M., & Kuhl, D. (1983). Naive physics: The curvilinear impetus principle and its role in interactions with moving objects. *Journal of Experimental Psychology: Learning, Memory, and Cognition, 9,* 146–156.

McCloskey, M., Wible, C. , & Cohen, N. (1988). Is there a special flashbulb memory mechanism? *Journal of Experimental Psychology: General, 117,* 171–181.

McCormick, D. A., & Thompson, R. F. (1984). Cerebellum: Essential involvement in the classically conditioned eyelid response. *Science, 223,* 296–299.

McCrae, R. R., & Costa, P. T. (1990). *Personality in adulthood.* New York: Guilford Press.

McCrae, R. R., & Costa, P. T. (1994). The stability of personality: Observations and evaluations. *Current Directions in Psychological Science, 3,* 173–175.

McCrae, R. R., & Costa, P. T. (1997a). Conceptions and correlates of openness to experience. In R. Hogan, J. Johnson, & S. Briggs, *Handbook of personality psychology.* New York: Academic Press.

McCrae, R. R., & Costa, P. T. (1997b). Personality trait structure as a human universal. *American Psychologist, 52,* 509–516.

McDonald, J. J., Teder-Salejarvi, W. A., & Hillyard, S. A. (2000). Involuntary orienting to sound improves visual perception. *Nature, 407,* 906–908.

McGeoch, J. A., & McDonald, W. T. (1931). Meaningful relation and retroactive inhibition. *American Journal of Psychology, 43,* 579–588.

McGuffin, P., Katz, R., Watkins, S., & Rutherford, J. (1996). A hospital-based twin register of the heritability of *DSM-IV* unipolar depression. *Archives of General Psychiatry, 53,* 129–136.

McGuire, W. (Ed.). (1974). *The Freud/Jung letters.* Princeton, NJ: Princeton University Press.

McGuire, W. (1986). The myth of massive media impact: Savagings and salvagings. In G. Comstock (Ed.), *Public communication and behavior* (Vol. 1). New York: Academic Press.

McGuire, W. J. (1961). The effectiveness of supportive and refutational defenses in immunizing and restoring beliefs against persuasion. *Sociometry, 24,* 184–197.

McGuire, W. J. (1985). Attitudes and attitude change. In G. Lindzey and E. Aronson (Eds.), *Handbook of social psychology.* Reading, MA: Addison-Wesley.

McKim, W. A. (1991). *Drugs and behavior* (2nd ed.). Englewood Cliffs, NJ: Prentice-Hall.

McKim, W. A. (1997). *Drugs and behavior: An introduction to behavioral pharmacology* (3rd ed.). Upper Saddle River, NJ: Prentice Hall.

McKinlay, J. B., & McKinlay, S. M. (1977). The questionable contribution of medical measures to the decline of mortality in the United States in the twentieth century. *Millbank Memorial Fund Quarterly–Health and Society, 55,* 405–428.

McNally, R. J. (1987). Preparedness and phobias: A review. *Psychological Bulletin, 101,* 283–303.

Meany, M. J., Aitken, D. H., Van Berkel, C., Bhatnagar, S., & Sapolsky, R. M. (1988). Effect of neonatal handling on age-related impairments with the hippocampus. *Science, 239,* 766–768.

Medin, D. L., & Ross, B. H. (1990). *Cognitive psychology.* Fort Worth, TX: Harcourt Brace Jovanovich.

Meehl, P. E. (1962). Schizotaxia, schizotypy, schizophrenia. *American Psychologist, 17,* 827–838.

Meehl, P. E. (1990). Toward an integrated theory of schizotaxia, schizotypy, schizophrenia. *Journal of Personality Disorders, 4,* 1–99.

Meeus, W. H. J., & Raaijmakers, Q. A. W. (1986). Carrying out orders to use psychological-administrative violence. *European Journal of Social Psychology, 16,* 311–324.

MeGargee, E. I. (1986). A psychometric study of incarcerated presidential threateners. *Criminal Justice & Behavior, 4,* 1–116.

Meier, R. P. (1991). Language acquisition by deaf children. *American Scientist, 79,* 60–70.

Meltzoff, A. N., & Moore, M. K. (1977). Imitation of facial and manual gestures by human neonates. *Science, 198,* 75–78.

Meltzoff, A. N., & Moore, M. K. (1989). Imitation in newborn infants: Exploring the range of gestures imitated and the underlying mechanism. *Developmental Psychology, 25*, 954–962.

Melzack, R. (1992, April). Phantom limbs. *Scientific American*, pp. 120–126.

Melzack, R., & Wall, P. D. (1982). Pain mechanisms: A new theory. *Science, 150*, 971–979.

Mendelson, W. B. (1993). Sleeping pills. In M. A. Carskadon (Ed.), *Encyclopedia of sleep and dreaming*. New York: Macmillan.

Menzel, E. W. (1978). Cognitive mapping in chimpanzees. In S. H. Hulse, H. F. Fowler, & W. K. Honig (Eds.), *Cognitive processes in animal behavior*. Hillsdale, NJ: Erlbaum.

Mersky, H. (1992). The manufacture of personalities. The production of multiple personality disorder. *British Journal of Psychiatry, 160*, 327–340.

Meyer, J., Huberth, A., Ortega, G., Syagailo, Y. V., Jatzke, S., Messner, R., Ulzheimer-Teuber, I., Schmitt, A., & Lesch, K. (2001). A missense mutation in a novel gene encoding a putative cation channel is associated with catatonic schizophrenia in a large pedigree. *Molecular Psychiatry, 6*, 304–308.

Micale, M. (1995). *Approaching hysteria: Disease and its interpretations*. Princeton, NJ: Princeton University Press.

Michaels, J. W., Bloomel, J. M., Brocato, R. M., Linkous, R. A., & Rowe, J. S. (1982). Social facilitation and inhibition in a natural setting. *Replications in Social Psychology, 2*, 21–24.

Miles, D. R., & Carey, G. (1997). Genetics and environmental architecture of human aggression. *Journal of Personality and Social Psychology, 72*, 207–217.

Miles, L. E., Raynal, D. M., & Wilson, M. A. (1979). Blind man living in normal society has circadian rhythms of 24.9 hours. *Science, 198*, 421–423.

Milgram, S. (1963). Behavioral studies of obedience. *Journal of Abnormal Psychology, 67*, 371–378.

Milgram, S. (1974). *Obedience to authority*. New York: Harper & Row.

Miller, D. J., & Kotses, D. J. (1995). Classical conditioning of total respiratory resistance in humans. *Psychosomatic Medicine, 57*, 148–153.

Miller, G. A. (1956). The magical number seven plus or minus two: Some limits on our capacity for processing information. *Psychological Review, 63*, 81–97.

Miller, J. G. (1984). Culture and the development of everyday social explanation. *Journal of Personality and Social Psychology, 46*, 961–978.

Miller, L. (1993). *Psychiatric disorders during pregnancy*. Washington, DC: American Psychiatric Press.

Miller, N. (1985). The value of behavioral research on animals. *American Psychologist, 40*, 423–440.

Millon, T. (1981). Personality disorders: Conceptual distinctions and classification issues. In P. T. Costa, Jr., & T. A. Widger (Eds.), *Personality disorders and the five-factor model of personality*. Washington, DC: American Psychological Association.

Milner, B. (1970). Memory and medial temporal regions of the brain. In K. H. Pribram & D. E. Broadbent (Eds.), *Biology of memory*. Orlando, FL: Academic Press.

Milner, B., Corkin, B., & Teuber, H. L. (1968). Further analysis of the hippocampal amnesic syndrome: 14 year follow-up of H. M. *Neuropsychologia, 6*, 215–234.

Miluk-Kolasa, B., Matejek, M., & Stupnicki, R. (1996). The effects of music listening on changes in selected physiological parameters in adult pre-surgical patients. *Journal of Music Therapy, 33*, 208–218.

Mischel, W. (1961). Delay of gratification, need for achievement, and acquiescence in another culture. *Journal of Abnormal and Social Psychology, 62*, 543–552.

Mistretta, C., & Bradley, B. (1977). Taste in utero: Theoretical considerations. In J. M. Weiffenbach (Ed.), *Taste and development: The genesis of sweet preference* (DHEW Publication No. (NIH) 77-1068). Bethesda, MD: NIH.

Mita, T. H., Dermer, M., & Knight, J. (1977). Reversed facial images and the mere-exposure hypothesis. *Journal of Personality and Social Psychology, 35*, 597–601.

Modestin, J., Ammann, R., & Wurmie, O. (1995). Season of birth: Comparison of patients with schizophrenia, affective disorders, and alcoholism. *Acta Psychiatrica Scandinavica, 91*, 140–143.

Moellering, R. C. Jr. (1998). Antibiotic resistance: Lessons for the future. *Clinical Infectious Diseases, 27* (Suppl. 1), 135–140.

Moerk, E. L. (1990). Three-term contingency patterns in mother-child verbal interactions during first-language acquisition. *Journal of the Experimental Analysis of Behavior, 54*, 293–305.

Moffitt, T. E., Caspi, A., Harkness, A. R., & Silva, P. A. (1993). The natural history of change in intellectual performance: Who changes? How much? Is it meaningful? *Journal of Child Psychology and Psychiatry, 34*, 455–506.

Moltz, H. (1963). Imprinting: An epigenetic approach. *Psychological Review, 70*, 123–138.

Money, J. (1987). Sin, sickness, or status? Homosexual gender identity and psychoneuroendocrinology. *American Psychologist, 42*, 384–399.

Money, J., & Ehrhardt, A. A. (1972). *Man and woman, boy and girl*. Baltimore: Johns Hopkins University.

Montagna, W. (1965). The skin. *Scientific American, 212*, 58–59.

Moore, C. I., Stern, C. E., Dunbar, C., Kostyk, S. K., Gehi, A., & Corkin, S. (2000). Referred phantom sensations and cortical reorganization after spinal cord injury in humans. *Proceedings of the National Academy of Science (USA), 97*, 14703–14708.

Moore-Ede, M. C., Czeisler, C. A., & Richardson, G. S. (1983). Circadian timekeeping in health and disease. *New England Journal of Medicine, 309*, 469–476.

Morey, L. C. (1988). Personality disorders in the *DSM-III* and *DSM-III-R*: Convergence, coverage, and internal consistency. *American Journal of Psychiatry, 145*, 573–577.

Morgan, C. L. (1891). *An introduction to comparative psychology*. London: Scott.

Morgan, C. L. (1928). Mind in evolution. In F. Mason (Ed.), *Creation by evolution*. New York: Macmillan.

Morris, D. (1967). *The naked ape*. London: Jonathan Cape.

Morris, J. S., Frith, C. D., Perrett, D. I., Rowland, D., Young, A. W., Calder, A. J., & Dolan, R. J. (1996). A differential neural response in the human amygdala to fearful and happy expressions. *Nature, 383*, 812–815.

Moschovakis, A. K., & Highstein, S. M. (1994). The anatomy and physiology of primate neurons that control rapid eye movements. *Annual Review of Neuroscience, 17*, 465–488.

Mullin, C. R., & Linz, D. (1995). Desensitization and resensitization to violence against women: Effects of exposure to sexually violent films on judgments of domestic violence victims. *Journal of Personality and Social Psychology, 69*, 449–459.

Munoz, M., Vazquez, C., Bermejo, M., & Vazquez, J. J. (1999). Stressful life events among homeless people: Quantity, types, timing, and perceived causality. *Journal of Community Psychology, 27*, 73–87.

Murdock, B. (1962). The serial position effect of free recall. *Journal of Experimental Psychology, 64*, 482–488.

Murphy, K. R., & Davidshofer, C. O. (1998). *Psychological testing: Principles and applications* (4th ed.). Upper Saddle River, NJ: Prentice Hall.

Murray, H. A. (1938). *Explorations in personality*. New York: Oxford University Press.

Narrow, W. E., Regier, D. A., Rae, D. S., Manderscheid, R. W., & Locke, B. Z. (1993). Use of services by persons with mental and addictive disorders: Findings from the National Institute of Mental Health Epidemiologic Catchment Area Program. *Archives of General Psychiatry, 50*, 95–107.

Nathan, P. E. (1993). Alcoholism: Psychopathology, etiology, and treatment. In P. B. Sutker & H. E. Adams (Eds.), *Comprehensive handbook of psychopathology*. New York: Plenum Press.

National Center for Health Statistics. (1995). *Family structure and children's health: United States, 1988*. (Vital and Health Statistics, Series 10, No. 178, DHHS Publication No. PHS 92-1232, Table 27). Washington, D.C.

National Commission for the Protection of Human Subjects in Biomedical and Behavioral Research. (1978). Washington, D.C.: National Academy Press.

National Institutes of Mental Health. (1999). Available: http://www.nimh.nih.gov/publicat/numbers.cfm.

National Vital Statistics Reports. (1996). Vol. 47, No. 9, National Center for Health Statistics, Centers for Disease Control and Prevention, U.S. Department of Health and Human Services.

Naveh-Benjamin, M., & Ayres, T. J. (1986). Digit span, reading rate, and linguistic relativity. *Quarterly Journal of Experimental Psychology, 38*, 739–751.

Neiberg, P., Marks, J. S., McLaren, N. M., & Remongton, P. (1985). The fetal tobacco syndrome. *Journal of the American Medical Association, 253*, 2998–2999.

Neisser, U. (1967). *Cognitive psychology*. New York: Appleton-Century-Crofts.

Neisser, U. (1976). General, academic, and artificial intelligence. In L. B. Resnick (Ed.), *The nature of intelligence*. Hillsdale, NJ: Erlbaum.

Neisser, U. (1998). *The rising curve: Long-term gains in IQ and related measures*. Washington, DC: American Psychological Association.

Neisser, U., Boodoo, G., Bouchard, T. J. Jr., Boykin, A. W., Brody, N., Ceci, S. J., Halpern, D. F., Loehlin, J. C., Perloff, R., Sternberg, R. J., & Urbina, S. (1996). Intelligence: Knowns and unknowns. *American Psychologist, 51*, 77–101.

Neisser, U., & Harsh, N. (1992). Phantom flashbulbs: False recollections of hearing the news about the *Challenger*. In E. Winograd & U. Neisser (Eds,), *Affect and accuracy in recall: Studies of 'flashbulb memory'* (pp. 9–31). New York: Cambridge University Press.

Nelson, C. A. (1999). Neural plasticity and human development. *Current Directions in Psychological Science, 8*, 42–45.

Nelson, K. (1993). The psychological and social origins of autobiographical memory. *Psychological Science, 4*, 7–14.

Nelson, R. J., Badura, L. L., & Goldman, B. D. (1990). Mechanisms of seasonal cycles of behavior. *Annual Review of Psychology, 41*, 81–108.

Nesse, R. M. (2000). Is depression an adaptation? *Archives of General Psychiatry, 57*, 14–20.

Nesse, R. M., & Berridge, K. C. (1997). Psychoactive drug use in evolutionary perspective. *Science, 278*, 63–66.

Nesse, R. M., & Williams, G. C. (1994). *Why we get sick: The new science of Darwinian medicine*. New York: Vintage Books.

Nettle, D. (2001). *Strong imagination: Madness, creativity and human nature*. New York: Oxford University Press.

Neugebauer, R., Dohrenwend, B. P., & Dohrenwend, B. S. (1980). Formulation of hypotheses about the true prevalence of functional psychiatric disorders among adults in the United States. In B. P. Dohrenwend, B. S. Dohrenwend, M. D. Gould., B. Link, R. Neugebauer, & R. Wunsch-Hitzig (Eds.), *Mental illness in the United States: Epidemiological estimates*. New York: Praeger.

Newcombe, F. (1987). Psychometric and behavioral evidence: Scope, limitations, and ecological validity. In H. S. Levin, J. Grafman, & H. M. Eisenberg (Eds.), *Neurobehavioral recovery from head injury*. New York: Oxford University Press.

Newell, A., & Simon, H. A. (1972). *Human problem solving*. Englewood Cliffs, NJ: Prentice Hall.

Nicholson, A. N., Pascoe, P. A., Spencer, M. B., Stone, B. M., Roehrs, T., & Rothe, T. (1986). Sleep after transmeridian flights. *Lancet, 2*, 1205–1208.

Nickerson, R. S., & Adams, M. J. (1979). Long-term memory for a common object. In U. Neisser (Ed.), *Memory observed*, 163–175. San Francisco: Freeman.

Nielson, S. L., & Sarason, I. G. (1981). Emotion, personality, and selective attention. *Journal of Personality and Social Psychology, 41*, 945–960.

Niemi , R. G., Mueller, J., & Smith, T. W. (1989). *Trends in public opinion: A compendium of survey data*. New York: Greenwood Press.

Nietzel, M. T., Bernstein, D. A., & Milich, R. (1994). *Introduction to clinical psychology* (4th ed.). Upper Saddle River, NJ: Prentice-Hall.

Nigg, J. T., & Gold, H. H. (1994). Genetics of personality disorders: Perspectives from personality and psychopathology research. *Psychological Bulletin, 115*, 346–380.

Norman, W. T. (1963). Toward an adequate taxonomy of personality attributes: Replicated factor structure in peer nomination personality ratings. *Journal of Abnormal and Social Psychology, 66*, 574–583.

Nottebohm, F. (1980). Testosterone triggers growth of brain vocal control nuclei in adult female canaries. *Brain Research, 189*, 429–436.

Nottebohm, F. (1991). Reassessing the mechanisms and origins of vocal learning in birds. *Trends in Neurosciences, 14*, 206–211.

O'Banion, M. K., Coleman, P. D., & Callahan, L. M. (1994). Regional neuronal loss in aging and Alzheimer's disease: A brief review. *Seminars in the Neurosciences, 6*, 307–314.

Okun, M. A., Stock, W. A., Haring, M. J., & Witter, R. A. (1985). Health and subjective well being: A meta-analysis. *International Journal of Aging and Human Development, 19*, 111–132.

Oldham, J. M., Skodol, A. E., Kellman, H. D., Hyler, S. E., Doidge, N., Rosnick, L., & Gallaher, P. E. (1995). Comorbidity of axis I and axis II disorders. *American Journal of Psychiatry, 152*, 571–578.

Olds, J. (1969). The central nervous system and the reinforcement of behavior. *American Psychologist, 24*, 114–118.

Olds, J., & Milner, P. (1954). Positive reinforcement produced by electrical stimulation of septal area and other regions of the rat brain. *Journal of Comparative & Physiological Psychology, 47*, 419–427.

Olfson, M., & Pincus, H. A. (1996). Outpatient mental health care in nonhospital settings: Distribution of patients across provider groups. *American Journal of Psychiatry, 153*, 1353–1356.

Oltmanns, T. F., & Emery, R. E. (1998). *Abnormal psychology*. Upper Saddle River, NJ: Prentice Hall.

Orne, M. T., Dinges, D. F., & Orne, E. C. (1984). The differential diagnosis of multiple personality in the forensic court. *International Journal of Clinical and Experimental Hypnosis, 13*, 118–169.

Ostrom, T. M., & Sedikides, C. (1992). Out-group homogeneity effects in natural and minimal groups. *Psychological Bulletin, 112*, 536–552.

O'Toole, B. I. (1990). Intelligence and behaviour and motor vehicle accident mortality. *Accident Analysis & Prevention, 22*, 211–221.

Oullette, S. C. (1993). Inquiries into hardiness. In L. Goldberger & S. Breznitz (Eds.), *Handbook of stress: Theoretical and clinical aspects* (2nd ed.). New York: Free Press.

Overmier, B., & Seligman, M. (1967). Effects of inescapable shock upon subsequent escape and avoidance responding. *Journal of Comparative and Physiological Psychology, 63*, 28–33.

Paikoff, R. L., & Brooks-Gunn, J. (1991). Do parent child relationships change during puberty? *Psychological Bulletin, 110*, 47–66.

Pallis, C. A. (1955). Impaired identification of faces and places with agnosia for colors: Report of a case due to cerebral embolism. *Journal of Neurology, Neurosurgery, and Psychiatry, 18*, 218–224.

Panksepp, J. (1998). Attention deficit hyperactivity disorders, psychostimulants, and intolerance of childhood playfulness: A tragedy in the making. *Current Directions in Psychological Science, 7*, 91–98.

Parsons, L. M., Bower, J. M., Gao, J. H., & Xiong, J. (1997). Lateral cerebellar hemispheres actively support sensory acquisition and discrimination rather than motor control. *Learning and Memory, 4,* 49–62.

Pateman, T. (1985). From nativism to sociolinguistics: Integrating a theory of language growth with a theory of speech practices. *Journal for the Theory of Social Behaviour, 15,* 38–59.

Patterson, F., & Linden, E. (1981). *The education of Koko.* New York: Holt, Rinehart, & Winston.

Patton, J. H. (1999, June 8). Personal communication.

Pavlov, I. (1960). *Conditioned reflexes.* New York: Dover. (Original work published 1927.)

Pedersen, P. E., Greer, C. A., & Shepard, G. M. (1988). Early development of olfactory function. In E. M. Blass (Ed.), *Handbook of behavioral neurobiology, Vol. 8, Developmental psychobiology and developmental neurobiology.* New York: Plenum Press.

Pelletier, K. R., & Herzing, D. L. (1988). Psychoneuroimmunology: Towards a mind/body model–A critical review. *Advances: Journal of the Institute for the Advancement of Health, 5,* 1–30.

Penfield, W. G., & Boldrey, E. (1937). Somatic motor and sensory representation in the cerebral cortex of man as studied by electrical stimulation. *Brain, 60,* 389–443.

Pennebaker, J. W. (1997). *Opening up: The healing power of expressing emotions.* New York: Guilford Press.

Peplau, L. A. (1982). Research on homosexual couples: An overview. *Journal of Homosexuality, 8*(2), 3–8.

Pepperberg, I. M. (1991). A communicative approach to animal cognition. A study of the conceptual abilities of an African gray parrot. In C. A. Ristau (Ed.), *Cognitive ethology: The minds of other animals,* 153–186. Hillsdale, NJ: Erlbaum.

Pepperberg, I. M. (1994). Numerical competence in an African gray parrot (Psittacus erithacus). *Journal of Comparative Psychology, 108,* 36–44.

Pepperberg, I. M. (1999). Rethinking syntax: A commentary on E. Kako's "Elements of syntax in the systems of three language-trained animals." *Animal Learning and Behavior, 27,* 15–17.

Pepperberg, I. M., & McLaughlin, M. A. (1996). Effect of avian-human joint attention in allospecific vocal learning by gray parrots (*Psittacus erithacus). Journal of Comparative Psychology, 110,* 286–297.

Perls, F. S. (1969). *Gestalt therapy verbatim.* Lafayette, CA: Real People Press.

Perls, F. S. (1970). Four lectures. In J. Fagan & I. L. Shepherd (Eds.), *Gestalt therapy now.* Palo Alto, CA: Science and Behavior Books.

Perry, A. R., & Laurie, C. A. (1992). Sustained attention and the Type A behavior pattern: The effect of daydreaming on performance. *Journal of General Psychology, 119,* 217–228.

Persinger, M. A. (1996). Subjective pseudocyesis in normal women who exhibit enhanced imaginings and elevated indicators of electrical lability within the temporal lobes: Implications for the "missing embryo syndrome." *Social Behavior and Personality, 24,* 101–112.

Pert, C. B., & Snyder, S. H. (1973). Properties of opiate-receptor binding in the rat brain. *Proceedings of the National Academy of Sciences, USA, 70,* 2243–2247.

Peterson, L. R., & Peterson, M. (1959). Short-term retention of individual verbal items. *Journal of Experimental Psychology, 58,* 193–198.

Petri, H. L., & Mishkin, M. (1994). Behaviorism, cognitivism and the neuropsychology of memory. *American Scientist, 82,* 30–37.

Petrill, S. A., Plomin, R., Berg, S., Johansson, B., Pedersen, N. L., Ahern, F., & McClearn, G. E. (1998). The genetic and environmental relationship between general and specific cognitive abilities in twins age 80 and older. *Psychological Science, 9,* 183–189.

Petty, R. E., & Cacioppo, J. T. (1986). *Communication and persuasion: Central and peripheral routes to attitude change.* New York: Springer-Verlag.

Petty, R. E., Schumann, D. W., Richman, S. A., & Strathman, A. J. (1993). Positive mood and persuasion: Different roles for affect under high and low elaboration conditions. *Journal of Personality and Social Psychology, 64,* 5–20.

Peyser, H. S. (1993). Stress, ethyl alcohol, and alcoholism. In L. Goldberger & S. Breznitz (Eds.), *Handbook of stress: Theoretical and clinical aspects* (2nd ed.). New York: Free Press.

Pfaffman, C. (1960). The pleasures of sensation. *Psychological Review, 67,* 253–268.

Phelps, J. A., Davis, J. O., & Schartz, K. M. (1997). Nature, nurture, and twin research strategies. *Current Directions in Psychological Science, 6,* 117–121.

Phillips, A. G., & Fibiger, H. C. (1989). Neuroanatomical bases of intracranial self-stimulation: Untangling the Gordian Knot. In J. M. Liebman & S. J. Cooper (Eds.), *The neuropharmacological basis of reward* (pp. 66–105). Oxford: Clarendon Press.

Phillips, M. I., & Evans, D. (1995). *Neuroimmunology* (Vol 24). New York: Academic Press.

Piaget, J. (1932). *The origins of intelligence in children.* New York: International University Press. (Reprinted 1952)

Piaget, J., & Inhelder, B. (1956). *The child's conception of space.* London: Routledge & Kegan Paul.

Piaget, J., & Inhelder, B. (1969). *The psychology of the child.* New York: Basic Books.

Piantanida, T. (1988). The molecular genetics of color vision and color blindness. *Trends in Genetics, 4,* 319–323.

Pillemer, D. B., Picariello, M. L., & Pruett, J. C. (1994). Very long-term memories of a salient preschool event. *Applied Cognitive Psychology, 8,* 95–106.

Pillemer, D. B., & White, S. H. (1989). Childhood events recalled by children and adults. In H. W. Reese (Ed.), *Advances in child development and behavior* (Vol 21). New York: Academic Press.

Pinel, J. P. J. (1997). *Biological psychology.* Boston: Allyn & Bacon.

Pinker, S. (1994). *The language instinct.* New York: Morrow.

Pinker, S. (1997). *How the mind works.* New York: Norton.

Pinneau, S. R. (1961). *Changes in intelligence quotient: Infancy to maturity: New insights from the Berkeley Growth Study, with implications for the Stanford-Binet scales, and application to professional practice.* Boston: Houghton Mifflin.

Plaus, S. (1996). Attitudes toward the use of animals in psychological research and education: Results from a national survey of psychology majors. *Psychological Science, 7,* 352–358.

Plomin, R. (1990). The role of inheritance in behavior. *Science, 248,* 223–228.

Plomin, R. (1994). *Genetics and experience: The interplay between nature and nurture in development.* Newbury Park, CA: Sage.

Plomin, R., DeFries, J. C., & Loehlin, J. C. (1977). Genotype-environment interaction and correlation in the analysis of human behavior. *Psychological Bulletin, 84,* 309–322.

Plomin, R., Fulker, D. W., Corley, R., & DeFries, J. C. (1997). Nature, nurture, and cognitive development from 1 to 16 years: A parent-offspring adoption study. *Psychological Science, 8,* 442–447.

Plomin, R., & Petrill, S. A. (1997). Genetics and intelligence: What's new? *Intelligence, 24,* 53–77.

Plumert, A. M., Pick, H. L. Jr., Marks, R. A., Kintsch, A. S., & Wegesin, D. (1994). Locating objects and communicating about locations: Organizational differences in children's searching and direction-giving. *Developmental Psychology, 30,* 443–453.

Plutchik, R. (1984). Emotions: A general psychoevolutionary theory. In K. R. Scherer & P. Ekman (Eds.), *Approaches to emotion.* Hillsdale, NJ: Erlbaum.

Poehlman, E. T. (1989). A review: Exercise and its influence on resting energy metabolism in man. *Medicine and Science in Sports & Exercise, 21,* 515–525.

Pons, T. P., Preston, E., Garraghty, A. K., Kaas, J., Taub, E., & Mishkin, M. (1991). Massive cortical reorganization after sensory deafferentation in adult macaques. *Science, 252,* 1857–1860.

Porter, R., & Teich, M. (Eds.). (1995). *Drugs and narcotics in history.* New York: Cambridge University Press.

Porter, R. H., Makin, J. W., Davis, L. B., & Christensen, K. M. (1992). Breast-fed infants respond to olfactory cues from their own mother and unfamiliar lactating females. *Infant Behavior and Development, 15,* 85–93.

Poulson, C. P., & Kymissis, E. (1990). Generalized imitation in infants. *Journal of Experimental Child Psychology, 46,* 324–336.

Pratkanis, A. R. (1992). The cargo-cult science of subliminal persuasion. *Skeptical Inquirer, 16,* 260–272.

Pratkanis, A. R., & Aronson, E. (1992). *Age of propaganda: The everyday use and abuse of persuasion.* New York: Freeman.

Premack, A. J., & Premack, D. (1972). Teaching language to an ape. *Scientific American, 227,* 92–99.

Prestrude, A. M. (1977). Some phylogenetic comparisons of tonic immobility with special reference to habituation and fear. *Psychological Record, 27,* 21–39.

Profet, M. (1992). Pregnancy sickness as adaptation: A deterrent to maternal ingestion of teratogens. In J. H. Barkow, L. Cosmides, & J. Tooby (Eds.), *The adapted mind: Evolutionary psychology and the generation of culture,* 327–366. New York: Oxford University Press.

Pullum, G. K. (1991). *The great Eskimo vocabulary hoax and other irreverent essays on the study of language.* Chicago: University of Chicago Press.

Rachlin, H. (1995). Self-control: Beyond commitment. *Behavioral and Brain Sciences, 18,* 109–159.

Rajecki, D. W. (1990). *Attitudes.* Sunderland, MA: Sinauer Associates.

Ramachandran, V. S. (1993). Filling in gaps in perception: Part II. Scotomas and phantom limbs. *Current Directions, 2, 56–65.*

Ramsay, D. J., & Thrasher, T. N. (1990). Thirst and water balance. In E. M. Stricker (Ed.), *Handbook of behavioral neurobiology, Vol. 10: Neurobiology of food and fluid intake.* New York: Plenum Press.

Rando, T. A. (1995). Grief and mourning: Accommodating to loss. In H. Wass & R. A. Neimeyer (Eds.), *Dying: Facing the facts.* New York: Taylor & Francis.

Random House Dictionary of the English Language. (1979). New York: Random House.

Rapee, R. M., & Barlow, D. H. (1993). Generalized anxiety disorder, panic disorder, and the phobias. In P. B. Sutker & H. E. Adams (Eds.), *Comprehensive handbook of psychopathology* (2nd ed.). New York: Plenum.

Rapoport, J. L. (1989). *The boy who couldn't stop washing: The experience and treatment of obsessive-compulsive disorder.* New York: Plume.

Rasmussen, T., & Milner, B. (1977). The role of early left brain injury in determining lateralization of cerebral speech functions. *Annals of the New York Academy of Sciences, 299,* 355–369.

Ray, W. J. (1997). EEG concomitants of hypnotic susceptibility. *International Journal of Clinical and Experimental Hypnosis, 45*(3), 301–313.

Razran, G. (1971). *Mind in evolution.* New York: Houghton Mifflin.

Reason, J., & Mycielska, K. (1982). *Absent minded? The psychology of mental lapses and everyday errors.* Upper Saddle River, NJ: Prentice Hall.

Recht, R. D., Lew, L. A., & Schwartz, W. J. (1995). Baseball teams beaten by. *Nature, 377,* 583.

Reed, T. E., & Jensen, A. R. (1992). Conduction velocity in a brain nerve pathway of normal adults correlates with intelligence level. *Intelligence, 16,* 259–272.

Rees, J. A., & Harvey, P. H. (1991). The evolution of mating systems. In V. Reynolds & J. Kellett (Eds.), *Mating and marriage.* New York: Oxford University Press.

Regier, D. A., & Kaelber, C. T. (1995). The Epidemiologic Catchment Area (ECA) program: Studying the prevalence and incidence of psychopathology. In M. T. Tsuang, M. Tohen, & G. E. P. Zahner (Eds.), *Textbook in psychiatric epidemiology.* New York: Wiley.

Reisman, J. M. (1976). *A history of clinical psychology.* New York: Irvington.

Renner, M. J., & Pierre, P. J. (1998). Development of exploration and investigation in the Norway rat (*Rattus norvegicus*). *Journal of General Psychology, 125*(3), 271–291.

Rest, J. R. (1979). *Development in judging moral issues.* Minneapolis: University of Minnesota Press.

Reynolds, D. V. (1969). Surgery in the rat during electrical analgesia induced by local brain stimulation. *Science, 164,* 444–445.

Rhodes, G., Proffitt, F., Grady, J. M., & Sumich, A. (1998). Facial symmetry and the perception of beauty. *Psychonomic Bulletin & Review, 5,* 659–669.

Rhodes, G., Sumich, A., & Byatt, G. (1999). Are average facial configurations attractive only because of their symmetry? *Psychological Science, 10,* 52–58.

Rhodes, N., & Wood, W. (1992). Self-esteem and intelligence affect influenceability: The mediating role of message reception. *Psychological Bulletin, 111,* 156–171.

Ricciuti, H. N. (1993). Nutrition and mental development. *Current Directions in Psychological Science, 2,* 43–46.

Richter, C. (1957). On the phenomenon of sudden death in animals and man. *Psychosomatic Medicine, 19,* 191–198.

Richter, C. P. (1936). Increased salt appetite in adrenalectomized rats. *American Journal of Physiology, 115,* 155–161.

Richter, C. P. (1942). Total self-regulatory functions in animals and human beings. *Harvey Lectures, 38,* 63–103.

Rimm, E. B., Giovannucci, E. L., Willett, W. C., Colditz, G. A., Ascherio, A., Rosner, B., & Stampfer, M. J. (1991). Prospective study of alcohol consumption and risk of coronary disease in men. *Lancet, 338,* 464–468.

Rimmele, C. T., Howard, M. O., & Hilfrink, M. L. (1995). Aversion therapies. In R. K. Hester & W. R. Miller (Eds.), *Handbook of alcoholism treatment approaches: Effective alternatives* (2nd ed.). Boston, MA: Allyn & Bacon.

Rinn, W. E. (1984). The neuropsychology of facial expression: A review of the neurological and psychological mechanisms for producing facial expressions. *Psychological Bulletin, 95,* 52–77.

Risley, T. R. (1977). The development and maintenance of language: An operant model. In B. C. Etzel, J. M. LeBlanc, & D. M. Baer (Eds.), *New developments in behavioral research.* Hillsdale, NJ: Erlbaum.

Roberts, R. J., & Aman, C. J. (1993). Developmental differences in giving directions: Spatial frames of reference and mental rotation. *Child Development, 64,* 1258–1270.

Robins, L. N., Tipp, J., & Przybeck, T. (1991). Antisocial personality. In L. N. Robins & D. A. Regier (Eds.), *Psychiatric disorders in America: The epidemiologic catchment area study.* New York: Free Press.

Robinson, T. E., & Berridge, K. C. (1993). The neural basis of drug craving: An incentive-sensitization theory of addiction. *Brain Research Reviews, 18,* 247–291.

Rochat, P. (1989). Object manipulation and exploration in 2- to 5-month-old infants. *Developmental Psychology, 25,* 871–884.

Roediger, H. L., III, & McDermott, K. B. (1993). Implicit memory in normal human subjects. In H. Spinnler & F. Boller (Eds.), *Handbook of neuropsychology* (Vol. 8). Amsterdam: Elsevier.

Roffwarg, H. P., Muzio, J. N., & Dement, W. C. (1966). Ontogenetic development of the human sleep-dream cycle. *Science, 152,* 604–619.

Rogers, C. (1942). *Counseling and psychotherapy.* Boston: Houghton Mifflin.

Rogers, C. (1951). *Client-centered therapy: Its current practice, implications, and theory*. Boston: Houghton Mifflin.

Rogers, C. (1959). *On becoming a person: A therapist's view of psychotherapy.* Boston: Houghton Mifflin.

Rogers, C. (1980). *A way of being*. Boston: Houghton Mifflin.

Rogot, E. (1974). Smoking and mortality among U.S. Veterans. *Journal of Chronic Diseases, 27*, 200.

Rohner, R. P. (1998). Father love and child development: History and current evidence. *Current Directions in Psychological Science, 7*, 157–161.

Rokeach, M. (1973). *The nature of human values*. New York: Free Press.

Rolls, B. J. (1986). Sensory-specific satiety. *Nutrition Reviews, 44*, 93–101.

Room, R., & Greenfield, T. (1993). Alcoholics Anonymous, other 12-step movements and psychotherapy in the U.S. population, 1990. *Addiction, 88*, 555–562.

Rosenfarb, I. S., Goldstein, M. J., Mintz, J., & Nuechterlein, K. H. (1995). Expressed emotion and subclinical psychopathology observable within the transactions between schizophrenic patients and their family members. *Journal of Abnormal Psychology, 104*, 259–267.

Rosensweig, M. R., Krech, D., Bennett, E. L., & Diamond, M. C. (1962). Effects of environmental complexity and training on brain chemistry and anatomy: A replication and extension. *Journal of Comparative and Physiological Psychology, 55*, 427–429.

Rosenzweig, M. R., Leiman, A. L., & Breedlove, S. M. (1999). *Biological psychology* (2nd ed.). Sunderland, MA: Sinauer.

Ross, C. A. (1997). *Dissociative identity disorder*. New York: Wiley.

Ross, C. A., Joshi, S., & Currie, R. (1990). Dissociative experiences in the general population. *American Journal of Psychiatry, 147*, 1547–1552.

Ross, L. (1977). The intuitive psychologist and his shortcomings: Distortions in the attribution process. *Advances in Experimental Social Psychology, 10*, 173–220.

Rotter, J. B. (1966). Generalized expectancies for internal versus external control of reinforcement. *Psychological Monographs, 80* (Whole No. 609).

Rotter, J. B. (1990). Internal versus external control of reinforcement: A case history of a variable. *American Psychologist, 45*, 489–493.

Routtenberg, A., & Lindy, J. (1965). Effects of the availability of rewarding septal and hypothalamic stimulation on bar pressing for food under conditions of deprivation. *Journal of Comparative and Physiological Psychology, 60*, 158–161.

Rovee-Collier, C. (1999). The development of infant memory. *Current Directions in Psychological Science, 8*, 80–85.

Rowatt, W. C., Cunningham, M. R., & Druen, P. B. (1998). Deception to get a date. *Personality and Social Psychology Bulletin, 24*, 1228–1242.

Rowatt, W. C., Cunningham, M. R., Rowatt, T. J., Druen, P. B., & Miles, S. S. (1999). *Deceptive tactics that people use and suspect other people use to initiate a dating relationship*. Manuscript under editorial review.

Rowe, D. C. (1997). Genetics, temperament, and personality. In R. Hogan, J. Johnson, & S. Briggs (Eds.), *Handbook of personality psychology*. San Diego: Academic Press.

Rowe, D. C., Almeida, D. M., & Jacobson, K. C. (1999). School context and genetic influences on aggression in adolescence. *Psychological Science, 10*, 277–280.

Rozin, P. (1967). Thiamine specific hunger. In C. F. Code (Ed.), *Handbook of physiology (Section 6): Alimentary Canal (Vol 1): Control of food and water intake*. Washington, DC: American Physiological Society.

Rozin, P., & Kalat, J. W. (1971). Specific hungers and poison avoidance as adaptive specializations of learning. *Psychological Review, 78*, 459–486.

Rubin, D. C. (1996). *Remembering our past: Studies in autobiographical memory*. New York: Cambridge University Press.

Rumbaugh, D. M. (Ed.). (1977). *Language learning by a chimpanzee: The LANA project*. New York: Academic Press.

Rumbaugh, D. M., & Gill, R. V. (1976). The mastery of language-type skills by the chimpanzee (Pan). *Annals of the New York Academy of Sciences, 280*, 562–578.

Rundus, D. J. (1971). Analysis of rehearsal processes in free recall. *Journal of Experimental Psychology, 89*, 63–77.

Rushton, J. P. (1995). Race, IQ, and the APA report on *The Bell Curve*. *American Psychologist, 52*, 69–70.

Russell, J. (1991). Culture and the categorization of emotions. *Psychological Bulletin, 110*, 426–450.

Russell, M. J. (1976). Human olfactory communication. *Nature, 260*, 520–522.

Russell, M. J., Switz, G. M., & Thompson, K. (1980). Olfactory influences on the human menstrual cycle. *Pharmacology, Biochemistry, and Behavior, 13*, 737–738.

Sacks, O. (1984). *A leg to stand on*. New York: Perennial Books.

Sacks, O. (1987). *The man who mistook his wife for a hat*. New York: HarperPerennial.

Sacks, O. (1990). *Seeing voices*. New York: HarperCollins.

Sacks, O. (1995). *An anthropologist on mars*. New York: Vintage.

Sagan, C. (1977). *The dragons of Eden: Speculations on the evolution of human intelligence*. New York: Random House.

Sagan, C., & Druyan, A. (1992). *Shadows of forgotten ancestors*. New York: Ballantine Books.

Salamé, P., & Baddeley, A. D. (1987). Noise, unattended speech, and short-term memory. *Ergonomics, 30*, 1185–1193.

Salamé, P., & Baddeley, A. D. (1989). Effects of background music on phonological short-term memory. *Quarterly Journal of Experimental Psychology, 41A*, 107–122.

Sandivk, L., Eridssen, J., Thaulow, E., Erikssen, G., Mundal, R., & Rodahl, K. (1993). Physical fitness as a predictor of mortality among healthy, middle-aged Norwegian men. *New England Journal of Medicine, 328*, 533–537.

Savage-Rumbaugh, S. (1987). Communication, symbolic communication, and language: Reply to Seidenberg and Petitto. *Journal of Experimental Psychology: General, 116*, 288–292.

Savage-Rumbaugh, S., McDonald, K., Sevcik, R. A., Hopkins, W. D., & Rubert, E. (1986). Spontaneous symbol acquisition and communicative use by pygmy chimpanzees *(Pan paniscus)*. *Journal of Experimental Psychology: General, 115*, 211–235.

Savage-Rumbaugh, S., Murphy, J., Sevcik, R. A., Brakke, K. E., Williams, S. L., & Rumbaugh, D. M. (1993). Language comprehension in ape and child. *Monographs of the Society for Research in Child Development, Serial No. 233, Vol 58, Nos. 3–4*, 30–170.

Scarr, S., & McCartney, K. (1983). How people make their own environments: A theory of genotype→environment effects. *Child Development, 54*, 424–435.

Schaal, B. (2000). Babies' taste established in womb. *Chemical Senses, 25*, 729.

Schacter, D. L. (1996). *Searching for memory*. New York: Basic Books.

Schacter, S. (1964). The interaction of cognitive and physiological determinants of emotional state. In L. Berkowitz (Ed.), *Advances in experimental social psychology* (Vol. 1). New York: Academic Press.

Schacter, S., & Singer, J. E. (1962). Cognitive, social, and physiological determinants of emotional state. *Psychological Review, 69*, 379–399.

Schaie, K. W. (1980). Cognitive development in aging. In L. K. Obler & M. L. Albers (Eds.), *Language and communication*. New York: D. C. Heath.

Schaller, G. B. (1964). *The year of the gorilla*. Chicago: University of Chicago Press.

Scheff, T. J. (1999). *Being mentally ill: A sociological theory* (3rd ed.). Hawthorne, NY: Aldine de Gruyter.

Schein, E. H. (1956). The Chinese indoctrination program for prisoners of war: A study of attempted brainwashing. *Psychiatry, 19*, 149–172.

Schiffman, H. R. (1972). Some components of sensation and perception for the reading process. *Reading Research Quarterly, VII*, 588–612.

Schiffman, H. R. (2000). *Sensation and perception* (5th ed.). New York: Wiley.

Schiffman, H. R., & Thompson, J. G. (1978). The role of apparent depth and context in the perception of the Ponzo illusion. *Perception, 7,* 47–50.

Schleifer, S. J. (1999). Psychoneuroimmunology: Introductory comments on its physics and metaphysics. *Psychiatry Research, 85,* 3–6.

Schleifer, S. J., Keller, S. E., & Bartlett, J. A. (1999). Depression and immunity: Clinical factors and therapeutic course. *Psychiatry Research, 85,* 63–69.

Schmidt, F. L., & Hunter, J. E. (1998). The validity and utility of selection methods in personnel psychology: Practical and theoretical implications of 85 years of research findings. *Psychological Bulletin, 124,* 262–274.

Schmidt, N. B., & Trakowski, J. H. (1997). Body vigilance in panic disorder: Evaluating attention to body perturbations. *Journal of Consulting and Clinical Psychology, 65,* 214–220.

Schmied, L. A., & Lawler, K. A. (1986). Hardiness, Type A behavior, and the stress-illness relation in working women. *Journal of Personality and Social Psychology, 51,* 1218–1223.

Schneider, D. M., & Watkins, M. J. (1996). Response conformity in recognition testing. *Psychonomic Bulletin & Review, 3,* 481–485.

Schneidman, E. S. (1966). Some essentials for suicide, and some implications for response. In A. Roy (Ed.), *Suicide.* Baltimore: Williams & Wilkins.

Schooler, C. (1998). Environmental complexity and the Flynn effect. In U. Neisser (Ed.), *The rising curve: Long-term gains in IQ and related measures,* 67–80. Washington, DC: American Psychological Association.

Schusterman, R. J., & Gisner, R. (1988). Artificial language comprehension in dolphins and sea lions: The essential cognitive skills. *Psychological Record, 38,* 311–348.

Schusterman, R. J., & Gisner, R. (1989). Please parse the sentence: Animal cognition in the procrustean bed of linguistics. *Psychological Record, 39,* 3–18.

Schwartz, G. E., & Weiss, S. M. (1978). Behavioral medicine revisited: An amended definition. *Journal of Behavioral Medicine, 1,* 249–251.

Scott, J. P., & Fuller, J. L. (1965). *Genetics and the social behavior of the dog.* Chicago: University of Chicago Press.

Seelye, K. Q. (1999, April 25). Clinton seeks to console students but falters. *New York Times on the Web.* (Search Seelye, K. Q)

Segal, N. L. (1997). Same-age unrelated siblings: A unique test of within-family environmental influences on IQ similarity. *Journal of Educational Psychology, 89,* 381–390.

Sejnowski, T. J., Koch, C., & Churchland, P. S. (1988). Computational neuroscience. *Nature, 241,* 1299–1306.

Seligman, M. E. P. (1975). *Helplessness.* San Francisco: Freeman.

Seligman, M. E .P. (1990). *Learned optimism.* New York: Pocket Books.

Seligman, M. E. P. (1995). The effectiveness of psychotherapy. The Consumer Reports study. *American Psychologist, 50,* 965–974.

Seligman, M. E. P., & Maier, S. F. (1967). Failure to escape traumatic shock. *Journal of Experimental Psychology, 74,* 1–9.

Selye, H. (1956). *The stress of life.* New York: McGraw-Hill.

Selye, H. (1973). The evolution of the stress concept. *American Scientist, 61,* 672–699.

Serpell, R., & Boykin, A. W. (1994). Cultural dimensions of cognition: A multiplex, dynamic system of constraints and possibilities. In R. J. Sternberg (Ed.), *Thinking and problem solving. Handbook of perception and cognition* (2nd ed.). San Diego, CA: Academic Press.

Seyfarth, R. M., Cheney, D. L., & Marler, P. (1980). Vervet monkey responses to three different alarm calls. Evidence of predator classification and semantic communication. *Science, 210,* 801–803.

Shams, L., Kamitani, Y., & Shimojo, S. (2000). What you see is what you hear. *Nature, 408,* 788.

Shapiro, A. K. (1971). Placebo effects in medicine, psychotherapy, and psychoanalysis. In A. E. Bergin & S. L. Garfield (Eds.), *Handbook of psychotherapy and behavior change.* New York: Wiley.

Shapley, R. (1986). The importance of contrast for the activity of single neurons, the VEP, and perception. *Vision Research, 26,* 45–61.

Shatz, C. J. (1992, September). The developing brain. *Scientific American, 267,* 60–67.

Sheldon, W. (1942). *The varieties of temperament: A psychology of constitutional differences.* New York: Harper.

Shepard, R. N., & Cooper, L. A. (1982). Mental images and their transformations. Cambridge, MA: MIT Press.

Sheppard, J. A., & Taylor, K. M. (1999). Social loafing and expectancy-value theory. *Personality and Social Psychology Bulletin, 25,* 1147–1158.

Shepperd, J. A. (1993). Productivity loss in performance groups: A motivational analysis. *Psychological Bulletin, 113,* 67–81.

Sherif, M. (1936). *The psychology of social norms.* New York: Harper.

Sherry, D. F., & Schacter, D. L. (1987). The evolution of multiple memory systems. *Psychological Review, 94,* 439–454.

Shibata, D. (2000, November 27). *The brain's basis for humor.* Proceedings of the Radiological Society of North America, 86th Annual Meeting, Chicago, 295.

Shulman, M. E. (1988). Cost containment in clinical psychology: Critique of Biodyne and the HMOs. *Professional Psychology Research and Practice, 19,* 298–307.

Shutts, D. (1942). *Lobotomy: Resort to the knife.* New York: Van Nostrand Reinhold.

Sibley, C. G., Comstock, J. A., & Ahlquist, J. E. (1990). DNA hybridization evidence of hominoid phylogeny: A reanalysis of the data. *Journal of Molecular Evolution, 30,* 202–206.

Sidman, M. (1953). Avoidance conditioning with brief shock and no exteroceptive warning signal. *Science, 118,* 157–158.

Siegel, P. Z., Brackbill, R. M., & Heath, G. W. (1995). The epidemiology of walking for exercise: Implications for promoting activity among sedentary groups. *American Journal of Public Health, 85,* 706–710.

Siegel, R. K. (1990). *Intoxication.* New York: Pocket Books.

Siegel, S. (1977). Morphine tolerance acquisition as an associative process. *Journal of Experimental Psychology: Animal Behavior Processes, 3,* 1–13.

Siegel, S., Hinson, R. E., Krank, M. D., & McCully, J. (1982). Heroin "overdose" death: Contribution of drug-associated environmental cues. *Science, 216,* 436–437.

Silverman, I., & Phillips, K. (1998). The evolutionary psychology of spatial sex differences. In C. Crawford & D. L. Krebs (Eds.), *Handbook of evolutionary psychology: Ideas, issues, and applications.* Mahwah, NJ: Erlbaum.

Simon, H. A. (1992). What is an "explanation" of behavior? *Psychological Science, 3,* 150–161.

Simon, H. A., & Gilmartin, K. (1973). A simulation of memory for chess positions. *Cognitive Psychology, 5,* 29–46.

Simoons, F. J. (1973). New light on ethnic differences in adult lactose intolerance. *American Journal of Digestive Disorders, 18,* 595–611.

Simoons, F. J. (1982). Geography and genetics as factors in the psychobiology of human food selection. In L. B. Barker (Ed.), *The psychobiology of human food selection.* Westport, CT: AVI Publishing.

Singer, J. L. (1975). Navigating the stream of consciousness: Research on daydreaming and related inner experiences. *American Psychologist, 30,* 727–738.

Singer, J. L., & Singer, D. G. (1986). Family experiences and television viewing as predictors of children's imagination, restlessness, and aggression. *Journal of Social Issues, 42,* 7–28.

Singh, D. (1993). Adaptive significance of female physical attractiveness: Role of waist-to-hip ratio. *Journal of Personality and Social Psychology, 65,* 293–307.

Singh, D., & Luis, S. (1995). Ethnic and gender consensus for the effect of waist-to-hip ratio on judgment of women's attractiveness. *Human Nature,* 6, 51–65.

Singh, D., & Young, R. K. (1995). Body weight, waist-to-hip ratio, breasts, and hips: Role in judgments of female attractiveness and desirability for relationships. *Ethology and Sociobiology, 16*, 483–507.

Sizemore, C. C. (1989). *A mind of her own*. New York: William Morrow.

Skinner, B. F. (1938). *The behavior of organisms*. Englewood Cliffs, NJ: Prentice-Hall.

Skinner, B. F. (1948). *Walden Two*. New York: Macmillan.

Skinner, B. F. (1957). *Verbal behavior*. New York: Appleton.

Skinner, B. F. (1963). Behaviorism at fifty. *Science, 140*, 951–958.

Skinner, B. F. (1971). *Beyond freedom and dignity*. New York: Knopf.

Skinner, B. F., Solomon, H. C., & Lindsley, O. R. (1953). *Studies in behavioral therapy: Status report I*. Unpublished report, Metropolitan State Hospital, Waltham, MA.

Slyper, A. H. (1994). Low density lipoprotein density and atherosclerosis: Unraveling the connection. *Journal of the American Medical Association, 272*, 305–308.

Small, M. F. (1999). Bringing back baby. *Natural History, 3/99*, 68–71.

Smith, J. W., & Frawley, P. J. (1993). Treatment outcome of 600 chemically dependent patients treated in a multimodal inpatient program including aversion therapy and pentothal interviews. *Journal of Substance Abuse Treatment, 10*, 359–369.

Smith, M. S., Glass, G. V., & Miller, T. I. (1980). *The benefits of psychotherapy*. Baltimore: Johns Hopkins University Press.

Smith, P. F. (1995). Cannabis and the brain: Recent developments. *New Zealand Journal of Psychology, 24*(1), 5–12.

Smotherman, W. P., & Robinson, S. R. (1990). The prenatal origins of behavioral organization. *Psychological Science, 1*, 97–106.

Smotherman, W. P., & Robinson, S. R. (1996). The development of behavior before birth. *Developmental Psychology, 32*, 425–434.

Snow, C. E., Burns, M. S., & Griffin, P. (Eds.). (1998). *Preventing reading difficulties in young children*. Washington, DC: National Academy Press.

Snyder, M., & DeBono, K. (1985). Appeals to image and claims about quality: Understanding the psychology of advertising. *Journal of Personality and Social Psychology, 49*, 586–597.

Spanos, N. P. (1986). Hypnotic behavior: A social-psychological interpretation of amnesia, analgesia, and "trance logic." *Behavioral & Brain Sciences, 9*, 449–467.

Spanos, N. P. (1996). *Multiple identities and false memories: A sociocognitive perspective*. Washington, DC: American Psychological Association.

Spanos, N. P., & Burgess, C. (1994). Hypnosis and multiple personality disorder: A sociocognitive perspective. In S. J. Lynn & J. W. Rhue (Eds.), *Dissociation: Clinical and theoretical perspectives*. New York: Guilford Press.

Spanos, N. P., & Chaves, J. F. (Eds.). (1989). *Hypnosis: The cognitive-behavioral perspective. Buffalo*, NY: Prometheus Books.

Spanos, N. P., Weekes, J. R., & Betrand, L. D. (1985). Multiple personality: A social-psychological perspective. *Journal of Abnormal Psychology, 94*, 362–376.

Spearman, C. (1904). "General intelligence" objectively determined and measured. *American Journal of Psychology, 15*, 201–293.

Spearman, C. (1927). *The abilities of man*. New York: Macmillan.

Spelke, E. S. (1988). The origins of physical knowledge. In L. Weiskrantz (Ed.), *Thought without language*. Oxford, UK: Clarendon Press.

Spence, J. T., & Helmreich, R. L. (1983). Achievement-related motives and behavior. In J. T. Spence (Ed.), *Achievement and achievement motives: Psychological and sociological approaches*. New York: Freeman.

Spence, M. J., & DeCasper, A. J. (1987). Prenatal experience with low-frequency maternal-voice sound influences neonatal perception of maternal voice samples. *Infant Behavior and Development, 10*, 133–142.

Sperling, G. (1960). The information available in brief visual presentation. *Psychological Monographs, 74* (Whole No. 498).

Sperry, R. (1964). The great cerebral commissure. *Scientific American, 210*, 42–52.

Sperry, R. (1968). Hemisphere deconnection and unity in conscious awareness. *American Psychologist, 23*, 723–733.

Spiegel, D., & Cardena, E. (1991). Disintegrated experience: The dissociative disorders revisited. *Journal of Abnormal Psychology, 100*, 366–378.

Spiegler, M. D., & Guevremont, D. C. (1998). *Contemporary behavior therapy*. Belmont, CA: Brooks-Cole.

Springer, S. P., & Deutsch, G. (1998). *Left brain, right brain* (5th ed.). New York: Freeman.

Squire, L. R. (1987). *Memory and brain*. New York: Oxford University Press.

Squire, L. R. (1992). Memory and the hippocampus: A synthesis from findings with rats, monkeys, and humans. *Psychological Review, 99*, 195–231.

Srull, T. K., & Wyer, R. S. (1994). *Handbook of social cognition: Vol. 1. Basic processes: Vol. 2. Applications* (2nd ed.). Hillsdale, NJ: Erlbaum.

Steiner, J. (1977). Facial expressions of the neonate infant indicating the hedonics of food-related chemical stimuli. In J. M. Weiffenbach (Ed.), *Taste and development: The genesis of sweet preference*, 173–187. Bethesda, MD: DHEW Publication No. (NIH) 77–1068.

Stemmer, N. (1989). The acquisition of the ostensive lexicon: The superiority of empiricist over cognitive theories. *Behaviorism, 17*, 41–61.

Stemmer, N. (1990). Skinner's *Verbal Behavior*, Chomsky's review, and mentalism. *Journal of the Experimental Analysis of Behavior, 54*, 307–315.

Sternberg, R. (1986). A triangular theory of love. *Psychological Review, 93*, 119–135.

Sternberg, R. J. (1985). *Beyond IQ: A triarchic theory of human intelligence*. New York: Cambridge University Press.

Sternberg, R. J. (1986). *Intelligence applied: Understanding and increasing your intellectual skills*. New York: Harcourt Brace Jovanovich.

Sternberg, R. J., & Detterman, D. K. (Eds.). (1986). *What is intelligence? Contemporary viewpoints on its nature and definition*. Norwood, NJ: Ablex.

Sternberg, R. J., & Wagner, R. K. (1993). The *g*-ocentric view of intelligence and job performance is wrong. *Current Directions in Psychological Science, 2*, 1–4.

Sternberg, R. J., Wagner, R. K., Williams, W. M., & Horvath, J. A. (1995). Testing common sense. *American Psychologist, 50*, 912–927.

Stevens, S. S. (1936). A scale for the measurement of psychological magnitude: Loudness. *Psychological Review, 43*, 405–416.

Stevens, S. S. (1962). The surprising simplicity of sensory metrics. *American Psychologist, 17*, 29–39.

Stevenson, H. W., & Stigler, J. W. (1992). *The learning gap*. New York: Summit Books.

Stickgold, R., Pace-Schott, E., & Hobson, J. A. (1994). A new paradigm for dream research: Mentation reports following spontaneous arousal from REM and NREM sleep recorded in a home setting. *Consciousness and Cognition: An International Journal, 3*(1), 16–29.

Stillion, J. M. (1995). Death in the lives of adults: Responding to the tolling of the bell. In H. Wass & R. A. Neimeyer (Eds.), *Dying: Facing the facts*. New York: Taylor & Francis.

Stoddart, D. M. (1990). *The scented ape: The biology and culture of human odour*. New York: Cambridge University Press.

Stone, V. E., Nisenson, L., Eliassen, J. C., & Gazzaniga, M. S. (1996). Left hemisphere representations of emotional facial expressions. *Neuropsychologia, 34*, 23–29.

Strauss, A. P., Spritzer, R. L., & Muskin, P. R. (1990). Maladaptive denial of physical illness: A proposal for *DSM-IV*. *American Journal of Psychiatry, 147*, 1168–1172.

Streissguth, A. P., Barr, H. M., Sampson, P. D., Darby, B. L., & Martin, D. C. (1989). IQ at age 4 in relation to maternal alcohol use and smoking during pregnancy. *Developmental Psychology, 25*, 3–11.

Strickberger, M. W. (1996). *Evolution* (2nd ed.). Boston: Jones & Bartlett.

Stroop, J. R. (1935). Studies of interference in serial verbal reactions. *Journal of Experimental Psychology, 18*, 643–662.

Strumwasser, F. (1965). The demonstration and manipulation of a circadian rhythm in a single neuron. In J. Aschoff (Ed.), *Circadian clocks*. Amsterdam: ASP Biological and Medical Press.

Strupp, H. H. (1996). The tripartite model and the *Consumer Reports* study. *American Psychologist, 51*, 1017–1024.

Strupp, H. H., & Blackwood, G. L., Jr. (1985). Recent methods of psychotherapy. In H. I. Kaplan & B. J. Sadock (Eds.), *Comprehensive textbook of psychiatry* (4th ed.) Baltimore, MD: Williams & Wilkins.

Studdert-Kennedy, M., Hurford, J. R., & Knight, C. (2000). *The evolutionary emergence of language: Social function and the origins of linguistic form*. Cambridge, UK: Cambridge University Press.

Stunkard, A. J., Harris, J. R., Pederson, N. L.. & McLearn., G. E. (1990). The body mass index of twins who have been reared apart. *New England Journal of Medicine, 322*, 1483–1487.

Stuss, D. T., Gallup, G. G., Jr., & Alexander, M. P. (2001). The frontal lobes are necessary for "theory of mind." *Brain, 124*, 279–286.

Sullivan, H. S. (1953). *The interpersonal theory of psychiatry*. New York: Norton.

Sulloway, F. J. (1979). *Freud: Biologist of the mind: Beyond the psychoanalytic legend*. New York: Basic Books.

Süskind, P. (1986). *Perfume*. New York: Alfred A. Knopf.

Swann, W. B. Jr., & Pittman, T. S. (1977). Initiating play activity in children: The moderating influence of verbal cues on intrinsic motivation. *Child Development, 48*, 1125–1132.

Swim, J. K., Aikin, K. J., Hall, W., & Hunter, B. A. (1995). Sexism and racism: Old-fashioned and modern prejudices. *Journal of Personality and Social Psychology, 68*, 199–214.

Symons, D. (1979). *The evolution of human sexuality*. New York: Oxford University Press.

Szasz, T. (1974). *The myth of mental illness*. New York: Harper & Row.

Szasz, T. (1990). Law & psychiatry: Problems that will not go away. *Journal of Mind and Behavior, 11*, 557–564.

Tabor's Cyclopedic Medical Dictionary. (1997). Philadelphia: F. A. Davis.

Tang, S. H., & Hall, V. C. (1995). The overjustification effect: A meta-analysis. *Applied Cognitive Psychology, 9*, 365–404.

Taylor, C. B., Sheikh, J., Agras, W. S., Roth, W. T., Margraf, J., Ehlers, A., Maddock, R., & Gossard, D. (1986). Self-report of panic attacks: Agreement with hear rate changes. *American Journal of Psychiatry, 143*, 478–482.

Taylor, S. E., & Brown, J. D. (1988). Illusion and well-being: A social psychological perspective on mental health. *Psychological Bulletin, 103*, 193–210.

Taylor, S. E., & Brown, J. D. (1994). Positive illusions and well-being revisited: Separating fact from fiction. *Psychological Bulletin, 116*, 21–27.

Taylor, W., Pearson, J., Mair, A., & Burns, W. (1965). Study of noise and hearing in jute weaving. *Journal of the Acoustical Society of America, 38*, 113–120.

Teitelbaum, P., & Epstein, A. N. (1962). The lateral hypothalamic syndrome: Recovery of feeding and drinking after lateral hypothalamic lesions. *Psychological Review, 69*, 74–90.

Tellegen, A., Lykken, D. T., Bouchard, T. J. Jr., Wilcox, K. J., Segal, N. L., & Rich, R. (1988). Personality similarity in twins reared apart and together. *Journal of Personality and Social Psychology, 54*, 1031–1039.

Terkel, J. (1988). Neuroendocrine processes in the establishment of pregnancy and pseudo-pregnancy in rats. *Psychoneuroendocrinology, 13*, 5–28.

Terman, L. M. (1916). *The measurement of intelligence*. Boston: Houghton Mifflin.

Terrace, H. S. (1979). *Nim*. New York: Alfred A. Knopf.

Thapar, A., Gottesman, I. I., Owen, M. J., O'Donovan, M. C., & McGuffin, P. (1994). The genetics of mental retardation. *British Journal of Psychiatry, 164*, 747–758.

Thigpen, C. H., & Cleckley, H. M. (1957). *The three faces of Eve*. New York: McGraw-Hill.

Thorndike, E. L. (1911). *Animal intelligence: Experimental studies*. New York: Macmillan.

Thorndike, E. L. (1932). *Fundamentals of learning*. New York: Teachers College, Columbia University.

Thurstone, L. (1938). *Primary mental abilities*. Chicago: University of Chicago Press.

Thurstone, L. (1947). *Multiple factor analysis*. Chicago: University of Chicago Press.

Tolman, E. C., & Honzik, C. H. (1930a). Degrees of hunger; reward and non-reward; and maze learning in rats. *University of California Publications in Psychology, 4*, 241–256.

Tolman, E. C., & Honzik, C. H. (1930b). "Insight" in rats. *University of California Publications in Psychology, 4*, 215–232.

Tomkins, S. S. (1991). *Affect, imagery, consciousness: 3. Anger and fear*. New York: Springer-Verlag.

Toscini, G., & Menaker, M. (1995). Circadian rhythms in cultured mammalian retina. *Science, 272*, 419–421.

Trafimow, D., Triandis, H. C., & Goto, S. G. (1991). Some tests of distinction between the private and the collective self. *Journal of Personality and Social Psychology, 60*, 649–655.

Triandis, H. C. (1994). *Culture and social behavior*. New York: McGraw-Hill.

Triandis, H. C. (1995). *Individualism and collectivism*. Boulder, CO: Westview Press.

Trivers, R. L. (1972). Parental investment and sexual selection. In B. Campbell (Ed.), *Sexual selection and the descent of man 1871–1971* (pp. 136–179). Chicago: Aldine.

Troop, N. A. (1998). Eating disorders as coping strategies: A critique. *European Eating Disorders Review, 6*, 229–237.

Tucker, D. M. (1981). Lateral brain function, emotion, and conceptualization. *Psychological Bulletin, 89*, 19–46.

Tucker, L. A. (1983). Muscular strength and mental health. *Journal of Personality and Social Psychology, 45*, 1355–1360.

Tulving, E. (1985). How many memory systems are there? *American Psychologist, 40*, 385–398.

Tulving, E. (1993). What is episodic memory? *Current Directions in Psychological Science, 2*, 67–70.

Tulving, E., & Psotka, J. (1971). Retroactive inhibition in free-recall: Inaccessibility of information available in the memory store. *Journal of Experimental Psychology, 87*, 1–8.

Tulving, E., Schacter, D. L., & Stark, H. (1982). Priming effects in word fragment completion are independent of recognition memory. *Journal of Experimental Psychology: Learning, Memory, and Cognition, 8*, 336–342.

Tulving, E., & Thompson, D. (1973). Encoding specificity and retrieval processes in episodic memory. *Psychological Review, 80*, 352–373.

Turkheimer, E. (2000). Three laws of behavior genetics and what they mean. *Current Directions in Psychological Science, 9*, 160–164.

Turner, J. A., Deyo, R. A., Loeser, J. D., Von Korff, M., & Forrdyce, W. E. (1994). The importance of placebo effects in pain treatment and research. *Journal of the American Medical Association, 271*, 1609–1614.

Turner, J. R., & Wheaton, B. (1995). Checklist measurement of major life events. In S. Cohen, R. C. Kessler, & L. U. Gordon (Eds.), *Measuring stress: A guide for health and social scientists*. New York: Oxford University Press.

Turner, R. J., & Wagonfeld, M. O. (1967). Occupational mobility and schizophrenia: An assessment of the social causation and social selection hypotheses. *American Sociological Review, 32*, 104-113.

United Nations. (1997). Information. United Nations Statistic Division Available: rsch.un.org.

U. S. Department of Health, Education, and Welfare. (1971). *Health survey questionnaire*. Washington, D.C.: HEW.

Uttal, W. R. (1973). *The psychobiology of sensory coding*. New York: Harper & Row.

Vaccarino, F. J., Schiff, B. B., & Glickman, S. E. (1989). Biological view of reinforcement. In S. B. Klein & R. R. Mowrer (Eds.), *Contemporary learning theories: Instrumental conditioning and the impact of biological constraints on learning*. Hillsdale, NJ: Erlbaum.

Vaillant, G. E., & Perry, W. (1985). Personality disorders. In H. I. Kaplan & B. J. Sadock (Eds.), *Comprehensive textbook of psychiatry* (4th ed.). Baltimore, MD: Williams & Wilkins.

Valdimarsdottir, H. B., & Bovbjerg, D. H. (1997). Positive and negative mood: Association with natural killer cell activity. *Psychology and Health, 12*, 319–327.

Valenstein, E. S. (1986). *Great and desperate cures: The rise and decline of psychosurgery and other radical treatments for mental illness*. New York: Basic Books.

Vallee, B. L. (1998). Alcohol in the Western world. *Scientific American, 252*, 56–59.

van Ijzendoorn, M. H., & Kroonenberg, P. M. (1988). Cross-cultural patterns of attachment: A meta-analysis of the Strange Situation. *Child Development, 59*, 147–156.

van Praag, H., Kempermann, G., & Gage, F. H. (1999). Running increases cell proliferation and neurogenesis in the adult mouse dentate gyrus. *Natural Neuroscience, 2*, 266–270.

Van Toller, C., Kirk-Smith, M., Wood, N., Lombard, J., & Dodd, G. H. (1983). Skin conductance and subjective assessments associated with the odor of 5-andrstan-3-one. *Biological Psychology, 16*, 85–107.

Vaughn, C. E., & Leff, J. P. (1976). The influence of family and social factors on the course of psychiatric illness: A comparison of schizophrenic and depressed neurotic patients. *British Journal of Psychiatry, 129*, 125–137.

Vernon, P. A. (1987). *Speed of information processing and intelligence*. Norwood, NJ: Ablex.

Vormbrock, J. K., & Grossberg, J. M. (1988). Cardiovascular effects of human-pet interactions. *Journal of Behavioral Medicine, 11*, 509–517.

Vygotsky, L. S. (1986). *Thought and language* (A. Kozulin, Trans.). Cambridge, MA: MIT Press. (Original work published 1934.)

Walker, K. (1994). Men, women, and friendship: What they say, what they do. *Gender & Society, 8*, 246–265.

Walker, L. J., & Taylor, J. H. (1991). Stage transitions in moral reasoning: A longitudinal study of developmental processes. Developmental Psychology, *27*, 330–337.

Walkup, J. T., Labellarte, M. J., Riddle, M. A., Pine, D. S., Greenhill, L., Klein, R. Davies, M., Sweeney, M., Abikoff, H., Hack, S., Klee, B., McCracken, J., Bergman, L. Piacentini, J., March, J., Compton, S., Robinson, J., O'Hara, T., Baker, S., Vitiello, B., Ritz, L. A., & Roper, M. (2001). Fluvoxamine for the treatment of anxiety disorders in children and adolescents. *The New England Journal of Medicine, 344*, 1279–1285.

Wallace, R. K., & Benson, H. (1972). The physiology of meditation. *Scientific American, 226*, 84–90.

Wallace, W. T. (1994). Memory for music: Effect of melody on recall of text. *Journal of Experimental Psychology: Learning, Memory & Cognition, 20*, 1471–1485.

Walster, E., Aronson, V., Abrahams, D., & Rottman, L. (1966). Importance of physical attractiveness in dating behavior. *Journal of Personality and Social Psychology, 4*, 508–516.

Walster, E., & Bersheid, E. (1974). A little bit about love: A minor essay on a major topic. In T. L. Huston (Ed.), *Foundations of interpersonal attraction*. New York: Academic Press.

Walton, G. E., & Bower, T. G. R. (1993). Newborns form "prototypes" in less than a minute. *Psychological Science, 4*, 203–205.

Walton, G. E., Bower, N. J. A., & Bower, T. G. R. (1992). Recognition of familiar faces by newborns. *Infant Behavior and Development, 15*, 265–269.

Washburn, M. F. (1908). *The animal mind*. New York: Macmillan.

Wason, P. (1968). Reasoning about a rule. *Quarterly Journal of Experimental Psychology, 20*, 273–281.

Wasserman, E. A. (1993). Comparative cognition: Beginning the second century of the study of animal intelligence. *Psychological Bulletin, 113*, 211–228.

Waterman, A. S. (1988). Identity status theory and Erikson's theory: Commonalities and differences. *Developmental Review, 8*, 185–208.

Watson, D., & Pennebaker, J. W. (1989). Health complaints, stress, and distress. Exploring the central role of negative affectivity. *Psychological Review, 96*, 234–254.

Watson, J. B. (1919). *Psychology from the standpoint of a behaviorist*. Philadelphia: Lippincott.

Watson, J. B. (1924). *Behaviorism*. New York: Norton.

Watson, J. B., & Rayner, R. (1920). Conditioned emotional reactions. *Journal of Experimental Psychology, 3*, 1–14.

Watson, R. I. (1960). The history of psychology: A neglected area. *American Psychologist, 15*, 251–255.

Weaver, C. A. III. (1993). Do you need a 'flash' to form a flashbulb memory? *Journal of Experimental Psychology: General, 122*, 39–46.

Weaver, C. W., & Kintsch, W. (1992). Enhancing students' comprehension of the conceptual structure of algebra word problems. *Journal of Educational Psychology, 84*, 419–428.

Wechsler, D. (1958). *The measurement and appraisal of adult intelligence* (4th ed.). Baltimore: Williams & Wilkins.

Wechsler, D. (1991). *WISC-III: Wechsler intelligence scale for children (manual)*. San Antonio, TX: Psychological Corporation.

Wechsler, D. (1997). *Manual for the Wechsler adult intelligence scale-III*. San Antonio, TX: Psychological Corporation.

Wegner, D. M. (1994). Ironic processes of mental control. *Psychological Review, 101*, 34–52.

Weinberg, R. A. (1989). Intelligence and IQ: Landmark issues and great debates. *American Psychologist, 44*, 98–104.

Weinstein, S. (1968). Intensive and extensive aspects of tactile sensitivity as a function of body part, sex, and laterality. In D. R. Kenshalo (Ed.), *The skin senses*. Springfield, IL: Thomas.

Weir, R. H. (1966). Some questions on the child's learning of phonology. In F. Smith & G. A. Miller (Eds.), *The genesis of language*. Cambridge, MA: MIT Press.

Weiskrantz, L. (1986). *Blindsight: A case study and implications*. New York: Oxford University Press.

Weiskrantz, L. (Ed.). (1988). *Thought without language*. Oxford, UK: Clarendon Press.

Weiskrantz, L. (1997). *Consciousness lost and found*. Oxford: Oxford University Press.

Weiskrantz, L. (2001, February). Personal communication.

Weiskrantz, L., Barbur, J. L., & Sahraie, A. (1995). Parameters affecting conscious versus unconscious visual discrimination without V1. *Proceedings of the National Academy of Science, USA, 92*, 6122–6126.

Wenger, J. R., Tiffany, T. M., Bombardier, C., Nicholls, K., & Woods, S. C. (1981). Ethanol tolerance in the rat is learned. *Science, 213*, 575–577.

Werker, J. F., & Tees, R. C. (1984). Cross-language speech development: Evidence for perceptual reorganization during the first year of life. *Infant Behavior and Development, 7*, 49–63.

Wesnes, K., & Warburton, D. M. (1983). Smoking, nicotine and human performance. *Pharmacology and Therapeutics, 21*, 198–208.

Whalley, L. J., & Deary, I. J. (2001). Longitudinal cohort study of childhood IQ and survival up to age 76. *British Medical Journal, 322*, 819.

Wheeler, M. A., Stuss, D. T., & Tulving, E. (1997). Towards a theory of episodic memory: The frontal lobes and autonoetic consciousness. *Psychological Bulletin, 121*, 331–354.

Whitely, B. E. Jr. (1999). Right-wing authoritarianism, social dominance orientation, and prejudice. *Journal of Personality and Social Psychology, 77*, 126–134.

Whites v. blacks. (1995, October 16). *Newsweek*, pp. 28–35.

WHO (World Health Organization). (1999). Non-communicative diseases. Available: http://www.who.int/ncd/.

Whorf, B. L. (1956). *Science and linguistics*. In J. B. Carroll (Ed.), *Language, thought and reality: Selected writings of Benjamin Lee Whorf*. Cambridge, MA: MIT Press.

Whybrow, P. C., Akiskal, H. S., & McKinney, W. T., Jr. (1984). *Mood disorders: Toward a new psychobiology*. New York: Plenum.

Wiberg, M., & Templer, D. I. (1994). Season of birth in multiple schlerosis in Sweden: Replication of Denmark findings. *Journal of Orthomolecular Medicine, 9*, 71–74.

Wilcox, A. J., Weinberg, C. R., O'Connor, J. F., Baurd, D. D., Schlatterer, J. P., Canfield, R. E., Armstrong, E. G., & Nisula, B. C. (1988). Incidence of early loss of pregnancy. *New England Journal of Medicine, 319*, 189–194.

Wiley, J. A., & Camacho, T. C. (1980). Life-style and future health: Evidence from the Alameda County study. *Preventative Medicine, 9*, 1–21.

Wilkins, L., & Richter, C. P. (1940). A great craving for salt by a child with a corticoadrenal insufficiency. *Journal of the American Medical Association, 114*, 866–868.

Wilkins, W. K., & Wakefield, J. (1995). Brain evolution and neurolinguistic preconditions. *Behavioral and Brain Sciences, 18*, 161–226.

Williams, J. E., & Best, D. L. (1982). *Measuring sex stereotypes: A thirty-nation study*. Beverly Hills, CA: Sage.

Williams, T. (1996). *The complete illustrated guide to Chinese medicine*. Rockport, MA: Element Books.

Williams, W. M. (1998). Are we raising smarter children today? School and home-related influences on IQ. In U. Neisser (Ed.), *The rising curve: Long-term gains in IQ and related measures*, 125–154. Washington, DC: American Psychological Association.

Wilson, E. O. (1975). *Sociobiology: The new synthesis*. Cambridge, MA: Harvard University Press.

Wilson, M. & Daly, M., (1992). The man who mistook his wife for a chattel. In J. H. Barkow, L. Cosmides, & J. Tooby (Eds.), *The adapted mind: Evolutionary psychology and the generation of culture*, 289–322. New York: Oxford University Press.

Winoker, G., Coryell, W., Keller, M., Endicott, J., & Akiskall, H. S. (1993). A prospective follow-up of patients with bipolar and primary unipolar affective disorder. *Archives of General Psychiatry, 50*, 457–465.

Wittenbrink, B., Judd, C. M., & Park, B. (1997). Evidence for racial prejudice at the implicit level and its relationship with questionnaire measures. *Journal of Personality and Social Psychology, 72*, 262–274.

Wolpe, J. (1990). *The practice of behavioral therapy*. Elmsford, NY: Pergamon Press.

Wolpe, J., Salter, A., & Reyna, L. J. (Eds.). (1964). *The conditioning therapies*. New York: Holt, Rinehart, & Winston.

Wolpoff, M. H. (1989). Race and human evolution. In P. Mellars & C. Stringer (Eds.), *The human revolution*, 62–78. Edinburgh: Edinburgh University Press.

Wood, W., Wong, F., & Chachere, J. G. (1991). Effects of media violence on viewer's aggression in unconstrained social interaction. *Psychological Bulletin, 109*, 371–383.

Woodward, A. L., Markman, E. M., & Fitzsimmons, C. M. (1994). Rapid word learning in 13- and 18-month-olds. *Developmental Psychology, 30*, 553–566.

Wright, P. H. (1982). Men's friendships, women's friendships, and the alleged inferiority of the latter. *Sex Roles, 8*, 1–20.

Wright, A. (1997). Concept learning and learning strategies. *Psychological Science, 8*, 119–123.

Wurtman, R. J. (1985, January). Alzheimer's disease. *Scientific American, 252*, 62–74.

Wyrwicka, W., & Dobrzecka, C. (1960). Relationship between feeding and satiation centers of the hypothalamus. *Science, 132*, 805–806.

Yost, W. A., & Nielson, D. W. (1985). *Fundamentals of Hearing* (2nd Ed.). Orlando, FL: Academic Press.

Young, J. Z. (1978). *Programs of the brain*. Oxford: Oxford University Press.

Zahorik, D. (1977). Associative and non-associative factors in learned food preferences. In L. M. Barker, M. R. Best, & M. Domjan (Eds.), *Learning mechanisms in food selection*, 181–200. Waco, TX: Baylor University Press.

Zahorik, D., Mair, S. F., & Pies, R. W. (1974). Preferences for tastes paired with recovery from thiamine deficiency in rats. *Journal of Comparative and Physiological Psychology, 87*, 1083–1091.

Zajonc, R. (1965). Social facilitation. *Science, 149*, 269–276.

Zhang, Y., Proenca, R., Maffei, M., & Barone, M. Positional cloning of the mouse obese/gene and its human analogue. (1994). *Nature, 372*, 425–432.

Zihl, J., Cramon, D., & Mai, N. (1983). Cerebral disturbances of movement vision. *Brain, 106*, 313–340.

Zimbardo, P. G., Haney, C., & Banks, W. C. (1973, April 18). A Pirandellian prison. *New York Times Magazine*, 38–60.

Zubieta, J. K., Huguelet, P., Ohl, L. E., Koeppe, R. A., Kilbourn, M. R., Carr, J. M., Giordani, B. J., & Frey, K. A. (2000). High vesicular monoamine transporter binding in asymptomatic bipolar I disorder: Sex differences and cognitive correlates. *American Journal of Psychiatry, 157*, 1619–1628.

Zucker, G. S., & Weiner, G. (1993). Conservatism and perceptions of poverty: An attributional analysis. *Journal of Applied Social Psychology, 23*, 925–943.

Zuckerman, M. (1998). Psychobiological theories of personality. In D. F. Barone, & M. Hersen, (Eds.), *Advanced personality*. New York: Plenum Press.

Credits

CHAPTER 1: 5 (left), Reuters/Mike Blake/Hulton/Archive, **(middle),** Corbis/Stock Market, **(right),** Will Hart/Photoedit; **7,** SuperStock, Inc.; **9 (left),** Ariel Skelley/Corbis/Stock Market, **(right),** Art Wolfe/Photo Researchers, Inc.; **10,** A.J. Deane/Bruce Coleman Inc.; **12,** David Young-Wolff/Stone; **14,** National Library of Medicine; **15,** Katsuyoshi Tanaka/National Museum of Anthro & Archeology/Woodfin Camp & Associates; **19,** National Library of Medicine; **20,** Hulton/Archive; **21 (left),** Partridge/Wellesley College. **CHAPTER 2: 34,** Allentown Morning Call, Catherine Meredith/AP/Wide World Photos; **35,** Stock Montage/SuperStock, Inc.; **38,** AP/World Wide Photos; **40 (left),** Ken Highfill/Photo Researchers, Inc., **(right)** Tom Brakefield/Corbis/Stock Market; **42,** Bob Daemmrich/The Image Works; **44,** Jose L. Pelaez/Corbis/Stock Market; **52,** Billy E. Barnes/PhotoEdit; 54, Steve Ruark/Syracuse Newspapers/The Image Works; **57,** Bob Daemmrich/Stock Boston; **60,** American Cancer Society; **62,** Frank Pedrick/The Image Works. **CHAPTER 3: 71 (left),** Willie Hill Jr./Index Stock Imagery, Inc., **(right),** Ken Lucas/Visuals Unlimited; **72,** Walt Anderson/Visuals Unlimited; **73 (left),** Bill Ruth/Bruce Coleman Inc., **(right),** B&C Alexander/Photo Researchers, Inc.; **74,** UN/DPI; **75,** CORBIS; **77,** Christopher Brown/Stock Boston, Inc./Picture Quest; **80,** Neg./Transparency no. K17271. (Photo by D. Finnin). Courtesy Dept of Library Services, American Museum of Natural History; 83, Spencer Grant/PhotoEdit; **86,** John Markham/Bruce Coleman Inc.; **87,** Jackson Lab/Visuals Unlimited; **90,** Nina Leen/TimePix; **92,** SuperStock, Inc.; **93,** Mitsuaki Iwago/Minden Pictures; **97,** Leland Bobbe/Stone; **100,** Anthro-Photo File. **CHAPTER 4: 106,** SIU/Visuals Unlimited; **113,** Bob Jordan/AP/Wide World Photos; **118,** Secchi-Lecaque/Roussel-USLAF/CNRI/Science Photo Library/Photo Researchers, Inc.; **123,** David Umberger/AP/Wide World Photos; **127,** John Moss/Photo Researchers, Inc.; **132,** Chuck Savage/Corbis Stock Market; **137,** ASAP/CNRI/Science Photo Library/Photo Researchers, Inc.; **141,** Laura Rauch/AP/Wide World Photos; **144,** SuperStock, Inc.; **145,** N. Myres/Bruce Coleman Inc. **CHAPTER 5: 150,** Elyse Lewin/The Image Bank; **162,** Lauren Goodsmith/The Image Works; **163,** Dr. Neal E. Miller/Yale University; **170,** Don Martinetti; **172,** The Centennial Museum, The University of Texas at El Paso; **176,** © 1975, Ekman & Friesen. Reprinted with permission. **CHAPTER 6: 187 (left),** Ulrike Welsch/PhotoEdit, **(right),** Spencer Grant/PhotoEdit; **188 (left),** A. Wright/The Image Works, **(right),** Bruce Hands/The Image Works; **190,** The Granger Collection; **205,** Bob Daemmrich/Stock Boston; **206,** Nina Leen/TimePix; **214,** Michael Newman/PhotoEdit; **218,** Rainbow; **220,** Dr. Bruce Moore. **CHAPTER 7: 229 (left),** Kjell Sandved/Visuals Unlimited, **(right),** David Hall; **238,** Ed Reschke/Peter Arnold, Inc.; **239,** Ralph C. Eagle/Photo Researchers, Inc.; **244,** Michael Newman/PhotoEdit; **245 (bottom right),** Fritz Goro/TimePix, **(left & right),** © Copyright Lowell Handler; **258,** Lee Snider/The Image Works; **259,** Triarch/Visuals Unlimited; **261,** Lewis M. Barker/Photo with permission of Ed Morrison and Richard Costanzo; **264,** Phil McCarten/PhotoEdit. **CHAPTER 8: 272,** Kim Taylor/Bruce Coleman Inc.; **277 (left),** © Historical Picture Archive/CORBIS; **280,** Photo by Rod Aydelotte. Reprinted with permission of the Waco Tribune-Herald; **281,** Eliza Houston Davey for the Chicago Architecture Foundation; **293 (left)** Hulton/Archive, **(right),** Kaiser Porcelain Company, Ltd.; **296,** Michelangelo Buonarroti. Tomb of Lorenzo de Medici. Medici Chapel, S. Lorenzo, Florence, Italy. Scala/Art Resource, NY. **CHAPTER 9: 306,** Tony Freeman/PhotoEdit; **312,** E.R. Degginger/Photo Researchers, Inc.; **316,** David Lassman/Syracuse Newspapers/The Image Works; **322,** Philippe Plailly/Science Photo Library/Photo Researchers, Inc.; **324,** Topham/The Image Works; **329,** Mary Evans Picture Library; **337,** Mike Gallitelli/Michael A. Gallitelli; **340,** Andrew Garn. **CHAPTER 10: 345,** Peter Menzel/Peter Menzel Photography; **349,** Ellis Herwig/Stock Boston; **362 (left),** Loftus EF, Miller DG, Burns HJ, (1978). Semantic integration of verbal information into a visual memory. "Journal of Experimental Psychology"; Human Learning Memory, 4, 19-31, **(right),** Loftus EF, Miller DG, Burns HJ, (1978). Semantic integration of verbal information into a visual memory. J. Expt. Psychology; Human Learning and Memory, 4, 19-31; **365,** Mike Chew/Corbis/Stock Market; **367,** Adrian Dennis/ AP/World Wide Photos; **371,** Gary Wagner/Stock Boston. **CHAPTER 11: 380 (left&right),** Photo Lennart Nilsson/Bonnier Alba AB, A CHILD IS BORN, Dell Publishing Company; **383,** Psychology Today Magazine; **391,** Enrico Ferorelli; **393,** Laura Dwight Photography; **397,** Judith Behling Ford; **408,** Katherine Lambert. **CHAPTER 12: 415,** Spencer Grant/PhotoEdit; **421,** Nigel J. Dennis/Photo Researchers, Inc.; **424,** Michael Nichols/Magnum Photos, Inc.; **425,** Michael Goldman/TimePix; **427,** Robin L. Sachs/PhotoEdit; **436,** Ian Shaw/Stone; **437 (left, middle, right),** SuperStock, Inc. **CHAPTER 13: 450,** Tony Freeman/PhotoEdit; **452,** CORBIS; **455,** National Archives and Records Administration; **461 (left),** © Timothy A. Clary/AFP/CORBIS, **(right),** © Chris Trotman/Duomo/CORBIS; **462,** Reuters/Eric Miller/Hulton/Hulton/Archive; **464,** Richard Lord/The Image Works; **468,** Courtesy of Harry and Larry Carothers. **CHAPTER 14: 486,** Michael K. Nichols/National Geographic Image Collection; **487,** Neg./Transparency no. K11228. Courtesy Dept. of Library Services, American Museum of Natural History; **494,** Albert Bandura, D. Ross & S.A. Ross, Imitation of film-mediated aggressive models. "Journal of Abnormal and Social Psychology", 1963, 66, P.8; **495,** Mike Greenlar/The Image Works; **504,** Yousuf Karsh/Woodfin Camp & Associates; **507,** © Roger Ressmeyer/CORBIS. **CHAPTER 15: 513,** Reuters/Jeff Mitchell/Hulton/Archive; **529,** Ryan McVay/PhotoDisc, Inc.; **532 (left & right),** Dr. Judith Langlois; **535,** Larry Fischer/Quad-City Times/AP/Wide World Photos. **CHAPTER 16: 546,** Esbin/Anderson/Omni-Photo Communications, Inc.; **549,** Mary Evans Picture Library; **556,** Corbis Digital Stock; **560,** AP/Wide World Photos; **564,** Claudia Kunin/Stone; **571,** Will Faller. **CHAPTER 17: 587,** Carmine Galasso/Carmine L. Galasso; **595,** Esbin/Anderson/Omni-Photo Communications, Inc.; **597,** Giraudon/Art Resource, N.Y.; **599,** Grunnitus/Monkmeyer Press; **582,** Courtesy of Dr. Nancy C. Andreasen, University of Iowa. **CHAPTER 18: 611 (left)** The Granger Collection, **(right)** Jerry Cooke/Photo Researchers, Inc.; **614,** Allen/AP/Wide World Photos; **618,** Robert Essel/Corbis/Stock Market; **625,** Richard T. Nowitz/Photo Researchers, Inc.; **629,** © Hulton-Deutsch Collection/CORBIS; **631,** N.H. Dunhill/Library of Congress.

Name Index

A

Abeche, A. M., 550
Abikoff, H., 633
Abrahams, D., 531
Abramov, I., 245–46, 389
Abrams, R., 630
Ackerknecht, E. H., 631
Adams, B. D., 529
Adams, H. E., 581
Adams, M. J., 357
Adams, R. J., 389
Adcock, G. J., 79
Addington, R. L., 421
Ader, R., 566, 568–69
Adler, A., 504–5, 506, 509, 615
Agras, W. S., 586
Ahern, F., 467
Ahlquist, J. E., 80
Aikin, K. J., 537
Ainsworth, M. D. S., 406, 410
Aitken, D. H., 300
Ajzen, I., 515
Akiskal, H. S., 594, 595
Albert, M. S., 375
Alborn, A. M., 129
Alcock, J., 421, 538
Aldwin, C. M., 564
Alexander, M. P., 308
Alexander, R. D., 404
Alexander the Great, 228
Allen, A., 4
Allen, W., 506, 615
Allport, G., 488–89
Almeida, D. M., 538
Aman, C. J., 396
Ambrose, S. H., 417
Amigo, S., 330
Ammann, R., 317
Anderson, A. K., 177
Anderson, C. A., 539
Anderson, C. D., 166–67
Anderson, D. C., 539
Anderson, J. R., 430
Andreasen, N., 596, 597
Angell, J., 21
Appelbaum, K. A., 619, 620
Arbib, M. A., 416
Archer, P., 387
Arcus, D., 407
Argyle, M., 553
Aristotle, 5
Armstrong, E. G., 380
Aron, A., 533
Aronson, E., 516
Aronson, V., 531
Asch, S. E., 521–22
Ascherio, A., 553
Aschoff, J., 310
Ashbridge, K. R., 569
Ashmore, R. D., 537
Askenasy, J. J. M., 323
Aslin, R. N., 388, 389
Atkinson, J., 389
Atkinson, R. C., 346–47
Averill, J. A., 175
Ayllon, T., 616
Ayres, T. J., 356
Azrin, N., 616
Azzopardi, P., 284

B

Baddeley, A. D., 347, 354–55, 358, 365, 372, 473
Badura, L. L., 317
Baer, D. M., 429
Baer, L., 587
Baggs, K., 619
Bahrick, H. P., 352, 399
Bahrick, P. O., 399
Baker, S., 633
Ball, G. F., 421
Ballentine, H. T., 629
Bandura, A., 215, 424, 431, 494, 496, 539
Banker, B. S., 537
Banks, M. S., 389, 391
Banks, W. C., 524
Bannister, R., 351
Banyard, V. L., 561
Barash, D., 96, 99, 165
Barbee, A. P., 530
Barber, T. X., 329
Barbur, J. L., 284
Bard, K. A., 179, 182, 416
Bargh, J. A., 307
Barker, L., 316
Barker, L. M., 618
Barkow, J. H., 96, 309, 538
Barlow, C. E., 556
Barlow, D. H., 587, 626, 627
Barlow-Brown, F., 416
Baron-Cohen, S., 308
Barone, M., 88
Barr, H. M., 473
Barrett, P. T., 472
Barron, K. D., 619, 620
Bartels, M., 308
Bartlett, F. C., 360–61, 363
Bartlett, J. A., 571
Bartoshuk, L, M., 258
Baskin, D., 327
Baudry, M., 375
Bauer, C. R., 136, 554
Bauer, R. M., 136
Baum, A., 544
Baum, A., 569
Baurd, D. D., 380
Baxter, D. W., 230
Bayley, N., 468
Bear, M. F., 273–74
Beck, A. T., 596, 621–22, 628, 635
Beckmann, H., 317
Behl, G., 384
Békésy, G. von, 252, 253
Bell, M. A., 391
Bellinger, L. L., 164
Belloc, N., 552
Belsky, J., 405
Bem, D. J., 515–16
Benassi, V. A., 564
Bendersky, M., 383
Benedict, H., 429
Benjamin, L. T., 423
Benjamini, W., 567
Bennett, E. L., 94, 128, 382
Benson, H., 331
Benson, P. J., 308
Ben-Zur, H., 572
Berg, S., 467
Berger, R. J., 320
Bergman, L., 633
Bergstrom, R. F., 78
Berk, L. E., 398
Berkeley, G., 14
Berkman, L. F., 552, 553
Berlim, M. T., 550
Bermejo, M., 561
Bernard, L., 228
Bernardis, L. L., 164
Bernstein, D. A., 616, 624
Bernstein, I. S., 317
Berridge, K. C., 333, 339
Bersheid, E., 532
Bertenthal, B. I., 391
Berzon, Y. W., 572
Best, D. L., 527
Best, P. J., 551
Betrand, L. D., 593
Betz, A. L., 234
Bhatnagar, S., 300
Biber, H., 327, 328
Bickerton, D., 308
Biederman, J., 585
Binet, A., 452–53, 457, 478, 482
Birley, J. L. T., 601
Bjork-Eriksson, T., 129
Blackwood, G. L. Jr., 615
Blair, R. J. R., 605
Blair, S. N., 556
Blakemore, C., 374, 375
Blanchard, E. B., 619, 620
Blaney, P. H., 372, 564
Blass, J. P., 375
Blehar, M. C., 406, 596
Bleuler, E., 598
Bloom, L., 430
Bloomel, J. M., 524
Bogen, J., 133–34
Boldrey, E., 123–24
Bolles, R. C., 258
Bombardier, C., 339
Bond, C. F., Jr., 334
Bond, R., 524

Boodoo, G., 451, 466, 472, 477
Boorman, G. A., 550
Booth, D., 160
Booth, R. J, 569
Bootzin, R. R., 324
Boring, E. G., 16, 19, 231
Bornstein, R. F., 234, 531
Bothwell, R. K., 536
Bouchard, T. J., Jr., 89, 407, 451, 466, 472, 477, 491, 492
Bouckoms, A. J., 629
Bovbjerg, D. H., 571
Bower, G. H., 130, 372
Bower, J. M., 129
Bower, N. J. A., 389
Bower, T. G. R., 389, 393
Bowers, D., 136
Bowlby, J., 405–6, 409, 410
Bownds, M. D., 309
Boyatzis, C. J., 539
Boykin, A. W., 451, 466, 472, 477
Brackbill, R. M., 556
Bradbury, J. W., 420, 538
Bradbury, T. N., 514
Braddick, O. J., 389
Bradley, B., 295
Bradley, R. M., 384
Bradney, N., 512
Bradshaw, G. L., 131, 438
Bradshaw, J. L., 417
Braid, J., 329
Brainerd, C. J., 397
Brakke, K. E., 425
Brammer, M., 308
Brand, C., 464
Brand, R. J., 553
Brannon, L., 545, 548, 562, 614, 620, 625
Braun, A. R., 417
Braun, E. W., 569
Braun, J., 284–85
Bray, G., 555
Breedlove, S. M., 153, 528
Breland, K., 216–17
Breland, M., 216–17
Brennan, J. F., 6, 19
Breslow, J. L., 554
Breslow, L., 552
Bresnick, B., 387
Breznitz, S., 572
Brigham, J. C., 536
Brill, P. L., 627
Broadbent, D. E., 349–50
Broadfield, D. C., 415, 417
Broca, P., 17, 18, 418
Brocato, R. M., 524
Brody, N., 451, 466, 472, 477, 486
Brooks-Gunn, J., 409
Brown, A. S., 360
Brown, B., 382
Brown, B. W., 601
Brown, E. N., 316
Brown, J., 589, 590
Brown, J. D., 565
Brown, R., 367, 371, 430–31
Bruce, D., 423
Brustrom, J., 564
Buccino, R., 416
Buchan, H., 630
Buchanan, M., 354–55
Buchwald, A. M., 563
Buchwald, H., 556
Buckley, K. W., 516
Bullmore, E. T., 308
Bullock, A. E., 337
Bullough, V., 529
Burger, J. M., 514, 564
Burgess, C., 330–31
Buring, J. E., 554
Burke, A., 555
Burns, H. J., 361–62
Burns, M. S., 385
Burns, W., 254
Burt, D. R., 600
Buss, A. H., 172–73, 407, 538
Buss, D. M., 530
Butler, S., 96
Butterworth, G., 416, 427
Butterworth, T., 561
Byatt, G., 532
Byrne, D., 531
Byrne, E., 405

C

Cacioppo, J. T., 517
Cain, N. G., 421
Calder, A. J., 177
Calkins, M. W., 20–21
Calkins, S. D., 391
Callahan, L. M., 375
Camacho, T. C., 553
Cameron, P., 327, 328
Camp, J., 629, 631
Campbell, C. B. G., 93
Campbell, G. S., 556
Campos, C. T., 556
Campos, J. J., 391
Candland, D. K., 171–72, 431
Canfield, R. E., 380
Cannon, W. B., 152, 154, 179, 182, 559
Cantor, N., 512
Cao, J., 337
Capafons, A., 330
Capaldi, E. D., 258
Cardena, E., 330, 591, 592
Cardena-Buelna, E., 330
Carey, G., 538
Carey, S., 428–29
Carlier, M., 473
Carlsmith, J. M., 518
Carmichael-Olson, H., 383
Carpenter, G. A., 311
Carpenter, L. L., 630
Carr, H., 21
Carr, J. M., 595
Carr, T. S., 538
Carroll, J. B., 468
Carron, A. V., 524
Carson, J., 561
Carter, F., 204
Cartwright, R., 326
Caspi, A., 468
Cassidy, J. F., 581
Cattell, J. M., 21–22, 24
Cattell, R. B., 488–91, 493
Ceci, S. J., 451, 460, 464, 466, 472, 477, 478
Cerny, J. A., 626
Chachere, J. G., 539
Chaiken, S., 515, 516
Chalmers, D. J., 308
Champoux, M., 405
Changeax, J. P., 142
Channon, S., 308
Chapin, R. E., 550
Chapman, J. P., 598
Chapman, L. J., 598
Chapman, M., 396
Charcot, J., 496–97, 558, 590
Chartrand, T. L., 307
Chase, W. G., 351
Chasin, J., 416
Chaves, J. F., 328
Cheney, D. L., 421–22
Cheriff, A. D., 571
Cherry, E. C., 349–50
Chess, S., 407
Ching, P. L. Y. H., 557
Chitnis, X. A., 598, 600
Chomsky, N., 423, 426, 428–29, 432, 446
Christensen, A., 627, 628
Christensen, K. M., 388
Churchland, P. S., 195
Cifuentes-Garcia, E., 549
Clader, A. J., 177
Clark, D. M., 252, 633
Clark, F., 605
Clark, L. F., 252
Clark, R. D., III, 530–31
Cleckley, H. M., 592
Clements, A., 561
Cohen, L., 604
Cohen, L. M., 543, 559
Cohen, N., 367, 566
Cohen, R. D., 553, 558
Cohen, S., 571
Colditz, G. A., 553, 557
Cole, C. S., 563
Coleman, P. D., 375
Coleman, R. M., 316
Colin, V. L., 406
Collinge, W., 545–46
Collins, A. C., 337
Collins, A. M., 365–66
Comer, R. J., 605
Compas, B. E., 620
Compton, S., 633
Comstock, J. A., 80
Conners, C. K., 578
Conners, B. W., 273–74
Conrad, C., 366
Cook, R. G., 222
Cook, W. L., 601
Coons, H. L., 561
Cooper, K. H., 556
Cooper, L. A., 434
Corkin, B., 374
Corkin, S., 265
Corley, R., 467
Coruzzi, G., 144
Coryell, W., 595, 596
Coslett, H. B., 136
Cosmides, L., 96, 298, 309, 538
Costa, P. T., 409, 490–91, 492
Costanzo, R., 261
Costigan, K. A., 384
Courage, M. L., 389
Courneya, K. S., 524
Cousins, N., 571
Cowan, W. M., 381
Cowey, A., 284
Cox, M., 550
Coyne, J. C., 562, 563
Craighead, L.W., 622, 625, 626
Craighead, W. E., 622, 625, 626
Craik, F. I. M., 357, 399, 400
Cramon, D., 286
Craske, M. G., 626
Crawford, H. J., 294, 330, 355
Creed, F., 561
Creese, F., 600

Creese, I., 600
Critchley, H. D., 164
Crits-Christoph, P., 615
Crnic, K., 405
Crook, T. H., 399
Cross, J., 522
Csikszentmihalyi, M., 464
Culbertson, F. M., 594–95
Cunitz, A. R., 354
Cunningham, C. E., 616, 618
Cunningham, M. R., 530, 531
Currie, R., 592
Curtiss, S., 403, 431
Cutler, W. B., 296
Czeisler, C. A., 316

D

Dabbs, J. M., 538
Daly, M., 97–98, 101
Damasio, A., 105–6, 178
Damos, D., 349, 353
Darby, B. L., 473
Darley, J. M., 525
Darwin, C., 17, 18, 21, 31, 70–75, 82, 87, 92, 102, 172, 174, 175, 182, 451, 496–97, 500, 502, 512, 530, 537–38, 589–90
Darwin, E., 82
David, A. S., 308
David, W., 572
Davidshofer, C. O., 459
Davidson, J. E., 435, 438, 445, 464
Davidson, R. J., 179
Davies, M., 633
Davies, N. B., 100
Da Vinci, L., 175–76, 178, 182
Davis, C. M., 158–59
Davis, J. L., 375
Davis, J. O., 473–74
Davis, L. B., 388
Dawber, T. R., 554
Dawkins, R., 96, 161, 187, 229–30, 299, 503
Day, R. H., 281
Deary, I. J., 453, 479
de Bono, E., 464
DeBono, K., 517
DeCaria, C. M., 604
DeCasper, A. J., 384, 388
DeFeo, V. J., 559
DeFries, J. C., 467, 470
deGroot, A. D., 371, 441
de Haan, M., 407
de Jong, W. W., 311
DelBoca, F. K., 537
DeLizio, R., 405
Dellarco, V., 550
Dement, W. C., 322–23
DeNeve, K. M., 175
Dennett, D., 106, 108, 147, 421, 425, 426, 433
Dennett, D. C., 206
Dennis, E. S., 79
DePaulo, J. R., 596
Dermer, M., 531
Derogatis, L. R., 561
Descartes, R., 5–6, 31, 546
Dethier, V., 157
Detterman, D. K., 451
Deutsch, G., 295
DeValois, R. L., 245–46
Dewey, J., 21
Dewsbury, D. A., 88
Deyo, R. A., 570
Diamond, J., 72, 81, 128, 186, 551
Diamond, M. C., 94, 382
Diehl, S. R., 600
Diener, E., 174–75
Dinges, D. F., 593
DiPietro, J. A., 384
Dix, D., 610
Dixon, R. M. W., 488
Dobrzecka, C., 163
Dobson, L., 389
Dodd, G. H., 298
Dodds, J., 387
Dohrenwend, B. P., 579, 601
Dohrenwend, B. S., 579
Doidge, N., 602
Doku, V., 598, 600
Dolan, R. J., 177
Dollard, J., 539
Donald, M., 415–16
Donnelly, J. P., 561
Doob, L. W., 539
Dovidio, J. F., 537
Dow, R. S., 130
Downs, T. J., 549
Dreary, I. J., 460
Dreifus, C., 463
Drive, J., 301
Druen, P. B., 530, 531
Drugan, R. C., 565
Druyan, A., 69, 151
Dryman, A., 584, 586
Duck, S., 532
Duffy, J. F., 316
Duflou, J., 555
Dufour, C. L., 564
Duman, R. S., 630, 632
Dunbar, C., 265
Dunbar, R. L. M., 415, 420
Dunnick, J. K., 550
Durrell, L., 486

E

Eagle, M. N., 613
Eagly, A. H., 529
Easteal, S., 79
Eaton, W. W., 584, 586
Ebbinghaus, H., 368–70, 374
Edwards, K., 517
Ehlers, A., 586
Ehrhardt, A. A., 528
Ehrlich, P. R., 97
Ehrlichman, H., 486
Eible-Eibesfeldt, I., 172, 173, 312, 313
Eich, J. E., 372
Eichen, E. B., 431
Einstein, A., 328, 443
Eisch, A. J., 630, 632
Ekman, P., 175
Elgert, K., 567
Eliassen, J. C., 178–79
Elizabeth, Queen of England, 293
Ellenberger, H., 503
Ellis, A., 621–22, 628, 635
Emerick, C. D., 627
Emery, R. E., 577
Endicott, J., 595, 596
Epstein, A. N., 163
Epstein, R., 438
Erickson, B., 296
Ericsson, A. E., 351
Ericsson, K. A., 440
Eridssen, J., 556
Erikson, E., 403–11, 410, 504, 527, 615
Erikssen, G., 556
Eriksson, P. S., 129
Erlich, A., 70
Erlich, H. A., 78
Erlich, P., 70
Eshleman, S., 584, 595
Ettinger, U., 598, 600
Evans, D., 512, 533, 566
Evans, D. D., 619, 620
Ewald, P. W., 549
Eysenck, H. J., 472, 473, 488–91, 628

F

Fabrega, H., 545–46
Fahrmeier, E. D., 397
Fairburn, C. G., 625, 626
Falconer, D. S., 86–87
Faloon, S., 351
Fancher, R. E., 14, 16, 19, 20, 189, 290, 451–53
Fannon, D. G., 598, 600
Fantz, R. L., 389
Faraone, S. V., 585
Farb, A., 555
Farrell, W., 530
Fechner, G., 231–36, 271
Fehr, B., 532
Fein, S., 522
Feingold, A., 531, 572
Feist, J., 545, 548, 562, 614, 620, 625
Felten, D., 568
Felton, D., 566
Feng, W. Y., 407
Ferland, R. J., 166–67
Fernandez, A., 372
Festinger, L., 518–19
Fibiger, H. C., 166, 167
Field, T. M., 554
Fifer, W. P., 385
Fincham, F. D., 514
Fink, B., 530
Fishbein, M., 515
Fisher, J., 85
Fiske, S. T., 513
Fitch, L. L., 556
Fitzsimmons, C. M., 430
Flaten, M., 571
Flatz, G., 162
Flavell, J. H., 397
Flaxman, S. M., 383
Fletcher, G., 514
Flora, J. A., 515
Florio, G. A., 561
Flourens, P., 16, 17, 18
Flynn, J. R., 471, 472, 475
Flynn, J. S., 167
Folkman, S., 559
Forrdyce, W. E., 570
Forster, K. I., 431
Foster, R. G., 310
Fouts, R. S., 415
Fowles, D. C., 600
Fox, N. A., 391
Frady, R. L., 538
Frances, A. J., 604
Francis, R., 511
Franco, R., 427
Frankenburg, W., 387
Franzek, E., 317
Fraser, S., 466
Frawley, P. J., 618

Frederick the Great, of Prussia, 339
Freud, A., 504
Freud, S., 24, 151, 298–99, 307, 309, 325, 326, 398, 487, 496–505, 505, 506–9, 537, 564–65, 566, 580–81, 613–15, 615, 635
Frey, K. A., 595
Friedman, D., 585
Frisina, R. D., 250, 253
Fritch, G., 17
Frith, C., 301
Frith, C. D., 177
Frith, U., 308
Frohman, L. A., 164
Fuchs, C. S., 553
Fulbright, R. K., 177
Fulker, D. W., 467
Fuller, J. L., 86, 172, 407
Funk, S. C., 564
Furman, M. J., 630
Furrow, D., 429
Fyer, A. J., 587

G

Gadow, K., 539
Gaertner, S. L., 537
Gage, F. H., 129
Gage, P., 105–6, 127, 134, 178, 419, 487
Gagné, G. C., Jr., 630
Galen, 111
Gall, F., 16, 18
Gallaher, P. E., 602
Gallese, V., 308, 416
Gallup, G. G., 307
Gallup, G. G., Jr., 308, 329, 462
Galton, F., 451–52, 457, 466, 472, 482
Ganellen, R. J., 564
Gange, J. J., 524
Gannon, P. J., 417
Ganong, W. F., 427
Gantt, W. H., 586
Gao, J. H., 129
Garcia, C. R., 296
Garcia, J., 218–20, 221, 449–50, 472
Garcia, R., 554
Gardner, B. I., 423
Gardner, H., 460–62, 465, 471, 482, 550
Gardner, R. A., 423
Garfield, C., 581
Garraghty, A. K., 265, 491
Garrison, R. G., 569
Gatch, M. B., 618
Gatchel, R. J., 563
Gauci, M., 569, 570
Gaziano, J. M., 554
Gazzaniga, M., 133, 135–36, 178–79, 629
Geary, D. C., 527, 538
Geen, R. G., 524
Gehi, A., 265
Geldard, F. A., 248
Gelman, R., 397
Gershon, E. S., 596
Gescheider, G. A., 250, 253
Ghandi, 515
Gibbons, L. W., 556
Gibson, E. J., 288, 391, 393
Gibson, H. B., 330
Gilbert, D. T., 514
Gill, R. V., 424
Gillan, D. J., 443
Gilligan, S. G., 372
Gilman, A., 631
Gilmartin, K., 371
Giordani, B. J., 595
Giovannucci, E. L., 553
Giriunas, I. E., 629
Gisner, R., 422
Glanzer, M., 354
Glass, G. V., 627
Glauberman, N., 466
Glenberg, A. M., 372
Glickman, S. E., 143, 166
Godden, D., 372
Goethals, G. R., 522
Gold, H. H., 605
Gold, H. S., 549
Gold, R. J., 327
Gold, S. R., 327
Goldberg, L. R., 488, 490–91
Goldblatt, J., 550
Goldhaber, S. Z., 554
Goldman, A., 308, 416
Goldman, B. D., 317
Goldman-Rakic, P. S., 600
Goldsmith, H. H., 407
Goldstein, A., 566
Goldstein, J., 327
Goldstein, M. H., 430
Goldstein, M. J., 601
Golin, E. S., 360
Goodall, J., 485–86, 487, 493
Goodglass, H., 419
Goodman, L. S., 631
Goodwin, C. J., 19
Gopnik, A., 428
Gordon, B., 633
Gordon, J., 389
Gordon, R. A., 478–79
Gordon, T. P., 317
Gorman, J. M., 587
Gortmaker, S. L., 557
Gossard, D., 586
Goto, S. G., 408
Gottesman, I. I., 382, 599, 600
Gottfredson, L. S., 464, 466, 471, 478, 479–81
Gould, J. L., 311
Gould, S. J., 74
Grady, J. M., 532
Graham, C. H., 241
Graham-Bermann, S. A., 561
Grammer, K., 530
Gray, D. S., 555
Green, D., 169
Green, D. M., 233
Green, S., 407
Greenberg, A., 572
Greenfield, P. M., 397, 417
Greenfield, T., 627
Greenhill, L., 633
Greeno, J. G., 435
Greer, C. A., 384
Griffin, D., 230
Griffin, P., 385
Grilly, D. M., 630, 631
Gross, J., 626
Gross, T. F., 397
Grossberg, J. M., 300, 554
Grossberg, S., 311
Grossmann, K., 407
Grossmann, K. E., 407
Gruen, R. J., 561
Gruenberg, A. M., 599
Grunberg, N. E., 564
Gruzelier, J., 330
Guarnieri, P., 619, 620
Guevremont, D. C., 616
Gulick, W. L., 250, 253
Gunnar, M. R., 407
Gunter, B., 539, 540
Gurevich, M., 562
Gutknect, L., 473
Guttley, G. A., 79
Gwynn, M. I., 330
Gyllensten, U., 77, 78–79

H

Haaga, D. A., 620
Haber, R. B., 370
Haber, R. N., 370
Hack, S., 633
Hacking, I., 452
Hackmann, A., 633
Hahn, R. A., 570
Hahn, S., 349
Haig, A., 517
Haimov, I., 315
Hainline, L., 389
Haldane, J. B. S., 551
Hall, G. S., 19, 23, 31
Hall, N., 566
Hall, V. C., 169
Hall, W., 537
Halpern, D. F., 445, 451, 466, 472, 477
Hamilton, W. D., 97
Haney, C., 524
Hankinson, S. E., 553
Hanlon, C., 430–31
Hanser, S. B., 294
Hare, R. D., 605
Haring, M. J., 174
Harker, L., 178
Harkins, S., 525
Harkness, A. R., 468
Harlow, H. F., 93–94, 95, 222, 299–300, 405
Harlow, M. K., 93–94, 95, 405
Harriman, A. E., 167
Harrington, A., 570
Harris, J. R., 409, 495, 496, 556
Harris, M., 188, 416
Harris, V. A., 514
Harsh, N., 367
Hartel, C., 27
Hartley, D., 14
Hartline, H. K., 241
Hartman, E., 321
Hartmann, T., 579
Harvey, P. H., 98
Hasert, M., 633
Hasher, L., 357
Hatfield, E., 529, 530–31
Hauchman, F., 550
Hay, D., 538
Hayes, C., 423
Hayes, J. R., 437
Heap, M., 330
Heath, G. W., 556
Heath, R. G., 167
Hecht, H., 434
Hecht, S., 243
Heider, F., 513
Heilman, K. M., 136
Heinreich, B., 421
Hellman, C., 571
Helmholtz, H. L. F., 16–17, 18, 250
Helmreich, R. L., 169
Hender, J., 407
Hendren, J., 512–13

Hendrick, S., 532
Hendrick, V., 532
Hendrickson, A., 389
Hendriks, W., 311
Hennekens, C. H., 553, 554
Henry VIII, King of England, 213
Hergenhahn, B. R., 453, 454
Hering, E., 245–46
Herman, L. M., 422
Hernandez, L., 164
Herrick, C. J., 110–12
Herrnstein, R. J., 464, 466, 474, 475, 477, 478, 479
Herzing, D. L., 566
Hess, E. H., 90–91, 121
Hester, R. K., 618
Hetherington, M. M., 160
Hewes, G. W., 416
Hewitt, K. L., 388
Heyser, C. J., 383
Highstein, S. M., 241
Higley, J., 633
Hilfrink, M. L., 618
Hilgard, E. R., 330–31
Hill, C. E., 627
Hillhouse, J., 619, 620
Hillier, L., 388
Hillyard, S. A., 301
Hilton, S. C., 384
Hinde, R. A., 85, 407
Hinson, J., 63
Hinson, R. E., 202
Hippocrates, 14, 488
Hirsch, J., 431
Hirschfield, R. M., 596
Hirshfeld-Becker, D. R., 585
Hitzig, E., 17
Hobson, J. A., 325, 326
Hockfield, S., 382
Hodges, T. B., 228
Hodgson, D. M., 384
Hodos, W., 93
Hoebel, B. G., 164
Hoffman, A., 338
Hofstede, G., 408, 514
Hogan, J., 158
Holden, C., 323
Hollander, E., 604
Holloway, R. L., 415, 417
Holmes, T. H., 560–62
Honzik, C. H., 217–18
Hood, B., 389
Hoogland, J. L., 404
Hooley, J. M., 601
Hoosain, R., 356
Hopkins, W. D., 416, 424, 435
Horn, J. M., 470
Horne, J. A., 321
Horney, K., 504
Horvath, J. A., 463
Houpt, K. A., 89
Hovland, C. I., 516
Howard, K. L., 627
Howard, M. O., 618
Howard, R. D., 404
Hsieh, M. H., 144
Hsu, L. K. G., 625
Hubel, D., 273–75
Huberth, A., 599
Huckeby, E. R., 430
Hudson, T., 445
Hugdahl, K., 330
Huggins, G. R., 296
Hughes, M., 584, 595
Huguelet, P., 595
Hull, C. L., 155, 156, 168
Hull, J. G., 334
Hulse, S. H., 421
Hume, D., 14
Humphrey, N., 307–8
Hungerford, L. R., 558
Hunt, E., 383
Hunt, W. A., 551
Hunter, B. A., 537
Hunter, D. J., 553
Hunter, J. E., 464, 480
Hunter, S., 550
Hurford, J. R., 415, 431
Hurvich, L. M., 245–46
Husband, A. J., 569, 570
Hyler, S. E., 602
Hyson, R. L., 565

I

Ingman, M., 78–79
Inhelder, B., 392, 396
Insko, C. A., 518
Isabella, R. A., 406
Isha, A., 434
Iskant, A. P., 479
Izard, C. E., 174

J

Jaccard, J., 619, 620
Jackson, D. N., 602
Jackson, R. L., 563
Jacobs, G. H., 245–46
Jacobson, K. C., 538
Jacobson, N. S., 627, 628
Jacoby, L. L., 399, 466
Jacoby, R., 466
James, W., 20–23, 23, 31, 179–81, 182, 306–7, 309, 320–21, 327, 332, 390, 450
Jameson, D., 245–46
Jamison, C., 622
Jamison, K. R., 596
Jang, K. L., 602
Jansen, A. S. P., 177
Janus, C. L., 529
Janus, S. S., 529
Jasiukaitis, P., 330
Jatzke, S., 599
Jaynes, J., 328
Jeacock, J., 561
Jemmott, J. B., III, 571
Jenicke, M. A., 587
Jenkins, H. M., 220
Jensen, A. R., 453, 464, 473, 478
Jerison, H. J., 108
Jermlin, L. S., 79
Jiang, N., 431
Johannsen, W. L., 77
Johansson, B., 467
John, O. P., 490
Johns, T., 618
Johnson, E., 630
Johnson, J. S., 431
Johnson, M. L., 387
Johnson, M. P., 316
Johnson, S. P., 389
Johnson, T. R. B., 384
Johnson-Laird, P. M., 443
Johnston, J. C., 348
Joliet, P. V., 479
Jones, E., 498
Jones, E. E., 514
Jones, H. E., 468
Jones, J., 522
Jones, L., 605
Jongbloet, P. H., 317
Joseph, R., 295
Joshi, S., 592
Judd, C. M., 535–36
Julien, R. M., 334, 335, 336
Jung, C. G., 503, 504, 506, 509, 615
Juscyzk, P. W., 389
Jussim, L. J., 234
Justesen, D. R., 569
Justine, S., 295

K

Kaas, J., 265
Kabat-Zinn, J., 331
Kaczynski, T., 462
Kaelber, C. T., 579
Kaessmann, H., 78–79
Kagan, J., 407, 495
Kahn, M., 614
Kahn, S., 564
Kalat, J., 158
Kalat, J. W., 220
Kalb, R. G., 382
Kalil, R. E., 382
Kamitani, Y., 301
Kanner, A. D., 562
Kant, I., 15, 18
Kaplan, E., 419
Kaplan, E. L., 427
Kaplan, G. A., 427, 553, 558
Kaplan, P. S., 480
Kaplan, R. D., 477
Karau, S. J., 525
Karni, A., 323
Karpitskiy, V., 177
Kassin, S. M., 522
Katz, R., 595
Katz, S., 160–61
Kausler, D. H., 400
Kaye, K. L., 393
Kazdin, A. E., 610, 616, 622, 625, 626
Keefe, F. J., 620
Keeley, L. H., 527
Keenan, J. P., 308
Keesey, R. E., 556
Keller, M., 595, 596
Keller, S. E., 571
Kelley, D. D., 322
Kelley, H. H., 513, 519
Kelley, K. W., 567
Kelley, S. J., 561
Kellman, D., 604
Kellman, H. D., 602
Kellogg, L. A., 423
Kellogg, W. N., 423
Keltner, D., 178
Kemperman, G., 129
Kendler, K. S., 584, 595, 599, 600
Kennedy, L. C., 529
Kenway, L., 324
Kermoian, R., 391
Kerr, B., 383
Kerry, T., 464
Kertesz, A., 433
Kessler, R. C., 584, 595
Keverne, E. B., 259
Keys, A., 554

Khachaturian, D. S., 375
Kiang, N. Y., 252
Kihlstrom, J. F., 330
Kilbourn, M. R., 595
Kim, K., 431
Kimeldorf, D. J., 218
Kimura, D., 132, 136
King, B. J., 424
King, B. M., 164
King, M. G., 569, 570
Kingsberg, S. A., 295
Kintsch, A. S., 396
Kintsch, W., 445
Kircher, T. T. J., 308
Kirk, R. W., 48, 61
Kirk-Smith, M., 298
Kirsch, C., 619, 620
Kirsch, I., 330
Kirshnit, C. E., 438
Kissin, B., 174
Kitayama, S., 514
Kit-Fong, R., 397
Kiwachi, I., 553
Klee, B., 633
Klein, R., 633
Kleinman, A., 577
Klevjord, T. A., 407
Klinger, M. R., 591
Klosko, J. S., 626
Knable, M. B., 600
Knebel, T., 330
Knight, C., 415
Knight, J., 531
Knowles, J., 549, 550
Kobasa, S. C. O., 563, 564
Koch, C., 195
Koelling, R. A., 218–20
Koenigsberger, L., 17, 18
Koeppe, R. A., 595
Koestner, R., 170
Koffka, K, 290–91
Kohl, H. W., 556
Kohlberg, L., 400–402, 403
Kohler, W, 290–91
Köhler, W., 437
Kohn, P. M., 561–62
Kolb, B., 126, 129, 141, 375
Kolb, F. C., 284–85
Koppenaal, R. J., 369
Kosslyn, S. M., 328
Kostyk, S. K., 265
Kotovsky, K., 437
Kotses, D. J., 570
Kottak, C. P., 476
Kramer, A. F., 349
Krank, M. D., 202
Kraus, L., 571
Krause, S. J., 515
Krech, D., 94, 128, 382
Krieger, A., 296
Kriegman, D., 503
Krohn, A., 604
Kronauer, R. E., 316
Kroonenberg, P. M., 407
Krosnick, J. A., 234
Krueger, T. H., 443
Kuffler, S. W., 272
Kuhl, D., 434
Kuhl, P. K., 429
Kuhn, C. M., 554
Kuhn, H. G., 129
Kulik, J., 367
Kumari, V., 598, 600
Kurtz, N. M., 632
Kymissis, E., 429

L

LaBarba, R. C., 295
Labellarte, M. J., 633
LaBossier, E., 389
Lacerda, F., 429
Lafreniere, K., 562
Lal, H., 618
Lam, H. M., 144
Lamarck, J. B., 73
Lamb, M. E., 406
Lamberg, L., 326
Lambert, M. J., 627
Landau, J. D., 360
Lange, 179, 182
Langer, E. J., 565
Langley, P., 438
Langlois, J. H., 530, 531
Lanza, R. P., 438
Lapml, M., 387
Larsen, K. S., 521
Larson, R. W., 512
Latané, B., 525
Laudenslager, M. L., 565
Laurie, C. A., 327
Lavie, P., 315
Lawler, K. A., 564
Lawley, H. G., 296
Lazarus, R. S., 559, 561–62
Leavens, D. A., 416
Lee, K. M., 431
Lee, Y. T., 514
Lefcourt, H. M., 571
Leff, J., 577, 601
Legge, J., 545
Leibnitz, G., 15, 18
Leiman, A. L., 153
Leiner, A. L., 130
Leiner, H. C., 130
Leitenberg, H., 620, 626
LeMagnen, J., 618
Lepper, M. R., 169
Lerner, M. J., 514
Lesch, K., 599
Leskowitz, S., 567
Leslie, A. M., 308
Le Souef, P. N., 550
Lester, D., 618
Lettvin, J. Y., 272
Levav, I., 601
Levi, N., 572
Levine, S. C., 428–29
Levitan, G., 572
Levitsky, D. A., 382
Levy, J., 136
Lew, L. A., 315
Lewis, M., 383
Lickey, M. E., 633
Lidow, M. S., 600
Lieberman, P., 425
Liebowitz, M. R., 587
Light, P., 397
Liker, J., 460
Lilly, J. C., 422
Lincoln, A, 271
Lindblom, B., 429
Linden, E., 423
Lindenberger, U., 396
Lindsay, E. W., 526
Lindsay, P. H., 240, 242, 247, 248, 343, 357, 365
Lindsley, O. R., 616
Lindy, J., 166, 167
Link, B. G., 601
Linkous, R. A., 524
Linnoila, M., 633
Linscheid, T. R., 616, 618
Linz, D., 540
Lipsitt, L. P., 384
Lischinsky, S., 572
Livesley, W. J., 602
Livingstone, M. S., 178
Locke, B, Z., 614
Locke, J., 14–15, 18, 190, 390, 432, 470
Locke, S., 568
Locke, S. E., 571
Lockhart, R. S., 357
Loeber, R., 538
Loehlin, J. C., 451, 466, 470, 472, 477, 492
Loeser, J. D., 570
Loewen, E. R., 400
Loewy, A. D., 177
Loftus, E., 345–46, 361–63, 440, 591
Lombard, J., 298
Long, J. M., 556
Long, M. L., 526
Lorenz, K., 89–90, 275, 405, 537
Lucas, R. E., 174–75
Luchins, A. S., 442
Ludwig, A. M., 596
Luis, S., 530
Lumsdaine, A. A., 516
Luria, A. R., 367–68, 370
Lutz, W., 627
Lykken, D., 407, 466, 491, 605
Lynch, M. P., 294
Lynch, N. R., 550
Lynn, A. R., 234
Lynn, R., 472
Lynn, S. J., 330

M

Macaluso, E., 301
Maccoby, N., 515
Macera, C. A., 556
MacKenzie, S. A., 89
MacKinnon, D. F., 596
MacNeilage, P. F., 416
Maddi, S. R., 564
Maddock, R., 586
Maffei, M., 88
Maher, B. A., 598
Mahoney, M. J., 622, 625, 626
Mai, N., 286
Maibach, E. W., 515
Maier, S. E., 565
Maier, S. F., 562, 563, 568
Mair, A., 254
Mair, S. F., 159
Makhijani, M. G., 529
Makin, J. W., 388
Malberg, J. E., 630, 632
Malina, R. M., 389
Malone, P. W., 514
Malpass, R. S., 536
Manber, R., 324
Mandel, D. R., 389
Manderscheid, R. W., 614
Manning, P. K., 545–46
Manson, J. E., 553
Manuck, S. B., 571
Marcel, A., 234
March, J., 633
Margraf, J., 586
Markman, E. M., 430

Marks, J. S., 383
Marks, R. A., 396
Markus, H. R., 514
Marler, P., 421–22
Marquez, S., 415
Marsh, R. L., 360
Marshall, G. N., 564
Marsland, A. L., 571
Martin, D. C., 473
Martin, L., 441
Martin, P. K., 295
Martinovich, Z., 627
Maslow, A. H., 23, 168, 170, 183, 506–9, 508, 563
Masterton, R. B., 230, 255
Matarazzo, J. D., 544
Matejek, M., 294
Mathews, D. B., 551
Matillo, G. M., 539
Matts, J. P., 556
Maturana, H. R., 272
Mayberry, R. I., 431
Mayr, E., 72
Mays, L. C., 168–69
McAleer, J., 539, 540
McAnarney, E. R., 300
McArthur, D., 416
McCall, R. B., 407
McCann, R. S., 348
McCartney, K., 470
McClearn, G. E., 467
McClelland, D. C., 169–70, 170, 571
McClintock, M. K., 295–96
McCloskey, M., 367, 434
McCormick, D. A., 129
McCracken, J., 633
McCrae, R. R., 409, 490–91, 492
McCulloch, W. S., 272
McCully, J., 202
McDermott, K. B., 360
McDonald, J. J., 301
McDonald, K., 424, 435
McDonald, W. T., 370
McGeoch, J. A., 370
McGeorge, E. I., 604
McGillis, J., 566
McGonagle, K. A., 584, 595
McGue, M., 407, 466
McGuffin, P., 382, 595
McGuire, W., 504, 539
McGuire, W. J., 516, 518
McKim, W. A., 335, 340, 631, 632
McKinlay, J. B., 550
McKinlay, S. M., 550
McKinney, W. T., Jr., 594
McLaren, N. M., 383
McLaughlin, M. A., 425
McLearn, G. E., 556
McManus, C., 544
McNally, R. J., 585
McNeill, D., 371
McPherson, K., 630
Meany, M. J., 300
Medin, D. L., 430
Meehl, P. E., 600
Meeus, W. H. J., 523
MeGargee, E. I., 604
Meier, R. P., 430
Meltzoff, A. N., 390, 428
Melzack, R., 264–65
Menaker, M., 311
Mendel, Gregor, 70, 74, 75–77
Mendelson, W. B., 324
Menzel, E. W., 435
Merler, P., 94
Mersky, H., 592
Mesmer, F., 329
Messner, R., 599
Mettenleiter, T. C., 177
Metz, 390
Meyer, J., 599
Meyer-Bahlberg, H. F. L., 528
Micale, M., 590
Michaels, J. W., 524
Michultka, D., 619, 620
Middleton, H., 633
Miklowitz, D. J., 601
Miles, D. R., 538
Miles, L. E., 313
Miles, S. S., 531
Milgram, S., 36, 522–23, 525
Milich, R., 616, 624
Miller, D. G., 361–62
Miller, D. J., 570
Miller, D. T., 514
Miller, G. A., 350, 354
Miller, J. G., 514
Miller, L., 559
Miller, N., 63
Miller, N. E., 539
Miller, T. I., 627
Miller, W. R., 618
Millon, T., 603
Milner, B., 374, 431
Milner, P., 33–51, 166
Miluk-Kolasa, B., 294
Minichiello, W. E., 587
Minsky, M., 463
Mintz, J., 601
Mischel, W., 170
Mishkin, M., 222–23, 265
Mistretta, C. M., 295, 384
Mita, T. H., 531
Mize, J., 526
Modestin, J., 317
Moellering, R. C., 549
Moerk, E. L., 429, 431
Moffitt, T. E., 468
Moltz, H., 90
Money, J., 528–29
Montagna, W., 263
Moon, C. M., 385
Moore, B. R., 220
Moore, C. I., 265
Moore, M. K., 390
Moore-Ede, M. C., 316
Moras, K., 627
Morey, L. C., 603
Morgan, C. L., 92
Morissette, P., 416, 427
Morrill, B., 619, 620
Morris, D., 80
Morris, J. S., 177
Morrison, E., 261
Morrongiello, B. A., 388
Moschovakis, A. K., 241
Moss, M. B ., 375
Mowbray, K., 415
Mowrer, O. H., 539
Mueller, J., 526
Muëller, J., 16–17, 18
Mullin, C., 540
Mundal, R., 556
Munoz, M., 561
Murdock, B., 354
Murphy, D. R., 360
Murphy, J., 425
Murphy, K. R., 455, 459
Murray, C., 464, 466, 474, 475, 477, 478, 479
Murray, H. A., 170
Muskin, P. R., 589
Musselman, L., 531
Muzio, J. N., 323
Mycielska, K., 371

N

Nachman, M., 618
Narrow, W. E., 614
Nathan, P. E., 618
Naveh, G., 601
Naveh-Benjamin, M., 356
Neiberg, P., 383
Neisser, U., 349, 367, 451, 462, 466, 471, 472, 477
Nelson, A., 308
Nelson, C. A., 382
Nelson, C. B., 584, 595
Nelson, K., 398, 429
Nelson, R. J., 317
Nesbitt, K. M., 539
Nesse, R. M., 333, 549, 550, 551, 596, 602
Nestler, E. J., 630, 632
Nettle, D., 597
Nettleton, N. C., 131
Neugebauer, R., 579
Nevo, E., 311
Newcombe, F., 433
Newell, A., 433, 436
Newman, S., 544
Newport, E. L., 389, 431
Newton, I., 14, 15
Nguyen, X. V., 177
Nicholls, K., 339
Nicholson, A. N., 315
Nickerson, R. S., 357
Nida, S. A., 525
Nielson, S. L., 349
Niemi, R. G., 326
Nier, J. A., 537
Nietzel, M. T., 616, 624
Nigg, J. T., 605
Nisbett, R. E., 169
Nisenson, L., 178–79
Nisula, B. C., 380
Noonan, K. M., 404
Nordborg, C., 129
Norman, D. A., 240, 242, 247, 248, 343, 357, 365
Norman, W. T., 490
Nottebohm, F., 94, 421
Nouriani, B., 330
Nuechterlein, K. H., 601
Nystrom, J., 554

O

O'Banion, M. K., 375
O'Ceallaigh, S., 598, 600
O'Connor, J. F., 380
O'Connor, M., 308
Odbert, H., 488–89
O'Donovan, M. C., 382
O'Hara, T., 633
Ohl, L. E., 595
Okun, M. A., 174
Oldham, J. M., 602, 604
Olds, J., 33–51, 142, 166
Olfson, M., 614
Olsen, H., 571

Olszewski, J., 230
Oltenacu, E. A. B., 89
Oltmanns, T. F., 577
O'Neal, S., 141
Orne, E. C., 593
Orne, M. T., 593
Ortega, G., 599
Ostrom, T. M., 536
O'Toole, B. I., 479
Oullette, S. C., 563, 564
Overmier, B., 562
Owen, M. J., 382

P

Paabo, S., 78–79
Pace-Schott, E. F., 325
Paffenarger, R. S., Jr., 556
Paikoff, R. L., 409
Pallis, C. A., 287
Palmer, J. C., 362–63
Palmer, R. L., 630
Panksepp, J., 577, 579
Panneton-Cooper, R., 430
Paradiso, M. A., 273–74
Park, B., 535–36
Parsons, L. M., 129
Pascoe, P. A., 315
Pascual-Leone, A., 308
Pateman, T., 430
Patterson, F., 423
Patton, J. H., 545–46
Pavlov, I., 22, 86, 189–204, 210, 212, 218, 307, 366–67
Peacock, J. W., 79
Pearce, M. B., 556
Pearson, J., 254
Pedersen, N. L., 467, 556
Pedersen, P. E., 384
Pelletier, K. R., 566
Pendleton, R. B., 569
Penfield, W. G., 123–24
Pennebaker, J. W., 561, 571
Peplau, L. A., 529
Pepperberg, I. M., 425
Perfilieva, E., 129
Perlis, M. L., 324
Perloff, R., 451, 466, 472, 477
Perls, F. S., 623–24, 628
Perrett, D. I., 177
Perrett-Clermont, A. N., 397
Perry, A. R., 327
Perry, M., 538
Perry, W., 604
Persinger, M. A., 559
Pert, C. B., 337
Peters, S., 94
Peterson, D. A., 129
Peterson, J., 626
Peterson, L. R., 352
Peterson, M., 352
Petri, H. L., 222–23
Petrill, S. A., 467, 469
Petty, R. E., 517
Peyser, H. S., 564
Pfaffman, C., 167
Phelps, E. A., 177
Phelps, J. A., 473–74
Philip, Prince, of England, 293
Phillips, A. G., 166, 167
Phillips, K., 538
Phillips, M. I., 566
Phillips, M. L., 308
Phillips, N. H., 320
Piacentini, J., 633
Piaget, J., 392–97, 402, 411, 434, 457, 502
Piantanida, T., 244
Picariello, M. L., 398
Pick, H. L. Jr., 396
Pierce, S., 407
Pierre, P. J., 218
Pies, R. W., 159
Pillemer, D. B., 398
Pincus, H. A., 614
Pine, D. S., 633
Pinel, J. P. J., 132, 417
Pinel, P., 581
Pinker, S., 106, 309, 414, 423, 427, 431, 495
Pinneau, S. R., 468
Pirenne, M. H., 243
Pisoni, D. B., 389
Pittman, T. S., 169, 234
Pitts, W. H., 272
Plaus, S., 62
Plomin, R., 89, 407, 466, 467, 469, 470
Plumert, A. M., 396
Plutarch, 228
Plutchik, R., 174
Poehlman, E. T., 556
Polt, J. M., 121
Pons, T. P., 265
Porter, R., 630, 631
Porter, R. H., 388
Poulson, C. P., 429
Powell, C., 516
Powley, T. L., 258, 556
Pratkanis, A. R., 234, 516
Premack, A. J., 424
Premack, D., 424
Preston, E., 265
Prestrude, A. M., 329
Preti, M., 296
Price, L. H., 630
Proenca, R., 88
Profet, M., 383
Proffitt, D. R., 434
Proffitt, F., 532
Proust, M, 260
Pruett, J. C., 398
Przybeck, T., 604, 605
Psotka, J., 370
Pullum, G. K., 441
Puska, P., 553

Q

Quillian, M. R., 365–66

R

Raaijmakers, Q. A. W., 523
Rabe-Hesketh, S., 308
Rabin, B. S., 571
Rabin, I., 555
Rachlin, H., 416
Radniz, C. L., 619, 620
Rae, D. S., 614
Rager, D. R., 329
Rahe, R. H., 560–62
Rajecki, D. W., 515
Ramachandran, V. S., 265
Ramsay, D. J., 155
Rando, T. A., 409
Rapee, R. M., 587
Rapoport, J. L., 588
Rasmussen, T., 431
Ravel, M., 295
Ray, W. J., 330
Raynal, D. M., 313
Rayner, R., 198, 562
Razran, G., 189
Reason, J., 371
Recht, R. D., 315
Reed, T. E., 473
Rees, J. A., 98
Reeve, C., 113
Regier, D. A., 579, 614
Reisman, J. M., 610
Relkin, N., 431
Remington, R. W., 348
Remongton, P., 383
Renner, M. J., 218
Rest, J. R., 402
Rethlingshafer, D. A., 88
Reyna, L. J., 616
Reynolds, D. V., 265
Rhodes, G., 532
Rhodes, N., 517
Rhue, J. W., 330
Riad, J. K., 538
Ricciuti, H. N., 382
Rich, R., 491
Richards, D. G., 422
Richardson, G. S., 316
Richman, S. A., 517
Richter, C. P., 149, 167, 559
Riddle, M. A., 633
Rimm, E. B., 553, 557
Rimmele, C. T., 618
Rinn, W. E., 179
Risley, T. R., 428, 429
Ritter, J. M., 530
Ritz, L. A., 633
Rizzolatti, G., 416
Roberts, R. J., 396
Robin, J. A, 585
Robins, L. N., 604, 605
Robinson, J., 633
Robinson, S. R., 384
Robinson, T. E., 339
Rochat, P., 393
Rodahl, K., 556
Rodin, J., 565
Roediger, H. L. III, 360
Roehrs, T., 315
Roffwarg, H. P., 323
Rogers, C., 506–7, 508, 509, 623–24, 628, 635
Roggman, L. A., 530, 531
Rogot, E., 59
Rohner, R. P., 405
Rokeach, M., 545
Rolls, B. J., 160
Rolls, E., 164
Ronda, J. M., 316
Room, R., 627
Roper, M., 633
Rose, R. M., 317
Rosen, J. C., 626
Rosenbaum, J. F., 585
Rosenfarb, I. S., 601
Rosensweig, M. R., 94, 128, 382
Rosenzweig, M. R., 153
Rosner, B., 553, 554
Rosnick, L., 602, 604
Ross, B. H., 430
Ross, C. A., 592

Ross, D., 494
Ross, L., 514
Ross, S., 494
Roth, W. T., 586
Rothbart, M., 407
Rothe, T., 315
Rotter, J. B., 563–64
Rottman, L., 531
Routtenberg, A., 166, 167
Rovee-Collier, C., 398
Rowatt, T. J., 531
Rowatt, W. C., 531
Rowe, D. C., 470, 471, 538
Rowe, J. S., 524
Rowland, D., 177
Rozin, P., 157, 158, 159, 220, 585
Rubenstein, B. S., 323
Rubert, E., 424, 435
Rubin, D. C., 366
Rubin, L. C., 438
Rudd, D., 625
Rumbaugh, D. M., 424, 425
Rundus, D. J., 356
Rush, B., 580
Rushton, J. P., 472
Russell, J., 175
Russell, M. J., 296–97, 388
Rutherford, J., 595
Ryan, S. M., 565

S

Sacks, O., 227, 269–70, 286–87, 301, 592
Saffran, J. R., 389
Sagan, C., 69, 85, 108, 151, 424
Sagi, D., 323, 434
Sahraie, A., 284
Salamé, P., 355
Salapatek, P., 391
Salili, F., 356
Salkovskis, P. M., 633
Salonen, J. T., 553
Salter, A., 616
Salvio, M. A., 324
Sampson, P. D., 473
Sandivk, L., 556
Sanyal, S., 311
Saoud, J. B., 604
Sapir, E., 441
Sapolsky, R. M., 300
Sarason, I. G., 349
Savage-Rumbaugh, S., 416, 424, 425, 435
Sawin, H. S., Jr., 556
Scafidi, F., 554
Scarr, S., 470
Schaal, B., 295
Schacter, D. L., 345, 360
Schacter, S., 179–80, 182, 570–71
Schaefer, C., 562
Schaie, K. W., 399
Schaller, G. B., 67–68
Schanberg, S. M., 554
Schartz, K. M., 473–74
Scheff, T. J., 634
Scheffield, F. D., 516
Schein, E. H., 516
Schiff, B. B., 143, 166
Schiffman, H. R., 247, 248, 280, 440
Schlaer, S., 243
Schlatterer, J. P., 380
Schleifer, S. J., 567, 571
Schmidt, D. P., 530
Schmidt, F. L., 464
Schmidt, N. B., 587
Schmied, L. A., 564
Schmitt, A., 599
Schneider, D. M., 521
Schneidman, E. S., 595
Schooler, C., 471
Schroeder, M. L., 602
Schumann, D. W., 517
Schusterman, R.J., 422
Schwartz, G. E., 544
Schwartz, W. J., 315
Scogin, R., 622
Scott, J. P., 86, 172, 407
Sears, R. R., 539
Sedikides, C., 536
Seelye, K. Q., 513
Segal, N. L., 407, 466, 468–69, 491
Sejnowski, T. J., 195
Seligman, M., 562–63, 566, 627
Seligman, M. E. P., 514
Selye, H., 559–60, 565
Senior, C., 308
Serpell, R., 477
Seurat, G, 277–79
Sevcik, R. A., 424, 425, 435
Seyfarth, R. M., 421–22
Shakespeare, W., 325
Shams, L., 301
Shapiro, A. K., 570
Shapiro, H., 387
Shapley, R., 279
Sharm, T., 598, 600
Shatz, C. J., 382
Shaw, R. J., 400
Sheikh, J., 586
Sheldon, W., 488
Shepard, G. M., 384
Shepard, R. N., 434
Sheppard, J. A., 525
Shepperd, J. A., 525, 565
Sherif, M., 521
Sherman, J. A., 429
Sherman, P. W., 383, 404
Sherry, D. F., 345
Shibata, D., 179
Shiffrin, R. M., 346–47
Shimojo, S., 301
Shrout, P. E., 601
Shulman, M. E., 634
Shutts, D., 178
Sibley, C. G., 80
Sidman, M., 214
Siegel, P. Z., 556
Siegel, R. K., 334
Siegel, S., 202, 372
Sills, R. C., 550
Silva, P. A., 468
Silverman, I., 538
Silvers, M. S., 415
Simmons, A., 308
Simon, H. A., 371, 433, 435, 436, 438, 440
Simon, R. J., 526
Simon, T., 453
Simonsen, T., 571
Simoons, F. J., 161–62, 536
Simpson, O. J., 535–36
Simson, P. E., 551
Singer, D. G., 539
Singer, J. E., 180, 570–71
Singer, J. L., 327, 539
Singh, D., 530
Siobe, B. S., 337
Sizemore, C. C., 592
Skinner, B. F., 22, 23, 24, 206–16, 217–18, 220, 221, 225, 429, 494, 496, 615–16
Skodol, A. E., 601, 602, 604
Slyper, A. H., 557
Small, M. F., 9
Smialek, J., 555
Smink, R. D., Jr., 556
Smith, E. E., 164, 517
Smith, H. L., 174–75
Smith, J. W., 618
Smith, M., 605
Smith, M. S., 627
Smith, P. B., 524
Smith, P. F., 338
Smith, R. L., 164
Smith, T. W., 526
Smotherman, W. P., 384
Snidman, N., 407
Snow, C. E., 385
Snyder, M., 517
Snyder, S. H., 337, 600
Solomon, H. C., 616
Spangelo, B., 566
Spangler, G., 407
Spanos, N. P., 328, 329, 330–31, 346, 593
Spear, L. P., 383
Spear, N. E., 383
Spearman, C., 450, 453, 457, 459, 466, 472, 482
Spelke, E. S., 433
Spence, J. T., 169, 619
Spence, M. J., 384, 388
Spence, S. H., 619
Spencer, D. D., 177
Spencer, M. B., 315
Sperling, G., 348, 354
Sperry, R., 133–34, 136
Spiegel, D., 330, 591, 592
Spiegler, M. D., 616
Spinoza, B., 6
Spitz, E., 473
Spitzer, M., 598
Spitzer, R. L., 589
Sprafkin, J., 539
Spretcher, S., 529
Springer, S. P., 295
Spritz, B., 405
Squire, L. R., 374
Srull, T. K., 494
Stampfer, M. J., 553, 557
Stangor, C., 515
Stark, H., 360
Stein, D. J., 604
Stein, J., 587
Steiner, J., 158
Stellar, E., 162–63
Stemmer, N., 429, 431
Stephens, K., 429
Stern, C. E., 265
Sternberg, R. J., 435, 438, 444, 445, 451, 462–65, 465, 466, 472, 477, 482, 532, 534
Stevens, S. S., 233
Stevenson, H. W., 477
Stickgold, R., 325
Stigler, J. W., 477
Stillion, J. M., 409
Stock, W. A., 174
Stone, B. M., 315
Stone, V. E., 178–79
Stoneking, M., 77
Strachan, A. M., 601
Strapp, C. M., 294, 355

Strathman, A. J., 517
Straub, R. O., 564
Strauss, A. P., 589
Strawbridge, W. J., 558
Streisand, B., 615
Streissguth, A. P., 383, 473
Strickberger, M. W., 79, 80
Stroop, J. R., 287–88
Strumwasser, F., 311
Strupp, B. J., 382
Strupp, H. H., 614, 615
Studdert-Kennedy, M., 415
Stueve, A., 601
Stunkard, A. J., 556
Stupnicki, R., 294
Stuss, D. T., 308, 398
Styron, W., 594
Suess, G., 407
Suffet, I. M., 549
Suh, E. M., 174–75
Sullivan, H. S., 504
Sulloway, F. J., 503
Sumich, A. L., 598, 600
Sumuch, A., 532
Suomi, S. J., 405, 633
Süskind, P., 227
Swann, W. B., Jr., 169
Swartz, C.M., 630
Sweeney, P. D., 564
Sweeney, M., 633
Swets, J. A., 233
Swim, J. K., 537
Switz, G. M., 296–97
Syagailo, Y. V., 599
Syme, S. L., 553
Symons, D., 531
Szasz, T., 579

T

Tang, S. H., 169
Tanne, D., 323
Tarcic, N., 572
Taub, E., 265
Taylor, C. B., 586
Taylor, J. H., 401
Taylor, K. M., 525
Taylor, S. E., 513, 565
Taylor, W., 254
Teder-Salejarvi, W. A., 301
Tees, R. C., 429
Teich, M., 630, 631
Teitelbaum, P., 163
Tellegen, A., 407, 466, 491
Templer, D. I., 317
Terkel, J., 559
Terman, L. M., 454, 457
Terrace, H. S., 423
Teuber, H. L., 374
Thapar, A., 382
Thaulow, E., 556
Thigpen, C. H., 592
Thomas, E. C., 252
Thomas, E. K., 629
Thomas, S., 571
Thompson, D., 371
Thompson, J. G., 280
Thompson, K., 296–97
Thompson, L. W., 294
Thompson, N., 354–55
Thompson, R. F., 129
Thorndike, E. L., 22, 205–6, 212, 435
Thorne, A., 79
Thornhill, R., 530
Thrasher, T. N., 155
Thurstone, L., 459, 460, 465, 482
Tiffany, T. M., 339
Tipp, J., 604, 605
Titchener, E., 19, 23–24, 31
Tolman, E. C., 217–18, 222
Tomkins, S. S., 174
Tooby, J., 96, 298, 309, 538
Toscini, G., 311
Tout, K., 407
Trafimow, D., 408
Trakowski, J. H., 587
Triandis, H. C., 408, 539
Trivers, R. L., 99
Troop, N. A., 564
Tsuang, M. T., 599
Tucker, D. M., 178–79
Tucker, L. A., 488
Tulving, E., 357, 360, 363, 364–68, 370, 371, 374, 398
Turkheimer, E., 88
Turner, J. A., 570
Turner, J. R., 561
Turner, R. J., 601

U

Ulzheimer-Teuber, I., 599
United Nations, 537
Unzner, L., 407
Urbina, S., 451, 466, 472, 477

V

Vaccarino, F. J., 143, 166
Vaillant, G. E., 604
Valdimarsdottir, H. b., 571
Valenstein, E. S., 178, 629
Valeri, C. R., 571
Vallee, B. L., 339
Van Berkel, C., 300
van de Loo, F. J., 144
VanDenburgh, M., 554
Vandergriff, J. L., 551
vanIjzendorn, M. H., 407
van Praag, H., 129
Van Toller, C., 298
Varco, R. L., 556
Vaughn, C. E., 530, 601
Vazquez, C., 561
Vazquez, J. J., 561
Vedak, C., 630
Vega-Lahr, N., 554
Vehrencamp, S. L., 420, 538
Veldhuis, J. D., 387
Vendemia, J. M., 330
Venter, Craig, 3
Vernon, P. A., 472
Virmani, R., 555
Vitiello, B., 633
Vogel, P., 133
von Helmholtz, H., 244, 246
Von Korff, M., 570
Vormbrock, J. K., 300, 554
Vygotsky, L. S., 397–98, 402

W

Wada, J. A., 132
Wagner, R. K., 463
Wagonfield, M. O., 601
Waits, T., 182
Wakefield, J., 416
Walk, R. D., 391
Walker, A. S., 393
Walker, K., 532
Walker, L. J., 401
Walkup, J. T., 633
Wall, P. D., 265
Wall, S., 406
Wallace, R. K., 331
Wallace, W. T., 373
Walpole, H., 44
Walster, E., 531, 532
Walters, R. H., 215, 494
Walton, G. E., 389
Warburton, D. M., 337
Ward, C., 514
Ward, C. M., 537
Washburn, M. F., 20–21
Wason, P., 443
Wasserman, E. A., 307
Watanbe, S. T., 252
Waterman, A. S., 409, 410
Waters, E., 406
Watkins, L. R., 568
Watkins, M. J., 521
Watkins, S., 595
Watson, D., 496, 561
Watson, J. B., 22, 24, 198–99, 203, 211, 307, 309, 494, 502, 516, 562, 565, 615
Watson, R. I., 14
Weaver, C. A. III, 367–68
Weaver, C. W., 445
Weber, E, 231–32, 236
Wechsler, D., 455, 457
Wedekind, C., 297–98
Weekes, J. R., 593
Wegesin, D., 396
Wegner, D. M., 591
Weinberg, C. R., 380, 469–70
Weinberger, D. R., 600
Weiner, G., 515
Weiner, H., 569
Weinman, J., 544
Weinstein, S., 234
Weir, R. H., 429
Weiskranz, L., 126, 241, 282–84, 308, 309, 433
Weiss, S. M., 544
Weissman, M. M., 584, 586, 596
Wenger, J. R., 339
Werker, J. F., 429
Wernicke, C., 17, 18, 417–18
Wertheimer, M., 22, 289–91
Wesnes, K., 337
West, R., 544
West, R. L., 399
Westbay, L., 533
Wever, R., 310
Whalley, L. J., 479
Wheaton, B., 561
Wheeler, M. A., 398
Whishaw, I. Q., 126, 141, 375
White, A. M., 551
White, E., 561
White, S. H., 398
Whiteley, B. E., Jr., 536
Whorf, B. L., 441
Whybrow, P. C., 594
Wiberg, M., 317
Wible, C., 367
Wickelgren, W., 343–44, 375
Widiger, T., 604
Wiesel, T., 273–75
Wilcox, A. J., 380
Wilcox, K.J., 491
Widiger, T., 604

Wiley, J. A., 553
Wilkins, L. H., 149, 337
Wilkins, W. K., 416
Willerman, L., 470
Willett, W. C., 553, 554, 557
William, K. A., 429
Williams, D. A., 620
Williams, G. C., 549, 550, 551, 596, 602
Williams, G. V., 600
Williams, J. E., 527
Williams, K., 525
Williams, K. D., 525
Williams, M. D., 166–67
Williams, R. M., 571
Williams, S. L., 425
Williams, T., 546
Williams, W. M., 463, 471, 478
Willis, J., 16
Wilson, E. O., 95–96
Wilson, M., 97–98, 101
Wilson, M. A., 313, 324
Windfelder, T. L., 421
Wing, J. K., 601
Winoker, G., 595
Wittchen, H. U., 584, 595
Wittenbrink, B., 535–36
Witter, R. A., 174
Wittlinger, R. P., 399
Wolitzky, K. L., 613
Wolpe, J., 616, 618
Wolpoff, M. H., 79
Wolz, J. P., 422
Wong, F., 539
Wood, N., 298
Wood, W., 517, 539
Woods, S. C., 339
Woodward, A. L., 430
Wright, A., 222
Wright, P. H., 532
Wundt, W, 19, 20, 23, 31, 307
Wurmie, O., 317
Wurtman, R. J., 375
Wyatt, J. K., 324
Wyer, R. S., 494
Wyrwicka, W., 163

X

Xiong, J., 129

Y

Yellin, A. E., 556
Yerkes, R., 454, 457
Yost, W. A., 255
Young, A. W., 177
Young, J. Z., 71
Young, R. K., 530
Young, T., 244, 246

Z

Zacks, R. T., 357
Zahorik, D., 159
Zajonc, R., 524
Zevon, M. A., 561
Zhang, Y., 88
Zhao, S., 584, 595
Zihl, J., 286
Zimbardo, P. G., 524, 525
Zinder, O., 572
Zubieta, J. K., 595
Zucker, G. S., 515
Zuckerman, M., 491
Zytkow, J. M., 438

Subject Index

A

A. *afarensis*, 79, 107
abnormal psychology, 36, 171, 574–607
absolute threshold, 232, 236
abstract thought, 396
abuse, 592
academic psychology, 28
accommodation, 392, 402, 409, 410
acetylcholine, 143, 145, 375
achievement, 169–70, 171
acquired immunity, 566, 572
acquired motivation, 155–56, 167–68
acquired pleasures, 170
action potential, 139, 145
activation-synthesis hypothesis, 325–26
adaptations, 41, 67–68, 71–72, 75
  cerebral cortex, 124–26
  emotions, 172–74, 182
  intelligence, 481
  memory, 344–46
  pleasure, 166
  reflexes, 229
  reticular formation, 122
  romantic love, 509–10
  sensation, 228–31
  smell, 295–98
  species-specific behavior, 85
  speech, 414
  touch, 299–300, 301
  See also evolution
adaptative behavior
  self-fulfilling prophecies, 622
The Adapted Mind: Evolutionary Psychology and the Generation of Culture (Barkow, Cosmides, & Tooby), 309
adaptive behaviors, 4, 106
  altruism, 98
  coping, 564–65
  crying, 426–27
  disease, 550–51
  gender roles, 527
  health, 544
  instrumental learning, 204–6
  law of effect, 206
  memory prompts, 400
  mood disorders, 596–97
  overeating, 556
  personality, 486–87
addiction, 339, 633
  See also drug use
additive color mixing, 244–45
adjustment problems, 611
Adler, Alfred, 504–5, 506, 509, 615
adolescence, 408–9
adrenal gland, 151–52
adrenaline, 560
adulthood, 409
adult intelligence tests, 454–56
aerobic exercise, 556–57, 558
affect, 599, 601
afferent nerves, 114
afterlife, 81
Age of Propaganda: the Everyday Use and Abuse of Persuasion (Pratkanis & Aronson), 516–17
aggression, 537–40, 540
aging, 249, 252–55, 402, 467–68
  Alzheimer's disease, 288, 375, 376
  memory and cognition, 399–400, 402
agonists, 145, 146
alcohol genes, 88
Alcoholics Anonymous (AA), 627
alcoholism, 317, 318, 618, 619, 627
alcohol use, 88, 333–34, 340, 630
  benzodiazepines, 633
  depression, 632
  health, 551, 553
  intelligence, 473–74
  smoking, 336–37
  SSRIs, 633
  stress, 564
  tolerance, 338
alertness, 310–13
algorithms, 436, 439
alleles, 75–77, 83
allergies, 568–70, 572
all-or-none principle, 140–41, 145
alpha waves, 320–21
alternate-form reliability, 61, 63
alternative medicine, 546–47
altruism, 98, 101
Alzheimer's disease, 288, 375, 376
ambiguous figures, 281
American College Test (ACT), 455
American Heart Association, 554, 555, 557
American Psychiatric Association, 582–84
  See also Diagnostic and Statistical Manual of Mental Disorders
American Psychological Association (APA), 19, 20, 27, 28, 30, 62
  guidelines, 198
  IQ scores, 466, 477
American Psychological Society (APS), 28–29
American Sign Language (ASL), 423–24
American Society for Clinical Hypnosis, 305–6
amino acids, 143
amnesia, 374, 591–92, 593
amphetamines, 335–36, 600, 602
amplitude, 247–49, 257
amygdala, 177–78, 182, 374–75, 376, 551
anal stage, 501, 505
analysis of dreams, 498, 505
analysis of variance (ANOVA), 48
analytic intelligence, 462, 465
analytic psychology. *See* psychoanalysis
anaphylactic reactions, 569
anatomical structures
  comparative, 80
  ear, 249–51
  epidermis, 262–64
  eye, 236–46
  nervous system, 113–21
  skin, 262–64
  See also brain structures
androgenital syndrome, 528
androstenone, 296–98
anesthesia, 119–20, 558
aneurysm, 127
Angell, James, 21
anger, 603–4
angular gyrus, 417–18, 419
The Animal Mind (Washburn), 20
animal models, 93–94
animals, 70–74, 85–86, 89, 92–95
  adaptation, 4
  aggression, 537–38, 540
  brain, 107–12, 124–26
  circadian rhythms, 310–11
  communication, 420–26
  consciousness, 307–8
  drug tolerance, 339
  emotions, 172–74
  feature detection, 272–75
  genetic factors, 80–82
  hypnosis, 329
  insight, 437–38
  research, 35, 62–63
  sensation, 121, 229–30
  sexual behavior, 98, 530
  sleep, 319–20, 326
  thought, 433
  touch, 299–300
  visual perception, 273–75
  See also primates
annoyers, 206, 211, 212
anomia, 295
anorexia nervosa, 625–26
Antabuse, 618, 619
antagonists, 145, 146
antecedent conditions, 37, 42
anterograde amnesia, 374, 376
anthropology, 6, 36–37
anthropomorphism, 92, 95
antianxiety drugs, 334–35, 340, 633
antidepressant drugs, 337, 340, 626, 632–33
antipsychotic drugs, 630–31
antisocial personality disorder, 604–5
anxiety, 499–500, 504, 505, 584–89, 611, 614
  borderline personality disorder, 603–4, 605
  children, 633
  drug treatment, 334–35, 633, 634
  panic disorders, 626
  surgery, 629
  therapy, 564–65, 621, 623–24, 634
APA Monitor, 449
The Ape and the Child (Kellogg & Kellogg), 423
apes. *See* primates
aphasia, 418–19, 420, 433
appetitive behaviors, 89, 95, 166
applied psychology, 27
aptitude testing, 21–22
archetypes, 504

arcuate fasciculus, 417–18, 419
Aristotle, 5–6
Armed Forces Qualifying Test (AFQT), 479–80, 481
Armed Services Vocational Aptitude Battery (ASVAB), 454–55
Army Alpha and Beta tests, 454, 457
art, 81
artificial selection, 72, 74, 86
artistic ability, 135
assertiveness training, 619, 620
assimilation, 392, 402
association cortex, 126, 130, 131, 307–8
associationism, 14–15
associations, 190, 353, 365–66, 368
asthma, 569–70, 572
asymmetry, 292
attachment, 300, 404–7, 409, 410
attention, 241, 328, 330, 331, 348–50
attention-deficit/hyperactivity disorder (ADHD), 577–79, 580
attitudes, 515–18, 519
attraction, 529–32, 534
attribution, 513–15, 519
audiological measurement, 232
auditory hallucinations, 598
auditory memory, 359–60
auditory nerve, 255–56
authority, 522–24, 525
autism, 308
autoimmune disease, 568
autonomic nervous system (ANS), 113–16, 120, 177, 179
autonomy, 408, 410
aversion therapy, 616, 618, 619, 620
aversive conditioning, 585
aversive stimuli. *See* punishment
avoidance, 409, 410
avoidance learning, 214, 216
avoidant attachment, 406, 410
awareness. *See* consciousness
axons, 117–18, 120
axon terminals, 118

B

babbling, 427, 429, 432
balance, 110, 250
barbiturates, 333–34, 633, 634
basilar membrane, 251, 252, 257
Beck, Aaron, 596, 621–22, 628, 635
Beck Depression Inventory, 60–61
behavior, 185–221
  abnormal, 576–77, 580
  appetitive, 89, 95, 166
  attitudes, 515–18, 519
  biological basis, 67–103
  brain-behavior relationships, 127
  catatonic schizophrenia, 599
  causes, 40–41, 61–62, 70–71, 96–97, 223–24
  consummatory, 89, 503
  controlling, 41–42
  disease, 551–57
  distal factors, 70–71, 97, 223–24
  dysfunctional, 576
  families, 97–98, 101
  fixed action patterns, 186
  genetics, 41, 83, 86–89, 101, 223–24
  groups, 520–26
  health, 58–60, 544
  homeostasis, 154–56
  human *vs.* non-human, 109–10
  hypnosis, 330, 331
  imitation, 390–91
  instrumental responses, 204–5
  learning, 186–89, 344–45
  locus of control, 563–64
  motivation, 96
  persuasion, 518
  plasticity, 100–101, 158
  proximal factors, 70–71, 97, 223–24
  responsibility, 408
  rituals, 587–88
  smell, 259
  social influence, 520–25
  sociopathic, 604–5
  species-specific, 85, 89, 91–92, 95, 186, 329
  stereotypes, 90
  violence, 38, 98, 537–40
  See also learning; sexual behavior
behavioral analysis, 618–19
behavioral control, 211–16
behavioral genetics, 36, 86–89, 95
behavioral medicine, 544, 547
behavioral plasticity, 100–101
behavioral regulation, 154–56
behavioral research, 40–42
behavioral therapy, 615–20, 627
behaviorism, 22, 206–11, 429, 494
behavior modification, 616–19, 620
belief in afterlife, 81
bell curve, 452, 458, 466–83
The Bell Curve (Herrnstein & Murray), 466–79
benzodiazepines, 633, 634
bereavement, 409
Beri Beri, 159
Berkeley, George, 14
beta waves, 320–21
between-groups design, 45, 51
Beyond Freedom and Dignity (Skinner), 216
bias, 57
  confirmation, 443, 445
  in-group, 536–37, 540
  response, 233–34
  self-serving, 10–11, 13, 514–15, 519, 565
big five personality factors, 489–91, 493, 494
Binet, Alfred, 452–53, 457, 478, 482
binocular vision, 276–77, 278, 281
biocultural evolution, 160–61, 165
biofeedback, 619–20
biological factors, 6, 36–37, 38
  aggression, 538
  behavior, 7, 8, 67–103, 186–89
  brainstem, 110–11
  clocks, 310–18
  gender roles, 526–27
  intelligence, 472–74
  memory, 374
  personality, 487, 489
  schizophrenia, 600–601
biological psychology, 101
The Biology of Mind: Origins and Structures of Mind, Brain, and Consciousness (Bownds), 309
biomedical model, 546–47
biopsychosocial model, 546–47
bipedalism, 392
bipolar disorder, 575–76, 582–83, 594, 596, 597, 631–32
birdsongs, 94, 96–97
bisexuality, 529
blindness, 287–88
blindsight, 282–84, 288, 503
blood pressure, 110
body language, 414, 416
body of knowledge, 39–40, 42
body types, 488, 493
books, 622
borderline personality disorder, 603–4, 605, 622
bottom-up processes, 271, 275, 301, 350
brain-behavior relationships, 127
brain functions, 108–12, 130
  amphetamine use, 336
  central auditory processes, 255–56
  consciousness, 307–8, 309
  emotion, 176–81
  genetics, 84–85
  hearing, 255–56
  intelligence, 452, 472–73
  language, 256, 416–19, 431
  memory, 374
  organization, 85, 108–10, 390
  pain, 264–65
  sleep, 320–22, 326
  smell, 259–61, 261
  vision, 239–46
  word problems, 445
brain injury, 105–6, 127, 134, 382–83, 385
  aphasia, 418–19
  emotions, 178–79, 182
  empathy, 308
  language acquisition, 431
  memory, 374–76
The Brain of the Tiger Salamander (Herrick), 110
brainstem, 110–12
  auditory nerve, 255–56
  behavior, 106
  emotion, 179
  taste, 259, 260
  vision, 241–42
brain structures, 6, 15–17, 83, 105–47
  amygdala, 177–78, 182, 374–75, 376, 551
  angular gyrus, 417–18, 419
  arcuate fasciculus, 417–18, 419
  brainstem, 106, 110–12, 179, 241–42, 255–56, 259, 260
  cerebellum, 108–11, 112, 129–30, 131
  development, 94, 107–13, 381–85
  forebrain, 108, 112
  frontal lobes, 106, 124–25, 130, 131, 177–78, 182
  hippocampus, 294, 374–75, 376
  hypothalamus, 110, 112, 151–52, 162–64, 165, 166, 311
  left hemisphere, 294–95, 416–18, 419
  medulla, 110–11, 112
  medullary pyramid, 127–28
  midbrain, 108, 112
  nerve conduction, 16–17, 19
  occipital lobes, 124–25, 130, 131, 238
  organic disorders, 581–82
  parietal lobes, 124–25, 130, 131, 284–86
  pituitary gland, 151–52
  planum temporale, 417, 419
  pons, 110–11, 112
  postcentral gyrus, 124–25
  precentral gyrus, 124–25
  primary auditory cortex, 256, 257, 417–18
  primary gustatory cortex, 260
  primary motor cortex, 126–28, 130, 131, 417–18
  primary sensory areas, 126, 130
  primary visual cortex, 417–18
  right hemisphere, 178–79, 182
  size, 107–8, 112

striate cortex, 239–41, 274, 281–86, 288
temporal lobes, 124–25, 130, 131, 285–87, 294, 374, 376, 416–17, 419
thalamus, 108, 110, 112, 122–23, 129, 131, 177–78, 239–42, 260, 261, 600
brainwashing, 516, 519
brightness contrast, 279, 282
Broca, Paul, 17, 18, 418
Broca's aphasia, 419, 420
Broca's area, 417–18, 419
bulimia nervosa, 625–26
bystander effect, 525

C

caffeine, 337
Calkins, Mary Whiton, 20–21
cancer, 568
Cannon-Bard theory, 179, 182
Carr, Harvey, 21
Cartesian dualism, 5–6, 31
case studies, 53–54, 63
catatonic schizophrenia, 329, 599, 601
Cattell, James McKeen, 21–22
causes of behavior. *See* behavior
cell body, 117–18, 120
cell membrane, 118
central attention, 348
central auditory processes, 255–56
central hearing loss, 255, 257
central nervous system (CNS), 113–21
central sulcus, 124–25, 131
centration, 394, 403
cerebellum, 108–11, 112, 129–30, 131
cerebral cortex, 108, 111, 112, 124–26, 131
cerebral hemispheres, 108, 110–11, 112
cerebrospinal fluid (CSF), 120
cerebrum, 112
challenges, 564
change, 518, 560
chemical dependency, 579, 580
chemistry, 36–38
chess, 371, 373
chi, 545–46
child abuse, 97
child development. *See* development
child-directed speech, 429–30, 432
child intelligence tests, 454–56
chimpanzees, 80–82, 84
See also primates
chlorpromazine, 610, 613, 630–31, 634
cholecystokinin, 143
cholesterol, 554–55, 557
Chomsky, Noam, 426, 428–32, 446
chromosomes, 77–78, 83
chunking, 350–51, 353
circadian rhythms, 310–16, 318
Civilization and Its Discontents (Freud), 504, 580
classical conditioning, 189–204
classification, 396
clinical depression, 594–96
clinical psychology, 27, 28, 30
clinical social workers, 612–13
clinicians, 611–13
closed feeding systems, 157, 165
closure, 292, 293
clozapine, 631
cocaine, 145, 167, 336, 382–83
cochlea, 249–52, 254–55, 257
cocktail party phenomenon, 349, 353
cognitive-behavioral therapy, 398, 625–26, 628, 633, 634
cognitive dissonance, 518–19
cognitive maps, 217–18, 221, 222, 396, 434–35, 439
cognitive processes, 221–22, 224, 432–46, 566–67
cerebellum, 130
development, 392–403
emotions, 180–81
personality, 494
speed, 472–73
See also intelligence
cognitive psychology, 28, 621–22, 627, 628
collective unconscious, 504
collectivism, 408
color, 237–38, 243–44
color blindness, 244–45, 245
color-opponent cells, 245
color vision, 245–45
Columbine High School, 512–13, 539
combined reinforcement, 214
common movement, 292–93
common sense, 9–11, 13, 463
communication, 230
animal, 420–26
persuasion, 516–17, 519
schizophrenia, 601
See also language
companionate love, 532, 534
comparative anatomy, 80
comparative psychology, 28, 92–95
compensation, 505
complementary colors, 244, 245
complementary medicine, 546–47
complex cells, 275
conclusions, 49
concrete operational stage, 395–96, 402
conditional sequential discrimination, 422
conditioned allergic responses, 569–70
conditioned compensatory response, 202–3
conditioned emotional response, 198, 203
conditioned immunosuppression, 568–69, 572
conditioned reflexes, 190
Conditioned Reflexes (Pavlov), 190
conditioned response (CR), 191–93, 197
conditioned stimulus (CS), 191–93, 197
conditioned suppression, 198, 203
conditioned taste aversion, 200–201, 203
conditioning, 189–211, 494
conduction aphasia, 418
conductive hearing loss, 253–54, 257
cones, 238–39, 245
confirmation bias, 443, 445
conformity, 521–22, 525
confounding variables, 46–47, 49, 51, 59
confrontation, 409, 410
congenital deafness, 255, 257
conscience, 408
The Conscious Mind: In Search of a Fundamental Theory (Chalmers), 308–9
consciousness, 134, 137, 305–41, 390, 505
definition, 306, 309
memory, 363–64
Consciousness Lost and Found (Weiskrantz), 309
conscious processes, 497
conscious sight, 282–89
conscious visual pathway, 245
conservation, 394–95, 402
conspecific communication, 230, 257
constructs of intelligence, 459
consummatory behavior, 89, 95, 109–10, 166, 503
contact comfort, 299–300, 301, 410
content validity, 458–59, 465
context effects, 371–72
continuity, 292, 293
continuity of species, 71–72, 74
continuous development, 386–87, 391
continuous reinforcement, 207–8, 211
control, 563–65, 566
control groups, 45, 49, 51
controlling behaviors, 41–42
convergence, 277, 281
conversion disorders, 496, 505, 590
cooing, 427, 432
cooperation, 98
coping, 564–65, 566
corpus callosum, 133, 136
correlation coefficient, 56, 63
correlations, 55–57
corticalization, 108, 112
cortisol, 407
counseling psychology, 28
counselors, 612–13
countertransference, 614
covariation model, 513, 519
cranial nerves, 110–11, 112
creative intelligence, 464–65
creativity, 596–97
criminal behavior, 604
criterion-related validity, 61, 64
critical periods, 89–90, 95, 431–32
Critique of Pure Reason (Kant), 15
cross-modal transfer, 393
cross-tolerance, 340
crying, 70–71, 432
cryptomnesia, 360, 363
crystallized intelligence, 400, 403
cultural factors
archetypes, 504
attachment, 406–7, 410
attraction, 530
depression, 594–95
emotion, 175–76
gender roles, 526–27
health, 545–47
individualism *vs.* collectivism, 408
intelligence, 475–81
personality, 492, 495
personal responsibility, 514–15
research, 397
schizophrenia, 598
smell, 298–99, 301
superego, 499
temperament, 407
See also memes
cultural knowledge, 400
curare, 145
cutaneous senses, 262–65, 299–302
See also touch

D

dark adaptation, 242–43, 245
Darwin, Charles, 82, 87, 451, 496–97, 500, 502
aggression, 537–38
comparative psychology, 92
emotion, 172, 174, 175, 182
evolution, 17, 18, 21, 31, 70–75, 102
hypochondriasis, 589–90
love and sexuality, 512, 530
See also natural selection
Darwin, Emma, 82
Darwin's Dangerous Idea (Dennett), 106
Da Vinci, Leonardo, 176, 178
daydreams, 327–28, 331

daylight savings time, 313–14
deafness, 252–55, 257, 428, 430
death, 409, 548, 549, 551–57
  Thanatos, 500, 505
  voodoo, 559
decay theory, 369, 373
declarative memory, 363–68, 374–75, 376, 385
decussation of the pyramids, 127–28
deductive reasoning, 396, 443, 445
deep processing, 357–58
defense mechanisms, 499–500, 505, 564–65, 566, 614
definition of psychology, 5, 13
definitions, operational, 44
degrees of relatedness, 78
déjà vu, 592
delta waves, 321
delusions, 598, 601
demand characteristics, 58
dementia, 288, 375, 376
dendrites, 117–18, 120
denial, 499–500, 505, 564–65
dependent variables, 44–45, 51
depersonalization disorder, 592, 593
depolarization, 139, 145
depressant drugs, 333–34, 340
depression, 564, 581, 594–96, 597, 614
  antidepressants, 632–33
  borderline personality disorder, 603–4
  electroconvulsive therapy, 630
  immune system, 571
  memory, 372–73
  stress, 561
  surgery, 629
  therapy, 621–22, 634
depth perception, 275–78, 281, 391
Descartes, René, 5–6, 31, 546
descriptive statistics, 52, 63
despair, 409, 410
destructive instinct, 500
determinism, 9
development, 85, 93, 379–411
  gender roles, 526–27
  infant psychosocial, 404–5
  language, 200, 201, 419, 426–32
  mental retardation, 385
  prenatal, 380–86
  punishment, 213
  touch, 299–300, 301
  See also parental roles
developmental/individual perspective, 7, 8
developmental psychology, 28
Dewey, John, 21
diagnoses. *See* abnormal psychology
Diagnostic and Statistical Manual of Mental Disorders (DSM), 582–84, 603, 610, 612
diagnostic terms, 581–83
diathesis-stress model, 563, 565, 601
dichotic listening, 132, 136, 349–50, 353
dichotomous traits, 75, 83
difference threshold, 231–32
differential reinforcement, 210, 211
digit-span test, 350
dinosaurs, 70, 74, 107
disconnection syndrome, 286–87, 288
discrimination, 195–97
discriminative stimulus (S^d), 212, 216
disease, 548–50, 557, 563–64, 568
  See also stress
disorganized schizophrenia, 599, 601
display rules, 175–76, 182
dissociative disorders, 330, 331, 591–93
distal causes of behavior, 74, 96–97, 223–24
disulfiram, 618, 619
DNA (deoxyribonucleic acid), 77–83, 83–84, 100
dominant alleles, 75–77, 83
dopamine, 37–38, 142–44, 146
  cocaine, 167, 170
  schizophrenia, 600, 602, 631
dorsal root ganglion, 118–20
double-blind experiments, 57–58, 63
dreams, 321–22, 324–26, 498, 505, 614
  daydreams, 327–28
drive reduction, 155, 156
drug treatment, 625–26, 630–35
  antianxiety, 334–35, 340, 633
  antidepressant, 337, 340, 626, 632–33
  antipsychotic, 630–31
  lithium, 631–32, 634
  MAO inhibitors, 632, 634
  narcotics, 202–3, 337–38, 340, 382–83
  psychoactive, 332–41, 340, 610, 630–35
  stimulants, 335–37, 340, 630
  tolerance, 202–3, 338–39, 340
drug use, 544, 610, 612
  alcoholism, 618, 619
  consciousness, 332–41
  dependence, 339
  depersonalization disorder, 592
  neurotransmitters, 144–45
  pleasure, 333, 340
DSM-IV, 582–84, 603, 610, 612
dualism, 5–6, 13
ducking reflex, 241
Dunker's candle problem, 438–39
dynamic exposure theory of intelligence, 469–71
dysfunctional behavior, 576
dysphoria, 594–96
dysthymic disorder, 594–96, 597

E

ear, 249–51
  See also hearing
ear-eye integration, 301
eating, 157–65
  disorders, 564, 625–26
  obesity, 555–56, 557–58, 564
Ebbinghaus, Hermann, 368–70, 374
ecological niche, 73, 75
edges, 281
education, 452–53, 458–59, 476–78
  assisted discovery, 398
  psychosocial development, 408
  training in psychology, 24–30, 43, 611
  See also learning
educational/school psychology, 28
The Education of Little Tree (Carter), 204
efferent nerves, 114
efficacy of treatment, 627–28, 633–34
ego, 498, 499, 505
egocentrism, 394–95
eidetic imagery, 373
Einstein, Albert, 328, 443
elaborative rehearsal, 358
Electra complex, 502–3, 505
electrical stimulation of the brain (ESB), 44–47, 166–67, 170
electric shock conditioning, 198–99
electroconvulsive therapy (ECT), 629–30, 634
electroencephalogram (EEG), 320–22, 326, 330
electromyogram, 619
Elemente der psychophysik (Fechner), 231
Ellis, Albert, 621–22, 628, 635
embryonic stage, 380, 385
emotional attribution theory, 180–81, 182
emotions, 150–51, 156, 171–82, 602
  adaptation, 182
  brain damage, 127
  eating, 157
  learning, 372–73
  physiology, 566–67
empathy, 308, 309
empirical methods, 14–15, 35–36
employment, 479–80
encoding, 354–59, 373
endocrine glands, 151–52, 156
endorphins, 143
environmental determinism, 212
environmental factors, 41
  aggression, 539–40
  attachment, 405
  cognitive development, 397–98
  creativity, 464
  depression, 595
  genetics, 84–95
  health, 544
  instrumental responses, 204–5
  intelligence, 467–71
  language acquisition, 429–31, 432
  learning, 186–87, 223–24
  natural selection, 74
  personality, 492
  reaction range, 468–70
  schizophrenia, 600–601
environmental niche, 106–12
epidemiological research, 58–60, 63, 552
epidermis, 262–64
epilepsy, 132–33, 374
epinephrine, 177, 335
episodic memory, 366–68
Erikson, Erik, 403–11, 504, 527, 615
Eros, 505, 537
escape, 214, 216
Essay Concerning Human Understanding (Locke), 14
estrogen, 528
ethical research practice, 35, 62–63, 64, 198
ethnicity, 475–81
ethology, 89–92
eugenics, 452
evolutionary factors, 4, 17, 67–103
  attention, 241
  attention-deficit/hyperactivity disorder, 579
  Charles Darwin, 70–75
  disease, 550–51
  feeding, 160–62
  gender roles, 527
  genetic variability, 82
  human brain, 106–12
  language, 415–16, 419
  memory, 344–46
  mood disorders, 596
  motivation, 503
  open feeding systems, 158
  phobias, 585
  sensation, 236
  sleep, 319–20, 326
  vision, 241–42
  See also adaptation
evolutionary psychology, 68, 95–101, 106, 151, 503
exceptional memory, 370–71
excitatory postsynaptic potential (EPSP), 139–40, 145
exercise, 556–57

experience, 186
  See also learning
experimental method, 31, 34–35, 42, 43–51
experimental neurosis, 196
experimental psychology, 19–20, 28
experimental research, 34–35, 43–51, 61–62
The Experimental Study of Intelligence (Binet), 453
expressed emotion, 602
The Expression of Emotions in Man and Animals (Darwin), 17, 92, 172
expressive language, 416, 418, 430
  See also language
external attribution, 513, 519
external inhibition, 193
extinction, 193, 197, 210
extragenetic information, 85, 95, 161
extrastriate cortex, 284–86, 288
extrinsic motivation, 168–69, 170–71
eye, 237–46
  See also vision
eye-ear integration, 301
Eysenck's personality theory, 489–90

F

face validity, 61, 64
facial expression, 175–76, 178–79, 182
facial features, 536
  attraction, 531–32, 534
  visual development, 389–90
factor analysis, 459, 465, 489–91
false memories, 345–46
False Memory Syndrome Foundation, 346
familiarity effect, 531–32
family experiences, 97–98
  genetic relatedness, 78–79, 96
  intelligence, 468–69
  See also parental roles
fat genes, 88
fear, 177–78, 198, 616, 627
feature detectors, 272, 275
feces, 298–99
feeding. *See* eating
feeding jags, 159–60, 165
feelings. *See* emotions
females. *See* gender
feral children, 171–72, 176
fertility, 317
Fetal alcohol syndrome (FAS), 382–83, 385
fetal stage, 380, 385
fever, 550
fighting. *See* violent behavior
fight or flight, 560
figure-ground relationships, 292–93
first words, 428–29
fitness, 72–73, 75, 96–97, 101, 187–88
fixation, 500–502, 505
fixed action patterns (FAP), 90, 95, 155, 186, 426–27
fixed interval (FI) reinforcement, 209, 211
fixed ratio (FR) reinforcement, 208, 211
flashbulb memories, 367–68
flat affect, 599
Flourens, Pierre, 16–17, 18
fluid intelligence, 400, 403
Flynn effect, 471–72, 474
follow-up experiments, 47
foot-in-the-door phenomenon, 516, 519
foraging patterns, 218, 221
forebrain, 108, 112
forgetfulness, 369–70, 373
  See also memory
formal operational stage, 396, 402
four goals of psychology research, 40–42
free association, 614, 615
free nerve endings, 264, 265
free recall, 354, 358
free will, 506–8
frequency, 247–49, 257
Freud, Sigmund, 23, 24, 537
  anxiety, 564–65, 566
  child sexuality, 298–99
  consciousness, 307, 309
  dreams, 325, 326
  memory, 398
  personality, 487, 496–509
  psychoanalysis, 613–15, 635
  psychosis *vs.* neurosis, 580–81
  unconscious, 151
Freudian slips, 498, 505, 614
friendship, 532–34
Fritsch, Gustav, 17
frontal lobes, 106, 124–25, 130, 131, 177–78, 182
frustration-aggression hypothesis, 539–40
functional disorders, 581, 584
functional fixedness, 438, 439
functionalism, 19–21
functional relationships, 46–47, 51
fundamental attribution error, 514, 519

G

Gall, Francis, 16
Galton, Francis, 451–52, 457, 466, 472, 482
ganglion cells, 238, 245
Gardner, Howard, 460–62, 465, 471, 482, 550
gate-control theory, 264–65
gender, 526–27, 534
  aggression and violence, 98, 538
  attraction, 530–31
  color blindness, 244
  daydreams, 327
  depression, 595–96, 597
  dissociative identity disorder, 592–93
  friendship, 532
  language, 132, 136, 427
  mating patterns, 98–101
  panic disorders, 587
  personality disorders, 603–5
  psychoanalysis, 614
  psychological practice, 29
  social isolation, 553–54
  stereotypes, 537
  stress, 564
  suicide, 595, 597
  treatment, 612–13
general adaptation syndrome, 559–60, 565
general intelligence *(g)*, 453, 457, 459–60, 473, 477
generalized anxiety disorder, 585–86, 588
generalized imitation, 429
general paresis, 581–82
generativity, 409, 410
genetic factors, 3–4, 67–103
  animal communication, 421
  antisocial personality disorder, 605
  anxiety, 585–86
  behavior, 41, 83, 86–89, 101, 223–24
  bipolar disorder, 596
  brain injury, 382, 385
  creativity, 464
  cross-species comparisons, 80–82
  depression, 595–96
  development, 379–80
  disease, 550–51, 554
  environment, 84–95
  feeding, 157, 161–62
  Gregor Mendel, 70, 75–77
  health, 555–56
  heart disease, 554
  homosexuality, 529
  hypochondriasis, 589–90
  intelligence, 451–52, 466–70, 474, 477
  language, 414
  memes, 187–88, 189
  mood disorders, 596–97
  open feeding systems, 158
  personality, 487, 489, 491–92, 493, 495
  phobic disorders, 584–85
  reaction range, 468–70
  schizophrenia, 599–600
  sexuality, 527–29
  smell, 299
  stress, 563
  temperament, 407
  variability, 82
genetic relatedness, 78
genetic variability, 84
genital stage, 501–2, 505
genotypes, 77, 83
germinal stage, 380, 385
Gestalt psychology, 22, 289–93, 624, 628
gestures, 416
glands, 151–52
glia, 116
glove anesthesia, 496–97, 558, 590
glucose, 164, 165
glutamate, 143–44, 375
goals of psychology, 40–42
good figure (pragnanz), 292, 293
Gould, Stephen Jay, 74
grammar, 430–31
grandiosity, 599
graphs, 46–47, 54–55, 63
gray matter, 119–20
Greek personality types, 488, 493
grief, 409, 410
grooming, 299–300
grouping, 291
groups, 98, 536
  pressure, 521–22, 524–25
  therapy, 45, 626–27, 628

H

habituation, 71, 193, 197, 223–24
hair cells, 251, 257
Hall, G. Stanley, 19, 23, 31
hallucinations, 598, 601
hallucinogens, 338, 340
Hamlet (Shakespeare), 325
handedness, 416–17, 427–28
happiness, 174–75
hard sciences, 36–37
hardy personality, 563–64, 565
Hartley, David, 14
Hassle scale, 561–62, 565
health, 58–60, 300, 301, 546
health psychology, 36, 543–73
healthy personality, 507–8
hearing, 230, 247–57, 387–88
  dichotic listening test, 132
  loss, 249, 252–55
  prenatal, 384
  Wada test, 132
heart disease, 554–57
heart rate, 384

hedonism. *See* pleasure
Helmholtz, Herman von, 16–17, 18, 250
hemianopia, 282–84
hemispheric specialization, 178–79, 182, 428
hemoglobin, 83, 84
Hereditary Genius (Galton), 451
heredity. *See* genetic factors
heritability, 88–89, 95
heterosexuality, 529
heterozygous alleles, 77, 83
heuristics, 435–36, 439
heuristic values, 50–51, 54
hidden observer, 330–31, 332
hierarchy of needs, 168, 170
higher cortical functions, 127
higher-order conditioning, 194–95, 197, 201
hindbrain, 108, 112
hippocampus, 294, 374–75, 376
Hippocrates, 14, 488
history, 187–88
history of psychology, 13–24
Hitzig, Eduard, 17
Holmes-Rahe Social Readjustment Rating Scale, 560–61, 565
homeostasis, 152–54, 156
  conditioned compensatory response, 202–3
  eating, 157
  light regulation, 241–42
home-team advantage, 524
Homo erectus, 78–79, 415–16
Homo ergaster, 79–80
Homo habilis, 107
homonculus, 123
Homo sapiens, 79, 81–82
  brain, 105, 107
  language, 415–16
Homo sapiens neanderthalensis, 79
homosexuality, 529, 534
homozygous alleles, 77, 83, 87
hormones, 116, 151–52, 156, 566
  aggression, 538, 540
  sexuality, 528
horseshoe crabs, 70
How the Mind Works (Pinker), 309
human brain. *See* brain functions; brain structures
human development. *See* development
humanistic psychology, 23, 487, 506–8
  stress, 563
  therapy, 623–24, 626, 628
human lineage models, 78–79
human nature, 84–85
human research, 35, 62–63
Hume, David, 14–15
humor, 179, 440, 498, 537, 571–72
hunger, 163–64
hyperactivity. *See* attention-deficit/hyperactivity disorder
hyperpolarization, 139–40, 145
hypnosis, 305–6, 328–31, 497, 593, 620
hypochondriasis, 589–90
hypomania, 594, 595, 597
hypothalamus, 110, 112, 151–52, 165
  biological clock, 311
  feeding, 162–64
  pleasure, 166
hypotheses, 43–44, 48, 51
hypovolemic thirst, 155, 156

I

I Ching, 545
id, 498–99, 505
identical twins. *See* twins
identity, 404, 408–9, 410
illness. *See* disease
illusion, 279–81, 282, 565, 566
imagination, 328, 331
imitation, 390–91, 424–25, 429
immune system, 566–70, 572
implicit memory, 359–60, 363
imprinting, 89–90, 95
impulsive and dramatic personality disorders, 603, 605
impulsivity, 106, 603, 605
incentives, 155–56
incidental encoding, 357, 358
inclusive fitness, 97, 101
incoherent thought, 598, 601
incus, 249–50, 257
independent variables, 44–45, 51, 58
individual differences, 52, 61–62, 63, 188, 189, 386, 397
individualism, 408
inductive reasoning, 396, 443, 445
industrial psychology, 28
infanticide, 97
infantile amnesia, 398
infant psychosocial development, 404–5
infection, 568
inferencing, 59
inferiority complex, 505
information-processing model of memory, 346–54
informed consent, 62
in-group bias, 536–37, 540
inherited traits. *See* genetic factors
inhibitory behavior, 106
inhibitory postsynaptic potential (IPSP), 139–40, 145
innate releasing mechanism, 90, 95
inner ear, 249–51
input attention, 348
insecure attachment, 406
insight, 437–38, 439
insight therapy, 621–29
insomnia, 324, 326
instinct, 70–71, 83, 85, 89–90
  attachment, 405
  reflexes, 190
  smell, 298–99
instinctive drift, 217, 221
Institutional Review Boards (IRBs), 62
institutions, 581, 610–11
instrumental learning, 204–6, 211
insulin, 164, 165
integration, sensory, 301
integrity, 409, 410
intelligence, 36, 449–83
  aging, 400
  ethnicity, 477
  IQ scores, 454, 457–65
  language, 441
  life experiences, 475–82
  multiple, 460–62, 465
  nonverbal tests, 433
  personality, 491
  persuasion, 517
  tests, 60–61, 433, 450–60, 479–80
intentional encoding, 357, 358
intentionality, 421, 426, 427, 435
interference theory, 369, 373
internal attribution, 513, 519
internal capsule, 127–28
internal inhibition, 193, 197
interneurons, 118–19, 120
interposition, 277, 281
The Interpretation of Dreams (Freud), 325
intimacy, 409, 410
intrinsic motivation, 168–69, 170–71
introspection, 19
inventories, 60–61
Inventory of College Students' Recent Life Experiences (ICSRLE), 562
IQ tests, 60–61, 433, 450–60, 475–82
irreversibility, 394–95
Ishihara colorblindness test, 244
isolation, 93, 409, 410, 553–54, 595–96

J

James, William, 20–23, 31
  altered consciousness, 327, 332
  consciousness, 306–7, 309, 320–21
  infant consciousness, 390
  intelligence, 450
James-Lange theory, 179–81, 182
jealousy, 538
jet lag, 313–15, 318
job performance, 464
Journal of Comparative and Physiological Psychology (JCPP), 50
journals, 49, 571, 572
Jung, Carl, 503–4, 506, 509, 615
jury process, 12
just noticeable difference (jnd), 231, 236

K

Kant, Immanuel, 15, 18
Kanzi, 424–25, 435, 441
kin selection, 97, 101
knowledge, 363, 368, 440
Kohlberg, Lawrence, 400–402, 403
Koko, 423

L

lactose intolerance, 161–62
Lamarckian evolution, 73, 75
language, 81, 85, 106, 413–47
  animals, 420–26
  aphasia, 418–19, 420, 433
  brain organization, 256, 416–18
  consciousness, 308
  development, 90, 389, 394, 397–98, 426–32
  dichotic listening test, 132
  emotion, 175, 182
  evolution, 414–17
  gender, 136
  genetic basis, 90
  intelligence, 400
  memes, 199, 415, 419
  memory, 294, 345, 365–66, 440
  perception, 292, 294–95, 301
  second-signal system, 199–200, 201, 203
  sign language, 255
  split-brain research, 135, 136–37
  stroke, 127
  thought, 396, 432–33
language acquisition device (LAD), 428, 432
The Language of Instinct (Pinker), 106
latency stage, 501–2, 505
latent learning, 218, 221
lateral fissure, 124–25, 131
lateral geniculate nucleus (LGN), 239–42, 245
lateralization of function, 131–37, 416–18, 428
lateral thought, 403, 464, 465

laughter, 571–72
See also humor
law of effect, 205–6, 211, 216–17, 435
leading questions, 362–63
lead poisoning, 382–83
learned behavior, 186–89
learned helplessness, 562–63, 565
learned stress, 562–63
learning, 36, 37, 85, 185–225
animals, 422–25
avoidance, 214
behavioral therapy, 615–20
brain damage, 374–75
conceptual, 221–24
conditioning, 189–204
environment, 223–24
instrumental, 204–6
language, 422–32
memes, 187–88, 189
memory, 344–45, 369
neuroethology, 94
nonassociative, 193
phobias, 585
placebo effect, 570
prenatal, 384
smell, 299
trial-and-error, 435, 439
See also development
learning disorders, 578, 580
left hemisphere, 294–95, 416–18, 419
A Leg to Stand On (Sacks), 592
Leibnitz, Gottfried von, 15, 18
levels of processing, 357–58
lexigrams, 424
libido, 500, 505
life experience variables, 552–57, 560–62
IQ testing, 475–81
schizophrenia, 601
stress, 560–62, 565
life span, 548, 553
light, 241–42, 312–19
lightness constancy, 279, 282
limbic system, 177, 182
Lincoln, President Abraham, 271
linear perspective, 277, 281
linguistic relativity hypothesis, 441, 445
literacy, 188, 416
literature searches, 49
lithium, 631–32, 634
lobotomy, 178, 182, 629, 634
localization, 256, 387
Locke, John, 14–15, 18, 190, 390, 432, 470
locus of control, 563–64, 566
logic. *See* reasoning
longitudinal fissure, 124–25, 131
long-term memory (LTM), 345, 347, 353, 359–64, 473, 474
loudness, 252
love, 509–10, 532–34
and friendship, 532
and kin selection, 97
and romance, 512
and transference, 614
as basic emotion, 198
as companionate, 533
as passionate, 533
as unconditional, 507, 623
evolutionary determinants of, 151, 512
of family, 97
by father, 404–405
in Freud's theory, 501–502
in Roger's theory, 507
in Sternberg's theory, 507
lunar rhythms, 317–18

M

The Magic Number Seven, Plus or Minus Two (Miller), 350
maintenance rehearsal, 356, 358
major histocompatibility complex (MHC), 297–98, 301
major perspectives in psychology, 7, 8
males. *See* gender
malleus, 249–50, 257
malnutrition, 382
mammals. *See* animals; primates
mania, 594–95, 597
manipulating images, 439
The Man Who Mistook His Wife for a Hat (Sacks), 286–87
MAO inhibitors, 632, 634
marijuana, 382–83
Maslow, Abraham, 23, 168, 170, 183, 506–9, 563
matched-groups design, 58, 63
matching hypothesis, 531–32
maternal roles, 93, 404–7, 410
mathematics, 356, 442
mating patterns, 98–101
meaning of life, 96, 409
means-end analysis, 436–37, 439
mean (statistical), 52, 63
Medical Inquiries and Observations on the Diseases of the Mind (Rush), 580
medical model, 580, 584, 612, 629–35
medication. *See* drug treatment
meditation, 331, 332
medulla, 110–11, 112
medullary pyramid, 127–28
meiosis, 82, 84
melatonin, 311, 315, 318
membrane potential, 138–42
memes, 161, 187–88, 189, 345, 400
behavior, 223–24
language, 199, 415, 419
smell, 299
memory, 36, 85, 343–77
aging, 399–400, 402
cognitive development, 398–400
dissociative disorders, 591–93
electroconvulsive therapy, 630
functional fixedness, 438
hippocampus, 294
infants, 398
language, 294, 345, 365–66, 440
literacy, 416
physiology, 566–67
problem solving, 435
REM sleep, 323–24
retrieval, 347, 353, 371–73
smell, 299
working, 347, 350–59, 473
See also long-term memory; short-term memory
Mendel, Gregor, 74, 75–77
menstruation, 295–98, 301, 317
mental disorders. *See* psychological disorders
mental health care system, 611–13
mental images, 433–34, 439
mental models, 434, 439
mental retardation, 385
mental rotation, 396
mental set, 442, 445
mesmerism, 329
metabolism, 310–11, 319, 331
method of constant stimuli, 232, 236
method of limits, 232, 236
method of magnitude estimation, 233, 236
midbrain, 108, 112
middle ear, 249–51, 253–54
midlife crisis, 409
mimesis, 415
mind-body interactions, 5–6, 13, 288, 558–59, 566–72
mirror neurons, 309, 416
mnemonic devices, 351–53, 371–72
modern synthesis, 72, 74
molar level of analysis, 36–37, 42
molecular level of analysis, 36–37, 42, 72
Mona Lisa (Da Vinci), 176, 178, 182
monism, 6, 13
monkeys. *See* primates
monoamine oxidase (MAO) inhibitors, 632, 634
monocular vision, 277–78, 281
monogamy, 98, 101
mood, 517
mood-congruent recall, 372–73
mood disorders, 593–97
moral development, 400–402
moral issues, 498
moral therapy, 581
morbidity and mortality, 548, 549, 552–57
Morgan's canon, 92, 95
morning sickness, 382, 385
Moro reflex, 92
morphine tolerance, 202–3
morphology, 427, 428
mosaic organization, 416, 419
motivation, 96, 149–71, 187, 503
motor cortex, 124–26
motor memory, 351, 365–66
motor neurons, 120
motor reflexes, 190, 191
movement, prenatal, 384
Muëller, Johannes, 16–17
Mueller-Lyer illusion, 280–81
multifactorial motivation, 157, 165
multiple intelligences, 460–62, 465
multiple personality disorder, 592–93
multiple sclerosis, 317, 318
multivariate regression methods, 62
music, 135, 294–95, 301, 433
hearing, 254–55
memory, 355, 372–73
prenatal development, 385
mutation, 82, 84
myelin, 117–18, 120, 141

N

The Naked Ape (Morris), 80
narcotics, 202–3, 337–38, 340, 382–83
National Commission for the Protection of Human Subjects in Biomedical and Behavioral Research, 629
National Health Occupations Students of America (NHOSA), 63
National Institute of Mental Health (NIMH), 558
National Institutes of Health (NIH), 62, 558
National Science Foundation (NSF), 62
nativism, 15
Natural Born Killers (movie), 539
natural history, 72
natural selection, 72–74, 548–51, 556
nature *vs.* nurture, 7–9, 13, 70–71, 187, 217
intelligence, 452

stress, 563–64
Necker cube, 281, 293
need for achievement, 169–70, 171
negative correlations, 56
negative discriminative stimulus (S^{Δ}), 212, 216
negative feedback, 153, 156
negative punishment, 212–13
negative reinforcement, 214–15, 216
neocortex, 108, 112, 126
neo-Freudians, 504–5, 509, 615
neophobia, 158–59, 165, 221
nerve growth factor, 382, 385
nervous system, 6, 113–21, 137–44
central auditory processes, 255–56
hearing, 249–55
nerve conduction, 16–17, 19
nerve impulses, 140–41
prenatal development, 382
taste and smell, 257–61
touch, 262–66
vision, 236–47
See also brain structures
neuroendocrine system, 116, 120, 151–56
neuroethology, 94, 95
neurogenesis, 128–29, 131
neuropeptides, 143
neurosciences, 6, 23, 28, 36, 397, 581
neurosis, 581, 584, 585, 611, 614, 615
neurotransmitters, 118, 120, 139–45, 145–46, 566–67, 634
Alzheimer's disease, 375
antidepressant drugs, 337, 632–33
anxiety, 633
depression, 595
drugs, 333–34, 337–38, 632–33
functional disorders, 581
lithium, 632
narcotics, 337–38
schizophrenia, 600
SSRIs, 632–33
stimulants, 335
neutral stimulus, 199
Newton, Sir Isaac, 14, 15
nicotine, 336–37
Nim Chimsky, 423
nocebo effect, 570–71, 572
nodes of Ranvier, 117–18
noise, 254, 255
nonassociative learning, 193, 197
nondirective therapy, 623–24
nonexperimental research methods, 35, 51–64
nonverbal communication, 416
nonverbal intelligence tests, 433
nonverbal processing, 135–36, 432–39
norepinephrine, 633
normal distribution, 52, 53, 63
normative development, 386–92
norms, 520
null hypothesis, 48, 51, 58
nurture. *See* nature *vs.* nurture
The Nurture Assumption: Why Children Turn Out the Way They Do (Harris), 495
nutrition, 158–59, 165, 472

O

obedience, 522–24, 525
obesity, 555–56, 557–58, 564
object permanence, 393–94, 402
observational learning, 215, 216
observation of behavior, 40
observer expectancy effects, 57, 63
obsessive-compulsive disorder (OCD), 587–88, 633
occipital lobes, 124–25, 130, 131, 238
occupations in psychology, 24–30, 611–12
odd and eccentric personality disorders, 603, 605
odor. *See* smell
oedipal complex, 501–3, 505
off-center cells, 272–73, 275
old age. *See* aging
olfactory bulb, 124–25, 260–61, 262
omnivore's paradox, 158, 165
on-center cells, 272–73, 275
one-word utterance stage, 428, 432
On the Origin of Species by Means of Natural Selection (Darwin), 17, 71, 496
ontogenetic history, 85, 95
open feeding systems, 158, 165
operant conditioning, 206–11
operational definitions, 44, 51
opium, 630
opponent-process theory, 245–46
optic nerve, 238–41
oral history, 187–88
oral stage, 500–501, 505
organic disorders, 581–82, 584
organizational psychology, 28
organ of Corti, 251, 257
orienting reflex (OR), 191, 197
original research, 49
osmotic thirst, 155, 156
outcomes, 627–28, 633–34
outer ear, 249–51
oval window, 249–51, 252
ovaries, 151–52
overachievers, 474
overjustification effect, 169, 171
overlearning, 369
oversimplification, 10–11, 13

P

Pacinian corpuscle, 264
pain, 121–22, 230–31, 264–65, 589
pair bonding, 93–94, 95, 410
pancreas, 151–52, 164
panic control treatment (PCT), 626, 628
panic disorders, 586–87, 588, 626, 633
parallel visual pathways, 284–86
paralysis, 119–20, 145
paranoid schizophrenia, 599, 601
parasympathetic division, 114–16, 120
parathyroid, 151–52
parental roles, 93, 404–7, 410, 477
anxiety, 585–86
attachment, 404–7
gender, 526
language acquisition, 429–31
personality, 495
schizophrenia, 601
sexuality, 98–99, 501–2
parietal lobes, 124–25, 130, 131, 284–86
partial reinforcement, 208, 211
partial reinforcement effect (PRE), 210, 211
passionate love, 532, 534
passive exposure theory of intelligence, 469–71, 473–74
paternal roles, 404–5, 410
Pavlov, Ivan, 22, 86
classical conditioning, 189–204, 210, 212, 218
memory, 366–67
Pavlovian conditioning, 189–204
peer influence, 495
peer reviews, 48–49, 51
penis envy, 502–3
perception, 36, 37, 231, 235, 236, 269–303
development, 387–91
pain, 264–65
stress, 565
perceptual/cognitive perspective, 7, 8
perceptual constancies, 278–79, 282
perceptual organization, 291–93
peripheral nervous system (PNS), 113–16
Perls, Fritz, 623–24, 628
persecution, 599
personal integrity, 409, 410
personality, 28, 484–509
attribution, 514
disorders, 602–6
immune system, 571–72
personal responsibility, 514–15
person-centered psychology, 508, 623–24
persuasion, 516–17, 519
PET (positron-emission tomography) scans, 132, 136
phallic stage, 501–3, 505
phantom limb, 265
pharmacological tolerance, 338–39
phenomenology, 507, 508
phenotypes, 77, 83
pheromones, 259, 262, 295–98, 301, 420
phi phenomenon, 290–91, 293
phobias, 584–86, 588, 616, 627
phonological loop, 354–56, 358
phonology, 355, 427, 428, 429, 432
photographic memory, 370–71, 373
photopigments, 70
photosynthesis, 229
phrenology, 16
phylogenetic history, 85, 95
physical appearance, 529–32
physical dependence, 339, 340
physical intelligence, 461–62
physical manifestations, 589–90, 599, 600
physics, 36–37
physiological psychology. *See* neurosciences
Piaget, Jean, 392–97, 402, 411, 434, 457, 502
pineal gland, 5–6
pituitary gland, 151–52
placebo effect, 570, 572
place theory, 252, 257
plagiarism, 360
planum temporale, 417, 419
plasticity, 128–29, 200
behavior, 100–101, 158
language acquisition, 432
pleasure, 150, 156, 166–71, 206, 301, 333, 340
pleiotropic genes, 551
pointilism, 277–78
pointing, 416, 427–28
polyandry, 98, 101
polygenic characters, 87, 95
polygyny, 98, 101
pons, 110–11, 112
Ponzo illusion, 280
population, 54, 63
positive correlations, 55–56
positive punishment, 212–13
positive reinforcement, 206–7, 211, 215
postcentral gyrus, 124–25
post-traumatic stress disorder, 611
postural reflex, 110
practical intelligence, 462–64, 465
pragnanz (closure), 292

precentral gyrus, 124–25
preconscious mind, 497, 505
Predator (movie), 292–93
prediction, 41–42, 396
predictive validity, 459, 465
pregnancy, 543–44
prejudice, 535–37, 540
prenatal development, 380–86
preoperational stage, 393–95, 402
preparedness, 220, 221
Presidential debates, 522
pressure sensation, 262–65
primacy effect, 356, 358, 518, 519
primary auditory cortex, 256, 257, 417–18
primary gustatory cortex, 260
primary mental abilities, 459–60, 465
primary motivation, 155, 156
primary motor cortex, 126–28, 130, 131, 417–18
primary punisher, 212
primary sensory areas, 126, 130
primary visual cortex, 417–18
primates
  brain, 107–12, 133, 417
  circadian rhythms, 310–11
  communication, 421–25, 426
  concept formation, 222–23
  drugs, 333
  emotions, 172–74
  intentionality, 435
  language, 419, 424–25
  reasoning, 443
  self-awareness, 307–8
  sexual behavior, 317
  social interactions, 93–94
  touch, 299–300, 301
  tribal tendencies, 536
  visual perception, 272–75
priming, 360, 363, 503
Prince of Tides (movie), 615
Principals of Behavior (Hull), 155
Principles of Psychology (James), 20, 450–51
prison population, 604
private speech, 398
proactive interference, 369, 373
probabilistic reasoning, 38, 42
problem solving, 326, 345, 396, 433–38, 442
procedural memory, 363–64, 368, 375, 376, 385
processing speed, 472–73, 474
productive language, 416, 418, 430
  See also language
professional organizations, 28
programmatic research, 42
progressive relaxation, 329, 331, 616, 620, 627, 633
projection, 170, 499–500, 505
promiscuity, 529, 534
prosopagnosia, 287
protolanguage, 420
proximal causes of behavior, 74, 96–97, 158, 223–24
proximity, 293
pseudopregnancy, 543–44, 559
psychiatry, 29–30, 580, 611–12
psychic blindness, 590
psychoactive drugs, 332–41, 610, 630–35
psychoanalysis, 23, 497–505, 612–15
  See also treatment
psychodynamic approach, 487, 496–505, 615
psychogenic origins, 592
The Psychological Corporation®, 21–22
psychological dependence, 339, 340
psychological disorders, 462, 575–606
  conversion, 496, 505, 590
  dissociative, 330, 331, 591–93
  eating, 564, 625–26
  functional, 581, 584
  impulsive/dramatic personality, 603, 605
  mood, 593–97
  odd/eccentric personality, 603, 605
  organic, 581–82
  panic, 586–87, 626, 633
  personality, 602–6
  phobic, 584–85, 586
  psychophysiological, 558–59
  psychosomatic, 558–59, 565, 589–90, 619–20
  seasonal effects, 317, 318
  somatization, 590
  somatoform, 589–90
psychological model, 581, 584
psychometrics, 60–61, 63
psychoneuroimmunology, 566–72
psychopharmacology, 630, 634
psychophysics, 231–36, 271
psychophysiological disorders, 558–59
psychosexual development, 500–503, 505
psychosis, 581, 584, 610, 614, 615
psychosocial development, 403–10
psychosomatic disorders, 558–59, 565, 589–90, 619–20
psychosurgery, 178, 182, 629, 634
psychotherapy, 506–7, 610, 613, 633–34
  See also treatment
puberty, 408–9, 502
publication of research, 50–51
punishment, 212–15, 216, 616

Q

quantitative psychology, 28
questionnaires, 60–61

R

racial stereotypes, 475–81, 536–37
rational-emotive therapy, 621–22, 628
rationalization, 499–500, 505
Raven's Matrices, 433
reaction formation, 499–500, 505
reaction range, 474
reading, 440–41, 445
  literacy, 188, 416
  memory, 355–56
Reason for Hope (Goodall), 485–86
reasoning, 38, 42, 325, 396, 443–44, 445
  See also problem solving
recency effect, 354, 358
receptive field, 272, 275
receptive language, 416–17, 430
  See also language
receptors, 235, 236
recessive alleles, 75–77, 83, 87
recombination, 82, 84
reductionism, 37–38, 42
referential pointing, 416, 419, 427
reflective processing, 119
reflexes, 90, 92, 190, 191, 197, 223–24
  classical conditioning, 204
  ducking, 241, 245
  postural, 110
  sensation, 229
  spinal cord, 118–19
  vital, 110
regression, 499–500, 505
rehearsal, 347, 358
reinforcement, 206–11, 616, 619
relatedness, 78
relative clarity, 277–78, 281
relative motion, 278, 281
relative size, 277, 281
relaxation training, 329, 331, 616, 620, 627, 633
reliability, 60–61, 63, 457
Remembrance of Things Past (Proust), 260
remission, 602
REM sleep, 321–25, 326
repression, 499–500, 505
reproduction, 97–100, 259, 295–98, 301
research methods, 33–65
  See also experimental research
research publication, 50–51
resistance, 614, 615
resistant attachment, 406, 410
response bias, 233–34
responsibility, 408, 514–15, 525
resting membrane potential, 138–42, 145
reticular formation, 122, 131
retina, 238–42, 245, 272, 275–78
retinal disparity, 276, 281
retrieval, 347, 353, 371–73
retroactive interference, 369–70, 373
retrograde amnesia, 374, 376
A Revelation of the Word (Fechner), 231
rhodopsin, 70
right hemisphere, 178–79, 182
rigidity, 599
Ritalin, 336, 579, 630
ritualized behaviors, 587–88
rod-cone break, 242–43, 245
rods, 238–39, 245
Rogers, Carl, 506–7, 508, 509, 623–24, 628, 635
role confusion, 408–9, 410
romantic love, 509–10
rooting reflex, 229

S

sadness, 594–96
Sagan, Carl, 69, 85, 108, 151, 424
sampling, 54, 63
Sapir-Whorf hypothesis, 441, 445
satisfiers, 206, 211
SAT (Scholastic Aptitude Test), 60–61
scatterplots, 54–55, 63
schedules of reinforcement, 207–11
schemas, 360–62, 363, 392
schizophrenia, 317, 318, 598–602, 630–31
Scholastic Assessment Test (SAT), 455
school. *See* education
school psychology, 28*t*
Schwann cells, 117–18
scientific method, 33–65
scores, 457–65
seasonal affective disorder (SAD), 317, 318, 594
secondary punisher, 212
secondary reinforcer, 168, 207, 211
second-signal system, 199–200, 201, 203
secure attachment, 406
seizures, 630
selective attention, 348–50, 353
selective pressures, 72, 74
selective serotonin reuptake inhibitors (SSRIs), 632–33, 634
self-actualization, 507–8
self-awareness, 307–8, 623–24

self-concept, 507, 508
self-correction, 42
self-help books, 622
self-help groups, 627
The Selfish Gene (Dawkins), 96
self-perception, 519
self psychology, 505
self-report methods, 60, 63
self-serving bias, 10–11, 13, 514–15, 519, 565
self-talk, 398
semantic memory, 365–66, 368, 440
sensation, 227–67, 271, 383–84, 385
sense of being, 81
sensitivity training, 626
sensitization, 193, 197, 223–24
sensorimotor stage, 391–93, 402
sensorineural hearing loss, 254 – 255, 257
sensory integration, 301
sensory memory, 346–48, 353
sensory-motor processing, 134
sensory-motor reflexes, 118–19, 120
sensory neurons, 16–17, 120, 121–22
sensory-specific satiety, 160, 165
separation anxiety, 406
serendipity, 44
serial learning, 369
serial position effect, 354–55, 358
serotonin, 595, 604, 622, 632–33, 634
set point, 152–53, 156
sex, as primary need, 167–168
sex hormones, 152
sex roles, 98–99
sexual abuse, 345–46
sexual advances, 11
sexual agendas, 98–99
sexual arousal, 116, 197
sexual attraction, 11
  role of smell, 297–298
sexual behavior, 98–101, 301, 516, 527–32
  and concealed ovulation, 317–318
  as genetically determined 96
  as instinctive, 93
  as stress, 561
  at puberty, 96
  choice of partner, and intelligence, 479
  daydreams, 327
  feces, 298–99
  Freud's stages of development, 500–503
  hormones, 152
  libido, 500
  love, 532–33
  seasonal rhythms, 317–18
  smell, 295–98
  SSRIs, 633
sexual content of dreams, 325
sexual fantasy in daydreams, 328
sexual harassment, 11
sexual jealousy, 97
sexual orientation, 528–29, 534
sexual patterns, 98–100
sexual reproduction, 82
sexual selection, 87–99
sexual stereotypes, 537
sexual urges, 23
sexuality, 100
Shacter's emotional attribution theory, 180–81
shallow processing, 357–58
shame, 408, 410
shape constancy, 279, 282
shaping, 207, 211, 516
shift work, 316, 318
short-term memory (STM), 137, 307, 345, 347, 350–53
  encoding, 354–59
  intelligence, 400
  object permanence, 393–94
  selective attention, 349
short-term psychodynamic therapy, 615
shyness, 407
sickle-cell disease, 83, 84, 161, 551
sight. *See* vision
signal detection theory, 233–34, 236
sign language, 255, 423–24, 428, 430
sign stimulus, 90, 95
similarity, 293
simple cells, 274, 275
16PF Personality Profile, 488–89, 493
size constancy, 278–79, 282
skin, 262–64, 265
Skinner, B. F., 22, 23, 24, 615–16
  environmental determinism, 212
  first words, 429
  nature *vs.* nurture, 217
  operant conditioning, 206–18, 220, 221, 225
  personality, 494, 496
sleep, 316, 318, 319–27
smell, 229, 259–62, 295–99, 301, 384, 387
smiling, 177–78, 182
social Darwinism, 466
social facilitation, 524, 525
social factors, 7, 8, 403–10
  Alcoholics Anonymous, 627
  IQ testing, 475–81
  isolation, 93, 409, 410, 553–54, 595–96
  language, 415
  schizophrenia, 601
social intelligence, 462
social-learning approach, 487, 493–96
social loafing, 525
social perception, 513
social psychology, 28, 36, 37–38, 509–41
social reinforcement, 215
social workers, 612–13
Society for Neuroscience, 23
sociobiology, 95–101
Sociobiology: The New Synthesis (Wilson), 95–96
sociocultural theory of cognitive development, 397–98
sociology, 6, 36–38
sociopathic behavior, 604–5
soft sciences, 36–37
soma, 117
somatic nervous system, 113–14
somatization disorders, 590
somatoform disorders, 589–90
somatosensory cortex, 122–25, 130, 131, 265
somatotopic organization, 122–23
sound, 247–49, 257, 294–95
  See also hearing
spatial processing, 136, 137, 145, 435
speaking, 418
Spearman, Charles, 450, 453, 457, 459, 466, 472, 482
specialized language, 441
species-specific factors, 70–74
  behavior, 85, 89, 91–92, 95, 186, 329
  genetic comparisons, 80–82
  phylogenic history, 85
  sexuality, 98–99
  See also animals
specific appetite, 155, 156
speech development, 90, 389
  See also language
speed of processing, 472–73, 474
spinal cord, 109–11, 112, 118–19, 121–22
spinoreticular track, 122
spinothalamic track, 122
Spinoza, Baruch, 6
spirituality, 627
spitting reflex, 229
split-brain procedure, 132–34, 136–37, 629
split-half reliability, 61, 63
spontaneous recovery, 193, 197
SSRIs, 632–33, 634
stagelike development, 386–87, 391
stages of psychosexual development, 500–502
stage theory of cognitive development, 392–403
stagnation, 409, 410
standard deviation, 52, 63
standardized tests, 52, 60–61, 63, 458, 465
Stanford-Binet intelligence test, 60, 454, 457, 458, 460, 482
stapes, 249–50, 257
startle reflex, 229
state-dependency effect, 372–73
statistical analysis, 48–53, 61–62, 63, 459
stepchildren, 97
stereotypes, 535–37, 540
stereotypic behavior, 90
Sternberg, Robert
  insight, 438
  intelligence, 451, 462–66, 472, 477, 482
  love, 533, 534
stimulants, 335–37, 340, 630
stimulus control, 212, 216
stimulus generalization, 195–97
storage, 356–57, 358
strange situation test, 406, 410
stream of consciousness, 20, 306–7, 309
stress, 551, 558–65, 581
striate cortex, 239–41, 274, 281–86, 288
string problem, 438–39
stroke, 127, 131
Stroop effect, 287, 288
structuralism, 19
structured interviews, 60, 63
study habits, 370
subcortical structures. *See* brainstem
subject expectancy effects, 58, 63
sublimation, 499–500, 505
subliminal perception, 234, 236, 503
subtractive color mixing, 244
suicide, 564, 579, 595–96, 597, 603–4
A Sunday Afternoon on the Island of La Grande Jatte (Seurat), 277–79
superego, 498–99, 505, 605
superior colliculus, 390
support groups, 627
suprachiasmatic nucleus (SCN), 311, 315, 318
surveys, 53–55, 63
survival of the fittest. *See* natural selection
Sybil (movie), 592
syllogism, 443
symmetry, 292
sympathetic division, 114–16, 120, 177
synapse, 117–18, 120
synaptic cleft, 118, 144, 145
syphilis, 581–82
systematic desensitization, 616, 617, 620, 627

T

tabula rasa, 14
talk therapy, 618–19
tardive dyskinesia, 631
taste, 159–60, 200–201, 229, 257–62, 295–99, 384

teaching. *See* education
telegraphic speech, 430, 432
television, 539–40
temperament, 404–5, 407, 410, 495
temperature, 230–31, 262–65, 620
  aggression, 539
  biological clock, 310–13
  disease, 550
  sleep, 319
temporal lobes, 124–25, 130, 131, 374, 376
  language, 416–17, 419
  meaningful sound, 294
  visual perception, 285–87
temporal summation, 145
teratogens, 382–83, 385
testes, 151–52
testosterone, 528, 538, 540
test-retest reliability, 60–61, 63
tests
  intelligence, 60–61, 433, 450–60, 475–82
  standardized, 52, 60–61, 63, 458, 465
texture gradient, 277–78, 281
thalamus, 108, 110, 112, 122–23, 129, 131, 177–78
  auditory nerve, 255–56
  lateral geniculate nucleus (LGN), 239–42
  schizophrenia, 600
  taste and smell, 260
Thanatos, 500, 505, 537
Thematic Apperception Test (TAT), 170, 171
theory of mind, 308, 309
The Psychological Corporation®, 21–22
therapy. *See* treatment
thermal feedback, 619
theta waves, 321
thiamine, 159
Thorndike, Ledward Lee, 22, 205–6, 212, 435
thought, 432–46, 566–67
  See also cognitive processes
The Three Faces of Eve (Thigpen & Cleckley), 592
thymus, 151–52
thyroid, 151–52
time, 68–69
time-outs, 213
tip-of-the-tongue phenomenon, 371, 373
Titchener, Edward, 19, 23–24, 31
tobacco, 382–83
To Know a Fly (Dethier), 157
tolerance to drugs, 338–39, 340
tonic immobility, 329, 331
tools, 417
top-down processes, 271, 275, 301
  language, 427
  music, 294
  short-term memory, 350
  temporal lobes, 286–87
touch, 121–22, 230–31, 262–65, 299–302, 410
  health, 553–54
  prenatal, 384
Tower of Hanoi (puzzle), 436–37
training in psychology, 24–30, 43, 611
trait approach, 487–93
tranquilizers, 633, 634
transduction, 238, 245
transference, 614, 615
trauma, 591–93, 611
traveling wave, 252–53, 257
treatment, 36, 45, 609–35
  anxiety, 564–65, 621, 623–24, 634
  aversion therapy, 616, 618, 619, 620
  behavioral therapy, 615–20, 627
  cognitive-behavioral therapy, 398, 622, 625–26, 628, 633, 634
  cognitive therapy, 621–22, 627, 628
  depression, 621–22, 634
  electroconvulsive therapy (ECT), 629–30, 634
  Gestalt therapy, 624, 628
  groups, 45, 626–27, 628
  humanistic therapy, 623–24, 626, 628
  insight therapy, 621–29
  moral therapy, 581
  nondirective therapy, 623–24
  person-centered therapy, 623–24
  psychoanalysis, 23, 497–505, 612–15
  psychodynamic approach, 487, 496–505, 615
  psychotherapy, 506–7, 610, 613, 633–34
  rational-emotive therapy, 621–22, 628
  relaxation training, 329, 331, 616, 620, 627, 633
  short-term psychodynamic therapy, 615
  talk therapy, 618–19
  See also drug treatment
trial-and-error learning, 435, 439
triarchic theory of intelligence, 462–65
triarchic theory of love, 533, 534
tribal tendencies, 536
trichromatic theory, 244, 245
tricyclic antidepressants, 632, 634
twins, 77
  aggression, 538
  eating habits, 555–56
  intelligence, 466–68, 473–74
  personality, 491–92, 495
  psychological disorders, 584–85, 595–96, 599
two-point limen, 234, 236
tympanic membrane, 249–50, 257
type, 489–90, 493

U

unconditional love, 507, 508
unconditioned response (UR), 191–92, 197
unconditioned stimulus (US), 191–92, 197
unconscious mind, 307, 309, 325, 326
  psychoanalytic theory, 497–98, 505, 614
unconscious vision, 282–89
underachievers, 474
unipolar disorder, 594, 597, 632
United Nations, 537
universal grammar, 430–31, 432

V

validation by consensus, 49, 51
validity, 60–61, 64, 458–59, 465
variable interval (VI) schedule, 209–10, 211
variable ratio (VR) schedule, 209, 211
variables, 44–45, 51, 58
ventricles, 120
vertebrates, 110–12
  See also animals
vertical thought, 464
vicarious trial-and-error learning, 435, 439
Vienna Psychoanalytic Society, 505
violent behavior, 38, 98, 537–40
vision, 229–30, 236–47, 269–93, 389–91
visual agnosia, 286–87, 288
visual cortex, 239–41, 274
visual displays, 420
visual fields, 282–84
visual memory, 359–60
visual perception, 269–93
visual problem solving, 444
visual processing, 68–69, 134, 272–75
visual sensation, 236–47
vital reflexes, 110
vocabulary, 430–31, 441, 458–59
Volkerpsychologie (Wundt), 19
voluntary retrievability, 415
voodoo death, 559
Vygotsky, Lev Semenovich, 397–98, 402

W

Wada test, 132, 136
Walden Two (Skinner), 212
Washburn, Margaret Floy, 20–21
Washoe, 423
Watson, John B., 22, 615
  behaviorism, 198–99, 203, 211, 502
  consciousness, 307
  stress, 562, 565
Weber's law, 231–32, 236
Wechsler Adult Intelligence Scale (WAIS-III), 60, 455, 458–61, 472–73, 475, 479–80, 482
Wechsler Intelligence Scale for Children (WISC-III), 60, 455, 458
Wernicke, Carl, 17, 18, 417–18
Wernicke's aphasia, 418–19, 420
Wernicke's area, 255, 257, 294, 417–18, 419
Wertheimer, Max, 22
Western medicine, 548–50
The Whisperings Within, 96
white matter, 119–20
Willis, John, 16
Wilson, Edward O., 95–96
win-stay, lose-shift strategy, 222–23, 224
wisdom, 85
Wisdom of the Body (Cannon), 152
wish fulfillment, 325
within-subjects design, 45, 51
Without Conscience: The Disturbing World of the Psychopaths Among Us (Hare), 605
Wonderlic Personnel Test (WPT), 479–80, 481
word problems, 396, 444–45
working hypotheses, 44, 51
working memory, 347, 350–59, 473
World Health Organization, 546, 547, 555
writing, 571, 572, 622
written history, 187–88
Wundt, Wilhelm, 19–20, 23, 31, 307

Y

yin/yang, 545–46
Yoga, 331
Young-Helmholtz theory of color vision, 244, 245

Z

zeitgeiber, 312–13, 318
Zend-Avesta (Fechner), 231
zoomorphism, 92, 95
zygotes, 82